The People, Politics, and the Politician

An Anthology of American Politics in Action

Revised

By

A. N. CHRISTENSEN
PROFESSOR OF POLITICAL SCIENCE
UNIVERSITY OF MINNESOTA

AND

EVRON M. KIRKPATRICK
DEPARTMENT OF STATE
WASHINGTON, D. C.

NEW YORK

HENRY HOLT AND COMPANY

PREFACE TO THE REVISED EDITION

DISTRUST of reason, of the intellect, and of things intellectual is widespread among Americans. As a people we have the power of sustained practical activity; and this is no small virtue. But we also have the vice of a reluctance to test the *quality* of that activity by reference to principle; and this is no small vice.

Americans have an aversion to theory. Among political scientists this has taken the form of emphasis upon constitutional, legal, factual and descriptive studies of governmental organization. There has, on the whole, been too little analysis, more learning than thinking. We have written histories of political theory but very little theory. This is due, in part, to dependence on a crude empiricism derived from false notions about the nature and methods of natural science. It has led to the beliefs first, that if you collect all of the relevant facts and classify them they will speak for themselves and, second, that preconceived theories or ideas about the facts are not only unnecessary but positively dangerous.

As a result, we Americans are inclined to take fundamentals for granted and too often collect what, in the end, are unanalyzed, unevaluated, and, in themselves, meaningless facts. Facts about political institutions are obviously essential but the analysis and evaluation that fit them into a total and meaningful mosaic is equally important.

It was with this in mind that the purpose, plan, and scope of the first edition of this book were formulated. Our experience with the book in our classes and the comments of colleagues, students, and general readers have confirmed our belief that it would be a valuable aid in the study *and understanding* of American government. The purpose, scope, and plan are unchanged, therefore, in this, the second edition. The contents of the book, however, have been thoroughly revised. We have tried to keep the emphasis on analytical and evaluative—not descriptive—materials. It is hoped that the book will continue to stimulate thought, provoke discussion and help the reader formulate a conceptual framework that will aid in the understanding of American political institutions, processes, and policies.

Since the publication of the first edition we have learned a great deal about American government. Our best teachers have been our own students.

Their constant desire to know not only the facts but also the meaning of the facts has encouraged us and guided us in assembling materials for the second edition. If this is a better book than its predecessor, our students are responsible. For its deficiencies, we alone are to blame.

A. N. C.
E. M. K.

Minneapolis, Minnesota
Washington, D. C.
March 8, 1950

PREFACE TO THE FIRST EDITION

THERE are a number of good books now available on American government. These books are, however, largely descriptive. They are concerned primarily with the legal, constitutional, and structural aspects of government. This means that those who seek analysis and criticism must turn, for the most part, to special books such as J. Allen Smith's *The Spirit of American Government* and Harold J. Laski's *The American Presidency* or to articles in journals of opinion. But there are obvious difficulties in making materials of this kind available to large groups of students. This fact led us to the conclusion that there was a need for a collection of such analytical and critical readings within a single volume.

The present volume was prepared to meet this need and includes materials that we have successfully used with students at the University of Minnesota and with general readers outside academic halls. We have found that essays which dare to argue are of great value in stimulating thought and provoking discussion. If a class discusses a selection with a point of view about such controversial questions as judicial review, labor regulation or economic planning and decides that the point of view is wrong, that discussion will be as valuable in the education of the students as if they had decided it was right. As a matter of fact, almost all persons will find themselves in disagreement with a few or with many of the viewpoints advanced in this volume. Indeed, we disagree vigorously with some of them and find ourselves in disagreement about some others. This, however, does not detract from their educational value. For, as John Stuart Mill pointed out long ago, the person who knows only his own side of the case knows little of that. To teachers with a firm grasp of their subject the presentation of critical and analytical materials in discussable form is of real value. If continuance of democratic institutions is to be assured, the student and citizen must not only have a picture of these institutions but also an insight into the fundamental problems with which they must deal. We are confident that the best assurance of the survival of democratic government lies in a citizen body that is keenly aware not only of the kind of institutions under which it lives but also of how and for whom these institutions work.

vii

This book, then, is not intended as a systematic and comprehensive treatment of the American system of government. It is intended as a stimulating and thought-provoking supplement to the textbooks on American government that are now available. It should be pointed out, however, that while designed primarily as a supplement to college textbooks on American government, we have kept the general reader in mind throughout. It is our hope that this volume will serve to stimulate his interest in, discussion of, and reflection upon the many aspects of government which so vitally concern those who wish to preserve and extend the democratic way of life.

To make this book a useful supplement to the textbooks, we have organized the material in such a way that it can be used in connection with almost any one of them. Each selection is numbered and reading assignments can be made either by chapter or by number to fit the needs of individual teachers. We have tried by brief introductions to the chapters in some cases and to the individual selections in others to suggest the problems involved and to give continuity to the whole. It should be noted, in addition, that some of the articles contain statements of fact that are now inaccurate because of events that have transpired since the articles were written. In no case, however, do these inaccuracies detract in a material way from the main point of the articles and, though we have let such articles stand as originally written, we have made corrections in brackets following the points in question.

For the benefit of students and general readers, we have included, at the end of the volume, a brief biographical note about each of the authors from whose writings we have made selections.

We cannot conclude without a special word of thanks: to the authors, periodicals, and publishers whose permissions to use material have made this volume possible; to the students whose frank criticisms have greatly aided us in the selection of materials; to our colleagues at Minnesota and elsewhere whose counsel was of great value; and to Mr. Ira Polley whose assistance was of greater worth than it is possible to acknowledge here.

We alone, of course, are wholly responsible for all errors or deficiencies in the book.

A. N. C.
E. M. K.

University of Minnesota
April 2, 1941

CONTENTS

CONTENTS

CONTENTS

Chapter I

THE AMERICAN CREED

[To review the history of the twentieth century is to review a series of great shocks to the liberalism with which the century opened. World War I, the communist and fascist dictatorships, the Great Depression, and World War II left no room for belief in inevitable progress toward world-wide prosperity, democracy, and peace. Had any basis for such optimism been left, events since World War II have destroyed it completely. Scientists moved on from the atomic bomb to create new and more terrible instruments of destruction. The Soviet dictatorship tightened its grip on the Russian people and established itself as the directing center for world-wide revolution. Communists ruthlessly seized power in Eastern Europe. Much of Asia, helpless and unaided, fell victim to the new tyranny.

To-day a black cloud of fear and insecurity casts its shadow over all our activities. Democracy is not safe; there is no peace.

In such a period, we need to see things in perspective, to take our bearings, to find our moorings. Victory for the free world cannot be won by money and material power alone. We cannot buy our way out of the troubles that confront us. The battle to-day is for the minds and hearts of men; our success depends upon the strength we derive from unity in a common vision, a common resolve, and a common and abiding faith in our moral and political values.

In this battle the United States has become a symbol of democracy and hope. What is this symbol, this hope? What are the beliefs, the ideals, the moral and political values that in America determine our relations with one another, with politics, with politicians, with the outside world? Do these values furnish a common bond of unity that has practical force in our political life? Do they constitute, in both symbol and reality, a weapon in the fight for the minds and hearts of our own and other people? Can we and will we use them as weapons of freedom and democracy?

Answers to some of these questions are found in the following essay by a famous Swedish social scientist, Gunnar Myrdal.]

1

No. 1

AMERICAN IDEALS AND THE AMERICAN CONSCIENCE [1]

by Gunnar Myrdal

I. UNITY OF IDEALS AND DIVERSITY OF CULTURE

IT is a commonplace to point out the heterogeneity of the American nation and the swift succession of all sorts of changes in all its component parts and, as it often seems, in every conceivable direction. America is truly a shock to the stranger. The bewildering impression it gives of dissimilarity throughout and of chaotic unrest is indicated by the fact that few outside observers—and, indeed, few native Americans—have been able to avoid the intellectual escape of speaking about America as "paradoxical."

Still there is evidently a strong unity in this nation and a basic homogeneity and stability in its valuations. Americans of all national origins, classes, regions, creeds, and colors have something in common: a social *ethos*, a political creed. It is difficult to avoid the judgment that this "American Creed" is the cement in the structure of this great and disparate nation.

When the American Creed is once detected, the cacophony becomes a melody. The further observation then becomes apparent: that America, compared to every other country in Western civilization, large or small, has the *most explicitly expressed* system of general ideals in reference to human interrelations. This body of ideals is more widely understood and appreciated than similar ideals are anywhere else. The American Creed is not merely—as in some other countries—the implicit background of the nation's political and judicial order as it functions. To be sure, the political creed of America is not very satisfactorily effectuated in actual social life. But as principles which *ought* to rule, the Creed has been made conscious to everyone in American society.

Sometimes one even gets the impression that there is a relation between the intense apprehension of high and uncompromising ideals and the spotty reality. One feels that it is, perhaps, the difficulty of giving reality to the *ethos* in this young and still somewhat unorganized nation—that it is the prevalence of "wrongs" in America, "wrongs" judged by the high standards of the national Creed—which helps make the ideals stand out so clearly.

[1] Gunnar Myrdal, *An American Dilemma* (New York: Harper and Brothers, 1944), pp. 1-25. Reprinted by permission of the publishers. The footnotes in the original version are omitted here.

America is continuously struggling for its soul. These principles of social ethics have been hammered into easily remembered formulas. All means of intellectual communication are utilized to stamp them into everybody's mind. The schools teach them, the churches preach them. The courts pronounce their judicial decisions in their terms. They permeate editorials with a pattern of idealism so ingrained that the writers could scarcely free themselves from it even if they tried. They have fixed a custom of indulging in high-sounding generalities in all written or spoken addresses to the American public, otherwise so splendidly gifted for the matter-of-fact approach to things and problems. Even the stranger, when he has to appear before an American audience, feels this, if he is sensitive at all, and finds himself espousing the national Creed, as this is the only means by which a speaker can obtain human response from the people to whom he talks.

. . . These ideals of the essential dignity of the individual human being, of the fundamental equality of all men, and of certain inalienable rights to freedom, justice, and a fair opportunity represent to the American people the essential meaning of the nation's early struggle for independence. In the clarity and intellectual boldness of the Enlightenment period these tenets were written into the Declaration of Independence, the Preamble of the Constitution, the Bill of Rights and into the constitutions of the several states. The ideals of the American Creed have thus become the highest law of the land. The Supreme Court pays its reverence to these general principles when it declares what is constitutional and what is not. They have been elaborated upon by all national leaders, thinkers and statesmen. America has had, throughout its history, a continuous discussion of the principles and implications of democracy, a discussion which, in every epoch, measured by any standard, remained high, not only quantitatively but also qualitatively. The flow of learned treatises and popular tracts on the subject has not ebbed, nor is it likely to do so. In all wars, including the present one, the American Creed has been the ideological foundation of national morale.

2. AMERICAN NATIONALISM

The American Creed is identified with America's peculiar brand of nationalism, and it gives the common American his feeling of the historical mission of America in the world—a fact which just now becomes of global importance but which is also of highest significance for the particular problem studied in this book. The great national historian of the middle nineteenth century, George Bancroft, expressed this national feeling of pride and responsibility:

In the fulness of time a republic rose in the wilderness of America. Thousands of years had passed away before this child of the ages could be born.

From whatever there was of good in the systems of the former centuries she drew her nourishment; the wrecks of the past were her warnings. . . . The fame of this only daughter of freedom went out into all the lands of the earth; from her the human race drew hope.

And Frederick J. Turner, who injected the naturalistic explanation into history that American democracy was a native-born product of the Western frontier, early in this century wrote in a similar vein:

Other nations have been rich and prosperous and powerful. But the United States has believed that it had an original contribution to make to the history of society by the production of a self-determining, self-restrained, intelligent democracy.

Wilson's fourteen points and Roosevelt's four freedoms have more recently expressed to the world the boundless idealistic aspirations of this American Creed. For a century and more before the present epoch, when the oceans gave reality to the Monroe Doctrine, America at least applauded heartily every uprising of the people in any corner of the world. This was a tradition from America's own Revolution. The political revolutionaries of foreign countries were approved even by the conservatives in America. And America wanted generously to share its precious ideals and its happiness in enjoying a society ruled by its own people with all who would come here. James Truslow Adams tells us:

The American dream that has lured tens of millions of all nations to our shores in the past century has not been a dream of merely material plenty, though that has doubtless counted heavily. It has been much more than that. It has been a dream of being able to grow to fullest development as man and woman, unhampered by the barriers which had slowly been erected in older civilizations, unrepressed by social orders which had developed for the benefit of classes rather than for the simple human being of any and every class. And that dream has been realized more fully in actual life here than anywhere else, though very imperfectly even among ourselves.

This is what the Western frontier country could say to the "East." And even the skeptic cannot help feeling that, perhaps, this youthful exuberant America has the destiny to do for the whole Old World what the frontier did to the old colonies. *American nationalism is permeated by the American Creed* and therefore becomes international in its essence.

3. SOME HISTORICAL REFLECTIONS

It is remarkable that a vast democracy with so many cultural disparities has been able to reach this unanimity of ideals and to elevate them supremely

over the threshold of popular perception. Totalitarian fascism and nazism
. . . [did] not in their own countries—at least not in the short range of their
. . . rule—succeed in accomplishing a similar result, in spite of the fact
that those governments, after having subdued the principal precepts most
akin to the American Creed, . . . attempted to coerce the minds of their
people by means of a centrally controlled, ruthless, and scientifically contrived apparatus of propaganda and violence. [The same techniques are
used, more ruthlessly and more successfully, by communism.]

There are more things to be wondered about. The disparity of national
origin, language, religion, and culture, during the long era of mass immigration into the United States, has been closely correlated with income differences and social class distinctions. Successive vintages of "Old Americans" have owned the country and held the dominant political power; they
have often despised and exploited "the foreigners." To this extent conditions in America must be said to have been particularly favorable to the
stratification of a rigid class society.

But it has not come to be. On the question of why the trend took the
other course, the historians, from Turner on, point to the free land and the
boundless resources. The persistent drive from the Western frontier—
now and then swelling into great tides as in the Jeffersonian movement
around 1800, the Jacksonian movement a generation later, and the successive third-party movements and breaks in the traditional parties—could,
however, reach its historical potency only because of the fact that America,
from the Revolution onward, had an equalitarian creed as a going national
ethos. The economic determinants and the force of the ideals can be shown
to be interrelated. But the latter should not be relegated to merely a dependent variable. Vernon L. Parrington, the great historian of the development of the American mind, writes thus:

> The humanitarian idealism of the Declaration (of Independence) has al-
> ways echoed as a battle-cry in the hearts of those who dream of an America
> dedicated to democratic ends. It cannot be long ignored or repudiated, for
> sooner or later it returns to plague the council of practical politics. It is
> constantly breaking out in fresh revolt. . . . Without its freshening influence
> our political history would have been much more sordid and materialistic.

Indeed, the new republic began its career with a reaction. Charles Beard,
in *An Economic Interpretation of the Constitution of the United States*, and
a group of modern historians, throwing aside the much cherished national
mythology which had blurred the difference in spirit between the Declaration of Independence and the Constitution, have shown that the latter was
conceived in considerable suspicion against democracy and fear of "the

people." It was dominated by property consciousness and designed as a defense against the democratic spirit let loose during the Revolution.

But, admitting all this, the Constitution which actually emerged out of the compromises in the drafting convention provided for the most democratic state structure in existence anywhere in the world at that time. And many of the safeguards so skillfully thought out by the conservatives to protect "the rich, the wellborn, and the capable" against majority rule melted when the new order began to function. Other conservative safeguards have fastened themselves into the political pattern. And "in the ceaseless conflict between the man and the dollar, between democracy and property"— again to quote Parrington—property. has for long periods triumphed and blocked the will of the people. And there are to-day large geographical regions and fields of human life which, particularly when measured by the high goals of the American Creed, are conspicuously lagging. But taking the broad historical view, the American Creed has triumphed. It has given the main direction to change in this country. America has had gifted conservative statesmen and national leaders, and they have often determined the course of public affairs. But with few exceptions, only the liberals have gone down in history as national heroes. America is, as we shall point out, conservative in fundamental principles, and in much more than that, though hopefully experimentalistic in regard to much of the practical arrangements in society. But the principles conserved are liberal and some, indeed, are radical.

America got this dynamic Creed much as a political convenience and a device of strategy during the long struggle with the English Crown/ the London Parliament, and the various British powerholders in the colonies. It served as the rallying center for the growing national unity that was needed. Later it was a necessary device for building up a national morale in order to enlist and sustain the people in the Revolutionary War. In this spirit the famous declarations were resolved, the glorious speeches made, the inciting pamphlets written and spread. "The appeal to arms would seem to have been brought about by a minority of the American people, directed by a small group of skillful leaders, who, like Indian scouts, covered their tracks so cleverly, that only the keenest trailers can now follow their course and understand their strategy."

But the Creed, once set forth and disseminated among the American people, became so strongly entrenched in their hearts, and the circumstances have since then been so relatively favorable, that it has succeeded in keeping itself very much alive for more than a century and a half.

4. THE ROOTS OF THE AMERICAN CREED IN THE PHILOSOPHY OF ENLIGHTENMENT

The American Creed is a humanistic liberalism developing out of the epoch of Enlightenment when America received its national consciousness and its political structure. The Revolution did not stop short of anything less than the heroic desire for the "emancipation of human nature." The enticing flavor of the eighteenth century, so dear to every intellectual and rationalist, has not been lost on the long journey up to the present time. Let us quote a contemporary exegesis [Charles E. Merriam] :

Democracy is a form of political association in which the general control and direction of the commonwealth is habitually determined by the bulk of the community in accordance with understandings and procedures providing for popular participation and consent. Its postulates are:

1. The essential dignity of man, the importance of protecting and cultivating his personality on a fraternal rather than upon a differential basis, of reconciling the needs of the personality within the frame-work of the common good in a formula of liberty, justice, welfare.

2. The perfectibility of man; confidence in the possibilities of the human personality, as over against the doctrines of caste, class, and slavery.

3. That the gains of commonwealths are essentially mass gains rather than the efforts of the few and should be diffused as promptly as possible throughout the community without too great delay or too wide a spread in differentials.

4. Confidence in the value of the consent of the governed expressed in institutions, understandings and practices as a basis of order, liberty, justice.

5. The value of decisions arrived at by common counsel rather than by violence and brutality.

These postulates rest upon (1) reason in regarding the essential nature of the political man, upon (2) observation, experience and inference, and (3) the fulfillment of the democratic ideal is strengthened by a faith in the final triumph of ideals of human behavior in general and of political behavior in particular.

For practical purposes the main norms of the American Creed as usually pronounced are centered in the belief in equality and in the rights to liberty. In the Declaration of Independence—as in the earlier Virginia Bill of Rights —equality was given the supreme rank and the rights to liberty are posited as derived from equality. This logic was even more clearly expressed in Jefferson's original formulation of the first of the "self-evident truths": "All men are created equal *and from that equal creation* they derive rights inherent and unalienable, among which are the preservation of life and liberty and the pursuit of happiness."

Liberty, in a sense, was easiest to reach. It is a vague ideal: everything turns around *whose* liberty is preserved, *to what extent* and *in what direction*. In society liberty for one may mean the suppression of liberty for others. The result of competition will be determined by who got a head start and who is handicapped. In America as everywhere else—and sometimes, perhaps, on the average, a little more ruthlessly—liberty often provided an opportunity for the stronger to rob the weaker. Against this, the equalitarianism in the Creed has been persistently revolting. The struggle is far from ended. The reason why American liberty was not more dangerous to equality was, of course, the open frontier and the free land. When opportunity became bounded in the last generation, the inherent conflict between equality and liberty flared up. Equality is slowly winning. The New Deal during the 'thirties was a landslide.

5. The Roots in Christianity

If the European philosophy of Enlightenment was one of the ideological roots of the American Creed, another equally important one was Christianity, particularly as it took the form in the colonies of various lower class Protestant sects, split off from the Anglican Church. "Democracy was envisaged in religious terms long before it assumed a political terminology."

It is true that modern history has relegated to the category of the pious patriotic myths the popular belief that *all* the colonies had been founded to get religious liberty, which could not be had in the Old World. Some of the colonies were commercial adventures and the settlers came to them, and even to the religious colonies later, to improve their economic status. It is also true that the churches in the early colonial times did not always exactly represent the idea of democratic government in America but most often a harsher tyranny over people's souls and behavior than either King or Parliament ever cared to wield.

But the myth itself is a social reality with important effects. It was strong already in the period of the Revolution and continued to grow. A small proportion of new immigrants throughout the nineteenth century came for religious reasons, or partly so, and a great many more wanted to rationalize their uprooting and transplantation in such terms. So religion itself in America took on a spirit of fight for liberty. The Bible is full of support for such a spirit. It consists to a large extent of the tales of oppression and redemption from oppression: in the Old Testament of the Jewish people and in the New Testament of the early Christians. The rich and mighty are most often the wrongdoers, while the poor and lowly are the followers of God and Christ.

The basic teaching of Protestant Christianity is democratic. We are all poor sinners and have the same heavenly father. The concept of natural rights in the philosophy of Enlightenment corresponded rather closely with the idea of moral law in the Christian faith [Ralph H. Gabriel] :

> The doctrine of the free individual, postulating the gradual escape of men from external political control, as they learned to obey the moral law, had its counterpart in the emphasis of evangelicism upon the freedom of the regenerated man from the terrors of the Old Testament code framed for the curbing of unruly and sinful generations. The philosophy of progress was similar to the Utopian hopes of the millenarians. The mission of American democracy to save the world from the oppression of autocrats was a secular version of the destiny of Christianity to save the world from the governance of Satan.

But apart from the historical problem of the extent to which church and religion in America actually inspired the American Creed, they became a powerful container and preserver of the Creed when it was once in existence. This was true from the beginning. While in Europe after the Napoleonic Wars the increasing power of the churches everywhere spelled a period of reaction, the great revivals beginning around 1800 in America were a sort of religious continuation of the Revolution [Guion G. Johnson] :

> In this way great numbers whom the more-or-less involved theory of natural rights had escaped came under the leveling influence of a religious doctrine which held that all men were equal in the sight of God. Throughout the Revival period the upper classes looked upon the movement as "a religious distemper" which spread like a contagious disease, and they pointed out that it made its greatest appeal to "those of weak intellect and unstable emotions, women, adolescents, and Negroes." But to the poor farmer who had helped to win the Revolution only to find himself oppressed as much by the American ruling classes as he had ever been by Crown officials, the movement was "the greatest stir of Religion since the day of Pentecost."

Religion is still a potent force in American life. "They are a religious people," observed Lord Bryce about Americans a half a century ago, with great understanding for the importance of this fact for their national ideology. American scientific observers are likely to get their attentions fixed upon the process of progressive secularization to the extent that they do not see this main fact, that America probably is still the most religious country in the Western world. Political leaders are continuously deducing the American Creed out of the Bible. Vice-President Henry Wallace, in his historic speech of May 8, 1942, to the Free World Association, where he declared the . . . war to be "a fight between a slave world and a free world" and declared himself for "a people's peace" to inaugurate "the century of the common man," spoke thus:

> The idea of freedom—the freedom that we in the United States know and love so well—is derived from the Bible with its extraordinary emphasis on the dignity of the individual. Democracy is the only true political expression of Christianity.
>
> The prophets of the Old Testament were the first to preach social justice. But that which was sensed by the prophets many centuries before Christ was not given complete and powerful political expression until our Nation was formed as a Federal Union a century and a half ago.

Ministers have often been reactionaries in America. They have often tried to stifle free speech; they have organized persecution of unpopular dissenters and have even, in some regions, been active as the organizers of the Ku Klux Klan and similar "un-American" (in terms of the American Creed) movements. But, on the whole, church and religion in America are a force strengthening the American Creed. The fundamental tenets of Christianity press for expression even in the most bigoted setting. And, again on the whole, American religion is not particularly bigoted, but on the contrary, rather open-minded. The mere fact that there are many denominations, and that there is competition between them, forces American churches to a greater tolerance and ecumenical understanding and to a greater humanism and interest in social problems than the people in the churches would otherwise call for.

I also believe that American churches and their teachings have contributed something essential to the emotional temper of the Creed and, indeed, of the American people. Competent and sympathetic foreign observers have always noted the generosity and helpfulness of Americans. This and the equally conspicuous formal democracy in human contacts have undoubtedly had much to do with the predominantly lower class origin of the American people, and even more perhaps, with the mobility and the opportunities— what de Tocqueville called the "equality of condition"—in the nation when it was in its formative stage. But I cannot help feeling that the Christian neighborliness of the common American reflects, also, an influence from the churches. Apart from its origin, this temper of the Americans is part and parcel of the American Creed. It shows up in the Americans' readiness to make financial sacrifices for charitable purposes. No country has so many cheerful givers as America. It was not only "rugged individualism," nor a relatively continuous prosperity, that made it possible for America to get along without a publicly organized welfare policy almost up to the Great Depression in the 'thirties but it was also the world's most generous private charity.

6. THE ROOTS IN ENGLISH LAW

The third main ideological influence behind the American Creed is English law. The indebtedness of American civilization to the culture of the mother country is nowhere else as great as in respect to the democratic concept of law and order, which it inherited almost without noticing it. It is the glory of England that, after many generations of hard struggle, it established the principles of justice, equity, and equality before the law even in an age when the rest of Europe (except for the cultural islands of Switzerland, Iceland, and Scandinavia) based personal security on the arbitrary police and on *lettres de cachet*.

This concept of a government "of laws and not of men" contained certain fundamentals of both equality and liberty. It will be a part of our task to study how these elemental demands are not nearly realized even in present-day America. But in the American Creed they have never been questioned. And it is no exaggeration to state that the philosophical ideas of human equality and the inalienable rights to life, liberty, and property, hastily sowed on American ground in a period of revolution when they were opportune—even allowing ever so much credit to the influences from the free life on the Western frontier—would not have struck root as they did if the soil had not already been cultivated by English law.

Law and order represent such a crucial element both in the American Creed and in the spotty American reality that, at a later stage of our argument in this chapter, we shall have to devote some further remarks to this particular set of ideological roots.

7. AMERICAN CONSERVATISM

These ideological forces—the Christian religion and the English law—also explain why America through all its adventures has so doggedly stuck to its high ideals: why it has been so conservative in keeping to liberalism as a national creed even if not as its actual way of life. This conservatism, in fundamental principles, has, to a great extent, been perverted into a nearly fetishistic cult of the Constitution. This is unfortunate since the . . . [164]-year-old Constitution is in many respects impractical and ill-suited for modern conditions and since, furthermore, the drafters of the document made it technically difficult to change even if there were no popular feeling against change.

The worship of the Constitution also is a most flagrant violation of the

American Creed which, as far as the technical arrangements for executing the power of the people are concerned, is strongly opposed to stiff formulas. Jefferson actually referred to the American form of government as an experiment. The young Walt Whitman, among many other liberals before and after him, expressed the spirit of the American Revolution more faithfully when he demanded "continual additions to our great experiment of how much liberty society will bear." Modern historical studies of how the Constitution came to be as it is reveal that the Constitutional Convention was nearly a plot against the common people. Until recently, the Constitution has been used to block the popular will: the Fourteenth Amendment inserted after the Civil War to protect the civil rights of the poor freedmen has, for instance, been used more to protect business corporations against public control.

But when all this is said, it does not give more than one side of the cult of the Constitution. The common American is not informed on the technicalities and has never thought of any great difference in spirit between the Declaration of Independence and the Constitution. When he worships the Constitution, it is an act of American nationalism, and in this the American Creed is inextricably blended. The liberal Creed, even in its dynamic formulation by Jefferson, is adhered to by every American. The unanimity around, and the explicitness of, this Creed is the great wonder of America. The "Old Americans," all those who have thoroughly come to identify themselves with the nation—which are many more than the Sons and Daughters of the Revolution—adhere to the Creed as the faith of their ancestors. The others—the Negroes, the new immigrants, the Jews, and other disadvantaged and unpopular groups—could not possibly have invented a system of political ideals which better corresponded to their interests. So, by the logic of the unique American history, it has developed that the rich and secure, out of pride and conservatism, and the poor and insecure, out of dire need, have come to profess the identical social ideals. The reflecting observer comes to feel that this spiritual convergence, more than America's strategic position behind the oceans and its immense material resources, is what makes the nation great and what promises it a still greater future. Behind it all is the historical reality which makes it possible for the President to appeal to all in the nation in this way: "Let us not forget that we are all descendants from revolutionaries and immigrants."

8. THE AMERICAN CONCEPTION OF LAW AND ORDER

While the Creed is important and is enacted into law, it is not lived up to in practice. To understand this we shall have to examine American attitudes toward law. It is necessary to discuss the legal tradition of America at the outset, since it gives a unique twist to each of the specific problems that we shall take up in ensuing chapters.

/ Americans are accustomed to inscribe their ideals in laws, ranging from their national Constitution to their local traffic rules. / American laws thus often contain, in addition to the actually enforced rules (that is, "laws" in the ordinary technical meaning of the term), other rules which are not valid or operative but merely express the legislators' hopes, desires, advice or dreams. There is nothing in the legal form to distinguish the latter rules from the former ones. Much of the political discussion has to do with the question of strengthening the administration of laws or taking other measures so as to enforce them. Between the completely enforced rules and unenforceable ones there are many intermediary types which are sometimes, under some conditions, or in some part, only conditionally and incompletely enforced.

To an extent this peculiar cultural trait of America is explainable by the fact that the nation is young and, even more, that it owes its state structure to a revolution—a revolution in the courageously rationalistic age of Enlightenment. Americans have kept to this custom of inscribing their ideals in laws.

The "function," from the legislator's point of view, of legislating national ideals is, of course, a pedagogical one of giving them high publicity and prestige. Legislating ideals has also a "function" of dedicating the nation to the task of gradually approaching them. In a new nation made up of immigrants from all corners of the world and constantly growing by the arrival of other immigrants, carrying with them a greatly diversified cultural heritage, these goals must have stood out as important to statesmen and political thinkers.

Another cultural trait of Americans is a relatively low degree of respect for law and order. This trait, as well as the other one just mentioned, is of paramount importance for the Negro problem as we shall show in some detail in later chapters. There is a relation between these two traits, of high ideals in some laws and low respect for all laws, but this relation is by no means as simple as it appears.

9. NATURAL LAW AND AMERICAN PURITANISM

On this point we must observe somewhat more closely the moralistic attitude toward law in America, expressed in the common belief that there is a "higher law" behind and above the specific laws contained in constitutions, statutes and other regulations.

The idea of a "natural law" has long been a part of our common line of legal tradition. When the elected "lawman" in pre-Christian times "spoke the law" to the assembled arm-bearing freemen, he was not assumed to make the law or invent it but to expound something which existed prior to and independent of himself and all others participating in the procedure. The idea of a "higher law," as well as the whole procedure of letting it become a social reality and, indeed, the entire legal system as it functioned and grew in the northern countries, had deep roots in primitive religion and magic, as is revealed by studies of the contemporary mythology and the peculiar formalistic mechanisms of the creation and operation of law. The distinguishing mark of the particular type of magical thinking in these countries was, however, that out of it developed what we now understand to be the characteristic respect for law of modern democracy.

When representative bodies, among them the English Parliament, emerged as political institutions, they also did not conceive of themselves as "legislatures" in the modern sense, but pretended only to state the law that already "existed." Even when these legislatures began to take on new functions and to make rules to meet new situations, they still kept up the fiction that they only "declared" or "explained" the law as it existed. The modern idea of creating laws by "legislation" is thus a late product in the historical development of Western democracy, and it was never totally freed from the connotation of its subordination to a "higher law" existing independent of all formally fixed rules.

In America the Revolution gave a tremendous spread to this primitive idea of "natural law" as it, in the meantime, had been developed in the philosophies of Enlightenment under the further influences of Greek speculation, Roman law, medieval scholasticism, and free naturalistic speculation since Francis Bacon, Thomas Hobbes and Hugo Grotius. American religion supported it strongly. The idea fixed itself upon the entire American state structure. "A peculiarity of American democracy had been from the beginning that it put its faith in a higher law rather than in the changing will of the people." The role given to the Supreme Court and the tradition of this tribunal not to "legislate," which as a court it could hardly have the right to do, but to refer to the higher principles back of the Constitution strengthened still more the grip of this old idea on the mind of the Americans.

The adherence even in modern times to this idealistic conception of the origin and reality of the judicial order undoubtedly, in one way, raised its moral prestige among the American people as it had done earlier in the history of the Old World. No careful observer of the present American scene should miss seeing, in spite of everything we shall discuss presently, the common American's pride in and devotion to the nation's judicial system and its legal institutions. Government authorities constantly appeal to this idealistic pride and devotion of the citizens in order to enforce the law. In America, there is a continuous endeavor to keep the judicial system orderly, and there is a continuous educational campaign on behalf of this idealism. Undoubtedly *the idealistic concept of American law as an emanation of "natural law" is a force which strengthens the rule of law in America.*

But, in another way, it is at the same time most detrimental to automatic, unreflecting law observance on the part of the citizens. Laws become disputable on moral grounds. Each legislative statute is judged by the common citizen in terms of his conception of the higher "natural law." He decides whether it is "just" or "unjust" and has *the dangerous attitude that, if it is unjust, he may feel free to disobey it.* The strong stress on individual rights and the almost complete silence on the citizen's duties in the American Creed make this reaction the more natural. The Jeffersonian distrust of government—"that government is best which governs least"—soon took the form, particularly on the Western frontier, of a distrust and disrespect for the enacted laws. The doctrine of a higher law fosters an "extra-legal" disposition towards the state and excuses illegal acts.

But the frontier was not, in this respect, fundamentally different from the old colonies. Without stepping outside the American tradition, Garrison could pronounce even the Constitution to be a "compact with Hell" on the slavery issue. This, by itself, would not have been dangerous to democracy, if he had meant to argue only for a change of the Constitution. But he and many more Northerners of conscientious inclinations found it a moral obligation not to obey the fugitive slave laws. Here the citizen does not stop to criticize the laws and the judicial system and demand a change in them, but he sets his own conception of the "higher law" above the existing laws in society and feels it his right to disobey them. It is against this background also that we shall have to study the amazing disrespect for law and order which even to-day characterizes the Southern states in America and constitutes such a large part of the Negro problem. This anarchistic tendency founded upon a primitive concept of natural law has never left American political speculation or American popular thought.

This anarchistic tendency in America's legal culture becomes even more dangerous because of the presence of a quite different tendency: *a desire to regulate human behavior tyrannically by means of formal laws.* This last tendency is a heritage from early American puritanism which was sometimes fanatical and dogmatic and always had a strong inclination to mind other people's business. So we find that this American, who is so proud to announce that he will not obey laws other than those which are "good" and "just," as soon as the discussion turns to something which in his opinion is bad and unjust, will emphatically pronounce that "there ought to be a law against . . ." To demand and legislate all sorts of laws against this or that is just as much part of American freedom as to disobey the laws when they are enacted. America has become a country where exceedingly much is permitted in practice but at the same time exceedingly much is forbidden in law.

By instituting a national prohibition of the sale of liquor without taking adequate steps for its enforcement, America was nearly drenched in corruption and organized crime until the statute was repealed. The laws against gambling have, on a smaller scale, the same effect at the present time. And many more of those unrespected laws are damaging in so far as they, for example, prevent a rational organization of various public activities, or when they can be used by individuals for blackmailing purposes or by the state or municipal authorities to persecute unpopular individuals or groups. Such practices are conducive to a general disrespect for law in America. Actually today it is a necessity in everyday living for the common good American citizen to decide for himself which laws should be observed and which not.

10. THE FALTERING JUDICIAL ORDER

. . . A low degree of law observance already became habitual and nationally cherished in colonial times when the British Parliament and Crown, increasingly looked upon as a foreign ruler by the Americans, insisted upon passing laws which the Americans considered unwise, impractical or simply unjust. The free life on the frontier also strained legal bonds. There the conflict between puritanical intolerance and untamed desire for individual freedom clashed more severely than anywhere else. The mass immigration and the cultural heterogeneity were other factors hampering the fixation of a firm legal order in America. The presence of states within the nation with different sets of laws and the high mobility between states were contributing factors. The jurisdictional friction between states and the federal government, the technical and political difficulties in changing the federal Constitution, the consequent great complexity of the American legal system, and the mass of legal fiction and plain trickery also are among the important factors. For example, it cannot be conducive to the highest respect for the legal system that the federal government is forced to carry out important social legislation under the fiction that it is regulating "inter-state commerce," or that federal prosecuting agencies punish dangerous gangsters for income tax evasion rather than for the felonies they have committed.

So this idealistic America also became the country of legalistic formalism. Contrary to America's basic ideology of natural law and its strong practical sense, "the letter of the law," as opposed to its "spirit," came to have an excessive importance. The weak bureaucracy became tangled up in "red tape." The clever lawyer came to play a large and unsavory role in politics, in business, and in the everyday life of the citizens. The Americans thus got a judicial order which is in many respects contrary to all their inclinations.

Under the influence of all these and many other factors the common American citizen has acquired a comparatively low degree of personal identification with the state and the legal machinery. An American, when he accidentally comes by the scene of a crime or of an attempt by the police to seize an offender, is, on the average, more inclined to hurry on in order not to get involved in something unpleasant, and less inclined to stop and help the arm of the law, than a Britisher or a Scandinavian would be under similar circumstances. He is more likely to look on his country's and his community's politics and administration as something to be indulged and tolerated, as outside his own responsibility, and less likely to think and act as a would-be legislator, in a cooperative endeavor to organize a decent social life. He is even inclined to dissociate himself from politics as something unworthy and to take measures to keep the worthy things "out of politics." This is part of what Lord Bryce called "the fatalism of the multitude" in America. This political fatalism and the lack of identification and participation work as a vicious circle, being both cause and effect of corruption and political machine rule.

The authorities, when not relying upon the idealistic appeal, will most often meet the citizen's individualistic inclinations by trying to educate him to obey the law less in terms of collective interest than in terms of self-interest. They try to tell the young that "crime does not pay," which, in some areas, is a statement of doubtful truth.

In the exploitation of the new continent business leaders were not particular about whether or not the means they used corresponded either with the natural law or with the specific laws of the nation or the states. This became of greater importance because of the central position of business in the formation of national aspirations and ideals. When Theodore Roosevelt exclaimed: "Damn the law! I want the canal built," he spoke the language of his contemporary business world and of the ordinary American.

We have to conceive of all the numerous breaches of law, which an American citizen commits or learns about in the course of ordinary living, as psychologically a series of shocks which condition him and the entire society to a low degree of law observance. The American nation has, further, experienced disappointments in its attempts to legislate social changes, which, with few exceptions, have been badly prepared and inefficiently carried out. The almost traumatic effects of these historical dis-appointments have been enhanced by America's conspicuous success in so many fields other than legislation. One of the trauma was the Reconstruction legislation, which attempted to give Negroes civil rights in the South; another one was the anti-trust legislation pressed by the Western farmers and enacted to curb the growth of monopolistic finance capitalism; a third one was the prohibition amendment.

11. INTELLECTUAL DEFEATISM

Against this background, and remembering the puritan tendency in America to make all sorts of haphazard laws directed at symptoms and not at causes and without much consideration for social facts and possibilities, it is understandable that the social scientists, particularly the sociologists, in America have developed a defeatist attitude towards the possibility of inducing social change by means of legislation. The political "do-nothing" tendency is strong in present-day social science in America. It is, typically enough, developed as a *general* theory—actually as a scientific translation of the old natural law idea in its negative import. The social scientists simply reflect the general distrust of politics and legislation that is wide-spread among the educated classes of Americans.

. . . A few critical remarks on the general theory that "stateways cannot change folkways" need to be made at the start. In this abstract form and as applied to various specific problems, the theory cannot be true, since in other parts of the world similar changes are effectuated by means of legislation. The theory must, therefore, be qualified in the light of specific American conditions. But even in America new legislation, infringing upon old customs and upon individual and local interests, is often made fairly watertight nowadays. The general explanation why some laws have been more successful than others in America is that *they have been better prepared and better administered.*

This means that, among the explanations for the general disrepute and deficiency of law and order in America, there are two other factors: *the habit of passing laws without careful investigation, and the relatively low standard of American administration of law.* To the latter point we shall return in a later chapter, where we shall point also to the new but strong tendency in America toward the building up of an independent and legal administration. On the former point we shall restrict ourselves to quoting a high authority [Dean Roscoe Pound]: "For nothing is done with so little of scientific or orderly method as the legislative making of laws."

These two factors are strategic. When the foolish attempts to suppress symptoms of ills while leaving the causes untouched become censored, and when lawmaking increasingly becomes an important task of scientific social engineering, and when, further, administration becomes independent, legal, impartial, and efficient, better laws will be made, and they will be better enforced even in America. It is a problem to explain why lawmaking and administration have been so backward in a nation where private business and also private agencies for public good are often excellently organized.

The mere possibility of change in these two factors shows the fallacy of the general theory that law cannot change custom. In the face of the tendency in American society toward more careful lawmaking and improved administration the theory appears politically as well as theoretically biased; biased against induced change. In this book we shall meet other dynamic tendencies in American society favoring the same development, the chief among them being, perhaps, the growing cultural homogeneity and the increasing political and social participation of the masses. Many social scientists tend not only to ignore these changes, but to deny them and, in some cases, to oppose them.

If in the course of time Americans are brought to be a law-abiding people, and if they at the same time succeed in keeping alive not only their conservatism in fundamental principles and their pride and devotion to their national political institutions, but also some of their puritan eagerness and courage in attempting to reform themselves and the world—redirected somewhat from the old Biblical inclination of thinking only in terms of prescriptions and purges—this great nation may become the master builder of a stable but progressive commonwealth.

12. "LIP-SERVICE"

The conflict in the American concept of law and order is only one side of the "moral overstrain" of the nation. America believes in and aspires to something much higher than its plane of actual life. The subordinate position of Negroes is perhaps the most glaring conflict in the American conscience and the greatest unsolved task for American democracy. But it is by no means the only one. Donald Young complains:

> In our more introspective moments, nearly all of us Americans will admit that our government contains imperfections and anachronisms. We who have been born and brought up under the evils of gang rule, graft, political incompetence, inadequate representation, and some of the other weaknesses of democracy, American plan, have developed mental calluses and are no longer sensitive to them.

The *popular* explanation of the disparity in America between ideals and actual behavior is that Americans do not have the slightest intention of living up to the ideals which they talk about and put into their Constitution and laws. Many Americans are accustomed to talk loosely and disparagingly about adherence to the American Creed as "lip-service" and even "hypocrisy." Foreigners are even more prone to make such a characterization.

This explanation is too superficial. To begin with, the true hypocrite sins in secret; he conceals his faults. The American, on the contrary, is strongly and sincerely "against sin," even, and not least, his own sins. He investigates his faults, puts them on record, and shouts them from the housetops, adding the most severe recriminations against himself, including the accusation of hypocrisy. If all the world is well informed about the political corruption, organized crime, and faltering system of justice in America, it is primarily not due to its malice but to American publicity about its own imperfections. America's handling of the Negro problem has been criticized most emphatically by white Americans since long before the Revolution, and the criticism has steadily gone on and will not stop until America has completely reformed itself.

Bryce observed: "They know, and are content that all the world should know, the worst as well as the best of themselves. They have a boundless faith in free inquiry and full discussion. They admit the possibility of any number of temporary errors and delusions." The present author remembers, from his first visit to this country as an inexperienced social scientist at the end of the 'twenties, how confused he often felt when Americans in all walks of life were trustingly asking him to tell them what was "wrong with this country." It is true that this open-mindedness, particularly against the outside world, may have decreased considerably since then on account of the depression, and that . . . [World War II] might work in the same direction, though this is not certain; and it is true also that the opposite tendency always had its strong representation in America. But, by and large, America has been and will remain, in all probability, a society which is eager to indulge in self-scrutiny and to welcome criticism.

This American eagerness to get on record one's sins and their causes is illustrated in the often quoted letter by Patrick Henry (1772), where he confessed that he had slaves because he was "drawn along by the general inconvenience of living here without them."

> I will not, I cannot, justify it. However culpable my conduct, I will so far pay my devoir to virtue as to own the excellence and rectitude of her precepts, and lament my want of conformity to them.

American rationalism and moralism spoke through Patrick Henry. America as a nation is like its courageous and eloquent son of the Revolution. It is continuously paying its *devoir* to virtue; it is repeating its allegiance to the full American Creed by lamenting its want of conformity to it. The strength and security of the nation helped this puritan tradition to continue. No weak nation anxious for its future could ever have done it. Americans believe in their own ability and in progress. They are at bottom moral optimists.

In a great nation there is, of course, division of labor. Some Americans do most of the sinning, but most do some of it. Some specialize in muckraking, preaching, and lamentation; but there is a little of the muckraker and preacher in all Americans. On the other hand, superficially viewed, Americans often appear cynical. Their social science has lately developed along a deterministic track of amoralistic nonconcernedness; but this is itself easily seen to be a moralistic reaction. As a matter of fact, this young nation is the least cynical of all nations. It is not hypocritical in the usual sense of the word, but labors persistently with its moral problems. It is taking its Creed very seriously indeed, and this is the reason why the ideals are not only continuously discussed but also represent a social force—why they receive more than "lip-service" in the collective life of the nation. The cultural unity of the nation is this common sharing in both the consciousness of sins and the devotion to high ideals.

Americans accuse themselves, and are accused by others, of being materialists. But they are equally extreme in the other direction. Sometimes an American feels moved to put the matter right, as Josiah Royce did when he explained:

> When foreigners accuse us of extraordinary love for gain, and of practical materialism, they fail to see how largely we are a nation of idealists. Yet that we are such a nation is something constantly brought to the attention of those whose calling requires them to observe any of the tendencies prevalent in our recent intellectual life in America.

The American problem to be studied in this book would, indeed, have an entirely different prognosis if this fact were forgotten.

13. VALUE PREMISES IN THIS STUDY

. . . "The American democratic faith is a pattern of ideals providing standards of value with which the accomplishments of realistic democracy may be judged," observes an author [Ralph H. Gabriel] surveying the historical trends of American thinking.

And there is no doubt that these ideals are active realities. The student of American history must be professionally near-sighted or blinded by a doctrinal belief in a materialistic determinism if he fails to see the significance of tracing how the Creed is gradually realizing itself. *The American Creed is itself one of the dominant "social trends."* "Call it a dream or call it vision," says John Dewey, "it has been interwoven in a tradition that has had an immense effect upon American life." Or, to quote a distinguished Negro thinker, the late Kelly Miller:

> In this country political, social and economic conditions gravitate toward equality. We may continue to expect thunderstorms in the political firmament so long as there exists inequality of political temperature in the atmosphere of the two regions. Neither Massachusetts nor Mississippi will rest satisfied until there is an equality of political condition in both States. . . . Democratic institutions can no more tolerate a double political status than two standards of ethics or discrepant units of weight and measure.

. . . The American Creed, just because it is a living reality in a developing democracy, is not a fixed and clear-cut dogma. It is still growing. During the Revolutionary epoch the interests of statesmen and philosophers and of the general public were focused on the more formal aspects of freedom, equality and justice. After a long period of material expansion but not rapid spiritual growth, the American Creed is in this generation again in a formative stage. It is now discovering its ideals in the social and economic sphere and in the realm of international organization.

While this is going on, there are great disparities in opinions even on fundamentals in these new fields of valuation—as there were during the Revolution concerning the ideals which then became crystallized. Some Americans see in trade unions a denial of the rights to human liberty; others see in the unions an expression of the common man's right to reach for greater equality and freedom. Some Americans want to tax property and nationalize public utilities in order to defend equality of opportunity for the masses of the people and to preserve their liberties; others see in such attempts an assault upon American principles of liberty. In the international field American ideals in recent decades and even to-day seem divided and rambling in the wide space of the triangle marked by the three points: absolute isolationism, an organized world democracy, and American world imperialism.

. . . Finally, in order to avoid possible misunderstandings, it should be explained that we have called this Creed "American" in the sense that it is adhered to by the Americans. . . . But this Creed is, of course, no American monopoly. With minor variations, some of which, however, are not without importance, the American Creed is the common democratic creed. "American ideals" are just humane ideals as they have matured in our common Western civilization upon the foundation of Christianity and pre-Christian legalism and under the influence of the economic, scientific, and political development over a number of centuries. The American Creed is older and wider than America itself.

Chapter II

THE RULES AND HOW THEY WERE MADE

[AMERICANS have a curious reverence and respect for the Constitution. We say "curious" because the reverence and respect do not result from any clear - and accurate knowledge of either the nature of our Constitution or the history of its formation. Instead it grows out of Americans' belief that the Constitution sanctions those policies with which they agree and prohibits those that seem dangerous or oppressive. It is a common belief of Americans that any action contrary to the conception they have of their own interest is unconstitutional.

This results, as we have said, partly from a lack of information and understanding of the real nature of a constitution and partly from the lack of a critical appraisal of the origin of our own Constitutions (national and state). It is essential, therefore, that those who wish to understand our governmental system recognize (1) that any constitution is something more than a written document; (2) that the early character of our Constitutions was determined to a great extent by men who wanted to make America safe against democracy; and (3) that the political genius of the American people is to be discovered in the way they, dominated by the American creed, have gradually but persistently democratized their Constitutions.]

No. 2

CONSTITUTIONS [1]

by Howard Lee McBain

IN the most generous sense of the term every country is and has been historically, except in time of revolution or other serious upheaval, governed under something that may be called a constitution. But governments vary greatly in pattern and principle, and their constitutions vary even more greatly in such matters as form and content, source and tangibility, stability and permanence. It is in consequence difficult to define a constitution save

[1] McBain, H. L., "Constitutions," *Encyclopedia of the Social Sciences* (New York: The Macmillan Co., 1930), Vol. 4, pp. 259-262. Reprinted by permission of the publisher.

in terms of rather precisionless and therefore rather useless generality. This difficulty has not daunted publicists and other commentators. Scores of definitions might easily be assembled. Some of these define with reasonable accuracy a particular constitution or group of constitutions. But few if any of them suffice to include all that may properly be regarded as constitution and to exclude all else. Yet constitutions are not generically unreal because they elude the grasp of words. Perhaps as safe and close a definition as any is that they are the fundamental laws and practises in accordance with which governments commonly operate. But manifestly the use of the word fundamental introduces a wide margin of indefiniteness in respect of which opinions will differ.

It has long been customary to distinguish between written and unwritten constitutions, and the constitutions of the United States and of Great Britain have usually been cited as the examples par excellence of these respective types. This aspect of the subject, although a matter of schoolboy erudition, no doubt requires some mention in any general consideration of constitutions. The written constitution is usually a single document, amended or unamended from time to time as the case may be. But no constitution in the form in which it functions is wholly written; for most of these documents are relatively brief and require supplementation in important particulars. In addition to this, time invariably weaves about them political customs that become durably fixed. Occasionally such customs very nearly belie the written words of the instrument. Well-known instances in point are the customs connected with the machinery of electing an American president and the custom of holding him politically responsible as the leader of national legislation despite his designation of chief executive and despite the doctrine and constitutional rule of the separation of powers.

Even so, in the case of most written constitutions a comparatively large number of the fundamental principles or arrangements upon which the government of the country is organized for operation are found in the words of the constitution itself. It is certain that from a study of the written constitution of the United States or the French Republic or the German Reich a person wholly ignorant of the politics of the particular country could form at least a blurred mental picture of its political and governmental outlines. For a picture of such outlines under an unwritten constitution he would be compelled to rely upon commentators and explanators.

The relative merits of written and unwritten constitutions have often been debated. But much of this debate appears to proceed from the specious assumption that a people can ordinarily elect to be governed under the one or the other type of instrument. It is easy to choose to be governed under a written instrument, but probably no people ever deliberately chose the unwritten type. Unwritten constitutions have invariably been evolved from absolute monarchies or autocracies. Indeed, this would seem to be an almost indispensable condition, for unwritten constitutions rest upon customs and time is a requisite ingredient of custom. Meanwhile, however, the power of government must be exercised by someone or some group. It must, so to say, be seized. Now while the seizure and direct exercise of power by an absolute monarch or relatively small group are not only conceivable but have not infrequently happened, it is very nearly inconceivable that a large group—all of the adult males, for example—could seize power and proceed to govern without committing to writing anything concerning the organization of the government. For in any sizable country government by the many involves of necessity the application of some kind of representation. And although more or less spontaneous and irregular conventions or congresses of delegates are not unknown to history, nevertheless the representative idea, if it is to continue any length of time, invites if it does not actually compel, written arrangements. While therefore an unwritten constitution may develop around a going monarchy or close aristocracy and may in the course of time become broadly democratized, it is difficult to see how a democracy, lacking these agencies, could carry on the necessary processes of government during the period that would be required for the gradual building up of customs.

In the case of federal governments, which have in most instances been dictated by expediency if not necessity, the imperativeness of a written instrument is even more obvious. The essence of federalism is that governmental powers are divided between a central or national government and certain definitive local units of government and that this division may not be altered by the independent action of either the one or the other. Such a division even when committed to writing usually involves a considerable number of legal and practical difficulties. That it should come into being in any true form by the evolvement of mere use and wont would be almost unimaginable.

"Flexible" and "rigid" are also terms that are sometimes applied to unwritten and written constitutions. At least Lord Bryce, who coined this classification, used these terms interchangeably. But surely this is to confound substance with legalistic appearance. An unwritten constitution may or may not be flexible; a written constitution may or may not be rigid. In legal theory the British Parliament may at a stroke alter the British constitution in any respect that it chooses or the prime minister may destroy the convention of cabinet government by the simple expedient of not calling the cabinet together. But such things do not happen. In the realism of history the British constitution is not flexible. It changes very slowly.

Apart from the several extensions of the suffrage, the subordination of the House of Lords in 1911 and the altered imperial status of the self-governing dominions since . . . World War [I] it has flexed very little in the course of a century. Indeed, despite the potentialities for change that exist under unwritten constitutions it is probably true to say that they tend toward rigidity rather than flexibility. Nor is this surprising, for they rest largely upon customs and customs commonly wax and wane but slowly.

On the other hand, written constitutions may prove to be very malleable instruments. Mussolini . . . had no difficulty whatever in warping to his wishes the written constitution of Italy. [Hitler had no difficulty doing the same thing in Germany after 1933.] In Russia under the Soviet regime, although there is a written constitution, it is completely subordinated to the Communist party. The Politbureau of this party, unmentioned in the constitution, is nevertheless the most powerful governmental agency in the country. It is a law unto itself above and beyond the constitution. It may be argued, however, that such instances are exceptional and probably ephemeral. But instances may be cited of other written constitutions which in practise have lent themselves readily to change. The constitutions of many of the American states are in this category. Some of them are amended with great frequency. . . .

The flexibility or rigidity of a constitution can best be tested pragmatically. If it is often altered it is certainly flexible. If it is rarely or never altered it probably should be classed as rigid. But the curious fact is that in many if not most instances the difficulty or facility of the amending process appears to have little to do with the matter of flexibility or rigidity. The French constitutional laws [under the constitution of 1875 could be] . . . amended almost as readily and as quickly as ordinary statutes. But the fact . . . [was] that they . . . [were] seldom changed and that no amendment was adopted from 1884 to 1926. This . . . [was] certainly not referable to the perfection of the French system of government. The constitution of the old German Empire which lasted from 1871 to 1918 was not difficult to amend but was infrequently amended. An amendment to the Constitution of the United States may be proposed by a two-thirds vote of the houses of Congress and must be ratified by the state legislatures or conventions in three-fourths of the states. History discloses that the difficulty of this process lies in the requirement of a two-thirds vote of the houses, for amendments are very rarely proposed to the states by Congress. Since the adoption of the three Civil War amendments [seven] amendments have been so proposed, and only one of these has failed of ratification. But the constitutions of a number of the American states also require that amendments be proposed by a two-thirds vote of the two legislative houses and in some of these experience has demonstrated that this requirement presents no obstacle whatever to frequent amendment. The test of rigidity in a constitution is therefore not necessarily to be found in the difficulty of its amending process. It is quite possible that amendments to the American constitution would not be frequently proposed even though an ordinary majority of the houses were empowered to propose them. It is also quite impossible to say how serious the obstacle of ratification by three-fourths of the states might prove to be if Congress proposed amendments more frequently.

Since the launching of the American nation under written constitutions both for the several states of the union and for the national government the practise of committing the fundamentals of governmental organization to writing has become increasingly common. These instruments, however, have sprung from a variety of sources. A few of them have been drafted and promulgated by more or less regular legislative bodies. Such, for example, were the American Articles of Confederation of 1781 and the Austrian Constitution and Austro-Hungarian Ausgleich of 1867. During the nineteenth century a number of constitutions were granted by kings and princes —the so-called octroyed constitutions—but these instruments, whatever their legal appearance of voluntary concession or gift, were usually wrested from more or less absolute monarchs by popular demand. Such were the French constitutions of 1814 and 1830, the constitutions of the several German states proclaimed prior to 1850 and the Sardinian constitutions of 1848 which by successive proclamations became the constitution of a united Italy in 1861. The vast majority of constitutions, however, have been formed and adopted by special constituent assemblies convoked for the express purpose of making a constitution, although as might be conjectured the popular basis of these conventions has varied widely. Practically all of the American constitutions have originated in such conventions, and among those in Europe of similar source may be mentioned the constitution of Belgium, 1831, of Switzerland, 1848, of Denmark, 1849 and 1866, and of France, 1875. The constitution of the North German Confederation of 1867, which substantially became the constitution of the German Empire in 1871, was drafted by the Prussian autocracy and was accepted by the governments of the other German states; but between these important steps in the process it was also ratified by a popularly elected assembly. All of the European constitutions that were adopted after . . . World War [I and II] were drafted by specially convened assemblies. Of similar origin are the constitutions of the British self-governing colonies, for although these are in ultimate law acts of the British Parliament they have in fact emanated from dominion conventions.

The practise of drafting constitutions by constituent assemblies was to some extent a logical outgrowth of the development of the democratic idea. Power to govern was regarded as proceeding from the people acting through a relatively wide electorate. A constitution embodying fundamentals came to be conceived as a superior kind of law. But in a country of size the people's power could be exercised only by representation. An ordinary legislature was scarcely an appropriate representative body for the enactment of an extraordinary law such as a constitution. Hence a special representative assembly was called into being. While this trend of thought—not to mention the more abstract theory of social contract—must have exerted considerable influence, the role of political expediency and practical necessity must not be disregarded. For not a few constitutions were liquidations of revolutionary movements that resulted in the shattering or undermining of existing institutions. In such emergencies if the principle of democracy was to find expression an ad hoc constituent assembly for the setting up of new or the remodeling of old institutions was certainly a rational, indeed almost an indispensable, mode of procedure. It is worth noting, however, that except in the diminutive state of Switzerland the democratic principle has nowhere prevailed to the point of submitting national constitutions to acceptance or rejection by direct popular vote.

The degree to which written constitutions are regarded as superior laws varies from country to country. It finds most complete acceptance in those countries in which the courts exercise the power of refusing to give effect to laws which they hold to be in violation of the constitution. The superiority of the constitution is thus vindicated in a practical way. By this process legal theory as well as popular sentiment is distilled into reality by the more or less frequent assertion and specific application of the principle of constitutional superiority. The exercise of such a veto by the courts arose in the United States, where it has played an important institutional role not only in molding the popular conception of the sacrosanctity of the "supreme law of the land" but also in influencing the course of economic, social, and political trends and events. Despite the long period of time during which judicial supremacy has flourished in the United States and despite the numerous constitutions that have been drafted and effectuated since it first took root in American soil, it has not been widely transplanted. It was servilely copied in a number of Latin American countries but the instability of their governments has deprived it of a suitable stage for adequate performance. It operates in Australia much as it does in the United States; and to a vaguely limited extent it was incorporated into the post-war constitutions of Austria and Czechoslovakia [after World War I].

Elsewhere the supremacy of a constitution over statutory law and execu-

tive order depends for its effectiveness largely upon the degree of deference
which the government of the moment accords it. Naturally this varies
with country, time and circumstance, and it affects and is affected by the
prevailing popular attitude. But generally speaking, at least in countries
of reasonably stable politics, the prescriptions of a written constitution are
not often ruthlessly ignored by those who hold the reins of government.
For the most part constitutions are in a very real sense supreme laws.

No. 3

THE AMERICAN GOVERNMENT OF THE REVOLUTIONARY PERIOD [1]

by J. Allen Smith

THE American colonists inherited the common law and the political institutions of the mother country. The British form of government with
its King, Lords and Commons and its checks upon the people, they accepted
as a matter of course. In their political thinking they were not consciously
more democratic than their kinsmen across the Atlantic. Many of them,
it is true, had left England to escape what they regarded as tyranny and
oppression. But to the *form* of the English government as such they had
no objection. The evils which they experienced were attributed solely to the
selfish spirit in which the government was administered.

The conditions, however, were more favorable for the development of a
democratic spirit here than in the mother country. The immigrants to
America represented the more active, enterprising and dissatisfied elements
of the English people. Moreover, there was no hereditary aristocratic class
in the colonies and less inequality in the distribution of wealth. This
approach to industrial and social equality prepared the mind for the ideas
of political equality which needed only the stimulus of a favorable opportunity to ensure their speedy development.

This opportunity came with the outbreak of the American Revolution
which at the outset was merely an organized and armed protest against
what the colonies regarded as an arbitrary and unconstitutional exercise of
the taxing power. As there was no widespread or general dissatisfaction
with the *form* of the English government, there is scarcely room for doubt
that if England had shown a more prudent and conciliatory spirit toward
the colonies, the American Revolution would have been averted. No sooner,

[1] J. A. Smith, *The Spirit of American Government* (New York: The Macmillan Co.,
1907), Ch. 2. Reprinted by permission of the publisher.

however, had the controversy with the mother country reached the acute revolutionary stage, than the forces which had been silently and unconsciously working toward democracy, found an opportunity for political expression. The spirit of resistance to what was regarded as unconstitutional taxation rapidly assumed the form of avowed opposition to the English Constitution itself. The people were ready for a larger measure of political democracy than the English Constitution of the eighteenth century permitted. To this new and popular view of government the Declaration of Independence gave expression. It contained an emphatic, formal and solemn disavowal of the political theory embodied in the English Constitution; affirmed that "all men are created equal"; that governments derive "their just powers from the consent of the governed"; and declared the right of the people to alter or to abolish the form of the government "and to institute new government, laying its foundation on such principles and organizing its powers in such form, as to them shall seem most likely to effect their safety and happiness." This was a complete and sweeping repudiation of the English political system, which recognized the right of monarchy and aristocracy to thwart the will of the people.

To what extent the Declaration of Independence voiced the general sentiment of the colonies is largely a matter of conjecture. It is probable, however, that its specification of grievances and its vigorous arraignment of the colonial policy of the English government appealed to many who had little sympathy with its express and implied advocacy of democracy. It is doubtless true that many were carried along with the Revolutionary movement who by temperament and education were strongly attached to English political traditions. It is safe to conclude that a large proportion of those who desired to see American independence established did not believe in thorough-going political democracy.

Besides those who desired independence without being in sympathy with the political views expressed in the Declaration of Independence, there were many others who were opposed to the whole Revolutionary movement. The numerical strength of the Tories can not be accurately estimated; but it is certain that a large proportion, probably not less than one-third of the total population of the colonies, did not approve the war.

"In the first place, there was, prior to 1776, the official class; that is, the men holding various positions in the civil and military and naval services of the government, their immediate families, and their social connections. All such persons may be described as inclining to the Loyalist view in consequence of official bias.

"Next were certain colonial politicians who, it may be admitted, took a rather selfish and unprincipled view of the whole dispute, and who, counting

on the probable, if not inevitable, success of the British arms in such a conflict, adopted the Loyalist side, not for conscience' sake, but for profit's sake,
and in the expectation of being rewarded for their fidelity by offices and
titles, and especially by the confiscated estates of the rebels after the rebels
themselves should have been defeated, and their leaders hanged or sent
into exile.

"As composing still another class of Tories, may be mentioned probably
a vast majority of those who stood for the commercial interests, for the
capital and tangible property of the country, and who, with the instincts
natural to persons who have something considerable to lose, disapproved
of all measures for pushing the dispute to the point of disorder, riot and
civil war.

"Still another class of Loyalists was made up of people of professional
training and occupation—clergymen, physicians, lawyers, teachers—a clear
majority of whom seem to have been set against the ultimate measures of
the Revolution.

"Finally, and in general, it may be said that a majority of those who, of
whatever occupation, of whatever grade of culture or of wealth, would now
be described as conservative people, were Loyalists during the American
Revolution."

These classes prior to the Revolution had largely shaped and molded
public opinion; but their opposition to the movement which they were
powerless to prevent, destroyed their influence, for the time being, in
American politics. The place which they had hitherto held in public esteem
was filled by a new class of leaders more in sympathy with the newly born
spirit of liberalism. This gave to the Revolutionary movement a distinctly
democratic character.

This drift toward democracy is seen in the changes made in the state
constitutions after the outbreak of the Revolution. At the close of the
colonial period, nearly all the state governments were modeled after the
government of Great Britain. Each colony had its legislative body elected
by the qualified voters and corresponding in a general way to the House
of Commons. In all the colonies except Pennsylvania and Georgia there
was also an upper legislative house or council whose consent was necessary
before laws could be enacted. The members composing this branch of the
legislature were appointed by the governor except in Massachusetts where
they were elected by the lower branch of the legislature, subject to a negative by the royal governor, and in Rhode Island and Connecticut where
they were chosen by the electorate.

The governor was elected by the voters only in Rhode Island and Connecticut; and in all the other colonies he was appointed by the proprietaries

or the Crown, and, though independent of the people, exercised many important powers. He was commander-in-chief of the armed forces of the colony; appointed the judges and all other civil and military officers; appointed and could suspend the council, which was usually the upper branch of the legislature; he could convene and dissolve the legislature and had besides an unqualified veto on all laws; he also had an unrestricted pardoning power.

The possession of these far-reaching powers gave to the irresponsible executive branch of the colonial government a position of commanding importance. This was not the case, however, in Connecticut and Rhode Island. Although the governor in these two colonies was responsible to the voters, inasmuch as he was elected by them, still he had no veto, and the appointing power was in the hands of the legislature.

The tidal-wave of democracy, which swept over the colonies during the Revolution, largely effaced the monarchical and aristocratic features of the colonial governments. Connecticut and Rhode Island, which already had democratic constitutions, were the only states which did not modify their form of government during this period. All the rest adopted new constitutions which show in a marked degree the influence of the democratic movement. In these new constitutions we see a strong tendency to subordinate the executive branch of the government and confer all important powers on the legislature. In the four New England states and in New York the governor was elected by the qualified voters; in all the rest he was chosen by the legislature. In ten states during this period his term was one year; in South Carolina it was two and in New York and Delaware it was three years. In addition to this the six Southern states restricted his re-election. Besides, there was in every state an executive or privy council which the governor was required to consult on all important matters. This was usually appointed by the legislature and constituted an important check on the governor.

The power to veto legislation was abolished in all but two states. In Massachusetts the governor, and in New York the Council of Revision composed of the governor and the chancellor and judges of the Supreme Court, had a qualified veto power. But a two-thirds majority in both houses of the legislature could override the veto of the governor in Massachusetts, or that of the Council of Revision in New York. The pardoning power of the governor was quite generally restricted. In five states he was allowed to exercise it only with the advice or consent of the council. In three states, where the advice or consent of a council was not required, he could, subject to certain restrictions, grant pardons except where "the law shall otherwise direct." The constitution of Georgia in express terms deprived the governor of all right to exercise this power.

The appointing power of the governor was also taken away or restricted. In four of the eleven states adopting new constitutions during this period he was allowed to exercise it jointly with the council. In six states it was given to the legislature, or to the legislature and council. The power of the governor to dissolve the legislature or either branch of it was everywhere abolished.

The supremacy of the legislature under these early state constitutions is seen also in the manner of the appointment, the tenure and the powers of the judiciary. In nine states the judges were elected by the state legis-lature, either with or without the consent of a council. In Maryland, Massa-chusetts, New Hampshire, and Pennsylvania they were appointed by the governor with the consent of the council. But this really amounted to indi-rect legislative appointment in Maryland, since both the governor and coun-cil in that state were elected annually by the legislature. The legislature also had a voice in the appointment of judges in Pennsylvania, New Hamp-shire and Massachusetts, since it elected the executive in the first and the council in the others. In nine states, then, the judges were elected directly by the legislature; in one indirectly by the legislature; in the other three the legislature participated in their election through an executive or a coun-cil of its own choosing.

In every state the judges could be impeached by the lower branch of the legislature and expelled from office on conviction by the senate or other tri-bunal, as the constitution prescribed. Moreover, in six states they could be removed according to the English custom by the executive on an address from both branches of the legislature. The term of office of the judges in eight states was during good behavior. In New Jersey and Pennsylvania they were appointed for seven years, and in Rhode Island, Connecticut, and Georgia they were chosen annually.

The legislature under these early state constitutions was hampered neither by the executive nor by the courts. It had all law-making power in its own hands. In no state could the courts thwart its purpose by declaring its acts null and void. Unchecked by either executive or judicial veto its supremacy was undisputed.

From the foregoing synopsis of the state constitutions of this period it is evident that their framers rejected entirely the English theory of checks and balances. The principle of separation of powers as expounded by Montesquieu and Blackstone, found little favor with those who controlled American politics at this time. Instead of trying to construct a state govern-ment composed of coordinate branches, each acting as a check upon the others, their aim was to make the legislature supreme. In this respect the early state constitutions anticipated much of the later development of the English government itself.

The checks and balances, and separation of powers, which characterized the government of England and her American colonies in the eighteenth century, resulted from the composite character of the English Constitution —its mixture of monarchy, aristocracy, and democracy. It is not surprising, then, that with the temporary ascendancy of the democratic spirit, the system of checks should have been largely discarded.

This democratic tendency is seen also in our first federal constitution, the Articles of Confederation, which was framed under the impulse of the Revolutionary movement. This document is interesting as an expression of the political philosophy of the Revolution, but like the state constitutions of that period, it has had few friendly critics among later political writers. Much emphasis has been put upon its defects, which were many, while but little attention has been given to the political theory which it imperfectly embodied. That it failed to provide a satisfactory general government may be admitted; but this result must not be accepted as conclusive proof that the principles underlying it were altogether false.

The chief feature of the Articles of Confederation was the entire absence of checks and balances. All the powers conferred upon the general government were vested in a single legislative body called the Continental Congress, which was unchecked by a distinct executive or judiciary. In this respect it bore a striking resemblance to the English government of to-day with its omnipotent House of Commons. But, unlike the English government of to-day, its powers were few and narrowly limited. Its failure was due, perhaps, not to the fact that the powers granted to the confederation were vested exclusively in a single legislative body, but to the fact that the powers thus granted were not sufficient for maintaining a strong and effective central government.

The reason for the weakness of the general government under the Articles of Confederation is obvious to the student of American history. It was only gradually, and as necessity compelled cooperation between the colonies, that the sentiment in favor of political union developed. And though some tendencies in this direction are seen more than a century before the American Revolution, the progress toward a permanent union was slow and only the pressure of political necessity finally brought it about.

As early as 1643 Massachusetts, Plymouth, Connecticut and New Haven formed a "perpetual confederation" under the name of the "United Colonies of New England." The motive for this union was mainly offence and defence against the Indian tribes and the Dutch, though provision was also made for the extradition of servants and fugitives from justice. The management of the common interest of these colonies was vested in a board of eight commissioners—two from each colony—and, in transacting the business of the confederacy, the consent of six of the eight commissioners was required. Any matter which could not be thus disposed of was to be referred to the four colonial legislatures. The general government thus provided for could not intermeddle "with the government of any of the jurisdictions." No provision was made for amending the "Articles of Confederation," and only by the unanimous consent of these colonies could any other colony be admitted to the confederacy. This union lasted for over forty years.

Again in 1754 the pressure of impending war with the French and Indians brought together at Albany a convention of delegates from seven colonies north of the Potomac. A plan of union drafted by Benjamin Franklin was recommended by this convention, but it was not regarded with favor either by the colonies or by the English government. The former regarded it as going too far in the direction of subordinating the separate colonies to a central colonial authority, while for the latter it was too democratic.

The union of all the colonies under the Articles of Confederation was finally brought about through the pressure of military necessity during the Revolution. Nor is it surprising, in view of the history of the American colonies, that they reluctantly yielded up any powers to a central authority. We must bear in mind that the Revolution was in a measure a democratic movement, and that democracy was then found only in local government. The general governments of all countries were at that time monarchical or aristocratic. Tyranny in the eighteenth century was associated in the minds of the people with an undue extension or abuse of the powers exercised by the undemocratic central government. It is not surprising, then, that the Revolutionary federal constitution, the Articles of Confederation, should have failed to provide a general government sufficiently strong to satisfy the needs of the country after the return of peace.

It must not be inferred, however, that the political changes which immediately followed the outbreak of the Revolution were in the nature of sweeping democratic reforms. Much that was thoroughly undemocratic remained intact. The property qualifications for the suffrage were not disturbed by the Revolutionary movement and were finally abolished only after the lapse of nearly half a century. The cruel and barbarous system of imprisonment for debt which the colonies had inherited from England, and which often made the lot of the unfortunate debtor worse than that of the chattel slave, continued in several of the states until long after the Revolution. Marked as was the democratic tendency during the first few years of our independence, it nevertheless left untouched much that the progress of democracy has since abolished.

No. 4

WRITING THE NATIONAL CONSTITUTION [1]

by J. Mark Jacobson

WE cannot hope to understand the political theory underlying the framing of the Constitution without an analysis of the conditions existing between the battle of Yorktown and the calling of the Philadelphia convention. No movement in world history is a better illustration of social and economic determinism; no accomplishment, a more complete rebound of the pendulum.

During the Revolution democratic political ideas had run rampant. The social contract theory, especially that of Paine, had glorified the "people." And under the leadership of such men as Samuel Adams in Massachusetts and Patrick Henry in Virginia, political control had passed from the aristocratic merchants and plantation owners to the petty traders and small farmers. In the struggle to determine who should rule at home, the conservative elements had lost ground. Revolutionary thought had looked upon government as a necessary evil. Government consequently became weak and decentralized. State governments had powerless executives and omnipotent legislatures. The central government under the Articles of Confederation was almost non-existent. Congress could act only through the states; it possessed no authority over individuals. It could raise no taxes; it could only request requisitions from the states. The Articles endowed Congress with authority over foreign affairs, but granted it no power to enforce treaties. The Continental Congress had carried the Revolution to a successful conclusion, but before long some states refused to send delegates or to pay their quotas. Congress remained only an ineffective symbol of a loose union.

As a consequence of this political disorganization, and as an aftermath of the war, economic chaos set in. Colonial independence from Great Britain meant withdrawal from the British mercantile system. The American

[1] J. M. Jacobson, *The Development of American Political Thought: a Documentary History* (New York: D. Appleton-Century Co., 1932), pp. 164-179. Reprinted by permission of the publisher.

merchants found the ports of England and the West Indies closed against them; and the impotent central government could not negotiate favorable trade agreements with other European powers. The loss of foreign trade threatened to wipe out those merchants who had cast their lot with the Revolutionists. Interstate trade became even more chaotic; jealousies developed among the states; each desired to keep money from going beyond its boundaries. Like modern nations, they endeavored to build up their own business prosperity at the expense of their neighbors. Thus New York taxed the produce of Connecticut farmers and destroyed their only profitable market. The seaport states financed their governments through imposts on European goods passing through their harbors, but destined for consumption in neighboring states. Madison thus picturesquely depicted the unhappy plight of those states not having seaports: "New Jersey placed between Phil^a and N. York, was likened to a cask tapped at both ends; and N. Carolina between Virg^a & S. Carolina to a patient bleeding at both Arms." The existence of different currencies in each of the thirteen states likewise hampered interstate trade. A Rhode Island merchant could not trade in Massachusetts without first exchanging his money into the currency of Massachusetts. The financial mechanism of present-day foreign trade did not then exist; even if the value of money had remained stable, the necessity of exchange would have discouraged trading. The continuous fluctuation of the depreciated state currencies, however, made commerce so hazardous as to be almost impossible. Furthermore, the attitude of the state courts toward non-resident creditors frequently prevented the collection of debts contracted in interstate trade. Truly, Madison wrote: "Most of our political evils may be traced to our commercial ones."

Chaotic finances likewise characterized the post-Revolutionary period. In an effort to finance the Revolution, the Continental Congress and each of the states had floated large bond issues and had printed much paper money. Both the securities and the money, unsupported save by the hope of victory and of possible payment, depreciated rapidly in value. In Virginia by 1781 the Continental notes "fell to 1000 for 1," wrote Jefferson, "and then expired, as it had done in other States, without a single groan." Jefferson records that he sold some land before the issuance of paper currency, but that he "did not receive the money till it was not worth Oak leaves."

The depreciation of money resulted in an interesting and important class struggle. The creditor groups suffered greatly. The merchants who sold on credit received upon payment a greatly decreased purchasing power; meanwhile, they had to pay their European creditors in gold or silver. The debtor groups, on the other hand, benefited from this situation. In the spring the farmer bought seed and provisions for repayment at harvest season; also, his farm usually had a heavy, long-term mortgage. With the declining value of money and the corresponding increase in farm prices, the farmer could repay his debts with fewer bushels of wheat or corn. Paper money thus proved valuable to him. It supplied the frontier com-munities for the first time with a sufficient medium of exchange. Consequently, the debtor groups opposed a stabilization in currency and favored further operation of the money presses.

The debtor-creditor conflict, which, as we have noted, began in the pre-Revolutionary days, now took an acute form. Constant agitation in favor of fiat money, lax bankruptcy acts, and installment laws punctuated politics. In some states, as Rhode Island, the agrarians dominated the legislature and enacted debtor laws. In Massachusetts the attempt of the courts to enforce debts and foreclose on mortgages led to a violent reaction on the part of the agrarian debtors. Led by Shays, the farmers of western Massachusetts rose in revolt. By armed opposition, they shut the courts—those pernicious institutions of aristocracy—and prevented the legal collection of debts. The militia, financed by the private subscriptions of Boston merchants, put down the rebellion. But the memory of Shays's attack struck terror into the conservative hearts of the commercial and financial class. This incident, more than any other, brought about the Constitutional Convention of 1787.

The depreciation of public securities and paper currency led to another important phenomenon. Just as after the World War heavy speculation occurred in the depreciated German mark and Russian ruble, so during and after the Revolution speculation took place in bonds, money, and land certificates. The moneyed men gambled on the possibility of repayment. But as long as the central government could not raise revenues, it could not redeem its issues. As long as agrarian debtors controlled the state legislatures, the value of their securities declined. And until the central government was sufficiently strong to build roads to the West and to afford protection against Indian attacks, settlers would move there in but small numbers, and the value of land certificates would not rise. The immediate outlook for the speculators was thus dark and uncertain.

These political and economic factors characterized the post-Revolutionary period and produced the American Constitution. The principal purposes to be served by the new government, according to *The Federalist,* were:

The common defence of the members; the preservation of the public peace, as well against internal convulsions as external attacks; the regulation of commerce with other nations, and between the states; the superintendence of our intercourse political and commercial, with foreign countries.

Edmund Randolph, in the opening address of the Constitutional Convention, expressed a similar view of the needs of the existing situation. Commercial chaos, depreciated currency, Shays's rebellion, loomed large in his mind.

> The character of such a governme(nt) ought to secure 1. against foreign invasion: 2. against dissentions between members of the Union, or seditions in particular states: 3. to p(ro)cure to the several States various blessings, of which an isolated situation was i(n)capable: 4. to be able to defend itself against incroachment: & 5. to be paramount to the state constitutions.

In speaking of the defects of the Confederation, Randolph professed:

> A high respect for its authors, and considered them as having done all that patriots could do, in the then infancy of the science of constitutions, & of confederacies,—when the inefficiency of requisitions was unknown— no commercial discord had arisen among any states—no rebellion had appeared as in Massts.—foreign debts had not become urgent—the havoc of paper money had not been foreseen—treaties had not been violated—and perhaps nothing better could be obtained from the jealousy of the states with regard to their sovereignty.

The existing political and economic conditions injured the large property groups. The merchants and manufacturers suffered through the loss of foreign trade and the chaotic obstacles against interstate commerce. The creditor class, in general, lost through the constant decline in the value of money. Speculators in securities, currency, and land desired a rise in values. A swing of the pendulum in that direction was impossible under the political situation of a weak central government and agrarian and popular control in the state legislatures. At this time, too, the large plantation owners of the South feared slave uprisings and preferred a strong central government for defense. And finally, possible repetition of Shays's rebellion of agrarian debtors frightened the conservative lovers of law, order, and security.

It was the representatives of these economic and social groups that convened in Philadelphia in May, 1787. They framed the American Constitution. Not one member represented, in his immediate personal economic interests, the small farming or mechanic classes. The agrarian legislature of Rhode Island refused to send delegates to such a capitalistic gathering. Patrick Henry, the populist leader of Virginia and a delegate from that state, "smellt a rat" and refused to attend. A majority of the delegates were lawyers by profession, and most of them came from towns, on or near the coast, where property was largely concentrated. Forty of the fifty-five members were public security holders. With the exception of New York and possibly Delaware, each state had one or more prominent representatives who held large amounts of securities. At least fourteen members held lands for speculation, and twenty-four had property in the form of money loaned at interest. Eleven delegates were interested in mercantile, manufacturing, and shipping lines. And fifteen were slave-owners. Beard, in his *Economic Interpretation of the Constitution,* has declared that:

> The overwhelming majority of members, at least five-sixths, were immediately, directly, and personally interested in the outcome of their labor at Philadelphia, and were to a greater or less extent economic beneficiaries from the adoption of the Constitution.

Beveridge, in his monumental study of Federalism, *The Life of John Marshall,* writes:

> Too much emphasis cannot be put upon the fact that the mercantile and financial interests were the weightiest of all the influences for the Constitution; the debtor and agricultural interests the strongest groups against it. It deserves repetition, for a proper understanding of the craft and force practiced by both sides in the battle over ratification, that those who owed debts were generally against the Constitution and practically all to whom debts were due were for the new Government.

The experience and the economic needs of the conservative propertied group that met at Philadelphia fashioned their attitudes. The delegates distrusted popular democracy and state legislatures, frequently agrarian in composition. Their main desire was for stability. Beveridge thus cogently depicts their mental state:

> Since the victory at Yorktown a serious alteration had taken place in the views of many who had fought hardest for Independence and popular government. These men were as strong as ever for the building of a separate and distinct National entity; but they no longer believed in the wisdom or virtue of democracy without extensive restrictions. They had come to think that, at the very best, the crude ore of popular judgment could be made to enrich sound counsels only when passed through many screens that would rid it of the crudities of passion, whimsicality, interest, ignorance, and dishonesty, which, they believed, inhered in it. Such men esteemed less and less a people's government and valued more and more a good government. And the idea grew that this meant a government the principal purpose of which was to enforce order, facilitate business, and safeguard property.

American historians have long written the story of the Constitutional Convention as an epic of conflict and compromise. They have devoted much attention to the struggle between the large and small states, with the resulting equal representation in the Senate. Attention, too, has been paid to the battle between the commercial North and the agricultural South, and to the compromises over the slave trade and the counting of slaves in connection with representation. But an examination of the realities of the proceedings at Philadelphia reveals, amidst the discord, a fundamental harmony. In the essential objectives of the Convention, virtual unanimity existed. The delegates differed only in the means of achieving their common ends. Not the conflicts and compromises, but the uniform distrust of democracy and the universal desire for stability, stand out in clear perspective.

The secret sessions of the Convention permitted the members utter freedom of expression. No speeches to the gallery, no orations for popular consumption, marked the meetings. With brutal frankness, the delegates passed judgment on the demerits of government by the people. Randolph of Virginia struck the keynote in the opening speech of the Convention:

> Our chief danger arises from the democratic parts of our constitutions. It is a maxim which I hold incontrovertible, that the powers of government exercised by the people swallow up the other branches. None of the constitutions have provided sufficient checks against the democracy. The feeble Senate of Virginia is a phantom. Maryland has a more powerful senate, but the late distractions in that State, have discovered that it is not powerful enough. The check established in the constitution of New York and Massachusetts is yet a stronger barrier against democracy, but they all seem insufficient.

Alexander Hamilton, a leader at the Convention and later the moving spirit in Washington's administration, "acknowledged himself not to think favorably of Republican Government." He addressed his remarks to "those who did think favorably of it, in order to prevail on them to tone their Government as high as possible." An economic determinism characterized Hamilton's speeches. In every community where industry is encouraged, he maintained, there will be a division into the few and the many, into creditors and debtors; hence separate interests will arise. If you give all the power to the many, they will oppress the few.

> To the want of this check we owe our paper money—instalment laws &c. To the proper adjustment of it the British owe the excellence of their Constitution. Their house of Lords is a most noble institution. Having nothing to hope for by a change, and a sufficient interest by means of their property, in being faithful to the National interest, they form a permanent barrier agst. every pernicious innovation, whether attempted on the part of the

Crown or of the Commons. No temporary Senate will have firmness en'o' to answer the purpose.

Inequality of property would, he felt, exist as long as liberty lasted, and would unavoidably result from that very liberty itself. This inequality of property constituted the great and fundamental distinction in society.

> All communities divide themselves into the few and the many. The first are the rich and well born, the other the mass of the people. The voice of the people has been said to be the voice of God; and however generally this maxim has been quoted and believed, it is not true in fact. The people are turbulent and changing; they seldom judge or determine right. Give therefore to the first class a distinct, permanent share in the government. They will check the unsteadiness of the second, and as they cannot receive any advantage by a change, they will ever maintain good government. Can a democratic assembly who annually revolve in the mass of the people, be supposed steadily to pursue the public good? Nothing but a permanent body can check the imprudence of democracy.

What is the remedy? "We ought to go as far in order to attain stability and permanency, as republican principles will admit." Hamilton was willing to grant life tenures to the senators and the President. At the very least, the Constitution should, he said, provide a seven-year term for the Senate in order that the upper chamber might have "a permanent will, a weighty interest, which would answer essential purposes." Thus did Hamilton express his distrust of democracy and his desire for stability.

James Madison played a leading role at the Convention; his influence was such that historians have labeled him "the Father of the Constitution." While he later became a follower of Jefferson, at this time he was an ardent nationalist and conservative. Madison frequently rose to demonstrate the necessity of checks upon the propertyless classes. In a speech on the suffrage, he felt that the freeholders of the country would be the the safest depositories of "Republican liberty." In future times, he feared, a great majority of the people would be not only without land, but without any sort of property. These would either combine under the influence of their common situation, in which case the rights of property and the public liberty would not be secure, or they would become the tools of opulence and ambition. In discussing the Senate, Madison's anti-democratic attitude again found expression. He argued that a limited number of enlightened citizens was a necessary defense against the impetuous counsel, fickleness, and passion of a numerous popular assembly. Like Hamilton, he held that in all civilized countries the people fall into different classes having a real or supposed difference of interests. Creditors and debtors, farmers, merchants and manufacturers, rich and poor—these classes divide society. In time a growth of population would of necessity increase the proportion of those who labor under all the hardships of life. While no agrarian attempt at a more equal distribution of property had as yet been made in this country, symptoms of a leveling spirit had, he claimed, appeared sufficiently in certain quarters to give warning of the future danger.

The government we mean to erect is intended to last for ages. The landed interest, at present, is prevalent; but in process of time, when we approximate to the states and kingdoms of Europe; when the number of landholders shall be comparatively small, through the various means of trade and manufactures, will not the landed interests be overbalanced in future elections, and unless wisely provided against, what will become of your government? In England, at this day, if elections were open to all classes of people, the property of the landed proprietors would be insecure. An agrarian law would soon take place. If these observations be just, our government ought to secure the permanent interests of the country against innovation. Landholders ought to have a share in the government, to support these invaluable interests and to balance and check the other. They ought to be so constituted as to protect the minority of the opulent against the majority. The senate, therefore, ought to be this body; and to answer these purposes, they ought to have permanency and stability. Various have been the propositions; but my opinion is, the longer they continue in office, the better will those views be answered.

A few other statements will indicate the existing distrust of democracy and the prevalent desire for stability. Elbridge Gerry was a leading Massachusetts merchant; a decade later he turned against the Federalists, and even in 1788 he found the Constitution drawn up by the Convention too aristocratic for his support. Yet, even Gerry admitted that heretofore he had been too republican; he had, he said, been taught by experience the danger of the leveling spirit. "The evils we experience flow from the excess of democracy. The people do not want virtue; they are the dupes of pretended patriots."
Governeur Morris of Pennsylvania held that there was as much reason to intrust the suffrage to children as to the ignorant and the dependent.

Give the votes to the people who have no property, and they will sell them to the rich who will be able to buy them.
The time is not distant when this Country will abound with mechanics and manufacturers who will receive their bread from their employers. Will such men be the secure & faithful Guardians of liberty? Will they be the impregnable barrier agst. aristocracy?

Roger Sherman of Connecticut was one of the few delegates who had risen from poverty through his own efforts; but with his rise in the economic scale, he had left behind all sympathy for the masses. The people, he held, should have as little as may be to do about the government. "They want information and are constantly liable to be misled."

John Dickinson of Delaware had written learned dissertations against British taxation of the colonies; at the Convention, however, he argued for vesting the rights of suffrage in the freeholders of the country. He considered them the best guardians of liberty, and felt that to restrict the suffrage to them was a necessary defense against "the dangerous influence of those multitudes without property & without principle, with which our country like all others, will in time abound."

Thus spoke the framers of the Constitution. Distrust of democracy, acquired through a decade of proletariat-agrarian-debtor control in local politics, dominated their thinking. A desire for stability, developed through commercial and fiscal chaos, directed their construction of the new governmental system. Benjamin Franklin, an aged delegate at the Convention, cynically remarked:

> Few men in public affairs act from a mere view of the good of their country, whatever they may pretend; and though their activity may bring real good to their country, they do not act from a spirit of benevolence.

The American Constitution is the resultant of two important factors: the economic and political situation after the Revolution, and the attitude which this situation inspired in the delegates at Philadelphia. The framers of the Constitution were not visionary idealists; they were practical men of affairs. They opposed popular democracy and desired upper class control in government. Naturally, they wrote their economic and social views into the document.

The Revolutionary theorists had glorified the "people"; the Convention delegates considered the masses, "turbulent and changing." The early state constitutions had trusted the legislature as the safest agent of the sovereign people; the Constitution of 1787 placed checks on the fickleness and passion of popular assemblies. Just as the Revolutionary state constitutions had accepted the thesis of the separation of powers, so likewise did the framers at Philadelphia; but in their equilibrium of departments, the scales weighed heavily against the legislature.

The Constitution minimized the role of the legislature and endeavored to prevent that organ from coming under popular domination. The Convention encountered considerable difficulty in framing the suffrage restrictions to operate in electing members of the House of Representatives. Finally, they adopted the provision that: "The Electors in each State shall have the Qualifications requisite for Electors of the most numerous Branch of the State Legislature." On its face, this section appears extremely liberal. But we must remember that almost every state had at this time property qualifications for voting. The turbulent masses were to play no role in the new regime.

Even after such restriction, the framers still distrusted the legislature. They adopted a bicameral system so that the permanency of the Senate might check the impetuous counsels of the lower chamber. Furthermore, to the independent executive they gave a strong veto; and no elected council shared the power with the executive, as was the case in several of the states. Congress could override a presidential veto only by a two-thirds vote of each house; and at the end of a congressional session the legislature could not check the President at all. Finally, the framers subjected Congress to judicial control. Critics of the Supreme Court frequently accuse Marshall of usurping the power of judicial review in the case of *Marbury* v. *Madison*. A careful analysis, however, of the debates at Philadelphia, of the proceedings of the state ratifying conventions, and of the Federalist Papers, shows that the framers of the Constitution intended that the Supreme Court should act as a check upon Congress. Suffrage restrictions, bicameralism, executive veto, judicial review—all were brought into play to guard against the dangers of populist or debtor legislation.

The Constitution-makers not only feared democracy, but also desired stability. Above all, the new government must render their property and social system secure. Consequently, they constructed a government of balances devised to prevent the majority from ever dominating "the minority of the opulent." They erected four separate units of government: a House of Representatives, a Senate, a President, and a Supreme Court. For each they provided a distinct method of selection. The qualified voters of each state were to elect the representatives; both branches of the legislature were to choose a state's senators. A specially constructed and entirely independent electoral college was to select the chief magistrate. The framers wanted no popular participation. Each state, through either its legislature or its electorate, was to choose a body of men; these colleges, each meeting in its own state, were to be uninstructed; they were to deliberate, to nominate, and to elect the President and Vice-President. Should this scheme fail, then the choice was to fall to the House of Representatives—the House, however, elected two years previously. And finally, the President was to appoint the justices of the Supreme Court, subject to senatorial confirmation. Similarly the framers established a different time-schedule of election for each unit. To the House of Representatives they gave a two-year term. The Senate was to stay in office for six years, one-third retiring biennially. The President's tenure was made four years; and the Supreme Court justices were to hold office during good behavior.

This scheme of balances, with its different methods and time-schedules of election, rendered the new government virtually safe from the dangers of popular, agrarian domination. In order for the debtor class to bring about issues of fiat paper money, they must now so dominate the state electorates as to win the House of Representatives, the state legislatures for a period of years as to win the Senate, and the electoral colleges as to win the presidency. Should the agrarians or the propertyless townspeople, by any chance, break through this carefully arranged system of different methods and times of election, the Supreme Court would still stand intact as the bulwark of property. The life tenure of the judges would render them independent and fearless in their opposition to the legislature. Later events actually demonstrated the foresight of the framers in this important matter. In 1800 the Jeffersonian Republicans captured the national government; but the judiciary, entrenched with staunch, conservative Federalists, acted as an effective check. Marshall and his associates, as we shall see, safeguarded the propertied classes.

A popular majority, during a period of temporary control, might, however, contrive to subvert this carefully arranged scheme. Against even this exigency the framers provided. They established a difficult method of constitutional amendment. A constitutional revolution must secure the sanction of two-thirds of the House of Representatives, two-thirds of the state-controlled Senate, and both legislative branches, or special conventions, in three-fourths of the states. The framers built well. Thus far only nineteen amendments [now twenty-one] have run this difficult gauntlet. Of these, the first ten, or the Bill of Rights, became law immediately as part of the bargain of ratification. The thirteenth, fourteenth, and fifteenth amendments were the aftermath of civil war. . . . two amendments passed Congress during the upheaval of the World War. Thus, only four [now six] constitutional changes have occurred during periods of normal political functioning. Truly, said Madison, "The government we mean to erect is intended to last for ages."

The powers granted to the federal government reflect the economic and political needs of the framers. The old Confederation acted only through the states; the new government could act directly upon the individual. The federal government was to have its own tax collectors, its own attorneys, its own marshals, its own criminal courts, its own army. The Constitution empowered Congress to lay and collect its own "Taxes, Duties, Imposts, and Excises"; no longer need it beg requisitions from the states. Direct taxes, however, Congress must apportion according to population—a provision included with a view to reconciling the rural interests. The taxing power and the immediate control over individuals formed the basis for all the other powers granted to the federal government.

Congress was given authority "to regulate Commerce with foreign Nations, and among the several States, and with the Indian Tribes." No longer was a labyrinth of state regulations to render trade chaotic. National commerce demanded national uniformity. The power "to coin Money, regulate Value thereof . . . and fix the Standard of Weights and Measures" likewise eliminated the previous obstacles to profitable interstate commerce. Thus did the mercantile and manufacturing groups at the Convention guard their interests.

Speculators, too, found protection. The Constitution provided: "All Debts contracted and Engagements entered into, before the Adoption of this Constitution, shall be as valid against the United States under this Constitution, as under the Confederation." This section guaranteed the repayment of the securities issued by the Continental Congress. To Congress the framers gave power "To dispose of and make all needful Rules and Regulations respecting the Territory or other Property belonging to the United States." Congress could admit new states into the Union and could establish post roads. By the exercise of these powers, the western lands would be opened, migration encouraged, and land certificates increased in value.

Still further, the framers provided for national peace and domestic security. Congress could raise and support an army, provide and maintain a navy, call forth the militia "to execute the Laws of the Union, suppress Insurrections and repel Invasions." These military provisions would enable the federal government to defend itself against foreign and domestic foes. The navy would defend our commerce, and the President might threaten its use to secure favorable trade treaties. The army and militia would put down class uprisings and slave revolts. The framers had not forgotten Shays's Rebellion. Shortly afterwards, the propertied Federalists were to use military force against a second agrarian revolt—the Whiskey Rebellion of the Pennsylvania corn growers.

In establishing the federal judiciary, the delegates at Philadelphia wrote into the Constitution safeguards for their commercial interests. Under the Articles of Confederation, New York merchants, for example, had experienced considerable difficulty in collecting debts in Connecticut; the state courts, often popularly controlled, had discriminated against non-resident creditors. To the new federal courts the framers granted jurisdiction in controversies between citizens of different states. Collection of interstate debts now rested in impartial courts. The federal judiciary also heard cases between a state and citizens of another state. Holders of state securities and land grants could now sue for the collection of their claims. All such grants of power to the federal government tended to eliminate those political and economic ills that had plagued the propertied classes. The new regime could maintain domestic peace and security, develop commerce and industry, and repay public security holders in full.

The framers, however, did not stop here. The populist state legislatures had attacked their property. This danger, too, they must eliminate. Article I, section 10, of the Constitution placed rigid restrictions on the states. No state hereafter should coin money, emit bills of credit, make anything but gold and silver legal tender in payment of debts, pass any *ex post facto* acts or laws impairing the obligation of contracts, or, without the consent of Congress, lay any taxes on imports or exports, or collect tonnage duties. Thus the Constitution-makers ruled out paper money, installment acts, lenient bankruptcy laws, repudiation of securities, and interstate tariff barriers. Thus they prevented any direct attack upon property. It is instructive to note that the Convention adopted these prohibitions with virtually no debate.

The framers of the Constitution distrusted popular democracy and desired stability. They built with their eyes well trained on their economic and political experiences. The structure of the new government eliminated popular rule and emphasized stability. The powers granted to the central government permitted it to eradicate the economic evils that oppressed the propertied groups. And the restrictions upon the states prevented future agrarian attacks.

The framers of this economic and social document naturally faced a serious problem in its ratification. In the first place, the state legislatures had authorized their delegates merely to amend the Articles of Confederation; the Convention, however, had drawn up a new document. In the second place, the Articles of Confederation had provided for amendment only by the unanimous consent of all thirteen state legislatures; and Rhode Island had refused to send delegates. And finally, the agrarians and urban wage-earners controlled some of the state legislatures; they would surely resent the restrictions on their authority. The Convention took the bull by the horns and engineered a peaceful revolution. It provided for ratification by nine states only and by special conventions. To the election of these conventions, the framers could more successfully devote their efforts.

Almost everywhere the people distrusted the new Constitution. They feared lest the new government would overawe the state sovereignties; they suspected that the new regime, being byond their reach, would prove subversive of their liberties. Four groups, in the main, were in opposition:

the small farmers, the town mechanics, the petty traders, and the politicians at the state capitals. The latter feared the decline of their importance and influence through the enlargement of the political pond; and they frequently became the leaders in expressing the more genuine popular fear of federal centralization. Amos Singletary, a rural member of the Massachusetts convention, typified the populist distrust of the new Constitution.

> These lawyers, and men of learning, and monied men, that talk so finely and gloss over matters so smoothly, to make us, poor illiterate people, swallow down the pill, expect to get into Congress themselves; they expect to be the managers of this constitution, and get all the power and all the money into their own hands, and then they will swallow up all us little folks, like the great *Leviathan*, Mr. President; yes, just as the whale swallowed up *Jonah.*

The speeches of Patrick Henry and George Mason at the Virginia convention likewise voice the popular fear of the political and economic domination of the propertied groups. Only through the superior ability of the Federalist leaders and the promise of numerous amendments—but ten of which later prevailed—could the supporters of the Constitution secure its ratification. The Bill of Rights thus resulted from the populist fears of the new oligarchic centralization. Rhode Island and North Carolina did not join their sister states until after the new government began operation.

No. 5

ADOPTING THE NATIONAL CONSTITUTION [1]
by Charles A. and Mary R. Beard

FULLY aware that their plan would be bitter medicine to a large part of the public, the delegates were puzzled about the best method of getting their instrument ratified. The lawful constitution, the Articles of Confederation, and the call under which the convention had been elected decreed that their project should be laid before the existing Congress for approval, transmitted to the states for ratification, and go into effect only after receiving unanimous consent. Now, the state legislatures, the Fathers knew by bitter experience, had been the chief assailants of public credit and private rights; they had repeatedly refused to indorse restraints on their own powers and their unanimous consent was hardly to be expected.

Having regard for realities rather than theories, the Fathers departed

[1] C. A. and Mary Beard, *The Rise of American Civilization* (New York: The Macmillan Co., 1934), Vol. I, pp. 328-335. Reprinted by permission of the publisher.

from the letter of the existing law in the interest of higher considerations. They did, indeed, provide that the new Constitution should be sent to the old Congress as a matter of form but they advised the Congress merely to pass the instrument along to the states with a recommendation that special conventions be called to decide the issue of ratification. Many citizens of the right sort, they reasoned, who would not take the trouble to serve in a local legislature, would be willing to participate in a ratifying convention; if once the barrier of the populistic state legislatures could be forced, they saw hope of victory.

Still the specter of unanimous ratification remained. After much debate on the point, the convention laid that ghost by an audacious proposal, namely, that the Constitution should go into effect, as between the states concerned, as soon as two-thirds had given their consent. This program, the learned commentator, John W. Burgess, makes plain, was a project for a revolution, a break with the prevailing legal order, a coup d'état, an appeal over the heads of established agencies to the voters, or at least to that part of the electorate prepared to overthrow the Articles of Confederation.

On September 17, after nearly four months of arduous debate, the convention brought its labors to a close. The Constitution was finished and the scheme for ratification formulated. Aggrieved by the decisions of their colleagues, some members had gone home in anger and some who stayed on refused to sign the document, denouncing it openly and opposing its adoption by the people. On the other hand, thirty-nine of the fifty-five members who had attended one or more sessions put their names on the parchment and sent it forth with their benediction, even though they differed widely among themselves in the degree of their enthusiasm for the common handiwork.

Hamilton thought the new government would not be powerful enough and entertained grave doubts about its success. While admitting that they were merely "making experiments in politics," and while expressing his disapproval of many provisions in the document, Franklin declared his faith in divine guidance in the matter. Standing then within the shadow of death, he wrote of the convention's achievement: "I can hardly conceive a transaction of such momentous importance to the welfare of millions now existing and to exist in the posterity of a great nation should be suffered to pass without being in some degree influenced, guided, and governed by that omnipotent, omnipresent, and beneficent Ruler, in whom all inferior spirits live and move and have their being."

With his customary practical view of things, Washington doubtless voiced the general sentiment of his fellow signers when he said: "The Constitution that is submitted is not free from imperfections. But there are as few radical defects in it as could well be expected, considering the heterogeneous mass of which the Convention was composed and the diversity of interests that are to be attended to. As a Constitutional door is opened for future amendments and alterations, I think it would be wise in the people to accept what is offered to them."

On receiving at Paris reports of the proceedings at Philadelphia, Jefferson was at first much troubled. He thought that the proposed House of Representatives would be incompetent to great tasks, that the President, aided by the army, might become a dictator, and that the convention should have been content to add a few sections to the Articles of Confederation, "the good, old and venerable fabric which should have been preserved even as a religious relique." Later, however, he changed his mind and on considering the possibilities of amendment came to the conclusion that the Fathers had done about as well as human circumstances permitted. In the end he came to view the whole operation as a noble triumph for humanity. "The example," he said, "of changing a constitution by assembling the wise men of the state, instead of assembling armies, will be worth as much to the world as the former examples we have given them."

Acting on the recommendations of the convention, the Congress submitted the Constitution to the states for their approval or rejection and in turn the local legislatures called upon the voters to choose conventions to pass upon the new project of government. In a trice the country was divided into hostile camps as all the engines of propaganda and political maneuvering were brought into play either to carry or to defeat the plan for a new government. With a bitterness that recalled the factional dispute in the revolutionary party a few years before, both sides resorted to strenuous tactics.

When, for example, certain opponents of the Constitution in the Pennsylvania legislature sought to win time for deliberation by leaving their seats and breaking the quorum, a federalist mob invaded their lodgings, dragged them through the streets, and pushed them back into the assembly room. Applauded by the victors, the vote was then taken and the election of delegates to the state ratifying convention was fixed at a date only five weeks ahead, reducing to the minimum the period allowed for taking "the solemn judgment of the people." Doubtless some gentlemen of the old school entertained regrets that the new law had been ushered in with disorder but the emergency was great.

Again when the New Hampshire convention met and a majority opposed to the Constitution was discovered, the assembly adjourned to prevent an adverse vote and give the friends of the new instrument a chance to work on the objectors. In one case haste, in the other delay, favored ratification.

As the winter of 1787-88 advanced into spring, the conflict was waged at close quarters, with steady gains among the supporters of the new form of government. Promptly and with little tumult, four states, Delaware, Connecticut, New Jersey, and Georgia—among the smallest and least powerful members of the confederation—ratified the Constitution. With similar promptness Pennsylvania added its approval following the events narrated above. Equally emphatic, Maryland and South Carolina, having given the voters ample time for deliberation, decided with a generous gesture in favor of ratification. In Virginia, where the popular verdict was doubtful, the weight of great names, such as Washington, Marshall, Randolph, and Wythe, finally carried the day. In New Hampshire, New York, and Massachusetts, where the election returned avowed majorities opposed to the Constitution, a great deal of clever engineering induced several delegates to depart from their apparent instructions and cast their ballots for ratification. But to the very end, two states, North Carolina and Rhode Island, refused to give their consent, allowing the new government to be erected without their aid and remaining isolated until the pressure of powerful economic forces brought them under the roof.

Intense as it was, the excitement that marked the struggle did not bring out an avalanche of voters to express their opinions at the polls. From the fragmentary figures that are available, it appears that no more than one-fourth of the adult white males in the country voted one way or the other in the elections at which delegates to the state ratifying conventions were chosen. According to a cautious reckoning, probably one-sixth of them—namely, one hundred thousand—favored the ratification of the new form of government. In any case, it is employing a juristic concept, not summarizing statistical returns, to say that "the whole people put restraints on themselves by adopting the Constitution."

Broadly speaking, the division of the voters over the document ran along economic lines. The merchants, manufacturers, private creditors, and holders of public securities loomed large among the advocates of the new system, while the opposition came chiefly from the small farmers behind the seaboard, especially from the men who, in earlier years, had demanded paper money and other apparatus for easing the strain of their debts. In favor of the Constitution, wrote General Knox to Washington from Massachusetts on January 12, 1788, was "the commercial part of the state to which are added all the men of considerable property, the clergy, the lawyers—including all the judges of all the courts, and all the officers of the late army, and also the neighborhood of all great towns. . . . This party are for vigorous government, perhaps many of them would have been still more pleased with the new Constitution had it been more analogous to the British constitution." In the opposition, General Knox massed the "Insurgents or their favorers, the great majority of whom are for the annihilation of debts public and private."

During the battle over ratification, advocates on both sides produced a large and, in the main, illuminating literature on the science of human government, a literature reminiscent of the grand style of the Revolution. Though time has sunk most of it into oblivion, especially the arguments of the defeated party, the noblest pieces of defense, namely the letters to the press written by Hamilton, Madison, and Jay in support of the Constitution, were rescued from the dust and given immortality under the name of *The Federalist.*

In the tenth number of this great series, Madison, who has been justly called the "father of the Constitution" and certainly may be regarded as a spokesman of the men who signed it, made a cogent appeal for ratification on practical grounds: "The first object of government" is the protection of "the diversity in the faculties of men, from which the rights of property originate." After enumerating the chief classes of property holders which spring up inevitably under such protection in modern society, Madison proceeded to show that "the regulation of these various and interfering interests forms the principal task of modern legislation and involves the spirit of party and faction in the ordinary operations of the government."

Then Madison explained how political strife involved economic concerns at every turn: "The most common and durable source of factions has been the various and unequal distribution of property. Those who hold and those who are without property have ever formed distinct interests in society. Those who are creditors and those who are debtors fall under a like discrimination. A landed interest, a manufacturing interest, a mercantile interest, a moneyed interest, with many lesser interests, grow up of necessity in civilized nations and divide them into different classes actuated by different sentiments and views. . . . From the protection of different and unequal faculties of acquiring property, the possession of different degrees and kinds of property immediately results; and from the influence of these on the sentiments and views of the respective proprietors, ensues a division of society into different interests and parties."

Of necessity, according to Madison's logic, legislatures reflect these interests. "What," he asks, "are the different classes of legislators but advocates and parties to the causes which they determine?" For this there is no help. "The causes of factions cannot be removed," and "we know from experience that neither moral nor religious motives can be relied upon as an adequate control." Since that is true, there arises a grave danger, namely, the danger that certain groups, particularly the propertyless masses, may fuse into an overbearing majority and sacrifice to its will the interests of the minority. Given this peril, it followed that a fundamental problem before the Philadelphia convention had been to "secure the public good and private rights against the danger of such a faction and at the same time to preserve the spirit and form of popular government." And the solution offered was in the check and balance system which refined and enlarged public views "by passing them through the medium of a chosen body of citizens." This, in the language of a leading Father, was the spirit of the new Constitution—the substance of a powerful appeal to all practical men of affairs.

By argument, by negotiation, and by the weight of personality the friends of the proposed revolution triumphed in the end. On June 21, 1788, the ninth state, New Hampshire, ratified the Constitution and the new system could then go into effect as between the parties that had sealed the contract. Within a few weeks, Virginia and New York, aware that the die had already been cast, gave their reluctant consent. With victory thus doubly assured, the Federalists could ignore the smoldering anger of the opposition that had proposed many amendments and could laugh at the solemn resolve of New York calling for another national assembly to modify the Constitution. Leaving North Carolina and Rhode Island still outside the fold unconvinced of its advantages, the old Congress made ready to disband by calling elections for the choice of men to constitute the personnel of the new government.

No. 6

THE STATE CONSTITUTIONS AFTER 1787 [1]

by J. Allen Smith

THE effects of the conservative reaction were not confined to the general government. The movement to limit the power of the popular majority was felt in the domain of state as well as national politics. Even before the Constitutional Convention assembled the political reaction was modifying some of the state constitutions. This is seen especially in the tendency to enlarge the powers of the judiciary which was the only branch

[1] J. A. Smith, *The Spirit of American Government* (New York: The Macmillan Co., 1907), Ch. 9. Reprinted by permission of the publisher.

of the state government in which life tenure survived. This tendency received powerful encouragement and support in the adoption of the Federal Constitution which secured to the judiciary of the general government an absolute veto on both federal and state legislation. For as the state courts were not slow in following the precedent set by the Federal courts, what had been before the adoption of the Constitution a mere tendency soon became the practice in all the states. This in reality accomplished a revolution in the actual working of the state governments without any corresponding change in their outward form. It effected a redistribution of political powers which greatly diminished the influence of the popularly elected and more responsible branches of the state governments and gave a controlling influence to that branch over which the people had least control.

Not only was the state judiciary allowed to assume the veto power, but their independence of public opinion was more effectually safeguarded by depriving a mere majority of the legislature of the power to remove them. The provision of the Federal Constitution requiring a two-thirds majority in the legislative body for removal by impeachment or otherwise was quite generally copied. Without some such safeguard the party in control of the legislature could prevent the exercise of the judicial veto by removing from office any judges who dared to oppose its policy.

New York and South Carolina were the only states adopting constitutions during the Revolutionary period, which included provisions limiting the power of the majority to impeach public officials. The New York constitution of 1777 required a two-thirds majority in the lower house, and the South Carolina constitution of 1778 a two-thirds majority in both houses. Pennsylvania copied the impeachment provisions of the Federal Constitution in her constitution of 1790; Delaware went even farther, and in her constitution of 1792, required a two-thirds majority in both houses; Georgia followed the example of the Federal Constitution in 1798; Virginia, in 1830; North Carolina, in 1835; Vermont, in 1836; New Jersey, in 1844; and Maryland, in 1851.

With the progress of this movement to restore the system of checks in the state constitutions the governor regained his independence of the legislature and also many of the rights and prerogatives of which the Revolution had deprived him. He was made coordinate with the legislature, set over against it and generally clothed with the qualified veto power, which made him for all practical purposes the third house of that body. Georgia increased the governor's term of office to two years and gave him the qualified veto power in 1798. Pennsylvania made his term of office three years and gave him the veto power in 1790. New Hampshire conferred the veto power on him in 1792 and New York in 1821.

This tendency to make the public official less directly dependent upon the people or their immediate representatives is clearly seen in other important changes made in the state constitutions during this period. Popular control over the legislature was diminished by lengthening the terms of the members of both houses and by providing that the upper house should be elected for a longer term than the lower. Georgia established an upper house in 1789 and made the term of office of its members three years. In 1790 Pennsylvania also added a senate whose members were to be elected for four years, and South Carolina increased the term of its senators from one to four years. Delaware extended the term from one to two years for members of the lower house and from three to four years for members of the upper house and made the legislative sessions biennial instead of annual in 1831. North Carolina increased the term of members of both houses from one to two years and adopted biennial sessions in 1835. Maryland in 1837 extended the term of senators from five to six years, and in 1846 established biennial sessions of the legislature. The responsibility of the legislature was still further diminished by the gradual adoption of the plan of partial renewal of the senate, which was incorporated in the Revolutionary constitutions of Delaware, New York and Virginia and later copied in the Federal Constitution. This ensured the conservative and steadying influence exerted by a body of hold-over members in the upper house.

With the exception of five states in which the members of one branch of the legislature were elected for terms varying from two to five years, the Revolutionary state constitutions provided for the annual election of the entire legislature. This plan made both houses conform to the latest expression of public opinion by the majority of the qualified voters at the polls. And since neither the executive nor the courts possessed the veto power, the system ensured prompt compliance on the part of the law-making body with the demands of the people as expressed in the results of the legislative election.

The influence of public opinion on the state governments was greatly weakened by the constitutional changes above mentioned. The lower branch of the legislature, inasmuch as all its members were simultaneously elected, might be regarded as representative of recent, if not present, public opinion, though effective popular control of that body was made more difficult by lengthening the term of office, since this diminished the frequency with which the voters could express in an authoritative manner their disapproval of the official record of its members. Under the plan adopted present public opinion as formulated in the results of the last election was not recognized as entitled to control the state senate.

These changes in the state constitutions by which the executive and judicial branches of the government acquired the veto power amounted in practice to the creation of a four-chambered legislature. By thus increasing the number of bodies which it was necessary for the people to control in order to secure the legislation which they desired, their power to influence the policy of the state government was thereby diminished. And when we reflect that not only was legislative authority more widely distributed, but each branch of the state government exercising it was also made less directly dependent on the qualified voters, we can see that these constitutional provisions were in the nature of checks on the numerical majority.

A consideration of the changes made in the method of amending the state constitutions leads to the same conclusion. During the Revolutionary period, as we have seen, the tendency was strongly toward making the fundamental law the expression of the will of the numerical majority. Difficulties in the way of change were reduced to a minimum. But under the influence of the political reaction which followed, and which produced the Constitution of the United States, the state governments were so organized as to make it more difficult for the majority to exercise the amending power. Georgia in 1789 changed the method of amending the state constitution by requiring a two-thirds majority in a constitutional convention, and made another change in 1798 by which a two-thirds majority in each house of the legislature and a three-fourths majority in each house of the succeeding legislature was required for the adoption of an amendment to the constitution. South Carolina in 1790 adopted a provision guarding against mere majority amendment by making the approval of a two-thirds majority in both branches of two successive legislatures necessary for any changes in the constitution. Connecticut in 1818 restricted the power of amending by requiring a majority in the house of representatives, a two-thirds majority in both houses of the next legislature, and final approval by a majority of the electors. New York in 1821 adopted a plan which required that an amendment should receive a majority in each branch of the legislature, a two-thirds majority in each branch of the succeeding legislature, and be approved by a majority of the voters. North Carolina in 1835 made a three-fifths majority in each house of the legislature and a two-thirds majority of each house of the following legislature necessary for changes in the constitution.

The judicial veto served the purpose of preventing majority amendment under the guise of ordinary legislation, while a safeguard against constitutional changes favored by a mere majority was thus provided in the extraor-

dinary majority required in both houses of the legislature to propose or
adopt amendments. This, as has been shown in the case of the Federal
Constitution, is a formidable check on the majority. In view of this restriction upon the proposing of amendments the provision for ratification by
a popular majority, which owing to the progress of the later democratic
movement has now been generally adopted, is no real concession to the principle of majority rule.

Assuming that a two-thirds majority in the legislature is required to propose an amendment, and that the principle of representation is so applied
that each party is represented in the legislature in proportion to its popular vote, it would scarcely ever be possible for any party to propose an
amendment to the state constitution, since it cannot be expected under any
ordinary conditions to control two-thirds of the popular vote. But inasmuch as the successful party often secures under our system much more
than its proportional share of representation in the legislature, it is by
no means unusual for a party to have a two-thirds majority in both houses
of a state legislature. This would appear to give the numerical majority
under such conditions the power to propose and adopt amendments. Such
would be the case if the party were really responsible to those who supported it at the polls. But this would assume the existence of a purely
state party, organized with reference to state issues only, and carrying
the election as the advocate of a definite state policy. Moreover, it would
presuppose all those means, political and constitutional, by which the majority in the legislature would be accountable to the popular majority in
the state. This is rendered impossible, however, as has been shown, by our
system of government.

The above-mentioned changes in the constitutions of the older states
may be attributed in large measure to the reaction against democracy which
brought about the adoption of the Federal Constitution. They may be regarded as an expression of that distrust and fear of democracy which
filled the minds of those who framed and set up our Federal government.
It is not contended, however, that they are now so regarded by the masses
of the people. The work of deifying the Federal Constitution was soon
accomplished. And when the people had come to venerate it as the most
perfect embodiment of the doctrine of popular sovereignty that the intelligence of man could devise, it was but natural that they should acquiesce
in the proposal to make the state governments conform more closely to
the general plan of that instrument. In view of the wide-spread sentiment
which amounted to a blind and unthinking worship of the Constitution,
it is not surprising that the political institutions of the general government
should have been largely copied by the states. The only surprising thing

in this connection is the fact that they did not follow the Federal model more closely, since every feature of it was the object of the most extravagant eulogy. Here we see, however, an inconsistency between profession and practice. The people who tolerated no criticism of the Federal Constitution showed nevertheless a distrust of some of its more conservative features. Much as the indirect election of President and United States senators was favored by the framers of our Federal Constitution, there has been no tendency to apply that principle in the selection of the corresponding state officials.

In all the states framing new constitutions during the Revolutionary period, except Massachusetts, New Hampshire, and New York, the governor was elected by the legislature. Pennsylvania abandoned indirect election and adopted election by the qualified voters in 1790; Delaware, in 1792; Georgia, in 1824; North Carolina, in 1835; Maryland, in 1837; New Jersey, in 1844; Virginia, in 1850; and South Carolina, in 1865. South Carolina and Maryland are the only states which have ever had indirect election of the upper house. Both adopted it in 1776, the constitution of South Carolina providing that the members of the lower house should elect the members of the upper house, and the constitution of Maryland requiring that members of the upper house should be chosen by an electoral college. This was abandoned for direct election in South Carolina in 1778 and in Maryland in 1837.

The conservative reaction was soon followed by a new movement toward democracy. This no doubt largely explains the failure of the people to reproduce in their state constitutions all those features which they professed to admire in the Federal Constitution. Not only did they not copy all the new features of that document, but they even discarded some of the then existing provisions of the state constitution which had been copied in the Federal Constitution. The principle of indirect election which was everywhere recognized in the choice of the state judiciary during the Revolutionary period was gradually abandoned for the more democratic method of direct popular choice which has now become the rule. The life tenure of judges which formerly existed in most of the states has almost entirely disappeared. In all but four states the judges are now chosen for terms varying from two to twenty-one years—the average length of the term being eight or ten years. The combination of direct popular choice with a fixed term of office has had the effect of making the state judiciary much more amenable to public opinion than the corresponding branch of the Federal government. By reason of the relatively long term for which the judges of the state supreme court are elected, however, and the plan of gradual renewal which prevents present public opinion from ever gaining the ascendency in that body, it is still the least responsible and most conservative branch of the state government.

We see, then, two motives exerting an influence in the remolding of the state constitutions, one being the desire to copy the Federal Constitution and the other the belief that the state government should reflect the will of the people. That the attainment of one of these ends would inevitably defeat the other was not generally recognized. The conviction which had become thoroughly rooted in the popular mind that the system of checks and balances was the highest expression of democratic organization ensured the embodiment of the general features of that system in the constitutions of the various states. The constitutional changes having this end in view largely destroyed the responsibility of the state governments to the people and thus prevented the very thing they were designed to accomplish. But however much this system was in reality opposed to the principle of direct popular control, it was adopted by the people with the idea of making the government more readily reflect their will. They were not conscious of any inconsistency in holding tenaciously to the doctrine of checks and balances and at the same time seeking to give the people more control over the state governments. The latter purpose is clearly seen in the constitutional changes relating to the tenure and manner of election of the judiciary and in the adoption of universal suffrage. Summing up the effects of these changes in the state constitutions, we may say that the suffrage was placed upon a democratic basis, the state judiciary was organized on a less irresponsible plan and the appearance of political responsibility secured by applying the principle of direct election to every branch of the state government. The longer term of office established for the legislative and executive branches of the state government, however, together with the increase in the authority of the judiciary and the adoption of the system of checks and balances has upon the whole had the effect of making the state government less responsive to the electorate.

. . . the framers of the Federal Constitution made use of the scheme of checks and balances for the purpose of limiting the power of the people. There is little evidence that they favored diffusion of authority except in so far as that authority rested upon a popular basis. Hence they carried the plan much farther in curtailing the power of the House of Representatives than a logical application of the doctrine would have justified, while at the same time giving more authority and power of independent action to the other branches of the general government than was consistent with their avowed, if not real, purpose.

They gave to the executive and judicial branches of the general government power to control the administration of Federal laws. The enforcement of all laws and regulations of the general government, in so far as the President and Senate might desire to enforce them, was guaranteed through the power to appoint and remove those who were entrusted with their execution, while the right of appeal from a state to the Federal courts precluded the possibility of enforcing a state law deemed to exceed the proper limits of state authority.

In the state governments on the other hand we find a high degree of administrative decentralization. The governor, unlike the President, was not given any adequate power to control those entrusted with the execution of state laws. A multitude of directly elected local officials are the agents of the state for this purpose. And since they reflect the sentiment of the various local interests to which they owe their election, it may and often does happen that a law to which those interests are opposed is rendered practically inoperative through the efforts of those local officials who are sworn to enforce it. The practical working of this system often gives to a local community an administrative veto on such general laws of the state as may be opposed to local sentiment. By this means the general executive authority of the state is weakened and its responsibility correspondingly diminished.

In still another respect the policy of dividing authority and parcelling it out between separate and distinct organs of government has been carried much farther in the state than in the Federal Constitution. Unlike the Federal government in which executive power is centralized in the President, the state constitutions have created a number of separate officials, boards and commissions, some directly elected and some appointed, independent of each other and irresponsible except in so far as a fixed term of office implies responsibility. This means that instead of one executive the state has many. Only one of them—the governor—has, it is true, a veto on the enactment of laws; but this, as we have seen, is really a legislative and not an executive power. Each of these has what may be termed an administrative veto; that is, the power to negative the laws which they are expected to administer by simply not enforcing them. The impossibility of securing an honest and faithful administration of the laws where the responsibility for their enforcement is divided between a number of separate and practically independent officials, is clearly shown in the experience of the various states. . . .

Under a system which thus minutely subdivides and distributes the administrative function, any effective control over the execution of state laws is made impossible. The governor, who is nominally the head of the executive agencies of the state, is not in reality responsible, since he has no adequate power to compel the enforcement of laws directly entrusted to other independent state officials. Any interest or combination of interests that may wish to prevent the enforcement of certain laws may be able to accomplish their end by merely controlling the one official or board whose duty it is to enforce the law in question. Their task would be a much more difficult one, if it were necessary to control for that purpose the entire executive arm of the state. The opportunity for the corrupt use of money and influence is thus vastly increased, since the people, though they might watch and judge fairly well the conduct of one state executive, can not exercise any effective censorship over a large number of such officials.

This irresponsibility which arises out of a wide diffusion of power is not confined to the executive branch of the state government. The legislature in the course of our political development has taken on the same elaborate committee organization which characterizes, as we have seen, our Federal Congress. The same sinister influences working through similar agencies oppose needed legislation. But although the good bills are frequently killed or mutilated in the secrecy of the committee room, the skilful use of money or other corrupt influence often secures the enactment of laws opposed to the interests of the people. Moreover, the practice known as log-rolling by which the representatives of various local interests combine and force through measures which secure to each of certain localities some advantage at the expense of the state at large are so common as to excite no surprise.

The relation existing between the executive and legislative branches under our system is another source of irresponsibility, since it does not follow simply because a law has been placed upon the statute books of a state that it can be enforced. An act may be passed in response to a strong public sentiment, it may be constitutional and the executive may be willing and may even desire to enforce it, and yet be unable to do so. The legislature may, and frequently does, enact laws under the pressure of public opinion while at the same time quietly exercising what is, in effect, a veto on their execution. In the case of much important legislation it can accomplish this by merely not appropriating the funds which are required for their enforcement. The laws against adulteration are a good illustration An official known perhaps as a dairy and food commissioner may be provided for, whose duty it is to enforce these laws. The nature of the work entrusted to him requires that he should have a corps of assistants, inspectors who are to keep a watchful eye on the goods likely to be adulterated and collect samples of such goods from the various places in the state where they are exposed for sale, and chemists who are to analyze the samples thus procured and determine whether manufacturers and dealers are complying with the law. Unless an adequate sum is appropriated for this purpose, and for prosecuting those who are violating the law, such laws can not be enforced.

In our state governments the subdivision of authority has been carried so far that no effective control over the enactment or enforcement of state laws is possible. Under the influence of the doctrine of checks and balances the policy of widely distributing political authority has inured to the benefit of those private interests which are ever seeking to control the government for their own ends, since it has supplied the conditions under which the people find it difficult to fix the blame for official misconduct. Indeed it may be said that wherever power should be concentrated to ensure responsibility, it has been almost invariably distributed.

Chapter III

CHANGING THE RULES FOR A CHANGING SOCIETY

[As J. Allen Smith long ago pointed out, all democratic constitutions are flexible and easy to amend. This follows from the fact that in a truly democratic government the people are in control, and a constitution must be a means of securing supremacy of the public will and not a means of thwarting it. Such a constitution must not be a check upon the people themselves. It must be an instrument for securing popular control over the agents and representatives of the people without which popular government is only a name. A government is democratic in the proportion that it responds to the people's will, and since one way of defeating the popular will is to make it difficult to change the fundamental rules, it follows that any constitution that is truly democratic must yield to changes in public opinion.

Now, if we examine American history we shall see that the society for which our original constitutions were framed has changed fundamentally since the late eighteenth century. With changes in society there have naturally been changes in the political needs and desires of the people, and the politician has accordingly sought to adapt the framework of government to the new conditions. It should surprise no one, therefore, that American constitutions have been materially altered in the last century and a half. But, have the changes been adequate? Have they met the needs arising out of changing conditions and changing desires? Are our constitutions of such a nature that they are readily adaptable to new situations in accordance with the wishes of the majority of citizens? These are questions that must be answered if we are to determine whether the formal and informal means of adapting our fundamental rules to changing conditions are such as to make our constitutions truly democratic.]

No. 7

OUR UNWRITTEN CONSTITUTION [1]

[Changing the Constitution without Formal Amendment]

by William Bennett Munro

THE written Constitution of the United States is a document that occupies five pages of print in the World Almanac and can be read in half an hour. But alongside it, and based upon it, there has developed during the past hundred and forty years an unwritten constitution of vastly greater dimensions. It fills the statutes-at-large, the law reports, the printed laws of the individual commonwealths, and constitutional treatises to the extent of a million pages or more. This unwritten constitution is made up of federal and state enactments, judicial decisions, usages, doctrines, precedents, official opinions, and points of view which have profoundly altered the implications of the original instrument. It has made the government of the United States a different affair from that which the framers of the written Constitution intended it to be.

So great has this divergence become at the present day that no one can now obtain even a silhouette of the American political system if he confines his study to the nation's fundamental law as it left the hands of its architects in 1787. Its words and phrases have been "twisted and tortured" during their journey down these fourteen decades, as Lord Bryce once said, until they now imply things widely remote from what they were originally thought to mean. Governmental powers of vast import have been nurtured from these few pages until we can now speak of the written Constitution as merely the taproot from which the tree of American nationalism has grown. Its branches increase their spread year after year. In a word the national government has become far more powerful in relation to the states than it was at the beginning—more democratic, more efficient, more far-reaching in its influence both at home and abroad.

The makers of the American Constitution neither began nor finished their work in the summer of 1787. Their ancestors began it at Runnymede and continued it at Westminster. Their descendants have kept bravely at the work ever since the Great Convention adjourned. It is often said that the last framer of the Constitution passed off the scene with Madison's death in 1836; but Marshall and Jackson were giving new significance to the supreme law of the land when Madison died. Nor were they the last of

---

[1] W. B. Munro, *The Makers of the Unwritten Constitution* (New York: The Macmillan Co., 1930), pp. 1-22. Reprinted by permission of the publisher.

the line. In the wider sense of the term the makers of the American Constitution form a great and still growing company. The list will not be closed until the end of time.

What has been said in the foregoing paragraphs is commonplace, or ought to be. Every textbook of American government adverts to the great discrepancy between what the government of the United States was intended to be and what it has become. This, moreover, in spite of checks and balances, limitations and prohibitions, and all the other artifices for preserving equilibrium that eighteenth-century minds could suggest. Such a phenomenon all the more deserves comment because it has not come to pass by reason of the nineteen [twenty-one] amendments. Among these additions to the original document only one enlarges the powers of Congress. All the rest impose restraints or change methods. The growth of the national government in strength and prestige has not been achieved by broadening the original foundation upon which it rests. Were there no other channels of federal expansion than that which the process of formal amendment has provided, the national government would now be relatively weaker than it was when it started. It has gained virtually the whole of its political and economic hegemony of to-day from statutes, from judicial decisions, and from usages. Together these make up the unwritten constitution, a structure which is the work of many hands, a rambling edifice to which successive generations of statesmen and jurists have each added wings and gables and pillars until only a semblance of the original architecture remains.

In this development of an unwritten constitution the United States has not been unique among countries which possess free government. All political systems are continually in process of change; like living organisms they must adapt themselves to an altered environment or die. You cannot encase a living organism in a marble urn and keep it alive. No more can one century be held in bondage to another. The written word, as a basis of popular government, must have the power to expand and contract. This adaptation will be by frank and formal change if the methods of constitutional amendment are easy (as they are in England and Italy); but it will follow other channels when the routine of amendment is roundabout and difficult as in the United States. The instinct of self-preservation in a government will impel it to find such channels, or to make them if need be.

Strange as it may sound to-day, the statesmen of 1787 intended to make the process of constitutional amendment an easy one. That is why they provided four alternative ways of putting an amendment through. They made it possible to initiate amendments in Congress, or without action by Congress. They provided for ratification by the state legislatures or without action by these legislatures if the occasion required. Hamilton devoted

almost an entire Federalist letter to proving the proposition that the amending process could not be made any easier without serious danger of constitutional instability.

Of course it was not anticipated that only one of the alternative methods
would ever be used. There was a feeling that the ratification of amendments by conventions in the states would often prove easier than ratification
by state legislatures. The situation in 1787 warranted that impression. If
the acceptance of the original Constitution had been left to the state legislatures, rather than to conventions called for the purpose, it would almost
certainly have been rejected by some of them. Nevertheless, after the Constitution had been ratified by these state conventions, the first series of
proposed amendments were initiated by Congress and sent to the state
legislatures as the quickest way of getting them into effect. This set a
precedent which has ever since been followed. But with this important
difference: that it required action on the part of only eleven state legislatures to add these first ten amendments, whereas it now requires affirmative
action on the part of thirty-six. [Since this was written the twenty-first
amendment was ratified by the convention method.]

The framers of the original Constitution anticipated, moreover, that from
time to time a national convention would be called for the purpose of
undertaking a general revision. If Thomas Jefferson could have had his
way he would have made such revision mandatory at least once a generation. Nothing, in fact, was farther from the expectations of Jefferson,
Madison, Franklin and the rest than that this roll of parchment would
remain unrevised to help govern their children's grandchildren, or that more
amendments would be added during the first ten years of its operation than
in the succeeding hundred and thirty. We are sometimes cautioned nowadays against a too-receptive attitude toward constitutional amendments;
but it would be difficult to find, at any subsequent stage in American history, a group of men more benevolently inclined toward amendments than
were the Fathers themselves.

In any case formal amendment has been only one of the agencies of
constitutional flexibility, and by no means the most important one. More
has been accomplished by statutory elaboration. The statesmen of 1787
did not desire or deem themselves competent to perform a task of encyclo-
pedic proportions. In eighty-one days they put together and agreed upon
only eighty-nine sentences; their four hundred hours of debate and deliberation eventuated in a document of only four thousand words. It was not
that they were lacking in vocabulary, but simply that they felt insistent
upon leaving the details of government as a hostage to the good sense of
those whom the people would elect as their representatives under the new

order. So they bequeathed an abundant legacy of problems to the state legislatures and the new Congress. To take a conspicuous example, they did not stipulate how the presidential electors should be chosen but merely dictated that "each state shall appoint, in such manner as the legislature shall direct, a number of electors equal to the whole number of senators and representatives to which the state may be entitled in Congress."

Again, they provided that members of the House of Representatives should be elected by the voters—but by what voters? The decision of that question they also devolved upon the state legislatures. To Congress they committed an even more formidable mass of routine to be worked out. The whole structure of the federal judiciary they left to be created by law. On the matter of administrative departments they said next to nothing. How many departments? Their functions? Their relation to Congress? On these and a score of other important matters of governmental practice the statutes have had to supply the omissions.

Some of the statutes which Congress has enacted during the past hundred years are, therefore, to all intents a part of the Constitution—for example, the Act of 1887 which supplements the Twelfth Amendment by fixing in detail the method of counting electoral votes and determining the way in which electoral controversies shall be settled. Another illustration is the Statute of 1886 which fixes the presidential succession in case both the President and the Vice-President are unavailable. In the French Republic these enactments would be called "organic laws," that is, laws which are theoretically open to amendment or repeal by exactly the same process as ordinary laws, but which supply certain important cogs in the mechanism of government and hence are virtually permanent and no more likely to be changed than is the Constitution itself.

Alexander Hamilton was the first to demonstrate how the words of the original Constitution could be given an expansive quality by legislation. His great fiscal statutes were the first of a series that has kept lengthening year by year. Congress has pressed its economic powers to the limit and at times has overstepped the bounds, as in the child labor laws. If the opponents of the Constitution could have foreseen the way in which Hamilton would wring economic domination out of its words by the process of statutory elabration they would have redoubled their opposition. Lawyers use the terms statutory and constitutional in antithesis; but if by a constitution we mean "all the fundamental rules which directly or indirectly affect the distribution and exercise of sovereign power," then there is no practical difference between some provisions of the American Constitution and some of our organic statutes.

The statutory provision for a Secretary of State is not less firmly anchored than is the constitutional provision for a Speaker of the House. The secret ballot, which rests on legislative enactment, would be harder to displace than freedom from unreasonable searches, even though the latter rests on a constitutional guarantee. The National Defence Act circumvents an implication of the Constitution and makes it possible for the President to call forth the militia of the states for service outside the United States (which clearly was not intended), by the artifice of "federalizing" these militia organizations overnight. Hence it is sometimes said, and with reason, that for governmental principles one may look in the Constitution, but that for governmental practice one must look in the statutes.

At any rate most of the things that the student of actual government desires to know are in the statutes, not in the four thousand words of the Constitution. Even the process of lawmaking itself has had to be built up without guidance from those who laid the foundations. The Constitution declares, for example, that the House of Representatives shall choose its own Speaker, but it does not say what his powers shall be. These are fixed by the rules of the House. It requires the assent of both House and Senate for the enactment of laws, but says nothing about how a disagreement between the two chambers shall be settled. The whole system of conference committees is based upon rules made by the two legislative bodies themselves. The Constitution does not even require that bills be given three readings, or referred to committees, or placed on the calendar. It says not a word about budgets, deficiency appropriations, filibustering, time-limits, lobbying, leave to print, riders, suspension of rules, and the countless other incidentals of the lawmaking industry which attract so much interest nowadays.

Judicial and administrative decisions form the second cornerstone of the unwritten constitution. It is one of the fictions of juristic philosophy that the courts do not alter constitutions. They only interpret them. But Justice Oliver Wendell Holmes blurted the truth when he declared that courts "do and must legislate," despite their professions to the contrary. Likewise administrators do and must make laws—notwithstanding Montesquieu, Madison, John Adams and their devotion to the theory of separation of powers. It must inevitably be so, for to give a rule a new interpretation is to give it a new meaning, and to give it a new meaning is to alter it.

The course of actual alteration has now proceeded so far that the student who desires to know the actual powers of Congress will get a very inadequate, and often a misleading idea of their scope and ramifications if he merely runs through the eighteen formal powers granted to Congress by the Constitution itself. Hundreds of judicial decisions have widened these original powers beyond recognition, yet never in a single instance has any

American court asserted its power to make actual changes in the phraseology of the Constitution or the laws. It is merely that the stretching of a phrase in one decision provides the basis for a further elongation in the next; the lines of alteration are pricked out gently by one adjudication after another until a great divergence appears between the finish and the start.

Let one or two illustrations suffice: The framers of the Constitution gave Congress power "to regulate commerce with foreign countries and among the several states," intending thereby to enable the nation to set up a tariff of its own while preventing the states from setting up tariffs against one another. Then, in 1824, the Supreme Court ruled that "commerce" included not only the merchandise but the carriers of commerce; thereby inaugurating a long series of decisions in which it has held that commerce also includes the transportation of passengers by land and water, the sending of messages by wire, and the transmission of electric power; but that the term is not flexible enough to include life insurance, or the making of commercial contracts, or the protection of migratory birds. Hence it is that a word which was put into the Constitution by men who knew only sailing vessels and stage coaches has been broadened to include steamships, railroads, trolleys and motor busses, telegraph and telephone lines, radio broadcasting and traffic by airplane.

Or, to give another example of this verbal expansiveness: The Constitution provides that Congress shall have power "to support armies." To the eighteenth-century mind these words meant feeding, clothing and paying armed men in the field. But during America's participation in . . . World War [I] they proved flexible enough to authorize the fixing of meatless and wheatless days for the whole civilian population, the stoppage of building operations, the cessation of industry on certain days of the week, and the taking over of the railroads. A vast amount of federal authority lies embedded in these three words! [World War II furnished many examples.]

The framers of the Constitution realized, of course, that differences of opinion would arise as to what the words and phrases of the Constitution expressed or implied, and they took for granted that the courts would resolve such difficulties just as they had been doing under the state constitutions. But they could not have foreseen the stupendous amount of interpreting that would be necessitated by the growth of the country, nor could they have envisaged the subtle way in which this interpreting process would redound to the advantage of the federal government. Most of the strength with which Hamilton unavailingly sought to endow Congress in 1787 has been imparted by Marshall and his successors. The stone which the builders rejected has become the chief stone of the corner.

And it is not the courts alone that interpret the words of the Constitution.

Administrative officers, from the President down, are almost daily confronted with the necessity of taking certain actions in virtue of what they deem to be their legal or constitutional powers. Such actions, although they may be challenged and subjected to judicial review, are for the most part allowed to pass without protest on the part of anyone and thus form precedents for the future. It is true, of course, that no administrative ruling, however long acquiesced in, is immune from reversal at the hands of the judiciary. Nevertheless when important private rights have been established under some such ruling, the courts are reluctant to disturb it. Executive orders and administrative regulations have been increasing at a rapid rate during the last twenty-five years. To-day they may be counted among the important agencies of constitutional development. Incidentally it ought to be explained that where there are any serious doubts as to the constitutionality or legality of an administrative regulation, the usual practice is to seek the opinion of the Attorney-General. The opinions of this officer are not given until after careful study has been made by his subordinates.

"Time and habit," said Washington, "are necessary to fix the true character of governments." Usage is merely habit long-continued and writ large. Governments, like men, adopt ways of doing things and in time these ways become traditional. In other words they become stereotyped in the national thought. To change a tradition involves re-educating a whole people, which is a long and difficult task. The written Constitution, for example, permits both the President and the Vice-President to be chosen from the same state. But that has never happened and probably never will. The usage is that they shall be chosen not only from different states but from different sections of the country, and any departure from this practice would be resented. So strongly is this usage entrenched that it would be easier to ignore a specific constitutional requirement (e.g., that a senator must be thirty years of age) than to place two Rhode Islanders, let us say, in the nation's chief executive posts at the same time.

Governmental usages are sometimes more constraining than the laws, and much has been written about the way in which the original Constitution of the United States has been modified by the influence of "time and habit." In general, however, too much emphasis has usually been placed upon usages which are, after all, of secondary importance. The example of an American constitutional usage most commonly cited is the one that now controls the method of choosing the President. Textbooks rarely fail to explain how the framers of the written Constitution desired the people to have no direct share in the choice of the chief executive and how usage has nevertheless given them a share which is both direct and complete. But such discussions regard the forms too much and the facts too little. It is true, no doubt, that some members of the Philadelphia Convention distrusted the competence of the electorate and were averse to the choice of the President by the people; but it was not out of deference to them that the plan of indirect election was finally adopted. Far more influential than any distrust of the populace was the argument that indirect election would give candidates from the smaller states a chance. Their merits could be much more easily made known to small groups of electors than to the people of the whole nation.

Moreover, it should be borne in mind that the men who framed the Constitution had scant expectation that the President would regularly be chosen by the presidential electors. On the contrary they assumed that these electors would in each case be likely to vote for someone from their own states and hence that no one would get a majority of all the electors, save in very exceptional circumstances. Mason of Virginia predicted on the floor of the Convention that not once in twenty elections would any candidate get a majority of all the electoral votes. This meant that under normal conditions the electors would merely nominate, and the House of Representatives would make the final choice from among the five highest nominees. In making this final choice, however, the House was to vote by states, each state having one vote irrespective of its size. That is where the small states scored in the Convention of 1787.

But their victory turned out to be a hollow one. Usage presently determined that nominations should be made by political parties, that the presidential electors should be pledged in advance, and that Mason's prediction should be almost exactly reversed. Since 1788 there have been . . . [forty] presidential elections and on only two of these occasions has the House made the decision. The last occasion was over a century ago, before the two-party system had become definitely established.

Many other usages have caused departures from the intent of the Fathers, and some of these usages will quickly come to the mind of anyone who is familiar with the practice of American government. The President's cabinet embodies one of them. Governor's councils were well known in 1787, but no provision was made for a President's council. Apparently it was the intention that the Senate to a limited extent should serve as one, and Washington tried to utilize it in that way, but his experience did not warrant a continuance of the attempt. So the heads of departments began to meet —occasionally at first and then regularly. The term "cabinet" was not applied to them collectively until the early years of the nineteenth century.

The usage which restricts a President to two consecutive terms has received new emphasis in recent years. Lord Bryce was hardly justified in his statement, a few years ago, that this tradition seems to have "lost nearly all its influence." The likelihood that it will ever be upset seems smaller to-day than at any previous time. [This passage was written in 1930.] So with the popular insistence on resident congressmen. In the written Constitution there is no requirement that a member of the House of Representatives shall live in the district from which he is elected. It was not definitely intended that there should be congressional districts. But as a practical matter the requirement is hardly less constraining than if it were a specific constitutional one; and unfortunately so, for it needlessly limits the range of popular choice and accentuates the spirit of localism in national politics. A dozen other examples of the influence of usage might be given; but this is not the place for them.

If the men who set up the political framework of 1787 were to rise from their narrow cells, after their long sleep of more than a century, what departures from their original conception would be the most astonishing to them? Without question they would be profoundly impressed by the far-reaching influence upon the nation's economic life which the federal government has been able to wrest from the first three paragraphs of Article I, Section 8. It would dawn upon them that what they intended to be a political instrument has become the basis for a vast endowment of economic authority and influence.

It is true, of course, that these paragraphs of the Constitution grew out of the economic necessities of the day. The whole document, indeed, was not so much a declaration of faith as of fears, for it was put together in an atmosphere of restlessness, at a time when business conditions in the thirteen states were about as bad as they could be. Independence had been gained by the war, but not prosperity. The war had burdened both the states and the Confederation with debt; the country had been deluged with paper money; prices were excessively high; trade was not reviving; and there were no agencies of credit able to cope with the situation. In their bewilderment the people of the various states were clamoring for the establishment of tariffs, each against the others, and seeking to better their own economic situation at the expense of the rest. There was a Congress of the Confederation, sitting at Philadelphia whenever it could muster a quorum; but it was without power to tax, without capacity to borrow, and without authority to enact the only measures that would secure economic prosperity.

The Philadelphia Convention of 1787 was called together for the purpose of dealing with this emergency. Its leaders had, as their primary motive, the desire to endow the central government with three powers which it did not possess, namely, the power to tax, the power to borrow (with means of repayment), and the power to regulate commerce. All else was incidental and subsidiary. Had it not been for the economic crisis it is difficult to believe that the states would have responded to the call for a convention.

Nevertheless, the framers of the Constitution did not venture to give the new federal government a single jot or tittle of economic authority beyond the limits of actual necessity. They gave Congress the power to tax, but circumscribed this taxing power with three severe restrictions. Federal taxes, they provided, must be uniform; must not be levied on exports; and if direct, must be apportioned among the states according to their respective populations. So with the commerce power. Trade with foreign nations and among the several states might be regulated by Congress, but no preferences among ports would be tolerated and the whole field of trade within each state was left to local self-determination.

The Constitution, accordingly, is eloquent in its economic omissions. There is no mention of banks or banking. It was assumed that the power to charter and to regulate banks would devolve upon the states along with all the other non-delegated powers. So with the issue of paper money. Congress was given exclusive control of the coinage, but no express authority to issue bills of credit. All this points to a full recognition of the jealousy with which the states regarded their own economic independence. Any attempt to set up a central government which obviously could exert a dominating influence over the financial and commercial affairs of the nation would have roused the states to a rejection of all that the convention proposed.

So the makers of the Constitution proceeded cautiously. They gave the new federal government, in express terms, that small modicum of economic authority that seemed to be imperative at the moment, leaving the rest to the individual commonwealths. Nothing could have been further from their minds than that even this small endowment of authority would enable the federal government in due course to control the prime interests of agriculture, manufacture, trade, communication, banking and credit throughout the length and breadth of the land. Certainly there is no such implication in the original document, especially when one joins with it the explicit declaration of the Tenth Amendment.

The government of the United States, at its inception, was a weak government. It was weaker than the leaders of the convention desired. The powers assigned to it were not those which they thought the federal government ought to have, but merely those which they hoped the states would consent to give. There were those who doubted that these powers were enough to produce any substantial amelioration in the existing economic confusion. Hence the first few years of the Constitution were its critical years. If Washington's first administration had failed to utilize every ounce of its power to improve the economic situation the revival of material prosperity would have been delayed and there would have been a general disillusionment. As it was the new government rode into the confidence of the people on a wave of economic prosperity which it helped in large measure to create. It found men who had the discernment to see that a union could not be strong unless its people were prosperous, and that national unity could be best promoted by a common interest in national economic legislation.

During the past hundred and . . . [sixty] years many minds have helped in the making of the unwritten constitution by drafting and enacting organic statutes, by framing administrative and judicial opinions, by setting precedents, and by developing habit into usage. Their number runs into the thousands. But among them there are four great historical figures whose work may be singled out as of conspicuous and enduring importance. These are Alexander Hamilton, John Marshall, Andrew Jackson, and Woodrow Wilson [and Franklin Roosevelt]. They, not less than Washington, Madison, Franklin, and Morris, are entitled to be known as Fathers of the Constitution in the broader sense of the term. Hamilton took hold of the economic provisions, gave them reality, and made them function. He seized the right psychological moment to start Congress on its way to supremacy in the economic life of the nation. A dozen years later it would have been too late. Marshall, during his long term as Chief Justice, reinforced Hamilton's work by widening the implied powers of the national government and making the Supreme Court their guardian. To Andrew Jackson we are indebted for having infused into the American political system a large part of the democracy which the framers of the original document did not intend it to possess. Finally, Woodrow Wilson [and Franklin Roosevelt] demonstrated the latent powers of the chief executive and set presidential leadership upon a new plane.

No. 8

AMENDING THE FEDERAL CONSTITUTION [1]

by Howard Lee McBain

WITHIN the calendar year 1933 two amendments were added to the Constitution of the United States. One of these abolished "lame duck" Congresses by changing the dates of the convening of Congress and of the inauguration of the President; the second repealed national Prohibi-

[1] H. L. McBain, "Amending the Federal Constitution," *The American Mercury* (February, 1934), Vol. 31, pp. 204-210. Reprinted by permission of *The American Mercury* and Mrs. Agnes Bartlett McBain.

tion. The event of amending the Constitution—never a common experience —is not without special significance at this time. For since March 4, 1933 our politico-economic structure has been undergoing swift, novel, and radical changes. Already the old Constitution finds itself groaning with the strain of stretching its terms to meet the new order [brought about by the depression and World War II]. It seems worthwhile, therefore, to take a new look at an old subject—the process by which the Constitution may be formally amended.

For a long time the difficulty of the amending process has been the subject of criticism. As everyone knows, an amendment must be proposed by a two-thirds vote of the members of each house of Congress—not two-thirds of the total membership, but of the members present at the time the vote is taken. Thereafter the proposal must be ratified by the legislatures or by conventions in three-fourths of the States as one or the other mode of ratification may be determined by Congress. This sounds formidable. It is. But what most people do not appear to know is that if history be taken as our guide, its formidableness consists in the two-thirds vote of the houses of Congress rather than in the extraordinary majority of the States that is required for ratification.

Literally hundreds of amendments have been introduced into one or the other or both houses of Congress. A few of them have run the gauntlet of one house but not of the other. Only . . . [twenty-seven] in all have run the gauntlet of both, and twelve of these were proposed at one time by the first Congress that assembled after the Constitution went into effect. Since 1789, therefore, a period of . . . [162] years, only . . . [fifteen] proposed amendments have passed the two houses of Congress, and three of these were of Civil War origin. It is thus evident that the big hurdle for amendments is the two-thirds vote. The difficulty that inheres in the ratifying process does not appear to have had any inhibiting effect upon Congress. Indeed, the contrary is probably true, since on doubtful proposals Congress would more readily pass the buck to the States, knowing how easily any proposal can be defeated by the action or inaction of a few of them.

I wonder, for example, how many members of the . . . [73rd] Congress, in spite of the apparent mandate of the election of November, 1932, voted to support the Prohibition repeal amendment with the covert thought and hope that it would have difficult sledding in at least the minimum thirteen States that could have prevented its ratification. Certainly few people thought in early 1933 that it would sweep the States as it did.

To emphasize the obstacle of the two-thirds vote is not, of course, to minimize the obstacle of ratification in three-fourths of the States. It is impossible to say how large this latter obstacle would have proved had

Congress been more prolific with proposals. Yet the fate which proposed amendments have met at the hands of the States is not without interest. Of the . . . [twenty-seven] amendments proposed by Congress only . . . [six] have failed of ratification. Two of these were among the original twelve amendments submitted in 1789. Both were inconsequential, one relating to the apportionment of representatives and the other to the compensation of members of Congress.

Likewise inconsequential was a proposed amendment of 1810 relating to titles of nobility. The fourth amendment which failed of ratification was one which on the very threshold of the Civil War sought to prohibit the abolition of slavery. The war killed its consideration. The fifth . . . [that failed] was the child labor amendment proposed in 1924. [The sixth that as yet has not been ratified—though it will be before the state legislatures until 1954—is the amendment proposed in 1947 limiting presidential tenure.] It thus appears that only . . . [three] amendments of any importance were ever defeated by the states, and one of these was a futile attempt to stem the tide of abolition at the peak of its flow.

Moreover, the States have usually acted with rapidity, especially when it is considered that few State legislatures meet annually and that they do not convene at any uniform time. The first ten amendments were under consideration by the States for less than two years. The eleventh, relating to suits against the States, required nearly four years for its adoption. The twelfth, dealing with the matter of electing the President and Vice-President, was ratified in nine months. The thirteenth, abolishing slavery, in ten months. The fourteenth, designed to protect the Negroes, in two years. The fifteenth, giving Negroes the right to vote, in one year. The sixteenth, authorizing income taxes, in three and a half years. The seventeenth, providing popular election of United States Senators, in one year. The famous eighteenth, in thirteen months. The nineteenth, providing woman suffrage, in fourteen months. The twentieth, abolishing "lame duck" Congresses, in one year. The twenty-first, repealing the eighteenth, holds the record of ratification in eight months, despite the fact that the procedure calling for ratification by State conventions required action not only by State legislatures but also by the voters and lastly by the elected conventions.

Another point of interest in this connection is that no proposed amendment has ever been positively turned down by one-fourth or more of the States. On the contrary, the necessary three-fourths have simply failed to ratify. Defeat has come by inaction rather than action. Theoretically, the . . . [six] unratified amendments are still before the States for their approval. Indeed, it may happen that revived interest in the subject of child labor may yet result in the ratification of that amendment, though this appears unlikely. [No time limit was put on the ratification of the child labor amendment. The amendment limiting presidential tenure in 1947 limited the ratification period to seven years.]

The rapidity with which most proposed amendments have been ratified by the States, thus indicating wide approval, is in itself perhaps a commentary on the reluctance of Congress to submit amendments. . . . The Federal income tax amendment proposed in 1909 had been actively agitated ever since the Supreme Court in 1895 had put the stamp of invalidity upon that form of taxation by Congress. For fourteen years Congress failed to propose the necessary amendment. Popular election of United States Senators had been urged for a generation or more and two-thirds of the House of Representatives had more than once approved a proposal to that end before the Senate finally yielded to public pressure in 1912. Indeed, a national constitutional convention was threatened if the Senate continued its obstinacy.

While the prohibition amendment and the woman suffrage amendment were not many years actually on the table before they were swept into the Constitution, it must be remembered that both propositions were unquestionably accelerated by . . . World War [1], and that support for them had been gathering strength by the steadily increasing roster of States that had adopted them as State policies. The evil of the "lame duck" Congress, curable only by process of amendment, had been the subject of popular complaint and demand for reform over a very long period of time. The repeal of national Prohibition, though it had advocates for a decade or more, was agitated as a serious possibility for a shorter period of time than was any other amendment of the modern era. Probably never before in our history was there such a swift change of popular sentiment on a contentious public issue. The very Congress that proposed it would not have dreamed of proposing it a year earlier than it did.

Before 1913 commentators had for a long time been saying that the Constitution of the United States was for practical purposes unamendable. History seemed to bear them out. In that year, however, the ratification of the income tax amendment broke the spell of inertia and proved the falseness of their criticism. Advocates of other amendments were heartened, and, as we have seen, five such were added in the next score of years. It seems clear nevertheless that, except in the event of some wide and sudden wave of public opinion, as in the case of sentiment for Prohibition repeal, it requires years of agitation and effort and apparently large popular demand to squeeze a proposal for amendment through the halls of Congress. This was true even of the child labor amendment, which to date has been defeated by the inaction of a sufficient number of States, perhaps proving thereby that public support was not as strong and general as many had supposed.

Should the amending process be made easier? The question might be and has in fact often been phrased thus: Should the amending process be democratized? The answer depends upon a larger number of considerations than are commonly advanced.

It is child's play to cite extreme figures of possibilities in denunciation of the present process. One-third plus one of the Senators can block any proposal to amend the Constitution. This would be thirty-three out of the ninety-six Senators, provided every Senator were present and voted. If these thirty-three chanced to be from the most sparsely settled States, they might represent only about 7% of the population of the Union. That is a ridiculously low representative percentage in which to vest such powers of obstruction.

But the fact is that Senators do not combine to vote on constitutional amendments in accordance with the census reports from their respective States. I suppose one might conceive of a proposed amendment in which the weight of the small States would be marshaled in opposition, but it would be highly exceptional in character. Despite the fact that the smaller States are much over-weighted in the United States Senate, some of the most conservative and reactionary of our Senators have come out of them. This goes to prove, if proof were necessary, that relative population figures are not a definitive factor in votes on constitutional amendments. In the election and the viewpoint of Senators sectional interests unquestionably play a part, but the comparative population of the several States has little relation to this except that most of the smaller States are predominately agricultural, Delaware and Rhode Island being conspicuous exceptions. In the votes of Senators numbers of dollars are sometimes more controlling than numbers of heads—by which I do not mean to imply bribery or corruption but merely an economic bent.

In the requirement of a two-thirds vote in the House of Representatives little complaint can be made of population inequalities since State quotas in the House are based on population. But the fact is that a two-thirds vote is difficult to get on any important matter in any non-homogeneous assembly. And certainly our houses of Congress, whatever the appearances and fictions of our two-party system, are sufficiently heterogeneous in character.

The answer to the question whether the two-thirds requirement should be reduced, say, to an ordinary majority appears to depend upon one's opinion as to how quickly responsive the Constitution should be to popular views of the moment. I can think of a lot of foolish amendments that have been introduced into Congress which luckily never got through.

In considering any proposal to ease the amending process it may be well to recall an historical fact or two. For example, from the era of Jacksonian democracy the doctrine impregnated our political philosophy for many years that a government was democratic in proportion to the number of officials that were chosen by popular vote. This doctrine, as applied, drove our State and local governments not only into administrative chaos but also into the almost unbreakable grip of machine politics. While it held sway amendment after amendment was introduced in one or the other house of Congress providing for the popular election of members of the President's Cabinet, of United States judges, and of a variety of Federal local officers, such as postmasters, district attorneys, customs officers, etc. Fortunately, the Federal government was saved this catastrophe and probably was saved by reason of the difficulty of the two-thirds vote. The appointive system has undoubted evils, but popular election would have been unthinkably worse. Ultimately the States and cities were impelled to retrace their steps in this matter.

Or to go back no further than 1912, Colonel Roosevelt apparently would at that time, if he could, have put through an amendment for the recall of judicial decisions, than which nothing could have been sillier, though no doubt the agitation on this whole subject of the recall of judicial decisions and of judges was wholesome in directing the attention of a good many judges to the seriousness of their public trust, and to the fact that the changing spirit of the times would not brook a too rigid Bourbonism on their part.

While I can recall these and other examples of foolish proposals that were forestalled, I cannot, on the other hand, think of any amendment which, having enlisted genuine and widespread interest and support, and having sustained that interest and support over a number of years, has been finally stifled by Congress. It is all a question of time. As matters now stand, a proposal for amendment cannot ordinarily be got through Congress unless a lot of people have done a lot of hard work in its behalf through a long number of years. If the requirements for proposals were reduced from a two-thirds to an ordinary majority this work would probably be lessened and the time shortened. For example, the Eighteenth Amendment was voted favorably by a majority of the House of Representatives as early as 1914; it mustered two-thirds only in 1918, in the midst of our participation in the war.

There are two points, however, that ought to be noted in connection with the consideration of any proposal to change in this respect the method by which the Constitution may be amended. In a country as large and diversified as is the United States the formation of positive public opinion on a national scale is difficult. The result is the formation of high-powered propaganda groups which in actual membership represent a small minority of the people. In our politics we are accustomed to the pressure of such groups. Their activities are widely denounced, especially, of course, by those who are opposed to their particular policies.

The Anti-Saloon League is probably the best example in recent history. The Women's Suffrage organization, of a wholly different character, was another. The wets have repeatedly declared that the Anti-Saloon League represented a minority of the people, even at the high point of its influence. Whether this was true or not it would be impossible to prove. Certainly there were large numbers of persons who adhered to belief in national Prohibition, whatever their relation to the League. The point is, however, that to reduce the majority required for the proposal of a constitutional amendment would manifestly increase the power of these fighting organizations. That should be recognized.

The second point to be observed is one that very few people appear to know. It is that the difficulty of the amending process seems often to have little to do with the number of amendments that actually triumph under it. This could be illustrated by reference to the actual practice of amendment under certain European constitutions. But we need go no further for illustration than our own States. A majority of the State constitutions require a two-thirds or three-fifths vote of the two houses of the legislature for the submission of an amendment to a vote of the people. Louisiana and Utah are two of these States. Contrast the results. The constitution of the former has been amended considerably over a hundred times in the twenty years of its existence. The constitution of the latter has been amended less than twenty times in the nearly forty years of its existence. The constitutions of about one-fourth of the States require that proposals before submission to the people shall be passed by two successive legislatures. New York and Iowa are in this group. The constitution of the former has been amended thirty-odd times in nearly forty years of its existence; that of the latter fewer than a score of times in a period of seventy-five years.

Though these figures are by no means conclusive, they at least illustrate that there are factors of importance other than the difficulty of amendment that determine the frequency of amendment. If we look only at the mathematics of the process, a two-thirds majority ought to be as easy to secure in Washington as in Baton Rouge. But it has not been. Nor would it be certain that the requirement of a simple majority in Congress would result in a marked increase in the number of amendments proposed.

Votes are often cast in Congress, as elsewhere, in the light of results that are known or closely guessed in advance of roll calls. The affirmative vote of a member under a two-thirds requirement might easily, in certain circumstances, become a negative vote under a bare majority requirement.

Let us look now at the requirement of ratification by the States. In spite of the fact that the States have failed to ratify only . . . [six] of the [twenty-seven] amendments that have been submitted to them by Congress, here again it is easy to cite extreme possibilities. One-fourth plus one of the States, that is, thirteen, can by mere inaction defeat any proposed amendment. If these thirteen States be those having the smallest populations, this means that fewer than 5% of the people of the country can defeat any proposed amendment. That seems absurdly small. Its possibility was greatly and naturally feared by those who promoted the repeal of the Eighteenth Amendment. But the point may again be made that it would have to be a very exceptional amendment that would unite in opposition only the smallest States in the Union.

Even so, in the last analysis both the proposal and the ratification of amendments is based upon an equality of the States, for each State has two Senators and each State has one ratifying vote. Considering the vast inequalities among the States in the matter of population as well as differences in economic and social interests, this extraordinary ratifying majority is certainly open to grave criticism. Ratification by a majority of the States containing a majority of the people would seem to be sufficient. But one has to attack the existing plan largely on grounds of theory, for the reason that there has been so little actual opposition in practice. The three-fourths vote has usually not been difficult to obtain, because proposals have seldom come out of Congress until the country as a whole has been thoroughly worked up to receive them.

In one most important respect democratization of the ratifying process has at length been achieved. The Prohibition repeal amendment was submitted not to State legislatures but to conventions elected in the several States for the sole and specific purpose of passing upon the proposal. This in effect amounted to a referendum to the people of the several States, though not, of course, a referendum to the people of the country as a unit. The vote was still by States. The referendum resulted from the fact that these conventions in the nature of things could not be deliberative assemblies. They could be nothing more than rubber stamps of the voters' will.

There was nothing to debate. National Prohibition had been discussed so freely and furiously throughout its short and inglorious existence that practically every numskull in the land was either for or against it. In most of the States the entire convention was elected on a Statewide ticket, there being a set of wet candidates and a set of dry candidates. The voters could scarcely have had the proposition put before them in a more direct "yes or no" fashion.

While this plan of submission to State conventions was before Congress a host of objections were raised: The State legislatures might not make provision for the call of conventions. The Governors might not call special sessions for this purpose. The plan would be expensive. It would delay the whole procedure. As usual, also, the legalists found grave difficulties: There were no precedents except the State conventions that ratified the original Constitution back in 1787-88. Did the Constitution authorize or require that Congress prescribe the time, place, manner, and all the other paraphernalia of procedure by which these conventions should be brought into being? or were all these matters left by the Constitution to the determination of the State legislatures?

Such were some of the bogies that raised their heads. They were definitely answered by swift-falling facts. Congress left all these matters to the State legislatures. Governors called State legislatures in special session where that was necessary. State legislatures provided for the call of conventions. Except for a very few matters, including the nomination of candidates, the ordinary election machinery of the State was employed. The voters voted and the conventions rubber-stamped. Precedents were established and a good many questions were answered, for the most part most sensibly. . . .

[Congress, therefore, has a satisfactory means at its disposal for submitting amendments to a popular vote and many people thought that no amendment would again be submitted to state legislatures. Congress, however, did not view the matter this way in 1947 when it passed and submitted to the state legislatures the proposed amendment limiting presidential tenure.

Senator Humphrey, Minnesota, along with a few other Senators advocated using the convention system again when the Senate debated a proposed amendment to abolish the electoral college in the Eighty-First Congress. And some students of constitutional law believe that Congress could go even further in providing for a popular referendum than it did when it submitted the Twenty-First Amendment. They believe that it might be possible for Congress constitutionally to provide for the state conventions in such a way that the elections would be held on the same day throughout the country and thereby actually hold a national referendum.]

[Given the fact that no constitutional change is necessary to secure a popular referendum on an amendment if Congress desires it] there remains only the possible abolition of the two-thirds vote in the Senate and the House and the even more desirable provision that ratification shall require a vote of a majority of the people of the country as a whole as well as a majority in a majority of the States. The latter requirement would probably be advisable not only as a sop to State equality but also because of the preponderant concentration of population in certain of the large industrial states. Such a change can be brought about only by amending the amending article itself, which has often been proposed. If it is ever accomplished, the useless conventions should doubtless be dispensed with and the respective powers of Congress and the State legislatures over the conduct of such referenda should be clarified in the newly phrased article.

No. 9

EVERYBODY'S BUSINESS [1]
[Changing the Rules in State Government]

NEVER before have so many states at one time been reconsidering their fundamental laws. In at least fifteen, constitutional revision is under way or being actively urged by political and civic leaders. This does not count Hawaii and Alaska, the two candidates for the honor of becoming the 49th state.

In short, American government is going through one of its great formative periods. What the people do with their state constitutions during the next five years may have as much influence on the future of our system as what they did during the first great period of constitution-making after 1776. This makes revision of state constitutions public business of first-rate importance—for all the people of all the states.

The people of each state have a vital stake in the quality of government in every state. Democratic federalism may be the only answer to the strong trend toward centralized dictatorships. The test of our federalism is not in the power and glory of the central government but in the vitality and effectiveness of the state and local units which make it up.

The current revival of interest in state and local government and the unprecedented effort to modernize constitutions and charters indicate that there is still plenty of life in the grass roots of our system. Whether this revival will prove only a flash in the pan or the beginning of a more vigorous democracy will depend on how resolutely and intelligently the people carry through. It would be a grave mistake to underestimate the dangers and consequences of failure.

[1] Editorial, "Everybody's Business," *The National Municipal Review* (March, 1948), Vol. XXXVII, No. 3, pp. 127-8. Reprinted by permission of *The National Municipal Review*.

Almost every state, except possibly those that have just gone through revision, desperately needs a new constitution. Few state constitutions ever were much good and fewer still have been fitted to the modern age of machine production, big cities and fast travel and communication.

The new American republic almost fell to pieces between the end of the Revolution and the adoption of the present Constitution of the United States. The disintegration was due not only to the ,lack of a sufficiently strong federal government but also to the incompetence and irresponsibility of the individual state governments.

The country was saved in 1789 not by the strengthening of the states but by covering them over with the protective tent of a stronger union. Although important changes have been made in state constitutions since that time, they have not produced a single document which approaches the federal constitution as a basis for responsible and effective government.

Here are some of the fatal weaknesses common to most state constitutions today:

1. A disintegrated executive branch, unable to provide responsible administration of the increasingly extensive and important services of modern government.

2. Complicated court systems manned by judges elected or appointed on terms which militate against the independence of traditional Anglo-Saxon justice and against the efficiency in administration required for the satisfactory performance of modern judicial business.

3. Bicameral legislatures almost impervious to reapportionment to meet shifts in population, especially the shift to the cities.

4. Limitations on legislative power which have so hog-tied state governments that the people are forced to turn to Washington for prompt and effective action on matters which should be handled locally.

5. Detailed provisions concerning county and other local governments which have seriously impeded the modern movement for home rule.

6. Inclusion in state constitutions of a mass of statutory details put there because of a fundamental distrust of the government of the day. Results have been the entrenchment of more and more vested interests and a blurring of the distinction between constitutional and state law which has confused the public and stymied healthy progress in law and government.

7. A long and indigestible ballot for the election of numerous state, county and local officers, including judges, which gives the voter an impossible and therefore disheartening task. This is a principal cause of public apathy and the substitution of government by private manipulators for government by the people.

8. Fantastic provisions for amendment and revision which in some cases have practically deprived the people of access to their basic law and in others have invited too frequent, even frivolous, changes.

This is an appalling indictment. One might reasonably ask, "How has our system survived?" The answer, already given, is that it could not have survived except by virtue of the federal government and at the expense of an unhealthy tendency to rely more and more upon Washington to compensate for failures at the state capitol and city hall.

The time is very late for a reversal of this trend but the signs in an increasing number of states indicate that it is still not too late. The next five or ten years may tell the story. The states *can* be rehabilitated and our federal system put on a firmer foundation than it has ever had. But this will require great determination on the part of citizens and civic leaders and rare statesmanship which disregards petty political and personal advantages on the part of public officials.

The discipline and determination required are surely not so great as those now demanded of the people of Great Britain and of other countries devastated and depleted by war. But the very fact that America is prosperous and intact means that we must display a political maturity remarkable, if not unprecedented, in human history in order to do what we must do.

No. 10

RESISTANCE TO CHANGE IN CITIES AND COUNTIES [1]

by Edward W. Weidner

CITIES and counties in the United States form the basic framework of our local government. In a country that is devoted to democracy, vigorous local government is of prime value, and it is therefore important that progressive changes be effected in these units. Yet while the national government has had its Hoover Commission of 1949 and its President's Committee on Administrative Management of 1937 and many states have had their little Hoover Commissions and reorganization plans from time to time, most local governments and especially counties seem to have stagnated in comparison, except for adoption by a city here and a city there of a council manager plan. Reform is more than a question of administrative reorganization, however. The scope of needed change in local government is much greater than that. It involves the number of units of local govern-

[1] Specially written for this book by Edward W. Weidner, Assistant Professor of Political Science, University of California, Los Angeles.

ment and the proper geographical area of each, the relationship of the citizen to his government, the role of the expert in local affairs, and the very nature of representative government.

It is common to blame the failure to effect a change in a particular local government on the inability to get out the vote on a particular day or on the failure of the legislature to pass a certain enabling act at a particular legislative session. But the real explanation involves the consideration of conditions that may be social or technological, personal or geographical, demographic or ideological.

We, of course, should never expect the same over-all achievement in obtaining change on a local level that is attained on state or national levels. The reason for this is simple. There is a far greater variety of people and conditions in local government than in the states and nation. Though there are poor states and rich states, small states and large states, extremes in wealth and size are much more disparate in cities and counties. The same may be said of almost all attributes of governments and people. Because of the very number of local government units, they exhibit more diversity in efficiency and inefficiency, innate conservatism and liberalism, apathy and drive, and numerous other special attributes.

If we were to plot the total picture of some one attribute of all local governments on a graph, we would find that the result would closely resemble the bell-shaped normal curve of distribution. Around the high center point of the curve (the norm) would fall the bulk of local governments, and from there their numbers would fall on a line tapering down and out from either side of the norm into the extremes mentioned above. The states and nation, on the other hand, would tend not to present such a normal cross-section. Partly because of their limited number and partly because of their superior position in the governmental hierarchy, the states and the nation attract the most capable leaders who, because of education, information and experience, tend to be more amenable to change than leaders in local governments. Though, again, we find extremes—very good and very bad—in leadership in cities and counties, the average is still not so good as that at state and national levels. It is to be expected, therefore, that change will be undertaken more quickly on state and national levels than on local levels.

We pride ourselves on the high value that we put on local government as an asset to democratic society. Part of the value inheres in the fact that groups that are minorities in a large constituency, such as a state or a nation, may become majorities in small units of local government. As a result, we get a vast governmental laboratory in our local governments. We can find our most efficient units of government in the United States at the local level, especially in certain cities. But we also can find our most inefficient units of government at the local level, especially in certain counties.

Such vast variety of people and conditions would lead one to conclude that a uniform pattern of reform for all units of local government is not acceptable. This is true, for example, when we consider the optimum physical area for a unit of local government, or the proper administrative organization, or the proper relationship of a city council to its people. There has been an unfortunate tendency among reformers, even firms of consultants who advise our local civic and official groups, to recommend a uniform pattern of organization and procedure for every locality. It is time to recognize that this is bad practice. In baseball each player develops his own stance in the batter's box from accepted basic principles. And so it should be in government. We must recognize that each locality has individual differences and must pick and choose its own particular adaptations of best basic principles. It must not apply the principles in rigid fashion; for, to the extent that a rigid pattern is adhered to, resistance to change is increased. There probably has been a wider adaptation of basic reorganization principles by the particular unit of government concerned on national and state levels than on local levels.

Resistance to change in cities and counties is further heightened by the fact that as a whole these units of local government are affected by fewer dynamic forces in our society than are states and the nation. Our nation is becoming more integrated. The most significant social and economic changes are taking place on a nation-wide or at least a region-wide scale. As a result, the adaptations that government must make to meet economic and social changes are made primarily on a national and state level and only secondarily on a local level. For example, while the population of the entire nation may grow tremendously, in many localities the population and population density may vary not at all or even decrease. The services citizens demand of some local governments may not be altered in the slightest by over-all changes in population or, say, by general depression or inflation; while at the same time, on national and state levels, the services demanded are enlarging or changing drastically.

More and more the national and state governments have been cushioning the shock of broad social and economic changes on local governments. To the extent they have been successful they have decreased the pressure for changes in local governments. This is a fact that needs underlining: Some of the most important stimuli to reform in cities and counties—indeed in any social institution—are extensive social and economic changes. Change does not take place in a vacuum. It is part of a chain reaction. To the extent that the national government and state governments are creating a semi-vacuum of constancy for local governments, they are draining off the demand for reform in localities.

Resistance to change also can be explained by a general lack of appreciation in local governments for the role of the expert. Professionalization of personnel has been a driving force for change on state and national levels, but the lack of professionalization in many local governments, whether through ignorance or lack of demand, is striking. To put the matter another way, the theory that any man can be a jack-of-all-trades, including that of public administrator, leads to a type of governmental organization quite different from that based upon a theory that policies, once democratically arrived at, are best executed by trained experts. It is not overstating the point to say that in many localities small government, indeed petty government, still exists. These localities employ no experts, no professionally competent individuals; and as a result, they cheat themselves of a vital source of change. Most of the localities which have recognized a need for technical advice have depended upon the states to supply it. Sometimes when states refuse such help and needs are so insistent, the local units are forced into employing experts themselves. But by whatever means the expert is brought onto the scene, the effect of his arrival is the same: The need for governmental reorganization becomes apparent almost immediately. It is not surprising that in states in which demographic changes are great, and hence the need for experts urgent, local government reform has proceeded at a rapid pace. California offers many excellent examples, as does Texas.

Much resistance to change can be traced to a lack of technical services. States and the national government and a few large cities can afford technical consultants to guide them in their decisions. But in many counties and in most of the smaller cities, the citizenry has no one to turn to for advice on improvements in its local government. Universities have been slow in extending the technical abilities and services of their staffs to the communities in their states, and the state governments themselves have been extremely slow in establishing central planning agencies that can extend advisory services to such groups. Voluntary organizations with adequate interest and knowledge in local government problems do exist but generally only in large urban areas. Without readily obtainable knowledge, we cannot expect change to be carried on at a satisfactory rate.

Even where knowledge, technical services and capable personnel exist, there are other factors which stand in the way of change. The more homogeneous and protected from the outside world a city or county is, the more likely it is that its tradition is impenetrable. Also, apathy tends to be rampant in such instances. As a matter of fact, the average citizen seems more interested in state and national issues than in those of local government. The relative number of votes cast in the elections for each level seems to bear out this contention. Intermingled with apathy and satisfaction with tradition is a spirit of live and let live. In purchasing supplies for local government, for example, it is considered good practice in many counties and cities to divide the purchases equally among the local merchants rather than to ask for bids or wholesale prices. This may be profitable for the local businessman, but it is not economical. Consequently, a tremendous resistance to change on the part of many influential members of the local populace is created because they have a stake in the status quo. Citizens usually do not become excited about such practices because they feel that local government needs to "favor" local citizens in every way possible. This is in part a question of values, of course. But such an attitude makes it difficult to uncover graft in instances where it does exist. In short, the friendly, easy, personal way of conducting most local governments is not conducive to modern organizational methods.

Resistance by vested interests, exemplified above by the stake of businessmen in purchases, has been one of the major deterrents to reform in local government. Vested interests are not limited to businessmen, however. The jobholders under any existing governmental scheme, the politicians or political groups in control of spoils or election devices, certain people with a stake in maintaining the current plan of rural-urban relations—all of these vested interests and many more may contribute to a feeling on the part of the individuals involved that they have a special advantage under the existing system, whatever that be. At any rate, whenever change is proposed in any local unit of government, whoever benefits from the existing system may feel that he must resist to the last any proposal to modify it.

The desire to resist is reinforced if the proposal is made by someone from outside the community. It may seem as if external forces are trying to obtain change for their own interests without regard to the interests of those who have some stake in the existing system. Consequently, those who have power under the existing system may feel that a proposal for change, made by a group not of their own, is a personal attack and resent it on such grounds. It may be that they lack adequate information or they may suffer from unwarranted fears. Nonetheless, their feelings are very real to them.

Unlike the higher levels of government which have open to them various avenues to change, local governments hardly ever can be reorganized by any means except a revision in the local charter. This in itself is difficult but often further complicated by the fact that many charters require more than a simple majority of votes to approve any amendment to them.

Errors in strategy during a campaign for a change sometimes create resistance to it. For example, taxpayers' groups frequently emphasize the economies that might be brought about by change. To a poor person, however, the cry of economy is not enough. There is a large segment of the population, including not only the poor but many other public-spirited citizens, who are less interested in economies than in adequate public services. They are more interested in education, parks and other services than in the tax rate.

Finally, we come to a series of barriers which, in the opinion of some observers, constitute the major obstacle to reform. They are the statutory, constitutional and judicial impediments to local reorganization. A thorough analysis of the situation indicates that though they may be of crucial importance in some states, they are of little or no importance in many others. Statutory and constitutional barriers simply mean the limitations in the statutes and in the constitution which prevent local governments from adopting reforms or provide an impossibly difficult procedure for effecting them. By judicial barriers are meant the restrictive judicial interpretations of statutes and constitutions limiting the power of local governments. The state legislature has the power needed to modify statutes but it generally fails to use that power. The reason why is a crucial point in the matter of local government reform. When a question of reorganization in some local unit is presented to the legislators, they inevitably hear also from those in opposition and arrive at the conclusion that the city or county is badly split. A cautious legislator then tends to take a hands-off attitude. If local officials and citizens cannot agree at least in large part upon a course of action, even upon home rule, it is not realistic to expect the legislature to jump at the chance of arbitrating local disputes.

There is little doubt that constitutional and statutory barriers have prevented reorganization in some cities and counties. However, if other and more basic factors preventing reorganization were neutralized or at least minimized, most constitutional and statutory barriers could be broken through, and judicial interpretations would no longer prevent the exercise of legally granted and greatly expanded powers by local governments.

If reorganization of local governments is to take place, those interested in furthering it must broaden and refine their attack. No single factor is responsible for the failure to achieve reform. If it is to be successful, it must be based, first, on a clear view of the ends to be achieved and, second, on an analysis of all the relevant aspects of the social, economic and political environment.

Chapter IV

THE SEPARATION OF POWERS

[IT is one of the dogmas of the American people that our governmental system does and should embody the theory of the separation of powers. They have accepted this dogma without critical thinking, and have given little attention to the real reasons for its adoption or the actual development of its operation. Perhaps the majority is of the opinion that the incorporation of this theory into our basic rules of politics was simply the result of a desire to avoid the tyranny of whatever politicians might be in control of either the executive or legislative branches of the government. Few perceived that, like the Constitution itself, the theory of the separation of powers was the product of the conservative reaction that followed the Revolution. Fearing control of government by the masses, the chief concern of the framers of the Constitution was to make the government stable and unresponsive to the popular will. They believed in a limited government, it is true, but it was popular rather than governmental aggression that they feared.

The theory of the separation of powers, however, was never as completely adhered to as many would like to believe. Its fundamental implications were, at the outset, violated by giving to each of the departments some controls over the other two; in other words the system of checks and balances was interlaced with the doctrines of the separation of powers. Furthermore, changes in our fundamental rules occasioned by basic changes in our society, have materially altered the application of even that part of the theory that was formally expressed in written constitutions. The emergence of the executive as a policy determining officer, and the enormous legislative powers exercised by the courts in the process of judicial review, amply illustrate these changes. With reference to the executive and the legislative departments, many have advocated further formal changes in their basic relationships in order to bring the two into closer harmony. While these proposals seemingly have much merit in them, they would involve very basic changes in our fundamental rules, changes which should be clearly and fully perceived before the step is taken.

The relationship of the judiciary to the legislative and executive branches of government is, of course, a part of the whole problem of the separation of powers. This relationship is, in the American system, however, so closely bound up with the problem of judicial review that a full discussion is reserved for a separate chapter. Those who wish to consider the problem at this point may refer to Chapter XXII.]

No. 11

THE SEPARATION OF POWERS IN AMERICAN GOVERNMENT [1]

by W. F. Willoughby

NO idea is more firmly held by the mass of the American people than that the most fundamental principle upon which their government is based is that of a separation of powers. It is in this separation of powers which they believe to exist that they find the greatest guarantee of their political liberties and safeguard against a despotic use of power by public officials. To this characteristic, on the other hand, is attributed many, if not most, of the evils which our system of government presents in actual operation; and in doing away with this separation of powers is believed to lie the only effective remedy against such evils. . . .

The fact of the matter is that our government represents one in which neither the theory of the union of powers nor that of a separation of powers has been consistently carried out. In framing our constitution, its authors proceeded upon the theory that all of the powers of government were divisible into the three great branches of legislative, judicial, and executive, and that separate provision should be made for each. They failed utterly to recognize, or to make any direct provision for, the exercise of administrative powers. In consequence of this failure, our entire constitutional history has been marked by a struggle between the legislative and the executive branches as to the relative parts that they should play in the exercise of this power. This is a matter to which we will give special attention in another place.

Disregarding this point for the present, we find that the framers of the constitution, in acting upon this theory that the powers of government fall into the three classes of legislative, judicial, and executive, proceeded to provide for three organs, a Congress, a Judiciary, and a President, which should constitute the three branches, or departments, of government corresponding to these three powers. Having made provision for these separate organs, they, however, refused to vest in them the exclusive exercise of the powers to which they correspond. On the contrary, they so defined the powers of each and so distributed the exercise of the three powers among them that

[1] W. F. Willoughby, *The Government of Modern States* (New York: D. Appleton-Century Co., 1936), pp. 241-249, 256-257. Reprinted by permission of the publisher.

no one can act independently in its own field. In almost all vital matters, the concurrence of one or more of the other two organs is required. A rapid survey of some of the more important provisions of our constitution bearing upon the exercise of the three powers will show to how great an extent this is true.

Though the first section of the constitution provides that "all legislative powers herein granted shall be vested in a Congress of the United States which shall consist of a Senate and a House of Representatives," active participation in the exercise of this power is in fact conferred upon the executive branch by the requirement that no bill shall become a law until it is referred to the President for his approval and by the power that is granted to the latter to veto such bills as do not meet with his approval. It is true that such veto may be overridden if a two-thirds majority vote for such action can be secured in both houses. This, however, does not negate the fact that the executive is given an active participation in the exercise of the legislative power and that this participation, in the great majority of cases, determines whether a given measure shall, or shall not, become a law. In this connection it is important to note that this veto power of the President, though negative in form, can be and is used to influence legislation in a positive way. This is done by the President letting it be known that if certain provisions are omitted from, or allowed to continue in, a measure it will receive his veto. In considering measures, Congress has constantly to bear in mind this contingency of a presidential veto. Through the possession of this power, the President thus exercises a very positive influence in determining the character of the laws that are drafted by Congress and sent to him for his approval.

This power to veto bills represents, moreover, but one of the ways in which the President participates actively in the exercise of the legislative power. The provision of the constitution that the President "shall from time to time give to the Congress information of the state of the Union and recommend to their consideration such measures as he shall judge necessary and expedient" has been interpreted as conferring upon the President, not only the authority, but the obligation, to propose legislation. In the early days of the Republic, it was believed that the President had exhausted his authority under this grant when he had brought to the attention of Congress action which in his opinion should be taken: responsibility for taking action upon these recommendations was deemed to rest wholly with Congress. Within recent years, however, a radical change of attitude towards this function has taken place. The people now look to the President, not only to formulate a definite legislative program, but to exert all his influence and power to secure favorable action upon it. A few years ago, Congress would have resented as an infringement of its function any attempt on the part of a President to embody his proposals in the form of definite drafts of bills. Now the President boldly puts his proposals in this form, declares them to be administration measures, and takes the position that support of them is a test of party fealty.

The President, moreover, does not stop with this formulation of a legislative program. He thereafter exerts himself to the utmost to secure favorable action upon his proposals. He is in constant consultation with the leaders of his party in Congress. By personal interviews and other means, he seeks to overcome the opposition of members not favorably disposed. If need be, he uses the great powers which he possesses to bring pressure to bear upon individual members to support his measures. Patronage can be liberally bestowed or wholly withdrawn, special action desired by members can be supported or opposed. In extreme cases, the fight can be carried into a member's district and his renomination or re-election to office can be supported or antagonized according to the position taken by him in relation to administration measures. The extent to which such a use of power by a President to coerce a member of Congress in the exercise of his function as a legislator is legitimate raises an important question which will be considered elsewhere. Here it is desired only to bring out the extent to which the President both has and uses the power to influence legislation and thus to make of himself one of the distinct organs through which the legislative function is performed. There can be little doubt that this increased participation on the part of the President in the field of legislation meets with popular approval.

The same demand that the chief executive shall formulate and seek to secure action upon a legislative program is equally evident in the administration of the affairs of the individual states. The assumption of this important function in relation to legislation by the chief executive, both of the federal government and of the constituent states, thus bids fair to harden into one of the firmly established conventions of our constitutional system. In virtue of this convention and the existence of the veto power by the President, it is thus not going too far to say that the President now constitutes an organ of legislation scarcely second in power and importance to Congress itself.

The chief executive is not the only organ, however, with which Congress has to share the legislative function. It has now become firmly established that upon the courts falls the function of determining whether the several branches of government in the exercise of their powers have kept within the limitations imposed upon them by the constitution through which they were established and their powers defined. Attention has already been called to the fact that one of the serious consequences of the attempt to define by constitutional enactment the extent of governmental powers and the manner in which these powers shall be distributed territorially and functionally is the establishment of a system under which many questions are bound to arise regarding the exact meaning and intent of these provisions and their application to particular concrete cases. This renders it imperative that authority shall be vested in some organ to pass upon these questions. In the United States, this power has been assumed by the courts as a part of their general duty to interpret the law of the land. The result is that all laws must finally pass the test of judicial approval if any question regarding their constitutionality is raised.

It might seem that this power possessed by the courts to construe laws is distinctly a judicial power and in no way partakes of the nature of the exercise of legislative power. Strictly speaking, this is so. Two facts, however, have made the exercise of this power by the courts one profoundly affecting the exercise of the legislative power. The first is the fact that, in practice the provisions of the federal and State constitutions determining the powers of government and the manner of their exercise have proved of such a character that it is almost impossible for Congress or a State legislature to depart in any way from the beaten path without giving rise to the question of the legality of their action. The result is that almost every attempt made by them to break new ground for the purpose of solving social problems has been questioned in the courts, and the latter have therefore the final say as to whether they should prevail. The second is that, in passing upon these questions, the courts have taken the position that it is a part of their function to determine the facts to which the laws are intended to apply as well as to interpret the language of the laws themselves. For example, the legislature, when it passes a law fixing the maximum number of hours of labor in a given industry, does so in the belief that the conditions are such as to bring such action within the police power of the State and thus to meet any objection that may be raised that it represents an improper infringement of the constitutional provision that no person shall be deprived of life, liberty, or property without due process of law. The courts, in passing upon laws of this character, have, however, assumed the power of questioning the soundness of this belief. If, in their opinion, such laws are not required for the proper protection of the individuals that may be affected by them, or the general public, they have not hesitated to declare such laws null and void, as not representing a proper exercise of the police powers and consequently as being instruments violating the constitutional provision just cited. The issue between the legislature and the courts is here one purely of fact and expediency. The propriety of the courts taking this position regarding their power is seriously questioned. This, however, is a matter into which we cannot here enter. We are concerned now merely with the fact that in our governmental system, as it actually works at the present time, the courts play a very large role in determining the character of legislation that the country shall have.

To sum up, it will thus be seen that our governmental system, instead of being one of the definite separation and segregation of powers, is, as far as the exercise of the legislative power is concerned, so decidedly the reverse that all three departments of government, the legislative, the executive and the judicial, participate in the exercise of this power. Authority and responsibility, instead of being concentrated in a single organ, are distributed among a number.

If we turn from the legislative to the executive power, we find here too a failure to vest the exercise of this power wholly in one organ. It is true that the constitution provides that "the executive power shall be vested in a President of the United States." Subsequent provisions, however, provide for the participation by Congress in the exercise of the power. The more important of these provisions are those which provide that the President shall have power to make treaties with foreign powers only by and with the advice and consent of the Senate and upon the concurrence of two-thirds of the Senators present, that Senatorial approval shall be had of the appointment of important officers, and that Congress and not the President shall be the authority to declare war and to provide for the calling forth of the militia.

Notwithstanding these provisions the principle of vesting the executive power in the hands of a single organ prevails to a far greater extent than it does in the case of the legislative power. The President, moreover, has been able effectively to protect himself from encroachment upon the exercise of his executive powers. The only possible exception exists in respect to the exercise of the treaty-making power. Here it is believed by many that the Senate has pushed its power to greater lengths than was originally contemplated. In this the author does not concur. It is significant that the provision granting the power to the Senate does not provide simply that treaties before becoming effective shall be approved by the Senate, but stipulates that they shall be made by and with the advice and consent of the Senate. Clearly this anticipated that the Senate should be consulted throughout the work of negotiating treaties. If anything, the practice on the part of Presidents of negotiating treaties without seeking the advice of the Senate and only bringing the treaties as negotiated before that body for approval or rejection represents an encroachment on the authority of the Senate as defined by the constitution.

Of the several powers, the judicial power is the one which has been most definitely concentrated in a single organ. The exercise of this power is vested solely in the judiciary. Neither the legislative nor the executive can be said to exercise this power in any way unless, possibly, the impeachment power of Congress be deemed to be judicial in character. Notwithstanding the dependence of the judiciary upon Congress and the President as regards the determination of its organization, procedure, and personnel, the judicial power itself is not distributed among two or more organs as is the case in respect to the executive, legislative, and administrative power, but is vested exclusively in one organ, the judiciary. In exercising its functions, the latter, moreover, enjoys a practical immunity from pressure of every sort from the other departments of government. This is due partly to the provision of the constitution that the judges shall hold office during good behavior and their compensation shall not be reduced during their terms of office, but chiefly to the tradition now firmly established that judges should exercise their judgment in an entirely independent manner. This tradition prevents the other departments from attempting to influence the judges and causes the judges to repel any such attempt should it be made. That in practice the United States has had a remarkably independent judiciary is beyond question. . . .

If now we seek to sum up and characterize in general terms the system of government of the United States from the standpoint of the manner in which this problem of distribution of powers functionally has been met, it will be seen that the system established, instead of being one of separation of powers, as is popularly supposed, is one which, while not embracing the principle of union of powers, in fact provides for a joint exercise of powers from both the organic and personal standpoints. It is true that special organs have been created for the exercise of legislative, executive, and judicial powers, and that general provisions have been incorporated in the constitution that the legislative, the executive, and the judicial powers respectively shall be vested in these organs. Actually, however, as we have seen, no one of these organs is independent and supreme within its own field. Especially is this true in respect to the two branches which are most directly concerned with the actual conduct of the internal affairs of government—the legislative and the executive.

This system under which each branch in its operations is more or less subject to the control of one or both of the other two branches is one which has been aptly designated as a system of checks and balances. The explanation of the adoption of a system of this character lies in the apprehension that existed at the time of the adoption of the constitution of the danger which was believed was inherent in any governmental system of the abuse of power by those in authority. One has but to read the discussions of the period to see how the framers of our constitution were dominated by the fear that either the popular branch of the government, the legislative, or the executive would so exercise its powers as to establish in effect a popular or autocratic tyranny. All governments, they believed, had to steer a difficult course between the Scylla of executive tyranny on the one hand and the Charybdis of democracy, or mob rule, as it was designated, on the other. Safety, they believed, could only be secured by making it possible for one branch of the government to check the other at all vital points. Due to this belief, the framers of our constitution were more interested in the negative than in the positive aspects of government, or at least gave undue prominence to the former. They were more concerned about preventing abuses and forestalling possible dangers than about establishing an efficient governmental organization.

No. 12

THE PRESIDENT AND CONGRESS [1]

by Wilfred E. Binkley

MUSTERED out after four years of service in the Union army Captain Oliver Wendell Holmes was back home in Boston. Presently he went out to call on his old philosopher friend at Concord. Emerson's conversation flowed on smoothly as he aired his transcendental abstractions of life and death, conscience and duty. The veteran of many a bitterly contested battle left convinced that Emerson was out of touch with reality. Battle experience had made Captain Holmes a stark realist who would henceforth translate life in terms of struggle. In 1872 Lord Justice Brett, under the Criminal Law Amendment of 1871, sentenced the London gasstokers' leaders to prison for a year for merely preparing to strike. Thereupon the act was condemned as class legislation, which criticism induced Holmes to expound his theory of legislation in a brief but illuminating article published in the *American Law Review* of which he was now editor.

The more powerful interests must be more or less reflected in legislation. . . . The objection to class legislation is not that it favors a class, but either that it fails to benefit the legislators, or that it is dangerous to them because a competing class has gained in power, or that it transcends the limits of

[1] Wilfred E. Binkley, "The President and Congress," *The Journal of Politics* (February, 1949), Vol. II, No. 1, pp. 65-79. Reprinted by permission of *The Journal of Politics* and the author. The footnotes in the original version are omitted here.

self-preference which are imposed by sympathy. . . . But it is no sufficient condemnation of legislation that it favors one class at the expense of another; for much or all legislation does that; and none the less when the bona fide object is the greatest good of the greatest number. . . . If the welfare of the living majority is paramount, it can only be on the ground that the majority have the power in their hands. *The fact is that legislation in this country, as well as elsewhere, is empirical. It is necessarily made a means by which a body, having the power, put burdens which are disagreeable to them on the shoulders of somebody else.*

When Holmes in the same article wrote that "whatever body (legislature) may possess the supreme power for the moment is certain to have interests inconsistent with others which have competed unsuccessfully," it sounds like a comment on American labor's serious set-back in the congressional elections of 1946. His observation on British labor legislation of the 1870's that "the more powerful interests must be more or less reflected in legislation" would be just as applicable to the Taft-Hartley Act three quarters of a century later. When the Farm Bloc induced Congress to establish a permanent policy of parity prices by which citizens, first as taxpayers, support the price of farm products by keeping them off the market even if the government must destroy valuable food supplies in order that these citizens, in the second place, as consumers, may be compelled to pay higher prices— there can be no doubt that legislation is "necessarily made a means by which a body having the power puts burdens disagreeable to them on the shoulders of somebody else."

Such then is how the Congress functions in the stage to which civilization has thus far advanced. Of course, the social structure of the United States is fundamental in the dynamics of congressional lawmaking and the constantly shifting strength of the competing interests results in ever changing points of equilibrium among them and consequently different kinds of legislation. One of our concerns here and now is the question as to how accurately the Congress, through its structure and habits, registers these balances of the competing forces of American society. Herein we may find fundamental causes of the recurring contests between President and Congress.

The persistent usage requiring a Representative in Congress to be a resident of the district that elects him makes him extraordinarily obsequious to his constituents. The reason is that the American member of Congress when defeated cannot, like the English member of Parliament, seek election in another district. When there is a near balance of parties in an American congressional district the Representative's function tends to become quasi judicial as he weighs the claims of competing interests. Thus he must seek to discover points of equilibrium when confronted with controversial issues on pending legislation. This signifies that the Congressman's legislative function is the translation of public opinion into public policy but as John Dickinson observes:

> The only opinion, the only will, which exists is the opinion, the will, of special groups. . . . The task of government and hence of democracy as a form of government, is not to express an imaginary popular will, but to effect adjustments among the various special wills and purposes which at any given time are pressing for realization.

The Congressman's calculation as to the point of equilibrium or the balance of forces in his district constitutes his bid for reelection which is an essential feature of the representative process as established by American usage. But there are 435 Representatives and 96 Senators, each presumably engrossed with his own problem of satisfying the dominant interests of his constituency while it remains for the President to seek for common denominators of national policy in the jig-saw puzzle of these 531 constituencies.

The problem of the President in dealing with Congress is complicated by the fact that the House of Representatives is so constituted that rural population not only has more than its proportionate share of Representatives in Congress but also because, as a consequence of the use of seniority in determining committee chairmen, the rural Representatives almost monopolize the chairmanship of the House committees. Thus urban constituencies not only fail to get their proper number of Congressmen but those they do elect largely fail to attain the positions of power in the organization of the House that control important legislation. The House of Representatives was established originally on the plan that representation should be approximately proportionate to population. The failure to maintain that principle is due to the delay of state legislatures in remapping congressional districts after a decennial reapportionment of Congressmen among the states. In many populous states the rural population, though a minority, can dominate the state legislature and thereby maintain an antiquated distribution of Congressmen. For example, Ohio was last redistricted for representation in Congress on the basis of the census of 1910, since which date population has concentrated intensively in a few urban counties. This leaves two thirds of Ohio's congressional districts with less than the national average of population per Representative and these sparsely settled districts are of course predominantly rural districts.

If urban population suffers from the mapping of its vast population in fewer than its fair share of congressional districts, even far more is it penalized by the rule of seniority in determining the leadership in the House of Representatives. The sovereignty in the House of Representatives is concentrated emphatically in the Speaker, the Rules Committee, the minority floor leader, and the chairmen of important standing committees. Long continuous service in Congress is an absolute prerequisite for occupancy of these places of power. Obviously this all signifies that these masters of the House represent the "safe" or practically one-party districts which are by no means confined to the Democratic party and "the solid South." An examination of the occupants of the top 76 positions of the Republican organization in the Eightieth Congress reveals an average previous tenure of 14½ years. Such a tenure spans the entire epoch of the New Deal despite its near total eclipse of Republican power. Moreover these 76 Republican Congressmen, with rare exceptions, represent agrarian districts. Their constituencies are intensely property and production conscious and consequently provide ready allies of business, industrial management and finance. The election of 1946 brought new Republicans to Congress from urban-industrial districts but their lack of seniority relegated them to unimportant committees. Indeed urban districts manifest a less stable party tendency, change Congressmen more frequently, and thus fail to attain commanding positions of power in Congress. As a consequence whenever the President urges upon Congress controversial measures in behalf of the urban masses such, for example, as rent or price control or housing legislation, he plays the game with Congress against heavily loaded dice.

Though based on French experience the observations of Emile Giraud are just as pertinent to the United States when he concluded that the legislature must be directed by the executive, the organ with "unity of thought," "capacity to acquire a view of the whole," and "possessing, by virtue of its participation in administrative and diplomatic activities, adequate information." "A feeble executive means a feeble state, one which fulfills badly its function of protecting the individual against political, economic, and social forces which, without the state, tend to swallow him up." The principle is easily stated but just how the executive is to "direct" the legislature or how the two great organs of government are to be integrated for the smooth and efficient functioning of government is a problem not yet solved by any nation—not even by Britain.

The evidence is conclusive that the fathers of the Constitution were far less fanatical devotees of the dogma of separated powers than their great-grandchildren. The framers did not specifically prescribe the separation of powers but merely implied it. The Courts have been compelled to resort to none too certain principles of jurisprudence in giving their judgments as to whether one or another branch of the government may "constitutionally" exercise a disputed power. Certainly the framers did not forbid the heads of the executive departments appearing in or even having permanent seats in the houses, although the Constitution does forbid their being members. The records of the first several Congresses provide incontrovertible evidence of the framers' assumption that the department heads would provide the initiative in legislation. At any rate eighteen delegates of the Constitutional Convention later sat unprotesting in the First Congress as one outstanding legislative problem after another was referred for study and report to the heads of executive departments. Congress had Secretary of the Treasury Alexander Hamilton, in his assumed role of the "prime minister," prepare and send to the House of Representatives the famous *Reports* on which were based the monumental statutes of the Hamiltonian program. Evidently these framers who sat in Congress thought it not improper that Hamilton use, as he did, his personal influence to persuade Congress to support these measures. So smoothly did this legislative-executive arrangement work that, to the Federalists, who were by and large the framers of the Constitution and who put it in operation, the relation of Congress to the executive must have seemed to have been properly, firmly, and finally established.

For better or for worse the Federalist adjustment proved to be transient. It was indeed but the first of many different adjustments of Congress to the executive that have come about as a consequence of the play of the forces of American society upon the national government. It can be set down as a fundamental principle that whether Congress or the executive is dominant in the government depends upon which of the two, in a given period, is the more adequate medium of governmental control for the dominant interests of the nation. The Federalist group combination had been so harassed by the "omnipotent" agrarians who dominated state legislatures that they had vested strong executive powers in the Presidency and then fortified those by the usage of executive initiative in legislation. Their opponents, the Anti-Federalists who had at first opposed the ratification of the Constitution, were infuriated by the Hamiltonian policies, rallied under Jefferson, captured the federal government and turned the Federalists out in 1801. These Jeffersonians had found the state legislatures satisfactory organs for their purposes and they consequently made the national legislature their peculiar organ by terminating its dependence upon executive departments. They established instead a system of congressional committees to take the place of the executive departments in shaping legislation, thereby setting a pattern that persists to this day. Under the Jeffersonians the Presidency gradually declined to an organ of relative insignificance in the federal government.

It was the awakening of the American masses in the 1820's, their revolt against what they considered the failure of a government dominated by Congress to satisfy their needs, and their consequent turning with passionate devotion to a party messiah in Jackson that ended the hegemony of Congress. Jackson proclaimed himself a "tribune of the people" and, through the veto power, made the Presidency practically a third branch of the legislature. A new dominant interest, that of the "common man," had found the Presidency to be the most convenient organ for achieving its desires and it has ever since turned to the Presidency for redress of grievances whenever stirred by a sense of crisis. Thus Jackson, Lincoln, and the two Roosevelts have been pre-eminently "tribunes of the people" and have brought to bear upon Congress the pressures of public opinion crystallized by presidential leadership.

When "the people" captured the Presidency under Jackson and made the office peculiarly their own it brought an about-face in the old group combination that had once been the Federalist party but which now constituted the Whig party. The President as a popular leader—demagogue was the favorite Whig epithet—was considered a potential dictator who ought consequently to be held rigorously subordinate to Congress. The present Republican party inherited the Whig attitude toward the Presidency. For more than a century now Congress has been the chief reliance of the industrial-finance-transportation complex of interests. Their conception of the proper relation of President to Congress was only too frankly expressed when, in the midst of the presidential campaign of 1864, the majority leaders of the two houses of Congress of Lincoln's own party in the notorious Wade-Davis Manifesto declared that "the authority of Congress is paramount" and informed their own presidential candidate that "if he wishes our support he must confine himself to his executive duties—to obey and to execute, not to make laws." It is significant that Theodore Roosevelt, the only other Republican President notable for vigorous executive leadership, had no happier time than Lincoln in dealing with the high command of his party. The Republican party consists of a group combination historically intolerant of executive leadership. It is scarcely improper to designate the Republican as a congressional party. The late Senator John Sherman knew thoroughly the genius of his Republican party when he advised President-elect Benjamin Harrison: "The President should have no policy distinct from that of his party and that is better represented in Congress than in the Executive."

The Republican dogma of congressional supremacy over the executive is almost certain to decline in practice, however much it may be proclaimed in theory. It was indeed a Republican President, Theodore Roosevelt, who gave the first marked impetus in this century to the practice of the legislative leadership of the President. "A good executive under present conditions of American life," he wrote in his *Autobiography*, "must take an active interest in getting the right kind of legislation in addition to performing his executive duties with an eye single to the public welfare." As a practical politician with previous legislative experience Theodore Roosevelt in the presidential office hit upon the expedient of occasionally inviting the master of the House of Representatives, Speaker Joseph G. Cannon, to the White House where the two conferred and came to an understanding on pending legislation, thereby establishing an organic integration of the two branches. Nor did he stop with this. Reminiscent of the Federalist liaison between the Executive and Congress is the comment of Senator Dolliver of Iowa in the fifth year of the Presidency of Theodore Roosevelt: "There are at least five acts of legislation, all of them referring to this and similar questions, that were put through Congress in the last five years practically without change, as they came from the office of the Attorney General of the United States." Shortly afterward it was admitted on the floor of the House that the pending Pure Food and Drug Act originated in a similar manner.

It was President Wilson who gave the first great demonstration in this century of executive leadership in legislation. As a student of politics he had become fascinated with the parliamentary system and he thought the Constitution provided both an opportunity and an invitation to introduce it in the national government in the clause that authorized the President to give Congress information on the state of the union and make recommendations for their consideration. In the fashion of a prime minister he appeared from time to time to address Congress in short but precise appeals for the passage of specific legislation. He made use of his party caucus and party organization in Congress to procure enactment of probably the most consistent legislative program since that of Hamilton. On the occasion of at least two important measures pending at different times in Congress Wilson stated privately his intention to resign if the vote were adverse to his recommendations, but he was sustained on both measures. The mental pattern of the parliamentary system can be seen between the lines of Wilson's ill-fated appeal for the election of a Democratic Congress in 1918. Even the election of 1920 was a "solemn referendum" on the Covenant of the League of Nations. Wilson set the pattern of legislative leadership for his chief disciple, President Franklin Roosevelt, no matter how very different the methods of the latter may have been.

In the full tide of the reaction against Wilson's leadership candidate Warren G. Harding mortgaged his presidential leadership by pledging himself to be a "constitutional" President only to find himself shackled in office when he sought to carry out party pledges. No matter how reluctant Calvin Coolidge was to assume legislative leadership, such had been the effect on the Presidency of Theodore Roosevelt and Woodrow Wilson that he admitted it to be "the business of the President as party leader to do the best he can to see that the party platform purposes are translated into legislative and administrative action." Coolidge even went so far in recognizing the legislative role of the President as to draw up legislation to apply the unexpended balance of the Deficiency Appropriation Bill of July 3, 1926, to the prosecution of litigation to cancel the Fall-Sinclair-Doheny oil leases. It was as an ex-President, however, that Coolidge expressed his most notable recognition of the President's appropriate function with respect to Congress when he declared, "It is because in their hours of timidity the Congress becomes subservient to the importunities of organized minorities that the President comes more and more to stand as the champion of the rights of the whole country."

According to Robert Luce, President Hoover "sent drafts of several important proposals to the Capitol to be introduced by leaders" despite the fact that later as an ex-President he declared the "militant safeguard of liberty" to be "legislative independence" and that "the weakening of the legislative arm does lead to encroachment by the executive upon the legislative and judicial functions, and inevitably that encroachment is upon individual liberty."

The twentieth century trend toward presidential leadership in legislation was greatly accelerated in the 1930's by the concurrence of a poignant crisis with the accession to the Presidency of a genius in the translation of current social forces into outstanding public policies. The studies of Lawrence H. Chamberlain indicate that almost half (8 out of 19) of the notable federal statutes of the last three quarters of a century that were mainly due to presidential leadership fall within the Presidency of Franklin Roosevelt. It is further striking evidence of President Roosevelt's leadership in legislation when Chamberlain found that of the thirty-five great statutes since the 1870's due predominantly to congressional initiative only two fell within the Presidency of Franklin Roosevelt.

After the rush and confusion of the first "hundred days," President Franklin Roosevelt gradually reduced the executive's participation in the legislative process to a quite definite pattern of procedure. Usually the way was paved for the introduction of new administration measures by having thorough preliminary studies made of the project. Relevant data were gathered and analyzed by nationally recognized specialists in the field of the proposed legislation. Meanwhile, appropriate publicity was being disseminated in order to inform the public and stimulate a pressure that might be brought to bear upon Congress. President Roosevelt knew from his own experience in the legislatures of New York that lawmaking is a slow and tedious process requiring hearings in order that those who might be affected by the proposed legislation can be heard. He had indeed himself practiced the legislator's difficult art of discovering the point of equilibrium among competing interests bearing on a pending bill. President Roosevelt had a habit of conferring frequently with what came to be known as the "Big Four," the Speaker of the House, the President of the Senate and the majority floor leaders of House and Senate. He took particular pains to see to it that an administration measure would not be referred to a committee inhospitable to legislation of the kind represented by a particular bill. When the bill reached the committee the information was at hand and the specialists prepared to answer the questions that might be raised.

President Truman was far less systematic than his immediate predecessor in promoting legislation, failing even to keep his own majority party organization in the Seventy-ninth Congress informed as to his plan. However, Congress had by this time become so accustomed to looking to the executive for legislative initiation that during the Eightieth Congress even with a Republican majority Senator Homer Ferguson of Michigan, an outstanding Republican leader, uttered this critical comment concerning President Truman:

> If the President wants to tell the people that he stands for a certain thing, he ought to come out with his proposal. He ought to come to the House and Senate with a message. And he ought to provide a bill if that is exactly what he wants.

Nothing can bring into bolder relief the generation's trend toward executive initiative in legislation than a Republican Senator's complaint that a Democratic President has failed to send a prepared bill to a Republican Congress. When President Truman sent Congress a proposal for certain legislation in the summer of 1948 a critical commentator remarked, "If President Roosevelt had recommended that legislation there would have been found lying right under the message a bill with the last 't' crossed and 'i' dotted."

Inch by inch then we seem to be resuming somewhat the original pattern of executive initiative in legislation with which the Federalists started off the government in 1789. At any rate over half the bills dropped in the congressional hoppers are said to originate in the executive departments so that "much legislation is tailor-made in the departments and sent to the Speaker or appropriate committee chairman for introduction in the House." Many of these measures are prepared in compliance with requests of congressional committees which is suggestive at least of the practice of the First Congress asking the departments for reports on projects. Before administration measures are transmitted from department to congressional committee they are routed through the Legislative Reference Division of the Bureau of the Budget to determine whether they conform with the

President's general program. Many congressional committees regularly refer bills to the department affected and report favorably only if the matter is approved by that department. Of course it is rather the routine and non-controversial measures by and large that can be handled by this procedure. This trend may be temporarily checked when Congress and President belong to opposing parties, a situation that might suspend but not reverse a trend so pronounced as to represent a wholesome developing usage.

It is in the enactment of such major matters of legislation as social security, or the Wagner or Taft-Hartley Labor laws affecting, as they do, powerful interest groups and sections of the nation, that the stresses and strains inherent in the American social structure become apparent. It is obviously erroneous to attribute the resulting clashes and deadlocks of President and Congress to party differences since alignments on such measures often manifest a tendency to ignore party affiliation. The enactment of Roosevelt New Deal legislation was stopped dead in its tracks in 1938 by the "unholy alliance" of Southern Democrats with Republicans. President Truman's program for domestic legislation encountered the same obstinate combination and it is significant that the Republican Congress that countered Truman's legislative program in 1947 served only to emphasize an executive-legislative deadlock already nine years old—nine years of Democratic Presidents and Congresses. Historically, Republican Presidents have, as a rule, been rather less happy than Democratic Presidents in getting Congress to enact their programs.

The clash of President and Congress is intensified by the striking differences between the ways in which pressures play upon the Congress on the one hand and upon the President on the other. For example, important elements such as labor, racial and certain other groups are peculiarly weak in urging their desires upon Congress. Consequently they quite naturally and properly seek to exert a leverage on the government through their voting strength as balance of power in presidential elections. Indeed, here is a counterbalance against the immense advantage the interests of property and production hold in Congress due to the under-representation of urban voters in Congress and to the fact that the practice of seniority in determining control of the House of Representatives reduces considerably the power of the urban voters. Such is the predominance of rural constituencies that the majority of Congressmen can ignore the desires of the urban masses with impunity while the President does so only at his peril. When the city voters are aroused on issues that affect them no presidential candidate can hope for election who does not pledge himself to heed their demands. More and more presidential campaigns are becoming competitions in bidding for the city vote and election returns reveal the reason. In 1944 Governor

Dewey appealed strongly, though in vain, for the metropolitan vote. His half million majority in up-state New York was more than cancelled by President Roosevelt's majority of three quarters of a million in New York City. And it was simply because the metropolitan majorities of President Roosevelt in half a dozen other key states with big electoral votes wiped out Dewey's majorities in the rest of those states that Roosevelt was elected for a fourth term. Thus a new President almost inevitably enters office pledged to issues and owing his election to elements that are inhospitable to the dominant groups in an overwhelming majority of the congressional districts. This explains why a leading Republican Congressman declared in 1945 that all the recent Republican candidates—Landon, Willkie, and Dewey—have been "too New Dealish."

In the nature of the case then the President, whether Democrat or Republican, comes face to face with a predominantly rural and hence potentially hostile Congress. The so-called presidential honeymoon turns out, in due time, to have been little better than an armistice. At any rate this has been the experience of every President in this century. The persistent growth of cities under-represented in Congress will certainly not reduce the tendency of Congress to clash with Presidents. A potential factor in intensifying this conflict has been the almost unnoticed restoration of the dictatorship of the Speaker of the House. It is to be doubted whether Joe Martin was, in effect, any less a "Czar," that is master of the House, than was "Czar" Joe Cannon in the heyday of his speakership. Joe Martin did not need to appoint and be Chairman of the omnipotent Rules Committee as Cannon had been when Martin could, through the power of recognition, block any move of that committee not to his liking. Martin was indeed, in effect, as one commentator put it, "ex-officio chairman of the Rules Committee."

No party member can play the "maverick" with impunity when the Speaker can casually call his attention to the fact that the party congressional campaign fund is at the Speaker's disposal to finance generously a rival candidate against the intransigent member of the next party-nominating primary. Republican party discipline approached an all-time high in the Eightieth Congress. For example, it was no accident that there were only three Republican votes against and 236 Republican votes for the Wolcott Housing Bill, or that on the motion to recommit the Knutson Tax Bill every one of the 236 Republican votes cast was in the negative. Speaker Cannon could have done no better. There is something to be said for a system like this. It is even an approach again to party government in the House such as enabled President Theodore Roosevelt to deal understandingly with Speaker Cannon as the responsible spokesman of the House majority.   The Republican majority cannot dodge responsibility for its record in the Eightieth Congress and the time may come when the electorate can pass decisive judgment on a Congress thus disciplined.   [Such judgment seems to have been passed on the Eightieth Congress in the 1948 elections.] And time will tell whether a President with qualities of leadership can effect a workable organic relationship with such a House as Theodore Roosevelt did under similar circumstances.

Formal changes in the mechanics of our government may ameliorate but can never solve the problem of conflict between President and Congress. Least of all can it be solved by adopting a parliamentary system.   What many an American enthusiast for such a solution overlooks is the fact that the essential features of the British system consist of a set of usages: the appeal to the country, the resignation of a ministry on an adverse vote, the King's asking the leader of the victorious party to form a ministry— these are mere habits institutionalized by long usage.   There are those who seem to believe that we might, by constitutional amendment and formal statute, make legally compulsory in America a set of British governmental usages.   We will undoubtedly be compelled to develop some better American procedures and habits to displace some bad ones.   But reliance upon organizational changes alone has proved pretty futile in the past.   The overthrow of "Czar" Cannon in 1910 was hailed as a great reform, but who to-day can say that Congress was markedly improved by the "Revolution of 1910"? Joe Martin's firm grip on the House [in the Eightieth Congress] brings us to-day "where we came in" in the first decade of the century and demonstrates the persistence of deep-seated tendencies with respect to American Speakers rooted originally in the experience of colonial legislatures.   The La Follette-Monroney Act was not in effect six months before profound disappointment was being expressed over how much Congress was still like Congress.   It was a Scholar-Congressman who expressed a philosopher's judgment upon this event: "It is those who magnify gadgets and seek to cure the grudges that attend their malfunctioning who will be disappointed at any and every reorganization of Congress."

Nor need it be assumed that we are in the clutches of inexorable fate. Improvements must be persistently sought with the understanding always that this is no age of miracles.   State legislatures must be put under the persistent pressure of an enlightened public opinion to remap congressional districts, give urban population their fair share of Congressmen and thereby remove the suggestion of rotten boroughs in rural constituencies.   As the urban pressures approached the point of explosion, the legislature of Illinois recently redistricted congressional constituencies near the end of half a century without change.   The evenly balanced congressional districts where the two-party system functions most healthily may yet become cognizant of how seniority reduces their share in the councils of the nation to little more than a shadow and become insistent that this distortion of representative power be corrected. The gross injustice due to seniority will ultimately doom it but the present difficulty is that no feasible substitute is in sight. Election of chairmen by the committees would doubtless precipitate demoralizing contests. Public opinion would scarcely support a return to the method in use before the introduction of seniority in 1910—that is, appointment by the Speaker of the House. However, this would restore a semblance of party government to the House and provide an opportunity for the electorate to pass stern judgment on the party in the majority which could scarcely dodge responsibility for sins of commission and omission.

Since cutting Gordian knots to solve the problem of executive-legislative relations is out of the question, why not direct our efforts to the adoption by the Federal government of an emerging genuinely American institution, the legislative-executive council . . . ? It might consist of designated members of the President's Cabinet and of congressional leaders, including possibly the Speaker of the House, the Vice-President, the party floor leaders of the two houses and the chairmen of some of the important committees. Meetings should be held regularly for the consideration of the formulation and execution of national policies. The council might be held responsible for setting up the agenda of Congress, that is the legislative program, in consultation with the President. Such a council could be established by joint resolution of Congress. The structure and formal provisions would be far less important than the usages that might develop in its actual operation. And this is as unpredictable as human conduct. "For most of the things that can be called evils," observed the late Justice Holmes, "the main remedy is for us to grow more civilized." This of course will afford little satisfaction to impetuous souls like the radical abolitionist Theodore Parker. When someone assured him that God in his own good time would end slavery, Parker remarked, "The trouble is God isn't in any hurry and I am."

No. 13

AN ANALYSIS OF THE PROPOSALS TO ALLOW CABINET MEMBERS ON THE FLOOR OF CONGRESS [1]

by Harold J. Laski

AS long ago as February, 1864, Mr. Pendleton, a congressman from
Ohio, sought to secure that "heads of executive departments may
occupy seats on the floor of the House of Representatives"; and his proposal
was strongly supported by James A. Garfield, then also a congressman from
Ohio, in a remarkable speech. The committee to which the resolution was referred then introduced a bill containing two proposals: (1) cabinet officers
were to have the right, in their own discretion, to attend debates when matters concerning their departments were under discussion; and (2) their attendance was to be made compulsory on certain days for the purpose of answering questions. An ardent discussion took place upon the bill, but it was
not voted on. Fifteen years later, Pendleton, then a member of the Senate,
raised the question a second time. The committee to which his resolution
was referred produced a long and valuable report; but, as in 1864, no vote
was taken upon the proposed measure. In 1886, Mr. J. D. Long, later a secretary of the navy, introduced a measure which permitted members of the
cabinet to attend and speak, at their own pleasure, in the House of Representatives; but, on this occasion, the bill was not reported out of committee.
The proposal then slumbered for twenty-five years. It was revived by
President Taft who supported the idea of cabinet representation in Congress with considerable vigor; but his proposal came to nothing. It was
renewed in 1921 and 1924; in neither case did it arouse any serious public
interest or discussion.

The case for the Pendleton proposal has been well stated by President
Taft. "Without any change in the Constitution," he wrote, "Congress
might well provide that heads of departments, members of the president's
cabinet, should be given access to the floor of each house to introduce
measures, to advocate their passage, to answer questions, and to enter into
the debate as if they were members, without, of course, the right to
vote. . . . This would impose on the president greater difficulty in selecting his cabinet, and would lead him to prefer men of legislative experience

[1] H. J. Laski, *The American Presidency* (New York: Harper and Brothers, 1940), pp. 96-
110. Reprinted by permission of the publisher.

who have shown their power to take care of themselves in legislative debate. It would stimulate the head of each department by the fear of public and direct inquiry into a more thorough familiarity with the actual operations of his department and into a closer supervision of its business. On the other hand, it would give the president what he ought to have, some direct initiative in legislation, and an opportunity, through the presence of his competent representatives in Congress, to keep each house advised of the facts in the actual operation of the government. The time lost in Congress over useless discussion of issues that might be disposed of by a single statement from the head of a department, no one can appreciate unless he has filled such a place."

The case is obviously a powerful one; and it has had the support of men so experienced as Mr. Justice Story, Senator Ingalls, and James G. Blaine. The case is the stronger with the immense growth, in recent years, of the congressional appetite for information from and investigation of the departments, much of which, if it is to be really effective, demands their friendly collaboration. There can be little doubt that it would greatly enhance the significance of congressional debate; and, thereby, it would give to it a character of responsibility and a popular significance which, compared to those of the House of Commons, are in considerable degree lacking. There is, too, much to be said for breaking down the antagonism between Congress and the departments; at present it is not untrue to say that many of the amendments each house makes to bills derive less from a knowledge of their value than from a desire to emphasize its power. I have myself heard Mr. Theodore Roosevelt insist that this method was not only likely to produce a wiser selection of cabinet officers; it was also, in his judgment, the best way to deal with the inherent difficulties of tariff legislation and of the "pork-barrel" bills which still remain a blot of no mean dimensions on the record of the legislature.

The argument, however, has not yet penetrated deeply into the popular consciousness. It is notable that in neither of his remarkable books on the American system did Woodrow Wilson think it worth while discussing, though he paid great attention to the relation between the executive and the legislature; while Lord Bryce, who knew Senator Pendleton personally, relegates it to a footnote in his *American Commonwealth*. The reason, I think, is clear. The change is not a superficial one. Its ramifications are, in fact, so wide that they might easily change the whole balance of power in the American system. They might change it, not merely as between the executive and the legislature, but within the elements of the executive itself. The failure to give the plan the consideration it deserves is not, I think, due to inertia, but rather, as Professor Cushman rightly suggests, to

"the vaguely uneasy feeling that the plan would unwisely upset the traditional and established relationship between the executive and legislative
departments with consequences that cannot be accurately foreseen and appraised."

Close analysis makes this at once apparent. If the cabinet is to sit in
Congress, the president must choose its members from those who are likely
to be influential with it. This at once narrows his choice. It makes him
think of the men who already have some standing in its eyes, and some
direct knowledge of its complicated procedure. But this means putting
a premium on the experienced members of either house as cabinet material.
It means, further, that the more successful they are upon the floor of Congress, the more independent they are likely to be vis-à-vis the president.
They will develop a status of their own as they become known as the men
who are able to make Congress take their views about the bills they promote. They are likely, in fact, to become rivals of the president himself
for influence with Congress. The problem, in this situation, of maintaining
cabinet unity would necessarily become a difficult matter. Congress might
easily tend to weaken the administration by playing off the cabinet, or
some part of it, against the president and some other part. The loyalty
of the cabinet officer would be divided. Is he, for example, to support the
president on a scheme like the Court plan, and thereby to weaken his
standing with Congress; or is he discreetly to make known his dislike for
the plan in the hope that he may thereby win approval for some bill in
which he is interested?

The president's problem of changing his cabinet would, moreover, be immensely intensified. Is he to keep an officer about whose full loyalty he
is dubious, but whose influence on Congress is clearly great? Can he prevent such an officer's so nearly rivaling his own authority as to make his
own position exceptionally difficult? Would not the position of a president like Lincoln, whose hold on his own colleagues was small when he assumed power, became virtually untenable if Congress were in a position to
play them off against him? Is there not, indeed, the danger of a powerful cabal of cabinet officers' becoming the effective mediator between the
president and Congress with a vital shift, as a consequence, in the present
delicate balance of power? Would it not, further, be likely that a tendency
would rapidly develop for any cabinet officer who became outstandingly
influential with Congress to become the rival of the president himself, and,
where the latter was weak, in actual fact his master?

More than even this is, I think, involved. There would develop the
tendency for the president to choose his cabinet from Congress in order
to maximize his influence with it, and thus to transfer the leadership of his

party there to a room, so to say, of which he only had the key. There would be a tendency for cabinet officers to use their relation with Congress as a platform from which to reach the presidency, with all the difficulties of colleagueship of this position, and more, that Polk emphasized. It is difficult, moreover, not to feel that, in these circumstances, the advice of the cabinet member upon questions of patronage would be given under conditions altogether different from and inferior to those upon which they now depend. The danger of trading posts for measures is already profound enough in the American system; it is difficult not to feel that it would be greatly intensified if a cabinet officer were independent of the president in his power to influence Congress. The coherence that is now given to administrative action by the supremacy of the president might easily be jeopardized by this aspect alone.

The Pendleton scheme suggested that cabinet members should have access to debates upon the floor of the House. But in fact, the main business of Congress is performed in secret committees to which the public has no access. No cabinet officer could adequately look after his measures unless he penetrated the committee rooms also. But were he to do so, the control over him of the president would be still further diminished; and the relation between him and Congress would rival in closeness that with the executive of which the president is the head. This seems scarcely desirable in a system where there is no collective cabinet responsibility, and where the unity of the executive structure is supplied by presidential control. In these circumstances, no cabinet member can be transformed into an automaton who merely reflects the presidential will. For first, in such transformation as this innovation portends, he would have been chosen just precisely because he is not an automaton; and second, to the degree that he seeks to act like one, he defeats the whole object of the innovation.

There are two further difficulties in the scheme, moreover, to which adequate attention has hardly been given in discussion of it. It raises most delicate and complicated questions of the relation between the cabinet officer, as a quasi-member of Congress, and the senator or congressman who is in charge of the bill in which he is interested. By whom is the concession to be made to a proposed amendment? How will chairmanships be arranged so as to secure a proper harmony in congressional proceedings between the cabinet officer and the chairman of his committee? On a bill, for example, like that of President Roosevelt's Court plan, the position of the attorney-general would be well-nigh intolerable unless he were at one with the chairman of the Judiciary Committee. The fact is that, on the present system, where the chairmen of the important committees of both houses form a kind of quasi-executive within the two branches of the legislature, the position of cabinet officers would be impossible at every point where they disagreed with that quasi-executive. Either they would be tempted into a position of continuous inferiority for the sake of agreement, in which difficult questions of loyalty to the president would be involved; or they would differ openly with the official chairmen of the legislative committees, in which case, they would greatly add, by that difference, to the burden the president had to carry.

Nor is this all. The Pendleton scheme seems to assume that each cabinet officer is to sit in Congress merely in relation to his own department. But the categories of government are far from being as simple as this view would make them appear. The range of modern legislation makes the secretary of the treasury as ubiquitously relevant as the chancellor of the exchequer in relation to most government proposals. The interrelations of modern problems of defense make half the issues which arise matters of coordination to which the secretary of the treasury, the secretary of war, and the secretary of navy are all relevant. On foreign affairs, every vital matter is at least a joint operation between the president and the secretary of state; the latter could hardly offer an opinion in Congress save as he affirmed that outlook for which he had prior approval from the president; and in matters of supreme importance it is the president only whose attitude it is vital for Congress to know. There, as the Wilson administration makes clear, he supersedes the secretary of state far more emphatically than, in an analogous situation, the prime minister of England supersedes (he rather supplements) the foreign secretary. Similar difficulties arise as between the Departments of Commerce and Labor; and the Department of Justice, especially in the context of prosecutions such as those under the Sherman Act, has a vital relation to many other departments. It is, in fact, difficult to see how any cabinet officer except the postmaster-general could be confined within any rigidly defined domain. In the result, most cabinet officers would—whatever the system started as—be bound to develop roving commissions of general relevance not very different from the part that a cabinet minister plays in the British House of Commons.

It must, moreover, be remembered that in the American system the initiative in legislation does not lie, as with Great Britain, for effective purposes in the government only. No doubt a special pre-eminence attaches to bills which have, so to say, the imprimatur of the president. But the source of a good deal of important legislative action lies in the hands of individual senators and congressmen; in this respect it is only necessary to remember how much has been done, often despite the administration, by men like the late Senator La Follette and by Senator Norris. It would be far from easy to adjust the delicate relations which would arise from this dual relationship, not least if the president were in a minority in Congress. And if members of the cabinet were admitted only to the floor of both houses, they would, for the most part, miss the chance of participation in the pivotal consideration of bills; while, if they were permitted their full share in the committee processes, the duality of leadership would create almost insoluble problems.

The Pendleton scheme, in short, does not meet the real problems created by the presidential system. The facts of American life have concentrated literally enormous power in the hands of the president; and it is no doubt true that the exercise of this power produces, above all in a second term, grave congressional doubts of the wisdom of its extent. At some time in the tenure of a president with a majority, the accusation of autocracy is almost bound to arise. But the real outcome of the Pendleton scheme, or any variant upon it, would be, I think, to transfer the essential features of presidential leadership to the cabinet. Its operations in Congress would be bound, sooner or later, to become the axis upon which the authority of the administration turned. I believe, indeed, that properly to perform its function in Congress the cabinet would be bound to try and discover the terms upon which it could become a unity; a unity, be it noted, not only against the Congress, but against the president also. The latter would be compelled to spend a good deal of his energy in maintaining his authority against colleagues who would have developed an interest and prestige at least parallel to his own, and, conceivably, different from it. None of them could fail to be aware that outstanding success in the handling of Congress was the highroad to the kind of reputation out of which a presidential nomination could be secured. Some of them, at least, would be bound to play for that nomination; and the problem, in those circumstances, of maintaining presidential supremacy would be at every point delicate and complicated.

The real result, in a word, of the adoption of such a scheme as Senator Pendleton proposed would be very rapidly to transform the president into a person more akin to the president of the French Republic than to that of the United States. He could not avoid the certainty that his colleagues who became pivotal in Congress would soon become indispensable to him. He could hardly avoid the concentration of public attention upon their activities in Congress rather than upon his relations with it. He would have to watch those activities with a jealous eye lest they impinge upon the sphere of influence that is at present his own. The man among them who became the congressional leader of the cabinet would soon become a figure akin in character and influence to the prime minister; the president would be dependent upon him for every legislative move in the fulfilment of his program. Indeed, I think it not unlikely that the president would become rather the adviser than the master of the man to whom Congress looked for the formulation and defense of the presidential program; he would be moved to second place. He would find it difficult to resist the pressure of a cabinet officer who was influential with Congress; he might well jeopardize his own position if he asked for his resignation. A hostile Congress might even play off the cabinet, or some section of it, against him.

On any showing, this is to say, the Pendleton scheme would wholly alter the balance of forces history has evolved in the American system of government. I do not say that it would necessarily alter them for the worse; any such estimate depends upon a comparison between the presidential and parliamentary systems that is here out of place. All I am concerned to argue is that latent in the scheme is a revolution in the historical conception of the presidency. As it now operates, the nation looks to the president for executive leadership, and, in the long run, circumstances make it difficult for that leadership to be found elsewhere. Such a scheme as Pendleton's inherently threatens that authority. While it separates him from his cabinet, on the one hand, it builds a bridge between the cabinet and Congress, on the other; and the president cannot walk across that bridge. It gives the cabinet an interest against him, not only with the legislature, but also with the party. A generation which has seen the vice-president of the United States use his influence in Congress to intrigue against the president should have no difficulty in seeing what his position might become if his influence were joined to that of any considerable part of the cabinet. At present, at any rate, when the president and Congress are at odds, the former's power of direct appeal to the nation makes the issue between them a clear one upon which public opinion can make up its mind. A cabinet that moved toward independence of him would make such a clarity of choice a difficult matter. It would, almost necessarily, divert a good deal of attention away from the case the president has to make. It would offer the possibility of great rewards to those about him who were prepared to risk the penalties of disloyalty to him. Anyone who reflects upon the position that might have arisen if Stanton had been able to utilize Congress as a platform against Andrew Johnson can see the potentialities that are latent in this change.

It may be, as I have said, that it should be attempted; for it may well be that the burden which the present situation imposes upon the president is greater than any statesman, above all in a democratic community, should be asked to bear. But the change should not be attempted without a full knowledge that it will profoundly alter the historic contours of the presidential system. It may not, in the first instance, transform it on the lines of the parliamentary system; it is bound, I have argued, in the long run to move it toward those lines. It cannot do so, on all experience, without two results. It must first depreciate the position of the man who cannot directly influence the congressional process; those, to use my earlier metaphor, are bound to be nearer to it who cross the bridge than those who stay on the other side. And if men are sought who can influence Congress, men are bound to be sought by whom Congress is prepared to be influenced. That does not only mean the device of a different kind of cabinet officer from those of the past. It means also, in the long run, men who realize that the way to influence a legislative assembly is to be responsive to its will; and that is the first step toward responsibility to its wishes. Fundamentally, this is to alter the whole balance of the American Constitution. It is to make it desirable to build a cabinet which can sway Congress. That makes the main lever of executive authority resident in the cabinet rather than in the president. While this may be a better scheme than the present one, its possible merits cannot conceal the fact that it is a constitutional revolution of the first magnitude. It is to dig into the foundations of the state; and that, as Edmund Burke insisted, is always a dangerous adventure.

Chapter V

THE GEOGRAPHICAL DISTRIBUTION
OF GOVERNMENTAL POWER

[As we have already seen, the fundamental rules under which any government is organized are embodied in its constitution. This constitution, written or unwritten, rigid or flexible, is the primary authority for the distribution and allocation of governmental power. But how should this power be distributed? Should one central government exercise all of the power to govern or should it be divided between a central government and major political subdivisions? If the latter, how should power be distributed within these subdivisions? These questions must be met by those who frame the rules. The British in the eighteenth century failed to meet them and the result was the American Revolution. Those who fought and won that war likewise failed to answer them and the result was the political failure of the Articles of Confederation. One of the major concerns of the Constitutional Convention was with these questions.

In the United States we chose to adopt what is known as a federal system of government; that is, a system of government in which there is a constitutional division of powers between a central government and major political subdivisions or states. The reasons for our choice were many and varied. They are found in the economic, religious, and racial differences extant in America of the late eighteenth century, and also in the antipathy of those who wrote the rules towards any strong and centralized government.

All federal systems show much the same strength and weakness, and in all similar problems emerge. Society is never static; consequently, a division of powers which is adequate for one generation may be totally inadequate for the next. One sees in all federal systems a constant readjustment in the original division of powers, and in almost every instance this readjustment has resulted in a flow of power from the major political subdivisions to the central government. Centralization is not a phenomenon peculiar only to our federal system.

Within our major political subdivisions, the American states, the problems are basically the same. On what principle should power be divided between them and the local units of government, such as cities, villages, counties and townships? Our choice in this field has been that of a unitary system of government; that is, we have constitutionally vested with the states complete power over all local units. Cities and counties are creatures of the state, their powers are given to and not reserved for them, and they may be abolished by the unilateral

action of the state. However, our tradition has departed from a strict application of this unitary principle. We have extended great power to local units in
the past but to-day one sees a trend towards centralization.

A third question also is daily becoming more important, namely, that which
concerns the relationship of the central or national government to the local
units in the states. Here, too, new relations of a centralizing character have
developed. Cities, counties, towns, and other local units are turning to or being
turned to Washington rather than to their respective state capitals.

Professor Laski, in the first of the following essays, makes a slashing attack
upon American federalism and argues brilliantly the case for centralization of
power. There is much of value in what he says, but it needs to be combined
with the sober examination and evaluation presented by Professor Anderson
and the effective argument for local self-government made by Mr. Miller. Taken
together these articles offer a solid foundation for the citizen genuinely interested in critically examining the geographical distribution of power in the United
States.]

No. 14

THE OBSOLESCENCE OF FEDERALISM [1]

by Harold J. Laski

NO one can travel the length and breadth of the United States without
the conviction of its inexpugnable variety. East and West, South
and North, its regions are real and different, and each has problems real
and different too. The temptation is profound to insist that here, if ever,
is the classic place for a federal experiment. Union without unity—except
in the Soviet Union and China, has variety ever so fully invited the implications of the famous definition? Geography, climate, culture, all of them
seem to have joined their forces to insist that, wherever centralization is
appropriate, here, at least, it has no meaning. Tradition demands its absence; history has prohibited its coming. The large unit, as in Lamennais'
phrase, would result in apoplexy at the center and anemia at the extremities.
Imposed solutions from a distant Washington, blind, as it must be blind, to
the subtle minutiae of local realities, cannot solve the ultimate problems
that are in dispute. A creative America must be a federal America. The
wider the powers exercised from Washington, the more ineffective will be
the capacity for creative administration. Regional wisdom is the clue to
the American future. The power to govern must go where that regional
wisdom resides. So restrained, men learn by the exercise of responsibility

[1] H. J. Laski, "The Obsolescence Of Federalism," *The New Republic* (May 3, 1939),
Vol. 98, pp. 367-369. Reprinted by permission of *The New Republic*.

the art of progress. They convince themselves by experiment from below. To fasten a uniformity that is not in nature upon an America destined to variety is to destroy the prospect of an ultimate salvation.

This kind of argument is familiar in a hundred forms. I believe that, more than any other philosophic pattern, it is responsible for the malaise of American democracy.) My plea here is for the recognition that the federal form of state is unsuitable to the stage of economic and social development that America has reached. I infer from this postulate two conclusions: first, that the present division of powers, however liberal be the Supreme Court in its technique of interpretation, is inadequate to the needs America confronts; and, second, that any revision of those powers is one which must place in Washington, and Washington only, the power to amend that revision as circumstances change. I infer, in a word, that the epoch of federalism is over, and that only a centralized system can effectively confront the problems of a new time.)

To continue with the old pattern, in the age of giant capitalism, is to strike into impotence that volume of governmental power which is necessary to deal with the issues giant capitalism has raised. Federalism, I suggest, is the appropriate governmental technique for an expanding capitalism, in which the price of local habit—which means, also, local delay—admits of compensation in the total outcome. But a contracting capitalism cannot afford the luxury of federalism. It is insufficiently positive in character, it does not provide for sufficient rapidity of action; it inhibits the emergence of necessary standards of uniformity; it relies upon compacts and compromises which take insufficient account of the urgent category of time; it leaves the backward areas a restraint, at once parasitic and poisonous, on those which seek to move forward; not least, its psychological results, especially in an age of crisis, are depressing to a democracy that needs the drama of positive achievement to retain its faith.

Before I turn to the case for this view, it is worth while to dwell for a moment upon the lessons of non-American experience. It is not, I think, accident that the heavy weather encountered by the federal system in the United States has been experienced also by the three major experiments elsewhere—by Germany, by Canada and by Australia. In the first, significantly, both federalism and democracy have gone. In the others the need for constitutional revision, the sense that the historic division of powers hampers the need for social and economic reconstruction at every turn, is one of the major themes of debate. Commissions seek to discover desirable terms of effective revision in both of them. Their literature speaks of "breakdown" and "collapse." In each, also, the federal government lacks, by its bondage to a past shaped in the faith of unlimited expansion, the power effectively to cope with its outstanding problems. In each, too, the older political parties are geared psychologically to that past; and their inability to escape from the framework in which it has imprisoned them, leads to the emergence of new political orientations which threaten alike their unity and their democratic foundation. Proportionately, I suspect, their problems are less susceptible of direct solution than those of the United States. But it is, I think, an expression, not of local circumstance, but of world-historical causes, which has made federalism everywhere in the world to-day a handicap and not a help to governmental progress.

(Giant capitalism has, in effect, concentrated the control of economic power in a small proportion of the American people.) It has built a growing contrast between the distribution of that economic power and the capacity of the political democracy effectively to control the results of its exercise. It has transcended the political boundaries of the units in the American federation so as to make them largely ineffective as areas of independent government. Whether we take the conditions of labor, the level of taxation, the standards of education, public health, or the supply of amenities like housing and recreation, it has become clear that the true source of decision is no longer at the circumference, but at the center, of the state. For forty-eight separate units to seek to compete with the integrated power of giant capitalism is to invite defeat in every element of social life where approximate uniformity of condition is the test of the good life.

The poor state is parasitic on the body politic. It offers privileges to giant capitalism to obtain its taxable capacity, offers escape from the impositions of rich states, in order to wrest from the wealthy some poor meed of compensation for its backwardness. It dare not risk offending the great industrial empires—cotton, coal, iron and steel, tobacco—lest it lose the benefits of their patronage. Their vested interests thus begin to define the limits within which the units of the federation may venture to move. And since the division of powers limits, in its turn, the authority of the federal government to intervene—the latter being a government of limited powers—it follows that the great industrial empires can, in fact, prevent the legislation necessary to implement the purposes of a democratic society. The situation may, briefly, be summarized by saying that the Constitution inhibits the federal government from exercising the authority inherent in the idea of a democracy; while the risk to a state government of attack upon the conditions exacted by those industrial empires for their patronage is too great to permit the states to jeopardize what they have by issuing challenge. Whether, therefore, it be the hours of labor, the standards of health and housing, the effective organization of the trade unions, at every point the formal powers of the states are rarely commensurate with the actual authority they may venture to exercise. And it is the common citizen of the United States who pays the price of that margin between formal and effective power.

Political systems live by the results they can obtain for the great mass of their citizens. A democracy is not likely to survive on formal grounds merely; it will survive as it is able to convince its citizens that it adequately protects their powers to satisfy the expectations they deem their experience to warrant. In the present phase of American capitalist democracy, the central government largely lacks the power to implement the ends it is essential it should serve if its democratic context is to be maintained. It cannot obtain adequate standards of government in many of the major fields it seeks to enter. It is hamstrung, partly by the division of powers from which it derives its authority; partly because the Constitution has not enabled it to develop the instrumentalities essential to the purposes it must seek to fulfill. Its effort to obtain the proper recognition of collective bargaining may be stricken into impotence by a state law against picketing. Its effort to produce proper control of public utilities may be rendered vain by local franchises granted in a period when the recognition of the need for uniformity in this field had not dawned upon the public consciousness. So, also, with conservation; with the provision of adequate educational opportunity; with the effective prohibition (a commonplace of any well-ordered state) of child labor; with the coördination of relief for unemployment; with public works, especially in the utilization of the possible sources of electric power; with public-health legislation, not least in the field of maternity and child hygiene; with a proper policy of public roads—witness the breakdown of federal-state cooperation in Arkansas in 1923, in Kansas in 1926 and Maine in 1929; with a proper policy in housing. I take examples only. The central point of my argument is the simple one that in every major field of social regulation, the authority of which the federal government can dispose is utterly inadequate to the issues it is expected to solve.

I do not think this argument is invalidated by the rise of cooperation between the federal government and the states, or between groups of states. That use has been carefully investigated in detail by Professor Jane Clark in an admirable and exhaustive monograph ("The Rise of a New Federalism," 1938). When all is made that can be made of the pattern she there reveals, I think it is true to say that, compared to the dimension of the problem, it amounts to very little. And set in the background of the urgent problems of time, it is, I think, clear from her account that in no fundamental matters will the pressure of political interests (behind which can be seen at every turn the hand of giant capitalism) permit the necessary uniformities to be attained by consent within the next fifty years. Not even the resiliency of American democracy can afford to wait so long. Professor Clark demonstrates admirably the inescapable interest of the federal government in a hundred subjects at every turn of which it encounters the power of the states; but she also demonstrates that the problems of dual occupancy of the same ground hinders at every turn the creative solution of the problems involved unless we conceive of those solutions in terms of geological time.

I am not arguing that the administration of government services ought to be centralized in Washington. It is true, as Professor Clark says, that "there is a line beyond which centralized administration cannot go without falling because of its own weight." My argument is the very different one: that (a) there are certain objects of administrative control now left to the states for which they are no longer suitable units of regulation. Economic centralization makes necessary at least minimum standards of uniform performance in these objects, e.g., health, education, unemployment relief; and in others, e.g., labor conditions, railroad rates, electric power, complete federal control without interference by the states; and (b) that the proper objects of federal supervision cannot any longer be dependent upon state consent. Where this dependency exists, state consent will be, in its turn, largely controlled by giant capitalism. That is why Delaware is merely a pseudonym of the du Ponts, and Montana little more than a symbol of the Anaconda Copper Corporation. That is why the people of the state of Washington, who ought long ago to have been permitted to have the advantage of the municipal electric-power plant of Seattle, still suffer from the division of its potential benefits through the survival of the Puget Sound Light and Power Company.

Nor would the problem be met if, instead of the states, America were divided, as writers like Professor Howard Odum suggest, into regions more correspondent with the economic realities of the situation. If America were to consist of seven or nine regions, instead of forty-eight states, that would still leave unsolved the main issues if they operated upon the basis of the present division of powers, and if their consent were necessary to any fundamental change in that division. Once again, it must be emphasized that the unity which giant capitalism postulates in the economic sphere postulates a corresponding unity in the conference of political powers upon the federal government. There is no other way, up to a required minimum, in which the questions of taxation, labor relations and conditions, conservation, public utilities (in the widest sense), to take examples only, can be met.

At this point, of course, the relation of a federal system to the power of judicial review becomes fundamental. No one now believes Marshall's famous assertion that "courts are the mere instruments of the law, and can will nothing"; it has been obvious, above all since the Civil War, that the Supreme Court is the effective master of federal legislation. And it is clear, further, that this mastery is exercised in the main not on obejctive tests of constitutionality (which do not exist), but upon the accident of a temporary majority's view of what it is "reasonable" for the federal government to undertake. The Court has become a non-elective third chamber of the government which may, as in the income-tax cases, defeat for many years purposes of which its members do not happen to approve. In an epoch of rapid change, it is a grave danger to any society that the will of a federal legislature should be subject to judicial control, and more especially when, as Marshall said, the amending process is "cumbrous and unwieldy." In a phase of liberal construction the difficulties of judicial review are obscured from the public. But the years before the controversy over the President's Court plan should be a sufficient reminder of the immense dangers lurking within it.

The view here urged, of course, looks toward a fundamental reconstruction of traditional American institutions. It is not impressed by the view, associated with the great name of Mr. Justice Brandeis, that the "curse of bigness" will descend upon any serious departure from the historic contours of federalism. The small unit of government is impotent against the big unit of giant capitalism. It may be that the very power of giant capitalism is no longer of itself compatible with the maintenance of a democratic political structure in society; there is much evidence to support this view. What, at least, is certain is this: that a government the powers of which are not commensurate with its problems will not be able to cope with them. Either, therefore, it must obtain those powers, or it must yield to a form of state more able to satisfy the demands that it encounters. That is the supreme issue before the United States today; and the more closely it is scrutinized the more obviously does its resolution seem to be bound up with the obsolescence of the federal system.

For that system presents the spectacle of forty-nine governments seeking to deal with issues for many of which they are inappropriate as instrumentalities whether in the area they cover or in the authority they may invoke. They are checked and balanced upon a theory of the state completely outmoded in the traditional ends upon which its postulates are based. Giant industry requires a positive state; federalism, in its American form, is geared to vital negations which contradict the implications of positivism. Giant industry requires uniformities in the field of its major influence; American federalism is the inherent foe, both in time and space, of those necessary uniformities. Giant industry, not least, requires the opposition of a unified public will to counteract its tendency to undemocratic procedure through the abuse of power; a federal system of the American kind dissipates the unity of public opinion in those fields where it is most urgently required. And, above all, it is urgent to note that giant industry, in an age of economic contraction, is able to exploit the diversities of a federal scheme, through the delays they permit in the attainment of uniformity, to reactionary ends. Thereby, they discredit the democratic process at a time when it is least able to afford that discredit. For, thereby, the confidence of the citizen body in its power to work out democratic solutions of its problems is gravely undermined.

Men who are deprived of faith by inability to attain results they greatly desire do not long remain content with the institutions under which they live. The price of democracy is the power to satisfy living demands. American federalism, in its traditional form, cannot keep pace with the tempo of the life giant capitalism has evolved. To judge it in terms of its historic success is to misconceive the criteria by which it becomes valid for the present and the future. No political system has the privilege of immortality; and there is no moment so fitting for the consideration of its remaking as that which permits of reconstruction with the prospect of a new era of creative achievement.

No. 15

FEDERALISM—THEN AND NOW[1]

by William Anderson

AMERICAN federalism as it is to-day cannot be understood without a complete revision of our ordinary thinking about it. Most of us have learned what we know about it through historical studies. Starting with the seventeenth century, if not farther back, our courses and books in American history filled our minds with a mass of facts about Massachusetts and New York, Pennsylvania, Virginia and other colonies that became States and declared their independence. As the story was developed, the stage was so filled with a multiplicity of characters and "props" and there were so many minor and incidental themes and actions that we could not fully master the grand plot or sense the completeness of its culmination

[1] William Anderson, "Federalism—Then and Now," *State Government* (May, 1943), Vol. XVI, No. 5, pp. 107-112. Reprinted by permission of *State Government*.

in our own day. When we try now to visualize the actual relations between national and state governments as they are to-day, we find that we have acquired a certain "set" or orientation of mind about them that is still largely eighteenth century. We know that there have been numerous changes in governmental organization and policies since independence was declared but we find it hard to view them all at once in their relationships one to another.

It is the thesis of what I am about to say that as a result of many changes American federalism to-day is different not only in degree but in kind from what it was in the beginning. There has been a virtual revolution in our system of government, an about-face almost as complete as can be imagined. The words we use, and the concepts that lie behind them, are still much the same as they were one hundred and fifty years ago, but the facts have been so drastically altered that nothing short of a complete reorientation will bring us up to date.

This revolution in American federalism is not the only drastic about-face that is crowded into the years since American independence was established. We have had one reversal after another in laws and in policies. From having been dependencies of a foreign land, the thirteen British colonies in America became States, a union of States, and soon a world power with its own dependencies. At one time this union opened its arms to the peoples of all lands. It was the promised land of freedom for the poor and oppressed in every clime. To-day it has immigration laws and quota regulations so strict that as a rule the outward flow of people almost or quite exceeds the inward movement. Then, too, there was a period when it was public policy to open nearly all public lands to private settlement and exploitation on very easy terms. In recent years the government's policy has been to discourage unwise settlement, to re-acquire lands for forest and conservation purposes, and to move many settlers off the very land that they and their forefathers acquired from the government. Need we mention other revolutionary changes—the about-face on slavery, the enfranchisement of women, the changed attitude of government toward labor unions, the complete nationalization of our armed forces, the drastic revision of the American tax system within a generation? Some of these and a number of others will inevitably be mentioned in the pages that follow. They appear to be cognate with the changes in federalism that are to be discussed. They are necessary results of the same forces that have been operating to change drastically our whole American way of life.

But it is unfortunate to use the past tense in describing these crucial modifications. "The revolution continues." Even . . . in . . . [the] critical time of our direct involvement in the Second World War, one . . .

[could] dimly foresee further changes in policy as being unavoidable. Our foreign policy, for example, once so negative, timid, and isolationist, obviously must become one of positive and bold participation in international controls. What impacts such a program in foreign policy will have, in turn, upon our federal system still remain to be seen.

The failure of a people, and even of trained scholars and statesmen, to see and to comprehend the changes that have gone on around them is nothing unusual. Such a lag in the comprehension of changes has been noted many times. It has been observed that even third- and fourth-generation colonists, far removed from the mother country, often continue to use an archaic language that came over with their forefathers, and to think of the home country in greatly outmoded terms. But this is not so surprising as the lag where a people fail to see and to comprehend the very changes that have taken place among themselves. We are linked to and dominated by the past. We remember and apply to-day as mature men what we learned in childhood. The more conservative our profession the farther back in time we go for our mental hitching posts.

CONCEPTION OF FEDERAL SYSTEM

It was not only Montesquieu, a foreign scholar, who in the mid-eighteenth century failed to understand the British governmental system. Many Americans, even some of the leaders in the federal convention of 1787, misunderstood it, and so no doubt did many Englishmen at the same time. George Washington continued to the end to misunderstand the nature of a party system; his denunciation of faction and party cannot be explained in any other way. Calvin Coolidge when retiring from the Presidency is said to have sensed vaguely that great changes had taken place that he could not comprehend. He is reported to have said, "I have lived beyond my time."

This essay is an attempt to bring the American conception of its own federal system up to date. That it will not succeed perfectly is just as certain as that many men, well-informed men, will disagree with its conclusions. It is the writer's prediction that he is more likely to be found to have understated than to have exaggerated the changes that have occurred.

By "federalism" and "the federal system" I mean especially the relations between the National Government and the States. In general the situation faced by the framers of the Constitution in 1787 will be considered as "Then," but in fact the description of Then will be applicable in part to a period of nearly a generation thereafter while the Founding Fathers remained in power. The adoption of the Constitution changed the legal status, but did not at once undo all factors in the previous situation. "Now" will be taken to include the late 1930's and the early 1940's, down to this date.

The many events between 1787 and 1942 that brought about the striking contrasts between the two periods can hardly be mentioned in this sketch. My interest is primarily in results. How is our situation to-day different from what it was then? Omitting details, the changes are as follows:

Then a small area, with a small and sparse population, mainly agricultural and poor. *Now* one of the world's great nations in both area and population, largely urban and highly industrial, with tremendous national wealth.

Then largely a debtor people and an exporter of raw materials. *Now* a great creditor nation and large exporter of manufactured as well as agricultural goods.

Then meager and slow transportation facilities, and even poorer provisions for communication. *Now* an equipment of railroads, steamship lines, highways, trucks and buses, air transport, and communications of all kinds unexcelled by any other nation and undreamed of in the past.

Then state citizenship, state and local loyalties, interstate suspicions and tariffs, localized business, and considerable internal disunity. *Now* a nation, with national citizenship, primarily national loyalties, a nationwide free market, and nationally-organized business, agriculture, labor, professions, press, and political parties.

Then an upstart and divided people, an international weakling, threatened from north and south, with very poor defense arrangements, and looking out over the Atlantic at an essentially hostile world. *Now* a great world power, an international leader, with a powerful army and navy, and with strong friends and interests (as well as enemies) across both the Atlantic and Pacific.

GROWTH OF FEDERAL ACTIVITY

Then inactive, negative, laissez-faire government with very few functions, and with only business leaders favoring a national government, and they desiring only to give it enough vigor to protect commerce, provide a nationwide free home market, and a sound currency and banking system. *Now* active, positive, collectivist government, especially at the national level, rendering many services with the support of powerful labor and agricultural elements, while many business leaders have reversed their position.

Then local law enforcement with state protection of the liberties guaranteed in bills of rights. *Now* increasing national law enforcement and national protection of civil liberties even against state and local action.

Then practically no employees of the National Government and very few state and local employees. *Now* a national civil service of normally over a million persons reaching into every county of the country, plus extensive state and local civil services.

Then small public budgets at all levels. *Now* public budgets and expenditures, especially for the National Government, that reach astronomical figures.

Then (before 1789) no national taxes at all and for decades after 1789 only customs and excise taxes on a very limited scale, with state and local governments relying almost entirely on direct property taxes. *Now* tremendously increased and diversified taxes at both national and state levels, with the National Government rising swiftly to a dominating position with respect to all taxes except those directly on property.

Then (before 1788) state grants to the Congress of the United States for defense and debt purposes. *Now* grants-in-aid by the National Government to the States in increasing amounts and with steadily tightening national controls over state action.

SUPPORTERS OF FEDERAL STRENGTH

Permit me to select a few of these profound changes for special emphasis. Those who planned and carried through the unification of the original States under the Constitution were for all practical purposes the business leaders of the time and their professional advisers. It is generally accepted that most farmers and laborers were either indifferent or hostile to the formation of a stronger union. But labor and agriculture, having learned that the States were incapable of satisfying their demands, also turned to the central government to increase their welfare and security and to enlarge their share of the national income. To-day organized laborers and organized farmers are among the strongest supporters of the National Government. They have become truly nationalist in their thinking. At the same time many business leaders, resentful of the new national regulations and taxes imposed upon them in the interests of labor and agriculture, preach a return to states' rights.

This partial reversal of positions is closely connected with the recent unparalleled increase in the activities of government, especially at the national level. An inactive government is necessarily a weak one. During the first century under the Constitution national government activities increased but little and the same was true of the States. For the nation the turning point came fifty years ago with the Interstate Commerce and Anti-Trust acts as the first important national regulations of business. Since the days of the Progressive Movement the increase has gone forward at an accelerated pace, and with each increase has come the further tendency toward centralization at the national level. To-day, even discounting the fact of war, the National Government is the strongest and most active it has ever been. Wartime controls only accentuate an established fact.

FEDERAL EMPLOYEES

To these we add one more consideration—the existence to-day of a nation-wide and national bureaucracy. In civilian employments alone the National Government now has over a million servants scattered throughout the length and breadth of the land. It has more employees than the forty-eight States combined. These men and women are engaged in rendering a host of services to the people everywhere. Their functions have become an indispensable part of the life of the nation, essential to the welfare of the people. It is almost unthinkable that any national administration, any Congress, or any Supreme Court for many decades to come would dare to undo or even seriously to threaten these national services to the whole population.

One other point. Since the adoption of the first national income tax a generation ago there has been what amounts to a revolution in American public finance. The revenues now available to the National Government under new and old forms of taxation are incalculably greater than anything in the past. While the States have also increased their revenues, they grow increasingly dependent upon the National Government for aid. Even now while state budgets are mostly in balance, state legislatures, under pressure from taxpayers, are proceeding to reduce existing state taxes. This act of retreat, however laudable its motives, is but a recognition by the States of the overwhelming superiority of National Government in the fiscal field.

For nearly one hundred and fifty years the emphasis in discussions of American federalism was on the division of powers between national and state governments. All readers of our history are familiar with the struggles of the States against the seemingly inexorable advance of the National Government. The theory of states' rights was discussed in the press and on the platform, debated in legislative bodies, pleaded in courts, and fought over on the battlefield. In spite of all these contrary efforts, the trend toward national control was never really checked. To-day it can be said that to debate national *versus* state powers is to raise one of the least important issues in American public life. For all practical purposes that issue has been settled. Numerous and influential sections of the American people—farmers, laborers, transportation interests, and others—have found that only through national action can their claims be satisfied. A nation has arisen that demands national action to meet national needs. Congress and the President have found that in one way or another they can satisfy most of these demands. The National Government is to-day regulating, promoting, and aiding agriculture, labor, and industry (which are not mentioned in the Constitution) as well as commerce (which is mentioned) in ways and to an extent obviously never visualized by the founders.

NATURE OF UNION MISUNDERSTOOD

And I might add parenthetically that the term "Federal Government" as applied to our central government is to-day more clearly a misnomer than it was even in the beginning. The Constitution nowhere uses the term "federation" or "Federal Government." It was a *union* that the people created through the Constitution; and, as the people have now become fully a nation, their union government has become their National Government.

The way in which the Supreme Court has been brought to the acceptance of the inevitable is indeed a curious history. Even while asserting a right to declare acts of Congress unconstitutional, in its first fifty years the court tended to be strongly nationalist. Meanwhile a theory had been developed that the Supreme Court existed in large part to police the boundaries between state and national powers and to prevent encroachments by either upon the other. The antagonism of national and state governments was assumed. Their interests were supposed to be always in conflict. Someone had to stand watch to prevent even the slightest trespass by either one upon the area marked out for the other.

Domestic as well as foreign publicists developed this idea. "Federalism is legalism," said Dicey. The Supreme Court was the great defender of the Constitution and of the federal system. By its legal decisions it would stop every leak in the dikes. No matter how high the waters of nationalism might rise, by its words it would turn them back.

RELATION OF STATES AND NATION

Then followed that period in the history of the court when it really tried to hold back a nation that was seeking means of national expression. Hamilton had said that "a nation without a national government is an awful spectacle" and so at times it was as the court again and again struck down important acts of Congress. Various theories of the relations of the nation and the States were developed in the court, including that defined by Professor Corwin as the theory of "dual federalism." But the trend of events was inexorable. Acts of Congress once struck down rose up again in new form. It became evident that some of these acts were needed in the public interest. The court began to yield a little, to distinguish one case from another, and finally to overrule its own prior decisions. In the early years of the "Great Depression" the court temporarily stiffened its opposition to new national regulations. It was hard to tell whether it was more interested in upholding states' rights or in protecting the sphere of anarchy that had been left to private business.

In 1937 this period came to an abrupt end. Recent volumes of Supreme

Court reports are filled with debris of old decisions that have been overruled by new. To many persons it seems a significant fact that the court has not since 1937 declared unconstitutional a single act of Congress. More important it appears to me are the battlefields from which the court has retreated. It no longer contends that Congress may regulate only commerce and not industry, agriculture, and labor. Quite the contrary is true. Without considering its war powers, the National Government is to-day in position to control all that is important in the whole economic life of the nation. In addition it may now tax the salaries and wages of state and local employees, may provide for the adjustment of local government debts, and may cooperate with state and local authorities in extensive programs of social legislation. These are but the most important of the national powers recently sustained. As the court says, the National Government is still one of delegated powers, but the delegations are so broadly construed that in effect Congress is now very much like the British Parliament in the extent of its legislative authority.

To speak of the recent reversal of the court's position as a retreat is in a sense to do injustice to its members. It would be more nearly correct to say that the new court since 1937 has had the statesmanship and the broad intelligence to recognize the facts of nationalism to which the old court had closed its eyes. It sees that many of the economic and social issues that confront the whole people cannot be dealt with successfully without national action. Of necessity this means also that the court accepts the need for collective or governmental action in many cases where that need was once denied. It is even willing to go far beyond the old court in upholding the actions of administrative bodies set up by Congress, because its members realize that a government engaged in many activities cannot do everything through the single channel of Congress.

INTERESTS OF STATE AND NATION IDENTICAL

The decisions of this court also reveal a new and constructive approach to the question of state and national relations. It rejects the theory of a necessary antagonism or conflict of interests between the States and the National Government. Peering through the fog of words thrown up by the endless and futile debate over states' rights *versus* centralization, it sees that the real interests of the nation and the States are common interests and that they call for cooperation, not conflict. Along with students and practitioners in the field of public administration, they visualize a new type of functional federalism, a relationship between the nation and the States in which the real issue is how best to perform the necessary public services. The old federalism that was legalism is dead. The old assumption that national and state governments are necessarily antagonistic and in perpetual conflict is dead. The old theory of two mutually exclusive spheres of action, one reserved for the states, the other delegated to the national government ("and never the twain shall meet") is also dead. Yes, and the old judicial theory of laissez-faire, that government should be merely negative and inactive, is dead.

The former constitutional barriers to cooperation between the national and state governments exist now only as memories. Both national and state governments have been freed to carry on jointly or separately, as they choose, their essential public functions. Acts of Congress are not struck down, if within the present broad range of express or implied powers, merely because they might conceivably impinge upon some state interest. Likewise the acts of state legislatures are in general not declared invalid merely because they occupy an area that might be, but has not been, covered by some act of Congress. The effort is usually made to sustain both state and national legislation.

This new approach to federalism that is coming to dominate our thinking does not eliminate all difficulties from our system of government. What it does is to change our focus, our point of view, and from this new vantage point we see new questions arising. If federalism is no longer legalism, as I believe to be the case, what about the future role of the Supreme Court? What importance will it have as compared with legislative and administrative authorities? Having in large measure renounced all pretensions to the right to overrule the economic legislation of Congress, can it continue to be, what once it seemed, a sort of continuous constitutional convention?

What about Congress and the state legislatures? Are they so constituted, so organized, and so implemented with procedures and internal restraints as to enable them to perform wisely the enlarged responsibilities that fall upon them in an era of active government and large scale administration? If they are not, must there be a still further shift toward executive leadership in both national and state affairs? Up to now it has been found easier for the President and Governors and administrative officers to cooperate than for Congress and the state legislatures.

FUTURE OF STATES

And finally, what is to be the real future of the States? An increasing dominance of the National Government in matters of policy cannot be seriously questioned. Furthermore, as to its major functions the National Government is free, if it so desires, to ignore the States and to set up its own administration, complete from top to bottom. Its regulations can be made to override those of the States. By its control in the field of taxation and to satisfy its own tremendous needs it might force the States into progressive diminution of their own revenues and a reduction of their activities. That way lies a rapid strangulation or at best a slow atrophy of the States.

It has been suggested that the National Government should lay down general policies and standards in each major field of service, that the state governments should set up the needed administrative organizations, and that the counties or other local governments should perform the necessary services. In times of great emergency like . . . [World War II] the cooperation of the States in such an unequal partnership can be expected, but hardly so in times of peace and prosperity. State administrations that are not in sympathy with the National Government will cause considerable difficulty; and it is doubtful whether United States Senators will favor administrative methods that give their potential or actual rivals, the state Governors, the power of patronage over national programs in their States.

In short it is one of the tasks of political scientists and statesmen for the next generation to work out a constructive and autonomous role for the States in the work of the nation. The right formula has not yet been discovered. The value to the whole nation of preserving the States can hardly be questioned and need not be elaborated. To keep them alive and strong they must be kept active in the performance of functions over which they have their own control. They should not be allowed to die of sheer inactivity, or to become mere administrative districts of the National Government. The problem is not simply one of maximum dollars and cents efficiency in performing particular services; that might be attained by complete centralization of functions in Washington. The question is: How, without impairing the power of the National Government to achieve all national purposes promptly and effectively, can the essential public services be rendered on a national scale, without undue waste, and in such a way as to preserve the advantages of state and local self-government?

To prove their value in the future in the face of a powerful national sentiment that has grown impatient with them, the States must show beyond a doubt that they can be effective and economical in their operations. More than this they must also demonstrate that they can be quickly responsive to local needs and sensitive to regional as well as national opinion. In short they must in the face of great odds win back again some of that great public favor that they once had, and re-create in their peoples that sense of regional loyalty that the States once represented. This will not be achieved by heated oratory about states' rights, or by legalistic attempts to obstruct the nation's actions. It is too late for that. What is needed is a deliberate reappraisal and demonstration of the role of the States in the national social order that now exists, and an attempt to re-educate the people in the values of self-government in state and local communities.

As de Tocqueville once said: "A democratic people tends toward centralization, as it were, by instinct. It arrives at provincial institutions only by reflection."

No. 16

THE WORLD DEMANDS PROOF [1]

by Spencer Miller, Jr.

HOW in the days ahead can we make state and local governments more effective and responsible—more competent for their tasks? Local government and world government may seem poles apart, but the success of the one is vital to the success of the other. If we are to achieve responsible world government, if we in America are to discharge in full measure our obligations in this great task, it will be because we have proved that we are capable of local self-government.

The most spectacular immediate result of the recognition of the moral and practical inadequacy of state and local governments about the turn of the century was an increase in federal activity. Both the "new nationalism" of Theodore Roosevelt and the "new freedom" of Woodrow Wilson called for action by the federal government to correct the failure of government to meet the requirements of the age. Theodore Roosevelt inveighed against the "twilight zone" or legal vacuum between the power of the state governments and the power of the federal government to deal with important economic problems.

To-day there is little "twilight zone" left. For a generation the federal government has extended vastly the outreach of its services and its functions and has appropriated, if not pre-empted, all new sources of tax revenues. In the same period new services have been superimposed upon the states though severe restriction of the tax bases has greatly limited the proper development of these services.

Congressional power has been extended further during the past three decades by grants-in-aid to the states. There can be no doubt that grants-in-aid speeded up social reforms throughout the country and provided a measure of equalization of economic opportunity for all sections of America. On the other hand, there can be little doubt that the net result has been

---

[1] Spencer Miller, Jr., "The World Demands Proof," *National Municipal Review* (February, 1947), Vol. XXXVI, No. 2, pp. 72-77, 82. Reprinted by permission of the *National Municipal Review*.

to extend federal control over local government by means of these subsidies and to weaken the initiative and responsibility of local government by further impairing the taxing powers of the state. Federal taxes on gasoline and alcoholic beverages provide two notable examples of this.

This extension of federal power and influence has been an inevitable concomitant of the increasingly national and international scope of economic and social forces. It certainly has not been without merit. But there are limits to beneficent centralization.

If we Americans had been as assiduous as we should have been in finding ways to make the governments at the grass roots responsible and effective, we should not have had to rely so completely on the federal government for dealing with the depression and with many of the problems of war and its aftermath. The federal government in turn might have been in a somewhat better position to concentrate its energies and attention effectively on the global problems of war and peace.

WEAKNESS AT GRASS ROOTS

In turning so readily to Washington we display a weakness in the American system which goes back to the days immediately following the Revolution. The writing of the constitution of the United States in 1787 was itself an answer, in terms of a greater central power, to the failure of the states either singly or by cooperation to deal adequately with the problems of the day.

One of the outstanding weaknesses of the first state governments was in the executive. Executive power, such as it was, was generally divided among a number of officers all of whom were dependent upon the legislature. There was neither personal nor corporate unity in the executive and little capacity for leadership or efficiency either in the formulation or in the execution of public policy. Recognizing, as Hamilton said, that energy in the executive is one of the principal ingredients of good government, the makers of the constitution of the United States departed from the state models and established the first independent American government with an adequate executive power. It was this difference between the federal and state constitutions which de Tocqueville later noted as one of the principal reasons for the generally superior character of federal government and administration.

This superiority was evident to thoughtful citizens almost from the beginning. It led to a certain amount of imitation of the federal constitution by subsequent state constitutional conventions. But the imitation invariably stopped short of a frame of government adequate to the real needs of the state. Partly because of the protecting and pervasive influence of federal power, the states have not been under the kind of pressure to recondition their own governments that led to the framing of the federal constitution. More often than not amendment or revision of state constitutions has been the result of an impulse to put some new limitations or shackles on a government already too feeble to be truly responsible for its action or its inaction.

So, while the legal and actual powers of the central government have been increasing, both by liberal judicial interpretation and by constitutional amendment, the powers of state governments have been restricted by the imposition of new limitations in both federal and state constitutions. The typical American response to an unsatisfactory exhibition of governing by state, county or city has been *not* to discover the fundamental cause of misgovernment but rather to forbid the act of misgovernment by the simple device of *forbidding government*.

State constitutions have become veritable catalogues of "thou shalt nots." Restrictions on the borrowing power, the use of the state's credit, and the raising and spending of state and local revenues have seriously limited the capacity of state and local governments to meet their own problems without federal aid.

STRAIT-JACKET LAWS

Provisions designed to prevent abuse of executive power, moreover, have so crippled it in many states that the people are forced to look to Washington for enforcement of laws and protection of rights which are the primary responsibility of the states.

Detailed constitutional provisions governing state departments and county and municipal governments have increased government costs and prevented the adaptation of state and local administration to changing needs.

So more and more, as Professor Henry Jones Ford of Princeton University pointed out in 1908, when the people have felt "the need of government" they have turned from the states to the national government in Washington. Reviewing the development of constitutional limitations on state government, Professor Ford summarized the situation thus:

The American state is unique in that the people not knowing how to control the government have reduced it to a condition of bare existence. America has created a form of polity the world has never seen before in producing the manacled state—the state that puts a strait-jacket and handcuffs upon government. And this at a time when there is an imperative social demand for extending the sphere of government and increasing its activities!

In this condition Professor Ford found one of the underlying reasons for "the tendencies towards aggrandizement of federal power now manifested in national legislation and in the decisions of the courts," an example of "the operation of the historical principle that sovereignty unprovided for in extant forms of government always seeks to embody itself in new forms."

Thus American political history had verified the warning Jefferson had uttered about a hundred years earlier, that it was important to revise state constitutions in order to strengthen state governments lest weak ones lose in competition for power with the federal government.

Belief in the importance of local self-government represents a profound and permanent truth which we have ignored to our peril. Even though we take this belief for granted, let us look at the reasons behind it. One has already been suggested. It is the lesson taught by all big administrative organizations that there are weaknesses and dangers in bigness.

There is another important reason for strengthening our state and local governments. These governments are recruiting and training agencies for a large proportion of the men and women who will ultimately be chosen to guide the destinies of the nation. Unfortunately, feeble government does not attract the best talent. We are rightly concerned at the distaste, the contempt even, that many Americans feel for political or public service as a career. I do not mean to disparage the many fine, not to say superior, men and women who have, despite these handicaps, made public service their profession.

All things considered, we have more of these people both in politics and in public administration than we realize, but if we would do the things we know we ought to do, politics and public service would be generally recognized as an honor and a privilege. In view of the importance of the role that American government must play in the world, we cannot longer be satisfied with any but the best talents in the higher reaches of our public service. We will never get that talent in the measure in which it is needed until we make the opportunity for real achievement in local and state government considerably greater than it is to-day.

NO CRACKER-BARREL DEMOCRACY

I have left to the last the chief reason usually offered for preserving local self-government. That is the supposition that the closer the government is in geographical and physical fact to the people the better will they understand it and the more readily will they be able to control it. The trouble with this supposition is that under present conditions it is often just not so. The national news services, national radio hookups and other media of communication enable the average citizen to feel that he knows more about candidates for president and about great national issues than he does about state, city and ward affairs.

In the old days, when it was possible for the voter to know personally most of his local functionaries, when he met them or their close associates in his ordinary daily or weekly round, he could know and control the conduct of local government in a manner much more direct than his remote control over Washington.   Unfortunately, we have allowed the neighborhood or community basis of this grass roots democracy largely to disintegrate while the national market for words and ideas has almost superseded the local markets for exchange of strictly local intelligence and ideas.

Yet, I think it is true there is no substitute for face-to-face dealings in private or in public business. If it is no longer true that people can understand their local governments better than their national government it ought to be. But it will not be true again unless we make a much more conscious effort than we do now to maintain means of communication on local problems. We need everywhere nonpartisan local citizens' organizations. We need in every neighborhood a regular meeting place to which citizens may come for information and exchange of views on problems and questions of all kinds. We probably need to spend time and money to re-establish valid media for communication via the printed word and the radio concerning local problems. And we need to reinvigorate the teaching of "community civics" to young and old.

Grass roots democracy is not an inevitable outcome of "progress" or of social change. It must be sought and worked for. What are the prospects? In spite of everything that has been said, there are many indications that the prospects may be better than they appeared to be 50 years ago.

We have entered what might be termed a new epoch of state and local government in this country. It is an epoch marked by a growing recognition of the great truth that government, like all other major institutions, exists to get things done. Consequently there has been less stress on constitutional limitations and more on rewriting state constitutions and municipal charters and reorganizing state and municipal administrations so as to permit these governments to do their share of the public business.

To be sure, the prescription for modern state government which appears in the *Model State Constitution* has not been taken whole by any one state. We have in Nebraska, however, one hopeful demonstration of the superiority of the unicameral legislature. We have an increasing number of legislative councils working to improve the quality of state legislation. We have made in many states varying degrees of progress toward integration of administration under a responsible chief executive.

We still have left largely unsolved the problems of finding satisfactory leadership in our legislatures and of achieving satisfactory working relations between the executive and legislative branches. Significantly, these are the two principal deficiencies in the organization of our federal government. It is to be hoped that the reorganization of Congress upon which a beginning has been made may be carried out to an ultimate solution of these problems at the federal level and that simultaneously more and more states will tackle these same problems.

More progress toward responsible government has been made at the local level. All but seventeen cities have abandoned the old bicameral city council. The charters of a majority of the major cities give at least some recognition to the need for concentration of responsibility.

If we really believe that self-government must begin at home we must learn to trust our state and local governments more than we have in the past. A failure to trust them indicates a fatal distrust of our own capacity for self-government. We now know that in the long run such distrust does not result in greater freedom from government, it simply means that government will be exercised from a more remote place, subject to more indirect controls and less susceptible to the bridle of a genuine public opinion.

SOME REMEDIES

So let us re-examine some of the constitutional limitations on state and local power. Let the states give genuine home rule, fiscal as well as legal, to soundly established county and municipal governments. This does not mean that every existing county or municipality, however inadequate it may be in area, population or resources, must necessarily be given home rule powers. In great metropolitan areas, for example, we must face the fact that there can be no such thing as self-government, or genuine home rule, in a central city which is deprived of the fiscal and intellectual resources of the more fortunate beneficiaries of its industry who happen to live in suburbs legally and politically isolated from the city. "One world" will become an empty dream if those of us who live in any of the more than 140 metropolitan areas in the United States are not ready to recognize their allegiance and responsibility to the "one city."

While we free our state governments of constitutional restrictions which help to drive people to Washington when they want to get things done, we must undertake the more fundamental job of reorganizing our state governments so that they have not only the power but also, as Professor Ford said, "the responsibility and efficiency essential to democratic government." This means that where the state legislature is dangerously unrepresentative that condition should be corrected. It indicates in practically every state the need for further progress toward a more responsible executive branch. It also means in many states a pretty substantial reorganization of the judicial branch.

COOPERATION ESSENTIAL

I have said a good deal about the necessity for making our state and local governments more efficient in order to fit them to assume a larger share of the burden of government. This does not mean that we can divide functions of government into three distinct categories, assign one set to Washington, another to the state capitol and another to city hall. More and more it is being recognized that many functions once thought of as strictly local have statewide, national or even international implications.

Consequently our state and local governments must become better cooperators, cooperators among themselves and with the federal government. Much progress is being made in this direction, thanks to the work of the Council of State Governments and to the examples of successful intergovernmental operations of such organizations as the Port of New York Authority, Interstate Commission on the Delaware River Basin, and others.

One other trend which points toward increasing effectiveness for state and local governments is the growing acceptance of planning. A government cannot do an intelligent job if it does not plan intelligently in advance for it. As the late Senator Dwight W. Morrow said on the subject of community planning: "I don't like to say that a plan does not cost anything, because anything that is worth while on this earth costs something. But I do think it is quite demonstrable that the real cost of building up a community is the cost of non-planning."

A major reason why the federal government is called upon to play so large a role in such matters as housing, urban development, and modern highway construction is the fact that we have allowed our large cities and metropolitan areas to develop, or rather to disintegrate, without local plan or direction to an extent that local resources and powers are frequently incapable of reversing the trend.

If we want our local communities to avoid having to go to Washington to save them from virtual destruction, we must greatly extend and accelerate the application of planning. And mere city planning is not enough. It must include metropolitan planning, planning at the state level and in many instances regional or interstate planning. It must embrace fiscal programming. Every plan must include the measures for its fiscal achievement. The only possible answer to the failure of such voluntary planning through state and local governments will be planning for an increasing number of regions enforced by federal authority or money.

In the last analysis, the success of any system of freedom must depend upon confidence—confidence in ourselves and confidence in one another.

The way to achieve confidence is to act confidently. If we are to continue to act confidently, we must correct the deficiencies in our American system and thus demonstrate both to ourselves and to the world that it works. The final proof of our capacity for responsible world government will be our demonstrated capacity to make state and local government both effective and responsible.

Chapter VI

INTERGOVERNMENTAL PROBLEMS—
CAN WE SOLVE THEM?

[WE have already seen that every political society is faced with the problem of distributing governmental power between a central government and some kind or kinds of political subdivisions. Once the distribution is made, other and equally vital problems arise. It becomes necessary, for example, to work out a way of life governing the relationships between the units of government that have been created. In a federal system, such as that in the United States, this is especially difficult because there is a constitutional division of power giving the major political subdivisions, or states, power to act independently of one another and independently of the central government in a number of fields.

As long as the United States was an agrarian nation with a poorly developed system of transportation and communication, the states could be relied upon to handle a great many of the social and economic problems independently. But this situation no longer obtains. It is now obvious that our social, political, and economic life is a vast, complex, and interrelated whole. There are few questions that are purely state or local in character. This means that we must submit to a greater degree of centralization or work out new means of interstate cooperation or both. Trends in both of these directions are observable.

Intergovernmental problems, of course, are not confined to relations between the states. Within the states we have a large number of local units of government—cities, towns, counties, school districts and the like. Problems involving the relationships of these units with one another are, if not as spectacular, just as important as interstate relations. Many of these units were unwisely established and badly planned. Much duplication of effort and considerable waste of public money attend their labors. Their existence makes the governmental machine more complicated and the task of the politician, who must keep that machine operating smoothly, more difficult. Yet it is also true that they perform in many, if not most, cases functions that are essential and vital to our society. The problems they raise, therefore, cannot be solved either by abuse of the politician or by the simple formula of consolidation and elimination. We must carefully examine the things the various governmental subdivisions do and how they do them. In this way only can we devise the necessary means for coordinating their work.]

No. 17

FEDERAL-STATE RELATIONS [1]

*by The Commission on Organization
of the Executive Branch of the Government*

I. THE PROBLEM

FEDERAL-STATE relations is the cardinal question of our Federal system of government. It is not a question that can be resolved once for all time. Emphasis shifts from generation to generation as the American people fashion their government to meet the needs of changing times and changing conditions.

Prior to 1900, the question was largely a legal problem. Since that time, it has become increasingly an economic problem.

Our Government to-day is very different in structure and in operation from that envisioned by the founding fathers. From a number of small semi-autonomous agricultural States, we have become a highly industrialized far-flung nation. We have become a world power with interests and responsibilities throughout the globe.

As we have grown as a nation, so have we grown as independent States; and government to-day—all of our governments—is a large social and economic mechanism designed to serve and operate for the welfare of the people.

As this development has taken place, two problems have been cast in bold relief:

1. How can the American type of democracy—a democracy based on individual liberty and extensive citizen participation in and control of government—be maintained and strengthened?

2. At the same time, how shall government provide the services which people increasingly demand and which are necessary for the general welfare?

These are not problems which can be solved by the States acting alone; nor can they be solved by the National Government without reference to the States. Their solution requires cooperation and teamwork on the part of the States and the National Government, with understanding and support from the people at large.

[1] The Commission on Organization of the Executive Branch of the Government, "Federal-State Relations," from *Overseas Administration; Federal-State Relations; Federal Research,* a report to the Congress by the Commission on the Organization of the Executive Branch of the Government. U. S. Government Printing Office, Washington, D. C., March, 1949.

II. THE DEVELOPMENT OF FEDERAL-STATE RELATIONS

In 1913, total expenditures of the National Government were approximately $700 million, an amount which represented about one-quarter of the aggregate cost of all levels of governments in this country. Then, to a very large extent, local, State, and Federal governments established, financed, and administered their own activities.

In that same year, the National Government entered the field of income taxation on a permanent basis, thus providing the central Government with a revenue potential of great magnitude.

Almost concurrently—in 1914—we embarked upon the first large-scale, continuing cooperative project, the agricultural extension program. The pattern established for this program has been widely followed in the development of highway, vocational education and rehabilitation, public health, hospital, social security, and similar programs until to-day there are few major public services which are not financed and administered to some extent on a Federal-State cooperative basis.

In effect, the National Government found not only a major source of revenue, but a field of expenditure commensurate with a broadened tax base was developed. The conjoining of these two forces carried important implications for the future of Federal-State relations.

The rapidly increasing demands upon government—growing out of the development of our industrial society, out of two world wars, and a major depression—have expanded and extended public services and governmental activities far beyond those contemplated a short generation ago; and the cost of all government—Federal, State, and local—has increased from approximately $3 billion per year in 1913 to about $55 billion in 1948.

The necessity for meeting public needs and the search for revenue to meet such needs are basic to the present-day problem of Federal-State relations. We have attempted to solve this problem by the development of an extensive program of so-called grants-in-aid, and this development has had a profound effect upon our tax, fiscal, and governmental structures.

III. GRANTS-IN-AID

"Grants-in-aid" is a term used to define a method of operation whereby funds derived from a tax levied and collected by one level of government are made available for expenditure and administration by another level, usually upon a matching basis, for some particular activity, and in accordance with definite and specific standards and requirements.

The grant-in-aid method is used extensively by both the State, with its political subdivisions, and by the Federal Government, with the States.

To-day, approximately 40 per cent of all funds expended by local governments, and approximately 15 per cent of all funds expended by State governments, are derived from grants-in-aid; and this trend toward using grants-in-aid for supporting public services is definitely on the increase.

Grants-in-aid are a part of the warp and woof of present-day government; but they cannot be considered separately from our tax and fiscal problems, nor from our Government plan and structure.

What are the assets and liabilities of this grant-in-aid method which is so large a part of the whole question of Federal-State relations?

Assets

a. The cooperative system based on grants-in-aid has provided needed standards of public services throughout the country in many fields—services that many States would be unable to supply. It has provided for some redistribution of resources from States that have superior means to those that lack them.

b. The plan has developed a division of responsibility: the National Government giving financial aid and establishing broad standards—the State governments sharing the fiscal burden and maintaining primary responsibility for administration. In addition to decreasing inequalities of service, the grant-in-aid method has raised the level of all aided services, without transferring functions entirely to the National Government.

c. The grant-in-aid method, in fact, has added to and expanded the activities of State governments by contributing to their resources and thereby enabling them to embark upon additional or more extensive public-service programs for their own people.

d. It has stimulated States and localities to provide a number of public services deemed necessary and desirable in the national interest.

e. The cooperative method has improved the administration of many State activities. National administrative standards, as in highway and welfare programs, and national advice, as in police work, have done much to increase the professional skill and effectiveness of State administrators.

Liabilities

a. Grant programs are unrelated; they are uncoordinated; and they have developed in a haphazard manner without any one agency—Federal or State—concerned with the over-all impact and the over-all effects of grants-in-aid upon the general operations of government.

b. The grant-in-aid method has removed large areas of discretionary power from the hands of State officials and has transferred a measurable degree of policy-making and ultimate responsibility and control for public services to the National Government.

c. Grants-in-aid have altered State service patterns and total State programs. Available Federal funds for matching purposes stimulate or "persuade" the States in many instances to expend large sums for an aided program while, of necessity, other needed services are neglected. The public assistance program as contrasted with the general relief program is one among many examples.

d. In order to provide funds for grants-in-aid, and to adjust to war and depression, the national system of taxation has been expanded until we have extensive overlapping and conflicts on the part of Federal, State, and local governments. Of greater importance to State and local governments, the national need for revenue has caused the Congress in some instances to utilize productive tax sources that could be used just as effectively by State or local governments. In this manner, the circle widens. Under pressure to meet needs, Congress appropriates more for grants. In order to secure necessary revenues, the national tax base is expanded which makes it more difficult for State and local governments to secure their own revenue, and hence stimulates pressure from more and more groups for more and more grants.

e. Federal grants-in-aid retard and repress the initiative of the States in financing the growing needs of State and local government, because such grants frequently result in rewarding those States which avoid their responsibility and in penalizing those which accept it.

IV. EFFECT UPON EXECUTIVE BRANCH OF GOVERNMENT

The development of cooperative government, based largely upon grants-in-aid, has had a far-reaching effect upon the executive branch.

It has enlarged the executive branch, requiring great expansion in many departments and the establishment of new administrative agencies.

It has increased national taxes.

And it has been responsible to some extent for the rapid development and extension of that fourth area of Government, known as the "regional area," serviced in large part by Federal regional offices.

Whether measured in terms of organizational set-up, personnel, or expenditures, a very large part of the executive and administrative task of the Federal Government is concerned with problems, functions, and services involving Federal-State relations.

V. RECOMMENDATIONS

Recommendation No. 1. We recommend that the functions and activities of government be appraised to determine which can be most advantageously operated by the various levels of government, and which require joint policy-making, financing, and administration.

Recommendation No. 2. We recommend that our tax systems—National, State, and local—be generally revised and that, in this revision, every possible effort be made to leave to the localities and the States adequate resources from which to raise revenue to meet the duties and responsibilities of local and State governments.

Many tax sources are exploited by both States and the Federal Government, and to-day there is even a triplication of taxation in the matter of incomes since many cities are now resorting to income taxes to meet their expenditures. The whole problem of duplicating and triplicating taxation is most difficult to resolve. But it is to be hoped that the Joint Committee of the Congress and the Governors' Conference will continue to explore the question of overlapping taxes.

Recommendation No. 3. We recommend that all grants-in-aid which are given to State governments directly be budgeted and administered on the Federal and State levels as are other Federal and State funds.

Recommendation No. 4. We recommend that the grant-in-aid plan and program be clarified and systematized.

A system of grants should be established, based upon broad categories—such as highways, education, public assistance, and public health—as contrasted with the present system of extensive fragmentation. There are now at least 3 separate and distinct grants in the realm of education, at least 3 in public assistance, and 10 in public health. Grants for broader categories would do much to overcome the lack of balance now readily apparent.

Recommendation No. 5. We recommend, in order to accomplish all of these things in an adequate and orderly manner, that a continuing agency on Federal-State relations be created with primary responsibility for study, information, and guidance in the field of Federal-State relations.

In cooperation with the Office of the Budget, this agency should develop a unified system of budgetary and fiscal control over the operation of all grants-in-aid. It should make available to the Congress data and information pertaining to the problem as a whole, as well as the many and various divisions and parts thereof. And it should be an agency which, on a continuing basis, would appraise our public needs, our resources, and ways and means for adjusting the one to the other in the interest of the American people.

The question of Federal-State relations, and the problems incident thereto, is a most important part of our governmental structure and our governmental operation. It should be studied and appraised in its over-all aspects carefully and continuously if public services are to be adequately rendered, if public administration is to be efficient and economical, and if we are to maintain a strong, vital, Federal system of government.

No. 18

INTERSTATE COOPERATION [1]

by Charles J. Calrow

IT is probably entirely pardonable for a Virginian to take his text from the writings of that master planner, Thomas Jefferson. Jefferson states in his autobiography: "but it is not by the consolidation, or concentration of powers, but by their distribution, that good government is effected. Were not this great country already divided into states, that division must be made, that each might do for itself what concerns itself directly, and what it can so much better do than a distant authority. Every state again is divided into counties, each to take care of what lies within its local bounds; each county again into townships or wards, to manage minuter details; and every ward into farms, to be governed each by its individual proprietor. . . . It is by this partition of cares, descending in gradation from general to particular, that the mass of human affairs may be best managed for the good and prosperity of all." The language of this statement is, in the light of to-day, highly significant.

In this statement Jefferson justified the division of the country into certain administrative areas on the grounds of necessity, realizing that even for the country, as it stood in his day, partition into administrative units was needed, if the public business was to be expeditiously conducted.

The language which Jefferson employed, in addition to saying that each of these administrative units might do for themselves that which a distant authority could not do so well, implies the passage of laws by these administrative units distinct from either amplification or extension of laws passed by a higher authority.

Jefferson's theories concerning government really involve two series of gradations, one downward, the gradation from "general to particular" in which the application of authority became more intensive as the area involved decreased, and one upward, with respect to the area over which

[1] Charles J. Calrow, "Interstate Cooperation," *National Municipal Review* (August, 1936), Vol. 25, No. 8, pp. 445-451, 464. Reprinted by permission of the *National Municipal Review*.

the authority should extend, the powers granted growing less as the so-called higher levels of government were reached.

But the form of government which we actually have fits neither of the Jeffersonian theories. We have neither the gradations downward from "general to particular" nor the gradations upward with the partition of cares proceeding from particular to general as the area increases.

Theoretically, the authority still flows from the people, but not through the lower levels of government controlling the minor geographical divisions to the higher, but directly from the people to the state, and from the people direct to the nation. In this last case it is, in certain particulars, restrained by the limitations erected by the same creators of authority acting in their capacities as citizens of the states. The tenth amendment to the federal constitution defines these limitations.

While Jefferson wrote in terms of geographical-political areas with their compartmentalization of authoritative control, the government which he administered was far from meeting his specification.

Under the present system there is really no series of planes of government. Such gradations as exist flow from "general to particular" both ways from the state, on one hand to the federal government, and on the other hand to the state's political subdivisions.

It is because the system of governmental levels described as desirable by Mr. Jefferson does not exist that, when problems which transcend state lines demand solution, the necessity for interstate cooperation appears. Interstate problems are all around us. Changing conditions in agriculture, industry, trade, transportation, and communication have transformed problems which were once localized into problems which refuse to be bounded by lines created by the King's Charter, Orders in Council, or determined by transit and compass. Many social, economic and physical problems arising in a single state cannot be solved by that state alone without a sacrifice of interests. Particularly is this true of those problems in which social and economic interests are simultaneously involved.

Of course, one method of handling such interstate situations is by the amendment of the federal constitution and the further delegation of particular authority to this unit of our governments. This is a form of interstate cooperation whereby three-fourths of the states may establish particular policies but of general application controlling in all states. Where this form is applicable it has many advantages, not the least of which is the designation of an authority with power to enforce and courts to adjudicate the disputes which may arise. Another advantage of this type of cooperation lies in the peculiar duality of relationship which the citizen of this country has, making him directly amenable to the laws of the United States as well as to laws of the state.

This method of cooperation has, however, certain limitations of desirability when the problems are not nation-wide but regional with reference to the area involved or particular with reference to type. For such cases interstate cooperation seems desirable.

We have recently had considerable discussion of the question of regions, and some of the supporters of the "region" concept have gone so far as to suggest the creation of regions having administrative and legislative power interposed as another level of government between the states and the federal government—a multiplication of governments. From a recognition of the fact that many of the social, economic, and physical problems are regional in character and not limited by state lines, and from the studies of this fact, it has been but a ready jump to the assumption that a regional governmental organization was a happy method of obtaining solutions of such group problems. But is it? How will such a region be delimited—by geography or function, by river basin, coal-bearing area, or maybe by particular type of agricultural production? If regions are delimited according to one of these characteristics, how will an area having a number of these types of characteristics be assigned? There is possibly some confusion of thought on this subject. Let us take Virginia as a case in point.

The economic, social, and physical problems of Virginia are shared with other states in many ways and many directions and in varying volumes. In the realm of agricultural economics Virginia shares with North Carolina, South Carolina, Georgia, Tennessee, and Kentucky the problems arising from the processes of tobacco production and tobacco marketing. With respect to mineral resources Virginia shares with Pennsylvania, Ohio, West Virginia, Kentucky, Tennessee, and Alabama, and to a certain extent with Indiana, Illinois, Iowa, Missouri, Kansas, and Oklahoma, in those problems arising in connection with the production and marketing of coal. In the realm of those resources taken from the sea Virginia shares with North Carolina, South Carolina, Maryland, Delaware, and New England the problems of distributing and marketing the products of commercial fisheries and in competitive markets meets the industries of the states on the Gulf. In the industrial world Virginia shares in production of rayon with the following states: Massachusetts, New York, Pennsylvania, Ohio, Tennessee, and eleven other states, and with New England, North Carolina, South Carolina, Georgia and Alabama in the cotton textile industry. It also shares its rivers with Maryland, North Carolina, Tennessee, and West Virginia.

The very plain fact is that in the case of Virginia the lines of certain regional area problems refuse to coincide with those of certain other regional area problems and for the problems of this state the region which would encompass them all would be so extensive that it would cease to be a convenient unit. Nor is this all, for in the territory included in such a region there would necessarily be other states which would have interlocking interest with still other areas outside of the region embracing the Virginia problems and thus a need for further regional extension.

The point may be taken further. Any division of the country into regions with limits fixed with relation to one set of problems would arbitrarily divide the areas of other problems and these last questions could only be handled by interregional cooperation or by some superior governing unit, so that all which would be accomplished by the new order of things would be a multiplication of problems both intra- and inter-regional.

A further point to be considered in connection with this regional doctrine is the question as to whether the regional authority is to be state-like with general sovereignty or to have only delegated powers like the federal government. If the former, then there is conflict of sovereigns and if the latter, nothing has been accomplished which could not have been done under the present constitutional forms.

The setting up of the regional organizations as additional levels of government between the states and the federal government is of course unthinkable under our present system but, if possible, it should not be done for the reason that it would tend to weaken the federal union.

It is believed that the regional government scheme as a method of interstate cooperation may be dismissed from further consideration and attention given to those methods which do not involve the creation of new governments.

As has been pointed out, the scheme of government outlined by Jefferson in the passage first quoted is far from being parallel with that under which we are operating. Our governmental system being what it is, our interstate problems, except in a relatively few cases, must be handled by the states severally as sovereign bodies or jointly through inter-state compacts approved by Congress, or by the federal government.

Interstate cooperation of this classification may be sub-classified under five heads:

(1) Under the first heading there may be placed that type of interstate cooperation which results in the establishment of uniform laws, uniform regulations, or uniform methods of administration. This cooperative effort toward standardization may spring from state action alone or as in the case of certain technical activities, cooperatively with federal departmental agencies.

As participation in such cooperative effort is entirely within the powers of the states and may be taken without action by the Congress, it has possibilities of expansion or limitation which permit its adaptation to any local conditions, social or economic, which may demand special consideration, thus meeting Jefferson's specification. With this plan of interstate cooperation there is, however, a possibility that some of the states, most in need of the beneficial results which may flow from its operation, may refuse to participate and thus destroy or at least weaken the cooperative plans, or else a state having once entered the cooperative plan may, for various reasons, withdraw and thus endanger the whole cooperative scheme. Lack of permanency, failure to attain or maintain sufficient coverage and, possibly, the lack of uniformity in enforcement are the weak points of this plan.

(2) In a second grouping are those state relations which are reciprocal in nature and are also without the necessity for federal approval. Many state acts of this type are on the statute books. Usually they take the form of a grant of privilege or license by the legislature of one state to the citizens or officers of other states in return for similar grants of privileges or authority for its own citizens or officers by the said other states. Reciprocity in recognition of professional registrations is an example.

An act of the Virginia General Assembly of 1936 providing for reciprocal agreement with consenting states as to the laws of "close pursuit" is another example of provision for this type of interstate cooperation.

Under plans for interstate cooperation of this type there are set up penalties for non-conformity; namely, the non-grant to non-conforming states of the rights and privileges given those entering into and holding to the agreement. This gives this cooperative effort an element of strength not possessed by the efforts grouped under the first heading.

(3) A third grouping of interstate cooperative activities is that under a plan for the conduct of a joint enterprise of a physical nature, as for example, the construction of a bridge over a boundary river. In this case a simple contractual relation exists between the states and neither functions as a governing unit. In this case while two states may by agreement regulate the use of the utility, the collective action proceeds no further. The relationship between the states is simply that of partners in a joint enterprise. This is not an exercise of sovereignty. Either party to the enterprise may sue upon the contract and such suits come within the jurisdiction of the federal Supreme Court, not because of the nature of the activity but because of the nature of the litigants.

A modification of this type of interstate cooperation is the joint agreement for the construction of certain kinds of public improvements such as roads with common points at the state line permitting the flow of interstate traffic. In this case each state would construct that portion of the road lying on its side of the state line and thus, despite joint agreements, the relation of any state to the enterprise is not that of a partner, and there is no controlling enforceable contract between the states. There is no authority to which appeal may be taken in case of failure to carry out the provisions of such an agreement.

(4) A fourth type of interstate cooperation is one in which the states may by treaty and with the approval of the Congress, engage in a joint enterprise administered by a governing body separate and distinct from the administrative departments of the cooperating states. The administrative authority may be of commission or corporation form and have, in so far as the particular enterprise is concerned, certain regulation-making authority. In this case the state acts creating the commission are, to a certain but minor extent, a degree of surrender of sovereignty by delegation of authority, as no state engaging in such an enterprise would possess the right to require the commission or corporation to commit acts in conflict with the rules laid down for its guidance in the approved treaty or compact.

This delegation of authority has, however, certain advantages, as the controlling unit thus set up acquires none of the general attributes of sovereignty and an aggrieved state has recourse through the courts without directly involving another sovereign in the proceedings. Needless to say, such a corporation or commission can have no power to enforce regulations except where it receives this authority by delegation from the states creating it; neither can its authority be extended or curtailed except with the approval of all of the parties to the original compact. In some ways, limited it is true, such a corporation or commission acquires, in relation to the contracting states, some of the same status as has the federal government.

It may be said in passing that the approval by Congress does not under the present constitutional limitations give to the federal government any administrative authority, and even though the approvals of compacts are required the so-called "upper level" of government acquires thereby no rights over the states.

(5) Still another class of interstate cooperative action is one of the Congress-approved compact type, in which each state reserves to itself the administration of the terms of the compact within its own borders. Here no authority or corporation is created. This form is generally applicable where the police powers of the states are to be employed and it is not suitable for enterprises in which the joint construction and operation of public works or public facilities are attempted.

An example of this type of cooperative effort is the Virginia tobacco control act, chapter 183 of the acts of the General Assembly of 1936, which in the draft of the proposed compact provides among other things that the states which are parties to the compact do jointly and severally agree "to cooperate with each other in formulating such regulations as will assure the uniform and effective enforcement of each of the aforesaid state statutes" and further "not to depart from or fail to enforce, to the best of its ability, any regulations concerning the enforcement of the state statutes, without the consent of a majority of the members of the tobacco commissions of each of the several states which is a party to this agreement."

It will be noted that while elsewhere within its stipulations the act provides for the enforcement of the regulations within each state and penalties for noncompliance therewith, nowhere does it provide penalties for the failure of the tobacco commission of any state to see that its own regulations are enforced; neither is there any recognition of a common authority before whom an appeal for such enforcement could be carried.

The failure of a superior state authority such as the governor, the legislature, or the courts to displace a recalcitrant commission would raise petty questions of conflict between interstate policies and constitutional law.

There may be other forms of interstate cooperation, but the list just given covers all the major types. Such others as may have developed will probably be found to be modifications of some one of these five.

Some of these interstate cooperation types are particularly applicable to certain joint enterprises having to do with things rather than with persons, and this is an important point. The problems arising from cooperative action by states as proprietaries are quite different from those which appear when joint action is taken concerning matters which call into play the police powers.

The time element is also another point which needs attention even in those cooperative plans involving only things. Certain affairs may be settled once and for all and the legislative acts providing for or ratifying the cooperative plan may well and fully provide for objectives complete within themselves and requiring no continuing administration. Where the project is one of a continuing nature the necessity for administration arises and with it troublesome questions. In all cases where the police power is invoked consideration of the time element is most important.

Despite the difficulties attendant upon interstate cooperation, the need for such action is so well recognized that every effort should be made to find a way to make cooperative effort effective. The number of matters in which joint action by two or more states would redound to the "good and prosperity of all" has vastly increased.

In summing up the weaknesses of various recognized forms of interstate cooperation it will be found that the chief of these is the failure to provide for uniform authoritative administration where the project is of a continuing nature or where it invokes the police powers of the cooperating states. The major problem, therefore, is one of providing for administration, and it must be admitted that none of the existing or suggested forms of interstate cooperation seem to provide this necessary element without some degree of conflict with "states' rights."

Even where the federal constitution has already provided for uniformity of enforcement, as it does under the provisions of section 2 of article 4, we have states refusing to recognize the extradition requisitions drawn by the executives of other states.

If it were not for the weakness due to lack of uniformity of enforcement, the uniform law plan (type 1) would, where police power alone is involved, be the easiest way out of the dilemma and, if the difficulties which arise from the tendency to delay and confuse the problem by bargaining for advantage could be overcome, the compact-commission form of cooperation (type 4) would probably settle the administration question for cooperative plans involving only things.

The reciprocity plan of cooperation (type 2) applies to only a few kinds of problems, and in the case of those problems involving economic as well as social questions it has an exceedingly limited application. This plan, however, may well be extended to cover those cases in which it would be useful. The administrative program here is not complicated and the question of states' rights does not arise.

The simple cooperative plan (type 3) has such limited application and only to specific physical problems that it needs no further consideration than already given it.

When we reach a discussion of the compact plan, which involves the use of the police power or seeks to control persons as well as things, we then enter a field in which the question of states' rights immediately comes to the front.

As has been stated, the present compact plan does not involve the federal government in the administration of the plan. It has, however, been suggested that this be changed and a three-point compact plan may solve the problem of regional controls. Under this changed plan the federal government or one of its agencies would supply the administrative authority for the cooperative region.

The plan involves first the adoption of suitable amendments to the federal constitution and next a limited delegation of authority to the federal government by interested states, and in this respect it departs from the present method of delegating authority to the federal government by constitutional provision chiefly by limiting the application of the authority thus granted to the subscribing states and omitting its application in the non-subscribing sovereignties. The delegation of authority, it is suggested, may also depart from the general constitutional form by limiting the scope of those laws needed to be passed by the federal legislature.

This form of provision for administration of interstate cooperative effort will be recognized as a modification of the compact plan heretofore described as type 4, the chief modification being that a federal agency would be substituted for the commission or corporation form of control.

The plan may also be considered as one in which the federal government places at the disposal of the states involved in the cooperative plan the facilities of the federal government for its administration. One example of such a plan, although not exactly parallel in form, was the municipal bankruptcy act. This particular act placed the facilities of the federal courts at the disposal of the municipalities of those states which by suitable legislation ratified the act. This act has been declared unconstitutional on the ground that it would lead to an invasion of states' rights, a view not shared by the minority of the United States Supreme Court.

Those upholding states' rights will object to this form of cooperative administration on the ground that it substitutes administration by federal bureau or department for that by state agency, and is thus a surrender of sovereignty, and so it would be. It is generally true that partners in a joint enterprise must waive the exercise of certain individual rights if they are to profit from the partnership.

It may also be said that the suggested plan tends to build up a federal bureaucracy at the expense of the states, and this may be true or not, depending on the nature of the enacted laws. It might be possible to so limit these laws by the acts of the delegating or ratifying states as to substantially give them the status of state-made laws.

Another plan proposed is one in which federal acts to accomplish specific purposes in limited areas are made applicable only to the areas of those states which, by suitable legislation, should permit the laws to be effective. In this case the ratification by two or more states would be a form of interstate cooperation, an interstate agreement to pass to the federal government the burden of taking care of specific problems. This transfer of burdens from the states to the federal government has been done in the case of specific purposes for the whole national area, as for example, in the case of the maintenance and government of the army, the navy, and the postal service. An extension of this system but with application only to those areas or states accepting it would be an innovation.

There is, however, one form of interstate cooperation which may be carried out without conflict with states' rights and this is cooperative planning by the states. In this case, as there are no administrative problems involved, there are none of the embarrassments arising from conflicts with state sovereignty. As the boundaries of the problem regions change, various combinations of states may join in the study of different specific problems and thus problems which transcend state lines may be completely covered. From such planning there should be developed such convincing evidence of need for state action that the several states interested in particular problems may be induced to enact suitable uniform legislation for remedying the troubles uncovered. Where uniformly capable administration is provided this is the least involved and may prove the most practicable method of providing for interstate cooperation.

The general purposes of the federal and state constitutions are to insure domestic tranquillity, promote the general welfare, and protect the liberties of the people. If to accomplish these purposes the people, in whom all powers are vested and from whom all powers are derived, find that in their capacities as citizens of problem regions having specific problems they are estopped from having these problems efficiently solved by reason of their own acts as citizens of the nation or as citizens of a state, then the people will in the end find a way out of this "no man's land" of government. Let us hope that this may be done without an increase in government.

No. 19

A PLAGUE OF SPECIAL DISTRICTS [1]

by Kirk H. Porter

A COMPLAINT frequently heard about local government is that there are altogether too many separate jurisdictions and too many local officers who have power to impose taxes for this, that, or the other purpose. In addition to the county, city, and township jurisdiction, the taxpayer is likely to find himself living within many other minor jurisdictions and subject to their taxes. There are school districts, park districts, drainage districts, forestation districts, road districts, mosquito abatement districts, sanitation districts, etc., etc. Each district has its own set of officials and its own precious tax rate, so that taxpayers come to feel that they are smothered with government, and lost in a maze of expensive complexities. Unfortunately, our American way of dealing with governmental abuses is

[1] Kirk H. Porter, "A Plague of Special Districts," *National Municipal Review* (November, 1933), Vol. 22, No. 11, pp. 544-547, 574. Reprinted by permission of the *National Municipal Review*.

to do nothing at all until the abuse has become well nigh intolerable and then to rise up in wrath and go at the trouble with radical remedies that promise dramatic changes but oftentimes no genuine correction of the real evil. Thus reformers want to sweep away all these special districts with bold gestures, to consolidate counties, to abolish popular elections, to set up county managers, or to establish full state control over local government and administration.

However, there is a reason for the special district; even though like many other useful institutions it has been grossly perverted, not only by corruptionists, but also by well-meaning people who have seen in it an agency of genuine democracy, and a safeguard against overweening power.

The special district was early designed to serve a purpose that existing governmental areas did not seem well adapted to serve. Thus, for instance, perhaps it becomes desirable to carry on a drainage project in a farm land area. But, it appears, the swampy lands involved, the streams that must be straightened or dealt with in some way, extend partially into the jurisdiction of two or three counties, to say nothing of a lot of townships. In a word, the physical, topographical, engineering problem does not conform to the rigid governmental areas.

One solution would be to turn the problem over to the state. But our devotion to old concepts of local self-government has stood in the way of this. Another method would be to get the governing authorities in the various jurisdictions to cooperate in the enterprise. But, when it comes to letting lucrative contracts, to employing workers, and most of all to levying the taxes to finance the undertaking, the good spirit of cooperation all too frequently evaporates; bickering, sharp practice, bitter rivalries and selfish interest creep in, and either the project is abandoned altogether, or else it goes forward accompanied with unwise compromises and much extravagance.

An obvious solution is the special district. Let the area of operation be marked out and surveyed. Let there be local referenda upon the broad question of going forward with the undertaking. If the popular vote be favorable let a special board of trustees be set up. Allow them to levy a certain rate upon all property within their district, and let them carry through the project, largely independently of all other local authorities. For good or for ill this type of special district has been resorted to for many years, and it does indeed seem to have served a good purpose, though many people to-day think such problems ought to be handled by the state directly.

But obviously, the justification for this particular type of special district exists only when the undertaking must needs reach into two or more existing jurisdictions,—that is, when it must cross county lines, or city boundaries.

But there are not many legitimate cases of this sort. Drainage projects are perhaps the clearest. The forest preserve, or large park project may present the same problem. But it is interesting to observe that for the most part, to-day, state departments are assuming full control of these undertakings. This is much to be preferred, and the practice would seem to make unnecessary for the most part any further application of the special district idea as applied in the past years.

Another type of special district appears when it is desired to get a given undertaking "out of politics." This reflects deep distrust of the "regular" governmental authorities, and a wish to get the project into the hands of a "better class" of people who presumably will have a keener interest in the work to be done, a minimum of ulterior motive, and a considerable spirit of noble self-sacrifice.

The school district is the classic example of this type. Specially selected school trustees, or directors, are elected. Their powers are prescribed in the law, they may levy a prescribed rate, and thus conduct school affairs independently of the "regular" governmental authorities. Not everywhere is this high degree of independence permitted, however. Sometimes mayors, or city councils, or county supervisors select the school authorities; but they usually are free in the matter of actual administration.

Here again, the *reason* for having a special district is clear enough. And there is something in it. And it is interesting to observe that criticism of the special school district system today is directed largely to the point that there are altogether too many districts, and not that the special district idea should be abandoned. Arguments against preserving the vast multitude of tiny school districts that spatter the land would seem to be overwhelming. And many educators would be only too thankful to see the county accepted as the unit of school administration. But there is by no means a unanimity of opinion as to the wisdom of abandoning the "special" district idea and turning school administration over to the "regular" authorities, i.e., county supervisors or commissioners, or city councils. Many a reform advocate would throw up his hands in horror at that, and would plead instead for completely centralized state control.

Now the reason that lies behind the special school district has been invoked again and again to set up special districts for other purposes. Thus, well-meaning people have wanted to get public libraries out of the hands of the "regular" city officials. City parks and playgrounds, it has been thought, ought to be taken "out of politics." One of the latest manifestations of this urge for exclusiveness and purity is seen in the practice of taking county hospitals "out of politics" and of setting up separate boards with their special tax rates to carry on this service independently of the so-called politicians.

Thus has come into being a considerable number of what may be called "disguised" special districts. This type of district is disguised because it is literally coterminous with an existing area—a city or a county. In this way a city virtually becomes a special district for library administration, and a special district for city park administration, and the county virtually becomes a special district for hospital administration. And each of these disguised special districts has its independent authorities,—its trustees, directors or commissioners, and its inevitable special, precious, tax rate. Furthermore it should be pointed out that often it has been the very "best" people in the community that have insisted upon this exclusiveness. These well-meaning people are deeply interested in the particular service—*for the time being, anyway*—and want to keep it "out of politics."

In addition to all this, the time-honored system of fixing special tax rates for specific purposes aggravates the situation, even though it does not bring into existence either the genuine or the disguised special district. And again it is often the deeply interested, well-meaning people who are responsible for it. In the case of the special rate they wish to coerce the regular authorities—the county governing board or the city council,—or to circumvent them, or to prevent them from curtailing a given service. Right there begins the procession of special rates for special purposes. A certain rate is made mandatory, and the funds must be spent for a certain purpose —highway patrol, for instance. Then a certain rate is fixed and *must* be applied for poor relief. Presently this is split and two special rates appear —one for institutional relief, one for out-door relief.

Then there must be the fixed mandatory rate for maintaining a cemetery, another for the care of old soldiers, one for the care of orphans, etc., until the list of special rates includes perhaps a score or more. To be sure, most of these rates are maximum rates. But the constant pressure that is brought by those who are particularly interested in each of these activities, makes it next to impossible for the governing bodies to keep these rates below the maximum. And it should be observed that the basic idea back of the special rate is to deprive the governing body of much discretion with respect to a particular service. Thus, suppose the council of a small city either cannot or will not maintain a municipal band. Music lovers want a band. The statutes afford an opportunity. A referendum is held—that glorious instrument of direct democracy! The people vote: Shall a special rate be applied to maintain a municipal band? A handful of people vote, and most of them vote "yes," and lo! there is a band! And another rigid tax rate is fixed upon the city.

Sometimes local governing authorities, county board members and city councilmen, are quietly active at the state house seeking themselves to have those special rates applied. To have them in the statutes relieves the officials of much responsibility. They can take refuge in the fixed rate, and honestly declare that it is beyond their power to economize with respect to the services thus bolstered.

The result of all this is an astonishing complex of overlapping jurisdiction: —the "regular" areas, i.e., counties, cities, towns, and townships, the legitimate special districts, a number of wholly unnecessary special districts, several disguised special districts, and overlaying the whole, a strangling net of special rates that makes it impossible for local governing bodies to budget their resources wisely, even when they have the best of intentions.

Reform is not easy. Mere sweeping away of the special districts will not solve the problem. In fact, the good that would come of this is often very much exaggerated. The citizen is told that he lives under so many separate jurisdictions, each with power to tax; and is led to believe that if the jurisdictions were not so numerous the costs would disappear. But this is in part a vain hope. If a government service is to be maintained it makes but little difference whether one body or another imposes the tax rate. If a county hospital is to be maintained it makes relatively little difference whether the necessary taxes for the purpose be levied by a board of county supervisors, or by a board of county hospital trustees. If a city park is to be supported, or a library maintained, or a mosquito abatement project carried through, or a municipal band subsidized, or a county poor farm supported, it makes little difference who applies the rate. A dozen given rates applied by one board would be about as heavy as a dozen similar rates applied by a dozen different boards.

"But," one is quick to say, "we would get rid of all these useless officials, we would cut down personnel and the salary burden." A little could be saved this way, perhaps, but not a great deal. Libraries, hospitals, parks, drainage projects, etc., cannot be conducted without people to give time and attention to them. In brief, we should not get the idea that by abolishing districts we abolish the basic costs of the services involved. This seems to be a great delusion of those who advocate county consolidation. They seem to forget that there would be just as many miles of highway to keep up, just as many bridges to build, just as many poor people to feed and clothe, just as many criminals to prosecute, just as many children to educate, just as many land transfers to record, etc., etc.; and after all, these are the basic costs of local government.

However, the prime evil of the special district is that it grossly decentralizes administration. It tends to exalt each little service. It tends to make those who are in charge lose their sense of proportion. It relieves the principal local authorities of the power and responsibility they ought to have. It helps to let large sums of money dribble through the fingers of woefully incompetent people who often give but scant attention to the problems with which they are supposed to deal. And it makes very much easier the nefarious work of grafting politicians and crooked contractors, every one of whom is in favor of local self-government to the last degree, and more and stupider special boards and commissions.

These complexities of local government make intelligent budgeting almost impossible. A very homely illustration will make this clear. Imagine a householder trying to budget his household expenses for a year. And imagine that the amount to be spent for most of the important items were rigidly fixed. His budgeting becomes a farce! If the sums that he must spend for clothing, for food, for recreation, etc., are all fixed, there is no point to budgeting. Furthermore the decentralization in the actual conduct of services through independent agencies makes for much trouble, lack of cooperation and duplication of effort;—not to mention the evils of the long ballot.

On the whole, county governing boards and city councils stand to acquire greatly increased power as a result of doing away with special districts—genuine or disguised;—and certainly they would gain greatly in power by abolition of many special rates. But increased power means increased opportunities for doing the things that need to be done—chiefly an opportunity for budgeting wisely. Any attempt to effect economies through a structure of many jurisdictions, and within the ambit of a complicated net of fixed rates is almost sure to fail. City and county officers must be released from their strait-jackets and given a chance to assume real power and responsibility. If we are afraid to give them such power because of the evil they might do, we are indeed afraid to put modern democracy to the test.

No. 20

[THERE is, in the United States to-day, much discussion of our public policy but little discussion of our politics; that is, little discussion of the organization and processes of government and their relation to democracy. By and large Americans accept their system of government and do not question its adequacy.

Yet the trend toward the centralization of both power and activities in Washington is contrary to the "great tradition" in democratic thought. Active and responsible local governments are, as was illustrated in Spencer Miller's essay, "The World Demands Proof" (No. 16), not only necessary but also a vital part of the growth and tradition of American democracy. Popular control over government is a technique that must be learned; it can be learned only in the context of situations that affect us vitally and intimately. It must be mastered, therefore, in the first instance, in the neighborhood in which we actually live and where the problems are close enough to us that we can hope to understand and cope with them.]

BIG GOVERNMENT NOT INEVITABLE [1]

by David E. Lilienthal

IF there is one proposition that I had supposed thoroughly well established and accepted it is this: that our democratic form of government depends for its vitality, its responsiveness to public need, on the development and strengthening and nourishing of local institutions of government.

To this proposition there is universal assent. But such approval is in part only lip service, for what has happened in practice? The policy of encouraging and nourishing the responsibilities of local government has given way to an increasing centralization of administration in the national capital. So far has this gone—by action as well as by default—that we now find a quite disturbing situation. Experts in administration and management have set out to persuade the American people that centralized "Big Government" is inevitable.

I deny that Big Government is inevitable, that we have no workable alternative. These prophets of a managerial revolution and those among public administrators who seek to persuade the American people that Big Government is inevitable are not measuring up to their high responsibility to the democratic faith. And, what is more serious, they are making more difficult the achievements and the works that make that faith the best hope of mankind.

We have two alternatives to Big Government which we should pursue. Experience in the Tennessee Valley is one kind of evidence—there are others, of course—to support the thesis that in respect to overcentralization there is no wave of the future before which we are powerless.

How is Big Government being sold to the American people? The story begins with full agreement that "of course" everyone desires strong, dynamic local government. The Big Government apologists never question that.

---

[1] David E. Lilienthal, "Big Government Not Inevitable," *National Municipal Review* (February, 1947), Vol. XXXVI, No. 2, pp. 65-71, 88. Also printed in *Reader's Digest* (May, 1947) under the title "An Alternative to Big Government." Reprinted by permission of the *National Municipal Review*, the *Reader's Digest* and the author.

Indeed, how could they? We are told that these are "fine ideals"—the ideal of home rule, of a flourishing community and state government. But following close upon this disarming prelude we are told that the complexities of modern living make this older ideal merely nostalgic. Our technical society, so they say, has made it obsolete and unworkable. The airplane, the telegraph, the telephone, swift transportation make it necessary, though regrettable, that the older ideal must give way to the facts of modern life.

Those who are trying to persuade us that Big Government is inevitable rarely if ever defend centralization. Their tack is to deplore centralization just as much as the rest of us. They usually admit that remote administration from Washington is not desirable. They will even agree that the withdrawal of more and more decisions out of local communities and the state into bureaus in Washington is unfortunate and corrodes our democratic institutions. But they say we must bow our heads before the inevitable trend.

Big Government is *not* inevitable. Many of our problems *are* national. Problems that once could be dealt with as a matter of local or state policy now require a national policy. But because Congress must and should determine upon a national policy in a particular field, it does not always follow that the administration of that policy must also be centralized. This distinction between a centralized or national policy and its decentralized or localized administration is one of fundamental importance which the apologists of Big Government persistently overlook. It is a distinction which unless observed and respected by corrective action can lead to the progressive atrophy of most local and state governmental functions.

The distinction between authority and its administration is a vital one. For a long time all of us—administrators, citizens and politicians—have been none too clear on this point. We have assumed that, as new powers were granted to the government in Washington, these powers must also be administered from Washington. We have taken it for granted that the price of federal action was a top-heavy, cumbersome administration. Clearly this is not true. The problem is to divorce the two ideas of authority and administration of authority.

THE TVA PATTERN

It is at this point that many of us as public administrators are falling short of our high profession of democratic faith. Effective techniques of decentralization—not better ways to centralize—should claim our first attention. The first question we should ask ourselves is: "Why cannot these federal activities be decentralized; if not in whole, why not in part?" The problem of first concern we must ever keep in mind is: Does this or that federal program really have to be centralized and to what extent?

The TVA is a concrete demonstration that ways and means can be devised to decentralize the administration of many of the functions of the central government. Indeed, one of the public's chief interests in TVA these days is in its practical, living proof that despite the interrelation of our vast country, despite the need for national policy on many matters heretofore local, the administration of those national policies can be placed in the hands of local community and state agencies. TVA's methods of decentralized administration may well prove to be one of the most important, if not indeed the most important, product of that experiment.

TVA, a public development corporation, is an agency of the central government. Its responsibility as defined by Congress is to develop or aid the people of the Valley to develop and to utilize their natural resources in a region of substantial size, embracing parts of seven states of the southeast. These functions are in general familiar and long-time responsibilities of the federal government—navigation, flood control, electric power, the problems of soils and forests, and research.

TVA is decentralized in more than one sense. First, it is a federal corporation directed not from Washington but from the Tennessee Valley. It is not incorporated within any Washington bureau or department.

LOCAL PERSONNEL USED

But there are other steps of even greater importance. The TVA has by persistent effort decentralized its functions so that most of them are carried out not by federal employees but by local and state personnel. This is effected by scores of contracts setting up joint partnerships between TVA and cities, towns, counties, state boards of health, state conservation commissions, city power boards, farmers' cooperatives, county extension services, state agricultural colleges, state geology departments—the list could be continued almost indefinitely. The widespread approval of the TVA among the people of Tennessee Valley region is attributed by the people themselves largely to this method of decentralization.

During a period of American history when centralization of administration in Washington has increased at a rapid rate, the fact is, I believe, beyond challenge that in the Tennessee Valley state and local functions of government have grown in diversity and strength more rapidly than in any other region of the United States during the same period.

Here are a few illustrations of TVA practice. In agricultural development and control of water on the land the TVA has a responsibility in respect to the development of land as one of its basic natural resources. Part of that responsibility arises out of the use Congress required TVA to make of the great laboratory and production plants at Muscle Shoals. TVA was directed to turn these plants, built during World War I for munitions purposes (and incidentally they again rendered service as munitions plants during World War II) to the benefit of agricultural development in the valley and elsewhere.

It was essential that there be made extensive practical tests and demonstrations of the value of new phosphate fertilizers we were developing in those laboratories. To carry out this responsibility TVA did not set up a large central staff. It did not send federal employees into the communities and onto the farms of the Tennessee Valley. TVA entered into a joint program with the state colleges of agriculture, the state extension services, the county agent system—existing agencies. Under this arrangement these agencies undertook to carry forward the actual demonstration and testing program, together with the agricultural education aspects involved.

In this federal activity of TVA the experts who deal with the farmers are members of the staffs of the state colleges of agriculture and of the state and county extension systems. They are selected by those agencies, which are reimbursed by the TVA for their salaries and expenses.

Another illustration is afforded by TVA's power system. TVA has a system of more than twenty dams on the Tennessee River which carry out familiar federal responsibilities—development of navigation and flood control on an interstate river. These are multiple purpose dams. They provide a navigable channel now being put to extensive use by the barges of commerce and also a measure of flood control unprecedented in this country. The same structures through their control of water generate huge amounts of electricity.

Congress directed that this electricity be sold. It is customary in private utilities that electricity be generated, transmitted and distributed to the homes and farms and factories by a single company. But in the Tennessee Valley the disposition of electricity is divided up. The TVA operates the generating plants and 6,000 miles and more of transmission lines that carry the electricity over an area as large as Great Britain. But its distribution is decentralized. One hundred forty locally owned, locally managed, locally financed distribution agencies carry the electricity from the city gates where TVA delivers it in bulk to the ultimate consumers. An agreement between TVA and these 140 cities, towns, and rural cooperatives fixes broad general policies of accounting, of general financial policy, of tax payments, and determines the level of rates subject to mutual adjustment. But the administration of electricity supply has been effectively decentralized.

Here is another illustration. Part of TVA's task is to aid in the development of private industry through research and exploration of the natural resources of the region so that they can serve in raising the level of income and economic activity of its citizens. This, too, as everyone knows, is not a novel function of the federal government. The Departments of Commerce and Agriculture, the bureaus of the Department of the Interior and others have had comparable objectives and responsibilities for a long time.

These activities are as fully as possible carried out by a combination of TVA sponsorship with actual execution in whole or part by state agencies. As a matter of legal authority all such activities could have been carried out by the TVA directly.

RECREATION POSSIBILITIES

A further illustration: When TVA began to harness the river by building a series of dams, many communities along the river were directly affected in many ways. The flooding of lands wrote new boundaries in place of the old trade areas; in many instances bridges, schools and churches had to be relocated or reappraised in their usefulness to the families which remained in the unflooded areas. Nearby TVA construction camps brought large numbers of people into counties whose health and school services were inadequate for the heavier load.

TVA urged the communities to see these problems as an opportunity to replan their facilities as a whole in the light of a new physical setting. But TVA did not want to make plans for a community It brought communities together with their state planning boards—and where they didn't exist it suggested to the state that a planning board be set up. TVA provided modest financial assistance through contracts with the state boards and encouraged the communities in turn to establish local planning boards to work with their newly created state agency.

LEGISLATIVE SUPPORT

One measure of the effectiveness of these contractual relations is the financial support given these agencies by their state legislatures. In 1935 there were no state appropriations for this purpose either in Tennessee or in Alabama. In 1946 the state planning agency appropriations in these two states amounted to about $200,000. And in these two states alone there was an increase in the number of local planning commissions from two in 1935 to 35 in 1946.

These relationships with state planning commissions have yielded other results. In several of the states where the development of industrial resources is a function of the state planning bodies, cooperative studies with

TVA have uncovered new industrial opportunities based upon the local resources of the region.

In a similar way several valley states are now showing leadership in recreation development from which a whole new industry is emerging. The Tennessee River is now a chain of beautiful lakes abundant with fish. As dams were built many towns and counties suddenly saw an unprecedented opportunity for water-front, park and water recreation development. To assure the public—the taxpaying owners of these beautiful lakes—the fullest opportunity to enjoy them, the TVA worked with the state departments of conservation (and in some cases helped the state establish such departments) to assist the communities in exploiting recreation possibilities.

In pursuing these decentralizing methods, the TVA has encountered plenty of resistance. There are those who would direct one or another phase of TVA's job from some centralized specialized bureau—in the interest, we are repeatedly told, of uniformity. As though uniformity were an end itself, regardless of the diversity which is one of the great sources of our national strength. But note, too, that the centralizer's control rests on a double assumption: not only that uniformity is desirable as an end in itself but also that similar practices can be obtained only by direct centralized supervisory control. Neither assumption is self-evident.

Overcentralization is to many attractively tempting. It has a special appeal to the administrator who quite conscientiously sees the complexity of his job in a coast-to-coast responsibility. The oversimplifications, the uniform rules and regulations, which centralization encourages, are convenient for him, however inconvenient they may be for the public.

Again, there are those managers who honestly doubt whether they can discharge their own vast responsibilities for nationwide programs if they should rely upon units of governments over which they do not have authority to hire and fire.

But it seems to me that as against the folly of centralized administration the risks involved in delegations and agreements with state and local agencies are clearly preferable. Indeed, these risks are implicit in our democratic faith.

Nor should we overlook the deeper question of how we can help our state and local governments gain in competence and in capacity. Surely we should not encourage state and local governments to escape from their duties or abdicate their responsibilities to Big Government, for this process merely perpetuates local weaknesses.

If we turn administration of localized problems over to Washington on the ground that thus we escape the inefficiencies and political shenanigans of state and local communities we are fooling no one but ourselves. Clearly, the fundamental solution is to crowd more, not less, responsibility into the community. Only as the consequences of administrational errors become more localized can we expect citizens to know which rabbit to shoot.

Most people are concerned about the way in which cities and states have lost functions to the federal government. Fiery speeches about states' rights and local home rule are easy to make; finding workable alternatives is harder and less showy. What is needed is not emotional outbursts but rather a clearer recognition of the dangers of overcentralization and persistent ingenious efforts to find ways and means of administering national policies through local and state agencies.

HAZARD TO DEMOCRACY

Overcentralized administration is not something simply to be made more palatable, more efficient and better managed. It is a hazard to democracy. It is a hazard to freedom. And for those interested more in results than in method overcentralization is a bungling way to do a job.

Many of us, as administrators, recognize this simple truth. But we are so prone to accept Big Government, to improve and refine it at the center to the sad neglect of the periphery where the people live and work, that the federal administrator who tries to reverse the trend is hailed as the exception to the rule. I cite one newsworthy illustration—would that there were many more.

Speaking in the northwest . . . , [when] Secretary of the Interior, J. A. Krug urged with forceful words the creation of a regional agency, decentralized and autonomous, to aid in the unified development of the Columbia River Valley. In explaining the decentralizing consequences of this proposal Secretary Krug said: "Final decisions would be made here (in the northwest) instead of in my department in Washington. Contrary to the charges frequently made of federal officials, I desire this. I would like to give up some of my power and authority exercised at Washington and see it exercised here." In such a spirit of self-imposed restraint as this lies true democratic statesmanship, and the road to a workable alternative to Big Government.

The cumulative effect of overcentralization of administration in a national capital is greatly to reduce the effectiveness of government. We are threatened, however, with an even more disastrous sequence, the loss of the people's confidence, the very foundation of democratic government.

When confidence of the community gives place to uneasiness, fears develop that the granting of further powers may be abused. Ridicule of the capriciousness of some government officials takes the place of pride. Democracy cannot thrive long in an atmosphere of scorn or fear. One of two things ultimately happens: either distrustful citizens, their fears often capitalized upon by selfish men, refuse to yield to the national government the powers which it should have in the common interest, or an arrogant central government imposes its will by force. In either case the substance of democracy has perished.

We face a dilemma; there is no reason to conceal its proportions. I do not minimize the complexities and difficulties it presents. We need a strong central government. But every important administrative decision need not be made in Washington. We must rid ourselves of the notion that a new staff, with every member paid out of the federal treasury, has to administer every detail of each new federal law or regulation.

We who believe devoutly in the democratic process should be the first to urge the use of methods that will keep the administration of national functions from becoming so concentrated at the national capital, so distant from the everyday life of ordinary people as to wither and deaden the average citizen's sense of participation and partnership in government affairs. For in this citizen participation lies the vitality of a democracy.

KEEP LOCAL RESPONSIBILITY

Big Government is not inevitable. True, the growth of our vast central administrative machines needs no encouragement from anybody. Big Government does get bigger and more highly centralized unless there is a conscious, continuous, creative administrative effort to reverse the trend. The community's impulse to hand its local problems over piecemeal to one remote agency after another feeds this hazardous push toward Big Government. The surrender of local responsibility for a part of the community's function generates further local weaknesses which furnish the reason for yet another surrender. Local communities and state governments can help by resisting these temptations to take the easy way out. They can help the administrators of federal programs to work out the methods of decentralization case by case. Local governments can resist surrender constructively by raising questions wherever the community or the state is able to do an executive job which the advocates of Big Government want to do themselves.

It will take a lot of such questions and a far greater awareness of the heavy price which centralization exacts before federal administrators and the management experts will find ways to decentralize. Here, indeed, is a great area of neglected administrative study of fruitful experiment. In this vital field of public management lies great opportunity for administrative ingenuity, a challenge to the joint interest and efforts of the experts in local, state and federal operations. The methods applied in the Tennessee Valley, and the results achieved there by the working partnership of public agencies engaged in a resource-development job, are not inconsiderable proof that Big Government overcentralization need not be inevitable.

Chapter VII

CIVIL LIBERTY AND DEMOCRACY

[THERE are, in the world today, two great classes of government: democratic or popular and autocratic or dictatorial. The autocratic or authoritarian system is one in which government is not responsible to the people, in which there is a concentration of the law-making and executive powers in the hands of a small group of irresponsible men, in which there is neither freedom nor equality before the law, and in which arbitrary judgments on the part of the rulers are substituted for rational consideration of cases according to the rule of law.

The autocratic system has been and is a powerful threat to democratic government. The proponents of this system ridicule democracy, destroy freedom, monopolize the press and the schools as agencies of propaganda, ruthlessly suppress free speech and assembly. The Soviet Union is the most powerful of such governments today.

The democratic system, on the other hand, is one in which government is founded upon the will of the majority, is responsible to the community, and governs in accordance with the rule of law. The individual, not the state or government, is an end; the state or government is a tool which the community uses through the process of majority rule. Freedom is planned for and protected in accordance with the will of the majority.

If we are to preserve and extend democracy in the United States, our citizens must examine and understand the character and value of freedom in our society. We say, for example, that freedom of speech is essential; but what does this mean? Does it mean complete and absolute freedom to say whatever one pleases wherever one pleases? Does it mean free speech for those who are committed to the destruction of free speech? What limits can the community place on the machinations of those who seek to destroy democracy? The following selections discuss some of these questions—questions which no responsible citizen can afford to ignore.]

No. 21

INDIVIDUAL LIBERTY AND GOVERNMENTAL AUTHORITY [1]

by J. Allen Smith

AMERICAN writers on political science, especially those with a conservative bias, take it for granted that the chief merit of our particular form of government is that it guarantees individual liberty through
an effective limitation of political power. The rights of individuals, being
expressly enumerated in our federal and state constitutions, are supposed
to be thus placed "entirely beyond the power of the government to curtail."
This viewpoint, which is quite generally presented in American textbooks
on political science, is merely an expression of the prevalent anthropomor-
phic conception of the Constitution of the United States as the guardian
and protector of the rights of the people.

That the notion of the Constitution as self-enforcing was not accepted
by the people in the early decades of American history, the emphasis on
the right of revolution abundantly proves. Gradually, however, under the
influence of skillful conservative propaganda, the fiction gained acceptance
that the government was powerless to disregard rights enumerated in the
fundamental law The Constitution, having come to be regarded as an
expression of the popular will, was relied upon to prevent the government
from interfering with the liberty of the individual.

The growth of the new conception of sovereignty as unlimited political
power, as well as the deification of the Constitution as the palladium of
democracy, tended to modify the popular conception of constitutional law
in its relation to individual liberty. The original idea of the Constitution,
as a check on the power of the people no less than on that of the government itself, was difficult to reconcile with the new doctrine of popular
sovereignty, which ascribed to the people untrammeled authority. The
rights of individuals, as they were understood at the time of the American
Revolution and in the period immediately following, constituted a recognized check on all political power, even that of the people themselves. This
original conception of individual liberty has, however, been supplanted by
the professedly more democratic one implied in the artificial distinction

[1] J. Allen Smith, *The Growth and Decadence of Constitutional Government* (New York:
Henry Holt and Company, 1930). Chapter XIV. Reprinted by permission of the
publisher.

between state and government. The chief significance of the attempt on the part of recent American writers to make this distinction is to be found in the need for some means of harmonizing a check and balance constitution with the notion of popular sovereignty. According to the supporters of this distinction, the people politically organized constitute the state, make and amend the Constitution, through it control the government, and are the final repository of unlimited power. Governmental authority is represented as being subject to the restraints imposed by a check and balance plan of organization, while the state, somewhat vaguely conceived as the people, is supposed to be subject to no limitation whatsoever. Although individual liberty is represented as effectually safeguarded against governmental encroachment, the individual, we are told, "has no rights which the state is bound to recognize."

To create belief in a human power that can legally override all restraints imposed for the protection of individuals is to supplant the basic idea in the theory of individual liberty by one which serves as a foundation for governmental absolutism.

It is interesting to note that the conception of the ultimate unlimited power of the people had a distinctly conservative origin; that its object was not to establish popular supremacy, but to ensure the subordination of the popular will to governmental authority. Superficially viewed, this interpretation of our political system seems to concede to the people, acting as the state, a degree of political power which would satisfy even the advocates of the most extreme form of democracy. But only in appearance is it a concession to the demand for an extension of the power of the people. Under the pretense of subordinating governmental authority, it in fact makes that authority supreme. By reason of the fact that the government controls the interpretation and enforcement of the fundamental law, it has the power in no small degree to remove, evade, or ignore the restraints by which its authority is supposed to be limited. The people having no part in the interpretation of constitutional law, except through the public officials who exercise this power, are as a matter of course bound by the Constitution as thus interpreted. Instead of controlling the Constitution, they are controlled by it as interpreted and enforced by governmental agencies.

No one can understand clearly the status of individual liberty in this country without bearing in mind the place occupied by the judiciary under our constitutional system. The effectiveness of our constitutional guaranties of individual liberty was greatly impaired when the government, and especially the branch of it farthest removed from popular influence, the Supreme Court, acquired the recognized right to interpret them.

The attempt to promulgate the idea that back of the government and the Constitution are the people organized as an omnipotent state, subject to no legal or constitutional restraints, tends to destroy the philosophic foundation on which the conception of individual liberty rests. Although the rights of individuals are supposedly protected against the government, they are represented as at all times subject to abridgment or abolition by this so-called state. And when we realize that this supposed political entity, in so far as it has any real existence, is only another name for purely governmental agencies, we can see that the natural effect of this fiction is to clothe the government itself with that unlimited power imputed to the mythical state.

That liberty for the individual is desirable would be readily conceded by the great majority of the people in all enlightened countries. Their practice, however, seems to be but slightly influenced by what they profess to believe. They may accept individual liberty as a purely abstract principle, and yet, in applying it, they may defeat its purpose, by giving it a narrow and illiberal interpretation. Everyone believes in individual liberty for those whose economic interests and whose opinions on social, political, and religious questions are identical with his own. What is meant by individual liberty, however, is not the right to conform, which no one questions, but the right to act as one's own judgment dictates where his opinion is opposed to that generally held. There is no need for the advocacy of freedom for individual conduct that conforms to generally accepted standards. Liberty for the individual means nothing if it does not imply the right to pursue a course of conduct and to hold and advocate views which do not have the approval of the majority and which may even be strongly condemned by that majority.

Individual liberty is inseparably connected with the theory of progress. Individuals must be free to advance new ideas and try new methods if a higher type of civilization is to be attained. The only possible guaranty of progress is the freedom of individuals and groups to criticize any belief or doctrine—religious, social, political, or economic—and to advocate any change in institutional arrangements which to them may seem desirable. Our beliefs at any given time are at best only partially true. We approach the truth only by a slow, laborious process in which competition between opposing views gradually eliminates error.

That which is established needs no special protection against that which is merely proposed. The old and generally accepted is always difficult to discredit and supplant with the new. The very fact that it has the stamp of social approval gives it a prestige which the advocates of change can not easily overcome. In actual practice the burden of proof is always, and of course ought to be, on those who attack the old. The almost universal tendency to be skeptical concerning the merit of any new idea or proposed innovation is a sufficient guaranty that there is not likely to be any undue haste in discarding the old for the untried.

The chief danger is not that false ideas and doctrines will supplant established truth, but that established error will seek to protect itself against the truth by suppressing all dissenters. That this is not a purely imaginary danger is easily understood when we reflect that, while the general mental inertia of the people disinclines them to accept new ideas, there are almost always important vested interests whose material prosperity largely depends upon the retention of the old. Every important idea or belief that has been long accepted has the support of influential classes whose interest in protecting it against attack has a more selfish basis than a purely disinterested desire for the truth.

Liberty for the individual is necessary if we are to realize the Christian ideal of personal responsibility or the democratic ideal of self-government. Men can not be morally accountable for their conduct or politically self-governing unless they possess the degree of freedom from external control which individual liberty connotes. The theory of individual liberty recognizes that there is a field of human conduct within which the coercive power of the state or of the organized church should not be allowed to intrude except for the purpose of guaranteeing this freedom by punishing those who abuse it.

It would be wholly incorrect to say that majority rule necessarily implies individual liberty. Both are the outgrowth of the struggle against irresponsible power. But the conception of individual rights as a check on governmental authority is not closely related to the growth of modern democracy, except in so far as the former was one of the influences which paved the way for the latter by limiting the power of king and aristocracy. Since the majority have come to regard themselves as the final source of political power, their attitude toward the theory of individual liberty has profoundly changed. It was to the advantage of the majority in the eighteenth century to defend the rights of individuals against the state. Having accepted the idea of popular sovereignty, however, they now regard individual liberty as a check on their own power.

We may concede that democracy is more desirable than any other form of government, and yet realize that individual liberty is not necessarily secure where the majority are in control. The rights of individuals are supposed, it is true, to be most respected in a society organized as a political democracy. As a matter of fact, however, the majority may be fully as intolerant of dissenting opinion as kings and aristocracies have always been.

Indeed, there is some justification for the conservative view that in a democracy personal liberty is more likely to be abridged than under a government in which the people have less influence. The reason for this is obvious. A government which is supposed to represent the majority, and has its support, is more confident of ability to override all opposition than one which does not recognize the right of the majority to rule and which must avoid the danger of arousing too much popular opposition. Since democracy is less exposed to the danger of effective popular resistance, it may with impunity invade the sphere of individual liberty. A strong government—one that has no fear of effective opposition on the part of the people—is almost certain to disregard the rights of individuals whenever the recognition of such rights would seriously hamper it in carrying out its policies. But where the state rests upon a basis generally recognized as undemocratic, those who exercise authority are constantly reminded of the need for a cautious moderate policy—one which will in so far as possible conciliate all important elements in the population and thus safeguard the country against the danger of revolution. Respect on the part of the government for the rights of individuals is due in much larger measure to this balance of opposing interests within the state than it is to formal constitutional guaranties. De Tocqueville in his *Democracy in America,* published in 1835, recognizes this fact when he refers to the tyranny of the majority in the United States.

I know no country (he tells us) in which there is so little true independence of mind and freedom of discussion as in America. In any constitutional state in Europe every sort of religious and political theory may be advocated and propagated abroad; for there is no country in Europe so subdued by any single authority, as not to contain citizens who are ready to protect the man who raises his voice in the cause of truth, from the consequences of his hardihood. If he is unfortunate enough to live under an absolute government, the people is upon his side; if he inhabits a free country, he may find a shelter behind the authority of the throne, if he require one. The aristocratic part of society supports him in some countries, and the democracy in others. But in a nation where democratic institutions exist, organized like those of the United States, there is but one sole authority, one single element of strength and of success, with nothing beyond it.

The old conflict between liberty and authority does not end with the emergence of democracy; it merely enters a new phase in which we must look to public opinion for the protection of individual rights. Political democracy is in no sense a substitute for individual liberty, which means the right of individual self-determination. Without individual liberty, political democracy is not likely to contribute much to the world's progress. If popular government is to free the world, it must exercise such self-restraint as may be required to keep it from encroaching on the rights of individuals. This, however, can not be ensured by formally proclaiming these rights in a written constitution. Such self-imposed checks are wholly ineffective, unless they are supported by a public opinion so clearly defined and so active that no government could afford to antagonize it.

Individual liberty in the United States to-day not only lacks the support of an active, intelligent public opinion, but often encounters a degree of popular hostility which renders constitutional guaranties wholly ineffective. The rights most likely to be abridged or denied by the government, or by the irresponsible and misguided groups who are constantly interfering with the constitutional rights of others by resort to mob violence, are those most fundamental—the ones our American constitutions have sought to preserve by express guaranties of freedom of speech, press, and assembly.

Although the hostility to free discussion in present-day society is, of course, not entirely due to any one single cause, it may be regarded as mainly economic. Wherever there is a conflict of interests we may expect to see some opposition to the recognition of this fundamental right. Let any class feel that it is enjoying advantages or privileges, of which society, if fully informed, would disapprove, and it will inevitably regard with disfavor any attempt to bring them to the attention of the public. No doubt, so far as the masses are concerned, the hostility to free discussion is largely due to a blind instinctive fear that it will undermine opinions and beliefs which they associate with the well-being of society and not to any consciously selfish interest. This is not true, however, of the opposition to freedom of speech and discussion which comes from the more intelligent classes, who take a leading part in every attack on this right.

The formal acceptance of the democratic idea by the modern world has emphasized the importance of public opinion. To-day it is conceived to be highly desirable, if not necessary, to have the support of public opinion for any economic arrangement which we wish to preserve. Quite naturally, then, every important economic group seeks to control public opinion where its material interests are involved. And since opinion is largely determined by what one is permitted to see, to hear, and to read, it can be controlled only through some form of censorship and propaganda, such as was formerly exercised by church and state—as the history of religious and political persecution clearly shows.

Propaganda, in the sense of an organized effort either to popularize or to discredit some idea, viewpoint, institutional arrangement, or economic system, has a sinister significance when through a monopolistic control of news sources it is accompanied by the suppression of all competing propaganda. The power to establish a monopoly of this sort is one that society could not safely entrust to any agency, public or private. Monopoly in such a field is infinitely more dangerous than monopolistic control of industry. There can be nothing worthy of the name of intellectual freedom without free competition between ideas.

The control of opinion by purely private interests, which modern capitalism has made possible, has come to supply an effective substitute for the old form of avowed class control. From the point of view of the capitalist class, this new form of control has some distinct advantages over the old system. It is indirect and not obvious to those who lack political and social intelligence, and, therefore, not recognized by many as class control. Concealed, as it is, under the outward form of political democracy, it is less exposed to the danger of popular attack than was the old avowed and generally recognized class rule. Moreover, it gives to capitalists the benefits of actual control without requiring them to assume any of the responsibility which should accompany it.

The efficacy of capitalistic control of opinion depends upon the extent to which organized wealth owns or controls the various agencies through which public opinion is formed. Ownership of the press, news associations, theaters, moving pictures, and broadcasting stations, as well as some measure of direct control over public school education, is prerequisite to an effective scheme of propaganda. Complete monopoly of these is perhaps not attainable, though a capitalistic control, sufficiently extensive to afford some of the advantages of monopoly, has actually been brought about.

The influence which the capitalist class may exert directly through ownership is, however, much less of a menace than the indirect pressure it may bring to bear upon those supposedly independent. The economic and financial power of this class may be used quite effectively to control those who are outside of its organization and legally independent. There are many kinds of discrimination possible against those who refuse to recognize its unjust and illegal authority. An independent paper will soon discover that one penalty for independence is the loss of all advertising controlled by this class; and this loss is usually sufficient to mean the difference between success and failure. Had any newspaper in any conservative American community during the last few years frankly defended the constitutional right of free speech, it could hardly have failed to lose its most profitable advertisements. Of course, it might have defended freedom of speech, press, and assembly as a purely abstract principle with suitable qualification, without incurring the active hostility of business—provided that it condoned the frequent interferences with the exercise of this right by mobs and by

equally irresponsible public officials. But this purely formal acceptance of
the principle of free speech is not to be confused with the defense of it as
a practical policy. No one can be regarded as a real supporter of this fundamental right, who is not ready to condemn the violations of it that are so
frequent in present-day society.

No. 22

[FREEDOM of speech is not an absolute and inalienable right. Almost everyone
recognizes the necessity for controlling libel, slander, treasonable utterances,
and incitement to crime. But, if some forms of speech may be abridged, what
principle is there for determining those forms that can be and those that cannot?
It is to this question that Mr. Meiklejohn addresses his essay.]

"EVERYTHING WORTH SAYING SHOULD BE SAID" [1]

by Alexander Meiklejohn

THE Government of the United States in the recent past has in many
ways limited the freedom of public discussion. For example, the Federal Bureau of Investigation has built up, throughout the country, a system
of espionage, of secret police, by which hundreds of thousands of our people
have been listed as holding this or that set of opinions. The only conceivable
justification of that listing is to provide a basis for action by the Government in dealing with those persons.

The legislative committees, Federal and State, which have been appointed
to investigate un-American activities, have the same implicit purpose. All
the inquirings and questionings of those committees are based upon the
assumption that certain forms of political opinion and advocacy should be,
and legitimately may be, suppressed. The Department of Justice, acting
on the same assumption, has recently listed some ninety organizations, association with which may be taken by the Government to raise the question
of disloyalty to the United States. And the President's loyalty order, moving with somewhat uncertain and wandering steps, follows the same road.
In these and other ways, we are officially engaged in the suppression of
"dangerous" speech.

Now these practices would seem to be flatly contradictory of the First

[1] Alexander Meiklejohn, " 'Everything Worth Saying Should Be Said,' " *New York Times
Magazine* (July 18, 1948), pp. 8, 32. Reprinted by permission of the *New York Times
Magazine* and the author.

Amendment to the Constitution. Are they? That amendment reads, in part, "Congress shall make no law abridging the freedom of speech." What does that statement mean? What is this "freedom of speech" which we guard against the men whom we have chosen to represent us? Why may not a man be prevented from speaking if, in the judgment of Congress, his ideas are hostile and harmful to the general welfare of the nation? Are we, for example, required by the First Amendment to grant freedom of speech to those who, if they had the power, would refuse it to us?

The First Amendment, taken literally, seems to answer "Yes" to those questions. It seems to say that no speech, however dangerous, may, for that reason, be suppressed. But the FBI, the un-American activities committees, the Department of Justice, the President, are, at the same time, answering "No." Which answer is right? What is the valid American doctrine concerning the freedom of speech?

Never in our history has the need of clear and reasonable answering of that question been so urgent as it is now. In the years following World War II our nation has taken, or has had thrust upon it by Fate, a new role. We have assumed leadership in the advocating of freedom of expression and of communication, not only at home, but also throughout the world.

Against our enemies in war, hot or cold, we have made many accusations. But our most serious and furious charge has been that they have suppressed, and are suppressing, the free exchange of information and of ideas. That evil drawing of the smoke-curtain, we have declared, we will not tolerate. We will not submit to it within our own borders. We will not allow it abroad if, by legitimate means, we can prevent it.

Now the assumption of this high and heavy responsibility for a principle requires that we think for it, as well as fight for it. What, then, do we, citizens under the Constitution, mean by the freedom of speech?

Toward the answering of that question I offer some suggestions.

First, to say that the freedom of belief and of expression as guaranteed does not mean, as we Americans often assume, that every individual has an unalienable right, granted by God, or by Nature, or by Reason, and confirmed by the Constitution, to talk as he pleases, when he pleases, where he pleases, about what he pleases, about whom he pleases, to whom he pleases, without legal hindrance or restraint. There is no such private right. Any well-governed society does, and must, prohibit certain kinds of speaking.

Libel must be forbidden and punished. So, too, slander. Seditious and treasonable utterances are subject to condemnation and penalty. Successful incitement to murder, to arson, to theft, and the like is itself criminal and must be dealt with as such. And, to take an example from another field, it is not allowable for a political enthusiast to rise up in a sick-room, without consent of doctor or nurse, to argue for his principles or his candidate.

Such speech is "out of order." If insisted upon, it becomes a "breach of the peace." Anyone who would thus wantonly interrupt, by speaking, the activities of a hospital, a lecture room, a concert hall, a church, a classroom, a football field, a home, does not thereby show himself to be a free man. Rather he reveals himself to be a boor, a public nuisance, who must be abated, by force if necessary. The First Amendment is not the guardian of unlimited talkativeness.

Second, if it be true, as we seem to have found, that there are many forms of speech whose freedom the Government may abridge or even suppress, a new question of principle is forced upon us. If some forms of speech are abridgeable while others are non-abridgeable, then we are inescapably faced by the task of defining the difference between these two kinds of utterance. And that definition must be made, not simply by listing cases, but by formulating a reason.

We must make clear to ourselves and to others why libelous, seditious, riotous speech is not protected by the First Amendment. And the same reason, on its positive side, must tell what forms of speech are protected and why that protection is given them. Unless that double-edged reason is definitely stated and applied, the principle of the freedom of speech has no usable meaning. We are defenseless against such seeming invasions of our freedom as are now being carried on by the FBI, by Congress and its committees, by the Department of Justice, and even by the President of the United States.

Third, as we start out in search for our principle, it is important to recognize that, in 1919, the Supreme Court added a new item to the list of speech activities whose freedom may be abridged. It declared that utterances which endanger the public safety may be suppressed. Giving unanimous support to an opinion written by Justice Holmes, the Court accepted the test of "Clear and Present Danger." It said that if "words used are used in such circumstances and are of such a nature as to create a clear and present danger that they will bring about the substantive evils that Congress has a right to prevent" they may be forbidden and punished.

The First Amendment, Mr. Holmes is telling us, does not protect such "dangerous" words. "When a nation is at war," he continues, "many things that might be said in time of peace are such a hindrance to its effort that their utterance will not be endured so long as men fight, and that no court could regard them as protected by any constitutional right."

Does this opinion of Mr. Holmes make clear the principle for which we are seeking? On the contrary, so far as it deals with the question at all, it seems to deny the principle rather than to interpret it. The Clear and Present Danger formula represents the Constitution as saying to Congress, "When the public safety for which you are responsible is clearly and immediately threatened by the words of a speaker, you may make laws to suppress such words and to punish such speakers." But, as against this, I am sure that the Constitution is saying to Congress, "When the public safety for which you are responsible is clearly and immediately threatened by words, you will be tempted to suppress those words. But you are forbidden to do so."

Congress has, it is true, both the right and the duty to prevent certain evils. And that may seem to mean that the legislators are authorized to do whatever is needed to prevent those evils. But the Constitution declares that inference to be radically false. It lists, one after another, actions which, however useful they might be in serving the general welfare, Congress is forbidden to take. Some preventions, it declares, are more evil than are the evils from which they would save us. And a primary instance of this doctrine of limited powers is the First Amendment. That amendment tells us that, when dangers arise from public discussion, the evils which they threaten must be endured if the only way of avoiding them is by abridging that freedom of speech upon which the entire structure of our free Government rests.

In the years since 1919, the Supreme Court has, it seems, found the Clear and Present Danger theory untenable. But the tragic fact is that, though the meaning of the phrase is gone, the phrase itself remains in legal and political use to befuddle and confuse the popular mind. Whoever, today, wishes to suppress dangerous debate, turns to that phrase for his final justification. The time has come when, by action of the Supreme Court, the phrase should be eliminated from the interpretation of the First Amendment.

Fourth, as we seek to separate speech which is abridgeable from that which is non-abridgeable, it is worth while to examine the methods and aims of the traditional American town meeting. That institution is commonly, and rightly, regarded as a model by which plans for political freedom may be measured. It is self-government in its simplest, most obvious form.

In the town meeting, the people of a community assemble to discuss and to act upon matters of common interest—roads, schools, poorhouses, health, external defense and the like. Every man is free to come. All meet as political equals. Each has a right and a duty to think his own thoughts, to express them, to listen to others, to make up his own mind. The basic intention is that the freedom of speech shall be unabridged. And yet, the meeting cannot be opened unless, by common consent, speech is abridged.

A chairman or moderator is, or has been, chosen. He "calls the meeting to order." And the hush which follows that call is a clear indication that restrictions upon speech have been set up. The moderator assumes, or arranges, that in the conduct of the business, certain rules of order will be observed. Except as he is overruled by the meeting as a whole, he will enforce those rules. His business, on its negative side, is to abridge speech. For example, it is usually agreed that no one shall speak unless "recognized by the chair." Debaters, also, must confine their remarks to "the question before the house." If one man "has the floor" no one else may interrupt him except as provided by the rules.

The meeting has assembled, not primarily to talk, but primarily, by means of talking, to get business done. And the talking must be regulated and abridged as the doing of the business under actual conditions may require. If a speaker wanders from the point at issue, if he is abusive or in other ways threatens to defeat the purpose of the meeting, he may be, and should be, declared "out of order." He must then stop speaking, at least in that way. And if he persists in breaking the rules, he may be "denied the floor" or, in the last resort, "thrown out" of the meeting.

The town meeting, as it seeks for freedom of public discussion of public problems, would be wholly ineffectual unless speech were thus abridged. It is not a Hyde Park. It is a Parliament or Congress. It is a group of free and equal men, cooperating in a common enterprise by means of responsible and regulated discussion. It is not a dialectical free-for-all. It is self-government.

These instances make clear that the principle of the freedom of speech does not forbid that the individual shall, on occasion, be prevented from speaking. What, then, does it forbid? To that question, also, the town meeting gives an answer. That meeting is called to discuss and, on the basis of such discussion, to decide matters of public policy. The community has agreed that such issues shall be freely discussed and that, when the discussion is ended, decision upon them shall be made by vote of the citizens.

Now in that method of political self-government the point of ultimate interest is not the words of the speakers but the minds of the hearers. The final aim of the meeting is action. It is the voting of wise decisions. The voters, therefore, must become as wise as possible. The welfare of the community requires that those who decide issues shall understand them. They must know what they are voting about.

The basic need of free discussion, therefore, is not that everyone shall speak but that everything worth saying shall be said. The vital point is that, though persons may, on other grounds, be barred from speaking, no one may be barred because his views are thought to be false or dangerous, are judged to be unwise or un-American. When men govern themselves, it is they—and no one else—who must estimate unwisdom and unfairness and danger.

Just so far as citizens are denied access to information or ideas which are relevant to an issue, just so far their planning for the general welfare must be ill-considered and ill-balanced. It is that mutilation of the thinking of the community against which the First Amendment is directed. It does not declare the Natural Right of a speaking individual. It is a deduction from our American agreement that public issues shall be decided by universal suffrage.

If, then, on any occasion in the United States, it may be said that our political institutions are superior to those of Britain or Germany or Russia, it may, with equal freedom, be said that those of Britain or Germany or Russia are superior to ours. And these conflicting views may be expressed, must be expressed, not because they are valid, but because they are relevant. To be afraid of ideas, of any ideas, is to be unfit for self-government.

The First Amendment, then, declares to us and to all men that Hitler's "Mein Kampf" or Lenin's "The State and Revolution" or the Communist Manifesto of Engels and Marx may be freely printed, freely sold, freely distributed, freely read, freely discussed, freely believed, freely denied, throughout the United States. And the purpose of that provision is not to protect a private right of Hitler or Lenin or Engels or Marx to say what he thinks. We are not defending the financial interests of a publisher, or a distributor, or even a writer. We are saying that the citizens of the United States will be fit to govern themselves under their own institutions only if they have faced squarely and fearlessly everything that can be said in favor of those institutions, everything that can be said against them.

The unabridged freedom of public discussion of public policy is the rock on which our Government stands. With that foundation beneath us, we shall not flinch in the face of any danger, however Clear and Present.

No. 23

[MANY who cherish freedom want to know how far it must be extended to Communists and other totalitarians. Mr. Meiklejohn argues that they must be given unabridged freedom of public discussion of public policy. Professor Loewenstein would agree so long as it remains a matter of individual discussion. But he argues that anti-democratic individuals should not be allowed to organize, form parties, run candidates for office, or hold office. In other words, he contends—and careful attention should be given to what he says—"the right to participate in one's government does not imply the right to destroy it."]

FREEDOM IS UNSAFE WITHOUT SELF-GOVERNMENT [1]

by Karl Loewenstein

ONE test of the essentialness of any right certainly is whether its absence can deprive men of other essential rights. To apply this test to the political right to participate in the government of one's country, we need only ask: Is freedom of speech, of the press, of religion, or freedom from arbitrary arrest safe in a dictatorship? The times answer for us. In whatever nation the keystone of political rights has been taken from free men, the whole arch of their freedom has collapsed.

It may be argued that an authoritarian government—that is, one which exercises political power without being dependent on popular participation —need not take away individual rights. History records no instance of a government not democratically organized and controlled which, in the long run, has respected men's liberties. Either men have had to alter such governments and make them politically responsive to the public will (usually by bloodshed), or the governments have ignored and flouted such liberties as men had. How can an authoritarian government allow men freedom of speech to criticize it? Human rights in a dictatorship are a contradiction in terms. There can be no security for the liberties of the individual unless the government is controlled by the people, unless the people can turn it out, and unless the opposition can freely protest if the government violates any man's rights.

It now appears clear, also, that men in every nation must have the right to control their government if there is to be any chance for peace. Unless democracy is made safe in the world, neither freedom nor peace will be safe. Admittedly the difficulties of planting effective political democracy in Germany and Japan and of extending it to the backward areas of the world are immense and will take time; but there is no reason for not recognizing the goal that must be reached. Certainly no statement of essential human rights that failed to include the right to participate in government would any longer be complete or practical.

In such constitutional democracies as the United States, though the right to take part in government is not specifically listed in the Bill of Rights, it is inherent in and guaranteed by the entire Constitution. Inclusion of the political right in the catalogue of fundamental human rights, equal in rank

[1] Karl Loewenstein, "Freedom is Unsafe Without Self-Government," *The Annals* of The American Academy of Political and Social Science (January, 1946), Vol. 243, pp. 47-49. Reprinted by permission of *The Annals* of the American Academy of Political and Social Science.

to freedom of religion and of assembly, has the immense psychological advantage of stamping political democracy not as a mere technical convenience but as a necessity. Moreover, raising the political rights to the level of other human liberties stresses the totality and mutual dependence of all rights. Freedom to hold political opinions, to organize in political parties, to assemble for political purposes, is inconceivable without freedom to elect a representative government and to hold it accountable; likewise, free elections are inconceivable without the other freedoms.

POLITICAL DEMOCRACY DEFINED

No one has found a better definition of political democracy than Lincoln's: "Government of the people, by the people, for the people." The achievement of this end does not mean that all nations must be poured into the particular governmental mold with which we are familiar in the United States. In classifying states and government, political science distinguishes between the form of a state (republican, aristocratic, monarchical, or theocratic) on the one hand, and the form of government (autocratic, authoritarian, dictatorial, fascist, totalitarian, or democratic) on the other. In our time the form of the state, as such, matters little. Great Britain is formally a monarchy, and yet she meets the requirements of political democracy. Italy under fascism, likewise a monarchy as to the form of state, was dictatorial in government. There are certain minimum standards for the form of government which, if satisfied, make a state a democracy regardless of its outward form; if absent, the state cannot be a democracy. Each state must have a democratic-representative organization, a parliament or national legislature. This representative body must be chosen through elections which are frequent enough to allow a reasonably continuous manifestation of the popular will. Political parties must be permitted to participate freely in elections by offering candidates and platforms. Elections must be based on suffrage sufficiently general to be a true expression of popular will; they must be secret and must be honestly conducted. No government is legitimate which perpetuates itself in violation of these principles. Perhaps one may add here the requirement that a democratically organized state must have a judiciary whose members exercise their functions without legislative or executive interference. The sum total of these institutional arrangements is political democracy.

UNDEMOCRATIC ACTIVITIES IN A POLITICAL DEMOCRACY

One purpose of guaranteeing human rights is to enable men to disagree, for disagreement contributes to growth and to a healthy society. An opposition party is essential to keep the antiseptic searchlight of criticism trained on governmental policies and actions. But in a political democracy, opposition cannot be permitted to degenerate into a denial of the principles on which political democracy is based. This is the evil of fascism. It abuses the privileges of freedom and democracy to destroy freedom and democracy. As indicated in Article 18 of the Statement of Essential Human Rights, individual rights find their natural limits in the rights of others. Those who wish to destroy these rights have no right to be protected in their aim to destroy. The difficulty, of course, is to find a practical means of curbing destructive and intolerant activities without weakening the value of the rights. But this difficulty may be more apparent than real.

It may be that some nations, for historical and psychological reasons, are more inclined toward authoritarian and dictatorial institutions than others which, with a longer experience in self-government, have acquired a broader basis of confidence in their own capacity to select and control their leaders. But even among the most authority-minded peoples, dictatorship could not have conquered the masses had it relied on the spoken word or propaganda alone. The success of totalitarianism is based on the masterly combination of mass propaganda and mass organization. This pernicious alliance between propaganda against democracy and organization to take power from democracy furnishes the technological conditions for modern dictatorial government. So we must forbid and prevent that alliance. The constitutional-democratic state is operated by a set of rules to which those in the game subscribe. If a team on a football field declares that it will win the game by shooting the opposing team, it will certainly win it; but it would seem wiser to exclude the team from the field before it destroys the game and the rules.

What this means practically is that antidemocratic, pro-totalitarian, or pro-dictatorial propaganda, as such, should be permitted only as long as it abstains from consolidating itself as an organization for the accomplishment of its nondemocratic aims. Antidemocratic propaganda should not be permitted to condense itself in a powder chamber. Consequently, while freedom of expression need not be withheld from antidemocratic individuals, antidemocratic parties must be denied protection under the right of free organization and assembly. They must be denied participation in elections for parliaments and offices. It would seem obvious that representatives of antidemocratic parties or movements must not be candidates or officials in a democratic state. The danger point is reached where propaganda begins to organize for the achievement of antidemocratic ends. If antidemocratic propaganda is deprived of the chance to organize itself in a political party and to participate in the government of the state, it becomes largely ineffective.

Article 3 on Freedom of Speech and Article 5 on Freedom to Form Associations, as well as Article 18 on Limitations on Exercise of Rights (all of the Statement of Essential Human Rights), seem effectively to make a workable distinction between permitting intolerant individuals full freedom to have their say and allowing them the right to do anything about effecting their destructive purposes. War and emergency legislation have rendered such self-defense of militant democracy less obnoxious than it might have been some years ago. Many democratic states have placed on the books legislation which prevents the translation of permissible antidemocratic opinion into illegal antidemocratic propaganda and organization. The degree of repression applied varies in intensity according to the stability of democratic traditions and institutions. Countries like Sweden, Belgium, Switzerland, and Great Britain were able during the war to deal with antidemocratic movements within their boundaries with less severity than others in which democracy was more exposed to internal danger. Even the United States could not avoid checks on subversive activities, though the technique applied was disclosure and not repression. Whatever may be the approach and the solution in the individual country, it should be clearly established that the right to participate in one's government does not imply the right to destroy it.

No. 24

HOW FREE IS OUR PRESS? [1]

by William Allen White

T O-DAY it is not considered at all significant that publishing a newspaper is a business, a legitimate business, which in certain of its higher realms may be reasonably called big business. But I came into the newspaper business fifty years ago and more, when journalism was passing out of its status as a trade and becoming a profession. As a profession it lasted for a generation or two. And in that period what once ideally might have been called a noble calling was transformed into a fairly safe 6 per cent investment.

Before the Civil War, back to Benjamin Franklin's time, an editor was generally an emeritus printer. The rules and traditions of his trade guided him, and the mechanical end of his day's work often interested the editor quite as much as his editorial policies. Which was natural enough. For

[1] William Allen White, "How Free is Our Press?" *The Nation* (June 18, 1938), Vol. 146, pp. 693-695. Reprinted by permission of *The Nation*.

often his editorial policy was a nice compromise between blackmail and begging. In my day, that is to say, beginning with the middle 1880's, the newspaper business began to merge into what was called in highfaluting terms "journalism." We reporters and editors fifty years ago scorned the term. But it prevailed over us. Journalism became a profession, not exactly one of the learned professions but a profession of sorts. It was still recruited, even at the turn of the century, largely from the composing-room of the printing office. Horace Greeley's festive phrase for college graduates—"other longhorn critters"—still echoed in the American newspaper offices in McKinley's day. Fifty years ago a fast-talking printer could borrow money from his friends or from a political banker and could establish a newspaper in a town for a sum that might be roughly estimated as a dollar for each five of the town's population. The country editor in a town of anywhere from a thousand to fifty thousand made about as much money as the local lawyer or doctor or grocer, not so much as the banker or the merchant prince of the drygoods store, and rather more but not much more than the preacher. The editor of McKinley's time belonged to the ruling class and took off his hat only to the town banker or maybe the men who owned the street cars and the waterworks. But he was a free man, this American editor of the last quarter of the old century. And being a free man, barring the tentacles of his mortgage, he ran a free press, restricted only by his courage, his honesty, and his intelligence. No outside influence restrained his powers.

With the turn of the century something new appeared in the country newspaper business. It was the linotype, the mechanical typesetter, and along with it came the rotary press, both expensive contraptions and both made necessary by expanding business which came to the editor's door. Common schools were increasing his subscription lists, and merchants found that by advertising they could create wants where no wants normally existed. So under the impulse of more subscribers and bigger and better advertisers, slowly in the first two decades of this century the costs of producing a newspaper began to rise. No longer could a man go to a county seat with $1,500 in cash and a good line of talk and buy or start a newspaper. When the armistice of the World War was signed, the business formula of the mechanical requirements of a country newspaper changed, and it required something like $10 for each head of population to buy the machinery, the typesetting machines, the press, and the stereotyping equipment, and to provide the working capital necessary to go into competition with the established newspaper in an American rural community, say a town of from one thousand to one hundred thousand population.

Obviously the young man whose father had breezed into town with a good line of talk and had persuaded the country banker to put up from $1,500 to $2,000 to start a newspaper could not get into the newspaper business himself as a proprietor in the machine age. And the old itinerant printer of Horace Greeley's day, who, according to the colloquialism of that ancient time, could start a newspaper with a shirttail full of type and a cheese press, had gone to join the troubadours, the mound builders, and the gay dancers in the Dionysian revels.

The trade which had become a profession turned into a business, and there it is to-day. And now an editor in a little country town all of whose inhabitants could be herded into a good-sized skyscraper comes before you as a small business man with a pay roll of $1,200 a week. When I bought the *Emporia Gazette* the pay roll was $45 a week, and twenty years before that the pay roll of the country newspaper in my town was less than $25 a week. Behold a miracle of the machine age.

In the next ten years the press may change again—certainly in its material aspect. Rotary presses, linotypes, stereotyping machinery may join the crossbow, the neckyoke, and the portcullis upon the ashheap of forgotten gadgets. But the merchandising of the news for a long while to come will be affected as it is now with a strong property interest. It will require machinery to assemble the news. It will require capital to distribute the news. And capital to-day or to-morrow always has a lively sense of its own advantage. Capital is instinctively, for all the noble intentions of us capitalists, class conscious. It is that class consciousness which is discrediting the press of the world to-day, particularly the press of the English-speaking democracies. Any newspaper in any American town represents a considerable lot of capital for the size of the town. The owners of newspaper investments, whether they be bankers, stockholders of a corporation, or individuals, feel a rather keen sense of financial responsibility, and they pass their anxiety along to newspaper operatives whether these operatives be superintendents known as managing editors, foremen known as city editors, or mere wage-earners known as editorial writers, copy-desk men, reporters, or what not. The sense of property goes thrilling down the line. It produces a slant and a bias that in time becomes—unconsciously and probably in all honesty—a prejudice against any man or any thing or any cause that seriously affects the right, title, or interest of all other capital, however invested. It is not the advertising department that controls the news. Newspapermen may lean over backward in their upright attitude toward the obviously unfair demands of advertisers and the moronic prejudices of subscribers, and still may be poor miserable sinners when they discuss problems affecting the stability of institutions that are founded entirely upon the economic status quo.

We editors realize that we have lost caste with the American people. We are on the bad books of public esteem, not heavily in the red but teetering back and forth between the right and the wrong side of the ledger. Labor as a class distrusts us. It wouldn't distrust us entirely without reason. The labor press sneers at us—that is to say, those class-conscious newspapers that are circulated entirely in what is known as labor circles. But one discounts frankly labeled class papers. It is a shame that the public also has, to discount certain areas of the plug-hat section of the newspaper gallery, which is supposed to be impartial, high-minded, absolutely dependable. One should quickly qualify this statement. It is not true of *all* papers or of any paper at all times. Moreover, in the last three years great improvement has been made by the metropolitan press as a whole. Trained reporters who know the implications of labor's struggle are now used by certain great newspapers to get at the exact truth, but reporters trained to handle labor struggles are few, and the struggles are many. And much room remains for improvement in the handling of labor news by the American press.

The deficiencies of American journals in treating the news of what we might as well frankly if regretfully call the class struggle in this country are found largely in unconscious political attitudes. It is so easy to "policy" the news. Indeed, it is so hard not to policy the news when the news is affected with a vital bread-and-butter interest to the capitalist who controls a newspaper, great or small. And strangely and sadly enough, capital is so fluid that a threat to the safety of any investment seems to be a threat to all investments. Therefore newspapers which represent sizable investments are tempted to shy off and shiver when in Congress, in the legislature, or in the City Hall a man or a group threatens an investment in any kind of patent medicine, in any kind of holding company, in any kind of misbranded food, in any kind of railroad security, in any kind of banking affiliate, good or bad. It is no longer the advertiser who puts on the pressure. It is not even the boss back of the pay roll who begins to quake. It is the whole middle and upper structure of society. Sooner or later the truth about any social abuse is gladly received by the middle class and by those who own and control newspaper investments. But off the bat, the newspapers representing the innate conservatism of property interests which crystallize middle-class psychology are sometimes unfair in their treatment of men or movements that threaten to disturb property in any form.

Which is only another way of saying that every new day produces its own peculiar threats to liberty. A decade or so ago it seemed likely that the direct pressure of large advertisers, as for instance department stores, might affect the press with a bias. Probably that danger is decreasing. The newspaper publisher stands the economic equal of his largest advertiser, and to-day the average publisher is wise enough to know that in the newspaper business it pays to be honest. But to-day we are faced with a new menace to the freedom of the press, a menace in this country vastly more acute than the menace from government. And this menace may come through the pressure not of one group of advertisers but of a wide sector of newspaper advertisers. Newspaper advertising is now placed partly, if not largely, through nation-wide newspaper advertising agencies. Some of these agencies have lately become advisers of great industrial corporations, which also advertise. These advertising agencies undertake to protect their clients from what the clients and agents may regard as real dangers from inimical social, political, or industrial influences. As advisers the advertising agencies may exercise unbelievably powerful pressure upon newspapers. There is grave danger that in the coming decade, as social, industrial, and economic problems become more and more acute, this capacity for organized control of newspaper opinion by the political advisers of national advertisers may constitute a major threat to a free press.

And while we are on the subject of a free press this black mark must be put down against editorial judgment in general: it rises in the circulation department—a low subconscious lust to acquire circulation and hold it in the moron latitudes of the population. It affects all editors more or less. I am guilty of this sin for all my noble protestations. And because I am guilty I realize that the circulation department of a newspaper is as dangerous as the advertising department in menacing the ultimate freedom of the press. It is not that we play up sex crime like Bernarr Macfadden or amplify the details of murder. Our sin lies deeper than that: we do not use the same talents to expand and elaborate good news that we almost instinctively use in writing and displaying human weaknesses and depravity. For instance, I had to find the news of the Scandinavian Neutrality Pact on the seventh page of my favorite newspaper, which is commonly accounted a decent newspaper. As far as I know, it was not in the press report that came to the Missouri valley. If it came here, the *Gazette's* telegraph editor, who is trained to look after such things and play them up, missed it. Yet the news that Sweden, Norway, Iceland, Denmark, and Finland had signed a declaration pledging their forces to a common neutrality policy in the event of war between other states was worth more than any rape in the country that day, worth more than the story of any lovelorn lady who shot her man to death, worth more than the news of capers cut by any Hollywood star or Long Island socialite. It is because we overlook opportunities like this that the people have a keen and accurate sense that much of editorial anxiety about the freedom of the press rises out of editorial greed.

The problem of the American newspaper to-day is to open its channels of cordial reception to new social ideals and to insure fair treatment for any reform or any reformer who is obviously honest, reasonably intelligent, and backed by any considerable minority of the public. How can this be done? How can the newspapers become open-minded? I don't know. They might try to hire as doorkeepers in the house of the Lord, at copy desks and in editorial chairs, men who are free to make decisions about newspaper copy, guided by their own instincts, following their own hunches, and not controlled by an itch to move to the next higher desk by pleasing his High Potency who sits in the mahogany-paneled room in front of the front of the front office. If owners would encourage a little chronic arthritis of the knee in the lower realms of reporting and copyreading we might come out from the clouds of suspicion that envelop our noble profession at the moment. But I suppose in the end newspapers cannot be free, absolutely free in the highest and best sense, until the whole social and economic structure of American life is open to the free interplay of democratic processes.

No. 25

[IN the preceding essay one of America's great editors discussed some of the problems of a free press. The problems that he raised are related not so much to government action or suppression as to internal problems of the press itself. It is to some of these same questions in the field of radio broadcasting that Mr. Flynn addresses himself in the following essay.

The problems of a free radio are, in many respects, even more difficult than those of a free press. The limited number of air channels makes regulation imperative. This regulation implies the power to determine who may broadcast, under what conditions they may broadcast, and, to some extent, what they may broadcast.

This, in turn, means that the government cannot avoid examining the internal affairs of the radio industry in a way it does not have to examine the internal affairs of the press. The relation between advertising and program content, the ownership of radio stations by newspapers, and the various uses to which broadcasting time may be put all are concerns of the government. It is in these that Mr. Flynn is particularly interested and with regard to which he makes suggestions that deserve consideration.

Though the development of FM, with the additional channels it opens up, may alter the role of government somewhat, the development of television is sure to raise new and still more difficult questions to which our democratic society must find democratic answers.]

RADIO: MEDICINE SHOW [1]

by John T. Flynn

A POSITIVE, defined, recognizable policy on radio broadcasting is one of those things the national government has not yet troubled itself to form. But attention to the problem cannot be very much longer deferred. The incredibly childish approach of the broadcasters to the problem of public discussion, the vague whisperings of plans for government entry into the business of broadcasting, the scandalous rumors about the commission set up to represent the public interest, the vulgarity, banality, sheer ignorance and immaturity of the advertisers who sponsor our daily ration of culture, have so irritated the public conscience that Congress is certain to get around presently to this very serious matter.

It is impossible to consider radio without discussing the problem of freedom of speech. It is impossible to conceive of radio broadcasting without government control. The air is a series of highways over which messages may be broadcast. The number of these highways is limited—less than 100. There is therefore a sheer traffic problem to be faced. Unless these radio bands or highways are allocated everybody would attempt to use the same bands and transmission would be impossible. These highways are not like public streets which countless vehicles can use at the same time. In the air every traveler must be kept off the aerial highway while the licensed user occupies it. There is, therefore, no escape from a system of government licenses.

The privilege of granting licenses and of renewing them comprises the right to refuse them, to cancel them, to deny renewal. Therefore an arbitrary or excessively political government can employ this power as a means of controlling the contents of the broadcast. And thus arises the old ghost of invasions of freedom of speech by the political authority. Everybody will agree that under no circumstances should the government be permitted to influence or dictate the social, economic, religious, political or other intellectual content of broadcast programs, save insofar as the rights of other citizens may be involved. The slander laws and, within properly defined limits, the police power to exclude obscenity cover the government's general sphere of control, so far as content is concerned.

But freedom of speech and of the press may have other enemies than

[1] John T. Flynn, "Radio: Medicine Show," *The American Scholar* (Autumn, 1938), Vol 7, pp. 430-437. Reprinted by permission of *The American Scholar* and the author.

the government. And this makes it necessary for us to be quite clear what we mean by freedom of speech and of the press. The man who owns a newspaper and who is free from every form of government restraint certainly enjoys freedom of speech so far as his newspaper is concerned. But we must distinguish between the individual newspaper and the press as an institution. There is a difference between freedom of the individual owners and freedom of the press as an institution. A group of men who severally own all the newspapers in a society may come together in an agreement to exclude all news and discussion of certain subjects of social concern. They do this in the exercise of their own freedom. But having done it, that society no longer enjoys a free press insofar as the censored subject is concerned. It is entirely possible, therefore, that the individual owners of the press may be free of all government restraint and yet the country be without a free press. It is this view of the matter which remains obscure in most discussions of the subject.

Every newspaper owner is subject to restraints which arise out of his own human weaknesses—fear of offending his community, fear of the hostility of its powerful leaders, fear of religious and social and political groups. These kinds of restraints can never be eliminated. They are in the order of human nature and must be accepted as inevitable. Freedom of the press and of course of the radio means freedom from such restraints as may be controlled. Against these human weaknesses there is but one safeguard—a multitude of journals and a multitude of editors who will not be subject to the same restraints. All will not be trying to please the same people. The very freedom—nay urge—of one man to print becomes a powerful corrective of the restraints upon another to omit the news. Political oppression of the press is so baleful just because it can exercise its influence over every editor, can terrorize and silence any editor who defies its interests.

The restraints upon the press which arise out of these private and social and commercial interests become a grave public problem when the powers which exercise these influences are so great and so united that their pressure may be applied to all editors and to the press as a whole.

Let us suppose that Editor Number One publishes his journal at a loss but makes up his loss through a subsidy granted by Mr. X. Editor Number Two also publishes a journal at a loss but meets his deficit by means of sums obtained for some service to Mr. Y. Editor One will feel at liberty to print what he chooses so long as he does not offend Mr. X. Editor Two will feel bound to print what pleases Mr. Y under penalty of losing Y's support. But Editor One will be hampered only by his dependence upon X and will be quite free to print what he chooses about Y. And Editor Two although restrained by Mr. Y will have no compunction about printing anything he wishes about X. But what will happen when Editor One and Editor Two are both dependent on Mr. X? If all the papers in a community are owned by Editors One and Two they constitute the press. In theory both editors are free to defy the powerful Mr. X. But in the nature of things they will not do so because the price of defiance is extinction. And therefore while these editors are legally free and voluntarily relinquish that freedom for a more highly coveted prize, namely solvency, the press is not free.

Something like this has happened to the press in this country. Few if any newspapers can publish their journals at a profit. They must employ those journals in another field than journalism—and that field is advertising, which is in no sense a part of journalism but rather a parasite upon it. It is the advertiser who makes up the editor's deficits.

It is not true, of course, that there is but one advertiser who holds in his hands the power of life and death over the editors. No one can deny, however, that the advertising interests in a community, although they have their special differences on points of religion and social principles and even of commercial policies, are generally a unit upon certain important essential principles. But even where they are not a unit there is a menace to the freedom of the press which arises out of the necessity laid upon the editor to court their favor. The publisher solicitous for the favor of Mr. X and of Mr. Y, even though these gentlemen differ upon a point, will exercise the greatest prudence in seeking to offend neither. The very number of the powerful persons who make up the patron element of the press merely multiplies the number of restraints upon the editor. Altogether it forces on him that conservative timidity which compels him to remain away from certain great areas of news and from the discussion of certain serious subjects which the commercial interests in a community as a whole and separately wish to remain untouched.

Thus it seems clear that before we can have a free press society must find means not only of protecting the individual editor from the invasions and restraints of government but of protecting the press as an institution from the editors themselves.

Thus far I have discussed this problem in terms of the press alone since that is an instrument with which we are more familiar. But the radio, like the press, is subject to the same observations. It is one of those instruments of public news and discussion which apparently cannot support itself as such and must turn to some other interest to pay its bills. Like the press it has turned to the advertiser. The advertiser is willing to pay the cost of assembling a great orchestra or of forming a troop of entertainers or supplying a dance band because he knows that millions will listen. All he asks is the privilege of interrupting the program at intervals to catch the ears of those millions of listeners. It is an old technique. The itinerant medicine man of former days carried about with him his banjo player and minstrel and clog dancer and magician to attract the crowd to his tent and to put them in a benevolent mood as a prologue to his own "high pitch" upon the wonders of his pills and lotions.

Now the radio is hopelessly committed to this form of operation. The advertiser is and doubtless for some time will remain the sponsor of the radio program. And because he pays the piper he is in a position to call the tunes. Thus the freedom of the radio as an institution of public discussion and news, not the freedom of the individual station, is threatened. The individual station is a commercial enterprise in the hands of an enterpriser who wishes to operate it as an instrument of profit derived from the commercial interests in the community. He has no wish to offend or battle or defy them. His only study is to please them to the uttermost, prove his usefulness to them and advance their interests. He has no liberty which he is deeply concerned in defending against them. But the grand result is that the institution of which he is but a part and which, as an institution, is a public and not a private function sees its freedom extinguished. Is it not clear that the freedom of the radio is destroyed if the government will not grant licenses unless it censors the programs? Is it not equally clear that that freedom is equally impaired if the advertising interests will not pay the bills unless they can impose a practical censorship?

But what then is to be done about it? There is obviously only one power with sufficient authority to do anything and that is the government, which is the trustee of the people for the adminisration of the air.

But no one will countenance a government-dominated news agency and forum. Men have not forgotten that the first struggle for freedom of speech and of the press was waged against political authority. That battle, certainly in this country, has been won. But a people vigilant for the preservation of its democratic freedoms will never cease to look with a certain suspicion upon political authorities, particularly in a world troubled as ours is to-day by so many ruling groups who assail the very existence of these rights. The radio is of necessity in the hands of the government. We cannot escape its presidency over the administration of the medium through which the radio operates. But every resistance should be offered the establishment of government-owned and -operated radio stations since these are liable to become the instruments not of the government but of the politician who operates the government. But equally we cannot tolerate unregulated private ownership of the air. And there is no regulating authority but the government. How far, therefore, may we trust the government with this function? I offer the following suggestions.

The advertising sponsor presents a twofold problem. First there is the abuse of the advertiser's privileges in the use of the air and secondly the abuse of his power to restrain free discussion over the air. On the first point the abuse arises when the advertiser is permitted to disseminate news and discussions of public questions. ' The advertiser wishes to advertise his product. He therefore desires to command a large audience. This is a purely practical matter of drumming up a crowd. To do this he uses the most attractive entertainment he can obtain. Having gotten his crowd he should be permitted within decent limits to advertise his product. But he should not be permitted to turn that crowd into a political, religious or economic meeting. He should not be permitted to employ the radio and the crowd to spread religious, social, economic or political propaganda. However bad the newspaper may have become it has not descended to this. It does not, as a rule, rent out its news or its editorial columns to advertisers. It does indeed succumb to the influence of commercial interests but it does not permit the editorial function to pass out of its hands. Its editorials and reports do not have to run the gauntlet of advertising agents, vice-presidents and presidents and managers of commercial corporations, as is the case in broadcasts. The handling of news and views in the newspaper is in the hands of a department separated from the advertiser. And although the advertiser's spirit broods over the editorial room the editorial room resents it, resists it as much as it can. Furthermore, thinking of its function in terms of editorial excellence and obligation, the editorial room does build up an ethical standard which stands as a barricade against the over-insistent business office.

I know too well the bad influence of the commercial spirit upon the press. I know as well as anyone how much better the press could be if it were emancipated from this influence. But I know also how infinitely worse it would be if the advertising agent and the advertiser had moved bodily into the editorial rooms. This is what has happened in the radio broadcasting station. This is what I wish to end.

I would not restrain the radio broadcaster from the dissemination of news or of discussions. But I would compel him to separate this function completely from the programs of the advertisers. To permit the advertiser to become a social and economic propagandist on the air is to give the advertising interest a disproportionate place in the great forum of public discussion. A great manufacturer can pay the immense sum required to support a great symphony orchestra on the air because he gets an advertising return for the expenditure. But having drawn together a vast audience to listen to the symphony orchestra and having subdued the mind by means of the melting music, he may then interrupt the concert for a precious five minutes while he pours into the ears of his guests his economic and political philosophies. There is no public group with sufficient financial resources to meet this kind of propaganda. The advertiser should be permitted to have his crowd and his concert and a brief period to sell his wares but no more. As a citizen with economic and social views to exploit he should have only the same right, so far as the air is concerned, as any other citizen. Although this would not free the air from the influence of the advertiser it would certainly tend to bring the distribution of the news and views of the broadcasting station under the administration of an editorial group capable of developing a far more civilized ethic with respect to the news.

I would divide the air into its three functions. In one it would be a great medicine show where advertisers, for pay, could put on entertainment and cry their wares, but the ballyhoo would be limited strictly to entertainment. In a second the air would be a great distributor of news and views which would be administered by a separate editorial board at the expense of the broadcaster. In a third I would consider the air as a great public hall which would be open to hire by persons, and by cultural and educational and other public organizations to hold meetings. And a part of this time I would compel the broadcasting station to give freely for educational and public purposes.

I would not permit any newspaper to own or operate a radio station. The newspaper is itself a dispenser of news and views. It tends to become more and more a monopoly in its community. One-paper communities, or communities dominated by a single owner, are growing in number. A multitude of journals and stations, and the inevitable competition between them, is the chief prophylactic against excessive surrender to the sponsoring advertisers in both press and radio. To permit the radio to fall under the dominion of the press as the press itself falls under the dominion of monopoly is to throw away this safeguard.

Regulations covering these points might well be made by the government without infringing the rights of anyone or without setting the government up as a menace to the liberties of the people themselves. No other agency of society can protect it from that usurpation of the instruments of communication by the great, predatory interests of the nation—which is coming to be one of the most sinister problems of the modern democratic state.

Chapter VIII

THE ALIEN—A POTENTIAL CITIZEN

[THE population of the United States, like that of any country, is made up of both citizens and aliens. Aliens, generally, have created special problems for governments. In America, the problem of the alien was intensified by Fascism, the war, and the spread of Communism.

Throughout most of our history we had a growing nation and an expanding economy; we could and did absorb a great influx of immigrants. But depression in the thirties and the dangers of international espionage and fifth column activities presented the alien problem in a new light. As a result, we have restricted immigration and have dealt with our alien population in ways no one would have prophesied a generation ago.

The United States has never closed its doors completely to the alien in the past; it is not likely to do so in the future. But the American people are going to have to give more attention to their immigration policy. Mr. Carter's essay furnishes the "perspective" for that attention.

The problem of the alien, however, extends far beyond the question of immigration policy. What shall we do with the immigrant after he arrives? How is he to be treated? We have, it is true, given these questions greater considerations in recent years than in the past. We have made special efforts to encourage the alien to become a citizen; we have tried to make the process of acquiring citizenship more meaningful. But there is need for much more to be done.

To be sure, in all of this, it is essential that we protect ourselves against the enemies of democracy. But we must devise such policies and procedures that we can do so without at the same time embittering those who are loyal friends and potentially good citizens. We must encourage the alien to become a citizen; we must encourage him to think of himself as a member and to become a part of the community. We want him to help give effectiveness and real meaning to our democratic institutions.]

No. 26

PERSPECTIVE [1]

by Hugh Carter

PERIODICALLY the American people reappraise their immigration policy. They are doing so at this time. The present basic immigration law of 1917, containing numerous qualitative controls including a literacy test, was enacted by Congress after prolonged debate. The quota legislation of 1924, establishing quantitative controls, was likewise preceded by widespread discussion.

Once the public had grown accustomed to the novel quota system, interest in immigration declined to a low level until near the end of the Second World War. Then began the public discussion of immigration that shows no signs of ending in the near future. The immediate cause of this debate was the urgent question of what to do about the displaced persons in Europe. Inevitably, such public discussion broadened to include all aspects of immigration policy.

DISPLACED PERSONS

Much of the present discussion of immigration is a direct result of the war. War inevitably uproots many people, but the conflict of 1939-45 was unprecedented in the number of persons that were impelled by forces beyond their control to leave their homes and seek temporary sanctuary elsewhere. Resettlement of these displaced persons is an urgent problem. In a war that engulfed the entire world, the advancing and retreating armies, the aerial bombings, the desires of political leaders to be rid of troublesome minorities, the insatiable demands of war industries for manpower, and the extermination policies of the Nazis directed against Jewish minorities combined to shift millions of persons about on the map of Europe.

The end of the war did not bring an end to this problem. Hundreds of thousands were left stranded, unable or unwilling to return to their former homes. They led a miserable existence in displaced persons camps or under the temporary shelter of international organizations.

SHORTAGE OF WORKERS

But while the displaced persons problem is the most dramatic of the immigration questions facing the United States, as well as one of strong

[1] Hugh Carter, "Perspective," *The Annals* of the American Academy of Political and Social Science (March, 1949), Vol. 262, pp. 1-4. Reprinted by permission of *The Annals* of the American Academy of Political and Social Science.

humanitarian appeal, the war also emphasized underlying demographic trends both in America and in western Europe that have a vital bearing on immigration policy. Many Americans were startled by the manpower shortages of the war years, for the preceding fifteen years had been a period of manpower surpluses, with millions unemployed. Suddenly all this was reversed. The press was filled with stories of delayed war production because of the lack of manpower. Needed crops rotted in the fields because no one was available to harvest them. A program of importing workers from nearby countries for work on railways and farms was instituted. Yet the shortages continued so acute that it was not unusual to see women working on the railroad rights of way.

Many persons attributed these conditions entirely to the millions of productive workers temporarily in the armed services, and dreaded the surplus of manpower that would exist as soon as the war ended. However, in the early postwar years industry began to clamor for more manpower. Press comments emphasized need for a great housing program, retarded by manpower shortages. There were numerous other shortages, as in steel and various basic materials, and there was the constant reiteration of the shortage of workers. How had these shortages come about, and what is their bearing on immigration policy?

POPULATION TRENDS

Population trends during the past century throw much light on the present situation and should be considered in any examination of immigration policy. During the nineteenth century and the early years of the twentieth century, Europe with its high fertility and low mortality had a substantial surplus of population for overseas migration, and millions of persons came to America. However, the long-time trend of birth rates, especially in western Europe, has been downward. (There was a marked rise in births associated with the war and early postwar years, but demographers do not expect an upward trend in fertility.) Death rates have fallen, but more slowly than birth rates. Consequently, the rate of population growth in the future may be expected to be more gradual than in the past. For certain areas careful studies point to a declining population within a measurable period of time. This indicates a decline in the migration potential of Europe. Moreover, the rapid growth of urban communities in Europe tends to absorb the surplus of rural population where fertility is highest. Temporarily, there is a source of migrants in the countries whose economies were wrecked by war.

Demographic changes in the United States have paralleled those of Europe. Here, too, fertility rates have tended downward, except for the war and early postwar period. The trend in death rates has also been downward, but these rates cannot be expected to go much lower, or, in any event, the rate of decline must inevitably be slower. Without immigration the population will probably level off within a few decades and will then decrease.

During most of the decades since the first census in 1790 there has been a high rate of population growth, the high fertility of the population being supplemented by substantial immigration. A dynamic, expanding economy needed more manpower. Immigrants helped to meet these needs, and by their presence added to the number of consumers. Many factors are involved in recent manpower shortages, but it may be pointed out that the immigrant, during most of American history, has added greatly to the labor supply. The total labor force of the past century was enlarged more by immigration than would appear at first sight, because of the high proportion of young adults among the immigrants, and the restriction on the growth of the labor force since 1930 has been substantial. Thus recent manpower shortages have come at a time when fertility and mortality trends have been moving toward an equilibrium and when for nearly two decades immigration has made only a slight contribution to the labor force.

ASSIMILATION OF FOREIGN BORN

Another important and frequently discussed factor in immigration policy is the assimilation of the foreign born. To what extent do the immigrants become assimilated and how rapidly does the process occur? One hears less to-day than in earlier discussions of the old and naive theory of the "melting pot," according to which assimilation is both complete and rapid. It is well known that numerous attempts to stimulate rapid assimilation have conspicuously failed. True assimilation involves changes more profound than can be measured by oaths of allegiance, and it occurs more gradually than changes in the manner of speech. The social process is more complex than a pot boiling over a fire.

From the standpoint of national welfare, however, it is obviously not essential that immigrant attitudes be made as nearly identical with attitudes of the native born as possible. On the contrary, if the newcomer supports the American form of government and makes a reasonable social contribution, he cannot be regarded as a social liability because he maintains certain variant culture patterns.

The term "cultural pluralism" has largely replaced "melting pot" in thoughtful discussions of the adjustment of the foreign born to American life. Numerous studies have been made of the assimilation of various nationality groups. These will not be reviewed here. It may be noted, however, that the great majority of European immigrants of the past fifteen years, judging from available evidence, seem to be making a good adjustment.

Two of the traditional areas of controversy regarding assimilation may be noted. First, there is the question of the relative assimilability of persons from northern and western Europe as compared with persons from southern and eastern Europe. The present quotas strongly favor the "old" immigration from northern and western Europe. The arguments advanced concern cultural differences, as no significant racial differences are involved. The second controversy concerns Orientals, who have been largely excluded under the immigration laws. Here there are racial differences as well as cultural differences. The familiar arguments, pro and con, on these controversies need not be reviewed. It may be observed that the recent widespread discussion of immigration policy has been concerned largely with European immigration. There is also a substantial stream of immigration from the Western Hemisphere.

Much insight is given into the processes of assimilation through a study of the various agencies organized by nationality groups in the United States. The churches, the newspapers and periodicals, and the fraternal organizations of immigrant groups satisfy fundamental human needs. At first glance these appear as barriers to assimilation, but in most cases, if assimilation is thought of as an adaptation that requires generations to complete, such agencies serve as a valuable element in the process. . . .

A PART OF FOREIGN POLICY

Increasingly there is discussion of the relationship of immigration policy to the over-all foreign policy of the country. It is obvious that any action taken by the Government affecting the nationals of another country is an act of foreign policy, whether the action admits a person, excludes him, or deports him. Traditionally, immigration has been regarded as exclusively a domestic matter; what was done concerned only the American people. During the nineteenth century this was the general viewpoint. To-day, the position of the United States as a major world power necessitates a careful re-examination of this position.

A case in point is that of the displaced persons. They are a major concern of the United Nations, and action by the United States will be closely followed by other member nations. Thus domestic consideration of the question cannot be divorced from its international implications.

One fact stands out as a result of a study of American immigration policy: it has been based on public opinion. On occasions the law and the attitudes of the majority have not been in accord, but this has changed with the passage of time. One may hope that the future policy, hammered out

through general discussion and debate, will be based on a mature consideration of all the major factors involved. . . .

No. 27

GOVERNMENT AGENCIES WORKING
WITH THE FOREIGN BORN [1]

by Ruth Z. Murphy

IN a country to which large numbers of persons of foreign birth have
come each year, it is to be expected that there will be social institutions
to assist the newcomer to a more satisfactory integration into the national
life.   Much integration, of course, is a result of a more or less natural
process.   It is part of the necessary adaptation to social pressures and the
general social organization.

The social environment in the United States is conducive to adjustment.
It is in our tradition to make the newcomer a part of our Nation.   There
have always been antiforeign attitudes, but these have seldom been official,
and they are counterbalanced by employment opportunities, by free schools
for the children and in many communities for adults, by the presence of
large groups of the same national background as the newcomer to help him
in understanding American ways, and by the opportunity for naturalization.
In five years, or less under certain circumstances, he may become a citizen
and secure the right to political participation and all other rights enjoyed
by citizens except that he may not become President or Vice-President of
the United States.

This liberal attitude toward the immigrant is important.   It gives him
a greater sense of security and results in a more rapid integration into our
national life.   This is essential, for we cannot have large groups in our
midst who feel themselves apart from us.   At the present time one in every
eight of our adult population is of foreign birth.   Of these, over 70 per cent
are citizens and, as such, suffer no legal handicaps.   They have the same
rights, the same responsibilities, and the same relations to our government
agencies as the native born.   Because of this, in a sense all government
agencies in the United States affect the foreign born.   But even our alien
population suffer few legal and governmental distinctions.   They, too, have
many of the rights and responsibilities of citizens, and consequently are

[1] Ruth Z. Murphy, "Government Agencies Working with the Foreign Born," *The Annals*
of the American Academy of Political and Social Science (March, 1949), Vol. 262, pp. 131-
138.   Reprinted by permission of *The Annals* of the American Academy of Political and
Social Science.   The footnotes in the original version are omitted here.

able to make many satisfactory adjustments. The distinctions that do exist have of course a bearing on assimilation, and insofar as governmental agencies are involved, should be considered here.

STATUS OF ALIENS

A major legal distinction is that aliens are denied the franchise by the states. This would seem to be fundamental. Voting is a right of citizens, and even their right is limited in some states by literacy tests or poll taxes. It is interesting to note that at the commencement of the First World War there were twelve states where persons could vote without citizenship, only "first papers" being required, but all states require citizenship now. Although the franchise is of basic importance in a democracy, the lack of it does not hinder the alien in his daily adjustments. In fact, a large part of our alien population are the older residents, men and women principally from peasant backgrounds, who have lived useful lives, doing some of our hardest and most needed work, who are parents of American children, but who have little background for political participation.

Work

Although the immigrant has the right to work, there are some occupations that are closed to him. Civil service positions usually carry a citizenship requirement. Almost every state excludes him from one or more professions and certain other occupations, generally those requiring licenses. There are also municipal ordinances restricting employment. Many of these laws, however, merely require "first papers" and so do not work undue hardship on most legally admitted aliens who are not members of one of the few races barred from citizenship. But the limitations as to work, although important and causing special hardship in the professions where long training is involved, do not greatly hamper most immigrants. There are still many jobs open to them.

Mobility and military service

The immigrant alien has always had the right to complete freedom of movement about the United States, and he may leave the United States and return if he gets a re-entry permit and meets other requirements of the immigration laws. Since the passage of the Alien Registration Act of 1940 he must notify the United States Immigration and Naturalization Service of any change of address. During the war there were restrictions on the travel of aliens of enemy nationality, and some were interned. Travel restrictions were removed, however, just as promptly as national security permitted.

Our armed forces accepted the alien for service under the provisions of the Selective Service and Training Act. Only the enemy alien was excluded, and he too could be inducted if found acceptable to our armed services. Statistics show that 26 per cent of the aliens that served were "enemy aliens." Any alien from a neutral country who did not wish to serve in the armed forces could be relieved of this obligation, but he was forever barred from American citizenship. Aliens who did serve were given special naturalization privileges, and from June 30, 1942, to June 30, 1946, there were 125,891 military naturalizations. Of these, 15,641 took place abroad and were performed by the representatives of the United States Immigration and Naturalization Service in all the remote places where our armed forces were to be found.

Social security

All Federal social security legislation includes the alien within its benefits. This gives him full coverage under the federally operated old age and survivors' insurance. In the public assistance provisions of the Social Security Act, the law is permissive, and states determine who should come under it. About half the states include aliens, although some laws also include long residence requirements. In 1943 New York and New Jersey amended their acts to include aliens. These are two states having large alien populations. The inclusion of aliens under the old age insurance benefits and in state programs for old age pensions is of particular importance, for it has been estimated that in 1944 over 30 per cent of the alien population was 60 years of age or over, and that 90 per cent of these had entered prior to July 1, 1924.

Deportation

The alien is also subject to the deportation laws. These affect but small numbers of legally admitted immigrants, for the careful selection that occurs under the immigration laws excludes most of the undesirables. In addition, for most causes for deportation there is a statute of limitations. In the year ending June 30, 1947, only 1,684 persons were deported for causes other than those associated with illegal entry, and this number was unusually large, for it represented a part of the accumulation of cases from the war years and the immediate postwar period when deportation to many countries was impossible. Although the likelihood of deportation is slight, still the possibility would greatly add to the immigrant's insecurity were it not that there is a statute of limitations for such causes as becoming a public charge and mental and physical ills.

General

In most other respects the alien immigrant has the same rights and responsibilities as the citizen—the right of protection of person and property, and access to judicial procedures. He may benefit from our public health services, our agricultural aids, and the many other governmental services. Public hospitals and schools are available to him and his children. On the other hand, he must obey our laws, pay taxes, send his children to school, and defend our country with the exceptions noted above.

In summary, the average alien may live here permanently and suffer only such hardships as arise from lack of knowledge of our language and our ways. Some develop a complete sense of belonging in the United States without ever becoming citizens. The long-resident alien Italian shoemaker who pointed with pride to the picture of his grandson, a first lieutenant in the Air Corps of the United States, illustrates this point.

On the other hand, some of the barriers to complete participation that are associated with alienage might profitably be removed in such cases where they work hardship and serve no useful purpose. Certain of the limitations of the right to work and exclusions in state social security and public assistance laws are unnecessary and undesirable. Even more important, the naturalization laws should be amended to remove technical obstacles to naturalization that serve no useful purpose, inasmuch as it is only through naturalization that the foreign born become fully integrated into our citizenry.

SPECIAL ASSIMILATIVE SERVICES

We shall consider now the activities of government agencies that more specifically affect the integration of the foreign born into American life.

The United States Office of Education has a specialist in adult education and offers advisory services to the foreign born. It was an important cooperating agency in the National Citizenship Education Program, which in the years 1941-43, under the leadership of Dean William F. Russell, prepared teaching materials and stimulated the interest of states in citizenship programs.

The Department of State also has functions affecting the integration of the foreign born. The most important is its responsibility for sending documents to consuls abroad enabling close relatives of permanent resident aliens or United States citizens to enter as non-quota or preference-quota immigrants. The uniting of families in the United States is important to the stability of the foreign born, and results in their becoming more deeply rooted in America. The Department of State and appropriate courts determine whether citizenship has been lost when foreign-born persons and their children have resided abroad for certain periods of time. These decisions may well affect foreign-born families here, as in the case of persons who could not return because of war conditions. During . . . [1948] the Department of State . . . had a Committee on Immigration and Naturalization and . . . studied dual nationality, statelessness, and expatriation. The State Department was one of three government agencies that prepared the draft for the codification of the nationality laws that became the Nationality Act of 1940.

During the war there was an effort on the part of government agencies to secure greater and more intelligent participation of the foreign born in the war effort. Committees of nationality leaders were organized in connection with programs for civilian defense, war bond drives, and other civilian activities. Materials were issued in foreign languages. The Foreign Language Division of the Office of War Information worked with the foreign language press and radio. Its Division of Educational Service concerned itself with ways of reaching the foreign born. The Office of the Coordinator of Inter-American Affairs participated in programs for Mexicans and other Latin Americans resident in the United States. The armed services had special educational programs for illiterates. These specially directed efforts ceased with the termination of the war. A study of them should be valuable in developing future programs for securing greater participation in peacetime.

IMPORTANCE OF NATURALIZATION

We shall now consider naturalization and the governmental activities associated with it. Naturalization, although not embracing the whole meaning of assimilation, serves as an index of it. Although certain groups seek naturalization almost immediately after entry, most persons who become citizens have been here twenty years or more. Of the persons naturalized in 1947, two-thirds had entered prior to 1930. The importance of naturalization to the foreign born is evidenced by the fact that of the 10,495,035 adult foreign born in the United States at the time of the 1940 Census, 7,159,643 had become citizens. Since that time an additional 1,783,938 have been naturalized. This is the largest number in any similar period since records have been kept, despite the fact that the naturalization potential was the lowest.

The great increase in interest in recent years is due to several causes: the desire of the refugee for citizenship, the desire of the long-resident Italians not to be classed as enemy aliens, the simplified naturalization for men in the armed forces, and the fact that the development of extreme political ideologies abroad has made American citizenship more meaningful than ever.

NATURALIZATION LAWS

The United States has always made provision for naturalization. The Constitution required that there be a uniform rule of naturalization, and in 1790 the first naturalization law was passed. This was repealed and replaced by the act of 1795, and this in turn by the act of 1802.

This act of 1802 remained substantially in force for over a hundred years and included many of the requirements of our present law. It provided for a declaration of intention, five years residence in the United States prior to naturalization, attachment to the principles of the Constitution, good moral character, citizenship for children, testimony of witnesses, and an oath of allegiance with specific renunciation of former allegiance. Naturalization jurisdiction was left to the courts. There were no specific educational requirements, nor did the concept of legal entry exist. These requirements and the provision for an administrative agency were not introduced till the passage of the Basic Naturalization Act of 1906. Separate naturalization for women was introduced even later, in 1922.

It was under the act of 1802, as subsequently modified, that large numbers of our foreign born were naturalized. The fact that it left naturalization entirely to the courts resulted in lack of uniformity in records kept, in documents issued, and in the interpretation of the requirements. Since even under our present law there are differences in judicial interpretation, despite the assistance given by the United States Immigration and Naturalization Service toward securing uniformity, it is not surprising that as the number of immigrants increased, chaotic conditions resulted. Certain courts made political football of their power and naturalized large numbers of aliens immediately before elections. One can but wonder what effect this had on the meaning of citizenship.

In an effort to eliminate abuses, a commission was appointed by President Theodore Roosevelt in 1905 to study existing conditions and make recommendations so that the intent of the Constitution might be carried out. This resulted in the passage of the Basic Naturalization Act on June 29, 1906. This act contained many of the provisions of the old law, but in addition it provided for an administrative agency. This administrative body brought about orderly naturalization procedures, although the actual granting of citizenship still remained a function of the courts.

Through the years this Basic Naturalization Law was amended, but it was not superseded until passage of the Nationality Act of 1940. This was principally a codification of existing law. It retains many of the provisions of the 1906 act, and shows the increasing administrative responsibilities of the United States Immigration and Naturalization Service.

At the present time the Immigration and Naturalization Service has sixteen district offices with numerous field offices handling naturalization. This Service prepares uniform records and forms, and has full responsibility for investigating the applicant for naturalization. It makes recommendations to the court as to whether he meets the technical requirements of the law, including the educational requirements, examines him and his witnesses under oath, and serves the court and represents the Government before the court, making recommendations concerning admission, continuance, or refusal. In over 95 per cent of the cases the courts accept the recommendation of the Service.

There has been considerable effort on the part of the Immigration and Naturalization Service to make its recommendations more uniform throughout the Nation. In recent years cases recommended for denial by any district office are first sent to the central office for review. Inasmuch as the granting of citizenship is a court function, and since there are many Federal district courts and state courts of record handling naturalization, the Service takes cognizance of the decisions that have been handed down by higher courts. However, for many types of cases there are no binding decisions by the courts, and the central review results in greater uniformity. In cases where the United States wishes to appeal a court's decision, the Service on request assists in preparing the case. This is also true in cases involving cancellations of citizenship.

There are certain activities associated with naturalization that are purely administrative. The Service is responsible for the issuance of certain documents, namely: certificates of arrival, certificates of lawful entry, certificates of citizenship for derivative citizens, duplicates of original certificates that have been lost or destroyed, certificates in changed names for persons who have had their names legally changed subsequent to naturalization and special certificates of naturalization to obtain recognition as a citizen of the United States by a foreign state.

EDUCATION OF THE FOREIGN BORN FOR CITIZENSHIP

Since the education of the foreign born for citizenship is a function of states and local communities, the Immigration and Naturalization Service can only stimulate and assist. Its educational program is carried on by its Office of Research and Educational Services, under the direction of Dr. Henry B. Hazard. Its areas of activity are defined by law and are limited to the preparation and distribution of a Federal citizenship textbook for use by students in the public schools, the sending of the names of applicants for citizenship to the public schools, and the encouragement of state and local boards of education to provide educational opportunities for the foreign born to prepare for citizenship.

Even before the passage of the act of May 9, 1918, under which the Service was first specifically authorized to carry on a program in this field, it had undertaken these responsibilities. As early as 1909 it urged the public schools to conduct classes in citizenship. Some school systems had already provided such classes, and there is a record of English classes in the Philadelphia public schools as early as 1872.

At the beginning of the First World War there was a sudden realization of the large number of non-English-speaking and unnaturalized persons in the United States. This led to an "Americanization" movement which resulted in the setting up of a number of state programs for adult education for the foreign born. The Bureau of Naturalization, as it was then called, played an active part. In 1916 it sent out invitations to attend classes to over 200,000 applicants for naturalization and their wives. It also distributed an outline course in citizenship.

Opportunities offered

The authority given by the act of 1918 was reaffirmed in the Nationality Act of 1940. In the years just prior to this act there had been an increase in educational opportunities, largely due to the Adult Education Project of the Work Projects Administration. In 1941 an additional impetus was given by the organization of the National Citizenship Education Program, which was a cooperative project of Federal and state agencies. When this project terminated in 1942, the Immigration and Naturalization Service took over a program of increased activities and added to its staff educational service men.

These educational officers stimulated the interest of educators, and some original programs were developed. The Chicago officer interested the states of Wisconsin and Illinois in forming county committees. These consisted of the county superintendent of schools, the county agricultural agent, and the vocational teachers, and worked to interest rural areas in courses for home study that the Service had developed. In the Detroit district the applicant was sent with his receipt for his application a statement concerning the educational requirements and a list of classes. The Service also cooperated in the Detroit citizenship rallies, to which applicants were invited and at which they were given the opportunity to register for classes.

The Service has developed its materials so that they are available at different literacy levels to meet the needs of the foreign born. It has also prepared manuals for teachers. In 1947, there were 190,354 copies of the various parts of the "Federal Textbook on Citizenship" distributed. In addition, the Service has developed "A Home Study Course in English and Government," and in 1947 forty-three states conducted such home study courses through the extension divisions of their universities or through their state departments of education. This has been of particular value to people in isolated sections and to many city people who could not attend classes. In the year ending June 30, 1947, approximately 10,000 persons were enrolled for home study.

For many years the Service has sent the public schools the names of the applicants for citizenship, and these have been used for recruiting classes. In January 1946 the Commissioner of Immigration and Naturalization started the practice of having the names of new arrivals sent to the schools, with the understanding that the information was confidential and that the school would exercise tact in approaching newcomers. This undoubtedly has helped to increase enrollments. In 1946 there were 2,632 English and citizenship classes in 496 communities, with about 85,549 students. In 1947 there were about 200 additional classes. Recently Commissioner Watson B. Miller has sent a personal letter to all newcomers in which he welcomes them to the United States and advises them that there are citizenship education opportunities available.

It is obvious that the Service merely supplements the educational opportunities offered by states and localities. Most of the large immigrant-receiving states have extensive programs, but unfortunately many states do not supply classes for the foreign born. The development of home study courses fills part of the need, but it is to be hoped that with the growing appreciation of adult education, suitable opportunities will be provided wherever needed in the United States.

WELCOMING NEW CITIZENS

The Service has also played an active role in the development of ceremonies for welcoming new citizens. Originally these occurred principally in the courts and in the schools at the time of completion of courses. However, civic ceremonies were held in New York and other cities prior to the first national "New Citizens Day" held in 1939. In 1940 a joint resolution of Congress provided for an annual "I Am an American Day" to be held the third Sunday in May. The Service has prepared "Program Aids for Citizenship Recognition Ceremonies" and distributes hundreds of copies annually upon request. It has in the past stimulated communities to conduct these ceremonies, and has continued to assist the courts in their ceremonies for new citizens.

In a sense, "I Am an American Day" symbolizes the relation of the foreign born and our Government. On this day the ceremonies are not only for the new citizens by naturalization, but also for those native born who come of age. As the President of the United States stated in his proclamation designating May 19, 1946, as "I Am an American Day," our Nation "derives its chief strength from the fact that its citizens, young and old, native born and foreign born, work together as one people."

No. 28

[BOTH collectively and individually, aliens in America often have been, and still are in many instances, the victims of ill-considered public policy and private prejudices. They often suffer the same kind of discriminatory treatment that minority groups of citizens—ethnic, religious, and racial—have suffered.

In the following article Professor Wirth discusses the treatment of minority groups in America. Though he does not specifically allude to alien groups, Professor Wirth's conclusions apply to alien as well as citizen minorities.

The "Unfinished Business of American Democracy" presents a challenge to those who believe that equality is an essential element of democracy and who wish to eliminate racial, religious and ethnic bigotry.]

THE UNFINISHED BUSINESS OF AMERICAN DEMOCRACY [1]

by Louis Wirth

AT the end of World War II the United States stands on the threshold of peace, victorious and powerful but troubled. The strategy of our enemies to play upon our internal tensions and conflicts and thus to divide and conquer has been frustrated. Our internal unity proved to be a military asset matched in importance only by our vast material resources. Had we not been able to close ranks within, we probably would not have been able to translate our industrial and military potential into the decisive instrument of Allied victory.

INTERNAL UNITY AND AMERICA'S ROLE IN THE WORLD

As we seek to harvest the fruits of that victory, for ourselves and for all mankind, it becomes ever more important to know whether this nation

---

[1] Louis Wirth, "The Unfinished Business of American Democracy," *The Annals* of the American Academy of Political and Social Science (March, 1946), Vol. 244, pp. 1-9. Reprinted by permission of *The Annals* of the American Academy of Political and Social Science. The footnotes in the original version are omitted here.

which has demonstrated such enormous strength in battle can be equally strong in peace. Having emerged from the war with fewer scars than any other nation, we must ask ourselves, as hopeful people everywhere are asking, whether we intend to use our newly found and overwhelming power wisely to heal the wounds of an ailing world and to build a peaceful and a better way of life for ourselves and for all. The opportunity exists. Its realization depends upon whether Americans will recognize it as a challenge. It is generally conceded that we can have a decisive voice in shaping the destiny of man on earth; but the future peace and prosperity of this country are a precondition for the effective exertion of our full influence upon the world at large. Our external strength is measured by our internal unity. Hence, our capacity to play the significant role which history has thrust upon us rests on our ability and our will to conquer the group prejudices which, if allowed to persist and flourish, will disappoint the hopes of the world.

THE HERITAGE OF WAR

The United States on the eve of World War II was far from being a unified and integrated nation. Our country, like other countries in the modern world, had its economic, political, regional, religious, and cultural lines of division. Because of the vast expanse of our territory and the size of our population, we perhaps would have been expected to manifest greater internal cleavages than most countries in the Western world. The peculiar racial and ethnic composition of the American people, however, and the historical background upon which the American nation rests presented us with problems of building national unity which were of a strikingly different character and magnitude than those faced by the other warring powers. In addition, because of our geographical position, the political forms of the United States were the scene of seemingly endless debate over the question of our vulnerability—a controversy which would have been utterly futile in countries less remotely situated from the center of aggression. Our political leaders realized that national security resting upon geographic isolation was illusory. They recognized that we could not be indifferent to the outcome of the mortal struggle between fascist and at least potentially democratic forces. Then, finally, the overt and direct aggression of our enemies ended the public debate over whether or not we should or could secede from the universe.

The outbreak of the war found us as a nation preoccupied with the many unsolved problems of democracy. These problems, in the years immediately preceding the advent of war, had been aggravated by mass unemployment and by large-scale nazi propaganda which sought to paralyze and neutralize our effective influence in the struggle which had been planned for years and which, at least in its initial stages, was so brilliantly and ruthlessly executed.

Government efforts

The efforts of the Roosevelt administration to minimize the disadvantages of minority status in a period of economic adversity were still under way as the war clouds gathered. Building upon the sound foundations of America's democratic creed, as embodied in our fundamental laws and our heritage of equality of opportunity for all, irrespective of race, creed, or origin, the New Deal had important gains to show in overcoming discrimination. Our policy toward our territories and colonial possessions was definitely beginning to be shaped by anti-imperialist principles. A more enlightened administration of the Office of Indian Affairs was encouraged. In the administration of relief and work relief, discrimination was kept at a minimum. The national public housing program paid particular attention to meeting the acute housing problems of Negroes. A policy of nondiscrimination in public employment was initiated. Public officials and leading personalities went on record and used their influence to gain popular acceptance for a program designed to aid minority groups to overcome their disadvantageous position in American life.

To implement these liberal policies, race-relations consultants were appointed and they met with an increasingly hospitable reception in the agencies of the Federal Government. No doubt was left in the public mind as to where our political leaders stood with reference to persecution of racial and religious minorities in the nazi and fascist countries, their doctrine of Aryan racial supremacy, and their aggressive intentions. Sympathy and aid were given to refugees from terror abroad, and our immigration regulations were liberalized to permit the entry of the victims of Nazi persecution into the United States.

In the states and local communities, too, there were signs of more acute awareness of the degree to which the promises of democracy remained unfulfilled. The very denial of the rights of man by the enemies of democracy abroad furnished an incentive for their reaffirmation and realization here. Even in sections of the country especially addicted to racial discrimination, such as the South and the Pacific coast, voices were raised in behalf of a policy more consistent with the tenets of American democracy. Campaigns to outlaw lynchings, the poll tax, and official discrimination took on renewed vigor and gained increasing support. Public-opinion polls and other indications of the state of the public mind revealed a growing consciousness of the extent to which we ourselves in our attitudes and practices fell short of living up to the American creed. The growth of organizations to stimulate remedial action programs gave promise that an ever larger portion of our citizenry were prepared to overcome their group prejudices.

Internal disunity

On the other hand, it should be noted that the efforts on the part of nazi and fascist propagandists to divide us were not entirely fruitless. Building on the pre-existing prejudices and the grievances which the depression had accentuated, large-scale and well-financed campaigns to arouse and aggravate racial, religious, and ethnic bigotry and tensions flourished. Once the war in Europe got under way, these movements were able to combine with the isolationist forces in this country and in some instances to make a common cause with them. But the march of events soon rescued the American people from confusion and internal division. The attack on Pearl Harbor was the signal for ending the long debate.

Our active entry into the war did not, however, automatically eliminate group prejudice and discrimination. Under the compelling stress of war the most extreme and blatant forms of organization and agitation to undermine national unity abated, took on the protective coloration of patriotism, or went underground. This was especially true of organizations and movements previously sponsored by enemy governments. But not a few leaders of such organizations continued to pursue activities which the Government felt were sufficiently subversive to call for Federal indictments.

Although organized intolerance movements subsided during the war, unorganized and sporadic group prejudice remained much in evidence. Indeed, the war itself and the measures invoked in the name of national defense provoked new antagonisms and accentuated existing or latent prejudices. The removal of Japanese nationals and, what is more important, American citizens of Japanese ancestry from the Pacific coast and their involuntary confinement in relocation centers gave official, though unwitting, support to racialist doctrine and was in part responsible for outbreaks of racialist feelings. The surveillance and, in some cases, the confinement of enemy aliens suspected of subversive intentions aroused little reaction, largely because of the unobtrusiveness with which it was accomplished. The professional bigots exploited the discomforts, the restrictions, and even the tragedies incident to war as propaganda devices to make invidious comparisons between the patriotism of one racial, ethnic, or religious group and that of another. The national slogans and symbols which were employed, though not always officially sanctioned, also contributed to the instilling and accentuation of racial and national prejudices. Even the old and overworked arguments that the war was being fought for the benefit of a small minority and that some were making all the sacrifices while others reaped all the profits were resuscitated and refurbished to play their part. But, on the whole, World War II was carried on with markedly less internal violence and probably also with less antiminority feeling than World War I, especially as far as the nationals of enemy countries and their descendants were concerned.

WARTIME GAINS AND LOSSES

It is yet too early to appraise the gains and losses to be ascribed to the war in respect to the status of minorities in the United States. Certain major facts and trends, however, may be tentatively recorded:

1. Many of the long-standing problems of prejudice and discrimination against racial, ethnic, and religious minorities remained unsolved during the war but were obscured by the urgent problems of the war itself.

2. Despite the pre-existing group prejudices toward racial, ethnic, and religious minorities and despite the assiduous efforts on the part of the enemy to cultivate these prejudices, the nation achieved and maintained a singular spirit of unity throughout the duration of the war, and this integration contributed immensely to victory.

3. Although our national policies regrettably violated the letter, and most certainly the spirit, of our laws in such instances as the treatment of the Japanese-Americans, our record of equity and self-restraint under the provocation of war is exceptionally good, especially as contrasted with World War I.

4. The urgent need for manpower for the armed forces, as well as for war production, initiated the greatest mass migration in American history since the settlement of the frontier, and furnished unprecedented opportunities for contact between racial, ethnic, religious, and regional groups. In the course of this intermingling in the armed forces, in industry, and in day-by-day living, there took place an extensive commingling of mores and attitudes. This diffused the racial prejudices of the South and the Pacific coast throughout the land, but it also made these sections of the country more conscious of their prejudices, if not actually more liberal. The nature of the war itself and the racial doctrines of our enemies virtually forced us into a position where, in order to fight effectively, we had to accent the democratic values of our heritage.

5. The frustrations and grievances induced by war in both the military and the civilian sectors of national life spontaneously led to, and were exploited to produce artificially, occasional violent antiminority outbursts in the form of race riots, lynchings, vandalism, work stoppages, school strikes,

and similar incidents. The inadequate housing conditions in congested areas, the high cost of living, the lack of recreational and other community services, and the absence of stable social ties furnished the fertile soil upon which pre-existing or induced group prejudices flourished.

6. The scarcity of manpower, coupled with the favorable public attitude toward full utilization of human resources in the war effort, irrespective of race, creed, or origin, provided the members of minority groups with new and enlarged opportunities in employment. The Negro in particular has been enabled to enter industries and occupations from which he was formerly excluded. He has benefited by upgrading, has found entrance into labor organizations, especially the Congress of Industrial Organizations unions, and has had at least some support in his claims for greater equality through national legislation and executive action, notably the Committee on Fair Employment Practice. While it cannot be said that the Negro and the Japanese-Americans were accorded equality of opportunity in the armed forces, especially the Navy, and while segregation was the general rule, nevertheless even there a closer approximation to democratic policy was made in the course of World War II.

7. The new areas of contact, stimulated and induced by the war, between the dominant group and minorities in the armed forces, in industry, in housing, in transportation, in community institutions and activities, and in politics may be viewed as new adventures on the frontier of democratic life which, whatever their outcome, serve as experiments in and examples of mutual adjustments and participation. They set precedents in action upon which new claims can be based and in the face of which old prejudices are impotent and will ultimately be reduced to mere ceremonial and rhetorical exercises. The war furnished many such demonstrations of democracy in operation.

Action postponed

8. The war confronted the leadership of minority groups as well as the advocates of democracy in the country at large with a serious dilemma. Considering the sinister forces against which the war was fought, the advocates of genuine democracy could be content with nothing less than its full actualization in our own domestic society. At the same time, they had to realize that to press the claims of minority groups to the full might produce fissions within our body politic and social which might jeopardize victory in battle. As a response to this situation there developed the general disposition on the part of responsible leadership, both within and without minority groups, to postpone the just solution of many problems until a more

propitious moment would arrive. Hence many unsolved problems of group prejudice are carried over into peace, when the incentive to deal effectively with them may be weaker, while the moral obligation to do so is all the greater.

Public policy re minorities

9. Public policy as embodied in Federal, state, and local legislation and administration in the course of the war has, on the whole, worked to the distinct advantage of minority groups. Even before the outbreak of war, in connection with the defense program, President Roosevelt issued Executive Order 8802 on June 25, 1941. This order states:

> It is the policy of the United States to encourage full participation in the national defense program by all citizens of the United States, regardless of race, color, creed, or national origin, in the firm belief that the democratic way of life can be defended successfully only with the help and support of all groups within its borders.

The principle to which this statement gave official expression became the basis for insertion of a nondiscrimination clause in defense contracts and for the establishment of the Committee on Fair Employment Practice. This agency, though always something of a governmental stepchild and limited in powers and resources, has through its very existence exercised a salutary influence on government, industry, and labor.

Although no permanent Federal fair-employment-practice legislation has been enacted, there has been considerable activity in this direction in the states. The recent New York and New Jersey legislation against discrimination in employment is particularly notable, and the recently adopted Indiana law, while less vigorous in its provisions, stands in sharp contrast to the previously prevailing view that discrimination against minorities in employment was of no concern to government. The "right to earn a livelihood" is declared under the New York law to be "a civil right." The New Jersey Supreme Court held that "the right to earn a livelihood is a property right which is guaranteed in our country by the fifth and fourteenth amendments of the Federal Constitution." In the last decade, thirteen states have taken legislative steps to forbid discriminatory practices of one kind or another. Even some cities have followed these precedents by adopting fair-employment-practice ordinances.

Since the beginning of the war, the courts have, on the whole, taken a more sympathetic view toward the disabilities from which members of minority groups suffer. Civil-rights legislation has generally been more respected and enforced, and public agencies have been made acutely aware of the watchfulness of an aroused public in case of violations of nondiscrimination laws and policies. Legislation abolishing the poll tax has made progress. Georgia abolished the tax in 1944, leaving only seven southern states in which payment is a prerequisite for voting. Texas and Tennessee have exempted members of the armed forces from their poll tax obligations, and have thus incidentally taken a step which redounds to the benefit of at least a portion of the Negro population.

In the armed services, in the Selective Service System, and in the management of veterans-care programs, the favorable influence of a sympathetic administration and public opinion has been felt. Despite many setbacks and local and sporadic cases of flagrant discrimination, and despite the obvious failure to integrate the Negro, the Nisei, and other minorities fully into the war effort, it appears that the record of World War II marks a distinct advance over that of World War I.

Organizations

10. One of the most notable trends of the war years has been the multiplication of national, regional, state, and local official and citizen organizations for the promotion of better race relations, for the improvement of the status of minorities, for combating racial, ethnic, and religious discrimination, for advancing civic and national unity, and for the fuller realization of the democratic ideal. The outbreak of a race riot in the summer of 1943 in Detroit served as a powerful stimulus to the establishment of many of these organizations. Their number is difficult to determine. Over two hundred such organizations have been established since 1943 alone. A recent directory lists over three hundred of them.

Some of these organizations are official, having been established by legislation or executive action and deriving support from public funds. Others are citizens' organizations established through and supported by private efforts. Some are devoted exclusively to race relations, minority problems, and the combating of discrimination; others, such as labor organizations of religious or racial groups, have the eradication of group prejudices as one of their many objectives, either with or without a special department devoted to this function. Some have come into being in response to and in an attempt to deal with a specific instance of discrimination. An illustration of this is the "Sleepy Lagoon Defense Committee" in California, which was organized to provide a defense for twenty-three Mexican-American boys charged with murder. Others, such as state inter-racial commissions or mayors' committees on civic unity, have wider scope and are expected to have greater continuity.

The efforts of some communities to carry out local programs have been widely advertised. Thus, for instance, the program of education for democratic living with particular reference to racial and cultural relations as embodied in the "Springfield plan" has been widely acclaimed. Although the unique contributions of this plan are by no means clear and although no objective evaluation of its effects on community attitudes and action exists, the publicity concerning it has aroused nationwide attention and there appears to be a disposition to copy it elsewhere, as if its success were already established in the community of its origin, and on the assumption that it would fit other communities equally well.

An aroused public

11. While it is difficult to estimate the effect of the activities of these official and unofficial bodies, their very organization is a symptom of the assumption, by at least the enlightened section of the citizenry, of a greater share of responsibility for the problems with which they seek to deal. That there is a more widespread awareness of the existence of group prejudices and of the facts of discrimination against minorities in all parts of the country and in diverse sections of the American people is also apparent from the responses to opinion polls, the evidence revealed by surveys, and the extent to which the subject of racial and cultural relations has been featured in the press, over the radio, and in motion pictures. The fact that discussion of these problems is increasingly open and frank is in itself an indication of a more wholesome state of affairs.

Despite many positive statements to the contrary, however, the evidence is too fragmentary and inconclusive to permit any generalization as to whether group prejudices have increased or decreased since the beginning of the war. The investigations carried out by the armed services will, when they are analyzed and published, probably afford the soundest base on the trends of group prejudices among the American people in recent years.

We cannot, however, and fortunately we need not, wait until all the facts are in. Action is proceeding from day to day and we must seek to guide it as far as we can in the light of the best knowledge and the wisest judgment of which we are capable under the circumstances.

AGENDA

The greatest danger as we enter a new era is that the compelling motives which held us together in war will speedily disappear and that we shall relax into complacency if not into a mood of cynicism when a common danger no longer seems to threaten us. The increased responsibility which our

Nation will have to bear for the course of the world lifts our problems of domestic peace, unity, and prosperity to the level of universal concern.

The problems we must face in the immediate future are primarily those of healing the scars left by the war, of weathering the unrest and disorder of the period of transition, and of consolidating the gains recently made. We must recognize that we have raised the hopes of all who were the objects of group prejudice and discrimination in our attempt to enlist their full participation in the national cause and in the attempt to achieve unity in the pursuit of our common aims. The time is now here to validate the ideals in behalf of which we asked for heavy sacrifices. They can be validated only by deeds. The circumstances which justified the postponement of certain policies are no longer present. Nor can we slide back into practices at variance with our ideals without serious repercussions from those to whom we made concessions while we were in danger from without. Not only, therefore, do we confront the agenda of the unfinished business of democracy at home dating back to the period preceding the war, but we also must find ways of meeting the grievances that have become aggravated by the war and the new expectations we created while fighting our enemies.

Employment

In the field of employment we face the urgent necessity of providing jobs for all who are able and wish to work, which will utilize the workers' highest skills and enable them to live at a progressively rising standard. Members of minority groups who during the war had their first opportunity to enter certain industries and occupations, who have been upgraded to positions of higher skill and responsibility and have demonstrated their ability to hold these positions, will not without a struggle relinquish their gains. This will be particularly true of those who have served in the armed forces and have a special claim to full economic opportunities. The meeting of this obligation may, however, prove difficult in a period when our economy is in a state of transition from war to peace and of general contraction. Hence it is of importance to achieve as rapid and orderly a transition from war production to a civilian economy as possible and to bend every effort toward reaching the goal of full employment.

In addition to the common interest of all in a prosperous America and the special interest of minorities in that economy, there is the further stake that minorities have in a national fair-employment-practice policy. To this end, the enactment of an adequate permanent Fair Employment Practice Bill and its vigorous enforcement is an essential immediate step. Such a law, moreover, is in need of effective support by labor unions, employers, and the general public. It will require intensive mass education to build this support.

Housing

Another part of the agenda of racial and cultural relations is the field of housing. Here, again, the interests of minorities largely coincide with the interests of the general population. However, minorities, particularly Negroes, face unique disabilities. Not only are they victims of the housing shortage and of slums by virtue of their concentration in the low income groups, but they have suffered also from especially vicious discrimination in the form of race restrictive covenants. The outlawing of the practice of using the courts to restrict Negroes and other minorities to racial and ethnic islands, which because of overcrowding inevitably tend to degenerate into slums, is a prerequisite for the solution of the minority housing crisis. Here, as in the case of employment, a vigorous and intelligent educational program must accompany enlightened public policy. The experience during the war with isolated experiments of mixed racial occupancy of war housing projects suggests the extension of the practice and its support by the example of mixed public housing projects.

Public services

We are already well on the way in most of our Federal programs and in many of the states and local communities toward providing approximately equal public services to all members of our society. Great inequalities in educational, health, welfare, recreational, and protective services still remain to be wiped out. The results of the Selective Service examinations have helped to call the tragic effect of these inequalities in public services to national attention. A concerted effort to attain approximate equality in public services for all, irrespective of race, creed, or national origin, requires not merely a sound public policy, but also a continued citizens' program of vigilance and support. A national housing act, a national health act, a comprehensive social security act, and large-scale national aid in the minimization of gross differentials in educational and cultural opportunities can be brought about only as a result of popular recognition of the compatibility of the special needs of minorities with the general welfare.

The achievement of a democratic public policy in these and other phases of public responsibility will not automatically erase private prejudices. It will, however, go a long way to minimize the adverse effects of such prejudices. The latter can be affected in the long run only by modifying attitudes which for the most part have nonrational foundations. By improving the objective conditions under which minorities are now forced to live, as a result of an undemocratic public policy and private prejudice, we at least provide the objective demonstration of the alterability of the character of men through deliberate intervention in their conditions of life, and thus set the stage for an effective educational program.

OUR WORLD RESPONSIBILITY

In her new role in the world, the United States is under a particularly heavy obligation to realize to a much fuller degree than ever before the ideals of a democratic order. Unless we can demonstrate in our domestic life that we mean to live by the tenets of the rights of man, we cannot very well hope to gain from other powers those concessions that we regard as necessary for ending the era of imperialism, for the establishment of self-government, for the abolition of exploitation of "backward" peoples, and for terminating the suppression of minorities in their own countries. We have but a short time to create a world community if we would avert the physical destruction of a large portion of mankind and a return to the jungle by the survivors. Henceforth the fate of all minorities everywhere is of concern to us. Our best propaganda is the example we furnish to the rest of the world.

Chapter IX

THE PEOPLE AND THE SUFFRAGE

[MODERN government consists, for all practical purposes, of a relatively small number of persons who formulate and execute policies which affect the lives of all who live within the territory it governs. It is the essence of its character that these people are legally bound by the policies it lays down. In a democratic government, those who formulate policies are chosen by and held responsible to the whole citizen body, and those who execute the policies must, in one way or another, share the same responsibility. In the United States this is in part obtained through the popular election of the chief executives as well as the legislative bodies in both the nation and the states.

It is important, however, to recognize the full implications of the necessity, in a democratic system, of providing direct channels by which the will of the ordinary man may have some influence on those who exercise political power. Most important of these is the right to the franchise. Every adult citizen must have the right to participate in the choice of those persons who undertake the task of making the rules under which he is to live. A democratic government has no alternative to universal adult suffrage. There are no practical tests for the exclusion of citizens from participation in the process of choosing those who are to rule. Neither sex nor lack of property, race nor creed, economic nor social position, ought to prevent the citizen from participating in the choice of his rulers. Whenever the body of voters is limited, those persons excluded do not receive their share of the benefits of government. A franchise based upon property limits the interests of the state to the owners of property. Educational qualifications are, in effect, partial substitutes for property-holding qualifications and, in addition, there seems to be no technique for correlating educational qualifications with political fitness. Exclusion on the basis of sex means inadequate protection of women where their interests conflict with those of men. To deprive those on the relief rolls of the right to vote is to stigmatize economic misfortune as a crime.

If it is argued that such an extension of the suffrage will result in unwise choices and mistaken policies, it must be answered that democracy is a process of trial and error. If it is argued that the common man does not have the knowledge to make a reasoned choice, the answer is that the state must make that knowledge accessible to him. If it is argued that the common man can not know enough about the intricate problems with which government must

231

deal to make wise decisions in the realm of public policy, it must be answered that widespread participation is not to give to all men the power to govern, but to give them an opportunity to prevent misgovernment. For, in the end, it must be realized that whenever a group of voters is excluded from participation in the franchise that group is also usually excluded from the welfare realized by the exercise of the power to govern.

Realizing the significance of the franchise, many have gone ahead to hold that those who fail to use it should be compelled to do so. A policy of this kind is built upon a failure to comprehend that there "can be no substitute for an alert civic interest on the part of those who vote." In addition, those who have argued the case for compulsory voting fail to realize the extent to which such argument diverts attention from the real problems of further democratizing our governmental system. To make government responsible we need to direct our attention to governmental organization. The federal distribution of power, the principle of separation of powers, checks and balances, and judicial review call for our serious consideration. We need to examine the possibilities for friction and deadlock which cause the voter to become lost; we need to shorten the ballot and to simplify governmental organization. The reduction of the number of elective officers to those concerned directly with policy determination would not only relieve the voter of a great burden but also enable him to see the effect of his decisions more directly. We do not need to compel men to vote. What we need is to make the system one in which the voter feels that his vote really counts for something. To divert attention from these important considerations by advocating compulsory voting is to divert attention from the essentials of our democratic system.

The following articles by Professors Smith and Eagleton and by Mr. Dumas discuss the problems of the suffrage, of voting, and non-voting in detail.]

No. 29

THE STRUGGLE FOR A DEMOCRATIC SUFFRAGE [1]

by J. Allen Smith

PROMINENCE was given in the public documents of the American Revolution to the social contract theory, the doctrine of natural rights, the idea of equality, and other conceptions more or less closely identified with the belief in political democracy. This tended to give to the Revolution the appearance of a genuinely popular movement, and thus aided

---

[1] J. Allen Smith, *The Growth and Decadence of Constitutional Government* (New York: Henry Holt and Company, 1930), Ch. 3. Reprinted by permission of the publisher.

materially in developing and crystallizing public opinion in support of the war for independence.

To proclaim that "all men are created equal" and that they are "endowed by their Creator with certain unalienable rights" which governments "deriving their just powers from the consent of the governed" are instituted to protect, may not be a positive and unequivocal statement of belief in the justice and desirability of a widely extended suffrage; but inferentially, at any rate, it constituted a solemn indictment of the then existing restrictions on the right to vote.

This Revolutionary enthusiasm for the rights of man, which found expression in the official pronouncements of representative bodies, did not commit the political leaders of that time, by any direct and specific statement, to the policy of democratizing the suffrage. It was no doubt clearly seen, however, that the doctrine of natural rights, which served the practical end of justifying the Revolution, could also be used effectively by those who wished to abolish property qualifications for voting and officeholding. That this was recognized is evidenced by certain qualifying statements, obviously designed to safeguard property qualifications against an attack based on the theory that suffrage is a natural right. Thus the Virginia Bill of Rights, adopted June 12, 1776, after declaring "that all men are by nature equally free and independent" and "that all power is vested in, and consequently derived from, the people," adds the saving clause "that all men, having sufficient evidence of permanent common interest with, and attachment to, the community, have the right of suffrage." Provisions identical in substance were incorporated in the Bills of Rights in Pennsylvania, Maryland, New Hampshire, and Vermont. The effort to reconcile the theory of natural rights with a restricted suffrage probably had little effect on the outcome of the suffrage controversy. Nevertheless, it was half a century after this outburst of Revolutionary enthusiasm for democracy in the abstract, before the movement to democratize the suffrage was well under way.

Neither at the beginning of the Revolution, nor later when the Constitution was framed and adopted, was the extension of the suffrage included in the list of proposed reforms. According to the viewpoint of the official and ruling class, government existed primarily for the protection of property and property rights. This was well expressed by John Adams at the beginning of the American Revolution:

> The same reasoning which will induce you to admit all men who have no property, to vote, with those who have, . . . will prove that you ought to admit women and children; for, generally speaking, women and children have as good judgments, and as independent minds, as those men who are wholly

destitute of property; these last being to all intents and purposes as much dependent upon others, who will please to feed, clothe, and employ them, as women are upon their husbands, or children upon their parents. . . . Depend upon it, Sir, it is dangerous to open so fruitful a source of controversy and altercation as would be opened by attempting to alter the qualifications of voters; . . . women will demand a vote; . . . and every man who has not a farthing, will demand an equal voice with any other. . . . It tends to confound and destroy all distinctions, and prostrate all ranks to one common level.

Forty-one years later, in a letter to James Madison, he said:

The questions concerning universal suffrage and those concerning the necessary limitations of the power of suffrage, are among the most difficult. It is hard to say that every man has not an equal right; but, admit this equal right and equal power, and immediate revolution would ensue. In all the nations of Europe, the number of persons, who have not a penny, is double those who have a groat; admit all these to an equality of power, and you would soon see how the groats would be divided. . . . There is in these United States a majority of persons, who have no property, over those who have any.

Adams expressed the ruling class conviction of the time, that government is, and ought to be, founded on property, and that only those who have sufficient property to ensure their support of the established order can with safety be allowed to vote. In the earlier statement of his reasons for opposing manhood suffrage, he based his objection on the ground that the propertyless laboring man is dependent on his employer, and consequently is not a free moral agent in casting his vote. On this assumption, the enfranchisement of the laboring class would not in reality place political power in their hands, but would merely increase the number of votes controlled by their employers, and thus have the effect of making government more oligarchical in character than it was before property qualifications were abolished. This argument was frequently used by the opponents of manhood suffrage, and was designed, no doubt, to influence the attitude of that large class of small landowning agricultural voters, who would not regard with favor any measure which would be likely to result in a substantial increase in the political influence of the wealthy employing class of the large cities. This particular reason for opposing the extension of the suffrage seems to have been a favorite argument of those who accepted the notion, then more or less prevalent among the ruling class, that political rights should be the exclusive privilege of landowners. Indeed, the idea that government should be controlled by landowners survived in many of the original states until well into the nineteenth century. After the Revolution there were ten states in which there was a freehold qualification for voters, though in five of these there was an alternative personal property qualification. The control of the state government by the landholding interests was still further safeguarded by means of substantial property qualifications for public office. The viewpoint of the ruling class at the time the Constitution of the United States was framed is reflected in the act of Congress providing for the government of the Northwest Territory. Under the provisions of this act, the governor was required to have a freehold estate of one thousand acres in the territory; the secretary of the territory and the territorial judges, estates of at least five hundred acres each. A freehold of two hundred acres was necessary for membership in the general assembly, and no one could vote who did not own fifty acres of land in the district.

By 1821 the suffrage question was receiving serious attention in the state of New York. In the constitutional convention of that year, the committee on the elective franchise reported in favor of giving the suffrage to every adult male citizen who contributed toward the support of the government by payment of taxes on real or personal property, by service in the state militia, or by work on the highways, provided he had resided within the state for a period of six months. This proposal was debated at length, being strenuously opposed by the conservative members of the body. In the course of the debate various amendments were offered, the object of which was to defeat the proposed extension or to nullify its effects. Two of the most active opponents of a liberal suffrage policy were Chief Justice Spencer and Chancellor Kent of the supreme court. Both believed that the proposal to extend the suffrage was revolutionary, and that it would destroy the security which property owners had up to that time enjoyed and in the end bring chaos and ruin upon the nation. Chief Justice Spencer thought the time not far distant when the agricultural interest would be in a minority. "And what," he asked, "is there to protect the landed interests of the state, the cultivators of the soil, if the wide and broad proposition on your table be adopted?" He predicted "that the landed interests of the state will be at the mercy of the other combined interests; and thus all the public burthens may be thrown on the landed property of the state." "Is it desirable," he asked, "that we should remove the safeguards of property, and destroy the incentive to acquire it, by rendering it insecure?" After attributing to the beneficence and liberality of property "all the embellishments and the comforts and blessings of life," he warned the members of the convention to take care, "whilst we nominally give the right of voting to a particular description of our citizens, that we do not in reality give it to their employers." On another occasion in the convention, he said: "Let me ask to whom this right will be extended? It will principally be . . . to those who work in your factories, and are employed by wealthy individuals, in the capacity of laborers. Now, I hold . . . that it will be one of the most aristocratic acts that was ever witnessed in this community— under the pretence of giving the right to them, we in fact give it to those who employ, clothe, and feed them."

Chancellor Kent expressed the fear "that our posterity will have reason to deplore in sackcloth and ashes, the delusion of the day." He contended that the landed interest of the state should retain the exclusive control of the senate, as a guaranty of protection to the owners of the soil. In reply to those who like Chancellor Kent desired special protection for property, David Buel, Jr., said:

> One ground of the argument of gentlemen who support the amendment (to retain the freehold qualifications for senatorial voters) is, that the extension of the right of suffrage will give an undue influence to the rich over the persons who depend upon them for employment; but if the rich control the votes of the poor, the result cannot be unfavourable to the security of property. . . .
>
> I contend, that by the true principle of our government, property, as such, is not the basis of representation. Our community is an association of persons —of human beings—not a partnership founded on property. . . . Property is only one of the incidental rights of the person who possesses it; . . . it must be made secure; but it does not follow, that it must therefore be represented specifically in any branch of the government. It ought, indeed, to have an influence—and it ever will have, when properly enjoyed. So ought talents to have an influence . . . but you surely would not set up men of talents as a separate order, and give them exclusive privileges.
>
> The truth is, that both wealth and talents will ever have a great influence; and without the aid of exclusive privileges, you will always find the influence of both wealth and talents predominant in our halls of legislation.

The effort to make men instead of property the basis of the state government was only partially successful. Several important changes were made in the plan submitted by the committee on the elective franchise which were designed to make the qualifications of voters less objectionable to the property holder. The residence requirement recommended by the committee, of six months in the state, was raised to one year, and a local residence requirement of six months in the town or county was added. The suffrage was given to adult male citizens who had paid taxes on real or personal property, or performed military service in the state militia within the year preceding the election. Adult male citizens who had not paid taxes on real or personal property, or had not served in the state militia, but who had been assessed and had performed labor on highways were allowed to vote, subject to a state residence requirement of three years and a local residence requirement of one year. No colored man was allowed to vote unless he had been for three years a citizen of the state, and owned, and had paid taxes on, a freehold estate of the value of $250.00.

The representatives of the landholding interest in the convention were unsuccessful in their effort to deprive non-freehold voters of a voice in the selection of the members of the upper house; but they did succeed in limiting the influence of this class of voters by retaining the freehold qualification for membership in that house.

The varying and conflicting opinions concerning the suffrage which were expressed in the New York constitutional convention of 1821, may be regarded as fairly indicative of ruling class sentiment at that time. There was an increasing number who favored the view that government was an institution established and maintained for the benefit of all citizens, and that to guarantee an equitable diffusion of the benefits derived therefrom, it was necessary to abolish the special constitutional protection given to property owners through property qualifications for voting and for holding public office. But only a small minority of the members of the convention, it seems, favored the abolition of all property qualifications. Martin Van Buren, afterwards President of the United States, declared that he did not believe that there were twenty members who, were "the bare naked question of universal suffrage put to them, would vote in its favor."

Broadly speaking, there are but two theories of the suffrage; one may be called the aristocratic and the other the democratic. The aristocratic theory, which found expression in our state constitutions during the first half century of our history as a nation, held that voting was a privilege to be conferred upon such of the adult citizens as were fit to exercise it. The advocates of this theory made use of it for the purpose of justifying the then existing restrictions on the right to vote. They did not really believe in the doctrine of equality or the theory of natural rights, nor did they accept Aristotle's definition of a citizen as one who shares in governing and being governed. A citizen, as such, was at the most, they thought, only a potential voter. Mere citizenship did not confer upon the individual, nor entitle him to claim, any active civic rights. The right to vote and to be elected to office did not belong to him as a citizen, but accrued to him incidentally as the owner of property. In order to justify this contention, it was necessary to make the assumption that participation in the political life of the state was but a privilege, which those in control might confer or withhold. The conservative believed then, as he does now, that men in their civic activities are very largely guided by what they consider to be their material interests. This stands out conspicuously in all the debates and other literature in opposition to the extension of the suffrage.

It has almost always been assumed, as a self-evident proposition, by the advocates of a restricted suffrage, that the poor, if granted the privilege of voting, would use the power thus given them to bring about a redistribution of wealth. It does not seem to have occurred to them that, if this contention has any merit, it could also be claimed with as much reason that under a property holding suffrage the material interests of property owners will be advanced at the expense of the classes who have little or no property. We are all too prone to assume that our particular interest is the best and most trustworthy indication of what is for the public good. It is, therefore, not difficult for any class to believe that its interests are representative of the general interests, and that legislation advantageous to it is also beneficial to the state as a whole. Without imputing, then, any consciously selfish motive to those in control, we may accept as true Professor Dicey's statement, "that from the inspection of the laws of a country it is often possible to conjecture, and this without much hesitation, what is the class which holds, or has held, predominant power at a given time."

The ruling class believed in the right of the politically fit to control the state. The test of fitness, however, was not personal worth, character, or intelligence. These qualities might make one respected and trusted as a man; but they furnished no assurance that political power, if placed in his hands, would be wisely and conservatively used. James Monroe in 1831, after he had been for eight years President of the United States, wrote:

> The danger is, if the right of suffrage is extended to the whole population, without any qualification, as to property, that as the difference of interest begins to operate, as it will soon do, that the mass of poor, which will be by far the most numerous, will elect persons who will be instruments in the hands of leaders who will overthrow the government. . . .

To the political liberal, citizenship implied the right to participate in the civic life of the community. To deny the individual the ballot was to deprive him of that which constituted the essence of citizenship in a democracy.

Those who believed in democracy repudiated the idea that government should be controlled by the property holding class. Citizenship, they maintained, implied the right to vote, which was a personal right of the citizen and not contingent on the ownership of a specified amount of property. Like any other right of the individual, it was subject to reasonable regulation for the common good. It was, however, a right, and not, as the conservative claimed, a mere privilege. It could and should be withheld from such as were clearly not fit to exercise it. But in determining the question of fitness, the state should not be guided by any external test such as the ownership of property. The grounds upon which exclusion from the suffrage could be justified were personal and such as clearly made one incapable of a wise use of political power. Thus naturally followed the exclusion of criminals, paupers, minors, and even women, who in the early days of democracy were classed with the politically unfit.

With the growth of democracy, the old or aristocratic view of the suffrage has been largely, though not entirely, abandoned. The idea that government exists primarily for the protection of property still survives in the thinking of the well-to-do classes; and, while property qualifications have in large measure disappeared, the influence of those who favor suffrage restrictions has been more or less effective. Even without property qualifications many adult male citizens are practically disfranchised. The chief substitute for the old property holding or taxpaying qualifications for voters is the more stringent requirement concerning residence. This is illustrated in the New York Constitution of 1821, which abolished the freehold qualification for the suffrage. The extent and character of the increase made in the residence requirement at that time clearly indicate an intention to make it serve the purpose of minimizing the effect of the non-property holding vote. While a residence requirement of one year in the state was added to the local residence requirement of six months for such voters as paid taxes or performed military service in the state militia, for all other voters, a residence of three years in the state and one in the locality was required, together with a highway tax to be paid in labor or its equivalent. For colored voters, a freehold qualification was retained.

No doubt the chief purpose of these more stringent residence requirements was to limit the wage earning vote, as may be most clearly seen in the case of the southern states. North Carolina, in the Constitution of 1876, increased the period of residence for voters from one to two years in the state, and from thirty days to six months in the county, and added a supplementary residence qualification of four months in the precinct or election district. Virginia, before 1850, required a residence of one year in the county, city, town, or borough. The Constitution of 1850, which removed property qualifications for voters, retained the local residence requirement of one year and added a state residence requirement of two years. After the Civil War this was reduced to one year in the state and three months in the locality. The movement to restrict the Negro vote, which culminated in the Constitution of 1902, restored the residence requirement of two years in the state and one in the locality. This increase in the residence requirement is an essential part of the suffrage restrictions contained in the more recently adopted constitutions of the southern states.

The Rhode Island Constitution of 1842 distinguished between two classes of voters, those who paid taxes on a freehold of a specified value and for whom a residence of one year in the state was prescribed, and those who paid taxes to the amount of at least one dollar on an estate. For the latter class of voters, a residence of two years in the state was required. When the property qualification for the suffrage was removed in 1888, the two years residence requirement was extended to all voters.

The effect as well as the evident purpose of these residence requirements is to diminish the influence of those who would have been excluded under the old property holding qualifications for voting. It is the tenant farmer and the wage earner who are most likely to be disfranchised by these restrictions. Even moderate residence requirements, under present-day conditions, disfranchise many members of the wage earning class.

Educational qualifications for voters may also be regarded as a partial substitute for property holding and taxpaying restrictions. They are, for the most part, a recent development, having little practical importance outside of the southern states, where they are utilized to limit the influence of the Negro vote. Until the adoption of the Fourteenth Amendment after the Civil War, the states could disfranchise the Negro, or, as in the New York Constitution of 1821, provide special and more restrictive qualifications for colored voters. The suffrage provisions in the recently adopted constitutions of the southern states, with the exception of the residence qualifications, which exclude many of the poorer class whether white or black, may be regarded as an attempt to accomplish by indirection a disfranchisement that is racial in purpose and effect. The restrictions upon the right to vote, such as the property owning, taxpaying, and literacy tests found in these constitutions, when viewed in connection with other provisions which have the effect of exempting white voters from their operation, are as clearly designed to limit the colored vote as were the direct and express provisions of this sort in some of the earlier state constitutions.

What the framers of the later constitutions did was to revive the old property holding and taxpaying qualifications, supplemented by an alternative educational test, and to make them apply in practice exclusively to colored voters. These provisions are an expression of the conviction that the political supremacy of the white voters must be maintained. The Fourteenth Amendment made it impossible for the southern states to retain the form of manhood suffrage without incurring the danger of political control at the hands of those elected by the colored vote. The expedients resorted to for the purpose of guarding against this possibility would probably have been adopted in any northern state confronted by similar conditions.

In many states where the right to vote for elective officials is not limited by property or taxpaying restrictions, these restrictions, nevertheless, apply to the more important matter of a vote on a proposal to incur public indebtedness for some specific purpose. In this way, the control over policies is kept very largely in the hands of the property owning class, though less obviously than was the case under the early state constitutions. The difference between total disfranchisement of non-property holders and the limitation of their influence by means of constitutional provisions of this sort, is only one of degree. Under the latter system we really have two classes of voters: those who, as property owners and taxpayers, have the unrestricted right of suffrage; and those who neither own property nor pay direct taxes and whose influence as voters is rigidly limited by constitutional provisions. Restrictions of this kind may be regarded as a compromise forced upon the advocates of manhood suffrage by those who were seeking to perpetuate the influence of property.

The demand for manhood suffrage as a political right paved the way for the woman suffrage movement. The mere fact that men had monopolized political power could not be accepted as a sufficient reason for denying women the right to vote. In an age when time-honored institutions and practices were being examined and criticized in the light of reason, it was inevitable that, with the extension of the suffrage to men, a further extension of the right to women should be demanded. Indeed, even under the theory which supported the system of property qualifications, there could be no logical defense of the practice which withheld from property owning, taxpaying women the right to vote. But the question of woman suffrage did not secure any recognition until the agitation for manhood suffrage had succeeded in breaking down the more obvious and direct barriers erected in the earlier state constitutions against popular control.

The rather close connection between the general movement for the extension of the suffrage to men and the woman suffrage is indicated by the fact that the first woman suffrage convention in the United States was called in 1848. The movement, however, made but little progress until after the Civil War. In 1869 women were granted the suffrage in the territory of Wyoming. The question of equal political rights for women was beginning to receive serious consideration in the early seventies. The Prohibition platform of 1872 demanded equal rights for women, and the Greenback platform of 1884 favored a woman suffrage amendment to the Constitution of the United States. Generally speaking, the woman suffrage movement has had the support of the more radical minor parties for the last fifty years.

In 1912 the Progressive party proclaimed its belief that "no people can justly claim to be a true democracy which denies people rights on account of sex," and in 1916 both the Democratic and the Republican parties included in their national platforms declarations favoring the extension of the suffrage to women by the states. Fifteen states had enfranchised women when the woman suffrage amendment to the Federal Constitution was adopted in 1920. Moreover, progress toward woman suffrage had been made in many other states by granting women the right to vote in school elections or on other local questions.

Women are citizens, and citizenship, to be real and effective, must confer the right to vote. One can hardly appeal to democracy in defense of manhood suffrage, without seeing that a further extension of the suffrage to women could be justified on the same grounds. From the viewpoint of democracy, suffrage is an essential right of the normal adult citizen, necessary in order that he may be guaranteed adequate protection under the laws of the state. Governmental policies are the resultant of the various interests which find expression in the votes of the people. A disfranchised class is deprived of the only means by which its interests can be adequately protected. A class thus divested of political rights is invariably discriminated against. We need not assume that this discrimination is in any sense conscious or intentional. It may be due to the more or less obvious fact that no group or class of persons having group or class interests peculiar to themselves are, or can be, adequately represented unless they have a voice in the making of the laws by which they are governed. The history of legislation shows that women as a class are no exception to this rule. Man-made laws, even in the most democratic communities, have failed to give women adequate protection where their interests conflict with those of men. The growth of democracy has brought about a much closer approximation to equality in the civil rights of men and women; but equal protection of women, where their interests as a class conflict with those of men, can be guaranteed only by an intelligent exercise of political rights by women themselves. "Men, as well as women," says John Stuart Mill, "do not need political rights in order that they may govern, but in order that they may not be misgoverned."

The democratic theory of the suffrage, which would grant the right to vote to every normal adult citizen, is regarded by those who oppose democracy as an unjustifiable attempt to establish an artificial political equality. Men, they say, are not equal in physical strength, intelligence, or moral character. Why should not this natural inequality be recognized in the organization of the state, by such restrictions on the suffrage as will keep political power in the hands of the fit? Those who emphasize inequality as an argument against democracy, however, always include themselves among the fit. The democrat might reply to them in the language of that advocate of monarchy, Thomas Hobbes, who after affirming that men are, all things considered, substantially equal, says: "From this equality of ability, ariseth equality of hope in the attaining of our ends." His argument is to the effect that whether men are equal or unequal, no man is willing to admit his own inferiority, nor will he be satisfied under institutions and laws which discriminate against him. Since every man thinks himself the equal of other men, it is necessary for the peace and safety of the state to treat all men as equals.

The conservative not only assumes the existence of marked inequality, but believes that such inequality is highly desirable. According to his system of political philosophy, only those whom nature has designated as the fit should be endowed with political rights. He fails, however, to recognize the important fact that any class or groups of classes that may happen to be in control of the state will always seek to justify their political privileges and to retain the material advantages derived therefrom. Moreover, the inequality that now exists is, as Hobbes says, very largely the product of unjust laws. Democracy could not, it is true, remove inequalities for which nature is responsible, but it is unalterably opposed to any policy which would make inequality more pronounced. A widely extended suffrage is necessary to safeguard society against an artificial, state-created inequality. One may be a firm believer in political democracy, without believing that men are equal in ability or worth. The conservative who conceives of democracy as a plan to establish and maintain an artificial equality is setting up a man of straw.

A democratic state with a widely extended suffrage is designed as a means of establishing and maintaining equality of political opportunity. It seeks to give to each man, not equal influence, but equal opportunity to exert such influence upon the state and its policies as is implied in the right to vote. The fact that each man may have one vote, and only one, does not make men politically equal, nor is it intended to do so. Qualities of mind and character which command confidence and respect will always give to their possessor an influence over the votes of others. True leaders, men of superior intelligence and worth, who have faith in democracy and are recognized as representing its aims and aspirations, may have far greater influence in a democratic society than would be possible under a restricted suffrage. In giving each individual the right to vote, a democratic system of government merely abolishes the political privileges which have made it possible in the past for the favored classes to control the state

without due regard to the wishes or interests of the disfranchised elements
in the population. With the extension of the suffrage, this power has, to
some extent at least, disappeared. Classes formerly disregarded, since they
had no means of registering an effective protest, must now be placated in
order to secure their political support. The extension of the suffrage abolished the form, if not the substance, of the political monopoly of the ruling
class. It left the members of this class, however, in possession of whatever
influence was due to their wealth, intelligence, or social prestige.

Closely connected with the influence of the dominant class was the
method of voting. To enfranchise the wage earning population without at
the same time ensuring a secret ballot was to give, in large measure, the
form without the substance of political power. This fact the wealthier
classes were quick to recognize. Long before the suffrage was extended,
indeed, conservatives appreciated the advantages of the *viva voce* form of
voting. Their point of view is well expressed by Montesquieu:

> The people's suffrages ought doubtless to be public; and this should be
> considered as a fundamental law of democracy. The lower class ought
> to be directed by those of higher rank, and restrained within bounds by the
> gravity of eminent personages. Hence, by rendering the suffrages secret in
> the Roman republic, all was lost.

The wealthy class clearly saw that its political influence might be endangered if secret voting should be established. A system of secret voting
would deprive the rich of the opportunity to use economic pressure for the
purpose of controlling the votes of those dependent upon them. Landlords
would have less influence over tenants; creditors, over debtors; and employers, over employees. Dependent voters, who under a system of public
voting could be counted on to be amenable to advice and influence, would
no longer be subject to these wholesome restraints. Even under a system
which limited the suffrage to property owners and taxpayers, the well-to-do
regarded the political influence of the rank and file of voters with more or
less apprehension, which was reflected in the high property qualifications
for the important offices under the early American state constitutions.

> In any political election [says John Stuart Mill], even by universal suf-
> frage (and still more obviously in the case of a restricted suffrage), the
> voter is under an absolute moral obligation to consider the interest of the
> public, not his private advantage, and give his vote, to the best of his
> judgment, exactly as he would be bound to do if he were the sole voter,
> and the election depended upon him alone. This being admitted, it is at
> least a *prima facie* consequence that the duty of voting, like any other
> public duty, should be performed under the eye and criticism of the pub-

lic. . . . Undoubtedly neither this nor any other maxim of political morality is absolutely inviolable. . . .

It may, unquestionably, be the fact that if we attempt, by publicity, to make the voter responsible to the public for his vote, he will practically be made responsible for it to some powerful individual, whose interest is more opposed to the general interest of the community than that of the voter himself would be if, by the shield of secrecy, he were released from responsibility altogether.

As a rule, secrecy in voting has accompanied or followed, and not preceded the extension of the suffrage. It was opposed by the same classes that defended property qualifications and for the same reason—the desire to keep political control in the hands of the well-to-do. A widely extended suffrage without the secret ballot, was, after all, less of an evil than it had seemed. The proposal, however, to make voting secret was clearly a plan designed to make it possible for members of the dependent classes to cast independent votes. A long period of agitation and discussion was required before the secret ballot in an effective form was finally and generally established. It was not until a full half century after the suffrage was extended in the American states that laws adequately safeguarding the secrecy of the ballot were generally adopted.

Even now, the fight for secrecy has not been entirely won. Under the election laws of some states, voters in primary elections must declare their party affiliations and receive a ballot on which are printed only the names of those from whom their party candidates are to be selected. This type of primary election prevents some voters, perhaps many, who would vote with a radical minor party, from voting with their party in the primary. The penalty for taking part in the selection of candidates for whom they expect to vote in the final election may keep many voters from the polls, or perhaps make it seem expedient to vote in the primary with a party which they do not intend to support. Among those who vote the Socialist ticket, for example, are many who would be made to feel the effectiveness of such discrimination as is often made use of to discourage radical voting by those economically dependent.

The opponents of the secret ballot professed to be the defenders of a high type of political morality. Those who are fit to vote, they contended, do not need nor desire secrecy; inasmuch as voters exercise a power conferred on them by the state, the public have the right to know how it is used; only harm would be the result of the secret ballot; fraud and deception would be encouraged.

It is difficult, for one reviewing this controversy from the standpoint of the present time, to credit the opponents of the secret ballot with a high order of political intelligence and not impute to them a certain amount of insincerity. Fraud in elections was often perpetrated under the old system of public voting. The fact that this method of voting encouraged fraud and intimidation was one of the most telling arguments for the secret ballot. Political corruption has not entirely disappeared with the introduction of secret voting; but the direct purchase of votes is no longer good business, since those who supply the funds for this purpose can have no assurance that the votes paid for will be delivered.

In England at the beginning of . . . World War [I], there was much dissatisfaction with the antiquated suffrage laws which permitted plural voting and excluded women from parliamentary elections. The plural voting system gave an undue share of political influence to the landowning class, since a landowner could vote in all districts in which he owned sufficient property to qualify him for the exercise of this right. This feature of the English suffrage laws made it possible for a minority of conservative voters to cast a majority of the votes and to control a majority of the members elected to the House of Commons. Naturally enough, the efforts of the Liberal party to abolish plural voting encountered determined opposition in the House of Lords.

The adoption of needed suffrage reforms was made possible by the abolition in 1911 of the veto power of the House of Lords. A comprehensive bill, systematizing and simplifying the qualifications of voters, was introduced in the House of Commons May 15, 1917. The enactment of this law increased the number of voters by extending the suffrage to about six million women. No woman . . . [could] vote, however, until she . . . [had] reached the age of thirty years, a discrimination against women which would seem to indicate that the members of the House were reluctantly recognizing the principle of woman suffrage. [In 1928 the age qualification was made the same for both sexes and in 1948 plural voting was abolished.]. . .

Belgium . . . had a system of plural voting . . . [from] 1893 [till 1918]. To every male citizen who . . . had attained the age of twenty-five years, . . . one vote [was given]. An additional vote . . . [was] conferred upon those who . . . [were] heads of families and [paid] as householders a tax of not less than five francs, or who [owned] land or securities of a specified value. Two additional votes . . . [were] given to such as . . . [were] presumed to have high educational qualifications. These [included] graduates of higher schools, members of the professional classes, and such as had held public office. Those who had more than one vote [in the period just before the law was changed] were 40 per cent of the total . . . and were entitled to cast 62 per cent of all votes.

Prussia, until the reforms instituted as a result of World War I, had a system of voting which distributed political power in the state according to the amount of taxes paid. The very wealthy class, which was numerically but an insignificant minority of the population, had one-third of the representation. The larger taxpayers among the remaining population constituted another political class having one-third of the total representation. The third class, which included an overwhelming majority of the people and which with manhood suffrage would have elected practically all officials, was allowed to choose but one-third of the representatives. In this way, the public interest in state and local government was effectively subordinated to the interest of the wealthy classes.

Various devices were resorted to for the purpose of restricting still further the influence of the third class of voters. They voted less frequently than the other two classes; property qualifications were required for a certain proportion of their representatives; and the absence of the secret ballot made it possible for the small minority included in the first two classes to augment their own political predominance through economic pressure.

On account of the size of Prussia and its peculiar relation to the German Empire, the spirit and character of the Prussian state government largely determined that of the Empire. Imperial elections, at which were chosen the members of the lower house of the Parliament of the Empire, were conducted on the basis of manhood suffrage and the secret ballot. This afforded some opportunity, it is true, for the expression of national public opinion. But on account of the subordinate place of this body in the general scheme of government for the Empire, it lacked the positive power which would have made it an adequate organ of public opinion. Moreover, the Reichstag was not a body which really represented the public opinion of the Empire inasmuch as the conservative rural districts were grossly over-represented.

The German system of government as it existed until 1919, in so far as it was elective, may be described as avowedly plutocratic. It would be difficult to contrive a scheme of voting that would more effectively ensure the political supremacy of the wealthy class. But although there was no adequate popular check on the power of this class, the hereditary element was a restraining influence. Moreover, the very fact that the ascendancy of wealth in the elective part of the government was legalized and generally recognized had a moderating effect. A wealthy class thus clothed with political authority, and recognized by the public as morally accountable for the use made of its privilege, is less of a menace than it would be if its control were less directly and obviously exercised and if in consequence it were less influenced by a sense of responsibility.

The suffrage may mean much or little. Its significance depends partly on the form of government and partly on the intelligence of the citizens. It may give to the people the appearance without much of the substance of political power. Where the state is of the check and balance type, the voters have less influence than under a governmental system in which the directly elected branch is supreme. Democracy, even in the negative sense of the term, would allow the people to exercise, either directly or through representatives chosen by them, a veto on all acts and policies of the government.

A government may, however, be thoroughly democratic in form without being democratic in its practical operation. According to the democratic theory of the state, public opinion should be a controlling influence. But the state as we think it ought to be is an altogether different thing from the state as it actually is. We have not yet reached the stage in political development where the people generally have sufficient civic intelligence to enable them to play the important and responsible part which is assigned to them in the theory of democracy. The extension of the suffrage to the masses does not mean effective popular control, even where the entire structure of the state has been democratized, unless the people have acquired an active and intelligent interest in the political and economic problems with which the government has to deal.

The idea that public opinion should be a determining political force is in fact a very recent development. Even in the Declaration of Independence, which formulated the most advanced political thought of the time, there is little to indicate that the people were expected to have more than a passive part in public affairs. Democracy in the active sense of the term is, even in this twentieth century, scarcely more than an ideal.

The growth of popular government by transforming subjects into citizens is supposed to have changed fundamentally their relation to the state. But this transition from subject to citizen, from passive submission to active participation, calls for a more radical change in the political outlook of the average individual than it is possible to bring about in a comparatively short period of time. Many of those upon whom the modern democratic movement has attempted to confer political power have not been able to adapt themselves readily and promptly to changes in political institutions which require them to abandon the ideas and habits that have become more or less fixed through centuries of experience. Consequently, a new system of government is always more like the old one in its actual operation and in its spirit and results than the differences in form would indicate.

The mere fact that a man votes does not prove that he is a good or useful citizen; his duty to the state is discharged only by voting wisely and with due regard to the larger social interests, to which his interests as an individual may at times be somewhat opposed. This ideal is impossible of realization, however, no matter what the form of government may be, unless the people have political convictions that are the result of civic intelligence. An unintelligent vote will always be a menace to popular government in that it tends to perpetuate, under the forms of democracy, all the evils which prevailed under the old political system of class rule with its restricted suffrage and its subordination of the general interests of society to the interests of the ruling few. The vote of the unintelligent citizen is likely to be counted against, rather than for, democracy.

Unless one can vote intelligently, it is his duty to leave the determination of public policies to such as measure up to the standard of civic intelligence which democracy has a right to expect of its citizens. It is not the number of votes cast but their quality that determines the success of democratic government. If a man lacks sufficient interest in public questions to vote when important matters are up for actual determination, it is obvious that he does not feel keenly enough his responsibility for the outcome to make his participation desirable from the viewpoint of the public interest. The citizen who understands what citizenship means in a democracy, who knows the extent to which individual success and well-being depend upon wise laws well administered, will no more think of ignoring his civic obligations than of neglecting his private business. No artificial devices are needed to ensure a full vote on the part of such as are fittest to share in democratic government.

There are some who believe that voting should be made compulsory. But this is, to say the least, a debatable question, whether we believe in a restricted or a widely extended suffrage. If we favor restricting the right to vote, our object is the exclusion of the unfit. But while no standard of fitness that could be adopted would exclude all of the unfit, they largely disfranchise themselves where voting is not compulsory. The view that suffrage is a right which may justly be claimed by every normal adult citizen furnishes as little justification for the policy of compulsion as does the theory that voting is a privilege. Compulsion is not needed for those who have an active interest in the outcome of the election, nor is the welfare of the state likely to be advanced by the votes of those whose chief motive in appearing at the polls is the desire to escape a legally imposed penalty.

Compulsory voting is not a recent innovation, nor should it be regarded as essentially democratic either in origin or purpose. It existed in some of the American colonies before the Revolution, along with a greatly restricted suffrage. Virginia had compulsory voting throughout the colonial period; Maryland had it in the beginning and revived it in 1715; Delaware also had compulsory voting. The constitution of Georgia (1777) imposed a penalty of not more than five pounds for failure to vote without reasonable excuse. Under the Belgian Constitution of 1893, compulsory voting is combined with a form of plural suffrage, while in some of the Swiss cantons it exists in connection with manhood suffrage.

Compulsory voting is an attempt to transform, through the imposition of penalties, the passive element of the citizenry into an active element. A policy of this sort fails to recognize the fact that there is no satisfactory substitute for an alert civic interest on the part of those who vote. It would be far better for the state if those who are not keenly alive to their civic responsibilities would stay away from the polls, than that they should vote under any form of compulsion. Indeed, democracy has far more to fear from, than to gain by, a vote cast for the purpose of securing some immediate personal advantage or avoiding some personal penalty. A vote cast under any form of compulsion, whether that compulsion comes from the state itself or from some powerful private interest, is a vote not for, but against, democracy. A free ballot is the foundation of free government, and means the right to vote without being influenced by any form of coercion, either political or economic. The chief danger to democracy lies not so much in its large non-voting citizenry as in the large proportion of actual voters who do not have sufficient information concerning the questions presented to enable them to vote wisely, or who, through pressure of some private or partisan interest, cast votes which do not represent their independent political choice. How to safeguard the ballot so as to ensure intelligent and independent voting is a problem for which democracy must find a solution.

It is no doubt highly desirable that all normal adult citizens should have the right to vote. Democracy in the true sense of the term can not exist where any considerable part of the population is outside the pale of political rights. Equality of opportunity is a principle which must be recognized in the organization of the state, or democracy will exist only in name. The right to vote and, through the vote, to share in determining the policy of the state is the indispensable guaranty of equality of economic opportunity, which it is the duty of every free government to establish and maintain.

The right to vote, properly viewed, is an opportunity extended by the state to the citizen, and he should be free to take advantage of it or ignore it. Sound public policy points not in the direction of compelling citizens to vote, but rather in the direction of making the exercise of this right purely voluntary by removing every influence which now militates against free choice. We can readily see that a man who must be paid to go to the polls is not likely to advance the welfare of the community when he votes; nor is that man actuated by a much higher motive, whose main interest in politics depends upon some concession, favor, or office at the hands of the party to which he is giving his support.

We should discourage by legislation when possible, and by every other practicable means, all efforts to influence the outcome of elections by bringing to bear upon the individual voter either the threat of individual punishment or the promise of individual reward. To allow intimidation or coercion, direct or indirect, or the promise of some personal favor or advantage, to be a factor in determining whether or not votes are cast and how they are cast, is to place such votes at the disposal of those interests against which it behooves democracy to be on its guard.

We should not be oblivious of the fact that the right to vote is of value to citizens only to the extent that it gives them the power to control the government. If the constitutional system be such as to tie the hands of the majority, as is the case in this country, the natural and inevitable result is, by limiting the influence of the vote, to discourage political activity on the part of citizens. An election must be the means of determining legislation, or intelligent citizens are likely to feel that suffrage is the empty form of a political right without its substance. A system of government which makes it possible for a small minority to prevent the enactment and enforcement of laws which a large majority may have endorsed at the polls naturally operates to discourage political interest and activity on the part of citizens.

No. 30

A DEFENSE OF THE NON-VOTER [1]

by Clyde Eagleton

MANY attacks are being directed nowadays against the American voter—a most reprehensible person, if one believes these critics, whose negligence is plunging democracy to ruin. At Albany a bill has been introduced imposing a fine upon all non-voters. The revered Elihu Root, the Vice-President of the United States, and others have emphasized the citizen's duty at the polls. And Mr. James Beck has gone so far as to compare the non-voter to the traitorous Man Without a Country, who damned his own fatherland.

Certainly statistics are sufficiently impressive to cause some reflection. It has been pointed out that in the last fifty years the percentage of the American electorate actually voting has diminished from 80 to 50; and it

[1] Clyde Eagleton, "A Defense of the Non-Voter," *The South Atlantic Quarterly* (October, 1928), Vol. XXVII, No. 4, pp. 341-354. Reprinted by permission of *The South Atlantic Quarterly.*

fell to 38 in the elections of 1922. At the same time, in England to-day [1928], the voting percentage is 80, in Germany, 89, and in France around 70. [More recent figures would vary somewhat from those cited, but the general point that is made would still be valid.] We rank, in this percentage, along with the illiterate Caribbean states. And when to this statement is added the significant claim of the ward boss, that he can count upon 85% of those who do vote to cast their votes as the party organization directs, it is a fair conclusion that the American voter is displaying but little of that intelligent judgment to be exercised at the polling-place upon which democracy is said to be founded. This, of course, is contrary to present democratic principles, as taught in citizenship courses and expounded from the Chautauqua platform. Unless each citizen thinks out for himself all the problems of government, and contributes his voice to the majority which instructs the legislators as to the best solution of these problems, the democratic system of which he is the foundation, cannot function properly. . . .

But is this, after all, true? or rather, is it possible? Would it serve any good purpose to compel the citizen to vote? It would be confusion worse confounded. It is an utterly hopeless waste of time for the average citizen to attempt to form an individual judgment upon the various questions which confront him; and if, by superhuman efforts, he does succeed in giving answers to them all, his vote, under the present system, is of little or no avail in determining what the action of the government will be upon those issues. If his opinion counts at all, it will probably be because he has expressed it in some manner other than voting.

Why, then, should he vote?

It must be recalled that life, and therefore government, is not nearly so simple a matter as it was in the days when our forefathers, freed from a monarchical form of government, made their proud way to the voting places, there to lay the foundations for the greatest democracy in history. The needs of government were few, so that the Supreme Court could run for several years with no cases upon its docket, and newspapers could print the oratorical efforts upon the floor of Congress and feel confident that they had reported the full legislative activity of the nation. But now the Supreme Court is several years behind in its efforts to hold the various parts of the governmental machinery within their constitutional boundaries, and to give constitutional protection to the individual; while the newspapers, despairing of discovering, much less of reporting, the obscure and multifold activities of Congress, content themselves with the conjectures of expert writers as to what is actually happening, or perhaps supply for our occasional delectation an especially luscious bit of governmental scandal. And in the meantime, department after department and bureau after bureau has been created, to care for interests the most of which the makers of the Constitution never heard of; and statutes pour from the legislative mills in such unceasing flood that it becomes no more than a vain hope for the citizen to know the laws under which he lives. He can only flounder about helplessly, wondering whether the Board of Estimate or the Transit Commission should be blamed for the subway *impasse*, or whether the exclusion of certain aliens as undesirable really represents the will of the people. And even more despairingly, he wonders what he could do about it if he did know!

It all results inevitably from the complexity and the interdependence of a social and economic system developed within the last century—that is to say, since the Constitution was made. The citizen who favored the ratification of the Constitution had no idea of the burden which was ultimately imposed upon his great-grandchildren. His life was simple, and government played but a small part in it. If he needed milk for his baby, he had not to concern himself with the establishment of an Interstate Commerce Commission, which would insure its safe delivery, nor with a national or state or local health bureau which would guarantee it to be Grade A when delivered. He could go out into his back yard and extract it for himself, or run over to his neighbor and purchase a pail-full. If he attempted such courses to-day, he might be subject to a penalty for maintaining a cow upon his premises, or his neighbor might be arrested for selling milk without a license. And he has about as little chance of supplying himself with other needed articles. The very glass of water which he draws from his faucet represents, perhaps, hundreds of millions of dollars, a governmental bureau, and a large technical staff for maintenance. He must to-day depend upon persons not only in his immediate vicinity, but throughout the nation and the world, to supply him with his everyday needs; and to protect him, the government has been forced to intervene more and more, to create vast organizations, to employ specialists to solve the problems therein arising, and to engage in international agreements and enterprises.

It has been said that the discovery of the germ revolutionized the science of government; and if this statement bears the distinguishing features of hyperbole, it is nevertheless true that the discovery of how one's own health might be affected by the personal hygiene of one's neighbor constituted a powerful wedge through whose use the government has been able to force its way into the domain of personal liberty, and has come to regulate the most intimate details of one's private life. Social measures of a thousand kinds have followed, until now one can not build a house or a factory, or carry on any sort of an undertaking, or even cross the street, without coming into contact with some department of governmental activities. Not even the inalienable right of the American citizen to expectorate where he pleases has been left to him! The average citizen does not pause to think of the source of any of the articles which he uses daily, much less of the governmental agencies which have made their use possible; yet he is expected to vote upon the intricate problems arising out of this complexity of life. It is a fascinating study, this great Juggernaut of modern civilization; but our question here is, Where does it leave the voter?

In the first place, there is far too great a number of, and an ever-increasing difficulty in mastering, the matters upon which the citizen must inform himself, if he is to perform the duties of his office with conscientious intelligence. The mere number of problems upon which he is supposed to reach a decision is appalling. In national affairs he can vote only for President, Vice-President and Congressmen; but in order to do this intelligently, under the American theory of representation, he must study questions involving almost every conceivable subject of human endeavor. For the Congressman, under this theory, is no more than a messenger-boy. He must vote, upon each bill as it comes up, as his constituency directs—which, of course, implies an ability upon the part of his constituency to direct him, and machinery for the expression of their desires. But in each term of Congress something like twenty-five thousand bills are introduced. It is worse in state government. In the last legislative year [1927], thirteen thousand statutes were actually passed and inscribed upon the books of the states; and this does not take into account those which were proposed—over three thousand in New York alone. Upon each of these the voter is—in theory, at least!—presumed to have instructed his legislators. Certainly he should have voted directly upon constitutional (state) amendments; and the increasing distrust of legislatures has led to hypertrophied constitutions full of details which the citizens dare not trust to their representatives. The constitution of Oklahoma contains over fifty thousand words, a fair-sized book, whereas the national Constitution requires only eighteen pages. So weary have voters become of this load that states have adopted special devices to compel their attention to constitutional amendments; but when one state forbade the proposal of new amendments until a certain percentage of votes should have been cast upon pending amendments, it was some fifty years before any change in the constitution of that state could be had!

Aside from the mere overwhelming number of matters upon which the voter must decide, the problems have themselves become so technical that only a trained specialist is competent, in each case, to render a fair decision. The average citizen must know economics, and decide what is the best fate for Muscle Shoals [now a part of the TVA], and whether a protective tariff on cotton is desirable; he must be acquainted with high finance, and instruct his representative upon the income tax; he must estimate the possibility of maintaining a five-cent subway fare, and calculate the roads upon which county bonds may most profitably be expended; he must understand the intricacies of international relationships, and determine whether to spend the national money upon submarines or warships or aeroplanes, or upon a World Court and a League of Nations. He should be able to pass judgment upon such abstractions as the doctrine of sovereignty, theories of socialism as against individualism, or federalism against states' rights; upon the more concrete questions of immigration, labor, farm relief, and an interminable list of others, upon any one of which a political scientist would habitually spend a lifetime of study. Yet to the illiterate Italian laborer of the East, or to the irresponsible Negro of the South, is entrusted the determination of problems which call for the best of technical training. What can they know—what, for that matter, does the average intelligent voter know?—of cycles of prosperity, or the causes of panics? Nothing, one may be sure; but if times are prosperous they vote confidently for the return of the current administration; and if money is scarce, they vote as confidently for the opposite party!

The burden of the voter is more directly in evidence in the number of persons for whom he must vote. Ballots sometimes contain several hundred names, in addition to constitutional amendments. It is manifestly impossible for the voter to become acquainted with more than a very few of those for whom he votes. And how, for that matter, is he to know who is properly equipped to become an efficient State Superintendent of Education, or a good County Judge? The greatest absurdity in American government to-day is the popular conviction that capable and responsible officials are to be obtained only through the elective process. There is no Republican or Democratic criterion for passing upon the qualifications of a tax collector; and yet most officials are chosen upon a party basis. A voter would probably consider himself incompetent to pass upon the qualifications of an electrical engineer for any ordinary purpose; yet Steinmetz, the electrical wizard, was defeated for the office of State Engineer in New York because of his Socialist tendencies! It is as absurd to think of the voter as capable of judging whether a man has the technical training necessary for a Supreme Court Judge, or to handle the records in a County Clerk's office.

If it be argued that the people have an innate ability to judge of the honesty and character of a candidate, it still remains to be discovered how they are to become sufficiently acquainted with the personal characteristics of the hundreds of persons whose names appear upon the ballots. What opportunity have they for reaching a fair and unbiased opinion, either upon candidates or upon issues? Without taking into account that we have not in this country learned to administer government upon a basis of efficiency apart from sentiment and passion and prejudice, it would be difficult for the most cool and detached intellect to make a fair judgment upon the basis of the information put before the voter. Certainly the material supplied by his party, or by propagandist institutions concerned with the questions, will not be unbiased; and he can hope for little better from his newspapers. If they do not frankly represent a party, they at least have their own well-fixed viewpoints. The paraphernalia or research is manifestly useless to the voter.

The question can not be resolved by deciding to vote exclusively for men or exclusively for measures: there are too many of either, and they are too far distant from the voter. It is quite impossible in most elections for the conscientious voter to go home from the polls, after having surveyed the long list of names before him, with his conscience clear in the belief that he has voted intelligently for every office. He is forced either to vote the straight party ticket, or else to leave many names unmarked. And if this be true, of what possible value could it be to compel him to vote, or even to place the names before him? He is expected to vote for a candidate not only upon the basis of acquaintance with his personal worth, but also on the expectation that when elected the candidate will represent his views. What possible views can he have as to how the books in the County Treasurer's office should be kept? Just how he is to instruct his representative upon problems which arise after election day, is not clear; but it is sufficiently clear that the average voter is not prepared to give instructions as to the best means of raising the national revenue, or of solving the coal-mining problem, or of supplying adequate transportation facilities in New York City. Perhaps it is his duty, as a patriotic citizen, to puzzle all such things out carefully; but if you tell him so, he will reply that he has a living to make. It is well enough to say that the success of democracy depends upon an educated electorate; but what is asked of the modern voter, absorbed as he is in the intricate struggle for existence—which must come first—is a physical and a mental impossibility.

But grant that the citizen is able to reach an intelligent decision, through some inconceivable educative process, and succeeds in conveying his will to his agent through his vote or in some other manner—of what use is it for him to do so in our present system? Democracy, if it means anything at all, means the control of government by the people; and yet there is no means provided in the American machinery of government by which the people can express their wishes upon any one given national issue. The

British have, even if they rarely use it, the opportunity of a general election upon a dissolution to ascertain exactly what the people wish on the point under debate; and other states use the referendum, or other devices. But we have no such opportunity—nothing except the national elections, in which issues are so jumbled together that it is impossible to say what the vote means when applied to any one question. Consider, for example, the famous election of 1920. Anti-Wilson, anti-Lodge, anti-League, anti-prohibition, anti-woman suffrage, and a thousand other negative impulses were thrown together into an utterly inextricable tangle. To say that a Presidential election means a popular majority upon any one issue, is mechanically impossible. Not even a constitutional (national) amendment is submitted to the people, but to state legislatures whose members are elected upon quite irrelevant pledges. [Only one national constitutional amendment, the 21st, has been submitted to state-ratifying conventions.]

Nor is there adequate machinery through which the citizen may instruct his representative after he has taken up his office. The latter is at a loss, for he may not be able to discover until the next election day, and then too late, what his constituency desired. It is not sufficient to do as one Senator admitted doing—to pile up letters and telegrams for one side in one pile, and for the other side in another pile, and then vote for the tallest heap. Only those who have a special interest at heart, or propagandist organizations formed to overcome the inertia of the average voter, will make such an effort. The great majority of the people may be opposed, and awake to express their opposition too late.

And even if the President (or other official) should be able to detect a clear mandate for a certain policy, there can be no assurance, with our present intricate distribution of governmental powers, that the policy indicated could be put into effect, granted the best of intention upon his part. In . . . [a recent textbook] upon American Government, Maxey remarks:

> The fact of the matter is that the American system is one of the most intricate and complex on earth; and it therefore requires a great deal more information and a great deal more mental effort to understand our system of government than almost any other. Compared to the intricate and highly involved scheme which we have in this country, the governments of such countries as Great Britain, France and Italy are simplicity exemplified.

The federal distribution of powers, and the principles of separation of powers, checks and balances, and judicial interpretation, provide ample opportunity for friction and deadlock; and in the process the voter loses track. The result is that if the will of the voter, initiated as a bill in Congress, successfully passes through the labyrinth of committees, bicameral action, and archaic rules of Senatorial procedure, and does not come out a monstrous malformation of amendments and reservations, it may still be killed by the President's veto, or by the decision of the Supreme Court. Even if the voter does not succeed in putting into Congress a majority of opposite party to the President, with a resultant deadlock, there can be no certainty that the two will work together. . . . [Presidents Coolidge, Hoover, Roosevelt, and Truman have had difficulties securing passage of their programs, even with Congresses controlled by their own party.] If the party, imposing a collective responsibility, is to be the answer to our problem, it must surely devise more effective machinery for harmonious action than this; and even more surely it must be brought under responsive control.

Why should one vote? The only reward for an honest attempt to vote intelligently is a vista of increasing trouble in the future, as the range of government widens; and there can be no assurance, as we are now organized, that the vote will be effective in the actual operation of the government.

This does not necessarily mean that democracy, as a theory of government, is a failure, as is so frequently being said to-day; but merely that the methods of American democracy are inadequate to meet modern conditions. The fact must be recognized that many people do not vote; and the fact may as well be recognized also that there is ample justification for their failure to vote. Even those who do vote are unable to do so intelligently; and this is true of the best educated as well as the most illiterate. Pure democracy was long ago admitted to be impossible with the huge populations of our day; but representative democracy will prove equally as unworkable so long as it is taken to mean that voters must form and express opinions for the guidance of their representatives upon all matters now thrust upon them. The very existence of the principle of representation implies a devolution of authority from the people to their representatives. Our problem is in large part the degree of devolution which the people should admit.

The answer is not to be found in coercive voting, nor in educating the people. The burden would be too great, under present conditions. We live in an age of increasing social and economic interdependence, in which the problems of government are more and more technical in character. They cannot be settled by the expressed whims of the people; they must be adjusted according to the laws of nature, interpreted and applied by experts. Many years ago Carlyle wrote:

Your ship cannot double Cape Horn by its excellent plans of voting. The ship may vote this and that, above decks and below, in the most harmonious exquisitely constitutional manner: the ship, to get around Cape Horn, will find a set of conditions already voted for, and fixed with adamantine rigor by the ancient Elemental Powers, who are entirely careless how you vote. If you can, by voting or without voting, ascertain those conditions, and valiantly conform to them, you will get round the Cape; if you cannot, the ruffian Winds will blow you ever back again.

So long as technical problems are left to be solved by the voter, he must, if he is bound by any sense of patriotic duty, stagger along under an ever-growing political burden, overwhelmed as he may be by his economic situation. We struggle to equip the voter with the requisite education for the performance of these duties; but as fast as we do, so fast is he loaded with new burdens. It is a hopeless race, a veritable Tantalus-task, in which the voter must always drag behind with lolling tongue.

What, one may ask, is the purpose of the elective process? Why should a person desire to vote? Apparently, there are two objects in view: to choose men for office in whom you have confidence, and who will, you believe, represent your own views in office; and to hold them responsible by failing to elect them again, if they have not proven satisfactory in office. Both rest upon the conviction that the people are capable of choosing capable men for office, and of holding them responsible for properly supporting the views of the voter. This conviction, under present day circumstances, is a fallacy. The number of men and of issues has increased to such a degree that the voter can no longer keep track of them; and the organization of the government has become so complex that it is impossible to allocate responsibility. The President blames it on Congress; the Senate blames the House; the Congressmen pass responsibility to the Committee, and the Committee to the sub-committee. The elective process, as now employed, has become unworkable. Nevertheless, it can not be discarded, if the people are to retain control.

The first need of the people is a shorter ballot; and this means, of course, far more than a reduced printing bill. It signifies a revised theory of representation on the part of the American people, who at present distrust their representatives and are convinced that the voter must himself oversee all the activities of the government. But this is no longer possible; and it is clear now that he must delegate some of his powers. Nine-tenths of the offices for which he now votes could be profitably removed from his control. By far the greater number of these are petty administrative or judicial offices upon which he is not competent to make a decision, and which could be more efficiently filled by appointment upon merit, through civil service machinery or in other non-partisan manner. If he fears this as risky, he may be reminded of the . . . [several] million now appointed, rather than elected, in the Federal Government, which is conceded to be more efficient than any other part of the American system. At any rate, the process of appointment could scarcely be more disappointing in its results than the present process of election; and the voter at least would be relieved.

We have not yet learned to distinguish between politics and administration. Legislative and constitutional action should be concerned only with the formulation of general principles of public policy in accordance with the will of the people, leaving methods to be worked out by trained men, independent of party machinations; and this is the more needed to-day when governmental action has become so specialized in nature that only experts can handle a great part of it. As it is now, legislatures and constitutions are so overburdened with useless trivialities and complexities of procedure that important measures are passed by for lack of time. It is within the competence of the voter, for example, to determine whether as a matter of policy a five-cent subway fare should be maintained, even if from the city treasury; but he is not capable of knowing whether the subways may be properly operated for a nickel fare, or of knowing what is the best method of organizing and laying out the transportation routes. The election of judges, who should be experts rather than demagogues, and the tying of their hands by legislative rules for judicial procedure, has made our judicial administration a laughing stock.

The reduction of the number of elective offices to those of a policy-determining nature—say, the legislative body and the chief executive in each governmental unit—would not only relieve the voter of a great many decisions which he is incompetent to make, but would educate him, and would lead automatically to further improvements in government. One of the chief defects in the American governmental system is its inability to attract the highest type of man into its service. At present, the tenure in office is too uncertain, dependent not upon merit but upon a demagogic ability to please a necessarily ignorant and uninterested constituency. A capable man can not therefore afford to choose government service as a career. If elective positions were made fewer, their attraction and prestige would be greater in various ways. Officials hitherto dependent only upon the will of the people would now be made responsible to the fewer elected officials. The result would be not only increased power for the latter, but less friction, a more centralized and efficient administration, and a better opportunity for them to work out their plans. Abler men would therefore be attracted to these offices, not only for the above reasons, but also because the electorate, having fewer offices to study, could take a greater and more intelligent interest in them.

This means, of course, the concentration of greater power in the hands of fewer men, and raises the question of securing responsibility. It is a question that needs to be raised, for it reveals the defect in our system which is in greatest need of correction. Responsibility, the most essential element in democratic government, is at present impossible to locate. It is scattered out between the States and the Nation, between the President, the Courts and Congress; it is hidden away in caucuses and committee rooms and floor leaders; it can be traced down to political parties and ward bosses and lobbyists. And if the responsible person could be found, there would be no means of dealing with him, except through the failing system of perennial elections, or the awkward and practically useless weapon of impeachment. Except in appointive offices, nothing can be done to remedy mere inefficiency in office, or to prevent discretionary action contrary to public will. The American people have recognized this, and have attempted to correct it by a wider extension of the direct control exercised by the electorate; but in so doing they have overburdened themselves. To-day, much greater efficiency and more responsibility is to be found in appointive than in elective offices. Instead of many offices separately responsible to the people, who would need to be Argus-eyed to watch over them all, it would be much simpler to have, as is done by the Federal Government, only two or three elected officials, with all administrative officials below answerable to them.

No business corporation—and the American Government should be regarded as one of the greatest upon earth—could live if organized in such haphazard fashion. The mighty motive power of public opinion which is supposed to run the government is dissipated to the four winds. But the prodigality of frontier days, when abundant resources were available and energy could be wasted, is no longer possible. Business organization points the way, and government becomes more and more a matter of business. The tendency everywhere is toward the concentration of power with corresponding responsibility. It is inevitable in government, as the cries of administrative tyranny occasionally to be heard in our country testify. To concentrate political power in the hands of a few elected officials will concentrate the attention of the people upon these offices, and will interest them in the problem of securing responsibility. Advances in the science of government are most successfully made by slow evolution. *Solvitur ambulando.* Radical reorganization of the governmental system is impossible in the present state of public opinion, and in all probability would be dangerous. A few simple changes to relieve the present intolerable situation of the voter would be the best guarantee of advance in the proper direction.

Why prod the voter? If he were compelled to vote, the problem would not be solved—it would merely be intensified. What we need is to put his power to work in the machinery of government, instead of dissipating it uselessly, as we now do, in trivial and unimportant tasks.

No. 31

APATHY—OUR FIFTH COLUMN [1]

by John N. Dumas

LAST June the Schenectady (New York) *Gazette* departed from news-paper tradition and criticized its own readers. The paper had found in a comprehensive poll that almost half the city's voters knew exactly nothing about their government. One out of four was prejudiced to the extent that he distrusted all politicians without exception. Many could hardly cast an intelligent ballot on election day.

Schenectady's 100,000 people, however, were told by the newspaper that, if the same poll were taken in almost any other city in the country, the results would probably be the same.

Schenectady represents a good cross section of greater America. Parent plants of the General Electric Company and the American Locomotive Company give the city better than its share of college-trained scientists, technicians and business executives. Its ratio of college graduates to non-college graduates is the second highest in the country. Approximately 40 per cent of its working population are unskilled and semi-skilled laborers; 20 per cent are white-collar workers. It is a miniature Detroit or Pittsburgh.

Schenectady's political organizations are far from corrupt; its last real machine was cleaned out years ago. Its two newspapers—the morning *Gazette* and the evening *Union-Star*—both independently owned, have kept constant tabs on the administration. During election week last year the *Gazette,* in six days, published 276 column inches of news and editorials devoted strictly to local government and politics—fourteen newspaper columns, nearly two full newspaper pages. Both papers, by and large inde-pendent in policy as well as ownership, average about eight columns of civic news each week.

On the surface Schenectady is far from lacking in civic consciousness. Last spring more than 210 organizations joined to accomplish a host of public improvements within a ten-year span. Their aim: to make Sche-nectady the "Town of Tomorrow."

But, as municipal affairs reporter for the *Gazette,* I saw the empty cham-bers in city hall when the city council held its bi-monthly meetings. I watched councilmen, under relentless pressure from minority groups, con-

[1] John N. Dumas, "Apathy—Our Fifth Column," *National Municipal Review* (October, 1947), Vol. XXXVI, No. 9, pp. 494-496, 502. Reprinted by permission of the *National Municipal Review.*

scientiously try to sound out public opinion without success. I boiled over when supposedly intelligent friends asked me what the "dirty politicians" in city hall were up to.

What was beneath the surface? What did the average man-on-the-street know about his local government—cornerstone of our democratic system? How many looked upon all public office holders as "dirty politicians"? Of those who voted, how many knew whom they were voting for?

A city-wide poll would give us a fairly reliable insight.

Preparation for the poll spanned a two-months period. In presuming to estimate public knowledge and opinion, a newspaper assumes great responsibility. Statistics were compiled showing existing occupational ratios in the city. On the basis of this persons to be polled were selected. They made up a cross section of the city and, I believe, a reasonable cross section of all American industrial centers where the great mass of the population is concentrated.

POLL REVEALS IGNORANCE

This is what the poll revealed:

One out of two did not know the name of the city manager—the chief administrative executive who is mentioned on front pages five days out of six.

One out of two could not identify his representative in Congress—although this man ran for reelection only eight months prior to the poll.

One out of two could not identify the legislative body that makes the laws for the city—yet virtually every city council meeting gets front page coverage.

Six out of ten would not want their sons to enter politics—a deplorable condition considering that more than ever before our government needs capable leaders.

One out of four thought it impossible for a man to enter politics and remain honest—even though it was explained that "honest" was being used in its broad sense as a synonym for integrity.

Thus we have a grim paradox: While we are loudly denouncing all the "isms," willing to defend our system with life and blood, a great many of us know nothing about our government and distrust those who set its policies.

To get at the basic causes for such apathy and misinformation—to make a start at eliminating them—is a huge task. But it must be undertaken. Otherwise there can be no real assurance that America will succeed in setting an example which the rest of the world will want to follow. Such a condition is, indeed, a real threat to our own democracy.

Without question some of the blame must fall upon our educational system. Perhaps our educators are putting the cart before the horse—dwelling on international affairs at the sacrifice of preparing tomorrow's voters for an active role in cleaning up their own backyards.

A portion of the blame must also rest upon the nation's press for neglecting to hammer home the necessity of citizen participation in politics and government under the democratic system.

The Schenectady *Gazette* to-day is pursuing a consistent, nonpartisan policy of public education aimed at ultimately attracting more voters—and better informed voters—to the polls.

How influential can one newspaper be in a direct effort to foster greater citizen cooperation in community affairs?

In so far as Schenectady is concerned, it is too early to estimate what effect the *Gazette's* consistent hammering will have. There have been some signs, however, which seem to indicate one important fact—the apathy is deeper, and will be harder to dispel, than many of us heretofore suspected.

On July 11, following a month of intense public service promotion aggregating more than 500 column inches, the *Gazette* and WGY, one of the biggest radio stations in the country, sponsored a "Civic Forum of the Air." The broadcast, originating from Union College and open to the public, was attended by barely 150 persons. And this despite the fact that 200 cards had been sent to the leaders of local civic groups while others were reached by telephone.

LITTLE INTEREST IN FORUM

Attendance was encouraged by the announcement of an open forum following the broadcast. The program had much to offer any truly civic-minded individual. Its speakers were Hon. Oswald D. Heck, speaker of the New York State Assembly and a possible candidate for governor in 1950; Chester H. Lang, General Electric Company vice-president and civic leader; Dr. Benjamin P. Whitaker, Union College economics professor and former budget officer for the state of Connecticut; and Anthony Barbieri, president of Local 2054, United Steelworkers of America.

The panelists agreed and emphasized during the broadcast that participation of local civic groups is essential. These groups were urged to devise their own programs to help reeducate the community to the benefits of an alert citizenry.

At this writing not a single civic organization has responded.

A few weeks after the *Gazette* poll was publicized, the newspaper began a heavily-promoted "Forum in Print"—an idea borrowed from the Yonkers *Herald Statesman.* Readers' views were sought on vital civic questions and it was intended as a means of tapping public opinion for the guidance of the city's lawmakers.

In view of the rising cost of government and the probability of a stiff increase in the city tax rate, the paper, at two-weeks intervals, asked: "Should the city discontinue cellar-to-curb waste collections?" and "Should a schoolboy patrol system be started to replace full-time patrolmen now at school crossings?" Because the board of education had been the object of much criticism, the paper asked, "Should the board of education be elected by the people, or should the mayor continue to appoint board members?"

All of these were vital questions, intimately affecting almost every taxpayer, but . . . "Forum in Print" died a lingering death because so few letters were received that the paper could not feasibly continue the feature.

During the week preceding primary day, July 29, the *Gazette* published a series of four articles entitled "The Truth About Our Primary Elections." The whole sorry story of the impregnability of a strong machine and its hand-picked candidates—able to remain in power only because the average voter ignores primaries—was laid before the community.

But on primary day, as in years past, less than 20 per cent of the eligible voters went to the polls. The articles apparently had little or no effect.

Working on public officials through its news and editorial columns, however, the *Gazette* did make progress toward better government this year. It criticized a police court system under which persons arrested for speeding were allowed to forfeit bail and escape having a conviction recorded on their licenses. Although it was a system of twenty years' standing, it has been changed. The paper criticized the city planning commission for its closed meetings during a six-months period, and the meetings were thrown open to the press only recently.

This is not to say that the newspaper should not continue acting as watchdog. But it is true that the results are partly nullified when an apathetic citizenry fails to maintain a companion vigilance.

This demonstration of civic apathy in one community, despite an all-out effort to reverse the trend, seems to indicate that there are deep roots to uncover. What has happened and is happening in Schenectady should serve as both a danger signal and a challenge to the rest of the country.

Chapter X

PUBLIC OPINION, PROPAGANDA, AND DEMOCRACY

[THE opinions people have, the beliefs they hold, the ideals they cherish have a real influence on government and public policy. As a consequence, those who wish to control that government or shape that policy seek to mold the opinions, beliefs and ideals of people.

In a modern dictatorship like the Soviet Union those who rule think this so important that they control and use the schools, the radio, the theatre, the arts, the press as instruments for maintaining power. In the United States no such monopoly exists; many people, many groups are seeking to create opinions, beliefs, ideals that will coincide with their own.

The student of government and those who believe in and want to extend the democratic system, therefore, must analyze and understand public opinion and propaganda. The enemies of democracy seek such understanding as an instrument of power; the democrat must seek it, too, as an instrument for strengthening democratic institutions and processes. Not praise or blame but knowledge and understanding are the effective weapons of a democratic people.]

No. 32

THE NATURE OF PUBLIC OPINION [1]

by Leonard W. Doob

THE Congress of the United States is discussing a bill involving a domestic problem. The debate inside and outside of the capitol building is prolonged and furious. Editorial writers, columnists, radio commentators, and cracker-barrel philosophers are stating their points of view. But, the question is asked, what do the American people think? How is "public opinion" really reacting?

From September 1, 1939, until December 7, 1941, almost every American was wondering whether or not the United States would enter the war. There

---

[1] Leonard W. Doob, *Public Opinion and Propaganda* (New York: Henry Holt and Company, 1948), pp. 33-43. Reprinted by permission of the publisher.

were some individuals and groups who believed that the conflict was no concern of ours and that therefore we should avoid becoming embroiled. There were others who felt that although Great Britain and then later the Soviet Union were fighting "our battle in defense of civilization," we should not actively participate but should help those countries defeat the Axis by becoming "the arsenal of democracy." And there were many who wanted this country to begin a shooting war immediately. Then the Japanese bombed Pearl Harbor. The next day war was declared on Japan and on December 11 the declaration by Germany and Italy was reciprocated. The American people, it was then felt, were no longer divided: "public opinion" was behind the war.

In a small American town in the Middle West the houses are made of wood. Architecturally they represent a variety of styles ranging from late nineteenth century to imitation classic and Cape Cod. On the whole people living there consider them neither outstandingly beautiful nor too depressingly ugly. The son of an old and wealthy resident comes home from an Eastern college, enters his father's business, marries a suitable girl, and begins building an ultra-modern dwelling for himself and his bride. At great expense rock is imported into the town and, as the construction progresses, it becomes evident that the house will have a completely flat roof. Most people in the community are outraged: they do not like the house and they say that it is ruining the beauty of the street on which it is being built. Feelings against the young man run high, there is talk of enacting some kind of zoning regulation which will prevent similar monstrosities in the future, and everyone says that "public opinion" is hostile toward the man and the architectural style he has selected.

A Negro is lynched in the Deep South. The members of the mob admit privately that he may not have been guilty but, they say, "public opinion" demanded that all Negroes be taught a lesson. Besides, a crime has been committed and the girl, before she died, stated that it was a Negro who attacked her. The governor of the state deplores the lynching and declares that "public opinion" is against this type of violence. Elsewhere editorial writers also point out that in general "public opinion" in the South is opposed to lynchings.

It is obviously unnecessary to belabor the point that the concept of public opinion is often employed. "Public opinion," it is stated variously, opposes or favors this or that, is expressed or repressed, is a source of wisdom or folly, or should or should not be heard. Perhaps the question may sound impudent, but it seems relevant to ask what the term means.

Like brushing one's teeth, the act of defining a word is both boring and essential. It is boring because it is more interesting and exciting to think and talk without stopping to decide on the meaning of words. Everybody knows what "water" is; why define the word? Everybody knows what "justice" and "truth" are; why—but is there really agreement on how such abstract words should be defined? Definitions are essential if communication is to be intelligible. Most people are aware of this. Modern semanticists consider themselves startlingly original when they repeat the truism in their own complicated terminology. But it remains pleasanter and easier simply to maintain that "justice is being upheld" or that "truth is being defended" than to indicate the precise meaning of such terms by means of less abstract words or specific illustrations.

Although most writers who use the term public opinion seldom indicate its referent and thus contribute to general confusion, it is possible to come up with numerous definitions by conducting a diligent search through various intellectual sources. Definitions begin with the simple word "people" and end with the semi-mystical idea of "a more or less rational collective judgment formed by the action and reaction of many individuals." No one can quarrel with a definition which is precise unless the question of its accepted usage is raised. "Public opinion," however, is such an ambiguous term that usage is no guide to clarity. Here is a definition that seeks to be precise and at least not sensationally different from the way in which the term is frequently employed: *public opinion refers to people's attitudes on an issue when they are members of the same social group.*

The key psychological word in this definition is that of "attitude." Before such a concept can carry the burden of the definition, it is necessary to recall from the previous chapter the characterization of an attitude as the socially significant, internal response that people habitually make to stimuli. Presumed, therefore, is a series of experiences which have produced within people more or less similar responses; various gradients of generalization and discrimination along which the evoking stimuli are arranged; and some connection with overt behavior. In this sense it might appear as though public opinion exists whenever people have attitudes. Most Americans, for example, drink coffee for breakfast and therefore may be presumed to have a favorable attitude toward this beverage; but should one say that American public opinion favors coffee?

According to common usage, it is fairly certain that this attitude would not be included in the category of public opinion. "American public opinion favors coffee"—no, it does not sound right. The definition of public opinion here proposed, moreover, also rules out the use of the expression to apply to coffee-drinking, *unless* an issue is at stake. An issue involves a controversy or conflict among people and therefore results in the interruption of a habit with consequent non-reduction of drives. If the price of coffee suddenly rises so high that it is beyond the budget of the average American family, then the attitude can no longer find its normal outlet in drinking the beverage but affects other behavior.   There are public demonstrations or there is petty grousing against the government, coffee merchants, or the capitalist system.   At this point public opinion regarding coffee arises.

In addition, the people who have attitudes more or less in common regarding an issue must be members of a social group before there is public opinion. Each group has a distinctive organization that regulates the behavior of its members. A crowd's organization is very simple: participants have face-to-face contact with one another and their behavior results from their pre-existing knowledge, attitudes, and drives as well as from mutual stimulation. Photographers scattered throughout the country belong to a social group, although they may not be members of a formal association: they are conscious of one another to a certain degree and they obviously share an interest in pictures.   Citizens of a country also are members of a social group, the nation, while simultaneously they belong to local groups as well as those also scattered throughout the land.

The social structure of a group, as Warner and Lunt have vividly demonstrated in the American society, assigns to each individual a status which in turn determines a large part but not all of his social behavior. The group, moreover, places at the disposal of its members certain media of communication through which public opinion can be expressed.   These media can be quite diverse.   Orally they range from the informal conversation of friends to the speaker whose voice is transmitted by a national hookup at one of the favorable evening hours. Visually they vary from a private letter received from a relative to a syndicated column reaching the more or less literate at their breakfast tables each day. They include the poorly focused snapshot in the family album as well as the most extravagant effusion from Hollywood.

The four illustrations given at the beginning of the chapter can now be critically examined in the light of this conceptualization of public opinion. Certain basic questions must be asked in connection with each:

1. *What group is involved?*   The reaction of "the American people" to a Congressional debate seems to include all citizens of the United States. But does it? Are the insane and children under six interested? Are non-voters?   In connection with the issue of American participation in the war before Pearl Harbor, it appears that many groups had varying viewpoints. What were these groups? Were they organized on a regional or an economic basis? It is said that "public opinion" looks with disfavor upon the young man who is building a modernistic home. Does this mean everyone in the community? "Most people," it is claimed, "are outraged"—well, who is not?

When the governor of the southern state claims that "public opinion" is opposed to lynching, is he referring to people like himself, to those with a college education, to poor whites, to Negroes? Certainly he cannot be thinking of the lynchers. Similarly, the mob is purported to claim that "public opinion" demands this form of pedagogy. Does the local minister advocate lynching? Do lawyers? Do Negroes? Who, moreover, opposes lynching in the South? Someone must, because editorial writers say they do. But who?

2. *What issue is involved?* The answer here seems easy at first glance: the bill being debated, America's participation in the war, the new style of house, and lynching. But are these the only issues? Maybe political or personal considerations enter into people's reactions to a Congressional debate. No doubt patriotism and social philosophy were involved before and after Pearl Harbor. Perhaps people are considering not only the man's new house but also his reputation in the community—could the "suitable girl" from the East or the "old and wealthy" family be the issue? It is conceivable that the issue for the governor of the state is not the lynching but the effect of the lynching on the state's ability to attract northern capital.

3. *Why have people responded to the issue?* Are people interested in the Congressional debate because the passage of the bill will affect their everyday lives or do they think that "matters of principle" are at stake? Why did isolationists who were opposed to American participation in the war suddenly become good soldiers or producers after Pearl Harbor? What happened to the isolationist attitudes? As a matter of fact, did all isolationists actually cooperate with the war effort? Why do people in a community worry about the appearance of houses when they are confronted with so many more pressing problems? For what reason do lynchers think that this kind of punishment will prevent Negroes from committing crimes in the future? Just who joins a lynching bee? Why do people in the South *and* the North take sides regarding lynching? This type of question could indeed be endless.

In fact, the series itself could be endless. It will be halted, however, at this point, though only three major questions have been asked. For these are the questions that are most relevant to the problem of understanding and analyzing public opinion. They are the questions which should be asked even before the term public opinion itself is employed.

A rough classification of public opinion is a first step in identifying some of the problems. Since there can be public opinion concerning any conceivable issue, the classification cannot be based upon the attitude content; instead the criteria must refer to the psychological and sociological significance of the attitude. The first type of classification distinguishes between public opinion that, at a given moment, is expressed and unexpressed. The second points out the difference between public opinion which is already functioning and that which conceivably may come into being.

The distinction between the attitudes people possess regarding a particular issue and the actual expression of these attitudes either as overt opinion or in overt behavior must be made in order to indicate the social role being played by public opinion in a particular situation. If those attitudes are not expressed, reference can be made to *internal public opinion*. If they are expressed and hence are the important but not the exclusive determinants of action, reference can be made to *external public opinion*. The conditions under which internal public opinion becomes externalized can usually be specified only in general terms. One important factor is the drive strength of the attitudes involved. When people are extremely enthusiastic or indignant, for example, it is difficult for them to conceal or repress their feelings; their overt behavior almost inevitably is affected by their attitude; and under these circumstances public opinion can be said to be externally effective. Another factor involves the rules of the social group to which the people belong. Under a modern dictatorship the secret police make it patently clear that certain types of expression are prohibited. As a result, individuals are afraid to express themselves in front of their neighbors or even in the presence of their own children, lest they be denounced to the authorities. Here public opinion remains internal and only those aspects are externalized which are countenanced by the regime. In contrast, the inhabitants of a rural area in the United States pride themselves on the freedom of expression which they consider a priceless privilege. Actually, their freedom is also restricted, not by the government but by the rules of their own group. An advocate of nudism, atheism, bolshevism, or any unpopular doctrine is not ferreted out by an official Gestapo, but he receives short shrift informally at the hands of his own contemporaries.

At other times, the expression of public opinion is limited by the available media of communication. One of the outstanding technological developments of the twentieth century has been the rapid growth of these media. Censorship permitting, most important events in the modern world can be described almost as they occur or—for those addicted to "dope" stories and for rumor-mongers—perhaps before they occur. Only the individual in our society who was disabled psychologically or the uncivilized man whose geographical isolation was left untouched by civilized warriors had not heard of Franklin D. Roosevelt or Adolf Hitler a few years ago. Under these conditions public opinion in theory has many more opportunities to express itself. In practice, however, it often happens that only a limited number of groups and of individuals within each group is able to employ these media.

When people react to an issue that has been presented to them, public opinion is either internal or external and it is also actual. *Actual public opinion,* consequently, indicates that attitudes have been aroused and that they are having some kind of effect upon internal or external behavior. Frequently, however, it is possible to anticipate public opinion before the issue arises, and so the term *latent public opinion* may be employed to refer to attitudes of people regarding an issue when those attitudes have not yet been crystallized or when they are not being evoked or are not affecting behavior. On the basis of their personality structure, it is likely either that potentially such attitudes can be learned and reinforced or that, being dormant at the moment, they can be aroused when and if the issue arises. During peace time public opinion about war tends to remain latent: the issue of fighting is not directly in front of people, although they continue to have attitudes which can be evoked by a conflict when it occurs and especially by the propaganda accompanying that conflict. Housewives have no specific attitude toward a new labor-saving gadget to be employed in their kitchens before that gadget is for sale and advertised. Potentially, however, they may be expected to express their approval, inasmuch as they are psychologically ready beforehand to learn to respond favorably: their desire to save labor and their readiness to accept gadgets are functioning attitudes which can be easily evoked.

Public opinion, however, should not be called latent unless certain attitudes which have not been previously learned or expressed are likely to be learned or expressed in connection with a future issue. It is perfectly true that potentially people can be made to approve or disapprove of any viewpoint or action, but there are also limits beyond which their behavior cannot be expected to range. Latent in the sense of potential should really mean probable or foreseeable. It is, for example, conceivable that Englishmen may some day change their form of government from a limited to an absolute monarchy. There is nothing in the English germ plasm, such a statement suggests, which precludes producing people on those blessed isles who could favor such a change. This state of affairs, however, is not likely to come to pass for a variety of reasons which either are obvious or else require a series of dull volumes to elucidate. English public opinion regarding an absolute monarchy, therefore, is both actually and latently unfavorable.

Another and final backward glance at the four illustrations in this chapter can reveal the applicability and utility of these distinctions:

1. *The Congressional Debate*

Public opinion of the American people on the question has not been ascertained. There is no way of knowing, therefore, whether that opinion is actual or latent. Since the debate is being reported in the mass media and since those media are perceived by people, there is presumptive evidence that public opinion has become actual. If the public opinion is actual, it certainly is internal rather than external; for the asking of the question—"How is 'public opinion' reacting?"—indicates that people's attitudes have not been expressed.

2. *Pearl Harbor*

Before the Japanese attack, the public opinion of various groups in this country was both actual and external. At the same time there was among the isolationists a latent public opinion, it must be assumed, which became actual after Pearl Harbor: almost all Americans are willing to immerse themselves in the war effort after war has been declared. The "my-country-right-or-wrong" element in the American tradition is then actual. Isolationist sentiment, however, did not die during the war: it remained either internal or potential and then tended to burst forth in a new form during the postwar period.

3. *The Modernistic Dwelling*

Those people in the community who previously have never seen an actual house with a flat roof were ready to be critical, although they themselves may not have been conscious of their attitude: their background and habits predisposed them in one way rather than another, and hence their public opinion could have been called latent. The inhabitants who disliked the young man or his family were internalizing their attitudes before the great crisis arose. Since some or many people are now enraged by the new dwelling, it may be said that public opinion has become actual and external.

4. *The Lynching*

People who approve or disapprove of lynching in the South represent actual public opinion: the issue of lynching tends to recur to Southerners again and again, even when no lynching takes place. This public opinion, however, remains internal until there is a lynching or talk of curbing lynchings in general. Then it becomes external and has an overwhelmingly important effect on their behavior.

In summary, it must be emphasized that public opinion is a term not to be employed either easily or carelessly. It is not a synonym for people. It presupposes a social organization or group as well as a series of more or less common experiences which people have had. It is a concept, therefore, which should creep into a sentence or a description only when these conditions have been ascertained and, if possible, only when they have been appropriately though approximately measured.

The delimitation of behavior called public opinion merely introduces the problem. Now it is necessary to relate public opinion to its context within a society . . . Then it will be possible to suggest the ways in which public opinion reacts as well as the basis for those reactions. Additional insight into public opinion can also be obtained as the problem of measurement is considered; for that which is measurable exists and that which exists is measurable. Finally, public opinion must be evaluated: how important are the actual, the latent, the external, the internal attitudes of people in modern society?

No. 33

PUBLIC OPINION AND POLITICS IN A DEMOCRACY [1]

by Leonard W. Doob

IN a democratic country the people are supposed to be supreme. This presumably means that important decisions depend, if only ultimately, on public opinion and that the day-by-day activities of government in some way or other reflect that opinion. The lip-service paid to public opinion by statesmen and politicians needs to be taken seriously: as a bare minimum, leaders must pretend that they are sensitive to the demands of their constituents.

A few years ago . . . 58 out of the 197 members of the New York State legislature were induced to respond to a questionnaire primarily on public opinion polls. One of the five questions was:

Do you consider it your public duty as a "representative" to reflect in official voting whatever preponderant sentiment your district displays on every issue, even if this is contrary to your personal conception of community welfare?

Significantly, 57 percent replied in the negative—39 percent were affirmative replies and the remaining 4 percent failed to reply at all or ran no risk by saying both "yes" and "no." Those who claimed they reflected the "preponderant sentiment" in their district were behaving—or so they asserted for the record—as they are popularly supposed to behave in a democracy.

[1] Leonard W. Doob, *Public Opinion and Propaganda* (New York: Henry Holt and Company, 1948), pp. 207-220. Reprinted by permission of the publisher.

Those who stressed their "personal conception of community welfare" were expressing a somewhat conservative viewpoint reminiscent of the distrust the Founding Fathers felt toward the masses of people: the legislators considered themselves experts and capable of making a distinction between actual public opinion ("preponderant sentiment") and latent but enduring public opinion ("community welfare"). Such replies, though of questionable reliability and validity, at least revealed a divergence of opinion even on the crude level of a survey.

Then, when thirteen Congressmen were interviewed and asked to state why they voted for or against the repeal of the Neutrality Act in 1939, twelve maintained that they were primarily exercising their own "independent judgment" and one gave as his reason the view of a public leader. These politicians, to be sure, must have been self-consciously talking for public consumption, but it is important to note that no one of them felt impelled to use "constituents' wishes" as his most prominent rationalization. Only seven in fact mentioned these "wishes" as a secondary reason. When the same investigator interviewed Congressional secretaries and newspaper correspondents concerning the reasons for the votes cast by ninety-six Congressmen on the same bill, "constituents' wishes" still ran a poor third after "independent judgment" and "party consideration." If these data are as "highly reliable" as the writer without proof says he "feels" they are, then public opinion in this instance was of relatively little importance to the law-makers.

According to a nationwide poll in 1944, moreover, 77 percent of a sample *acquainted with public opinion polls* believed that "generally speaking . . . Congressmen should be guided by the thinking of a majority of the people in their districts on important questions." Twenty percent thought that "Congressmen should vote as they think best without regard to what a majority of the people feel." The remaining 3 percent had no opinion on this question. But 31 percent of the very same people who had heard of polls claimed they would be influenced against a candidate if they knew that he "waited to see from polls what the majority of people thought before he expressed his own point of view on an issue." Only 11 percent would be influenced in his favor and the rest—58 percent—could not decide how or whether they would be influenced or maintained that they would not be affected one way or the other.

It would seem that public opinion is only one of the many factors determining political judgment. Government officials, therefore, inevitably are—and, according to many citizens, should be—much more than what has been called the "office boys" of their constituents. They do more than identify themselves with the people who have elected them. For they are human beings, and human beings are almost always variously motivated. There are political factors not directly related to public opinion: adherence to the principles of the party, sometimes regardless of their popularity at the moment; intelligent or blind opposition to the rival party or parties which perhaps only they as politicians vent; or deference to influential rather than typical groups in the community. There may be social factors arising out of the voting situation: the crowd spirit which sometimes pervades the debate in a legislature; pressure from lobbyists or some vocal minority; the influence of a powerful leader. There may also be individual factors in addition to "the personal conception of community welfare": the attempt to secure publicity for other than political reasons; the influence of a friend, a wife, or a mistress; some form of a *quid pro quo,* including straight bribes; an idiosyncratic impulse arising from an aggressive streak, a mother-fixation, a poorly digested meal, etc.

Government officials sometimes claim that they can adequately represent and reflect public opinion because they are people "like the rest of us" and consequently their attitudes are the same as their constituents. Any man, however, can be typical of a group only in relatively few respects and then merely in terms of that group's average. A politician whose age is forty-two does represent a community whose average age is likewise forty-two so far as age is concerned; but even this is only statistical representativeness, inasmuch as some of his constituents are older and some younger. The laws which legislators make, moreover, affect all age ranges; and yet the constitution of the states or of the country prevents younger people from choosing one of their number by barring them from voting and requiring that prospective candidates attain some minimum age. If the most prominent occupation in a community is farming, then a politician who has been a farmer is typical. He is a farmer of a particular economic and social status, which may or may not be the average in the community and, in addition, he is definitely not occupationally representative of hired hands, shopkeepers, and professional men. As a matter of fact, the representatives of the people in the Congress of the United States tend to come from white-collar groups, like lawyers, who are in the numerical minority. Since relatively few citizens have political ambitions, it follows that those who do must be unusual or not typical in respect to whatever psychological drives are reduced by being elected to public office. A representative can be slightly more representative on a particular issue involving public opinion if the attitudes of people are distributed in the form of a J-curve and if his own attitude conforms to that of the vast majority—in this case he represents everyone except the individuals whose non-conforming attitudes give rise to the J's tail.

The unavoidable unrepresentativeness of representatives has at least two important political consequences. Firstly, it may mean that politicians have a degree of expertness higher than that of some, most, but not all of their constituents. They may be more intelligent or influential; they may be better educated or more economically secure. As a result, they can be in a more advantageous position to envision the results of political decisions —or they may simply conclude that they are. Sometimes, too, the representatives acquire expertness after being elected: members of Congressional committees in the United States, for example, learn procedures and facts which enable them to function more effectively. Then, secondly, the judgments of representatives are certain to be affected by their own unrepresentative personalities or by their own not necessarily typical social-class interests. It does not inevitably follow that such judgments are not "beneficial" to the majority of the people or even to groups and individuals whose status is different from that of their representative. Franklin D. Roosevelt's upper class status, for example, apparently did not prevent him from adopting a policy of aiding labor unions, although that status doubtless had a marked effect on his foreign policies, especially those relating to the British Empire. Representatives, in a word, represent not only public opinion *en masse* but also themselves and the specialized forces within the community.

Lippmann, having established the unstable grounds on which public opinion is formed, then suggests that people should be and in fact only are consulted when an issue has already produced its protagonists. This view appears to be a rather accurate description of the state of affairs in democratic society, but it could be debated on the level of political philosophy. Ordinarily it is recognized that in politics as in all other fields, men and women do not have, or cannot be made to have, central attitudes on every issue. A revision of the tax rate, for example, interests only those who are immediately affected, even though such a change in the government's fiscal policy may begin a trend which eventually involves almost everyone. A factual study of non-voters in the United States—and about one-third of those eligible to vote do not go to the polls in a presidential year—reveals that these individuals tend to have relatively little formal education and to be economically less secure; to be more satisfied than are voters with American politics, with the established form of government, and in general with the status quo; and perhaps to have less knowledge about political affairs. Evidently there is some relation between non-voting on the one hand and interest and knowledge on the other.

In practice, each problem of government cannot be submitted to the people. There are day-by-day decisions which have to be made with dispatch and there is simply no time to consult public opinion. Only a few experts inside the government possess the required technical knowledge concerning certain matters. Even the citizens of a democratic country have few formal and established ways of expressing themselves. Election day is one such way. In the United States the practice of the initiative and the referendum exists in twenty states and that of recall in twelve; in theory such machinery enables people to be consulted between elections and on a greater number of proposals at election time. In England unscheduled elections, which occur when the party in power feels it is no longer receiving the parliamentary support it requires, give the electorate an opportunity to pass judgment on the broad, general policies of the contending political parties. Before the last war there was considerable agitation in the United States to have people make the most crucial decision of all—whether or not to go to war. The Ludlow Amendment which would have given Americans that right, however, was killed in the House of Representatives. Events after Pearl Harbor moved so quickly that there was little time for public opinion to become articulately external.

Since a continuous series of referenda in a democracy is obviously impractical and since people frequently demand to be heard, public opinion expresses itself and representatives become acquainted with public opinion in less formal ways. The political party, it has been pointed out, arose in the United States as a device for people to band together in order to achieve their own self-appointed objectives. It continually offers the average citizen, who hesitates to see government officials, the opportunity to complain to someone—the ward boss, for example—whose recognized duty it is to listen to complaints and, if possible, to take appropriate action. Groups with money and power seek directly to influence the decisions of government by employing lobbyists whose function it is to exert direct pressure upon officials; or as an organization with some prestige they make known their desires to those officials with or without the implied threat of "do as we say or else we'll vote you out of office." Elected officials, moreover, deliberately talk informally with their constituents. American voters are supposed to avail themselves of the privilege of writing their Congressional representatives to make known their views on governmental activities. Then, in addition, ordinary people have some effect on the viewpoint expressed by the mass media of communication which in turn are consulted by officials interested in "the public reaction" to events. Finally and more recently, there are the public opinion polls whose status among legislators and administrators has been discussed.

There is some question, however, whether public opinion is really expressed through these informal devices. Results from polls may be truly representative in a sampling sense but, as has been indicated, instrument errors make those results misleading or at least ambiguous. According to a Gallup poll in the summer of 1946, only 14 percent of Americans had ever written their Congressmen or Senators, and 36 percent of these letter-writers claimed they communicated in this fashion because some other "person or organization suggested it." A study of a sample of mail received by all Congressmen on the issue of repealing the Neutrality Act in 1939 and one of a sample of mail received by a small number of Congressmen on the issue of the Selective Service Bill in 1940 revealed that the letters gave a very distorted impression of public opinion as measured by polls. In general, according to one study, these very letters from the public are considered by Congressmen to rank first among ways open to them to determine the state of public opinion. Pressure groups by definition can represent only the organized and not public opinion in general. The knowledge of public opinion that government officials possess, therefore, may be inaccurate, biased, or inadequate.

It is in the voting procedure and in political parties where the more important short- as well as long-run effects of democratic public opinion must be sought. Why people vote as they do is a question which fascinates both the candidate or politician and the voters themselves. Politics in fact is the art of finding the devices which will gain the support of the electorate, that is, of public opinion or of important segments thereof. Stimuli are employed which will arouse favorable responses in people who, consequently, will vote for one individual or party rather than another. In a democracy like England or the United States—and to a lesser degree in all countries where free elections prevail—one of the most effective stimuli is the party label. Between 1940 and 1946, Gallup polls in the United States reveal, about 20 percent of the American people considered themselves "independents" at a given moment and probably their preferences, therefore, determined the outcome of presidential elections. The rest, according to their own testimony, were Republicans, Democrats, or members of minority parties. Very few of the self-styled party members actually participated in a party organization; nevertheless they felt themselves favorably disposed toward one party rather than another. Approximately half of a panel of voters in Erie County, Ohio, had decided in May 1940 for which party they would vote in November, even though at the time neither of the two major presidential candidates had been nominated.

Naturally party leaders seek to build up the prestige of their labels by frequent references to past and present accomplishments and by the kind of petty but very significant personal services rendered by the ward boss and others higher up the line. This record may be exaggerated by the politicians, it may be misinterpreted by the electorate, but it nevertheless must be quite decisive in determining voting preferences. Some individuals vote the party ticket because their families have done so for generations; or there may be regional traditions (as in the South and in many rural areas) from which few deviations occur. Yet the political complexion of an area or the country does change over a period of time, which means—aside from the important consideration of the merits or demerits of the particular candidates running for office—that the fluctuating rewards and punishments incurred from the domination of one party eventually have their effects upon the party labels. The differences between the major American parties may be of the tweedledum-and-tweedledee variety, as they tended to be in the era from the end of World War I to the time of Franklin D. Roosevelt, but eventually they impress themselves upon the electorate.

At a given moment the stimulus "Democratic party" or "Republican party" arouses a series of responses which leads to a favorable or unfavorable attitude. Consider, for example, the responses aroused by those labels in the month of February 1946—six months after the war against Japan had ended and ten months after Mr. Truman had succeeded Mr. Roosevelt. According to Gallup polls at that time:

1. Fourteen percent of Americans believed that the Democratic party was "most interested in persons of above average," 46 percent in those of "average income," and 61 percent in those of "below average income." The corresponding figures for the Republican party were, respectively, 57, 21, and 10 percent. These figures seem to show that the Republicans tended to be identified with the wealthy and the Democrats with the poor. Democrats in the polling sample agreed that Republicans were most interested in the wealthy and Republicans that the Democrats showed most concern for the poor. A larger percentage of Democrats than the Republicans, moreover, was convinced of its own party's interest in persons of average income.

2. Most Americans believed that the Democrats rather than the Republicans could handle the following problems: "dealing with world affairs," "keeping wages high," and "keeping farmers' income high." Conversely, more people had greater faith in the Republicans regarding: "encouraging new business to start," "keeping taxes from getting too high," and "keeping business profits high." Opinion was almost evenly divided as to which party could cope more effectively with: "reducing strikes and labor troubles" and "running the government efficiently."

That the responses to these political labels vary with events is shown by the reactions of Americans to the one problem of "reducing strikes and labor troubles" over a short period of time. Asked by Gallup which party had the advantage in dealing with the problem, successive samples responded as follows:

Party having advantage	Oct. '45	Feb. '46	Oct. '46
Democratic	41	38	23
Republican	31	36	46
Neither	28	26	31

In October of 1945 the great postwar strikes were just beginning, and so the Democrats' reputation in respect to reducing labor problems was still intact. Then as strikes continued during Mr. Truman's administration the Republican label gained in prestige.

The specific devices employed by politicians to impress the electorate are variations of general propaganda techniques and will be considered . . . [by the author] as propaganda is analyzed. They range from the general promises of reward which the political platform offers to the kind of vague ego-satisfaction or identification which parents feel when their baby has been kissed by a candidate. They include the appeal to tradition and idealism as well as transporting the voter to the poll and purchasing his vote. They are based on the plea of love-me-because-I-love-you as well as on the cry of hate-him-because-he-means-only-misery. They vary from a voice on a national hook-up to one behind a soap box on a street corner. Politics is propaganda in the best and worst buckshot tradition.

Every politician and campaign manager knows, in addition, that he cannot trample upon public opinion in his effort to seduce people to vote as he wishes. He must keep his ear to the ground, his finger on the public pulse, his nose in the air, his eyes on the target, and so on until even his brain is aware of what people want and do not want. Patronage, the well-timed favor, and the political club room are employed to impress specific people in the hope that they will then spread the appropriate word to their friends. On a national scale in the United States, the climax of diagnosing the public comes in the formulation of the party platform. Here every effort is made to use the cliché-stimuli which will touch off the greatest number of responses favorable to one party and unfavorable to the other; to state the issues of the day in such general terms that almost all of the heterogeneous groups which compose the United States will somehow be vaguely pleased; to tailor the promises to the most promising candidates but to make them so unspecific that the party commits itself virtually only in favor of virtue and against sin; and to suggest with a rhetorical flourish that the victory of one party will mean a virtual state of Nirvana and its defeat the kind of chaos only otherwise produced by the explosion of the atomic bomb.

Public opinion in a democracy, moreover, may be contemptuously thought of as a kind of putty by fascists, but it cannot be considered quite so malleable when its effects on politics and politicians are observed. The representative of the people realizes constantly that he must be re-elected and, even when he has decided to retire or is ineligible for re-election, he knows he has an obligation to his friends and party; therefore he reminds himself again and again that ultimately he or his associates are dependent upon public opinion. If he favors one type of legislation rather than another, he cannot forget that his vote will be part of the public record and will influence people's attitudes toward him. Periodically while in office and permanently afterwards he must return to the community which has elected him. Privately he may view with great cynicism the letters from his constituents or the conversations he holds with some of them, but publicly he must show the greatest respect for their words. The party itself may be controlled by a small clique of bosses, but even their smoke-ridden conclaves must frequently be devoted to the problem of what people want. Since a party, moreover, is a social group with particular rules of organization, it is always possible for a collection of malcontents to bore from within and for the grassroots to smother the vermin.

The overall result of the political process in a democracy seems to be a kind of compromise. People seldom pick the candidates to be placed on the ballot, but they have an effect on the preliminary steps leading to the election. They seldom determine the precise nature of the platforms confronting them, but their needs are catered to as the documents are written. They are confronted with pre-established alternatives when they vote, but they have played some part in establishing the alternatives. The results of most elections are ambiguous because usually so many issues are involved, but even the most unscrupulous politician must make some effort to interpret what he calls "the mandate of public opinion" for the sake of his own future.

The dominant belief of democracy is that government exists for the people and that the people do not exist in order to serve the state. The available facts, however, indicate that public opinion is not the decisive factor in all situations and cannot be. In general, some people are listened to when they are determined to be heard, and all people are determined to be heard only when they feel that a crisis is at hand and that they themselves are personally involved. Government-by-public-opinion-only-in-a-crisis can be dangerous since it tends to relieve people and their representatives of important responsibilities. The people then have only a segmental interest in governmental affairs and their representatives have only a segmental concern for public opinion. Both await the crisis and may forget that most crises are the result of previous events whose impact in the preliminary stages is not always so striking. Democracy succeeds or fails as it manages to discover some point between government-by-public-opinion—which is not feasible and perhaps not desirable—and the crisis-approach.

To strive to reach such a point, the leaders and interested citizens place stress upon education. They believe that the electorate must become more completely aware of the issues which confront the country and should acquire as much of the relevant information as possible. What is discouraging about democracy in the modern world and what elsewhere has helped give rise to alternate forms of government is the increasing complexity of the affairs with which government must deal. If the forces of democracy have enabled information to be spread at an arithmetically increasing rate, it can be said without much exaggeration that technology and social changes have increased at a geometrical rate the amount of information which needs to be known for the electorate to be intelligent and reasonably expert.

Makeshift and ever-changing devices are employed to improve the relation between public opinion and government. Discussions and announcements of governmental decisions, for example, are placed on the public record, so that people will have an opportunity to pass judgment. Unfortunately some but not all of the most crucial decisions of government—those involving foreign relations and war itself—cannot be revealed for security or strategic reasons. Then efforts are made to equalize the unequal strength of the contending factions in a country by having citizens who are not members of organized groups testify before legislative committees; by requiring that all political candidates (including the small minority parties in the United States) be given an equal opportunity to use the radio; and by stimulating public forums at which everyone is encouraged to express himself.

Many Americans appear to display greater interest in a national campaign than they do in local politics and they are more likely to know the names of cabinet members than of the Congressmen from their own state or of the officials in their own county. This means many things. The popular media of communication give more publicity to cabinet members than to Congressmen. Americans are drawn to a contest: some of the attitudes aroused by national politics resemble those associated with prize-fighting and horse-racing. The interests of the electorate in state, county, or local government are segmental, whereas those involving national politics—while not central—at least can be more easily and more frequently aroused.

At the same time, when a community is small, well organized, and politically conscious, public opinion has a more direct effect upon politics. The American prototype of such a community is the small New England town where public opinion is vividly expressed at an annual meeting. There the problems requiring political action, the individuals who perform the action, and the electorate itself are so well known that the dividing line between public opinion and political policy becomes very thin. The issues to be decided are ones affecting people directly and usually include some in which almost everyone has a rather high degree of expertness. Should a garbage-disposal truck be purchased? Should a kindergarten be added to the local school? Should the tax rate on property be raised so that a new community center can be constructed? In like manner the skills and the defects of the candidates for local office are generally well known, though they may be misappraised as a result of people's prejudices. Such an ideal relation between knowledge and attitude of course cannot be achieved on a national scale, but it can be argued that only by approximating this condition can the long list of names and proposals confronting the voters in the voting booth become more intelligible. To expect a well-informed electorate on every issue or candidate is just as wishful a bit of thinking as it is to anticipate that a smart dictator can completely disregard the people he rules. Neither is possible. Perhaps governmental activities in a democracy can become more meaningful to greater numbers of people through decentralization along regional lines.

No. 34

DO THE POLLS SERVE DEMOCRACY? [1]

by John C. Ranney

MOST of the current controversy over public opinion polls has centered about the question of their accuracy: the reliability of the sample taken, the impartiality of the sponsorship, the honesty of the interviewer and the person interviewed, the fairness of the questions, the measurements of intensities or gradations of feeling, and the validity of the analysis or interpretation. These are all, admittedly, important questions; but they tend to ignore or to beg one which is both more important and more theoretical: Assuming that the polls were to attain a miraculously perfect and unchallengeable accuracy, would they, even then, contribute significantly to the working of democracy?

One's first inclination is to take it for granted that the answer is "Yes." No principle, in democratic theory, has been more fundamental than the belief that political decisions ought to be made by the people as a whole or in accordance with their desires. Yet no principle, in democratic practice, has proved more difficult of precise application. In theory, even when

[1] John C. Ranney, "Do the Polls Serve Democracy?", *Public Opinion Quarterly* (Fall, 1946), Vol. X, No. 3, pp. 349-360. Reprinted by permission of *Public Opinion Quarterly* and the author. The footnotes in the original version are omitted here.

doubts are entertained as to the rationality, the objectivity, and the capacity of the ordinary citizen, modern democratic writers have continued to find the essence of democracy in popular participation in policy-making. But in practice, it has long been apparent that our electoral system, as a reflection of popular wishes and as a channel for popular activity, leaves a good deal to be desired.

Various improvements have been suggested, ranging from the initiative and the referendum to proportional or functional representation. But none of these devices, except by placing an intolerable strain on the voter, has solved the problem of how to reflect simultaneously the great diversity of his interests and attitudes on different issues. The result, under our present system, is that even if one assumes that the voter does anything more than choose between the personalities of rival candidates, an election approximates what has been called "plebiscitary democracy." It is a way of approving or disapproving in the most general terms the policies of the party or individual in office and of renewing or transferring this exceedingly vague mandate for the coming term of office.

Such a check and consultation is much better than none at all. Notwithstanding its resemblance to some of the dictatorial plebiscites, it permits, in a free society, the expression of at least the major discontents. But consultations which are so sweeping and which occur at such rare intervals are only the thinnest caricature of the democratic belief that the health of the community depends upon the personal, active, and continuous political participation of the body of its citizens.

It is here that the polls are supposed to make their great contribution. By separating the issues from one another, by stating them simply and clearly, and by covering the electorate completely and continuously, they avoid the most obvious obscurities, strains, and distortions of the older procedures. If to these virtues one might add unchallengeable accuracy, the well-known dream of Bryce would be realized: the will of the majority of the citizens could be ascertained at all times; representative assemblies and elaborate voting machinery would be unnecessary and obsolete.

ATTACKS ON THE POLLS

Not everyone has rejoiced over this possibility. Anyone who agrees with Hamilton, for example, that the people are turbulent and changing, seldom judging or determining right, is hardly likely to welcome a device to make the voice of the people (which decidedly is not the voice of God) more audible than ever. Nor is this attitude likely to surprise or disturb the genuine democrat.

What should disturb him, however, is the fact that there are many people who consider themselves good democrats and who nevertheless consider the polls a menace to democracy. The objections of this second group deserve more systematic attention than they have yet received.

THE DESTRUCTION OF LEADERSHIP

The first and most frequent of these objections is that the polls destroy political courage and leadership. Every adequate government, it is maintained, requires these qualities in its officials. They can exist, however, only where there is freedom and flexibility and where the statesman is not bound, either in form or in fact, by rigid instructions from the voters. The government official, whether Congressman or administrator, has access to information which is beyond the reach of the ordinary voter, and he has something more than the ordinary voter's leisure in which to consider it. To subject his judgment to the ill-informed and hasty judgment of the electorate is to commit the political crime of rendering a decision before considering the evidence on which it ought to be based. It is true that the polls have no official standing and cannot bind any office-holder. But, the charge runs, the official who wants to keep his job will abandon his duty of analyzing and judging proposed policies in favor of the simpler, and safer, device of deciding as the polls tell him to decide.

So far as the legislator is concerned, there are several weaknesses in this argument. Simply as a matter of fact, it would be extremely difficult to show that the polls have had a decisive effect in determining the voting habits of any substantial number of representatives. It is one of the dubious advantages of the American system that it is extremely difficult to allocate responsibility; and even in those cases in which responsibility can be fixed, the ordinary voter is only too likely to be ignorant of the voting record of his representative. The average Congressman on the average issue need not worry too much about the opinion of his constituents in the mass. What he does need to worry about is the opinion of specific organizations and individuals inside his constituency, especially the political machines and organized pressure groups. Any Congressman who is concerned with political realities knows that it is more important to appease a well-disciplined minority, which can deliver the votes on election day, than to gratify an unorganized and casual majority, the intensity of whose convictions and the efficacy of whose action is far less likely to be decisive. If the polls exert any influence at all, therefore, they tend to moderate or deflate rather than to reinforce the special pressures already influencing legislators.

The absence of scientific methods for measuring opinion, moreover, has never prevented politicians from trying to guess what it is. The representative, if such there be, who follows the polls slavishly would have his ear well to the ground under any circumstances. It is hard to see how democracy is undermined or its moral fibre destroyed simply by providing him with more reliable methods of judgment. It can hardly be urged that so long as a representative is going to vote according to public opinion anyway, the more distorted his picture of it, the better. Nor would it be easy to show that, among those restrained by the polls, the idealists seriously outnumber those who would otherwise follow the dictates of selfish and limited interests.

Finally, it should be remembered that public opinion is not so definite and rigid as the argument implies. In some instances, changes have been both rapid and extreme, and political leaders have often been in a strategic position to influence or shape it. In addition, men of intelligence and foresight who understand the probable effects of an unfortunate policy or the misconceptions on which it is based can anticipate the ultimate revulsion of public feeling and act accordingly. Voters, it should be remembered, do not always show great tolerance for the Congressman who excuses his own past mistakes with the plea that most of the electorate, at the time, shared his way of thinking.

Although the argument concerning the destruction of leadership is usually made with the legislator in mind, it actually has somewhat more factual strength in the case of the policy-making administrator. Surveys indicate that he is more likely to pay attention to the results of the polls, and he is also more likely to have expert or specialized personal knowledge as an alternative basis for decision. There is a possibility, at least, that his interest in the polls may indicate a tendency to subordinate his own well-informed judgment to the opinion of the electorate; and there is a further possibility that he may become so dependent upon it that he will take no action at all when that opinion is confused or divided or simply non-existent.

On the other hand, the administrator is, if anything, subject to even greater and more numerous pressures than is the Congressman. For him, therefore, the polls may be even more important as a basis for resisting minority pressures in the public interest. Moreover, like the legislator, he has considerable power to influence public opinion, although his methods are somewhat different; and a precise knowledge of what that opinion is can be an important help in enlightening or changing it.

The factual basis, or lack of basis, for the argument that the polls destroy leadership is less important, however, than two of the argument's theoretical implications.

The first of these is that government officials, whether legislators or administrators, constitute something of an expert body, possessing unusual intelligence, information, and skill, and that to this body the voter, because of his personal inadequacy, should delegate his power.

This argument, however, proves too much. If expertness is to be the criterion for the right to participate in government, the ordinary Congressman would himself have difficulty in qualifying. Even the policy-making administrator, in an age of increasingly voluminous and technical legislation, is likely to be an expert only in the most attenuated sense of the term. To be sure, both he and the legislator must make use of the knowledge and experience of the expert, especially in determining the technical means to achieve broader and predetermined objectives. But when it comes to determining the objectives themselves—and it is with objectives rather than with means that the polls are primarily concerned—the democratic theorist who would free leaders from the restraint of less well-informed public opinion is, consciously or unconsciously, on the road to what, since the days of Plato, has been the radically undemocratic position of urging rule by some elite.

The second theoretical implication is the even stranger one that ignorance of what the people want and feel is a positive advantage in a democracy. Yet few defenses of democracy have been more persuasive than the one which insists that democracy alone provides the government with adequate information about the desires and attitudes of the people and that, even if these prove to be ignorant or irrational, it is only on the basis of such information that a government can act intelligently. Legislation cannot be separated from the practical problem of administration and enforcement; and it is of fundamental importance, in framing and administering laws with intelligence, to understand, as one of the vital factors in the situation, the state of public feeling. This is not to say that opinion is the only factor to be considered. It is saying that it is an essential element in the rational analysis of any political situation. People will not refrain from having opinions and acting upon them simply because they are not asked what they are. Yet statesmen, whether legislators or administrators, are unlikely to have direct personal knowledge of these feelings; and the weaknesses of elections, the press, and other methods of identifying them have been obvious for decades. Here, therefore, if anywhere, the polls, far from being a menace to democracy, give substance and meaning to what has always, in theory, been one of its outstanding advantages.

In short, so far as this first set of criticisms is concerned, the polls are neither, in fact, so destructive of leadership and courage as critics suggest nor, in theory, so incompatible with the traditional meaning of democracy. On the contrary, the unstated assumptions of the critics tend logically to a conclusion which is itself basically undemocratic.

THE POLLS AS A BRAKE ON PROGRESS

A second set of charges is remarkable for the way in which it parallels Hamilton's way of thinking for purposes which are quite un-Hamiltonian. Its authors agree that the intelligence and judgment of the people is to be distrusted—not because of their radicalism, however, but because of their conservatism and complacency. Far from being a source of turbulence and unrest and a menace to private property and traditional ways of doing things, the people are so conventional and so contented with things as they are that they constitute a formidable brake upon progress, slow to see the need for drastic social changes and slow to take the necessary steps, always doing too little and always doing it too late. Public opinion polls, by giving publicity to these attitudes, increase their force. In addition, the attention and deference paid them intensify both the complacency of the people and their confidence in their own mystical rightness. What the people need, however, is to develop some realization of their own shortcomings and some willingness to leave to the expert those matters of which he alone can judge.

Here, as in the case of the first set of criticisms, it would be difficult to prove that the people are actually more conservative than their representatives. Some observers, in fact, contend that the polls have repeatedly shown the people to be far readier than Congress to accept progressive ideas. But even if the people proved, as a regular matter, to be a hindrance to progress, certain theoretical difficulties would remain. It is undoubtedly true that the process of modern government is too technical and complex to be directed in detail by the ordinary citizen and that the skill and knowledge of the expert must be tapped in a responsible fashion. Yet this argument is too easily confused with the very different argument that the "responsible" expert must be given the power to introduce, according to his own judgment, drastic social changes. There is, to begin with, a certain lack of logic in an argument which speaks of ultimate responsibility to the public while maintaining that "trained intelligence" must none the less be free to introduce the drastic changes which the uninformed public is not prepared to accept. And the more one tries to avoid this dilemma by limiting responsibility to the voter in favor of government by a disinterested, wise, and public-spirited elite, the more the criticism becomes one, not of the polls as a hindrance to the operation of democracy, but of democracy as a hindrance to progress.

The defense of democracy, which is as old as Aristotle, does not need to be elaborated here. But it is essential to point out, as Plato himself came to recognize, that no government, however well intentioned, can force a community to move in directions in which it does not want to move, or to move much more rapidly than it would otherwise move, without resorting to instruments of force and tyranny which are incompatible with both the spirit and the practice of democracy.

THE POLLS AS A MISCONCEPTION OF DEMOCRACY

The third, and by far the most valid, criticism which can be made of the polls is that they represent a fundamental misconception of the nature of democracy. Bryce's picture of a society in which the will of the majority of the citizens would be ascertainable at all times is neither a very profound nor a very realistic picture of democratic society. Democracy is not simply the ascertaining and the applying of a "will of the people"—a somewhat mystical entity existing in and of itself, independent, unified, and complete. It is the whole long process by which the people and their agents inform themselves, discuss, make compromises, and finally arrive at a decision.

The people are not the only element in this process, and they are not necessarily the agent which is best suited to each part of the task. In general the executive and the administrative services are best fitted to see policy as a whole and to prepare a coherent program as well as to handle the technical details of legislation. The legislature provides a forum in which the different interests within the country can confront one another in a regularized way, as the people cannot, and acquire something of the mutual understanding and comprehensive outlook which is essential for the satisfactory adjustment of interests. The people themselves, finally, can express better than any other agency what it is they need and want.

None of these functions, it is true, belongs exclusively to any one agency, nor can any be separated rigidly from the others. The process of discussion and adjustment is a continuous one, carried on on all levels. There is a constant interweaving and interpenetration of talk and action subject to no precise demarcation but in which it is none the less essential that each agency refrain from functions which are beyond its competence. In this process the operation of the polls may be positively harmful, not in interfering with "government by experts" as more frequently charged, but in emphasizing the content of the opinion rather than the way in which it is formed and in focussing attention on the divergency of opinion rather than upon the process of adjusting and integrating it.

To say this is not to urge a restriction on popular participation but to emphasize its real nature and function. Popular participation in government is thin and meaningless if it is nothing more than the registering of an opinion. It becomes meaningful to the extent that the opinion is itself the product of information, discussion, and practical political action. There is something not only pathetic but indicative of a basic weakness in the polls' conception of democracy in the stories of those who tell interviewers they could give a "better answer" to the questions if only they had time to read up a bit or think things over. It is precisely this reading up and thinking over which are the essence of political participation and which make politics an educational experience, developing the character and capacity of the citizens.

The polls, however, except as their publication tends to stimulate political interest, play almost no part in this process. They make it possible for the people to express their attitude toward specific proposals and even to indicate the intensity of their feeling on the subject; and they can distinguish the attitudes of different social and economic groups from one another. But they provide no mechanism on the popular level for promoting discussion, for reconciling and adjusting conflicting sectional, class, or group interests, or for working out a coherent and comprehensive legislative program.

In fact, far less perfect instruments for discovering the "will" of the voters are often much more effective in arousing popular participation. The initiative and the referendum, for all their weaknesses, stir opponents and advocates of measures to unusual activity and stimulate a large proportion of the voters, rather than a small selected sample, to consider and discuss the issues. Similarly, the privately-conducted British Peace Ballot proved to be an educational experience for the entire British people. Even the much maligned *Literary Digest* Poll performed a greater service in arousing thought and discussion than did its more accurate competitors.

In short, the polls are not concerned with, and provide no remedy for, the gravest weaknesses in the democratic process. If one thinks of democracy in practical terms of discussion and political activity rather than of a disembodied "will," the great need is to get rid of the obstacles to popular education, information, debate, judgment, and enforcement of responsibility. To do this, there must be a multiple effort directed against a multiplicity of evils. To mention only a few of these, the political education in most of our schools, handicapped as they are by conventional school boards and the fear of controversy, is wretchedly inadequate. In too many cities the sources of information are insufficient, the news itself distorted, and the free competition of ideas seriously restricted. In general, our facilities for discussion—clubs, unions, pressure organizations, forums, round-tables, and the radio—provide no adequate successor to the town meeting in the sense of active and responsible personal participation. More fundamentally, the undemocratic character of much of our economic and social life is a real hindrance to the growth of political democracy.

Moreover, even if our political education were magnificent, the channels of information completely clear, the facilities for discussion abundant, and the spirit of democracy universal, the obscurity and confusion in our political system, resulting from its checks and balances and its lack of party discipline, would make it almost impossible for the ordinary voter to understand what is going on, to pass judgment intelligently, and to place responsibility. Yet any government in which the people are to share must at a minimum be comprehensible. Obscurity and anonymity kill democracy. These defects, however, are present in our government, and about them the polls can do very little.

SUMMARY

The chief advantage of the polls is that, in an age of increasing strain upon traditional democratic procedures, they have made a constructive technical contribution by reflecting sensitively and flexibly the currents of public feeling, by making this information available to political leaders in a way which is neither rigid nor mandatory, and by testing the claims of special interests to represent the desires of the people as a whole. These are services performed by no other agency, and they should not be underestimated.

But if, in a democracy, the health of the community depends upon the personal, active, and continuous political participation of the body of its citizens, this contribution is a limited and even a minor one. Even when used with the greatest accuracy and intelligence, the polls cannot achieve any fundamental improvement until our political system itself is simplified, until the lines of responsibility are clarified, and until devices are discovered for increasing the direct participation of the people, not simply in the registration of their aims, but in the deliberative procedure which is the real heart of democracy.

Chapter XI

THE POLITICAL PARTY

[WE have already seen that a democratic government is one in which the mass of the adult citizens have the opportunity to choose and hold responsible those charged with the formulation and execution of public policy. One of the vitally important organizations in that process is the political party. The parties help formulate the issues, choose the candidates, and conduct the campaigns that are indispensable parts of the democratic political process.

Admittedly the parties do not function perfectly in the performance of these functions. Most important, perhaps, is the fact that there is so little participation by the mass of people in party activities. The parties tend to become controlled by small groups and one of the main opportunities for the average citizen to have a hand in his government seems denied to him. Yet, when every criticism of the party system has been made, the service that it renders to the democratic state is still tremendous. It does enable the electorate—even a passive electorate—to choose between alternatives, to change its rulers without recourse to violent means. The value of the party system to democracy is sufficiently great that modern dictatorships have lost no time in abolishing the *party system* and establishing a one-party monopoly in which the party is in reality the government. Fascists, nazis, communists all follow the same strategy. They abolish the *party system*, establish a one-party monopoly of power, and deny the people any opportunity to choose effectively and hold that one party accountable for what it does.]

No. 35

[THE literature of American government and particularly the American party system is replete with attacks on the vagueness of party platforms and on the failure of the major parties to take clear and positive stands on policy issues. Although these criticisms are, in general, soundly based, the critics have frequently overlooked the stabilizing influence of our party system and its great contribution in effecting compromises between divergent views. This is not the case with Professor Nevins who does discuss in the following essay the great value of our not-too-widely differentiated parties as a stabilizing influence in our political life.]

THE STRENGTH OF OUR POLITICAL SYSTEM [1]

by Allan Nevins

THE pageantry of the Republican and Democratic conventions is over. Now comes the discipline, the semi-military marshaling of forces and the hard campaign work. It is all distinctively American, and in most respects it is all comparatively new. Though political parties are as old as our Government, the tremendous mechanism of national, state and local party organizations, pivoted upon local, state and national conventions, dates only from the second administration of Andrew Jackson. We have little over a hundred years of history to illustrate the function of fully developed parties in general and the two-party system in particular.

Have they a healthy function? Some of the principal leaders of Washington's era (a theoretical era, given to abstract speculation upon government) thought not. They held that parties simply bred factions and discord. Virtuous citizens of the new republic should abjure them, and return to the fine Roman spirit later hymned in Macaulay's Lays: "Then none was for a party, then all were for the state." The unanimous election of Washington as first President seemed to vindicate this ideal. But realities, described by Jefferson in a trenchant passage, sheared through this utopian theorizing. Parties were essential to express political aims, to educate the people, to carry on government, and to criticize the Government. In short, wrote Jefferson, parties were vital to liberty:

> In every free and deliberating society, there must, from the nature of man, be opposite parties, and violent dissensions and discords; and one of these, for the most part, must prevail over the other for a longer or shorter time. Perhaps this party division is necessary to induce each other to watch and to relate to the people at large the proceedings of the other.

Probably few Americans realize just how important the instant emergence of parties in the United States was, and how inevitable it was that the division between Federalists and Republicans should follow the two-party model of Great Britain. Our Constitution was so drawn that it might as readily have been given an anti-democratic as a democratic cast; it might long have been the instrument of one-party class control. The electoral college, as first devised, was anti-democratic. The Senate, chosen by the

[1] Allan Nevins, "The Strength of Our Political System," *The New York Times Magazine* (July 18, 1948), pp. 5, 31. Reprinted by permission of *The New York Times Magazine* and the author.

state legislatures (in which property seemed at first supreme) was anti-democratic. The Federalists who, with Washington as nonpartisan head, came into executive power, and who showed a remarkable genius for efficient administration, were anti-democratic. The question whether the Constitution might be given a permanently anti-democratic character had to be settled within ten or fifteen years.

Inevitably, the dominance of the men who wished to see the national Government powerful, well-centralized, and anti-democratic called into existence a counter-party who wished the Government kept weak, uncentralized, and democratic. Washington in the selection of his first Cabinet recognized two parties. On the national and aristocratic side he chose Hamilton for the Treasury and Henry Knox for War; on the democratic side he selected Jefferson for the State Department and Edmund Randolph for Attorney General. The divergence of opinion in Cabinet meetings was paralleled by an even more passionate divergence in the nation at large. Within a few years the two parties were formally reorganized, and every American knew that their struggle would decide the course of constitutional development. Federalist and Republican fought to put Government within their particular molds just as Whig and Tory fought to shape the unwritten British Constitution.

Here was a difference in principle. The dominant purpose of the Federalist party was to place such a construction on the letter of the Constitution as to broaden the powers of the Federal Government and restrict those of the states. The essential purpose of the Jeffersonian party was to interpret the Constitution in such wise as to limit the national and foster the local power. Two rival ideologies were in frontal collision. In France of the period this meant battles and guillotines. In America, however, from the very beginning three factors operated to lessen the violence of the party clash.

What were they? First, principle itself was interpreted with a saving grace of reservations and modifications, and was subject to sudden changes dictated by expediency. Thus Jefferson, once in power, actually made more far-reaching use of the central Government, as in the Louisiana Purchase and the embargo, than John Adams had done, while that good Democrat, Andrew Jackson, proved the sternest nationalist in our history. Second, both parties took up all manner of subsidiary issues, ranging from tariffs and internal improvements to foreign policy; and as they did so, both appealed to a wide variety of constantly fluctuating groups. Third, each party had such a healthy respect for public sentiment that, following the old Anglo-Saxon rule of compromise (undoubtedly the most vital single element in our Government), the majority abstained from abusing its authority, and the minority yielded to the majority on the tacit understanding that no abuse would be practiced.

For a variety of reasons, from Hamilton to Truman the two-party system has perpetuated itself. For one, in a populous democracy the costs of maintaining a party on a national scale, quadrennium after quadrennium, are so great that splinter parties cannot meet them. Also, most great leaders rise to influence within the two main parties. But, above all, the two-party system suits the genius of the people. They want a responsible authority, on which they can count for stability; they want it closely watched by a strong opposition; they want to use its power, but to do so in the spirit of compromise, with a due regard for minority rights.

Is such a party system democratic? "A party," William H. Seward once remarked, "is in one sense a joint stock association, in which those who contribute most direct the action and management of the concern." Accepting this definition, we can see why great parties sometimes fall under an undemocratic control.

Just before the Civil War the Democratic party, as Seward complained, was dominated by a comparatively restricted body of slaveholders who contributed more money, determination and brains to its direction than any other group. After the Civil War the Republican party fell, for a long period, under the domination of big business. But party machinery (through the direct primary, better publicity, restriction of campaign gifts and so on) has been improved to permit of broader controls. If much still remains to be done, as James Reston has pointed out, it *can* be done. And the very heterogeneity of our parties makes for democracy.

If any lesson is written in our history, it is that an undemocratically controlled party sooner or later pays a heavy penalty. Elements of revolt gather within its ranks. Reform groups rise up against the slavery oligarchy, or the Tammany-Bourbon alliance, or the special privilege corporations, or whatever other group has become dominant. They join the opposition party, in such a tremendous accession of "independent" strength as that which in 1884 elected Cleveland over Blaine, for example; or they stage a revolt within their own party, like Bryan's revolt against the Tammany-Ryan combination in 1912; or they organize a third party, as the Progressives did. In one way or another, they strike a decisive blow for a more democratic management of party affairs.

So little is the American system understood that some people are constantly asking: "Why don't the parties stand for hard and fast principles? Why is it so difficult to tell Republican aims from Democratic aims? Why are they so much alike?" Bryce wrote about 1880 that the abiding object of the Democratic party was still to oppose a unitary and much-interfering Government in Washington; but under Woodrow Wilson and Franklin D. Roosevelt the traditional party role on this head seemed reversed.

And so little is the system appreciated that some critics continually repeat the question: "Why can't we have a Conservative party and a Liberal party? Why can't we have parties on economic lines?"

Such statements ignore the cardinal utility of our two great parties. They are an amalgam, not a solvent; their fundamental value in the United States is in pulling together an immensely varied mass of social groups, economic constituencies, racial stocks, and local and sectional interests for the purpose of governing by consent.

The greatest disaster that ever befell the nation in the past resulted from a temporary division of parties along sectional lines. The worst disaster that could possibly happen to it in the near future would be a division along economic and class lines. We have the utmost reason for rejoicing, not for regretting, that the Republican and Democratic parties are so much alike that the scepter can pass from one to the other without perceptible shock.

It is of the first importance that each party represent a fair cross-section of the nation, with rich and poor, farmers and city clerks, Catholics, Jews and Protestants, old stock and immigrant stock. Our wide diffusion of property prevents any division between rich and poor. But if we did have a Conservative party of the propertied and a Radical party of the unpropertied we might at last be within sight of the day when the losers in an election would begin throwing up barricades in the streets.

Our type of two-party system has its manifest disadvantages and defects. Obviously, two big, loose, heterogeneous parties are always exposed to schism. Obviously, too, such mammoth parties, making constant compromises within their own ranks, must be guilty of a good deal of time-serving, trimming and hypocrisy. We have seen the spectacle of one Republican Administration after another uttering bright platitudes about Negro equality while courting the "lily whites" in the South. We have seen the Franklin D. Roosevelt Administration preaching noble political ideals while accepting the partnership of Boss Hague and Boss Crump. The alliance of low-tariff Iowa farmers and high-tariff Pennsylvania ironmasters under the Republican aegis, and the alliance of Tammany Hall with Alabama agrarians under the Democratic banner, have not made for political honesty of the austerest type.

At a grave crisis in the Civil War, just after the defeat of Fredericksburg, Lincoln kept the disharmonious Republican party together by obtaining written resignations from Secretary Seward, pet of the conservatives, and

Secretary Chase, pet of the radicals; not to be used, but to be balanced against each other. It was an effective stroke, but it did not illustrate the highest kind of political forthrightness.

Nevertheless, the benefits of the existing system far outweigh its draw-backs. We, like the British, and for basically the same reason, find a multi-party system almost unthinkable. Our whole tradition is built on government by a strong and responsible majority, which will wield power effectively but will at the same time respect minority rights. The spectacle of irre-sponsibility, confusion and intolerance presented by some Continental Euro-pean nations of multitudinous parties may be exciting, and some of their parties may suggest an intellectual rigor unknown in our politics; but the practical results do not commend themselves to us.

We feel the safer in trusting to two major parties because, unlike the British, we have surrounded minority rights with an elaborate system of checks and balances. We feel the safer because even our strongest Presi-dents—Jackson, Lincoln, Wilson, the two Roosevelts—have never, despite much short-lived partisan talk to the contrary, shown any really dictatorial tendencies.

Nor are we willing to give up the vast benefits we reap from the fact that the two great parties are ponderous cross-sections of our varied society, representing every element. Third parties have never been that. They have usually been parties of one idea—abolitionism, prohibition, populism—and hence one group. In a nation so large and so variegated in resources and climate, so widely differentiated in economic and social interests, so complex in its stocks and faiths, it is essential that our parties promote unity. In a population which does now and then grow hotly emotional over changing issues, a party organization built on principles of cohesion and compromise is obviously invaluable.

The fundamental character of our political organism has changed aston-ishingly little between the days of Hamilton and Jefferson, and the days of Truman and Dewey. To that fact we may ascribe much of our national stability.

No. 36

[If we are to fulfill our obligation to examine critically the role of people, politics, and the politician in American life we must begin with a re-examination of the role of the politician who, in the final analysis, is the practitioner of political science. It is safe to affirm, with Mr. Davenport, that the number of persons in this country who would regard this as important is not large; for Americans have traditionally held the politician in low esteem. The labeling of an individual as a "politician" is with but few exceptions an act of opprobrium. This is partly due to the lag in the social sciences and it is also based on the almost universally accepted belief that politicians are, as a general rule, incompetent and probably not incorruptible. A few dead political leaders may be canonized and admitted to the ranks of statesmen but even they were labeled "politicians" by their contemporaries and their now respected policies were regarded as cheap political gestures. An editorial writer in 1793 believed that Washington should "retire immediately; let no flatterer persuade you to rest one hour longer at the helm of state. You are utterly incapable to steer the political ship into the harbor of safety." The now respected Jefferson was described, in his time, as "a man without religion, a statesman without principle, and a patriot regardless of his country's welfare and entirely devoted to raise himself and his partisans upon the nation's ruin." One of the leading papers of the nation portrayed Lincoln as "an uneducated man, a vulgar village politician, without any experience worth mentioning in the practical duties of statesmanship."

This tendency to damn "politicians" is therefore an old American custom. The descendants of the writers just quoted are probably now busily at work keeping it alive. The results are, of course, unfortunate. We have contented ourselves in blaming the "politician" instead of investigating—and reconstructing—our political machinery. For the poor performance of badly organized legislatures, we blame legislators; if the administration of public policy is badly done, we find some administrator to blame; when the courts fall behind in their dockets, undoubtedly a judge is at fault. Basic faults in our governmental machinery have long been perceived by a few who were not too enmeshed in the crude empiricism of American political thinking. But their attempts to point out and correct these faults have been thwarted by the popular disposition to blame only the "politician."

A democratic society cannot long endure if little attention is given to the defects in its institutions and if we unthinkingly feel we can exorcise the evil spirits who plague our political practices by frequently chanting the word "politician." A full appreciation of the process of American government can be obtained only by a knowledge of the intricate structure of American government and the highly complex interrelationships that characterize this structure. And it is on the "politicians" we place the heavy burden of making it work. A fuller realization of the magnitude of his task will lead not only to a greater appreciation of his real contribution to American life and culture but also to a keener insight into the basic processes of American government.]

THE MAGNITUDE OF THE TASK OF THE POLITICIAN [1]

by Frederick M. Davenport

IT is a safe venture to affirm that the number of persons in the country, who would regard as important a discussion of the task of the politician, is not large. A much more popular and intelligible topic would be the task of ridding ourselves of the politician. Very few lift hand or pen or voice in his defense. In recent times Wallas, Lippmann and Frankfurter have given more than fugitive evidence of an appreciative understanding of him, but it has been left for F. S. Oliver, in the opening chapter of his work upon the endless adventure of governing men, a chapter in praise of politicians beginning with Walpole, to present in terms of whimsical, yet profound social, insight the service and function of the politician under any government, particularly a democracy.

It is true about politicians in general that there is much that is unlovely. The public has in mind the unintelligent, brawling, municipal wardheeler, who preys upon the widespread helplessness of large elements in the population, whose economic underpinning is graft and corruption, who fattens upon the incompetence and failure of the underprivileged. The public has in mind the machine boss who is mentally pictured as seeking and gaining power for his own upbuilding, and as pursuing at all times his own selfish interest. The public thinks of the legislator as one who is likely to lack courage, to prove the proverbial opportunist, the temporizer, the arrant compromiser. The public thinks of a political organization as built upon the lowest instincts which human beings possess, and of the politician as the man who must, in order to win, fall in with the method and the technique associated with the management and mastery of the baser qualities of mankind.

The public knows the evil in politicians, and very little about the good in them. The press attends to that. Virtue is rarely worth a headline.

Formerly the banker, the financier and the captain of industry were merciless critics of the politician. This criticism has not been so severe recently, since glass houses became more common habitations. The wholesale condemnation of the public men known as politicians, whether in high place or low, has become shallow and menacing. It has helped to undermine the

[1] F. M. Davenport, "The Magnitude of the Task of the Politician," *Harvard Business Review* (July, 1933), Vol. XI, No. 4, pp. 468-477. Reprinted by permission of the author and the *Harvard Business Review*.

prestige of the public service and to weaken the leadership of the country. It is not without reason that we take stock afresh of the real function of the able and useful type of politician and his place in the governmental order.

As a matter of fact, the politician is the person who actually brings things to pass within the fabric of government. Nothing much would happen in that field without him. He is the expert in the political behavior of the electorate. He understands human nature. He charts human prejudices and prepossessions and emotions. He knows his social psychology. The political thinker, the advisory counselor, may furnish the idea. The politician knows whether the idea is practical and can be maneuvered through the channels and past the reefs of public sentiment and into safe harbor in the Law and the Constitution. He is the navigator of the Ship of State. No one can take his place in a storm. What Lincoln did in the years 1861-1865 was to bring into safe harbor the idea of Webster that the Union must be preserved. When Lincoln entered the presidency, his position on slavery was Webster's position: it must not extend into any new territory. Lincoln navigated Webster's ideas through to success and broadened them into the policy that all men everywhere under the American flag should be free. Lincoln was the master of his country's fate and the captain of her soul, because he was the master politician of her history.

The most successful presidents have been the best politicians in a high sense—but politicians. The American people do not appreciate administrative capacity in the presidency to anything like the degree that they appreciate a sense of human contact with the President: that he is par excellence, their voice, their spokesman, their friend.

Contrary to the usual belief, a great part of the success of the American Revolution and of the new government of 1789 was due to the amazing political instinct of George Washington. If you wish a picture of the politician who became our first President, hear this description of him in Philadelphia—as a member of the Continental Congress, accompanied by loyal Virginians ready to join with the other colonies in a martial adventure which might lead to infamy or renown. His latest biographer writes:

> When Colonel Washington strode through the streets of Philadelphia, his imposing ways, his tall form in his handsome uniform . . . attracted a great deal of notice. He went here and there everywhere in the city, buying provisions, arms and munitions for his Virginians. He did not talk, but quietly purchased and paid. He made a profound impression. He was seen everywhere. In the morning and afternoon in Congress, in the evening at the tavern with the merchants, or dining in society . . . with the ostentatious banker Morris or with the well-known lawyer Dickinson, with Mayor Fisher,

with the leading Quakers. . . . He was untiring. One Sunday morning he appeared at a Quaker meeting. In the afternoon he attended the service in the Church of England. On the Sunday following he went to hear a morning sermon in the Presbyterian Church, and attended benediction at the Catholic Church after lunch. He frequented the taverns where the New England delegates were lodged, as well as those where the delegates from Carolina were dined, and going everywhere, wherever he went he gave the same telling impression of force, resolution and calm.

There was your political genius. In the living room at Mt. Vernon and in the House of Burgesses he met and learned to influence his own aristocratic class, and after his campaign around Boston and his association with the free and independent Yankees, who went off home whenever it struck their fancy and came back when they were ready, he learned to understand and to manage the peculiarly free and easy traits of that inchoate and loosely organized body of human beings, later to be known as the American people. Washington and the Declaration of Independence were at the moment the only genuinely fusing forces in the population.

Theodore Roosevelt was a great public leader because he was a great political craftsman. His genius, as I observed it when he was President, lay in his capacity to listen to a half dozen differing views upon a problem which he himself did not yet understand; and when the experts were through, he then knew which one of the various ideas was practical and would pass muster with the informed sentiment of the country. He took the Government of the United States out of a rut for the first time in a generation, and the country liked it.

The able and useful type of politician is the man who persuades people to behave like rational human beings when they are in danger of milling around like muddle-headed cattle, something that now and then happens in the best-regulated democracies. He understands the management of the gregarious instinct in mankind. He has a peculiar sensitivity to the mental, and particularly to the emotional, processes of the popular mind. He knows how to mellow and mollify, if anybody can, the pressure groups, such as the newspapers, the financiers, the labor leaders, the veterans, the farmers. His is the task in a modern democracy of moulding these disparate and often hostile interests into something like mutual understanding. It is his business to refine and combine the two kinds of energies which are ever fighting for the mastery in a democracy—the ignorance, the folly, the envy, the passion, the prejudice and the self-interest on the one hand, and the virtue, the kindliness and the idealism of the masses of the people on the other.

The mind of the able politician is a social laboratory. There he tests social experiments by his intuitive reactions. There are no laboratories for the social sciences in the sense that there are for the natural sciences. There is past experience, but that is no demonstration of future experience, because too many social variables are constantly appearing. The changes going on all the time within the consciousness of a mighty, turbulent democracy such as we now have in America, the shifting of effective motives, the transitoriness of sentiment, the social forces on the march which are dimly forming and cannot be resisted, these the true type of politician detects and respects, even when he seeks to alter their course or clarify their objectives, or perhaps attempts to thwart them altogether.

It is in this field that the politician completely overtops the academic thinker upon public affairs. It is his awareness of new premises and of invincible psychological realities which leads him sharply to check up on the policies of the university expert, the advisory counselor or the member of a brain trust. For example, it was upon the rock of the inner feeling and bitter economic necessity of distraught mankind that the successive agreements about reparations and war debts came to wreck. It was the sense of injustice in the breasts of German youth, faced with the black cloud of 62 years of economic despair, which produced Hitler instead of payments on account. Expertly well-wrought-out plans they were, but they paid little attention to the processes of human nature in vast populations. In the midst of many intricate devices proposed in Washington to create a rise in the price level, we are obliged to remember that if schemes are framed without the divination of political genius, they are sure to fail. Whether it is the economic rule of supply and demand or the subtler psychological behavior of human nature in an emergency, if the rule or the trend is violated, there always remains the law of gravitation to bring the schemes to earth.

So far as it is necessary for us to go on employing the method of trial and error in the social process, and that is still likely to be for a good while, the politician will continue to be a useful individual. He will even change his mind, and that is painful business, as every academic person knows. In a changing world there is much to be said for such a practical mental trait. So far as we can bring ourselves to provide in advance against our catastrophes and miseries, we shall find the predictive capacity of the true politician to be of inestimable advantage in determining what method of defense and adjustment will work, and what will not. In helping to bring the right thing to pass, there is nobody who can gauge so well the probable political behavior of masses of men.

Even in what we regard as the submerged areas of municipal politics, which have their foundations in graft and the spoils system, the politician and his organization perform indispensable services. In ordinary times as well as in critical times, the political machine in New York City or Boston or Philadelphia is busily finding employment for those who are out of work, is feeding the hungry without ostentation, is maintaining the morale of the plain citizen in difficulty whose actual government seems to be far away from him. There is an intimate friendliness about the neighborhood political clubhouse which, alas, government cannot match. It is true that warm shoes against the winter slush and happy picnics for the district are no fair shield for governmental incompetence and political exploitation and corruption. But it is also true that there are real human traits in these political organizations which are deep and true; and that is the reason, I take it, that the shifting masses of our metropolitan populations in the long run respond more naturally to the humanness of the machine than to the mechanical shortsightedness and cold efficiencies of reform governments. As a bulwark against proletarian revolution in certain large cities of the United States, I put the politician and his organization at the head of the list. At least where he is in the flower of his control, men will never riot because they are hungry.

There is another point. The large municipalities of the country have built up a complicated system of government. There are certain functions within their borders exercised by the Federal Government, certain by the states, certain by the counties, certain by the boroughs perhaps, certain by the municipal entities themselves. In the city of Chicago there are scores of independent local governments operating within the limits of the city. There are boards of estimate and aldermen and sinking funds and taxes and assessments, and many more. In order to get effective government there must be a correlation in action, in planning, in progress. The parts must fit together and work reasonably smoothly, if the man on the street is to get anything out of it. For example, the plain citizen is interested in good health. He wants the Federal Government to quarantine the plague cases in the port. He expects the municipality to inspect the milk. He depends upon the state to deal with river pollution. But it is the invisible politician, and he only, who establishes unity and coherence of protection for the common man.

The government of the state and nation has become a vast, technical tangle of activities, necessarily administered by bureaucratic competence or incompetence, as the case may be. But the contact of bureaucracy with the desires and ambitions, the hopes and the needs of the average man, no one supplies but the politician. That is practically one-half the task of the conscientious member of Congress. The human relation of a genuine representative with hundreds of his constituents is as intimate as that of the doctor, the lawyer, the priest or the minister. The taxpayers, the veterans, the immigration derelicts, the citizens with business troubles, job-hunters and information seekers, not to mention the postmasters—the political representative in Congress has these groups always with him, sleeping or waking.

The Congress of the United States, made up largely of politicians, is sometimes a very foolish body, but it is a true cross section of the American people. Its very faults and blunderings are the faults and blunderings of the American people. Its aspirations and ideals, its yearnings for a better economic and social order, are the yearnings, the aspirations and the ideals of the American people. It has given evidence of futility in the presence of pressure groups and crises, but the way out in the long run in America, let us hope, is not through dictatorships within or without the Constitution. Pouring difficult and dangerous problems into the lap of the President of the United States, in the hope that the zeal and toil of his advisory experts will prevent his being overwhelmed, is not an inspiring sight. It is not the way of hope or courage or intelligence in the long run. The way out is through more and better politically and socially minded leaders in Congress, recruited especially from the young men and women to whom the country has given the higher training at great cost, looking appealingly to them to support this country with their intelligence and character in the hour of her need. Instead of contemptuously sniffing at politicians and denouncing those who occupy positions of authority and power, we should look to them to give a fair portion of their energy, their time and their integrity to the development of political talent and genius in the rough and tumble reality of citizenship. The American people, their humorists, their editors, their critics, ought to teach the young men and women of the present generation that, next to enlisting in war in a great emergency, there is nothing more difficult or more important than enlisting and fighting in the public service.

In my opinion there is no more alarming symptom in the American democracy than the tendency on every hand to point the finger of scorn at the Congress of the United States. There is nothing which has had more certain effect in enfeebling that body, burdened as it is with complexity of problem and gravity of decision. If the sentiment of millions at home is hostile to the army, the army must collapse. If the sentiment of the people at home is hostile to their public servants, consciously or unconsciously their public servants cannot do their best. If the American people expected more from the Congress of the United States, they would receive more.

America never stood in greater need of exponents of social wisdom. Such persons, I suppose, are university experts, and others. Also the country never stood in greater need of leaders with practical judgment and skill to put wisdom into action. Such persons in a democracy are and always will be politicians. And it is no easy job. In modern governments we have entered upon the path of attempting the deliberate direction of human affairs by conscious intelligence. There is no other way; certainly not for America, in spite of the contention of Burke and Disraeli that the reason of men is inadequate for any great political or social achievement. The study of Recent Social Trends by a Federal commission indicates clearly enough that the only hope is in a new leadership of social wisdom. In that report we find abundant evidence, if it were needed, that "the capitalist economic system is collapsing under pressure and that problems of great variety and complexity are upon us—the poverty of the marginal farmer; the insecurity of wage earners; the perplexity of consumers; the plight of the railways; the speculative instability of the banking system; the failure of the flow of credit and purchasing power to synchronize with the flow of production; the weakness and dishonesty of the corporate structure; the chaos of international relations, communication among peoples proceeding more speedily than the reorganization of goodwill; great strain and tension resulting from changes in phases of national and world economy at different rates of speed." Furthermore, there is no likelihood that the issues will grow less complicated with time. There is no evidence that the problems can be solved or even analyzed without technical knowledge of the highest order.

Government is called upon to ease the tension, to lessen the strain, to mend the broken circuits, to stimulate social invention so that it may keep pace with mechanical invention. Private initiative and intelligence have failed. The quality of instruments of government is imperfect. Above all there still remains in the American population a dangerous amount of heterogeneity, unintelligence, inertia, indifference. Inventive social ideas are not enough. They are valueless except when combined with knowledge of the principles and practice of political navigation. None can pilot the Ship of State in such mounting seas except those possessed of the highest type of political talent and genius. But the attitude of public opinion is hostile to the normal functioning of such individuals, highly unfavorable to the breeding or training of the kind of leaders we need most. The traditional ill-repute of the politician is so firmly fixed in the popular mind that it is difficult to secure the enlistment of the most intelligent and the ablest.

Democracy is in trouble. Other forms of government like fascism or bolshevism look like temporary expedients, useful though they may be in their place and time. The only way out appears to be through a better government by better politicians, supported by a better quality of trained intelligence. And let me now speak up for the expert. It is very evident that I put the politician ahead of him. The place of the expert, as somebody has said, is "on tap and not on top." The university expert who has not associated much with politicians is a dangerous person in public affairs, but he learns a great deal from association with politicians. He learns that it is one thing to spawn ideas and another thing to keep them alive and potent. He learns that the field of theory may be on a different planet from the field of reality. He learns that it is one thing to invent a political policy and another thing to make Congress or the country believe in it or vote for it. The expert learns from the politician that he must keep his premises up to date. The consent of the governed is no more an infallible political principle than the theory that all men everywhere follow the line of their own self-interest is an infallible economic principle. The politician must deal constantly with social variables. Sometimes the expert learns that, too.

When he is able to find his way around in public affairs, it is true that the university expert is able to furnish a rich background of fertile and alternative suggestions to the politician. For example, the politician could never interpret and discuss the gold and credit and price-level problem without the expert at his ear. The politician would be quite out of his depth in the midst of the agenda of the world economic conference without the self-same life preserver buoying him up. So it boils down to the point that good experts can make good ammunition, but it is the politician who shoots it and knows when. The politician takes dough from the expert, but if it ever becomes well-baked bread, it will be in the politician's oven.

Business leaders are constantly being importuned to be more active in the political field. It is important that they should be, but they have equally to remember with the academic expert that business acumen and political skill are quite different characteristics. Business men in political affairs may fail because they may not possess, or even succeed in developing, this particular political skill. They may have neither the indirect technique nor the camaraderie of the politician. Unless they, too, have come along the path of a reasonable amount of everyday political experience, they are pretty certain to get into hot water unless escorted about by a lieutenant who does understand political human nature.

Having thus prepared the way, I hasten to say that day-by-day government at Washington would be paralyzed without the expert. There are ten thousand civil-service positions scattered throughout the departments of the Federal Government which are nearly all filled by college and university men and women—medical experts, legal experts, engineering experts, chemists, physicists, biologists, economists. . . . [The extent of turnover in the civil service in the United States following a shift in party control of the administration generally has been greater than in England. Following the

British Labour party victory in 1924, it has been said that the shift in personnel was less than a hundred persons in the British government. The shift after the Labour victory in 1945 also was less than has usually been the case in the United States. The situation in this country in recent years, however, has been moving in the direction of that in Britain as more and more Government workers are brought under the merit system and given greater security of tenure.]

The houses of Congress gingerly employ the expert. Of course Congress has an excellent staff of legislative draftsmen. But at the most important point of testimony-taking before committees, there is a curious futility. The committee advertises a hearing upon an important measure and opens it wide to all who come. Those who have especial interest on one side or the other appear and overwhelm the committee with statistical tables and reams of alleged information and *ex parte* material. The university expert is heard if he is interested enough to appear, and occasionally he is sent for, but he is usually under the suspicion of some member of the committee as having been planted for a purpose. Far better results would be obtained, I think, if the committees of Congress themselves habitually called in trained university experts, from various fields, whenever needed, and paid them from contingent appropriations. These experts might well meet in advance of the hearings, in executive session with the committees, to aid in marking the bounds of useful inquiry. There is now a vast waste of time and energy in excursions far afield. It would be good practice, I think, if these experts called by the committee were to sit throughout the hearings and listen to the testimony, master it, help to evaluate it, and interpret it finally in executive session with the committee. Such a use of experts would be more helpful to Congress than the system which now prevails.

There is a feeling in this country that advisory commissions appointed by executive or legislature are likely to be unproductive. If there were a better tradition, like the tradition which supports the British Royal Commission, the plan would be less objectionable. When the Government of England asks the King to appoint a Royal Commission, it is practically the delegation of the matter to arbitration—the relation at least borders upon the arbitrative—and the Government is bound to take favorable notice of the report. This tradition about it is generally accepted in English political thought. Of course it is not so in this country because we have no fixed nonpolitical authority like a king. Without some such tradition, the expert member of a commission in this country often finds himself in an unpleasant dilemma. Before he knows it he is in danger of becoming a tame expert, chained to the person of the executive who appointed the commission or to the majority-party organization in the legislature. The self-respecting individual finds himself unable to accept this relationship and is driven either to run the commission or write his own report. A commission of this kind must be free from political pressure or its purpose fails.

It requires some refinement of method to fit the university expert into the structure of American Government, but, nevertheless, his service is indispensable. In a world increasingly dominated by economic and techno-logical methods and forces, there is no getting on without his trained intelli-gence. The passions and imaginations of men still startle us in political crises with bursts of instinctive power, but they are far less sure-footed than they were in simpler times with simpler issues.

If the question were asked whether popular government on the whole has grown stronger and more effective in the last 25 years in the United States, I do not think it could be answered whole-heartedly in the affirma-tive. A good deal of democratization of society is clear enough. Dress and fashion are for all, or nearly all. They no longer establish a line of demarcation between economic classes. Public education is for all, although we are by no means sure that public education is what it ought to be. The motor car, the moving picture, the radio are for all. But of democracy as a way of government, not so much that is favorable can be said.

Twenty-five years ago we entered upon a crusade to break the politician and the party machine. They had developed forms of autocracy and rela-tions with corporate wealth which were obnoxious to the American people. We established the direct primary, not as a far-sighted student of govern-ment like ex-Governor Hughes of New York would have had us do it, with organized leadership at the heart of it, but in a heedless and irresponsible form. We were through with politicians and bosses and machine managers who had led us astray and left us in the wilderness. We sought to strip political parties and political organizations of their power. We idealized the common man in the direct primary. We assumed that he would do right under all conditions, that he would show himself unselfish, unpreju-diced, unbiased. It is difficult to conceive that the popular primary will ever be taken away from the common man. No power of that sort, once granted is ever withdrawn. Sometimes the common man has made good use of it. But having learned the trick of popular organization, he has more or less left the direct primary to shift for itself or to be run by the politician behind the scenes, and has gone off to form blocs and willful minorities and pressure groups to confound representative popular govern-ment and to land it in a political morass.

The American people have been startled at the ineffectiveness of their Congress in recent emergencies. The houses of Congress themselves have recognized their own helplessness and have delivered their authority to the executive to exercise for them. There are, I think, two outstanding causes of the present weakness of congressional government in Washington. The first, of course, is the presence of widely heterogeneous elements in the population itself, as well as diverse sectional backgrounds and interests. Representatives in Congress are dependent for their political lives upon the diverse and heterogeneous temperaments and sentiments of their own districts. Out of such extreme divergence of viewpoint upon many questions, it is hard to get a national program even in time of dangerous stress and strain.

The other cause of the present weakness of Congress is the influence of pressure groups which are no longer secret lobbies of the old order, but open organizations of men and women out to punish any Representative who opposes the particular special interest of their own enthusiasm and desire. The number of these open associations, which are bent on ending the career of members of Congress whom they cannot control on some one issue, is large and increasing. The most independent and far-sighted Representatives from the standpoint of the nation are most exposed to the ravages of these pressure groups.

I do not believe that the effective corrective of this growing menace to American nationality and liberty is to be found in the movement, which is now going on apace, to organize pressure groups on the other side of these issues to do battle with their adversaries for the voting bodies and souls of their elected Representatives. The transfer of the field of political conflict to this extra-legal area of voluntary associations pitted against each other, will not, it seems to me, help the Government or the country, but will make confusion worse confounded.

We must come back to the business of strengthening and improving the genus politician. He is the man who knows how in a democracy. Only there must be more of him, possessed of higher intellectual and moral quality than at present. He can make democracy work and nobody else can. In order to widen the field of selection of the politician, there must be many thousands of recruits from the younger citizenship who, as a part of their regular and ordinary lives, begin the practice of politics at the grass roots.

Many persons have learned to be politicians by seeking office. That is a good method of finding out whether a man or woman has political intuition, but it is economically a hazardous way unless the individual can afford it. Politicians are of little use to the country unless they are willing occasionally to lose elections for their own convictions. But there must be at least a willingness to set aside a reasonable portion of one's time to learn to practice the political process, to gain, as Oliver says:

> an understanding sympathy with one's fellow creatures, to mix and fight and fraternize with all sorts and conditions of men, to have the good fortune

to meet people face to face whose opinions you abhor, and be buffeted by them, and give as good as you get, and know how to take it.

It is in this rough and tumble that politicians are made. When they are made and have the right quality, they can do swiftly for the country more than the clash of pressure groups can ever accomplish. They can establish personal loyalties which will mellow and melt even racial heterogeneity into national unity. For what is politics but courage and common sense and the capacity to understand people, to harmonize and compromise, and yet have strength of character enough to stick to what you believe is right for the community and the country?

You may win very little appreciation and you are sure to win almost no gratitude, but there is nothing comparable with it as a field of potent endeavor for one's country and mankind. The chief reason, next to softness of fiber, that far larger numbers of the young men and women of the country do not employ their energies in this field, and that the best brains of the country are not enlisted in its political defense, is the almost universal and shameless denunciation of public servants in America, which has made it impossible for the right tradition to grow.

Once more, a supporting comment from Oliver:

> Politics is the most hazardous of all professions. There is not another in which a man can hope to do so much good to his fellow creatures, neither is there any in which by a mere loss of nerve he may do such widespread harm, nor is there another in which he may so easily lose his own soul, nor is there another in which a positive and strict veracity is so difficult. But danger is the inseparable companion of honor. With all the temptations and degradations that beset it, politics is still the noblest career that any man can choose.

No. 37

[ASIDE from the examination and analysis of the character and value of the party system in its broadest sense, it is important to examine the detailed character of the organization of political parties. This is even more important at the local level than at the national.

It is in the local community that the day-to-day work of the political party is carried on; it is in the local community that the citizens have the power to control that work. Yet it is in the local political organizations that most of the graft and corruption have been and are to be found.

The following selection discusses one of the most important features of local political organization, namely, the local political club. It was written by one of the great political figures in American history, Alfred E. Smith. Having been both governor of New York and a candidate for the Presidency of the United

States, Al Smith knew politics and offers here a first-hand view of this important aspect of American party life. He knew that it was through participation in local politics that the young man or woman could play a vital role in the development of a more effective democracy.]

THE POLITICAL PARTY AND THE LOCAL POLITICAL CLUB [1]

by Alfred E. Smith

THE first thing to consider in a discussion of "the citizen and his government" is the smallest and most basic unit of political organization under our party system—that is, the local political club. Naturally, and because of geographic rather than any other influence, local political clubs find their greatest development in the cities and in the areas of cities where the population is most concentrated. The fact that country or suburban dwellers maintain a more natural sort of neighborliness than the city man who lives in an apartment or tenement house probably has something to do with this. Farmers or suburbanites usually know their next-door neighbors and a good many others within a short distance of their homes well enough to mingle with them socially and secure companionship or, if need be, assistance.

In the cities, however, the great variance in the backgrounds and living habits of the millions of citizens, as well as the very closeness with which they are packed into the houses in which they live, has resulted in an almost complete lack of the quality of neighborliness. Most city people do not even know the names of those living in the same house with them, much less have much social contact with their close neighbors.

Therefore the local political clubs, which in the last analysis exchange social contacts and political and economic services for votes, offer a natural and much used gathering-place for the citizens, young and old, of the cities and particularly of the neighborhood in which each club may be located.

When young Johnny Brown reaches the age to possess a night-key of his own he is going to be attracted to the local political club. In spite of the fact that the city in which he lives may offer a thousand and one different attractions, amusements, and educational opportunities, the local political club is going to seem a natural center of interest and excitement for everyone in the neighborhood. In it Johnny will see the people of his own district, sharing his own economic and social interests, given an oppor-

[1] Alfred E. Smith, *The Citizen and His Government* (New York: Harper and Brothers, 1935), pp. 3-19. Reprinted by permission of the publisher.

tunity to enjoy contact with their friends and neighbors which they could not otherwise enjoy; and in it he will especially realize that he and his family may obtain the highly prized "favors" and services of the political leader and his assistants.

At some stage in Johnny Brown's career he has probably attended a picnic under the club's auspices in the summer. In the fall, especially in the exciting pre-election weeks, he has seen great activity and much to interest him around the clubhouse. Bands play and parades carrying the traditional red fire, political signs, and orators set out to stump the neighborhood for votes. Many other social and political events of great glamour to a young fellow center around the club.

Johnny may have an older brother or father who is a member, and if he is an alert young man who watches what is going on about him he will inevitably look forward to the day when he will be able to join the club and himself take part in the political meetings. When Johnny comes of age there will be no trouble about becoming a member of his local political club. There is nothing exclusive about it. The most necessary qualification for membership is simply the ability and legal qualification to vote. Johnny's name will almost automatically be added to the rolls of eligible voters and placed in its proper alphabetical order. This may be done at the suggestion of one of his relatives; or perhaps one of his pals who is active in the club and anxious to receive the credit for bringing in a new member may see to it that he is properly enrolled.

From this point on Johnny's prominence in local affairs and city, state, or nationwide politics will be entirely dependent upon himself: first upon his natural ability for politics and for developing friendships and a following; and second upon his desire to make politics a career or on the other hand to use the club simply as a social meeting-place.

Johnny Brown will unquestionably be anxious to become acquainted with the district leader himself. This leader will be a man of whom he has heard much, a man who takes the position of a sort of neighborhood idol, interested in all affairs, personal and political, large or small, of the people in his neighborhood; a man able to accomplish things in a very definite manner and a man looked up to by a large number of people in the neighborhood who depend upon the political organization for assistance in a thousand and one different matters.

Johnny soon finds that the district leader is a busy man, probably to some extent a fairly mysterious individual—most of his club members believe there is some occult political power through which the leader moves to perform his wonderful acts and favors for his people. But yesterday or to-day, the district leader's primary responsibility is to deliver as many solid and definitely countable votes as possible for his party from the neighborhood around his clubhouse. Upon his ability to deliver at every election and to repeat unfailingly his delivery of a definite and preferably growing party strength, depends his survival as a leader, because a man who cannot keep his people in line cannot qualify as a leader in any sense of the word, political or social, and will not last long as a political power.

Contrary to the belief of Johnny Brown and a great many others un-schooled in the political system, the district leader's job is not entirely con-fined to securing employment for those in the district who may be in need of it. On the other hand, we do find that a great many people in the district turn to the leader for every sort of assistance and advice, particu-larly on many matters that have nothing to do with government. It is through these services that the district leader gains the loyal following which enables him to deliver votes that make him a power to be reckoned with and considered in the larger party organization.

Therefore, the district leaders set up in their clubhouses a sort of modern organized counterpart of the old trade guilds or other community centers where the people of earlier days were able to find advice, counsel and assist-ance. The difference is that the trade guilds of the middle ages were simply social organizations designed to set up a system whereby families might share prosperity and assist one another. The man who had steady work and a good income for a long period might be able through a common organization to help another member of the same craft who was destitute and had not been able to make enough money to keep his family in food and clothing. There was no necessity in those past centuries for a political organization. Such activities were either forbidden or seriously discouraged because the ruling powers wanted no interference with their own govern-ment and did not wish the people to have any organized voice.

To-day under our democratic system, it is very necessary that the people have these local political units where they may gather and where the politi-cal thoughts and aims of individuals may be consolidated into an organized powerful voice of the group or the political party. Just as the score or more of neighborhood clubs in a big city combine their views and their sentiments to make the sentiment and power of the Democratic or Republi-can party of the city as a whole, individuals within the district clubhouse and its leader express the wishes, thoughts, and aspirations of all the voters of the neighborhood.

The clubhouse provides almost everything that a poor man may need and which he cannot find elsewhere. No loyal member within the district will ever be forgotten in the apportionment of assistance. A destitute family in one tenement house may be noticed and sought out by a captain in the next house who is responsible for the votes of the families in his immediate block or street. The clubhouse will be notified and coal, food, cash, or medical aid obtained through the district leader or his assistants. This applies whether or not that family includes actual members of the club.

Every clubhouse of any prominence has a lawyer or local judge present most of the time, and citizens of the district, irrespective of their membership in the club, can come to these people for free legal advice. Small business men come to the leader with their business troubles. I have myself seen the secretary of a local organization making out a statement of loss because of fire for a storekeeper unable to read or write English.

The local clubhouse can make no distinction between citizens or aliens. If the alien does not vote this year, he may become a citizen and have a vote next year, and certainly if he is helped while an alien and learns to depend upon the district organization for assistance in earning a living and becoming an American, the club can count on his support when he receives his citizenship papers.

The district leader is a slave to his voters from morning until midnight and for three hundred and sixty-five days in the year. No exertion is too great, no favor too insignificant, to obtain his attention, and in return he asks only loyalty and a measure of help at election time from his people.

District leaders are not paid for their political or community services. They draw no salaries from their clubhouses or local organizations, and to the best of my memory I cannot recall a clubhouse which made a profit or which was even able to meet its expenses. Therefore most district leaders are unable to devote all of their time to clubhouse activities and must engage in other businesses to support themselves and their families. Between the two functions of earning a living and retaining political leadership by service to the party and its people, the leader finds more than enough to occupy the working hours of each day.

A considerable part of the district leader's time has to be spent in attending to the many personal affairs of his neighbors and club members. It is a necessary part of his efforts to cement and foster the warm feeling and personal friendship of the people in his neighborhood which are essential in his political work. Therefore the district leader attends funerals, wakes, marriages, and christenings. He makes himself a leading figure at any neighborhood dance or social function. In some districts the summer picnics and winter balls given by the district club under the personal auspices of the leader are notable affairs that are awaited the year round by the people of the neighborhood, both young and old.

One organization holds a yearly party in Central Park at which several thousand mothers and children get a day in the open, free milk and ice cream, sandwiches and athletics, and at which a money prize is awarded for the most beautiful children, the most freckled boy and girl, and so on.

Another neighborhood organization holds a great yearly dance at the Hotel Astor in New York, where the grand march is always led by the leader, and at which the attendance includes many of the notables and officials of the city and state.

In a great many cases the interest of the leader and his organization in the personal affairs of a family means a great deal more than just participating in their social affairs. There is the concrete and specific matter of supplying the means to live. Families in distress because of death, sickness, or unemployment are aided in thousands of instances by the local club, and it is through such activities that our young friend Johnny Brown learns to count on the district leader and his clubhouse for warmth and friendly spirit in any trouble he may come up against in the conduct of his daily life, or that of his family.

Of course, one of the great features of the club is that if functions all year round. The leader or his representative is available at any time, Sundays and holidays included, and this means much in meeting the inevitable emergencies that will arise in the lives of the several thousand families concentrated in a crowded city district. A friend or relative may get in some sort of trouble in the middle of the night. Perhaps he is arrested and the family does not know where to turn for bail money. The district leader, if he knows the family and has faith in their honesty, will find a bond and obtain the prisoner's freedom until the case comes up and the district club can provide a lawyer to help defend him against the charge.

It is easy to see why the district leader becomes a sort of neighborhood idol, a real figure of pure sympathy and help in human form, and why he is able to command political loyalty in return for the manifold acts he is able to perform for his people.

Along about this point I can hear our friend Johnny Brown asking how the district leader gets to be in such a position, how he becomes leader, and why he retains the job.

It must be borne in mind that while political parties have their form of organization, selection of officers, time of meetings, and such provided by law, the district club itself has no official standing in the governmental set-up. The organization of the Democratic and Republican parties as well as the minor parties, the manner in which their meetings are to be held and their officers elected, are all specified in state laws. The district club is only a unit of a larger party, and its operations and the manner in which it elects its officers, collects its dues, and conducts its activities are governed entirely by tradition and by the wishes of the club members and their leader.

The district leader, as such, holds no political office, has no power of an official nature, but most of them are appointed to public position, and therein lies their aid to clubhouse activities.

The district leader is usually someone who has been active and well liked in the social and business and political life of his neighborhood long before his actual participation in official party activities.

The district club is made up of two classes of membership—first, those who belong by actual and official registration to the political party represented by the local club; and second, those who, while not actually enrolled on the lists of the party, support the policy of the party and generally may be expected to adhere to its ticket on election day.

Since the district leader's position and the manner of attaining it are not defined by law, it is up to these club members to select from their ranks a person in whom they are all willing to repose confidence and whom they wish to elevate to the post of leader. The method of doing this has become so basic a part of the modern political picture that everyone should thoroughly understand it. The state law provides that in each county there shall be a County Committee made up of as many members as the rules and regulations of the party provide. This rule is usually based on a ratio of one representative in the County Committee for a given number of votes cast for the particular party at the preceding general election. That would mean that in a strong democratic district in New York City there would probably be two hundred or two hundred and fifty members of the County Committee. In another county of the state the ratio of one representative for only twenty-five party votes may be adopted, and in still another the ratio may be one for each fifty votes. Therefore the size of the membership of the various county committees throughout the state varies with the wishes of the local organization.

The Democratic County Committee of New York County (Manhattan Island) is composed of more than six thousand people, and the membership is kept at a large figure intentionally in order to bring as many of the voters as possible into prominence in party affairs. The County Committee is made up of delegations from the Assembly Districts, with each individual delegate representing a few voters in his immediate neighborhood in the selection of candidates and in the guidance of party policies.

The district leader is always a member of the County Committee and meets with this committee, at a time specified by law after the members are selected by the voters at the primary election, to elect a chairman and other officers. These officers are charged by law with the conduct of the party's affairs.

Obviously the great number of members from each district makes the

County Committee as a whole too large to transact all its business directly. Therefore the members of the County Committee in each district meet and select a representative to sit on a central committee known as the Executive Committee, which conducts the party affairs. The members of this Executive Committee are the district leaders, and their continuance as members of the Executive Committee is only an official symbol or notice of the fact that they are continuing as leaders of their own local political organizations.

The law, of course, does not provide for the existence of an Executive Committee. It is a voluntary body representing the wishes of the larger committee, and the men selected to sit in the Executive Committee have in turn control over the election of a county leader, who becomes the most publicly known of his party in the larger city organization. Obviously the Executive Committee, unofficial as it is, is a more powerful body than the County Committee, although the County Committee enjoys a legal standing which is denied to the Executive Committee.

In the event that any considerable number of the party members of a political district become dissatisfied with their leader and wish to oust him and place someone else in his position, it is necessary for them to contest at the next primary election his candidacy for membership in the County Committee. If the incumbent leader is unable to marshal enough votes in his own district to keep his place on the County Committee, he is considered to have lost control of his district and is replaced by a new delegate to the Executive Committee from his district. Thus we see that the present political system in New York City is a mixture of legal and traditional practice, with only a part of the party organization specified and supported by law and the rest of the system created and continued under rules of usage rather than those of law.

The social activities of political organizations of the lower East Side were more important in the time of my boyhood than they are to-day. Any boy or girl of my generation will remember most vividly from his New York childhood the political chowder parties, ox-roasts, picnics, and banquets sponsored by the local political clubs. Every man, woman, or child of the district, irrespective of party affiliations, was invited to attend, and there would be a great junket up the river to some resort or beach point on Long Island.

It must not be thought that all political activity either in the old days or to-day is restricted to the Democratic party. The Republicans, as well, have their noted leaders, their district clubhouses, their parties and parades, and although they seldom win an election in New York City they keep up the local organization.

All in all, district leaders of old New York, and those of to-day as well, have done perhaps more than any other individuals to promote the welfare of their communities and to give opportunity for political and personal advancement to deserving young people.

If it had not been for Tom Foley, leader of the Second Assembly District, in which I was born and raised, and for the genuine care he took in fostering my career and giving me an opportunity to get ahead in public affairs, I should certainly never have been able to travel the long road of politics which I have seen in my lifetime. I think that most men in public office, or men who have gained prominence partly or wholly through politics, will bear me out when I say that without the help of their old-time district leaders they would never have been given the chance to show their mettle and to place their feet upon the first rung of the ladder of success. Tom Foley did no more for me than many another leader has done for other young men of his district. He gave me my chance at election to the Assembly because he thought I was capable and well enough known in the district to get the winning vote.

Leadership in a district is really a matter of the survival of the fittest. No leader gets or keeps his position without a genuine understanding of and sympathy with his own people—the people that make up his district and who are members of his club. Successful leaders spring from the rank and file, practically all of whom are struggling for power—practically every one of the rank and file hopes to become a leader himself. Leadership in a political organization, as in every other field of human endeavor, must be reached by hard work, brains, and a thorough ability to deal with people. There is no other way in which the ambition to become a leader can be achieved or a position of leadership retained.

My remarks about the district leaders would be incomplete if I did not record the fact that some of them, in the past, have been unfaithful to their trust and have used the power of their leadership to benefit themselves in a manner with which nobody could concur, but the answer to that is they only hold their positions by and with the consent of the majority of the members of the County Committee which they represent.

All that I have written upon this subject has reference to the past. I am firmly of the opinion that the younger generation now coming into power, because of numerical strength, are not going to be so easily led by the old-time political methods that I have herein described. I feel very strongly that consideration will in the future be given for service to the whole city by the political party rather than the ability of the district leader to hold his forces by personal favor. Shifting of population, change in conditions, make it difficult to operate under the old-time methods, and I feel that our younger people growing up will look to party achievement in the city as a whole rather than to the favor, friendship, or whatever you may desire to call it of the local political leader. Both of the major political parties lose their power when the great masses of the people became dissatisfied with their administration, and in that event I do not believe that the power or the influence of the district leader can avert political disaster. No matter how highly organized a political party may be, the people, when given a definite issue, decide elections without any consideration of political leadership. As far as patronage is concerned, it means nothing when there is an issue that appeals strongly to the people themselves. That fact has been demonstrated times without number in elections within the last twenty years. In other words, the younger people want the leadership of thought, the thought that means the betterment of the whole city.

No. 38

[THE preceding selection by Alfred E. Smith gives a good indication of the character and importance of the local political clubs. The following selection, presenting the views of a typical district leader in New York City, throws further light upon the character of the activities of local political leaders and their influence upon elections.]

TO HOLD YOUR DISTRICT—STUDY HUMAN NATURE AND ACT ACCORDIN'[1]

by W. L. Riordon

"THERE'S only one way to hold a district; you must study human nature and act accordin'. You can't study human nature in books. Books is a hindrance more than anything else. If you have been to college, so much the worse for you. You'll have to unlearn all you learned before you can get right down to human nature, and unlearnin' takes a lot of time. Some men can never forget what they learned at college. Such men may get to be district leaders by a fluke, but they never last.

"To learn real human nature you have to go among the people, see them and be seen. I know every man, woman, and child in the Fifteenth District, except them that's been born this summer—and I know some of them, too. I know what they like and what they don't like, what they are strong at and what they are weak in, and I reach them by approachin' at the right side.

---

[1] W. L. Riordon, *Plunkitt of Tammany Hall* (New York: McClure, Phillips and Co., 1905), pp. 46-53. Reprinted by permission of Doubleday, Doran and Company.

"For instance, here's how I gather in the young men. I hear of a young feller that's proud of his voice, thinks that he can sing fine. I ask him to come around to Washington Hall and join our Glee Club. He comes and sings, and he's a follower of Plunkitt for life. Another young feller gains a reputation as a base-ball player in a vacant lot. I bring him into our base-ball club. That fixes him. You'll find him workin' for my ticket at the polls next election day. Then there's the feller that likes rowin' on the river, the young feller that makes a name as a waltzer on his block, the young feller that's handy with his dukes—I rope them all in by givin' them opportunities to show themselves off. I don't trouble them with political arguments. I just study human nature and act accordin'.

"But you may say this game won't work with the high-toned fellers, the fellers that go through college and then join the Citizens' Union. Of course it wouldn't work. I have a special treatment for them. I ain't like the patent medicine man that gives the same medicine for all diseases. The Citizens' Union kind of a young man! I love him! He's the daintiest morsel of the lot, and he don't often escape me.

"Before telling you how I catch him, let me mention that before the election last year, the Citizens' Union said they had four hundred or five hundred enrolled voters in my district. They had a lovely headquarters, too, beautiful roll-top desks and the cutest rugs in the world. If I was accused of havin' contributed to fix up the nest for them, I wouldn't deny it under oath. What do I mean by that? Never mind. You can guess from the sequel, if you're sharp.

"Well, election day came. The Citizens' Union's candidate for Senator, who ran against me, just polled five votes in the district, while I polled something more than 14,000 votes. What became of the 400 or 500 Citizens' Union enrolled voters in my district? Some people guessed that many of them were good Plunkitt men all along and worked with the Cits just to bring them into the Plunkitt camp by election day. You can guess that way, too, if you want to. I never contradict stories about me, especially in hot weather. I just call your attention to the fact that on last election day 395 Citizens' Union enrolled voters in my district were missin' and unaccounted for.

"I tell you frankly, though, how I have captured some of the Citizens' Union's young men. I have a plan that never fails. I watch the City Record to see when there's civil service examinations for good things. Then I take my young Cit in hand, tell him all about the good thing and get him worked up till he goes and takes an examination. I don't bother about him any more. It's a cinch that he comes back to me in a few days and asks to join Tammany Hall. Come over to Washington Hall some night and I'll show you a list of names on our rolls marked 'C.S.' which means, 'bucked up against civil service.'

"As to the older voters, I reach them, too. No, I don't send campaign literature. That's rot. People can get all the political stuff they want to read—and a good deal more, too—in the papers. Who reads speeches, nowadays, anyhow? It's bad enough to listen to them. You ain't goin' to gain any votes by stuffin' the letter boxes with campaign documents. Like as not you'll lose votes, for there's nothin' a man hates more than to hear the letter-carrier ring his bell and go to the letter-box expectin' to find a letter he was lookin' for, and find only a lot of printed politics. I met a man this very mornin' who told me he voted the Democratic State ticket last year just because the Republicans kept crammin' his letter-box with campaign documents.

"What tells in holdin' your grip on your district is to go right down among the poor families and help them in the different ways they need help. I've got a regular system for this. If there's a fire in Ninth, Tenth, or Eleventh Avenue, for example, any hour of the day or night, I'm usually there with some of my election district captains as soon as the fire-engines. If a family is burned out I don't ask whether they are Republicans or Democrats, and I don't refer them to the Charity Organization Society, which would investigate their case in a month or two and decide they were worthy of help about the time they are dead from starvation. I just get quarters for them, buy clothes for them if their clothes are burned up, and fix them up till they get things runnin' again. It's philanthropy, but it's politics too—mighty good politics. Who can tell how many votes one of these fires bring me? The poor are the most grateful people in the world, and, let me tell you, they have more friends in their neighborhoods than the rich have in theirs.

"If there's a family in my district in want I know it before the charitable societies do, and me and my men are first on the ground. I have a special corps to look up such cases. The consequence is that the poor look up to George W. Plunkitt as a father, come to him in trouble—and don't forget him on election day.

"Another thing, I can always get a job for a deservin' man. I make it a point to keep on the track of jobs, and it seldom happens that I don't have a few up my sleeve ready for use. I know every big employer in the district and in the whole city, for that matter, and they ain't in the habit of sayin' no to me when I ask them for a job.

"And the children—the little roses of the district! Do I forget them? Oh, no! They know me, every one of them, and they know that a sight of Uncle George and candy means the same thing. Some of them are the best kind of vote-getters. I'll tell you a case. Last year a little Eleventh Avenue rosebud whose father is a Republican, caught hold of his whiskers on election day and said she wouldn't let go till he'd promise to vote for me. And she didn't."

No. 39

[IN every case the political boss must have some source of income to aid him in maintaining power. He may sell political favors; he may exact tribute from gamblers, houses of prostitution, dope peddlers, and the like; he may loot the public treasury and he may take advantage of his inside knowledge of governmental activities to profit by that information. The views of George Washington Plunkitt, a former Tammany district leader and State Senator in New York, on honest and dishonest graft give an interesting and unusual insight into some of the sources of the income of political bosses.]

HONEST AND DISHONEST GRAFT [1]

by W. L. Riordon

"EVERYBODY is talkin' these days about Tammany men growin' rich on graft, but nobody thinks of drawin' the distinction between honest graft and dishonest graft. There's all the difference in the world between the two. Yes, many of our men have grown rich in politics. I have myself. I've made a big fortune out of the game, and I'm gettin' richer every day, but I've not gone in for dishonest graft—blackmailin' gamblers, saloon-keepers, disorderly people, etc.—and neither has any of the men who have made big fortunes in politics.

"There's an honest graft, and I'm an example of how it works. I might sum up the whole thing by sayin': 'I seen my opportunities and I took 'em.'

"Just let me explain by examples. My party's in power in the city, and it's goin' to undertake a lot of public improvements. Well, I'm tipped off, say, that they're going to lay out a new park at a certain place.

"I see my opportunity and I take it. I go to that place and I buy up all the land I can in the neighborhood. Then the board of this or that makes its plan public, and there is a rush to get my land, which nobody cared particular for before.

"Ain't it perfectly honest to charge a good price and make a profit on my investment and foresight? Of course, it is. Well, that's honest graft.

"Or, supposin' it's a new bridge they're goin' to build. I get tipped off

[1] W. L. Riordon, *Plunkitt of Tammany Hall* (New York: McClure, Phillips and Co., 1905), pp. 3-10. Reprinted by permission of Doubleday, Doran and Company.

and I buy as much property as I can that has to be taken for approaches. I sell at my own price later on and drop some more money in the bank.

"Wouldn't you? It's just like lookin' ahead in Wall Street or in the coffee or cotton market. It's honest graft, and I'm lookin' for it every day in the year. I will tell you frankly that I've got a good lot of it, too.

"I'll tell you of one case. They were goin' to fix up a big park, no matter where. I got on to it, and went lookin' about for land in that neighborhood.

"I could get nothin' at a bargain but a big piece of swamp, but I took it fast enough and held on to it. What turned out was just what I counted on. They couldn't make the park complete without Plunkitt's swamp, and they had to pay a good price for it. Anything dishonest in that?

"Up in the watershed I made some money, too. I bought up several bits of land there some years ago and made a pretty good guess that they would be bought up for water purposes later by the city.

"Somehow, I always guessed about right, and shouldn't I enjoy the profit of my foresight? It was rather amusin' when the condemnation commissioners came along and found piece after piece of the land in the name of George Plunkitt of the Fifteenth Assembly District, New York City. They wondered how I knew just what to buy. The answer is—I seen my opportunity and I took it. I haven't confined myself to land; anything that pays is in my line.

"For instance, the city is repavin' a street and has several hundred thousand old granite blocks to sell. I am on hand to buy, and I know just what they are worth.

"How? Never mind that. I had a sort of monopoly of this business for a while, but once a newspaper tried to do me. It got some outside men to come over from Brooklyn and New Jersey to bid against me.

"Was I done? Not much. I went to each of the men and said: 'How many of these 250,000 stones do you want?' One said 20,000, and another wanted 15,000, and another wanted 10,000. I said: 'All right, let me bid for the lot, and I'll give each of you all you want for nothin'.'

"They agreed, of course. Then the auctioneer yelled: 'How much am I bid for these 250,000 fine pavin' stones?'

" 'Two dollars and fifty cents,' says I.

" 'Two dollars and fifty cents!' screamed the auctioneer. 'Oh, that's a joke! Give me a real bid.'

"He found the bid was real enough. My rivals stood silent. I got the lot for $2.50 and gave them their share. That's how the attempt to do Plunkitt ended, and that's how all such attempts end.

"I've told you how I got rich by honest graft. Now, let me tell you that most politicians who are accused of robbin' the city get rich the same way.

"They didn't steal a dollar from the city treasury. They just seen their opportunities and took them. That is why, when a reform administration comes in and spends a half million dollars in tryin' to find the public robberies they talked about in the campaign, they don't find them.

"The books are always all right. The money in the city treasury is all right. Everything is all right. All they can show is that the Tammany heads of departments looked after their friends, within the law, and gave them what opportunities they could to make honest graft. Now, let me tell you that's never going to hurt Tammany with the people. Every good man looks after his friends, and any man who doesn't isn't likely to be popular. If I have a good thing to hand out in private life, I give it to a friend. Why shouldn't I do the same in public life?

"Another kind of honest graft. Tammany has raised a good many salaries. There was an awful howl by the reformers, but don't you know that Tammany gains ten votes for every one it lost by salary raisin'?

"The Wall Street banker thinks it shameful to raise a department clerk's salary from $1500 to $1800 a year, but every man who draws a salary himself says: 'That's all right. I wish it was me.' And he feels very much like votin' the Tammany ticket on election day, just out of sympathy.

"Tammany was beat in 1901 because the people were deceived into believin' that it worked dishonest graft. They didn't draw a distinction between dishonest and honest graft, but they saw that some Tammany men grew rich, and supposed they had been robbin' the city treasury or levyin' blackmail on disorderly houses, or workin' in with the gamblers and law-breakers.

"As a matter of policy, if nothing else, why should the Tammany leaders go into such dirty business, when there is so much honest graft lyin' around when they are in power? Did you ever consider that?

"Now, in conclusion, I want to say that I don't own a dishonest dollar. If my worst enemy was given the job of writin' my epitaph when I'm gone, he couldn't do more than write:

" 'George W. Plunkitt. He Seen His Opportunities, and He Took 'Em.' "

Chapter XII

NOMINATIONS AND ELECTIONS

No. 40

[POLITICS is a complex and time-consuming enterprise and it is difficult, even under the best of conditions, for the millions of members of our political parties to participate effectively. Yet, such participation by the rank and file is essential to a healthy democracy.

Professor Myrdal, in the following essay, examines the relation between leadership and mass participation in American society. As he points out, the problems of leadership and rank-and-file participation in American politics have not been the object for much reflection in America, and we seem to be only slightly aware of the oligarchic character of our churches, trade unions, clubs, business organizations, and political parties. Yet, if we are to preserve and make meaningful to the world the democracy we symbolize, we must constantly use our creative imagination to devise new ways to secure fuller and more effective participation of all our citizens in the process of democratic self-government.]

THE AMERICAN PATTERN OF INDIVIDUAL LEADERSHIP AND MASS PASSIVITY [1]

by Gunnar Myrdal

DESPITE the democratic organization of American society with its emphasis upon liberty, equality of opportunity (with a strong leaning in favor of the underdog), and individualism, the idea of leadership pervades American thought and collective action. The demand for "intelligent leadership" is raised in all political camps, social and professional groups, and, indeed, in every collective activity centered around any interest or purpose—church, school, business, recreation, philanthropy, the campus life of a college, the entertaining of a group of visitors, the selling of a

[1] Gunnar Myrdal, *An Amerian Dilemma* (New York: Harper and Brothers, 1944), pp. 709-719. Reprinted by permission of the publisher. The footnotes in the original version are omitted here.

patent medicine, the propagation of an idea or of an interest. As a standard demand it appears with great frequency in public speeches and newspaper editorials and will seldom be absent even when the social reformer or the social scientist speaks.

If an ordinary American faces a situation which he recognizes as a "problem" without having any specific views as how to "solve" it, he tends to resort to two general recommendations: one, traditionally, is "education"; the other is "leadership." The belief in "education" is a part of, or a principal conclusion from, the American Creed. The demand for "leadership" plays on a different plane of his personality. It is a result less of a conscious ideological principle than of a pragmatic approach to those activities which require the cooperation of many individuals. For this reason it is also much less a part of Americans' self-knowledge. While the democratic Creed and the belief in education are an ever present popular theory with highest national sanctions—held conscious not only by affirmative references in practically every solemn public utterance, but also maintained by an ever growing literature—it will be found that Americans in general are quite unaware that the leadership idea is a particular characteristic of their culture. Since the leadership concept—though, with a quite different import—has recently become associated with fascism and nazism [and communism], it is understandable that Americans regularly show a marked reluctance to admit the fact even when it is pointed out by the observer.

What Americans display in their demand for leadership are primarily the general traits of their culture which may be referred to as individualism and romanticism. The ordinary American has a liking for the personal and the dynamic in collective activity, a longing for the uniquely human, the unexpected, the adventurous. He wants changes, and he likes to associate them with new faces. He hopes for individuals to step out of the mass, to find the formulas for directing the course of events, to take the lead. And he is prepared to create room for the exceptional individual's initiative. He is willing to gamble quite a bit on his choice. Not least important in his attitude toward the "outstanding" person is the inclination to be hopefully experimental. James Bryce observed:

> I doubt if there be any country (except the United States) where a really brilliant man, confident in his own strength, and adding the charm of a striking personality to the gift of popular eloquence, would find an easier path to fame and power, and would exert more influence over the minds and emotions of the multitude. Such a man, speaking to the people with the independence of conscious strength, would find himself appreciated and respected.

In retrospect the American becomes rather pronouncedly a hero-worshiper. He usually conceives of the American Revolution as the deed of a group of outstanding, courageous and resourceful individuals. The Republic has its "Founding Fathers," such as few other democratic nations have. In fact, the American dramatizes and personifies the entire history of his country and of the world. Social changes are rarely looked upon as the outcome of broad trends and deep forces. The long toils and seemingly blind moves of anonymous masses are pushed into the background of his world view.

Like no other people, Americans have continually succeeded in creating popular heroes—national, local and professional. Outstanding individuals may become heroes while they are still living. In no other part of Western culture is it less true that "no one is a prophet in his own country and his own time." A rising leader in America has quite commonly the backing of his home town and his own group: the American ideas of "favorite son" and "local boy who made good" are significant indications of this trait of American culture.

American individualism and romanticism have, in this particular respect, a personality basis to operate upon, which, for want of a better term, we shall call "personal generosity." On the average, Americans show a greater kindness and patience with others than Europeans do. This attitude is a natural product of the opportunities on the frontier and, more generally, in a rapidly expanding economy. Americans worship success. This peculiarity has been the object of their own and others' ironical and often scornful comments. What has less often been pointed out is that this success cult in America is not particularly self-centered; instead it is generous. *Usually it is not in his own but in other persons' success that the ordinary American rejoices and takes pride.* He identifies himself with those who succeed. He is inclined to "jump on the bandwagon," as the American expression runs, to "be on the winning side."

Americans have thus come to develop an unmatched capacity for vicarious satisfaction in watching others fight. The immense and agitated crowds of spectators, who can always be counted on to fill the stadiums when a hard struggle is staged, testify to this, as does also the manner in which international and national news is presented by press and radio to suit the American public. In America, as everywhere else, ninety-nine out of a hundred do not "succeed," of course—or "succeed" only if the standards are set low. But the extraordinary fact is that these ninety-nine less successful individuals in America, when they see their own hopes disappointed and their ambitions thwarted, are less likely than similar individuals in other countries to retreat into sour chagrin. The individual who is rising in

America is not held back much by the mortification of his fellows and compeers. Occasionally he may even be pushed ahead.

Let us not be misunderstood. Of course there is personal envy in America, too. But there has been decidedly less of it than in the more static, less "boundless" civilizations of the Old World. Luck, ability and drive in others are more tolerated and less checked in America. Climbing is more generally acclaimed. Leadership is more readily accepted.

So it becomes more natural, and more possible, in America, to associate the dynamic forces of society with individuals instead of with masses. In the Negro problem it is evident to the observer that the "community leaders" are given an astonishingly important role. When the white people want to influence Negro attitudes or behavior in one direction or another—to get the Negro farmers to plant a garden around their shacks, to screen their windows, to keep their children in school, to cure and prevent syphilis, to keep Negroes more respectful to the whites, to prevent them from joining trade unions, and to frighten them against "outside meddlers" or "red" seducers—the natural device (besides the long-range one of "education") is to appeal to the "community leaders." These leaders are expected to get it over to the Negro masses, who are supposed to be rather passive.

There are, as we shall point out, special reasons in the caste situation for this practice. *But more fundamentally this is a common American culture pattern.* Caste accentuates it, but in the sphere of the Negro problem both whites and Negroes display a general attitude toward leadership and followership which permeates the entire American nation. It is incorrect to discuss Negro leadership except in this general setting. If we should study Negro leadership as an isolated phenomenon, we should be inclined to ascribe to the Negro people certain cultural characteristics which are simply American. Actually the Negro, in this as in so many other respects, because of the peculiar circumstances in which he lives, is an "exaggerated American."

For in all America it is assumed that every group contains leaders who control the attitudes of the group. Everywhere—not least in idealistic pursuits—the method of reaching a goal is assumed to be the indirect one of first reaching the leaders and, through them, influencing the masses. The leaders are organized locally in civic clubs of all sorts, and they are conscious of their role. They create a "public opinion," the peculiarity of which becomes apparent when, for instance, it is said about a strike which has failed, in spite of the fact that practically all the workers—making up the majority of the population—participate, that "local opinion did not favor the strikers," or even more explicitly that "public opinion suppressed the strike."

The other side of this picture is, of course, the relative inertia and inarticulateness of the masses in America. The remarkable lack of self-generating, self-disciplined, organized people's movements in America is a significant historical fact usually overlooked by American historians and social scientists.

The new continent has always offered fertile soil for "isms," including every possible "European-ism" and, in addition, a great variety of home-grown ones. Communist societies have been built by Shakers, Rappites, Zoarites, True Inspirationists, and other sects, and by secularized Owenites and Fourierists. The Mormons experimented with polygamy, as well as with communism, and the Oneida Community with idealistic unchastity. Fantastic slogans of easy money and cheap credit, "ham and eggs," "thirty dollars every Thursday," "share the wealth," "every man a king," have inflamed local sections of opinion and startled the world.

America has had its full share of utopians and idealists, and much more than its due of charlatans and demagogues. America is also the country of countless associations. For every conceivable "cause" there is at least one association and often several. De Tocqueville and Bryce observed this, and it is true to-day. Americans in the upper and middle classes are great "joiners" and "supporters" of all sorts of schemes for the common good. If a proposal makes sense to people, their participation and purse can be counted on. But somehow the associations seldom reach down to the masses of people. In spite of all this lively organizational activity, America has had few protracted zealous movements among the people. There has frequently been popular unrest among farmers and workers in America; they have been dissatisfied and have dimly felt the need of one reform or another. Occasionally there have been bloody clashes; resort to violence both by employers and by workers in settling labor disputes has, until recently, been rather characteristic of America. Undoubtedly a general influence on the course of national and local politics has been exerted by the masses through democratic elections. But for some reason these forces, working in the masses, have seldom crystallized into orderly mass organizations.

The trade union movement is one of the oldest in the world, but in America it has always been comparatively inconsequential. Even with the active support of the federal government during the 'thirties, instituting protective legislation unmatched in other democratic countries, it has not even reached the size of the peak unemployment. The observer is struck by the importance played by salaried "organizers" and the relative unimportance of, or often the lack of, a spontaneous drive from the workers themselves. There has never been much of a cooperative movement in

America. Often cooperatives are still petty neighborhood organizations based on the activity of the individual idealists—the "leaders"—more than on the concerted effect of cold economic reasoning and of the desire for independence and economic power on the part of the mass of consumers. The diverse activities collectively known as "adult education" in America are often laudable strivings to disseminate education among the common people by universities, philanthropic organizations, state and federal agencies, radio companies, or groups of enlightened community leaders. There is still little concerted drive for self-education in civic affairs. There is no spontaneous mass desire for knowledge as a means of achieving power and independence.

The passivity of the masses in America is, of course, a product of the nation's history. The huge immigration through the decades has constantly held the lower classes in a state of cultural fragmentation. They have been split in national, linguistic, and religious sub-groups, which has hampered class solidarity and prevented effective mass organization. Folk movements require close understanding among the individuals in the group, a deep feeling of common loyalty, and even a preparedness to share in collective sacrifices for a distant common goal. Only on a basis of psychological identification with the interest group is it possible to ask the individual to renounce his own short-range interests for the group's long-range ones. The immigrants have felt social distance to other lower class persons with different cultural origin. Also because they have difficulty in communicating with other Americans, immigrants have had to have leaders for this purpose. Bent on accommodation to social and economic pressure and on individual climbing, they have been conditioned to be even more individualistic than the native Americans.

The open frontier and the relatively good prospects for every able and energetic individual to rise out of the lower classes kept down social discontent. Perhaps even more important, this social mobility drained the masses in every generation of most of their organizational catalysts. Few potential "leaders" remained in the lower classes to stimulate their loyalty and to organize their resistance against pressure. Since American industry was organized as it was, it required no sinister intention of the industrial executive to promote the rising labor leader to personnel expert or labor manager to the great advantage of the enterprise, but at the expense of weakening the energy of the workers. The way into independent business was even more open. If the workers wanted to keep a man under these circumstances, they had to give him a salary which raised him much above their economic and social level. A similar process worked on the potential organizers of cooperatives, farmers' movements and, indeed, every germ of concerted action on behalf of the lower classes in America.

Cultural fragmentation, the division of interest of the lower classes, and their loss of leaders, thus stamped the masses with inertia. They are accustomed to being static and receptive. They are not daring, but long for security. They do not know how to cooperate and how to pool risks and sacrifices for a common goal. They do not meet much. They do not organize. They do not speak for themselves: they are the listeners in America. They seldom elect representatives from their own midst to Congress, to state legislatures or to city councils. They rather support friendly leaders from the upper strata, particularly lawyers. Labor politics in America has constantly held to the common minority pattern of support-. ing parties and individual candidates who favored them and of assailing candidates who opposed them. Labor has never—except in a few localities— successfully sought political power for itself. It has never seriously tried to plan to utilize its large potential share of the electorate to capture the government of the country. Farmers' politics has, in the main, followed the same minority scheme. Farmers' organizations in America have constantly been in danger of being run by the small top group of big farmers, who, most of the time, have different interests from the mass of small farmers. Generally speaking, the lower classes in America have been inarticulate and powerless.

This is the more striking when the lower classes are compared with the "Pullman class," which had greater cultural homogeneity, more self-confidence, and more of a tendency to pool its power than a similar class in most other countries. There are closer ties and a more easy understanding between upper class persons in the various professions and businesses in this country than anywhere else. They travel more than in other countries; being together on a Pullman train brings people together intimately. They meet constantly for conferences. They are accustomed to being dynamic and courageous and to taking big risks. They know how to cooperate and even how to sacrifice for a common cause. They feel responsibility for the whole nation, as they view its interests, partly because they usually have a long line of American ancestry. The "Pullman class" has been fairly open to talent from below and has contained a disproportionate amount of the nation's brains and courage. Its members have been willing and prepared to take the leadership made so easy for them by the inertia of the masses.

For judging future possibilities, it is important to note that the era of mass immigration has ended. The proportion of foreign-born white persons in the population is decreasing from decade to decade: it was 12.5 per cent in 1920, 10.9 per cent in 1930, but only 8.7 per cent in 1940. The other main factors behind the political inertia of the American masses—the open frontier and the easy escape out of the lower classes—are also disappearing. There is no longer any free land, and agriculture is depressed and likely to remain depressed. The modern organization of American industry is not favorable to small independent enterprise, and no lower class person can accumulate the huge capital necessary to start a large enterprise. The control of production from Washington during the . . . War . . . inevitably . . . [stepped] up this movement to eradicate small independent business. The growth and improvement of education and the trend toward professionalization in all desirable occupations also has helped to eliminate the "self-made man" even in America. Ambitions for children are real, but they cannot compensate entirely for the lessened possibilities for climbing of the parents themselves.

The class barriers are thus becoming higher and more unyielding, at the same time as the cultural heterogeneity within those barriers is continuously decreasing. The masses receive a steadily improved general education and keep a greater number of their own potential leaders. These trends might make them active and articulate. For the time being, however, there are only minor indications of such a change. If and when it comes, it is destined to remake the entire public and social life of America.

The present observer is inclined to view the American pattern of individual leadership as a great strength of this nation, but the passivity of the masses as a weakness. These two cultural traits of America have, in their historical development, been complementary. But individual activity and mass activity are not necessarily antagonistic principles. It is possible to envisage a future development where the masses in America participate more intensively in political activities of various sorts, but where, nevertheless, outstanding individuals are permitted to have wide space for their initiative according to the great American tradition. Such a social system, if it ever developed, would realize in the highest degree the age-old ideal of a vitalized democracy. It would result, not only in a decrease in the immense class differences in America, but more fundamentally, it would effect a higher degree of integration in society of the many millions of anonymous and atomized individuals; a strengthening of the ties of loyalty running through the entire social fabric; a more efficient and uncorrupted performance of all public functions; and a more intense and secure feeling on the part of the common citizen of his belongingness to, responsibility for, and participation in the commonwealth as a great cooperative human endeavor—a realization of a fuller life.

This is a dream—and a dream well in line with the ideals contained in the American Creed—but the American patterns of individual leadership and mass passivity are a reality that can be studied in all social spheres. They are, of course, particularly apparent in the political life of the nation. In both local and national politics the individual officeholder is—for the period he is in office—awarded much more power than he would be in democratic European nations. What is even more important, he is allowed and, indeed, expected to follow the inclinations of his personal drives and ideas much more unhampered by laws and regulations or particularly by continuous and democratic participation from the people.

In local politics, America has, on the whole, not spread political responsibility upon countless citizens' boards, as have, for example, the Northern European countries (including England), thereby widening political participation and making politics more anonymous and less dependent on outstanding leadership. Much more, not only of broad policy-making, but also of detailed decisions, are, in America, centralized in the offices of salaried functionaries. *Political participation of the ordinary citizen in America is pretty much restricted to the intermittently recurring elections. Politics is not organized to be a daily concern and responsibility of the common citizen.* The relative paucity of trade unions, cooperatives, and other civic interest organizations tends to accentuate this abstention on the part of the common citizens from sharing in the government of their communities as a normal routine of life. In this essential sense American politics is centralized. The same is even more true of national politics.

The basic democracy, however, is maintained in spite of the extraordinary power awarded to the individual officeholders and the equally extraordinary lack of participation by the common citizens in the running of public affairs. *While American democracy is weak from the aspect of the citizens' sharing in political action and responsibility, it is strong in the ultimate electoral controls.* And there is logic in this. Several elements of what, from the other side of the Atlantic, looks like "exaggerated democracy" in American measures of popular control may be explained as having their "function" in preserving for the common man the ultimate political power in this system of government where he participates so little in its daily duties. It is this trait which prevents the delegation of such tremendous power to leaders and the hero worship from degenerating into fascism.

Americans have thus such "exaggerated" democratic devices as frequent elections, long ballots (so that even minor officers can be elected), the initiative and referendum, short terms of office, prohibitions against running for a second or third term. The intensive and ruthless publicity focused upon all officeholders—which does not even spare their private life—serves the same "function" of making officeholding precarious. Finally, the American system of "checks and balances" has not only gone into the federal and state constitutions but has become deeply entrenched in the American attitude toward all power problems even outside politics proper. Americans are inclined to give not only much power but *overlapping power* to two or more officials or agencies and then leave it up to them to work out a *modus vivendi* through cooperation, mutual hamperings and occasional stalls.

The Roosevelt administration, with all its duplication of offices for the same or similar functions, exaggerated only somewhat an American tradition. In a lesser degree this is a trait which runs through the whole gamut of social institutions in America.

To the foreign observer this American pattern of power control, built upon systematic friction and actual competition of competent people, looks sometimes not only cumbersome but wasteful of energy and dangerous to reasonable efficiency of government. In a system where such extraordinary powers are constantly being delegated to the functionaries and where so little is held for the participation of the common men, this device, like the others mentioned, serves the "function" of keeping the executives within popular control. For when competing holders of power come in conflict and eventually stall, the ultimate arbiter is the electorate at the next election. It is to this arbiter—and, in advance, to "public opinion"—that they plead when they are in danger of getting stuck.

The patterns of strong and competitive personal leadership and weak followership, which we have exemplified for politics, permeate the entire social structure. In most of these other fields the popular check on the system—that is, the strong electionary system—is much weaker. This gives much greater power to leaders. In large sectors of the labor union movement it is thus a problem of how to avoid complete boss rule and how to preserve that minimum of democracy which consists in the leaders' being regularly elected and having to report to meetings of the common union members. When in recent years the question of industrial unions *versus* craft unions finally was brought before the public, it appeared as a fight between William Green and John L. Lewis. Cooperatives, when they infrequently managed to get securely established in America, often degenerated into ordinary business partnerships. Universities in America have never been controlled by the professors but by their presidents—not elected by the professors—and their appointed deans, subject to the control of boards of trustees who are outside and above the university. In modern business corporations in America, shareholders have lost their power to directors and other "insiders." Even in small groups—civic committees, research projects, or Sunday schools—the same pattern prevails: the leaders run the show, the masses are passive except for an occasional election.

The general public interest in personalities and in short-run developments manifests itself in government and business as well as in other phases of life. In Washington and in Wall Street, as well as in the other American centers of power control, the perspective is predominantly that of actual happenings yesterday and to-morrow and of individual persons in the spotlight: What effect will this minor event have? What one person is behind what other person? What idea has caught whom?

One earlier observation should be reiterated. The idea and reality of leadership is not an object for much reflection in America; indeed, it is almost not part of conscious knowledge. There is no popular theory to explain it or justify it. It is not a fortified and preached ideology like the American Creed. Not only the unsophisticated common citizens but also the social scientists have observed these facts without much questioning or evaluation. The patterns of leadership and followership simply exist as things which are a matter of course. They have not yet been detected to be important problems. . . .

No. 41

[ONE of the major objectives of a political party is to secure control of the personnel of government. One of the steps in attaining this goal is for the parties to offer candidates to the voters for their approval or rejection. The average voter tends to regard the final election as the crucial point in the process and gives comparatively little thought to the process by which the parties choose the candidates they will offer to the voters. But the nominating process by which the parties choose their candidates is vital in democratic government.

In America we have experimented with many types of nominating procedure. Each new scheme that has been proposed has grown out of a desire to secure to the rank and file a greater control in party affairs. Few have recognized this more clearly than Professors Merriam and Overacker who discuss the relation of the direct primary to democracy in the following essay.]

DEMOCRACY AND THE DIRECT PRIMARY [1]

by Charles E. Merriam and Louise Overacker

THE nominating system is a phase of the American party system; . . . this is in turn a phase of the larger problem of modern democracy. And democracy is a phase of the political order now existing, and this in turn of the economic and social order of the present day and the Western

[1] C. E. Merriam and Louise Overacker, *Primary Elections* (Chicago: University of Chicago Press, 1928), pp. 351-358. Reprinted by permission of the University of Chicago Press.

world. All of these are under fire and all are subject to rapid change. We do not know whether the party system may be materially modified; whether the democracy we now know is destined to survive; whether the modern political or economic order can resist the revolutionary forces that are hammering at its gates; what science will do to the whole social order in another generation.

Only the most enthusiastic and inexperienced would therefore expect that changes in the nominating system would produce a fundamental effect, whether through an indirect or a direct method.

The primary is a phase, an important phase, of our political life, and significant advances might be made in its processes, but it should not be expected that these will contribute the last word to our political problems. Too much was expected of the mongrel caucus when it was established; too much was expected of the convention when it overthrew King Caucus; too much was expected of the regulated convention; and too much was expected of the direct primary in its day. Perhaps there must always be a myth as a preliminary to progress, but the myth must not become a tradition, a memory rather than a hope. My wise colleague, Dr. Herrick, warns us to beware of making our hypothesis a religion.

The level of politics is in the long run the level of intelligent public interest in men and affairs political. Under any system the largest and most skilful group of interested and active citizens will determine public policies and will select the persons to formulate and administer them. The uninterested, or the spasmodically interested, or the ineffectual who wish well feebly will be the governed, not the governors. It was Montesquieu who said that "A slave people can have only their chains," and it is impossible to escape the conclusion that only an intelligent and interested electorate habituated to political practice can use the mechanism of democracy or the systems of nomination in use here.

There are those who foresee the decline of parties, of democracy, of politics itself, in the development of modern life. But they deceive themselves with words, for when politics is destroyed the set of relations formerly called politics emerges under some other name, whether economics or what not. Men may not be vitally interested in the mere mechanisms of government, but they were never more intensely interested than now in the patterns of human leadership, domination, cooperation; and there were never more fascinating types of political leaders in the social and political worlds than in our day. Roosevelt, Wilson, Lloyd George, Clemenceau, Stresemann, Lenin, Trotzky, Mussolini, Gandhi—these are great figures of vivid interest to mankind. In America urban and rural leaders of many colors attract the interest of millions of citizens and outshine even movie stars, boxers, base-ball heroes.

Nor was there ever a time when the functions of government were more important in the field of social relations than at the present time. Not-withstanding the furious denunciation of governmental activity and inter-ference, it advances at a rapid rate, usually with the support in one field of those who condemn it in another. There is likely to be more government and politics before there is less, and political crises and tensions are likely to become increasingly significant. Likewise, political leaders are likely to become more important in the near future than in the past.

All systems of government require some form of general judgment on leaders and policies, and some method of indicating toleration or approval of the dominant leaders and their policies. This is necessary in times of peace as well as of war, for the sake of morale if for nothing else. Murmur-ing, discontent, unwillingness, scattered protest, outbreaks, resistance, rebel-lion, revolution—these are the classic methods of expressing these popular judgments. Democracy provides an orderly way of passing judgment upon leaders, replacing them with others, and of indicating approval or disap-proval of public policies as well as of types of leaders; and further pro-vides that practically all of the adult population shall be eligible to partici-pate in the process. Those who are satisfied or not much dissatisfied, or lazy, or incompetent, or careless, either do not participate, or are ineffective in their participation. An election and a primary election reflect this situ-ation. They present the issue which is basic to modern democracy, namely, Are the people interested enough and competent enough to choose leaders and determine policies? The well-known answer was, "Let them vote until their stomachs ache, but do not let them decide anything." Our political order is based upon the democratic assumption that there is material in the electorate for the formulation of sound policies of state and the choice of wise leadership, and difficulties found in this direction are on the whole less than those met with in alternative directions of dictatorship, hereditary monarchy, military or theocratic rule. We are engaged in testing this assump-tion.

Most of the objections raised against primaries apply to elections as well as to universal suffrage, and to the whole plan of democracy. Disbelievers in popular government are constantly asserting that many are ignorant, that many are incompetent, that many are indifferent, that many are lax, lazy, and drifting, that nothing can come from this mediocre mass of yokels and boobs, that the mass should abdicate in favor of the few and kiss the rod that condescends to rule them, thanking God that they are allowed to live and be cared for by their betters—these are common charges among those to whom modern democracy is unwelcome.

All these criticisms should be examined, and the wheat carefully sifted from the chaff, but for some time to come it is clear that the democratic experiment will continue, and the broad outlines of the basic political order will not be changed. What the outcome of the experiment may be, no one can safely predict. It seems to me that there are more signs that democracy will succeed than any of the alternatives suggested; but I do not know this and can only register my own judgment that the interests of society will be best served by the continuance of the democratic assumption and the political order based upon it.

It is quite true that there may be democracy without primaries, or without conventions for that matter. It is also possible that primary devices may develop later in the political life of a larger number of modern states. It may logically be contended that political parties should not be subject to any legal regulation of any description, but should be left to the political rebuke of the electorate. But if the objection to the primary system is to democracy itself, that should be clearly understood. And the remedies proposed need not be simply reversion to an earlier type of nomination, but should be constructive attempts to make the democratic assumption more readily workable. The short ballot, organization of conspicuous responsibility, development of technical public administration, sounder civic training, better organization of political prudence, more fundamental study of the science of politics, elimination of maladjustments in our economic and social life—all these are significant.

There is nothing sacred about our American nominating systems, direct or indirect, regulated or unregulated. They are all parts of the larger democratic experiment and should be subject to change and adaptation, as new experience or new conditions may indicate. The caucus, the convention, the regulated convention, the direct primary, the nomination by petition only, the double election, proportional and preferential voting—these are all phases of an attempt to organize the system of selecting leaders and determining policies more and more effectively, under constantly shifting conditions, rural, frontier, urban, with shifting systems of education, industry, intercommunication.

Experienced, intelligent, and disinterested men and women differ on the details of the nominating system and upon the areas within which the direct or indirect system is preferable. In so far as this represents intelligent difference of opinion and is intelligently supported, it is beneficial. It would be unfortunate, however, if this discussion were to distract interest, intelligent and persistent, from the broader problem of the reorganization of our whole electoral system, the raising of the standards of political practice, and the possibility of improvements of such types as have been discussed in previous pages of this study. The success of the democratic experiment will not be determined primarily by the direct or indirect system of nomination, but by our attitude toward the wider problems of political organization and practice which affect much more fundamentally our political future. Whether we cling to the spoils system or adopt some more scientific system of public administration; whether we retain the ballot's burden or adopt the short ballot; whether we centralize more closely authority and responsibility in cities, counties, and states; whether we develop sounder standards of leadership or fall into the hands of bosses and demagogues; whether we are able to work out a more effective system of civic training better adapted to a changing society, looking to the future as well as the past; whether we are able to adapt our representative system to modern needs and escape the gerrymanders of tradition; whether our political system reflects the deeper trends down under the surface of social and economic life and the still more revolutionary tendencies of modern science—these and many other like problems are pressing hard upon our political order, and require the united effort of those interested in the development of our political system. As these questions are attacked it is not improbable that other and better types of nomination may emerge and take their place in the political world, competing with the older for survival under new conditions.

No. 42

[THE presidential election system devised by the framers of the constitution made no provision for the nomination of candidates. This was partly due to the anti-democratic presuppositions of those who drafted the constitution and partly due to their failure to foresee or understand the beginnings, in their own day, of the party system and the effect it would have on the electoral college. From the beginning, the election scheme, of which they were so proud, failed to work as they had planned. Some method of nomination became essential and the nominating convention was developed.

Ever since its inception, in the 1830's, the convention system has been maligned. It has been compared to a four-ring-circus and described as the epitome of the smoke-filled-room and behind-the-scenes character of American politics. First radio and then television brought the opportunity for Americans to hear and see much that gave weight to these comparisons and descriptions. As a result, many Americans have concluded that the system never produces the able man but always the "available" man.

Critical evaluation is of course desirable, but this necessitates looking at both sides of the ledger. It is important to know and understand the facts about the whole process. The way delegates are apportioned among the states, the method of selecting delegates, the way the convention is organized, the rules of convention procedure, the behind-the-scenes activity, the deals and trades that are an inevitable part of politics, the noise and show of convention meetings, the routine work of committees—all are part of the picture. Some of it is bad, some of it is good. But an evaluation must be based upon knowledge and understanding of it all.

In addition, before pronouncing judgment, it is desirable to consider what the alternatives would be, to compare nominating procedure with systems of nomination practiced in other countries, and to see what kind of a record our system has on the basis of its results. This will give us the additional perspective that is needed for evaluation. The following essay by Professor Laski will contribute to that perspective. Professor Laski is a well-known English political scientist; he examines our presidential nominating system, compares it with the British system, evaluates the results of both, and concludes that the American system achieves the results that the needs of the people require and that "anyone who knows the life of a political party from within Great Britain will not feel inclined to cast a stone at the American system."]

THE CONVENTIONS AND THE PRESIDENCY [1]

by Harold J. Laski

THE founders of the Constitution were especially proud of the method they adopted for choosing the president; none of their expectations has been more decisively disappointed. The presidential candidates are now chosen at national conventions of the respective parties; and the decision is made by the electorate at large, with the reservation, as shown by the famous Hayes-Tilden case, that a plurality of votes does not necessarily carry with it the certainty of election. It is, indeed, a desirable thing that the method should be made to correspond to the facts. A constitutional amendment which simply stated that the candidate with the most votes should be deemed to have been elected would be a wise safeguard against possible difficulties in the future.

An American presidential convention is like nothing else in the civilized world; and the critics of the system—which, in its modern form, is just a hundred years old—have exhausted the language of vituperation in attack upon its character. The power of money; the persuasive power of hidden

[1] Harold J. Laski, "The Conventions and the Presidency," *Harper's Magazine* (July, 1940), Vol. 181, pp. 166-171. Reprinted by permission of *Harper's Magazine*.

and corrupt influence; the undue authority of the "doubtful" State; the overt and hidden prejudices against particular types of candidates, as, for instance, members of the Roman Catholic Church; the "deals" which accompany the capture of a delegation for one candidate as against another; the mythology of the "favorite son"; the casual influence, notable in the case of Lincoln's selection, the choice of the convention city; the undue impact, as in the Democratic Convention of 1896, of a single speech by a potential nominee; the operation of the technic of the "dark horse" candidate; the exploitation of the "stalking-horse" behind whom some well-organized group has its carefully prepared selection whose name is put forward at the right moment; and, finally, the raucous, complex, and hectic atmosphere of the convention itself; its well-improvised enthusiasms; its fantastic horse-play; its immunity to thought; its wild rumors; its incredible conspiracies—all these characteristics, none of which can ever suffer exaggeration, seem to the outsider, and especially to the European outsider, about the worst possible way in which to choose a man to occupy the highest executive post in a democratic commonwealth.

The convention itself is of course predominantly an organ for registering decisions that have been made behind the scenes. Occasionally an utterance upon its floor may exercise a real influence upon its outcome. Senator Conkling did Blaine irreparable damage in 1880; and the contrast between his speech and that of Garfield, who nominated Sherman, had a good deal to do with the emergence of Garfield as the Republican candidate. So also the famous speech of Bryan in 1896 turned the balance of opinion in his favor. But in general the actual nomination is decided in part by the pre-convention campaign and in part by bargains actually concluded in and around the convention itself. The pre-convention campaign is of great importance. It was decisive, for instance, in the selection of Franklin Roosevelt in 1932; the spadework done by Mr. Farley in the two preceding years was the condition precedent to his nomination. Bargaining at the convention is of course a special art. Its importance emerges either when there are a number of outstanding candidates between whom choice is difficult— as with the Republicans in 1880 and 1920, and with the Democrats in 1924, —or when a powerful group has made up its mind to try to force a "dark horse" upon the convention.

Accident in fact plays a much smaller part in the choice of the candidate than is imagined. The public, for example, expected either Governor Lowden or General Wood to be the Republican candidate in 1920; and immense sums had been expended in promoting their interests. But the skilful proponents of Senator Harding's name had long foreseen that the acuteness of their rivalry would make neither possible, and they had long foreseen the probability of Harding's success. "At the proper time after the Republican convention meets," said Mr. Daugherty, Senator Harding's manager, "some fifteen men, bleary-eyed with loss of sleep, and perspiring profusely with the excessive heat, will sit down in seclusion round a big table. I will be with them, and will present Senator Harding's name, and before we get through, they will put him over." That is precisely what occurred.

Out of all this complexity there has emerged the doctrine of "availability." The party needs a candidate who, positively, will make the widest appeal and, negatively, will offend the least proportion of the electorate. On the whole, he ought to come from a doubtful State; a Democrat from New York is more "available" than one from the solid South because he is likely to win votes which might otherwise be uninterested. It seems still to be true that it is difficult to elect a Roman Catholic; even the solid South refused to vote for Governor Smith in 1928. He must not be anti-religious; that would offend the great vested interest of the churches. He must be sound on the tariff; he must be against wild currency adventures; he must not be too overtly internationalist in outlook. Administrative experience, like the governorship of a State, is important. It is helpful, if he is a self-made man; the "log cabin to White House" tradition is still, despite the two Roosevelts, an influential one. He ought not to possess any nostrum which can be represented as extreme. In the aftermath of a war period it is important that he should have played his part in the army; from Jackson and Taylor onward, the military hero has had an immense appeal to the electorate. It is undesirable that he should have too close an association with the big interests, especially Wall Street; Wilson, in 1912, owed his nomination to Mr. Bryan's famous pronouncement that he would not support anyone under obligation to "Morgan, Ryan, Belmont, or any other member of the privilege-seeking, favor-hunting class." He must have a sufficiently flexible mind to accept the implications of the trading necessary to build his majority. He must not be the kind of man whom it is obviously easy to ridicule in a campaign, either because he is "viewy," or for any other reason.

All of which means, as a general rule, that the outcome of a presidential convention is likely to be a compromise of some kind. But it is important to realize that it is not a compromise in which, without cause, the outstanding candidate is certain to be defeated. Henry Clay never became president because the admirable instinct of his party warned it against choosing a man whose avidity for the office was so patently excessive. Blaine never became president because even many of his admirers profoundly felt that his association, to say no more, with dubious political methods left too much to be explained away. [Clay, however, was nominated in 1831 and 1844 and Blaine in 1884.]   Governor Fuller of Massachusetts could not be nominated because, as Senator Borah said, Sacco and Vanzetti would thereby have become issues in the campaign.   Senator Lodge was for forty years an outstanding figure in the Senate.   But he could not have secured the Republican nomination simply because his own party realized that, whatever his qualities, those years in politics were a continuous demonstration of his unfitness for high executive office.   Mr. Hoover was undoubtedly the leading Republican in 1936; and, on the precedent of Cleveland's nomination in 1892, was the natural recipient of the candidature.   But he was unavailable because the party leaders felt, quite rightly, that he was too closely associated with Republican failure in the depression to be an acceptable candidate.

It is notable, in short, that whenever an obvious contender for the nomination does not receive it there is usually a quite adequate explanation for his failure.   It is notable, further, that when a "dark horse" nominee emerges he has been held in reserve for just such an opportunity by powerful influences which are waiting for their moment.   It is possible for someone, like Franklin Pierce, who is unknown to the general public, to emerge from the ordeal.   But it is to be noticed that if he does his emergence is always due to special circumstances, and that there is to be detected behind him a substantial cohort who know precisely what they are doing.   A "dark horse," that is to say, is a compromise candidate in much the same way as Mr. Bonar Law was a compromise between Mr. Austen Chamberlain and Mr. Walter Long in 1911, or Sir Henry Campbell-Bannerman as Liberal leader after 1895.   Much the same situation obtains in the complicated intrigues of French politics.   It is difficult for the outsider to follow the tortuous internal events which make now Mr. Herriot, now M. Chautemps, and now M. Daladier the leader of the Socialist Radicals.   Immediacy on the basis of "availability" there also explains the result that is reached.   It is as natural for Henry Clay or James G. Blaine to have missed the presidency as it was for Mr. Churchill or Sir Austen Chamberlain to have missed the premiership in their country. [Churchill later became premier.]

The real difference of course lies in the prior experience of those who are chosen as nominees.   Other things being equal, a prime minister in Great Britain or France will have served a long apprenticeship in the legislative assembly before obtaining the supreme office.   He will be a figure in the House.   He will be known to the party.   He will probably have had considerable administrative experience in a lesser office.   He will be pretty intimately known to those whom he is to lead.   In the United States none of this is necessarily true.   Since the Civil War a distinguished career in Congress has rarely been a passport to the nomination.   Attainment of

cabinet office has had no direct relevance to a candidature in any except
two cases; and, of these, Mr. Hoover's name was made rather by his war
record than by his experience in the Department of Commerce. A State
governorship has counted for much. But it is pretty true to say that most
of the chosen candidates have been names in the nation rather than in
Washington. They have not known with any intimacy those with whom
they would, as president, be expected to work.

The position is in curious contrast with the pre-Civil War period. The
first four presidents of the United States almost nominated themselves; and
among their successors there was hardly a candidate for the nomination
who was not a person of considerable political consequence. One feature,
indeed, is constant. No presidential candidate in the whole record has been
a business man. [Mr. Willkie, Republican nominee in 1940, was a business
man.] The vocation, clearly, is a full-time one; and the qualities which make
for business success make also against the possibility of nomination. It is true
that in his engineering period Mr. Hoover was mainly a company organizer.
But after his return to America all his energies were devoted to politics.
Business men have played a not inconsiderable part in the conventions as
king-makers; but it is a curious fact that in a civilization perhaps more
dominated by business men than by any other they have had to surrender
the hope of being king. The lawyer, the soldier, the rentier, and politician
—these are the types from whom the candidates have been chosen. The
business man may hope for cabinet office. He is likely to be important
in negativing ambitions the realization of which would not be regarded with
favor by the big interests. But, on the record, he must be the power
behind the throne; he cannot hope to occupy it.

The reason, I think, is simple. The small man cannot hope to afford
the risks of a political career. The great one, a Rockefeller, a Vanderbilt,
even an Owen D. Young, would not be an "available" candidate simply
because he would arouse the suspicion that the party which nominated him
was in bondage to the money-power. The influence of the business outlook
upon the parties must, therefore, be indirect. It is real enough, as the election of McKinley makes clear. But it must always seek to veil itself in a
decent obscurity if it is not to prove a source of violent opposition from
the interests of labor and the small farmer. Franklin Roosevelt gained
great strength from both these sources by the fact that the Liberty League,
an organization dominated by the great business interests, was opposed to
his re-election.

The big problem that is raised by the American method of nominating
presidential candidates is whether it puts a premium, as Lord Bryce argued,
against the opportunity of first-rate men to receive consideration. I do not

think his case is proved by making a list of first-rate men, Calhoun and Webster, for example, who missed nomination. The answer to that argument is, first, that many first-rate men have become president by reason of the system; and second, that the reasons which stopped others would have been powerful reasons against their elevation in any representative democracy. It is, I think, at least doubtful whether the elevation of a Roman Catholic to the premiership would be regarded favorably in Great Britain. A great business man, both in England and France, will operate mainly behind the political scene rather than in front of it; of our three business men who have become prime ministers one was, in fact, a rentier, and the others had long retired from active participation therein. Few people could easily explain the nuances that account for the failure of one man to reach the top, and the success of another. And in estimating the meaning of "availability" we must remember always that there is a real sense in which the more strong the candidate, supposing that he represents a special point of view, the more strong also are likely to be his enemies. Not infrequently an easy nomination—so long as the renomination of an existing president is not involved—merely means, as it meant with Horace Greeley in 1872, with Judge Parker in 1904, with Governor Landon in 1936, that rival candidates do not consider there is much prospect for their party's success, and they are not anxious to be associated with a dismal failure at the polls, with a view of a later nomination.

Granted, this is to say, the greatness of the prize and the necessity of popular election, it is difficult to see what other method than the nominating convention is available; more, it is true to say that, on balance, it has worked well rather than badly. The criticisms that are brought against it are rather, in their real substance, criticisms of the place of the presidency in the American constitutional scheme than of the method whereby the president is chosen. It is regrettable that an inexperienced man may come to reside in the White House; the answer is that few of those who have reached it have been inexperienced men. If it be said that men like Harding and Coolidge were unfit for the great post they secured, the answer is that the first had considerable experience both in the Ohio legislature and in the Senate, while the second had been a successful Massachusetts politician, twice occupying the governorship. If we take the presidents of the twentieth century, there is not one who had not been prepared for presidential office by a long experience of politics; and, with the possible exception of the Democratic candidate in 1904, that is true also of their defeated rivals. What is lacking in their training is mostly the art of handling Congress; and the rules of that art are only partly dependent upon the character of the president for the time.

It must be remembered that in making the choice there are two fundamental considerations in the background of which the meaning of "availability" must be set. The first is that the party choosing a candidate wants, if it can, to win; and second, it knows that if it does win, and its nominee becomes president, there is great likelihood of its having to adopt him a second time, since not to do so is to condemn an Administration for which it has to bear responsibility. While, therefore, it is quite true that a party convention provides an opportunity for the art of such a wire-puller as Mr. Daugherty, it is also true that the managers of a great party are anxious to avoid, if they can, the consequences of success in that type of manipulation. One has only to read the account of an experience of conventions like that of Senator Hoar of Massachusetts to see that a scrupulous and honorable man will approach the task of selection with all the seriousness that its consequences require.

All in all, I doubt whether the methods of the system are very different from those of other countries. They are perhaps more open and crude than in Great Britain. There is no generosity in the fight for power. There is a passionate determination on the part of organized interests to get the "safe" man who can be relied upon to live up to the commitments exacted from him. There is the fierce conflict of rival ambitions. There is the organization of every sort of cabal to win a victory for its man. Press and radio and platform are vigorously manipulated to this end. Immense promises are made, pretty ugly deals are effected. Yet I suggest that anyone who knows the life of a political party from within Great Britain will not feel inclined to cast a stone at the American system. It fits well enough the medium in which it has to work. It achieves the results that the needs of the people require.

For there is at least one test of the system that is, I think, decisive. There have been five considerable crises in American history. There was the need to start the new republic adequately in 1789; it gave the American people its natural leader in George Washington. The crisis of 1800 brought Jefferson to the presidency; that of 1861 brought Abraham Lincoln. The War of 1914 found Woodrow Wilson in office; the great depression resulted in the election of Franklin Roosevelt. So far, it is clear, the hour has brought forth the man. It is of course true, as Bagehot said, that "success in a lottery is no argument for lotteries." I agree that no nation can afford a succession of what Theodore Roosevelt termed "Buchanan Presidents"— men whose handling of the issues is uncertain and feeble. But the answer is that the nation has never had that succession; an epoch of Hardings and Coolidges produces, by the scale of the problems to which it gives rise, its own regeneration. The weak president, as I have argued, comes from the

fact that a strong predecessor has set the ship of state on an even keel. He
is chosen because after a diet of strong occasions a nation, like an individual, turns naturally to the chance of a quiet time. "Normalcy" is always
certain to be popular after crises.

The issue is whether, when crisis comes, the system can discover the man
to handle it. On the evidence, this has so far been very remarkably the
case. To urge that it is chance is, I think, a superficial view. It is the
outcome of the national recognition that energy and direction are required,
and the man chosen is the party response to that recognition. The more
deeply we penetrate the working of the system the more clearly does it
emerge that the result is inherent in its nature.

No. 43

[As soon as the candidates are nominated, the details of the campaign must
be mapped out. This task not only involves decisions on broad issues but also
careful attention to every last detail of the appeal for votes. The voters are
familiar with but a part of the magnitude of this work. To many of them a
campaign involves little more than the choice of the issues which are to be
emphasized and the subsequent delivery of speeches and distribution of campaign literature in which these issues are discussed. In general the public has
little information relating to the *minutiae* of an electoral campaign.

These small but highly important details are discussed in the following selection by Alfred E. Smith. It will be seen that the failure of a candidate to visit
a given state in his campaign tour may result in the loss of that state, whereas
an appearance in another area may be a complete waste of the time and energy
of the candidate. If a presidential nominee fails to see a prominent local party
leader, or if he has even a brief chat with the wrong leader, he may lose the
whole-hearted support of a local organization and thus jeopardize his chances
of carrying that locality and perhaps the state. It is indeed true in politics
that "for the want of a nail" the campaign may be lost. Few persons in American
public life were better qualified to write on this subject than was Mr. Smith.
As a state legislator, governor of New York, and presidential candidate he had
a long and intimate contact with every phase of local, state, and national politics
and campaigning.]

BACKSTAGE IN A NATIONAL CAMPAIGN [1]

by Alfred E. Smith

FROM the instant of his nomination the candidate is plunged into a frenzy of time-wasting, harassing work, publicity operations, speech-preparing and other activities—all mingled with the brief opportunity given him to seriously plan and consider his campaign. Naturally, every voter in the country is interested to the extent that they want the newspapers, radio, and moving pictures to describe to them every minute of the daily habits of the candidate and his family. As a result the candidate is immediately surrounded by an army of newspaper reporters. Two daily press conferences must be planned and held, one for the morning and one for the evening representatives. Time must be devoted to picture-taking, meeting delegates, hand-shaking, talking for the talking pictures, making radio speeches, and signing autographs for well-meaning but bothersome voters. Questions of all kinds from the press and the public, covering every conceivable subject interesting to various localities but about which the candidate may actually know little or nothing, must be received, answered, or parried by members of a staff who know that it is important that no local leader or voter be offended or get the impression that the candidate is not giving his personal attention to that section of the country. Thousands of letters pile up daily. Every one must be answered and it takes a vast organization of skilled workers to sort, read, digest the contents of, and answer a presidential candidate's correspondence, particularly since it is through this correspondence that he must learn to a great extent the individual opinions and wishes of the voters whose favor he is seeking.

There is no real rest for a candidate. If he desires a few days off for himself and goes to some country spot which he had previously found lonesome and restful, he will find camera men, movie men, newspaper reporters, and the radio broadcasters his constant companions. There is no use trying to avoid it or to rebuff these representatives. They are doing their job and are under the orders of their editors or other bosses, who in turn are simply carrying out the desires of their millions of readers to know every detail of a candidate's life while he is before the public in a pre-election campaign.

But during this period the swirl of activity that immediately surrounds the candidate himself is only part of a large organization that is being arranged and set up in the various sections of the country to carry on the

[1] Alfred E. Smith, *The Citizen and his Government* (New York: Harper and Brothers, 1935), pp. 119-139. Reprinted by permission of the publisher.

vote-getting campaign. Each local political committee has definitely fixed its mind upon the fact that its particular community will respond vigorously on election day to the plea of the candidate.

To organize these committees through a central office, supply them with money, campaign literature, and enthusiasm, is a tremendous job which must be handled by a central organization which in recent years has almost always been set up in New York or Washington. A vast labyrinth of campaign departments must be set up to cater to the wishes and needs of every conceivable class or race of voters. There must be departments to deal with various races of people, departments to handle fraternal organizations, to handle war veterans, the farmers, the labor-union members, the first voters, the colleges, and many others.

Each of these activities must be placed in the hands of some one skilled and familiar with the work, and the whole thing headed by responsible executives who will represent the candidate and who can be trusted not to place him in any embarrassing situation.

It is a job in itself for the people at campaign headquarters just to see and handle the thousands of people who wander in for one reason or another, and in doing this to avoid offending anyone, thus saving the important executives from the necessity of wasting their time seeing the various types who seem drawn to a campaign headquarters as flies are to sugar.

There is a widespread impression that political parties have practically unlimited funds to spend on campaign activities, and although nothing could be more erroneous, especially in recent years when money-raising has been one of the most difficult parts of a political campaign, there are still thousands of people who think that all they have to do is go to campaign headquarters, convince some one that they can get votes, and be handed a check.

All the world's "unemployables" are among the thousands who come around looking for some sort of hand-out. People who never seem to exist at all except during campaign time reappear. They fill the reception-rooms and take up endless time of the personnel managers, volunteer assistants, chairmen of committees, and bureau heads. They claim to know how to do everything from typing to publicity and public speaking. They offer to sell valuable secrets which will demolish the opposition, or to make an investigation of the opposing candidate that will bring out such damaging facts about his character and record as to make further campaigning unnecessary.

There are always hundreds who offer to deliver vast blocks of votes, practically without further effort, if they are paid a suitable sum which may range anywhere from ten to ten thousand dollars. This sort of thing is not peculiar to any one party. They appear in every campaign head-quarters.

For a person interested in personalities or humanity in general a few hours spent in a national campaign headquarters is a lesson in the handling of human beings. Here are the dignified, courtly gentlemen with their big black "senatorial" hats and heavy Southern accents, wearing thick gold watchchains, laden with fraternal emblems, each one announcing his ability to deliver the vote of an entire Southern state, if not the whole of the South and Southwest. Sometimes these gentlemen are so impressive that campaign managers hesitate to offer them compensation, but these fears are usually dispelled by a request for a little recompense for the effort and expense involved.

Then there are the Western people, attired in a sort of citified cowboy fashion and guaranteeing to deliver their cattle-raising sections of the country. The agricultural experts are likewise on hand, as well as the inevitable labor-union official who is willing to accept a well-paid position to organize the labor vote.

Most of these people have nothing genuine to deliver. The most one can say for them is that they imagine they have, but I do not hesitate to state that there are many conscious fakers among them. Nevertheless, they come to campaign headquarters with every kind of claim and sometimes succeed in getting themselves on the payroll. If they are successful in this, they often look upon a campaign job simply as an opportunity to loaf. Few expect to work hard and they all expect salaries that will enable them to live for a few months in the sunshine of campaign prosperity, after which they can retire somewhere for another four years, perhaps being able to make a few dollars in local campaigns between times.

As a way to waste money, nothing exceeds the employment of this type of people. Even the important political leaders, the members of the National Committees, local or state officials, and others who come to campaign headquarters or are in touch with the guiding minds of the campaign are troublesome to deal with, consuming a great deal of time uselessly, and must be taken with a grain or two of salt.

Every political leader has the notion that he will be unable to carry his locality alone. Notwithstanding that their candidate may speak nightly on the radio, supply them with vast quantities of literature or even money, they insist that real results can be accomplished only if the people of the locality can see the candidate, have him smile at them, ride through their city and wave his hand in friendly greeting while engaging in personal conversation with the local leaders. This brings to the presidential candidate the same problem faced by a candidate for Governor who finds that there are just not enough days in the campaign period for him to be transported to every locality where he is informed that his presence is indispensable, and it will be realized that when this is applied to the nation as a whole the problem is an impossible one.

The question of what states and cities the presidential candidate should really visit, and what subject he should discuss when he arrives there, is one of the most troublesome and trying parts of the campaign, both for the candidate himself and for his managers. It takes people with real political acumen and a genuine knowledge of the needs and interest of the voters in various parts of the country to decide on these points. But some one must spend a lot of time listening to the claims and arguments of all these local leaders. In the end there must be a considerable amount of heartlessness in making these decisions. Old friends and stanch supporters must be firmly and definitely turned down, and the candidate's itinerary carefully planned so as to enable him, with a minimum of time and effort expended, to cover the really necessary ground and to show himself and talk in the places where the real campaign-planners feel that there will be a genuine chance of changing votes.

Of course, the radio has made this situation a little easier. If a candidate cannot appear in a particular town he can at least arrange through the speakers' bureau and the radio department for a near-by broadcasting station to be hooked on to the network carrying his speeches, so that this locality may hear his voice.

But even this is not a complete solution. There are still some places at which a candidate must actually show himself, where perhaps there may be such doubt as to his personality or his convictions that he and his advisers may honestly feel that the only way to gain votes and change sentiment in his favor is to circulate in person, shake hands with the proper people, and show himself in a large hall to as many of the citizens as possible.

But when the campaign is all over and the candidate sits back in his easy chair and looks back over his experiences, he will usually find that ninety per cent of the political committees who urged him to appear in their towns or states, and whose requests were granted, were really more eager for local glory and the benefit they might gain for their individual organizations, than they were for the ultimate success of the party in the entire nation. I cannot say that this is done deliberately, but nevertheless it is often the case.

It is practically impossible, during the heat of the actual national campaign, for a candidate to find time enough really to think out the speeches he is about to make. Particularly is this true of a candidate who cannot or does not wish to rely upon some other person who is willing to spend his time preparing the material for his speeches, but who desires to take a personal and individual responsibility for everything that he says. When you get right down to it, a candidate on tour does not have a single moment to think out the things that represent his own thoughts unless he is prepared to satisfy himself and try to keep going with only a couple of hours' sleep every night.

An amusing anecdote illustrating this is told of Bryan's first campaign for President. A newspaper man asked former Governor Hill of New York what he thought about Bryan. Mr. Hill said, "Well, I guess he is all right." When the newspaper man replied, "Why, he makes sixteen speeches a day," Mr. Hill inquired, pointedly, "Yes. But when does he think?"

The trouble with campaign trips, while they accomplish something worth while in the way of exhibiting the candidate to the people, is that the trip is more of a general reception than a business proposition aimed at intelligently discussing the issues of the campaign before the people. Countless thousands of people who have no real interest or reason for meeting the candidate are anxious to shake his hand and gain the glory of a personal introduction.

About the most trying and tiring part of the whole 1928 campaign trip was the necessity of spending most of every day shaking hands with people whose only desire was to meet the candidate and who could not by any stretch of the imagination be supposed to be capable of materially helping the cause of my election. Nevertheless, it is impossible to offend any one of the thousands of local leaders, politicians, and just plain friends and admirers who make these requests, even if their fulfillment means occupying almost all of the candidate's time. Well-meaning railroad men conspired to help aggravate this situation. Even if the local political committees had not arranged receptions, the train could be sure of a waiting crowd at every water-tank or other stop along the line because the railroad men wired ahead word of the campaign train's arrival.

Of course, every village, town, and hamlet wants a speech from the traveling candidate, and none of them takes into consideration the fact that the candidate may have nothing left to say after days or even weeks of active campaigning, and that he must save the discussion of important matters for the nightly radio speeches broadcast to the entire country.

All in all, I found it next to impossible to get enough sleep or even to keep up with the necessary campaign work of my 1928 trip through the country.

But, nevertheless, the tour goes on. The better organized a candidate makes his personal staff, the easier things will be for him. Good publicity men, secretaries, research assistants, and others can assume a considerable part of the vast burden of campaign work, but no one can take over the job of personal meetings and greetings, hand-shakes, autographs, impromptu speeches and receptions to local political people who will be gravely offended if they have no opportunity to meet the candidate personally.

Another job the candidate has to assume for himself is meeting the press in daily conferences. The candidate must depend upon the press to be helpful to him in carrying his utterances widespread to the people, and he must hope for the press to be friendly enough to support him editorially, as well as to carry his speeches and activities in the news columns. That is necessary, but it takes a great deal of the candidate's time and energy to attend one, or usually two, daily press conferences, answer or parry the questions of anywhere from ten to one hundred eager and intelligent reporters, among whom there are sure to be many who represent hostile newspapers. In addition to these conferences there is the continual necessity of meeting feature writers, artists, photographers, and pen sketchers, who have been assigned by their editors to use their artistic talents in writing about the more personal life of the candidate and his family, or to picture him in the various activities of a campaign.

The campaigner for the Presidency had better be ready to accept with good grace every conceivable type and kind of gift. The well-meaning Democrats of the United States loaded the baggage-cars of my 1928 campaign train with every sort of present from pipes, tobacco, clothing, and underwear, to animals, such as large dogs and even a live donkey meant to represent the Democratic emblem.

Of course, one genuinely useful function of the campaign tour is the opportunity it gives a candidate to hear and sense at first hand the sentiment of the parts of the country through which he passes and the feeling of the voters toward his candidacy. One of the most difficult, and at the same time useful, political attributes is a genuine sense of perspective in such matters. It is extremely hard for a candidate to look with proper abstraction upon the noisy, cheering, and vast signs of approbation he may see around him every time his train stops, and yet to penetrate through the noise and the flattery and cheering and music and see dispassionately what impression he is really making on the voters and how the country feels toward him. It must be remembered that the crowd that usually turns out to see a candidate upon his arrival in town, or to listen to and cheer his speech, is usually largely composed of people who intended to vote for him anyhow, whose very attendance was prompted or encouraged by the local organization of his party, and who would scarcely be expected to do anything but show the highest approval of the candidate's every word, no matter what the sentiment of the voters as a whole or of the majority of them may be in that town or state.

•

It is worth remembering that in the 1928 campaign, when my tour through the South and West attracted the largest and most enthusiastic crowds that had ever greeted a Democratic candidate in those parts of the country, I nevertheless learned a different story when the votes were counted on election day. It takes a trained and experienced political sense to know what really lies behind the cheers of the crowd.

None the less, a candidate who has the ability to sense what is really going on and see back of the noisy receptions will gain much by his tour, for he will learn from day to day and week to week what issues can really swing votes in any given part of the country, and can thus decide what he really means to do or say about such issues.

Of course, if the local leaders would be willing to meet some intelligent member of the candidate's staff and explain their needs and desires to him and enable the staff member to digest and pass on the information in more readily usable form to the candidate, a great saving in time and effort would be effected on the part of the candidate himself. But the wise men and party wiseacres are not thus easily satisfied; each of them has an entirely different system for the candidate to follow if he is to finally enter the White House, and each of them has an insatiable desire to tell his story in person, shake the candidate's hand, and receive his personal thanks for the information, whether or not it is useful.

Therefore, even when he stops for a day or two to visit some locality and address a meeting, the candidate finds little rest and no solitude. If he dines in a public dining-room, the back-slapping and handshaking will not only prevent the consumption of any food, but will undoubtedly delay the candidate to such an extent that he will be late for the public meeting. If he attempts to dine in his own room, he is equally unlikely to get any dinner because of poor service in the unusually jammed hotel, and the persistent attentions of callers anxious to see him for one reason or another.

After the meeting there is still little rest for the harassed candidate. More and more people of the locality insist on a personal hand-shake and an opportunity to express approval of the speech or to make suggestions for the next one. But out of it all the keen-minded candidate can gain political information of vast value to the conduct of his campaign; information which must, however, be combined with the news which reaches him from the nerve center at national headquarters, where the personal communications, letters, and visits from political leaders and plain voters in every part of the country are continually being digested and prepared by a competent staff into information easily translated into oratory or statements calculated to win votes.

But the activities immediately surrounding the candidate are only a small part of the whole campaign organization. At national headquarters hundreds, even thousands, of people are laboring to gather in a harvest of votes in various specialized fields. The publicity bureau must grind out a continual grist of statements, not only by the candidate, but by the party chairman, local leaders, members of Congress, and every person prominent in the public eye whose support is worthy of publicity.

Scores of specialized bureaus which I have mentioned previously must continue their specialized appeals to special racial, fraternal, or other groups of voters. The speakers' bureau must function in a business-like and efficient manner to supply the necessary personal oratory or material for speeches to every locality that feels it needs that sort of support.

The life blood of political campaigning is money. One cannot conceive the vast number of demands made upon the party treasurer during national campaigns. Every party worker and every voter from one end of the country to the other feels that the party treasury is fair game. Letters, telephone calls, and personal requests for places on the payroll or just plain hand-outs of money pour into the national headquarters by the thousands. Naturally these tremendous demands for funds place upon the party treasurer and his organization one of the most important duties of the entire campaign organization.

Of course, one of the most difficult parts of a money-raising campaign in recent years has been the necessity for a swift, almost instantaneous, organization of all the vast facilities necessary for money-raising on a national scale, and the necessity for creating such an organization practically out of a clear sky within a very few weeks. This was the case right up to the 1932 campaign. Previous to that date it was customary for the party committees to lapse into almost complete inactivity for the period between the presidential election and the date on which it was necessary to make plans for the next presidential nominating convention.

But between 1928 and 1932 all this was changed. Mainly due to the activity of John J. Raskob, as party chairman, and his willingness to supply funds for the cause and to help raise them from other sources, the Democratic party entered on a program of real minority activity, even though the Republicans were in power. An aggressive, efficiently organized office was opened in Washington under the able direction of Jouett Shouse, and the policies and activities of the Republican administration and Republican Congress systematically exposed for the inspection of the people of the country. Naturally, such activity on behalf of one of the great parties caused the opposition to enter into an equally aggressive program—a change in political tradition that I feel has meant a great deal for the betterment of our party system.

But to return to the question of money-raising. The first decision to be made by the campaign managers is how much money will be needed and where it is to come from. Where no plans have been made in advance, the situation is just that much more difficult, but where the National Committee has been in active operation for years ahead of the presidential campaign, it is not too difficult a job to organize an appeal to the public for funds. Practically every form of money-raising activity has been tried at one time or another by the various parties. Newspaper advertising on a national scale in 1928 did not bring enough return to pay for the advertising expenditure; but on the other hand, appeals over the radio for financial support brought immediate and startling results. On one occasion $5,000 expended for radio time brought in contributions of $85,000, and in the whole 1928 campaign over $1,500,000 was raised by radio appeals directly from the party leaders to the people.

Personal solicitation, letter-writing by men prominent in party circles or in industry, women's committees, hundreds of other forms of activity, are used to raise money. The cost of the national campaign in 1928 was approximately $6,000,000 for the Democratic party, and $8,000,000 for the Republican party. But in 1932 the stress of economic conditions brought the capacity for money-raising, and necessarily the capacity for spending, down to $1,638,177.58 and $1,916,640.93, respectively.

Of course, the business management of a campaign must be vitally concerned with the expenditure of this money. What is it used for and why? Campaign managers must become hard boiled and dispassionate in their considerations of the thousands of proposals that are made for the expenditure of campaign money. There is no sum on earth that could be raised during campaign time sufficient to cover the expense of every one of the proposals that reaches a national headquarters.

But there are certain necessary and definite things that must be done. The candidate's tour costs a lot of money, the purchase of radio time a great deal more. (In the 1928 campaign $600,000 was paid to the radio companies.) The printing of literature, posters, campaign manuals, and other such material is another large item; the rental of vast office space, furniture, and salaries of clerical help another big item of expense.

The vice-presidential candidate must be helped in his campaign. The expenses of his tour about the country are met by the National Committee, even though his activities may attain only a small place in the national party picture. High-priced services of experts in publicity, research, economics, and other lines must be retained to insure the accuracy of the party's utterances and claims.

According to party tradition, divisional headquarters must be opened in three or four sections of the country, each duplicating in its small way the larger activities of the national headquarters and each spending a considerable sum which must be supplied from the central party pocketbook. If I had my way future campaigns would eliminate these divisional headquarters, as well as a great many of the expenses connected with them, particularly those in the way of supplying them with vast quantities of literature, buttons, and other campaign paraphernalia which cannot in the long run really make votes, but only serve to add to a general atmosphere of ballyhoo, and which in some cases are not even distributed by lazy or uninterested local leaders.

Most important of all, and perhaps the only really vital expense of all the campaign, is the sending into the various states of money to be expended during the last few days of the campaign at the discretion of the leaders, to get out the vote and see that it is recorded in the right way. Under this heading also come efforts in various cities in which the party must contend with a corrupt opposing machine and where it is necessary to hire a large number of watchers in order to insure the honesty of the vote and its counting.

The man who rules the party treasury must be equipped with an iron hand and a clear head if he is not to be fooled by the cupidity of local leaders who flock to the national headquarters and insist that the lack of additional funds stands between them and the loss of their locality to the party. Only a well-grounded political experience and ability to resist oratory and all sort of cajolery will prevent the party treasurer from being almost literally robbed of hundreds of thousands of dollars by leaders who claim, almost with tears in their eyes, that for the lack of anywhere from a thousand to one hundred thousand dollars, as the case may be, the candidate and his party may lose out in their home town or state.

The treasurer must know where to draw the line. Each state is entitled to something, some more than others, and the sum cannot be determined only by the size and population of the area affected, but by its past political complexion and the treasurer's personal knowledge of the party's vote-getting possibilities, as well.

It is inevitable that some of the funds will be wasted, for, unfortunately, the chief interest of some local leaders is simply to line their own pockets at the expense of the national campaign; but most of them are loyal and honest and use the campaign funds to the best possible account to bring out the votes.

Adding all these items up, one quickly reaches the vast total of money collected for national campaigns, and in most years even more. This deficit must be met by money raised on the part of the National Committee from

banks or individuals willing to advance some money. Of course, it is traditional that the winning party has little difficulty in wiping out this deficit.
Collections are comparatively easily made from those among the wealthy
and well-to-do who always want to be on the band wagon of the winner,
no matter what. The losing party must often go through a painful period
of years gradually collecting a few dollars here and a few dollars there
before the deficit is cut down to such a point that the party will not be
hampered in its activities during the next election.

No. 44

[IN the preceding article Mr. Smith raised some questions concerning the raising and spending of party campaign funds. Such problems have long been
before the American people, and have frequently been the subject of legislative
action. Generally this legislation has dealt with such matters as the amount
of money that may be spent in any given campaign, the sources of campaign
contributions, and the legal and illegal objects of expenditure.

The problem of party finance, however, has a much deeper significance than
legislation of this kind indicates; it has a vital relationship to democratic government. In such a government we assume that all parties may place their
policies and candidates before the voter and thus may have an equal opportunity to claim his attention and support. The huge costs of campaigning,
however, deny to all but a few parties this equality of opportunity. A campaign is, of necessity, a costly enterprise. In an American presidential election
over eighty million potential voters must be reached by the radio, the press, and
the motion picture. These channels of publicity are expensive and, whatever
the issues of an election may be, it is clear that only the two major parties can
raise the necessary millions of dollars. This means that third parties, regardless
of the merits of their policies or the abilities of their candidates, can never compete on a basis of equality with their richer rivals. Furthermore, the existence
of huge war chests may lead to reckless and questionable expenditures, and thus
may affect not only the outcome of an election but also the whole operation of
the democratic process.

In the following essay, Professor Charles A. Beard discusses the significance
of the whole problem of campaign finance and outlines the federal legislation
in this field. Since this article was written, new federal legislation has been
passed which places a limit upon the sum which may be expended in a presidential election and limits the size of campaign contributions. The problems
of enforcement that are noted in this essay, however, remain much the same as
they were when Professor Beard wrote "Money in Federal Politics."]

MONEY IN FEDERAL POLITICS [1]

by Charles A. Beard

PERIODICALLY the country is shocked by investigations revealing the expenditures of huge sums of money by candidates for Congress; these shocks have been intermittent since the close of the Civil War. A great deal of heat has been generated, escaping usually in talk, and Congress has skirted around the edges of the subject in several statutes. Generally speaking, "nothing has been done about it"; yet there are signs of change. Not long ago the Senate in the Vare case added a new qualification for membership in that body: a citizen presenting his election credentials to the Senate must show that he has not spent too much money in an irregular fashion in winning his seat. A short time before this significant incident, Senator Bronson Cutting forcibly raised the whole question of political expenditures in a searching speech in the Senate and introduced a program of legislation designed to cope with some of the worst evils in the present practices. Judging by his pertinacity, we may assume that Mr. Cutting will not let the matter rest and that Congress, in its next session, will have to face the issue of money in federal politics.

Under the prevailing system of popular elections, thousands and even millions of voters must be reached through various agencies, such as the press, meetings, the post, telegraph, radio and party workers. Huge expenditures are necessary even for legitimate purposes, to say nothing of bribery direct and indirect. To win party nominations for offices in large jurisdictions, individual aspirants and their supporters must ordinarily make considerable outlays of money, and to win elections, party organizations and candidates must do likewise, if they have any formidable competitors. Here the American theory of democratic equality absolutely breaks down in fact. Although it is not true that the longest purse always wins, it is certainly true that without a purse of some kind to aid him, no citizen can expect to win the office of President or a seat in Congress.

Ordinarily money for such expenditures comes from four prime sources —disinterested persons of wealth, office holders, office seekers and citizens with economic undertakings which may be benefited by action or inaction on the part of the government. Attempts to raise large sums through petty contributions by the masses are not usually crowned with success. Inevitably this brings about a concentration of immense power in the hands

[1] Charles A. Beard, "Money in Federal Politics," *The New Republic* (July 30, 1930), Vol. 63, pp. 305-307. Reprinted by permission of *The New Republic*.

of a relatively small number of people. And recent investigations, not to say scandals, have revealed a widespread use of money by individuals and groups in primaries and elections—money derived from sources economically interested and sometimes expended in a fraudulent manner. In 1928 and 1929, two men were excluded from the United States Senate on the ground that their campaign expenditures were highly irregular, if not tainted with corruption. In recognition of such facts, the most advanced states have enacted elaborate campaign-practices laws and Congress has tardily but gingerly dealt with the subject.

Federal legislation in this field is of four types:

First of all, Congress has imposed certain limits on the collecting and giving of money in connection with elections. According to the terms of a law originally passed in 1883, no Senator, Representative or federal officer may solicit or receive any contribution, subscription or assessment from any officer, clerk or other employee drawing a salary from the federal treasury. Thus, an effort was made to dry up one of the prime sources of political funds. Cut off from this assistance, political leaders came to rely more and more on the contributions of great financial and industrial corporations. To counter this movement, Congress has made it unlawful for any national bank or any corporation whatever to make any money contribution in connection with elections at which presidential and vice-presidential electors, Senators or Representatives are chosen; furthermore, candidates, political committees and all other persons are forbidden to receive any contributions from these sources.

While attempting to combat the collection of political funds from three interested groups in society—office holders, national banks and business corporations—Congress has placed limits on the amount which candidates for Congress may spend in elections. In no case can they exceed the sum set by state legislation in this relation. In the absence of a state law fixing a smaller figure, a candidate for the Senate may spend $10,000 and a candidate for the House of Representatives, $2,500. However, if the size of the constituency permits it, this amount may be increased to a figure obtained by multiplying by three cents the total number of votes cast at the last general election for all candidates for the position in question—that is, for Senator, or Representative. Even then, no matter how large the vote, no candidate for the Senate may spend more than $25,000 and no candidate for the House more than $5,000.

But highly significant exceptions must be recorded. In summing up all his expenditures under the federal limit, a candidate may omit outlays for his necessary personal, traveling and subsistence expenses. He may likewise leave out of the reckoning money spent for stationery and postage, for distributing circulars and for telephone and telegraph service. Also excepted from the accounting are all assessments, fees and charges levied on him under the laws of the state in which he resides.

Meager as are the provisions of federal law on political contributions and candidates' expenditures, they are still more meager with respect to the purpose of outlays—the uses which may be made of money and other objects of value in elections. It is unlawful for any candidate for Congress to offer directly or indirectly any public or private employment in exchange for support, or to promise his influence to secure such employment on this condition. It is likewise unlawful to offer to make, or to cause to be made, any expenditures to any person with a view to inducing him to vote for or against any candidate or to withhold his vote. The acceptance as well as the offering of money for these purposes is also prohibited. In some measure, no doubt, the comparatively slight federal limitations on the uses of money are due to the fullness of state laws dealing with bribery and other corrupt practices in elections.

A further restraint on the collection and use of money is supposed to be afforded by a federal law providing for the publicity of campaign funds. Every candidate for Senator or Representative must file with the secretary of the Senate or the clerk of the House, as the case may be, both before and after election, a statement showing in detail contributions received in support of his candidacy and itemized expenditures made by him or by any person with his knowledge and consent. And, curiously enough, he must add a statement of pledges or promises made by himself, or with his consent, relative to offering public or private employment in exchange for support.

Besides requiring candidates for Congress to file reports of their outlays, the law prescribes publicity for political committees. Within the scope of the law is every committee, association and organization which accepts contributions or makes expenditures for the purpose of influencing or attempting to influence the election of candidates or presidential or vice-presidential electors in two or more states. The law does not stop here. It also applies to every other committee, association or organization engaged in influencing elections, whether it operates in more than one state or not, if it is a branch of a subsidiary of a national committee, association or organization—excluding duly organized state and local committees of political parties. All political committees covered by this legislation must file periodically fully itemized statements containing receipts and expenditures. The list of outlays must show in great detail the purposes as well as the dates and amounts of the expenditures.

After the federal legislation respecting the use of money in elections was consolidated and amended in 1925, some of the most extraordinary scandals in the long history of campaign funds occurred. Coupled with independent criticism from the outside, the discussion of these scandals in Congress has raised anew the question of providing a complete national code regulating and restricting the use of money in politics. In this relation numerous deficiencies of the existing laws have been pointed out and remedial bills proposed.

Perhaps the greatest gap in federal legislation is the total exclusion of primaries from the scope of control. The publicity act of 1911 covered both primaries and elections, but the Supreme Court in the Newberry case in 1921 held that the power of Congress to regulate the manner of holding elections did not extend to senatorial conventions and primaries. Subsequently Congress, in consolidating the corrupt-practices acts, expressly provided that the term "election" does not include a primary election or convention of a political party. Yet it is doubtful whether this exception is required by the Constitution. In the Newberry case mentioned above, only four of the nine judges of the Supreme Court agreed that Congress had no power over primaries. Another judge joined them in holding invalid a part of the law enacted previous to the adoption of popular election of Senators, but reserved judgment as to whether the authority of Congress in this respect had not been increased by the subsequent change in the Constitution. Thus, in fact, the power of Congress over primaries and political conventions is clouded with uncertainty.

And yet in a large number of cases it is the primary, not the election, that counts in the choice of Senators and Representatives. Wherever one political party continuously dominates a state, as, for example, the Democrats in Alabama or the Republicans in Pennsylvania, the real fight is over the nomination; the election is secure. It has been estimated that in a majority of the congressional districts the chief contest is the primary. It was in the primaries in Pennsylvania and Illinois that a part of the enormous expenditure was incurred which led to the exclusion of two men from the Senate on grounds of corruption or misuse of money. . . . [Recent Supreme Court decisions indicate that Congressional power to regulate elections extends to primary elections and a constitutional amendment to give Congress such power is not necessary as once was thought.]

A second criticism of the present corrupt-practices legislation bears upon the clause which exempts from the limits fixed on expenditures money spent by candidates for stationery, postage, printing, personal uses and publicity in general (except for newspapers and billboards). Under this rule a candidate may spend as much as he pleases for effective campaigning—letters, telegrams and circulars, for instance. Thus, outlays for most of the purposes which may be called "legitimate" are in fact not at all restricted in amount, and the man or woman with a long purse is given a decided advantage.

Besides leaving the candidate absolutely free to spend as much as he likes for such publicity purposes, the law allows his friends and supporters to spend all they please on his behalf without accounting for it. It is in this connection that some of the worst abuses have arisen. Frequently it is not the candidate but some powerful economic interest behind him that makes huge outlays in primaries and elections. As long as the candidate is not held personally responsible for all expenditures in support of his candidacy in primaries and elections, and the amount not strictly limited, wealth has a decided advantage in every contest.

Through another hole in the corrupt-practices law money may creep. Political committees may have large deficits in their funds at the end of the campaign and raise the money to meet these deficits long after the period for making public their accounts of the election has expired. As Senator Cutting once remarked: "A contribution made to a preëlection fund would have been in the nature of a gamble, but a contribution made to a deficit, and particularly to a deficit of the party which had been successful in the election, was simply putting . . . money over the counter and getting a return for his investment. That is a danger which is not dealt with under our present statutes at all." This practice was illustrated in connection with the campaign of 1920, when a big deficit in the Republican fund was covered by Mr. Harry Sinclair, who was later charged with fraudulently obtaining oil leases from the politicians who benefited from his campaign contributions. Mr. Sinclair stated at the time that he did not know whether he was a Republican or a Democrat, but at all events he staked his money on the winning horse.

In addition to its structural defects, the corrupt-practices law is weak on the side of enforcement. The provisions for publicity are not effective. Statements of campaign receipts and expenditures are carelessly filed in irregular form, they are not published, and after a period of two years they may be destroyed. Most of them merely accumulate dust. Eager newspaper reporters may dig out certain figures that will make news or a sensation, but as a rule candidates and committees can be fairly sure that little will be heard or known of their "public" statements. While the national committees of the great political parties report in detail, other political committees and many candidates for Congress are, to say the least, extremely careless in making their returns. It is doubtful whether the news of their publicity statements often reaches their respective districts. In this relation the law has no teeth.

Furthermore, no agency is responsible for enforcing its terms. A de-feated candidate may attack his opponent in the federal courts for some infraction, but there is no permanent machinery to investigate charges of irregularity. Committees on elections in both houses of Congress and special committees for inquiring into campaign expenditures do go into specific cases as they arise, or make hurried searches when scandal breaks out, but they are almost always partisan in character and concerned pri-marily with immediate issues. It is not the business of any non-political federal officer or agency to maintain constant scrutiny over the operations of the election laws.

From these criticisms it follows that any thoroughgoing revision of the corrupt-practices acts should include primaries and conventions as well as elections within the scope of the law. It should fix limits to all expendi-tures, define the purposes for which they may be made, place full responsi-bility for expenditures on candidates and committees and abolish exemp-tions in accounting for campaign outlays. If publicity is to be more than a farce, then provisions must be made for giving effect to it in a form that will reach the voters. Deficits present a knotty problem, but committees that incur them can be made accountable and conditions may be prescribed for meeting unpaid bills. With reference to the issue of enforcement, Sena-tor Cutting has proposed the creation of an election commission to audit reports, investigate credentials, deal with contested cases, serve as a fact-finding body, and report results of its inquiries to Congress for final deter-mination.

If the defects in the present laws are cured by new legislation, the prob-lem of money in politics will not be entirely solved. Indeed, there are Sena-tors who hold that it cannot be solved until the use of private money in primaries and elections is forbidden entirely. But this involves heroic action. Especially does it throw upon the federal government the burden of providing machinery by which all aspirants and candidates may present their claims to constituents on an even plane at public expense. It will take more thought than has yet been expended on the subject to evolve a scheme that will place the long head on a parity with the long purse. Perhaps it can and may be done. But no matter what restraints the law may put on the use of money in politics, it cannot by that process separate politics and economics.

Chapter XIII

THE JOB OF THE LEGISLATOR

[EVERY individual and every association of individuals are constantly faced with the problem of making decisions about matters they feel to be important. The individual must ultimately make these decisions himself and most associations can make them at a meeting of their entire membership. But there are a great many associations, of which the state is one, that have so many members and extend over such a wide territory that it is impossible for the members to meet together. Under such circumstances it becomes necessary to establish some kind of a representative body to act for the association as a whole. In the state this body is known as the legislature.

We have already seen that in a democratic government the legislature or legislatures are elected by the great body of adult citizens and held accountable to them. This immediately raises a number of important questions. What is the legislative function? What role does the individual legislator play? What is the relation of the legislator and the legislature to politics? What does the legislator do in his various roles as representative of his constituency, member of his party, member of legislative committees?

Unfortunately, the legislature and the individual legislator often suffer unjustified attack. There are, of course, grounds for attack. But, in general, Americans have spent too much time in pointing out the vices and too little in determining the merits of the legislative way. For, besides the functions normally ascribed to it and performed with a much higher degree of competence than much criticism would lead one to believe, the legislature plays a valuable role in a democracy. It offers a forum where, after the heat of election campaigns, representatives of different parties and different interests can meet face to face to work on common problems. In the give and take of daily work, the members confront each other, compare thoughts and speeches, and discover how to obtain the maximum welfare with the minimum of coercion.

The job is a complex one and neither its difficulties nor the demands it makes upon time and patience are very well appreciated. The legislator, if conscientious (and most of them are), can only do the legislative job by being a scholar, a politician, a parliamentarian, and a party member—all at the same time.

The legislator must be sensitive to the problems of the world in which he lives. He must have sufficient knowledge—or know where to get it—to challenge the opposition as well as the executive and administrative officials. He must be adept in the ways and means of legislative procedure. He must have a stout heart, a mature wisdom, an insight into human nature, and a general power of judgment. That is a large order, to be sure, but one that is more nearly filled than is generally realized.]

No. 45

[PROF. T. V. SMITH is exceptionally well qualified to discuss the legislature and the legislative way. As a professor of philosophy he has always had an interest in politics and has written numerous books and articles on government and democracy. In addition, he has been a member of the Illinois State Legislature and Congressman at Large from Illinois in the national House of Representatives. "In Praise of the Legislative Way" is the result, therefore, not only of study and reflection but also of practical personal experience.]

IN PRAISE OF THE LEGISLATIVE WAY [1]
by T. V. Smith

THERE is an elementary fact about politics which is not well understood. It is this: that conflict here is the normal, not the abnormal, state. Men talk of, even talk against, power-politics; there is in essence no other kind of politics. Though peace be its goal, war is the differential of politics. This is only half the story, the easier half at that. The other half, the harder half, is that in politics the strife which prevails is normally between honest men. Honesty, we seem to think, ought to beget amity; and amity, we surely believe, ought to cure strife. Why should it be baffling to meet honesty as obstacle? And yet it is so. Dishonest men you can scare into acquiescence; not so the honest opposites. Honest men are of all men the most obdurate. They have been martyred, of course; but even the martyrdom of such men but unites others behind their honesty, to make it more obdurate still. And when it is honesty that is at odds with honesty, as in politics, the conflict is rendered worse by efforts to subvert, divert, or even to convert. That is what makes politics so difficult.

This conception of politics—as a crown of thorns woven by idealists for others to wear, but worn in the event by those who wove them—I do not present as an hypothesis to be discussed. I submit it as a characterization to be accepted before we can even talk intelligently about politics.

If you cannot bring yourself to accept the hypothesis that ideals themselves are inharmonious, or at least provoke their devotees to open conflict

[1] T. V. Smith, "In Praise of the Legislative Way," *The Antioch Review* (March, 1949), Vol. IX, No. 1, pp. 46-59. Reprinted by permission of *The Antioch Review*.

in the name of the ideals, then I can throw little light upon any such questions; I can only leave you where you have stationed yourself: waiting at the wayside of life to be picked up by some candidate for dictatorship, be he but recommended to you in the warm axiological insignia of your particular provincialism. Together you will make fanatics, you and he; and together you can, and probably will, do great harm to mankind, though honestly of course in the name of your joint sectarian good.

II

With so much plainly before us, let us repair now to the place prepared for such a conflict, to the legislative assembly. A fit meeting place it is; for the legislature, by identification, is the organ of the function in question: it is the place where honest men meet to argue over, and to adjust if possible, their differences as to honesty, where just men meet to quarrel over justice. You will expect it to be a noisy place, for there honest men will at first stand aghast at the audacity of other men who claim to be equally honest. Such men aghast are not usually silent about it. It is, in the Anglo-Saxon tradition, not as noisy a place, however, as you might well expect. The noise is mitigated by the fact that it is not the honest men of the original differences who meet there; it is rather their agents. The distance from the original differences lends, from the outset, a certain dispassion to the scene. These agents are the elected representatives, altogether representing—if the system be just and wise—all citizens with their divided interests. Rising out of this noisy void of politics, our subject now achieves form, and takes this shape for systematic discussion of the tragedy of reason in the domain of action. To contain this tragedy, we must first consider the relations of these agents, organized as the legislature. But since they are agents, not principals, we must consider the relations between them and their principals: "the people" in theory, "the party" in well-regulated practice, and "the interests" in all too frequent suspicion. Since, furthermore, the conflicts which are so noisy between the agents are but the tighter-meshed conflicts that smolder behind the scenes in the interest-groups involved, our final discussion must be of the people themselves banded into competing groups and represented by historic parties.

We are lucky to begin with the most humanely pleasant of our interrelationships. In the legislative domain of life you will find human relations at their best. You may have thought differently upon your last visit to a legislative gallery. But what went ye for to see—good men all agreed on goodness, honest men all agreed on honesty, just men all agreed on justice, holy men all agreed on holiness? Such agreement is not on earth, not yet, not soon. What saw ye—articulate simpletons intent upon minimum business, to the tune of maximum noise, in an atmosphere of partisan strife? Come, now! Go again! Look again from the legislative gallery!

Do you not notice how courteous the interruptions? Do you not notice that they go by protocol through the Speaker, that the interruptions are tended in courtliness and received with grace—whether accepted as interruptions or declined for lack of time or merely postponed, more likely, out of a sense of orderliness? Having looked again to see what you did not at first see, go again to hear what you did not at first hear. Go when great issues impend, when action upon issues is imminent. If you return at such a time, you will see the chamber packed, party lines marshaled, time fairly divided and carefully assigned, amendments efficiently argued and quickly voted up or down. You will see, for example, 435 orators and egoists behaving as neither is popularly supposed to behave, as disciplined adults intent upon collective action.

Look closer still and you will isolate two elements in that impressive view: one, the individual component; the other, the traditional factor. Individually, the representatives are for the most part treating each other with respect, even with deference. The approach is seldom rude. Not "that so and so from such and such a district." It is usually all too urbane: "the distinguished representative of a great constituency from a noble state. . . ." When occasionally the approach is strident, you will see, if you stay to observe, the member attacked walk out arm in arm with the attacking member, as if they were close friends, which more than likely they are.

A "political apprentice" of mine once sat in the gallery of the senate of Illinois to keep analytic tab upon the pattern of all interpersonal relations, by charting every call of one member upon another member over several weeks. It was a beautiful chart, but I forget what it proved, if anything. Politics is more esthetic than scientific, and more responsive to the synthetic than to the analytic approach. As one who has always enjoyed the game, whether fully understood or not, I here hazard only the main conclusion: that nowhere on earth is the inescapable human factor more fruitfully or more beautifully handled under conflict conditions than in legislative halls. Responsible men (but their responsibility is owed to different sections of the people) meet and mingle and enjoy each other as full plenipotentiaries—of the whole people.

The reason for all this both trenches upon and transcends the personal factor. The rationale reaches into the traditional for its main support. Parliamentary usages are what make meetings possible from what would otherwise be mobs. "Rules of Order" are literally what give order to any and every effort to pool human insight, to each endeavor to compose adult differences. The rules for all sorts of public occasions have grown out of legislative procedures. Legislatures are both the source and the continuing beneficiaries of this marvelous invention whereby mind meets mind to ends constructive. In America, the rules of our national House of Representatives are built upon British experience in the House of Commons. Thomas Jefferson gave us our first systematic manual. This as elaborated by experience and implemented through many volumes of decisions by the Speaker of the House upon "points of order" constitutes the seasoned wisdom of our race in collective procedure. The respect by each member for this priceless legacy, this supplement to his shortsightedness, makes progress in legislation possible because it makes order actual in deliberation. Those who have not learned that tradition is the backbone of all effective individualism are no good at the democratic process. This respect for procedural authority makes operative in each representative the great principle of liberty under law.

So much for the dual factor in human relations between elected representatives of a democratic people functioning in legislative halls. This brief allusion can serve to remind us that liberty is not a gift of the gods but an achievement of resolute men; that progress is not rained from heaven but is raised from the depths by patience, sagacity, ingenuity—in a word, by operative reason. Civilization is more a matter of discipline achieved collectively than of rights claimed individually. Such observations lead us into our second topic through an avenue as natural as it is fruitful.

III

The avenue between representatives and represented is the political party. What was not foreseen as inevitable by our American fathers, was indeed deprecated by some of them; what was for a fact publicly dispraised by Washington in his Farewell Address, this has become head of the corner of our political system. I would raise your respect for our two-party system by calling attention to its function; and in order to do this, I shall not hesitate to speak with candor of omens now portentous in American party skies.

The individual citizen can never be certain how his elected agent will vote until the party influence is assessed. Some critics grieve over this, but in general it is a deviation from our historic process as desirable as it has proved to be inevitable. The political party by playing its role in the disciplining of members steadies policy. Indeed, in advance of steadying policy, it makes policy possible. There is room for a few, but for only a few, genuinely independent representatives in the democratic process. As the percentage of party independence rises, the possibility of policy declines, until if you had all independents, you would probably have no policy at all. This conclusion proceeds from the surmise that the more intelligent men are, the more they disagree upon important matters; and that the more honest they are, the more stead they set on their disagreements. This means that politics is mediocre in product not because its participants are bad but because they are good: so good indeed that each rises in moral dignity to insist upon his own brand of goodness. Such insistence is ruinous to policy, for legislation comes from agreement to agree, whatever the temptation be to insist upon one's own view in the premises. It is this implied agreement to agree for the party's sake which is the normal warp of political loyalty; and it is the further agreement to agree as between the two parties that constitutes the warp and woof of our common citizenship.

The desirability of parties in our democratic system arises not from the historical fact that we wanted to, but that we could not, get along without them; it arises from the moral fact that the parties wean us away from our individual narrowness, that they sublimate our economic commitments, and that they facilitate the superagreement to agree in every national pinch of which our American patriotism is woven. Politics is thus not primarily a science; it is a sportsmanship. It is not (a matter of) proof; it is (a thing of) patriotism.

Provincialism is the prime enemy of sportsmanship, the deadly foe of patriotism. Anything which weans us from the little and wins us to the large is so far forth politically good. The party weans us from whatever holds us back from the bigness of the consensus of, say, one half our common kind; and there is much that holds us back. There is race, there is creed, there is economic interest; and, in between these, there are a thousand and one concerns which tempt and would reward our unswerving loyalty. But loyalty to the little is treason to the large. Above all there is conscience, individual conscience, which allies us, upwards, with the angels of amity, which connects us, downward, with all the devils of fanaticism. (I beg you to remember, in moments the most sober, the sagacity of the sharp current wisecrack: "The fanatic is only the man who does what God would do, if God had all the facts!") When we have surmounted all that is less than party loyalty and have come to terms with all which such loyalty portends, we have emancipated ourselves from what is little and we have prepared ourselves for two things that are larger than party loyalty. We have prepared ourselves, that is, for interparty cooperation as testament to our patriotism and for international cooperation as the fuller meaning of what we have always vaguely intended, though never yet fully meant, by nationalism.

Leaving aside the matter of internationalism for the time, we must here see how the business of patriotism is involved in party politics, if we are rightly to understand the relation between the representative and those represented by him. When a Republican has come to terms with all who pass as Republicans—it is a motley gang, East and Midwest—he will not find it too hard in a congressional pinch to stomach Democrats. Equally, when a Democrat has come to terms with all that squeeze into his party— it is a motley gang, North and South—he will not find it too hard in a congressional pinch to stomach Republicans. I speak not of theory, but of daily practice in Congress. And as I speak, I think of the friendship which has grown at the top between veterans like Sam Rayburn and Joe Martin, of gallantry which survives demotion by each at the hands of the other, as public opinion fluctuates back and forth.

But for the discipline which political parties afford, no policy could ever be steadied for implementation when agreed upon, or could even get agreed upon. Surmounting our prejudices and previous commitments by party halves, we achieve now and then the whole of a national policy on matters that become sufficiently pressing. Men who have grown from childhood under the warm parental praise for the Grand Old Party (whichever one he means); men who march to the banner of a favorite candidate in national convention only to achieve the discipline perhaps of seeing another chosen; men who campaign to the tune of a common platform and rise to the level of a great, though partisan, purpose—such men and such alone are prepared for something bigger. The common symbol of a national party suffuses divergence with a glow warm enough to subordinate differences within the party. This, in turn, enables leaders in Congress to transcend whatever differences remain between the parties. Nonpartisanship is born and bred of a partisanship growing from more to more through the discipline which conditions the growth itself.

The smallness of the differences obtaining between our two great parties many deprecate, and some would repair through the medium of a third party. Now, it is not becoming intelligence to speak against a third party as such, for through such pedagogy from without, our two parties have in the past been at times disciplined to advancement. But that is the proper role, not the purpose proclaimed by supersensitive idealists. That purpose, as usually proclaimed, is to achieve the realignment in which, say, all sincere "liberals" (those who agree with *us?*) would be in one party, and all "conservatives" (those reactionary to our purposes?) would be in the other party. To such extent as this realignment can be achieved, to that extent the party-system itself gets undermined. Broaden the gulf *between* the parties, artificially abridging the gulflets obtaining within each party, and you make more difficult, if not at last impossible, the final compromises that synthesize differences into national policy—and as chief unearned increment thereof you discipline an individualistic citizenry into a patriotic citizenship.

Any help a third or fourth party can contribute toward a clarification of issues is to the good. But the net result of such effort, if not to be pernicious, is to strengthen, upon whatever improved foundations, the two-party system. And the genius of that system is what at once yields it strength and offends the sentimental idealist: that genius is *not* to make so clear the distinctions between parties, and so deepen conscientious devotion on each side to such clarity, as to render accommodation impossible between the parties.

I do not go so far as to advise strategic obfuscation of issues, but I do recommend it. What cannot be virtuously advised as conscious intent, can be and must be accepted with natural piety as the major discipline which political activity affords. Third-party movements must, in the name of patriotism, be prepared to die into another party, or to become the other, at the price which the other has paid to become itself: the price of confused purpose if not also of bedimmed conscience. Only the politically powerless can ever be morally pure, in the sense initially intended by leaders of reform movements. In politics, it is better to have moderate power (power shared, i.e., with an equal party) with moderate compromise of purpose than to have maximum purity and minimal power. It is power which action requires. But justice requires the pluralizing of power. Religions are kept humble only through this pluralizing of power, and only through the dualizing of power are political parties kept moral.

One party is too few for liberty; more than two are too many for democratic discipline. Two is the right number for both liberty and discipline. Such a system allows enough liberty for self-respect and growth, and it furnishes sufficient discipline to inform persistent consciences that no amount of feeling a thing to be right makes it right until convictionism has met equally insistent commitment halfway and has come to terms with it. This is the great discipline of political life, and it is the final moral justification of a party system of politics as well as the culminating glory of the two-party system. Thus is the personal factor (some would say peculiarly moral factor) in politics, transformed by the exigency of party life into what is more truly the ethics of democracy. This traditional role furnished by the party to the political person is the genuinely conservative basis in any dependable liberalism.

The broadening factor has to do with the relations between the elected persons as such and the citizens whom he represents. He represents those who voted against him as well as those who elected him. It pays him to remember this. Abraham Lincoln, a good politician before he became a statesman through death, promised his constituency in Illinois that he would represent all of them, "those that oppose as well as those that support me." That was his first promise. And that is the prime commandment of American sportsmanship in politics. It is that spirit which keeps party politics patriotic. What the politician deals with is, as Lincoln said, "too vast for malice." But it was his second promise that goes to the heart of our present concern. Is the elected person a deputy to follow merely the will of another, or is he truly a representative, who will use such talents as he has, with certainly superior opportunities for information, to do the right thing for his constituency, whether they have indicated a given "line" or not? This is an old controversy; and, like all such controversies, has merit no doubt on both sides.

At the level where the politician projects himself, Lincoln again made as deft a statement as one could wish. It is profound in its balance, and highly strategic in its ambiguity. He said: "While acting as (all the people's) representative, I shall be governed by their will on all subjects upon which I have the means of knowing what their will is; and upon all others, I shall do what my own judgment teaches me will best advance their interests." As if anybody could know, even with public opinion polls, precisely what "their will" is on any specific issue at any given time!

Both the theories of the proper relation between elected and electors are historically respectable. Both are morally defensible. There is room for individual differences and for choice in the given premises. Each theory is dangerous if monopolistic or self-righteous. The delegate conception can cover spinelessness with a mantle of respectability, the representative doing what any articulate group makes appear at any time the will of the whole electorate. The representative conception, on the other hand, can cover fanatical conscience with a mantle of democratic leadership, and let a delegate set himself up as a little god, until the election day of reckoning sets all things right. Railed once a very high-minded woman to a very light-hearted representative of my acquaintance: "We want somebody down there who will obey us, not one who will be always obtruding his own convictions." She did him perhaps more honor than he deserved, but her outburst makes my point. I personally doubt whether we have room for serious complaint in America as to the balance between the two theories which we seem to have struck in our national politics. There are a few politicians who follow their own consciences; and, as I have said, too many such independents are not compatible with the need of national policy. There are more, as there should be, who do their best to find out what their districts want. With the party standing between the electors and the elected, as already indicated, fanaticism is made too dangerous dependably to survive the next election; and with the party intervening, as suggested, to give focus to a widening fringe of popular concerns, the pluralism of regional desires, is given pattern eventuating in crises as national policy.

In this way, the egoistic factor in American legislation seems to me to achieve and to maintain a fair balance in practice. Lincoln provides us, again, the pattern for our summary. The conception of government "for the people" could easily yield a paternalism benevolent in intent but utterly fanatical in its outcome. The conception of government "by the people" could give us the anarchy of "pure democracy" in which, every man following his own desires or even his own conscience, all order would disappear, and with it all dependable liberty. But Lincoln's mediating conception of government "of the people" connects extremes and yields us in general what we have: representatives who honor their constituencies and yet, as mediators of regions and partisan interests in the name of the nation, discipline themselves through party loyalty to regularity within the party and to unity above the party.

It is a remarkable system, this two-party arrangement of ours—with resiliency as between social order and individual liberty; with leeway of a legislature also to maintain *ad hoc* what the theory calls for in general. This leeway would, however, not be effective were there not a larger leeway provided by the relations which obtain beyond legislative halls between the various competing elements of our multi-group society represented in legislatures by those upon whom the spotlight plays. These men are but symbols, even in their stridency. The substance is off the boards, behind the lights, in the conflicts of various groups whose failure to adjust necessitates politics, foredooms it to the noisy business it is, and requires that its fruitage should never be fully satisfactory to any. Contrasting pure democracy with what he calls a republican government like ours, James Madison declares, on the democratic side, that "if the impulse and opportunity [of partisanship] be suffered to coincide we well know that neither moral nor religious motives can be relied on as an adequate control." But he also adds, on the side of republican representation, that "under such a regulation, it may well happen that the public voice, pronounced by the representatives of the people, will be more consonant to the public good than if pronounced by the people themselves, convened for the specific purpose."

IV

We should never fully understand the paradox of the happy relation between representatives and the unsatisfactoriness of their joint yield to those represented, if we did not go behind the scenes and see what the factors are, personal and corporate, that obtain in general between human beings both as natural individuals and as banded together in corporate competition.

One does not have to rely on Hobbes's dark view of man's inherent struggle for advantage and power, nor have to go beyond Hobbes to the religious view of human nature as totally depraved. He has only to look around him to discover that all is not sweet and well as between human beings. Or, if disinclined to believe possible what he sees to be normal, he seeks American authority, he need not go beyond the Founding Fathers. Not to Hamilton, known to be extremist against human nature, do we appeal, but to Madison, the equable temperament and the constructive statesman. "So strong," says he in measured words, "is this propensity of mankind to fall into mutual animosities, that where no substantial occasion presents itself, the most frivolous and fanciful distinctions have been sufficient to kindle their unfriendly passions and excite their most violent conflicts."

Not only by their wills are men competitive, but even more inevitably beyond their wills. Since wants are practically limitless and the means of satisfaction often quite limited, men are hurled by their very location against each other; and conscience invests with high sanctions whatever is deeply enough required. Organization intensifies conflicts by erecting walls of social distance to shut out the assuaging common touch of face-to-face contacts. The legislature typically handles problems which every intermediate agency of accommodation, from private conscience to governmental conciliation, has failed to solve and in failure has confirmed opposing consciences and deepened frustrated aggressions. It is no wonder that the best legislators can do is but to forefend violence.

Fair failure of ideal fulfillment is brilliant success, in the face of such odds. The agency of these odds—politics, that is—is naturally deprecated by good men; and the agencies of man's moral oddities—politicians, that is—are naturally reprobated by high-minded citizens. It is not merely, as Winston Churchill has said, that politicians "wash the dirty moral linen for the soldiers"—who disdain them—but the deeper and sadder fact that they play this role of moral midwifery to the parturition of every high conscience.

It is partly in compensation for this their common lot, more or less as pariahs, that legislators achieve the splendid personal relations which, as we have said, characterize legislative assemblies. But this compensation must be allowed to work both ways. If legislators find their constituents a trial, how do you suppose constituents—who admit themselves the moral if not intellectual superiors—find their legislators? "Trial" is too mild a word. "Terror" will not deliver even the simple demand of "justice." It is indeed no light business to go asking only bare and simple justice, and come chronically away with some miserable half loaf of hodgepodge—and it moldy with reeky compromise. And to have this happen time after time, in the estimation of both or all parties to the deal, no one of whom even closely approximates what he regards as but elemental right—this is the red-raw moral stuff of which civic rebellion could well be made. The avoidance of downright disorder is no poor achievement of order in such an unordered world.

Just, however, as the politicians compensate through fraternization among themselves for their inability to make the ideal prevail against the quarreling idealists, so the citizen, frustrated by politics to which he was forced to repair, compensates by tightening the bonds of the like-minded group whose expanding interests drove him into politics in the first place. This like-mindedness is a mighty compensation. Each frustrated group, while licking its chops over the latest defeat and repairing its lines for another try at success, can swear at the politicians and can reassure one another of their joint rectitude and deserts. It is a majestic system in which like-minded groupings can compensate all alike, including the politicians who also make their own "we-group" to double their little joys and cut each other's griefs in half. Moreover, such compensation makes the ideal itself to prevail mightily. There is perfection for every organized like-mindedness: "Perfection 1," "Perfection 2," "Perfection 3," and so on; and there is no necessity for them to conflict with one another or with parent-perfection itself, so long as the politician can keep the power pluralized through mutually respected social distances.

Thus we have more than two hundred religious denominations in America, each of which in its own way regards itself as custodian of the truth, guardian of the way, and dispenser of the life. The suspicion that there cannot be hundreds of agencies of perfection, since indeed there can be but one, does not drive to desperation those who claim themselves to be that one—and whose bond of brotherhood is the daily reassuring of one another that the joint claim is true. The same principle holds with art groups, with sport groups, with professional groups, with college groups. Idealistic absolution by getting thus pluralized through spoken or written bills of rights becomes safe for society, and not only safe but also fruitful. Such relations in a democracy make it possible to maintain against all its odds the interpersonal relations we have seen in the legislature. The extreme pluralism that prevails in our multi-group matrix requires and rewards the division of power in the government itself. And this division in turn preserves, through civil rights, the variety which compensates in pluralistic intensity for the absence of unlimited unity around any and every ideal.

The American separation between church and state—long may it continue unimpaired, in spite of the presently growing number of sacerdotal saboteurs—completes the symbolism of our sacred pluralism. Out of this conflict of ideals, regulated by law which is created by legislators, comes the self-renewing solution of problems which constitutes our most secure progress. It is not this advance or that advance to which we should point with most pride. It is, rather, the process of self-renewal through continuous self-correction that democracy has discovered and knows how to maintain. By pluralizing our power we purge it of its indigenous poison. And by pooling our idealistic impulses, purged of fanaticism by good sportsmanship, we render sacred the roomy secularity of our variety. Not until the sacred is thus pluralized, can the "sacred" become safe for free men. So purged, competition becomes the source of morale and the prod to progress.

Against this magnificent background of unmeasured variety which our society enshrines, we return for a final word upon the legislative foreground. The legislature is of course the very center of our cyclone of divided powers. But at the heart of the storm is a sort of dynamic calm. The judiciary, above the storm, of it but not in it, is ideological, concerning itself not with power but with meaning as perfected through interpretation. The executive of our government is power personified, devoting itself to efficiency of means for ends already prescribed and now interpreted. But it is the legislative branch which is most dynamically instinct with aspiration—seeking justice through a moving equilibrium of conflicts. It is also informed of power, but limited in results to the little which conflicting ideals permit to emerge as consensus. Uniting thus the heart and the head of humanity in the name of such ideality as can become practical, the legislature compounds the variety of our diverse national life and exploits for common policy the underlying unity thus arduously disclosed.

It is little wonder that the cynics of democracy are not often found among the legislative has-beens. "Lame ducks" are not "soreheads" in American politics, not for long at least. Men's moral instincts get deeply involved in and rewarded through political action; for in politics little happens that does not palpably hurt or harm, or at least does not clearly convenience or inconvenience fellow men and fellow citizens. If, however, the moral nerve come to ache from overuse, let the esthetic sense take over. And what a show is here, what a magnificent show is here, to be gathered as the harvest of any eye quieted with mellow humor. The spectacle of democratic politics ranges from the humble level of the Russian proverb, "Only he who tickles himself may laugh as he likes," to the austere heights of Plato's "institutional beauty." What a story that would be, but clearly another story: the beauty of democratic design. That story, could it here be told, would yield us an esthetics that is moral and a morality mellowed on patience, maturing as progress, and all the while instinct with joy. There are radicals who resent our smiling at that design while their own souls are unfulfilled. Let them for solace bay at their pale moon. There are reactionaries who cringe at the noise and disorder of this democratic variety. Let them bay, and let them cringe. Those who cannot bring themselves to take life neatly, just as it is, while working to make it what it ought to be, can never make it what it ought to be. They themselves are not right with life. Look again, for yourself, at this magnificent system in which we live and move and have our freedom—a system in which, with or without you, we still sail on, like the gallant ship of state this system is.

I see, as I look with you, I see a free people who can laugh at their own infelicities. I see a confident people who can admit their faults without interrupting plans for future perfection, because they have inherited and are preserving a political process wherein sportsmanship matures its daily fruitage. We can, that is, swing from Right to Left, from Left to Right, without liquidating the center as we swing in the zodiac of any electoral season. I see, for all their dynamism, a patient people who know that the radical's uncompromising Best is always enemy of the modest man's Better; who know that the reactionary's lust for *returning* is the graveyard of the decent man's hope. I see, indeed, beyond its vulgarities, over which we smile; beyond its blunders, for which we repine; yes, beyond its injustices for which we repent; beyond them all I see operative a technique of self-criticism which will serve our children's children as it has served our fathers' fathers. Such is the legislative way of life, whose timeless esthetics we can well afford to enjoy as we turn its dynamic ethics into endless self-corrections.

No. 46

[LIKE T. V. Smith, Paul H. Douglas is a rare combination of professor, politician, and legislator. He has taught economics at the University of Chicago, written many books, been elected to the Chicago City Council and the United States Senate. He makes clear the arduous nature of a Senator's work.]

REPORT FROM A FRESHMAN SENATOR [1]

by Paul H. Douglas

THERE is a moment on election night when a new Senator feels himself to be a new Adam, the first of his breed. But on that score, as on a number of others, he begins to change his mind when he comes to the Senate. For one thing, he senses that giants like Clay, Calhoun, Benton, Webster,

[1] Paul H. Douglas, "Report from a Freshman Senator," *The New York Times Magazine* (March 20, 1949), pp. 10, 72 ff. Reprinted by permission of *The New York Times Magazine* and the author.

Stephen A. Douglas, Davis, Sumner, John Sharp Williams, "Fighting Bob" La Follette and George Norris have been there before him.

For example, I am now filling the identical Illinois seat occupied a century ago by the "Little Giant" who bore the name of our clan, Stephen A. Douglas. The realization of this tradition humbles a freshman at first. In time it should prove a source of strength and reassurance.

For another thing, a freshman Senator learns that the sense of a living tradition is perhaps one of the reasons for the almost exquisite courtesy which prevails in the dealings of Senators with each other. Our political campaigns are indeed rough and a candidate has to develop a tough hide to withstand the poisoned spears which are driven into him. But on the floor of the Senate, however much Senators may differ, they behave like gentlemen. In a world of sharply differing interests and ideas, this is no mean achievement. This, also, makes the freshman anxious to be worthy of his fellows, the many able men of both parties now in the United States Senate.

Before I came to Washington I thought I knew what I would be up against because my wife had previously served a term in Congress and because, in addition to my experience in local government, I had frequently testified before Congressional committees. But only the toad beneath the harrow can really feel the sharpness of the prongs. One must live the life of a Senator to know its pains. It is relatively easy to offer advice. But it is a soul-trying experience after weighing evidence and conflicting claims and interests to be compelled to decide what is best for the people of the United States and then, as one must, to assume full responsibility for that decision. And the strain is intensified by the fact that one is forced to make many such fundamental decisions in the midst of a crushing burden of routine work.

The Labor Committee, for example, has been holding two and three hearings a day on the repeal of the Taft-Hartley law and this in itself has taken from five to eight hours of my time each day. Then there are the hearings of the Banking and Currency Committee and the Joint Committee on the Economic Report on which I am also serving, and where I am trying to pull a laboring oar. But in addition to all this, I must also help to answer the mail which now averages over 700 communications a day, and which one morning reached 1,700, and meet callers and delegations. Let me chronicle a fairly representative day when the Senate was *not* in session:

7-8:30 A.M. Rise, breakfast, read two morning papers and study memoranda for hearings.

8:30-9:30 A.M. Look over mail, answer some of the most important letters and block out to-day's policy with the staff.

9:30-11 A.M. Hearings on the Taft-Hartley repeal.

11-12. Hearings on the housing bill.

12-1 P.M. Work on correspondence and see visitors.

1-2 P.M. Lunch with constituents.

2-2:30 P.M. See delegations and telephone Government departments.

2:30-5 P.M. Hearings on the Taft-Hartley repeal.

5-6:30 P.M. Sign 250 pieces of mail, send telegrams on pressing matters of business.

6:30-7:30 P.M. Dinner with group which wants to consult on legislation.

7:30-10 P.M. Hearings on the Taft-Hartley repeal.

10-12. Read two evening papers and several weekly journals. Clean up correspondence and study more material on Taft-Hartley law and housing problems, block out radio speech for next day.

12:30 A.M. Go to bed.

I am frank to say that I do not know for how long a man can keep up such a pace. Thus far, it has not seemed to slacken. I thought I had reached the ultimate in work when I ran for election in a way which I described last fall in this same magazine. But the job of serving as a Senator is no less strenuous than running for the office.

It is not merely work, however, but also worry which characterizes a Senator's life. One feels the tug not merely of conflicting forces but also of sharply opposing ideas, in each of which one recognizes some element of truth. On which side does the greater merit lie? Is there a way of resolving the sharp and bitter conflicts into some higher synthesis which will enable the national life to proceed upon a higher level and if so, how can it be found and put into effect?

Interspersed with these worries there come the reproaches of old friends who feel neglected by decisions which I have had to make concerning appointments and patronage; the criticisms of home newspapers who do not like my votes, and the irate letters of citizens who disagree with my real or fancied opinions and acts. Is it small wonder, therefore, if beneath the surface of a Senator's life there is a deep loneliness and also many inquietudes which at night interfere with sleep and which, were it not for the reassurance of my wife and friends, would seem overpowering? Never does a man realize the need for fellowship, for religious faith and for a sense of humor more than when these worries and decisions pour in upon him as a Senator.

A Senator is not suffering from a persecution complex when he recognizes the sober fact that he has a multitude of enemies who are not only ready to shout to the world when he slips on a banana peel, but who are quite capable of strewing them in his path. And there are also a certain number of correspondents who, with the best will in the world, nevertheless regard a freshman Senator as fair game to fill their columns.

In all innocence, I have already stumbled into one such booby trap. I was asked by a small group of reporters whether I thought the Labor Committee could complete its hearings on the new labor bill within a set period of time. "Yes," I said, "if the Senators would only work late afternoons and evenings and forego the cocktail hour." And then I innocently added that I thought Washington cocktail parties were too time-consuming.

These words were no sooner spoken than the air was filled with debris and scent of cordite. From somewhere behind a pall of smoke I heard shrill voices tell me through the press that if I didn't like the Washington cocktail hour, all I had to do was to say, "No, thank you, I can't come today." And to this moment, I cannot understand why a few sentences about the schedule of labor hearings should have set off such a hubbub in which everyone purged himself of bile on a lot of irrelevant subjects. But that is what happened. It is why, when I am now asked what day of the week it is, my instinctive reply is "No comment."

The whole of this trivia summons to my memory Shakespeare's observation that "Honor alone doth not make a good surgeon." Neither, I add, doth it make a good Senator or keep him out of trouble. Something more— and a great deal of it—is needed; something in the way of caution, physical endurance, a sense of selection, a sense of maneuver, and the inner tinkle of a bright hell's bells air. Some of these traits may be inherent in a person prior to his induction into the Senate. Some of them can be absorbed from the memories which hover in the place. And some of them can be acquired through the senior-junior tutorial system.

Let me say here that I had arrived in Washington full of misgivings about the Senate's seniority system. Yet the operation of that system, as it has unfolded in the committees to which I have been assigned, has brought home some of the practical ends which it serves. Stated negatively, I am convinced that no new Senator can or should be the chairman of a Senate committee, even if that unlikely prospect were ever opened to him. Outside of the Senate, he may be the world's foremost expert in a particular field of interest, but knowledge for its own sake, and knowledge woven into a policy of legislative action, are, unfortunately, two different things.

The seniority system provides the Senate with a steady flow of leaders who know the past record of the legislative proposals under their jurisdiction, why they were accepted or rejected, who advanced them or blocked them, who testified on their behalf or remained silent, who gave way and compromised and who stood firm under fire. And though the junior Senator can applaud himself for the splendid purity of a scheme he had once devised to remove at least one of the nation's ills, the older hands around the place may know that this same scheme has been examined in detail before, and for very practical reasons was turned down flat. In all these matters, the senior Senator or the senior member serves the junior as a file of memories dealing with the whole catalogue of legislative cunning.

For all their wear and tear, the committee hearings themselves are of incalculable importance to a new Senator. These hearings are indeed one of the principal means by which a new Senator can educate himself.

If one reviews the Senatorial day, it becomes evident that there is not much chance for a Senator to undertake a profound or cloistered study of a problem. The research personnel in the departments may be of some help to him. His own staff will be of greater help. But in the final analysis, he must learn for himself what is true or false. And he can only find that out in the committee hearings. Here, he must argue out his thoughts publicly even as the facts on which they are based are presented to him. Sometimes, he gets tripped up by his improvisations in committee sessions and feels like a fool because of it. Sometimes, his head spins under an attack from an unexpected quarter which tramples down his hastily built defenses. But once his injured pride is mended, the net result is both self-education and a more enlightened public opinion.

What, then, about the effect and conduct of lobbies in shaping legislative decisions? I regard it as my duty to listen both courteously and with a judicial mind to the representatives of every responsible group. For every group in a democracy has the right to present its case both to the public and to the Legislature. To this degree lobbies are of distinct aid. But it is a very different thing for a legislator to vote with a pressure group either because of fear or because of favors he has allowed himself to receive.

Even a brief experience with the lobbying of special interests makes a Senator wish, however, that the members of these groups would practice a greater degree of self-restraint and a lesser degree of group selfishness. Not only do groups ask for more than they expect to get, but even the sum of all their bed-rock demands amounts to far more than the country can afford. It is properly the job of Congress to select the most urgent of these needs and to discard those which are less acute.

There are, of course, a number of questions which a Senator, new or old, can only answer by seeking the inner light of conscience. They may involve such matters as the obligations one owes to one's party as against those which are owed to personal convictions. Or they may involve such questions as a reconciliation of the national interest with a state interest.

As to the first question, my tentative answer takes this form: Support one's party in all procedural matters everywhere. Argue substantive programs within party councils in the hope of gaining a majority within the party. But when the chips are down in the Senate, a Senator should vote his profound individual convictions on substantive matters regardless of who is with or against him.   Fortunately, I do not expect any sharp conflict between my conscience and party policy, since I believe in the principles of our Philadelphia platform and in the general foreign and domestic program of President Truman.

As to the second question, the answer to it demands that the Senator try to become a teacher, instructing the state as to its function in the nation, and instructing the nation as to the nature of at least one of its states.

One further point: Edward Everett Hale is known to present-day Americans as the author of "The Man Without a Country."   But at the turn of the century he was also known as the wry-tongued chaplain of the United States Senate.   One day, as he walked to the Senate Chamber to do his duty and offer his noonday prayer, one of his friends fell in step with him and said, "I suppose, Mr. Hale, that you first look at the country and then pray for the Senate."   "On the country," Hale replied, "I first look at the Senate and then I pray for the country."

In the day when this barb was first voiced, the Senate seemed little more than a millionaires' club whose members used it as though it were a board of directors' room for the corporations which they served.   As against what happened in Hale's day, the private vocations of to-day's Senators offer no clue as to where any one of them will stand on any public issue.   The lawyers still hold a comfortable majority of the Senate seats, with former university professors in second place, and a scattered assortment of business men, newspaper publishers, doctors and farmers sharing third place. Some of these men are rich.   Some of them have no more wealth than is represented by their government pay.   What marks their conduct as a group is their relative independence from the pat views which are commonly identified with fixed classes.

For all the seeming petty bickering, the vying for partisan advantage and even filibustering, the present Senate has a great sense of its function as the supreme forum in the world for free discussion.

No. 47

[WHY did my Congressman vote that way?   This is a question many of us often ask but few of us can answer.   The explanation is never simple but Mr. Phillips sets us on the path to finding it.]

WHY A CONGRESSMAN VOTES THAT WAY [1]

by Cabell Phillips

A CONGRESSMAN'S mind and his emotions are under a continual state of siege from people who want him, if not to believe as they do, at least to do as they wish. They call upon him in droves, individually and in delegations. They shower him with letters, telegrams, petitions and resolutions. They send their lobbyists to buttonhole him in the corridors or on the golf course, persuasive spellbinders who try to seduce him with logic or cocktails. They appeal to his vanity with expensive junkets or the flattering attentions of tycoons and dignitaries. They play adroitly upon his patriotism, his religious scruples, his prejudices, principles and ambitions.

In addition a Congressman is pressed by his own conscience. He wants to do what is right, not alone for his own state or district, but for the nation at large. Yet he knows that just as he is elected by his constituents so can he be retired by them if he incurs their displeasure.

How, then, does the average Congressman, beset by propaganda from all sides and with more work than there is time for, make up his mind about how to vote? What factors influence his decisions? How well informed is he on legislative matters, and how does he inform himself?

In their order of importance, these seem to be the prevailing forces upon which Congress relies for guidance:

(1) The opinion and the wishes of the people back home, including such "special interest" groups as may be represented in his constituency.

(2) Party policy.

(3) Reports of committees or other special reports.

(4) Newspaper and radio comment, general conversation, etc.

(5) Floor debate.

I. OPINION BACK HOME

Every member of Congress at some time puts to his conscience this query: "Do I represent my constituency or the nation?" He rarely gets a clear-cut answer. His conduct usually represents a compromise.

Most members of Congress feel they know their local opinion. It is instinctive, the sum of their environment and experience. But this is not always a safe guide. There are controversies which split families and neigh-

[1] Cabell Phillips, "Why a Congressman Votes That Way," *The New York Times Magazine* (May 29, 1949), pp. 14, 37, 39. Reprinted by permission of *The New York Times Magazine* and the author.

borhoods as well as states and nations. To disregard, or to be unaware of, these differences could easily prove fatal to a member's re-election prospects.

Mail is the readiest means for tapping back-home sentiment. Individual members average anywhere from a few hundred to as many as a thousand letters daily. Most letters ask favors or seek information. A good many are of the "pressure" variety—appeals or demands inspired by some organized campaign. Most "organized" mail is disregarded; if it comes in excessive quantity, it is likely to have an opposite influence from that intended.

"I'm a lot more impressed," one Congressman said recently, "by a letter written by a poor farmer in pencil on a sheet of ruled tablet paper than I am by the inspired propaganda letters that are delivered by the sackful. I know that man wouldn't write to me unless he really had something on his mind."

But unsolicited mail is not always reliable. Rarely is it channeled toward the problem on which the member needs enlightenment. Nor does it always come from the sources which could be most helpful to him. It is a valuable but undependable source of guidance.

A few members have adopted systems of polling their constituencies by mail. They send out questionnaires to cross-sections of the voting lists and tabulate the answers that are received. Representative Robert J. Corbett of Pennsylvania does this every two or three months, sending out from 15,000 to 20,000 questionnaires at each mailing. His returns have run as high as 37 per cent, but average about 18 per cent.

"If the results of the poll on an individual question," he says, "don't run more than 55 per cent for or against, I don't feel that I have any clear mandate. If they are much above that, though, I figure I've either got to conform to it in my vote or else be mighty well prepared to explain why I didn't. Checking over the last four years, I find my voting record has been consistent in every particular with the majority opinion expressed in these polls."

All members of Congress have "organizations" back home. They may be nebulous and transient, coming to life effectively only at election time. Or they may be of a more durable character, with an office and permanent staff; a "branch," more or less, of his headquarters in the Senate or House office buildings in Washington.

In any event, a Congress member is certain to have spotted throughout his constituency certain key men and women upon whose insight into local conditions and attitudes he can rely. He taps these sources constantly.

Also within each constituency there are likely to be roots of one or more of the important "special interest" groups. If it is a coal-mining state, the member is particularly attentive to the problems of the mine workers and operators. He may be from a "silver state" or a "wool state" or a "tobacco state." Or he may come from a region that is peculiarly concerned with public power development, soil conservation or shipping. Perhaps his district has a heavy foreign-born population, or large concentrations of union labor, or great sums invested in a particular type of manufacturing or other industrial enterprise.

Whatever the nature of this "special interest," if it is a predominant concern with the people of his state or district, the member of Congress who represents them will be an advocate of the special causes they sponsor. He is not only attentive to the lobbyists they send to Washington, but is more often than not their most conscientious co-worker.

2. PARTY POLICY

Both parties in Congress have steering or policy committees in each house which lay down a party "line" with respect to most controversial legislation. In the case of the present Democrats, this line theoretically originates in the White House and is handed down through the Vice-President and the Majority Leader, on the Senate side, and through the Speaker in the House. . . .

It is well known, however, that these official party lines are honored almost as much in the breach as in the observance. There have been several spectacular examples recently of Democrats rebelling against the . . . leadership and refusing to support measures in the Administration's program. And there is a hard core of Republican "Young Turks" in each house who habitually flout their party's leadership with equal disdain.

Thus, party discipline is not hard and fast. But a reasonable record of party regularity is a cherished possession at election time. And most members, when no great sacrifice of principle is involved, are willing to accept the party line.

3. COMMITTEE AND OTHER REPORTS

Few members of Congress read the texts of any but the most urgently important bills. Legislative English probably is the most incomprehensible gibberish in the language, anyway, and the perusal of a forty-page bill is likely to leave all but the drafting experts hopelessly confused. But all bills before they reach the floor have been subjected to deliberation in committee, and the committee issues a report of its findings and recommendations. The conscientious member who wants to find out what the bill is about can do so by studying the committee report, by reading the printed transcript of the hearings, if he is so moved, and even, *in extremis,* by reading the bill itself.

This is the simplest and most effective means of informing himself about individual measures. Most members study as many committee reports as they can, often occupying themselves in this manner while debate on some other subject is proceeding on the floor. Where the documentation is particularly voluminous they will often have a secretary summarize the committee reports.

Another source of information upon which Congress leans with increasing dependence is the special and periodic studies produced by the Legislative Reference Service of the Library of Congress. Enlarged and strengthened under the Reorganization Act of 1946, the service has a staff of about seventy scholars and specialists who undertake factual and objective studies of a wide range of subjects arising on the Congressional calendar.

The Public Affairs Bulletin, of which ten or a dozen editions are issued during an average session, covers broad policy matters in domestic and foreign affairs, giving all pertinent background, historical data and analysis of pending proposals. These are sent to all members as they are published and have won high prestige for their lucidity and accuracy.

In addition, all the committees of Congress and each member of the House and Senate are free to call upon the service for special reports on virtually any subject under the sun. Sometimes these inquiries can be handled by a quick reference to an almanac. Again, a major research project through the library stacks and the executive departments downtown may be involved. The service handled 2,900 such individual requests during one recent month.

4. NEWSPAPER AND RADIO COMMENT

Members of Congress, like lesser mortals, vary widely in their reading habits. On the whole, they keep fairly well abreast of the current views. Nearly all read *The Washington Post* and *The Evening Star.* At a fair guess, about half of the Senate and a third of the House get, in addition, either *The New York Times* or *The Herald Tribune* each morning. A great many of them subscribe to *Time* and *Newsweek.* And each of them, without exception, is on the mailing list of two to a dozen papers from back home.

How much of this they read, and how well they read, it is impossible to say. But Congressmen as a whole are better informed on national and international affairs than the general run of citizens of a comparable level of intelligence. The events that make news are often events which they have had part in or observed at close range. They reinforce their own knowledge through newspapers and the radio. And in turn they inevitably are influenced in their opinions by the opinions of columnists and commentators they admire, or editorials from the papers they respect.

5. FLOOR DEBATE

Last, by all accounts, in the factors which help the member make up his mind is floor debate. In the great majority of cases he has already decided what his stand on a given measure is by the time that measure reaches the floor. He has reached that decision, perhaps, through tapping the sentiment in his home state; by talks with his party leaders; by scanning the committee reports, and by the general comment and discussion which have appeared in the public prints. The debate, he knows, is likely to be a formality, designed more to project the question into the public consciousness than to analyze its strength and weaknesses. Or if he is inclined to cynicism, he knows that the debate is no more than an opportunity for partisan forensic exercises by some of his colleagues.

Debate is important to him only when important amendments to a bill are being hammered out. If it is an appropriation bill, or another in which he has a close interest, he will be alert to discussion on the floor. Often he will be swayed by the arguments he hears at the time. But in general, legislative oratory is as tedious and boring to the Congressman at his desk as to the reporters in the press galleries—boring, indeed!

*   *   *

In summing up the problems of the legislator recently, Senator William Fulbright of Arkansas said:

> My greatest enemy is that clock on the wall. There just aren't enough hours in the day to do all the things you are expected to do, and do your "homework" on legislation, too. I don't think the average member knows nearly enough about the bills—and I mean important bills as well as the unimportant ones—that he is expected to vote on. Yet, I don't know what can be done about it in the face of the enormous amount of legislation each Congress is called upon to enact. It's just a human impossibility to devote the amount of time to studying them that they deserve.

Most members of Congress, suffering such a sense of frustration, are deeply concerned with means to become better informed and to free themselves from over-burdensome detail. What is being done and what can be done to effect such an improvement?

The problem could be alleviated if the Congressmen would vote themselves more generous allowances for clerk hire. Senators already are authorized to hire one $10,000-a-year executive assistant. Members of the House should accord themselves the same privilege, and perhaps each should expand the number to two. These aides not only relieve the members of a great deal of routine office labor, they also digest important bills and other issues on which the member must render a final decision.

Another important step would be to further increase the effectiveness of the Legislative Reference Service by enlarging its staff. Properly manned, this agency could prepare synopses on all legislative questions and that would materially cut down the personal labors of the members.

Finally, if the members of Congress could summon the courage to say an emphatic "No!" more often to the trivial and inconsequential importunities of their constituents, they would save themselves a lot of time which could be put to more useful purposes.

No. 48

[ALTHOUGH most of us think of the legislature in America as a purely lawmaking body, a closer examination would reveal to us that it performs constituent, judicial, electoral, and executive functions as well. American legislatures—state and national—have an important part in changing American constitutions, have the power of impeachment, take part in the election of certain public officers, and play an important role in the making of administrative appointments. All of these are an important part of the legislator's job. It is important, therefore, in evaluating the work of a legislator to keep in mind that he is not simply a lawmaker in the usual sense of the term. The voter who wants to pass judgment on his legislative representative must examine all of his representative's activities, if he is to judge him adequately at election time.

It is unfortunate that the doctrine of separation of powers has served to conceal this fact from us. Having divided governmental power (in our minds at least) into legislative, executive, and judicial and having set up legislatures, executives and courts to exercise these powers, we tend to think that each of the powers is granted to and only to the corresponding branch of the government.

Of course, as noted above, the power is not divided this way. Not only does the legislature have other than legislative functions but the executive and the courts have other than executive and judicial functions. Each of the branches is given some of the powers possessed by the others. This allows each to serve as a check upon the other two. One of the least understood checks of the legislature on the executive is senatorial participation in appointments.

In the national government, the President has the power, with the advice and consent of the Senate, to make a great many appointments. The normal process is for the President to nominate an individual to the Senate and, if the Senate consents, the appointment is made. Actually, of course, the President in making such nominations must seek advice from many quarters. There has grown up, however, a tradition that the members of the Senate will not consent to an appointment that is objected to by a Senator from the state in which the appointment is made if the Senator is a member of the President's own party. This tradition is known as "Senatorial Courtesy."

An example of the operation of Senatorial courtesy is to be found in the Senate's rejection of President Roosevelt's nomination of Floyd H. Roberts as Federal District Court Judge in Virginia. The following opinions by President Roosevelt and Senator Glass, occasioned by the above case, throw some light on the full meaning and character of this constitutional tradition]

THE SENATE AND THE APPOINTING POWER— SENATORIAL COURTESY [1]

(President Roosevelt's letter to Floyd H. Roberts, whose nomination as a Federal Judge was rejected by the Senate, precipitating a controversy over the appointive powers of Senate and President, follows in full text:)

MY DEAR JUDGE ROBERTS:

I feel that in justice to you and your family I should write to you in regard to the refusal of the Senate to confirm your appointment as United States District Judge for the Western District of Virginia.

First of all, I tender you my thanks for the honorable, efficient, and in every way praiseworthy service that you have rendered to the people of the United States in general and to the people of the Western District of Virginia in particular.

Second, I wish it known that not one single person who has opposed your confirmation has lifted his voice in any shape, manner or form against your personal integrity and ability.

In order that you may know the full history of what has occurred, I take this opportunity to summarize the story.

On March 17, 1938, I received a letter from Senator Glass enclosing a clipping from a local Virginia paper. This newspaper article, quoting an editorial in another local Virginia paper, made the assumption that it would henceforth be necessary to receive the backing of Governor Price of Virginia before any Virginian could hope for a Federal appointment.

---

[1] The letter from President Franklin D. Roosevelt to Floyd H. Roberts and the statement by Senator Carter Glass are reprinted from the *United States News* (Feb. 13, 1939), an independent magazine on national affairs issued weekly at Washington, D. C.

Senator Glass in his letter asked if Federal appointments, for which Senate approval was necessary, would be subjected to the effective veto of the Governor of Virginia.

To this I replied on March 18, explaining to the Senator the difference between the appointive power, which is in the President, and the power of confirmation, which is in the Senate. I pointed out to the Senator that time-hallowed courtesy permits Senators and others to make recommendations for nomination, and, at the same time, that every President has sought information from any other source deemed advisable.

On March 19 Senator Glass wrote me again, covering his construction of Article II of the Constitution, and asking me again as to the accuracy of the newspaper statement. He winds up by saying "the inference is, of course, that you approve the offensive publication which was the basis of my inquiry."

I replied to this letter from the Senator on March 21 in a personal and friendly vein. I stated that I was glad that we seemed to agree in our construction of the Constitution. I told him that I was not in the habit of confirming or denying any newspaper article or editorial. Obviously if I were to begin that sort of thing, I would have no spare time to attend to my executive duties.

I told the Senator to go ahead as before and make recommendations; that I would give such recommendations every consideration; but that I would, of course, reserve the right to get opinions from any other person I might select. I ended by asking the Senator to forget the newspaper article and wished him a good vacation and expressed the hope that he would come to see me on his return.

Subsequent to this date, I received a number of recommendations for the position of United States District Judge for the Western District of Virginia —among them recommendations in behalf of two gentlemen from Senator Glass. I am not certain whether these recommendations were at that time concurred in by the Junior Senator from Virginia, but this is possible. Other recommendations were received from citizens of Virginia to a total number, as I remember it, of five or six.

The Attorney General was asked by me to report on these recommendations, paying attention as usual to the qualifications of each person suggested. I might add that your name was on this list but that at no time, to my knowledge, did you seek this office of Judge.

The Attorney General and I held several conferences with the result that we concluded that you were best fitted to fill the Judgeship.

As a result, I wrote on July 6 to both of the Virginia Senators stating that I had concluded to appoint you, that a number of gentlemen had been suggested for the place, but that I believed you to be the best fitted.

The following day, July 7, I received a telegram from Senator Glass stating that he and his colleague would feel obliged to object to your appointment as being personally objectionable to them, and that a letter would follow. A few days later I received a letter from the Senator stating that he could not conceive any fair reason why one of his candidates had not been appointed.

It is worth noting that neither Senator on July 7 or subsequently raised any question as to your integrity or ability, and the only objection was that you were personally objectionable.

In regard to the original newspaper article suggesting that Governor Price had been given the veto over Federal appointments, this and similar stories are, of course, not worth answering or bothering about, for the very simple reason that no person—no Governor, no Senator, no member of the Administration—has at any time had, or ever will have, any right of veto over Presidential nominations. Every person with common sense knows this.

Your appointment followed, you took the oath of office, and have been serving with great credit as District Judge since then.

Your name was sent by me to the Senate in January, 1939, together with many other recess appointments.

We come now to the last chapter. Your nomination was referred to the Judiciary Committee of the Senate and by the Chairman of that Committee to a subcommittee of three. It appears from the record that both Senators from Virginia registered their objection with the subcommittee, saying "this nomination is utterly and personally offensive to the Virginia Senators whose suggestions were invited by the Department of Justice only to be ignored."

The subcommittee reported back the nomination to the full Committee without recommendation, stating the raising of the matter of Senatorial courtesy and saying that this matter had not been a direct issue since 1913.

At a special meeting of the full Committee on the Judiciary and before the Committee went into executive session, attention was invited to the presence of the Governor of Virginia, to the presence of two former Governors of Virginia, and to the presence of the nominee and his counsel.

After lengthy discussion the Committee went into executive session, re-opening the doors an hour later.

The record shows that at this time the Committee heard the Governor of Virginia in favor of the nominee and also former Governor E. Lee Trinkle and former Governor Westmoreland Davis; also, George M. Warren, Esq., counsel for nominee.

Thereupon the Committee, instead of hearing other witnesses in behalf of the nominee, many of whom were present, moved that a list of these further witnesses be incorporated in the record without hearing them. The Committee also agreed to receive certain letters and editorials in behalf of the nominee, and, finally, a record of designations you have received from former Governors of Virginia to sit in other judicial districts, this list including many designations of you made by former Governor Harry F. Byrd.

That was followed by your own testimony.

The privilege of making the closing and sole arguments against you was accorded to the two Senators from Virginia.

Senator Glass stated that neither he nor his colleague had formally or definitely made any statement affecting your capabilities.

He proceeded to review the newspaper reports of last March, stated that he had not communicated with the Governor to ascertain whether or not the latter had authorized the publication, and spoke of his letter to me. He went on to state that the President had not answered his question up to this date, except by sending the nomination to the Senate.

You will recognize from what I have written you that as far back as last March, in reply to Senator Glass' letters, I told him categorically that I never answered any questions relating to the credibility or otherwise of newspaper articles or editorials, and I asked him to forget the newspaper article altogether. Therefore, the statement of Senator Glass to the Committee does not square with the facts.

Continuing, the Senior Senator from Virginia referred to other newspaper articles which spoke of "rebukes" to the Senators. It is almost needless for me to suggest that neither you nor I pay any attention to such excuses.

Finally, Senator Glass stated "as a matter of fact, the President of the United States did give to the Governor of Virginia the veto power over nominations made by the two Virginia United States Senators."

I am sorry, in view of my long personal friendship for the Senior Senator, that he has made any such statement, and I can only excuse it on the ground of anger or forgetfulness.

At the end of his speech Senator Glass says "Mr. Cummings never had the slightest idea of giving consideration to the recommendations of the two Virginia Senators because the Governor of Virginia had been promised the right of veto on nominations that they made." Neither of these statements is true.

Senator Glass was followed by Senator Byrd, who stated that your nomination was personally offensive to both Senators, in fact, "personally obnoxious."

At the very close of the Judiciary Committee hearing Governor Price stated "Senator Glass has made a charge against me. He is entirely mistaken about it." The Governor further stated that he was not involved in the newspaper story.

The Committee thereupon abruptly closed the matter and went into executive session, with the result, as you know, that your nomination was reported adversely to the Senate.

This brief history repeats several episodes in the history of the United States, which have occurred from time to time during the past one hundred and fifty years. In other cases nominations by former Presidents of men of outstanding ability and character have been denied confirmation by the Senate, not on the plea that they were unfitted for office but on the sole ground that they were personally obnoxious to the Senator or Senators from the State from which they came.

During this whole period Presidents have recognized that the constitutional procedure is for a President to receive advice, i.e., recommendations, from Senators.

Presidents have also properly received advice, i.e., recommendations, from such other sources as they saw fit.

Thereupon Presidents have decided on nominations in accordance with their best judgment—and in most cases basing their judgment on the character and ability of the nominee. In many cases, of course, the recommendations of Senators have been followed, but in many other cases they have not been followed by Presidents in making the nominations.

Thereupon, under the Constitution, the Senate as a whole—not the Senators from one State—has the duty of either confirming or rejecting the nomination.

It is, of course, clear that it was the intention of the Constitution of the United States to vest in the Senate as a whole the duty of rejecting or confirming solely on the ground of the fitness of the nominee.

Had it been otherwise, had the Constitution intended to give the right of veto to a Senator or two Senators from the State of the nominee, it would have said so. Or to put it another way, it would have vested the nominating power in the Senators from the State in which the vacancy existed.

On somewhat rare occasions the Senate, relying on an unwritten rule of Senatorial courtesy, which exists in no place in the Constitution, has rejected nominees on the ground of their being personally obnoxious to their Senators, thus vesting in individual Senators what amounts in effect to the power of nomination.

In the particular case of which you are the unfortunate and innocent victim, the Senators from Virginia have in effect said to the President—

"We have nominated to you two candidates acceptable to us; you are hereby directed to nominate one of our two candidates, and if you do not we will reject the nomination of anybody else selected by you, however fit he may be."

Perhaps, my dear Judge Roberts, the rejection of your nomination will have a good effect on the citizenship and the thinking of the whole nation in that it will tend to create a greater interest in the Constitution of our country, a greater interest in its preservation in accordance with the intention of the gentlemen who wrote it.

I am sorry, indeed, that you have been the victim. Against you not one syllable has been uttered in derogation of your character or ability in the legal profession or your record on the Bench.

Very sincerely yours,

FRANKLIN D. ROOSEVELT.

Honorable Floyd H. Roberts,
Bristol, Va.

(A statement by Senator Carter Glass (Dem.), of Virginia, on President Roosevelt's letter to Floyd H. Roberts, whose appointment as a judge was rejected by the Senate, follows in full text:)

The only reason I think the President's extraordinary letter to his rejected nominee for judge of the Western District of Virginia deserves the slightest notice is the fact that some of the covert implications should be brushed away.

The Senate itself is amply able to attend to his attack upon the time-honored custom of respecting the reasonable objections of its members to executive nominations intended to be offensive to them; but I think it pertinent to summarize the relative facts in order that the public may determine the exact truth of the matter at issue.

On last March 16, under a two-column picture of Governor Price and Hon. James A. Farley, characterized as "chief patronage dispenser in the Federal Government," thus obviously to accentuate the significance of the subjoined announcement, there appeared in heavy headlines in *The Richmond Times-Dispatch*, an article captioned "Price Backing Seen Necessary for Federal Job."

The body of the article, being largely quoted from an editorial of the chief proponent of Judge Roberts, printed at his home, stated that: "Henceforth the indorsement of Governor Price will be necessary before any ambitious Virginian may hope to land an important Federal job."

Stating that the editor of the paper quoted from had "conferred with the President in Washington the preceding Monday," the paper stated without reservation that "President Roosevelt himself has made this decision, which means the Governor is to have the veto power on all appointments of any consequence in Virginia."

As incredible as this publication seemed, it did not shock the Virginia Senators, because they had previously learned that Governor Price, eagerly accepting the delegated function of Federal patronage dispenser in Virginia, had theretofore communicated with certain Federal officials recommended by the two Senators for reappointment on their assured record as "among the most outstanding officials of their class in the United States."

To their credit it must be said that not one of these officials had sought the Governor's proffered indorsement and none had been willing to join in the effort to discredit the Virginia Senators.

After waiting a day for Governor Price to contradict this extraordinary statement published right under his nose, I addressed the President a note on March 17, drawing his attention to the obnoxious publication. In this note I ventured to say: "I desire to ask if recommendations made by me as a Senator of Virginia for important Federal appointments, requiring the advice and consent of the United States Senate, are to be subject to the effective veto of the Governor of Virginia?"

It seemed to me then, as it does now, that this was a perfectly reasonable and simple question which might be answered directly and, of course, without evasion of any kind. It was not answered then, directly or otherwise. Instead, the President wrote me a page essay on the requirements of the Constitution as to Federal appointments, whereupon I ventured to reply that I had a fairly intimate knowledge of the fundamental law and nowhere discovered anything in it requiring Federal appointments to be made by and with the advice and consent of a State Governor.

Failing to get anything of a pointed nature, beyond this lecture on the Constitution, it seemed to me then, and in my mind is now confirmed, that the President approved the offensive publication which was the basis of my inquiry. This I stated in another note.

The answer of the President to this note, which he now thinks was "in a personal and friendly vein," still failed utterly to deny or affirm whether recommendations by the Virginia Senators were to be subject to the veto of the Governor of the State. True, I was told to go ahead in the usual way; but the President added that he would reserve the right to consult "Nancy Astor, the Duchess of Windsor, the WPA, a Virginia moonshiner, Governor Price or Charlie McCarthy." I cheerfully absolve Charlie Mc-Carthy from giving the advice designed to discredit the Virginia Senators, and the record shows that none of the persons named was consulted except Price.

The President, indulging in this trivial evasion and having disdained a frank answer to my simple question as to whether he proposed to subject the recommendations of the Virginia Senators to the veto power alleged to have been delegated to Governor Price, my colleague and I hesitated to make any suggestions at all. We did not do so until specifically asked by the Department of Justice to send in a nomination at once, as it was desired to submit the name to the Senate for confirmation before adjournment.

We desired to present the name of former Governor George C. Peery, but I was told by the President he would not appoint a man over sixty years of age. By the Attorney General I was urgently advised to name a man between forty and fifty years of age, with prospect of long service. Incidentally, this only piece of advice by the Department of Justice was totally disregarded in the nomination made by the President.

The Senators prevailed on Judge A. C. Buchanan, forty-eight years old, of the Virginia Circuit Court, to permit the use of his name, and also on Frank Tavenner, forty-three years old, an assistant United States District Attorney, saying that either would be acceptable to the Virginia Senators. Can any human being conjecture why any one or the other of these men was not appointed, except that the Governor of Virginia, in conjunction with the only hostile Congressman of the six whose districts are embraced in the Western Judicial District, were promised the appointment regardless of the Senators and with the ill-disguised purpose to discredit them?

Tavenner is one of the brightest young lawyers in the Western Judicial District, of fine antecedents and himself a splendid character, with useful experience in Federal court practice. He was indorsed by every Bar Association in the second largest Congressional district of the State.

Judge A. C. Buchanan is a notable character on the bench and Supreme Court records attest that he is incomparably superior in legal knowledge to the nominee rejected by the Senate. Time and time again, as I pointed out to the Senate Judiciary Committee, the State Supreme Court had adopted Buchanan's opinions textually in important cases as its own.

Some years ago, when it was thought desirable to revise the State's judicial procedure, Buchanan was by the Supreme Court put on the judicial council to do this work. There is no man in Virginia, on or off the bench, who stands higher in reputation for probity and learning.

Although petitions for the President's nominee were circulated through the Congressional district before the ink was dry on the bill creating this judgeship, scores of lawyers indorsed Buchanan when he was reluctantly induced by the Virginia Senators to permit the use of his name. Every lawyer of his circuit indorsed him and lawyers in every county of his Congressional district. George Peery, Governor until last January; the presidents of outstanding colleges and universities, judges on the bench, members of the General Assembly as well as many men of character and great worth, approved the recommendations of the two Senators.

What objection was there to his appointment except that he had been recommended by the two Virginia Senators, charged by the Constitution with advising and consenting to such Federal appointments?

Did the President ever open his lips or communicate directly or indirectly with either of the Virginia Senators concerning their recommendations for the judgeship? He did not. Did his Department of Justice discuss with them in any wise the relative fitness of the six applicants for the position? It did not.

Was not Judge Roberts promptly brought to Washington for a conference? I am reliably told he was. Was any one of the other six persons mentioned for the judgeship brought to Washington or communicated with in any respect? Not one of them, I am told. Governor Price's own testimony, of official record, shows an admission that he was called over long-distance phone by the Department of Justice and asked his opinion of Roberts. Was he asked his opinion of Buchanan or Tavenner, or any other one of the six persons mentioned for the judgeship? He was not.

Was Governor Peery, four years ago, asked about the qualifications of Judge Pollard for the Eastern District of Virginia? He was not, nor, in my belief, was any other Governor since the foundation of the State invited to project himself into a scheme to "purge" the two United States Senators from a State by practically vetoing their recommendations for executive appointment.

Before the Judiciary Committee, I ventured the opinion that the Attorney General "never had the slightest idea of giving consideration to the recommendations of the two Virginia Senators because the Governor of Virginia had been promised the right to veto on nominations that they made."

The President says neither of these statements is true; but, with as much deference as the occasion requires, I believe the record demonstrates that both statements are true. If the Attorney General had any such intention, he never made the slightest effort to carry it into effect, not even the common courtesy of communicating with either United States Senator on the subject.

If the President did not delegate the veto power on Senatorial nominations to the Governor of Virginia, why did not the latter deny the offensive assertion published in all Virginia papers and by nearly all of them condemned, and why should the President of the United States have declined to answer a simple question propounded to him by a United States Senator for whom he had repeatedly professed friendship?

Governor Price, as may be seen from the stenographic report of the proceedings before the Senate Judiciary Committee, virtually, if inadvertently, admitted he had been given the privilege of vetoing Senatorial nominations when he said: "It was an empty honor. All the patronage had been distributed."

What was an "empty honor"? Why, of course, the delegated power to veto Senatorial recommendations. And why was not the privilege immediately exercised?

Governor Price says because the Federal patronage had already been distributed; but he failed to say he immediately projected himself into the matter of Federal appointments by trying to make the officials renominated by the Senators understand that his indorsement was essential. And his chief newspaper advocates boasted that the names of these four officials were held up by the Justice Department until Price gave his approval. This is a record of that point which I confidently submit to the public for its own intelligent conclusion.

The President in his unprecedented letter to his rejected nominee expresses the opinion that "every person of common sense knows" that "no Governor, no Senator has at any time had or ever will have the right of veto over Presidential nominations."

This is as inaccurate as many other statements and inferences made by the President are. Ninety-six Senators have the right of veto over Presidential nominations in specified cases, and on last Monday seventy-two of them against nine to the contrary exercised their right of veto on the President's nominee for judge of the Western District of Virginia, and I am assured that others would have done likewise had they been present at the vote.

But, of course, persons of common sense or uncommon sense will readily understand that the Virginia Senators were not primarily discussing veto by the Governor of "Presidential nominations." We were discussing the delegated power of the President's political vice-regent in Virginia to veto Senatorial nominations, exercised so conclusively in the case of Judge Buchanan and Frank Tavenner.

The most extraordinary statement in the President's lament to his rejected nominee is contained in the forty-fifth of his forty-six paragraphs. He states that the Senators from Virginia have in effect said to the President: "We have nominated to you two candidates acceptable to us; you are hereby directed to nominate one of our two candidates; if you do not we will reject the nomination of anybody else selected by you, however fit he may be."

Of course, everybody knows that this implication has not the shadow of fact to support it. The Virginia Senators neither said nor intimated anything of the kind and in making such a statement the President must have been actuated by a vastly greater measure of anger than he was pleased to ascribe to me.

As the record shows, his Department of Justice asked the two Virginia Senators for a recommendation. For years this courtesy has prevailed, and a reading of the debates shows that the writers of the Constitution intended it to be perpetual. Complying with the request, the Virginia Senators named two men against whose eminent capabilities and character no man has dared utter a word.

The President not only ignored the recommendations of these men, but did not extend to the two Virginia Senators the common courtesy of discussing with them the appointment of a Federal judge in their State.

We were prepared to accept any capable man who was not deliberately intended to be offensive to us, by himself completely ignoring us and willingly making himself the beneficiary of an attempt to dishonor us in our State and among our colleagues. The Virginia Senators are still perfectly willing to accept any capable nominee of the President who is not willing to concede to the Governor of Virginia or a bitterly hostile Congressman the right to veto suggestions by the Senators of men of the highest character and capability.

This is no fight for patronage. I do not care a tinker's dam for patronage. I do not recall that I ever met Judge Buchanan. I do not know, nor have I ever inquired, whether or not he approved my course in the Senate. I inferred his appointment would not get either Senator a vote he would not receive anyhow, because I know Buchanan has too much character and too great a sense of propriety to be a judicial "sniper" or to permit politics of any description to enter his court.

I was looking for a judge, not for a job. I was not seeking a man under my political patronage, nor one under the patronage of any politician.

Buchanan would have been an ornament to the Federal bench, as he has been to that of the State, and it is to be deplored from every point of view that he should have been rejected by the appointive power merely through a desire to "purge" the junior Senator next year and the senior Senator of Virginia later should I live longer than the intriguers hope.

Chapter XIV

LEGISLATIVE ORGANIZATION AND PROCEDURE

[How legislatures are organized and how they carry on their business are puzzles to most Americans. Yet, if we are to have a healthy democracy, citizens must acquaint themselves with legislative organization and procedure. And they must constantly renew this acquaintance, for an organization and procedure that will do the job to-day may not do it satisfactorily to-morrow.

We must, therefore, not only learn how legislatures are organized and function now but we must also analyze how well the organization and procedure are adapted to the job at hand.]

No. 49

[ALTHOUGH the advantages of the unicameral legislature are, for the most part, undoubted, all American states except one have two chambers. The original reasons for bicameral legislative bodies in the United States are easy to discover. The framers of the Constitution had the model of the British Parliament before them, and they were faced with the problem of reconciling the views of those who believed the new Congress should represent states with the beliefs of others who felt that it should represent groups of persons. Furthermore, their lack of confidence in the full democratic process led them to erect a second chamber which could check the feared excesses of the more representative house.

These same factors were influential in the original adoption of the bicameral system for state legislatures. The early state constitution makers had both the British Parliament and the new Federal Congress to imitate. They too had to reconcile opposing views of representation. They also had a desire to check the more popularly elected house by a second chamber, chosen by a more restricted electorate. Although most of the reasons for the adoption of the bicameral system have now disappeared in our states, the structure still stands. Cities in the United States, however, have generally reorganized their legislative bodies in accordance with the unicameral principle.

Students of American government must understand not only the bases upon which the bicameral-unicameral argument rests but also the full theoretical implications of both systems. The following selection offers penetrating insight into these theoretical factors.]

A COMPARISON OF THE BICAMERAL AND UNICAMERAL SYSTEMS [1]

by W. F. Willoughby

ALTHOUGH, as has been shown, the general adoption by states of the bicameral legislative system has been due to historical accident, to the necessity believed to exist for meeting certain special conditions, or to a mere copying of existing institutions, rather than to a reasoned belief in its superiority as an instrument of legislation, there is nevertheless a strong body of opinion that this system has certain intrinsic merits which, apart from all other considerations, justify its employment.

As a preliminary to a consideration of the extent to which this opinion has a sound basis of fact, it is desirable first to point out what are the undoubted advantages of the unicameral system. Briefly to recapitulate them, they are: it is simple; it entails less expense in its operation; it permits of expeditious action; it furnishes the means for a direct, authoritative representation of the electorate; and that, under it, responsibility for action is definitely located. To these may be added the fact that it represents the system generally adopted in making provision for the exercise of other governmental powers, and that it is the one invariably employed by private corporations in making provision for the exercise of general direction and rule-making powers. In marked contrast with this, the bicameral system is one which is complicated and entails additional expense. It leads to delay in action. Two separate bodies have to be brought into accord before any action can be taken. In many cases this means that proposed action will be defeated, while, in almost all cases, the result is a compromise. And, finally, it has the serious disadvantage that, under it, responsibility is divided.

As regards these relative advantages and disadvantages of the two systems there can be, and is, no question. What then are the advantages claimed for the bicameral system that would lead to its being preferred to the unicameral system. Generally speaking, they are that such a system compels delay and deliberation; it makes it impossible for a legislature to be swept from its feet by a sudden wave of unreasoning emotion; it ensures that opportunity will always be given for a sober second thought; it ensures that measures, before their adoption, will undergo a careful revision; and

[1] W. F. Willoughby, *Principles of Legislative Organization and Administration* (Washington, D. C.: The Brookings Institution, 1934), pp. 222-234. Reprinted by permission of The Brookings Institution.

that it furnishes a means of preventing the legislature from being dominated by a single city or metropolitan area embracing a majority or a
large proportion of the population of the state.

All of these are, undoubtedly, desirable ends. It remains, however, to
be considered whether the bicameral system, as it obtains in modern states,
and particularly in the United States, is so devised as effectively to achieve
these ends; whether adequate means for securing them are not already provided by other features of the political machinery; whether these ends are
not more than offset by the disadvantages that have been pointed out, and
which are inherent in the system; whether these ends are, in fact, achieved
by the system in practical operation; and whether, even if they are, the
system does not give rise to other difficulties in the operation of the political system which more than counterbalance the advantages that the system
is supposed to afford.

As regards the first of these functions, it has already been pointed out
that, whatever may have been true in the past, the bicameral system as it
now exists, in both the national government and those of the states, no
longer is so constituted as to give separate representation to different interests; nor is it any longer the desire of the American people that special
provision should be made in this way for the representation and protection
of property rights. Such protection, it is believed, and properly so, is
afforded by the numerous safeguards set up in our constitutional documents
such as those which prohibit the taking of property without due compensation, the requirement of due process, the prohibition of bills of attainder
and the like, and the provision for an independent judiciary.

Turning now to a consideration of the second important function that a
second chamber is supposed to perform, namely, that of acting as a brake
or curb upon democracy, there can be no doubt but that it does act in this
way, since anything that makes more difficult the carrying out of the popular will cannot but have this effect. It is more than a question, however,
whether in so doing, it renders a valuable service. When our government
was first established popular government as applied to any large body of
people was in the nature of an experiment and it was but reasonable that
serious apprehensions should exist as to how it might operate in practice
if adequate safeguards against an abuse of powers were not provided. This
system, however, has not justified itself upon that ground. If our political
system is open to criticism from this standpoint, it is to be found in the
difficulty that exists in giving expression to the popular will rather than in
making it possible for such will to find too free expression. In considering
this matter it is important to realize that a profound transformation has
taken place with respect to the demands made upon governments. The old

belief that that government is best which governs least has long passed away. The requirements of the present time are, not so much the prevention of unwise action, as the securing of wise action. The harm that may be done by unwise action is more than outweighed by the damage that may result from failure, or delay in, taking action that is urgently needed. One of the most significant political developments of recent times is the disrepute into which the parliamentary system in European countries has fallen and the constant criticism that is made of our own legislative bodies. This disrepute is due in no small degree to the dilatoriness with which legislative bodies respond to popular demands.

It is important to note that, in our own system at least, the second chamber does not constitute the only means available for the prevention of undesirable action. There exists, in the first place, the great safeguard against an abuse of powers resulting from the numerous constitutional limitations upon the powers of our legislative bodies, limitations which exist to a like extent in no other political system. Secondly, and of still greater importance, is that characteristic feature of our legislative system which requires that all acts of legislation, before becoming effective, must be submitted to the executive for his approval. As regards the importance of this method of preventing unwise legislation, in comparison with that provided by the provision that the acts of one chamber must be ratified by another, Mr. Colvin, who made an exceptionally careful study of the working of the bicameral system in the State of New York, has the following to say:

> A comparison of the bills checked by the executive with those checked by the second house shows that the quality of the check exercised by the governor was far superior. Many of the bills defeated in the second house, especially those defeated by the assembly, suggested a hit-or-miss method of dealing with the bills and that there was little discrimination between those which passed and those which were left, other than that they were subject chiefly to the discrimination measured by the political influence behind them. On the other hand, the check of the governor showed a careful choice and a comprehensive grasp of the needs of the State, and a wise elimination of the undesirable and unnecessary, hasty, or ill-considered bills. . . . There seems to have come to be a dependence upon the governor to act as an efficient check rather than upon the second house.

That these two features greatly weaken, if they do not entirely do away with the need for a second chamber as a brake upon legislative action can hardly be questioned.

As regards the argument that a second chamber furnishes the means for securing a careful revision of legislative proposals as first formulated careful examination of the system, as it actually exists and operates, shows that the advantage thus claimed is more theoretical than actual. In the first place, it must be evident that, if a second chamber is really to perform this function, it should be specially constituted with this end in view. Preferably, its members should be selected in some manner other than that obtaining for the selection of the members of the lower house, the emphasis being laid on securing members of high technical qualifications rather than the giving expression to the representative principle, to the end, not merely of securing greater competence in the exercise of the revising function, but of putting such members in a position where their action will be determined by the technical merits of the propositions coming before them rather than by purely political, party considerations. No such special qualifications, however, are provided for in the United States. The members of both houses are selected in practically the same manner; they have the same representative character; they are equally dominated by political considerations, and there is no assurance that members of the upper house will be more technically qualified or be actuated by higher motives than those of the lower chambers.

Secondly, it should be noted that this need for one chamber to exercise a revising function with respect to the acts of the other is not so great as at first thought might appear. As has elsewhere been pointed out, the tendency is more and more for all important general legislative proposals to originate with the administration where they receive careful consideration both as regards their substantive character and their technical formulation. In the federal government at least, it is, moreover, the general practice to have all bills affecting governmental action in any way referred to the proper administrative authority for its consideration and recommendation. As a result of these two practices, all bills of real general importance already undergo the examination and scrutiny of two independent agencies.

Finally, it should be observed that the system of having the acts of one chamber reviewed by another has the serious defect of tending to induce lack of care on the part of the chamber first acting, and to lead it to pass bills that it would not pass if it knew that its action would be final. Often a chamber will shirk the duty of making needed changes in a pending bill on the ground that it is not necessary to do so since such changes can be made in the other house. In other cases, the responsibility for the defeat of an undesirable measure is shifted to the other chamber.

There remains for consideration the final argument brought forward in favor of the bicameral system that, through it, means are provided for meeting the special problem of preventing the legislature from being dominated by a single large city or metropolitan area containing a majority or a large proportion of the state's population. Undoubtedly, provision for a second chamber can be made to serve this purpose, but the complicating of the legislative structure and the legislative process in this way would seem to be an excessive price to pay for achieving this end, especially in view of the fact that it can be equally well attained by so apportioning representation in a single chamber among the political subdivisions of the state as to prevent any one city or metropolitan area from having a majority or an undue proportion of the total representation provided for. That action in this way is quite possible is demonstrated by the fact, as is later pointed out in our special discussion of the problem of apportionment, that, in practically all states having a city or metropolitan area embracing a majority or a large part of the population of the state, the principle of apportioning representatives in the lower house according to population is departed from, and such areas are given a smaller representation than they would have were strict adherence had to this basis of representation.

Before leaving this subject of the relative merits and demerits of the two systems, a further feature of the bicameral system which, in practice, has produced results far from satisfactory, should be commented upon. An essential feature of the bicameral system is that means shall be provided by which differences arising between the two houses with respect to legislation may be adjusted. In the United States, as is elsewhere pointed out in our consideration of the problem of the organization and procedure of legislative bodies, this means is provided by the setting up of what are known as conference committees; that is, committees composed of representatives of the two houses to which bills as passed by them are referred for the purpose of recasting in a form which will meet the approval of both houses. An essential feature of this system is that the measures as so redrafted must be either accepted or rejected by the two houses substantially without modification. This not only means that the character of much of the important legislation enacted is determined by these committees, but that other conditions of a highly undesirable character are set up. The defective working of this system is pointed out in a forcible way in the following quotation from a contribution to the *New York Times* of January 28, 1923, by one who has had exceptional opportunities to observe them. Writing under the title of "One Branch Legislature for States Would Improve Results," Senator George W. Norris, of Nebraska, says:

> In every legislature composed of two branches . . . the only thing that emerges from the conference is the final agreement. The individual legislator must then vote upon a conference report without any opportunity of expressing by his vote his opposition to anything that the bill in this form contains.

The citizen is deprived entirely of an opportunity to pass a just and fair judgment upon the result. In conference provisions are often put in and other provisions taken out, where an entirely different result would be obtained if the action took place in the open, where a record vote could be had upon all provisions of the bill. . . . Experience has shown that it is within the privacy of the conference committee room that jokers get into legislation, and that provisions of law demanded even by a majority of both branches of the legislature are sometimes not included in the finished product. . . . It very often happens that the most important features of legislation are put into the bills while they are being thus considered. Members of conference committees are often compelled to surrender on important items where no surrender would be even demanded if consideration of the legislation were in the open where a public record could be had of the proceedings. When the bill emerges from conference it is not then subject to amendment. It must be accepted or rejected as a whole. The conference is held in secret. There is no record vote on any proposition decided at the conference. . . .

A one-branch legislature would obviate all these difficulties. There would be no way for any member of the legislature to conceal his opposition upon any legislative proposition that comes before the body. The citizen would be able to absolutely and without difficulty place responsibility where it properly belonged for every act of the legislature. It would thus be easy to punish those whose records are unsatisfactory and to reward those whose services are meritorious.

There remains yet another objection of a practical character that can be raised against the bicameral system. The bicameral system came into existence before the development of political parties in the modern sense. This is true of the United States as well as of England where it took its rise. With the rise of the party system, an entirely new element was injected into the problem of legislation. Opinion is now fairly unanimous that this system gives its best results where what is known as party government obtains, that is, where responsibility for action can be definitely placed upon the party commanding the majority support of the people. Even in a state having the responsible type of government, the effective operation of such a system is seriously interfered with where the legislature consists of two houses, one of which is not directly representative of, and responsible to, the electorate. In England, this difficulty was only in part met by the development of the principle that majority support in the lower house alone should determine the continuance in power of a ministry representing the majority party, since, under that system, it was still possible for the upper house to prevent such majority party from having its way. It was finally overcome only by the passage of the Parliament Act of 1911, which, in effect, abolished the bicameral system, though it retained the upper house as an organ for the exercise of what is in effect a qualified veto power. In France, where no such modification of the bicameral principle has been effected, the complications introduced into the working of party government are constantly in evidence.

It is when one turns to the United States, however, that the extent to which the effective working of the system of party government is interfered with by the existence of two co-ordinate branches of the legislature is most apparent. As is well known, under our system of government, the contingency that the two houses of the legislature may be of different political complexion is not always present but is in fact of frequent occurrence. When this is the case, it is impossible for the principle of party government to find proper expression, and when party differences and animosities are acute it may result in a practical deadlock so far as the enactment of legislation of general importance is concerned. At best, it means that the whole process of legislation is slowed down and that much of the legislation that is enacted will be of a compromise character thoroughly satisfactory to no one. That such a condition constitutes a serious defect in our political system can scarcely be doubted. That it exists is wholly due to the existence of the bicameral system, and its correction is only to be found in the abolition of that system or its modification in such a way as will destroy the position of the upper house as co-ordinate with the lower house.

The foregoing critical study of the bicameral system has, it is believed, established, not only the disadvantages inherent in that system, but the further fact that the particular objects sought by its adoption, are either not achieved, or are amply provided for by other features of our political system. This being so, the conclusion inevitably follows that the system is one that should only be adopted where very special conditions exist rendering its employment desirable. No such conditions exist in the case of our states. Few things, in the opinion of the writer, would contribute more to the improvement of the whole system of state administration than the abolition of this system and the substitution in its place of a single chamber with a comparatively restricted membership. By such action the structure of government would be materially simplified, responsibility for action would be more definitely located, the establishment of effective cooperative relations between the legislature and executive would be rendered easier, and the whole process of legislation would be facilitated and made more responsive to public opinion. Added advantages would be a reduction in the cost of government and an increased probability of securing as legislators those persons who are best fitted to perform the duties of that office. One of the gravest criticisms of our state legislatures, as they now exist, is the mediocre character of their memberships. Their failure to attract to themselves persons who, as the result of their personal attainments or experience in other walks of life, are specially qualified to participate in the conduct of public affairs, is undoubtedly due in part to the difficulties that such persons would encounter in making their influence felt under conditions now existing where responsibility for action is so widely diffused. With a single chamber of comparatively small size, the post of legislator would become one of greatly enhanced power and prestige, and, as such, could not fail to make a greater appeal to men of ability, and a knowledge of this changed condition on the part of the electorate could not but tend to make it exercise greater discrimination in selecting its representatives.

In thus arguing for the abolition by the states of their bicameral systems, the writer voices the conclusions that have been reached by those students of political science who have given special attention to the problems of state government. Thus the distinguished group of scholars which cooperated under the auspices of the National Municipal League in the drafting of a model state constitution, made the unicameral chamber the central feature of their recommendations regarding the set-up of the legislative branch. Both on account of the weight of the authority carried by them, and because they summarize in an exceptionally forcible way the considerations previously presented, the comments of the committee upon this feature of their recommendations are here reproduced:

The committee believes that a single body, chosen by proportional representation and not too large in number, will be at once more representative and efficient than the present two-chamber system. The old arguments for two houses claim that they are more representative and more deliberative than a single body can be. But state senators are now chosen in the same manner as state assemblies. The senatorial district may be larger but the qualifications and weight of individual voters are the same in both districts. They represent the same people in the same way as the lower house does. As long as European nations accepted an aristocracy of higher degree than the multitude there was a reason for an upper chamber. But the many now no longer concede special privileges to the few; and the upper house, although perhaps retained in law, has abroad been rendered almost impotent in fact. The state senators likewise are not now regarded as rational checks upon legislation. Doubtless they increase the effort necessary to pass legislation just as a rough road impedes the passage of an automobile, but mere obstruction is not a virtue. Intelligent obstruction may be, but the upper house rarely renders such obstruction because it is merely a pocket edition of the lower house.

A division of power between the two houses leads to a division of responsibility, to political trades, to "passing the buck." Measures often pass one house with the understanding that they will be killed in the other and from such transactions the people get a false impression as to the checking influence of the bicameral system. As former Governor Hodge of Kansas said: "About the only purpose I have ever been able to see for the two-house system is that it enables a legislator to fool his constituents by getting a measure demanded or promised them through his branch of the legislature and then using every effort to have it killed in the other branch."

A distinct advantage of the single-chamber system is the encouragement that it affords to the development of public, responsible leadership within the legislature, and to closer cooperation between the governor and the legislature. We are all familiar with the situation which arises when the two houses are of different political complexions, or when the governor and a branch of the legislature are at odds. And yet the governor by reason of his grip on the administration and his knowledge of the working of law is naturally the one person whose work the legislature should be able to enquire into with the greatest ease. The governor should be closer to the legislature, both as a leader and as a servant, but this can only come about if there is real centralization of authority within a well organized and smoothly running body. The voters can keep track of such a legislature. We mistrust our present legislatures because they so easily slip out of our grasp.

In view of these manifest advantages of the unicameral over the bicameral legislature, it is rather remarkable that proposals looking to the changing from the latter to the former have made so little headway in the various conventions in recent years for the revision of the constitutions of the states. The only explanation of this is to be found in the inherent conservativeness of the American people in political matters. There is great reluctance to depart from any long established practice. Should one state, however, make the break and go over to the new system of a single chamber it might easily result that others would speedily follow the example. [Since this was written one state, Nebraska, has established a unicameral legislature.] It is not so long ago that the bicameral system was the prevailing one in providing for the exercise of the ordinance-making, fund-raising, and fund-granting power of our municipalities. With the movement once started for the substitution of the unicameral system, the change over to this system took place with great rapidity until at the present time the bicameral system is found in few of these governments.

No. 50

[CONGRESS, in 1946, provided for a comprehensive congressional reorganization that was long overdue. The Act of 1946, however, did not deal with all of the problems that called for action, and time and changing conditions will create still others. Professor Outland, who served four years in Congress, discusses in the following essay the form further reorganization might take.]

CONGRESS STILL NEEDS REORGANIZATION [1]
by George E. Outland

ACCOMPLISHMENTS OF THE 1946 ACT

1. *Considerable improvement in the committee system.* The number of standing committees in the House was reduced from forty-eight to nineteen; in the Senate from thirty-three to fifteen. Even granting the validity of the criticism that there have since been established too many subcommittees, still the reduction in permanent standing committees is a most important step forward. The jurisdiction of these committees has been more clearly defined. Conference committees cannot write new legislation (as they formerly did). There has been a much greater regularization of committee hearings and in the keeping of committee records.

2. *Improvement in the staffing of Congress.* Both for individual members and for the committees has there been marked advance in quantity and quality of skilled help. All but five of the Senators have taken advantage of the act permitting them to appoint skilled assistants. (This provision for House members was omitted from the Reorganization Act and added for Senate members later in a special bill.) Both Houses have seen their committees add to their personnel trained investigators and consultants, as well as needed clerical help. The importance of this step can hardly be overestimated.

3. *Some reduction in the unnecessary work load.* While there is still a considerable problem here, it has been noticeably lessened by the Reorganization Act. The private bill problem, for example, has been markedly reduced. The committee reorganization in both Houses has effectively lowered the assignments of members.

4. *Miscellaneous gains.* The provision for the regular adjournment of Congress at the end of July is a noticeable improvement. Not only does

---

[1] George E. Outland, "Congress Still Needs Reorganization," *The Western Political Quarterly* (June, 1948), Vol. I, No. 2, pp. 156-164. Reprinted by permission of *The Western Political Quarterly*. The footnotes in the original version are omitted here.

it permit members to plan regular visits to their districts, but by setting a time limit it stimulates a greater amount of work earlier in the session than was formerly accomplished.

The increase in Congressional salaries to $12,500 and the addition of an annual expense account of $2,500 are much-needed advances; further steps in the same direction are indicated. Similarly, the Reorganization Act did make a start on a Congressional retirement system, though much more remains to be done.

One of the most important gains of the Act was the requirement that lobbyists register and make financial statements. While this provision is still not completely clear, it is certainly a progressive move.

FAILURES OF THE 1946 ACT

Besides the preceding achievements, there were included in the 1946 Act provisions which it was hoped would meet many of the other deficiencies. To date this hope has not been realized. Probably the most important of these failures has been that of the legislative budget. Traditionally, there has been practically no relationship in Congress between taxation and appropriation; Section 138 of the Act attempted to meet this problem by providing for a "legislative budget." Partly because of lack of advance staff work before the meeting of the 80th Congress, and partly because of irreconcilable difficulties between the conferees of the House and the Senate, this part of the act has failed completely, to date.

Other provisions in the bill designed to bring about fiscal reforms have also failed, including those calling for open hearings by the House Appropriations Committee and its subcommittees, the expenditure analyses by the Comptroller General, the establishment of "show-case" accounting of their expense items by Government agencies, and the studies for reduction of permanent appropriations. In general the items of the Act dealing with financial reform taken together constitute the most important failure of the Reorganization Act.

Among the other items which have not been adequately carried out to date are the provision against the Senate's including substantive legislation in appropriation bills, the requirement that witnesses file written statements three days in advance of oral testimony before committees, and the provisions for adequate appropriations for the Legislative Reference Service and the Office of Legislative Counsel, for a three-day interval between the report and the hearing on appropriation bills, and for complete abolition of individual claim cases. (As to the last named, while the old Claims Committee has been abolished, much of its former work has simply been transferred to the Judiciary Committee.) While most lobbyists appear to be registering, many are not filing adequate financial accounts as required. [The] Attorney General . . . has announced that his office will investigate thoroughly all violations of this provision of the Act. General legislative supervision of the Executive branch, as authorized in Section 136, has likewise been inadequately carried out.

NEXT STEP IN CONGRESSIONAL REORGANIZATION

If Congress is to play its full part with the other two branches of our check-and-balance system, several further important steps need to be taken immediately. Without attempting to discuss them at any length, it is suggested that the following constitute a minimum program:

1. *Continued improvement of committee structure.* Great gains were made in committee structure by the 1946 Act; but much still remains to be done. Four points stand out: the discontinuance of all special committees, the elimination of the seniority method of choosing chairmen, an overhauling of the Rules Committee, and provisions for parallel committees in the two houses, to hold joint sessions so far as possible.

There can be no justification for the continuance of special committees; if investigations of any nature are necessary, this can be done through a special subcommittee of one of the existing committees. Special committees tend to be political in nature, to duplicate the work of standing committees, to be inefficient, and, in general, to be wholly unnecessary. Their liquidation is indicated.

As pointed out by an expert in the field there are at least six other methods of selecting committee chairmen than by the antiquated method of automatic seniority:

1. Appointment by the Speaker of the House and the presiding officer of the Senate (or the majority leaders in each chamber).
2. Secret election by committee members.
3. Secret election by party caucus.
4. Selection by a committee on committees (or the Rules Committee).
5. Automatic rotation in office at periodic intervals.
6. Election from the floor.

All of these alternatives have drawbacks. One may, perhaps, agree that the best method would be appointment by the majority leadership in each House. This would further strengthen party responsibility, would insure the choice of men of ability and would tend to speed up the legislative program. These advantages would be even more certain were the leadership likewise empowered to remove chairmen who were uncooperative.

The executive power concentrated in the hands of the House Rules Committee has become notorious. Even after the Norris-led revolt of 1910 . removed the Speaker as one of its members, this unusual House group continued to possess, for all practical purposes, the power to emasculate or kill a measure coming from any standing committee. Certainly there should be completely removed from it the ability to thus frustrate committee action; it should be only "the traffic director on the legislative highway," not the collective reincarnation of Joe Cannon.

Another major step toward congressional efficiency would be achieved through further reduction in the number of standing committees in each House, and provision for truly parallel functions and frequent joint sessions of these committees. Galloway's suggestions, amended by Kefauver and Levin, would provide for thirteen such parallel committees, each having jurisdiction over specific executive agencies. As these authors point out, "Sound administration requires that the same number of committees exist in both bodies and that they have identical functions."

2. *Continued improvement in Congressional staffing.* Section 202 of the Act authorized increased staff personnel for congressional committees. While this authorization was inadequate to meet the increasing demands for specialized, technical assistance, even these provisions have not been fully carried out thus far. If Congress is to meet on an equal plane with the specialists of executive departments and special interest groups, it must have considerably more trained advisory help than has been the case to date. The additional expense would be infinitesimal in proportion to the increase in committee efficiency.

Originally, it was contemplated that the Reorganization Act would include a provision authorizing an administrative assistant for each Congressman, to take from his shoulders much of the detailed non-legislative work. This provision, although subsequently authorized for Senators in another bill, was not included in the final Act. Representatives too need such assistance. There is a danger, of course, that if the position of such an administrative assistant were authorized it might degenerate into another patronage job; but that danger could easily be overcome by providing that such assistants should be selected from a special civil service list.

3. *Adequate provision for controlling federal expenditures.* It has already been pointed out that the legislative budget, for which such high hopes were held, has not worked. There are some thoughtful students of Congressional machinery who contend that it cannot work and should not work. For example, David Cushman Coyle contends that

Liberals might do well to drop the idea of the legislative budget, since it only confuses Congress, which ought rather to be discussing the really critical questions: Do we want a surplus, a deficit, or a close balance next year? Once that is decided, the others must follow, and any attempt to promise either the budget total or the tax rate in advance is liable to make those who do it ridiculous.

On the other hand, the principle of the legislative budget has been endorsed by spokesmen for the U. S. Chamber of Commerce, the National Planning Association, and the Committee for Economic Development. In his recent statement before the Senate Committee on Expenditures in the Executive Departments, Galloway speaks in favor of the budget principle, but points out eight specific safeguards which should be enacted if it is to function.

The writer cannot speak with authority on this particular problem. He does believe emphatically, however, that there must be considerably more coordination of government taxation and government spending than there has ever been before if our national economy is to survive. Congressional reorganization on a broad front in this field is imperative; the specific proposals, however, still await additional study.

4. *Continued reduction of the "busy work" of Congress.* Some progress in removing from Congressmen the petty details of their daily work was accomplished by the Reorganization Act of 1946. Much, however, remains to be done. Home Rule for the District of Columbia which has been advocated for years might be mentioned as an example. At the present time there is a bill pending before the Congress to accomplish this end. It has been estimated that in the first regular session of the 80th Congress, approximately 3,000 congressional man-hours were consumed by the members of the House in committee meetings on District legislation. For these members, it was a waste of time so far as their district and national responsibilities were concerned; for the citizens of the District of Columbia it signified a continuation of a status of disenfranchisement. The passing of . . . [a home rule bill for the District of Columbia] would be a definite step forward not only in congressional reorganization but in the extension of democratic principles.

Congressmen would likewise have less busy work if they were relieved of the necessity of making appointments to postmasterships and to the two service academies. No justification can be seen for continuing these portions of the old spoils system; they are inefficient and excessively political, and consume all too much time which could better be devoted to national legislation. Whatever may have been the reasons advanced for such practices in the past, they can no longer be held to be valid.

Plugging the holes in the 1946 Act so that claims bills and similar ones of a private nature could not be referred to the Judiciary Committee would likewise aid the overworked members of that particular committee. As suggested above, the appointment of a special administrative assistant for each Representative would be a further means of removing responsibility for detail from the shoulders of overburdened members of the Lower House.

5. *Improved relations with the Executive Department.* While the American system of checks and balances contemplates that no single branch of government shall dominate the other two, it does not imply that each must constantly be in conflict with the other two. The struggle between the White House and Capitol Hill has been marked since the days of George Washington; at times it has been so bitter as practically to stalemate the processes of government.

The creation of a joint Legislative-Executive Council (a proposal originally recommended by the Joint Committee on the Reorganization of Congress) would probably help considerably to bridge the gap between the two departments of government. Such a committee, to consist of the President and his Cabinet, on the one hand, and the Vice-President, Speaker, majority leaders of both Houses, and the leading committee chairmen, on the other, could do much to remove present suspicions and misunderstandings, and to plan cooperatively vital national legislation. It has also been suggested by the writer and others that the minority leaders might well be included in such a council.

Section 136 of the Reorganization Act specifically instructs the standing committees of Congress to "exercise continuous watchfulness of the execution by the administrative agencies concerned of any laws, the subject matter of which is within the jurisdiction of such committees. . . ." To date this important legislative function has been most inadequately performed. This failure has been due to several factors, among which are inadequate committee personnel, lack of clarity as to specific committee jurisdiction, and general inertia. The practice of the old House Committee on Public Buildings and Grounds, during the war, of calling monthly meetings with the executives of the National Housing Agency, and jointly threshing out problems of policy and practice, could well be emulated by all standing committees of both Houses. Such joint meetings, when partisanship is minimized, have a wholesome effect on both executive and legislative branches. This practice could easily be formalized by supplementary legislation.

For years, Representative Kefauver, one of the most thoughtful students of Congressional procedure, has been advocating that our government utilize the "question-period" practice, as is done in the House of Commons in the English Parliament. He has repeatedly pointed out the advantages of having Cabinet heads appear before Congress to answer questions pertaining to national policy, and he has built a strong case. It is doubtful, however, whether this innovation would accomplish much to bridge the gap between executive and legislative departments.

6. *Improving of floor procedure.* Congressmen have frequently criticized "the bureaucrats" for inefficiency; the American people can well level the same charge at Congress. For example, it has been estimated that in the past three years the House alone has wasted the equivalent of one legislative month each year for roll calls alone. How simple it would be to remedy this waste by the installation of electric voting machines such as are now used in some eleven state legislatures! But the quorum calls and roll call votes, each of which requires more than half an hour in the House, continue. Remedying of this single lag in Congress would in itself increase efficiency inestimably.

The friends of civil rights need not hope for, and the enemies need not fear, any results from the President's courageous message *To Defend These Rights* so long as the filibuster is unchecked in the Senate. The right of unlimited debate in the Upper House is an excellent example of the right of freedom of speech without the corresponding responsibility. As long as a two-thirds vote is necessary to invoke cloture, i.e., to limit debate, it is doubtful if the filibuster menace can be alleviated. Since 1917, cloture has been brought to a vote some twenty times; four times only was it successful. The amending of the rules of the Senate to provide that cloture may be invoked by a simple majority vote would not abolish the filibuster, but it would go far toward minimizing it.

Floor procedure in the House would certainly be improved by reorganizing the rules of "general debate" to prevent out-of-order speeches for home political consumption, and by forcing roll call votes when the House is in Committee of the Whole. If the latter were done, it would enable the American people to have a much clearer picture than at present as to where their representatives really stand on issues.

Unless the executive powers of the Rules Committee can be otherwise checked, it would be in order to so amend the House Rules as to revert to the practice of permitting bills to be brought to the floor when a petition is signed by 100 names, rather than requiring a minimum of 218 as at present.

The intriguing suggestion that the proceedings of Congress, or parts of them, be broadcast, has been frequently advanced. Whether such broadcasts would interfere with such "important programs" as soap operas, swing "music," and "you-guess-the-answer" programs is questionable. It would be interesting indeed to try it for a year as an experiment and have Mr. Gallup tally the results.

7. *Abolition of the two-thirds Senate vote for treaty ratification.* This radical suggestion, frequently made by students of our government, would require a constitutional amendment, which in turn would necessitate a two-thirds vote of the Senate, so any discussion of it is probably academic. If it were possible to change procedure here so as to authorize ratification of treaties by a majority vote of both houses, there is little doubt that such a step would constitute a tremendous gain. Some of the obvious advantages are that it would be more democratic and practical by including the House of Representatives, which has the power of purse strings in many phases of foreign policy anyway; that it would lessen the presidential tendency to bypass Congress by negotiating executive agreements; that it would bolster the hand of the State Department by affording greater advance certainty of legislative approval; and that it would expedite policy formation in foreign affairs. There is almost no objection to it except that the Senate is exceedingly jealous of its traditional prerogatives, and would doubtless defeat the proposal overwhelmingly. Even the Senate, however, has been known to alter its position when public opinion has become sufficiently persuasive.

8. *Miscellaneous suggestions.* Certain it is that if only half of the above suggestions could obtain favorable action, most students of Congressional structure would be gratified, even though many additional improvements are needed too. Among the latter would be a further increase in Congressional salary to $20,000, or even $25,000; provision for a more adequate retirement plan for Congressmen; a constitutional amendment to change the term of Representatives from two to four years; and further regulation of political campaigns and expenditures.

OBSTACLES IN THE WAY OF REFORMS

The casual observer will ask, "Why are these things not done? They seem so obvious." The answer is that the same old enemies of any social change are responsible for this situation. Inertia and habit, tradition, lack of interest inside Congress and outside too, failure to realize the necessity for modernization—all of these are influential opponents of all reorganization plans. More important is another traditional enemy of social change— vested interests. Committee chairmen do not wish to give up their cherished prerogatives and power. The Speaker and the Rules Committee can certainly be counted on to oppose any diminution of their authority, and to convert many others to the same point of view. The Senate will not lessen its power over foreign affairs, and individual Senators are loathe to consider any regulation of their complete freedom of speech. Opponents of such legislation as civil liberties, minimum wages, fair employment, etc., who have traditionally found refuge in the complex rules and procedures of both houses, will not willingly stand by and see those rules altered. Fear of public censure will prevent Congress from raising salary standards and retirement provisions to adequate levels. The general complexities of our check-and-balance system will give aid and encouragement to such vested interests and assist in preventing needed reform in budget procedure, supervision of the executive department, and joint committee hearings. . . .

No. 51

[BELIEVING that legislatures make mistakes and that legislators are not too well qualified to do their work, the American people have severely restricted the frequency and length of state legislative sessions. This problem is primarily a problem of the states. Congress now meets in annual sessions beginning January 3 each year—and each session may run until the following January 3. The Legislative Reorganization Act of 1946 provides that the session run only until July but Congress can extend the date at will. City councils in our larger cities meet weekly or bi-weekly. Only on the state level do we adhere to the belief that we can get along without fairly frequent and extended sessions of the policy-determining branch of government. The problems raised and difficulties encountered because of this belief are the subject of the following article.]

PROBLEMS PECULIAR TO THE SHORT-SESSION LEGISLATURE [1]

by William E. Treadway

WHETHER the legislative session limited by organic law in frequency and duration should be abrogated in favor of one unlimited in times of convening and of indeterminate length, is a question wholly apart from this discussion. The short-session legislature, where it exists, is so firmly imbedded in tradition and so generally accepted that to propose its abandonment at this time would be to precipitate a highly controversial debate. It will be assumed, therefore, that the constitutional limitations upon the legislative department of government in a number of states will continue. An effort will be made to point out some of the problems existing under such limitations, and to suggest their remedies where possible.

[1] William E. Treadway, "Problems Peculiar to the Short-Session Legislature," *The Annals* of the American Academy of Political and Social Science (January, 1938), Vol. 195, pp. 110-115. Reprinted by permission of *The Annals* of the American Academy of Political and Social Science and the author. The footnotes in the original version are omitted here

Indiana is fairly typical of the states having short-session legislatures, and for reasons of familiarity and convenience will be drawn upon for occasional illustrations. Prior to the constitutional convention of 1850 the Indiana Legislature had met annually, and the frequency of its meeting seems to have been one of the outstanding questions upon which delegates to the convention were elected. A proposal to limit the General Assembly to triennial instead of biennial sessions mustered a now surprising vote of 43 for the resolution to 83 negative votes. Only 5 of the 129 delegates voting upon the adoption of this section of the constitution favored a retention of annual sessions.

The successful argument advanced at the time was that the laws of the state had been continually fluctuating.

> The changes made were of such frequent occurrence that the people did not know what the laws were; and, of course, they could not be obeyed by men who did not know when they had violated them. That was impossible. And a further evil resulting from this continual change was, that they were not administered a sufficient length of time for the people to ascertain whether their effect was good or evil.

Section 9 of Article IV of the Constitution of Indiana as adopted in 1851 provides:

> The sessions of the General Assembly shall be held biennially at the capital of the state, commencing on the Thursday next after the first Monday of January. . . . But if, in the opinion of the governor, the public welfare shall require it, he may, at any time by proclamation, call a special session.

An amendment offered at the convention seeking to limit the matters to be considered at such special session to subjects specified by the governor in his proclamation was defeated.

Section 29 of the same Article limits the duration of regular sessions to a maximum of sixty-one days, and of special sessions to a maximum of forty days. There is no limitation upon the number or the frequency of special sessions, other than that their convening is only upon the call of the executive, and under such a constitutional arrangement it is conceivable that the legislature might remain in continuous session should a governor see fit to issue his proclamation prior to the constitutional adjournment. The experience of years, however, has demonstrated as strong a reluctance on the part of the executive to prolong the assembly as was shown in the convention. Hence, certain problems have arisen inherent in the short session.

A lack of continuity from session to session is one of the major problems. A heavy turnover in membership is noted at each assembly. New members constituted 62 per cent of the Indiana House of Representatives in 1935, and 43 per cent in 1937.

This enormous turnover is accounted for probably more by voluntary withdrawals than by primary and general election defeats. The short-session legislature is the one department of government to which no one can afford to devote himself exclusively and continuously. All members must, of necessity, have superior outside interests upon which to depend for a livelihood and to which they must direct their energy and thought during the time between sessions. The irritating interruption from the normal pursuits of professional and business men and the physical strain accompanying the short session are the reasons most frequently given for voluntary retirement. While a rapid turnover in the legislature may appear in keeping with democratic theory, in practice it will be seen that this phenomenon operates for inefficiency.

This disruption is most damaging within standing committees. The life of the committee is limited to that of the session. Experienced chairmen and committee members, if available, could give invaluable counsel upon numerous questions that recur at each succeeding session. Not infrequently, during a session an industrious committee may gather a wealth of information upon a subject of great public concern, only to have its knowledge dissipated for all practical purposes by a substantial if not complete change in personnel of the committee at the ensuing session.

This situation might be materially improved if such important committees as those upon the subjects of taxes and finance, judiciary, public safety, and interstate and Federal cooperation were empowered to meet from time to time, as their business requires, during the interim between sessions, and to maintain a continuous secretariat.

A single legislative council composed of representative members of the more important committees of the House and the Senate and supplemented by certain lay members having special knowledge of problems of government, is another possibility.

The experience in Indiana with special study commissions appointed at the close of one session with a mandate to report its findings at the beginning of the next has been disappointing. Selections to such committees have been made more upon the basis of geographical or political distribution than upon the personal fitness or the special interest of the appointees. The result has been a disorganized and unscientific attack upon the problems assigned. Such a commission appointed in 1935 spent considerable time in touring eastern states in a superficial "study" of tax laws. No analysis of comparative legislation was made, and as a result the commission was unable to make an intelligent report of its findings. Conversely, a similar delegation from an eastern legislature visited Indianapolis during the same year, and while it did actually publish a report, its findings disclosed that Indiana was operating successfully with the income from a 2 per cent sales tax, whereas Indiana has never had a sales tax. Except in a few isolated instances, it has been fairly well demonstrated that little value may be expected from such special commissions.

Possibly the greatest single problem presented by the short-session legislature is that of an economical and efficient use of the time allotted to lawmaking. Much of the physical and mental exhaustion which has been so inseparably associated with the closing days of the session could be alleviated and the chaos of adjournment avoided by a more orderly conduct of the assembly's affairs from the beginning.

As much as several days' time may be consumed at the start of a session in the matter of reorganization. The election of officers and the appointment of employees and committees cannot precede the opening of the session, constitutionally. However, with the more-and-more accepted theory of party responsibility, it is possible for the members-elect of the party naming the largest membership in a legislature to meet in advance of the constitutional day of opening and to complete the organization of each house in caucus, subject to a formal ratification on the first day, thus being prepared for normal functioning from the hour of convening.

With the typical legislature meeting a few weeks after an election, the membership of the house and of that part of the senate up for election cannot be known long in advance of the session to the members themselves or to others. While in theory the legislators arrive freshly instructed from the electorate, in reality there has been little opportunity for a mature consideration of desirable legislation in advance. Comparatively few members bring with them any bills prepared beforehand. Soon the congestion of the short session makes heavy demands upon the time of all. And while many legislators avail themselves of the facilities of legislative drafting bureaus during a session, the fact remains that a very considerable number of bills are prepared by outside interests, both public and private, and are introduced, in fact, by request. Thus many legislators suddenly find themselves the "authors" of measures which they had not the slightest idea of sponsoring, prior to the session. This accounts for the inability of so many to give an intelligent and satisfactory explanation of their bills on the floor.

A lack of time for the proper consideration of bills in committees is deplorable. A number of committees, by reason of the subjects with which they are concerned, are idle much of the time, and designations of membership thereon serve principally as handy vehicles in making committee assignments go the rounds. Other groups may be known, notoriously, as "graveyard" committees, to which measures are consigned with a tacit understanding that they are not to be reported upon. For the most part, the other committees are greatly overworked. It is not uncommon for some committees to have as many as fifty bills on hand for consideration.

A lack of some systematic arrangement for committee hearings is a cause of endless confusion. Rules ordinarily prohibit the meeting of committees during sessions. Announcements of meetings frequently are made just prior to a daily adjournment, and are often for an immediate convening of the committee without other notice to parties interested in bills to be considered. Some fairly important committees seldom, if ever, actually meet, the chairmen "explaining" such bills as are desired "out" to a majority of their committee members and filing their reports. Committee amendments are not frequent, and minority reports are rare except upon bills of highly controversial subjects. The pressure exerted upon committee chairmen to release or to hold bills during the short session might be compared to the display of conflicting interests in a football game with a limited time to go. A "pocketing" disposition of a bill by a chairman is made relatively easy by the excuse of lack of time for consideration. Motions to discharge one committee from further consideration of a bill, with a request that the bill be recommitted to another, are seldom heard.

Under the ordinary situation, only one typewritten copy of a bill is available for the study of an entire committee. To "save time" the bill is usually "explained" by its proponent. Unless the subject matter is such as to draw the attention of an adversely affected party, there is seldom anyone present to make any explanatory remarks in opposition.

A sufficient amount of time of a session should be definitely allocated for work in committees. Certainly every member of a committee should be furnished a copy of all bills under consideration. Without an opportunity for an actual study of bills in committee an intelligent report is impossible, and legislators in the short session must of physical necessity rely to a large extent upon committee reports in determining their votes.

In Indiana, a bill ordinarily is printed before being placed on second reading, and at no other time. As a result, by the time it is eligible for a vote upon final passage, the bill may contain far-reaching amendments that are not apparent on the members' printed copies. Upon third reading, the bill, as amended, is explained meagerly on the floor by its sponsor, who, under pressure of time if not also from a want of facts, may often preface his brief remarks by saying, "This bill merely provides for . . ." It would seem obvious that all amended bills should be reprinted as amended or that a rule should be adopted requiring all amendments not so printed to be read in full before such bill is placed upon its final passage. No member is in a position to cast an intelligent vote upon a measure which he has had no opportunity to read or to hear read in its final form, and such a change in rules would conserve the time of the conscientious and energetic member who makes an effort to inform himself upon amendments during the short session.

Bills are not actually read in full upon any one of the three "readings" required by the constitution. It would be physically impossible for most members to read and digest every bill up for consideration, as long as the volume of legislative business keeps its present stride. No limit is placed upon the number of bills that may be considered for final passage in one day. It is not unusual, toward the close of a session, for thirty or forty bills to be passed in a few hours. In fact, a member may often consider himself lucky to have thumbed through the sheaf of bills upon his desk and to have found his copy of the one under final consideration by the time the polling clerk calls his name.

During a day on which the legislative mill is geared to high speed, a great many bills may be passed "on faith." Confusion is generally apparent, with even veteran members striving with some difficulty to keep abreast of the day's rapid developments. Time and again during rapidly succeeding roll calls are heard the questions: "What are we voting on now?" "Is this bill all right?" "How should I vote on this bill?" At times the situation would furnish a most interesting laboratory study for the mob psychologist. Rumors may be the means of passing or killing some measures even after a roll call has been commenced. Anonymous whispers such as: "This is a bad bill," "This is a dangerous bill," or "This bill will bankrupt the tax-payer," have been known to kill many meritorious bills through a stampede of a sufficient number of uninformed, uninterested, or exhausted members; while a last-minute whisper of some word of popular appeal, similarly, has made possible the enactment of some questionable legislation.

This extremely chaotic condition would be greatly improved if an impartial, printed synopsis of every bill introduced were made available to all members as an additional service of the legislative bureau. Such a synopsis should be sufficiently concise to be readable, but at the same time sufficiently informative to convey the full import of the bill. This service could be rendered daily by a cumulative looseleaf system. A daily calendar might also be made available, showing the current status of every bill introduced, the committee action if any, and the legislative day upon which the bill will be open for amendment on second reading or for final passage on third reading.

Mutual "back-scratching" seems to be almost inevitable in the short session. But little business ordinarily is transacted during the first few weeks. The tendency is for bills to accumulate in committees and in the various channels of enactment. Short-session legislators are all conscious of the disastrous consequences of delay upon bills of their introduction. Usually by mid-session a wave of resentment on the part of all those having bills unacted upon has reached such proportions as to offer a potential threat of retaliation. The jam is then broken by a series of bargains and concessions, express or implied, and the race against time moves into the home stretch. This situation can best be remedied by a forceful demand from the chair for a prompt and routine expedition of business from the very beginning.

An attempt has been made in Indiana to ease the pressure of the closing days of the session by a rule requiring unanimous consent for the introduction of bills after the expiration of the first forty-five days. In operation, this rule has failed to accomplish its purpose. The member desiring to present a bill during the period covered by the rule merely asks consent of the house to introduce the measure, and no one ever voices objection.

Approximately one-third of the time of a lower house in each session is consumed in roll calls. The roll of the Indiana House of Representatives was called 518 times during the session of 1935. The usually estimated time for taking and verifying a roll call is twelve minutes, and the average legislative day is five and one-half hours in duration. Thus it will be seen that of the total of sixty-one days allotted by the constitution as a biennial season for lawmaking, which incidentally includes Sundays and two holidays, about nineteen legislative days were required for calling the roll.

Roll calls are not to be discouraged. They are much more satisfactory than a mere voice or division vote, and a roll call upon every step of the progress of important measures would tend to make of the legislature a more responsible body. Members frequently hesitate to demand a roll-call vote on a question of consequence, solely because of the time required in calling the roll.

In several states the roll-call problem seems to have been solved satisfactorily by the installation of mechanical voting devices. By means of electrical switches upon members' desks they are enabled to cast their votes simultaneously and with a minimum of confusion. The vote is displayed immediately upon an indicator in full view of the members, and at the same time is permanently recorded by means of a photostatic impression or by perforation upon a specially designed ballot. The complaint of frequent errors in the hasty recording of oral votes by clerks is overcome by mechanical precision. In Wisconsin and Virginia, with lower houses identical in size to that of Indiana, a complete roll call is now taken and recorded within one minute by mechanized voting. Thus science now makes available the use of several additional legislative days for committee study and for a more intelligent consideration of proposed legislation. The adoption of such a device should expedite business to a point where the frenzy of the last days could be avoided and perhaps even an earlier adjournment could be made possible.

An effort has been made herein to paint an authentic picture of the short session with some of its more apparent problems. A pessimistic note has not been intended. The short-session legislature is a time honored institution in state government and is likely to continue in substantially its present constitutional form for some time. However, a frank consideration of its shortcomings as they exist will convince the observer that a correction of the two major problems, that of a lack of continuity between sessions and that of an economical and efficient use of the limited time within sessions, should be expected to result in fewer and better laws.

No. 52

[MR. TREADWAY's article has spotlighted one of the serious limitations under which state legislatures labor. There are many others. The following article sets forth some major defects in state legislative organization and procedure and suggests remedies that would give us more effective democratic government.]

STRENGTHENING STATE LEGISLATURES [1]

by Lynton K. Caldwell

DECLINING prestige of legislative bodies has recently prompted inquiries looking to self-appraisal and reform in Congress and in legislatures of a number of the states. Dissatisfaction with the traditional organization and procedure of state legislatures has grown among legislators, who

[1] Lynton K. Caldwell, "Strengthening State Legislatures," *The American Political Science Review* (April, 1947), Vol. XLI, No. 2, pp. 281-289. Reprinted by permission of the American Political Science Association. The footnotes in the original version are omitted here.

undertake the perplexities of present-day law-making with inadequate assistance and ineffective machinery. Legislation was seldom a simple problem, but it is to-day more difficult than at any time in our national history. As the responsibilities thrust upon legislatures are increased, so must the tools and processes of legislation be improved if the quality of legislation is to meet the needs which call it forth.

To assist in the reappraisal and review of state legislative organization and procedure, twelve general suggestions for strengthening state legislatures have been reported to the Council of State Governments by a committee of state officials. Appointed in November, 1945, by the Board of Managers of the Council, the Committee on Legislative Processes and Procedures developed its report after broadly surveying legislative theory and practice and selecting for recommendation to the states those measures of most general application. Dealing with the problems of state legislatures generally, the committee decided at an early date to direct its attention to the strengthening of state legislatures as presently constituted. Questions of reapportionment, of representation in the legislature, proportional representation, unicameralism, and certain mechanics of procedure such as electrical voting were not treated in the final report. The committee held that any attempt to develop a program covering all phases of the legislative process would diffuse its efforts to the extent of defeating its purpose. Certain questions, notably legislative reapportionment, of particular interest in several states were not issues of primary concern to the greater number of states. Recognizing that no program could be drafted which would answer the needs of all states, the committee chose to limit its recommendations to those measures which might be expected to bring greatest benefit to the greatest number of the states.

Following are the recommendations of the committee, with brief comment on their application:

1. *Legislative Sessions.* Restrictions upon the length of regular sessions should be removed. If legislatures may be called into special session by governors or by a majority of their members without undue restrictions upon the measures to be considered, the question of annual versus biennial sessions is largely resolved.

The increasing number and complexity of public questions requiring legislative consideration have made obsolete traditional restrictions upon the length of legislative sessions. That constitutional and statutory limits upon the length of sessions do prevent legislatures from sitting as long as the effective discharge of their duties might require is suggested by a comparison of the average length of sessions in states which have restricted duration and those that do not. In 1943, the average length of sessions in twenty-six states limiting duration was approximately 73 days. In the twenty-two states having no restrictions, the average length was 114 days. Allowing for differences among the states with respect to how the actual number of days of a legislative session is calculated, and recognizing that for some states all legislative business may be adequately dispatched within the limits imposed upon the length of the session, the committee concluded that little was to be gained by restricting session length, whereas much was likely to be lost.

After considering annual versus biennial sessions, the committee concluded that no general recommendation could be made to the states with respect to this question. Six states—California, Massachusetts, New Jersey, New York, Rhode Island, and South Carolina—now have annual sessions; but provisions for special sessions permit the legislatures of all states to meet annually, or even more frequently if necessary. During 1946, seventeen state legislatures convened in special session, and in California, Illinois, Michigan, and New Jersey two special sessions were held; three were held in Arizona and four in Ohio. In a number of states, restrictions upon the agenda of special sessions limit their value as a substitute for annual sessions. The committee concluded that although regular annual sessions might not be necessary for a considerable number of the states, consideration should be given to liberalizing the rights of the legislature with respect to the measures to be considered in special sessions, thus in large measure resolving the question of annual versus biennial sessions.

2. *Legislators—Compensation.* From the viewpoint of good public service, the compensation of state legislators is now too low. Annual salaries sufficient to permit competent persons to serve in legislatures without financial sacrifice should be provided by statute. Salaries should not be fixed by constitutional provision.

Whether increased compensation for legislators will result in a more competent and independent legislature is a moot question. The committee believed increased legislative compensation justified upon the basis of the present responsibilities of legislators. Obviously, no uniform level of legislative salaries could be prescribed for all states. Nevertheless, the committee felt that in most states a review of the compensation of the legislators was in order, and particularly that the method of fixing salaries by constitutional provision should be abandoned. It was believed that the sensitivity of legislators to unfavorable public response to increased legislative salaries would provide adequate check upon the legislature, and that it is unwise to freeze a particular pattern of compensation by writing it into the state constitution.

3. *Legislators—Terms.* In order to strengthen legislatures by increasing continuity of membership, the lengthening and staggering of legislative terms should be considered. In representative government, frequent elections are necessary. Experienced legislative leadership and smoothly operating legislative machinery likewise contribute to the attainment of democratic objectives.

There appears to be growing feeling among legislators that the variety and complexity of contemporary legislative problems places a higher premium on experience in the legislature and on continuity of legislative membership than in earlier days. Offsetting this consideration is the traditional reliance upon frequent elections to hold a legislature accountable to public opinion and responsive to changing public views. It was the belief of the committee that the possibilities of increasing continuity of membership and length of terms and, at the same time, providing for frequent elections had not been sufficiently explored by American legislative bodies. The staggering of legislative terms was therefore suggested as one way to reconcile these several desirable objectives.

Although no recommendation was made with respect to specific methods by which new legislators might be assisted in preparing for their responsibilities, the committee directed the attention of legislators to pre-session legislative conferences such as have been held with some regularity in Arkansas, Colorado, Connecticut, Georgia, Massachusetts, and North Carolina. Attention was called to the publication of legislative manuals in 35 states. These booklets describe the organization, rules, procedures, and reference and research aids of legislatures, and they have been found particularly useful in helping new legislators prepare to meet their responsibilities.

4. *Legislative Employees.* Skilled and essential full-time legislative employees should be appointed on the basis of merit and competence. The tenure of key legislative personnel should be unaffected by changes in party control, and as far as circumstances permit, the working conditions of legislative employees generally should not be less advantageous than those of employees in the executive and judicial departments.

Although the committee did not think that employees of the legislature should be appointed on the basis of merit system or civil service rules, it believed that methods should be explored to insure that legislative employees, however appointed, should be honest and competent, and should enjoy reasonable security of tenure. The application of scientific personnel administration with respect to legislative positions was viewed sympathetically, and the committee believed that in so far as possible the compensation and work conditions of employees in the legislative branch should not be less favorable than those obtaining elsewhere in state government. With respect to all questions concerning legislative employees, however, the committee kept in view the need for "closest confidence and cooperation between the legislator and his assistants," and emphasized that "adequate and competent service should be secured by methods which do not unduly restrict the legislator's choice of persons who are to work with him."

5. *Legislative Committees—Organization and Procedure.*   Committees should be reduced in number wherever practicable and organized with regard to related subject-matter, equalization of work, and cooperation between legislative houses.

Committee meetings should be scheduled and announced so as to prevent conflicting duties for committee members, and a permanent and public record of committee action should be kept.

In the sixteen years since Winslow's study of state legislative committees, little progress has been made in reducing the number of committees so as to be commensurate with the time, energy, and information of individual legislators. A survey in 1946 by the Council of State Governments indicated that senate committees averaged slightly over 32 and house committees slightly less than 40. Although numerous inactive committees may not seriously encumber the legislative process, there is general agreement that the committee system in a majority of the states needs consolidation and reorganization.

The Committee on Legislative Processes and Procedures favored the reorganization of a reduced number of committees around topics of major legislative concern, and in so far as practicable, the provision of equivalent house and senate committees. Substantially equivalent committees not necessarily bearing the same title, nor in all cases having identical jurisdiction, will greatly facilitate joint legislative hearings, permit economies in the provision of research facilities, and may simplify relations between the legislature and the governor. Systematic administration of the committee system was urged, with schedules of committee meetings established and published so as to be fully available to committee members and to the public. Moreover, the records of committee action should be permanently preserved, so that the disposition of measures by committees and the vote of each committee member on each bill could be a matter of public record. The Committee on Legislative Processes and Procedures did not believe that committees should be required to report all bills, but it agreed that a record of committee non-action upon bills should be reported to the legislature before the close of each legislative session.

6. *Legislative Committees—Public Hearings.* Provision should be made for public hearings on all major bills, and advanced notice of hearings should be published and made readily available, giving time and place of hearing and subject-matter of legislation to be heard, and wherever possible indicating the number and title of bills. Rules of procedure by committees governing hearings should likewise be published and made readily available.

A major aspect of the legislative process is the representation of public views. Public hearings on major legislative proposals strengthen and supplement the representative character of legislative assemblies. Public hearings may have an educational value to legislators and to the public at large. Where hearings are properly announced, conducted impartially, and testimony and findings made widely available, they add greatly to public confidence in the legislative process.

Although hearings on all bills are held in Connecticut, Massachusetts, Nebraska, Wisconsin, and in the Illinois Senate, the Committee on Legislative Processes and Procedures considered that while hearings on all bills might be desirable, the essential requisite was that there be hearings on those measures of major public concern. In some states, hearings on all bills would diffuse the energy and attention of legislators to the detriment of legislation generally.

The importance of records, transcripts, and unpublished testimony to the legislative history of a bill was recognized by the Committee, and it was recommended that on the completion of hearings all committee papers and records be delivered to the legislative reference library for indexing and preservation. The committee urged that "regular records should be kept of all committee meetings . . . should cover time, place, committee members present and absent, the names of all persons appearing at hearings in favor of or against a measure, whom each represents, and a summarized statement as to the disposition of the measure by the committee in executive session."

7. *Legislative Councils and Interim Committees.* Provision for legislative councils or interim committees with adequate clerical and research facilities deserves serious consideration. These services can be provided most readily and effectively through a legislative reference bureau.

Although at least fifteen states have now established legislative councils or comparable agencies, the original legislative-council idea has been modified considerably as it has spread among the states. In the view of the committee, this adaptation of the council idea to the particular needs of the several states has been as desirable as it has been inevitable. States with long-established interim committee traditions may not need the type of council which has been notably successful in Connecticut, Kansas, and Maryland. There is room for further experiment among the states with councils or committees to provide for the establishment of priorities in the legislative program, to give focus and direction to legislative research activities, and to represent the legislature generally during the interim between regular sessions. The committee commended the council "idea" rather than a particular pattern of organization.

8. *Reference, Research, Bill Drafting, and Statutory Revision Services.* Legislative reference, research, bill drafting, and statutory revision services should be reviewed in each state, and strengthened wherever necessary by improved organization and more adequate staffing and appropriations.

Concomitant to the council idea is the provision of adequate fact-finding —research and technical legislative services of which bill-drafting and statute revision are particularly important. Although the legislative reference bureau actually antedates the legislative council and is considerably more widespread (32 states now have some form of legislative reference service), states have increasingly established or expanded legislative reference services as primary research agencies for legislative councils or advisory committees.

9. *Introduction of Legislation.* Consideration should be given to limiting by rule the period during a legislative session when new bills may be introduced. Provision should be made for the drafting, filing, and printing of bills before the opening of the session. All bills and important amendments introduced during a session should be printed promptly after introduction, and whenever possible they should be inspected before printing by bill drafters or revision clerks.

Publication of manuals covering the form, style, and grammatical construction of bills is suggested.

Pre-session bill-drafting is provided in at least thirty-two states, and pre-session filing is permitted in Massachusetts, New Hampshire, Vermont, and Nebraska, and has been recommended in New York by the Joint Legislative Committee on Legislative Methods, Practices, Procedures, and Expenditures and in Connecticut by the Legislative Council. Coupled with a limitation by rule on the period during which new bills may be introduced into a legislature, these provisions should go far toward regularizing the flow of measures into the legislature, and should reduce the so-called "jam" of legislation at the close of sessions.

The committee believed that the inspection and printing of bills does not receive adequate attention in most states. With respect to the printing of bills and major amendments, the committee concurred in the view of the Connecticut Legislative Council that "there is no other way in which legislature, press, and the public can be guaranteed prompt and easy access to every proposed measure." In order to encourage better preparation of proposed legislation, the committee suggested the publication of bill-drafting manuals, covering the form, style, and grammatical construction of bills. Arizona, Illinois, Maine, Mississippi, New Jersey, New Mexico, Oregon, Texas, Washington, and Wisconsin have to date prepared or published manuals of this sort.

10. *Legislative Rules.* The rules of legislative houses should be reviewed and revised wherever necessary to expedite legislative procedure, with due regard for adequate deliberation on measures and fairness to minority parties.

Permanent standing committees or a joint committee on legislative organization, rules, and procedure should be established in some form by each legislature.

Recognizing the impracticality of any effort to review the legislative rules of the states generally, the committee urged that the legislative houses of each state regularly reconsider their rules and revise them to expedite procedure, provide for adequate deliberation, and insure fairness to minority parties.

11. *Legislative Finance.* The legislature should provide for a budget adequate to meet all probable expenditures during a fiscal period. Provision for a fiscal officer responsible for the centralized custody of legislative personnel, payroll, and expenditure records of each house, and the supervision of legislative expenditures, should be considered.

In dealing with problems of legislative finance, the committee drew heavily upon the experience of the New York Joint Legislative Committee which had made similar, but more detailed, recommendations to the New York legislature. The objective of the committee recommendation was to provide order and accountability for legislative fiscal affairs. How the states could best regularize their legislative fiscal activities was left to them to decide, but with the suggestion that a legislative fiscal officer be designated or appointed. It was believed that existing budgetary and accounting machinery within the executive branch might be utilized for this purpose by the legislatures of some states.

12. *Local and Special Legislation.* Consideration and settlement of claims against the state should be delegated to judicial or to administrative agencies, and general, optional, or home-rule legislation should provide positive sub-

stitutes for special legislation affecting cities, counties, and other political subdivisions of the states, particularly in matters of purely local concern.

Although Illinois, Michigan, and New York have established courts of claims, and although in several states certain categories of claims may be settled by the attorney-general or secretary of state, most states continue to burden their legislatures with an excessive amount of private legislation. The committee urged the states to delegate this time-consuming function to designated administrative or judicial agencies capable of rendering decisions on merit and making, within reasonable limits, monetary awards.

With respect to local or special legislation, the committee concurred with the Council committee on state-local relations, which has recommended the adoption of general, optional, or home-rule legislation in place of the large volume of law enacted every session in many states specifying in detailed terms the authority and obligations of local government.

Concluding Observations. Although legislative organization and procedure customarily receive more attention among the states than in the federal government, the recent reorganization of Congress has renewed interest and stimulated action in the legislatures of many of the states, and the recent report by a committee of experienced state legislators and officials should give added impetus and direction. The states have not been afraid to experiment with the structure and operations of their legislative houses, but the accelerated tempo of contemporary life requires that their legislatures more rapidly than ever reorganize themselves to meet a seemingly ever-increasing volume of problems and responsibilities. . . . The report of the committee of the Council of State Governments should be of constructive assistance in the framing and consideration of measures intended to strengthen all legislatures.

Chapter XV

ADVISING THE LEGISLATOR

[ANYONE who is familiar with the job of the legislator knows it is impossible for him to be an expert on all the subjects with which he deals. Also, anyone who is familiar with the character of a free, democratic political system knows that many individuals and groups are anxious to advise the legislator. It is important, therefore, to see both how individuals and groups seek to advise and influence the legislator and how he, in turn, seeks and gets independent, impartial and expert advice.]

No. 53

[PROFESSOR SABINE, in his penetrating essay "What Is the Matter with Representative Government?" analyzes the basic nature of the representative legislature and shows why an ever-growing number of Americans have come to rely more and more on the lobby to represent them and their views.]

WHAT IS THE MATTER WITH REPRESENTATIVE GOVERNMENT? [1]

by George H. Sabine

HARDLY more than a century ago, the hopes of liberals were centered in the creation of representative legislatures. Popular assemblies were established where none existed, and everywhere the assembly was made representative of a larger part of the population. In the end the suffrage was extended in many countries to approximately the whole adult population, of both sexes and of all degrees of wealth, education, and rank. And yet, with this process now practically complete, success has brought disillusionment rather than elation. In the United States we have the last

[1] George H. Sabine, "What Is the Matter with Representative Government?", *The North American Review* (May, 1921), Vol. 213, pp. 587-597. Reprinted by permission of the author and *The North American Review*.

step still fresh in mind, the enfranchisement of women. It is safe to say that the great majority even of those who favored it were rather listless; certainly few believe that it solves any serious political problem or that most legislation will be appreciably better because women have the vote. Broadening the basis of representation has ceased to seem a very important gain in the progress of government.

The fact is that as representative assemblies have become matters of course, we have very generally lost confidence in them as organs for making law. It is natural that in war-time, legislatures should decline in popular estimation, but I am not referring merely to that. The change was going on long before the War. Americans had long been accustomed to holding their legislatures in rather slight esteem, to thinking that the member of Congress or of the State legislature is not a very intelligent or a very important person. In fact, one would have to go a long way back in American politics to reach a time when election to Congress was an honor eagerly sought by men of ability and standing. The case of the State legislatures is much worse. If anything is written large across the histories of our states, it is popular distrust of the legislature. Our State constitutions, with their detailed restrictions upon legislative power, are monuments to this distrust.

The freedom of our legislatures has been limited in two chief ways. It has been partly lost through the assumption of legislative functions directly by the people, but still more has it been hampered by the ascendancy of executive officers, who have had to assume more and more responsibility for getting laws framed and passed.

It was natural for Americans to assume that the democratic way to settle a question was to leave it to the people, and the more they distrusted their representatives, the more they tended to think that leaving it to the people meant letting the people vote on it. Since they did not trust the legislature to pass the laws they wanted, they invented ways of initiating legislation. And since they feared that the legislature would pass laws they did not want, they reserved to themselves the right to pass upon an enactment before it became law. More and more of our State law was written into the State constitution, which as a rule could be amended only by a referendum. Thus the initiative and the referendum were symptoms of the low opinion which Americans had of their State legislatures, but they were also causes of the further decay of those bodies, for the surest way to make a place unacceptable to an able man is to make it a place where little or nothing can be done.

In the case of the Federal Government, Congress lost power mainly to executive officers. Not that it tamely surrendered, or that its legal powers were restricted. Except in unusual circumstances, Congress has been tenacious of its Constitutional independence, and has rather enjoyed waging guerilla warfare against a President or Cabinet officer. But in the long run, circumstances have been too much for Congress. The power of the President, even over legislation, has steadily increased, and more and more Congress has had to accept his leadership. No theoretical independence could free Congress from the results of the President's superior strategic position. He could bring public opinion to bear upon them in a way they dared not neglect. For there can be no doubt that the public by preference sides with the President. It may grow tired at times of what orators call "one-man government," but when some action is definitely wanted, the public rather likes to see the President put it through. It is in fact a definite gain in popular government to be able to hold some one person responsible for legislation, as for other results. The President, paradoxically enough, has become the people's agent for keeping the people's representatives up to their job. Our most successful Governors in the last twenty years have been men who could deal with State legislatures in the same fashion.

The public esteem in which the legislature is held has thus tended to decline in comparison with that given to other parts of the Government. Indeed, it is not too much to say that our legislatures have come to be distrusted, and that a very large number of persons feel that our so-called representative bodies are the part of the Government which least represent them in those matters which they deem of the greatest importance. It should be noted, however, that distrust of legislatures has not meant distrust of legislation. Particular acts may be condemned, but so far as methods are concerned, we look to legislation for the remedy of abuses almost as much as ever we did. In fact, this faith is inevitable. Social and economic relations in an industrial society have refused to become stable and social processes have undergone a steady and amazing acceleration. Such changes call for corresponding changes in the legal relations of the parties interested. Hence the law has had to change much faster in the last fifty years than ever before in human history. And some sort of legislative machinery has to labor at this task. Hence the appalling volume of law that our national, State, and municipal legislatures have poured upon the world. One may believe in particular cases that much of this law was ill-made, but he cannot escape the fact that one way or another most of it had to be made. There is no reason to suppose that the next fifty years will see any diminution of the need for revising the law.

The two outstanding features of the present situation are the need of legislating and our loss of confidence in the agencies by which legislating is done. Since there is no possibility of doing away with the need for legislation, the only question is the possibility of more satisfactory agencies. In particular we need to get at the seat of our distrust of elected representatives. Representation, doubtless, we must have, since direct lgislation is out of the question both by reason of the size of modern States and equally by reason of the complexity of the questions involved. Along what lines may we expect our law-making institutions to move under the stress of the present discontent? But first, can we explain more clearly *why* representatives have lost touch with their constituencies and lost the confidence of those who elect them?

The general notion of representation is of course very old. For English-speaking people especially it was not at all an invention of the age of democratization. There was one element, however, in the early notion of representation which has been almost wholly lost in the course of modern political evolution. In earlier times it was a *community* which was represented. The representative was the spokesman for a unified group which might not unreasonably be expected to express itself with one voice. It was a unit in fact, in the sense that the interests of the members really were for the most part confined to the local group, and it was a unit also in the minds of the members. The community was relatively small. It was economically self-sufficing to a very large extent, and there was relatively little communication with other communities. In consequence, the interests of every person in it were almost exclusively local and were very largely bound up with the welfare of the locality. Its social and economic organization was exceedingly simple, compared with modern communities. There really were group interests and these interests really could be represented.

Moreover, the members were definitely conscious of the community as a real being. If we were to borrow a modern idea, we should say that the units of representation were corporations. The local bodies acted in all respects as if they were persons. A county was in no sense merely the indefinite number of persons who happened to live in a given area. In fact, though the word county (*comitatus*) does refer to a geographical district, it means equally the county court, or local representative body, which chooses members to sit in Parliament. The county has duties, rights, guilt, judgment, will, and organs for performing or expressing these. The looseness of the individual from the locality in which he lives, which is natural to our way of thinking, is essentially a modern idea. The correlated notion of the locality as merely a square mile of land inhabited by some indefinite number of persons is equally modern. In the past the local group was a community. Sometimes it was a guild with a definite unity of economic interest, but in any case the members were united by ties which seemed to them entirely tangible and the group thus formed was in their eyes a permanent, living, acting entity. Representation always involved the idea of such a unified group which spoke through its sworn mouthpiece.

The evolution of modern social and economic conditions, and the accompanying growth of modern government, have conspired, one might almost say, to crush the life out of the smaller units and localities which were once its living elements. It was inevitable under the circumstances that government should become more and more highly centralized, and that localities should be subjected more and more to centralized control. In the nature of the case the small local group could not preserve its individuality and self-sufficiency. More and more politics became a relation between two sharply contrasted extremes. On the one hand is the very powerful national state which knows no limit to its legal competence, which claims the power, —and sometimes exercises it,—of regulating all phases of the citizen's life, from his religion to his industry and from his education to his hygiene. On the other hand there is the citizen himself whose local attachments and communal bonds often have singularly little to do with his political activities and relationships. No doubt he still belongs to a community of some sort, but the community has largely ceased to be local and is not at all a political entity; on the other hand, the local political districts in which he votes have never become communities in any real sense of the word.

Thus we come to our present notion of representation, which is purely geographical and numerical. The constituency has become merely the indefinite number of heterogeneous individuals who happen to live inside an arbitrary line. If a State has sixteen members in Congress, a Congressional district is merely an area containing one-sixteenth of the population of the State. By no stretch of the imagination can the Congressional district be called a community: it need have no common interests; its people are held together by no conscious social bonds; and they may in fact be heterogeneous to any extent. The other units of local government are no different. Our cities are divided mechanically into wards; our States are divided mechanically into counties; and the States themselves, if they ever had any real unity, have ceased to have it. By this I mean that there is little or nothing in the social and economic relations between the people that correspond to the legal and political distinctions imposed upon them by the existence of the State.

Thus it is true almost universally that the local units of government have little real significance; the local governments do not stand for functionally active communities conforming to the interests and sentiments of the people. When we have wished to make really effective administrative units, such for example as the districts of the Federal Reserve Bank, we have had to neglect the legal frontiers between our local governing units. Is not this the

fundamental reason why the claim to States' rights and local self-government, which has been acclaimed persistently as an ideal in American politics,
has had so little practical effect? But more especially is it not at the root
of our difficulty with representation? How can one man represent that
which has no unity and stands for no definite purpose? Is it not easy to
see why men feel that a representative who is shared among a heterogeneous mass is no representative at all? In the nature of the case he
cannot stand for that which vitally interests anyone, for if he does, he
becomes antagonistic to someone else who has an equal claim upon him.
Thus he is smoothed down to the level of the man who is everybody's friend
—the very symbol of futility. In a word, our political representation has
lost touch with the social and economic relations which make up most of
the life of the community.

The fact is that while political representation has adhered rigidly to the
locality in the mere geographical sense, the general tendency of social and
political development has been to make human communities independent of
locality to a degree that would have been utterly inconceivable a century
ago. Stripped of their traditional associations in the local community,
men have set themselves to the making of new ties and new associations
which are for the most part not local. Wide and easy communication make
it practically certain that human associations will never again depend so
much upon locality as they have in the past. What is essential to an association is not that the members should be in the same place, but that they
should be convinced of a common interest in uniting, a common purpose to
be attained, a common cause to be served. If this interest is a permanent
one and if it is one which can obtain the adherence of large numbers of
men, great and enduring associations can result which awaken a high degree
of loyalty in their members. There is one such association which has
played a great part in human life and which is by no means modern, viz.,
the Church, but the last generation has seen an amazing proliferation of
associations of this sort. We have, for example, all the manifold associations
with an economic basis,—the chambers of commerce, the employers' associations, the federations of labor, the cooperative consumers' leagues, the
farmers' marketing and purchasing associations. It is extraordinary how
easily and rapidly men ally themselves in these ways when the conditions
are right to make them aware of a community of interest. Moreover, by
no means are all these modern associations economic in origin. The lawyers'
bar associations, the physicians' medical associations, and the engineering
associations appeal in part no doubt to an economic motive, but certainly to
many other motives besides. The many associations of scholars are for the
most part not economic at all. In general, any permanent basis of common

interest that can be furthered by cooperation offers the ground for an association of this sort.

The great number of these non-local associations that are based on common interests, and the rapidity with which they grow in size and power, make a striking phenomenon of present-day society. They have increased as the local community has declined, and for the same reason: under modern conditions it is simply impossible that interests should be confined within the bounds of local groups. Modern men in increasing numbers are but loosely attached to local groups and on the other hand have more and more interests in common with other men who are widely scattered. The interests which unite them with other persons of the same occupation outside their locality may easily be more vital than those which unite them with their neighbors, and the associations which result may command a correspondingly larger share of their attention and loyalty. In short, they feel that this association, or its agents, is a more adequate representative of their real interests than the political representative whom they must share with all sorts and conditions of men because of the merely external identity of residence.

Though non-local associations based upon common interests have become a serious social phenomenon, it should be noted that they have not as yet attained the standing of a political phenomenon, at least in the United States. By this I mean that they are wholly outside the law, though of course not contrary to it. They are private associations and nothing more. Government does not recognize them or make any use of them, except under unusual circumstances. Indeed, it has sometimes tried to hinder them, especially in the case of labor organizations, though with no great success when many persons were convinced of their utility. I do not say that they have played no part in government. They have, for in many cases an important part of their purpose is to influence legislation. They try to supply indirectly the representation which their members do not feel that they get from their political representatives, but such activity is extra-legal; it is no part of the organized agencies by which our laws are made.

This extra-legal influence upon law-making, though it doubtless always existed in some degree, has grown to be one of the paradoxes of representative government. We solemnly elect our representatives and send them to the State or National capital to make our laws. But when we want something, or believe that something needs doing, we show little confidence that our representative will know about it or give his help if he knows. We forthwith begin to devise ways of convincing him that we want it and of putting pressure upon him to help us get it. What we actually rely on is the extra-legal, voluntary association which we feel can really be trusted to look after our interests. The merchant or manufacturer looks to his chamber of commerce or his employers' association to secure the legislation he needs or to prevent the legislation he fears. Even the citizen who wants nothing more from the legislature than an adequate provision for the public schools, finds that he must work through associations organized to bring political pressure to bear upon State officials. We are in the position of the man who kept a dog but had to do his own barking.

Thus every legislative assembly is attended by a great pulling and hauling of interests, but this in itself is not what makes the paradox. The purpose of law is to harmonize and adjust conflicting interests in behalf of the whole community. It is right and proper, therefore, that all interests should be represented and heard. The paradox lies in the fact that the real representatives are not the responsible legislators, that the most decisive part of the session is likely to take place in the lobby, and that the duly elected "representative" constantly tends to become a puppet whose strings are pulled by someone in the background. And the public generally expects that results will be got by pressure or persuasion, by methods which it vaguely hopes will be legitimate but which it knows often are not so. Thus our laws are passed under conditions which are merely another chapter in the old story of bad government: power without responsibility and responsibility without power. The real representative who commands the support of an organized and interested part of the voters is a private person who need only keep on the right side of the corrupt practices act, while the man who is elected ostensibly to make law is politically responsible to an unorganized constituency which has no unified purpose to be represented. Is it strange that men with real ability and serious purposes should be loath to undertake such a job?

In the meantime, organization for the cooperative furthering of common interests grows steadily and rapidly. It is idle to blind ourselves to the fact that there are great possibilities of danger in this. A powerful association to promote a particular interest becomes a public menace when it uses its power in an irresponsible or purely selfish manner. But of course it is equally idle to suppose that we can influence such associations by treating them as if they were somehow abnormal. The danger lies not so much in the fact that they are powerful, as in the fact that they are irresponsible. Both labor unions and employers' associations as we know them have been organized mainly to wage war on their enemies and to win advantages for the interests they represent, whatever other interests may suffer in the process. So long as they remain of this sort they are seeds of disorder; it is just this which no statesmanlike solution of the problem can tolerate. Conflict of interests we shall always have and these conflicts will call for continual readjustment. But the adjustment must itself be an obligation upon the organizations which exist to maintain the interests. They must be made responsible for the adjustment of conflicts and for a due regard to other interests.

When an organization reaches a certain degree of power, it is really a pretense to go on treating it as if it were merely a private and more or less casual association. Already there exist associations both of labor and of capital able to exercise a power of life or death over the industries upon which the community has to live. Though nominally voluntary, they exert a control over their members which is sometimes more binding than law itself. In fact, they have at their command much of the psychological apparatus that goes to the making of law. In a word, they are institutions, or at least they are clearly on the road to becoming institutions, though they lack recognition. In one way or another, government must take account of these vast organizations; it must utilize them as responsible agencies in the public control over the vital organs of the community.

The problem of representative government is to get back to a representation of vital interests by responsible representatives. It is not my purpose to discuss the plans by which it has been proposed to bring this about. Proportional representation would at least permit men to group themselves as their interests might dictate. The representation of industrial interests permitted by the German Constitution [of 1919] is a recognition of the problem, if not a solution. Perhaps in the end we shall be driven to the much more radical expedient of organizing our basic industries as self-governing units having more or less of legal competence and subject more or less to some kind of outside regulation. Such plans for the future contain necessarily a large element of speculation. But it is not speculation to say that representative government as it now exists is far from being an unequivocal success or that it has grievously disappointed the hopes which liberals built upon it. It is not speculation to hazard the forecast that representation will never again be made effective upon a merely local or geographical basis. The modern community has outgrown the limits of locality, which, from the beginning of man's experience down to the end of the eighteenth century, were natural to all communities. When essential human interests and the associations built upon them have ceased to be local, it is idle to suppose that locality can continue to serve as a sufficient basis for political representation. We cannot go on forever with a twentieth century society and an eighteenth century system of government.

No. 54

[SHOULD the lobby be abolished? Does it serve any function in the American political system? Are those who engage in lobbying the representatives of evil interests engaged in subverting the democratic system? In other words, should the "pressure boys" be abolished or do they represent a valuable part of American political life? Too often the lobby, the "pressure boys," and lobbying have been the object of an ill-considered attack by newspapers, magazines, and reformers. There is another side of the case to be considered before any final judgment can be made.

Mr. Henry A. Bellows, the author of the following article, was at one time a member of the Federal Radio Commission. Following this work he was engaged as the legislative counsel for the radio industry of the United States. In this latter capacity he frequently appeared before Congressional committees and gained much firsthand information on the contributions of the lobby to American politics. His article "In Defense of Lobbying" is based on his close association with the federal government as an administrator and as a member of the "third house."]

IN DEFENSE OF LOBBYING [1]

by Henry A. Bellows

NO other trade in America to-day is subject to such widespread vilification as that of the lobbyist. The departed gangster is at least deemed worthy of a flamboyant funeral, and uproarious crowds cheer the acquittal of a confessed beer runner, but for the lobbyist nothing is audible but scorn and contumely. Ordinarily a Congressional investigation is a ready road to popularity; the man who has been quizzed by a Senatorial committee emerges a hero. But the pilloried lobbyist has no such consolation. Before his testimony is fairly out of his mouth, he is on the front pages of the newspapers, a hapless target for national reviling. Whenever any form of financial interests conceives that it has a right to present its views on pending legislation, and to try to convince Senators and Congressmen that they ought to give fair consideration to those views, then the hue and cry begins.

There is a natural reason for this. The financial interests have, or are supposed to have, lots of money, and some of them have been found none

[1] Henry A. Bellows, "In Defense of Lobbying," *Harper's Magazine* (December, 1935), Vol. 172, pp. 96-107. Reprinted by permission of Mrs. Philip W. Pillsbury and *Harper's Magazine*.

too scrupulous in its employment, particularly in connection with State and municipal affairs. There have been ugly revelations in connection with expenditures for propaganda. A well-filled "war-chest" inevitably evokes the horrid specter of bribery, and even though in recent times there have been no proved Congressional instances of such corruption, the public is prone to believe that where there is so much smoke there must be some fire. Above all, a single egregious blunder, such as the fraudulent York telegrams (although no lobbyist deserving of the title would be stupid enough to countenance such practices) casts its black shadow over every effort to affect by whatever means the legislative process.

The very term "lobbying" is in itself suggestive of sinister methods. It paints a grim picture of a furtive individual lurking in the byways of the Capitol, buttonholing a Senator here, a Congressman there, whispering secrets into quivering ears, a stealthy, malevolent perverter of truth. And in recent years this hideous figment of the imagination has grown to gigantic proportions. Not content with his pernicious activities beneath the dome of the Capitol, the lobbyist must needs reach out into every city and hamlet, and there stir up tornadoes of propaganda that writhe their way back to Washington in the form of myriads of letters and telegrams.

All very horrible, no doubt, but far from the whole story. Go to any committee hearing on an important bill. Who is that man in the witness chair, answering innumerable questions, generally of a technical nature, and, as he finally withdraws, receiving the cordial thanks of the committee chairman? He, strange to say, is a lobbyist. He is paid to represent a group or an industry for the express purpose of affecting the course of legislation. It is quite possible that he will ultimately urge those whose interests he represents to communicate with their Senators and Congressmen regarding the pending bill. The members of the committee know all this, and yet it is clear that they look upon him, not as Public Enemy Number One, but as a serviceable and trustworthy ally.

The plain fact is that lobbying, properly conducted, is not only a perfectly legitimate exercise of a Constitutional right, but a direct benefit both to Congress and to the country at large. Most important bills involve the consideration of complex problems, which can be solved only on the basis of long practical experience and careful research. The lobbyist places at the disposal of Congress the collective experience of those whom he represents. That in so doing he is unbiased he would be the last to claim. Of course he is biased, but so are all the other witnesses, including, be it noted, such representatives of the government itself as may testify. The whole business of Federal law-making is, in this respect, remarkably like the functioning of the courts. An attorney is not expected to be nonpartisan, and the judge does not condemn him because he brings out the strongest points in favor of his client. Rather, the ends of justice are considered as best served when both sides are fully and ably represented, when all the evidence is clearly set forth, and when judge and jury have the benefit of whatever technical guidance the issues in the case may require.

The analysis and discussion of a proposed law, if it is to amount to anything more than superficial guesswork, normally requires weeks or months of intensive preparation. It cannot be done adequately by untrained persons, or even by experts who can devote to it only their spare time. Many a capable executive makes a lamentable witness before a Congressional committee because he neither speaks nor understands the special language of legislation; many an eloquent lawyer falls down when searching questions reveal his limited familiarity with practical details. The experienced lobbyist, on the other hand, intimately acquainted with his subject through long association with the people he represents, and fully cognizant of the special complexities of legislative procedure, including the peculiarly difficult technic of phraseology, frequently can and does render invaluable assistance in the shaping of proposed laws.

Proof of this is spread all over the pages of the published records of legislative hearings. Obviously there is nothing secretive or surreptitious about a type of lobbying that is thus publicly recorded, and yet lobbying within the ordinary definition of the term it certainly is. It is an effort to affect the course of pending legislation; it is openly conducted in the interests of some particular group, and not infrequently it costs a good deal of money. And yet the records show both its value to the public and the almost invariable cordiality with which it is welcomed by committee members.

During the past eight years I have appeared many times on behalf of one industry before committees of both Houses. I have yet to experience anything other than the utmost consideration, and I have never left the witness stand without the friendly thanks of the chairman, and frequently of other members of the committee. Even when the questioning was incisive, as it frequently was, the purpose remained perfectly clear: the committee collectively was trying to elicit whatever information might help it in drafting a satisfactory bill. I never pretended to be anything but what I was—the legislative representative of a single industry; but whenever legislation affecting that industry was under consideration, I always found that Senators and Congressmen were eager to understand its point of view and the reasons therefor. If, in the end, I did not always succeed in convincing them, it was never for lack of ample opportunity. I am quite sure that this summary of personal experience can be duplicated by almost everyone who has practiced this form of lobbying.

It will, of course, be argued that this is not the type of lobbying to which anyone seriously objects, that it is a far cry to the activities which warn Senators and Congressmen of dire consequences at the polls if they do not vote in such and such a way, that shake down avalanches of telegrams and letters on their defenseless heads, and, going one step farther, in the ominous vocabulary of practical politics "put pressure" on them.

After all, however, our entire system of government is based on the principle of representation, and each legislator must consider all questions of national scope as they may affect both the general welfare and that of the locality which has empowered him to represent it. A keen and constant interest in what people think "back home" is by no means, as is so often inferred, exclusively indicative of vote-counting spinelessness. It is distinctly and properly a part of the job, inherent in the provisions of the Constitution itself. The lobbyist in Washington, from the very nature of his residence and work, is commonly without immediate State affiliations; he must study pending legislation from the national rather than from the local point of view. Is he, therefore, to assume that Senators and Congressmen will disregard their direct accountability to those whose special interests they are required to safeguard?

The people "back home," however, normally have very limited access to detailed information about legislation. It is seldom that an issue is so sharply defined that the question is simply one of voting for or against a bill in its entirety. Even those whose interests are directly involved are, as a rule, far from clear in their own minds as to the precise things that they do or do not want. And yet, with complete propriety, every Senator and Congressman is eager to know what his constituents, and particularly the better-informed among them, really think about the matters on which his vote will be recorded.

At this point the lobby inevitably broadens its scope. Consider any extended group which may be directly affected, either favorably or the reverse, by some pending item of legislation. Its lobbyist has painstakingly analyzed the bill; he knows, as well as anyone can know, what effect it is likely to have on those whom he represents. He understands what amendments will increase the benefits or mitigate the hardships. From all over the country he receives urgent calls for information and advice, in order that the members of his group—and it does not matter whether they are producers or consumers, employers or labor, lenders or borrowers—may more intelligently transmit their own views to their Senators and Congressmen.

And so the lobbyist perforce launches a service of information. If he knows his business, his reports attempt no concealment of their frankly partisan nature. They do not try to hide their origin by masquerading as impartial news. They are careful never knowingly to misstate facts, and clearly distinguish between established facts and the inferences drawn therefrom. Above all, the wise lobbyist sees to it that his reports never contain a single line that cannot invite the widest publicity, and that is not actually, in substance at least, a matter of record. Provided such legislative service is honest within the requirements just set forth, it may be intensely partisan.

"Propaganda!" shout the hot-heads. Of course it is propaganda, and why not? How long since it has become a crime to disseminate legislative information? Is the political education of the American people to be left entirely to public agencies with an itch for self-perpetuation? The lobbyist's report is no whit more selfishly motivated than many a departmental press release or franked Congressional speech. Admit that it is not the whole truth; its openly proclaimed source is a virtual guarantee of that. Nobody is capable of telling the whole truth about any important legislative matter; otherwise there would be no debates in Congress. The legislative news service sent out by lobbyists, provided always it makes no concealment of its origin, is a definite and wholly legitimate contribution to public education, and to brand it as in any way improper is rank injustice.

Such information is sent out for the manifest and admitted purpose of influencing public opinion "back home." What are the recipients to do with it? File it, read or unread, in the wastebasket? By all means, if it does not coincide with their views. But if it provides satisfactory answers to the questions they have been asking themselves, and if they feel that they are in any way personally concerned in the matter, then it is not only their right, but actually their duty, to see that their chosen representatives are made acquainted with their opinions.

Occasionally some Congressional sleuth makes the amazing discovery that since many of the communications he receives are similar or identical in wording, they must have had a common origin. Certainly they had. How many good citizens and conscientious voters know enough about the details of any significant piece of pending legislation to frame a really helpful letter or telegram regarding it? Even the relatively well-informed and actively interested are commonly inarticulate when it comes to giving specific recommendations for action. And yet, as the numerous insertions in the Congressional Record demonstrate, Senators and Congressmen are keenly interested in such communications from their constituents as evince genuine understanding and provide logical reasons for the opinions set forth. It is, therefore, quite understandable that the lobbyist is constantly being asked to suggest the most effective wording for such letters and telegrams.

This, of course, leads into the dark side of the picture—the obvious opportunity for fraud. The evidence in the matter of the York telegrams is conclusive, and there have been other instances in which there has undoubtedly been a greater or less degree of falsification. Any mass appeal for signatures, even if it is conducted with the utmost scrupulousness—which it generally is not—always involves some element of deception, as anyone who has ever dealt with widely circulated petitions well knows. The things that otherwise sane men and women will sign, and the uses to which they will lend their names, mostly from an easy-going inability to say "No," are unbelievable. And when the request is coupled with an offer to pay for the telegram—a wholly vicious and indefensible practice—the result is an appalling distortion of the truth. Moreover, it is impossible to undertake any task of this kind without entrusting the actual work to canvassers whose ethics may be on a level even below that of their intellects.

The answer—as the York telegrams proved—is that such tactics almost always defeat themselves, and that no lobbyist of experience, let alone integrity, sanctions them. Fraud in such matters is peculiarly easy to detect, and irretrievably damning when exposed. Most Congressmen, and their secretaries, know their home districts pretty well, and in any batch of unauthorized messages there are bound to be a few that instantly disclose their fraudulent character. A message from even a defunct Legionnaire has caused embarrassment. The lobbyist who indignantly and truthfully denies ever having had anything to do with such methods proclaims not only his honesty but still more his common sense.

Furthermore, there are relatively few legislative proposals regarding which mass communications are effective. In practice the thing generally works just the other way round. When a Senator or Congressman finds his desk littered with telegrams from people who, in the nature of the case, cannot possibly have a considered opinion, he is instantly and naturally suspicious, and his tendency is to swing sharply in the opposite direction. No one who has noted the customary fate of petitions to Congress, fortified as some of them are with thousands and hundreds of thousands of signatures (on one occasion I was confronted by documents aggregating well over two million names, most of which I believe to have been authentically signed) retains much faith in the general efficacy of mass communications, except, indeed, in those rare cases wherein the issue immediately and obviously affects vast numbers of people, and where advice can be simplified down to a flat "Yes" or "No." It is safe to say that ninety per cent, and more, of this kind of activity is engineered, not by the much-abused Washington lobbyists, but by people on the outside whose zeal atrophies their brains, and also occasionally their ethical sense. This is not because the lobbyist is purer than his fellows, but because he knows Washington and they don't.

Any form of legislative propaganda, however, undeniably opens the way for the sort of thing that has brought lobbying into such evil repute. Money can be and has been viciously used, and direct financial pressure of all sorts exerted, to color the views and actions of those who have influence either at home or with their Congressional friends. It may be impossible to buy a Senator or a Congressman, but it is sometimes quite feasible to purchase those to whom Senators and Congressmen must listen—the local political bosses who control the machinery of nomination and election. The most honest legislator who values his job—and the majority of them do—has his vulnerable spot, and if he owes his office to the support of crooks, money will talk to them and they to him. Many of the most outrageous political scandals have been of this type, with the elected representatives of the people, and still more, the appointed incumbents of high offices, mere pawns in the unscrupulous hands of local politicians who cynically offered themselves for sale to the highest bidder.

When, recently, Mr. H. C. Hopson testified that Associated Gas & Electric had attempted to influence editorial opinion by placing or withholding advertising, he gave an excellent illustration of anti-social methods of propaganda. It may be hard sometimes for a corporation to see why it should go on spending its money to support a publication which attacks it; but any use of financial pressure for the purpose of controlling editorial expression is clearly an outrage against public decency. This sort of thing, be it observed, is not lobbying or the work of lobbyists. It is something much more far-reaching and infinitely more pernicious than lobbying at its very worst—the secret use of money to buy public opinion. It is closely akin to the methods formerly charged against certain of the power interests, whereby the very children in the grade schools were supposed to learn from their teachers the iniquities of government ownership.

The seamy side of all attempts to influence legislation is, in truth, the ugly background of our entire politico-economic system of conventions, nominations, and elections, of the whole complex relationship between wealth and public service. With most of this the legislative lobbyist has little or nothing to do. In the scandals of the Ohio ring in its palmy days, for instance, lobbying was a relatively unprofitable side-issue; there was far more to be made out of the administrative branches of government. Any State or community which permits its elections to be dominated by bosses or gangs will inevitably face corruption, and that corruption will show itself in attempts to influence legislation as in everything else in which there is a possible shake-down. But it is utterly unjust to blame lobbying for such a condition.

To what extent, and through what channels, it may be legitimate to spend money—in the long run the people's money—for the purpose of affecting public opinion is wholly problematic. It costs money, for instance, to be elected to Congress. The laws provide, not that a candidate shall spend only a specified sum, but that he shall fully and truly account for whatever he does spend—and also tell where he got it. A like rule would help to eliminate many of the evils in the employment of money for purposes of propaganda, and, incidentally, would relieve the lobbyist of much of the opprobrium now thrust upon him because of acts for which he is seldom responsible.

In all this matter of seeking to influence public opinion, whether legitimately or otherwise, there is nothing of the traditional activity to which lobbying owes its repulsive name. The man who appears at public hearings, generally by express invitation, as the representative of some particular group, who assists, again commonly by invitation, in the drafting of legislation or of amendments thereto, and who sends out legislative information for the guidance of his clients or for distribution to the public, has so far done nothing which would require him ever to ask whether the Capitol has any architectural features denotable as lobbies. But the lobbyist is likewise accused of conversing privately with individual Senators and Congressmen. Well, why shouldn't he? Usually he calls on them, like any other visitor, in their offices, but there are times when he does have to earn his title by seeking them in the fusty purlieus of the Senate and House chambers. It is no indictable crime—though it may well prove an error of judgment—to talk with a Congressman even amid the blended aromas of the House restaurant, or to confer with a Senator on that scenic railway that careens underground between the north wing of the Capitol and the Senate Office Building.

This—this holding converse with legislators individually—is lobbying in all its pristine nakedness. It is excoriated as if it were a consorting of habitual criminals. And yet its hideous immorality is singularly hard to discover. Practically everyone who goes to see a Senator or Congressman "wants something"—a job, an introduction, a departmental favor, a card to the galleries. Why should it be perfectly proper to talk to him about anything else, but indecent to confer with him about his most important duties.

The lobbyist, indeed, is often at a peculiar disadvantage in this respect; he has a far harder time in capturing ten minutes with any legislator who doesn't want to see him than the camel had in squeezing through the Needle's Eye. He lacks the "Open Sesame" of the voter from the home district, and if he is, or is guessed by the secretary to be, in the least unwelcome, he will cultivate the patience of Job in the outer office while the magic doors fly open to those who, on election day, may remember. And if he seeks his prey in the Capitol itself, though from the gallery his own eyes may have told him that the gentleman is safely in his seat reading the comic page of the morning paper, the attendant who condescends to bear his card into the sacred precincts of the Senate or House chamber returns with the curt advice, "Isn't there."

Most lobbyists waste very little time in seeking to make possibly undesired calls, nor is there ordinarily much occasion for it. After all, legislation is made largely in committee, not on the floor. The members of the two committees, one in each House, to which any particular bill is referred, and frequently just the members of special sub-committees of these committees, are the persons whose opinions will be guiding, and probably determining. Even in debate on the floor, the lead in almost every instance is taken by not more than half a dozen members, most of whom have already had the advantage of studying the proposal in committee. These are the people whom the lobbyist makes a point of seeing personally, and he frequently does so by express invitation.

As typical of many such conferences, I recall a hearing several years ago at which I had to testify, largely on technical matters, at a length which completely exhausted both the committee and me. Just when I thought I was through answering questions, and the chairman was about to dismiss me with evident relief, one member, who had hitherto remained absolutely silent, piped up. "I've been listening to this witness," he said, "for hours, and I've been listening to other witnesses for days, and they've all used lots of words I don't understand, and what's more I don't believe the rest of the members of this committee understand them any better than I do. Now I wish this witness would just start in now and explain what some of these words mean."

There was a bewildered pause. The request was reasonable enough, and yet to grant it meant compelling the whole committee to sit and listen to me for at least another hour. The chairman gazed at me forlornly. The other members squirmed uncomfortably in their seats. And then I caught in the chairman's eye—though he would deny this—the faintest suggestion of a wink.

"I should be delighted to do the best I can," I said, "but the committee has already been so patient and considerate that I hate to trespass further on its time"—at this point the tension began palpably to relax—"and so if the Congressman will be good enough to give me a few minutes in his office I will try to answer any questions he may care to ask me."

Whereupon I departed with the benediction of the chair, and that afternoon I strove to answer the Congressman's questions for a solid hour. I had reckoned him as certainly among the opponents of the amendments I was advocating—so much so that in our talk I made no effort to discuss them—but when the committee reported, there, to my astonishment and delight, was my Congressman with the majority—a small one and not on party lines—recommending the adoption of the amendments in question.

The trouble with the personal conference, as distinct from most of the other phenomena of lobbying, is that since it is not a matter of record, it gives occasion for all sorts of sinister inferences. I remember once, in the Senate waiting-room, overhearing a conversation between two women, one evidently a Washingtonian, and the other a friend from afar who was being shown the sights.

"That's Senator So-and-so," said the Washington lady in the stage whisper with which one refers to marvels at the Zoo, "and that"—indicating the man with whom the Senator was in earnest conversation—"is Mr. Blank—you know—the lobbyist for the What's-its-name."

"O-o-oh," responded the visitor in awed tones. "Is he bribing him now?"

This state of mind is lamentably common. The lobbyist is supposed to go about bearing a brief-case stuffed with currency, or at the very least to do his nefarious work by the alternate application of financial threats and promises. Now, it would be absurd to claim that such things never have happened—there have been black sheep in Congress, as everywhere—but by and large there is amazingly little evidence of it. It must be remembered that every legislator who faces re-election, as most of them periodically do, lives in the most transparent of glass houses, with opponents goggle-eyed for any chance to "get the goods on him." Even for a legislator with an itching palm the risk is too great.

Of course, Senators and Congressmen are always being told that certain actions will win—or lose—untold numbers of votes, but it is hard to see what is inherently wrong in that. After all, we live in a democracy, and the only way in which a legislator can free himself from the tyranny of the ballot is by death or not choosing to run. "Pressure" of this sort is inevitable, but most of it comes, not from the lobbyist, but from the politically-minded friend from home. As for direct bribery, most of the talk about it is utter nonsense. I am told that somebody once prepared what purported to be a current market price list of Senators and Congressmen—a document which, if it ever really existed, which I doubt, would have made good reading. Washington is a hotbed of wild rumors on every subject, and anyone who has lived there awhile learns to discount them heavily. One would think, from the absurdities that periodically gain currency, that a

Congressman could not so much as dine with an old friend without thereby selling his immortal soul. Nobody with a grain of intelligence imagines that one can buy a legislative vote with a dinner. If there is ever more direct bribery than this, the secret is unbelievably well kept, and that in an environment where secrecy is almost impossible.

Back in the Hoover era, on one of Washington's hottest summer days, I encountered a certain distinguished Senator in a corridor of the Senate Office Building, and we went to lunch together. It was too hot for appetite, and our combined meal—for which, after some altercation, I paid the total sum of twenty-five cents—consisted of one order of shredded wheat and two glasses of milk. In the course of this Spartan fare, I mentioned a bill which was scheduled to come up that afternoon, and told the Senator what I thought of it, and why. Afterward, as we were walking across to the Capitol, he suddenly stopped. "What," he said solemnly, "do you suppose the Great Engineer would think if he knew there was a United States Senator who could be bought with a shredded wheat biscuit?"

It is quite true that many of the lobbyists are on friendly terms with a considerable number of Senators and Congressmen, and that this personal relationship is sometimes assisted by a certain amount of entertaining. But, here again, why not? In every other sphere a reasonable amount of luncheon- or dinner-giving is regarded as entirely fitting, and an attorney may offer a cocktail to a judge without being in contempt of court. Accepting such an invitation occasionally does not put a legislator under the slightest obligation to vote as his host wants him to. Such entertaining as is done— and for obvious reasons it is seldom lavish or costly—is partly for the purpose of establishing friendlier personal contacts, but far more because the lunch or dinner hour is often the only time when Senators or Congressmen can get away from their tasks. Even legislators have to eat, and many a conference takes place over the luncheon table. It was at just such a luncheon—given and paid for, incidentally, by a Senator who wanted me to discuss a certain legislative matter with some of his colleagues—that I last met the late Will Rogers, whom our host had run into on his way to the dining room. Mr. Rogers knew and cared nothing about the subject of the conference, but his wit gave me the best-humored audience I ever hope to have.

Not long ago I was guilty of what now appears to be a heinous crime— I gave a cigar to a Senator, and the worst of it is that I did it in public. A hearing was just getting under way, and I happened to be the first witness. As I sat down, I noticed that the Senator sitting opposite me —a warm personal friend, but notoriously likely to disagree with everything I was there to say—was fumbling in his pockets, and then making unmistakable but unavailing pantomime in the direction of one of his colleagues.

Brazenly I took a cigar from my pocket; shamelessly, in the sight of all, I handed it across the table. The official record immortalizes the sin with the one significant word "Laughter."

Admittedly, however, the personal friendliness which exists in some cases between lobbyists and members of Congress, and which it is manifestly part of the lobbyist's business to maintain, opens the way to certain grave abuses. There are, unfortunately, plenty of people in Washington who seek to trade unscrupulously on alleged present or past "influential connections." Former Senators and Congressmen, lawyers or specialists who have been associated with administrative departments of the government, publicity agents, people of all kinds who claim to be somehow "on the inside," can be found among the ranks of those who undertake to render mysterious services for their prospective clients.

The trouble, of course, lies in the abuse rather than in the use of such contacts. It is exceedingly important, and indeed essential, for anyone who has dealings with any branch of the government to be fully posted as to procedure, to know whom to see and how to see him. The person who comes on business to Washington without a competent guide and adviser is likely to waste hours and days which could easily have been saved by a little timely counsel and a few entirely proper introductions. The moment, however, any person claims to have "influence" for sale then it is time for everyone concerned to look out. This is the most flourishing of all the Washington rackets, and, like all rackets everywhere, it fattens chiefly on the gullible. Nobody knows how much money is annually wasted in fees for this sort of "service," any more than we know how much is lost in any other form of confidence game. Here, indeed, are the frayed and tattered fringes of lobbying; here are the people who have done most to bring lobbying into disrepute.

Experience of governmental methods, a wide acquaintance among Washington's official population, long and special training in the analysis and interpretation of bills, laws, and regulations, and an established reputation, all these are parts of the wholly legitimate stock-in-trade of the attorney or other representative who does work in Washington on behalf of clients elsewhere. It is likewise legitimate that these qualifications should, in some instances, command exceedingly high prices. The experienced lobbyist, whether or not he is a practicing lawyer, is a specialist, and not infrequently is paid as such. Even if he happens to have gained some of his experience in the service of the government itself, it is certainly no crime subsequently to use that experience openly for the benefit of his clients. But as for the self-advertised venders of "influence," they continue to exist only because there is apparently no end to the supply of credulous and stupid people who believe in miracles.

Many of the ablest lobbyists in Washington to-day are Republicans, whose present political influence, as former Secretary of War Hurley recently stated, is "not worth anybody's nickel." Lobbying, indeed, has always been a special prerogative of the party out of power, by reason of its much larger number of politically prominent persons who no longer have government posts. Nobody with a grain of sense supposes that a Republican ex-official collects large fees on the strength of his influence with the New Deal. Among the Democrats who are now active as lobbyists, only the least reputable—and least successful—claim to be able to exercise any "personal influence." The large majority, like their Republican colleagues, make it perfectly clear that what they have to sell is experience in a field in which long and intimate observation is peculiarly necessary.

Enough has been said to indicate that the large fees sometimes paid to Washington attorneys and others for guidance and assistance in legislative matters—in simple language, for lobbying—do not necessarily imply the slightest impropriety. A man who, in an important civil suit, pays his attorney fifty or a hundred thousand dollars is not therefore assumed to be seeking to corrupt the judge or bribe the jury. Whether the attorney's services are actually worth that much is for the client, and for him alone, to decide. In exactly the same way, there are Washington representatives who, without having or claiming a particle of "influence," and without a single word or act that will flinch beneath the spotlight of publicity, are sufficiently experienced and capable so that they are fully entitled to charge high prices for their services.

Nobody would contend that all the money used for the purpose of affecting the course of legislation is wisely or honestly spent. Some part of it is at times diverted into wrong channels, above all when it gets into the hands of irresponsible underlings far removed from Washington itself. Expenses for general propaganda, whether legitimate or not, are always open to challenge, but the mere size of some of the amounts revealed whenever there is a lobby inquiry is not of itself enough to justify such an outcry. Any adequate legislative campaign costs money, even assuming, as is generally the case, that every cent of it is spent properly. A single item, such as the preparation and printing of a brief, may easily run into many thousands of dollars, and every lobby swells the receipts of the Post Office Department. The public ultimately pays the bill, of course, just as it pays the cost of the very active and efficient lobbies maintained by the various administrative departments of the government. In both cases the essential thing is full and accurate publicity as to how the money is spent; the fact that the amount involved may be large is no indication of improper use.

But what of the poor man in all this? The corporation may be able, with its customers' money, to hire expensive lobbying counsel, but how about the consumer, the man in the street, the housewife? The answer to that is that the strongest and most effective lobbies in Washington to-day are essentially "poor men's" lobbies. The American Legion campaign for the bonus bill, compared to which the efforts of the utility holding companies have been as the crackling of thorns under a pot, was certainly no plutocrats' party. To this day people recall the efficiency of the lobby which presided over the passage of the Adamson Bill. The lobby maintained by the American Federation of Labor, which is always on the job, has no support from millionaires. As for the farmers' lobby, it has been getting bills for the relief of agriculture passed in almost every session of Congress since the World War; if the farmers have not reaped the benefits thereof, it has certainly been from no lack of lobbying pertinacity. Anyone who thinks that lobbying unduly favors the rich has only to survey the laws enacted by Congress during the past five years—the period, we are told, of the lobbies' most insidious efforts.

Furthermore, the lobbies representing "the masses" have a tremendous head start. To begin with, they have the votes. When a labor representative tells a Congressman that his support of a certain bill will infallibly cost him the labor vote in his district, that Congressman pricks up his ears. When a consumers' organization advises a Senator that every woman in his state wants a certain thing done, that Senator is going to think twice before refusing to do it. There is, too, an enormous psychological advantage in championing what appears to be the cause of the people, even though the people may be in the end the chief sufferers. And nobody need imagine that the lobbies representing the consumers, labor, and the smaller producers are inefficiently staffed. True, they seldom go out and hire expensive counsel, but they more than make up for it by keeping their people on the job permanently. The intimate knowledge that some of them have of their business makes the highest-priced attorneys look like novices.

There are abuses in lobbying, of course. There are lobbying crooks who swindle their clients with fabulous tales of the wonders they can accomplish through mysterious channels. There are blunderers with distorted moral senses who fake telegrams and advocate whispering campaigns. There are subterranean workers who intimate that every legislator has his price. Above all, there are the people whose business is to squeeze money out of every phase of politics—the bosses who control elections and therewith the men they elect. Just so in every field; there are shyster lawyers, quack doctors, absconding bankers, labor racketeers, venal office-holders. But because these elements exist, in lobbying as elsewhere, it is grossly unjust to single out for public denunciation an occupation which not only exists by legal right but which—when properly conducted, as it commonly is— is a benefit and a necessity to the American people. It is largely through the instrumentality of lobbyists that legislation is adequately studied before enactment, and it is chiefly by way of the lobbyist that detailed information regarding such legislation reaches those who are most deeply concerned with it.

There can be no serious objection to having lobbyists registered as such, with full publicity as to their relations with their clients and with the public in all matters affecting legislation—provided there is a clear realization that the badge of the lobbyist is not a Scarlet Letter of crime. When a President of the United States referred publicly to the "lobbyists who, like a swarm of locusts, infest the halls of Congress," there was more than an intimation that the people had no longer the right of petition guaranteed by the Constitution, and that our laws ought to be enacted in Star Chamber secrecy. Until that right is denied as contrary to the mechanism of dictatorship, the lobbyist has a legitimate, necessary, and honorable place in any system of government by the people.

No. 55

[IN the following essay Stuart Chase tells us who the important groups are that advise the legislator, describes the techniques they use, and seriously questions whether the general public is effectively represented.]

THE PRESSURE BOYS IN ACTION [1]

by Stuart Chase

MY friend Richard Neuberger, a West Coast journalist, got himself elected to the Oregon legislature a few years ago. As a new member he was fair game for lobbyists. He was waited on by a group of earnest women who wanted a law passed to restrain billboards on the highways. They were reformers interested in scenery, order and safety. The bill made sense to Mr. Neuberger and he endorsed it—just as you would, or I would. It was clearly in the public interest.

Poor innocent! The advertisers' lobby began to teach him the facts of

[1] Stuart Chase, *Democracy Under Pressure* (New York: The Twentieth Century Fund, 1945), pp. 21-29. Reprinted by permission of the publisher. The footnotes in the original version are omitted here.

life. Here were no fine questions of public safety and order, but a vested interest threatened with pecuniary loss. The next thing Mr. Neuberger knew, the lobby had got the Signpainters' Union to denounce the measure and call him an "enemy of labor." This is a fearsome charge to levy against any legislator. Then came a torrent of letters from "widows and orphans" who would starve if rents from the beneficent billboard companies were cut off. Then telegrams rained in, and editorials in the papers.

The legislature ran to cover, and the bill was quashed. Mr. Neuberger believes that a large majority of the citizens of Oregon would support it, but citizens are not organized, and the lobby gets there fustest with the mostest. In the course of time the bill is certain to be passed, for it is on the trend curve; but not before a lot of beautiful country has been needlessly blighted, and a lot of cars needlessly wrecked.

MASSED BATTALIONS

Every state legislature is under similar pressure, while in Washington the heat often becomes fantastic, as Raymond Clapper sadly pointed out.

The TNEC found more than four hundred lobbies in Washington—not counting the bright boy who collected $60,000 during one session of Congress by writing big executives every time a law they liked was passed, and admitting he was solely responsible. We might roughly classify the four hundred into:

The Big Three—official business, labor and farm organizations. . . .

Specialized producers, such as cattlemen, publishers, citrus growers, broadcasting stations, telephone interests.

Professional and occupational groups, such as the bankers, insurance companies, advertisers, real-estate men, exporters and importers, doctors, teachers, lawyers.

Reformers, such as the conservationists and the birth controllers.

The governments in exile, who are now protesting loudly against actual or anticipated injustices to Ruritania. Never forget that Ruritania's sons can swing a tight election in a number of Congressional districts.

WHAT THEY REALLY WANT

It is interesting to tunnel under the exalted verbiage and find the simple wants which animate some of the four hundred lobbies. For instance:

Shoe manufacturers want a higher tariff.
Farmers want parity prices.
The merchant marine wants subsidies.
So do the airlines.
The silver bloc wants 71 cents an ounce, and would take $1.00.

Teachers want federal aid.

Unions want the closed shop.

Dairymen want a prohibitive tax on oleomargarine.

Railways want to weaken the waterways and the bus lines.

Cattlemen want Argentine beef plainly labeled not fit to eat.

Insurance men do not want too much social security.

Medical men want to scuttle socialized medicine.

Coal operators want hydroelectric projects halted.

Drug men would like food and drug reformers quietly chloroformed—which would not displease the publishers either.

The aluminum interests want no nonsense at all about competitors getting hold of new government plants.

One could continue the list until it became a saga. The objective behind these wants is usually a direct subsidy for the interest itself, or a hand grenade for a competitor. Practically all the labors of the economic pressure groups revolve around these twin goals. Observe, however, that such goals are often in violent conflict as among the several groups. This is no harmony chorus.

ALL IN THE WEEK'S WORK

The TNEC describes a typical week of lobbying in the 1930's:

The American Legion pushes a war widows' pension bill through the House

The Veterans of Foreign Wars, however, cannot get their bonus bill out of committee.

The National Federation of Federal Employees stops a pay cut in the House omnibus economy bill.

The American Automobile Association, after unheard-of efforts, fails to block a Senate increase in the automobile tax.

The petroleum lobby wangles a special tariff into the general tax bill.

The druggists' lobby—sometimes called the Pain and Beauty Boys—fights off a tax on cosmetics.

SLOGANS

Pressure groups make good use of slogans. The AFL marches to legislative battle behind "The American Standard of Living." Who would be low enough to attack that? The Chamber of Commerce runs to "Free Enterprise," and the National Association of Manufacturers to "The American System." The investors' lobby works wonders with "Widows and Orphans," while the American Publishers can get away with practically anything in the name of "Free Speech and Free Press."

When a bill is to be killed, however, the accredited method is to label it "communistic," "socialistic," "fascist-inspired," "bureaucratic," "regimented," or "controlled by politicians."

All pressure groups protest that they are concerned with the "public interest." This comes as naturally to them as for a parson to declare himself against sin. They let it be known that they are making this splendid fight for the common good at great personal sacrifice to themselves. This makes it hard for the rest of us to discuss the public interest without acute nausea.

When a price-fixing job is under way, the boys call it "preventing unfair competition," or "eliminating trade abuses," or "getting rid of cutthroat competition," or "regulating chiselers." It is an awful thing to be called a chiseler. A competitive price cutter, to be sure, is the hero of Adam Smith's atomistic society. But when the Cattle Growers want to break through the OPA price ceilings in wartime, they piously advocate the "restoration of the law of supply and demand."

STRATEGY AND TACTICS

Lobbying has been going on so long that it is now almost as formal a ceremony as the tango. All the motions are known to the professional, and are endlessly repeated. Political action can take place on four fronts:

First, get the "right" Congressman elected. He will vote for our bills. This means campaigning in the field.

Second, turn the heat on Congressmen already elected.

Third, influence an administrative agency to interpret bills in the "right" way. This is usually harder than influencing Congress.

Fourth, fight the constitutionality of unfavorable bills through the courts, right up to the Supreme Court. It is said that the electric power lobby used to count on an average delay of seven years after the passage of a law affecting utilities adversely, before the final decision by the Supreme Court. This gave the gentlemen quite a lot of time to turn around.

A Washington lobby normally consists of a professional agent and a staff of research workers. The agent gets up the strategy, and the research workers get up the figures. Either or both may draft the bill they want passed. Congressmen seldom prepare their own bills. The strategy is as elemental as an army's: to take more territory, and to kill off the opposition. Sometimes, as already noted, the strategy accidentally does run parallel to the public interest. The labor bloc lobbied for the Child Labor Amendment to the Constitution. It kept children from competing for union members' jobs, and at the same time it was a good thing for the children of the nation. The doctors have campaigned from time to time for pure food and drug legislation. The farmers have sometimes got behind conservation measures.

The agent's primary task is to build up a bloc of votes in Congress, to be backed with appeals from home at the psychological moment. This is known as "hearing from the people." The agent stands at the amplifier to megaphone the appeals. He also uses his professional abilities on the press, the columnists and the radio. His men in Congress can use their franking privilege to good advantage. A large part of the *Congressional Record* is free propaganda for pressure groups.

Congressmen are rarely influenced by debates on the floor. The best way to prove this is to take a look at them when a debate is on. Of the few who are present, those who are not reading the papers seem to be taking a nap. What really stings a Congressman into activity is (1) mail from home, (2) testimony at committee hearings, (3) high pressure from the agent.

The dangerous lobbies are not out in the open. They work in the half-light or in the dark. The techniques of entertainment, dinners, cocktail parties, subtle flattery, are often exquisite. Since the corruption law of 1911, there has not been much direct bribery. The crude buying of votes has given way to more subtle blandishments. Congressmen as well as administrative officials are shy of little black bags.

CONTINUITY

A few lobbies operate intermittently. The Fair Trade League makes a play for fixing retail prices when in the mood. At other times it hibernates like a woodchuck. Per contra, certain manufacturers have had somebody on the job in Washington day and night for practically a hundred and fifty years. The professionals favor continuity—if for no other reason than that it stabilizes their own jobs. It gets better results than the hit-and-run method.

I once joined a pressure group to oppose the building of a reservoir in my town. The water was for Bridgeport, not for us, and there was a mean smell of a real-estate racket mixed up in the project. We were an enthusiastic crowd of amateurs, numbering such virtuosos as Franklin P. Adams, Jascha Heifetz, E. J. Steichen, the late Frank Hawks, Roger Burlingame, Louis I. Dublin, R. L. Duffus, Rollin Kirby. We worked our heads off. To hire us at space rates would have cost a million. We never got to first base. We worked only when we had the time. The water company, a private outfit, worked all the time.

A GREAT BIG PUBLIC UPRISING

When a vote is to be taken, and the moment comes to turn on the electrons, it is inspiring to watch a big lobby in operation. Constituents arrive by train, air and motor car. Sometimes they walk, or ride in buggies, or even on high-wheeled bicycles. Telegrams pour in like autumn leaves. Strong men stagger down Senate corridors under bursting sacks of mail. Editorials blossom in the local papers, duly canned for the occasion in crisp, short sentences. The wires and airwaves crackle with radio speeches and long-distance phone calls.

Young Voters' Leagues, political clubs, Independent Citizens' Committees swing into action, apparently with utter spontaneity. Movie queens, sob sisters, local celebrities get in front of flashlights. The wretched legislator is made dizzy by these activities. A big uprising, he concludes; a Great Big Public Uprising!

The agent lies low while the uprising is on. Some professionals advise getting out of Washington altogether.

A modern lobby would be unthinkable without modern technology, specifically telephone, telegraph, radio, rotogravure press and telephoto. The words often fall in the nostalgic cadences of Jeffersonian agriculture, but the technical devices which transmit these cadences are strictly up to date.

THE LEADER AND THE LED

For all this expert technical performance, it is not always clear how far the technician really represents his flock. Mr. George Gallup finds that sometimes the two are wide apart. He says:

> During recent years, polls of organized workers have, on many occasions, found them taking exactly the opposite view from the spokesman of labor organizations. Likewise they have found farmers going contrary to the claims of their leaders, business men taking opposite views from the heads of business associations, war veterans failing to see eye to eye with American Legion officers.

While labor leaders were recently fighting a bill to make unions disclose their financial condition, a poll showed 80 per cent of union members actually in favor of publicity for union accounts. Perhaps they too wanted to know where their money went.

As for mail to Congressmen, Mr. Gallup presents a striking case in connection with the Selective Service bill of 1940. As you remember, the uproar over the first draft law was prodigious. Into the offices of a group of fourteen Senators came 30,000 letters. A tabulation disclosed that 90 per cent were against the draft. Meanwhile a poll of the nation showed 68 per cent of all citizens for the draft, 27 per cent against it, and 5 per cent with no opinion.

A skilled lobbyist has an economic interest in his job. Like the rest of us, he prefers to have it seem important. Sometimes he grows worried when the opposition weakens. He wants to give the impression of being in there swinging all the time. Thus if he is an agent for a safe-and-sane business group, he may not only welcome communist scares, he may prod the comrades a little so they will start one. If lobbies represented only the common denominator of their members, and not the personal ambitions of the lobbyist as well, they might be less of a menace.

Meanwhile, when a big campaign fills the papers and warms the airwaves, it is well to remind ourselves that a lot of the heat is synthetic.

No. 56

[LEGISLATORS and legislatures are by no means completely dependent on the lobbyist. They have tried to provide impartial and expert advice and assistance for themselves. Congress has made a start by establishing the Legislative Reference Service in the Library of Congress. What the state legislatures have done is discussed below.]

TECHNICAL SERVICES FOR STATE LEGISLATORS [1]

by Edwin E. Witte

THE major technical services for state legislators which have developed in this country are legislative reference, bill drafting, and statutory revision. . . .

All these three types of technical services are universally acknowledged to be very necessary to the reasonably efficient functioning of state legislatures; where established, they function without arousing serious opposition, and legislators do not hesitate to make use of them; from time to time additional services are created in states without them. But very certainly, bill drafting, legislative reference, and statutory revision services have not fulfilled the high hopes expressed by their champions when they first attracted public attention in the pre-war decade.

At that time they were hailed as a "really far-reaching reform in our legislative life." There was expectation that through such services legislation could be placed upon a scientific plane and freed from the baneful influence of the lobbyists.

It is now evident that too much was expected of the legislative reference bureaus. No matter how efficient the technical services may be, they cannot guarantee good legislation. Much more fundamental changes are re-

---

[1] Edwin E. Witte, "Technical Services for State Legislators," *State Government* (February, 1938), Vol. 11, pp. 32-34. This is a shorter version of an article by the same title that appeared in *The Annals* of the American Academy of Political and Social Science (January, 1938), Vol. 195, pp. 137-143 and is reprinted here by permission of *The Annals* of the American Academy of Political and Social Science and *State Government*.

quired to make the state legislatures function at maximum possible efficiency.

It is also very clear that legislative reference work has suffered from administrative reorganization in many states. When a legislative reference bureau is attached to a large administrative department, it becomes more difficult to preserve the reputation for neutrality, which everyone agrees is vital in services of this kind.

Occasionally, also, legislative reference services have become involved in contests between legislatures and governors, with resulting disastrous consequences to them. Such services should serve both, but it is often difficult to do so without arousing the suspicions of one or the other, when they are in conflict.

Most of all, technical services for state legislators have suffered from too narrow a conception of their purposes and from second rate leadership. A few legislative reference executives, perhaps, attempted too much and forgot that their function was to serve the legislatures, not to boss them. Much more commonly, however, the executives of technical services have been content to conduct them in such a way that they would not arouse opposition. There is far more danger that legislative reference bureaus will do too little than that they will attempt too much. Services of this kind will, indeed, be continued if they are content to go on as they have been, but if they make their continued existence their major objective, they will fall far short of accomplishing what they should.

Many legislative reference services are merely "highly specialized libraries," as Professor Leek described them a decade ago, but they should be something very different. It was unfortunate that the bill drafting and legislative reference service which Dr. McCarthy built up in Wisconsin was called "the legislative reference library" and was attached to the free library commission. In Wisconsin this title has made no difference, and the connection with the library commission has been advantageous; but it was the Wisconsin service that first attracted attention, and other states in trying to establish a similar service made the mistake of regarding it as a specialized library.

Legislative reference work does not consist of collecting books or even the very miscellaneous fleeting literature of current legislative questions; nor does it consist merely of indexing bills and making accessible prior legislative proposals. The essence of legislative reference work is the furnishing of information in response to inquiries, primarily from legislators and secondarily from others interested in legislation. The information furnished should be accurate and as complete as possible. No less important is it that the information should be in such concise and understandable form that it can and will be used by the legislators. A library consisting mainly of materials compiled in answer to prior or anticipated inquiries will be helpful; but it is a hindrance, not a help, if it absorbs too large a part of the energies and appropriations of the service.

Likewise, bill drafting must concern itself with more than the technical details. It is not the draftsman's job to tell the legislator what sort of legislation he should introduce or support. It is for the legislator to decide all questions of policy. But it is the draftsman's responsibility to translate the decisions of the member into statutory provisions as consistent as possible with the existing body of law and the structure and functioning of the government. To do so, the draftsman must understand the member's proposal and all its implications, and it is his duty to acquaint the member with all its effects upon the existing law and government, so that the member can make intelligent decisions on alternative methods which are open to him in working out the details of his proposal.

All this means that "technical services for legislators" are fraught with many difficulties. In the last analysis, how well these services are performed depends upon the man in charge and the competency of his assistants. This is truly, as Dr. McCarthy said, "a man's work"—one that calls for all the ability that any man possesses. At one and the same time the director and his staff must have "a passion for anonymity," unusual tact, a broad knowledge, and tireless energy. But if well done, services of this kind are worth all the effort that anyone can put into them; and, while they cannot guarantee good legislation, they can be very valuable in helping legislators to do their work more efficiently.

Chapter XVI

THE EXECUTIVE IN AMERICAN GOVERNMENT

[THE executive in modern government has, in general, two functions. In the first place, he is concerned with a legislative program. His business is to translate the complex pressures of public opinion into legislative recommendations. In the second place, the executive is concerned with the management of a large body of public employees who are applying legislation. His business is to see that the public services apply the legislation, in letter and in spirit, as the legislative assembly intended. The executive is responsible, therefore, not only for the character of most of the matters considered by the legislature but for the detailed and day-to-day application of legislation enacted. Errors that are made are ultimately his errors; the blame is, to a large extent, upon his shoulders.

This means that the President, the governors, the mayors, and the city managers are among the focal points of study for one who wishes to know about American government. These executives have great powers (the American President is one of the most powerful political figures in the modern world). And the recent trend in American government has been toward increasing, not decreasing, their power.

One interested in maintaining and extending democratic government in America will immediately ask, therefore: Does the system work in such a way that these executives are responsive to the will of the people and accountable to the people for the way they exercise their power? It is important, of course, that government be efficient, that the job be done with the least cost. But the question of efficiency is not the only question and, to the democrat, not the most important one. Therefore, each aspect of executive power, executive organization, and executive action must be examined to determine its relation to democratic principles. What is the relation of the executive to the legislature? What sort of control does Congress, the state legislature, the city council, and ultimately the people have over the executive?]

No. 57

[IN many ways the President of the United States symbolizes the American government to the American people. Every speech he makes, every action he takes is national, even international, news. He is certainly the most important and most powerful single figure in any democracy in the world to-day. How has this come about? Has the power of the President in American political life developed to the point at which it is a threat to democratic government? Is there adequate legislative and popular control over the President? What can be done to insure a presidential office compatible with democratic principles? It is such questions that Professor Corwin raises in the following article. He deals with them in a penetrating way.]

THE PRESIDENT AS "DICTATOR" VERSUS THE PRESIDENT AS LEADER—A NEW TYPE OF CABINET [1]

by Edward S. Corwin

THE growth of presidential participation in legislation, and indeed the vast expansion in recent decades of the President's role in all the departments of national power, invites our attention afresh to a question which has been repeatedly raised regarding the Presidency in the past, but never with more insistency than in recent years, nor for more cogent reasons. This is the question whether the Presidency is a potential matrix of dictatorship; and, if it is, whether there is a remedy.

"Dictatorship," I hardly need to point out, is a word with a highly ambiguous connotation, so much so in fact that I propose to dismiss it at the outset in favor of a less colorful word, "domination." "A nation," it has been well said, "does not have to have a genuine dictator in order to suffer some of the evils of too great executive domination." Imagine a historically minded member of the 81st Congress seeking to emulate Henry Dunning's exploit in 1781 in bringing George III's domination of Parliament to an end and with it, ultimately, British resistance to American independence. It would be the part of such a member to move a resolution declaring that "the power of the President has increased, is increasing, and ought to be diminished," and he would have little difficulty in making out an arresting case.

[1] Edward S. Corwin, *The President: Office and Powers,* Third Edition (New York: New York University Press, 1948), pp. 353-364. Reprinted by permission of the publisher. The footnotes in the original version are omitted here.

First off, he would point out that impeachment, the weapon which the Constitution provides against presidential "high crimes and misdemeanors," is, as Jefferson early discovered, a "scarecrow," and that to galvanize this scarecrow into life would be to run the risk of reducing the Presidency to a nullity, as almost happened in 1868. Then, noting the decision in *Mississippi v. Johnson* shortly after the Civil War, he would assert, and quite correctly, that the President has no judicially enforcible responsibility either for nonperformance of his duties or for exceeding his powers. Congress' power of the purse, to be sure, still offers, he would concede, an obstacle to presidential usurpation which only an outright *coup d'état* could entirely overcome. Nevertheless, as Dr. Wilmerding points out in his volume on *The Spending Power,* not only have Presidents been able repeatedly to break over statutory controls on expenditure, but such controls are usually much abated by Congress itself in times of emergency, exactly when expenditures are heaviest and presidential dominance is at its zenith. Indeed, generalizing from what happened during the Great Depression, the honorable member might urge that congressional largess in such situations, by the hold which it gives the executive branch upon millions of votes, enables the President to tighten his hold also upon Congress, and so creates a vicious circle whereby Congress pays for its own slow enslavement. And, continues our orator, when war activates the President's powers as Commander-in-Chief, the situation is still more disastrous from the point of view of opposing the power of the purse to presidential dominance. The sums which Congress is at such times under every compulsion to vote are colossal. The needs which they are designed to meet are forcefully represented, and are believed by the public to be most urgent, while itemization is put out of the question by the demands of military secrecy; and unexpected turns in the military situation may aggravate all these difficulties. Moreover, the criticism which overworked congressional committees of varying competence can offer to the demands of the executive branch under such conditions will be haphazard in the extreme—an item of $50,000 may get more consideration, and certainly far better informed consideration, than a presidential demand for billions.

Turning then to the course which constitutional interpretation has taken more and more pronouncedly in consequence of our participation in two world wars and under the stimulation of economic crisis, our fictioned Dunning will sketch a system of constitutional law which attributes to Congress a legislative power of indefinite scope, and the further power to delegate this indefinite power to the President *ad libitum,* and which attributes to the President in his own right an indefinite power to proclaim "emergencies" and thereby appropriate an indefinite "aggregate of powers" in meeting them. At the same time, he will show that the President, not without judicial encouragement, has been able to cut loose from the two most important controls which the Constitution originally imposed upon his direction of foreign policy. With our four greatest wars directly ascribable to presidential policies, the exercise by Congress of its power "to declare war" has become, he will assert, an empty formality; while by means of the executive-agreement device the President has emancipated himself from his constitutional partner in pledging the national faith.

And at this point our hypothetical member will perhaps devote a word or two to the advantages which a President to-day enjoys in appealing to the multitude. Propaganda, he will point out, once the casual art of a gifted few, has been within recent times converted into a skilled technique, which is supplemented by the most ingenious gadgets of mechanical science. To-day the President of the United States can at any time request that the nation's broadcasting channels be cleared so that he may "chat" with the people, and the request will be granted pronto, for are not all the available frequencies allocated to companies on federal licenses which terminate every six months? Besides, every member of his administration is a propagandist and has access to the radio at will, although a first-class radio voice may not be the heaven-sent gift of all.

Finally, our orator will note certain of the consequences of the demise of the anti third-term tradition. A third-term—a fortiori a fourth-term—President is bound to dominate not only his party, and Congress through it, but the executive agencies, most of whose chief personnel he will have appointed, and even the courts, a large proportion of whose judges will be his appointees. And in proportion as a President displays reluctance to quit office will the strength of the vested interests supporting his continuance in it wax greater.

The picture is unquestionably overdrawn in some of its details. Thus, if it is true that impeachment is no longer to be reckoned with as an effective weapon in the arsenal of liberty, this is partly due to the fact that Presidents have in the past kept pretty clear of courses which might make people think seriously of so extreme a discipline. Again, although there is no court which is entitled to order a President to perform his duties or to enjoin him from exceeding his powers, yet the subordinates through whom he must ordinarily act do not share his immunity in this respect; and his orders are at all times subject to judicial inquiry into their validity when anybody bases on them any claim or justification whatsoever. Also, his subordinates are, ordinarily, liable at any time to be summoned before a congressional investigating committee and put to the question regarding their official conduct.

Nor is it by any means the case that Congress' control of the purse strings is ineffective as a restraint on the executive branch. To the contrary, it is potentially a highly effective restraint, which with improved machinery within the power of Congress to provide could be made actual. Again, our orator did not find it to his purpose to mention that in the "concurrent resolution" a device to-day exists by which sweeping delegations of power to the President can be recalled by the houses without the necessity of obtaining presidential consent; nor that ordinarily executive agreements, unlike treaties, do not have the force of law unless they have been sanctioned by Congress. And other lesser exaggerations or omissions might be indicated were it worthwhile.

What is more, that is a seriously contracted point of view from which presidential domination appears as solely a *menace* to democratic institutions. Why, in the face of our democratic institutions, has presidential domination attained its present proportions? Indeed, must not this development be considered as a fulfillment in a measure of those institutions, and as an answer to some demand from public opinion, on which by hypothesis they are grounded? Without doubt, such is the case, and especially as regards presidential leadership in legislation; nor is it difficult to identify this demand—it is the demand that government assume an *active* role in matters of general concern, and especially in matters affecting the material welfare of the great masses of the people. This may eventually turn out to have been a demand impracticable of beneficial realization in the long run; but of its existence there can be no present question.

So we are not free to blame presidential leadership as such for those intrusions upon "liberty," as it has sometimes been understood, which present expanded theories of governmental function entail. This at least must be conceded. We are free, on the other hand, to ask whether presidential leadership, as we know it, is as good an instrument of the demand which brought it into existence as conceivably it might be. Presidential leadership sets itself the task of guiding legislation; and the critics are numerous who say that it does the job badly. To make the indictment more specific, it is asserted that presidential leadership is discontinuous, not to say spasmodic; that it is too dependent on the personality of the President rather than on the authority of the office; that it is often insufficiently informed, especially as regards the all-important matter of administrative feasibility; and, finally, that the contact between the President and Congress is most faulty, being, in fact, at the mercy of either's whim. These contentions also have too much obvious validity to make it worthwhile to attempt to refute them or even to qualify them nicely.

In short, we are confronted, not with a *single* problem, but with *two* problems: first, the problem of bringing presidential power in *all* its reaches under some kind of institutional control; secondly, the problem of relieving presidential leadership in the legislative field of its excessive dependence on the accident of personality and the unevenness of performance which this involves. Is it possible that these two problems admit of a common solution? At least, so far as they do, it is evident what form the solution must take—the *provision, namely, of some kind of improved relationship between President and Congress.*

It is not irrelevant in this connection to recur for a moment to the argument which the President's Committee on Administrative Management advanced a decade ago in support of its recommendation that the independent agencies be brought within the departments whose heads compose the President's Cabinet. It was upon these agencies, the argument ran, that the most novel, most controversial, most interesting activities of the National Government had been lodged in recent decades, with the result that the President had been constrained to look increasingly outside the Cabinet for advice in shaping his legislative program. But let the Committee's recommendation be adopted, the argument continued, and the President would be forced, or at any rate would have incentive, to return to the bosom of his "official family" instead of consorting with this, that, and the other anonymous adviser or dispenser of happy ideas. Thus, on the one hand the Cabinet would be revitalized, and on the other hand the President would become "the spokesman for the 'administration' in the real sense of the word, not merely the interpreter of his own fancies." He would be at all times what he had always been in times of his greatest power, the representative of the public.

The argument overlooked certain facts, one of which is that "Kitchen Cabinets," far from being recent phenomena, on the contrary long antedate the first "independent agency." Nor is the reason far to seek. It is because the Cabinet seraglio has been recruited from an early date on principles which make it fairly certain that an active presidential imagination will frequently stray beyond its decorous precincts. One of these—the one which is of chief importance for the present discussion—is the idea that the heads of the great majority of the departments ought to be administrative experts, or at least capable of quickly becoming such. Unfortunately, an expert in a particular area of governmental activity is not likely to possess the breadth of outlook which is most desirable in a political adviser, or the time or inclination to interest himself in the problems of other departments or of the country at large. And obviously the Committee's proposal to increase his departmental duties was badly calculated to overcome these handicaps, if that was one of the ends in mind. The argument overlooks the fundamental distinction between Politics and Administration, between determining *what* government ought to do and *how* it should do it, and the exigent need of a President for responsible counsel in relation to the former. It overlooks too the considered opinion of competent critics that, even as an agency for the development of a unified *executive* policy among its own membership, the Cabinet has to-day "become an administrative anachronism."

Two other plans for stabilizing presidential leadership, while also pivoting on the Cabinet, are directed primarily to the problem of creating a permanent link between the President and Congress. The less radical of these would give the Cabinet members the right to attend the houses in order to participate in debate on matters of official interest to them and impose upon them the obligation of doing so in order to impart information desired by the houses. The proposal, far from raising any constitutional difficulties, has the countenance of early practice under the Constitution. The first volume of the *Annals of Congress* records that "Secretary for Foreign Affairs Jefferson attended agreeably to order, and made the necessary explanations." Actually, it was Secretary for Foreign Affairs Jay, for this was on July 22, 1789, and Jefferson did not become Secretary of State till March 1790. Secretary of War Knox later visited the Senate Chamber with the President on at least one occasion . . . and by himself on two others. The Act of 1790, organizing the Treasury Department, provided that the head of the Department should digest plans for improving the revenue and public credit, and "make report and give information to either branch of the legislature, in person or in writing, as may be required," etc. That Hamilton, the first Secretary of the Treasury, was never asked to report in person was due, as we saw earlier, to the opposition of the rising Jeffersonian party as voiced by Madison.

And so matters rested till near the end of the Civil War when George H. Pendleton of Ohio began an agitation, the principal result of which was a report many years later by a distinguished Senate committee supporting the idea both on grounds of policy and of constitutionality; and since then at least four future or past Presidents are on record as having expressed themselves in its favor. Why then has the suggestion never produced tangible fruit? Chiefly because most of the legislative work of Congress is done by committees, and before such a body a head of a department can always obtain a far more satisfactory hearing than would be conceivably possible before either of the houses in open session. Conversely, if it is Congress which is seeking information, it can do so through the investigatory process much more effectively and thoroughly than by the wasteful and pretentious methods of parliamentary interpellation.

We come now to the more radical proposal referred to above. *It is simply that the President shall construct his Cabinet from a joint Legislative Council to be created by the two houses of Congress and to contain its leading members.* Then to this central core of advisers may be added at times such heads of departments and chairmen of independent agencies as the business forward at the moment naturally indicates.

That the creation of a Cabinet with legislative members would not encounter constitutional difficulties was pointed out in an earlier chapter. Nor would it amount to supplanting forthwith the "Presidential System" with the "Cabinet System." The President would not become a prime minister, bound to resign when outvoted in Congress, although circumstances might arise in which it might be expedient for him to do so, as Mr. Wilson contemplated doing in 1916 in the event of Mr. Hughes' election. Nor yet would he be a figurehead like the King of Great Britain or the President of Italy, for he would still retain all his constitutional powers and prerogatives although, again, he might choose to use them at times less for pushing a program of his own than for the purpose of mediating between the programs of others, as did Washington at the beginning.

The new Cabinet would, in other words, still be a body of *advisers*. But there are advisers *and* advisers. The proposed Cabinet would comprise men whose daily political salt did not come from the presidential table, whose political fortunes were not identical with his, who could bring presidential whim under an independent scrutiny which to-day is lacking, and yet who, by putting the stamp of their approval upon his proposals, would be able to facilitate their enactment into law. It would be a body both capable of *controlling* the President and of *supporting* him; of guaranteeing that the things needing to be done would be done on time, but that, on the other hand, the judgment that they needed to be done represented a wide consensus, a vastly wider consensus than the President can by himself supply.

But it may be objected that such an arrangement could not long be adhered to, or if it was it must at times cut athwart the two-party system, and so weaken the political responsibility of the President. The objection has reference to the evident possibility of the President's belonging to the party which is a minority in Congress. Actually, the supposed situation has obtained comparatively rarely—only four times since the turn of the century, covering eight years out of forty-eight. Furthermore, the objection overlooks the fact that the advantage which is supposed to accrue from President and Congress both being of the same party rarely outlasts the first two years of an administration, when indeed it lasts that long, while some of the bitterest feuding between the two branches has often occurred when both were of the same party. Such conspicuously was the case in the latter days of "F.D.R.," as I was at pains to point out earlier in this chapter. What kept the two branches cooperating at all was the common compulsion of a great emergency; and at such times, even under present arrangements, cooperation between President and Congress does not stop at the party line. *But why should it require a crisis to bring forth best methods, especially as with best methods operative crisis might often be avoided?* Suppose one takes the position that government is normally a species of *nation-keeping;* then it is clear that much of the fuss and fury of politics is really factitious and a sheer waste to the community; that the chief objective to be sought in political discussion, whether carried on in Cabinet council, on the floors of Congress, or elsewhere, is *consensus*—in what light does the above proposal then appear?

Furthermore, it would seem that the principle of cycle holds in the matter of legislation, and especially of reform legislation, as it does in so many other things mundane. The mere enactment of laws is only the first step toward incorporating them in the social order; following it ensues a process of gradual absorption into the general institutional setup and outlook of the community; and this process is apt to be hindered rather than helped if reforms are pressed forward too fast and furiously. A wise legislative leadership will, therefore, reckon on a certain amount of reaction against its measures as inevitable and seek to forestall this. In such an endeavor the advice of potential political foes may easily be of more value than that of overenthusiastic supporters.

Kept within bounds, the power and prestige of the Presidency comprise the most valuable political asset of the American people; they are, moreover, in a very true sense the creation of the American people. But centering as they do in a single individual who is free to advise, or to refrain from advising, with whomsoever he chooses, this power and this prestige are apt to become unduly *personalized,* thus inviting two dangers: the slowing down of the legislative process to an extent that unfits it for a crisis-ridden world in which time is often of the essence, and—in consequence—autocracy. It is, therefore, an additional merit of the suggestion advanced above that it is calculated to meet, or at least abate, both these dangers. Effective presidential leadership is essential to the ready availability of the national lawmaking power; this ready availability reduces to a minimum the excuse for autocratic courses.

To sum up: What is sometimes termed the question of "presidential responsibility" is not a single problem, but presents two quite different, even opposed, aspects: (1) that of concern for the *responsiveness* of government, and particularly the legislative branch of it, to public opinion; (2) that of concern for the *accountability* of the executive branch to the existing constitutional structure, which also presumably embodies public opinion. I am here suggesting that these two aspects admit of a common solution.

Practice under the Constitution clearly demonstrates that the legislative process requires presidential guidance. But it shows too that no President can long shape policy in any field without legislative support, or—as happened during the Civil War—an obvious breach of constitutional forms. The problem for which a constitutional solution is sought is, therefore, really the problem of equating easily, and without constant jar to society, the political forces which Congress at any time represents with those which the President represents at the same time, and of putting the relationship of the two *on a durable and understood basis*. For this purpose a reconstruction of the Cabinet, which in its present form has proved but an indifferent success for more than a century, is at least a promising expedient, and one to which the Constitution interposes no obstacles.

No. 58

[THE tasks and responsibilities of the executive in our state governments are not fundamentally different from those of the executive in the national government. It is true, however, that governors are generally more hampered by the constitutional organization and distribution of executive power than is the President. And, it is true also that the governors are neither felt to be as important nor are they as closely subjected to public scrutiny in their actions as is the President. This latter fact is important because the states are extremely vital parts of our political system and, in many respects, much closer to the people than the national government. The efficacy with which the states deal with problems and the effectiveness of popular control of the state governments will do much to determine the character of American political life.

The following article by the late George Dern, who was at one time governor of Utah and later Secretary of War, gives us the reflections of a successful politician and executive officer upon the operation of the executive office in the states. Though the main emphasis is upon the administrative rather than the legislative aspects of the office, the article is valuable for the insight it provides into the difficulties besetting a governor who wishes to be an effective administrator. In addition, it raises the question as to whether the present organization of state government is such as to enable the people to hold the politicians in the executive offices responsible for the efficient administration of the public's business.]

GOVERNORS AND LEGISLATURES [1]

by George H. Dern

THERE is a considerable degree of misapprehension in the popular mind with respect to the proper functions of a governor. Some critics might add that occasionally there is also a considerable degree of misapprehension in the mind of a governor with respect to his own proper functions. But at any rate, it is important to have a clear conception of a governor's duties, and of his relationship to the legislature in administrative matters.

Without wasting time on non-essentials, let us dive head-first into the vital question of where governmental responsibility is situated in the American system.

It is not front page news that each state government, as well as the national government, is divided into three departments—legislative, executive and judicial. The Judicial Department is usually an orderly, well-behaved group which knows its place and keeps in it. To be sure the national legislative branch once in a while thinks the Supreme Court is poaching upon its private preserves, but as a general rule there is a satisfactory line of demarcation between the Judicial Department and the Legislative and Executive Departments, especially in the States.

This seems to leave the quarrel, if there be one, between the Legislative and Executive Departments. Do these brethren always dwell together in harmony? Do legislators work overtime praising the executive for his fairness and scrupulous regard for the rights and powers of the co-ordinate branch? Does the executive lie awake nights thinking up new ways to tell the public that the legislative branch knows its place and stays in it? Oh, we get along with each other pretty well, and the little clashes help to make life interesting. Such clashes as we have are, of course, due to the cussedness of legislators who persist in playing politics, a vice which never even enters the purer mind of the executive.

Nevertheless, there are honest differences of opinion as to the distribution of authority between the Legislative and Executive Departments. The general public is prone to hold the Governor responsible for everything that happens during his term of office, including the acts of all elective and appointive officials, if not the actions of the Legislature itself. Popular opinion thinks of him as an officer of vast power and clothed with authority

[1] George H. Dern, "Governors and Legislatures," *State Government* (August, 1931), Vol. 4, pp. 7-16. Reprinted by permission of *State Government*.

to tell everybody else what to do and what not to do. With such an impression abroad I say, "Come let us reason together."

The Governor has two functions, executive and administrative. When a Governor goes into office he ought first to get it firmly fixed in his mind that there is a vast difference between these two functions. His executive functions are inherently his own, being vested in him by the Constitution. His administrative functions, on the other hand, are all delegated to him by the Legislature, for the legislative branch is the source of all administrative authority. This distinction is of such fundamental importance that it is worthy of amplification.

A State constitution usually provides that "the Governor shall see that the laws are faithfully executed." That is his executive function, with which the Legislature has nothing to do. On its face it looks like a fine cloak of authority, but upon examination it is a flimsy garment, because the actual enforcement of the laws is in the hands of various State and local officials.

Although the Governor is denominated the chief executive, in most States he is only one of a group of constitutional executive State officers elected by the people, all independent of each other and, in their executive capacities, responsible only to the electorate, whilst in their administrative capacity they are responsible to the Legislature. The Constitution of my State, which is typical, provides that "the Executive Department shall consist of Governor, Secretary of State, State Auditor, State Treasurer, Attorney-General and Superintendent of Public Instruction." In many States the number of elective officers is much larger. Oklahoma fills 14 State offices by popular election, Mississippi 13, and Arkansas, Louisiana, Michigan, Nebraska, New Mexico and North Dakota 10 each. On the other hand, lucky Maine and New Jersey only elect one. The Governor, of course, has certain constitutional powers peculiar to his office. He is commander-in-chief of the militia; he may convene the Legislature; he may fill certain vacancies in State and district offices; and he has the appointive power. However, he has little authority or supervision over the other elective officers of the Executive Department, each of whom has his own constitutional duties. Indeed, it might almost be said that Utah, for instance, has six Governors instead of one.

Not only has he scant supervision over the other elective State officers in their executive capacity, but he is in substantially the same position with respect to them in their administrative duties and also with respect to the appointive State officials. These have their functions specifically prescribed by law, and it is their duty to obey the law, not to obey the Governor.

At the most the Governor, in his executive capacity, only has authority to see that they perform those duties faithfully.

Perhaps the Governor has come into office on a promise to enforce certain laws which are being flagrantly violated. When he gets on the job he finds that the enforcement of such laws is the duty of local officers over whom he has no control. If a complaint reaches him that the peace officers of some community are winking at law violations, about all he can do is to call the complaint to the attention of the officers who are doing the winking.

Thus he becomes disillusioned about his great executive powers, and he finds that instead of having law enforcement in his hands he is little more than a figurehead in this respect. If he is a philosophical student of our form of government he will not find fault with this arrangement. So far as the general principle is concerned he will doubtless approve the good old theory that this is a government of laws, not of men, and that law enforcement should be kept close to the people.

So much for the Governor's executive function, which, as I have attempted to show, consists of a general supervision over the law-enforcing agencies of the State government. We come now to the administrative function, which consists of actually administering the laws as enacted by the Legislature and interpreted by the Judiciary. In this field the Governor has a much wider influence. Although it is still the duty of the administrative officers to perform the duties laid upon them by the Legislature, and although the Governor is not in a position to exercise his own judgment and discretion in enforcing the laws, he will find that through his power of appointment he has a very substantial, though intangible, influence upon the manner in which many laws are enforced. In this field of administrative functions, if we except his influence upon legislation, he will find most of his own activities and most of his opportunities for useful service, provided the laws of his State invest him with the authority which he needs in order to render the services. All his administrative powers must be delegated to him by the Legislature.

Let us examine his legal powers in this field a little more closely. The National Government is the same as the State governments in that all administrative authority is derived from Congress. Because the President is the only executive officer, and since the members of his cabinet are appointed by him, there is a common belief that he is legally responsible for all their acts. That this view is erroneous was clearly explained in a Senate report during the 46th Congress, which, after enumerating the President's constitutional executive powers, used this language:

The departments and their principal officers are in no sense sharers of this power. They are the creatures of the laws of Congress exercising only such powers and performing only such duties as those laws prescribe. . . . The Secretaries were made heads of departments; they were charged by law with certain duties, and invested by law with certain powers to be used by them in the administration confided to them by the laws. They were in no sense ministers of the President, his hand, his arm, his irresponsible agent, in the execution of his will. There was no relation analogous to that of master and servant, or principal and agent. The President cannot give them dispensation in the performance of duty or relieve them of the penalty of non-performance. He cannot be impeached for their delinquency; he cannot be made to answer before any tribunal for their inefficiency or malversion in office; public opinion does not hold him to stricter responsibility for their official conduct than that of any other officer. They are the creatures of law and bound to do the bidding of the law.

The foregoing doctrine has been sustained by the Supreme Court, as witness the following extract from one of its decisions:

The executive power is vested in a President, and as far as his powers are derived from the Constitution, he is beyond the reach of any other department, except in the mode prescribed by the Constitution through the impeaching power. But it by no means follows that every officer in every branch of that department is under the exclusive direction of the President. Such a principle, we apprehend, is not, certainly cannot, be claimed by the President. There are certain political duties imposed upon many officers in the executive departments, the discharge of which is under the direction of the President. But it would be an alarming doctrine that Congress cannot impose upon any executive officer any duty they may think proper, which is not repugnant to any rights secured and protected by the Constitution, and in such cases, the duty and responsibility grow out of and are subject to the control of the law and not to the direction of the President. And this is emphatically the case where the duty enjoined is of a mere ministerial character.

The same rule, of course, applies to State governments, and hence the plan of centralized administrative control does not mean at all that the Governor will become an autocrat who will try to run every State office and activity. Personally, I have no use for dictators, whether they be of the Mussolini type or of the Lenin type. They all look alike to me, and I should be the last to advocate a scheme that would defeat or impair our representative form of government. But I do think that, in the interest of the taxpayer, our State governments should be organized in such a fashion that they may be able to approach private enterprise in efficiency.

To illustrate the statement that the legislative branch is the source of all administrative authority I need only cite one or two concrete illustrations.

Whether or not the State shall have a system of State highways is for the Legislature to decide. What roads shall be State highways is also for the Legislature to decide. Who shall construct the highways and how much money shall be expended are likewise questions for the Legislature to decide. If the Legislature prescribes a highway program, and creates a highway commission to be appointed by the Governor to carry out the program, it is the commission's duty to build the highways, not the Governor's. The Governor has nothing to do with how, when and where the roads shall be built. His duty is to appoint the commissioners, and see that they carry out the program prescribed by the Legislature. He should, however, have administrative power to see that the commission sets up an efficient organization and does not waste the State's money. He should therefore have the power of removal as well as the power of appointment.

The regulation of rates charged by public utilities is a proper function of the Legislature, but it is not feasible for the Legislature itself to perform that function in a satisfactory manner. It therefore creates a Public Utilities Commission, and authorizes the Governor to appoint its members. The Public Utilities Commission is an arm of the Legislature, not an arm of the Governor, and it would be usurpation on his part to attempt to dictate to the commission with respect to its duties. Nevertheless, even with a punctilious respect for the official powers and duties of the commission, it is entirely appropriate for him to scrutinize the organization and operation of the commission from a business or financial standpoint, with a view toward preventing waste or extravagance.

I need not multiply examples to prove that it is the function of the legislative branch to decide what activities the State shall undertake; to dictate how and by whom the activity shall be carried on; to give the necessary directions and prescribe rules of procedure; to furnish the money to carry on the activity; and to exercise control, by means of adequate accounting, audits, reports and other devices, over the persons to whom the work is entrusted. These are all the administrative functions, and constitute the means by which the Legislature confers administrative authority upon its agents.

Notwithstanding the fact that the Legislature is the source of all administrative authority, there is no reason why the Governor should not be the most important administrative officer, particularly in matters of finance. On the contrary, there is every reason why he should be. For the past 20 years or so the cry has been for greater efficiency and economy in government, both National and State. We are told that Government should adopt the methods of private enterprise where efficiency and economy have been most highly developed. The advice is good, and we ought to study the organization of private business and pattern after its good features. How does a successful corporation function?

In the first place, it has a body of stockholders, who own the business, and who are in it to make money. They elect a board of directors to run the business for them, giving it broad powers as to policies and methods. Once a year the directors report back to the stockholders. If their steward-ship is approved they are usually re-elected. If not, they are superseded by another board.

The directors, however, do not pretend to manage the business. They only determine policies and authorize projects, and they elect a general manager to carry out those policies and projects. Within the limitations imposed by the directors he has authority to conduct the business of the corporation, and he is held responsible for the results. If the Board elects other officers, such as a treasurer and a secretary, their duties are of a subordinate character, and they have no voice in the general management of the business. They have nothing to do with making profits except in so far as they are of assistance to the general manager.

How nearly analogous is the organization of most State governments to this approved type of business organization? If we consider the State as a corporation, the people are the stockholders. They own the business, but they are not in it to make money. They are in it to get certain services as cheaply as possible. They elect a board of directors, known as a Legislature, to run the business for them, giving it broad powers as to policies, direction, supervision and control. Obviously the Legislature, consisting of a large number of members, and meeting only every two years, cannot pretend to manage the business directly; hence it must delegate its authority to others. It therefore farms out its authority to sundry officers, boards and commis-sions. These should all be under the supervision of a general manager who would be responsible to the Legislature. The Legislature, however, does not elect a general manager to act as its agent. The general manager, in the few states which have one, is elected by the people and he is called the Governor. If the Governor were given full authority to supervise the finan-cial administration of the policies and projects of the Legislature, and if he were held responsible for the results, the cases would be nearly parallel, for the mere circumstance that the Governor is elected by the stockholders in-stead of by the directors does not necessarily militate against successful operation of the proposed set-up.

However, there are only a few States where the analogy is approximately complete. In my State, as I have said, we have six managers, all elected by and responsible to the people, and all independent of each other. Many States have a longer list of constitutional elective officers. Although the Governor is nominally the Chief Executive, the other officers are not subordinate to him, and if they do not like his orders they can tell him where to go. Each of these officers usually has important administrative functions added to his constitutional functions, but they are not co-ordinated under one head. They may antagonize each other and all pull in different directions. How long could a private business enterprise survive with that sort of internal discord? How long would such foolishness be tolerated by the stockholders?

It seems anomalous that in our National Constitution we should be willing to say that "the executive power shall be vested in a President of the United States of America," whilst in most of our State Governments the executive power is spread out wide and thin, and the Governor is the Chief Executive in name only. But it is far worse to spread the administrative authority all over the lot, with no centralized control over the spending of the taxpayers' money.

The Secretary of State of the United States, to whom we entrust international affairs of tremendous import, is appointed by the President, but the Secretary of State of most of the States of the Union must be elected by popular vote.

The Attorney-General of the United States, who is the lawyer for the National Government, is appointed by the President, and is therefore in harmonious relationship with the Chief Executive, but in most of the States the Attorney-General is elected by the people, so that he is not only independent of the Chief Executive, but may actually be hostile to him. Why should not the Governor select his own legal adviser, so as to be sure of having a lieutenant of whose ability he is satisfied and upon whose co-operation and loyalty he can depend?

Why should we tolerate a system under which the Governor may be pulling in one direction whilst his fellow officers are pulling in the opposite direction and frustrating his efforts? How can we enforce efficiency under such a system? I do not speak out of any personal grievance. It happens that I am receiving cordial cooperation from my fellow officers of the Executive Department, and they are my personal friends. Unfortunately, this happy condition does not always exist, and the form of organization actually is important. If the other State officers, instead of being elected by popular vote, were appointed by the Governor, they would naturally be his trusted advisers and the State would reap the advantages of the cabinet form of government.

I suppose Utah is not the only State that has worked out a fairly satisfactory form of centralized financial administration despite a multiplicity of elective State officers.   The State has a budget system and the formulation of the budget is the duty of the Governor, as it should be.   The Governor, the Secretary of State and the Attorney-General constitute the State Board of Examiners, who must approve all claims before payment, thereby exercising financial control.   These officers also comprise the State Board of Supplies and Purchase which supervises the purchasing department and performs some of the functions of a department of finance.   This triumvirate therefore exercises broad administrative powers, and we virtually have a commission form of government, instead of the Governor being the real adminstrative head of the State Government.   Perhaps there is something to be said for a multiplicity of counsel.   It is obvious, however, that the same system could be used with appointive officers, and also have the other advantages of the cabinet system.

There is nothing novel in this suggestion that the States should take a leaf out of the Federal Government's book, and centralize administrative authority in the Governor, because several States have already done so.

There is nothing undemocratic about it.   Why should it be considered more democratic to vote for half a dozen candidates, five of whom the average voter does not know, than to vote for one whom the voter does know?   For there is no conceit in the plain statement that in a State election the candidates for Governor are the ones who arouse public interest and around whom the campaign centers, whilst the rest of the candidates are usually just so many more party nominees.   Democracy means that every voter uses his individual judgment and makes his own choice of candidates. In a State election not more than one voter in a thousand even knows the names of the candidates for, say, State Treasurer, and so instead of making a choice he merely registers his political party affiliation.   What is there so democratic about that?   What does the voter gain by it?

As Governor Alexander once said,

A modern business institution is a true democracy, controlled and conducted by those who own its stock yet who know little about the details of the business they conduct.   The American people are said to elevate the dollar above all else, including even their patriotism, yet they are content not to meddle in the details of the business in which their dollars are invested and which returns them other dollars.   They never suspect that in selecting a competent manager to conduct their business they are waiving any of their rights.

This is a good place to put more business into government.   Certainly one officer can be held accountable much better than can six who may all pass the buck to each other. The system of checks and balances is wholesome as between the three departments, but to let one executive officer check another leads to confusion and inefficiency.

The practice of curtailing the powers of the Governor is a relic of colonial times, when the Governor was appointed by the British Crown. The colonists had no voice in his selection and he was seldom chosen from their number. He was regarded as an outsider over whom they had no control, and who administered affairs not for the best interests of the colonists but as the agent of the mother country. There were frequent conflicts between the Governor and the Legislature, and the people invariably sided with the Legislature, especially when the arbitrary will of the Governor prevailed. The result was that the people became embittered and prejudiced against executive and one-man power.

This prejudice remained after the Revolution, and it was deemed necessary to do away with executive tyranny. The Governor was therefore generally elected by the Legislature, and shorn of all but a semblance of power, while the Legislature became supreme.

Gradually, however, the practice grew up of electing the Governor by popular vote. The people learned that when he, no less than the Legislature, was selected by and responsible to them the fear of tyranny was groundless. Furthermore their implicit confidence in the Legislature was shaken by specific cases of legislative corruption and extravagance, and it became evident that the great powers of the Legislature should be curtailed and that some of them should be transferred to another body. During the first half of the nineteenth century there came a wave of extreme democracy, which resulted in frequent elections of almost all public officials, from dog catcher to Governor and Supreme Court judges. While the Governor became independent of the Legislature his power for several decades was not appreciably increased. In fact, in some of the States his duties were so slight that it was not even deemed necessary for him to live at the seat of government.

Since the Civil War there has been a decline in public confidence in the efficiency of popular elections, and simultaneously there has been a great increase in the number of the functions undertaken by the States, which has resulted in the creation of very many new offices. When it became almost a physical impossibility to place on the ballot the names of all the officers to be chosen, many of them were made appointive by the Governor. There has come about a gradual increase in the power, prestige and influence of the Governor, until to-day there is probably more distrust of Legislatures than of Governors. Nevertheless the decentralized type of administration in the American States is still the rule rather than the exception. The object of the framers of the American Constitution was to prevent the government from becoming so strong as to jeopardize the rights and liberties of the individual citizen, and our State constitutions are still cluttered with the efforts in that direction. The inertia of governmental organization is hard to overcome.

There can be no doubt that if we want our State governments to approach the efficiency of private business, we need a more unified, concentrated and efficient type of administrative organization. All competent students of the subject are agreed on this point, and also in the conviction that it can be achieved without any sacrifice of individual liberties.

How can it interfere with individual liberties when all we are talking about is financial administration? The powers of the Legislature will not be affected at all, and the only object is to save money for the taxpayers.

It is not proposed to infringe upon the responsibility of the Legislature in determining what the State shall do and in what activities it shall engage. This does not necessarily mean that the Legislature should specify every detail. In my State, for example, the Legislature designates certain State roads, and makes certain funds available for their construction and maintenance. It is left to the State Road Commission to determine the precise location of each road, the type of construction, and the order in which the several projects shall be built. The system works admirably, and I have recommended a similar arrangement for State buildings. The Legislature, during its brief session, is poorly equipped to make adequate study of the building needs of the State institutions. I think it would be advantageous to have a State building commission make a thorough survey of the State's building needs, and report its recommendations through the Governor to the Legislature. The Legislature might well use these recommendations to aid it in authorizing a building program to meet the State's estimated needs for a period of years, and determine how much money should be spent from time to time. The building commission could then determine the order in which the buildings should be erected and the type of construction, and proceed to carry out the program. Legislative log-rolling would be eliminated, and a higher type of construction could be had at a minimum cost.

The centralized administration herein suggested does not contemplate taking away from the Legislature the function of prescribing the agencies and organizations which shall carry on the activities which it has created. Here again efficiency might be promoted if the Legislature did not attempt to be too specific in the details of internal organization of an activity. Decisions in this field made in advance of actual experience are likely to be productive of harm.

The Legislature should also be left with authority to determine the personnel of the agencies which it creates, particularly the officers who are to be responsible for the direction of the activities. That is, it should determine their number, character, compensation, powers and duties. How far it should go in specifying the subordinate personnel is doubtful, but it can impose a limit by the size of the appropriation. It is for the Legislature to say that the Industrial Commission shall consist of three members, but it is difficult for it wisely to prescribe the number of inspectors, statisticians, reporters and other necessary employes. Centralized administrative control, however, contemplates that the Chief Executive shall prepare a budget of the financial needs of the service and submit it to the Legislature. In the formulation of this budget a careful study of the subordinate personnel would be made for the information and guidance of the Legislature in making appropriations. A businesslike control of expenditures by the Chief Executive is another administrative function that the Chief Executive would perform for the Legislature.

The Legislature, as the source of all administrative authority, must obviously have power to determine means for legislative supervision and control, and it should exercise that right. It can do so by requiring proper records, regular reports, accurate accounts, periodical audits, and such other means as it may deem proper.

With all these safeguards and reservations of power in the Legislature there can be no reason why the Chief Executive should not be invested with the duties and powers of a general manager, and made the real business head of the administration, whom the Legislature will hold responsible for carrying out its declared policies in an efficient manner. The line of administrative authority should run through the Governor to the Legislature, which means that the purely administrative officers should be the subordinates of, and subject to, the superior authority of the Governor. In his administrative capacity, as distinguished from his executive capacity, the Governor will therefore be the subordinate of the Legislature, and will be acting as the agent of the Legislature in controlling financial affairs.

I have tried to convey the idea, and I now repeat it, that there is a fundamental distinction between the responsibility of the Governor in respect to the organization and management of the government and his responsibility in respect to the technical work done by the operating units. What I mean by that is that the Governor should be held responsible for the government being well organized and well run from the business standpoint, but that he should not meddle with the technical work that has been delegated to the operating units by the Legislature. The general manager of an industrial plant does not tell the chemist how to make his analyses, but he does regulate the wages and hours of assistants, and he sees that supplies are economically purchased. If the Governor finds that the operating units are not functioning efficiently from the business standpoint he should have power to interfere, but his responsibility should be restricted to the appointment and dismissal of officers.

I summarize by quoting from an excellent bulletin issued by the Chamber of Commerce of the United States entitled "The Financial Administration of Government." This bulletin states that a proper system of financial administration should be based on certain fundamental principles. The first of these is "The definite recognition of the Chief Executive as the responsible head of the administration, and as such having general responsibility for directing, supervising and controlling the conduct of administrative affairs and particularly those having to do with finance." The second is, "The provision of adequate means through which the Chief Executive may, in fact as well as in name, meet and discharge these responsibilities."

If we accept the principle that the Governor shall be the general manager we must also adopt the rule which is inviolable in private business that he should have the right to hire and fire. A general manager who cannot select his own subordinates is a joke in the business world. Of course, this only refers to the responsible heads of departments, and would not interfere with civil service.

To give the Governor this power will generally require several important changes in constitutional as well as statutory provisions. In the first place in most of the States the chief administrative officers are elected by the people. In the second place, the Governor can only make appointments with the advice and consent of the Senate, and in some States he can only remove them with the concurrence of the Senate. The approval and consent of the Senate may be salutary in connection with the appointment of judges, but when it comes to the appointment of administrative officers to be the subordinates of the Governor it is out of place. It is absurd to hold the Governor responsible and then tie his hands.

It seems proper for Governors to seek more power in order to make themselves more useful to their States. But I have not suggested anything in this article that is not already in successful operation in several States and advocated by competent authorities on State government.

I have not tried to cover the whole field of the Chief Executive's functions. For example, the most conspicuous service rendered by the Governor is often in connection with his influence upon legislation. Through his powers of recommendation and veto he has both a positive and a negative influence upon the enactment of new laws. Moreover, if he assumes the position of leadership which his people expect of him, he can make himself a strong force in behalf of new policies which he considers wise and salutary. While this function is among his chief powers, duties and responsibilities, yet it is not a part of the theme of this article. I have intentionally limited myself to the administrative side of his office, where his usefulness apparently can be increased.

No. 59

[POLITICAL scientists have long urged the adoption of the city manager plan of local government. But some seem to have done so less in the interest of democracy than in the interest of efficiency. In any event, the role of the city manager in his relation to politics and as a community leader is a feature of local government that needs examination. Following is a provocative discussion of the problem.]

THE CITY MANAGER AS A COMMUNITY LEADER [1]

by C. A. Harrell

ONE of the most perplexing problems facing the council-manager movement is the determination of the proper relation between the city manager and the council. In its simplest form the question can be stated thus: To what extent should the city manager attempt to assume the status of a leader in his community? In discussing this problem I shall try to point out what appears to be the desirable road for managers to follow.

The city manager is, of course, already an acknowledged leader in other fields. He is the chief administrator of his municipality. Within the framework of the government he is the leader in personnel matters, in budgetary affairs, in the over-all direction and coordination of the several departments. These leadership functions are taken for granted. But how far should the city manager assume additional leadership functions outside the framework of internal administration?

In the first place the city manager has never been considered only as the administrator of policy. The council makes the final decision on what the policy should be and the council also should defend its action. The manager carries out the policy adopted by the council. But in the process of determining the policy the manager can and should play a most important role. City managers cannot be concerned only with developing better techniques and methods. Such administrative tools are not an end in themselves, but merely serve as means to a much broader end.

[1] C. A. Harrell, "The City Manager as a Community Leader," *Public Management* (October, 1948), Vol. XXX, No. 10, pp. 290-294. Reprinted by permission of *Public Management* and the author.

The ideal city manager is a positive, vital force in the community. He spends a great deal of his time thinking of broad objectives which would greatly improve community life. Why should he hesitate to initiate policy proposals and submit them to the council. Neither the mayor nor individual councilmen can give much time to this task and if the manager also shies away from such leadership the community stands still and important matters are allowed to pass by default.

I believe therefore that we as city managers owe it to our communities to exercise more imagination and vision in initiating policy proposals for action by the council. We have the best interests of our cities at heart. That is our job and that is what we work for. We must broaden our concept of managerial duties and not wait for the council or even citizens to propose actions which we believe the council should consider.

City government is getting to be bigger and more complex every year and numerous problems must be met with vigorous leadership based on experience. The nonpartisan council usually is composed of well-meaning businessmen who have all too little time to give to the constantly increasing details of municipal enterprise. The city manager, a full-time experienced executive responsible to the council, can provide advice, suggestions, and arguments which will give the council a basis for decision.

POSITIVE PROGRAMS

Thus the city manager has a moral obligation to devise careful plans, policies if you will, for submission to the council. He is more than a mere adviser, he is a formulator of action, and a planner. He does not limit himself to worship of the gods of techniques, procedures, and implementation. Rather he visualizes broad objectives, distant goals, far-sighted projects. This done, he presents his explorations in the field of policy to the council for acceptance or rejection. Is this usurping the logical domain of elected representatives? I do not believe it is. It is impossible for the city manager to say what the policy will be.

I hold that it is the manager's solemn duty to say what in his judgment the policy ought to be. He does this by presenting a positive program and by supporting it with logical argument. The manager who aggressively takes such a program directly to the people is of course endangering the principles of the type of government which we represent. But the manager who submits positive programs with definite recommendations directly to the council is making our profession a dynamic force for community good.

This is not to say, or even to intimate, that the council should not initiate policy on its own behalf. I say that it is a joint responsibility. The point I want to make is that since managers are generally better equipped they should never hesitate to recommend specific councilmanic actions by presenting completed paper programs for approval or disapproval.

I say that managers are better equipped to visualize broad objectives because they have surrounded themselves with the proper tools. Many of them have research staffs, almost all have planning agencies, and most know what other cities are doing and have learned to profit from their experiences. And all who cherish their work spend hours dreaming of ways that their city can be improved.

In Norfolk we follow the principle of completed staff work. When one of my assistants tackles a problem, often on his own initiative, he bothers me only once and that is when he presents his solution. And not only the solution. I am handed at the same time the statement of the problem, the facts underlying it, the recommended solution and the letters, already drafted for my signature, which will implement the recommendations contained in the report.

In other words, if I sign my name to this completed staff work, I am formally making the ideas of the assistant my ideas. In my own sphere I have instituted a policy and acknowledge complete responsibility for it, even though I may not have originated it at all. On the other hand, I am perfectly free to reject it in its entirety or to utilize whatever portions I like.

I draw this picture of completed staff work because I think there is, in this instance, an analogy between the assistant and the city manager and the city manager and the council. The principle of completed staff work has merely to be moved up one rung in the organization.

Should this recommendation of positive programs be considered as community leadership? Very definitely, for by his actions the manager is consciously attempting to shape the future development of his community.

All well and good, you may say, but what about the loss of the type of leadership that the elected mayor was able to furnish? How could the city manager possibly hope to assume these aggressive functions and still retain his nonpolitical position?

COMMUNITY LEADERSHIP

The answer to this question lies in the distinction between "community" leadership and "political" leadership. In their *City Manager Government in the United States,* Stone, Price, and Stone very clearly recognize this distinction and make the following notable comment: "Community leadership . . . includes explaining the work of the city government, and proposing new policies for it to the members of the council and the general public, either in private conversation or by public speaking. It includes negotiation with private citizens and community organizations in order to get them to support particular aspects of the work of the city government. . . ."

Conversely, the authors interpret "political" leadership as actively participating in election campaigns, and promoting policies "by offering special favors or threatening political opposition or punishment." An appeal by the manager to the voters over the heads of the councilmen would most certainly constitute political leadership.

The community leadership approach, then, obviously excludes participation in anything which is identified with factional interests. It is intended rather as a positive, factionless approach which has as its purpose the best possible service to the community as a whole.

Well, you may say, just how far should we go with this leadership idea? The fact is many of us have been operating under this principle for years. Each time we give an interview to the press, each time we accept membership in a civic organization, each time we try to "sell the government" to the people, we are openly using features of the community leadership plan.

PUBLIC RELATIONS

How many of you, for instance, have instituted, or have thought of instituting, full-fledged public relations programs in the past several years? How many are interested in trying to develop active support for the community improvement functions which your government may be sponsoring? As city managers we are certainly not concerned with trying to perpetuate any single group, or to lavish any particular segment of the population with favors. But we are, we must be, vitally concerned with creating understanding and support for those policies which will determine the future of our cities.

In most cities the council is no longer looked upon as the leader in public relations. Aside from appearing before civic clubs at irregular intervals and giving occasional interviews to the press, council members seldom attempt to build popular support for municipal programs. Nor is this lack of activity something new. Nonpartisan councilmen, busy with private business affairs, simply cannot give more extensively of their time to the conduct of municipal affairs.

Should we merely take this situation for granted and do nothing about it, or should we consider that public relations can logically be made a function of the administrative branch? I think the whole thing can be boiled down to this: Our broad civic policies either get positive public support, or they fail; either the public is carefully informed, instructed even, or we'll surely watch our programs crumble; either we actively build popular approval for our projects, or we inevitably cultivate destructive criticism and opposition.

There are some city managers who say that popular support is sufficiently generated simply by perfecting a kind of mechanical efficiency; that the visual results of well-handled programs furnish the most effective public relations in themselves, and that no other attempts to develop approval are needed.

I disagree wholeheartedly with this philosophy. Doubtless the civic-minded, the public-spirited, and the more intelligent of our citizens need little more than this. But what about those strata of society which outnumber all others: the lower economic levels, the *un*civic-minded, the indifferent?

In the past we have neglected these groups, and by our neglect we have perpetuated their indifference. We can no longer afford to ignore them if we truly desire good government. We cannot wait for them to appraise intelligently the results of our technical skill, for if we do we wait in vain. On the contrary, we must seize the initiative by taking the government directly to them, and by presenting it in symbols they know and understand.

One thing we must never forget. The average citizen is not technically minded. He has no intimate knowledge of government, nor is he able to absorb the impressive statistical figures that we use so often. In taking the government directly to the people we must always simplify and personalize it; we must try to make it real and tangible; we must try to make *all* our citizens feel that the government belongs to them, that the city programs are *their* programs. These goals can only be achieved by a well-planned, year-round administratively directed public relations program. They can be achieved only by direct action on the part of the city manager and his staff.

Public relations as such means numerous popularized reports, the use of motion pictures and the radio, the publication of featurized leaflets, the pressing into service of private citizen committees, the substitution of informative picturized advertisements for cold legal notices, and so on.

Several months ago we were hard at work in Norfolk devising a new zoning ordinance. Realizing that most people normally feel antagonistic toward any regulatory law, we did not wait for the ordinance to come up before the council unheralded. We built up a careful public information campaign, not around the minute features of the proposed law, but on what the principle of zoning means, what the broad advantages are, how our city would profit from increased zoning regulations. As a result we had far fewer complaints from people who thought they were against something simply because they did not understand it.

CONCLUSION

Such plans of action, I think, should be a part of every city manager's job. The sum total, of course, adds up to this intangible thing called community leadership. Is it desirable? I think it is. Admittedly, it must find its greatest expression indirectly through the council. I have never contended otherwise. I have never contended that we should attempt to become political leaders. To do so would destroy the council-manager plan. But it is my firm conviction that we should use our every effort to inject into our local governments the imagination and vision which they have lacked in the past.

Community leadership on the part of the manager does not detract from the political leadership which derives from the council. Rather, they are parallel leaderships, each enhancing the strength of the other. The city manager cannot possibly be likened to the inconspicuous British career civil servant we've all heard so much about, or to a career administrator in the federal government, whose duty it is to implement impartially major policies which are decided upon by *career* policy-makers. We cannot apply these inappropriate patterns to the conduct of American municipal government.

The city manager can never forget the basic principles of a representative democracy. He cannot lust for political power. But he can and should prescribe for the council desirable community goals which should be achieved. He does not make an issue of his proposals; if the elected representatives of the people cannot be convinced of the logic of his plan, then he devises another, or simply does what the council tells him to do. But he never waits, as a matter of course, for the council to develop initially their own plans for community improvements. To do this would almost invariably subject his city to erratic growth. His stand must be positive, not negative.

And once the Council has acted, he assumes the responsibility, *as an administrative duty*, for selling the policy to the people, for developing, by means of his public relations program, popular approval through education.

These are the fundamental principles, then, of community leadership. The city manager—a community leader or not? I say yes.

Chapter XVII

ADMINISTRATION—ORGANIZATION AND REORGANIZATION

[THE work of government falls into two broad categories: (1) the formulation of policy and (2) the execution of policy. The first of these may be called politics, the second, administration. As we have already seen, the chief executive has duties and carries on activities closely related to both of these phases of governmental activity. He has become chief legislator and has long been, in name at least, chief administrator. Although the Congress, state legislatures, or city councils actually approve or adopt policies, create the machinery of administration, provide for its maintenance, prescribe its duties, and examine its results, the chief executive and members of the administration supply information, make suggestions, draft legislation, and in many other ways take part in the process of formulation of policy. Thus, it should be clear that the doctrine of separation of powers is not carried out in any complete or systematic fashion in American government, and that various parts of the governmental machine do not operate in splendid isolation from each other.

None the less, the administrative organization of government, at some risk to be sure, can be singled out for purposes of description and evaluation. Not only can it be separated for these purposes, but such separation, description, and evaluation are essential for those who wish to improve the American system of government. We should not be misled by Alexander Pope's couplet:

> For forms of government let fools contest
> Whatever is best administered is best.]

No. 60

[ONE of the most common charges brought against the administrative branch of government is that it constitutes a bureaucracy. Those who bring this charge do not usually define what they mean by the word "bureaucracy." They generously imply, however, that the powers of the executive branch of government have been expanded too rapidly at the expense of the legislative and judicial branches and to the danger of the liberties of the people. Furthermore, they intimate that government, at all levels, is attempting to perform too many functions, with the result that the number of governmental employees increases beyond all reason and that taxes become too great a burden.

Each of these three charges is a serious one. If the evidence supports the filing of any one of them, it should be carefully considered by the American people. Democratic self-government may be endangered by an unthinking reliance on executive action; liberty may be threatened by a sudden and unplanned expansion of governmental functions. However, the accusations must be carefully and exhaustively considered. As Professor Dickinson points out, one neither proves the charge nor encourages careful consideration of its implications by raising "The Perennial Cry of Bureaucracy."]

THE PERENNIAL CRY OF BUREAUCRACY [1]

by John Dickinson

NO more frequent charge is brought against some of the activities of the federal administration than that they involve a dangerous and unwarranted increase of bureaucracy. Behind and apart from the merely disparaging implications of the word, this charge of bureaucracy seems more or less reducible in the minds of those who bring it to three specific charges: first, that there is too great an enhancement of the functions and powers of *executive* agencies of government at the expense of the legislative and judicial agencies; second, that the government is undertaking to perform too many functions; and, third, that for the foregoing or other reasons there is too great an increase in the number of governmental employees, and consequently in the expenses of government and the resulting burden on the taxpayer.

These three charges are seldom clearly distinguished by those who fear bureaucracy, and when thus cumulated into an undifferentiated mass impression, they constitute a disquieting picture, each part serving to heighten the lurid shadows of the rest. Naturally, no part of the total impression is more portentous than that which implies violation of supposed constitutional principles through the vesting in executive agencies of powers which belong properly to legislature or judiciary.

This last charge is not new. In being urged against the so-called New Deal legislation, it is simply being made to do a fresh turn of duty after having served steadily for fifty years against most of the important legislation enacted during that period. As a preliminary to examining the merits

[1] John Dickinson, "The Perennial Cry of Bureaucracy," *The Yale Review* (March, 1935), Vol. 24, pp. 448-463. Reprinted by permission of the author and *The Yale Review,* copyright Yale University Press.

of the charge, it will be helpful to look at some special reasons which give it a perennial appeal to certain elements of American opinion.

The first of these is the tendency to distrust and disparagement of the executive branch of government merely as such, which results from an oversimplified and conventionalized reading of English and American governmental history during the seventeenth century. During that period the English executive was the Crown, a hereditary governmental organ not chosen by any process of election, and still claiming to rule by inherent right rather than by delegation of authority from the people. In the American colonies there was the additional fact that the executive in the person of the colonial governor represented in most colonies the alien power of the mother country, three thousand miles away, in opposition to the will of the local legislators. It was primarily for these reasons that the struggle for liberty took the form of a struggle against the executive, rather than because of anything inherently hostile to liberty in the nature of executive power. However, the result was to create in men's reading of history a bias against the executive branch, which disclosed itself forcefully when our new States came to shape their constitutions during the Revolution. "What power have you given to the governor?" a North Carolinian was asked. "Only the power to draw his salary," was the famous reply, and it has always remained easy to rouse those Americans who pride themselves on some historical knowledge to a distrust of any increase whatever in the powers or responsibilities of the executive department, even though that department is, and under our constitutional system has long been, as fully representative and as responsible to the electorate as is the legislature, and even though it has been made fully dependent on the legislature for many of its powers and all its funds. Identification of executive power under our Constitution with the position of an English king like Charles the First, or James the Second, and an attitude towards executive power, based on such identification, represent a misleading perversion of historical knowledge.

Just as oversimplified understanding of history constitutes one reason for disparagement of the executive, so a second reason is supplied by an oversimplified conception of the so-called theory of the "separation of powers," which has become a fixed dogma in the minds of many Americans who have had the benefit of an elementary course in political science. A number of years ago a high school teacher was discussing with me the fact that President Harding had made a point of having the Vice President attend Cabinet meetings, while President Coolidge after his election had given up the practice. "At first," said my friend, "I was inclined to blame President Coolidge for the abandonment of the practice, but on reflection I saw that he was perfectly right because the Vice President, as presiding officer of the Senate, is closely connected with the legislative branch of the government and, therefore, his sitting with the President and Cabinet, who constitute the executive branch, would be a clear violation of the separation of powers and, consequently, unconstitutional."

The separation-of-powers doctrine apparently implies in the popular mind a government rigidly organized along the following simple lines. In the first place, the legislature, consisting of a body of elected representatives, must formulate of its own initiative, and enact in the form of laws, all state-enforceable rules and regulations governing conduct. At this point the executive steps in, in the person of the public prosecutor and the sheriff or marshal with their deputies, and undertakes to discover any infraction or supposed infraction of these laws. In the event of discovery of a supposed infraction, the individual under suspicion is brought by the executive before a court representing the third, or judicial, branch of the government, and the question of the occurrence or non-occurrence of the infraction must be exclusively for the courts to establish. Should the courts find the fact of an infraction, it is their function to pronounce the penalty prescribed by law and turn the offender back to the executive in the person of the sheriff or marshal for the execution of the sentence by way of imprisonment or forfeiture. This is the outline sketch of government which seems to lurk, consciously or unconsciously, behind the thinking of a large body of more or less informed Americans, and supplies the standard by which they are tempted to judge whether or not the legislative measures to which their attention is called are constitutional.

Of course, no government functioning exclusively along these lines could satisfy the needs of even the simplest frontier community. In the first place, they omit all provision for any public-service, as distinguished from purely regulatory, functions of government. In even the simplest and most individualistic communities such public-service functions are represented by the construction and maintenance of roads and bridges, if not of schools. Indeed, in our American communities of colonial times, they sometimes extended to maintenance of such service agencies as sawmills, grist-mills, breweries, and the like.

The discharge and oversight of public-service functions of this character find no place in the framework of government outlined above. Necessarily the agencies performing such functions are "executive" in character. Necessarily also it is impossible in the nature of things for the legislative body to lay down in the form of statutes all the rules and regulations in accordance with which such service agencies must operate. However detailed the legislative mandates might conceivably be as to the width and grading of roads, the materials and type of labor to be used, and so on, there would still inevitably arise for decision possible alternatives within the terms of the legislative mandate which the administrative agency would have to resolve. The legislature itself could not dictate these decisions unless it chose to act itself directly as the road-building agency, that is, as an executive or administrative agency actually carrying out the job.

Nor does the foregoing picture give even an adequate conception of the operation of the regulatory, or police, functions of government. Here again, the executive arm cannot act as simply a mechanical intermediary between the legislature and the courts. Since in the drafting of statutes, as in other human activities, prevision is limited, situations always emerge which raise a doubt as to whether or not they fall within the statutory language. In such cases law enforcement officials will inevitably exercise a power of statutory interpretation to determine whether or not they shall bring the matter into the courts. This is particularly true after public business increases to the point where the official must emphasize certain aspects of his work at the expense of others.

It can be laid down as a basic governmental fact that as public business increases in volume, through the mere increase in the population of the community if for no other reason, the amount of detail which can be directly handled by the legislative body itself will necessarily decrease, and correspondingly the amount of discretion which will be exercised by enforcement and other administrative officials will necessarily increase. This is a plain matter of physics and physiology, wholly apart from considerations of constitutional law or theory. Our colonial legislatures looked into and decided by statutory enactment countless matters which we should to-day regard as of a detailed administrative nature. As the colonies increased in size and became States, the legislatures had to content themselves with laying down rules for the guidance of officials, with the inevitable result that a field for administrative construction of these rules, and hence of administrative discretion, came into being.

Nor is it mere increase in the size of a community which restricts the sphere of detail open to direct action by the legislature. An even greater factor is the increase in the number and variety of human activities and interests. In a simple community the number of things which people do, and which may have to be regulated at certain points in the public interest, is relatively limited. They plough and sow and reap; grind grain into meal or flour, or brew or distil it into strong drink; breed and slaughter animals; cook, spin, weave, and sew within the home; cut timber and build houses; trade a little by way of barter or for cash; marry, bring forth children, make wills, die, and are buried. How different from this short yet almost exhaustive catalogue is the list of activities which men carry on in an advanced modern community, with its systems of credit and banking and insurance, its multiplicity of corporate organizations, its network of transportation facilities, its complicated forms of merchandising and advertising and distribution, its accounting systems and variety of intangible forms of property.

If any legislative body to-day were to undertake to give not an increased, but merely the same, measure of attention to the life of the community which legislatures gave a hundred years ago, it would find the task completely beyond its physical capacities. Unless, therefore, as the size of our communities and the complexity of our social and economic dealings increase, we are to have a progressively *decreasing* amount of governmental intervention and control, our legislatures must act in progressively less and less detail, which means that they must more and more utilize the agency of administrative officials.

One device to which American legislatures early resorted in order to increase their ability to cover the necessary field of action has been to handle their business almost exclusively through committees. The members of each committee devote practically their whole time to a special class of questions, either banking, insurance, public utilities, or the like, and, except in the case of measures of unusual public interest, the results of the labors of these specialized committees are accepted and ratified with very little question by the entire legislative body. This delegation of the functions of the entire body to a small part of the membership illustrates the same physical necessity as the further delegation to administrative officials. Even, however, after it has been carried to the utmost limits, it does not eliminate the necessity for, but still requires to be complemented by, such further administrative delegation.

Just as the inevitable increase of public business presses upon the human limitations of the legislative body, so before long it exhausts the effectiveness of the district attorney and the sheriff as the sole and exclusive agencies of law enforcement. While enforcement is limited to elementary rules of conduct, like those against murder and theft, these officials, if provided with a staff of assistants increasing in rough proportion to the population, might, no doubt, supply all the enforcement needed. When, however, with the economic progress of the community it becomes necessary to administer rules relating to sanitation and public health, transportation facilities and practices, banking, insurance, security issues, conservation of natural resources, pure food, unfair advertising, and similar matters, district attorneys and sheriffs, unless their staffs were increased to unwieldy numbers, would prove entirely inadequate enforcement agencies.

Nor in many of these fields can enforcement with justice to the individual or advantage to the public be confined to the infliction of penalties after the offense has been allowed to occur. We have learned the advantages of prevention. It is better to require that, in advance of being admitted to practice, doctors and dentists should submit to examination and be licensed than that competence should be tacitly assumed and that the protection of the public should rest wholly upon subsequent prosecution and suits by injured persons. It is more effective to require a building permit in advance than to deal with fire hazards or unsanitary structures after the erection has been completed. This system of administrative permits and licenses, which has accordingly spread in response to the need for regulation in new fields, is rooted in an old one. Even in the frontier stage of our culture we required liquor dealers to have licenses and we set up boards to grant them, and no one raised any question of a violation of the separation-of-powers doctrine.

The need for saving the time of the legislature, and the need for other enforcement devices than mere prosecution or civil suits in the courts, led as long ago as the Tudor period in England to the invention of what may be called the administrative method of law enforcement, the application of which to a new field is always met with the cry of bureaucracy. This administrative method may be described in outline as follows. When the legislature decides to provide protection for the public in some such matter as purity of food or drugs, it does not attempt the impossible task of defining specifically in the statute what particular combination of ingredients constitutes impurity in the case of each and every article of food or medicine, but indicates its purpose of requiring that the foods and medicines offered for sale shall be pure and unadulterated, and defines the broad sense in which these terms are used. The legislature then sets up a specialized agency to enforce this statute, whether by granting permits or licenses, or by receiving and passing upon complaints, or by making inspections and orders, as the statute may provide.

In the exercise of these functions the administrative agency, as its work develops, must necessarily bring the comparatively broad provisions of the statute down to specific cases by deciding, for example, whether or not the presence of certain foreign matter in a particular food, or the inclusion of a certain ingredient in a medicine, renders the food or medicine impure or adulterated. In other words, it has to interpret or construe the statute and lend it greater particularity in applying it to specific cases. This process of interpretation is precisely what the courts are continually doing every day when they apply statutes in their decisions. When the administrative body performs the same task, and announces in advance in the form of a rule or regulation that it will consider the inclusion of a particular chemical as constituting an impurity, it is said to be exercising quasi-legislative power and to be making one of those "rules having the force of law," which are so often represented in any argument against bureaucracy as an invasion of the power of the legislative branch of government.

Of course, no invasion of legislative power exists if the rule constitutes a fair and reasonable interpretation of the statute and lies within the field of construction which the legislature intended to leave to the administrative agency. Such construction, as has already been pointed out, must inevitably be performed by whatever agency enforces a law, in view of the limitations on human prevision and legislative prescience. The question is always one of degree—of whether or not the administrative delegation reasonably conforms to the legislative purpose and standard, and whether or not the expression of that standard is sufficiently clear to afford a reasonable guide to administrative action. Under our American practice, the administrative body is on both these points always subject to control by the courts at the instance of any individual alleging actual or threatened injury. Where an administrative body has made a regulation claiming to have the force of law, it is always in the last analysis for the courts to decide whether the legislature has provided a sufficiently definite standard for the administrative body to follow, and whether the administrative ruling reasonably conforms with that standard. If either of these questions is decided in the negative, the administrative regulation is invalid. These safeguards, which exist in our American practice, do not exist in England, and this lack therefore renders inapplicable to our situation the arguments against delegation of legislative power which have been urged with so much force by Lord Hewart and others in England in recent years.

It must also be remembered that, apart from the protection of the courts, any interpretation of a statute laid down in an administrative regulation is subject to correction or repeal by the legislature itself. One of the purposes sought to be accomplished by the delegation of power to make administrative rules and regulations is to provide greater flexibility and adaptability of the law to changing conditions of technology and the arts than would exist if too detailed regulations were permanently frozen into the statute itself. If, however, an administrative regulation, even when sustained by the courts, is, nevertheless, thought by the legislature to be at variance with the then legislative purpose, it can be wiped out as effectively as if it had been originally written into the statute, and in all probability more promptly. There are thus two great safeguards against abuse of administrative rules and regulations—the legislature and the courts.

Administrative power exercised under such safeguards is a vastly different thing from the bureaucratic power of the Ministries of an absolute monarchy which John Stuart Mill had in mind in the famous passage in which he contrasted bureaucratic with representative government. Furthermore, it must be remembered that our administrative officials are as much servants of the people as are our legislative officials. In the state governments many of them are chosen by popular election. Even where appointed, they are designated by a popularly elected chief magistrate, whose policies must be brought to the test of approval by the people at the polls. This removes them altogether from legitimate comparison with the bureaucracies of the Roman empire or of the absolute monarchies of Continental Europe in the eighteenth and early nineteenth centuries.

It is curious that on this point those who bring the charge of bureaucracy against administrative regulation blow both hot and cold. On the one hand, they use arguments forged against irresponsible bureaucracies not subject to popular control. On the other, they frequently urge against our own administrative agencies that they are not impartial and independent but "political" because subject to a chief executive who must justify his conduct at the polls. If it be an argument against administrative agencies to say that they are political, surely the same charge could be brought with at least as much effect against the legislative bodies whose powers these same administrative agencies are accused of wrongfully invading.

The final and complete answer to the argument that delegation to administrative authorities involves an unconstitutional violation of the separation-of-powers doctrine is that this argument has been repeatedly urged upon our highest courts and in every instance rejected. It is valid only on an oversimplified, school-book interpretation of what the separation-of-powers doctrine means. Our courts, following Madison in "The Federalist," have interpreted it in a more realistic sense, so as to render it compatible, rather than inconsistent, with the effective functioning of government. All that the maxim means, says Madison, is "that where the *whole* power of one department is exercised by the same hands which possess the whole power of another department, the fundamental principles of a free constitution are subverted." Where an administrative agency is authorized to make rules and regulations having the force of law, it does not exercise the *whole* legislative power, since those rules and regulations must conform with, and fit within the outlines of, a statute enacted by the legislature.

It is, therefore, no argument against the constitutional validity of legislation, new or old, that it delegates to an arm of the executive department broad authority to determine the details necessary to effectuate legislative policy. All that can be attacked are specific case-to-case instances, where it may be alleged that the particular administrative agency in question has overstepped the limits of the legislative grant or has acted where the legislative mandate is too vague and uncertain to supply a sufficient guide. The broad policy of delegation to the executive, whether or not we choose to disparage it by the word "bureaucracy," has been an integral part of our governmental system since the first statutes enacted by the first Congress under the Constitution.

Nor is there substance to the charge that the administrative system of regulation invades the proper province of the judiciary. No administrative order can be brought home to an individual except through the instrumentality of the courts, or under circumstances which permit court review. A condition of the validity of such an order is that the parties affected must have ample notice and full hearing either before the administrative body or in court. No doubt, in the initial phases of the work of any new administrative agency, there will be certain informalities in procedure until permanent forms can be worked out. If these informalities go so far as in the opinion of the reviewing court to amount to a denial of a fair and full hearing, the administrative order will be set aside.

The criticism is often made that administrative procedure is inherently unfair because not infrequently the same agency both presents a charge and hears it. This claim the courts have never sustained as amounting to a violation of the guarantee of due process or invalidating the constitutionality of administrative procedure. In so far as it has any practical justification, the tendency at present in the organization and reorganization of federal administrative units is to effect so far as possible a separation within each unit between the personnel which initiates proceedings and that which passes upon them in a quasi-judicial capacity.

From all that has been said, it is apparent that the constitutional argument used to support the charge of "bureaucracy" is without substance. The additional arguments, that government is performing too many functions and that it is increasing too greatly the number of governmental employees, are usually employed in a circular fashion. Government is said to be undertaking too many tasks because to perform them it must increase its personnel to the size of an enormous bureaucracy. On the other hand, it is said that the army of government employees constitutes a dangerous bureaucracy because they are employed in unnecessary and superfluous tasks which are a menace to liberty. Each argument rests on the other; separated they lose most of their effectiveness.

It has long become apparent that no abstract formula other than the public convenience and welfare at a given time can determine the proper scope of governmental activities. The liberty of individuals in our Anglo-Saxon tradition means not immunity from government but liberty under law, and law means restraint for the common welfare. Under the increasingly congested and interdependent conditions of modern living, new governmental restrictions are being continually introduced, often in substitution for older forms of restriction which have become obsolete and are abandoned. We are not permitted to operate motor vehicles on the highways without an examination to determine competency. We are not permitted to sell milk or meat without an inspection to determine its purity and fitness for human consumption. We are not permitted to erect buildings without a permit and inspection to determine their safety. Will anyone claim that such restrictions are an invasion of liberty in any real sense, or in any sense that men have fought for? Will anyone claim that we would be better off without them?

The principal argument against many of these governmental regulations sometimes seems to be that they must be administered through governmental officials, who, for the purpose of the argument, are thereupon opprobriously termed "bureaucrats." Here again the circular argument recurs. The regulations are criticised because of the officials, and the chief ground of criticism of the officials is that they administer the regulations. Senator Borah warned us a short time ago of the "deadening hand of bureaucracy." More recently another distinguished statesman has spoken of the "slow strangulation of an engirdling bureaucracy." Are we being "strangled" and "engirdled" by motor vehicle inspectors, or building inspectors, or medical examining boards? Is the "dead hand of bureaucracy" upon us because pure-food inspectors examine the meat we eat and the milk we drink? And, if so, is not the "dead hand of bureaucracy" preferable to the death-dealing bacilli of ptomaine or typhoid?

It may, of course, be granted that some of the regulations introduced by the recent federal recovery legislation are different in degree, if not in kind, from the types of regulation which have just been mentioned. No doubt, plausible arguments could be advanced to support the charge that for one reason or another some of these forms of regulation are not truly in the public interest. With that question we are not here concerned. What we are concerned with is that it is not a valid argument against a new regulation that it must be administered by government officials who, because they have to administer the regulation, can be impugned as an "engirdling" and "deadening" bureaucracy. Whether or not officials constitute a "deadening" bureaucracy depends entirely upon whether or not they perform with promptness, efficiency, and fairness the governmental functions entrusted to them, assuming that those functions are, on their merits, required by the public welfare. There is no reason why governmental officials, just because they are governmental officials, should be regarded as necessarily always acting inefficiently and oppressively any more than the employees of a private corporation or of any other large and important body. To believe that they must always so act is a pure assumption inherited from the days of irresponsible types of government when hereditary hordes of personal servants of an absolute monarch exercised the powers of government without any obligation to satisfy public opinion, and free from the pressure which public opinion can bring. Those conditions are gone. Under a constitution like our own, no government can remain in power if the acts of its official subordinates displease public sentiment. To deny that government officials can act as promptly and justly as men in other stations is not merely to accept the anarchist denial of the possibility of reasonably good government, but is substantially to deny the effectiveness of all corporate action.

It is, of course, conceivable that the field of governmental regulation might be extended to the point where the number of officials needed to administer it would become so large as to constitute an intolerable burden on the rest of the community. If that point were reached, it would no doubt be an indication that the scope of governmental action has been unduly enlarged. That it has been reached is the impression frequently sought to be produced by those who warn us of the dangers of bureaucracy. The figures disprove this contention. The total number of persons employed to-day in the combined service of the state and local as well as the federal governments amounts to . . . [less than 4% of the population. This includes all such civil employees, national, state, and local, as school teachers, lawyers, doctors, clerks, stenographers, judges, engineers, firemen, policemen, and administrators.] This proportion would have seemed slight to our New England ancestors with their multiplicity of fence viewers, hog reeves, hay wards, surveyors, sealers, and other town officials. If to-day the cost of government is high and the annual budgetary outlays large, these expenditures are not primarily for the payment of an army of officials. They are, in great part, payments of interest on sums laid out in the construction of roads and public buildings, and payments to contractors, material men, laborers, and the like. [In state and local governments the largest part of the expenditure traditionally has gone for education and public highways. Both of these are vital to the public welfare.] In the federal government . . . [the major part of the budget is for past wars, present and future national defense, and the international welfare of the nation. This includes interest on the debt, payments and services to veterans, the maintenance of military forces, and programs like Marshall Aid and Point IV. The part of the budget that goes to government employees in salary is a small proportion of the total.] . . .

No one would deny that it is well for a democratic government to be on its guard against bureaucracy in the sense of an inefficient, irresponsible, and overgrown army of public employees. The weakness in the charge of bureaucracy which is so steadily dinned into our ears is, that like the cry of "wolf," it may deaden us to the danger should the danger really come. And, in the meanwhile, it serves to prevent a frank and fruitful examination of many measures on their merits by dragging a false scent across the trail.

No. 61

[HOLDING those who formulate and carry out the policies of government accountable for what they do is one of the basic tenets of democracy. In the nineteenth century the primary struggle in the extension of democracy was that of securing broader and more effective control of the legislative bodies by the people. In the twentieth century the primary struggle is to secure broader and more effective control of the executive by the legislature.

The job of government has become so big and the executive and the administrative agencies have become so important, both in formulating policies and in carrying them out, that the legislature occasionally appears to be at the mercy of the executive. Realizing this, we attempt to do something about it from time to time by administrative reorganization. Both President Roosevelt's Committee on Administrative Management and the more recent Hoover Commission were attempts of this kind. But some of those committed to securing more effective democracy feel that neither of the above committees tackled the fundamental problem of popular control. Further, there are some who, having seen "big government" in operation, believe the task almost insuperable.

Certainly no one alert to the major problems of democracy in our times can afford to ignore the question: "Our Super-Government—Can We Control It?"]

OUR SUPER-GOVERNMENT—CAN WE CONTROL IT? [1]

by James MacGregor Burns

DURING a campaign talk in 1920 Warren G. Harding said airily that "government is a simple thing." A year in the White House was enough to change his mind. "I can't make a damn thing out of this tax problem," he exploded to a secretary one day. "I listen to one side and they seem right—and then—God!—I talk to the other side and they seem just as right, and here I am where I started. God, what a job!"

Stronger Presidents than Harding have had trouble managing "the toughest job on earth." Much of the difficulty has stemmed from the creaking

---

[1] James MacGregor Burns, "Our Super-Government—Can We Control It?", *The New York Times Magazine* (April 24, 1949), pp. 7, 28 ff. Reprinted by permission of *The New York Times Magazine* and the author.

machinery, the fuzzy organization and the sheer bulk of the executive branch of the National Government. For decades our Chief Executives have been trying to overhaul and modernize the administrative apparatus, which Franklin D. Roosevelt once termed a "higgledy-piggledy patchwork of duplicate responsibilities and overlapping powers." Since McKinley's time distinguished committees have been appointed, elaborate studies made, reforms recommended. But our administrative structure has remained sadly out-of-date; the Chief Executive's job has become more grueling than ever.

Guided by an ex-President who had wrestled with the problem in his own day, the latest excursion into the Dark Continent of the national bureaucracy is now coming to an end. The reports of the Hoover Commission on Organization of the Executive Branch indicate that our Federal Government has become the most colossal and complicated enterprise on earth. It employs over two million persons. It spends over forty billions a year—more than the total income of all Americans hardly a generation ago. It employs over half the types of skills found in all private enterprise. It owns one-fifth of the area of the United States.

The Government is big because its jobs are big. The Treasury Department handles almost fifty million individual income tax returns every year, the Postoffice Department almost forty billion pieces of mail. The Veterans Administration manages about forty billion dollars of insurance policies. Sometimes work failures come in proportion to work accomplished. A medium-sized agency confessed to the Hoover Commission last year that it had on hand a backlog of over a quarter-million cubic feet of wartime records that had not yet been processed.

Many Americans eye this burgeoning giant with suspicion, if not with open repugnance. Some of them look eagerly to the day when large parts of it can be dismantled. But the extraordinary fact seems to be that the commission on organization—headed by Herbert Hoover himself and sprinkled with conservative business men and Congressmen—has supplied the most convincing evidence we have yet had that our super-Government is here to stay.

In setting up the commission Congress emphasized an interest not only in economy and efficiency but also in "abolishing services, activities and functions not necessary to the efficient conduct of government." Here was a mandate to the commission to track down the hundreds of worthless bureaus that—according to popular notion—make up a large part of the National Government. But the commission took no such tack. Its efficiency experts found waste—duplication of effort, lack of order, poor control. It has urged the consolidation of activities and the adoption of sweeping reforms. But after sixteen months of exhaustive investigation the commission has not recommended the abolition of any significant function. Indeed, the commission has urged the expansion of a number of Government services.

How can this result be explained? The answer is that the commission and its staff carefully studied the facts of governmental life instead of contenting themselves with generalities about "bureaucracy rampant." They discovered—if they did not already know—that government is not a single entity that can be easily deflated like a balloon. It is a collection of hundreds of separate agencies, rendering a tremendous variety of services to "clients" who depend heavily on those services. It is a collection of human beings with many tasks: a hoof-and-mouth disease inspector in Texas; an economist in Washington; a weather forecaster in New York; a veterans' counselor in Seattle; an expert on Korean affairs in the Pentagon, and thousands of others.

Very few of these functions compete with private enterprise; on the contrary, almost all of them are responses to needs that only government can meet. It has long been agreed that our Government should deliver the mail, wage war, regulate interstate commerce, take the census, and the like; few seriously argue that such tasks could or should be turned over to private individuals.

Our super-Government, in short, has become a fixed part of the "American way of life." It has become a vital instrument for social progress. But its very size and importance make it a costly and dangerous instrument if not properly managed. It is precisely on this point that the Hoover Commission, while recognizing that big government is here to stay, has raised storm warnings.

The American people directly hire and fire only one person—the President —out of the two million in the Executive branch. The Chief Executive must serve as a firm link between the people and their bureaucracy. His office is the funnel through which their needs and urges are translated into administrative action. Everything depends on the responsiveness of the bureaucracy to the President's—and hence to the people's—direction.

That is where the trouble lies. By far the most significant finding of the Hoover Commission is that the Chief Executive does not have full control of his own establishment. Authority is scattered about; lines of control are tangled and broken. Broad policy does not flow from the White House to the agencies as clearly as it should, but is confused and dissipated.

For one thing, the agencies are not set up in well-defined, cohesive groupings. President Truman has shown visitors a huge chart on his office wall picturing well over 100 officials required by law to report to the Chief Executive alone, and has complained that "I cannot even see all these men, let alone actually study what they are doing." Even if the President were able to ignore his legislative, political and ceremonial duties and concentrate wholly on administration—which he cannot do—he would have only a few minutes a week to meet with these officials.

With an adequate staff the Chief Executive might give a measure of direction and coordination to this labyrinth of departments and commissions. But he is lacking some of the indispensable tools of good management. Control of personnel is not fully in his hands, and he lacks the means to check on the performance of the agencies. The President cannot choose his own staff as freely as he would like. Nor can he rely on his Cabinet for disinterested advice, because the members are concerned mainly with their departmental duties and often represent warring factions in the party. A dozen years ago President Roosevelt's Committee on Administrative Management summed up the situation simply: "The President needs help." The need is even greater to-day.

The strong chain of command that should tie the bureaucracy to the President and thus to the people is broken at other points. Subordinate officials have been given power by law to act independently of the Chief Executive. For example, the Secretary of the Interior can handle the sale of helium to foreign nations, and the Army Chief of Engineers can prepare river development plans without referring to superior authority. Independent boards make vitally important decisions that are beyond Presidential reach. The Maritime Commission's control of shipping can sharply affect our foreign relations. Yet the President must negotiate with the Maritime Commissioners almost as with foreign plenipotentiaries.

The chain of command is also weakened at the departmental level. Often the departments are mere "holding companies" for semi-independent bureaus that go their own way. Such a situation breeds administrative slackness and aloofness, and what Pendleton Herring called "quiet sabotage by unsympathetic technicians and genteel blackmail by high policy officials." Delay and fumbling are hard enough to curb under any conditions. Harry Hopkins complained during the war, according to Robert E. Sherwood, that after important decisions had been reached by Mr. Roosevelt and Mr. Churchill and by the generals and admirals, months-long delays would occur—"and then you start investigating and it takes you weeks to find out that the orders have been deliberately stalled on the desk of some lieutenant commander or lieutenant colonel down on Constitution Avenue."

If failures of top control are serious in the civilian agencies, they are positively dangerous in the military. Traditionally, Americans have had a healthy fear of military cliques and of the "man on horseback." Knowing something about military oppression, the framers of the Constitution carefully put the Army and Navy under civilian control. The safeguards they provided are all the more important under conditions of modern war, whether of the atomic, bacteriological, or "push-button" variety. The fact that the per capita cost of defense is now $100 annually has given taxpayers a tremendous stake in the efficiency of the military as well as its responsibility.

On this score, too, the Hoover Commission has uttered an urgent warning. It reports that centralized civilian control "scarcely exists." It has found a weak link in the chain of command between the Secretary of Defense and the service departments—the Army, Navy and Air Force. The basic trouble here arises from the manner in which the new military establishment was tacked together as a federation of competing services rather than as a unified, integrated system with clear control in the hands of the President and the Secretary of Defense. The Joint Chiefs of Staff—composed of military chiefs—are virtually a law unto themselves.

To clear up the disorganization and irresponsibility in both the civilian and military parts of the Executive branch, the Hoover Commission has proposed some old-fashioned remedies. Among these are intelligent grouping of agencies in major departments, centralization of authority in the President, clear lines of command and accountability, and adequate staff services. These suggestions are, indeed, so obvious that the question arises: Why is it that after a decade or two of big government we are still trying to apply first principles to the running of our administrative machinery?

If our Chief Executives had had the power to manage the Executive branch as they wished, they long ago would have applied these first principles in an effort to lighten their own heavy burdens. But the Constitution, while vesting the "executive power" in the President, does not give him exclusive authority over his own branch of government. Under our system of checks and balances Congress has considerable control of administration, just as the President in turn takes part in lawmaking through his veto and other powers.

Congress determines whether a new function of government will be placed firmly under the President or will be somewhat independent of him. It can give the President a good deal of leeway in setting up agencies, or it can specify provisions that bind the President at every turn. Congress, in short, has the power to organize the Executive branch—and to reorganize it. Even more important, the Senate and House of Representatives hold the "power of the purse" through their appropriations committees.

Along with these constitutional powers are others that have grown up by custom and usage. The House and Senate have expanded their investigating power into strong tools for influencing administrators. Sometimes the probes are full-dress committee inquiries conducted amid exploding flash bulbs; sometimes they are quiet "fishing expeditions" by one or two Congressmen with special interests. In any event, they help to make the harassed administrator watchful of his Congressional relationships. Finally, Congress has considerable weight in the selection of officials. Under the Constitution the Senate must confirm major appointments; moreover, the President, by the unwritten rule of "Senatorial courtesy," must clear thousands of selections with interested Congressmen.

Inevitably Congress has come to wield day-to-day influence over large parts of the Executive branch. Inevitably, too, the bureaucrat has come to look not simply to the White House for orders and support, but also to Capitol Hill. Administrators are quick to see that Presidents may come and go, political parties may rise and fall, but the committee chieftains in Congress seem to go on forever.

What is the result? Not only is control of the bureaucracy divided between President and Congress. In Congress it is further divided among Senate, House, legislative blocs, committees, subcommittees and individual members. As a result of this fragmentation of power in Congress one finds lines of authority running horizontally from committee or Congressman to department or bureau chief, so that authority is shifted from the President and dispersed throughout the bureaucracy.

Under such conditions any hope of pinning responsibility for mistakes or achievements on the proper officials often becomes forlorn indeed. The source of administrative direction often seems to be far underground, lost in a maze of subterranean channels among President, administrators, Congressional blocs and committees. "There is no danger in power," Woodrow Wilson said, "if only it be not irresponsible. If it be divided, dealt out in shares to many, it is obscured; and if it be obscured, it is made irresponsible."

The Hoover Commission wants to pin on the President as much executive responsibility as the Constitution will allow, and thus to make him strictly accountable to Congress *as a whole* and to the people. Its pleas for a stronger chain of command from the President downward stem from its conviction that singleness of control is the essence of both responsibility and efficiency.

Unhappy experience indicates, however, that any move to reorganize the Executive branch will run head-on into the opposition of the groups that profit from the present state of affairs. Every major function of government is carried on amid intense pressures from the interests affected. Agency heads are often caught squarely in the storm center of labor politics, farm politics, transportation politics, medical politics, as the case may be. They cultivate close ties with interests they promote or regulate. Sometimes they find it hard to mediate between the national welfare and the interest of a particular group.

Congress as a whole genuinely favors responsibility and efficiency in government. But individual Congressmen and blocs in each chamber are likely to demand that their own agencies be left out of any plan for firmer control by the President. They prefer the agencies to be more vulnerable to Congressional control, to be more responsive to the affected interests. The Congressmen cannot be blamed for holding such views, for they too are under pressure from the groups dominant in their states and districts. The Hoover Commission had only to suggest the shift of some public works functions from the Corps of Engineers to the Interior Department for a storm of protests to descend on Capitol Hill.

A sizable group of Congressmen opposed to reorganization can log-roll the proposals to death. The process is much like the traditional handling of tariff bills, when Congressmen forgot their free-trade principles in their zeal for protection for the "folks back home" and busily swapped concessions with one another. The only remedy for such log-rolling is to delegate extensive power to the President to draw up proposals. In 1912 Congress granted President Taft power to make reorganization changes without referring back to the Legislative branch.

More recently Congress has been niggardly in giving the President reorganization powers. Changes proposed by Presidents Coolidge and Hoover failed in the face of stout resistance. In 1937, after hearing the advice of his Committee on Administrative Management, President Roosevelt asked Congress for broad reorganization authority. Along with specific changes he proposed that the President have the power to draw up reform proposals; these would become law unless disapproved by both Senate and House within sixty days.

This proposal provoked a great hue and cry from groups that feared the effect of the plans on their favorite agencies. Although Taft had received far greater reorganization power, the President's bill was soon dubbed the "dictator bill." The violent fight over the Supreme Court reform proposal had just taken place, and many Americans swallowed the charge that the reorganization bill was but another move toward executive tyranny. Deluged by telegrams, the House killed the bill. In 1939 a far weaker act was passed, later to be renewed in about the same form until 1948.

President Truman recently asked Congress to re-enact and broaden the power to initiate reorganization plans. The Hoover Commission heartily supports this request. It has warned, moreover, against putting limitations on the President's power, for "once the limiting and exempting process is begun," the commission says, "it will end the possibility of achieving really substantial results." No safeguard is necessary other than the right of Congress to veto Presidential reorganization plans as a whole.

The renewal of the Reorganization Act—and the form in which it is renewed—will be one of the important issues facing Americans during the immediate years ahead. Already a sharp battle seems to be shaping up. Last January Congressional leaders told President Truman flatly that no reorganization bill could pass unless several independent commissions were exempted. More "grasshopper bites," as Chairman Hoover called them, were taken out of the bill before it passed the House. Recently Congressmen have complained of lobbying against proposed reforms by pressure groups and even by agency heads.

Much will depend on the ability of Americans to understand that granting the President more power over the Executive branch is a move not toward dictatorship but toward more responsible government. Years ago Lincoln stressed the need of maintaining a Government strong enough to fulfill its obligations but not too strong for the liberties of the people. A Chief Executive accountable to people and Congress and firmly in control of the bureaucracy is a first step in meeting that need. For in the age of super-Government, nothing can last very long without skillful and responsible management—not even our own democracy.

[In 1949, the Congress granted the President fairly broad reorganization powers. Under the grant, President Truman submitted a series of reorganization proposals to Congress based on the Hoover Commission Report. With the exception of the first proposal—for a new Welfare Department— the Congress approved. The job of reorganization is a continuous one, however, and calls for the constant consideration of citizens and public officials.]

No. 62

[If holding the administration accountable to the people is basic to democracy, every proposal for administrative reorganization must be examined not only to see how it increases efficiency but to see what it does to accountability. The student of government must be as much interested in the location of power as in the efficiency with which power is exercised. The following selection by Professor Hyneman is especially valuable because it helps us evaluate the administrative machinery we already have, as well as the proposals that are made for changing it.]

ADMINISTRATIVE REORGANIZATION [1]

by Charles S. Hyneman

·   ·   ·   ·   ·   ·   ·

THE pattern of state administrative reorganization which came to be generally accepted was shaped by many hands. The most systematic and one of the most doctrinaire justifications of the integrated administrative structure was Mr. W. F. Willoughby's *Principles of Public Administration,* published in 1927. Mr. Willoughby wrote this book, he said, to establish the position that "in administration there are certain fundamental principles of general application, analogous to those characterizing any science, which must be observed if the end of administration, efficiency in operation, is to be secured." While many writers, before and since this work appeared, have suggested that different ills may require different remedies, almost everyone entitled to professional consideration who wrote on public administration from 1915 to 1936 accepted the "principles" which he announced; and most of them appeared as convinced of their incontestability as Mr. Willoughby himself. With virtually all students of public administration "efficiency in operation" was the end of government and integration through reorganization the only path to that goal.

As early as 1922 Mr. Francis W. Coker filed his dissent from the prevailing theory, but his essay seems not appreciably to have stayed the march to orthodoxy. In 1927, the year of Mr. Willoughby's *Principles,* Mr. W. H. Edwards published a series of articles in which he audaciously characterized the prevailing program of reorganization as the concoction of "political medicine men," and a "cure-all" which would soon "be buried in the potter's field of political panaceas." His attack, incisive and scathing, was ignored. Three years later Mr. Harvey Walker questioned whether boasted achievements were due to integration and disputed the reasoning of orthodox reorganizers so far as seemed necessary to justify a competing program of reorganization which he has had on the market ever since.

I find nothing in the literature of public administration from 1930 until 1936 that could be said to challenge the orthodox position in respect to administrative reorganization. In 1936 Mr. Leonard D. White applied a "scrubbing brush" to Mr. Willoughby's "principles" and, when he had freed them of "the layers of surface associations," found (I convert Mr. White's

[1] Charles S. Hyneman, "Administrative Reorganization," *The Journal of Politics* (February, 1939), Vol. 1, pp. 62-65. Reprinted by permission of *The Journal of Politics* and the author. The footnotes in the original version are omitted here.

clear implication into positive assertion) that they were "hopes, assertions, and opinions."

Mr. Porter's departure from the approved pattern of organization has already been noted. It remains to record the most significant challenge to orthodoxy since the blistering attack by Edwards—that currently made by representatives of the Institute of Government Research of Brookings Institution. In their report to the Byrd Committee in 1937, the Brookings group managed to challenge nearly every one of the tenets of orthodox administrative theory. Since they were concerned with national administration, their remarks constituted at best an oblique attack on the state reorganization movement. What the report to the Byrd Committee lacked in directness was supplied, however, by Mr. A. C. Millspaugh in his contribution to the *Essays in Political Science in Honor of Westel Woodbury Willoughby*. The volume contained two essays on public administration. In one Mr. W. F. Willoughby reidentified his "hopes, assertions, and opinions" as "fundamental principles" and pointed to state reorganization as their triumph in practice. In the other Mr. Millspaugh condemned the reorganization program as "theoretically unsound," suffering from "unimaginativeness, impractical theorizing, and, of course, inadequate factual support."

The "fundamental principles" which Mr. Willoughby arrived at by "rigid application of scientific methods" were found by Mr. White to be merely "hopes, assertions, and opinions," and by Mr. Millspaugh to be "theoretically unsound." What, then, is the scientific character of the state reorganization movement?

Judgments arrived at intuitively may be sound though not supported by recitation of evidence or convincing argumentation. It is nevertheless worthwhile to examine the quality of the literature which fortifies a position. That can best be done in this instance, I think, by testing the argument against a series of questions; the reasoning which supports reorganization will be convincing to one, it seems to me, only as it satisfies him on the following points.

1. *Is "efficiency" acceptable as the first objective of reorganization?* Mr. Willoughby clearly states that "efficiency in operation" is "the end of administration"; the literature makes it abundantly clear that many other writers and consultants are concerned first of all to accomplish savings in materials and effort.

There are many grounds for discontent with American state government besides its inefficiency and wastefulness. What does the administrative reorganization program, designed to achieve efficiency and economy, offer to the man whose chief concern is for certain other qualities in his government —whose chief concern is that vision, imagination, and courage predominate in the execution, adaptation, or modification of policy? "An administrative organization," says Mr. Porter, "which is designed wholly in accordance with the theory that the sole function of an administrative department is to *do* things may not be suited to the task of deciding *what* shall be done." Apparently there is a good deal of feeling in non-academic circles that organization for efficiency, by way of integration, is pretty sure to be destructive of vigorous, far-sighted development of policy.

I find nowhere in the literature dealing with state reorganization a single statement designed to put Mr. Porter's doubts at rest—nowhere a statement designed to demonstrate that a broader "social efficiency" necessarily follows upon the achievement of "efficiency in operation."

The rationalization of reorganization is addressed to the taxpayer; it makes no promise to the laboring man concerned about revision of the industrial rules and regulations nor to the investor demanding that great capitalists be forced to respect the blue sky law. If such people are led intelligently to embrace the reorganization program it is because they have themselves conceived that devices for efficiency will effectuate the policy they desire.

2. *Can work of administrative character be divorced from control of policy?* The literature supporting the reorganization movement is thick with statements that work of an administrative character should be separated from policy determination and the administrative work entrusted to officials controlled by the chief executive. If such a severance is possible, the dilemma of reconciling "efficiency in operation" with vision and courage in policy determination may be solved. In very few instances, however, does one find in the literature of reorganization either evidence or argument designed to demonstrate that such a severance is practically possible. The proposition is certainly not self-evident; indeed there is a body of experience to suggest that it cannot be accomplished. Every one of the Illinois code departments, for instance, exercises important control over persons and property; every one makes rules and regulations having the force and effect of law; every one makes adjudications in which matters vital to the livelihood of individuals are determined.

The formulation of rules and regulations and the conduct of adjudications can of course be taken from the department head and entrusted to a board. But even if this is done the department head will retain important control over policy for he will decide whether the law is to be the same for the rich as the poor; whether one interest group is to use government to enthrone its advantage at the cost of other groups. If the department head is stripped of such control over policy he becomes a mere office-manager; if such control over policy is vested in a board, then the kind of department which Mr. Porter recommends is thereby created and the departmental situation which reorganization was designed to terminate is reestablished.

3. *What evidence is there that single officers are preferable to boards for work of an administrative character?* Conceding for the moment that the chief objective of reorganization is "efficiency in operation" and that it is possible to separate work of an administrative character from policy determination, what evidence is there to establish the superiority of the single officer over the board for administrative work? The answer is—nothing that need be convincing to a skeptical mind. I find no record of an extended experience in careful observation. There is a great deal of convincing testimony that boards have proven unsatisfactory, but in no instance have I found these statements accompanied by the assertion that single officers in the same state or single officers heading like departments in other states were any more satisfactory. It is pointed out that continental European countries prefer single officers to boards; I have nowhere encountered the statement that this is the cause of some superiority of their government over ours.

It is customary to point to the business corporation as an organization that achieves efficiency through the use of single rather than plural officers. The analogy will not be of much value, however, unless the decisions made by the officer of the corporation are comparable to those entrusted to the state department. Is it not true that most of the important "administrative" decisions of the corporation go to the board of directors—the validation of major purchases, determination of pay increases, location of new plants, establishment of a basic advertising program? But these decisions are of a kind with those which confront the state department head, whether single officer or board. And what of the use of committees of officers in the business corporation? Several of the leading retail merchandizing corporations will not permit the department head to select a store site, commit the corporation to lease or purchase of real estate, or make a contract for any major alteration of store properties; such decisions go to a committee of administrative officers where to quote one department head, "they take nothing for granted; you have to satisfy them on every point." Is this not grist for Mr. Porter's mill?

The supporters of reorganization certainly have not shown their readers all facets of the corporate analogy.

Action is the imperative need in state government, says Mr. Austin Macdonald; single officers are the key to action, say all the supporters of reorganization. When [certain dictators] cry that the day for deliberation is past and the time for action is at hand they are urging a nation to a program; they are not denying leaders the opportunity to consult with one another. When Mr. Macdonald cries for action, he demands that major policies be formulated before leaders can get together. His picture of government in action is perhaps fairly accurate for the emergency ward of a hospital; has it any validity for government where one is likely to encounter it? Can Mr. Macdonald and other proponents of the integrated state have misconceived that the need of firmness in enforcing compromise is, instead, a necessity of avoiding compromise?

4. *Do we need the whole reorganization program in order to obtain central direction of administration?* All students of administration are agreed, I believe—including Coker, Edwards, and Millspaugh—that the governor ought to be given more supervisory power than he possesses in many of our non-integrated state administrative systems. But in order to get a satisfactory central direction of administration, is it necessary that the governor have power to appoint and remove department heads at will? It is Mr. Porter's contention that if the governor had adequate financial control and a dependable force of men to handle that and other staff functions he would possess "the instruments through which a governor could dominate all the administrative activities of the state if he wished to do so." My reading of Mr. Harvey Walker and the Brookings report to the Byrd Committee indicates that Mr. Porter is not alone in his views.

Mr. Porter offers much argument but little evidence to support his point. In this he is matched by those who demand the most thorough implementation of executive control—there is a surfeit of "reason dictates," a dearth of "this occurrence demonstrates."

5. *What is the truth as to administrative accomplishments under reorganization?* "Where sound consolidation plans have been adopted," said the unrepentant and unreformed Brookings Institution in 1930, "there has resulted almost universally an improved type of public service at a decreased public expenditure." On the other hand, Mr. Harvey Walker asserts that "it is very difficult to point to any concrete financial advantage gained through the adoption of a reorganization plan." Mr. Buck accredits some praiseworthy accomplishment to reorganization in practically every state that has been reorganized. Some of the accounts appear to differ little from campaign boasts. One, at least, is a story of mid-depression reduction in the cost of government, no effort having been made, so far as Mr. Buck enlightens us, to determine whether these economies were not being paralleled in every other state in the union.

Nearly all the economies which Mr. Buck recounts are supposed to have occurred during the administration of the governor who initiated reorganization, yet at most only two or three writers have pointed out that possibly these men were strong executives who would have achieved the same economies, with or without a budget, under a non-integrated system of semi-independent departments. I have encountered only two conscientious efforts to evaluate the accomplishments of reorganization. One frankly admitted inability to determine what accomplishments were due to reorganization; from the other I could gather nothing which need alter any man's prejudices on the subject.

6. *Can the governor be made responsible for the conduct of administration?* It is now more than . . . [twenty-five] years since Mussolini marched on Rome; a good deal of the world's population is in the grip of dictatorship. Yet the literature of administrative reorganization is filled with contempt for those who warn against overarming the chief executive with power. Not until 1935 did the literature of public administration (except for the critics of reorganization) reveal anything approaching concern to subject the chief executive to effective popular control.

The customary reconciliation of democratic ideals with concentration of power is presented in the following paragraph:

> If the plan here proposed is adopted, the Governor would stand out in the limelight of public opinion as never before. The economies of his administration would redound to his credit, while waste and extravagance could be laid at his door. He would become in reality the responsible executive of the State, whose duty it would be to serve the best interests of the people; and if he did not do this he would have to put his political aspirations forever behind him.

Unfortunately for the persuasiveness of the foregoing argument, the quotation is preceded by the statement that, "As a matter of fact, the voters really look to the Governor at the present time as the responsible head of the State administration, although they elect several other administrative officers." If the people already believe the governor is chief of the administration, what difference does it make, so far as they are concerned, for him actually to assume that position? What reason is there to suppose that voters will assert a new vigilance simply because an official has assumed a power which they already thought he possessed?

Can this supposed transformation of the voter's attitude be explained by the fact that formerly he had divided his attention between so many candidates for state office that he was unable to scrutinize the records of the candidates for the governorship? Evidently not, since one frequently encounters the statement that prior to reorganization the voter gave little or no attention to the candidates for subordinate administrative positions. What relief, in that case, does the voter obtain when the ballot is shortened? Concede that the voter did divide his attention between the candidates for the various elective offices prior to reorganization, concede that he is freed of a part of that burden so that he can give his whole attention (so far as not drawn off to national and local issues) to the candidates for the governorship, how much wiser will he be on election day? What facts or gossip concerning the candidates for governor can be expected to come his way because of the elimination of other offices from the campaign?

Perhaps there is something to the statement that the battle for the governorship, under long or short ballot, will regularly be fought out on a legislative or political issue—rarely if ever on an issue of honest, enlightened and economical conduct of administration. Perhaps the market for news and the agencies for its distribution and dramatization in many of the states are such that the public can never expect to be reliably informed on the conduct of public administration. Perhaps popular control of the executive can be achieved only when there exists a representative assembly which can match power with power—such an assembly as now exists in none of the forty-eight states.

Mr. Coker, Mr. Edwards, and Mr. Millspaugh are concerned about this. A few other students of administration are aware that the problem of popular control exists. Most of the rationalizers of state reorganization, however, appear to proceed blithely on the assumption that God looks after fools, drunkards and the liberties of the people.

It has been my intention to show, as accurately and adequately as the space at my disposal permits, to what extent the literature supporting the reorganization movement deals in demonstrable truth as distinguished from supposition born out of wish. I find my own view of the argument adequately expressed in John Locke's remarks on Filmer's *Patriarchia*.

> If he has in that chapter, or anywhere in the whole treatise, given any other proofs of "Adam's royal authority" other than by often repeating it, which, among some men, goes for argument, I desire anybody for him to show me the place and page, that I may be convinced of my mistake and acknowledge my oversight. If no such arguments are to be found, I beseech those men who have so much cried up this book to consider whether they do not give the world cause to suspect that it is not the force of reason and argument that makes them for absolute monarchy, but some other by interest, and therefore are resolved to applaud any author that writes in favour of this doctrine, whether he support it with reason or no. But I hope they do not expect that rational and indifferent men should be brought over to their opinion, because this their great doctor of it, in a discourse made on purpose,

to set up the "absolute monarchical power of Adam" in opposition to the "natural freedom" of mankind, has said so little to prove it, from whence it is rather naturally to be concluded that there is little to be said.

My complaint, up to this point, has been directed against a betrayal of the intellectual obligations of a learned profession; the evidence will also sustain an indictment of the profession on ethical grounds. Men invited to recommend a program which promises efficiency and economy for a state, as I see it, have not only mistaken supposition for fact and hypothesis for principle; they have failed to warn their clients (in the printed report at least) of the enormous risk involved in creating a powerful chief executive in a state which has no responsible legislature and in many instances no effective opposition party.

Text-book writers, while admitting that the accepted pattern of reorganization is disputed by men entitled to respect, have nonetheless proceeded, through the use of sweet and sour words, to prejudice the immature student by strictly emotional as distinguished from intellectual appeals. Senatorial confirmation of appointments is a "vicious arrangement"; efforts to transform the impeachment process into a device for establishing legislative supremacy over the executive in matters of policy are "both ridiculous and deplorable"; a "comprehensive plan" prepared by "experts" for Maryland was rejected in favor of a "makeshift scheme"—the author not mentioning that the adopted arrangement was carefully studied by responsible persons and was quite as "comprehensive" as the one rejected.

To my complaint and to this indictment it is possible, however, to enter a general demurrer. Perhaps the ideal of our profession is the faith of a priesthood rather than the skepticism of a science; if so, it is no offense to dogmatize assumptions and eschew inquiry. Perhaps a code of ethics is too dear a luxury for a profession still driving hard to establish prestige; if so, who shall condemn us if we indulge occasionally in cozenage or venture close to barratry?

No. 63

[Professor Hyneman has made it clear that proposals for reorganization of the administrative machine should be subjected to careful scrutiny before they are accepted. Professor Edwards looks into a related matter: Have reorganizations succeeded where they have been made?

In answering this question, Professor Edwards reviews what had been accomplished in state administrative reorganization up to the time he wrote. Although there have been some further efforts since that time, his general observations still stand. They bring out factors that should be taken into account in any analysis of administrative reorganization.]

HAS STATE REORGANIZATION SUCCEEDED? [1]

by William H. Edwards

THE nation-wide controversy aroused by the President's plan to reorganize federal administration has revived interest in state reorganization. The federal plan is said to be based upon state reorganization principles. For that matter, state reorganizations were based upon federal principles, and were advanced as the "federal plan for states." Such mutual admiration signifies that what is good enough for the federal government is good enough for the states, and vice versa. At this turn of the federal-organization-state-reorganization-federal-reorganization wheel, information is needed concerning results in the states as a basis for evaluating the federal plan. In 1931 Charles A. Beard said: "No one has taken the trouble to examine in minute detail the achievements of the machinery which has been installed in fifteen states." The present writer has since attempted such an examination. Only a few facts and conclusions, reached by a study of what happened in the first fifteen states to be reorganized, can be cited here.

The first question to consider is: To what extent have the states actually been reorganized in accordance with the basic reorganization principle? That principle is to centralize administrative control in the governor by consolidating many agencies into a few large functional departments, each headed by one individual appointed by the governor.

Consolidation of agencies by abolishment and assignment of their functions to new code departments was not as great as has been claimed. The actual reduction ranged from thirty-seven in Illinois to three in Maryland. The average number of agencies reduced by consolidation in the fifteen states was seventeen. The average number absorbed by each code department was one and one-half. The Massachusetts consolidation, according to Mr. A. E. Buck, was so insignificant that it accomplished no reduction. Yet it leads ten other states. South Dakota, with only two reorganized departments, accomplished a greater reduction than nine other states. Thus the reductions in most states were insignificant and were not large in comparison with the number existing before reorganization, which we were informed ran into the hundreds. Now as a result of the tendency toward decentralization, there are almost as many agencies as before reorganization.

Concerning the nature of agencies abolished, many were of minor ad-

[1] William H. Edwards, "Has State Reorganization Succeeded?" *State Government* (October, 1938), Vol. 11, pp. 183-184. Reprinted by permission of the author and *State Government*. A fuller statement of the author's views may be found in the *Southwestern Social Science Quarterly*, June, 1938.

ministrative importance. Some were inactive before reorganization. Others, whose functions were important, were abolished and their functions were not given to any other agency. This was not consolidation but cessation of desirable government activities. Some proper government functions were eliminated apparently because they were performed by plural-headed agencies—the disapproved type of overhead organization.

With regard to the scope and nature of the reorganized departments, whole functional fields were left outside the code structure in nearly every state. Numerous "reorganized" departments absorbed no functions of abolished agencies, but were merely the same old departments, which were placed bodily within the code structure without alteration. Some departments are departments in name only, such as headless departments, departments composed primarily of semi-independent bodies, and departments in which divisions are in practice separate agencies. Consolidations have frequently united totally unrelated functions. Departments have also been overloaded with too many functions for one director to oversee. In short, even on paper there are fewer consolidations than claimed, and the codes as administered are more decentralized than they seem from the law, so that the administrative structure, in fact, is still a diffuse organization.

Consolidation was achieved to a greater extent by attaching semi-independent agencies to code departments than by abolishing agencies and merging their functions in integrated departments. In the fifteen states as a whole over twice as many agencies were attached as were abolished. In each of nine states the number of attached agencies exceeds the number abolished. In Maryland the proportion of attachment to abolishment is over fifteen to one. New York has 120 attached agencies. Almost all attached agencies are plural-headed and largely independent of the governor. When agencies are attached to departments which are independent of the governor, he is farther removed from control than if they had been left unattached. Departments with attached agencies are often departments in name only. Many "attached" agencies are unattached in practice. Frequently so much confusion of authority has resulted from attaching agencies to code departments that administrative functions have been seriously impaired. A device, similar to this of attaching agencies to functional departments, was adopted to give the appearance of consolidation, i.e., the creation of a "governor's office" or "executive department" to serve as a top bureau drawer. By this process five states corralled unrelated agencies which often perform operating rather than staff functions. This expedient accomplished no consolidation and no change in the relations of the governor to these agencies.

The basic reorganization principle requires code departments to be headed by individuals appointed by the governor. Otherwise the resulting structure will be worse than the former decentralized system. In only six states, however, are all code departments so headed. In six other states from one-half to less than one-sixth of their code departments are so headed. Comparing totals of all code departments in the fifteen states, plural-headed or other disapproved types are three-fourths as great in number as the governor-appointed single-headed type. Not all single-headed departments are re-organization achievements. In Minnesota all single-headed departments were such before reorganization, while all four new departments were placed under plural heads in violation of the basic principle. Divisions of headless code departments are in most instances under plural heads or elective officers. Elective officers frequently occupy positions of large influence under the codes, and the code sponsors have aided in the retention of elective officers in contradiction of the basic reorganization in principle.

The codes have not reduced the governor's burden of appointing a mass of petty subordinates. In Pennsylvania he appoints some 670 code officers. In Nebraska he must appoint every officer and employee under the code. Some reasons for this burden are: the limited scope of reorganization; consolidation by attachment rather than abolishment; the existence of large numbers of plural-headed code departments, plural-headed divisions of headless departments, plural-headed attached agencies, and many unreorganized agencies most of which are plural-headed; and the requirement that the governor appoint subordinates within reorganized and unreorganized agencies. Because the codes require him to appoint department heads and employees, and because of his opportunity to dictate the appointment of employees generally, one authority has stated that political parties support the codes to secure "a rapid allocation of spoils while retaining the fiction of efficiency and civil service."

Since reorganization, "the natural tendency toward decentralization" has reasserted itself. The selfish motives for decentralization are manifested by "ripper bills" and partisan tinkering with the administrative machine; the altruistic ones by reaction against overloaded departments and confusion of authority arising from attached agencies and by the desire of professional and reform groups to take particular services out of spoils politics. As a result, some codes have been virtually obliterated and others largely disorganized.

Reference should be made to such other reforms as the use of modern methods of budgeting, accounting, and purchasing because they are sometimes confused with the central purpose of reorganization—the concentration of power in the governor. Such reforms may be a part of many other forms of governmental organization and are not an inherent part of the one-man-control plan. Space does not permit consideration of the impact of state reorganizations upon other reforms. I submit, however, that the most useful contribution of the reorganizations is not in partially establishing the basic principle of one-man-control but in helping to install other reforms, namely, centralized purchasing and modern fiscal practices.

The major benefits expected from reorganization were "efficiency and economy." Those claiming economies gave no direct evidence that economies resulted from increasing the governor's authority. When specific claims were cited, they were generally the result of central purchasing. Indeed a major weakness of the efficiency claims is that benefits have been attributed to the one-man-control plan which should have been attributed to related reforms, such as central purchasing, fiscal improvements, or unifunctional departmentalization. Enthusiastic advocates asserted that reorganizations have saved in some states hundreds of thousands of dollars and in other states millions. More cautious advocates have repudiated such claims. Thus Charles A. Beard holds that it is impossible to show "gains in efficiency and economy," and that support should be based upon the "logic" of "lines of responsibility from bottom to apex."

Thus it seems that reorganizers have swung from exaggeration to modesty as regards evidence of efficiency and economy. But perhaps something can be said of the advantages and disadvantages accruing from reorganization. What then can and what cannot be evaluated? Specific effects can be and have been determined: the extent to which the reorganizations have helped to install other reforms, namely, modern fiscal and purchasing methods and unifunctional departmentalization; the effect of reorganizations upon civil service laws and the merit system; and the effect upon particular functional departments where the overhead organization has been changed from plural to single heads. But on the other hand, the general economy and efficiency of reorganized versus unreorganized states cannot be estimated for several reasons. One is that many reorganized states are no more reorganized than unreorganized states so far as the basic test, the preponderance of single-over plural-headed agencies, is concerned. Another reason is that accounting techniques will probably never be developed to the point where the general proposition of concentrating authority in an elective chief administrator can be evaluated in dollars and cents. Even though such an evaluation might be made, it would still be more useful to calculate this concentration in terms of representative democracy and political liberty.

In conclusion: the facts concerning reorganization, a few of which are cited here, indicate that the reorganization movement has not been able to carry through or maintain its fundamental principle of concentration of power in the governor by consolidation of many agencies into a few large

integrated departments headed by governor-appointed individuals. Consequently, it is difficult to evaluate the one-man-control plan. It is possible,
however, to make piecemeal evaluations to the extent that functional departments have been changed from plural to single heads. *If* there are any
lessons for the federal government in state reorganizations, they are: that
the limited scope of reorganizations makes general conclusions useless;
that federal reorganization will probably not carry through the basic principle; that the President will probably not be much, if any, more of a chief
administrator than now; that powerful independent agencies will probably
remain such; that, therefore, opponents of reorganization need not be unduly
alarmed because a comprehensive reorganization will probably not materialize; and that, as Dr. Beard says, it will be difficult or ·impossible to prove
tangible benefits from reorganization, except "logical assumptions" which
can be proved as well beforehand.

Chapter XVIII

THE GOVERNMENT AND ITS EMPLOYEES

[THERE are in the United States to-day more than five million public employees. There is almost an infinite variety in the work that they do. Some of them are legislators, some executives, some judges; but these three groups constitute only a small fraction of the total number of public employees. The overwhelming number of public workers is found in the hundreds and thousands of public offices in which the everyday work of government is done. Here every profession, trade, occupation, and skill is represented. Accountants and zoologists, janitors and pharmacists, radio operators and carpenters, teachers and actors—these, and a host of other occupational groups, are employed by us to do our public work and thus constitute our civil service.

In a broad sense the term "civil service" includes all of the civil, that is, all of the non-military and non-naval, employees of government. But the term has another and inexact meaning; many use it as a synonym for "merit system." When used in this sense it implies that the civil servant secures his position through some procedure which tests his training, aptitude, and skills, and that once he has his job he is protected from political interference. This is an incorrect usage of the term. If all of the stenographers or bacteriologists of a city public health department are chosen because of their friendship for the department head, or because of their perspicacity in backing the right mayoralty candidate, this department has a civil service in spite of the absence of a merit system.]

No. 64

[THE struggle for the attainment of a merit system for public employees has been a long and strenuous one in the United States. The "spoils system" has shown, and continues to show, a remarkable tenacity. The reasons for its ability to withstand the movement towards a real merit system are several. Not the least of these is the current but erroneous attitude which we, the American people, have towards our civil servants and the work they do. The following selection discusses these fallacies in our thinking. As long as Americans retain these points of view there is little possibility of securing that energetic and thoughtful action without which we cannot hope to substitute merit for spoils.]

FALLACIES IN AMERICAN THINKING ON GOVERNMENTAL PERSONNEL [1]

UNDER the American system, our governments, federal, state, and local, constitute a cooperative enterprise through which we endeavor to maintain freedom; sustain law, order, and property; protect the individual against exploitation; conduct essential public services, such as highways, water supply, fire protection, postal service, and sanitation; guard the public welfare through the promotion of health and the care of the sick, the handicapped, the poor, and the unemployed; conserve our national resources for the benefit both of the present and of the future; furnish and encourage universal education through schools, colleges, universities, libraries, and other agencies; cooperate with private individuals and associations for economic advance through the expansion of domestic and foreign markets, the improvement of agricultural and industrial practices, the study of practical and scientific problems, the protection of patents and copyrights, and the development of standards and standard practices; provide for the creation of corporations, and regulate those which deal with the necessities of life or are by nature monopolies; protect public health, decency, and morals with controls over child labor, hours of labor, wages, foods and drugs, alcohol and narcotics, medical and other practices, housing, and the use of land; create and regulate the banking and currency system; conduct foreign relations, and maintain our national independence.

During emergencies certain of these powers and services are greatly expanded: in time of war, to mobilize men and resources and protect the nation against the enemy; in time of flood, earthquake, fire, or drought, to prevent starvation, epidemics, or further destruction and encourage quick recovery; and in time of economic collapse, to feed, clothe, and house the destitute, find work for unemployed men, restore credits, start in motion again the complicated mechanism of our economic life, and lay broad plans so that the full energies of the nation, public and private, may work to the same constructive ends.

In brief outlines, these are the responsibilities and work of the American national, state, and local governments to-day. Government is a cooperative enterprise exceedingly complicated and difficult, and supremely important to every one of us, rich or poor, employed or unemployed, wherever we

---

[1] Commission of Inquiry on Public Service Personnel, *Better Government Personnel* (New York and London: McGraw-Hill Book Company, 1935), pp. 13-22. Reprinted by permission of the publisher.

live. We must have government to live, to work, to advance, to enjoy the fruits of our labor.

The success or failure of that government, and the kind of service which it renders, will rest in the last analysis upon the capacity and character of the men and women who constitute it. We must therefore maintain a governmental system under which the government attracts to the public service its full share of the capacity and character of the man power of the nation. This we do not accomplish in the United States under existing conditions. The American people know it, and demand a change, though they do not clearly see the way out. The whole work of the Commission of Inquiry on Public Service Personnel has therefore been directed, first, toward finding out what are the reasons for our nation-wide failure to attract enough men and women of the finest capacity and character into state, local, and national governmental services; and, second, toward devising, on the basis of experience, a constructive program for the future which will correct this failure.

The inquiry and the program of the Commission are confined to the appointive administrative services, and do not include the elected legislators and councilmen, boards and commissions, mayors, governors, and other elected officials, nor the judiciary and military forces. These limitations have been adopted because it is apparent that the weakest link in American democracy, the point at which we fall most conspicuously behind the other self-governing peoples, is in the appointive services where the great bulk of the work of modern government is carried on. Moreover, permanent advances can be achieved in this field by united effort in a relatively short time.

The selection of appointive administrative personnel for governmental service in the United States, especially in the state and local fields, is profoundly influenced by a number of common fallacies. Though men and women of experience have repeatedly called attention in the hearings of the Commission to the falsity and absurdity of these conceptions, they nevertheless prevail in many of our public appointment policies. The evidence we have taken indicates that these wrong ideas, accepted without thought, are in large measure responsible for the failure of our national, state, and local governments to attract to the public service their due share of men and women of capacity and character.

Among these fallacies, the following may be listed:

1. The false notion that "to the victor belong the spoils." From this it is inferred that it is right and necessary for a newly elected administration to discharge incumbents regardless of their merit and appoint its own party workers regardless of *their* merit to any salaried posts which can be found, vacated, or created. This was not the doctrine of the fathers of the Con-

stitution. It is a corruption of democracy, introduced into American government between 1810 and 1824. It is of no value to government nor, in the long run, to political parties, and has been abandoned in many parts of the United States, and in most of the democracies of the world.

2. The mistaken idea that the duties of governmental employees are, as President Jackson said, "so plain and simple that men of intelligence can readily qualify themselves for their performance." Whether or not this was true in 1829, it is certainly not true to-day. On the contrary, certain of those duties are now so difficult, so complex, so technical as to require the recruitment of highly trained specialists and the training in the services of the best administrative talent which the nation produces. Moreover, experience and science demonstrate that men have different physical and mental and moral capacities, and that these differences must be recognized in their education, in their work, and in many of their other relationships, not only from the standpoint of their usefulness to society, but from that of their own happiness as well.

3. The false idea that charity begins on the public payroll. All over the United States men and women are elected or appointed to office or kept on the payroll because they need the job: someone has died, there are twelve children in the family, a leg has been lost, or some other misfortune has befallen them. The employees appointed for these eleemosynary reasons draw the pay while others do the work, or else the work is botched and neglected. The cost to the public is not only the salary involved but also the much larger social cost of poor and bungled service and of lowered morale among the other employees.

4. The erroneous assumption that "patronage is the price of democracy," that the parties which we need for self-government cannot exist without spoils. This fallacy, more than any other, is responsible for the hopeless, defeatist attitude of good citizens, deterring them from advancing to the annihilation of the spoils system. There are, it is true, large cities, certain states, and other areas where political parties and political activity are *at present* sustained by patronage. But in great sections of the United States, and in other democracies of the world, democracy exists, political life is maintained, parties thrive, without the spoliation of the appointive administrative services. The truth is, as Theodore Roosevelt once observed, that patronage is the curse of politics. It is the selling-out price of democracy, because of itself it turns the political party into a job brokerage machine, creating a mercenary army of occupation, which, under the guise of democracy, robs us of self-government.

5. The idea that "the best public servant is the worst one. . . . A thoroughly first-rate man in public service is corrosive. He eats holes in our

liberties. The better he is and the longer he stays, the greater is the danger." Though this was the printed statement of a past president of the United States Chamber of Commerce in 1928, the Commission of Inquiry on Public Service Personnel could find no support for the idea in 1934. Springing in part from the same fallacy, much vilification of public employees as "tax eaters," "payrollers," and "bureaucrats" is, however, indulged in by certain groups in certain areas. The evidence indicates that these groups either are thoughtless or else have selfish reasons for desiring bad government. Indiscriminate vilification lessens the morale of all public officials, dissuades capable persons from entering the public service, and discredits the authority of government. Such efforts to change government through personal abuse of public servants as a class, rather than through the advocacy of specific reform measures, must be recognized as thoroughly subversive. No one who goes through the country from coast to coast examining the public service, as did this Commission, can fail to be impressed by the many evidences of marked ability and loyalty in those who now serve the public. To transfer to these worthy employees the abuse earned by a few bad ones is a most unwholesome piece of demagogy.

6. The erroneous thought that "tenure is the cure of spoils." This was the central idea of early civil service reform, and is the chief objective of certain organizations of public employees. American experience shows that guaranteed tenure for public employees is, when standing alone, a dangerous thing. It tends to produce poor service and low morale, to lessen the standing and prestige of the "protected" classes, to prevent the advancement of efficient personnel, and to keep deadwood on the payroll. It is used in many jurisdictions by the politicians as a dugout for spoilsmen. The evidence presented indicates that tenure should not be established except as a part of a merit system which selects with care those who are to be given tenure, establishes a definite retirement system, and sets up the method of getting rid of deadwood. Responsible employees' organizations both in this country and abroad have not only recognized these facts but have insisted that they cannot afford to ask for the protection of incompetent personnel, as this will not only result in bad service but will undermine public confidence in all public servants.

7. The superficial thought that the way to eradicate spoils and favoritism is to begin at the bottom with clerks, stenographers, and policemen, and work up, and that the success of reform can be measured by the percentage of the total service which is placed "under civil service." All the evidence presented shows clearly that the top posts are of supreme importance, and that chief administrative officers who are spoilsmen can demoralize the rank and file and wreck the service in spite of any law.

8. The belief in "home town jobs for home town boys." Tariff walls around individual city, county, and state payrolls are a bad thing not only for the public service and the taxpayer, but also for those who desire to work for government. Residence requirements, particularly for technical, skilled, and other higher posts, restrict the opportunity for selection by the employer, that is the government, and they limit the opportunities for a career on the part of the person entering the service. No such restrictions have, as a rule, been imposed with regard to school teachers, nor in private business, and they should not be imposed in connection with other appointive government positions. Residence qualifications are a benefit only to incompetent applicants and petty politicians.

9. The notion that "the public service is always less capable and efficient than private enterprise." The best businesses are more efficient than the average government; while the most efficient governmental units are more efficient than the average business. At many of the hearings of the Commission the opinion was expressed that businesses and governments are apparently about on a par—what business gains through the profit motive and elasticity being apparently lost in many instances through hereditary management, labor difficulties, and outside control. It was pointed out also that in America, governments have, as a rule, undertaken no services except after private agencies have proved themselves incapable or powerless to conduct them. To achieve any measure of success under such conditions is a remarkable accomplishment for public management. Businesses and other private agencies, too, have their problems of nepotism, favoritism, sharp practice, low morality, embezzlement, insolvency, and decay, as well as the difficulties which arise from useless competition. The criticism of the public service arises by comparison not so much with the superiorities of business as with the higher standards which we expect and have a right to demand from our governments.

10. The erroneous idea that the spoils system, the eleemosynary system, and the other corrosive influences can be driven out of the public service through the prohibition of specific abuses. Time and again, the Commission has been told that laws will not cure the situation. What is clearly required is not negative laws, but the positive and militant handling of the problem of personnel with the active backing of the public and the press.

These are among the fallacies which have been more or less dominant in American thinking during recent generations, which have an important effect upon the problem of public personnel policy. The fact that the American people are now beginning to recognize the falsity of these ideas clears the way for a new constructive approach to the problem of attracting to the public service men and women of capacity and character.

No. 65

[THE Civil Service Commission and its administration of the federal civil service have long been subject to criticism. John Fischer diagnoses a number of the ailments and prescribes some cures.]

LET'S GO BACK TO THE SPOILS SYSTEM [1]

by John Fischer

THE good citizens slapped each other on the back on the evening of January 16, 1883, and their hosannas were heard throughout the land. A reluctant Congress had just passed the Civil Service Act, which would guarantee an honest, efficient, and economical government forevermore. The corrupt political bosses finally had been routed; their thieving henchmen would be shooed away from the public trough; and from then on federal jobs would be filled strictly on merit by the ablest men the country could produce. It was a major victory for Righteousness, Liberalism, and Good Government.

But somehow, in the . . . years since that glad day, the Great Reform has gone sour. To-day Washington is filled with good citizens who lie awake nights thinking up new and sulphurous curses to hurl at Civil Service. Nearly every agency pays a large staff to figure out ingenious schemes for carrying on the public business in spite of Civil Service regulations. (These rules and regulations, couched in language that would gag a Philadelphia lawyer, fill a 524-page book, plus 46 pages of reference tables. Probably no living man wholly understands them; but they govern every waking hour of the three and a half million people in the federal service, including—*especially* including—their behavior off the job.) Thousands of typists, who might be doing useful work in a hand laundry, waste their dreary lives filling out stacks of Civil Service forms, usually in quintuplicate. A responsible executive officer in the War Department recently offered (very privately) his considered judgment that the Civil Service system had been the greatest single obstacle to the war effort.

Even Congress finally has recognized the failure of Civil Service. Whenever our lawmakers want to set up a really effective and businesslike agency —for example, TVA or the Federal Farm Mortgage Corporation—they always provide that it shall operate "without regard to the provisions of Civil Service."

[1] John Fischer, "Let's Go Back to the Spoils System," *Harper's Magazine* (October, 1945), No. 1145, pp. 362-368. Reprinted by permission of *Harper's Magazine* and the author.

II

What's gone wrong with Civil Service is easy enough to find out. You can get the story, in almost identical terms, from anybody who has ever held an executive job in Washington.

First of all, it's too slow. If you were an administrator in urgent need of a new assistant, you might hope to get somebody on the job—with luck and infinite finagling—in six or eight weeks. (He wouldn't be the man you want, of course.) In wartime the pace was a little faster—there were even cases in which a man was hired within a week—but even then par for the course was at least a month. If you wanted to beat that, you had to "hand process" the appointment, personally carrying the sheaf of papers through the maze of the agency personnel office and the Civil Service Commission, and mobilizing all the pressure you could, including telephone calls from the applicant's Congressman.

When you want to fire a man, the procedure naturally is more tedious. In theory, it is as easy to get rid of an incompetent in the government service as it is in private industry; in practice, the ordeal may drag on for six or eight painful months. If you are an experienced administrator, you will never try to fire anybody—you will foist him off on some unsuspecting colleague in another bureau, or transfer him to the South Dakota field office, or reorganize your section to abolish his position.

I once spent a whole winter trying to "terminate," as Civil Service puts it, an elderly female clerk who had become so neurotic that no other woman could work in the same room with her. This involved written charges, interviews with my tearful victim, protests from her Senator, indignant union delegations, and formal hearings before a panel of personnel experts. In the end I gave up and arranged for her transfer, with a raise in pay, to the staff of a trusting friend who had just joined the government. She is there to this day, chewing paper clips, frightening secretaries, and muttering to herself as she misfiles vital documents; I think of her every time I pay my income tax. My friend, who no longer speaks to me, is trying to get her transferred to the Veterans Administration before General Omar Bradley learns how Washington works.

Even worse than the Civil Service Commission's leisurely gait is its delight in harassing the operating officials who are responsible for running the government. The typical administrator may spend as much as a third of his time placating the commission and the hordes of minor personnel specialists who infest Washington. He draws organization charts, argues with classification experts, fills out efficiency ratings, justifies the allocation of vacancies, and listens to inspiring lectures on personnel management until he has little energy left for his real job. He may search for hours for those magic words which, properly recited in a job description, will enable him to pay a subordinate $4,600 instead of $3,800. (The phrase "with wide latitude for exercise of individual initiative and responsibility" is nearly always worth $800 of the taxpayers' money; but it took me two years to find that out.)

No bureaucrat can avoid this boondoggling. If he fails to initial a Green Sheet or to attach the duplicate copy of Form 57, the whole machinery of his office grinds to a halt. If he deliberately flouts the established ritual, or neglects to show due respect for the personnel priesthood, his career may be ruined and his program along with it. In a thousand subtle ways the personnel boys can throw sand in the gears. They can freeze appointments and promotions, block transfers, lose papers, and generally bedevil any official who refuses to "cooperate." If they bog down a government project in the process, that is no skin off their backs—nobody can ever hold them responsible.

Nor can the administrator escape the Civil Service investigators, who drop in once or twice a week to question him about the morals, drinking habits, and possibly treasonable opinions of some poor wretch who has applied for a federal job. These investigators often are amusing fellows. I got well acquainted with one who formerly had been a small-town private detective; he had an uncommonly prurient mind, which led him to handle every case as if he were working up adultery charges for a divorce suit. Nearly all of them operate on the theory that anybody willing to work for the government must be a scoundrel, probably with Communist tendencies, who could never hold a job anywhere else. They have a boundless appetite for gossip, and they waste a lot of other people's time. What purpose they serve is obscure, because their investigations often are not completed until five or six months after the new employee starts work. If he actually were as villainous as they seem to suspect, he would have plenty of time to sell the country's secrets to a sinister foreign power before the investigators caught up with him.

These are minor indictments, however. The really serious charge against the Civil Service system is that it violates the most fundamental rule of sound management. That rule is familiar to every businessman: when you hold a man responsible for doing a job, you must give him the authority he needs to carry it out. Above all, he must be free to hire his own staff, assign them to tasks they can do best, and replace them if they don't make good.

In peacetime, at least, no agency operating under the trammels of Civil Service has this authority. Suppose, for example, that Congress sets up a special Flood Control Agency, with urgent orders to harness the rampaging Ohio River. The new FCA administrator, full of zeal, asks the Civil Service Commission to give him the best chief engineer the merit system can supply.

After some argument whether a first-class engineer—capable of earning $30,000 a year in private practice—is worth $6,500 to the government, the commission finally tells the administrator to take his choice of three men. They head its list of people who once took a Civil Service engineering examination. All the best men on the list have already been snapped up by other agencies, of course, because the last examination was held five years ago. And it wasn't a very good list in the first place, because few people in the profession knew that such an examination was being held. (It had been announced in a bulletin, printed in the kind of type used for Bible footnotes and displayed on postoffice notice boards between the Marine recruiting posters and the FBI photos of escaped kidnappers.)

Of the three "referrals," one turns out to be a professor at Freshwater Academy who never poured a yard of concrete in his life. The second is afflicted with a personality which makes it impossible for him to work in any organization. The third actually has had some practical experience— he once designed a garbage disposal plant—but he has no sympathy with the flood control program; he is a firm believer in Free Enterprise and non-interference with acts of God. The administrator has to take him anyway, although he personally knows a dozen better-qualified men who are eager to tackle the job.

During the next six months, while the administrator tries desperately to recruit the rest of his staff from Civil Service registers, the chief engineer surveys the Ohio River. He reports that flood control is neither practical nor desirable, and that in any case it should be left to private industry. Meanwhile, a flood wipes out Cincinnati, Louisville, and Paducah. With one voice the press denounces the administrator as a bungling bureaucrat, and a Senate investigating committee demands his head.

The Civil Service Commission, of course, is unperturbed. It has done its duty in preserving the merit system free from all taint of patronage. The sacred regulations have been kept intact. If a few thousand unfortunates have been drowned in the Ohio Valley, that is none of its concern.

Fantastic? Not in the least. In the past twelve years a number of government programs have been hobbled in precisely this fashion.

III

Although the defects of Civil Service are plain enough, the reasons for them are not so easy to find.

By no means all the blame rests on the Civil Service Commissioners.

They are three earnest, well-meaning people, who grieve sincerely over the flaws in their organization.

The chairman of the commission is Harry B. Mitchell, a ruddy-faced Montana rancher and publisher, who once served as mayor of Great Falls. His health is none too robust, he has had no special training in large-scale management problems, and even his admirers do not describe his leadership as dynamic. Perhaps his chief interest has been the improvement of the retirement system for decrepit government employees. Appointed in the early months of the Roosevelt regime at the suggestion of the late Senator Tom Walsh, he serves—like his colleagues—at the pleasure of the President. Since his son recently was elected Senator from Washington, no one doubts that the President will be pleased to keep him on indefinitely.

The other Democratic member is Mrs. Lucille Foster McMillin, widow of a former Congressman and governor of Tennessee. Her husband was the boon friend and political mentor of Cordell Hull, and she herself once represented Tennessee on the Democratic National Committee. So long as Hull's influence is felt in the Administration, her seat presumably is safe. A Southern gentlewoman of the old school, Mrs. McMillin devotes much of her energy to the protection of the federal working girl. Every fresh outbreak of rape in the Washington parks fills her with alarm, and she labors tirelessly to improve housing and working conditions for women. [Mrs. McMillin was replaced by Frances Perkins.]

Paradoxically, the commission actually is run by its lone Republican member, Arthur S. Flemming, the youngest, most progressive, and best qualified of the three. Roosevelt drafted him six years ago from the American University School of Public Affairs, which Flemming had directed with marked ability. To him belongs the credit for most of the wartime improvements in the commission's operations. [Mr. Flemming resigned to become president of Ohio Wesleyan University.]

His major reform was a temporary relaxation of the regulations to give the war agencies considerable freedom in recruiting their own staffs, subject to a review of each appointment by the commission. He also has decentralized a good deal of responsibility to the field offices, brought in a number of able assistants, improved the techniques of examination, and cleaned out most of the witch-hunters and hayseed dicks from the investigation staff.

In these and other efforts to shore up their rickety machine, Flemming has won the assent of his Democratic colleagues by the exercise of unmeasured patience and tact. They now leave to him the day-to-day chores of management, and even permit him to speak for the commission before congressional committees. He has had less success, however, in gaining the support of the commission's permanent staff—the most inbred, tradition-ridden clique in Washington.

These veteran bureaucrats know that their bosses come and go, while they endure forever. They are skilled in the art of passive resistance, and they have no intention of letting any upstart commissioner tamper unduly with their time-hallowed procedures. Their idol is Theodore Roosevelt, the only Civil Service commissioner who ever attained national prominence —his desk is enshrined in the central hall of their F Street lair—and they look with grave suspicion on any ideas which he did not sanction in 1895.

The tight inner circle of the permanent staff is made up of men who started with the commission as messengers or clerks some twenty years ago, and rose to positions of power on the seniority escalator. Few of them have had any experience in private business or other government departments; they have little conception of the problems of an operating agency.

They have two guiding principles. The first is Keep the Rascals Out. Civil Service, in their view, is a kind of police force designed to keep political patronage appointees from creeping into federal jobs. This they do well— but they rarely feel any responsibility for positive action to make the government work, or to persuade the best possible men to enter the federal service.

The second aim of the commission bureaucracy is to increase the dignity and power of the personnel profession. To this end, they have developed a special jargon which no outsider can understand, plus an elaborate structure of regulations, red tape, and ritual which can be mastered only after years of study. They demand of the whole government what Dr. Floyd W. Reeves, professor of administration at the University of Chicago, has described as "an almost idolatrous worship" of the commission's "detailed and antiquated rules."

It is hard to blame them for this—after all, they are only doing what the legal and medical professions did centuries ago. The result, however, is a vested interest in complexity and formalism which is largely responsible for the ill-repute of the Civil Service system.

But the greatest share of guilt falls on Congress. Lacking any real enthusiasm for the Civil Service idea, it has never bothered to work out comprehensive legislation for a modern, effective system of personnel administration. Instead, over the course of years it has encrusted the original act of 1883 with scores of piecemeal amendments and special statutes. This has resulted in a legal patchwork which would baffle even the ablest and most aggressive commissioners. One law, for example, sets up special qualifications for coal mine inspectors; another provides that employees of the Farmers' Home Corporation must be residents of the states where they work; a third specifies that superintendents of national cemeteries must be disabled Army veterans—no sailors or Marines need apply. All of these laws, and many more like them, undermine the principle that the best man ought to get the job; each one is intended to confer special preference on some particular group of job-hunters. They are simply devices for legalizing favoritism and patronage on a large scale.

In addition, Congress has steadfastly refused to give the commission enough money to hire a proper staff or to run its business efficiently. (Until a few years ago, one of the field offices got along with a single telephone and borrowed chairs from the federal jail whenever it had to hold an examination.) Nor have there ever been funds to develop scientific testing methods, or to keep the registers fresh with frequent examinations.

It is true, of course, that the commission seldom fights aggressively for the money it needs, and that it sometimes has actually encouraged Congress to pass bad legislation. Only a few months ago, for example, the commission managed to have written into law one of its most hampering regulations —the so-called "Rule of Three," which limits choice in appointments to the three names at the top of the register. Dr. Reeves, a leading authority in the field of public administration, characterized this step as "a major disaster."

Nevertheless, such blunders would be impossible if Congress took an intelligent interest in the problems of federal employment . . . The attitudes of the . . . [Congressmen] range from indifference to frank contempt. As a result, government pay scales are notoriously low, and any bill designed to harass or discriminate against government workers is almost sure to pass with whoops of glee.

Worst of all, Congress has perpetuated the basic flaw in the original Civil Service Act. The commission is still an independent agency, entirely divorced from the normal structure of government. Although it wields great power it is responsible to no one. It serves only as a kind of decrepit watchdog, which growls at the regular departments, but seldom tries to help them get their job done.

IV

It can be argued, in all seriousness, that Congress would do well to wipe out Civil Service, hide, horns, and tallow, and go back to the old-fashioned spoils system.

Any political party which believes intensely in its program presumably would choose the ablest men in its ranks to put that program into effect. Each administrator would be in sympathy with the project he is assigned to run, and he could expect loyal support from every subordinate. Moreover, he could count on fast action; no ward heeler could survive unless he handled appointments more promptly than the present Civil Service machinery.

Naturally every Congressman would slip a few of his maiden aunts and broken-down henchmen onto the public payroll. But they could hardly be more useless or expensive than the thousands of personnel men now roosting in Washington. Indeed, the treasury might well save a few millions, since most political hacks are harmless creatures, who merely draw their pay and don't bother anybody, while personnel experts take great zest in pestering the working officials.

And if the party in power should ever load the payroll with too many thieves and incompetents, then a healthy democracy would throw out the whole gang at the next election. The constant threat of a change in administration would help keep all government employees on their toes; they would never dare sink into the smug mediocrity which now afflicts so many civil servants who are sure of indefinite tenure.

Such a forthright return to the patronage system would, however, be a pretty drastic step—probably more drastic than is actually necessary. Before junking Civil Service entirely, maybe Congress should consider replacing the 1883 jalopy with . . . [an up-to-date] model.

The blueprint for a modern and workable Civil Service is already at hand. It was drawn up in 1937, after months of careful study, by a group of experts from outside the government known as the Committee on Administrative Management. The committee's suggestions were warmly endorsed by most of the recognized authorities in this field, and the President urged Congress to put them into effect immediately. As usual, Congress wasn't interested, and nothing happened.

These proposals are still as sensible . . . [now as then] and even more urgently needed. They call for four major reforms:

1. The present commission should be abolished, along with its whole collection of red tape and the senescent bureaucrats who weave it. (These gentlemen should be permitted to leave Washington quietly, in spite of a widespread demand among other government workers that they be tarred, feathered, and ridden out of town on their own filing cabinets.)

2. Each agency should be permitted to hire its own help. They should be chosen strictly on merit, with all political influence ruled out, on the same basis which TVA now is using so successfully. Every department would then be able to get a competent personnel staff to replace its present herd of second-raters—it could attract good men because it could give them real responsibility.

3. A single Federal Personnel Administrator, responsible directly to the President, would lay down over-all policies for the various agencies, and see

to it that they are carried out. (He would *not* try to enforce a multitude of petty rules.) His office also could carry on the few functions of the present commission which really need to be centralized—such as handling retirement funds, arranging transfers, and pooling the recruitment of minor employees.

4. A part-time, unpaid, non-political board should be set up to keep a wary eye on the administrator and on the personnel operations of the agencies. From time to time it might suggest general policies or standards. Its main job, however, would be to look out for the public interest, and make sure that the new, decentralized merit system actually worked with a minimum of political interference. (It would of course be impossible, and probably undesirable, to get a scheme which would be entirely free of politics. The present setup certainly is not—the whims of a Senator now are treated with religious deference by nearly all Washington personnel men, from the commission down.)

These changes, plus a number of minor reforms suggested by the Committee on Administrative Management, should result in an immediate and substantial saving for the taxpayer. By eliminating the present overlapping and duplication between the functions of the Civil Service Commission and those of the agency personnel offices, it should make possible a sharp reduction in the total number of personnel men in Washington. What Dr. Reeves describes as the "elaborate, time-consuming, and costly reports" now prepared at the commission's behest could be dispensed with; every week, according to my rough estimates, this should save 1,328,772 forms, Green Sheets, affidavits, and classification charts, thus releasing from bondage whole regiments of typists. Moreover, many an expensive subterfuge could be abandoned. A department could put a new man on the regular payroll the day it needed him, for example, instead of hiring him as a "temporary consultant" at $25 a day during the months it takes for his appointment papers to trickle through the commission.

Far more important, however, would be the gains in speed and efficiency throughout the entire government. Officers no longer would be demoralized by the annual ordeal of efficiency ratings. Transfers and promotions might come through on schedule. Administrators could spend their time administering, instead of practicing the mumbo-jumbo of the Civil Service liturgy. Men of stature might then be more willing to enter the public service, and the machinery of government perhaps could cope a little more adequately with the unprecedented loads which are being thrust upon it.

No. 66

[IN many American communities citizens have been faced with what appears to them to be a most perplexing problem. Shocked by the waste and inefficiency of a politically appointed public service, they have in scores of instances demanded and won the adoption of the merit system. Believing the battle to be won, they thereupon have relaxed their interest and happily awaited the coming of a well-trained and well-directed group of public servants—a corps of workers that inexplicably failed to materialize. These citizens made the mistake of assuming that the policy decision was the only battle of the war. In their concern over this battle they overlooked the equally important and decisive engagement which revolved about good administration of the personnel program.

These perplexed people can find the explanation of their predicament in this article by Professor V. O. Key, Jr. As Professor Key shows, the ingenuity of the spoilsman has kept pace with the fervor of the reformer. If the people in any community want a civil service based on the merit system, they must be vigilant to see that methods of evasion of merit legislation are not practiced. Groups of citizens who organize to secure the enactment of legislation must remain organized and use their power to compel the enforcement of the law.]

METHODS OF EVASION OF CIVIL SERVICE LAWS [1]

by V. O. Key, Jr.

ANY systematization of the techniques of political machine formation must include an analysis of the methods of evasion and avoidance of merit system legislation. The electoral power of the "machine" depends in large measure upon the efforts of disciplined and loyal party workers who may be recruited most readily through the distribution of patronage. Almost uniformly legislators and practical politicians have opposed, at least privately, the enactment of laws providing for the recruitment of public employes upon the basis of merit. Militant reform movements compelled the enactment of such legislation and ways and means came to be devised to mitigate the requirements of the law. Without attempting an extensive survey of the present status of the merit system, examples of evasion in various jurisdictions may be brought together to indicate the more frequently recurring general types.

[1] V. O. Key, Jr., "Methods of Evasion of Civil Service Laws," *The Southwestern Social Science Quarterly* (March, 1935), Vol. 15, pp. 337-347. Reprinted by permission of *The Southwestern Social Science Quarterly* and the author.

Limiting the Scope of Merit Laws.—By framing legislation to exclude certain classes of employes from the application of merit requirements and procedures, many positions have been saved to be dispensed at the discretion of the organization. Practically every proposal in Congress for the creation of a new administrative agency is marked by a fight to exclude its employes from the provisions of the civil service regulations, and often the effort meets with success. The disastrous effects of such a step on prohibition enforcement are too well known to require comment.

Although there are some exemptions of specific administrative agencies in states and cities having merit laws, more positions are affected by the exemption of classes cutting horizontally through all the administrative departments. Heads of departments and their immediate subordinates, such as deputy commissioners, are generally open to selection upon the basis of political considerations. These jobs are extremely valuable from the patronage standpoint, for it may be said that the value of a job for this purpose increases with its altitude in the administrative hierarchy. The place which their holders occupy in the public eye serves as a constant reminder to the Italians, the Brotherhood of Locomotive Engineers, the Poles, the Catholics, the Negroes, the American Legion, or other pressure group that the administration has recognized them by placing one of their number in a post of power and honor. Furthermore, the possession of a large number of such positions greatly simplifies the matter of discipline within the organization. The leader is constantly being challenged by men who are almost his equal and the astute distribution of positions of this type among the more dangerous contenders for power helps mightily in checking insubordination.

Every important official must have his confidential assistants, personal investigators, private secretaries, or other attachés possessed of a title of relatively high prestige value. Due to the intimate relationship and the delicate matters handled by these persons, it is argued that they should be selected by their superior completely free of any requirement for competitive examination. This contention is often groundless, but after the places are created and exempted from examination requirements they may be used as rewards for deserving members of the organization.

Some positions which for other reasons are thought not to be susceptible of being filled by competitive examination are governed by pass or noncompetitive examination provisions. This type of examination gives much greater discretion to the appointing authority than the ordinary open competitive test. In effect, complete freedom may be given to the appointing officer. At the other extreme, laborers are usually exempt from the operation of the competitive procedure. There are loafers and workers, able and disabled persons, whose characteristics could be determined by a personnel officer, but the merit system was introduced with emphasis upon the academic type of examination which precluded the inclusion of this type of employe. This leaves a large number of jobs for unskilled workers which can be used with extraordinary effectiveness in building up organization support. The possible effect of all these exemptions may be seen from the fact that in 1929, of the 86,509 employes of the City of New York, 246 belonged to the unclassified service, which number included heads and deputy heads of departments; 1,024 to the exempt class; 11,694 to the non-competitive class; and 24,200 to the labor class. Over 40 per cent of the employes of the city were thus exempt from merit procedures.

TABLE I

TEMPORARY APPOINTEES OF WEST CHICAGO PARKS SYSTEM

Year	Number of Positions	Salary Paid to "Temporaries"	Percentage of Total Payroll Paid to "Temporaries"
1915	79	$ 5,021.86	0.0071
1920	234	35,132.93	3.3
1925	636	473,350.33	26.3
1928	1725	1,202,616.90	42.5
1929	1305	984,867.82	39.9
1930	1798	872,777.00	27.4
1931	2212	1,748,501.65	61.2
1932	2122	1,142,163.90	46.7

Slightly different from permanent exemptions from the merit laws is provision for the appointment of temporary employes to fill positions otherwise subject to examination. Legislation usually provides that vacancies in such positions may be filled for thirty or sixty days by temporary employes pending the holding of an examination. By filling competitive positions with temporary employes and repeatedly renewing these appointments merit laws may be practically nullified. As an example of what may be done by this method the West Parks system of Chicago may be cited. Table I shows the progressive increase in the number and proportion of temporary appointees over a period of years. About 1,900 of the 4,500 Cook County (Chicago), Illinois, jobs are subject to the merit laws. During 1928 at least 40 per cent of these positions were filled by temporary appointees. In 1923 approximately 5,000 of the 22,000 positions in the Chicago classified service were filled by temporaries. During the Cermak administration in Chicago the general trend in the number of temporaries was upward with aperiodic fluctuations nicely synchronized with the occurrence of elections. The total number of temporary employes was reliably estimated at between five and six thousand. In Cleveland in 1922 it was found that more than 2,000 of the 5,000 positions subject to examination were occupied by "thirty-day" appointees. The practice was carried to its logical conclusion in Kansas City, where at one time all positions in the city service were held by temporary appointees. In Cuyahoga County (Cleveland), Ohio, in 1929, 58 per cent of the county's 1,466 positions were either exempt, unclassified, or filled by temporaries. By renewals these positions became in effect permanent, at least for the duration of the party's power. Such appointees, however, may be removed at will, thus greatly simplifying the problem of maintaining organizational discipline.

Under certain circumstances the civil service commission usually has the authority to exempt positions from examination and this is often done, sometimes for the benefit of the organization and at other times for legitimate reasons. Without the complicity of the commission, positions in the classified service may be left unfilled by the appointing authority and the duties performed by persons appointed under some title not subject to examination. In the federal service it was found at one time that a large number of persons appointed as laborers without examination at the request of various politicians had been assigned to classified duties.

Under the civil service laws of some jurisdictions it is possible to evade the requirement of competitive examination prior to appointment by contracting for services. This exception, designed to provide for the employment of attorneys, accountants, architects, and experts of various kinds on a contractual basis, was used in New York City to furnish a berth for Dr. William H. Walker, brother of the former mayor. The Board of Education contracted for his services as a "medical consultant" to render the same service as a "medical examiner" in the competitive class. When the Court of Appeals nullified this evasion, about 250 employes hired under the contract system in New York City were affected. In Boston contracts were made for the services of laborers. The contractor made a profit in furnishing these men who could have been employed directly by the city. In Chicago it was alleged in a legal proceeding that political employes of the West Parks board were not on the personnel payroll, but were paid with vouchers for materials.

Clerical employes and other attachés of the courts on all levels of government and in practically all jurisdictions remain subject to the patronage system. Due to the insistence upon the independence of the judiciary as a coördinate branch of government, its employes are more often excluded from the operation of civil service laws than not. This action has not been unconnected with the fact that court functionaries are often in a position to render services of peculiar value to the organization, particularly in the

lower courts handling minor criminal cases. Similarly, employes of legislative bodies—clerks, pages, stenographers, and the like—are in most cases
selected on a patronage basis. In some instances the committees making
the selections are frankly named the "patronage committee."

"Right Guys."—The early advocates of civil service reform—affectionately
referred to by the "pols" as the "goo-goos"—envisaged civil service commissions as agencies independent of the administrative departments applying the merit laws stringently and without fear or favor. This conception
was readily demolished by appointing "right guys," i.e., loyal organization
men, to the commissions. "If the mayoralty of the city falls into the hands
of the spoilsman who appoints the civil service commission, it is an easy
thing to take all the starch out of the civil service requirements. The manifold ways in which this was done under the Walker administration (in New
York City) revealed the abuses incident to the commission being appointed
by the mayor and owing its allegiance solely to him." In Illinois during the
regime of Governor Len Small the chief examiner of the civil service commission quoted one of its members as saying that "there will be just examinations enough to keep up appearances." Even when the commission is
constituted of men firmly committed to the policies of the merit law and is
assisted by a staff of technically proficient personnel officers, it can accomplish little without the voluntary cooperation of the chief executive and the
heads of the administrative departments.

An excellent example of what can be done by appointing the "right" men
to a commission occurred during Mayor "Big Bill" Thompson's first two
terms in Chicago. The two Republican positions on the commission were
held by three individuals at various times during his administration. Charles
E. Frazier, a prominent member of the Thirty-third Ward Republican organization, was appointed, he said, with the understanding that he should
"do nothing unjustified." Alex J. Johnson, vice-president of the William
Hale Thompson Republican Club, replied to a query as to the relationship
between his political activities and his appointment to the commission:
"What of it? You don't think the Mayor would appoint an enemy, do
you?" Percy B. Coffin, the third Republican holding membership on the
commission during this period, served as a handy man for the mayor in
various capacities, including a stint as unofficial patronage dispenser.

The appointment of loyal organization men to the commission is undoubtedly the most effective means for bringing the civil service under the
control of the organization. This can be done, of course, only when there
is no effective opposition to such a policy. To placate opposition to spoils
practices frequently a minority of the commission consists of effective but
harmless "window dressing." Or appointments of weak men without mal-

odorous records, easily subject to manipulation, may be made for the same purpose.

Legislative Sabotage.—Control of appropriations for the work of the personnel agency may serve as a means for mitigating the severity of the enforcement of merit laws. However disposed the commission may be, without ample staff to carry on the voluminous and complex work of testing, classification, *et cetera*, it can accomplish little. By reducing the appropriations for the personnel agency the legislative body may effectively draw its fangs. The Chicago Civil Service Commission may be cited as an example.

TABLE II

STAFF AND APPROPRIATIONS FOR CHICAGO CIVIL SERVICE COMMISSION, 1915-1922

Year	Staff	Appropriation
1915	74	$101,000
1916	63	74,520
1917	37	65,640
1918	37	61,930
1919	39	74,420
1920	31	82,070
1921	31	87,580
1922	33	104,820

When Mayor Thompson first took office in 1915 the commission had an average staff of 75 employes and an annual appropriation of about $100,000. It was recognized as one of the best personnel agencies in the country. Table II shows what happened to its staff and appropriations. Other factors contributed, but by 1923 the commission had sunk to a position of very low repute. The financial strangulation of the personnel agency has been carried to the logical conclusion in Kansas, where no appropriations are made and the state civil service law remains dormant. Short of actually cutting appropriations pressure may be brought to bear upon civil service agencies by members of the legislative body. One can not very well deny a legislator a favor one day and ask him to vote for an appropriation the next.

The Process of Selection.—In the process of examination there is opportunity for maladministration. Although safeguards are usually employed to prevent the identity of the examinee from being known to the rater, they may be evaded. Furthermore, a considerable latitude of discretion in the evaluation of papers is possible due to the type of questions often used in civil service examinations. A Cook County, Illinois, grand jury in 1922 compared the markings of papers by the civil service commission examiners and by the persons who had been brought in by the commission to prepare the questions. Although no proof of abuse of discretion was presented except by inference, the range of variation as indicated by Table III indicates the possibilities.

Numerous instances of unfair grading of examination papers are available from a study of the Cuyahoga County, Ohio, civil service commission. An examinee, who had not had the experience required to enter the examination, was asked: "When would you permit the addition of sand above the amount called for in the specifications in a batch of concrete?" The answer was: "When the weather is wet, before the engineer has been able to make a

TABLE III

COMPARISON OF RATING PAPERS BY EXAMINERS AND BY PERSONS
PREPARING CERTAIN EXAMINATION QUESTIONS

Paper	Mark by Civil Service Examiners	Mark by Person Preparing Questions
A	90	70
B	60	80
C	40	85

test." He went to the head of the eligible list. In an examination for dirt street foreman the following question was put: "Describe in detail and illustrate with a diagram a case where a drain across a street is needed." The reply was: "A drain should be placed under roadway." No drawing was furnished. Although the applicant had not had the required experience for entrance to the examination, he passed and was appointed to the service. In another examination for the same position a man who had been a barber most of his life said in his application: "I did not have any practical experience of this position, but I have a number of barber shops." He was given 70 per cent for experience. Two years' experience in dirt highway construction work was required. In an examination for sewer maintenance foreman answers totaling fourteen lines to five questions earned a mark of 98.4 per cent. A close check of 1,175 names on the eligible lists resulting from 73 examinations by the Cleveland city commission showed that 22 per cent of them had actually failed in the tests.

Members of the organization may take the examination and be appointed with or without chicanery in the ratings. Being appointed, they may do their political work "on the side," assuming, as is customary, a weak enforcement of the rules prohibiting political activity by permanent employes. In some cases positions requiring technical training and practical experience are filled by inexperienced political temporaries who acquire experience at the expense of the public and then secure permanent appointment after examination.

In case of necessity, when the examining authorities are careless, a substitute may take the examination for the applicant. Occasional instances of this have been uncovered. "James M. Curley and Thomas F. Curley were convicted," according to Foulke, "of impersonating two candidates at a civil service examination in Boston and were sentenced to two months in jail." In some cases little publicity is given to coming examinations. This may leave the organization practically free to appoint its candidates through the forms of competition.

Members of the civil service commission or its employes may be bribed to give an applicant a favorable rating. When the examinations are fairly conducted, but an atmosphere of suspicion exists, persons with "inside" information can pick up a little pin money. A municipal civil service commissioner once said that "someone would accidentally or in some improper manner" discover the results of the examination "and would go and obtain money" in return for an assurance that the examinee "would get the rating which he had already earned by his own ability." In other cases persons claiming the power to influence the selection from among the three highest in an examination have collected money from as many as possible of those likely to be appointed, keeping the amounts paid by the successful ones and repaying "those not selected, with the explanation that counter influence was too strong."

Movement of Personnel.—The control of promotion, discipline, and assignment may be employed to persuade recalcitrant members of the administrative personnel, recruited into the service by an open and aboveboard system of examinations, to serve the purposes of the organization in the same way as those appointed by an out-and-out spoils procedure. Criteria of achievement or failure of achievement in the political organization may be substituted for similar criteria within the administrative hierarchy in the management of personnel. A man may be promoted within the administrative service for gloriously carrying his precinct or he may be made to "go along" with the organization by actual or threatened disciplinary measures.

Because of the difficulty of developing an objective measure of relative merit for promotion in the administrative service, promotion is peculiarly susceptible to manipulation for political purposes. In some cases no effort is made to promote as the result of examinations. Discretion in selecting persons to be promoted is left to the head of the department or some other administrative superior. This discretion may be exercised upon the suggestion of party officials. By its power to determine the classes of employees eligible to take promotional examinations, the Chicago commission was able to favor particular individuals.

Persons entitled to promotion on the results of an examination under some laws may waive their right to someone lower down the promotional list. Pressure may be brought upon them to compel them to do so. In 1915, one Weideling, a sergeant in the Chicago police department, took the examination for police lieutenant ranking forty-fifth on the examination results. Forty-three men waived and Weideling, then becoming one of the three highest, was promoted to a lieutenancy. "It was directly charged in the press that these forty-three men were compelled to waive their rights by pressure and influence brought to bear by the head of the police department in order that Weideling's name might be reached." Control of assignments is a method often used in police departments to defeat the purpose of the merit laws among other things. Police who persist in political indifference may be sent to the "prairies" or to the "sticks." Assignment to a post far away from home is a powerful persuasive. Continual application of such measures will usually bring the most obstinate person into line.

Positions in the classified service may be abolished as an "economy" measure or on some other basis. New positions with different titles but similar duties may then be created and filled by temporary political appointees. In Chicago the license bureau which had charge of the collection of business and occupational license fees was abolished by council action. A short time later fifty clerks, selected in fact by the fifty Democratic ward committees, were stationed in police station houses to perform similar duties at a much higher cost and a reduction of license revenue. The chief function of these clerks appeared to be to sound the alarm when the police brought in persons charged with crime and to call to their rescue the ward committeemen or other party functionaries. Similarly in Columbus jobs held by classified employes were abolished and later re-created under new titles and filled by political appointees. In Troy, New York, competitive positions were abolished and new jobs exempt from examination, "executive secretaries," were created to handle the work.

It would be a grave error to say that the movement for civil service laws beginning with the passage of the Pendleton Act by Congress in 1883 has not limited to a considerable extent the patronage available to political organizations in many jurisdictions. Nevertheless, ways and means have been found to weaken in varying degrees the efficacy of the administration of these laws. The explanation is simply that the groups of citizens interested in combatting the patronage system have not been powerful enough to compel the enforcement of these rules.

No. 67

[Our first attempts at reform of the public service were directed at only two or three objectives. It was believed by many that if we could obtain capable persons in the civil service, through merit examination, and protect them from political interference, the problem of public personnel would be solved. In the long period that has elapsed since the passage of the Pendleton Act we have learned that a sound personnel system involves much more than these two steps. The attainment of a real merit system necessitates the adoption of sound systems of promotion and advancement, the provision of adequate means of discipline, suspension, and removal from the service, and the attainment of a high morale among the civil servants. Furthermore, the relationships between the adoption of a sound personnel policy and the functioning of democratic government must be clearly perceived. These and other considerations are the concern of "Essentials of a Model Personnel System."]

ESSENTIALS OF A MODEL PERSONNEL SYSTEM [1]

by Floyd W. Reeves

THERE is no such thing as a personnel system that can serve as a model for all types and sizes of governmental jurisdiction. There are, however, certain basic principles of personnel administration that are relatively uniform for all jurisdictions, irrespective of size or scope of operations. Any personnel system, to be effective, must be organized and administered in a manner consistent with these principles and with the basic objective of personnel administration. This basic objective is to secure and retain in the public service a quality of personnel that corresponds to the responsibilities of the service, and to achieve standards of competence that are as high as available human resources will permit.

The first essential of an effective personnel system is that it be a part of an effective system of government.

Laws, rules, and regulations providing that the personnel system operate on a merit basis are essential to secure efficiency in personnel administration, but they will not in themselves produce it. They must be enforced by a well-established tradition of good government, a tradition of merit in per-

[1] Floyd W. Reeves, "Essentials of a Model Personnel System," *The Annals* of the American Academy of Political and Social Science (January, 1937), Vol. 189, pp. 134-141. Reprinted by permission of *The Annals* of the American Academy of Political and Social Science. The footnotes in the original version are omitted here.

sonnel administration, and an enlightened public opinion. Unless they are so enforced, they will not result in a merit system. Tradition is more important, however, than the laws, rules, and regulations. The latter constitute a negative attack upon the problem. Building a tradition of merit in public service requires postive, constructive action. The administration of the personnel function in a model personnel system will be designed to increase the prestige of the public service. Unless there is prestige attached to the service, it is difficult to secure efficient public servants, and when they are secured, it is difficult to retain them.

A tradition of merit in government administration recognizes such administration as a profession. Public administration cannot become a profession, however, in a jurisdiction in which a large number of the major administrative officers are elected for specified terms. A short ballot is a requisite for an effective system of government. Elected officials will include only those engaged in major policy-forming activities. This group may include the chief executive officer and a very few immediate assistants. It will never include officers whose principal function is administration.

The legislative body is the major policy-determining agency in government. When this body is small, as in the case of many city councils, the chief executive will not need to assume major responsibility in connection with the determination of broad policies. In such cases, the chief executive may well be a part of the professional staff, selected upon a merit basis. Such a plan now operates effectively in many cities with the city-manager form of organization. When the legislative body is large, as in the case of state governments, the chief executive and a few immediate assistants will not be members of the professional staff, since they will be called upon to participate actively in policy formation.

The complexity of modern government requires a high degree of competence, particularly at the levels at which the higher administrative officers function. It also requires a high degree of devotion to the public service. These requirements can best be met through training for and experience in government service. A corps of career administrators in charge of operating departments and responsible to policy-forming officials is essential to the successful functioning of the executive branch of the government. This is the only means whereby the quality of personnel in public service may be made to correspond to the large responsibilities of that service.

The effectiveness of the personnel system is affected by the soundness of the organization of operating departments. To as large a degree as possible, each operating department will administer closely related functions. It is seldom possible, however, to organize an operating department in a manner such that some of its functions will not impinge upon functions performed by other departments. The successful administration of such functions requires close inter-departmental cooperation. This, in turn, requires machinery for coordination at all major levels where these functions operate. Often this coordination can best be achieved by means of inter-departmental committees, composed of staff members of the departments affected, and reporting back to the department responsible for the administration of the function concerned.

An effective organization requires that the number of major coordinate administrative officers responsible directly to the chief executive shall not exceed a reasonable span of control. This implies the assembling of all functions of a governmental agency into a few large groups. In a state or city government, this number should probably never exceed six or seven, and might well be smaller.

Over a period of many years the activities of government have constantly expanded and become more complex. To provide for this expansion and the increased complexity of government, a heavy strain has been placed upon personnel administration. In its earlier stages of development, public personnel administration was conceived to be a function designed primarily to eliminate spoils. This idea has given way to a broader conception that places major emphasis upon developing incentives, increasing morale, and stimulating employee efficiency. The promotion of the merit system has not decreased in importance, but new methods for accomplishing this purpose, methods that do not interfere with the development of a constructive and positive personnel program, are now recognized as essential and are being employed in many jurisdictions.

Personnel functions of an administrative nature include such matters as attendance control, checking pay rolls, administering pensions, care of records, and preparing reports. Most personnel agencies also participate in one way or another in the classification of positions in the service, the determination of salaries, and the formulation of salary schedules. The negative controls on recruitment have not decreased in importance, but the technique employed to accomplish the ends sought is being constantly improved.

Personnel agencies are increasingly participating in quasi-judicial functions in connection with appeals from decisions relating to demotion, separation from the service, classification and salary status, and compensation for injuries received in line of duty.

Many of the newer and more constructive functions of personnel administration are primarily advisory in their nature. Their purpose is to stimulate desirable action on the part of employees and management. Functions of this type relate to such matters as discipline; employee-management relations; working conditions; and health, safety, welfare, and recreation

These matters are primarily the concern of the heads of the operating units, but an effective personnel service can render valuable assistance in studying such problems and suggesting means for their solution.

No exhaustive analysis of the functions mentioned above is necessary to make it clear that a continuous program of research is essential if personnel problems are to be dealt with adequately. Personnel management is not static in any of its aspects. Because this is true, no one of the personnel functions may well be excluded from the research program. This implies a personnel research agency in every jurisdiction except those that are very small. Small units may find it advisable to utilize the assistance of some outside agency in carrying on necessary research activities.

Most of the essentials of a model personnel system relate to the two major aspects of the personnel function—entrance to the service, and increasing efficiency within the service. Both of these aspects will be discussed briefly.

Effective public administration requires throughout the service men and women with adequate training for the work they are to perform and with qualities of character adequate for the positions they are to occupy. The best laws that may be devised may be virtually annulled if they are administered by an incapable or unsympathetic staff. The requirements mentioned are particularly important for those charged with the responsibility of administering the personnel function, since pressures, political and otherwise, are frequently concentrated at that point.

Within the general service, as distinguished from the major policy-determining group, the judiciary, and the military service, merit appointments will not be confined to the lower positions in a model personnel system, but will extend throughout the service. No appointments will be made for political purposes, or on the basis of personal friendship, family relationships, religious affiliations, or other non-administrative reasons. There will be no attempt to find jobs for individuals, but a constant endeavor will be made to find qualified and efficient persons to fill necessary jobs. There will be no discrimination because of the marital status of employees or applicants. Resident requirements will not be set up for technical, skilled, or higher posts, because such requirements restrict opportunity to secure the best talent for the public service, and limit the opportunity to develop a career service. For economic reasons, such requirements may be applicable for temporary positions or for unskilled labor. The conditions set forth above are necessary in order that all appointments may be made upon the basis of merit, which is a requirement of an effective personnel system.

The technique employed in the recruitment of personnel will be in accord with the democratic principle of equality of opportunity in accordance with merit. Examinations will be widely advertised and the duties and responsibilities of the positions for which the examinations are held will be adequately explained. The personnel administration will not wait passively for applicants to apply, recruitment will be active. Well-qualified persons will be sought out and urged to file applications. Cooperative arrangements for the certification of candidates will be developed with other governmental jurisdictions, with accredited professional associations, and with educational institutions.

Few personnel agencies can afford to have a permanent staff of examiners qualified to pass finally upon the qualifications of candidates for some of the more important positions requiring high technical, professional, or administrative ability. In certifying eligibles for such posts, therefore, use will be made of special boards of examiners. Such boards may well consist of a major staff member of the personnel division, a representative of the operating agency for which the candidate is to be certified, and one or more persons either from within or from without the service, qualified to pass upon the eligibility of candidates for the position.

The procedures employed in selecting personnel for entrance to the service will be in accord with the requirements for the development of career services. A career service has been defined as a "life work . . . an honorable occupation which one normally takes up in youth with the expectation of advancement, and pursued until retirement." The establishment of effective career services is essential to the development of an effective personnel program.

For each major type of service there will be an appropriate method of entrance based entirely upon qualifications to render effective service. These qualifications include not only ability to render effective service immediately after entrance, but, what is even more important, capacity for continued growth in the service. This implies that a majority of those entering each type of service will be relatively young, will enter at the lower positions within that service, and will be promoted to vacancies at higher levels entirely on the basis of merit.

It would seem inadvisable to restrict entrance to higher positions in the service exclusively to those who entered the service at the lower levels. No matter how effectively a career service system may operate, no agency is likely to secure a monopoly upon persons well qualified to fill the higher positions. It may be conceded that opportunity for promotion within the service is essential to a career service and to an effective personnel program. It may also be conceded that employees within the service, when they are equally qualified, should be given preference over candidates from without the service. An effective career service, however, does not imply filling important positions from within the service when better trained and better qualified personnel can be secured from other sources. Such action would not assist in creating a true career service, but would tend to prevent the attainment of that goal.

In personnel management, as in recruitment to the service, the techniques employed should exemplify the democratic principle of equality of opportunity in accordance with merit. Employees in a model personnel system will receive just treatment and be given reasonable security. This requires that they be placed in positions where they can render the largest service, in accordance with the total needs of the governmental units of which they are a part; that they be protected against arbitrary dismissal, demotion, or discipline; that their positions be properly classified as to duties and responsibilities; that they receive fair compensation for services rendered; that adequate provisions be made for supervision and in-service training, with opportunities for advancement or demonstrated merit; that they and their dependents be protected against the hazards of sickness, old age, and death, disability, or injury in line of duty; and that working conditions be as conducive to health, safety, and efficiency as the nature of the work and the requirements of the public interest permit.

Upon entrance to the service, every employee will be placed on probation for a definite period of time, ranging from a few months for positions of a routine nature to one or two years for important positions requiring diversified talents and involving large responsibility. During this probationary period the supervisor of the employee, in cooperation with the personnel agency, will give the employee careful supervision, assist him to become more proficient in his present work, and encourage him to take additional training when such training seems advisable. Service records will be kept, and at stated intervals throughout the probationary period, reports will be made by the supervisor to the personnel agency. At the end of this period the supervisor will be required to make a definite recommendation with reference to the future placement of the probationer in the service. He will recommend that the employee be retained in his present position, that he be transferred to some other position of equal or lower grade, that he be dismissed, or, in rare cases, that he be promoted to a position of greater responsibility. In any case, the recommendation will be definite. The employee will not be retained in his present position merely because of a lack of positive action.

Supervision and training will not cease with the end of the period of probation. Both are important throughout the entire service, and at all levels.

In-service training is of two general types—training for the position which

the employee now occupies, and training for some other position in anticipation of transfer or promotion. The governmental agency, through the
stimulation of its personnel division, will be encouraged to provide both
types of training when such facilities are not adequately provided by
the educational system or are not easily available. When agencies of public
education are easily accessible to employees, such agencies will be encouraged to provide facilities for in-service training.

In filling positions that become vacant above the lower grades, it is a
matter of major importance that appointing officers give proper consideration to employees already in the service. Consideration will first be given
to employees in direct line within the same department and unit. Next in
order will come employees available for transfer and promotion from other
departments. Failing to find suitable candidates within the service, well-
qualified former employees available for reinstatement will be considered
before turning to existing examination registers. New open competitive
examinations will be given only after failure to secure eligibles through the
procedures mentioned above. Classification of positions as to duties and
responsibilities is a technical function of great importance to the building
of morale within the service. It is one of the major factors affecting the
compensation of employees. As such, it becomes particularly important
that this function be performed efficiently and fairly, in order that high
morale may be achieved. As a highly technical function, classification cannot be performed effectively unless it is administered and conducted by
trained experts devoting full time to such work.

Good working conditions and some degree of security are essential to
high morale. The attainment of these objectives is a joint responsibility
of the operating departments, the personnel agency, the chief executive of
the government, and the policy-forming body responsible for the government. The central personnel agency will administer the accident compensation and retirement services. It will also cooperate with and encourage the
departments to provide other services for the improvement of working conditions.

In addition to activities of the type mentioned above, an effective personnel agency will perform many functions of a broad, developmental nature.
It will keep itself well informed concerning methods, policies, and procedures
of personnel management throughout the service. It will encourage and
support constructive personnel development, and will disseminate knowledge concerning such development to other parts of the service. It will
provide machinery for the coordination of personnel policies and plans
within the service. It will develop advisory relationships with personnel
administrations of other governmental jurisdictions and of industries, and

with students of personnel administration wherever they may be found. It will utilize every legitimate means to stimulate better personnel practices throughout the service. It will encourage officials to recognize the importance of high morale, and to become familiar with the means whereby such morale may be developed. To accomplish these ends, emphasis will be placed upon positive, constructive action rather than upon negative, restrictive measures of control.

One of the most effective ways for government to improve the development of its personnel function is through the cooperation of representative groups of employees and the supervisory staff. To secure such cooperation, recognition should be given to the right of employees to participate actively in the development of policies and plans whenever they are in a position to make a contribution. Members of the management staff and the supervised employees, together, comprise an organization for public service. To obtain the objective sought, the whole-hearted cooperation of all members of this organization is essential.

The management of personnel is and must continue to be a major function of all administrators. Some aspects of the personnel function, however, are so highly technical that general administrators are rarely found who are equipped with the technical knowledge or skill now available for personnel work. Furthermore, the burden placed upon administrators in administering the operating functions under their direction is usually so heavy that it does not permit them to devote the time and attention necessary to the successful performance of technical personnel functions. Because of this situation, specialized personnel agencies are essential at all major levels of administration.

Good personnel in charge of the administration of the personnel function is an essential of good administration. But good personnel may be rendered relatively ineffective unless it is placed in an organization framework that is structurally sound. Furthermore, good personnel is not attracted to an organization that is structurally unsound, and when secured, can seldom be retained. Therefore, the personnel administration must be given its proper position in the structural organization of the agency of which it is a part.

Personnel administration is a part of management. Functions such as selection of employees, efficiency rating, promotion, demotion, and removal from the service, are essentially management functions. Negative controls may be secured in part if these functions are performed by an independent civil service commission, but only in part. It is easy to find ways and means whereby restrictive laws, rules, or regulations may be overcome. Furthermore, such negative controls as may be necessary are more effective when operated as a part of management. Any other arrangement violates sound principles of administration, in that it robs management of initiative, and undermines responsible leadership. Consequently, negative controls can never be wholly effective if administered by a civil service commission operating as an independent agency outside of the management structure. Positive, constructive action in the performance of the personnel function almost never develops through an independent civil service commission.

The personnel agency is one of a group of service agencies established to assist operating agencies through the performance of technical functions. Other agencies of a similar type include those for fiscal control, purchasing, management of physical facilities, research, and long-range planning. Of this group, the agency for fiscal control and the personnel agency are of major importance. Their functions are closely related. At the level where the chief executive operates, these agencies constitute the major instruments through which he performs his managerial functions. Therefore it is important that the heads of these agencies be made responsible directly to the chief executive. Both functions are so important that no chief executive can afford to delegate their performance completely to others.

There is another reason, and a major one, why agencies for the performance of functions such as personnel administration and fiscal control need to be attached directly to the office of the chief executive. These agencies must be given large responsibility for the performance of their specialized functions, but these functions are performed in connection with activities for which line officers are responsible. The service agencies can never be given authority over the operating agencies commensurate with the responsibility that the service agencies have for the successful conduct of the functions with which they are charged. Therefore the service agencies need the active support of the chief executive and the prestige that will come from being attached to his office, in order that they may function in a satisfactory manner. No specialized function of major importance should be administered by a specialist primarily concerned with the administration of another specialized function. Both personnel administration and the administration of the budget are highly specialized and important functions. Therefore neither of them will be made subordinate to the other, but they will be given coordinate positions in the structural organization of the government.

Some governmental jurisdictions are so large that it is not advisable to concentrate all personnel functions in a central personnel agency. Many of these functions can be administered more effectively if placed in the operating agencies where the functions are to be performed. Some of them, such as the classification of duties and responsibilities of employees, need to be administered in part by the central agency and in part by the operating agency under the supervision and control of the central agency. In the case of functions administered directly by the central agency, such as examinations for entrance to the service, the active cooperation of the department is essential. Therefore, in each of the larger departments or other administrative units, personnel offices will be established with a relationship to the head of the department similar to that described for the head of the central personnel agency with the chief executive of the entire governmental jurisdiction.

Since in the larger jurisdictions there will be both a central personnel agency responsible to the chief executive, and departmental personnel offices responsible to the departmental heads, coordinating machinery is essential. Possibly the best way to secure such coordination is to organize the heads of the personnel offices in the departments into an advisory council, with the head of the central agency serving as chairman.

Personnel functions may be classified as quasi-judicial, administrative, and developmental. The hearing of appeals from decisions of administrative officers is quasi-judicial. Activities such as the giving of examinations or the classification of employees are administrative. Stimulating others to perform their personnel functions more effectively is developmental. The question arises as to the best type of agency through which to perform personnel functions. Should the personnel agency be headed by a board, or by an individual? There are advantages and disadvantages in both arrangements.

In the case of quasi-judicial functions there are some advantages in placing responsibility upon a board composed of three or more persons. But it is generally conceded that administrative functions can be performed best by an individual. Likewise, an individual is more effective than a board in the performance of developmental functions.

The quasi-judicial functions are important, but the administrative and developmental functions are of equal if not greater importance. The model personnel system will have a central personnel agency headed by an individual to care for administrative and developmental functions. Within this central agency it will establish a board which will be charged with responsibility for the quasi-judicial aspects of the personnel function. In this way the advantages of both forms of organization may well be secured without the disadvantages attached to either form of organization.

Chapter XIX

THE COURTS AND THE LAW

No. 68

[IT requires very little reflection upon the circumstances of our everyday lives for us to see the necessity of some kind of rules if people are going to live together peacefully.   The following article by Professor Radin illustrates this point in describing the origin, necessity, and nature of law.]

THE HAPPY ISLAND [1]

by Max Radin

THE Island Mas-a-tierra, some centuries ago, was a wholly deserted member of the group called Juan Fernandez, about four hundred miles off the coast of Chile.   There, in the month of September, 1704, a Scottish sailor named Alexander Selkirk was marooned and there he lived quite alone for five years, till he was rescued and taken back to his home.   His adventures gave Defoe the idea of *Robinson Crusoe* and became the subject of a great many poems, essays, and sermons.   Perhaps the most famous poem about him is the one by the English poet, William Cowper, of which the first stanza runs:

> I am monarch of all I survey—
> My right there is none to dispute;
> From the centre all round to the sea,
> I am lord of the fowl and the brute.

If Alexander Selkirk had been given to thinking hard and carefully about his surroundings, he would have realized that his condition was even stranger than he supposed.   Instead of everything on the island belonging to him,

---

[1] Max Radin, *The Law and Mr. Smith* (Indianapolis: Bobbs-Merrill and Co., 1938), Ch. 1, pp. 1-5. Reprinted by permission of the publisher.

the truth was that nothing belonged to him. He had no rights, because there was no one against whom he could claim them. He had no privileges, because there was no one who disputed them. Whatever he did, he had no duties and no liabilities. So far from being a monarch or lord, he no more ruled or owned the place he occupied or the things he used, than the sea-gull owns the portion of the ocean over which it flies. Whether he moved or stood still, ate or walked or slept, hunted or planted, he was completely lawless.

Now, mark how different all this would be if he had found another human being there or if another human being had joined him. Perhaps we shall understand it if we recall the delightful ballad by W. S. Gilbert, entitled "Etiquette," which tells the story of the *Ballyshannon,* which foundered, drowning all the passengers but two, Gray and Somers:

> These passengers, by reason of their clinging to a mast,
> Upon a desert island were eventually cast.
> They hunted for their meals, as Alexander Selkirk used,
> But they couldn't chat together—they had not been introduced.
>
> And somehow thus they settled it without a word of mouth
> That Gray should take the northern half while Somers took the south.

These two perfect Englishmen managed their living together on the island in their own way, but the most important thing was that there had to be some way. The moment two persons are in the same place, where they might conceivably run into each other or where the one might want what the other had, they must in some fashion decide how to avoid conflicts. If they do not, the only possible result will be that the stronger will kill the weaker or make him his slave.

When there are only two, the way to avoid conflicts is simple. One way is to act like our two Englishmen, each keep to his own side and never so much as nod to the man on the other side. There are other ways, of course, but they are all pretty easy to understand and pretty easy to follow.

But when, instead of two, there get to be a great many people on our island, the ways that have to be arranged so that people do not run into each other, interfere with each other, take things away from each other, hurt and abuse each other, are much more complicated. We cannot simply let Somers take the southern side and Gray take the north, because there are only four points of the compass and there are, let us say, many thousands of persons. We must, therefore, manage it so that everybody can go somewhere, live somewhere, get something to eat and something to wear, assuming that there is enough to go round in all these matters, as there generally is.

We could manage it easily enough, with or without "word of mouth," if we could divide the island up into exactly equal parts, each one of which was in every respect as good as the other, and if we could then divide the commodities in the island, the things that could be used and enjoyed, into exactly equal portions. Then, if everyone would remain perfectly satisfied with his share and never want any other or any more, our way of living together on our island would be simple enough. The rules of our society would be easy to understand and there would be no difficulty about keeping the rules, because no one would have any reason for breaking them.

Obviously, what we have assumed is impossible. In the first place, no region can be divided into exactly equal parts; and, if it could be so divided, these parts would not have the same qualities. For many purposes, one could not possibly be as good as another. The same is probably true for the commodities on the island. Secondly, it is impossible to suppose that all the islanders would be satisfied or remain satisfied. The strong, the good, the industrious, the competent, would feel that they ought to have more things or better things than the weak, the bad, the lazy, the incompetent; and the greedy, the avaricious, the selfish, would certainly wish to have more, whether they ought to have them or not.

We might be willing to admit that those in the first group ought to have more than the others and we might even assist them in getting it, but we should certainly not do so in the case of the second group. On the contrary, we should do everything we could to prevent them from getting what they wanted. The simple rules of living together would, consequently, have to be modified. We should have to find some way of discovering who the good, the strong, the competent, the industrious, are. We should then have to keep in restraint the greedy, the selfish, the avaricious. The rules would no longer enforce themselves, because there are now many people who might want to break them, and we should have to do more than establish rules; we should have to get some sort of force to compel those who wish to break the rules to keep them.

Our Happy Island has already got to be a pretty complicated place, but real life is far more complicated. After all, our island is imaginary. No country we know ever began with even a pretense that all its inhabitants had an equal share of the good things in the country. Every country has rules about living together, established long ago, and the first thing we note about these rules is that they have nothing to do with either the deserving or the undeserving classes of the community.

There is one further thing which we must try to understand. Let us go back to our Happy Island for a moment. We have discovered that we need rules. Gray must know that Somers will not be found on the northern side—that is, on Gray's side—and he must know that this arrangement is lasting. Or else he must know that Somers will not be there on Monday, Wednesday, and Friday. In any case, the rule means that the situation is to be repeated; it is something that happens many times in the same form. If Gray could never know whether Somers would be there or not, life under the circumstances would, we are told, be intolerable to him.

So also when there are thousands of persons instead of two involved. If anything might happen any day, there would be no rule, and living together would be really impossible. John Smith, peering out from his refuge, might see Thomas Brown and Brown might rush on him to kill him, or he might leave him alone. Smith might exchange goods with Brown and Brown might take his goods back again or leave them. Smith could never be sure about his safety or his property. Life would be one constant terror-ridden anxiety. Rabbits might live that way, but certainly not men.

And it is almost as bad when there are rules but we do not know them. Suppose Smith comes to a wholly foreign and previously unknown country —let us call it Laputa. He sees from a hiding-place people acting in a way that seems entirely without rule or method. Sometimes one Laputan attacks another and sometimes he leaves him alone. If Smith knew Laputan, he would have understood that the Laputans always attacked each other unless one of the two made a certain gesture, and that if he wished to go about peaceably he had only to make that gesture.

In other words, there are two things necessary. There must be rules, and there must be some way of finding out what they are. In most countries, in our own country particularly, most people have somewhere to go, some place to live in, and some means of getting the commodities necessary for living. How much they can get, and the number and variety of things they can do, depend upon rules which number over a million and which are some-times extremely hard to understand.

Of these rules, some, for reasons we shall try to discover, are called legal rules, and the sum of all of them is called THE LAW, a phrase which we often write in capitals, but which is not half so awe-inspiring as it sounds.

No. 69

[WE have already seen that government has two main functions: (1) the formu-lation of the rules under which the community is to live and (2) the enforcement of those rules. We have seen, also, that these two functions are carried out by a variety of governmental agencies and that there is no clear-cut division and separation of powers relative to them.

It should be no surprise to us, therefore, to learn that the functions of the judicial branch are not confined wholly to the execution or enforcement of public policy, but that they include the actual determination of what the policy shall be in many cases. In other words, while it is the job of the court to investigate and determine facts and apply the law to the facts thus determined, there are many cases in which there is doubt as to what the law is and its applicability to the case at hand. Laws are, of necessity, general in character. They are, in many cases, worded so that their exact meaning is in doubt. Conditions arise which present issues not considered when laws were framed. Laws often conflict, and there is doubt as to which is applicable; in some cases there seems to be no clear-cut law at all. As a result, courts have the important task of determining what the law is, what scope and meaning it is to have, what law shall prevail when there is conflict, and what the law shall be when there is no rule available to fit the case at bar.

These functions are of great importance in any country, but in the United States they are particularly important because we have a system of jurisprudence known as the "common law." This means that the rules governing the relations of individuals have not been reduced to statutory form to a very considerable extent and that the law has come into existence as a result of a long line of judicial decisions in particular cases. This in turn produces certain results. The law built up in these decisions comes to be looked upon as composed of a body of "deathless truths" to which those who interpret it can turn for a solution of their problems. It comes to have a meaning and significance, especially for lawyers and judges, of more importance than any other kind of law. Both statutes and constitutions come to be interpreted in the light of it; it becomes, in a sense, the high priest and oracle of our legal system It becomes "THE LAW"; and an understanding of this fact is a valuable aid in the evalua tion of our whole judicial system.]

"THE LAW" [1]

by Fred Rodell

THE Law is the killy-loo bird of the sciences. The killy-loo, of course, was the bird that insisted on flying backward because it didn't care where it was going but was mightily interested in where it had been. And certainly The Law, when it moves at all, does so by flapping clumsily and uncertainly along, with its eye unswervingly glued on what lies behind. In medicine, in mathematics, in sociology, in psychology—in every other one of the physical and social sciences—the accepted aim is to look ahead and then move ahead to new truths, new techniques, new usefulness. Only The Law, inexorably devoted to all its most ancient principles and prece-

---

[1] Fred Rodell, *Woe Unto You, Lawyers!* (New York: Reynal and Hitchcock, 1939) pp. 23-38. Reprinted by permission of the publisher.

dents, makes a vice of innovation and a virtue of hoariness. Only The Law resists and resents the notion that it should ever change its antiquated ways to meet the challenge of a changing world.

It is well-nigh impossible to understand how The Law works without fully appreciating the truth of this fact:—The Law never admits to itself that there can be anything actually new under the sun. Minor variations of old facts, old machines, old relationships, yes; but never anything different enough to bother The Law into treating it otherwise than as an old friend in a new suit of clothes. When corporations first came on the legal scene, The Law regarded them as individual persons, in disguise, and so, for most legal purposes, a corporation is still considered, and even talked about, as a "person." A transport airplane, so far as The Law is concerned, is nothing but a newfangled variety of stagecoach. Such things as sit-down strikes, holding companies, Paris divorces, were treated with almost contemptuous familiarity by The Law when they first appeared, and the same fate undoubtedly awaits television when it grows up and begins to tangle with The Law. For all this is part of a carefully nurtured legend to the effect that The Law is so omniscient that nothing men may do can ever take it unawares, and so all-embracing that the principles which will apply to men's actions five hundred years from now are merely waiting to be applied to whatever men happen to be doing in 2439 A.D.

What The Law purports to be is a tremendous body of deathless truths so wide in scope and so infinite in their variations that they hold somewhere, and often hidden, within their vastnesses the solution of every conceivable man-made dispute or problem. Of course the truths are phrased as abstract principles, and the principles are phrased in the strange lingo of The Law. And so only the lawyers—especially those who have become judges or ordained interpreters of The Words—can ever fish the proper solution out of The Law's vastnesses. But it is the very keystone of the whole structure of legal mythology to insist that all earthly problems can and must be solved by reference to this great body of unearthly abstractions—or, in short, that they can and must be solved by the lawyers.

The chief reason why it is so hard for the ordinary man to get the lawyer's picture of The Law—as a supreme mass of changeless abstract principles—is that the ordinary man generally thinks of law as a composite of all the little laws that his various governments are forever passing and amending and, occasionally, repealing. Congress and state legislatures and city councils keep laying down rules and changing rules. Is this not clear proof that The Laws moves with the times? Briefly, it is not.

To the lawyer, there is a vast difference between The Law and the laws. The Law is something beyond and above every statute that ever has been or could be passed. As a matter of fact, every statute, before the lawyers allow it to mean anything—before they let it have any effect on the actions of men—has to be fitted into The Law by "Interpretation" of what the statute "means." And any apparently harmless little statute is likely to mean plenty to a lawyer, just as a statute which seems to carry dynamite in its words may mean nothing by the time the lawyers are through with it.

A few decades ago when the famous Clayton Act was passed, which was intended to preserve competition and crack down on monopolies, a strong labor lobby got Congress to write Section 20 into the new law. Section 20 had practically nothing to do with competition or monopolies. Section 20 was intended to restrict federal courts from granting so many injunctions against union activities. Samuel Gompers, who was then the head man of the unions, called Section 20 "labor's Magna Charta." But Samuel Gompers was no lawyer.

By the time the lawyers, headed by the Supreme Court, got through with Section 20 it meant exactly nothing. Chief Justice Taft, speaking for the lawyers, said it was *intended* to mean exactly nothing. Referring to The Law as authority, he said that it was clear that Section 20 was no more than a restatement of The Law as it had existed before the Clayton Act was passed. Now, Chief Justice Taft was in no position to know, and would have considered it irrelevant if he had known, that the Clayton Act might not have been passed at all if it had not seemed clear to labor that Section 20 gave strikers the right to picket without constant interference by the federal courts. But Chief Justice Taft and his court of lawyers had the last word. They made of labor's "Magna Charta" something strangely resembling Germany's "scrap of paper." And all in the name of The Law.

Of course, Chief Justice Taft and his court would have found it far more difficult to do this if other lawyers had not played a leading part in writing the Clayton Act. Section 20 was full of those typically meaningless legal words, like "wilfully" and "maliciously." It said, for instance, that federal courts could not stop strikers from picketing "lawfully." "Lawfully," according to Chief Justice Taft, meant in accordance with The Law before the Clayton Act was passed. Before the Clayton Act was passed, the lawyers had ruled that just about all picketing was against The Law. Therefore it still was Q. E. D. And, incidentally, the Supreme Court did almost the same thing with the whole of the Clayton Act by picking on other meaningless legalistic words to prove that most trusts were not trusts and most monopolies were not monopolies—according to The Law. You can change the laws all you please, but you can't change The Law. And The Law is what counts. It would, moreover, be a mistake to jump to the conclusion that Chief Justice Taft and his court "interpreted" Section 20 of the Clayton

Act into complete oblivion merely because they didn't like unions or strikes or picketing. For Taft, in the course of explaining at great length why Section 20 did not really mean a thing, went out of his way to include in his opinion a rousing defense of labor unions. Of course, this defense did not do the unions any good, any more than Section 20 did the unions any good after Taft got through with it. The point is that Taft was insisting to his fellow-lawyers—the only people who ever read or understand judicial opinions—that in disappointing the unions he was merely following The Law. The choice, however distasteful, was forced upon him. For it is part of the legal legend that no lawyer—not even when he becomes a Supreme Court justice—ever does any more than explain what The Law is and how it applies. He is merely the voice through which the great gospel is made known to men.

Moreover, The Law can do strange things to man-made laws even when, as very rarely happens, such laws are not so full of "wilfullys" and "maliciouslys" and "lawfullys" that they practically invite the lawyers to write their own ticket. For example, there was the Guffey Coal Act, involving federal regulation of the coal industry. The Supreme Court first said that most of the important parts of the Act were unconstitutional. Now, saying that a law is unconstitutional is really no more than a convenient way of saying that it goes against The Law. But the whole idea of constitutionality and unconstitutionality is so mixed up with notions like patriotism and politics, as well as with the most sacred and complicated of all legal rules, that it deserves and will get full treatment a little later on. The point here is that, after saying part of the Guffey Act was unconstitutional, the judges went on to say that the good part had to be thrown out with the bad part. Not unreasonable perhaps, on the face of it. Not unreasonable until you learn that Congress, foreseeing what the Supreme Court might do with part of the Act, had taken particular pains to write very clearly into the Act that if part of it should be held unconstitutional, the rest of it should go into effect anyway. And so in order to throw out the whole Act, the Court had to reason this way:—Part of this law is unconstitutional. The rest is constitutional. Congress said the constitutional part should stand regardless of the rest. But that is not our idea of a proper way of doing things. We do not believe Congress would want to do things in a way that does not seem proper to us, who really know The Law. Therefore, we do not believe Congress meant what it said when it said to let the constitutional part stand. Therefore, we will throw it out along with the unconstitutional part. In the name of The Law.

That reasoning is not a burlesque. It is a shortened version of part of what the Supreme Court actually said, though the Court phrased it in multisyllabic legal language, in the case of Carter against the Carter Coal Company. And the result is an example, more obvious but no more extreme than thousands upon thousands of others, of how little the laws written by our so-called lawmakers really mean until the lawyers have decided what those laws mean—or don't mean—in the light of The Law.

Thus, the common man is dead wrong when he thinks of law as a conglomeration of all the laws that are passed by legislatures and written down in books—even though it is true that practically all those little laws are phrased by lawyers in legal language. Those little laws, those statutes, are, to a lawyer, the least important and least respectable of three kinds of rules with which the lawyers deal. The other two kinds of rules are those that make up what lawyers call "the common law" and those that make up "constitutional law."

Now, the common law is actually closer to The Law with a capital L than any constitution or statute ever written. The common law is the set of rules that lawyers use to settle any dispute or problem to which no constitution or statute applies. There is, for instance, no written rule to tell the lawyers (or anybody else) whether a Nevada divorce is good in Pennsylvania. There is no written rule to tell whether a man who orders a house built with a bathroom between the kitchen and the pantry has to take the house and pay the builder if everything else is fine but the bathroom is between the living-room and the coat closet. In both cases, the lawyer-judges write their own answers without interference from any constitution or statute. In both cases, the answers are said to be fished directly, non-stop, out of the mass of abstract principles that make up The Law.

Constitutional law is something else again. A constitution, in this country at least, is halfway between The Law and an ordinary statute. Like a statute, it is phrased by men, a few of whom are usually not lawyers, and is written down in definite if often nebulous-meaning words (though in England the Constitution isn't written down anywhere and so is indistinguishable from The Law of England). But like The Law, constitutions, except where they deal with the pure mechanics of government—as in giving each state two senators or listing the length of a governor's term of office—are made up of abstract principles which mean nothing until brought down to earth by the lawyers. If this sounds like heresy, consider, for instance, the U. S. Constitution's well-known guarantee of freedom of speech. What does that guarantee mean, practically speaking? It did not stop the federal government from putting people in jail during the World War [I] because they talked against war. It did not stop the police of Harlan County, Kentucky, from beating up people who tried to make speeches in favor of unions in Harlan County. On the other hand, that constitutional guarantee does prevent the extreme restrictions of free speech which are common abroad to-day. How tell, then, which free speech is good and which is bad, under the Constitution? Only by asking the lawyer-judges. And how can they tell; how do they decide? Simply by referring to our old friend, The Law, in order to "interpret" the Constitution.

The Law is thus superior to constitutions, just as it is superior to statutes. And according to the legal legend, it is neither constitutions nor statutes which finally determine the rules under which men live. It is The Law, working unimpeded to produce the common law, working through the words of constitutions to produce constitutional law, working through the words of both statutes and constitutions to produce statutory law. All three kinds of law are merely obedient offspring of that great body of abstract principles which never changes and which nobody but a lawyer even pretends to understand.

Justice Holmes was in effect talking about The Law as a whole, when he said of its nearest and dearest offspring: "The common law is not a brooding omnipresence in the sky." But Justice Holmes, as he well knew when he said that, was dissenting not only from a decision of the Supreme Court but from the opinions of most lawyers about The Law. For practically every lawyer thinks and talks of The Law as a sort of omnipotent, omniscient presence hovering around like God over the affairs of men. Yet every lawyer purports to be able to understand and interpret a large part of that presence for the benefit of those who are not lawyers—at a price.

The strange thing is, however, that lawyers, for all their alleged insight into the great mystery, are never able to agree about the presence or its interpretation, when it comes down to applying The Law to a simple, specific factual problem. If the lawyers agreed, there would never be a law case, for every law case results of course from a legal dispute as to what The Law is. If the lawyers agreed, there would be no dissenting opinions. If the lawyers agreed, we would not have appellate courts reversing the judgments of trial courts and super-appellate courts reversing the judgments of appellate courts, and super-super-appellate courts—or supreme courts— reversing the judgments of super-appellate courts. The fact is that every lawyer claims to know all about The Law *until* it comes down to applying The Law to a specific dispute. Whereas no non-lawyer cares in the slightest degree what The Law is until it comes down to applying The Law to a specific dispute.

It is all very well for a lawyer to say, out of his knowledge of The Law, that a "mortgagor" has "legal title" to a building. That is very pretty and sounds very impressive. But if the mortgagor then wants to know if he can sell the building, and on what terms, and if he has to pay taxes on it, and if he can kick the mortgagee out if the mortgagee comes snooping around, the lawyers will begin to disagree. It is all very well, too, for a lawyer to say that The Law forbids "interference with the freedom of contract." But when fifty-seven respectable lawyers of the late Liberty League declare unanimously that employers need pay no attention to the Wagner Labor Act, because it interferes with freedom of contract, and then the Supreme Court tells them they are one hundred per cent wrong, the fifty-seven lawyers' undoubted knowledge of The Law begins to look just a trifle futile.

The Law, as a matter of fact, is all things to all lawyers. It is all things to all lawyers simply because the principles on which it is built are so vague and abstract and irrelevant that it is possible to find in those principles both a justification and a prohibition of every human action or activity under the sun.

And how does The Law, then, ever get brought down to earthly affairs? In what way does it actually succeed in building regulatory fences around men's conduct? The answer is just as simple as it is complex. The answer is that the last bunch of judges which gets a shot at the solution of any specific problem has the decisive word on The Law as it affects that problem. The solution which that last bunch of judges gives to that problem *is* The Law so far as that problem is concerned—even though every other lawyer in the world might suppose The Law was different. It might not then be irrelevant to ask just what a judge is. And it was an unusually candid judge who recently gave the best answer to that question. "A judge," he said, "is a lawyer who knew a governor."

The lawyers who knew governors—or who knew presidents—or who knew enough ward-leaders (where judges are elected)—bring The Law down to earth in all sorts of different and conflicting ways. A home-owner who beats up a trespassing hobo may be a hero in one state and a criminal in another. But no matter which he is, the legal appraisal of his actions will fit perfectly into the great and ubiquitous framework of The Law. For, no matter how differently different judges in different places may decide the same human problem, or decide it differently in the same place at different times, the great legend of The Law as steadfast and all-embracing is always adhered to. Decisions may change or differ or conflict, but The Law budges not.

And it is necessary to understand this keystone of legal reasoning—and to accept it as a fact no matter how silly it may sound—before it is possible to understand the strange processes of The Law. It is necessary to realize that The Law not only stands still but is proud and determined to stand still. If a British barrister of two hundred years ago were suddenly to come alive in an American court-room, he would feel intellectually at home.

The clothes would astonish him, the electric lights would astonish him, the architecture would astonish him. But as soon as the lawyers started talking legal talk, he would know that he was among friends. And given a couple of days with the law books, he could take the place of any lawyer present—or of the judge—and perform the whole legal mumbo-jumbo as well as they. Imagine, by contrast, a British surgeon of two hundred years ago plopped into a modern hospital operating room. He would literally understand less of what was going on than would any passer-by brought in from the street at random.

The Law, alone of all the sciences, just sits—aloof and practically motionless. Constitutions do not affect it and statutes do not change it. Lawyers talk wise about it and judges purport to "apply" it when they lay down rules for men to follow, but actually The Law—with a capital L—has no real relation to the affairs of men. It is permanent and changeless—which means that it is not of this earth. It is a mass of vague abstract principles —which means that it is a lot of words. It is a brooding omnipresence in the sky—which means that it is a big balloon, which has thus far escaped the lethal pin.

No. 70

[PROFESSOR RODELL has given us a general picture of The Law. Mr. Hibschman, in the following article, brings some of the details of that picture into focus by a discussion of specific cases.]

HUMPTY DUMPTY'S RULE IN LAW [1]

by Harry Hibschman

"WHEN I use a word," said Humpty Dumpty, "it means just what I choose it to mean—neither more nor less."

But Alice objected, "The question is whether you can make words mean so many different things."

And Humpty Dumpty airily replied, "The question is which is to be master, that's all."

We are not living in Wonderland, as we have reason to know every time we come to grips with actualities; and yet in this very real world what Humpty Dumpty said is true—words mean what their masters say they mean. And the masters are the courts of last resort, the Supreme Court

[1] Harry Hibschman, "Humpty Dumpty's Rule in Law," *The Atlantic Monthly* (April, 1932), Vol. 149, pp. 470-474. Reprinted by permission of the author and *The Atlantic Monthly*.

of the United States and the appellate courts of the various states. This statement a study of their decisions will speedily confirm; and it will at the same time show what a myth is that certainty of the law which laymen are assured exists.

To begin with the highest court in the land, it held many years ago that the expression "high seas" includes the Great Lakes, though the question arose in connection with the interpretation of a statute written originally by a Congressman who later became a judge, and who as a judge declared that the Great Lakes were not included. A dictionary in common use even now, in defining the words "high seas," uses the Great Lakes as an example of what the words do not cover; and to ordinary folks the dictionary definition for "high seas" as the open ocean seems still to be good.

But would it occur to you that a fence is a building? A New York court said it was. And the highest court of Massachusetts has held a tent to be a building. A railroad car is a building in Nebraska, but not in Arkansas. A corncrib is also a building in Iowa, but not in Florida—perhaps because they raise corn in the former state and not in the latter. At any rate the Florida Supreme Court argued, "We have been unable to find this word 'corncrib' in Worcester's Dictionary; and it is not necessarily a building, a ship or a vessel. . . . 'Crib' has various meanings, as the manger of a stable, a bin, a frame for a child's bed, a small habitation, and it is used in the latter sense by Shakespeare. Nowhere else do we find it used in the sense of a building." That was in the year of the Lord 1882, and as a consequence of the court's conclusions a defendant who had been convicted of burglary went free.

On the other hand, a Texas court, in order to sustain a conviction of burglary, held that an office in one corner of a hardware store, made of pickets about four feet high, three inches apart, with a plank on top used as a shelf, was a building, though it is clear that it was nothing more or less than a corner fenced off within a building. By the same reasoning the part of a court-room railed off from the public is a building.

A jackass is a horse. The Tennessee Supreme Court settled that many years ago. And, according to the Illinois Supreme Court, asses are cattle. So are goats under a ruling of the North Carolina Supreme Court. The latter court cited in support of its conclusions the well-known case of Laban and Jacob.

Snakes are "implements, instruments, and tools of trade," at least when Uncle Sam is collecting his revenues. For the same purpose a new metal called "bouchan," used in watches, is a jewel. In Georgia a minor who has a separate estate is an orphan. In Pennsylvania a bicycle is an animal, and in the Federal courts it is also a business vehicle.

Chinamen in California were formerly held to be Indians, which disqualified them as witnesses against white folks and made it possible for good white men to rob and assault them with impunity. A Chinese merchant sent to the penitentiary is no longer a merchant, but a laborer, so that the exclusion acts may be applied to him. For the same purpose a gambler is a laborer. According to a very recent decision, however, an air pilot is not a laborer.

In New York, under the sanitary code, candies are vegetables; and in Georgia a watermelon is both a fruit and a vegetable. Pipes, tobacco, cigars, and newspapers are not "articles of comfort" for a poor husband, but mere luxuries. So says the Alabama Supreme Court, which might be expected to have a deeper sympathy for the downtrodden male. In Massachusetts a college education is not a necessary under present-day conditions, according to a decision rendered last year.

In Michigan a dentist is a mechanic. In Mississippi he is not a mechanic. And in North Carolina he is not a physician, within a statute allowing the sale of liquor on the certificate of a physician. Otherwise, says the court, "toothache would be more welcome and more prevalent than snake bite."

A gelding is not a horse. At least both the Montana and the Kansas Supreme Courts have held that, where an indictment charges a defendant with having stolen a gelding, his conviction cannot be sustained if the evidence merely shows that he stole a horse. And a charge of stealing a hog cannot be supported by testimony of the stealing of a dead hog. In other words, a dead hog is not a hog. We have the word of the Supreme Court of Virginia for that.

A question that often arises in connection with certain crimes is the meaning of the term "daylight," or "daytime." This is also an important matter in connection with the service of search warrants. In such a case decided in 1923, it was held by a Federal court that a search warrant providing for a search in daytime only was no justification for a search made at 5.15 P.M. on December 22. In another case decided in 1927, however, it was decided that thirty-eight minutes after sunset was "daytime" in Georgia. The test applied was the so-called burglary test, which is whether there is sufficient light from the sun to recognize a man's features. Judge Sibley said in that case: "Daytime does not in law or by common understanding begin at sunrise, and end at sunset, but includes dawn at one end and twilight at the other."

But in 1929, in a case involving a search under a daytime warrant, Judge Norton, another Federal district judge, reached a conclusion directly contrary to that of Judge Sibley. Judge Norton said:

"Daytime" in this statute is used in its ordinary meaning at the present time. . . . What seems to me to be the correct rule is stated in Murray's Dictionary, where "day" is defined as "in ordinary usage including the lighter part of morning and evening twilight, but, when strictly used, limited to the time when the sun is above the horizon." This rule has great practical advantages. . . . Sunrise and sunset will make a much better working rule than the vague and shadowy boundaries adopted for humanitarian reasons in defining burglary.

So there you are. Which is right? I confess that I do not know.

Is an airplane a "self-propelled vehicle"? A Federal district court held it was and convicted a defendant of the crime of having transported a "self-propelled vehicle," which had been stolen, from one state to another, where the facts showed that he had flown a stolen plane across the state line. But the United States Supreme Court held only a few months ago that the district judge was mistaken—that an airplane is not "a self-propelled vehicle."

In Missouri a pistol so defective that it could not be discharged even if it were loaded is a firearm. In New York it is not.

Nowhere is it more evident that the prejudices and predilections of the courts determine the meaning of words than in the decisions interpreting Sunday laws, particularly with reference to baseball. Thus, the Supreme Court of Kansas has held that baseball is not a game under a statute forbidding "games of any kind." The Missouri Supreme Court has laid down a similar rule, saying that baseball is a sport. But the Nebraska Supreme Court has held baseball to be a game within a statute forbidding "sporting" on Sunday. The New Mexico Supreme Court, on the contrary, has held that baseball is neither a sport nor labor. But it is labor in Virginia, at least when played by professional players, though no admission is charged. In Tennessee it is not the exercise of "any common avocation of life"; and in Oklahoma it is a public sport and banned if played by professionals, but a private sport and not within the statute when played by amateurs.

Turning away from the criminal law for a moment, let us take a look at the exemption laws and the laws of estates. How would you define the words "household effects"? In Vermont it was held some years ago that they did not include a piano. In Michigan there has been a similar holding; but in Missouri, Oklahoma, and Texas the term "household effects" has been held to include a piano. In New York it has recently been held that "household effects" included two automobiles, a riding horse, and a speedboat; and an earlier New York decision was to the effect that wines in a well-stocked cellar were "household goods." It may be interesting in this connection to note that the Iowa Supreme Court held in 1929 that a radio had "no likeness or kindred relationship with a musical instrument."

Another word that has puzzled the courts from time to time and led to conflicting rulings is the word "accident." According to a Pennsylvania court, the bite of a dog is an accident. So is being shot by an assailant or robber; and so was the shooting of a husband by his wife, when, following a quarrel, the husband approached the house, swearing and carrying an axe, and the wife took a pistol and killed him. The latter holding was made to enable the wife to recover on an insurance policy containing a provision that there could be no recovery by the beneficiary if the insured met his death at her hands other than by accident. Suicide in a fit of delirium or insanity is an accident; but electrocution following a conviction of murder is not an accident according to a decision of the United States Circuit Court of Appeals handed down last June. However, death by lynching is an accident in the opinion of the Kentucky Supreme Court, whatever it may appear to the victim.

"Colored person" in Virginia means one having one-fourth or more of Negro blood. In North Carolina, on the other hand, it means a person having Negro blood of any degree. In Oklahoma it is held to mean Negro so clearly that a white person charged with being colored can maintain an action for libel. But in Mississippi it has been held that the term "colored races" includes all races except white. The Court of Appeals of the District of Columbia, on the other hand, held in 1910 that "colored" referred only to persons of the Negro race, and that, regardless of the slight amount of Negro blood that might be in their veins,—the determining factors being "physical touches, whether of shade, hair, or physiognomy,"—they were "colored" if there was the least admixture of Negro blood.

The word "collision" is another that has demanded a great deal of attention on the part of the courts, and their conclusions as to its application have been varied and conflicting as usual. The Michigan Supreme Court, for instance, held in 1920 that "an object coming from above" might be considered as constituting a collision, the object in that case being the shovel of a steam shovel that fell upon a loading motor truck. The Texas Court of Civil Appeals, on the contrary, decided in a somewhat similar case that an object falling from above could not be considered as constituting a collision, the object being the upper floor of a garage that gave way and crushed a car standing on the floor below.

In New Jersey a recovery on an insurance policy on the ground of a collision was allowed where the car went through the guard rail of a bridge and was damaged by falling to the ground below. Where a car was backed into an open elevator shaft and fell to the floor below it was held to be a collision by the Pennsylvania Superior Court. But in Wisconsin it has been held that where a car ran off the road, and down an embankment into a river, the facts did not justify recovery as for a collision. In Missouri, on the other hand, recovery as for a collision was allowed under almost identical circumstances. Where, in order to avoid striking an approaching car, a driver turned out and his car left the road, fell down an embankment, struck a rock, and turned over, it was held in New York that the injury to his car was due to a "collision," the court saying, "In simple words it is a striking together of two objects. The road is an object, likewise the earth. Whether vertical or horizontal makes no difference." But the Washington Supreme Court held in 1924 that it was not a collision where a car skidded off the road and rolled and bounded down a mountain side, striking stumps and trees as it went. Again, on the contrary, the Alabama Supreme Court held that same year that where a car was left standing on a hill and started by the force of gravity, going over a cliff and hitting the ground a number of feet below, damages were recoverable as for a collision.

There is one other troublesome word that needs to be noted—namely, the word "drunkenness." The Nebraska Supreme Court held that a man might be under the influence of liquor without being drunk, and gave as the test the one of whether or not he had lost control of his bodily and mental faculties. But the Iowa Supreme Court in a case involving the removal of a mayor on the ground of intoxication, after saying that intoxication and drunkenness meant the same, held, "It means not necessarily that he is so drunk as to be unable to walk straight or show outward signs to a casual observer, but is satisfied if he is sufficiently under the influence of liquor so that he is not entirely himself."

A Texas court more wisely said, "A person may be intoxicated and not drunk. One drink will not ordinarily make a man drunk. Defendant had the appearance of a man who was drinking some but able to attend to his business." But the same court had said previously with even a greater exhibition of wisdom, "It is extremely difficult to draw the line on a 'drunk.' There are various stages, such as quarter drunk, half drunk and dead drunk. There are the stages of being vivacious, foxy, tipsy, and on a 'high lonesome,' and it is as difficult to determine when a young lady gets to be an old maid as it is to tell when a man has taken enough alcoholic stimulant to pass the line between 'jolly sober' and 'gentlemanly drunk.'"

And now, approaching the end, let us see what "end" means according to an august appellate tribunal. Said the Virginia Supreme Court: "It imports what will be when the Apocalyptic Angel, with one foot on the sea and the other upon the Earth, shall lift his hand to Heaven and swear, by Him that liveth forever and ever, that there shall be 'Time no longer.'"

It is well, however, to note that at least in one instance a high court was stumped by a problem of definition. It was the Supreme Court of Georgia, which in 1925 admitted and explained:

> From the days of Socrates and Xantippe, men and women have known what is meant by nagging, although philology cannot define or legal chemistry resolve it into its elements. Humor and threats are idle. Soft words but increase its velocity and harsh ones its violence. Darkness has for it no terrors, and the long hours of the night draw no drapery of the couch around it. It takes the sparkle out of the wine of life and turns at night into ashes the fruits of the labor of the day. In the words of Solomon, "it is better to dwell in the corner of the housetop than with a brawling woman in the wide house."

And further deponent sayeth not.

No. 71

[THE nature of the rules applied in particular cases, as we have seen, is determined to a considerable extent by the judges who find the rules by peering into the crystal ball of The Law. Unfortunately the rules that are to be seen there are often archaic, but tradition coupled with a reactionary judicial psychology makes reform difficult. This situation is made clear in the following article by Mr. Hibschman.]

LEGAL COBWEBS [1]

by Harry Hibschman

JAMES HARRIS, a gentleman of color, was indicted in the State of Delaware in 1841 for having stolen "a pair of boots." But at the trial it appeared that, in the excitement of acquiring new footwear in violation of the law, he had seized and asported, not two boots that were mates, but two that were both for the right foot. He was convicted as charged in the indictment; but on appeal the high and honorable Superior Court reversed his conviction on the ground that a charge of stealing a pair of boots could not be sustained by proof of the stealing of two boots that were not mates. "The object of certainty in an indictment," said the court, speaking didactically, "is to inform the defendant plainly and precisely of what offense he is charged. This certainty must be not merely to a common intent but to

---

[1] Harry Hibschman, "Legal Cobwebs," *The American Mercury* (December, 1931), Vol. 24, pp. 455-460. Reprinted by permission of *The American Mercury* and the author.

a certain intent in general, which requires that things shall be called by their right names." (3 Harrington 559.)

To be sure, that was ninety years ago. But the rule applied in the Harris case has not yet been sent to limbo. In fact it still works. For, in law, rules and precedents are like musty bottles in old wine cellars—they are esteemed for their age. In 1881, for instance, the Kansas Supreme Court decided with all due judicial solemnity that evidence of the stealing of a gelding would not sustain a charge of stealing a horse. (State v. Buckles, 26 Kan. 237.) In 1912, the Alabama Supreme Court held that a charge of a violation of a statute making it a felony to steal "a cow or an animal of the cow kind" could not be sustained by evidence of the stealing of a steer. (Marsh v. State, 57 So. 387.) And in 1917 it was decided in Missouri that a conviction under an indictment charging a man with stealing hogs would have to be reversed where the evidence showed that the hogs were dead when taken. The august appellate tribunal that handed down this illuminating decision went across the seas for its main precedents and cited three English cases as authority, two of them decided in 1823 and the other in 1829. It reached the conclusion that "the carcass of a hog, by whatever name called, is not a hog." (State v. Hedrick, 199 S. W. 192.)

A very recent example of a reversal of a conviction because of "variance," as the courts call the vice condemned in the cases already cited, is the Texas case of Prock v. State (23 S. W. (2nd) 728), decided last year. Here the complaint on which the defendant was arrested and bound over for trial described him as a "male person," and the information filed against him and on which he was tried described him as an "adult male." It was held that this difference required the reversal of his conviction of aggravated assault on a female, though where the harm to him lay is beyond the imagination of an ordinary man.

Another Texas case was reversed in 1910 on the ground that the indictment in which the defendant was accused of burglary described the burglarized premises as being occupied at the time of the crime by six Japanese mentioned by name, while the evidence was to the effect that there were only five. (Grantham v. State, 129 S. W. 839.) In 1917 the Illinois Supreme Court reversed a conviction for embezzlement because of a mistake in the name of one partner out of more than thirty named in the indictment as the injured parties. (People v. Dettmering, 116 N. E. 205.) And in 1919 it similarly upset a conviction in a liquor case because in one count out of forty-nine, under all of which the defendant was found guilty, his name was spelled Holdburg instead of Goldburg. (People v. Goldburg, 123 N. E. 530.)

Judges whose morning prayer is, "Keep my feet in the paths of Coke and Blackstone, for precedents' sake!" may, of course, find complete satisfaction for their souls in such decisions. But if one dares to be captious and ask what difference it can make to a defendant—what rights of his are jeopardized—if two unmated boots are described as a pair, a gelding as a horse, a steer as of "the cow kind," or a dead hog as a hog, or if he is proved to have burglarized the premises of only five Japanese instead of six, or embezzled from thirty men properly named and one misnamed, or has the first letter of his last name given wrongly in one count out of forty-nine, one is moved to repeat with the Oklahoma Criminal Court of Appeals that a technicality is "a microbe which, having gotten into the law, gives justice the blind staggers" (Ryan v. State, 129 Pac. 685.), and to exclaim with the Wisconsin Supreme Court that "there is little wonder that laymen are sometimes heard to remark that justice is one thing and law is another!" (Gist v. Johnson-Carey Company, 158 Wis. 204.)

With many American appellate tribunals the point of view, regardless of the breakdown of the judicial machinery and the increase of serious crime, is still that expressed long ago by the Supreme Court of Massachusetts in the case that is said to have driven William Cullen Bryant from law to literature as his life's work. "In a matter of technical law," said the court, "the rule is of more consequence than the reason for it." (Bloss v. Tobey, 19 Mass. 320.)

American courts have been especially fearsome of permitting one jot or tittle to be taken from, or changed in, indictments. This attitude is due to the supposedly sacred character of the Grand Jury as an institution and of the indictment as its solemnly begotten child.

Thus, it has been held within the last five years that a Federal court is absolutely without power to amend an indictment—even to strike out by stipulation of the defendant's counsel the words "and feloniously" as surplusage. (Stewart v. U. S., 12 Fed. (2nd) 524.) The leading Federal case on the subject was decided by the Supreme Court in 1886, when it was held that, if a change is made in the indictment, "the power of the court to try the prisoner is as much arrested as if the indictment had been dismissed or a nolle prosequi had been entered." (In ex parte Bain, 121 U. S. 1.)

Applying this rule, our appellate courts, both State and Federal, have handed down decisions that seem the height of folly if justice is really the end sought by the judicial process and if individuals are expected to retain a modicum of respect for the law and for the tribunals established to administer and interpret it.

Among the most notorious are the "the" and the "did" cases. Of the former the best known is a Missouri case, decided in 1908, in which a verdict of guilty was set aside because the indictment read "against the peace and dignity of State of Missouri" instead of "the peace and dignity of *the* State." (State *v.* Campbell, 109 S. W. 706.) But there had been a similar holding in Texas as far back as 1883. (Thompson *v.* State, 15 Tex. App. 39.) The leading "did" case was decided in Mississippi in 1895, when a conviction was reversed because the word was omitted from the indictment. Then in 1907 this original case was followed as a precedent in a murder case. In the murder case the fact that the word had been omitted in the indictment before the words "kill and murder" was discovered in the lower court at the time of the trial, and its insertion was permitted by the trial judge. In spite of this amendment, the defendant's conviction was reversed and the case ordered dismissed. (Cook *v.* State, 17 So. 228; and Hall *v.* State, 44 So. 810.)

The "the" cases have been overruled in Missouri, and there have been no recent "did" cases; but that does not mean that the technical approach to the consideration of indictments has been rejected, not by any means. That reversals still continue in many jurisdictions as of old will be evident from a few cases out of many decided during the year 1930.

In South Carolina, for instance, it was held that, where an indictment for murder charged that death occurred in the same county as the assault but the evidence showed that death occurred in another county, though the assault causing death occurred in the county in which the trial was being held and, therefore, the defendant was properly brought to trial there, still it was error to permit the indictment to be amended at the trial to show that death occurred in the other county. (State *v.* Platt, 151 S. E. 206.) In Louisiana an indictment charged the defendant with forging a certain order for $6 on a corporation and, on motion of the State's attorney, the indictment was amended to give the value of the forged order as $4 instead of $6. This was held to be reversible error. (State *v.* Sylistan, 125 So. 859.)

In Illinois a conviction was set aside because the indictment charged an attempt to open a showcase with intent to steal its contents but failed to allege that the attempt was unsuccessful. (People *v.* Donaldson, 173 N. E. 357.) In Texas an indictment was held fatally defective because it alleged that the defendant deserted his complaining wife "unlawfully and willingly" instead of "unlawfully and wilfully." (Carter *v.* State, 27 S. W. (2nd) 821.)

And in a New Jersey case, where an indictment for larceny was amended by striking from it the name of the party found by the grand jury to be the owner of certain alcohol alleged to have been taken and by substituting the name of another as owner, the appellate court held that the trial judge was without authority to permit such change, saying: "There can be no conception of the crime of larceny without ownership of the property alleged to have been stolen being in someone. It is therefore quite clear that the allegation of ownership in an indictment is a matter of substance and not of form." (State *v.* Cohen, 147 Atl. 325.)

But there are a number of late cases in which it is held that such amendments as those just mentioned are permissible. The substitution of a different name for that given in the indictment in connection with the ownership of the property taken, for instance, was upheld in Iowa in 1922 and in Mississippi in 1929. (State *v.* Luce, 191 N. W. 64; and Wood *v.* State, 124 So. 353.)

The difference of opinion in these cases lies largely in varying conceptions by the courts of what is a change in substance and what merely a change in form. That is the rock on which they split, one stream of decisions flowing in the most ancient channels and the other breaking through the banks of hoary precedent and cutting new passageways through the legalistic débris of the centuries.

The strange thing about American adherence to outworn doctrines and practices is that we claim to have inherited them from England. And yet England and her dominions have long since cast most of them overboard as so much rubbish. The judge who sits in an English criminal court may wear an ancient garb, but the procedure he follows has been modernized until an American hardly recognizes its semblance to what we are supposed to have derived from the same source. Since 1851 such defects in the indictment as have been discussed above have been of no importance whatever in English jurisprudence. The insertion of words like "the," "did," and "against the peace and dignity," or amendments to show true ownership or description of property or identification of persons are permitted as a matter of course.

The fundamental difference between present-day English criminal jurisprudence and American criminal jurisprudence may be graphically illustrated by quoting the indictment in the famous Sacco-Vanzetti case and comparing it with a similar indictment in Canada. The Sacco-Vanzetti indictment read as follows:

COMMONWEALTH OF MASSACHUSETTS

Norfolk, ss.

At the Superior Court, begun and holden within and for the County of Norfolk, on the first Monday of September in the year of our Lord one thousand nine and twenty, the Jurors for the Commonwealth of Massachusetts on their oath present That Nicola Sacco of Stoughton in the County of Norfolk and Bartholomeo Vanzetti of Plymouth in the County of Plymouth on the fifteenth day of April in the year of our Lord one thousand nine hundred and twenty at Braintree in the County of Norfolk did assault and beat Alexander Berardelli with intent to murder him by shooting him in the body with a loaded pistol and by such assault, beating and shooting did murder Alexander Berardelli against the peace of said Commonwealth and contrary to the form of the statute in such case made and provided.

In Canada that indictment would have read:

In the Supreme Court of Ontario

The Jurors for our Lord the King present, that Nicola Sacco and Bartholomeo Vanzetti murdered Alexander Berardelli at Ontario on April 15, 1920.

Compare this last, too, with an indictment returned by a grand jury in the District of Columbia in 1891. It charged that the defendant

did cast, throw, and push the said Agnes Watson into a certain canal then situate, wherein there then was a great quantity of water, by means of which casting, throwing, and pushing of the said Agnes Watson in the canal by the aforesaid Frederick Barber, in the manner and form aforesaid, she, the said Agnes Watson, in the canal aforesaid, with the water aforesaid, was then and there mortally choked, suffocated, and drowned.

This indictment was held defective on the ground that it did not allege that Agnes Watson died by reason of "the defendant's homicidal act." (U. S. *v.* Barber, 20 Dist. of Col. 79.)

If England and Canada have been able to modernize and simplify indictments and other elements of their criminal jurisprudence, why can't we? Do our inflexible constitutions stand in the way? Are we helpless in the face of the rising tide of criminality?

The answer is that what our co-heirs of the English common law and English jurisprudence have done, we can do. And we have already made a beginning in some states. California is, despite the Mooney case, perhaps the most striking example; and her accomplishments are worth noting as proof that we are not altogether helpless.

California's record of reversals in criminal cases, while not among the highest, was formerly, unlike her climate, nothing to brag about. In the period extending from 1900 to 1909, for instance, 22.5% of all criminal cases appealed were reversed. True, the record for Illinois for the same period was 37.3%; but that of New York and Massachusetts was under 15% each.

The old attitude of the California courts is evidenced by a case decided in 1880. It involved an indictment charging "entry into a stable to commit *larcey*." This was held not to describe any offense because of the simple omission of the letter *n*, notwithstanding the fact that there was a provision in the Penal Code, reading: "No indictment shall be deemed insufficient, nor shall the trial, judgment, or other proceedings thereon be affected by reason of any defect or imperfection in matters of form which shall not tend to the prejudice of the defendant." (People *v.* St. Clair, 55 Cal. 524; 56 Cal. 406.)

All of which goes to show that judges, like horses, may be led to the trough but can't be made to drink by mere legislative enactment. Judicial reform by statute can be, and repeatedly has been, thwarted and prevented by the wrong kind of men on the bench. One thing the layman groping for something better in the field of law needs to realize is that in the end, regardless of what the law-makers may say, it is the judges who determine what the law is and how, if at all, it shall operate.

But in 1911 the following section was added to the California constitution:

No judgment shall be set aside or new trial granted in any criminal case on the ground of misdirection of the jury or the improper admission or rejection of evidence, or for error as to any matter of pleading or procedure unless, after an examination of the entire cause including the evidence, the court shall be of an opinion that the error complained of has resulted in a miscarriage of justice. (*Constitution, Art.* VI, *Sec.* 4½.)

The first case involving this provision to reach the Supreme Court of the State seems to have been approached somewhat doubtfully and apprehensively. The court did, however, go so far as to say that "Section 4½ of Article VI must be given at least the effect of abrogating the old rule that prejudice is presumed from any error of law." (People *v.* O'Bryan, 130 Pac. 1042.)

That was in 1913. But by 1924 the Court had become bolder, and now it laid down this rule: "It is now incumbent upon the complaining party to make an affirmative showing that prejudice followed from the error relied upon." (People *v.* Mahach, 224 Pac. 130.)

The result of the recognition and application of this new constitutional provision is manifest from the fact that, while from 1910 to 1912, over 23% of the appeals in criminal cases were reversed, the percentage from 1916 to 1918 was only 12 and from 1918 to 1920 only 11.

Then in 1927 the Penal Code was amended so as to permit a short form of indictment or information and so as to make many other radical changes. The former crimes of larceny, embezzlement, false pretenses, and kindred offenses, for instance, were amalgamated into one crime, theft. And many of the old, technical rules were wholly abrogated. All these provisions have been sustained by the higher courts, and the spirit in which they were adopted was completely recognized in People *v.* Campbell, 265 Pac. 364, where the Supreme Court said:

Much of the time of courts has been consumed in the consideration of technical objections to pleadings in criminal cases; yet it is probable that few judges are able to recall a single case in which a defendant was actually in the slightest doubt as to the crime with which he was charged. Modern legislation is endeavoring to cut the Gordian knot by which the trial of criminal cases has so long been fettered, and the courts ought not to thwart that laudable effort by an adherence to mere technical precedents which regard form rather than substance.

The short form referred to has also been adopted in Maryland, Massachusetts, Alabama, Iowa, New York and other states and has the endorsement of the American Law Institute. So we are making some progress, and there is some reason for hope. But before we can travel very far, the comparatively few enlightened jurists and members of the bar who are striving for a better judicial system must be supported and reinforced by an awakened, insistent and clamorous laity. Tradition, the self-interest of certain groups, indifference, conservatism, and a reactionary judicial psychology constitute almost insuperable barriers to even the degree of reform attained in England. And a sane system, truly modernized and humanized, must carry us far beyond it.

No. 72

[THE two preceding selections present the case against "The Law." It is a case that has much merit and deserves serious consideration. But, before we deliver our verdict, we must hear the arguments of the counsel for the defence. "The Law" is neither all bad nor all good. Only when we see it in the perspective of the whole case can we render a balanced judgment.]

COMMON SENSE AND THE LAW [1]

by William A. Stern, 2nd

IN the sense of a fixed body of rules which, correctly interpreted, should bring about a single outcome to any matter coming before a court, there is no law. Despite lawyers' verbiage and judges' solemn obeisances to precedent, practically all lawsuits are decided on the basis of judges' and juries' simple convictions of what is right and what is wrong; moral sentiments lie between the lines of the most learned, long-winded decisions. Far from creating confusion, this essentially ethical approach affords greater assurance

[1] William A. Stern, 2nd, "Common Sense and the Law." *The American Mercury* (February, 1949), Vol. LXVIII, No. 302, pp. 145-152. Reprinted by permission of *The American Mercury* and the author.

of justice than could a collection of black or white pronouncements generally considered to be The Law.

Seldom, of course, does a court frankly state in an opinion that in the light of the facts no other outcome would be just; the myth of The Law is maintained, and prior decisions are cited as supporting authority. It does not seem to matter that a precedent may not be to the point, or that more apposite precedents would bring about a different result. Far-fetched analogies and devious reasoning can accomplish wonders in justifying an opinion apparently based on established rules but actually on plain horse sense.

Rarely, too, do lawyers admit what the ablest of them really try to do: present the facts so the tribunal will be convinced their clients are in the right. Once a Court reaches this conclusion, it is unimportant what precedent is cited, for even a dubious one will be welcomed. Since tons of tomes of law reports contain decisions, many contradictory, on nearly every question, finding appropriate precedents is the least of a lawyer's job.

If my law school made any attempt to teach this fundamental of applied law, that decisions go to the parties who present the most convincing factual demonstration of the rightness of their causes, it must have been on a day I was absent. I was assigned case after case to study, and though I found many whose principles conflicted, I was always given the idea that one case expressed the true law while its opposite was not the law. Had all these cases been in different jurisdictions it would have been easy to understand why they were so divergent, but for almost any decision it was possible to find a conflicting one in the same state. It then became part of my duty as a law student to "distinguish" cases; that is, to learn why the facts in one made it unnecessary to follow the principle laid down in another apparently similar. Though distinctions were usually without substantial difference, I managed to learn my hair-splitting well enough to be admitted to the bar.

Then bewilderment really struck me. The courts seemed to be all wrong. Juries would not follow the law and judges acted as though they had never gone to law school. Matters on which I had confidently advised clients, after careful research, went in the opposite direction in court. Other suits, which I won, according to the books should have been lost.

II

To-day, after a quarter of a century of experience in the courts, I am a wiser man but by no means sadder. I have found out that law, as actually, not theoretically, practiced in these United States, embodies the will of living people, not of those long buried; that it comes closer to what is in to-day's newspapers than what is in moldering pages on law library shelves;

that facts are strong and technicalities weak. Above all, more often than not, an innate sense of justice triumphs over legalistic obfuscation.

From the beginning, American jurists, though they always headed straight into the letter of the law, usually came out with decisions in the spirit of a self-willed, individualistic people. For instance, John Marshall, Chief Justice of the United States Supreme Court in the years 1801-1835, consistently acted in accordance with his firm Federalist, anti-states'-rights outlook. He upheld the Supreme Court as final interpreter of the Constitution, restricted the power of a state legislature to impair the obligation of a contract, denied the power of a state to tax a national bank and freed interstate commerce from state interference. His successor, Roger Brooke Taney, with equal sincerity and conviction acted along quite different lines. He held that a state which authorized a free bridge competing with a previously chartered toll bridge did not impair the obligation of a contract. Without disputing Marshall's opinion that a charter is a contract, he proceeded as he, a Democrat and states'-rights advocate, thought right. Since nowhere in the toll bridge charter had it been stated there would be a monopoly, he held there was no impairment. Thus, by the typical fillip of "distinguishing," in order to strike a blow against monopoly he justified a state's destruction of a contract's benefits.

In the *Dred Scott* case, Taney's propensities showed up even more clearly. The facts were simple enough. Scott, a slave, had been taken into territory where slavery was forbidden by the Federal statute known as the Missouri Compromise. Upon being returned to slave territory, he sued for his freedom on the ground that he had been in free territory. The first part of Taney's decision was simple, too; Dred Scott, he said, because he was a Negro and had never been made a citizen, was not entitled to sue in a Federal court. Though this clearly decided the case Taney did not stop here. For the first time since Marshall had proclaimed the power of the Supreme Court to pass upon the constitutionality of acts of Congress, 54 years before, the principle was exhumed. Scott had never been free, Taney maintained, because Congress had no power to forbid slavery in the territories and therefore the Missouri Compromise was unconstitutional. This wide excursion beyond the immediate grounds of the lawsuit was, of course, accompanied by elaborate ratiocinations and many solemn references to the Constitution.

At the beginning of the disturbed period immediately following the Civil War, finance and industry had markedly diverse views about how best to get the country out of financial chaos. So did Supreme Court judges. Within a year, the identical Legal Tender Act was declared unconstitutional by a four to three decision and—in an enlarged Court—constitutional by a vote of five against the original majority of four.

During the 1870s, the Court several times approved state regulation of business when protection of citizens' health and welfare was involved. This pathway for social gains had been followed only a short time when with booming industry the nation embraced the doctrine of laissez-faire in a kind of religious fervor. In 1905 a New York statute prohibiting employment in bakeries more than ten hours a day was declared unconstitutional. The statute was termed "a meddlesome interference"; the right to purchase or sell labor was part of the liberty of the individual guaranteed by the Fourteenth Amendment and the New York law was, therefore, unconstitutional. The usual genuflection, of course, was made to precedent. The Court piously agreed that a state could act to protect health. But the spirit of this law was "deplorable." It had only the remotest connection with the protection of health; its primary motive was to regulate hours of labor and "it might seriously cripple the ability of the laborer to support himself and his family."

Until the disillusionment of the Great Depression, almost unanimous national faith in laissez-faire continued. A District of Columbia minimum wage law for women was invalidated in the case of *Adkins v. Children's Hospital*.

Meanwhile, a more liberal though still minority trend in social thinking was being expressed in the dissenting opinions of Justices Holmes, Stone and Brandeis. By the time the New Deal came into power with the overwhelming support of the voters, enough members of the Supreme Court were sensitive to the country's desperation to find a way to sanction measures that upset a long line of prior decisions. Minnesota passed an act giving mortgagors two years in which to redeem their property from foreclosure, where they had had only one before. As dissenting Justice Sutherland correctly pointed out, the constitutional clause prohibiting a state to pass a law impairing the obligations of a contract had as its object the prevention of just such a statute; nevertheless, by a five to four vote, it was upheld. Although Minnesota farmers were on the verge of revolution, Chief Justice Hughes, who gave the majority opinion, carefully disclaimed any emergency power of the Supreme Court. But with the beautiful illogic of men who must find legal reasons for doing what they feel is morally right, he went on to save the distressed farmers by saying, "While emergency does not create power, emergency may furnish the occasion for the exercise of power."

Even more striking evidence that necessity is the mother of decision were the 1935 *Gold Cases*. The amount of gold in a dollar had been decreased by about 40 per cent, currency was no longer redeemable in gold, and we were not permitted to have any gold coin or certificates. Yet holders of government or other gold bonds had been promised payment in gold coin of the value it had at the time the obligation was incurred. Plaintiff creditors realized they could not now be paid in gold; but they did demand equivalent value in the now devalued dollars.

The Court was faced with a poser. The debtors' promises were clearly worded, but if keeping them was insisted upon, $1.69 for every dollar borrowed would have had to be paid by all gold debtors and our whole credit system would have collapsed. It was relatively simple for the Court to find a way out for private debtors by holding that the gold clauses in their contracts infringed upon the constitutional power of Congress to fix the value of money and were therefore invalid. To rescue the government from meeting its gold obligations in old-value dollars took a deal more legalistic wriggling. The majority opinion unequivocally stated that Congress could not repudiate its own obligations; of course the plaintiffs were entitled to receive exactly what the government had promised to pay them! But—and it was a big but—plaintiffs could not recover because they had suffered no damage. This conclusion was reached *via* mental acrobatics to the effect that if plaintiffs were paid in gold coin they would immediately have to surrender it in exchange for present value dollars.

A rare instance when precedent was unabashedly overruled occurred in *West Coast Hotel Co. v. Parrish,* 1936. The issue, the validity of a state of Washington minimum wage law, was identical with the one in *Adkins v. Children's Hospital* thirteen years before. Mrs. Parrish's attorney, who wanted the law upheld, diligently attempted to differentiate between it and the invalidated District of Columbia law. The Court said frankly there was no difference between them, but held that the Adkins decision had been incorrect. It approved the Washington statute.

In 1941 the Court approved Federal regulation of child labor, which it had disapproved in 1918. Altogether, the long record of Supreme Court decisions shows hundreds of contradictory opinions which are not only the expressions of its justices' personal beliefs, but also the history of the social and economic thinking of the people.

III

As jurors, the people have more immediate opportunity to apply their conceptions of right and wrong. Juries are supposed to evaluate testimony and determine what are the true facts; then to take the law, as explained in the judge's instructions, apply it to those facts, and bring in a general verdict such as "Not guilty" or "Plaintiff should recover $5000."

From the beginning, as now, judges and lawyers tended to mistrust juries: laymen without benefit of knowledge of precedent, all too likely to be swayed by sentiment and prejudice, incapable of understanding complex issues. And so rules of evidence were laid down as safeguards against common men's fallibility. To-day, though these rules have been considerably relaxed, and their application is much more at the discretion of the judge, we still go through some of the futile motions of building a formal framework proof against human reactions.

Judges' instructions to juries are less an attempt to prevent mistakes in judging the facts than one to ensure decisions in accordance with legal principles. But it makes little difference whether the instructions are correct—in the sense that they will not be reversed by an appellate court—or incorrect; regardless of what the judge tells them, jurymen come to their own conclusions. I remember one New York suit on a very harsh contract. In that jurisdiction, as in most, mailing the acceptance of an offer constitutes a contract and the only issue in this case was whether the plaintiff had actually mailed a letter. Carefully the judge instructed the jury that if they found plaintiff had placed a stamped, properly addressed letter in the mail a contract had been executed and plaintiff was entitled to recover; but if they found that the letter had not been mailed, no contract existed and they should bring in a verdict for the defendant. The jury returned a verdict for the defendant and as the proof of the mailing had seemed much stronger to me than the doubts defendant had attempted to cast on it, I asked one of the jurors whether he really thought plaintiff was lying when he testified he had personally put the letter in a post office mailing slot. The juror answered, "No, none of us thought he lied. I guess he mailed the letter all right, but we wouldn't bring in a verdict for that bloodsucker."

To the great majority of my colleagues such typical disregard of instructions is appalling. Many, indeed, think juries should be abolished because of their unaccountable verdicts. Jurymen, like robed judges, bring their ideas of justice with them into the courtroom and, with a remarkable consistency that one has to be trained in the law to find inconsistent, fit their picture of the facts into these.

Surely it is more than coincidence that in the majority of retrials verdicts go to the same parties favored in the original trials; evidently there is method in the madness of which juries are accused. What is more, since in most states verdicts must be unanimous, agreement by twelve individuals must have some common basis. And what is more common than the ideas of right and wrong shared by people living under the same mores?

Henry Weihofen, in an article on Colorado state hospital examinations of criminal defendants before trial, gives some striking illustrations of the way juries act according to what they think is best. In 37 out of 42 cases where insanity was a defense, juries accepted the diagnoses made by state hospital officials. In the five cases where they refused to follow the recommendations of the hospital they had their own reasons for the verdicts. In a case of rape against an infant, diagnosis was "psychosis with mental deficiency," but the plea of insanity was disregarded because the community was very bitter. A woman who had murdered her husband's mistress was found sane by the doctors, but not by the jurors, who shared the whole community's sympathy for her; and so, apparently, did the judge, for after the verdict of insanity he did not commit her. Also found insane by the jury, against hospital diagnosis, was the murderer of a brutal deputy sheriff; "It was common gossip that the community was benefited by the act," Weihofen notes. The perpetrator of a peculiarly savage murder was found guilty, and hanged, despite a diagnosis of "dementia praecox, paranoid type." An embezzler, diagnosed as having "psychosis, with cerebral arteriosclerosis," was nevertheless convicted: his criminal career had started before he was insane.

Not only will juries ignore instructions and facts but even statutes repugnant to their idea of what should be. There is, for example, the attitude of New York juries toward the crime of adultery. Annually, in their state, at least 10,000 divorces are granted, and as the sole ground for divorce is adultery, that means at least 20,000 criminal acts. Until recently, however, few indictments for adultery were ever attempted because it was practically impossible to get a jury to give a verdict of "guilty." And it seems hardly necessary to recall how in prohibition days juries in wet communities refused to convict unmistakable violators of the Volstead Act.

It is because of, not in spite of, the kind of standards for judgment jurors use that I believe the jury system works, and works well. Juries are a cross-section of the population, the community in microcosm, and they therefore reflect the mores. If the jury system is a failure, so is democracy.

Judges in lower courts are not quite as free as either juries or Supreme Court judges to follow their own lights, because their decisions are subject to possible reversal by appellate courts; but by and large, they too—amply fortifying themselves with citations of authorities—adapt facts and principles to what they believe the desirable result. To a certain extent, they and appellate judges share with juries the responsibility for verdicts. They can, and according to the rules should, set verdicts aside when these are "against the weight of the credible evidence." That this is seldom done is one more indication of the homogeneity of our ethics.

In my opinion any intelligent twelve-year-old, given a set of facts within his comprehension, is likely to decide upon them in the same way as the most learned judge. When I said this to one of my colleagues, he acted so appalled at this lese majesty to our profession that, as an experiment, I drew up fifteen problems involving legal principles upon which all courts agree, and had them presented to a group of average youngsters aged ten to twelve. "You promise a man to mow his lawn free of charge," read one. "You fail to keep your promise. If the man has to pay someone else to mow the lawn, will a court make you pay him what it cost him?" Correctly, the children answered, "No," although they had never heard of the legal argument that a binding promise requires a consideration to support it. Another problem read: "Because of illness, a tenant has no money to pay his landlord. Will a court permit the landlord to evict him?" They correctly answered, "Yes," though some of them added, "But somebody ought to take care of the sick man." Despite the familiar childish expression, "Finders keepers," the answer was also "Yes" to "You find a gold watch in the street. The owner discovers you wearing it a few weeks later. Will a court make you return it to him?" This, too, was in accordance with the law books: title is not divested by loss. Altogether, in all but two of the questions— and these I mistakenly based on matters outside youngsters' immediate experience—the children's consensus tallied with accepted legal principles.

IV

Much of what I have said is counter to the writings of great jurists and legal philosophers, but inasmuch as they disagree among themselves I feel less trepidation at voicing what, to most of my colleagues, will be heresy. I must, however, acknowledge a debt to the writings of Justice Oliver Wendell Holmes, Justice Benjamin Cardozo, Justice Harlan Fiske Stone, Rudolf von Jhering, Munroe Smith, Arthur L. Goodhart, Dean Roscoe Pound, Judge Jerome Frank and others. Many of their ideas have been the springboard for my jumping to my own conclusions. In affirming that our juridical system is flexible, personal, subject to the influence of public opinion and not fixed to the past, I am not alone; in my conviction that this is a good thing, I may be.

I must not give the impression that I think our way of administering justice is without its sore spots. Wherever a judge is given the sole decision, his personality and his conditioning must, to a certain extent, affect his viewpoint and hence his decisions. Certainly occasional miscarriages of justice occur when a judge because of disposition or bigotry, departs from the mores, but not nearly as often, I believe, as the "What did the judge have for breakfast?" school thinks. Again, justice may be thwarted by sectional prejudices. Or a flare-up of public indignation against an individual, a nationality or a race or the holder of certain political and economic views may adversely affect judgment. Or, as in the Dred Scott case, when partisan passions are rampant, a decision is bound to seem wrong to a large part of the people.

The great majority of decisions, however, seem fair, because they meet general approval—or, I could put it, they meet general approval because they seem fair. The people know little and care less about The Law, but they do care about justice; and whenever they are aroused to injustice, they effect a change through legislation forcing the reinterpretation of decisions, or war. It is the saving grace of our juridical system that the weasel words, the Latinisms and citations which clutter decisions, are mere window dressing for fundamental promptings of conscience. Its glory is that that conscience is as sound as the nation's.

Chapter XX

THE COURTS AND PUBLIC POLICY

[IN addition to participation in the formulation and execution of public policy as discussed in the preceding chapter, the courts in the United States have the power to invalidate acts of the legislature on the ground that they are contrary to the constitution. This is known as the power of judicial review and, in the form in which it is now exercised, amounts to actual participation in the legislative or policy-determining work of government. The claim is made that much of the social and economic legislation invalidated by the courts throughout our history has not been held void because it was in clear and unmistakable conflict with the constitution but because it was in clear and unmistakable conflict with the economic and social views of a majority of the court. Thus the court exercises what is essentially a legislative veto and, in essence, does the legislature's job over again.

In order to understand the role of the judiciary in American government, it is essential to appreciate the nature of the power of judicial review and the way in which it has been exercised by American courts. The following articles will give to anyone who will reflect upon the material they present a better understanding of the processes of American Government.]

No. 73

THE ROLE OF THE SUPREME COURT IN A DEMOCRATIC NATION [1]

by Robert E. Cushman

BACK in 1801 Jefferson wrote to a friend: "The Federalists have retired into the judiciary as a stronghold—and from that battery all the works of republicanism are to be beaten down and erased." Some people to-day believe that in a democracy no court should have power to invalidate

---

[1] Robert E. Cushman, "The Role of the Supreme Court in a Democratic Nation," Edmund Janes James Lecture at the University of Illinois, March 9, 1938. Reprinted by permission of the University of Illinois and the author.

laws passed by the representatives of the people. Many others believe that we need a Supreme Court with power to declare laws unconstitutional; but they also feel that in the use of that authority the Court has dangerously assumed powers which belong to the legislature, powers which in a democratic government ought not to be exercised by a court of law. This is the problem which I wish to explore. What is the rôle of the Supreme Court in our constitutional democracy?

I should like to divide my discussion into three parts. I should like *first* to show the nature and growth of the Supreme Court's power to invalidate laws. *Second,* I wish to show that the Court in reviewing legislation determines not merely the constitutionality of law but the wisdom and desirability of legislative policy. *Third,* I shall explain how I think the Supreme Court can best be restored to its proper rôle in a democratic government.

I. *The nature and growth of the Supreme Court's power over legislation.* Let us turn to the first of these three topics,—the nature and growth of the Supreme Court's power over legislation. I do not enter here upon any analysis of the theory of judicial review. I do not wish to make any comment upon the old, old dispute as to whether the framers of the Constitution intended to have the Supreme Court invalidate acts of Congress. We may accept judicial review as a going concern without worrying about its lineage. I should like, however, to trace the stages in the development of the power of the Supreme Court to declare laws unconstitutional, from the rather modest beginning in John Marshall's famous decision in the case of Marbury *v.* Madison, to the broad and drastic power which the Court now enjoys. This will make more clear the actual working relations between the Supreme Court and the Congress. There are at least four stages in this evolution of the Court's power, and these I wish to discuss.

First, let us examine briefly the case in which the Supreme Court first declared an act of Congress unconstitutional. This was the case of Marbury *v.* Madison, well known to every college student. President John Adams, about to retire from office, had appointed some sixty loyal Federalists to judicial positions created two weeks earlier by the Judiciary Act of 1801. The commissions of all these appointees had been signed and sealed, but John Marshall, Adams's easy-going Secretary of State, had not gotten around to deliver them when at midnight on March 3rd Thomas Jefferson, the newly-elected President, took office. Jefferson regarded these so-called "midnight" appointments to be an outrageous assault upon the principles of democratic government and common decency and ordered his Secretary of State, James Madison, not to deliver the commissions still left in the office. One of these had been destined to make James Marbury a justice of the peace in the District of Columbia, and Marbury, not wishing to be done out of his job, brought an action in the Supreme Court of the United States to compel Madison to give him his commission. He brought his suit under a section of the Judiciary Act of 1789 which authorized the Supreme Court to issue writs of mandamus and prohibition in the exercise of its original jurisdiction. After much delay the case reached the Supreme Court in 1803 and Marshall, as Chief Justice of the United States, was confronted with the fruits of his own negligence. The Court's decision and Marshall's opinion announcing it made history. Marshall began by scolding the Administration for not delivering Marbury's commission to which he was clearly entitled. This was just the kind of case in which it would be proper to mandamus Madison to deliver the commission. Unfortunately, however, this could not be done because the section of the Judiciary Act purporting to give the Supreme Court the power to issue a mandamus in the exercise of its original jurisdiction was unconstitutional. The Constitution clearly states the limits of the original jurisdiction of the Supreme Court and those limits Congress may not change. It could not, therefore, authorize the issuance of mandamus in original actions. The law purporting to give this new jurisdiction conflicts with the Constitution, and the Supreme Court, sworn to uphold the Constitution, must refuse to enforce the invalid statute. Thus was the doctrine of judicial review announced by the Supreme Court.

Now there are two facts about Marbury v. Madison which should be carefully noted. In the first place, the act of Congress held void was an act in which Congress had, in the Court's opinion, unconstitutionally tampered with the Court's own jurisdiction. It had tried to give to the Court powers which could not validly be given and the Court had protected itself against this legislative assault on its own integrity. Jefferson himself could not logically quarrel with the basic theory of the Court's action. He believed that each of the three departments of the Government must interpret the Constitution in so far as it bears upon its own powers and status, and may properly follow its own interpretation. No department is bound by the constitutional interpretation of any other department. In Marbury v. Madison the Court is simply saying to the Congress, "You must keep your hands off from us. You cannot enlarge our jurisdiction beyond constitutional limits." While some of Marshall's language is more generous, the case of Marbury v. Madison, viewed on its facts, does not establish the power of the Court to reach over its own fence and pass upon the validity of Congressional or Presidential acts which in no way affect the prerogatives or jurisdiction of the Court itself. Marshall nowhere asserts the superiority of the Court over Congress or the Executive, nor does he lay claim on the Court's behalf to any general power of supervision over the other two departments. In the second place, no other act of Congress was invalidated until the Dred Scott case in 1857. If the Supreme Court, under the doctrine of Marbury *v.* Madison, was supposed to enjoy the broad power to supervise the constitutional correctness with which Congress and the President exercised their own powers, it is rather surprising that during the fifty years following no attempt was made to seek the Court's decision as to the constitutionality of the Bank of the United States, a protective tariff, the acquisition of Louisiana, the annexation of Texas, and numerous other legislative or executive acts which aroused bitter constitutional dispute.

The second stage in the development of the power of judicial review was reached in the Dred Scott case decided in 1857. We cannot go into the fascinating story of this great case. It is enough for our purposes to know that the Court held that a Negro slave could not become a citizen of the United States, and that the Missouri Compromise Act of 1820, which forbade slavery in the federal territories north of 36° 30″, was unconstitutional. In thus forbidding slavery in the territories Congress had exercised a power not granted to it in the Constitution, a power which could not validly be implied from the delegated power to govern the territories. This represents an important enlargement of the scope of judicial review over the doctrine of Marbury *v.* Madison. Marshall's early decision had held that the Court could refuse to enforce laws purporting to change its own jurisdiction when the Court believed those laws to be invalid. In the Dred Scott case Taney and his colleagues go much further. They hold that the judgment of Congress as to the scope of one of its own legislative powers, this time a power in no way concerning the Court, is wrong and that the act so passed is unconstitutional. The Court, in other words, takes on the task of determining whether Congress has exercised powers which the Constitution has not delegated to it. Congress must stay in its own constitutional backyard and the Supreme Court, not Congress, is to determine whether it has done so.

The third stage in the growth of judicial guardianship over legislation came in the late eighties with the emergence of the Court's modern doctrine of due process of law. Here the Court added to its power of deciding whether Congress exercised undelegated power the much more far-reaching power of deciding whether Congress has exercised delegated power in an improper manner. Due process of law is a test, not of the existence of legislative power, but of the method of its exercise. The story back of this can be sketched only in the briefest way. The guarantee of due process of law traces its ancestory back to Magna Charta. After many permutations we find it set forth in the Fifth Amendment of the Federal Bill of Rights. There we read, "no person shall be deprived of life, liberty, or property without due process of law." Similar clauses are found in most state constitutions, and in 1868 the Fourteenth Amendment included an identical due process clause which applies to the states. The early history of due process of law was not spectacular. For a hundred years due process was held to be a limitation upon governmental procedure and not upon the substance or content of legislative policy. It required notice and hearing and a fair trial, but it did not forbid the legislature to regulate a social or economic problem. After the Fourteenth Amendment was adopted the Supreme Court, in its first case construing it, held that the due process clause had no relevance to, and could not, therefore, forbid an arbitrary state police regulation setting up a slaughterhouse monopoly in New Orleans. Due process seemed destined to remain the "forgotten clause" of the Constitution. But vast economic changes were taking place. The states began to deal with social and economic problems through more drastic exercises of their police powers, while the regulatory powers of Congress, especially under the commerce clause, were pushed far beyond previous limits. All this legislative activity was a sharp challenge to our American pioneer philosophy of *laissez faire*. Vested interests felt keenly the need of a constitutional weapon with which to combat the onward march of the new social control, and after a period of some wavering and uncertainty the Supreme Court, abandoning the precedents of a hundred years, converted the due process clauses of the Fifth and Fourteenth Amendments into judicial yardsticks by which to measure the validity of the substance and content of social legislation. Under the new rule a state or federal law was void as a denial of due process of law if in the opinion of the Court it impinged in an "arbitrary" manner upon the liberty or property rights of the individual. This step, taken without ostentation, constituted the greatest expansion of the Court's power to review legislation which has thus far occurred. Let me give a single illustration of the way in which the new doctrine enlarged judicial power. In 1898 Congress passed the Erdman Act regulating interstate railroads. One section of that act, aimed at the promotion of collective bargaining, forbade any interstate railroad to discharge one of its men because he belonged to a labor union. The Supreme Court held the act void on two grounds. It held first that this provision was not a regulation of interstate commerce because the relations between the railroad and its men had nothing to do with interstate commerce and did not, therefore, fall within the delegated power of Congress to regulate that commerce. It held, secondly, that, even if Congress had exercised its commerce power in passing the act, it had exercised it in so arbitrary and unreasonable a manner as to deprive the railroads of their liberty and property without due process of law. Congress had tried to exercise a power it did not have; but even if it had had the power, it had exercised it in an unconstitutional manner.

There is a fourth step in the development I am tracing. By it the Court has added to its scrutiny of the constitutional propriety of the *method* by which a granted power has been exercised by Congress, the further job of judging the constitutional propriety of the *purpose* for which the power has been used. (This new technique was first employed in invalidating the first federal child labor act in 1918 in the case of Hammer v. Dagenhart.) This act had forbidden the shipment in interstate commerce of the products of mines and factories in which children were employed in violation of standards set up in the act. In a five-to-four decision this was held void on two grounds. First, child labor is not closely enough connected with interstate commerce to make the statute a bona fide exercise of the delegated power to regulate commerce. Secondly, even if the statute were a bona fide exercise of the commerce power, it was an exercise of the commerce power for an unconstitutional *purpose,* namely, the regulation of child labor, a matter lying within the powers reserved to the states by the Tenth Amendment. Three New Deal measures of importance were invalidated on this same ground, that they constituted exercises of valid federal powers for invalid purposes. These acts were the Agricultural Adjustment Act, the Municipal Bankruptcy Act, and the Guffey Coal Act. In invalidating the AAA in the Butler case Mr. Justice Roberts did not hold the processing taxes and the paying of crop reduction benefits void on the ground that Congress was not exercising its delegated power to spend money. He held it void because the tax was levied in order to raise money to be spent for financing a scheme for the regulation of agriculture, an object which lies outside the delegated powers of Congress. The power was there, the method was regular, but the purpose was wrong. The Court has thus extended its supervision to the *motives* which have led Congress to exercise its delegated powers. "Thus," as Mr. Justice Cardozo put it, "the process of psychoanalysis has spread to unaccustomed fields."

To summarize this whole growth of judicial power, we find the Court at the outset protecting itself and its jurisdiction from unconstitutional interference by Congress. It next assumed the power to keep Congress from exercising powers not delegated to it by the Constitution. By a third step, the Court took over the authority to see that Congress and the States do not exercise their admitted powers by methods which seem to the Court to be arbitrary. Finally, the Court has undertaken to scrutinize legislative motives and to invalidate exercises of valid powers, by valid methods, but for wrongful purposes. Thus the judicial camel has got himself pretty completely into the legislative tent.

II. *The legislative and policy-determining character of the Supreme Court's power to declare laws void.* This brings me to the second major part of my discussion—the substitution, through the Court's power of judicial review, of judicial for legislative judgments on major questions of legislative policy. Has this come about in any large measure? If so, how has it come about, and with what practical results? My own view is that the Supreme Court now exercises wide power over the actual content of legislative policy. A very large proportion of the social and economic legislation invalidated in recent years has been held void not because it conflicted clearly and unmistakably with the clauses of the Constitution, but because a majority of the members of the Supreme Court believed the legislation to be economically unsound and objectionable. The Court exercises what I believe to be essentially a legislative veto. It is doing the legislature's job over again.

I am well aware that this charge would be sternly denied by the Supreme Court. As Professor Thomas Reed Powell has neatly put it, the Court has a very keen appreciation of "the rôle of rigmarole" in the judicial process. Proceeding on the theory "let not thy left hand know what thy right hand doeth," the Court continues to insist that the invalidating of a statute is an almost mechanical judicial process in which there is no room for personal opinion as to the social or economic merits of the legislation involved. In the very process of holding the Agricultural Adjustment Act void on grounds so strained and loosely reasoned as to reach almost a new low in judicial technique, Mr. Justice Roberts takes time out to restate the old orthodox incantation:

> When an act of Congress is appropriately challenged in the Courts as not conforming to the constitutional mandate, the judicial branch of the Government has only one duty—to lay the article of the Constitution which is invoked beside the statute which is challenged—and to decide whether the latter squares with the former. All the Court does, or can do, is to announce its considered judgment upon the question.

All of which sounds as though the justices, with the aid of compasses and slide rules, should reach a perfectly accurate result with which there can be no disagreement.

Now, certain clauses of the Constitution can be interpreted by the Supreme Court in this coldly mechanical manner. If Congress should fix federal income tax rates at a higher level in Illinois than in New York there could not be the slightest doubt that such an act violates the requirement of geographical uniformity in accordance with which the Constitution states that such taxes must be levied. It would be impossible for Congress to regulate criminal procedure in the federal courts in such a way as to violate the provisions of the federal Bill of Rights guaranteeing trial by jury, or protection against compulsory self-incrimination. It may be readily agreed that in such cases the Court could put the statute and the constitutional provision side by side and see at a glance that they do not jibe. Cases of this kind are exceedingly rare. They are rare because legislatures are not likely to indulge in self-advertised violations of the Constitution.

But these are not the cases in which the validity of social and economic legislation is involved or in which broad questions of legislative policy are at issue. If we examine the cases in which important legislative measures have been held by the Supreme Court to be valid or to be invalid over the last twenty years, we shall see that the constitutional provisions which these laws are supposed to violate do not have any clear, certain, and established meaning. What, for instance, are the major constitutional issues on which the validity of the principal New Deal measures turned? They are three in number. *First,* has Congress exercised some power not delegated to it? Or, concretely, can you reasonably hang the National Industrial Recovery Act on the constitutional "peg" of the commerce power, which Congress thought it was exercising when it passed the statute? *Second,* has Congress, or have the states, exercised some power in a manner so arbitrary or unreasonable as to amount to a deprivation of liberty or property without due process of law? *Third,* has Congress exercised some delegated power, such as the commerce power or the taxing power, for a purpose believed by the Court to be unconstitutional? There are no sharp, clear lines here between the constitutional and the unconstitutional, no categories of black and white, and in settling these issues the Court has come to exercise a type of judgment and discretion which is essentially legislative in character. Let us examine more closely just how the judicial process actually works in dealing with problems of this sort.

Let us turn first to the Minimum Wage Cases. In 1923 the Supreme Court by a five-to-three decision held that the due process clauses of the Constitution guarantee the right to pay women and children starvation wages. The Court clung to this shocking doctrine until last year when it held by a five-to-four vote that its previous decision was wrong and that minimum wage laws for women and minors do not deny due process of law. Now what actually happened here? A minimum wage law is an exercise of what we call the police power. The police power is that vital power of the American states to legislate for the public welfare. More specifically it is the power of the state to restrict individual freedom of action, or the free use of private property, in order to protect the health, morals, good order, convenience, or general welfare. A parking regulation, a quarantine of contagious disease, or an act forbidding gambling is each an exercise of the police power. Each exercise of the police power contains two elements. It restricts individual liberty and it protects or promotes some public social interest. The Court's task when it applies the test of due process of law to a legislative exercise of the police power is to weigh these two conflicting interests one against the other. If, in the opinion of the Court, the restriction upon individual liberty outweighs the social advantage claimed for the act, then it denies due process of law. Thus a majority of the Court prior to March, 1937, believed that minimum wage laws imposed upon employers and employees a burdensome restriction of their right to make free contracts with each other about wages, and that this restriction was not offset or compensated for by any equivalent social gain. The valued right of women and minors to work for next to nothing was at stake, and there was no substantial advantage to the community in having them paid a living wage. Then suddenly light came to one of the members of the Court and this balance between social advantage and restricted bargaining power was reversed. There were now five justices who believed that starvation wages for women and children were a sufficient social menace to warrant a legislative restriction on the free bargaining power of employers and employees, and as a result minimum wage laws suddenly became constitutional.

Now in reaching these important decisions the words of the Constitution have played no real part. The Constitution does not mention minimum wages and it does not explain what it means by due process of law. The Court therefore must decide whether or not a minimum wage law is valid without any direct help from the Constitution itself. The question is in essence not a legal question at all. It is a question of individual judgment and opinion and the answer which the individual judge makes to it will depend upon his social and economic philosophy, which, in turn, will depend upon his early environment and education and his business or professional associations. This is what Mr. Justice Stone was driving at when he said, "It is difficult to imagine any grounds, other than our own personal economic predilections," for holding a minimum wage law void. And when the Supreme Court invalidates important legislation on the basis of its "own economic predilections" it is doing the work of a legislature and not of a court; it is determining questions of legislative policy and not questions of law. Minimum wage laws were unconstitutional for fourteen years not because the Constitution forbids them but because a majority of the Court believed them unsound and objectionable.

Let us examine next the Schechter case in which the Supreme Court held void the National Industrial Recovery Act. We may pass by that part of the Court's decision holding that the NIRA invalidly delegated legislative power to the President, because the statute could easily have been amended to avoid that constitutional defect. The crucial issue in the case was whether Congress in the exercise of its delegated power to regulate inter-state commerce could validly authorize the application of a code of fair competition to a Brooklyn wholesale poultry market and punish violations of that code. The Court, in a unanimous decision, held that it could not. The Government urged that the transactions in the Schechters' poultry market, and other similar establishments covered by the code, vitally affected the stream of interstate commerce in poultry in the metropolitan area. Congress therefore could properly take measures to protect that inter-state commerce against the harmful effects of bad labor conditions and unfair competitive practices prevailing in the local markets. In a substantial number of cases the Court had permitted federal power to penetrate into local affairs in order to protect interstate commerce from the effects of local evils or local discrimination. The Supreme Court did not repudiate these earlier decisions. It did not even deny that conditions prevailing in the Schechters' poultry market had an influence upon the interstate commerce which Congress might lawfully regulate. It merely held that that influence was "indirect" and not "direct" and therefore the code could not be sustained under the commerce power. Here is an important act of Congress stricken down by the Court because it falls on the wrong side of the line by which the Court separates those transactions and interests which are "directly" connected with interstate commerce from those which are only "indirectly" connected with it. It is perfectly clear that in making such a decision and in drawing such a line the Court translates into a rule of constitutional law its own opinions as to how far the policy of federal centralization under the commerce power should be permitted to go, again a question of policy, a question of expediency, thinly disguised as a question of law.

There is a third type of decision in which the Court even more clearly assumes the rôle of the lawmaker. These are the cases in which the Court invalidates acts of Congress because delegated powers have been used for what the Court regards as wrongful purposes. Some of the best illustrations have arisen under the federal taxing power. In 1902, Congress, under pressure from the powerful lobby representing the dairy interests of the country, drove colored oleomargarine out of the market by levying on it a prohibitive tax of ten cents per pound. Two years later in the McCray case the Supreme Court upheld the statute against the charge that it was an abuse of the federal taxing power since its purpose was not revenue but destruction. The Court refused to inquire into or worry about the motives which had led Congress to pass the act. Such motives cannot properly be made the subject of judicial scrutiny. The oleomargarine tax is "on its face" a revenue measure. It is, in short, "objectively" constitutional, and whether it is "subjectively" unconstitutional, whether Congress had an ulterior and unconstitutional purpose in levying it, is none of the Court's business. A year ago this doctrine was reaffirmed in a case in which Congress had imposed a special license tax of $200 per year upon those engaged in selling machine-guns, sawed-off shotguns or rifles, and silencers. "On its face," says Mr. Justice Stone, "it is a taxing measure" and "inquiry into the hidden motives which may move Congress to exercise a power constitutionally conferred upon it is beyond the competency of the Court." The good faith of Congress is evidenced by the fact that twenty-seven people paid the tax in 1934 and twenty-two in 1935, so it must have been a revenue measure. In 1919, however, Congress imposed a tax of ten per cent upon the net income of those employing children in violation of the standards set up in the act. It had also passed the Future Trading Act by which a tax of twenty cents a bushel was laid upon all grain sold on future contracts upon grain exchanges which were not registered with the Secretary of Agriculture and subject to his regulations. The Supreme Court held both of these statutes unconstitutional. The taxes levied were not really taxes at all. They were penalties imposed on those who indulge in practices which Congress objects to but may not directly forbid. Speaking of the child labor tax Chief Justice Taft declared, "Its prohibitory and regulatory effect and purpose are palpable. All others can see and understand this. How can we properly shut our minds to it?" How indeed, except by just following the sound and wholesome doctrine of the oleomargarine tax case that the motives leading Congress to exercise a delegated power are not a proper subject for judicial examination. But this the Court was not willing to do. Last year the court applied the rule of the Child Labor Tax Case to a federal statute imposing an annual license tax of $1000 upon anyone engaging in the business of selling liquor in violation of the laws of a state. This, again, is a fiscal penalty and not a tax and encroaches, therefore, upon state power.

Now the Court in these tax cases has very deftly managed to eat its cake and keep it too. It invalidated the child labor tax without overruling its decision in the oleomargarine tax case. It has, therefore, both rules to play with and can select with a good deal of freedom which prohibitory or regulatory federal taxes it is going to hold valid and which it is going to hold void. Looking at them realistically there is no essential difference in the nature of these taxes or the privileges or interests upon which they fall. Congress taxes the privilege of making colored oleomargarine, the privilege of employing children, the privilege of selling the kinds of weapons with which gangster crimes are usually committed, or the privilege of operating as a bootlegger within a state. Congress could not directly forbid anyone to exercise any of these privileges on which it has laid its tax. In every case the tax is for a non-fiscal purpose and everybody knows it.

When the Court approves of the regulatory policy involved in the tax it turns a blind eye to the obvious effect of the tax and applies the test of "objective constitutionality." But with equal ease it can invalidate a similar regulatory tax, by taking into account "what everybody knows" and applying the test of "subjective constitutionality." In deciding which formula to use the Court is able to give effect to its own views as to the expediency of the legislative policy involved, it is able to exercise a policy-determining power.

I have no patience with the pious verbal expressions and legal epigrams by which certain judges and lawyers seek to camouflage or to conceal the essentially legislative power which the Court exercises in the handling of these three groups of cases and many others. In applying these vague and general clauses of the Constitution to concrete cases the Court has the opportunity, and it embraces the opportunity, of giving effect to its hunches, its predilections, and its prejudices. In interpreting due process of law it may read into the Constitution either a progressive social philosophy or a Mid-Victorian theory of "rugged individualism." In setting the limits to the commerce power it may swing the balance toward an aggressive federal centralization or toward an equally vigorous protection of state rights. In my judgment the legislative power which the Supreme Court now wields in the exercise of its power of judicial review of legislation is far greater than can be soundly adjusted to the principles of democratic government. Our constitutional system rests on the principle that the legislative power of the United States is vested in the Congress. It is not vested in the Supreme Court. It seems to me one of the vicious paradoxes of our national democracy that so many vital questions of national policy are determined in the last analysis by the "personal economic predilections" of Supreme Court justices.

III. *Can the Supreme Court be divested of its undemocratic assumption of legislative power?* This brings me to my final and very practical topic— Can the Supreme Court be divested of its undemocratic assumption of legislative power? How can we establish a sounder and more democratic balance between the legislative and judicial powers under the American Constitution? I have two answers to this question, but before explaining them, may I mention some proposals which I do not favor? I do not believe that the Supreme Court should be deprived of its power to declare acts of Congress unconstitutional. I do not attach much importance to the suggestions that Congress should so alter the appellate jurisdiction of the Supreme Court as to reduce substantially the number of chances the Court would have to pass on the validity of laws. I have never been enthusiastic about the proposal to require seven or more of the nine members of the Supreme Court to concur in declaring a statute void. Such a rule does not go to the root of the problem and I doubt if it would accomplish any very important results. I am not in favor of giving Congress the power to override decisions of the Supreme Court declaring acts of Congress void, although I should be glad indeed to see rather similar results attained by making our clumsy process of federal constitutional amendment simpler and more democratic. I merely state my views on these points as I do not have time to explain my reasons for holding them.

The first of my proposals is a very simple and wholly unspectacular one. It does not upset anything and it would, I believe, increase rather than weaken the Court's prestige. It is the simple proposal that the Court shall of its own volition abandon the job of legislating and confine itself to the task of judging; that in reviewing legislation it shall accord what Mr. Justice Washington over a hundred years ago called "a decent respect due to the legislative body by which any law is passed." This is, of course, exactly what the Supreme Court officially claims that it does, and no one would endorse my suggestion more heartily, in all probability, than those justices who have been among the most ruthless in overriding legislation on the basis of "personal economic predilections."

But what I have in mind is not a matter of words. It is a thing of the spirit, a positive and aggressive determination on the part of the Court to encroach just as little as possible upon legislative discretion, a complete unwillingness to invalidate a statute if any reasonable ground can be discovered upon which it may be sustained. This was the life-long judicial philosophy of Mr. Justice Holmes. Justices Brandeis, Cardozo, and Stone . . . [also upheld] this doctrine of judicial tolerance. It claim[ed] the adherence of Chief Justice Hughes not infrequently and of Mr. Justice Roberts once in a while. This attitude is peculiarly necessary in applying the nebulous test of due process of law to social and economic legislation. Whether such legislation is "arbitrary" or not, is, after all, a matter of opinion and the legislature is entitled to its opinion even if that opinion be mistaken or foolish. "There is nothing that I more deprecate," said Mr. Justice Holmes, "than the use of the Fourteenth Amendment beyond the absolute compulsion of its words to prevent the making of social experiments that an important part of the community desires, in the insulated chambers afforded by the several states, even though the experiments may seem futile or even noxious to me and to those whose judgment I most respect." There is certain irony in the fact that Holmes came to be universally regarded as a great liberal. Every advocate of social and economic reform regarded him as an ally. And so he was—but not always in the sense in which they thought him to be. There is reason to believe that Holmes had little use for a large amount of the social and economic reform which he voted to hold constitutional. In his own social philosophy he was a fairly conservative man. But he believed firmly in two things—first, as he neatly put it, "I am not God"; second, an American legislature possesses what Lowell called in the Bigelow Papers "the right to be a cussed fool," and that right must be respected and protected by the Supreme Court. Holmes's liberalism was the liberalism of tolerance, often a disgusted tolerance, a tolerance grounded on respect for the integrity of the legislature's own job no matter how stupidly that job was done. That attitude on the part of the Court is vitally necessary at the present time. Its attainment and the development of a tradition which would make it permanent would do more to restore the Supreme Court to its proper place in the American Constitutional system than any of the drastic proposals which I mentioned and discarded a moment ago.

Is there any hope of securing such an attitude upon the part of the Court towards legislation? I believe there is even if results of this somewhat intangible sort may not be achieved all at once. There are two ways in which progress may be made. One is by the slow process of education. This means education within the legal profession so that lawyers who attain seats on the Bench will have a sound and wise understanding of the nature of the judge's job with respect to legislation. It means education on a broader base so that there may be an increasingly well-informed public opinion to insist upon the appointment to the Bench of men who have this attitude. We are beginning to profit from the results of this educational movement which has been going on for twenty years or more. A second way in which progress may be made is by focusing attention and public pressure upon the Presidential appointment of judges of the right kind and upon their confirmation by the Senate. I cannot develop this in detail. Our existing system of choosing Supreme Court justices does not give us as good results as it should. We get a few distinguished men, a good many able men, and now and again somebody definitely below par. The country is entitled to have on the Bench judicial statesmen. The traditions surrounding Supreme Court appointments must be so shaped as to secure them. It must be made good politics for the President to name such men and for the Senate to confirm them. The making of these vitally important appointments should never be casually inadvertent. It might be wise if the rules of the Senate should forbid the confirmation of major judicial appointments in less than thirty days so that full and open hearings may be had upon the qualifications of the men named by the President. Progress along these lines may be slow and erratic, but I believe that public opinion in this country is coming to see the importance of securing the right kind of Supreme Court justices and that we shall build up the kind of traditions which will insure their appointment.

I have a second proposal to make. This we may fall back on if we fail to persuade the Supreme Court to abdicate voluntarily its legislative and policy-determining functions and to adopt the wise tolerance toward legislative discretion which Mr. Justice Holmes preached and practiced. This proposal is that we adopt clarifying amendments to the Constitution which will sharpen the meaning of its clauses, make clear the scope of its delegations of power, and the impact of its limitations. The Court in construing the commerce clause or the due process clause is engaged in making broad decisions of policy which do not properly belong to a judicial body. We could relieve it of that power by clarifying those clauses so that their meaning and application is no longer a matter of honest dispute. If we wish to make sure that the power of Congress under the commerce clause includes the regulation of laboring conditions under which goods are made for the interstate market, then let us say so with definiteness and precision. If we are tired of having the due process of law clause used by conservative judges to throttle needed social legislation, let us make clear what we wish the due process limitation to mean, or discard it altogether. I believe that the Court itself would welcome such a change. I believe we should all be better satisfied if, without impairing the integrity or the traditions of our judicial system, we left to the Court the task of applying constitutional clauses which have reasonably definite meaning, instead of attacking it for giving what we feel is the wrong meaning to clauses so vague as to have no clear and concrete meaning of their own. Our whole judicial system would gain in efficiency, and in public confidence, under such a change.

I have traced the stages through which the Supreme Court has gradually acquired the vast and far-reaching power over legislation which it now exercises. I have undertaken to show that this power has enabled the Court to dominate wide ranges of legislative policy in the light of the opinions and prejudices of the justices, and I have suggested that this exercise of essentially legislative power by a court of law conflicts with the democratic principle upon which we have built our governmental system. I have no patience with the attitude of constitutional ancestor-worship which rejects as sacrilege any change in the Constitution or in the Supreme Court's power of judicial review, but I have no desire to see the power of judicial review pulled up by the roots or mutilated. Let the Supreme Court clean its own house. Let it replace an arrogantly ruthless attitude toward the exercise by Congress of its legislative discretion, by the tolerant aloofness which bespeaks the judge and not the lawmaker. Let the President and the Senate place on the Supreme Court men who appraise correctly the relation between the Court and Congress. If the Supreme Court cannot or will not do this let us, instead of changing the Court or changing its power

of judicial review, change the concrete nature of the job which we give it
to do. Let us withdraw from the reach of its interpretation those vast
uncharted ranges of discretion which come from vague and general clauses
of the Constitution. Let us sharpen and clarify the sections in the construction of which the Court now finds it possible to impose its policy judgments upon the country. By following this course we shall preserve and
strengthen the best features of the American system of judicial review of
legislation. We shall get rid of its weaknesses and its dangers. The Supreme
Court of the United States will become not an obstacle but an aid to the
smooth and efficient working of democratic government in a great nation.

No. 74

THE DIVINE RIGHT OF JUDGES [1]

by Max Lerner

A LONG view of the power of the Supreme Court is difficult to
achieve . . . , [Mr. Lerner points out that this is particularly true
in the midst of immediate issues and angry passions that arise in periods
when the courts are smashing the best legislative efforts of the community.
But he notes that such action by the court, as well as attacks upon it, have
been no novelty.] It would try to get at the nature, the psychological roots,
and the economic consequences of the power of judicial review—presumably
America's most beautiful and original gift to the art of government.

Judicial review is a political device by which the court passes on the
constitutional validity of legislative and executive acts. It enables the judges
to apportion powers between the states and the national government, and
between the legislative, executive, and judicial branches. This is a power
nowhere to be found expressly granted in the Constitution itself. But it
has by this time written itself into the Constitution by court interpretation,
and although only a custom it has become as commonly accepted as if it
were clearly granted in the document.

There are two opposing theories as to how the power grew up. One is
the usurpation theory. It goes back to Jefferson and is repeated afresh in
every period of constitutional crisis. It holds that judicial review is sheer
usurpation and that the Supreme Court has deliberately filched powers
belonging to other departments. This point of view is generally highlighted
with charges of tyranny that transport us back into the pages of Plutarch.

[1] Max Lerner, "The Divine Right of Judges," *The Nation* (January 29, 1936), Vol. 142
pp. 121-123. Reprinted by permission of *The Nation*.

The other is the Federalist view that the judicial power flows inherently from the nature of our federal system, and that without it our government would be unworkable and our democracy unthinkable.

I shall confess I cannot subscribe to either of these theories, although they both offer fragments of the final answer. It is true that there have been some men on our court with a will to power. And it is true, on the other side, that given our federal-state governmental system, if both the states and the nation try to ride the same horse someone must finally decide who shall ride in front. But a clearer answer than either would be that the court's power is a natural outcome of the necessity for maintaining capitalist dominance under democratic forms; that judicial review has proved to be a very convenient channel through which the driving forces of American economic life have found expression and achieved victory. Such a view could be documented by reference to the history of the judicial power since Marshall first established it in 1803 by his decision in Marbury vs. Madison. The high points in the story would be Marshall's use of the judicial power to give enlarged scope to the expansion of business enterprise, the development of the doctrine of due process of law after the Civil War, and the reading of a laissez faire social philosophy into the Constitution in the decades around the turn of the century.

. . . [in the early 1930's the Court reenacted] the role it has always played whenever a resurgence of popular feeling has threatened to sweep away some of the established power of business enterprise. Nor has there been in all this any consistency of judicial doctrine or political theory. When the people have gained control of the state legislatures, as happened in Marshall's day and in the decades of agrarian revolt, the court has denied power to the states and concentrated it in the federal government. But when, as . . . [was true in the 1930's], the people have captured the federal offices, then the court denies power to the federal government and reserves it where it must be ineffective in the task of business regulation—with the state governments. The Republicans now find themselves amazingly the devoted adherents of states' rights, and the Democrats (shades of the Jeffersonian tradition!) are earnestly seeking to increase the national power.

There are several rather striking misconceptions to-day about the court's power and function. One is that judges decide as they do because they can do no other—that they follow an inflexible path of constitutional doctrine. Only a little less far from the truth is the second and opposite misconception—that the judges are untrammelled in the expression of their own social attitudes and that they can play ducks and drakes with judicial precedent. What are actually the limits within which the Supreme Court has to work? It can decide only specific cases and not abstract questions

—the case of the Schechter brothers, for example, and how they sell their chickens—and out of those specific judgments the body of constitutional law grows up. Once a case is settled, however, a rule of law is established for future decisions, and every judge must abide by it (*stare decisis*) regardless of his previous views. The court works, moreover, within a difficult technical tradition, under a limited jurisdiction, and with severe procedural regulations. Finally, its role with respect to legislation is negative and passive. It can initiate nothing of itself. But after you have said all that, the fact remains that the judge retains a great latitude of decision. On the same set of facts in the Hoosac case, after hearing the same arguments and reading the same briefs, with the same body of precedent to draw on, possessed of the same degree of integrity and patriotism, Mr. Justice Roberts comes to one constitutional conclusion and Mr. Justice Stone to exactly the opposite one. What can explain this? Only the hypothesis that the judge works within limits and with material flexible enough to allow for personal choice. The *determining* factor becomes not some rigorous rule but the judge's own social philosophy. This in turn is shaped by his class roots, his education, his experience, and the elements in the contemporary climate of opinion to which he is responsive.

There is another misconception. We tend to believe that the court shows its power only when it declares an act of Congress unconstitutional. Actually the court has exercised this judicial veto only on some sixty occasions, many of them of slight moment. The judicial veto represents the outer limits of the court's power. It shows how far that power can go. But usually the court influences the shaping of an act even before it is passed, for the knowledge that the act will have to run the gauntlet of judicial review is a sovereign acid for eating away features that the court will predictably disallow. Once the act is passed it may be whittled into ineffectiveness (as happened with the antitrust legislation) without any actual declaration of unconstitutionality, or the agency set up (like the Federal Trade Commission) may be crippled by court interpretation without being destroyed outright. Thus the court's power is broader and more continuous than the exercise of its veto. Even when it upholds legislation it is directing our economic life. The entire landscape of life as it is lived to-day by the common man is ultimately at the mercy of the court's action or sufferance.

The essence of the court's position in our system is that it takes problems that are primarily economic and clashes of interest that are economic, and translates them into terms of legal doctrine. It thus becomes the bottleneck of economic policy. I believe that is the one overwhelming fact that we must face to-day. As long as economic issues are fought out frankly as such, their solution lies with the people and with their representatives in the legislature. But when economic issues are translated into legalistic terms, when the question of the fate of the farmers and workers and housewives and working children becomes a matter of hosts of none-too-angelic lawyers dancing on the needle of due process of law, then the big electoral battalions are left helpless. If we face it clearly, looking beyond the tangle of our traditional usages, the question of what we shall do with our farms and our factories is not ultimately a question for lawyers or judges to settle. It is a question of economic and social policy. To allow our economic policy to be shaped by the judges is wrong whichever way you look at it. If they decide, as is often claimed, on purely legal grounds, then those are the *wrong grounds* on which to decide questions of economic policy. If they decide, as is sometimes admitted, on economic and social grounds, then they are the *wrong people* to be intrusted with decisions on these grounds, for they are judicial and not economic technicians.

In passing thus on economic policy the Supreme Court has throughout our history functioned as the last bulwark of the possessing classes. It has always been a final line of defense for them, a sort of Hindenburg line that would stand fast when all else crumbled. Beaten at the polls, in danger of having the economic institutions of a plutocracy leveled by the political forces of a democracy, the defeated group has always turned to the court for shelter and has found it in the safe haven of constitutional law. Jefferson discovered this fact when he and his party of small farmers and mechanics turned the Federalist propertied interests out of Congress and the Presidency in 1800, only to find them dug in again behind the earthworks of the court. Jackson discovered it in the 1830's, Lincoln in the 1850's, the agrarian leaders in the eighties and nineties, the Progressives such as La Follette and Theodore Roosevelt as the century ended. And . . . Franklin Roosevelt . . . discover[ed] it afresh. It seems to be the fate of American reformers to conduct their education in public.

Each of these men sought to attack the court. In no case has the court's power been successfully limited. What accounts for this extraordinary toughness and viability of the court? The defenders of the court answer that its survival indicates the hollowness of the attacks on it. What is involved is evidently a medieval ordeal by fire, proving innocence. But the successive crises of the judicial power can no more be exorcised by this sort of mumbo-jumbo than can the crises of the economic system. Each attack on the judicial power in America has not been merely an unaccountable bit of behavior of the democratic mass. It has been the expression, in constitutional terms, of the inability of our state to adjust its own power-relations and resolve its own contradictions. And for that reason each successive crisis of the judicial power has taken its color, its substance, its tension from the contemporary stage of the struggle of economic groups and classes.

This . . . [happened in the 1930's too. And then], as in the past, the court . . . [survived] the attack on it, not because of any inherent rightness in the judicial power, but because the larger number of our people still have a sense of the sanctity of the court. What used to be the divine right of kings has now been replaced by the divine right of judges.

There are several elements in this pattern of divine right as it exists in the popular mind. One is the fact that we have been encouraged for over a century to make a fetish of the Constitution. Every people needs some form of anchorage, some link with the invariant. The Rock of Ages is as essential to political as it is to religious life. In fact, the habits of mind begotten by an authoritarian Bible carry over to an authoritarian Constitution; and a country like ours, in which our early tradition had prohibited a state church, ends by getting a state church after all. To be sure, not all who make a fetish of the Constitution believe in it. There are many newspaper and political groups which appeal to the sanctity of the Constitution with their eyes fixed on the immensities and their hands reaching out for their own special interests. And yet with the larger number of our people the belief that the Constitution is sacred beyond change is a genuine belief, and must be reckoned with.

The second psychological element in the tradition of the divine right of judges is the belief that the Supreme Court is the special guardian of the Constitution—and a better guardian than Congress or the President. Part of John Marshall's genius lay in his skill in pushing into the background the power that the court was gaining over economic policy, and thrusting into the foreground its role of guardianship. This the later judges have encouraged by their continued utterances, and it has become the official theory of the court's power. The judges have thus been associated in our minds with the function of protection rather than with the struggle for power.

The third element has been the tradition of judicial neutrality. We have somehow placed the judges above the battle. Despite every proof to the contrary the common man attributes to them the objectivity and infallibility that are ultimately attributes only of godhead. The tradition persists that they belong to no economic group or class; that they are not touched by economic interests; that their decisions proceed through some inspired way of arriving at the truth; that they sit in their robes like haughty gods, unaffected by the prejudices that move common men.

How long a myth built of such baseless fabric can continue is another matter. It is undoubtedly weakening and may be expected in the end to crumble. Meanwhile, however, its force and its hold on the popular mind . . . [were] enough to daunt Mr. Roosevelt and keep him from making an open attack on the court's power. In the end it will not be the Roosevelts who will restore to the popular will the power of deciding on economic issues. The Supreme Court may be expected to be its own bitterest enemy. Even the myth of the divine right of judges will not survive many more decisions like Mr. Justice Roberts's masterly essay in obfuscation in the Hoosac case.

No. 75

THE INCIDENCE OF JUDICIAL CONTROL OVER CONGRESS [1]

by Henry W. Edgerton

JUSTICE HOLMES said: "I do not think the United States would come to an end if we lost our power to declare an Act of Congress void. I do think the Union would be imperilled if we could not make that declaration as to the laws of the several States." It may be necessary to national survival that some national tribunal have authority to decide that acts of state legislatures are inconsistent with the Federal Constitution. Judicial supremacy over national legislation rests on no such necessity. Whether to preserve, restrict, or abolish the power of courts to hold acts of Congress void is a pure question of policy, the answer to which should depend on the character of the results which the present system has produced and is, therefore, likely to produce. How and when the system originated, what were the attitudes of the founding fathers toward it, whether it is in some sense a usurpation are questions with which scholars have dealt. There has been much discussion of the relation in which particular constitutional decisions stand to other decisions and to the original Constitution and its amendments. Little serious attention has been paid to the practical question of the incidence of the courts' control over Congress, i.e., its effect or tendency,

---

[1] Henry W. Edgerton, "The Incidence of Judicial Control over Congress," *The Cornell Law Quarterly* (April, 1937), Vol. 22, pp. 299-301, 246-248. Reprinted by permission of *The Cornell Law Quarterly* and the author. As the analysis of specific cases and the footnotes are omitted from this material as reprinted here, everyone is urged to read the article in full as it appeared in *The Cornell Law Quarterly;* Reorganization of the Federal Judiciary: Hearings before the Committee on the Judiciary, United States Senate, 75th Congress, 1st Session, on S. 1392, A Bill to Reorganize the Judicial Branch of the Government (1937), pp. 1881-1912; or *Selected Essays on Constitutional Law,* published under the Auspices of the Association of American Law Schools (1938), Book 1, pp. 793-844.

as between different social groups and interests. On that point there has been much summary assertion but little proof.

A full treatment of this subject would deal with all reported cases in which any court has held an act of Congress void; the number and character of the acts which Congress has been deterred from enacting, or encouraged to enact, by the prospect of judicial review; the uncertainty which often exists between the passage of a law and the Supreme Court's disposition of it; the question whether the relative abstinence from political effort of American as compared to European intellectuals is due to the knowledge that desired legislation, even if its passage is secured, may not become "law." With most of this the present article will not deal. It will consider only the cases in which the Supreme Court has held an act, or part of an act, of Congress unconstitutional. Decisions of the same sort by other courts which were reversed or not passed on by the Supreme Court are too many to be treated in an article; moreover, they have been relatively local in their effects. The difficulty of dealing objectively at present with the Supreme Court's disposition of "New Deal" legislation, and the inherent uncertainty regarding the effects of much of it, seem sufficient reasons for not considering statutes passed after March 4, 1933. This article aims to consider briefly all the cases in which earlier acts of Congress have been annulled by the Supreme Court.

Congress does not contravene the black-and-white clauses of the Constitution, like that which allots two Senators to each State. The conflicts between Congress and the Court have related to the indefinite clauses, like those which deal with interstate commerce, due process, and executive power. It is familiar that the relation of a law to these broad clauses is not a matter of fact but a matter of opinion. Congress in all the cases to be considered, and members of the Court in many, differed in opinion from the majority of the Court. This paper is not concerned with the question whether the congressional or the judicial opinion seems, in general or in a given case, the more reasonable. In other words, it is not concerned with the soundness or propriety, from a technical point of view, of the decisions. It does not discuss the commerce clause or any other clause of the Constitution. Neither is it concerned with the backgrounds, beliefs, and desires that led Congress to pass the laws, or the Court to annul them. There is no question, in my mind, of the high motives of the Court. I am concerned only with the practical effects and tendencies of the nullifying decisions. What interests, individual or social, do they protect; and, conversely, whose ox is gored? Has judicial supremacy been, on the whole, neutral in its incidence; or has it tended to protect the interests of a relatively poor and unprivileged majority on the one hand, or of a relatively well-to-do minority on the other?

It is always difficult, and usually impossible, to determine how different things would be if they were not as they are. The effects of the decisions cannot be fully known. The possibilities in that direction cannot be exhausted in one article, or by one man. A vast amount of contemporary material would need to be studied. Treatises would have to be written, from a special angle, on all the topics with which the various decisions deal, including, for example, taxation and trial by jury. This paper is offered as an introduction to a neglected subject. It deals, for the most part, with direction rather than distance. If the tendencies of the decisions fit into a pattern, conclusions not too tentative can be drawn regarding their collective incidence.

[The detailed analysis of the acts of Congress held unconstitutional by the Supreme Court is omitted here. Everyone interested in the subject, however, is urged to read the examination of these cases in the original article.]

CONCLUSION

To repeat, with motives, and with the relative reasonableness of conflicting congressional and judicial views on vague standards like interstate commerce and due process, this paper is not concerned. It is concerned only with the practical effects and tendencies of judicial supremacy. The discussion might be expanded by considering acts of Congress which the Supreme Court has upheld against attack. But apart from the period of uncertainty which precedes the decision, judicial supremacy produces, in connection with a statute which is upheld, no effect whatever, since the statute would necessarily be upheld if there were no such thing as judicial supremacy. Some of the cases in which the Supreme Court has annulled state legislation have had more effect than many in which it has annulled acts of Congress. But cases involving state legislation, besides being too many to be treated in an article, are foreign to the subject of this one. The supremacy of courts over state legislatures and the supremacy of courts over Congress stand on different ground. If the one sort of control is a practical necessity, it does not follow that the other is; and if the one sort has protected certain interests it does not follow that the other has protected like interests. In the control of state legislation there have been deviations, including certain free speech cases, from the pattern of the federal cases. What should be done about the one sort of control and what should be done about the other are different questions.

Exhaustive investigation would reveal more than this brief inquiry about the effects of many of the decisions. It might modify the views expressed here regarding some of them. It is unlikely that it would seriously qualify the conclusions which follow.

Of the pre-New Deal cases in which the Supreme Court annulled acts of Congress, one group protected mistreatment of colored people; another group protected businesses or business methods hurtful to the majority; another, comprising employers' liability, workmen's compensation, minimum wage, child labor, and union membership cases, protected owners of business at the direct expense of labor; another protected owners of business against taxation; another protected the recipients of substantial incomes, gifts, and inheritances against taxation; and other cases protected the interests of property owners in other ways. Not many cases of any importance fall outside these categories. A few decisions were approximately neutral in their incidence as between different social groups. Rich and poor were given theoretically equal assurance that for various offenses they must be indicted before they are tried, and must be tried by a jury of twelve. But few persons ever find themselves in a position to be affected by such decisions, and any benefit which they may confer is uncertain, slight, and probably less equal in practice than in theory. Moreover, the statutes which those decisions annulled were limited to Chinese, to Alaska, or to the District of Columbia, and there is no reason to assume that their principle would have been extended, as the principle of the minimum wage would obviously have been extended, if its local application had been upheld. There is not a case in the entire series which protected the "civil liberties" of freedom of speech, press, and assembly; on the contrary, over the protest of Holmes and Brandeis, the Espionage Act was not merely upheld but extended by the Court. There is not one which protected the right to vote; on the contrary, congressional attempts to protect the voting rights of Negroes were defeated by the Court. There is not one which protected the vital interests of the working majority of the population in organizing or in wages; on the contrary, congressional efforts to protect those interests were frustrated by the Court.

So much is objective, more or less. Subjectively, according to one's social philosophy, it may follow that judicial supremacy over Congress is good, bad, or indifferent. The cult of "the Constitution," which contemplates chiefly this power of the courts, illustrates the connection between conventional standards and the interests of dominant groups. In one who identifies the country with the well-to-do minority of its population, enthusiasm for judicial control over Congress is as logical as enthusiasm can be. It is hard to see why, apart from convention, one who does not make that identification should share that enthusiasm. When a legal scholar says,

"I am for continuance of the Supreme Court's power of review. I think that it has proved its worth. . . . I think that over the long haul the Court has done a superb job," I wonder what cases seem to him so valuable as to outweigh the *Dred Scott* case, which helped to entrench slavery; the *Civil Rights* and related cases, which protected the oppression of Negroes; the employers' liability and workmen's compensation cases, which denied relief to injured workmen; the child labor and minimum wage cases, which protected the hiring of women and children at starvation wages; the income tax cases, which prevented the shifting of tax burdens from the poor to the rich; and the many minor instances in which the Court's review has done harm to common men.

No. 76

THE FATE OF THE SUPREME COURT [1]

by Max Lerner

IN the halcyon days before the Schechter decision Professor Corwin of Princeton had the courage to write a book under the title *The Twilight of the Supreme Court*. He said that the court was on its way to a dignified but ineffectual old age, and that its sun was setting. The book was a good book and a learned book. It was well reasoned, and its conclusion should have been a sound one. But scarcely was the ink dry on its pages when the court handed down the first of its series of hostile decisions on the Roosevelt legislation. Instead of subsiding into twilight, it shone forth with the blaze of noonday strength.

The moral is, I suppose, that it is always bad policy to compose a man's obituary before he is for certain dead. Yet Professor Corwin was less wrong than would appear. During the next decade or more the power of the Supreme Court will undoubtedly be challenged as never before. But if there is a decline in the court's power it will not come about by any gentle slipping into euthanasia. It will come about only after a stiff fight. There are any number of evidences that the fight has already begun. The court is now entering its iron age.

For one thing we are witnessing the first signs of a crack-up in what I called in my first article the sense of the divine right of judges. While Americans are still strongly imbued with it, they are no longer in a complete innocence about such matters. They are beginning to learn that judicial decisions are not babies brought by constitutional storks but are

[1] Max Lerner, "The Fate of the Supreme Court," *The Nation* (March 25, 1936) Vol. 142, pp. 379-381. Reprinted by permission of *The Nation*.

born out of the travail of economic circumstance. The poll held after the Hoosac decision by the American Institute of Public Opinion showed that some 53 per cent of those polled were in favor of requiring more than a Supreme Court majority to invalidate an act of Congress. That is in itself almost a revolution in American opinion. And the crack-up in opinion will grow every year as economic collapse makes legislation on a national scale more necessary.

But the court will have ample support in the struggle that lies ahead. It will have of course the driving force of the vested interests with all their control over the molding of public opinion. But it will have even more powerfully the strongest support that any tribunal or institution can have— namely, fear. I do not mean fear of the court, fear of the judicial power, the fear that one has of the whiplash of tyrants. I mean fear of not having the court. I mean the terrible fear of change and the unknown, which is to so many people more powerful than the felt needs and pressures of to-day. It is fear and not will that underlies a good part of our politics— the creeping fear of people who do not want to make decisions, and prefer to surrender their decisions to others. This sort of womb-retreat is no unknown thing to political psychology. It is a phenomenon familiar enough in fascism. We are just beginning now in America really to explore and understand the length and breadth and depth of the middle-class mentality in our politics. For that mentality the court's ancient sureness seems something not to be abandoned, lest we confront an uncharted future. If this is only a social myth it has thus far been a necessary one. It will have to do until we build a new set of necessary myths that are emotionally rooted not in fear but in the collective will, and economically rooted not in the class power of the dominant group but in an expanding economy for all. When that has happened, the struggle over the judicial power will be over, and the Supreme Court's iron age will be at an end.

Proposals for dealing with the court have been thick as blackberries. They have come from professional and amateur constitutionalists of every kind. They fall into three general groups: the remedial proposals, those looking toward a Congressional curb on the court's power, and those looking toward a constitutional amendment.

The first group, the remedial, implies the existence and desirability of the court's power. They are more concerned with lopping off the excrescences of that power than with challenging it. Perhaps the simplest proposal is that of a eugenics program for the court. Just as the vitality of the race is held by some to depend on selective breeding and thus getting the right babies, so the proper functioning of the judicial power is held to depend on getting the right judges. And that of course goes back to getting the right Presidents, who will appoint the right judges, who will in turn render the right decisions. This view, of course, sees judicial decisions as almost entirely a matter of the personnel of the court. Everything depends on the individual judge. In this sense, such a view is too optimistic. Individual judges are themselves products: their minds and their direction have been shaped by the dominant institutional forces of our life. Another difficulty is that getting the right President does not seem to insure getting the right judge. Examine the . . . composition of the court [in 1936] and you will find that Justice Brandeis, leader of the liberals, and Justice McReynolds, the most inveterate tory of them all, were appointees of President Wilson. Justices Roberts and Cardozo, confronting each other in opposite judicial trenches, were appointees of President Hoover.

More drastic than the pious hope that better justices will be appointed is the movement for advisory opinions. At present a law is enacted, administrative machinery is set up to enforce it, taxes are levied, government and business expenditures are made on the strength of it, men are set to work—only to have the court, in passing finally on a specific case, declare the whole thing unconstitutional. The proposal for advisory opinions would have Congress get from the judges their opinion on the constitutionality of a projected law before it had come into force and economic interests had become entangled with it. The great merit of this proposal is that it would do away with our present uncertainties. And one of the refreshing things about it is that, like the child in the Hans Christian Andersen tale, it innocently announces the nakedness of the king. It recognizes frankly that the court is a third legislative chamber, and insists that since this is so we ought to know the fate of our legislation as quickly as possible.

But for that very reason the proposal runs counter to the entire tradition of the court. That tradition is the tough, concrete tradition of Anglo-Saxon case law, in which the individual case has to bear the freightage of weighty issues. An issue of constitutional law does not arise until a specific case has arisen that involves it. Until then the heavens may fall, but the court knows no generalizations and will give no advice. Its wisdom is a pragmatic one. There is a good deal to be said in support of this approach. The true meaning of a law is not to be found in the bare statute. The statute must take root, like a tree, in the soil of actual circumstance, it must bear a leafage of functioning and consequence before it can be seen as a reality. "How do we know what we think," the judges may ask, "until we see how things work out?"

The proposal from the liberal members of the court is the exact opposite of advisory opinions—namely, judicial self-limitation. This tries to carry the implications of case law all the way. It denies that the court has anything to do with legislation directly, and insists that the judges must restrict themselves to the narrowest issues in the cases that arise. Judicial self-limitation of this sort was an integral part of Justice Holmes's entire philosophy of judicial tolerance. It . . . [was] part also of Justice Brandeis's philosophy that a case cannot be torn out of its context—and that context includes the impulsions to the legislation, its consequences, and the entire economic and procedural history of the case itself. Judicial self-limitation has always been given some lip-service by the court, as in the rule that the judges will consider no "moot" cases, nor any cases raising only "political questions" (blessedly vague phrase). The deliberately adopted strategy of Justices Brandeis, Stone, and Cardozo . . . [was] to push this form of judicial hara-kiri much farther. It has found its best expression in Justice Stone's dissent in the Hoosac case, Justice Cardozo's dissent in the Mayflower Farms case, and Justice Brandeis's concurring opinion in the TVA case. These opinions not only made the general plea of judicial restraint (in Justice Stone's words, "The only check upon our own exercise of power is our own sense of self-restraint") but pointed out the two directions in which it is to be exercised: always passing on as few issues as the court can get away with, and always giving the legislature the benefit of any reasonable doubt.

It may well be asked how dependable such a method is in solving the problem of the court's power. It involves not only the selection of extraordinary judges who will be willing to limit their own power. It involves the shaping of a new method, a new mood and temper, a new conception of the scope of the court's power. . . . The court has never operated in a social vacuum. It has always been an integral part of the social struggles of every period in our history. It has taken its temper from the prevailing ideology of an aggressive individualist capitalism. It has been part of the fiber of a culture dominated by business enterprise. It is terribly hard to expect the court to generate a new humility now. The whole idea of judicial humility is strikingly like the plight of the gigantic Serrovius in Shaw's "Androcles and the Lion," whose powerful frame shakes with all the passions of a healthy beast, yet whose Christian principles bid him stay his hand whenever it is raised to strike. How can a court cultivate this sort of humility when issues are at stake throughout our national life that touch the justices as much as they touch anyone else? . . . [The Supreme Court has exercised a great deal of self-restraint since the middle 1930's.]

I have mentioned the remedial proposals at some length partly because it is unlikely that we shall get anything more than that in the immediate future, partly because they go to the heart of the problem of the judicial power. But the most discussed proposals are the group that seek directly to curb the court's power. These are the proposals that rouse Liberty Leaguers to the highest pitch of fury. But they are not new. Although they have never been advanced in such profusion until . . . [1936], they have cropped up periodically when the court was under attack.

The simplest way to curb the court would seem to be to "pack" it. Congress has undisputed power to determine the size of the court. In Jackson's Administration the number of judges was increased from seven to nine in order to counterbalance the influence of the Marshall tradition. Under Lincoln, during the Civil War, the court was conveniently increased to ten, to make it safe for the war powers of the President. There seems to be ample proof that Grant packed the court in order to get a favorable decision on the Legal Tender cases. This is a technique that Mr. Roosevelt might have used if an unfavorable NRA decision had come down earlier than it did, while the country was still under the spell of the New Deal; and especially if the court had been closely divided on the issue. . . . Eventually of course an Administration with enough temerity may do what the liberals did in England to the House of Lords—threaten the creation of so many new justices that under the threat the court would yield up some of its power.

The most frequent suggestion for a judicial curb is to regulate not the numbers on the court but the manner of their voting. It would provide that a majority of the justices were not enough to invalidate an act of Congress. Some number such as seven or eight or more than two-thirds of the court is usually suggested. The obvious answer is of course that, granted the existence of the judicial power, this would leave the decision on constitutionality in the hands of one or two justices. The answer to that answer is that just such an event is intended: that since you can usually count on one or two justices who will vote on the side of Congress, this leaves the decision on economic issues where it belongs—with Congress and the President. Another device, intended to have somewhat the same effect, would be to provide that unfavorable court decisions could be overruled by a two-thirds vote of Congress. Still another would be to abolish entirely, by Congressional action, the court's right to invalidate acts of Congress; or to take certain types of cases or certain issues of legislation out of the jurisdiction of the court.

About all of these the same three questions arise. Are they constitutional? Would they be effective? Could they be accomplished? A strong case could be made out, on the basis of precedent, that Congress has the power to set the conditions under which the Supreme Court shall function, and that such a power would include the regulation of its numbers, voting, jurisdiction. The supreme irony of the whole situation is of course that whether Congress has such a power would have to be finally decided by the court itself. . . .

One proposal for dealing with the court's power that has the amazing distinction of being favored by both sides is the amending process. The liberals and radicals want it because it seems to them a fundamental attack on the whole problem. The conservatives don't object to it because they don't really think an amendment has any chance of being adopted. The idea is therefore one calculated to assuage them in their present constitutional agony, and postpone a reckoning to the dateless future.

The questions that have been most often raised as to what form a constitutional amendment would take seem to me comparatively unimportant. We are not lacking in the political inventiveness and legislative draftsmanship adequate to solve the problem. More serious is the question whether the court will not interpret away any amendment, no matter how skilfully and shrewdly drawn, just as it has interpreted away many a statute in the past. But most serious of all are the issues of power. An amendment giving Congress the right to legislate on all issues affecting agriculture, industry, labor, and finance on a national scale would be so direct a path to the control of business enterprise by the state that it would meet the massed force of opposition from business enterprise. What lengths that opposition would go to it is now difficult to say. But it is clear that such an amendment could be carried through only as part of a larger movement not only to curb the court's power but to establish a controlled economy. Such a movement involves a greater degree of organization of the productive groups in our society than has yet been achieved, and a new political alignment. Into it the best democratic energies of the country will be poured. The court and the country are both entering on an iron age. The struggles of that age will determine whether the promise of American life can be made constitutional.

Chapter XXI

JUDICIAL ORGANIZATION AND PROCEDURE

No. 77

[PROFESSOR RADIN, in the first selection in this chapter, carries on the discussion of the role and function of the courts. In addition, he points out what a court is, how and from what group the judges are chosen, and gives us a brief and general description of the hierarchical arrangement of American courts, federal and state.]

WHO SAYS IT IS THE LAW? [1]

by Max Radin

IF an observer with a telescopic eye powerful enough to see things some two hundred and fifty thousand miles away as clearly as though they were right at hand, were to seat himself in the moon and turn that eye of his on our Earth, he would see, moving about chiefly on the land, some eighteen hundred millions of beings who would puzzle him greatly. He would see them walk or run, or refrain from any action whatever. He would see them put things together and pull them apart, work side by side in some cases and in others violently attack each other, and he would certainly make little sense of what they were doing if he tried to keep all the eighteen hundred millions in view at the same time. He might note that they all ate and breathed and slept, but otherwise he would find it hard to discover anything that they all did, or even anything that nearly all did.

But if he gave up trying to keep track of the entire eighteen hundred millions and directed his gaze at some smaller part of the world—the United States, for example—he would discover, if he watched carefully, that there were a great many things after all that nearly everybody in that region did,

[1] Max Radin, *The Law and Mr. Smith* (Indianapolis: Bobbs-Merrill and Co., 1938), Ch. 2, pp. 6-13. Reprinted by permission of the publisher.

626

and he would further note that the same people were likely to repeat certain of their actions over and over again. And if our observer with the monstrous eye were a reflective kind of person, who liked to arrange his knowledge and put it in order, he would soon be busy with these repetitions, classifying them and working out some scheme to explain them to himself.

Now let us leave the moon and get back to Earth, particularly to our part of the Earth, the United States. Nothing can be more obvious or significant than the similarity among the actions of most of us. Men, for example, all dress in almost exactly the same style and use in their clothes only black, brown, gray, or blue colors, almost never red, green, yellow, or purple. Women's clothes vary more but still in a general way follow a common, if new, style every year. Almost everybody eats set meals at about the same time. In the city, men leave their homes after breakfast and go to a different place where they do nearly the same kind of work every day and return about 6 P.M. to eat their dinner. When letters are written, they begin and close with set phrases which are very like each other. People in speaking to each other use the same language; that is, they use the same words for the same ideas and utter them in a fixed order which they would not think of changing. People walking or riding on the street keep to the right, and so avoid colliding with each other. A great many men raise their hats when they see women whom they know. When they are told to stop or keep in a certain direction by a uniformed policeman, they obey his orders. If they want anything displayed in a shop window, they know they will have to pay money for it and they usually do.

These are only a small selection of the number of acts that all or most men in any one country do. Many of these things they do without thinking about them, and some of them they do consciously but still without objection on their part and without any reluctance. Some of them they do because they see other people doing them and have fallen into the way of imitating them. Some of them they have been told to do by parents, employers, foremen, teachers, friends, policemen, or even casual strangers who seem to know. If they do these acts unconsciously they are apt to call them habits; if they do them consciously they may think of them as *rules;* that is, as things which for some reason they feel they ought to do, or ought to do in a particular way.

Their reasons for thinking they ought to do them vary a good deal. Sometimes they think so because everybody else does them, sometimes because they are the easiest way of getting a certain purpose fulfilled, or because someone they respect told them to do them, or else because they are satisfied that some Higher Power would like them done. And among all these rules, there are some of a peculiar sort which are called *rules of law.*

What is peculiar about them? A great many persons have said wise and rather mysterious things on the subject and have phrased the difference in words that are a little hard to follow, but to the Ordinary Person the difference does not seem a particularly mysterious matter. If you asked this Ordinary Person why he raises his hat to a lady of his acquaintance, he would probably reply in a lofty tone that all gentlemen do, and he would not be impressed if you proved to him that in many parts of the world gentlemen do not, and that in western Europe they have been doing so for only some three or four hundred years. He would retort that what gentlemen do here and now is a good enough rule for him.

If, on the contrary, the Ordinary Person were asked why he does not snatch a desirable tie from a haberdasher's shop and make off with it, there can be no doubt that the first reason which would occur to him would be that he might be arrested and imprisoned for acting in that way. It is not the only reason, surely, but it is a good one and, I think we may say, it is the one most likely to be given. We might take another example. If the Ordinary Person were asked to put on green silk knickerbockers and go to work daily in them, he would surely decline, and his reason, if he condescended to give one, would be that he did not wish to make himself ridiculous. Again, if he wished to buy a house, he would not be satisfied with an oral promise on the part of the seller, but would insist on having one in writing. And in this case the reason would be, not that an oral promise is ridiculous or unmannerly, but that without a written promise he would be unable to prove in court his right to the house, if it should come to that.

We could follow this through. There are a great many rules of all sorts—rules of morals, of fashion, of manners, of religion, of convenience, of common sense, and any of them may be rules of law as well. But we think of them as rules of law only when and if they call up in our mind a court or else a policeman, a sheriff, or other officials who have some connection with a court. That is not quite the whole story, but it is much the greater part of it, and it answers well enough to what in most people's minds is the test of whether a rule is a legal rule or not. It is not a legal rule to refrain from wearing green silk knickerbockers in our daily routine of business, because a court will not care whether we do or not. But we had better not come to work in no clothes at all, because a court is very likely indeed to care about that.

What is this court which we have to keep in mind so much? Why should our plans have so frequently to depend on what this court will do or will say? And how do we know what it will do or say? For I hope it has been noted that we have been using the future tense. In describing whether a thing is *now*, at the present time, a rule of law, we are indulging in prophecy.

We are imagining a future situation in which the rule will be considered by a court, and we are forecasting the result of that consideration. If the court will enforce it, when in the future it has occasion to, it is a rule of law *now*. We cannot get this too early in our minds or keep it there too firmly.

It is therefore highly important to know what a court is. And though it may sound childish to start out by saying what a court is not, it is on the whole well to remember that a court is not a building or an institution, but a man or else a very small group of men, practically never more than nine. The court is the judge or judges, and the judge—there is usually but one—is the court. Everything else is secondary. And this judge is a human being and a citizen, extremely like the rest of us in character, feelings, manners, and habits. He is in no sense inspired; he possesses no mysterious powers which the rest of us do not have, and, to do him justice, he does not pretend to have such inspiration or such powers—at least the vast majority of courts do not. For that reason, sensible courts would be very glad if people stopped speaking of them in figures of speech or in grand and high-sounding phrases. They are not Priests of Justice, or Bulwarks of the State, or the Foundations of Society, or Lighthouses, or Rocks, or Anchors, or any of the other things that eloquent and well-meaning people have called them, but merely fellow citizens who have been elected by the people or appointed by Presidents and Governors to do a certain particular job. They are almost always selected from among lawyers, a class of people of whom we shall have to say a great deal later, but whom we shall describe for the present as men who for a number of years have educated themselves intensively by study and practice, so that judges—that is to say, courts—can be selected from them.

Our courts, then, are men who have had a particular kind of education and who spend most of their lives in close association with lawyers; that is to say, with men who have had the same kind of education. Not only are they subject to error, but they may properly assert—in spite of popular notions to the contrary—that they are readier to admit their mistakes than other professional groups and have created more ways of correcting themselves than have other professions. And surely it does no possible good, and may do a great deal of harm, if these particular public officials are separated from all others and considered to be sacred or holy or somehow entitled to a particular kind of reverence, over and above the respect which they may claim by reason of their abilities, education, and character.

Having settled in our minds what courts are not and in a very general way what they are, let us look at them more closely. These men about whose words or actions we must prophesy, if we wish to know what the law is, are not very numerous. They number about one in thirty thousand of the population, or, if we include justices of the peace or police judges, about one in twelve thousand. In most of the United States, they have been elected by the people; in a very few of them they have been appointed by the Governor with the consent of the State Senate. There are, besides, Federal Courts, which have been appointed by the President of the United States with the consent of the United States Senate.

Evidently we cannot, in a book like this, learn all the details of the organization of all the courts. Nor if we could learn them, would it do us much good to remember them, because changes so frequently occur in details. But we might get some notion of how these things are managed, because we shall have to refer to certain special courts again and again.

First of all—in order to get them out of the way—there are the United States Courts. Certain things are reserved for them; things we had better omit for the present. They are not many, although, as we shall see, they are important enough. If we wish to know what the law is on one of these matters, we must put the following question: "What would Judge Blank of the Federal District Court decide about it, since we live in his District?" We should have to ask that, knowing that if he does not say what we think he should say, we could "appeal," i.e., take the matter to a higher court, consisting of three judges higher in rank than Judge Blank, called Judges of the Circuit Court, who sit often in a distant city. The law, instead of being as Judge Blank will say, will turn out to be as the Circuit Court will say. There, we shall have to stop in most cases. In a very few cases— highly important ones—we may get a chance to correct even the Circuit Court. We may get permission to go to the United States Supreme Court at Washington, where nine judges will make up their minds whether Judge Blank was right after all. That often takes a great deal of time; we sometimes do not discover until many years after an event has happened what the law *was,* according to which it should or should not have taken place.

Except for this small number of important things which are reserved for the Federal Courts, everything else, large or small, may come before the State Courts. If we live in Chicago and wish to know the law of the state of Illinois on a particular question, we ask ourselves what Judge Bracton of the Superior Court will say about it, since we have reason to think the matter will come before him. If the arrangement in the city is such that we cannot be at all sure it will be Judge Bracton, but know merely that it will be some one of the forty or fifty Superior (or Circuit) Judges in the city, we must try to imagine what any one of them would say. That will be harder, but if they are all sensible persons and we are sensible ourselves, it will not be impossible.

And just as in the case of the Federal Courts, we shall have a chance of "appealing," first to the District Appellate Court, in which three judges sit, and finally to the State Supreme Court of seven; and we can usually do so without asking anyone's permission. In this way, just as in the case of the Federal Courts, it will sometimes take many years before we can find out whether we were right or wrong when we said, about a particular thing that happened, that it was or was not in accordance with a rule of law.

Not only does it take time but it takes money to find out. Judges, being public officials, are paid salaries. They do their work in buildings that often cost a great deal of money to build and a great deal of money every year to keep in order. In every case there are many records which must be kept, and it costs much money to make these records and take care of them. Now, most of this money is taken from the public treasury, but some of it—a very small amount—comes from the fees which people must pay to get a case decided by the court. They must pay a small fee when they start, a larger one while the case is in progress, and further fees when they appeal. All these fees together do not amount to very much but they may run in a simple case to as high a sum as $150, which for extremely poor people is a large sum of money.

This, then, is the way our courts are organized, and it is not a very complicated matter. It used to be far more complicated and may soon become so again. For, while we have described two systems of courts running more or less parallel, we have not described them all. For small matters, where small sums are involved or slight injuries done, we do not go to a Superior Court at all, although we sometimes may if we want to, but we usually find ourselves before a justice of the peace or a police judge. He does not have to be a lawyer but he usually is. We generally do not spend much time in conjecturing what he will say about a rule of law, because if there is doubt about it we are pretty sure to appeal to the Superior Court. None the less— although once more we must wait till later to discuss the question—this court of small matters has a great power and can do a great deal of good and a great deal of mischief.

We are not yet through with courts. If the question is whether under a legal rule an injured workman is entitled to compensation and how much, that will not go before the ordinary court at all, but before a Compensation Commission which is really a court under another name. Similarly in some states, questions of workmen's wages, rates for gas and electricity or railroad rates—all these things will go before special commissions, not before the regular courts. That makes things fairly complicated; and, as it is likely that there will be more commissions rather than fewer, what with Federal

Courts, State Courts and Commissions, it will be something of a problem to know just which court we are to have in mind when we try to foretell what the law is. Evidently we shall need guidance.

Where this guidance comes from is the subject of a later chapter. For the present, let us ask ourselves a more important question. These judges have as their sole task that of stating whether an act was or was not in accordance with a rule of law. How do they know?

No. 78

[THE organization and jurisdiction of the federal constitutional courts are familiar to all who are interested in the study of American Government. Not so well known, either with reference to their organization or to their highly specialized jobs, are the legislative courts. The Court of Claims is one of the oldest of this latter type but, as Miss Stern points out, it is so unknown that many Congressmen and lawyers are unaware of its existence and work.]

THE UNKNOWN COURT [1]

by Edith M. Stern

"THE sovereign cannot be sued" is an axiom of law, a corollary of the ancient doctrine that "the king can do no wrong." Every school child knows that the United States repudiated kings and their infallibility in 1776, but comparatively few citizens know that the United States, alone among all the sovereign states of the world, may be sued by right and with-out special permission. The special court which keeps hard at work on such cases alone attracts so little notice that long ago it was dubbed The Unknown Court.

Its shabby red brick and brown-stone home, a block from the White House, is never pointed out to sightseers. Yet it disposes of claims running into hundreds of millions of dollars annually. Its decisions have established vital principles of law, and there is no appeal from its findings of fact. Only the Supreme Court can reverse it on points of law.

In this U. S. Court of Claims an inventor can sue the Government for infringement of a patent that the very same government has granted. Even the humblest citizen may seek justice from the "sovereign." Duke Stubbs, for instance. Duke and his wife had been on relief for some time. But he

---

[1] Edith M. Stern, "The Unknown Court," *Current History* (November, 1938), Vol. 49, No. 3, pp. 35-36. Reprinted by permission of *Current History and Forum*.

won a judgment of $50,000 from the Court a few months ago because the government had ruined his silver fox farm in Alaska.

Duke Stubbs' suit against Uncle Sam followed extension by the Government of the boundaries of McKinley National Park. Forest rangers, tramping across his premises, made breeding impossible; foxes are such temperamental animals that even a change in the wearing apparel of their attendants is said to keep them from mating or make the vixens miscarry. Mr. Stubbs and his wife had sunk everything they had into their venture, and just when it was beginning to pay handsomely it had to be abandoned. Responsibility for compensation, the Court decided, lay with the Government.

Duke Stubbs was fortunate in getting the right lawyer. He might easily have failed to hear of the Court of Claims. Even the dean of a midwestern law school told a building contractor that his only recourse was to write to the Treasury when he complained that his costs had been increased because the Government had held the plans submitted for approval an unreasonably long time. A congressman not long ago told a constituent that the Court had no power to award damages. One of the leading lawyers of New York didn't know where to seek justice for a client who had a claim against Uncle Sam.

But though the Court is a stranger to most people and even to some lawyers, enough cases are brought before it to keep judges and clerks busy the year round. Many of the suits seek indemnities far out of proportion to actual damages, for Uncle Sam is not only vulnerable but rich. When army bombers miss their target and set fire to a farmer's crops, he may be tempted to place a value of $10,000 upon the destroyed hay and wheat, or more than what his entire farm may be worth. So that in addition to being a boon to the humble citizen who has an honest grievance against the Government, the Court is a careful guardian of the public funds, saving the taxpayers from paying millions of dollars to satisfy unjust claims.

Recently, an Illinois landowner claimed $1,000,000 because his lands were flooded by a new federal spillway. The Court decided that his lands had been flooded often before the spillway was built, and that he was therefore not entitled to recover. The verdict ended at the same time 80 similar lawsuits, involving tracts of fifty to thousands of acres, and sums of $10,000 to $60,000,000.

That decision, involving millions of Government money, got not a line in the Washington newspapers the day it was handed down, though the papers gave plenty of space to police court items. But the Court is accustomed to being ignored, and it goes on quietly doing its work without expecting public recognition.

The Government's interests before the Court of Claims are represented by the Department of Justice. Skilled attorneys of the Department resist unjust claims to the limit—and with remarkable success. Last year they defended action in 1600 cases and succeeded in limiting recoveries to one-half of one per cent of the amounts sued for—the finest record they have made to date.

Claims against the Government are nothing new, but in the early days of the Republic they could be settled only upon passage of special legislation by Congress. This meant confusion, caprice, corruption. There was the notorious Fisher case that Mark Twain immortalized, in which it is said that the heirs of a farmer whose crops were destroyed by troops during the War of 1812 milked the Government of $67,000. The widow, during her lifetime, would have been content with $600.

To relieve this situation, the Court of Claims was established in 1855. Originally it merely reported its recommendations to Congress. Lincoln, in his first annual message, 1861, urged an enlargement of the Court's powers. "It is as much the duty of Government," he said, "to render prompt justice against itself in favor of citizens as it is to administer the same between private individuals." Since 1866 the Court has been empowered to render judgment. Now its findings of fact are final; they cannot be reversed by appeal to any higher tribunal. And only the Supreme Court can reverse it on the law.

The three judges who sat first soon found themselves overburdened with the handling of intricate cases "involving enormous amounts in a country of 25,000,000 people." The Court was expanded to five judges in 1863, and in 1925 seven commissioners were added to assist in sifting evidence.

The claims that come before it are of many kinds. The Government is not an abstraction, but an aggregate of federal employes who, like other human beings, make mistakes. A navy vessel collided with a fishing boat, and the owner sued. During . . . [World War I], when the Government was running the railroads, a spark from an engine started a great forest fire in Minnesota. A Government dredge, deepening a harbor on the Atlantic coast, ran over a man's oyster bed and destroyed the breeding mollusks. An army post had been using coal for fuel; the heating system was changed to oil, and the coal company whose contract was cancelled sued for damages.

Formalities and technicalities are few in the Court of Claims. Suit is started by a petition, to which the Government replies. Then follows a unique procedure for taking testimony. Instead of witnesses coming to court, the Court—in the person of a commissioner—goes to the witnesses. Both sides may select the places most convenient or economical for the examination of witnesses.

A contractor, for instance, claimed that the Government should have informed him that the "borrow pit" (place from which earth is removed), used in the construction of a levee near New Orleans, was over what was once a cypress swamp. A dozen engineers were prepared to testify, for the Government, that the possibility of buried stumps is characteristic of the lower Mississippi and that the contractor should have calculated the chances of running into them. Oldest inhabitants averred that the existence of this particular swamp was not a matter of common knowledge, and that there was no reason why the Government should have known about the obstacle. To move such a crowd to Washington would have been costly for the Government, so a commissioner and the attorneys on both sides trekked to Louisiana.

The process of fact-finding often goes on for years when the matters involved are immense and complex. When inventors have claimed, for example, that the War Department infringed upon their patents for a tin helmet, an airplane propeller, or a potato-peeling machine, the Court had to determine the validity of the patent, the actuality of the infringement, and the extent of the damages. In patent and contract cases 5000 pages of printed records are not uncommon; 10,000 not unheard of.

Indian claims— 98 of them are pending—involve staggering sums and intricate details. The Sioux entered suit 17 years ago and to-day their claim, with interest at six per cent since 1876, amounts to over $900,000,000. During the course of westward migration the Government appropriated their lands, and promised that it would use any money from the sale of such land for the benefit of the tribe. That it has failed in its trust is the subject matter of a petition that runs 4835 printed pages—eight bound volumes —and during the course of the suit, not yet decided, 162,899 claim settlements, 600,000 vouchers and 1900 appropriations have been examined.

Once the evidence is complete the Court considers the findings of fact and then the five judges assemble to hear the argument. Often the argument takes no more than an hour. Since there is no jury, there is little oratory. Later the Court renders judgment. And though a claimant may at times feel that a verdict is mistaken, at least he knows that its side of the story has had thorough consideration by judges appointed for life, free of political influence—judges who never since the beginning have been touched by the slightest breath of scandal or corruption.

Only a small part of the cases affected by the Court's decisions are ever tried. Sometimes by agreement a suit for a small amount is instituted as a test case for a whole class of similar claims. At the moment 1400 soldiers are claiming $75 to $300 allowances for re enlistment in the U. S. Army. Soldiers who leave the army, and then re-enlist, are given a gratuity for every year of previous enlistment. During the economy legislation following the depression, these allowances were not paid. Only one of these claims will be tried. If the claimant wins, all other soldiers with similar claims will get their money. If he loses, none of them will. . . .

It is a demonstration of democracy-in-action when a corporation claims and recovers $16,000,000 in taxes and a clerk in the Department of Agriculture claims and recovers $1.50 for lunch money.

True, the Court does not cover personal-injury cases. If you are run over by an army truck, you have no legal right to sue the Government. All you can do is entrust your claim to your senator or representative. If he has the time, the inclination, and the influence, he may get Congress to pass a private act for your benefit, which can take the form either of a direct appropriation or special permission to sue.

But even with its limitations the Court of Claims is something for Americans to regard with pride. It is a living negation of the dangerous doctrine that the state can do no wrong. And it is an evidence of high national morality that, in a world of increasing arbitrary dictatorships, to sue the United States rests upon a right and not a prayer. [The Congressional Reorganization Act of 1946 provided that all claims arising after January 1, 1945 will be settled in the administrative agencies or the courts, depending on whether the amount involved exceeds one thousand dollars.]

No. 79

[It is difficult to classify the courts which are found in our state governments. Their number, type, and jurisdiction, and the manner in which their judges are selected vary widely from state to state, even though they follow, in general, the pyramid arrangement which Professor Radin outlined. One state court which is almost universal in the United States is the justice of the peace. Overlooked because of the petty nature of the cases which he hears and decides, the justice of the peace is nevertheless an important judicial officer. His work and how he performs it are the subject of the following article.]

J. P.[1]

RECENT studies of the justices of the peace indicate that the people's courts are frequently neither popular nor judicial. Investigators in as widely separated states as New York and California, Michigan and Mississippi, conclude that the present system of rural justice is uneconomical and inefficient, and that it should undergo drastic reorganization.

[1] J. P., *State Government* (March, 1934), Vol. 7, pp. 69-71. Reprinted by permission of *State Government*.

One of the most striking points brought out by these studies is the large surplus of justices. For example, Professor Sunderland found that, out of the 290 justices who had been elected in six Michigan counties, only 21 ever did any judicial business—the other 90 per cent never tried a case. The New York Commission on the Administration of Justice, in its report this year, states that "out of a total of some 3,600 justices of peace, only 1,500 perform judicial functions of any kind." In the metropolitan region of Chicago, Dr. Albert Lepawsky reported that one-tenth of the justices never hear a case, and that about one-half of them try the great bulk of the cases. This situation is not due solely to the fact that these three states are among the half dozen in which the justices perform some slight administrative duties in addition to their judicial functions. Dr. Douglass found that two of the 26 justices in Hamilton County, Ohio, handled two-thirds of the garnishment and attachment suits, while three justices heard 91 per cent of the speeding cases.

The reports also indicate that, in some of the states at least, there is justification for the old saying the "J. P." stands for "judgment for the plaintiff." The report of Dr. Sikes on the justice courts in Mississippi, for example, contains the statement that only two per cent of the civil cases in those courts were decided in the defendant's favor. In criminal cases the defendants were almost equally unsuccessful.

In Ohio, however, the defendants seem to have a somewhat better chance of a favorable decision. A study of 5,820 civil cases and 1,239 criminal cases revealed that defendants were successful in four per cent of the former and that they were discharged in 21 per cent of the criminal prosecutions. However, half of the discharges, it should be noted, were for want of prosecution.

Among the 926 civil cases brought before the justices in the six Michigan counties which Professor Sunderland studied, only seven—or less than one per cent—resulted in judgments for the defendant. In contrast, the defendant succeeded in more than a third of the cases brought before the circuit or superior courts of these same counties. A study of criminal cases confirmed the findings of the civil cases—the defendants were adjudged guilty 95 per cent of the time.

A much greater problem than this monotony of judgments for the plaintiff is the distortion of justice directly traceable to the fee system. Dr. Sikes, for instance, contends that the administration of justice should not be on a competitive basis; that the judges who receive fees for each case decided can scarcely be expected to remain strictly impartial in their decisions. Many states have remedied the evils of the fee system, but some still retain this method of remuneration in spite of a denunciation of it by a Chief Justice of the United States Supreme Court.

Unfortunately, however, the mere removal of the fee system is apparently not a complete solution for all of these problems. A recent survey of the justices of Los Angeles county—where these officers are paid an annual salary—shows that even there many of them are inactive. There were 46 justice courts which heard no cases during the year 1931-1932, and the number of cases heard by individual justices ranged from seven per year to 3,000 per year. Per capita expenditures for these courts ranged from 26 cents to 61 dollars.

Several of the investigators criticized the records—or rather, the lack of records—covering the work done in the justice courts. For example, Professor Sunderland pointed out that some justices kept no records at all, and that the few records which *were* kept were inaccurate, inadequate, unsystematic, and lacking in uniformity. Such records are, of course, worthless for supervisory purposes. Those whose official duty it is to superintend and inspect the work of the justice courts are blocked at the outset by inadequate reports.

Private "supervision" of an efficient and effective character, however, may —as Dr. Lepawsky states—step in to take the place of nonexistent public control. He found that, in the metropolitan region of Chicago, agencies like the larger department stores, mail order houses, and motor clubs have taken active interest in these inferior courts in order to insure favorable decisions for their cases.

Qualifications for the office of justice of the peace are not specified by most of the states. In fact, only one state requires that such officers have even modest pretensions to learning: in Louisiana a justice must be able to read and write the English language. Under such circumstances, one would not expect to find many lawyers among these minor officials, and the studies by Dr. Douglass in Ohio and Professor Manning in Kentucky reveal that the percentage is not, indeed, very large. One-third of the justices of peace in Hamilton County, Ohio, are members of the bar, but less than one per cent of the Kentucky justices are lawyers.

A composite picture drawn from all of these studies shows the typical rural magistrate as a man of between forty and sixty years, with only a common school education, who has never held any other political office. The judicial duties are, of course, assumed in addition to the regular "private business" of the justice which, in three-fourths of the cases, is farming. Although the office frequently possesses a certain popular appeal, the typical justice serves only one or two terms.

The facts presented in these studies are by no means new developments, nor were they previously unknown. *State Government* cannot refrain from quoting a few lines from the interesting volume by Bruce Smith, entitled *Rural Crime Control,* in which he recalls the colorful Roy Bean, who

> . . . was born one day near Toyah
> Where he learned to be a lawyer
> And a teacher and a banker and the mayor,
> He was cook and old shoe-mender,
> Sometimes preacher and bar-tender,
> And it cost two bits to have him cut your hair.

Mr Justice Bean was the sole peace officer in the 35,000 square miles, more or less, lying west of the Pecos River in Texas. A photograph, dating so recently as 1900, shows him holding court, in shirt sleeves and a five-gallon hat, on the "veranda" of his establishment in Langtry. Three signs adorn his one-story shack. One, over the door, reads "Justice Roy Bean, Notary Public." A second, placed just below, but in much larger capitals, declares for "Law West of the Pecos." A third and comparatively modest shingle bears the legend "Beer Saloon." While it may seriously be doubted whether the same combination of callings would produce satisfactory results in more settled communities, it seems to be agreed among those most likely to know that "Cold Beer" and "Law" labored together amicably in establishing order throughout the vast territory "West of the Pecos."

Quite as significant as the general dissatisfaction which is expressed with these rural justice shops are the suggestions for their improvement. Professor Sunderland recommends: "a county court, properly organized and housed, having a trained judge, a competent clerk, office equipment sufficient for the keeping of proper records, and sitting at such times and places as the needs of the community should indicate," to replace the obsolete justice courts.

But a mere consolidation may be only a first step. Bruce Smith concludes:

> The lessons of English experience with local courts will in large measure be lost if we do not make some provision for a justice's clerk. In many instances this will prove to be the only effective means for bringing administrative competence and some degree of procedural expertness into the conduct of daily routine of rural justices' courts. Moreover, if such course be followed, it will prove possible to attract to the rural bench men of local standing and ripe wisdom who are now unwilling to serve because of the burden imposed by petty detail. If the personal qualifications of justices were improved there would need be less concern about their professional training, and other problems surrounding the justice of the peace would have a fair prospect of early solution.

No. 80

[FOR more than a generation American jurists, lawyers, and scholars have been subjecting our judicial machine to a careful and critical examination. These inquiries have followed several channels and from each have come suggestions for change and proposals for reconstruction. As was the case in the field of public administration, these proposals must themselves be subjected to examination, and Professor Haines does this in the following article.]

THE GENERAL STRUCTURE OF COURT ORGANIZATION [1]

by Charles Grove Haines

THE present system of court organization presents certain characteristics which are the natural outgrowth of the common law background of American law.

In the first place, a hierarchy of courts was established with relatively little in the way of cooperation or mutual adjustment among the courts, whether of different or of the same grade. Each court or group of courts had, as a rule, an independent status incased in the provisions of the constitution and statutes providing for its organization and jurisdiction. Higher courts, of course, reviewed the decisions and judgments of lower courts in accordance with well-defined statutory requirements and common law procedure; but administratively, each court was a separate entity and was seldom subject to direction or control by any superior body.

In the second place, as judicial business increased or new types of controversies arose, new courts were established or additional judges were authorized. The change from a pioneer, rural type of life where a few judges acted as community arbiters, to an urban industrial economy with a multiplication of cases to be settled, resulted merely in more courts and more judges. These judges continued to apply what Mr. Justice Cardozo termed "a system of case law, with powers of innovation cabined and confined."

Though a detailed analysis of state judicial machinery is impractical and would serve no useful purpose in this connection, it is well to recognize that much greater diversity prevails in the state judicial establishments and their practices than is generally recognized. Little progress will be made

[1] Charles Grove Haines, "The General Structure of Court Organization," *The Annals* of the American Academy of Political and Social Science (May, 1933), Vol. 167, pp. 1-11. Reprinted by permission of *The Annals* of the American Academy of Political and Social Science. The footnotes in the original version are omitted here.

in the scientific study of the administration of justice until broad generalizations regarding state administration are replaced by observations and conclusions resulting from thorough and independent investigations in many states. Some investigations of this type, such as those of the Johns Hopkins Institute of Law, are under way and promise interesting revelations regarding the operation of courts.

Realizing that details vary in the systems of courts established in the states, certain common features usually belong to the structure of court organization as formulated in constitutions and statutes. Thus, there are as a rule four grades of courts: first, local peace magistrates and inferior courts for petty causes; second, county and municipal courts with a limited jurisdiction in civil and criminal matters and a variety of duties administrative in nature, such as the disposal of probate matters, and in certain communities a separate tribunal for the trial of equity cases; third, superior, district, or circuit courts of general jurisdiction at law and equity, with authority to try more serious offenses and to review the decisions of inferior magistrates; fourth, a supreme court of review.

A marked increase in the causes to be disposed of, both in the trial courts and in the appellate tribunals, resulted in only two significant changes during the latter part of the nineteenth century—the establishment of more trial courts or provisions for additional judges, and, to relieve the strain on appellate courts, the authorization of intermediate appellate tribunals. As a rule the constitution prescribed the system of courts for the state, defined in a general way their jurisdiction, and surrounded court procedure with some specific limitations. It was this general type of court organization which was challenged when, at the beginning of the present century, the administration of justice in the states was subjected to serious criticisms on the ground of inefficiency.

In a report of a special committee of the American Bar Association "to suggest remedies and formulate proposed laws to prevent delay and unnecessary cost in litigation," two principles were proposed as involving the central issues in the reform of court organization and procedure in the United States. These principles were as follows:

I. The whole judicial power of each state (at least for civil causes) should be vested in one great court, of which all tribunals should be branches, departments, or divisions. The business, as well as the judicial administration of this court, should be thoroughly organized, so as to prevent not merely waste of judicial power, but all needless clerical work, duplication of papers and records, and the like, thus obviating expense to litigants and cost to the public.

II. Whenever in the future practice acts or codes of procedure are drawn up or revised, the statute should deal only with the general features of procedure, and prescribe the general lines to be followed, leaving details to be fixed by rules of court, which the courts may change from time to time, as actual experience of their application and operation dictates.

These suggestions for reform in the field of court organization were made for the committee by its chairman, Dean Roscoe Pound, who summed up the situation in relation to court organization in the comment that

> with respect to anachronisms in the machinery of justice generally, I submit that relief is to be sought in a modern, unified, flexible, judicial organization in which judicial power is conserved, the administrative activities of the tribunals are systematized, and provision is made for expert and responsble supervision.

The English Judicature Act of 1873 and the administrative arrangements which developed therefrom served as a model for the proposed reforms.

The changes suggested, which were intended to bring about a unification of the existing scattered and more or less independent state and local judicial tribunals, were expected to involve large powers of general direction, supervision, and control over the work of the courts, including authority to establish divisions, control assignment of judges, formulate rules of procedure, and supervise the types of records and reports, and to insure a more definite standardization of practices in the administration of justice.

Dean Pound's proposals for reorganization of judicial machinery, which soon received the support of bar associations, of the American Judicature Society, and of numerous other organizations, took concrete form in the establishment of special municipal courts.

The first city to secure a partial unification of its court system was Chicago. The court established in that city, and placed under the direction of Chief Justice Olson, involved the following features: first, a single court in place of numerous justices of peace and police magistrates; second, the chief justice as an administrative head acting as a general manager; third, the chief justice and associate justices constituting an administrative council for the general supervision of rules and regulations and of the administrative activities of the court; fourth, rules of procedure to be formulated by the court, with their preparation largely in the hands of the administrative council; fifth, provision for specialization and accordingly for the establishment of separate branches (among the branches established were the following: domestic relations, traffic, morals, boys, and small claims courts); sixth, a psychopathic laboratory, in charge of an expert who was expected to act as consultant and adviser to the justices. For a number of years this court performed its functions so successfully that it was deemed a model for similar courts to be established in other metropolitan centers.

Among the cities which followed Chicago in the effort to unify the judiciary was Detroit, where a single court was established for the handling of criminal cases. A number of reforms were instituted, such as the establishment of special divisions, the elimination of unnecessary steps in trial procedure, and improvements in the keeping of records. The first years of this court resulted in noteworthy improvements in the administration of criminal justice in Detroit.

Only a few cities have adopted the plan of a unified court system, but the principles of consolidation, specialization, and flexibility in administration have been accepted and applied in varying degrees in a number of cities. The scope and significance of the application of these principles are exemplified in the Philadelphia Municipal Court. This, according to a recent appraisal, is

a court with jurisdiction to hear initially the smallest case, yet manned by judges learned in the law, as compared with the magistrates' courts, with their lay judges, before whom it was practically compulsory to bring small claims prior to the establishment of the municipal court; a court "of record" in which trial of civil cases without a jury is encouraged and before which a number of minor criminal offenses not requiring jury trial are regularly tried; a court in which thousands of juvenile offenders are handled with a view to their welfare and in disregard of the requirements of the criminal law; a court which begins desertion and nonsupport proceedings with a letter asking for a conference rather than by an arrest plus imprisonment or bail; a court which helps the unmarried mother to get not only the father's support, but prenatal care and medical and hospital service at the birth as well; a court which has ordered the dispensing of thousands of dollars of public money to widows, that they might keep their children with them; a court which adjusts many of its cases without formal court proceedings; a court with investigators to supply the judges with information which might not be forthcoming from the parties themselves; a court with physicians and psychiatrists to diagnose the ills of its wards and recommend treatment; a court specializing in sex offenses, in which the presence or absence of venereal disease is a fact of great weight; a court which hears its juvenile and domestic relations cases without the preliminary hearing before a magistrate that once was necessary; a court which uses probation and parole extensively, and has many probation officers to aid in the rehabilitation of individuals and families; a court which has experimented with a "poor man's court" and has established a "conciliation, small claims, and legal aid division," a labor bureau to find employment for its wards, and a statistical department to interpret the court's work to the court and to the public.

These steps toward unification for a metropolitan community were followed by attempts to unify and centralize the entire judicial system of a state. Constitutional conventions in New York, Illinois, and Missouri incorporated in draft constitutions all or part of the program for unification. New York adopted only part of the unification plan. Illinois proposed to unify the courts of Cook County and granted the rule-making power to the Supreme Court. The draft constitution of Missouri included the essential features of the model unification plan as proposed by the American Judicature Society. The entire judicial system of the state was to be under a single administrative direction. With the rule-making power in the courts and a judicial council established, the process of central control and supervision was to be rendered effective. But these draft constitutions were rejected by the voters, in state-wide political contests waged only in small part around the changes in the judicial systems.

The model state constitution prepared by a committee of the National Municipal League also includes a plan for consolidation. Under this plan a general court of justice is to be established, comprised of three departments to be known as the supreme court, the district court, and the county court. The supreme court is authorized to sit in two or more divisions and to make rules for the distribution of cases between divisions and for the hearing of certain cases by the full court. The district court is to have original jurisdiction in certain cases, and such appellate jurisdiction as shall be conferred upon it by the judicial council or by law. County courts are granted original jurisdiction to try all cases heretofore considered within the jurisdiction of county courts and those cases which formerly were tried by justices of the peace or local magistrates.

Provision is also made in the model constitution for a judicial council consisting of the chief justice, the presiding justices of the supreme court, and two county court judges to be assigned each year by the chief justice. The chief duties of the council are to make rules and regulations respecting the business of the courts and to assist in the division of business and the assignment of judges in the various tribunals. All of the judges of these courts are to be appointed by the governor, subject to approval, in certain instances, by a majority of the legislature. This plan provides for a unification and centralization of the judiciary which has appeared on the whole too revolutionary to be adopted by any state.

In the general discussions over these and similar plans for structural reorganization of the courts, there is rather general agreement upon certain fundamentals; namely, that there should be:

First, a General Court of Judicature for the state.
Second, three main divisions of the court:

I. A supreme court, with two divisions, criminal and civil, and other divisions if necessary.

II. District courts—intermediate courts of appeal—with original jurisdiction in a limited number of cases.

III. County courts—with original jurisdiction over civil and criminal cases and appellate jurisdiction over cases from local magistrates; with special supervision and control over local magistrates or justices of peace (certain plans do not make any provision for local magistrates); with authority to establish divisions for probate, juvenile cases, and so forth.

Third, establishment of a judicial council

(a) To make rules of practice and procedure.

(b) To control the business of the courts, supervise judicial statistics, assign judges, and generally exercise administrative supervision.

The grant of the rule-making power, which is a significant feature of all plans according to Mr. Justice Roberts, should be so broad in its scope

> that the question of forms of action, the question of the initiation of an action, the question of pleadings, the question of proofs, the question of trial procedure, the question of appellate procedure and the whole genus of procedural things, from the start to the end of a litigation, ought to be in the hands of those who know best about it and who, from time to time, can make rules to meet situations as they arise in the actual practice of law.

The extent to which the courts of a state can be unified is one on which opinions differ widely. Though few would defend the existing arrangements in most of the states, it is doubtful whether so thorough a centralization as designed in the above plans would be practicable. In the first place, it must be recognized that conditions in the states vary to such an extent that generalizations on the matter of unification should be made with due caution. The problems of states like Connecticut and Rhode Island are scarcely analogous to those in Texas, Montana, and California; so that general principles of centralization cannot be applied without doing violence to local conditions and requirements. The abolition of local magistrates or justices of peace may be desirable where a county covers no more acreage than a great many farms in the states of the West. But when a county has a population of a million or more inhabitants and comprises a territory almost equivalent to a small state, a single county court scarcely meets the situation. Nor does the proposal to have the county court sit in different parts of the county meet every condition.

Some direct control and supervision over the entire court system, such as is being developed through the judicial councils, is undoubtedly desirable and can be applied to advantage in most of the states. On the other hand, if the results of centralization in other fields can be taken as indicative of what is to be anticipated from this movement, it is doubtful whether the authority to appoint judges for the entire judicial system should be placed in the hands of the governor without more definite restrictions and limitations than the model constitution or other plans for judicial reform provide.

Neither the system of appointment of judges nor that of election has worked satisfactorily. If appointments are to be made by the governor, it is believed that an eligible list should be prepared by committees of judges and lawyers who can form estimates of the professional qualifications of those recommended. Or, if the state judicial system is placed under the direction of a minister of justice or chief judicial superintendent, judges may be appointed by this officer with the advice and consultation of the judicial council. But there are good grounds to question too great a concentration of power as to the appointment and control of judges in all the cities and local communities of a state. After all, much is to be gained by placing special responsibilities in the administration of justice upon local communities, provided a flexible plan of judicial organization and administration is adopted and limited central control and supervision are established.

Certain guiding formulas in court organization and administration which may be adapted to a variety of conditions are: first, centralization and general administrative control in the making of rules of procedure, in the distribution of cases among the various courts, and in the assignment of judges; second, specialization in court trials and administration for the handling of those cases where peculiar technique and intimate understanding of conditions are imperative; third, flexibility in the establishment of separate departments or divisions and in the provisions which are made for the handling of various types of cases. These formulas can be carried out with a limited amount of central supervision and control, and with the placing of greater responsibilities on local communities for the conduct of judicial administration.

It is doubtful whether general approval can be given to the proposal that the centralization of courts under a strong chief justice is desirable, though certain gains are likely to follow from unification. Centralization may readily be carried too far, so that the special interests and circumstances involved in such fields as juvenile offenses and probate matters may be forced into mechanical and undesirable channels. Administrative unification has distinct advantages in preparing uniform and flexible rules of procedure for all courts, in developing an effective system of reports and of the use of reliable judicial statistics, and in adjusting the personnel of the bench in order to expedite the disposition of cases; but it cannot be deemed as a corrective of some of the most serious ills which now affect our administration of justice.

There is a point in the process of centralizing administrative responsibilities where an increase in duties results in a diminution of efficiency. This has been rightly termed "the inherent vice of centralized authority." Professor Laski says:

It is so baffled by the very vastness of its business as necessarily to be narrow and despotic and overformal in character. It tends to substitute for a real effort to grapple with special problems an attempt to apply wide generalizations that are in fact irrelevant. It involves the decay of local energy, taking real power from its hands. It puts real responsibility in a situation where, from its very flavor of generality, an unreal responsibility is postulated. It prevents the saving grace of experiment.

Another difficulty with unification of the courts lies in the fact that a mere change in organization cannot be effective unless it involves also an improvement in the personnel of the judiciary. After a number of years in operation, Professor Moley remarks that the municipal court of Chicago is

still as inefficient and confused and political as most unreformed courts in other cities. . . . The majority of the judges now sitting are fitted neither by experience, education, nor, what is more important, sufficient professional standards to discharge with credit the great responsibilities and powers which they possess under the law. The court is full of incompetence, of political influences, of lamentable laxness in meeting an unprecedented tide of crime. In the hands of such a staff the court, technically well organized and full of possibilities for good, yields a sorry product.

In Detroit a deterioration of the personnel of the court had similar, though not as serious, results. Other cities with less effective organization and a better personnel on the bench have secured more effective results than either Chicago or Detroit. It not infrequently happens that the results secured by a court depend more on the ability, the courage, and the independence of the judges than upon the particular form of court organization.

With proposals for improvement in the administration of justice, as with reforms in other divisions of government, there has been an overemphasis on the mechanics of court organization, and too much has been expected from mere changes in the organization and administrative arrangements of the system of courts. In the advocacy of both the commission form of city government and the commission-manager type of organization, claims have been made assuring improvement in city administration which have not been satisfactorily or permanently fulfilled unless other important factors were favorable to the new administration. So enthusiastic proponents of reorganization of the administrative services of the states, coupled with an executive budget, predicted a transformation in the control of the public business which has not been realized, except in a few conspicuous instances where forceful personalities secured remarkable improvements in the state public services, or other fortunate combinations of circumstances gave to administrative centralization a success only partially to be attributed to structural reform.

Though there may well be no diminution of effort to eliminate weaknesses in organization, whether in the legislative, the executive, or the judicial branch of the government, little is gained by giving attention to faults of organization unless other factors vital to successful administration are given equal scrutiny.

A consideration of the structure of the courts in the American states involves also certain questions which require brief observations, namely: whether there are too many courts, and hence a reorganization should mean the abolition of some of those now functioning; whether civil and criminal cases should be considered by separate tribunals; whether misdemeanors and felonies should be merged in the trial process and be dealt with by the same court; and whether greater flexibility can be secured both in the trial of cases and in the administrative arrangements among the several courts.

It is difficult to give an answer to the question whether there are too many courts under existing arrangements. As cases are now dealt with in our judicial tribunals, there certainly are not enough courts; but apparently the increase in judicial business is so great that the mere multiplication of courts is creating a situation which from many standpoints is both impracticable and intolerable. In Los Angeles County the number of superior court judges has been doubled in a five-year period, with approximately fifty judges trying cases, and considerably behind in the docket. At the same rate of increase, it is difficult to imagine the situation in the next fifty years.

Instead of an increase in the number of courts functioning as they are at the present time, it would undoubtedly be advisable to reduce the number of trial courts and judges. Other and more effective methods must be devised, however, to take care of the increasing number of controversies which come to the courts for trial, if the judicial system is to be saved from functional paralysis.

On the other hand, if the reduction of the number of courts would mean the concentration of judicial business in a few centers and the removal of the trial of minor and petty offenses a considerable distance from the litigants, with increasing delays and expense, the expedient of a reduction of courts would indeed be questionable.

There are serious doubts whether the proposals to eliminate the justices of peace or petty magistrates is a step in the right direction, provided measures may be adopted to secure more competent justices in the minor courts and improvements may be inaugurated in the procedure followed.

In both England and France, important and effective use is made of the justices of the peace in the disposition of minor causes. The main function of the French justice is to bring parties to an informal conference and to adjust disputes by methods of conciliation and to pass on minor infractions of the laws and ordinances. Those selected for this position must have a degree of license in law and two years' practice or experience in a law office, and must pass a professional examination.

Though the English justices of peace as a rule are not professionally trained, they develop a successful technique as a result of experience, and, with the aid of competent clerks, render a type of justice which is generally deemed satisfactory. Even in graver offenses a trial may be had in "petty sessions," a court of summary jurisdiction composed of at least two justices usually residents of the immediate neighborhood.

In both countries, an inexpensive and informal justice is kept close to the people, rather than removed to distant courts with a high degree of formality and expense.

Ultimately the issue as to the number of courts is tied up with the introduction of more effective methods in the handling of minor cases, in the sifting of evidence by informal examination, by affidavits, and by the discovery of documents, and the determination of issues involved, in advance of trial, so that only controverted points need to be proved in court. In civil cases, much more extensive use of arbitration and conciliation may well be made before the controversy reaches the stage of trial. The problem of the determination of the number of courts must also be adjusted in accordance with the marked differences in the size of the states, the necessary distances to be traversed, and the complexity of conditions which arise over an extensive territory such as is comprised in many of the states.

As in the answer to other questions, the separation of civil from criminal jurisdiction can scarcely be dealt with in general terms. The practice prevails in the United States and in foreign countries for the same court to try both civil and criminal cases. The Municipal Court of Chicago, deemed a model for court organization, combined the trial of both civil and criminal causes. On the other hand, the Detroit plan separated the trial of civil from criminal business.

The main argument for the combination of civil and criminal trials is that the arrangement provides a more effective use of the personnel of the bench. It is a question, however, whether better results may not be secured by greater specialization, whether under a unified court arrangement or in separate courts. So many fields of trial work to-day require a special knowledge and technique that it seems unwise to expect judges to be familiar with the details and the technique necessary for the trial of all kinds of civil and criminal causes. Better results would undoubtedly be secured so far as the dispatch of business is concerned if the judges were given definite assignments either to the civil or the criminal division of the court and thus put into a position where they could acquire specialized knowledge and skill. Though there are advantages in having judges broaden their interest and activities by the trial of different types of cases, most of the advantages thus secured can be gained by the separation of the civil from the criminal business, with an occasional exchange of judges in divisions or branches involving similar facts and circumstances.

Unfortunately, too much dependence has been placed upon the necessity of structural changes in court organization to secure an informal and flexible type of justice. Without any specially planned or advertised reorganization, a chief justice was placed at the head of the Common Pleas Court of Cuyahoga County, Cleveland, and by this simple device one of the most efficient and successful trial courts in the country has been functioning for a number of years.

Whether the trials of misdemeanors and felonies may appropriately be merged under a single tribunal also depends to a considerable degree upon local conditions and interests. The general attitude of neglect and indifference toward justices of peace and minor courts, it is often claimed, can be changed by putting all courts on a basis of equal importance. Why tolerate inferior courts? is the query often raised. The term "inferior" attaches to the courts the stigma of unimportance, and hence neglect and contempt on the part of the public. Should not all courts be potentially equal in importance? And as these are the final courts for the majority of the people, should they not be placed on a par with the higher courts? Thus, it is contended, the stigma attached to courts of inferior jurisdiction may be removed and the disposal of petty misdemeanors may be placed on the same plane as the trial of serious felonies. Since able judges will not accept positions on existing inferior courts, the trial of petty offenses is to be combined with the hearing of charges of graver importance.

Much as it may seem commendable to make this kind of a combination, in practice, results come therefrom which are not so favorable as are usually predicted. Where the trials of felonies and of misdemeanors have been combined, it frequently happens that men of force and character will not accept positions on the courts. They are unwilling to devote their time to the hearings in petty conflicts. The doctrine that all courts are potentially equal in importance, though a well-sounding phrase, does not seem to work out well in practice.

It is frequently not realized that much greater flexibility, both in the methods of trial now in use and in the administrative adjustments among courts, could be secured without drastic changes in the legal arrangements now prevailing regarding court organization. Some of the most important and effective changes in law enforcement can be accomplished by the adoption of simple, reasonable, and effective administrative devices with a minimum of permissive legislation. Effective as the administration of criminal justice is in England, it is carried on through a set of courts which have not been seriously changed for generations. Such devices as have been evolved in England and Continental European countries for securing and sifting the evidence prior to the trial of a case could be adopted to great advantage in this country.

Without any marked changes in the structure of courts, it would be possible to accomplish the result which was thus described by Lord Bowen as applicable to the administration of justice in England. In every cause, whatever its character, said Lord Bowen,

> every possible relief can be given with or without pleadings, with or without a formal trial, with or without discovery of documents and interrogatories, as the nature of the case prescribes—upon oral evidence or affidavits, as is most convenient. Every amendment can be made at all times and all stages in any record, pleading or proceeding, that is requisite for the purpose of deciding the real matter in controversy.

Could not the English plan of summons for direction before a master, by which the vast scheme of discovery is largely administered, be utilized without waiting for the adoption of an elaborate scheme of court organization?

Three significant factors account in large part for the efficiency which prevails in the administration of justice in England and in France. They are: first, the central position and the authority of the judge; second, the lack of technical rules of evidence and the relative informality of procedure which prevails in the actual trial and consideration of cases; third, the subordinate position of the lawyer, who is deemed primarily an agent and assistant of the court, aiding the judge in securing accurate data regarding the case and the selection and determination of the vital issues involved. Most of these advantages could be gained in the actual administration of justice in the United States with relatively few important changes in court organization. In practice, individual judges assume the functions comparable to those of a French or an English judge, with results that are considered satisfactory to all parties concerned.

Principles which require special consideration in any plan to revise existing judicial machinery may be briefly summarized as follows:

First. Flexible constitutional provisions for court organization. The Federal plan vesting judicial power in a Supreme Court and such inferior courts as Congress may establish, which has been followed in a few states, is preferable to the usual clauses of the state constitutions covering the details of court organization and jurisdiction. Progress in remolding judicial machinery is always slow, and is greatly retarded by the difficulties involved in the adoption of frequent constitutional amendments.

Second. Establishment through constitutions and statutes of a certain degree of unification of the court system involving a limited supervision over all inferior tribunals by the Supreme Court and a judicial council authorized to prepare and issue rules of procedure, to assign judges for special duties in accordance with the pressure of causes to be determined and the special capabilities of the judges, and to develop uniformity in records and statistical information.

Third. Expeditious procedure in the preparation of affidavits and in the discovery of documents, with greater use of masters and judicial assistants, to dispose of issues before the stage of trial is reached, as is done in a large percentage of cases in England.

Fourth. Flexible administrative arrangements, to permit specialization where required, to provide for conciliation and arbitration as well as other devices to secure informal and inexpensive proceedings in the adjustment of small claims, and to facilitate the settlement of controversies by summary judgments, declarations of right, or any other device which serves to secure the ends of justice.

The adoption of the above principles will require not a few structural changes in court organization, but they can be applied by degrees, without a radical reconstruction of present judicial machinery. A considerable part of such a program will necessarily have to become a part of American law and practice if we are to accept Elihu Root's challenge to put our judicial house in order.

No. 81

[To understand the American judicial system, it is necessary to know not only what the courts are but also how they carry on their business. Professor Radin, in the following selection, outlines the procedures of both a civil and a criminal trial.]

CIVIL AND CRIMINAL PROCEDURE [1]

by Max Radin

A CIVIL TRIAL

JUST what the course of legal procedure is in most American states at the present time can be illustrated best by a brief history of an action at law.

Suppose John proceeding on his lawful occasions is run into by an automobile driven by Richard and feels that he ought to be compensated for the injuries he has received. His complaint will run as follows:

The plaintiff complains of the defendant, and alleges:

1. That on or about the —— day of ——, 19—, the plaintiff was crossing a public highway known as —— street in the city of ——, in the above-named county and state, at the point where —— avenue intersects with said —— street, and at the same time the defendant (or a servant of the defendant in the course of his employment and while transacting the defendant's business) was driving an automobile in an easterly direction along said —— street near the point where the plaintiff was crossing the same.

2. That the defendant (or the defendant's said servant) then and there negligently and carelessly drove and managed said automobile in this, that he drove the same at an excessive rate of speed, to wit, at the rate of —— miles per hour, and that he failed to sound the horn on approaching the plaintiff.

3. That by reason of the negligent driving and management of said automobile by the defendant (or the defendant's said servant) as aforesaid he ran the same against the plaintiff and thereby knocked him down, and that the plaintiff was by means of the premises bruised, injured and disabled and suffered great bodily and mental pain and will for an indefinite time be disabled from continuing his ordinary activity and occupation.

4. That by reason of the injuries aforesaid, the plaintiff has been put to great expense for care and medical treatment and has been unable to attend to his affairs and has thereby suffered great losses of income and has been otherwise injured in his business.

5. Wherefore plaintiff demands judgment against the defendant in the sum of —— dollars with interest and costs.

(Signed) John Doe

---

[1] Max Radin, *The Law and You* (New York: The New American Library of World Literature, Inc., December, 1948), pp. 101-118. Reprinted by permission of the publisher.

This complaint will be written out for John by a lawyer, and John will sign and swear to it. The complaint will then be "served" on Richard, the defendant, that is to say, someone in the lawyer's employ will hand it personally to Richard if he can find him. If he cannot do so after reasonable effort, a way will be sought to get the complaint to Richard.

This complaint, the defendant, Richard, will answer in a formal way. Evidently the answer will likewise be written out by a lawyer, just as the complaint was, and the answer will go to the plaintiff's lawyer, not to the plaintiff himself.

Even if Richard is willing to admit his negligence, he may regard the demand for compensation as far too large. Like most owners of automobiles, he may carry insurance, in which case he will probably turn the matter over to the company agent to adjust, since it is the insurance company and not he who will have to pay. Or if not insured, he will himself select a lawyer, Mr. Olivier, to negotiate a settlement with Mr. Rowland, John's attorney.

If he claims not to have been negligent at all, or if he is sure that John was also negligent, he will be advised by Olivier that he legally owes nothing whatever to John and that he should defend the suit on that theory. Olivier will draw up an answer for him, which will be served on Rowland since, once an attorney is selected, the parties themselves need do nothing more about the case till the actual trial.

The answer will be headed precisely as the complaint was, and may run somewhat as follows:

The defendant, answering the complaint of the plaintiff, herein denies each and every allegation in said complaint contained. And

For a further separate and distinct answer and defense, defendant alleges that the plaintiff himself did not exercise ordinary care, caution and prudence to avoid said accident and the resulting injuries, if any, complained of, were directly and proximately caused by the fault, carelessness and negligence of the plaintiff in the premises.

Wherefore, the said defendant demands judgment dismissing said complaint with costs.

Evidently there is a clear issue of fact here. The issue is about the conduct of Richard. Either Richard was in fact negligent, or else he was not.

After the answer has been served, the case will be set for a certain day, generally some months later. On that day, plaintiff and defendant, John and Richard, their attorneys and their witnesses, will repair to the courtroom of the judge to whom the case has been assigned—an assignment, if there are several judges, which is likely to be determined by lot.

How will the facts be presented in the case between John and Richard? John has already told his story in outline in his complaint, which the judge has read. John will now be required to tell it again, this time to the judge and jury together. The first thing therefore is to select a jury.

There are present in the courtroom a large number of persons, men and women, who are among those selected for jury duty for this term of the court. There are many more than would be necessary for this particular case, since some of the jury panel may be rejected or excused. Twelve of the panel will take their seats—more or less by lot—in the jury box as the tentative jury. Since this is a civil case and not a criminal one, far less difficulty will be made about accepting the jurymen.

But they will not be accepted as a matter of course. It may be that each one will not be specially and personally examined. It probably will suffice to ask whether any of the tentative jury is personally acquainted with the litigants or their attorneys, or whether any of them is a shareholder in an insurance company that insures against public liability. Sometimes it may be asked whether any of the jury has himself brought an action for damages for negligent driving.

Persons who indicate that they belong to any one of these groups will in all likelihood be excused for that case. The reason is the obvious one that, because of their association as indicated by these questions, they are likely to be prejudiced for or against either plaintiff or defendant.

When a jury is once agreed on, the trial proper will commence.

Witnesses will be heard. Doubtless the first witness will be the plaintiff himself. But he will not be permitted to tell his story in his own way as he did when he consulted his lawyer. He will be required to answer questions, and after examination by his own lawyer, he will be cross-examined by the defendant's lawyer. And the questions put by both lawyers must be in accordance with what is called the "law of evidence."

There are two basic requirements under this law of evidence. The testimony given must first be "relevant and material," and second, it must be "competent." The first requirement is a matter, one would say, of common sense. The jury must make up its mind from what it hears. The jury may be allowed access to the written record of part of the testimony if it asks for it, but a jury cannot demand that as a right. Under these circumstances, it is desirable that a jury should not be presented with a mass of irrelevant detail which may be hard to separate in its recollection from what is relevant. And some of the irrelevant will have a tendency to color the narrative improperly.

When we deal with competence, we have a much more difficult problem. Under the law of evidence, certain things must not be stated at all. The witness must testify only as to facts—things he knows of his own knowledge about what he did, things he actually saw and heard himself. He must not testify about what someone else told him—there are of course exceptions to that—and he must not utter opinions, except as an expert, or conclusions from what he observed rather than the observed fact itself.

The picture of lawyers, springing to their feet and crying out "I object," is one that occurs to most spectators as the most striking and irritating part of a trial and contributes in large measure to making the trial seem like a continual wrangle between opposing counsel. The reason for the objection is often a technical matter of law quite beyond the comprehension of the ordinary spectator or juryman, and the need of deciding these objections promptly makes serious demands on the judge. An erroneous decision may furnish the ground of an appeal and therefore of prolongation of the suit, which even without appeal will consume a great deal of time. And it interrupts the course of the witness' testimony sometimes so substantially that both the court and the jury find it difficult to follow the train of the narrative.

Cross-examination has as its purpose that of discrediting a witness before the jury, by bringing out contradictions and improbabilities in his testimony, by suggesting doubts to him, or trapping him into admissions that will injure his case. It is cross-examination by hostile counsel that witnesses dread as the most trying element in the case, and if the cross-examination is carried on in a sneering, hectoring, or bullying tone, a sensitive witness is often reduced to tears or even to hysterics, or is tempted into retaliatory outbreaks which generally will not help him before the jury.

It may be said that the abuse of the right of cross-examination is one of the most serious defects of our method of trial. It is lessened partly by the objections offered by opposing counsel and by rigorous conduct of the trial by a competent and authoritative judge. Unfortunately, interference by the court with the cross-examination might seem, or be made to seem, partisanship of the judge with the side whose witnesses he seeks to protect. The result is that the cross-examination to which inexperienced men and women may be subjected is presented as so great an ordeal that they do their utmost to avoid appearing as witnesses, even when, without them, just claims can only with difficulty be established or unjust claims repelled.

After testimony on both sides is concluded, the attorneys will "sum up" before the jury. The judge's share in the trial has so far been unspectacular. He has maintained the discipline of the courtroom, which at times is very much like the discipline of a schoolroom and calls for much the same type of personality as a schoolteacher, but the judge has vastly greater power at his disposal than any schoolteacher. Discipline is not confined to the task of preventing any disorder or rowdiness. A good deal of it consists in enforcing the rules about the method and the sequence with which evidence is presented. In addition, as we have seen, the court is required to make prompt decisions of law whenever the competence or relevance of evidence is challenged.

But it is after the testimony is in that the most important function of the judge begins. He must instruct the jury on the law applied to the case before him, and his task is all the more difficult because there is no way in which he can compel the jury to heed his instructions, and in many instances, there is no way to discover whether they have paid the least attention to what he has said.

The jury system grew up in England during the Middle Ages and passed through a number of changes before it became the institution we know. It became a symbol of freedom and popular government because in criminal cases it seemed to protect an accused person against arbitrary punishment by people in power. This function it still performs, and the fact that it gives this protection will ensure its continuance in democratic communities permanently in spite of the attempts constantly renewed to abolish it.

Evidently in civil suits like the one between John and Richard here described, the function of protection against arbitrary exercise of power disappears, and we are left with an institution which is not particularly well adapted to perform the task assigned to it.

The task of the jury is to determine the facts, just as the judge's task is to decide points of law. The difference between law and fact seems a simple and easy one, and in many situations it presents few problems. It is often, however, extremely difficult, all the more so because there are legal rules which assume the existence of facts without proof of them.

In the case of John against Richard, what is a question of law and what a question of fact is not particularly hard to decide. But the particular question of fact involved is one of the most difficult of questions. It resolves itself into determining whether, under all the circumstances of the case, once the jury has made up its mind what the circumstances were, Richard has acted with proper care. Just what is proper care is something for which one cannot make rules. And the result must be that each member of the jury will put himself in Richard's place and ask himself whether, if he acted as Richard did, would he feel that he had been careful. But if he follows the judge's instructions, he will have to do more. He will have to put himself in John's place and ask himself whether, if he had acted as John did, he would have been guilty of even slight carelessness.

The judge's instructions or "charge" to the jury will present the law on the subject of negligence, as it has been developed in that particular jurisdiction, chiefly by decided cases. It will be fairly complicated, and only the barest outline of the law has so far been given. This charge will be given orally, and the jury must try to remember all that has been said. The jury may take notes and sometimes ask for further instructions on points of detail, but it is only rarely, and certainly not as a matter of right, that the judge will give them his entire charge in writing, although this would seem an obvious advantage.

The jury need give no reason for finding, that is, determining the issue, for one or the other, and there is nothing to show whether they have paid the least attention to the judge's instructions. Although thousands of people have in a period of ten years served on juries, we have extremely little authentic or reliable information on what goes on in a jury room. The verdict may have been determined by a general feeling of sympathy with John as an injured man, whether he was negligent or not. The jury may have discovered that Richard is insured or is much better off than John, although they are warned by the court that such matters are wholly irrelevant. Indeed, an actual effort is made to prevent the fact that Richard is insured from reaching the jury at all, an effort that, as we can guess, is generally quite unsuccessful.

Or the jury may have been impressed by John's or Richard's appearance. If on the basis of that impression they decide whether John or Richard is telling the truth, they are acting within their legal functions. Where witnesses contradict each other, it is the jury's task to decide which is to be believed, and doubtless a casual group of twelve persons can do this as well as it could be done. But even if it is a mere prejudice in favor of a person acting or talking like Richard or John, there is no way to prevent this prejudice from determining the verdict.

The verdict does not end the trial. The end of the trial is the judgment of the court based on the verdict. The losing party will undoubtedly ask to have the verdict set aside and a new trial ordered, or even for a judgment in spite of the verdict. It is only in extremely rare cases that this request will be granted. It will only be granted if the verdict was plainly and clearly against the evidence. It will not be granted merely because the judge, who has heard the evidence as well as the jury, has reached a wholly different conclusion about who was negligent in this case.

While the request to set aside the verdict is granted only in very rare instances, it is not uncommon for the court to reduce, rarely to increase, the damages to which John, if he has won the verdict, is entitled. These damages are not wholly a mere matter of calculation. They are in part purely a matter of arithmetic so far as medical expenses and loss of earnings are concerned. But John has a right to claim something beyond this for the pain and suffering caused him, and this amount the jury must estimate without the aid of arithmetic. Nor will the court disturb this estimate unless it is absurdly excessive or inadequate.

This is the end of the trial, but not quite the end of the case. It is possible to appeal. These appeals in civil cases may suspend final judgment for a long while. The majority of cases are not appealed. The majority of appeals are rejected. But until the appeal is decided, or until the time for appeal has expired, we cannot tell whether John has established his right to damages or not.

The length of time between the offense and the final determination of the case in criminal trials will be referred to in the following sections. In civil, that is, noncriminal cases, this interval is likely to be even greater than in criminal matters. That is partly due to the press of business and the insufficient number of appellate judges. Partly, however, it is due to the opportunities still present in appeal procedure to gain delay after delay and to postpone final decision for an unconscionable time. Efforts to reform this situation are more and more successful. The cases of litigation that last for more than a generation, of which there were several in the seventeenth, eighteenth, and early nineteenth centuries, are practically impossible to-day.

A CRIMINAL TRIAL

The trial which we have been following is in a much simplified form, a civil trial, perhaps the commonest example of civil trial. It will end in a judgment that Richard owes John nothing or that he owes him a specified sum of money. What John will do with his judgment is to try to execute it, which in this case has none of the gruesome connotations of the word. It means simply he will attempt to find property belonging to Richard which can be sold to satisfy the judgment. If he finds none, nothing can be done about it, since he cannot have Richard arrested or summarily ordered to pay the judgment. The judgment simply declares that Richard owes this amount, and this obligation of Richard's cannot be again drawn in question unless the higher court reverses the judgment. But that is as far as the judgment goes. It declares the obligation and no more.

It is a different matter in a criminal trial. In many respects the form of a criminal trial is like a civil one. In fact, the two types of trial were not distinguished in early law. Just as in a suit between John and Richard there is a plaintiff and a defendant, so in criminal trials the Crown is the plaintiff in England, and the People or the State or the Commonwealth is the plaintiff in the United States.

The plaintiff is represented by a lawyer just as the defendant is, only in this case the lawyer is a public official, generally called the district attorney, and popularly known by the abbreviation of D.A. In England and in many of our states, the prosecution cannot proceed in the case of felonies or serious misdemeanors, unless the grand jury, a body of twenty-three men sitting permanently for at least a month, and sometimes for an entire year, brings an accusation, an indictment which takes the place of the complaint in a civil suit.

In indictments the utmost precision formerly was required. To meet the ingenuity of lawyers, greater and greater complexity of form was developed, and until very recently it grew into a curiously involved document indeed. But we give here an indictment in a modern form, which itself indicates how much must have been done in the way of simplifying and clarifying even that part of the law in which lawyers are wont to be most tenacious of traditional forms.

The Grand Jury of the County of Kings, by this indictment, accuses the defendant of the crime of murder in the first degree, committed as follows:

The defendant on March 1, 1921, in the County of Kings, wilfully, feloniously and of malice aforethought, shot and killed Jane Roe with a revolver.

In some states, while the grand jury still functions, it has lost a great deal of its importance, since the district attorney can begin the case with a simple "information" which does as well as the indictment. But whether it is an information or an indictment, it must describe the act which is charged against the accused as a crime, with great particularity, and if it is incorrect in any important detail, the accused cannot be found guilty, no matter what other criminal acts incidentally appear from the testimony at the trial. He has either done what the indictment or information charges him with, or he must be acquitted.

After being accused, the defendant will be arrested. He has a right to be brought at once before a magistrate, which in our system generally means a judge of inferior rank. The magistrate must examine the accused to determine not whether he is guilty but whether there is enough evidence against him to justify ordering a trial. After all, the indictment is merely an assertion. If the district attorney cannot satisfy the magistrate that he will have enough evidence to convince a jury, the magistrate will order the prisoner discharged, which would not prevent a new indictment and a new arrest whenever the prosecutor thinks he has a better case than he had before.

The accused on examination may by his own statements indicate that there might well be a case against him when it comes to trial. These statements are wholly voluntary. He need say nothing at all. Or else he may waive this examination before the magistrate altogether, and declare his willingness to go to trial before a judge and jury at a time which under the Constitution should be as soon as it conveniently can be. Until the trial, the accused may demand to be freed temporarily on bail, except in the case of a capital crime, like murder or treason or any other crime punishable by death. Bail is a constitutional right, and it is further provided in the Constitution that the bail must not be excessive, since if the amount is obviously beyond reason, the right to bail is valueless.

The examination before the magistrate is the first time the accused has been heard at all. When the grand jury considered the indictment, they had before them only the prosecutor and the witnesses he intended to summon to the trial, or some of them. In fact, the grand jury normally will consider nothing except what the prosecutor presents to them, since he is their legal adviser. The accused has no access to the grand jury at all.

In England, when the person is arrested, he is formally warned that anything he says will be taken down in writing and used against him at his trial. This warning is no longer necessary in the United States and is as a matter of fact somewhat uncommon. But in all common law countries, he is assumed to have the privilege of saying nothing. He need not incriminate himself, and if he does or if he confesses, the law sternly demands that his incriminating statements or his confession must be entirely voluntary and must not be the result of coercion, or torture, or be elicited by promise of leniency.

Unfortunately for our professions and protestations in the matter, as well as in spite of the clear mandate of the law, it is notorious that persons arrested for crime frequently are subjected to pressure to make them confess or to get from them evidence damaging to their case. Prisoners are often held by the police for an appreciable time before they are brought before a magistrate, and in nonbailable offenses, they are very much under the control of the police and the prosecution.

It is impossible to shut our eyes to the fact that this coercion in many instances takes the form of torture, which is only in degree different from the torture used in the Middle Ages and continued in Continental Europe until relatively recently. A special name has been found in popular speech for this type of illegal coercion. It is called the third degree. There is credible testimony that it often takes the form of savage beating. Even if it takes the form of keeping the accused awake for continuous questioning over periods of twenty-four and even forty-eight hours, it does not cease to be an atrocious misuse of power which ought never to have received the half-ashamed tolerance of the public.

It is a matter of fact that the notorious inadequacy of our police methods first occasioned the use of the third degree and then extended it. The inadequacy of our police is less to be charged to the police themselves than to the public. Our police are in far too many instances sufficient neither in number nor in training for their tasks, nor are they well enough paid to attract the sort of men that police work needs. It is encouraging to be able to state that the situation has improved vastly in recent years, but great strides still have to be taken before we reach standards already attained elsewhere. And these standards can easily be attained without sacrificing any of the guaranties of personal liberty on which our particular system of political organization is based.

Once the trial begins, the procedure is much like that of a civil trial. But selecting a jury is much more difficult. Both sides have the right of challenging a certain number of prospective jurymen without giving any reason, and any juryman who can be shown to be biased for or against the accused will be excused by the court. It often takes many days to select a jury in an important case, especially one that has been much discussed in the newspapers.

Otherwise, the process of summoning witnesses, examining and cross-examining them is the same in both types of procedure. Since the issue involves such serious consequences, objections to the competence and relevance of the questions are much more frequent and are likely to be more hotly contested than in civil trials.

The matter of "the burden of proof" has already been mentioned. A sharp distinction is made between this burden in the two kinds of trials. In civil trials, it is merely necessary to have the balance of probability in favor of one side or another. The plaintiff must prove his case, and if he fails altogether to do so, his claim will be dismissed without calling on the defendant at all. But if both sides have given all the testimony they possess, the jury will be instructed to find for the party that on the whole seems to have more in its favor.

In criminal trials, however, it is declared that to convict the accused the proof must be "beyond a reasonable doubt." This is based on the presumption of innocence, to which reference has already been made.

Modern historians of law have analyzed the presumption of innocence very carefully and have found that it does not furnish quite the sort of protection which popular speech assigns to it. In practice, if casual statements of jurymen can be relied on, it does not help the accused very much. It has been half-cynically declared that it is nonsense to say that a person accused is presumed to be innocent when a grand jury has already declared that he is probably guilty. And it may be that the attitude of jurymen is described correctly by the apocryphal story of the juryman who, on hearing of the presumption from the court, retorted, "If he's innocent, how does he come to be here?"

What the presumption of innocence or proof beyond a reasonable doubt amounts to is therefore something less than what the words seem to mean. The court will in a criminal case give the jury careful instruction on this very point, and while these instructions will vary with the instructing judge, they will in the main seek to enforce in the jury's mind the duty of being surer in a criminal case than in a civil case before they find against the defendant, in this instance, the accused. It is hard for the jury to estimate degrees of proof and hard for the court to explain them. He can remind them, however, that the kind of inner conviction that might justify conduct in the ordinary affairs of life would not be enough in a criminal case, where so much depends on their verdict. They need not seek to imagine farfetched and fantastic situations under which the accused might be innocent. On the contrary, they would be justified in finding him guilty if he could not be innocent except by imagining such highly unusual and improbable circumstances.

The power of a criminal jury is greater than that of a civil jury. Their verdict is always a "general verdict." They find the accused guilty or not guilty, and they give no reasons. If they find him not guilty, that is the absolute end of the case. The prosecutor cannot move to have the verdict set aside, nor can he appeal. That is due to the constitutional rule that no one may be "twice put in jeopardy for the same offense." Even if it should be proved that the jury had been bribed, or even if the accused later confessed the crime or boasted of it, nothing could be done about it.

In many crimes there are "degrees." This is especially the case in murder, where there is murder in the first degree and in the second degree, and where there is even a third degree, usually called manslaughter. The punishment for second-degree murder and for manslaughter is less than for murder in the first degree. The jury is perfectly aware of this fact, and since in any case of homicide, it can bring in a verdict of guilty of any degree it chooses, it can determine not only whether the accused is guilty but what punishment he shall receive, and can do so despite the careful discrimination which the judge's charge makes between the degrees as a matter of law.

Because the jury in criminal cases is the real arbiter of life and death, of freedom and liberty, and because the jury's verdict of acquittal cannot be set aside or reversed on appeal, the function of advocates in criminal cases much more decidedly takes the form of eloquent appeal than is the case before a civil jury. The custom of using every form of impassioned oratory in the final address to the jury is the one that gives criminal trials an especially dramatic character and looms even larger in fictional accounts of such trials than is the case in fact. There is a marked decrease in recent times in the importance attached to this type of eloquence, but it still plays a large part, and the public is more likely to know the names of advocates famous for their eloquence than of lawyers distinguished in the profession for their skill and learning in the law.

The jury in criminal cases must be unanimous whether for acquittal or conviction. If it cannot agree, it reports its disagreement to the court and will be discharged. This does not release the defendant, who may be tried again and even a third and fourth time if the following juries fail to agree. It is likely, however, after a second disagreement and almost certainly after a third disagreement that the prosecutor will come to the conclusion that there is no prospect of a conviction and will have the prisoner released. Subsequent rearrest and trial are possible but highly unlikely.

The rule of unanimity formerly governed civil trials as well as criminal and still does in England, in the federal courts, and in many states. In a number of states, on the other hand, it has been abandoned for civil trials and has been replaced by the requirement of a two-thirds or three-quarters majority. From time to time, an effort is made to make the same changes in criminal trials. This, however, would probably be unconstitutional if it permitted conviction by two-thirds instead of by a unanimous jury. Whether acquittal by a two-thirds vote would be unconstitutional is more doubtful. It is hard to see how the question could be raised. The rule that the jury must be unanimous in an acquittal as well as in a conviction has always seemed harsh and is in fact extremely hard to justify.

Naturally, most persons convicted of crimes appeal. There is a popular belief that the higher courts go out of their way to reverse judgments and do so on the basis of futile and silly technicalities, such as misspelling of names, or the omission of some phrase in the complaint, or a slight and insubstantial error in the trial. It is quite true . . . [as can be seen in original book] that courts until quite recently did lay stress on these technicalities and sometimes did reverse cases because of them. But at no time did this happen in the majority of instances. And within the last generation, statutes have specifically required courts to affirm a judgment, even if errors were made in the trial, unless these errors could be shown to be substantial and likely to have rendered the trial unfair.

This is particularly the case in criminal appeals. Whatever was once the situation, reversals of criminal convictions are now very rare indeed, and must be based on really important errors committed in the trial to the prejudice of the defendant. At no time may the prosecution appeal if the accused is acquitted.

DELAYS OF JUSTICE

The foregoing description of what actually happens at a trial inevitably raises the question whether this complicated and formal method is the best way of going about it and whether a better way could not easily be found. Any reflection will show that some procedure is necessary. But is our particular procedure necessary?

The attack on our procedure is based on its uncertainty, its expense, its length, its employment of terms and devices which are remote from those of everyday life, and so far as the jury is concerned on the complete and fundamental inadequacy of the jury as a method of determining facts.

The fact that the outcome of a lawsuit is necessarily uncertain has serious consequences for the law. A person who has what seems to him an incontrovertible claim, or who receives a preposterous and unjust demand, is strongly tempted to avoid a suit at law at any cost, no matter how just he feels his position to be, unless the property is large. It will take time; it will interfere with his affairs; it will cost him some money whether he wins or loses. And the terms win and lose are significant, since they represent the way in which a lawsuit appears to most peaceful citizens, that is, as a game of chance in which one or the other of the contestants has an equal chance of being successful. Both the purpose and the effect of legal procedure is thus completely frustrated, and we find intensified the unhealthy situation of suspicion and hostility to everything that is associated with the law.

One thing, however, is clear. The occasions on which a totally unjust claim is made or a totally just one refused are rare. In the great majority of cases, people fulfill their obligations as a matter of course and, one may say, as a matter of habit. Social and commercial intercourse would be impossible if that were not the case, and social and commercial intercourse does in fact exist in our communities. But what also happens is that the opinions of persons in controversies about what is wholly and completely just are inevitably colored, both by their interest in the matter and by matters which by their nature are known to only the person affected. This applies particularly to those many situations in which the intentions of the parties are integral parts of the facts on which legal claims are based, or in which the meaning attached to words used is in issue.

In such cases, however crystal clear the justice of the matter appears to either party, there is an inevitable uncertainty when a third person, who is wholly dissociated from either side, must be convinced of its justice. Such a third person is a judge or jury. Obviously, there is no way in which a person can be assured that he rather than his adversary will persuade a court, and the uncertainty of which men complain in these extremely common cases is the uncertainty that is part of the nature of the human mind and the complexity of social relations. No system of law could possibly remove it.

This assumes good faith on both sides. But there are instances in which this good faith is lacking, and in which the complaint that a plainly unjust claim has been allowed by the court or a plainly just one rejected is well founded. The fact that this is relatively rare affords little consolation to the person to whom it happens. No means of surely detecting falsehood have ever been devised, and there is no present prospect that such means will be discovered. That the court will sometimes err and take a lie for the truth and the truth for a lie is an inevitable incident in human society. And that the result is harm suffered by an innocent man is equally inevitable. Only a marked increase in personal and social morality will decrease the number of these instances.

If there is no way to remedy the uncertainty of the law, the same cannot be said for those objections to legal procedure which are based on its expense and its length. The cost of obtaining justice even in the simplest matters is one of the oldest grievances. Throughout history, it has been repeated with increasing bitterness and with greater bitterness in highly organized than in unorganized societies.

The expense of litigation has often been ascribed to the excessively large number of persons—lawyers, court officials, clerks, recorders, and the like—who are in part responsible for the fact that litigation is expensive. So far as attorneys are concerned, however, it is at least as likely that a diminution in numbers will create, as they have created in the past, a monopoly which is likely rather to increase costs than to reduce them.

For persons of small means, the fact that litigation, which is necessarily uncertain in its results, is far more expensive than it need be is beyond denial. At the present day, earnest efforts to remedy this abuse have successfully established small claims courts, in which claims for sums such as fifty dollars or less can be litigated quickly at a nominal fee without the intervention of lawyers. Other reforms have fixed the fees which can be demanded by lawyers in common types of litigation, such as those arising out of industrial accidents or in the probating of wills. It is on the whole no longer a fact that litigation is prohibitively expensive, and if other objections could have been met so readily, the cost of a suit at law can hardly be taken as a serious grievance in the United States.

The same cannot quite be said for the time spent in litigation, outside of the small claims courts already mentioned. It is true that compared with litigation in older times recent litigation has been substantially expedited. Undoubtedly much more could be done, and the recurrent reforms in procedure have this goal in mind more than any other.

The fact that criminal trials are likely to be long affairs, has been the occasion of some of the sharpest criticism of our procedure. The English practice is contrasted with that of the United States. In England, it is not at all unusual, even in murder cases of great notoriety, to have the case begun within a month after the offender is arrested. The trial rarely lasts more than a few days. If there is an appeal, it will generally be decided within a month, and execution will follow shortly after.

Against this in the United States, the person accused in a murder case is rarely put to trial within six months of the offense; the trial may last several weeks; the appeal is not likely to be decided within six months; and execution will not follow for as much as a year thereafter. So in the case of Bruno Richard Hauptmann, the arrest took place on September 18, 1934, and the trial began on January 2, 1935. Hauptmann was convicted on February 13, 1935, and executed on April 3, 1936.

That these delays are not necessary may be seen in the fact that in 1901 in the case of Czolgosz, the assassin of President McKinley, the trial took two days, and Czolgosz was electrocuted within two months of the death of his victim. Similarly, when Mayor Cermak was shot in the attempt to kill President Roosevelt in 1933, the assassin Zangara was even more speedily convicted and executed. In neither case was there an appeal. To be sure, the nature of the crime was such that public sentiment would not have tolerated the use of dilatory or technical devices, and evidence of mental incompetence, which seemed available, would have been considered a pure technicality.

In this demand for speedy justice, there is probably at work the vindictiveness which the general public feels in the case of an atrocious crime like murder. The normal identification is with the victim. But a part in this is also played by the public sense of insecurity. The crime has imperiled this security, and a quick elimination of the offender has the psychological effect of minimizing if not eliminating the danger.

Chapter XXII

THE PLACE OF GOVERNMENT IN THE SCHEME OF THINGS

[IN the preceding chapters we have examined the structure and operation of the governmental machine; it is now time to examine the nature of the load it pulls. Government is not an end in itself; it is an instrument for the accomplishment of certain common purposes of the community. Its character is determined not only by its organization but also by what it does, and to-day it is doing more than ever before.

Whether the organization of government is democratic or autocratic, whether rule is by majority or by dictator, a world-wide trend is observable. The role of government is constantly expanding. The load it is pulling is getting bigger and bigger. The reasons for this are many, but among the most important is the rapid transformation of our society from a rural agricultural to an urbanized industrial one. If we were still living under eighteenth-century conditions, we would have little need for many of the things now being done by government. Slum clearance is essentially a problem of an industrial and urbanized community; the protection of the rights of labor is not of primary importance in an agrarian nation; the question of old age insecurity is primarily a problem of urban industrial workers. If each family lived on its own farm, the simple activity of securing a pure water supply would be a concern of each family. When millions of us live in small areas, it becomes a concern of the whole group and government takes over the task.

Advances in science and technology have forced the government to assume many jobs never before considered as properly within its sphere. When evidence was obtained that yellow fever was carried by mosquitoes, control of these insects became an essential function of government. When we became aware that impure milk was an important factor in the spread of such diseases as typhoid fever and tuberculosis, we insisted that government regulate the production and sale of milk. One only needs to examine the relationships of the radio, the automobile, the railroad to the community to see still further tasks for which government has had to assume responsibility.

In other words the American people no longer believe that that government is best which governs least. More and more they are inclined to look upon government as a huge service agency and to judge that government best that serves best. This must not be allowed, however, to lead uncritically to the view that the government can and should undertake every kind of activity. But this raises the question, discussed by Professor Groves, "What is the place of government in the scheme of things?"]

No. 82

THE PLACE OF GOVERNMENT IN THE SCHEME OF THINGS [1]

by Harold M. Groves

INTRODUCTION

MOST treatises on public finance begin with some discussion of public expenditures and of government's place in the scheme of things. The relevance of this subject is obvious: if governments were not so ambitious, the tax problem could be relatively simple. Moreover, the proper role of government is of vital consequence in postwar policy generally. Until recently, at least, nearly every newspaper brought us reports from Europe of further trends to the left—and toward more government. Our own people . . . are none too sure of themselves. Thus an exploration of the sphere of government seems a fitting task. . . .

There are many possible approaches to a study of public expenditures and the scope of government. One is to consider the effects of public outlay on such aspects of the economy as production, consumption, and the distribution of income. Another is to explain the many classifications into which public expenditure can be divided (such as outlay for self-liquidating projects versus that for those not self-liquidating). A further approach is to analyze the principle of maximum advantage, which tells us that governments should undertake what they can do more efficiently than private individuals or groups. A still different tack is to explain the causes for the skyrocket advance in public expenditure. Here one observes the voracious appetite of the war-making function and concludes that the really big prizes for the economy-minded lie in the field of international relations; but he also observes that while the state was once conceived to serve mainly as our policeman and warrior, it is now expected to play the role of cooperative, promoter, equalizer, and balance wheel. This leads into the approach here chosen, that of examining the role of the state. Even then one has alternatives: he might delve into political science and philosophy and wrestle with the definition and concept of the state; or he can lead off from an economic

---

[1] Harold M. Groves, *Trouble Spots in Taxation* (Princeton: Princeton University Press, 1948), pp. 26-50. Reprinted by permission of the publisher. The footnotes in the original version are omitted here.

angle and examine the role which the state should play in the economy. Being an economist, the author will take the latter of these alternatives.

One's view of the state is coupled so closely with his general economic philosophy that it is possible to consider the two together. Perhaps we can best proceed, therefore, by sketching several economic philosophies of life— and, of course, of the role of government. They are based on different views of what is required to make an economic system function satisfactorily. No claim is made that these categories cover the ground exhaustively. It is recognized that there are many shades of opinion within each philosophy and that an individual can espouse more than one simultaneously.

DEEMPHASIS OF CONCERN FOR ECONOMIC VALUES

Said John Maynard Keynes: "The economic problem, the struggle for subsistence . . . has been . . . the primary, most pressing problem . . . not only of the human race, but of the whole of the biological kingdom from the beginnings of life in its most primitive forms." There are many, however, who feel that man's preoccupation with wealth-getting—especially beyond the point of subsistence—is unworthy and corrupting. There have been many critics, both at home and abroad, of the so-called overemphasis of materialism in the United States. Thus, Lin Yutang depicts us as ruled by the slogan: "The greatest goods to the greatest number." André Siegfried went much further to say· "In America, the dominant force that is threatening to carry everything before it, Protestant, Catholic, and Jew, is the obsession for tangible and material accomplishment." "It is a materialistic society, organized to produce things rather than people, with output set up as a god." And our own Dorothy Thompson rounds off with: "The world envies our technical and scientific achievements but no country in the world envies or admires the kind of society we have."

These criticisms, though aimed at the United States, could be applied with equal validity to Communist Russia.

The philosopher Henry Thoreau was convinced that poverty, at least voluntary poverty, is not incompatible with the good life and that many spirits are imprisoned by the things they own.

The critics of this alleged overemphasis of economic concern advocate more attention for individuals and less for institutions. Real reform, they hold, must come the Chinese way—by cultivating the moral quality of the individual. Social reform without individual reform is likely to prove a mirage. Says Koestler: "The Second and Third Internationals got into the blind alley because they fought capitalism in its own terms of reference, and were unable to ascend to the spiritual climate the longing for which we feel in our bones."

There is undoubtedly much to be said for the view that a nation can become too prosperous for the good of its own soul. Satisfactory living is more likely to be built upon moral rules and promises faithfully kept than upon economic achievement. The blessings of mass production are very considerably overrated! Prophets who cry out against "the production of goods, more goods, more things, mountains of things—to what purpose?" deserve to be heard. The least we can do in response is to improve the quality of our consumption. *What* we produce should concern us as well as *how much*. Here the government enters, since "socialized consumption" is a main avenue for improving our utilization of wealth.

It seems unlikely, however, that we shall pass up an economy of abundance and further conquests of nature on the ground that they might prove demoralizing. We must somehow learn to live with plenty. Also there is the grim fact of widespread poverty in the midst of much abundance. This poverty, too, is demoralizing. Every social worker knows that along with the bad housing and malnutrition which mark poverty go crime, delinquency, bad health, perverted views, and other ugly social consequences. Economic progress is only one weapon for attacking poverty but it is the one that is least controversial.

LAISSEZ FAIRE AND INDIVIDUALISM

The second philosophy to be considered is based on the view that the economic world is a self-regulating system kept in order by a balance of forces as are the heavenly bodies in the physical universe. Free competition and supply and demand are the economic equivalents of mass and gravitation. Tinkering with the handiwork of Providence is likely to prove harmful. Economic laws yield a natural brand of justice; the system tends to distribute to each of the factors of production the amount of wealth it creates. By his pursuit of self-interest the individual unwittingly serves the public good.

This laissez-faire doctrine was so well established in 1850 that it could be prescribed without qualification or apology by the Society for Promoting Christian Knowledge. The endorsement included, of course, the idea that men do the greatest service to the public when they are thinking of nothing but their own gain. This identification of economics with self-seeking, John Ruskin attacked as a libel upon the businessman. Perhaps the ultimate in the self-interest doctrine was reached by the Supreme Court of Michigan when, in the case of *Dodge v. Ford,* it sustained the view of minority stockholders that reducing prices and increasing wages is philanthropy rather than business and is beyond the pale of legitimate business policy.

Related to the laissez-faire philosophy, but stemming from different roots, is the view of life that may be described as "rugged individualism." One root of this doctrine can be found in Herbert Spencer's adaptation of Darwinism to economics. Growth and progress in both natural and social realms are a matter of survival of the fittest. This view was swallowed whole by Professor William Sumner of Yale, who taught that "without inequality the law of the survival of the fittest could not operate."

Perhaps a more enduring root of individualism can be traced to Puritanism. In the Puritan view, poverty was to be condemned rather than pitied or relieved; a sound whipping was an appropriate punishment for incorrigible idlers. The rich must regard their wealth as a stewardship and avoid gain at the expense of others; if they met this test they were to be honored. *Poor Richard's Almanack* extols the economic virtues as the Puritans saw them. Even to-day, success stories make excellent magazine copy. Orison Swett Marden sold his theme of how to get ahead in the world in many books, many editions, and millions of copies. One of the most outstanding and indigenous of America's intellectuals, Ralph Waldo Emerson, is best known for his essay on self-reliance.

The views of the laissez-faire proponents and the rugged individualists are vulnerable enough. The laissez-faire doctrine took a beating during the thirties when we were confronted by a deep depression which seemed only aggravated by a do-nothing policy. The Spencerian approach has been attacked by John Dewey, among others, on the ground that the unfit may be the anti-social rather than the physically weak or the economically dependent. The businessman often survives by fraud and chicanery rather than by able administration. The Puritan creed gave scant if any recognition to the view that the strong have obligations to the weak—a view increasingly stressed as the conscience of humanity becomes more sensitive.

Yet there surely is something in the old individualism that is worth preserving. Perhaps it is the element which holds that the individual is the object of all social endeavor and only in the degree to which he can develop creatively is a system successful. In these days of much paternalism and statism, when a full stomach for all, however attained, is so frequently exalted as the end product of reform, it is well to recall that it is better to help an individual help himself than only to help an individual.

Moreover, it seems unwise to conclude that we have said farewell entirely to laissez-faire. The idea that economic forces can operate with benevolent results, unchecked or unaided by extensive government policing, does seem indeed to have failed the test of experience. However, a coordinated system regulated to follow the design of political leaders may not prove a panacea either. In the second next phase of economic development, at least, we may concentrate our efforts on the achievement of a more successful automatic sphere. We may find, as Walter Lippmann predicts, that government can become too large to be well managed by finite men and that the efforts of intelligent statesmanship once more will be devoted to limiting the role of government. Instead of attempting to reform institutions we may try to develop wisdom in individuals and groups. Certainly it is high time that private business developed a new type of leadership with some understanding and appreciation of the public interest. There are signs that this leadership has begun to appear. It is significant that even Karl Marx envisioned a final stage of evolution in which the state was destined to "wither away," and James Peter Warbasse, intellectual of the cooperative movement, came from a different angle to the same conclusion.

After the above has been said, however, it is still in order to applaud the passing of unbridled individualism. The extremists of laissez faire, such as Herbert Spencer, probably did more to pave the way for socialism and economic planning than the proponents of these philosophies.

THE ANTIMONOPOLY PHILOSOPHY

The antimonopolists are somewhat akin to the individualists but they have a much keener appreciation of the need for positive governmental action to preserve effective competition. Judged by the degree of change they advocate and by their sympathy for the underdog, some of them might be labeled "radical." There is a wide range among them, however, in this respect.

It is said that the soul of a nation can be perceived in its choice of heroes. Perhaps the American statesmen who are honored and revered above all others are Lincoln and Jefferson. The former embodied the American view of the dignity of the common man. Jefferson is identified with that potent strain in American thought and tradition which might be called the antimonopoly philosophy.

Above all else, Jefferson exalted the rural aspect of American life. He had a profound distrust of everything urban including the working class of the cities. Here certainly, he was at the opposite pole from Karl Marx, who distrusted everything rural, referred to farmers as "yokels," and looked forward to the industrialization of agriculture as a prelude for his social revolution. Said Jefferson: "Those who labor in the earth are the chosen people of God, if ever He had a chosen people, whose breasts He has made his peculiar deposit for substantial and genuine virtue."

Jefferson also gave strong support for the strain of anarchy in American thought. It is to this patron saint of liberals that we owe the slogan: "That government is best which governs least."

The antimonopolists fear centralized power, whether exercised by private or public authority. They hold that rich and democratic living requires small and autonomous units whether of school, city or business. They seek a system that aspires to abundant living through the spontaneity of its constituent parts. They may dislike and distrust inequalities and the "money power" quite as much as the socialist, but they are also profoundly skeptical of the latter's propensity for singleness of organization. They see safety and the preservation of values in a plural universe—the maintenance of alternatives. As one of them puts it: "When I can no longer tell my employer to go to hell and know I can always find another, my kind of a world will have disappeared." For the antimonopolists the federal system is admirably adjusted to the needs of a democratic society; it is a great achievement, one of the greatest "ever struck off by the mind of man." But in our day the central government tends to encroach upon "home rule" mainly because it must control business, which itself has been allowed to grow "too big." Big business has necessitated big labor as well as big government, and the combination seems to be leading us straight to omnipotent statism.

A classic statement of the antimonopolists' fear of bigness is that of Professor Carver:

> If, without the slightest change of character or disposition . . . (the common house cat) were suddenly enlarged to the dimensions of a tiger, we should at least want her to be muzzled and to have her claws trimmed, whereas if she were to assume the dimensions of a mastodon, I doubt if any of us would want to live in the same house with her. And it would be useless to argue that her nature had not changed, that she was just as amiable as ever, and no more carnivorous than she always had been. Nor would it convince us to be told that her productivity had greatly increased and that she would now catch more mice in a minute than she formerly did in a week. We should be afraid . . . that in her large-scale mouse catching she might not always discriminate between us and the mice. . . .

Similarly bigness of a corporation is definitely a matter for the law to take into account.

The growth of chain stores is ordinarily either applauded or accepted with equanimity by a socialist. An antimonopolist may find such a development quite alarming. Justice Brandeis, in his classic dissent in the Florida chain store tax case, expressed the opinion that a legislature may not unreasonably view this centralization of the distribution business as a menace, converting independent tradesmen into clerks and sapping "the resources, the vigor and the hope of the smaller cities and towns."

The antimonopolist rejects the contention that there is an inevitable trend toward concentration in business. He believes that the modern corporation has been allowed to go "hog wild," with no adequate check as to financial structure, business practices, or size. The "trusts" did not evolve out of a natural order; many of them were fostered by discriminations that could and should have been prevented. The government's antitrust division has always suffered from malnutrition, and the courts have given it only half-hearted support. The fact that the same administration could offer N.R.A. and Thurman Arnold in close succession is evidence of the government's vacillation on this vital issue. "The so-called failure of capitalism (of the free enterprise system, of free competition)," wrote Henry Simons, "may reasonably be interpreted as primarily a failure of the political state in the discharge of its minimum responsibilities under capitalism. This view may suggest reasons for skepticism with reference to the currently popular schemes for curing all our ills."

The antimonopolist pins his hopes on such measures as reduced tariffs, federal incorporation, more vigorous anti-trust enforcement, and perhaps taxes on size. Improvement of the charters governing private corporations is regarded as an aspect of the economy at once highly neglected and extremely promising.

Although the antimonopolist would like more competition in business, he may also concede that competition is far from a "dead duck." Private enterprise is not hopelessly monopolistic. Indeed, many will argue that competition was never so lively as now. It has been furthered by the development of alternative products. Besides actual current-price competition there is service and quality competition, in addition to potential competition. It is argued that without some check on competition, businesses with high overheads would face chaos. What constitutes "workable competition" under these circumstances has been the subject of much speculation.

The antimonopoly movement has passed its heyday, perhaps, and exercises less influence upon American thought than formerly. Many intellectuals now heap scorn upon it and describe its proponents as reactionaries who would have been liberals had they lived a half century earlier. However, the philosophy is sound in its view that government, along with business, can develop the evils of bigness—arrogance, incoordination, and blindness at the center for the needs at the periphery. It is also sound in its view that there is safety in numbers and richness of living in the spontaneity of men and communities. It remains to be seen if these values are compatible with the equally significant ones of full employment and the progressive elimination of poverty. It is to be fervently hoped that they are. The antimonopoly movement deserves a new birth of vitality.

THE COOPERATIVE MOVEMENT

Many proponents of the antimonopoly movement are also interested in consumer cooperatives. Some socialists, too, favor the cooperative movement. Nevertheless, the movement has a distinct tradition and philosophy of its own. Many cooperators see in it a check on the growth of the state— a means by which an overgrowth of political power and machinery can be avoided.

The cooperative movement is by no means new in this or other countries but it has only recently grown strong enough here to capture more than passing attention. The movement urges consumers to go into business for themselves. On the foundation of numerous grass-roots local ventures, a super-structure of wholesale and manufacturing business can be developed.

Objectives of consumers' cooperation include, of course, protecting the consumer from the waste and abuses of non-cooperative business and from his own ignorance and gullibility. Also included is protection from monopoly. In the United States, the movement, though young, has ventured into the production (directly or under contract) of petroleum products, farm machinery, and tobacco—all monopolistic lines. The movement is also said to be an end in itself—a "way of life."

The cooperative movement lays great stress on the means with which it proposes to accomplish its ends. The means are described as voluntary, peaceful, evolutionary, and democratic. Probably it can truthfully be said that the cooperative movement is the only form of radicalism which involves no social risks whatever.

Perhaps the limitations of the movement are related to this lack of risk. The achievements of cooperation develop slowly, and feverish radicals are likely to feel that reform will not wait so long. Business administration may be simpler and easier under autocratic than under democratic auspices. Quite frequently those most interested in the cooperative movement do not have the capital required for rapid expansion, and even though the movement is mature in Europe, it has made little attempt to invade the heavy industries there. Nevertheless, the cooperative movement appeals to many as the golden mean between the excesses of capitalism on the one hand and the dangers of socialism on the other. The least to be said for the movement is that it provides a valuable alternative for monopoly capitalism. Freedom in no small part consists of the availability of effective alternatives.

If the farm-machinery trust holds up prices and is slow to adopt new ideas, as alleged, let the farmers produce their own tractors and milking machines. If the manufacturers of razor blades deliberately use poor steel in order to sell their wares, let the consumers themselves prove this. If the tobacco trust is knee-deep in unjust enrichment, let the consumers try their hand at producing and distributing cigarettes. Of course, the road is not easy, but one is entitled to hope that not all the courage and skill are on the side of the monopolists. At least, the road for alternative forms of organization should be kept as open as possible.

SOCIALISM

Not all socialists are Marxists, but all have been influenced considerably by the intellectual stimulation and leadership of Karl Marx. We cannot attempt here to explain his famous doctrines: the economic interpretation of history; surplus value; class struggle; growing concentration of industry; increasing severity of crises; progressive misery of the exploited classes; inevitable revolution, with the state falling heir to the important means of production; dictatorship of the proletariat; and ultimate economic democracy with a decreasing role for the state. Very few accept this body of doctrine to-day without qualification: some consciously accept it with qualification; and many more borrow from it unconsciously. One writer sizes up Marx's contribution with the observation that whatever may have been the blind spots in his doctrine, he was "irresistibly right in his prophecy that the civilization of his epoch was built upon the sand." Socialists would add that the foundation has improved little, if any, since his time.

Among the weaknesses and contradictions in present-day capitalism, stressed by socialists, is the unemployment of men and resources. The chronic tendency toward unemployment might be disputed but at least, it is said, the wave motion known as the business cycle represents a cross which capitalism—and only capitalism—has to bear. The only sovereign remedy for unemployment yet devised by the democracies is total war. While we have relied on competition to control prices, the large-scale business corporation has developed and it is the acme of irresponsible power. An attempt to atomize these corporations would be only trying to make the clock run backward. Increasing cynicism and distrust, it is argued, are manifest on all sides. The complications of our uncoordinated economic system and its unheralded gyrations have proved too much for even professional economists to explain, and probably to understand. Monetary and fiscal reforms seeking stabilized full employment are inflationary and opportunistic. Since the early days, at every crisis a host of soft-money cranks have appeared, offering to save a rotten institutional structure by pumping in credit. When will we learn that the patient requires a more fundamental operation?

Defenders of capitalism are frequently unimpressed by these charges. They cite the impressive record of achievement which capitalism has to its credit. Taking the offensive, they point to an alleged blindness of their opponents to the dangers and difficulties in a greatly enlarged political sphere. Here they have on their side the long-standing American distrust of government. They point out that the President and Congress are already overloaded and that the level of personnel manning the elected branches of our federal, state, and municipal governments is none too high. Says Schumpeter: "No responsible person can view with equanimity the consequences of extending the democratic method, that is to say, the sphere of 'politics,' to all economic affairs."

Socialism is, of course, a matter of degree as indicated by the fact that our present economic order is often described as a "mixed economy." Quite possibly evolution may take the form of enlarging the portion of government ownership in the mixture. As attractive precedent for this trend, Sweden is often cited. Anticipating a later discussion, we may observe that a mixed economy of the Swedish type has an important strategic advantage in its control of business cycles. In such an economy, public investment for compensatory purposes may take the form of expansion in the capital and equipment of public industries. A common criticism of self-liquidating public works as a depression measure is that there are not enough prospective works to counteract unemployment. Sweden need have less concern than some other countries on this score. The commonly accepted rule that governments should undertake what they can perform more efficiently than private enterprise is satisfactory only if the term efficiency is construed to include all the social results. Under this rule one can often make a plausible and convincing case for the expansion of government ownership and operation in the area of public utilities and some natural resources.

It is also true that collective ownership is open to a variety of institutional forms. The Tennessee Valley Authority, rather than the post office, might serve as a model of a public corporation. A mixed corporation, with the government exercising a majority vote in the control, has possibilities. These alternatives are not necessarily incompatible with the anti-monopolist's hope of maintaining a pluralistic universe.

The socialists have scored impressive gains in Europe and their program seems much less remote and unattainable in America than it once did. The pragmatic progressive who has constituted the traditional opposition to the *status quo* in this country has never taken to the "isms." But Americans do insist that their economic system shall make progress against the age-old problems of unemployment and poverty. Looking toward the future they will insist on rapid progress, for popular articles on the potentialities of the new technology have taken hold. The typical American now has his fingers crossed regarding the economics of the future. He would prefer progress along familiar roads involving no risk of traditional values. However, if these roads become blocked and lead only to frustration, the socialists might yet have their day.

OVER-ALL PLANNING

There is an alternative to socialism little if any less inviting to the opponents of capitalism and one that might prove more attractive to the American people. It is known as "over-all economic planning." The planners agree with the socialists that steady economic progress is not to be expected from *uncoordinated* private production. However, the socialists are wrong, it is said, in their view that collective ownership is necessary to achieve coordination. Control is the meat of ownership; the government has already helped itself to some of this meat and it can take more. Our economy is impressive in many respects but it lacks direction. Thus, says George Soule: "We have magnificent muscles in our great industrial plants; efficient arteries in our railroads and highways; sensitive nerves in our lines of communication. But we have only a trace of gray matter in our economic cranium." Planning looks moderate but it can have radical implications; what the planners propose to do in effect is to leave the body of private enterprise in Detroit and Pittsburgh but take the soul to Washington. Growing concentration in industry is an open invitation to over-all planning. A large part of the economic system could be brought under control with a very few orders. Let it be shown that "the two hundred" corporations have deliberately chosen to restrict output for their own good and at the expense of the public and the private character of these companies could disappear quickly. Again it may be observed parenthetically that the "wave of the future" may be in the area of mixed control of the corporate institution.

In some respects the planners are considerably more radical than the socialists. When the time is ripe to center all important authority in the federal government, they intend "to act fast." Alfred Bingham, in his advice to planners, observes that "you can't jump over a ditch by a series of short tentative jumps."

Just how far the planners would have to go in achieving coordination is discussed with frankness and discernment by Mrs. Barbara Wootton in her *Freedom Under Planning*. Cultural freedom must and can be preserved. It is possible "to coordinate the time tables of the different railway lines without controlling the topics of conversation inside the carriages." Freedom of choice may also be allowed in consumption and vocation. On the other hand, prices and wages would need to be controlled and labor unions would have to accept this fetter. Mrs. Wootton would be the last to contend that even the lowest income recipients have nothing to lose but their chains. She concedes that the program would require long-term commitments and hopes that all political parties might agree eventually to inaugurate such a step.

The planners in this country are now in full retreat following the death and burial of O.P.A. However, if and when the time comes for another W.P.A. with its wasteful utilization of labor resources, the alternative of planned production of essential goods and services—the "organization principle"—is sure to prove attractive.

PARTIAL PLANNING THROUGH FISCAL AND MONETARY POLICY

Some would draw no distinction between over-all planning and so-called fiscal planning. Others espouse fiscal planning as a means of avoiding wholesale regimentation and at the same time of ensuring adequate employment opportunity. The state, says Sir William Beveridge, is in a different position from private citizens in that it can control *money* rather than be controlled by it.

The economic doctrine of the fiscal-control philosophers is largely the work of John Maynard Keynes. Keynes attacked the traditional doctrine that unemployment is due to excessive wages—to labor "pricing itself out of the market." He also attacked the traditional view that the volume of saving and investment is nicely adjusted by a fluctuating interest rate. Reducing wages during a period of unemployment might aggravate rather than relieve the problem. Automatic changes in the interest rate might not occur nor lead to full employment if they did. Saving and investment will be brought into balance instead, perhaps, through a curtailment of the national income, which in turn affects the ability to save. The real cause of unemployment is the fact that the propensity to consume and invest runs short of the propensity to save. The problem is one of money flow. The real remedy must be found in augmenting either consumption or investment.

However, there are many ways to augment "outlay." Beveridge lists five points at which consumption or investment might be expanded: (1) private investment; (2) private consumption; (3) subsidized private consumption (such as food subsidies); (4) public investment in public business (such as government utilities); (5) socialized consumption (government outlays for public services). In periods of unemployment, outlay might be encouraged by expanded public expenditures financed with deficits; by expanded public expenditures financed by progressive taxes; or by reduced taxes (expenditures remaining constant).

Of course, we must distinguish between cyclical and chronic unemployment. It has long been recognized that fluctuation in outlay for new capital and inventory is one of the factors that generate the ups and downs in business and employment. Many Keynesians, going further, contend that there is a persistent tendency in a rich and highly industrialized country toward oversaving and underinvestment or underconsumption. This so-called stagnant-economy thesis is usually associated with Professor Alvin Hansen, who argues that declining investment is due to a decreasing rate of population growth, the passing of the frontier, a dearth of great new industries, and the increasing ability of business to finance itself by depreciation reserves and reinvested earnings. All of Hansen's fears are belittled by his critics, especially George Terborgh, who argues that population trends and the closing of the frontier are by no means new phenomena nor is there any evidence that industries are more able now than formerly to finance their own needs. As for new industries, no one knows what inventions may be knocking at the door and, moreover, many small innovations may be as effective in absorbing capital as a few large ones.

No doubt there is wisdom to be had from a study of economic history but its lessons are far from apparent and unambiguous. It is argued with plausibility that oversaving and excessive profits caused the depression of 1929 and with equal plausibility that deficit spending, when given a trial during the thirties, was a failure. It is also argued that the late twenties were characterized by overinvestment, that is, by overdevelopment of productive capacities in relation to the prospective market. Of course, we had had severe depressions before, even when income levels were lower and when investment opportunities were apparently more abundant.

The fear of oversaving is based largely on deductive analysis which suggests, at least plausibly, that a static economy could absorb little if any saving. Replacements would appear in the accounts as costs, before net income was totaled. Saving is required to finance an *expansion* of demand and to develop innovations. The innovations also result in some loss of old capital. The rate of innovation may vary to some extent fortuitously, to some extent according to the institutional environment. A rich economy will insist on saving substantially whether or not there is any demand for new capital. The conclusions are: (1) that a dynamic and progressive economy is essential to full employment in a rich country, and (2) that public policy should be set to a mold that either discourages saving or promotes its absorbents. This doctrine is not verified by enough experience or evidence to justify unlimited confidence; but it does have sufficient plausibility to justify a public policy framed accordingly, especially since such policy would be in harmony with other social interests.

Let us return to the problem of coping with the business cycle. Obviously this is a large order and our treatment must necessarily be extremely sketchy. During the twenties the favorite tools of the stabilizers were in the realm of central banking policy—rediscount rates, open-market operations, changing reserve requirements, and the like. The central banks were expected to check booms by making it more difficult for commercial banks to lend, reversing this procedure when times were bad. These tools are still valued and many would make them more effective now by raising reserve requirements substantially and by counting government securities held by banks as reserves. This would help to restore to the federal government its power of control over "credit money." But such controls are much weakened by the fact that private loans now account for only a minor part of the assets of commercial banks.

More popular currently is the proposed use of taxation to check expansion and contraction. Taxation can influence the Keynesian "propensities" in two ways: the general level at which purchasing power is shunted into the treasury will affect the ability to spend and invest; and the distribution of taxes among taxpayers (upper and lower brackets) will affect all the factors—spending, investment, and saving.

Historically, taxation has seldom if ever been used as a device to control business cycles. The policy has been to lower taxes when times were good and revenue easy to raise and then to "get tough" when conditions reversed themselves. Such, with qualifications, was our procedure during the twenties and thirties. Now the proposal is to give the government a compensatory role. It is expected to be optimistic, so to speak, when private business is pessimistic, and vice versa. Some would go only so far as to try to stabilize tax rates, allowing tax yields to fluctuate with cyclical trends. Others recommend the bolder course of applying lower effective rates when the base itself drops.

The ultimate in the conception of taxation as a fiscal-control device has been expressed by Abba P. Lerner as follows: "The purpose of taxation is never to raise money but to leave less in the hands of the taxpayer." "The government can raise all of the money it needs by printing it if the raising of money is the only consideration." Those who suppose that taxation exists to provide a meal ticket for government are simply behind the times!

The idea of using taxation as a countercycle control has not gone unchallenged. There are those, Professor Lutz, for instance, who believe that the budget should be balanced every year or at least that a break-neck effort should be made toward this end. They hold that a cyclical budget, in practice, will be all deficits and no surpluses and that this will inevitably lead to an ever-mounting national debt and inflation. They reject the idea that inflation of prices will wait until we reach full employment.

As previously suggested, the business cycle is the great conundrum of capitalism, and so far we have made little progress in getting it under control. We can afford to reject no device that is at all promising. At the very least, we might try keeping the rates of taxation stable while the tax base fluctuates over the cycle.

In a sense, taxation and public expenditure are but opposite sides of the shield. Instead of or in addition to tax measures to cope with deflation, we could inaugurate public spending or public investment. Compensatory spending or investment encounters the difficulty that unless it is so done as not to shake business confidence, it continually enlarges the deflationary gap with one shovel while it fills in with another. The psychological factors in business recovery are extremely important, and no one stressed this more than John Maynard Keynes. Some of this circular motion was in process, perhaps, during the thirties.

Two things might be done to increase the effectiveness of compensatory spending. One is monetary education; businessmen still remain who are not convinced that it is one thing for the government to go into the red (as a monetary measure) and quite another for a state or individual to do so. The second is to set up a public investment program so creative in character that it can be paid for out of fees and a future improvement in the tax base. This would put the expanding productive debt of the government in the same class with expanding bank loans.

The following ten tenets supported by some Keynesians, either directly or by implication, may be listed in conclusion. The first five seem tenable to the author but he is skeptical of the last five:

1. It is possible for a nation to save too much; that is, to overindulge in thrift.

2. This would mean an obstruction in money flows; quite possibly depression and unemployment; quite certainly a lowering of national income.

3. In a rich and highly developed country, a shortage of markets is likely to be more of a problem in the long run than a shortage of goods. We are much more likely to encounter unemployment relief than rationing.

4. When a tax-rate adjustment is being contemplated, important consideration should be given to its effect on inflation and deflation.

5. Governments from now on will be forced inevitably into the assumption of responsibility for the unemployed; if these governments do not spend beyond their current means during a severe depression in order to promote a revival, they will and should do so anyhow to make life bearable for the unemployed.

6. The relationships between spending, saving, investment, and income are very inelastic and do not change substantially over even long periods of time; oversaving, accordingly, is certain and inevitable except as it is corrected by government action.

7. A proper interpretation of recent economic history leads to the conclusion that the thirties are typical of what we can expect in the future.

8. It is possible and desirable for governments to discount unemployment in advance, so to speak, and thus prevent it from ever appearing.

9. There can be no inflation and rise in prices until our human and other resources are fully employed.

10. One can prove a thesis so completely by deductive logic that he can rest assured thereafter of having all the answers.

CONCLUSION

In concluding this essay, we observe first that the state seems destined to play a very large role in the immediate future, no matter who wins elections. Several economic philosophies of life are competing for adherents. In addition to these is the pragmatic tradition of the American people. It rightly insists that we make rapid progress against the age-old problems of poverty and unemployment but commits itself to no dogma as to how this must be done. The author has indicated his preference for a mixed economy, which leaves a large sphere to self-governing forces (free enterprise plus cooperatives), but he has emphasized that in our day this means a positive program and not a mere abnegation of government. Public ownership and operation in the zone of public utilities and some natural resources are often desirable on direct analysis and may have further advantage as an outlet for compensatory investment. Almost any experimentation, not clearly incompatible with democracy, is preferable to chronic unemployment. Our progress in understanding the business cycle is not a cause for self-congratulation among economists: at present, some of the Keynesian (compensatory) tools are the best we have and should be applied accordingly.

All of this may seem to involve some hedging and compromise and opportunism; but then again it may be common sense. The pragmatic tradition is the dearest and best established of any we have in America.

Chapter XXIII

RAISING THE MONEY FOR GOVERNMENT

[As noted in the preceding chapter, the field of governmental activity is rapidly expanding both in scope and intensity. The remaining chapters of this book are devoted to a consideration of old and new governmental functions. Our concern here, however, is with the relationship of these functions to the problems of public finance. If the people demand schools and highways, policemen and health officers, regulation of business and protection of the consumer, and if these demands on government continue to increase, it is clear that the government must, by some means, raise more money to-morrow than it is securing to-day. If revenues fail to meet proposed expenditures, any of several consequences may follow. It may result in an increase of taxes, either by increasing the rate of taxation or broadening its base. A second possibility is to curtail or reduce the activities of government. A third is to borrow. No magic formula can be found, in spite of the desires of candidates for public office, which will enable government to continue its services and not at the same time force it to continue its programs for the raising of sufficient revenue. The question of taxes is consequently directly related to public policy on governmental activities. The complaint over high taxes cannot be divorced from it.

If we can decide on what we wish government to do for us, and how much this will cost, we have by no means solved our tax problems. Taxation, although the major, is not the sole source of public revenues. Government derives income, for example, from borrowing and from the earnings of its enterprises. Taxation is, however, the most important item on the revenue side of the governmental ledger. If we know how much we wish to spend, and what portion of this sum must come from taxes, we must then determine what kinds of taxes should be levied and which should be avoided. Furthermore we must decide which level of government shall use, exclusively or in conjunction with other units, the various kinds of taxation. Our federal system of government and the number and complex structure of local government units make this latter problem a particularly difficult one in the United States.

There is finally the problem of evaluating the tax structure we now have with reference to the possible demands that may be made on it in the future. If reconstruction or reform is needed, the issue must be faced directly and now. The essays in this chapter throw light on all of these questions of tax policy.]

No. 83

TAXES AND THE TAXPAYER [1]

by Donald B. Marsh

Taxes need not be merely a necessary evil. Many of our fears concerning postwar taxation derive from an ancient view of the functions of a tax system, the truth of which seems at first to be self-evident. We are taxed, so tradition has it, because the government *needs* the money. Taxes can be lowered only by reducing government expenditures. Government borrowing can postpone taxation, but it cannot remove the ultimate necessity of covering the government's expenditures by imposts upon its citizens. In so far as minimum outlays are required, taxes become, on this view, a necessary evil, which results from that other necessary evil, government expenditure.

The literature of taxation provides many exceptions to the last of these propositions. In a *laissez-faire* economy, large government expenditures are *prima facie* evidence of waste. But the broadening of governmental functions, in the social services and elsewhere, has made greater expenditures necessary. One may repudiate social legislation, but otherwise one must put up with the fiscal consequences. Moreover, acceptance of the broader functions of the state has led to the concept of "productive" governmental expenditure. The state becomes a partner in productive processes; and taxes may be more than offset by its contribution.

But this is only part of the case. Taxes may make a contribution in themselves, even apart from the expenditure of the funds. The effects of taxation upon employment, the direction of production, and the distribution of income are major problems in public finance. They were recognized as major problems before the emergence of the modern fiscal view and the theory of "functional finance." But recent discussion has emphasized certain effects of taxation which it is desired to achieve, while the traditional theory was concerned quite often to point out certain effects of taxation which it was desired to avoid. In general, traditional theory set out to discover ways of minimizing the effects of a tax upon the balance of the system in equilibrium. Taxes in the traditional view are supposed to be economically neutral devices for raising governmental revenue.

[1] Donald B. Marsh, *Taxes Without Tears?* (New York: The Ronald Press Company, 1945), pp. 1-10. Reprinted by permission of the publisher. The footnotes in the original version are omitted here.

"Taxes for revenue only" are less important than they used to be. In practice, the mere raising of revenue is seldom the only consideration. This may result in part from the pressure of interested groups, and in part from the general movement away from strict *laissez-faire* principles. Mere efficacy in raising revenue has been superseded in many cases by other *criteria;* and there is probably no cause, however slight, for which tax revenue would not be sacrificed or subordinated, given the appropriate pressures. One might argue, indeed, that taxes are levied for almost every conceivable purpose *except* revenue. Taxes promote equality, or they prevent inflation, or they discourage undesirable practices, or they provide incentive for certain types of activity. Raising revenue becomes incidental to these main functions. Some taxes may achieve their purpose best without raising any revenue at all. The federal tax upon state bank notes, first imposed in 1866, has resulted in their disappearance from circulation, as the law intended. The law is still in effect, but it would be something of a shock to the Treasury if the tax were suddenly to begin yielding revenue. Here is a tax which is one hundred per cent effective only when revenue is zero. And there are many less extreme cases.

The two purposes of revenue and control may upon occasion become cross purposes. They are almost certain to become so if economic effects are not carefully investigated. But any tax is bound to have some economic effects, and policy makers must choose between neutralizing these, so far as possible, or using them as positive means of control over the economic system.

And all taxes have other than revenue effects. There are three important ways in which tax policy may affect the economic system for good or ill.

First, taxation may affect the volume of employment; and employment, other than make-work, means output of goods and services. A movement towards full employment (or a higher level of employment) means that more goods and services can be produced with the same amount of capital and natural resources. Human resources which would otherwise be idle are put to work and, as a result, there is more real income to go round. Whether the movement at any time is towards higher or lower employment may depend to a significant extent upon the government's tax policy.

Second, taxation may alter the allocation of economic resources. In established economic usage, this is a way of saying that tax policy may affect not only the volume of output but its *character*. Some goods will be produced in greater quantities because of the tax, while the output of others will be reduced; or new varieties of goods may be produced while others disappear. This function of taxation may prove especially useful in the control of monopoly. For, under monopoly conditions, too few of the monopolized commodities are produced, at unnecessarily high prices, while competitive industry may be experiencing a glut which is forcing prices down. Where, as under monopolistic conditions, the price system under capitalism fails to perform its function, tax policy may be used to supplement it. Tax policy might even become a substitute for the more direct control of production which is usually associated with economic planning in the socialist state.

Third, taxation may be expected to alter the distribution of wealth and income. Adam Smith's canon of equality may justify the effect on distribution, if the re-distribution of income is considered more equitable than before the tax.

In general, traditional theory has urged that the first two effects be minimized, on the ground that the ends of true economy are best served by the operation of the free market; but of course actual policy has very often been aimed directly at securing a higher volume of employment or at shifting resources from one industry to another. The tariff, for example, aims at both: it is supposed to increase home investment and employment, as well as to allocate more of the community's resources to the making of certain protected commodities.

Only the third objective (that of the redistribution of income) has been officially canonized in tax literature; but the others are at least equally important in the framing of tax laws. It is likely, therefore, that further movement away from *laissez-faire* principles will follow practice in this connection. Taxes for other than revenue purposes will be devised to achieve generally accepted ends of policy and this, perhaps, will counteract the present tendency to use such taxes largely for furthering the ends of special interest groups.

Other ends of taxation may be subordinated to revenue. Whether or not non-revenue ends are *in fact* dominant in modern tax policy, revenue has until recently remained the ultimate end. This accords at once with the popular view, with the statements of legislators, and with the wisdom of most of the experts in public finance. The revenue end may be achieved directly or through a multi-purpose system of taxes, but revenue must at some stage be achieved and in sufficient quantity. That at least would seem to be received opinion, whatever actual performance may indicate.

If this is true, the non-revenue ends of taxation may have to be subordinated at some point. It might be impossible, for example, to use effectively the government's discretion in tax policy for the purpose, let us say, of obtaining the desired level of employment. Before the employment goal is reached, something might happen requiring a revision of the tax structure to meet revenue requirements.

But revenue needs can be postponed, or made flexible. If revenue needs are unavoidable, tax policy for non-revenue ends is inhibited; but even so there are alternatives. The same amount of revenue can be raised with different kinds of taxes. Some of these taxes would be neutral, or even conceivably of positive help, in the employment program. For example, unemployment insurance taxes could be directly geared to the level of employment instead of being flat taxes on payrolls. A tax on the employer's payroll is likely to depress employment or wages or both. It becomes a cost to the businessman which may not (like ordinary wages, interest, etc.) be reflected in anyone else's income; in other words, the net effect will be to reduce the community's available spending power unless benefit payments are at least equal to the tax. This reduction of spending power would be helpful during periods of threatened inflation, as in war, when social security tax rates (especially those on individuals) might well be increased. But, ordinarily, the economy cannot afford this additional drain, and it has been suggested that unemployment insurance taxes (or social security taxes generally) be assessed at rates just sufficient to balance benefit payments and costs during periods of "full" or "standard" employment, but that they be raised if employment rises above this level and lowered if employment falls below it. Thus the fund would show a surplus during booms, and a deficit during depressions, and this, it is hoped, would help to counteract cyclical unemployment. The idea is now being expounded by men of affairs, and it may soon lose enough of its academic taint to become acceptable in practice.

It is possible, therefore, that even a conservative view of the fundamental character of "revenue requirements" may be reconciled with the use of the tax system for economic control. The cleavage here is not in the theory of public finance, but in social attitudes towards governmental regulation of economic processes.

It must be remembered, however, that piecemeal methods of this nature are inadequate for an all-out attack upon general unemployment. Social security taxes are not large enough in the aggregate to have a very significant effect upon employment, even if they are eliminated entirely during a slump. The general principle of flexible social security taxes is sound, but quantitatively it takes a reduction of taxes in general or the substitution of direct government outlays in excess of total government expenditure (negative taxes) to counteract the powerful forces which, if uncurbed, are certain at times to depress the level of employment.

Borrowing may be resorted to. An obvious alternative (not always squarely faced) is not to tax at all, and to raise the needed revenue through borrowing. This expedient will at least postpone the evil day when taxes must be levied and that may be enough to restore full employment.

It may, of course, be urged that government expenditures have to be met sooner or later by taxation, and that borrowing may complicate matters in the future if it leads to the piling up of a huge national debt. But complications are not altogether inevitable, provided certain fiscal devices are adopted. Some of these devices may be unthinkable as practical policies, at least for the present. Perhaps they will have to continue a furtive existence in the realm of pure economics, but this is not necessarily the case. With a reasonable amount of amiable hypocrisy some of these unorthodox devices might be applied in practice without ever being accepted in principle. This is the usual path of fiscal progress.

The least controversial position, *i.e.*, the one most likely to succeed, is that the absolute size of the national debt is less important than its size relative to the national income. An austere policy of debt reduction may therefore prove unwise if there is threatened or actual unemployment on a large scale. But if debt reduction is postponed where possible until national income is approaching boom levels, taxation to reduce the debt has a two-fold advantage. In the first place, it reduces the debt at a time when the productive system can best afford to do so; and, in the second place, the heavier taxation required prevents an inflationary boom.

Or purchasing power may be created directly. The most controversial position, at present, is to urge that the *only* function of taxation is to prevent inflation; and the national debt, or interest charges on the debt, should never be paid out of current income unless inflation threatens. Higher incomes and higher (anti-inflation) tax rates will yield a budget surplus which may be applied to reducing the national debt. The debt itself is harmless, during unemployment and "normal" times, regardless of its size; and if inflation threatens the debt can be reduced with a minimum of discomfort to the community. This is A. P. Lerner's "functional finance": but only in its milder form. An apotheosis of heresy is reached when he declares that the debt itself need never be incurred (or increased); for the same objective can be obtained if, instead of borrowing, the government engages in the direct creation of purchasing power.

Revenue is always revenue for a purpose, not an end in itself, and it may be subordinated to other ends of policy. "Functional finance" carries to its logical conclusion the widely accepted premise that revenue must not be regarded as an end in itself. It differs only in degree from the "least controversial" position, above. But the difference in degree is significant politically; and in any case the most respectable connections will never win those who oppose on principle any use of taxation as an instrument for social control. Nevertheless, once the first step is taken, and taxes are deliberately used for other than revenue purposes, it is difficult to find a logical basis for being timid about it. It is possible, therefore, that, with the appropriate amount of orthodox dilution, "functional finance" may become part of the complex of public policy. Indeed, in a mild form, "functional finance" is already here. Taxation to prevent inflation is an accepted end of wartime fiscal policy. And no government can afford to face another 1932 with even a half-hearted attempt at a balanced budget.

Fortunately, we do not have to take a position on thorough-going "functional finance" so early in the discussion. We need only accept the proposition that taxation can be used for certain desired ends of policy; we can then inquire what kinds of policy seem most likely to be furthered by tax measures and how effective are tax measures in furthering them?

A fiscal system in which taxes, not merely expenditures, are used to promote social well-being differs greatly not only from a medieval sovereign's personal imposts upon his subjects, but from the more recently approved tax policy appropriate to the *laissez-faire* police state.

"The Taxpayer" is not always ill-used, although he may fail to see general effects because of preoccupation with his own problems. What will happen to the tearful little man in his barrel, whom many readers of a well-known newspaper identify with "the taxpayer"? He is unlikely to become less tearful, nor is he likely as a fiscal theorist to exert less influence on the man in the street. He owes his reputation to the indisputable fact that people have less money after paying taxes than they had before. But it is real income that counts, as the economist has known, and the man in the street should have learned by experience in wartime. It is barely possible that the taxpayer's tears may become less bitter, if it can be shown that in peacetime, as in wartime, a coherent tax policy may be used in various ways to swell the real income of a country.

The effect of taxation on real income will be our main concern in the chapters to follow. But one problem will always lurk in the background: the taxpayer may remain unconvinced that he has any personal interest in a rise in community real income. The personal interest of the taxpayer in community welfare may be accepted intuitively, but it cannot be demonstrated without elaborate argument, mainly beyond the realm of economics. The "political objections" which realists urge against any economic reform are likely to spring from some variant of this essentially ethical conflict between socially desirable ends and the selfish interests of individuals or politically powerful groups.

This book does not propose to compromise with current economic stupidity for the sake of political realism. To that extent it is "pure economics."

Political realists emphasize the well-known truth that not all who know the good will seek it. It is possible nevertheless to make the not improbable assumption that most people have good intentions. This book is written in the faith that many evils (and "political problems") will disappear when, through an extension of knowledge, these well-meaning people are prevailed upon to do less harm.

No. 84

THE PROBLEMS OF DUPLICATING FEDERAL AND STATE TAXES [1]

by James W. Martin

FOR a long time the United States government and the governments of the states financed themselves almost without duplicating taxes. The central government in the nineteenth century derived revenues mainly from import duties and from consumption excises on the sale of alcoholic beverages, tobacco products, and a few other commodities. The states and their agencies and subdivisions taxed property, polls, corporate franchises and other business privileges, and, more recently, transfers of property at the death of its owner. In some parts of the country, states and cities collected alcoholic beverage taxes or licenses. Also a few states imposed income taxes which were duplicated by the federal measures of the Civil War era. Until a comparatively recent date, however, the degree of overlapping was negligible.

In 1909 Congress imposed a corporation tax measured by net income; four years later, with adoption of the Sixteenth Amendment to the Constitution, income taxation became a standard practice for the central government. Meantime, the enactment of the modern Wisconsin income tax of 1911 gave state exploitation of this revenue source marked impetus. During and shortly following World War I other duplications in federal and state taxes became numerous. The federal government and many states imposed death taxes, corporation taxes, tobacco taxes, and other excises; and each maintained separate administrative machinery to enforce the independently enacted laws. With the depressions of 1921 and 1931, the problems became intensified by the addition of other areas of duplication. Not only were there duplicating taxes on the same income, the same inheritance, the same sale, and so on—but there was also an increasing number of conflicts in

[1] James W. Martin, "The Problems of Duplicating Federal and State Taxes," State Government (March, 1944), Vol. XVII, No. 3, pp. 287-289. Reprinted by permission of State Government.

technical provisions. In the main, the elements of friction or inconsistency as between federal and state taxes fall into three categories, and each of these will be sketched in the paragraphs which follow.

The Congress of the United States in formulating tax legislation appears to take inadequate account of the kindred revenue measures of the several states. The states likewise seem largely to ignore federal revenue legislation when formulating their own. As to the former, it is fair to say that the central government would be unable, even if it gave adequate attention to the problem, to adjust satisfactorily to take account of state policy, because each state is likely to have a different plan.

CONFLICTING RATE POLICIES

For example, state income tax rates range from none at all in a third of the states to a maximum of fifteen per cent in one or two states. How may the national government adapt its rates? Again, the gasoline tax rates range from two cents a gallon in some states to seven cents in others; and in addition some high-rate states have local rates which still further complicate the picture. As the United States uses practically all of its revenue sources as elastic elements subject to rate variations as conditions change, the states which would impose their own tax measures in the light of federal policy are equally at a loss. For example, had a state legislature in 1940 imposed a state income tax with full consideration of the federal plan, the weight of 1942 taxes might have been entirely out of keeping with the intended impact on taxpayers—not because the state changed its mind but because Congress revised the national government requirements. For a long time, as recently emphasized by the special committee designated by the Secretary of the Treasury to conduct a study in intergovernmental fiscal relations in the United States—the Groves committee—the consequences of this difficulty were merely irritating and did not necessarily effect any serious inequity in taxation.

In the recent past, with justifiable federal demands for war revenues, the situation has become more serious. In fact, in the opinion of many informed persons, the integrity of state finances is now imperiled. At the National Tax Conference in Chicago in November, 1943, for example, a table reflecting calculations made by the California state franchise tax commissioner showed that allowing a deduction of federal taxes in computing the state income tax liability would have cost the state about fifty-eight per cent of its revenue. (Skepticism was expressed with regard to the accuracy of the figure, but nobody suggested that the proportion lost would be small.) Moreover, the California authorities estimated that, of the indicated loss, more than half would ultimately accrue to the Treasury and less than half to the taxpayers concerned. As the state views the situation, present federal income taxes are in large part taking away the tax base of the state. At the same time, the central government, confronted by the greatest public debt in all history and by staggering present public expenditure requirements, is wrestling with unprecedented deficits. Even those federal technicians and officials most acutely aware of the loads imposed on taxpayers and of the impairment of state tax bases must wonder what, in the light of the necessities, can be done about the nation's fiscal problem.

CONFLICTING TECHNICAL PROVISIONS

Historically much more serious than the type of "tax conflict" just discussed are the inconsistent provisions of federal and state tax laws and regulations. The difficulties on this score are twofold: confusion and added expense for taxpayers, and increased administrative cost for the public. Some of the conflicting provisions have been constitutionally unavoidable. For example, the federal government has not been able to tax the interest on state and local securities, and the state governments have not been able to tax the interest from federal bonds. Thus the income bases were inevitably different. Formerly, the same kinds of difficulties were confronted with respect to public salaries.

TAXPAYER CONFUSION

But, as a matter of policy, many diversities having no legal basis are found. For example, one state, to plug an evasion loophole, provided that interest should be deductible only if income from the asset provided through the loan were subject to tax, that is, only if the interest were in principle a business expense. The difference between this and the federal deduction was so great that the state subsequently changed the plan. In another instance, the state, seeing no good reason for subsidizing charities of other states, provided in its income tax law for the deduction of gifts to charity within but not to similar beneficiaries without the state. Although entirely logical, this provision, because it differs from the federal, has caused much taxpayer confusion and has involved the state in perhaps sufficient additional cost to use up most of the added revenue collected.

Another sort of kindred misunderstanding and expense arises from taxpayer uncertainty as to the tax base. For example, in administering the federal sales taxes on cosmetics there has been confusion in some states as to whether the face-cream price, the basis of the tax, includes or excludes state sales tax. Conversely, and more seriously, it has been questionable whether the price forming the basis for a state sales tax included or excluded the amount of cosmetics tax due the federal government. In computing the federal estate tax, is the amount paid the state in inheritance tax deductible? In figuring the state inheritance tax, is the amount paid the United States deductible?

The illustrations cited, except for the death tax example, are concerned with laws not relatively complex. The difficulty, of course, is greatest in connection with involved measures which necessitate numerous decisions as to detail and the exercise of a considerable degree of discretion. Perhaps the corporation income and excess profits taxes are those which conflict most seriously. Even the individual income tax and the estate tax occasion substantial difficulties. Although the latter introduces many technicalities, the difficulties it causes are not as great as might be assumed because the Bureau of Internal Revenue audits every case—in the instance of the federal tax—and a specialist handles nearly every case in behalf of the taxpayer.

As has been hinted already, this type of statutory or administrative inconsistency between federal and state revenue measures presents two kinds of difficulty. In the first place, it provides headaches for taxpayers, especially. if the individuals characteristically concerned are unskilled in taxation, as in the case of the individual income or retail sales taxes. It adds other troubles if the complications are serious even in the event the taxpayer's case ordinarily is handled by an accountant or an attorney. The inevitable difficulties from non-uniform federal and state provisions may be intensified if the administration in either government or in both governments is inclined to be meticulously technical. In the second place, due to taxpayer confusion, the cost to the state is increased unduly. Incidentally, the problems of public relations, which are always important in tax administration, are rendered doubly difficult by inconsistent federal and state legal provisions which affect the tax base. Not only are money costs advanced and relationships with taxpayers entangled, but resentment against the tax concerned is aroused and the need for compulsion in administration rendered more frequent. Thus, on the whole, the conflicting measures bring about much discrimination between individual taxpayers even if there is no inequality due to double taxation as such.

CONFLICTING DUAL ADMINISTRATION

Much has been said about the wastes of duplicate administration. Although from a monetary viewpoint the losses to the government are perhaps not as great as those due to the types of conflict already sketched, nevertheless they are considerable. In a recent study of *Cost and Efficiency of Tax Administration,* made for the Groves committee appointed by the Secretary of the Treasury, I estimated that the total out-of-pocket administrative expense exceeded a quarter of a billion dollars a year. Since that time, as a result of the wartime tax measures, there has been an increase in the federal costs. More arresting, because largely neglected in the past, the cost to taxpayers of complying with tax requirements is very material— perhaps approaching the public administrative costs. If the expense of tax administration, public and private combined, reaches a total of between four hundred thousand and five hundred thousand dollars, then the figure is far from negligible. Those parts of the cost due to avoidable duplication should undoubtedly be regarded *prima facie* as representing unwise policy.

But the money expense involved in dual administration is not the only objection. The fact that both governments handle the same tax brings other inevitable difficulties from inconsistencies. The taxpayers' adverse reactions—often without logical basis, it may be granted—are nonetheless undesirable from the point of view of rendering the tax load as palatable as possible In other words, the divergent methods of computing tax liability originate largely in the fact that there are two separate sets of officials and employees. All differences from inconsistent interpretations, or at least practically all, arise thus; and a considerable number of conflicting statutory provisions could be unified if one management administered both federal and state taxes.

Dual federal and state administration is thus the source of material increase in aggregate public and private costs of administration. It brings about some of the diversities in tax base which cause taxpayers and public officials alike no end of difficulty. It may even lead to duplicating and excessive levies on particular classes of taxpayers. So anything that can be done to alleviate the evils from two sets of administrative officials for the same tax is, on the face of it, to be desired.

WHAT PHYSICIAN SHOULD BE CALLED?

Numerous proposed remedies for the difficulties sketched above have been advanced. The most obvious is: Let us return to the practice of separating federal from state and local sources of revenue. There is no disagreement as to what the federal government should give up and what the states should sacrifice; there is a consensus among the advocates of this view that the revenue sources exploited by one government should not be employed at all by the other (though some advocates would apply the notion only to certain taxes). H. C. Adams over fifty years ago advanced a simple proposal akin in its conception to the plans of those persons who to-day favor segregation of sources. He said: Let the national government have the revenue from import duties, from selective excises and, so far as the business engaged in is interstate commerce, from corporation taxes; and let states and their subdivisions use all other revenue sources. Some other prescriptions leave the states and localities little beyond the property and license taxes. The two fundamental questions which obtrude themselves as this plan is examined are: (a) Exactly what means of raising revenue shall be turned over to the central government, and what to the commonwealths; and (b), having decided the first question, how shall the turning-over be accomplished and how shall it be maintained or guaranteed?

A second proposal is that Congress grant taxpayers a credit for federal tax obligations on account of state taxes of similar character. The advocates of this plan usually do not propose that it be applied in every case, but only in the instance of particularly suitable taxes. The idea has been invoked for more than fifteen years in the case of death taxes, and for over half a dozen years in the instance of employment taxes measured by payrolls and enacted to finance unemployment compensation. Opinions differ as to the achievements of the device in these two cases, but critics would generally admit that it has not prevented statutory and administrative diversities, that it has not eliminated dual administration, and—as to the death taxes—that it has not prevented unduly high rates in some cases if both federal and state taxes are taken into account.

A third plan would provide for centralization of administration by one or the other of two or three possible means. Some advocates propose federal tax administration with a direct division of the revenues among the states from which they were collected, that is, a sharing with states. Others favor a similar tax administration plan coupled with great increases in federal grants-in-aid of state activities instead of simple return of the collections to the states of origin. Still other persons favor central tax administration with provisions for state supplementary levies on the same base as that defined by Congress for the federal tax. A few individuals would seek a thorough reshuffling of governmental functions and so accompany increased centralization of tax administration with a transfer of many state tasks to the central government. For instance, it is urged that unemployment is caused by national factors, and so all unemployment relief activities should be the responsibility of the federal government. As tax administration is more feasible for the nation than for the states, this argument continues, the transfer of welfare work away from states altogether would save friction and conform more exactly with the logic of the situation. Of course, advocates of "states' rights" cannot follow such a line of reasoning.

Without condemning any one of the three varieties of solutions for conflicting taxation for particular applications, and without denying that all the proposals may have limited valuable uses, some realistic students of tax policy believe most of the practical "cures" for conflicts are more likely

to come from administrative and other small-scale readjustments. Even
advocates of implementing coordination by means of separation devices,
credit provisions, and some form of centralized administration may accept
the view that some remedies for tax conflicts lie in the administrative
area. . . .

No. 85

MEETING THE NEEDS FOR STATE AND LOCAL REVENUES IN THE POSTWAR ERA [1]

by W. Brooke Graves and Karl W. H. Scholz

I. THE PLIGHT OF THE LOCAL UNITS

Limitations on Local Taxing Powers. In the face of the multiplicity of
taxing jurisdictions, the base on which these agencies may levy taxes has
become increasingly narrow. Local communities in Pennsylvania are not
permitted to tax sources of tax revenue pre-empted by the state. Moreover,
the state constitution prohibits levying any taxes which are not uniform
on a given class of subjects. A progressive tax on net personal incomes
based on ability to pay, recognized by tax authorities as an equitable tax,
cannot be levied even by the commonwealth of Pennsylvania, let alone by
local communities within the state.

Results of Inability to Raise Adequate Local Revenues. Parallel with
the increase in the number of units of local government, there has been a
tremendous increase in the number and scope of the functions of government
performed, with a corresponding increase in the total expenditures incurred.
Because of the narrow tax base available to meet these expanding local
needs for public expenditures, local communities have been hard pressed
to find sources of revenue adequate to meet the financial burden imposed
on them. They have increased the tax on real estate values, often beyond
the point of fairness and equitability. They have tried, within the constitutional limits imposed upon them, to devise new tax forms. They have
made extensive use of their constitutional or statutory borrowing power,
many of them rushing headlong into debt. Not least important of the
methods which they have tried has been the appeal to the larger units of
government for financial assistance; and thus have grown up the extensive
systems of federal and state grants-in-aid. In view of the perplexing problems which face the local communities in the postwar era, it becomes

[1] W. Brooke Graves and Karl W. H. Scholz, "Meeting the Needs for State and Local
Revenues in the Postwar Era," *American Political Science Review* (Oct., 1944), Vol. XXXVIII,
No. 5, pp. 904-912. Reprinted by permission of the *American Political Science Review*.

important that we analyze now the effects of the grant-in-aid system, and that we consider ways and means of meeting the state and local needs for revenue.

II. FUNDAMENTAL ASSUMPTIONS

Any proposal for meeting the financial needs of the state and local units . . . must of necessity be based on certain assumptions, of which three are here important:

Trend toward Centralization. We may as well accept the fact that the development of modern science has made it not only possible but necessary for government to function in larger units than heretofore. Machinery and new methods of transportation and communication have changed our way of life. The diminishing importance of space has made government at long range possible; the increasing significance of the time factor has stimulated the demand for speed in governmental activity. Power has passed from one unit to the next successively higher, in one jurisdiction after another, both here and abroad. Counties, cities, and towns have lost to the states, the states to the nation; and now it seems likely that the nation will likewise shift some power to some international organization designed to maintain peace and order in the family of nations. Politicians have denounced this trend, while scholars have expressed apprehension about the speed with which centralization has advanced, if not about centralization as such. Whether we like it or not, it is here, and as far as can be seen, it is likely to be more rather than less in evidence in the immediate future.

It is not meant to imply either that this trend toward centralization will go on forever or that it cannot be reversed. Certainly there is a point beyond which it cannot go, although no mortal may be wise enough to tell us precisely where it is. It may not be so far ahead as some are inclined to believe. Neither is it to be concluded that centralization has been an unmixed blessing; the verdict of the future may be that, in some of its forms, it has already gone too far. Since, however, the end is not yet in sight, we may well, for the present purpose, concern ourselves less about the fact of centralization and more about making adjustments essential to the operation of free institutions within the new and somewhat different framework which results from centralization.

Expanding Scope of Governmental Activity. In the second place, we may as well accept the idea that government will undertake more activities and assume more functions designed to promote the general welfare, and that it will enlarge many of the programs that are already under way. One may call it bureaucracy, if he chooses, but that does not in any way diminish the significance of the fact that the people are constantly demanding— and getting—more and better service from government at all levels—national, state, and local. While this trend, also, may not go on forever, no one knows where it will stop. If there is to be left a sizable sphere within which the individual is free to do as he likes, the trend should stop—one may even say, it must stop—somewhere well on this side of the assumption by government of control over all forms of human activity. Perhaps, even here, we may be nearer than we realize to the outermost boundaries of that expansion.

Nor should one forget that many of the supposed losses of power occurring through centralization have been offset, in whole or in part, by the development of new activities and the expansion of older functions already being performed by the very units which centralization is supposed to be destroying. New standards of administrative management demand not only that governments do more things, but that they do them better; and governments are meeting that challenge.

Continuance of Federal Financial Assistance to State and Local Governments. Finally, we must assume that, by some device or other, the amount of financial assistance given to the states by the federal government will continue to be very large and that it may even increase. Grants-in-aid for established state activities have grown from the small beginnings made in the Morrill Land Grant Act of 1863 to very considerable proportions. The number of purposes to which the subsidy system has been applied has steadily increased, along with the amounts appropriated. When periods of emergency have arisen, enormous additional grants have been made, regardless of the party in power. The Republicans established the Reconstruction Finance Corporation; the Democrats continued this agency and added many others—the Civilian Conservation Corps, the National Youth Administration, the Works Progress Administration, the Public Works Administration, etc. It seems reasonable to assume that, in the critical postwar period, old established grants will be continued as in the past, and that new ones will be made in large amounts, the purposes and conditions of which will be dependent upon the nature and proportions of the emergency.

(One observer takes exception to this assertion. His views are best stated in his own words: "In the first place, the federal government will have financial difficulties of its own; and, in the second place, unless the law of the pendulum has been repealed, there will be a political reaction to the recent policy of increasing federal financial aid to the states. In short, I am not at all sure that the trend as here stated will inevitably continue; but even if I were, and I believed it boded ill, I would resist it rather than hasten it. I recall the famous retort of the late Senator Penrose to a committee of suffragettes who asked his espousal of their cause on the ground that woman suffrage was inevitable. He replied, 'So is death, but I don't see anyone hastening to meet it.' Lest I be misunderstood, let me hasten to remark that I never shared the late Senator's distaste for woman suffrage.") It behooves us now, therefore, to take thought for the morrow, before the pressure for immediate action in a critical situation precludes the possibility of careful analysis.

III. POSSIBLE SOLUTIONS

Continuance of the Grant-in-Aid System. Grants-in-aid by both the federal and state governments for specific purposes have become an important source of "public funds" in states and local communities during recent years. In the present discussion, consideration will be confined chiefly to federal aid payments to the state and local governments which, during the fiscal year 1938, for only three forms of public assistance, amounted to over a quarter of a billion dollars. Just before the outbreak of the war in 1939, federal aid to states and local communities, in the form of regular, permanent grants, reached approximately one-half billion dollars. Substantial increases in these grants may be expected in the years to come, particularly for public assistance grants under the Social Security Act, for public health, and for public housing.

In the light of this expansion in the use of so-called "federal funds" to help meet local needs, it would appear advisable to examine into possible alternatives, perhaps resulting in a radical change in the past and present policy of granting federal aid. The states and local communities, being either unable or unwilling to pay for new programs of governmental activity, have appealed to the federal government for more and more aid for more and more purposes. While the amount appropriated for such aid has been increased from year to year, this has not been done in accordance with any plan. The amount of increase has depended upon the resourcefulness of lobbyists and on the success with which their techniques have been applied in the sponsoring of new programs of increases in existing programs. No attempt has been made, either to determine how much federal aid should be given to the states and local communities, in relation to their over-all needs or to the total national income, or to allocate in some equitable and systematic manner the total federal funds to be apportioned among the various governmental purposes for which subsidies are desired.

Federally Collected, State-shared Taxes. A system of federally collected, state-shared taxes might be used to supplement, or at least in part as a substitute for, the existing grant-in-aid system; the means test, which is widely applied in the allocation of such aid, might be in part dispensed with, so that the amount of funds agreed upon would be made available to the states as a matter of legal right. Where the grant-in-aid system was continued, some means test of eligibility for such grants should be required, with a view to maximizing the community benefits derived from funds made available by the federal government for state and local purposes. The term "federal funds" is an unfortunate misnomer, for in the last analysis, these funds are collected by the federal government in the form of taxes levied against the income of the people. Because federal taxes, under present laws, can be more equitably apportioned than locally levied taxes, the possibilities of extending the principle of centrally-collected, locally-shared taxes should be carefully explored.

Under this proposal, the federal government would serve as the collecting agency for a portion of the local taxes, which would be refunded in accordance with an acceptable formula, considering population, federal taxes paid, or other similar criteria to be agreed upon in advance. In highway appropriations, for instance, the old formula allotted equal weight to population, area, and post-road mileage. Extensive controversy has developed out of the current proposal to allot such funds by a formula in which one-half of the funds appropriated are allocated on the basis of population, one-fourth on area, and one-fourth on post-road mileage.

If the federal government were . . . to refund annually to the state and local governments for some years to come ten dollars of taxes per capita, paid by the people in the form of federal income taxes, this would represent, in the case of the city of Philadelphia, a fund of $20,000,000. A similar refund of ten dollars per capita throughout the country would mean $1,300,000,000 annually, or less than one week's cost of financing our war effort. But if $20,000,000 additional tax revenue had to be raised locally by increasing the levy on real estate values in Philadelphia, it would necessitate increasing the city tax rate, which many regard as too high already, by practically 50 per cent.

The differences between obtaining grants-in-aid and obtaining federal tax refunds by the states or local governments are rather obvious. So-called "federal funds" would come to the states and their subdivisions without strings attached, and without wirepulling and political maneuvering to get them. A broad provision that these funds should be used for local capital expenditures, as planned and recommended by the local planning commission, might be considered, but it is believed that control over the allocation of the refunds should be under local authority and not centered in the federal government. Funds collected by the federal government would be refunded as a matter of legal right, and not by requiring definite proof of need, as is the case with many of the current federal grants-in-aid.

Modernizing the State Tax System. It has been argued that it would be sounder procedure to aim at state and local tax reform, through constitutional amendments if necessary, in the interest of efficiency, economy, and equity in levying state and local taxes, rather than to centralize the taxing power in the hands of the federal government. Certainly the effort to achieve such reform should not be diminished; on the other hand, the solution of immediate postwar financial problems cannot be suspended while further efforts at reform are carried on. Constitutional revision in the states proceeds at a snail's pace. Few movements for revision ever get to the convention stage, and of those that do, very few indeed actually result in the adoption of revised constitutions. The prescribed processes for piece-meal amendment are so difficult to operate that, in most states, progress by this method is equally difficult. The proposal for change, by whatever method, arouses such determined resistance on the part of entrenched groups that the prospect of solution of the tax problem by the time-honored processes of state and local action seems extremely remote.

Our inquiries into overlapping taxes and possible ways of allocating sources of revenue to the three levels of government should go on, and undoubtedly will result ultimately in a more orderly and equitable revenue system than we now have. Once we have arrived at some degree of agreement on the broad outlines of such a system, there is likely to be more rapid progress toward state and local revision than we have had in the past.

IV. WHAT COURSE SHALL WE FOLLOW?

An effort has been made to indicate the framework within which a choice of method or methods in the handling of the . . . needs of state and local governments for funds will have to be made. Many of the states have not, in recent years, been able to provide the revenues they need, under the shackles of outworn constitutional provisions affecting their taxing powers. As a substitute for making the necessary changes in their constitutions, they have sought federal aid. Former Governor Pinchot of Pennsylvania, for instance, was among the first—if not the first—of the governors of the states to appeal for federal assistance in the relief crisis of 1932, and Pennsylvania, a populous and wealthy state, might, if it had had a modern tax system, have met its own needs fairly easily. By seeking aid from afar, the states have to a large extent forfeited their control over their own affairs. Their citizens pay the tax bill anyway, in the form of federal taxes, if not in that of states taxes, and in so doing, they have surrendered to Senators and Representatives from other states the determination of the kinds and amount of taxes to be raised from their citizens, and the disposition which shall be made of the funds so obtained. . . .

There are, as has been shown, three ways of meeting the financial problem which . . . confronts the states and many local communities. . . . Which one shall they adopt? The course that they ought to follow is perfectly clear—they ought to put their financial houses in order. This they have made no serious effort to do in the past; if they should do it now, they could, in all probability, get along reasonably well without wholesale financial assistance from the federal government. Perhaps one way of accelerating tax revision at the lower levels of government would be to remove Santa Claus from the upper level. A strong case might be made for a federal policy that would force state and local governments to bestir themselves in the matter of revenues rather than for pursuing, as in the past, or as seems likely in the future, a policy that would lull them to sleep. From that sleep there might be a dreadful awakening!

It is probably merely wishful thinking, however, to expect either that the states will themselves reform their financial policies and procedures in time to meet the postwar needs, or that the federal government will compel them to do so. We are confronted, then, with an unwelcome choice between a continuance of the haphazard grant-in-aid system and the adoption of a federally collected, state-shared tax program. The subsidy system is, in a sense, a bribe to the states to increase their spending. It may, in some cases, be wasteful. It has been systematic and consistent only in its adherence to the principle of raiding the federal treasury. But it is not likely soon to be abandoned. The politics of the situation points clearly to its continuance. The senators and representatives from the many states that have the votes and that need the money are not likely to settle for less than they have been getting. But always the amount of federal aid should be kept at the minimum necessary to aid states with limited resources to maintain essential services at a minimum acceptable standard, and the states and local communities should be required to carry as much of the burden themselves as they can. Locally raised money is less likely to be spent lavishly than money received as a "gift" from the federal government.

There are many objections, also, to federally collected, state-shared taxes, one of the most important of which is the possibility that the plan might lead to further centralization of the taxing power in the hands of the federal government. As Chief Justice Marshall said in quite a different connection, "the power to tax is the power to destroy"; increasing concentration of the taxing power in the federal government might lead ultimately to the complete destruction of the state and local tax autonomy. Moreover, to accept the principle of centrally collected and locally shared taxes as a matter of legal right is an implied admission of failure to achieve state and local tax reforms, designed to make possible levying equitable taxes by the state and local governments.

It has been argued also that, unsatisfactory as the subsidy system is, to go from it to federally collected, state-shared taxes is to jump from the frying pan into the fire. Under a system of federal grants for specific purposes, the amount of federal aid has to bear some reasonable relationship to specific purposes and specific needs, while under the latter, the grants would be for general purposes of the states only, and the sky might be the limit. Much larger sums might come back to the states under this plan than under the grant-in-aid system, and, it is argued, the evils inherent in having "gift" money to spend would be correspondingly magnified.

Another possible objection arises from the difficulties likely to be encountered in devising an acceptable formula for the distribution of the shared taxes. It will prove immeasurably more difficult, says one writer, to devise an appropriate formula than to say that there should be one. If such a formula were devised by Congress, it might be written by a pen guided by sectional interests rather than by considerations of justice, and it might change with the changing political complexion of Congress, thus introducing a high degree of instability into state finances. While every proposed change of major policy should be examined with a view to foreseeing the worst possible outcome of its adoption, this dire prediction exaggerates the instability of Congress and suggests a too ready willingness to expect the worst.

Not all taxes, of course, can be centrally collected to advantage. Careful selection must be made of the taxes to be so handled. Obviously, a tax on real estate values should not be centrally collected, nor should a mercantile license or other tax on the privilege of doing business. On the other hand, a sales tax—either general or specialized—should, if it is to be effective, be so collected. Central collection of such a tax insures lower costs and a minimum of evasion due to the making of purchases in areas not included within the area in which the tax applies. Similarly, an income or wage tax can be best collected centrally.

In spite of the many objections to and limitations upon the centrally collected, locally shared principle, it seems definitely preferable to the subsidy system—the alternative that seems most likely to prevail. It is more economical in collection costs than duplicate collection systems in the individual states. The federal collecting machinery is more efficient than that in most states; hence there is less opportunity for tax evasion. The use of the graduated income tax principle assures fairness and equitability in the distribution of the tax burden. Most important of all, it makes possible the exercise of some control over the amount of federal aid given to state and local governments, and restores to them the opportunity to determine the uses that shall be made of the money. As such, it constitutes a move in the direction of the restoration of the vitality of the state and local governments in the management of their own affairs.

If such a plan is adopted, care must be taken to establish a situation in which the federal government will not take advantage of its position as collecting agency to force conditions upon the states, as has been done on many occasions in the past. The Hayden-Cartwright Act of 1934 well illustrates this practice. Here, funds appropriated to the states for highway purposes were made available only to those states which refrained from an "excessive" diversion of the funds raised by gasoline and motor vehicle taxes. While an amendment to the federal Constitution would give greater assurance of continued freedom from federal interference in the use of the funds, it will be necessary, in the absence of such an amendment, to rely upon the integrity of Congress. . . .

No. 86

CAN MUNICIPAL TAXES BE REDUCED? [1]

by Carl H. Chatters

FEW municipalities can reduce their taxes. A decreasing proportion will be able to finance the growing list of public services and social welfare payments. This inability to reduce taxes and support services results generally from an increasing level of costs, a growing number of public services primarily in the social welfare groups and from a spotty and illogical distribution of the total public revenue.

First, let me observe that the number of public services required of local governments has grown in number and cost, particularly since 1920, and the sources and amount of *local* revenues have been comparatively constant, while state revenues have been increasing rapidly and the *number* of state functions has not appreciably increased. Between 1926 and 1942 the states increased their tax yields thirteen times as rapidly as localities. If the period were extended to 1946 the discrepancy would be even greater.

Now about the services of government. The quantity and quality of these public services determine the amount of money really needed by a municipality. For several years I have been working on "An Inventory of Governmental Activities in the United States." It's shocking even to one who has lived intimately with government all his life. It's shocking, not in a

[1] Carl H. Chatters, "Can Municipal Taxes Be Reduced?", *State Government* (March, 1947), Vol. XX, No. 3, pp. 80-81 ff. Reprinted by permission of *State Government*.

bad sense, but just because it shows so clearly how much government does—and how much more it does now than it did earlier in the century. For instance, in the list of public service enterprises operated by municipalities you will find railroads, street railways, bus lines, electric power plants, water works plants, gas plants, liquor stores, airports, ferries, bus terminals, markets, grain elevators, abattoirs, cemeteries and crematories, broadcasting stations, telephone systems, and ports and harbors. But these might all be self-supporting, so look at another list. Local police departments now prevent and investigate crimes, keep custody of their prisoners, maintain identification records and crime statistics, have extensive communication systems, supervise morals through suppression of prostitution, liquor control, narcotic control, and the regulation of dance halls and amusement places. The police also maintain traffic signals, patrol city streets and highways, inspect motor vehicles and conduct drivers' examinations. The protective inspection services of a municipality are numerous and their necessity has been well justified by recent fires and other tragedies. There are municipal building inspection, plumbing inspection, electrical inspection, gas inspection, boiler inspection, elevator inspection, inspection of weights and measures, smoke inspection, and numerous health inspections. Local services related to public health, social services, hospitals, and public recreation could be listed even more at length. Then there are the two areas where expenditures have been so great: namely, highways or streets and public education. This catalog grows tiresome so it will end with two pertinent observations: one, that the states have also increased their activities but in many less fields and, two, that the increased number and cost of services tend to make small, local areas of government much more inadequate for performing and financing these services.

Let us look again at the question "Can Taxes Be Reduced?—To What Extent Can Municipalities Support Their Public Services?" Assume that municipalities are required to carry on only those services they had in 1926. Assume also that these services are performed as honestly and economically as possible. How can municipalities spend less for these services when salaries and wages are so much higher . . .

Several general lines of direct attack can be used to reduce municipal taxes. Taxes *can* be cut without reducing expenditures. That's a good old political trick with which you are all familiar. But it doesn't help in the long run. Next, taxes *can* be reduced by doing nothing new or constructive, by failure to maintain present facilities or to build new ones. However, genuine tax reduction is possible in many municipalities by at least three devices. First, genuine economy will be aided by removal of political deadheads or other incompetents. They are a material factor in only a few places. Second, greater state grants-in-aid will reduce local taxes if properly administered. Otherwise they stimulate and increase municipal spending. Third, great savings may be made by proper arrangement of the areas for collecting taxes and conducting public services and by other changes in the form of government areas and administration.

The events which would aid municipalities to support their public services or to reduce local taxes are divided here into two groups: what the state could do and what the municipalities could do.

WHAT MUNICIPALITIES CAN DO

Municipalities can act independently in many ways to improve their ability to support their public services. Some of these follow:

1. Get rid of political appointees, useless workers and deadheads. Civil service must be used to get qualified persons on the payroll and neither political interference, civil service, or union action should keep on incompetent or unnecessary employees. Retention of incompetents by any means is just as deadening as political interference is demoralizing. The salaries of top personnel in government should be increased greatly to attract capable, practical administrators and technicians.

2. Recognize the high cost of municipal debt. Avoid it where possible. Debt fixes municipal costs for a generation and makes reduction of taxes or the increase of services impossible. The greatest municipal waste may be found in this area. Sometimes it comes through inability to sell bonds properly. At other times bonds are sold when it is unnecessary to do so.

3. Municipalities can now and in the future support *some* services but not *all* services. They can support *more* services when their debts are low and the income of the community is high. They cannot be expected to support from local funds, services which spread unequal burdens such as social services or services which increase out of proportion to municipal income such as unemployment relief, education, unusual construction projects and many of the newer social services.

4. A consistently balanced budget over a long period of years is the best guarantee that a municipality will be in the best position to meet its obligations. But there must be included as expenditures all vital maintenance, all necessary capital improvements, and actual payment currently of all obligations incurred.

5. Municipalities need a more flexible and a more dependable revenue system so that their revenues will increase with the price level or with added services and will not contract too greatly in times of depression. The

states and the national government should be prepared to finance or take over the services which expand unduly or supplement the revenues which shrink where they are most needed. Remember that local taxes generally are tied to an inflexible base while state and federal taxes, primarily on incomes and sales, automatically give more revenue as prices and incomes rise. Probably the states get less tax complaints than municipalities because the latter must increase *tax rates* to get more money while the states, without a change in the rate of the income tax or sales tax, just sit by and watch the money roll in.

6. Municipalities that are homogeneous, that grow gradually, that build community wealth as population increases, that are not surrounded by parasitical communities, these municipalities have few troubles and generally can support their public services.

7. On the other hand, rapidly growing municipalities that must finance improvements by debt, municipalities that construct uneconomic facilities, school districts that share unequally and unfairly in revenues such as that from railroad property in Illinois, municipalities surrounded by small communities which draw on the central city for many services but contribute little, if anything, and the very large cities where the state syphons off their income and returns too little; these municipalities cannot now and never will be able under similar conditions to finance their services.

8. Municipalities should endeavor to strengthen their local revenues by every means which is legally, socially, and economically sound. But the failure to do this does not give the state an excuse to impose unfair burdens by new services, nor does it give the state the right to absorb an unfair share of the total public revenue. But the failure of municipalities generally to handle their financial affairs as well as they might, gives the state the excuse for interference in local affairs.

WHAT THE STATES CAN DO

State governments can do many things which will make it possible for the municipalities to work out their own financial problems or which will remove municipal financial burdens.

1. The states can and should refrain from granting exemption from real property taxes and expect the municipalities to carry the entire burden of the exemptions. Exemptions granted pursuant to state law are an unbelievably large part of total property and the exemptions are unevenly distributed throughout the state. The question should be examined and most exemptions removed or modified.

2. The states should finance, in part, those municipal expenditures which are not constant, which are distributed unevenly over the state, which

result from acts of God or national economic disasters or which cannot be fairly borne by the areas of government as presently constituted. I mean to include among others a great share of unemployment relief costs, funds to equalize educational costs within a state, removal of unusual snows in cities, suppression of epidemics and relief from disaster. The work of the so-called Moore Commission in New York state is an admirable application of this idea.

3. The states can refrain from passing laws which require expensive municipal services unless (a) the state investigates to determine that municipalities can bear the burden or (b) the state pays the cost of such services.

4. No state government at any time, anywhere in the United States, should have the right to fix the salary or hours of work of any municipal employee or official or any group of employees.

5. Many states can profitably examine their systems of grants-in-aid and shared taxes. In most cases, grants should replace shared taxes, but the grants should not be given solely to stimulate a particular type of expenditure, nor should the grants always be related to a particular expenditure. Grants should be given to increase local revenues and not to stimulate municipal expenditures.

6. The states should abandon the granting of special charters to municipalities but should govern through a municipal home rule law which gives specified responsibilities and privileges to every municipality and within specified limits permits each municipality to adopt and amend its own charters. . . .

7. The gasoline tax should be more fairly distributed to the municipalities by the states. The greatest financial travesty of this century is the collection of the gasoline tax by the states, the use of the tax for rural roads, and the construction of city streets by real estate taxes or special assessments.

8. For the protection of municipalities as public corporations and for the protection of municipal property owners, the states need to strengthen their laws relative to the use of land both in and adjacent to cities so that the cities will not be surrounded by jerry-built houses on small plots of swamp land nor by types of buildings which the municipalities would not permit to be built. Municipal, county, and state officials share the responsibility for protecting present and future home owners from exploitation or depreciation.

9. A committee like the national "Baruch" committees with their simple, direct reports is needed to study and report on the areas of government, their number, their size, and their ability to finance and perform services. How can a rural township in an urban area be expected to function in any way? It has no effective organization, no money, no technical or profes-

sional services. How can a city or village with one square mile of area properly function in a metropolitan region? Yet there are many of them. How can a modern industrial city, particularly a one-industry city, be expected to care for its unemployed when nearly everyone is unemployed? Why should so many Illinois cities or townships have plenty of money for schools because there's a railroad track in the town, while a neighboring city or township with equal or greater need cannot have good schools because an accident placed the railroad elsewhere? Why should the accidental or premeditated location of an industry give money and privilege to a small area, money and privilege to the particular industry, while denying services to equally worthy governments? Why should the accident of location give a government or industry privilege while the accident of birth in the United States is supposed to confer special privilege to no one? Sometimes these small areas of governments are knights that fight off the lords of the surrounding territory; more often they are vassals subject to the whim of economic chance, neglected by the state and existing in political poverty. At the other extreme, why should a great city like Chicago have to ask the state of Illinois for money? The city has the wealth and the income. Give it reasonable powers to tax and it will solve its own problems. To return to the question of areas. Examine the statutes, activities, revenues, officials, and geographic boundaries of all the local governments in your state and see if this question is not the most fundamental any state can tackle.

CONCLUSION

How can these recommendations to the states and municipalities be carried out? Try this. Establish a *state department* of municipal affairs equal in rank to the departments of highway, education or health. Give it authority to conduct research, gather statistics, prepare municipal laws and serve as the contact point between state and municipal officials just as other departments do now in other fields. You need the facts which can come only from uniform statistics. You need the laws which can emerge from intimate departmental contacts. Augment this department with legislative committees or interim commissions. The Pennsylvania local government commission has done notable work in eliminating a network of confusing legislation and substituting statewide laws relating to debt and taxation. The Moore Commission in New York brought wide reform last year in the distribution of state aid and state grants. More recently the Maryland Commission on the Distribution of Tax Revenues has reported. Finally, obtain the active cooperation of local government officials with the state department, state commissions and legislative committees.

If all of these work together, your actions may bring solutions to aggravating problems of tax reduction and financing of services.

If you want a dogmatic answer to the question "Can Taxes Be Reduced— To What Extent Can Municipalities Support Their Public Services?", it would have to be "Municipal taxes cannot be reduced substantially—municipalities can support their normal traditional services if the areas of government are large enough and state revenues are distributed equitably." But a dogmatic answer is never the best, so I recommend a careful rearrangement of areas, better distribution of state taxes, and a state agency for municipal affairs.

Chapter XXIV

MANAGING THE PUBLIC'S MONEY

[DURING the nineteenth century and even in the early part of the twentieth the activities carried on by government were so limited and inexpensive, and public revenues were so ample, that the government had little reason to worry about meeting a deficit. In fact, at times, the government (particularly at the national level) had a surplus. The result was laxity and carelessness in handling public finances and the failure to develop a systematic budget system.

But, as the nation grew and the responsibilities of government increased, it became more and more evident that careful planning of taxes and expenditures, close supervision of the disbursement of funds, and adequate accounting and auditing would be essential if the resources of the nation were to be used soundly and wisely. There arose, therefore, a definite movement to establish budget systems in national, state, and local governments designed to make them more efficient in the raising and spending of public funds. This movement got under way in local government shortly after the turn of the century, moved quickly to the state level, and proposed budget measures appeared in Congress in the second decade of this century. A budget and accounting act was passed by Congress and signed by President Harding in 1921.

Budget procedure, established as a consequence of this legislation, attempts to provide a systematic and efficient method of handling the public's money and relating it to the public's needs. It is a procedure beginning with estimates of the revenues and expenditures for the fiscal year, general planning of the relation of public needs to income, enactment and enforcement of tax and appropriation legislation. As Professor Anderson outlines it in his *American Government,* "The preliminary *budget estimates* are those prepared by the several administrative agencies that spend the money while the *final budget estimates* are those embodied in the book that is laid before the legislative body by the budget-planning agency. The *budget proper* consists of the entire enacted program of work, expenditure, revenues, and borrowing for the period under consideration; it includes appropriation acts, revenue acts, borrowing measures, and incidental legislation."

The following selections discuss some of the problems involved. The article on "The Management of the Budget" deals with the preparation and administration of the budget, primarily at the national level. The article by Lillian Ross describes the preparation of the budget in our largest municipality, New York

714

City, and gives a vivid picture of the kinds of activities that a major city engages in and on which it spends the public's money.   Professor Merriam advances some ideas that citizens and taxpayers who are concerned about a sound handling of public money should keep in mind and that are often lost sight of by well-intentioned citizens who are sincerely worried about the high cost of government.]

No. 87

THE MANAGEMENT OF THE BUDGET [1]

by The Committee on Postwar Tax Policy

BUDGETARY balance at the desired level should be the normal and regular policy to be followed by the federal government.   The country cannot afford to trust to the course of circumstances to produce that result. It must be planned for and worked for, if it is to happen with any consistency and regularity.

To the present time there has been no definite responsibility upon either the President or the Congress for balancing the budget.   The executive budget is not required, by law, to show a balance of receipts and expenditures.   Under the American system, which created a federal government composed of three coordinate branches—legislative, executive, and judicial—governmental power is distributed among the three branches, each of which is supposed to function as a check and balance against the other two.   All authority to initiate legislation is vested in the legislative branch, and no member of the other branches may also be a member of the legislative branch at the same time.   In this respect our system differs from that which is ordinarily described as a "parliamentary system," under which the heads of the several administrative departments are also members of the legislative branch.   As members of the latter, the department heads of the English cabinet, for example, sit in the House of Commons, participate in its debates, vote on all legislative proposals, and jointly, as a cabinet, introduce all public legislative measures.   The English budget comes before the Commons with all the standing of a legislative proposal and is acted upon as such.

The President's budget can never be more than a series of recommendations.   The Congress is entirely free to modify, up or down, the budget proposals as to both appropriations and revenues.   The direct check which the chief executive may apply to Congressional action is the veto, but even

---

[1] The Committee on Postwar Tax Policy, *A Tax Program for a Solvent America* (New York: Committee on Postwar Tax Policy, 1947), pp. 26-32.   Reprinted by permission of the publisher.

this becomes ineffective if the Congress be sufficiently determined upon a certain course to enact a bill over the veto.

The management of the budget involves two aspects, its preparation and its application or execution.

PREPARATION OF THE BUDGET

The legislative reorganization act of 1946 takes a first and most important step toward the establishment of Congressional responsibility in the preparation of the budget. There is to be an authoritative legislative budget, in addition to the President's advisory budget. While due consideration is to be given to the latter, the two need not, and probably will not, agree in all respects. The legislative budget becomes an advance commitment as to the over-all total of expenditures and, it is to be hoped, of receipts. Its great merit lies in the fact that there will be established a broad framework within which the spending and the taxing are to be determined, each with reference to the other.

The new legislation obviously does not require that the budget shall ever be balanced, but it does require that if a deficit be estimated Congress shall specifically authorize a corresponding increase in the public debt. The level of the budget is a matter of policy, as is the question of surplus or deficit. The best hope for progress toward a lower total lies in the fact that, for the first time in our history, the proposed spending must be directly related to the necessary taxing. Under this arrangement, any disregard of the standard of budget balance will be brought more and more into the open and will be freely and fully discussed, in and out of Congress. As this procedure becomes better established in public thought it should lead to more effective and complete budgetary control.

It is too early to foresee the extent to which the new procedure may modify the practices that have hitherto been followed by the appropriations committees. A valuable feature of these practices has been the publication of the record of hearings before the several subcommittees on the various appropriation bills. While the review which these subcommittees conduct of the departmental request necessarily duplicates, to a considerable extent, the review which the budget bureau has already conducted, the absence of any published record of the proceedings before the bureau means that the only public information regarding the proposed expenditure program is to be found in the reports of the subcommittee hearings. If the contribution which the two appropriations committees are to make to the joint statement on the legislative budget is to be based upon the kind of investigation which has been conducted in the past, it will be necessary to begin earlier and proceed more expeditiously with these hearings. Without them, much greater reliance than heretofore must be placed upon the President's budget recommendations.

One possibility would be to accept the President's budget as a series of maximum proposals, with the Congressional investigation and action pointed at the case for sustaining, or reducing, but not increasing, the expenditure totals proposed. In this connection the procedure followed in New York, largest of the states in population and resources, may be of interest. The following passages are from Article VII of the New York Constitution:

Section 2. Annually, on or before the first day of February, the governor shall submit to the legislature a budget containing a complete plan of expenditures proposed to be made before the close of the ensuing fiscal year and all moneys and revenues estimated to be available therefor, together with an explanation of the basis of such estimates and recommendations as to proposed legislation, if any, which he may deem necessary to provide moneys and revenues sufficient to meet such proposed expenditures.

Section 3. At the time of submitting the budget to the legislature the governor shall submit a bill or bills containing all the proposed appropriations and reappropriations included in the budget and the proposed legislation, if any, recommended therein.

The governor may at any time within thirty days thereafter and, with the consent of the legislature, at any time before the adjournment thereof, amend or supplement the budget and submit amendments to any bills submitted by him or submit supplemental bills.

Section 4. The legislature may not alter an appropriation bill submitted by the governor except to strike out or reduce items therein, but it may add thereto items of appropriation provided that such additions are stated separately and distinctly from the original items of the bill and refer each to a single object or purpose.

Section 5. Neither house of the legislature shall consider any other bill making an appropriation until all of the appropriation bills submitted by the governor shall have been finally acted upon by both houses, except on message from the governor certifying to the necessity of immediate passage of such a bill. . . .

Section 11. Except the debts specified in sections 9 and 10 (relating to short term debts in anticipation of revenues and of permanent bond issues, and on account of invasion, insurrection, war, and forest fires), no debt shall be hereafter contracted by or in behalf of the state unless such debt shall be authorized by law, for some single work or purpose, to be distinctly specified therein. No such law shall take effect until it shall, at a general election, have been submitted to the people, and have received a majority of all the votes cast for it at such election nor shall it be submitted to be voted on within three months after its passage nor at any general election when any other law or any bill shall be submitted to be voted for or against.

These provisions give the executive budget the predominant place in fiscal procedure. They do not entirely stop the introduction of appropriation bills by members, but the strictness of the debt provisions tends to hold the total spending within the available revenues.

Under such an approach as this there would be little opportunity of voting a larger total than was contained in the budget, and the question of surplus or deficit would turn on the degree to which the Congressional action may have resulted in a reduction of expenditures within the proposed budget total or in the adjustment of taxes to provide the needed revenue. The plan would not allow sufficiently, perhaps, for those purposes which appear after the budget has been prepared, except as they might be incorporated into supplemental budget statements which were regularly transmitted as amendments to the main document. As the federal experience . . . [has shown], however, unlimited leeway to appropriate for purposes not covered in the budget can lead to serious disorganization of a financial program.

THE ADMINISTRATION OF THE BUDGET

The expression "administration of the budget" includes (1) the administration of the revenue laws and other laws under which the taxes and other revenue receipts are collected and covered into the Treasury; and (2) the application of the funds appropriated to meeting the costs of governmental operation. Revenue collection has been established since the beginning of the Republic. Executive control of the application of appropriated funds was made possible through the creation of the budget bureau by the Budget and Accounting Act of 1920.

The bureau's control is, in one sense, a routine which is generally regarded as no more than an orderly adjustment of the rate of spending to assure that a given appropriation will last out the fiscal year. In this capacity, the several appropriations are apportioned and the funds are released to the various departments and agencies on a monthly basis suitable to the rate of their respective operations. There is no authority for apportioning sums in excess of appropriations, but the number and volume of deficiency appropriations indicate that the practice of making apportionments at a rate which necessarily involves overspending is fairly common. The new legislation, now effective as to the future, requires that the legislative budget carry such provision as may be deemed necessary for deficiencies.

The precedent for executive action dates from the early days of the present budget procedure. Shortly after the organization of the budget bureau it was made responsible for securing the compliance of all executive agencies with the provisions of the anti-deficiency act. President Harding inaugurated the practice of requesting the heads of the spending agencies to set aside a portion of their appropriations at the beginning of each fiscal year as possible savings. President Hoover undertook by similar methods to effect a 10 per cent reduction of expenditures for the fiscal year 1932. President Roosevelt effected salary reductions in 1933 and 1934 by executive order.

Thus, there has been ample precedent for the following statements by President Truman in his budget review message of August, 1946, referring to the increases in appropriations:

> I have directed the Secretaries of War and Navy to curtail military expenditures to the level contemplated in the January budget, except for terminal leave pay, and certain additional naval programs which the Congress authorized upon my recommendation. . . .
>
> I am addressing letters to the heads of those agencies which have direct charge of public works, and also to those which have responsibility for grants-in-aid or loans, requesting them to take all measures to secure the postponement of public works at the present time so that the Government competes as little as possible for scarce labor and materials. I have also given instructions to postpone all purchases of automobiles, office equipment, and other items in short supply except in emergency cases.
>
> Furthermore, various agencies will absorb the major part of the recently enacted pay increases.

The version of the legislative reorganization bill which was passed by the Senate contained a provision which would have authorized the President to make reductions in the non-mandatory appropriations sufficient to keep the total within the budget as approved by Congressional joint resolution. This provision was eliminated in the House. It would have given statutory regularity to a procedure which is now applicable only under the control which the power of appointment and dismissal gives the chief executive.

Under the Legislative Reorganization Act of 1946 unexpended balances, which have been troublesome in the past, will no longer present a problem. Section 139 (c) of that act is as follows:

> (c) No general appropriation bill or amendment thereto shall be received or considered in either House if it contains a provision reappropriating unexpended balances of appropriations; except that this provision shall not apply to appropriations in continuance of appropriations for public works on which work has commenced.

Another paragraph of the same section provides for a study, by the two appropriation committees, of existing permanent appropriations with a view to limiting their number and determining which, if any, should be discontinued, and also for a study of the disposition of funds resulting from the sale of government property or services by all departments and agencies with a view to designing a uniform system of control of such funds.

The excerpt just quoted from the reorganization act evidently has no retroactive effect, for the budget for the fiscal year 1948 proposed to use a large carry-over of unexpended balances. Against total expenditures of $37,528 million, the new appropriations to be asked for total only $31,300 million. The excess of expenditures over new appropriations is to be covered from appropriations previously authorized. In the budget message the following statement was made regarding these prior appropriations:

> Existing appropriations available for obligation in 1948 and subsequent years are again under review. As these appropriations become unnecessary, their withdrawal will be recommended to the Congress.

Since the appropriations in question were voted during the war years, at a time when the termination of the war emergency was not predictable, it is proper to suggest that they should be cancelled at once. Their extension into 1948, or even some later fiscal year, is contrary to the purpose of the reorganization act. Their continuing availability, under conditions utterly different from those under which they were originally provided, is conducive to extravagance. The fact that upward of one-sixth of all expenditures can be supported by authorizations of this character, as was the case in the President's budget for 1948, limits by so much the responsibility of the present Congress in its determination of a federal expenditure program. It really means that one-sixth of that program has already been determined by previous Congresses with no consideration having been taken of the vast change in circumstances between the time of enactment and that of ultimate application.

Notwithstanding the road block set up by unrescinded prior appropriations, the present situation reflects a gratifying degree of progress toward better coordination of spending and taxing and toward the plain and direct assumption, by the Congress, of a significant degree of responsibility for budget preparation. The problems involved in the application or execution of the budget have been unaffected, as yet, except for the elimination of the carry-over of unused balances of appropriations. The failure to retain a provision directly authorizing the President to adjust appropriation totals under certain conditions leaves unsettled his legal right to do this, although there could hardly arise a serious doubt as to the validity of presidential influence exerted upon the persons whom he had appointed as administrative heads.

The success of a balanced budget policy requires the positive support of both the Congress and the executive branch. The total expenditures and the total revenues must be considered as parts of a whole, and there must be recognition of the fact that increased taxation must be provided when necessary to balance the budget. Under the new legislation we have the fortunate prospect that this correlation will occur. A surplus of revenues for debt reduction, or a state of budget balance, should not be simply a fortuitous outcome. The President and the Congress have a joint responsibility for the careful preparation of the budget, and the former has the principal, if not the full responsibility for producing the expected result in the application of the budget program. He should have clear and express authority to get this result by such control over apportionments as may be necessary. He should not be expected or required, however, to shoulder the responsibility of drastic adjustments such as would be required to correct large scale discrepancies between revenue and expenditure.

All of these problems of budgetary management are of greatest importance when they are related to the policy of budget balance. If deficits are incurred deliberately, control of the rate of spending becomes more difficult. Once we have taken the essential first step of declaring for the balanced budget as the foundation of normal fiscal policy, we shall be in a position to perceive and develop such measures, supplemental to existing procedures, as the achievement of the main goal may require.

No. 88

$1,031,961,754.73 [1]

by Lillian Ross

A LONG about last Thanksgiving, Mayor O'Dwyer gave a luncheon at Gracie Mansion to which he invited a few of his associates for an informal thrashing out of some of the municipal problems that weren't making it any easier for him to sleep nights. Afterward, while coffee and cigars were being served, he remembered something he had intended to mention and, turning to his Director of the Budget, Thomas J. Patterson, he asked him if he was all set to start drawing up the city's budget for the 1947-48 fiscal year. Patterson replied that he and his staff at the Bureau of the Budget were indeed all set. As a matter of fact, he said, he was just about to draft a form letter to the heads of all departments—the usual way of referring to the hundred and nine branches into which the municipality's complex structure is broken down for budget and administrative purposes—

[1] Lillian Ross, "$1,031,961,754.73," *The New Yorker* (July 12, 1947), Vol. XXIII, No. 21, pp. 27-36. Reprinted by permission of *The New Yorker Magazine, Inc.*

asking them to submit their annual requests for money. "Fine, Pat, fine," said the Mayor. "But take it easy on every penny. It's going to be a tough budget. We'll have the usual blather from people who think they're not getting enough and from people who think we're spending too much, but blather doesn't pay bills. We'll have to get along without a lot of things we need." He gave his Budget Director a friendly clap on the back. "Find a way to allocate the few pennies we get so that the two ends will meet," he said.

The two ends of the budget that went into effect last week do meet, in the sense that from July 1, 1947, through June 30, 1948, it is the plan of the city to spend no more money than it takes in. The 1947-48 budget calls for the expenditure of $1,031,961,754.73, which, even not counting the seventy-three cents, comes to quite a few pennies. It is the largest budget in the history of the city—or of any city, for that matter—being some $166,000,000 more than the one approved a year ago, which was a record breaker itself, and in its full printed form, a condensed version of which is the one in general use, it is also the heaviest (twenty-one and a half pounds). It fills a 1,425-page book, which stands as high as the Manhattan Telephone Directory and is twice as wide and almost twice as thick. Patterson and a staff of fifty budget examiners worked on it intensively for six months. The examiners, who busy themselves the rest of the year checking up on where the money goes, sought to outdo one another in lopping dollars and cents off the requests of the various departments to which they were assigned, but they tried not to let penuriousness get the better of sound judgment. Largely as a result of their efforts, for instance, the budget assures the finches, canaries, and conures at the Staten Island Zoo of $6.50 worth of bird gravel during the next twelve months, and it provides $45 for wood-chip bedding for whatever skunks and monkeys come down sick there. It allots $2,750 to pay the salary of an upholsterer for the Fire Department and $508,134,356.54 to pay the salaries of the 157,418 other individuals who, if everything goes according to plan, will work for the city during the coming year. It also allots $10 for two sapphire phonograph needles to see the municipal radio station, WNYC, through its duller moments; $96,500 to heat the American Museum of Natural History and $4.80 for cannel coal for the fireplace in Mayor O'Dwyer's office; $30 for a pair of electric clippers to shear the mice, rats, and rabbits used by the Department of Health in antitoxin experiments; $250,000 for bread and $1,735,000 for meat to feed the inmates of the city's eight prisons and twenty-five hospitals; and $5 for rice and salt to perk up the five police dogs that accompany cops on particularly tough beats.

For the last six months, I've been dropping in every now and then on the people responsible for preparing the budget, and in the course of my visits I've seen a good deal of how it grew from a mere problem on the minds of the Mayor and his Budget Director during their chat at Gracie Mansion to a book of remarkable proportions. Early in January, I went down to the Bureau of the Budget, which occupies half of the twelfth floor of the Municipal Building, just east of City Hall, and had a talk with Mr. Patterson. He is a thin, nervous man of sixty-three, who never has the slightest idea how much money he has in his pockets. He went to work for the city in 1906 as a bookkeeper in the Comptroller's Office, of which the Bureau of the Budget was then a part. Later, the Bureau was set up on its own, and Mr. Patterson stayed with it. Promotions came slowly but with comforting regularity, and in 1943 he became director. He is addicted to chewing gum and has a low opinion of people who don't consider budgets enchanting. (An unselfish man, he permits his wife the pleasure of keeping the family budget, the backbone of which is the $15,000 salary allotted him by the city budget.) Mr. Patterson loses patience when he comes across a city councilman he has reason to suspect has not so much as riffled through the Bureau's master-work. "Read it, read it, for gosh sakes! It's a good book!" he shouted one day last May while discussing the budget with a legislator whose conversation showed plainly that he had not familiarized himself with such engrossing matters as items 196, 197, and 198 on page 1258, wherein it is disclosed how many inspectors of pipes and castings the Board of Water Supply may employ during this fiscal year (one at $3,650, three at $3,230, and three at $3,050). Mr. Patterson's temperament is such that he is rarely able to finish a long sentence. "Say, this year's budget is no lemon," he told a city official who was pondering the results of his efforts a while ago. "It's tough, neat, reasonable, and ninety-nine per cent of it will remain unchanged by the Board or the City Counc . . . Say, what's happened to all the chewing gum around here, anyway?"

Mr. Patterson occupies a large office with a distant view of the Hudson. As I entered the room on my first visit, he was poring over a copy of the 1946-47 budget. "Just opened the book," he said, when I had introduced myself. "I'm trying to get a general idea of what the departments are going to ask for. I read the smallest departmental appropriations first and move on to the big ones. Find it makes better reading that way." At his invitation, I drew up a chair while he unwrapped a stick of gum. The smallest departmental appropriation for 1946-47, he said, had been $3,700 for the Public Administrator of Richmond County. "It's only a one-man department, but he'll ask for more this year," he told me grimly. "They'll *all* ask for more." Shortly after his talk with the Mayor at Gracie Mansion,

Patterson said, he had sent out a letter and a folder of instructions to the heads of all departments, cautioning them not to use abbreviations or ditto marks in their requests; to be sure to fill in the cents columns, even if only with ciphers; and not to be "over-optimistic regarding the financial outlook for next year." He was waiting now for the requests to come in. For the time being, he said, things were rather slow around the office, because most of his examiners were out making on-the-scene studies of departmental needs. When the requests arrived, the examiners would go over them carefully, pruning as they saw fit, and then, after Patterson had approved the results, the Bureau would call in the department heads for separate hearings.

"We're here to help the Mayor figure out what he ought to spend," Patterson said. "The Comptroller is the one who tells him how much revenue he'll get to spend. He'll have *his* estimates ready next month—the conservative ones, that is. Comptrollers are always conservative in the beginning. We've got to have our figures ready for the Mayor by the middle of March. That's when a mayor always goes into what we call the annual budget retreat —right here, in a conference room next door. Takes about two weeks, all day every day." After the Mayor has approved the budget, Patterson told me, the Board of Estimate gets a crack at it, and then the City Council. "But they won't change it much," he said. "Actually, all the work on the budget is done right here. My examiners know more about the departments than the departments know themselves. You might say they help me piece this book together. Come back in a month or so, when we've got something good to show you." As I left, he was unwrapping a fresh stick of gum.

I stopped by to see Patterson again about the middle of February. This time, I found him standing before his desk looking agitated and chewing gum at an accelerated clip. "Can't spare a minute," he said, pommelling himself on the temples. "Got to go over estimates with eight examiners to-day. The Comptroller just sent us his revenue estimates, and now we've got to revise some of our figures downward. Hardly a month before the Mayor comes over for his retreat, and we've got to be ready for him. He'll want to know why we can't do without this and why we can't do without that. It was nerve-racking under LaGuardia and it's nerve-racking with this man." He sat down and sighed heavily. "It was *especially* nerve-racking under LaGuardia," he said. "Fiorello moved right into my offices for two weeks. I had to move out and sit with Miss Pray—that's my secretary. Fiorello never went out to lunch. Sent out for hot dogs, which he ate with mustard provided by us. We never got an appropriation for it, either. Tell you what. You talk to a few of my examiners. I'll get you some who've already gone over their estimates with me, and then you'll know what we're going to tell the Mayor."

He picked up his phone, asked for a Mr. Fitzpatrick, and told him to come in for a minute. Then he turned back to me. "One of our oldest and stingiest men," he said complacently. "You couldn't do better than talk to Fitzpatrick. Let me tell you, the departments asked for a total of eighty million dollars more than they got last budget. We'll give them ten or eleven. On top of that, though, there'll be about a hundred and twenty-five million of what we call mandatory, or inescapable, increases— for debt service, pensions, things like that." He shook his head gloomily. "Even the Public Administrator of Richmond County wants more. Remember I said he would? Well, he wants two thousand more. We *need* stingy examiners. Not that we're trying to deprive the departments or anything. Take Grant's Tomb, for instance. We're giving the Tomb seven thousand in this budget. That's two hundred and fifty dollars over last year. Well, our Grant's Tomb examiner is satisfied that they really need that extra two-fifty for repairs, new flags, keys, fuses, furniture polish, and uniforms— for the caretaker, I mean, not Grant."

The door opened and an elderly, white-haired man with a high stiff collar came into the office. "This is Mr. Fitzpatrick—Libraries, Museums, and Gardens," Patterson said. "Mr. Fitzpatrick will show you how the examiners work." Mr. Fitzpatrick nodded gravely and asked me to come with him. I followed him down a long corridor to his office, where he introduced me to two other examiners, named Walsh and McEneney, assigned, respectively, to the Police and Fire Departments. Both of them were working in their shirtsleeves at desks piled with papers. These, and two more desks that were unoccupied at the moment, pretty well filled the room. Mr. Fitzpatrick walked over to one of the vacant desks. "I work on several departments," he said stiffly. "Mr. Walsh and Mr. McEneney, they are concerned wholly with a single department each."

"Cops keep you busy," said Walsh, a stocky, square-jawed, middle-aged man with bright pink cheeks, who was smoking a cigar in a long holder.

McEneney, a dour, six-foot, sandy-haired man in his fifties, looked at him thoughtfully. "Firemen keep you busier," he said.

"We enjoy quite a bit of friendly rivalry," Mr. Fitzpatrick said as the other two returned to their work. He pulled a chair over beside his desk, arranged it precisely parallel to his, and bowed slightly in its direction. I sat down. "I think we'll run through the Botanical Garden first," he said, choosing his words carefully and speaking in a slightly querulous voice. "They were pretty good this year." From the top drawer of his desk he took a folder containing several sheets of paper covered with figures.

"The Botanical people didn't exaggerate their circumstances very much," he went on. "They requested three hundred and fifty-three thousand two hundred and eighty dollars, and we're giving them within six thousand of that. And in the case of many items, I must say I didn't have to restrain them very much." He consulted his folder before continuing. "Let's see. They wanted a hundred and fifty for bamboo poles for plants to climb up on, forty-five for pot labels, a hundred and ten for fish-oil soap, seven hundred and fifty for cow manure, and three hundred and twenty-five for a motor scythe to work on rocky and rough ground a regular mowing machine can't operate on. All those sounded reasonable to me and I gave them exactly what they asked for. But they also wanted two hundred for two new typewriters, and I said no. I'm not very liberal on typewriters." I asked him what happened when a department and he disagreed on how much was needed, and he replied that some officials complained directly to Patterson. "But the Budget Director and I, we usually have a meeting of minds on the question," he added.

"Some Commissioners go crying to the Mayor," said Walsh, pushing his papers aside. "But not my Commissioner. Not Wallander. That I'll say for him." A band down in the street, twelve stories below, started to play "My Old Kentucky Home," and the music came clearly through the windows. "My cops are getting medals over at City Hall," Walsh said. "That's their band. Don't it play loud and nice?"

Mr. Fitzpatrick cleared his throat noisily, gave Walsh a cool look, and started to tell me why he was going to recommend increasing the salary of the lady in charge of the picture collection at the Public Library from $3,120 a year to $3,660, but before he got very far, his telephone rang. When he had hung up, he said I'd have to excuse him. The Budget Director wanted to go over his estimates on the Metropolitan Museum of Art with him. He put the folder carefully away in his desk, adjusted his collar, took another folder from a cabinet, bowed to me, and left.

"That's O.K.," Walsh said to me. "McEneney and I will tell you what goes on. But don't get me wrong. Fitz is all right. Nothing gets past him." Without turning around in his chair, he pointed behind him to a big green calendar on the wall. On it was printed, "Official Calendar, Police Department, City of New York, Arthur W. Wallander, Commissioner." "I've been taking care of cops these past fifteen years, so I guess I've got a right to it," Walsh said. "A four-bit calendar. We're giving the cops five hundred of them in the new budget. Cops got to have their own calendars, because it wouldn't look proper, now, to walk into a station house and see one put out by a beer company or something the butcher gave out for Christmas."

McEneney, who had been listening to all this with a skeptical look, remarked dryly, "Fire gets along all right with calendars from the butcher."

"The Mayor is more particular about cops," Walsh said. "They're asking for ninety-two million. We'll give them about ninety—maybe more. We're even giving the mounted cops two vans to carry horses in. Each van costs ninety-five hundred. Holds eight horses in stalls and eight mounted cops in a section of their own up front. For five years I've been saying no on those vans. Now the Budget Director's got himself convinced that the Mounted Division needs them. Horses get all tired out, he says, walking all the way from their barn in Queens to scenes of emergency, like I Am an American Day. I was overruled, but I still say horses can walk. They don't need taxis."

McEneney remarked that he didn't give money away that easily to the Fire Department. For one thing, he had turned down a request for $688,200 to pay the salaries of a hundred and forty-four additional lieutenants, and the Budget Director had backed him up. "Fire can get along without *any* new lieutenants," McEneney said. "They've already got a lot of lieutenants posted in theatres and night clubs. They say they've got to be there to reassure the public in case of conflagration. I say nonsense. I say theatre ushers can reassure the public. What Fire can do is inspect the theatres and night clubs, so that conflagrations won't break out. All those lieutenants can be released and go to work. Patterson agreed with me. Fire wants fifty six million. We'll give them about fifty-three, maybe less."

A short, swarthy man came into the room. "Look who's here," Walsh said. "Carlo Montecalvo—Licenses, County Clerks, City Register, City Sheriff, Board of Elections, City Record. The stingiest examiner in the office."

"I'm the stingiest," McEneney said mildly.

Montecalvo pulled up a chair in front of McEneney's desk and straddled it. "Always fighting about who is the stingiest in getting up the good book," he said amiably.

I asked whether any of the department heads had been making much fuss over the allotments at their hearings with the Budget Director, and Walsh replied that, speaking for himself, the Police hearing had taken all of twenty minutes. The Police Commissioner had simply read a statement summarizing his requests. "He said he wanted two hundred and thirty-two new motorcycles and so forth," Walsh told me. "We're giving him fifty new motorcycles and so forth. But the Commissioner don't know it yet. I didn't want to start any discussion. You start a discussion and it goes on for days."

Montecalvo said he had had no trouble at all with Licenses. Among other things, he had allowed the Department five additional inspectors (twenty requested), one fluorescent desk lamp for the Commissioner's office (one requested), three wall clocks (five requested), and no typewriters with Gothic type (five requested). He had allotted twenty-six dollars for paper towels. "Licenses used roll towels before, but paper towels cost about the same," he said. "They got a right to change their tastes."

The Board of Elections and the City Sheriff, on the other hand, had not been so easy. "The Board is going to cost us two million two hundred and thirty-four thousand nine hundred and ninety dollars," Montecalvo said, rattling off the figure as easily as if he were telling me the price of a pair of shoes. "We got two election primaries for this budget—the primary next fall and the spring Presidential primary—and the cost of printing ballots is way up." He suddenly looked forlorn. "We had to give the Board three hundred thousand more than what we did a year ago," he said. The two other examiners shook their heads sympathetically. "I cut them down thirty thousand, though," Montecalvo continued, brightening. "They wanted a lot of things I turned them down on. And if I can persuade the Budget Director that the canvas voting booths don't need a cleaning this year, I'll save another sixty-two hundred."

In the case of the City Sheriff, Montecalvo confessed, he had been overruled by the Budget Director on two or three counts. "I gave the Sheriff a new washing machine for the New York County Jail," he said. "The machine they got now, it's so old and dilapidated, even when it works it tears apart all the sheets and cooks' aprons they put in it. But then the Sheriff wanted a seven-hundred-and-fifty-dollar set of law reports, and I gave that a big zero, because I figured he could go on using the Bar Association's reports, just like he's been doing all along. But the boss didn't agree with me. Oh, well, I can take a rebuff the same as the next man."

"My Aunt Minnie," Walsh said, grinning at his two colleagues.

On my way out, I stopped in at Patterson's office to thank him for his help. He was there alone, going over Water Supply, Gas, and Electricity's requests, and I asked him what had become of Mr. Fitzpatrick. "Gone up to the Metropolitan Museum," he replied, adding that both he and Mr. Fitzpatrick had decided they needed more information about the duties of a $2,640-a-year steamfitter there. "Got to keep our noses to the grinding stone," he went on, chewing his gum furiously. "Got to have everything in order for the Mayor when he comes over for his retreat." I said I'd like to sit in on some part of the retreat, and he told me that to do so I'd have to get in touch with Louis Cohen, Assistant to the Mayor. "Cohen was over just the other day," Patterson said. "Encouraging us to get our estimates lower. So the Mayor can see our figures without seeing red, if you catch what I mean."

By the middle of March, Mayor O'Dwyer was ready for his retreat, and the Budget Bureau was ready for him. On the day the retreat began, I got in touch with Cohen, who said he'd try to get me in. There probably wouldn't be any vetoing of appropriations while I was there, he said, as differences of opinion on such controversial matters are usually kept confidential. "We don't want to hurt a department's feelings any more than necessary," Cohen explained. He added that he was going to be present at the retreat himself that afternoon and said he would take me along if I came down to his office at City Hall at one o'clock. When I arrived there, he was sitting at his desk, adroitly eating a cheese sandwich and talking into the telephone. He waved me to a chair and went on talking. Cohen is a careworn, cynical Democrat from the Bronx who started as an office boy in the Health Department in 1908 and worked his way up to Deputy Commissioner of Hospitals under Mayor Walker. He was elected a City Councilman during the LaGuardia regime and served as chairman of the Council's Finance Committee, in which capacity he found many pleasurable opportunities to hack away at the Fusion Mayor's budgets. "The Mayor can raise or lower the budget, and so can the Board of Estimate," Cohen once told me. "But the Council can only lower it. And that's what we always tried to do. LaGuardia was always claiming that he had cut his budget to the bone, and I'd always thunder at him, 'Send in the bone! We'll cut it!'"

Upon finishing his phone call, Cohen jammed his hat on his head and led the way outdoors. It was a warm day, the sun was shining, and a peanut vender in City Hall Park was doing a fine business with the lunch-hour crowds. The benches in the park were filled with men and women sitting with their coats open and their faces lifted to the sun. "Municipal Civil Service workers," said Cohen, with elaborate sympathy. "Look at them. They're so pale. They're just getting over twelve years of horror." He changed his tone abruptly. "Listen, you sure you know where the city gets its money?"

"Taxes?" I suggested.

"That's what they all think," he said, glancing at me pityingly. "But how about forty million from water rates, thirty million in federal aid, a hundred and forty million in state aid? A million here, a million there – licenses, market rentals, student fees, ferry tolls. They all bring in money. Remember that. Sure, there are taxes, too—the Comptroller estimates a hundred million from the sales tax, three million from the hotel-room tax. Whatever we need in addition to all such steady income we have to make up by taxing real estate. But, except for whatever's needed to service the city's debt for capital improvements, you can't tax real estate more than two per cent of the average assessed valuation for the last five years. That's the law, and that's one reason you've got to keep the budget down."

A patrolman was guarding the door to Patterson's conference room. He greeted Cohen, and just then two men, one in a Fire Department uniform, came out of the door, looking flushed and unhappy, and hurried away. Cohen identified them as the Fire Commissioner and his Chief and said that he suspected they had just heard the Mayor veto a number of their pet projects. Then he excused himself, explaining that he'd better go ahead and see if this was a good time for me to sit in. In a moment, he reappeared in the doorway and beckoned to me. I walked into a spacious room with a table running almost its entire length. The Mayor and Patterson were sitting side by side about halfway down it and there were eight or ten other men seated around it—budget examiners, Cohen said. The table was heaped with documents, and in front of the Mayor stood a tumbler holding seven or eight cellophane-wrapped cigars. O'Dwyer, I thought, looked heavier and more fatigued than he had when I had first met him, about a year before. He nodded as I took a chair on the opposite side of the table, and, helping himself to one of the cigars, put it in a holder and lit it. At that point, my old friend Mr. Montecalvo came into the room and advanced toward an empty chair at the table. "Boys, I know this man," Cohen said. "Montecalvo. Examiner of Licenses. He wouldn't give away the right time of day." Montecalvo grinned self-consciously as he sat down, and the Mayor looked at him approvingly. "Now," said Patterson, "the Department of Licenses is going to cost two hundred and seventy-two thousand one hundred and seventy-five dollars this year, Mr. Mayor. It's up forty-five thousand over last year, but it's eighty thousand less than the Department wanted. We gave them five new inspectors, for one thing."

"Have they increased the number of licenses to be inspected?" the Mayor asked, in such a low voice that I could hardly hear him. Montecalvo replied that inspection work was expected to increase considerably because it looked as if licenses were going to be issued to at least four new categories of business.

"This department brought in sixty thousand more than last year," Patterson said quickly. "And the inspectors, they're . . . That right, Montecalvo?"

"Yes, the inspectors are absolutely necessary," the examiner said. "In fact, I've been very miserly with Licenses, Mr. Mayor. The Commissioner asked for a lot more inspectors, but I told him he could use the Police Department for the rest."

"Now, is that sound?" the Mayor asked, studying his cigar holder. "Is it sound for the License Commissioner to be so short of his own men that he has to use the police?"

"Why, Mr. Mayor, he'd need a *thousand* new men if he didn't use the police," said Montecalvo.

"Didn't *you* have to help out with license inspections when you . . . ?" Patterson asked, looking at the Mayor in amazement.

The Mayor leaned far back in his chair. "Oh, that's right," he said. "Come to think of it, in the days when I was on the police force, you had to turn in a report on every hole in the street. You had a card with a list of things to look for on your tour of patrol, and if you failed to report an unlicensed junk wagon or something, and the sergeant came along and spotted it, you were subject to discipline. All right, Pat," he said, straightening up and tapping the ashes off his cigar. "Licenses looks all right to me. Believe me, friend," he said, turning to me, "all the departments aren't as reasonable as this one." Then he nodded at Montecalvo, who left, looking flattered.

"Now, how about Debt Service, Pat?" the Mayor asked. "Debt Service— the mortgage on the home," he went on, while Patterson placed some papers in front of him. "Before we can move, before we can buy so much as a lead pencil, we've got to provide the money for Debt Service—amortization and interest payments on what the city owes. How much is it, Pat?"

Patterson said it came to $201,583,273.69 and was, as usual, the biggest item in the budget. "And how much does the city owe altogether?" the Mayor asked, as if he were leading the recital of a catechism, and Patterson chirped, "Two billion eight hundred and fifty-seven million twenty-three thousand nine hundred and ninety dollars and forty-eight cents."

After a properly respectful silence, Cohen grumbled that the city's indebtedness was the fault of earlier regimes and that nobody could do anything about it now. "It's like that time around 1870," he said, "when they went and issued two hundred and seventy-eight thousand dollars' worth of seven-per-cent non-callable bonds so they could lay some wooden planks on a street up in the West Farms section of the Bronx. The last of those aren't going to mature until March 1st, 2147. A hundred and ninety-eight thousand dollars' worth of them are still outstanding, and they're going to cost us nearly fourteen thousand in interest this year."

"You mean we still don't own the Bronx, Louie?" the Mayor demanded.

"Just two hundred years more and it'll be ours," Cohen assured him. "But for that matter, practically all the bonds the city has ever issued were non-callable because the bankers say they won't take any other kind. Why, only back in 1940, when the city took over the subways, it issued more than three hundred million dollars' worth of three-per-cent bonds that won't mature until 1980. To-day we could borrow that money at two per cent or less, but we can't call those bonds in."

"Most of the subway equipment the city bought with that money has already been discarded," the Mayor said. "But we'll still be paying for it for the next thirty-three years. How much is the interest on all the city's non-callable bonds, Pat?" About a hundred and two million dollars this year, Patterson told him. "I wish I knew who thought up the idea of non-callable bonds," the Mayor said. "I'd heave every plank in West Farms at him. But I suppose most of the planks are worn out by this time."

"All of them are," said Cohen.

On April 1st, Patterson sent me a copy of his twenty-one-and-a-half-pound book, printed (at a cost of $32,575.20) in advance of approval or amendment by the Board of Estimate and the City Council on the assumption that whatever alterations were to come would involve nothing more than changing some of the figures and then running another edition off the presses. With it, he enclosed a copy of the Mayor's budget message (three ounces) to the Board and the Council. I read the message first. In it, the Mayor lamented that the budget did not provide for all the services that he considered essential but declared that it was the best he could do within the city's financial limitations. He noted that he had pared $68,400,000 from the total requested by the various departments. He did not mention horse vans, voting booths, or typewriters with Gothic type. The total sum he felt obliged to spend during the coming fiscal year, he said, was $1,029,120,314.73. (Upon reading the message, a conscientious representative of a taxpayers' organization sat right down and figured out that at this rate the city would be spending $32.54 a second.)

I then read enough of Patterson's book to discover that the Mayor had decided that the Police Department needed about half a million less than Examiner Walsh thought it did and that the Fire Department needed about a hundred thousand less than McEneney thought it did.

During the second week of April, public hearings were held at which a hundred and sixty-seven of the 7,835,000 citizens of New York City appeared before the Board of Estimate to argue for changes in the budget. They had their say for five fairly fruitless days—the longest series of hearings on the subject in the city's history. The official steno-typist for the Board, who has been recording budget hearings for the last nineteen years and estimates that all told they have run to a total of at least forty million words ("Maybe it's fifty million," he says. "All I know is I've got a broken back"), took down 620,000 words during those five days.

On the morning of the first hearing, I went around to Patterson's office beforehand to catch up on the latest developments. Patterson told me that several days after the session of the retreat I had attended, the Mayor and he had totted up totals and discovered that the budget was something like twelve million dollars more than the revenue anticipated by the Comptroller. So they had gone back over most of the large departmental appropriations and after several hours of anguish had cut out those twelve million. "We had to cut a lot of items we still think are essential," Patterson said as we walked over to City Hall together. "The Mayor was very unhappy about it. Much as I hate to admit it, we even had to cut Education a million and a half—fuel, salaries for substitute teachers, and a hundred thousand dollars' worth of school supplies. We had to take away two inspectors from Licenses, too." I asked him how about the horse vans for the Police Department and he said Police would get only one van, instead of two. I asked him what had been done about the sixty-two hundred dollars the Board of Elections wanted to clean its voting booths. "Well," he said, "I thought we ought to clean them, but that looked like a good way to save a little. As a matter of fact, you know, Montecalvo was against it all along. Well, here we are, just in time for the start of the great debate."

The hearings were held in the Board's large, drafty chamber on the second floor of City Hall. The members of the Board are the Mayor (three votes), the Comptroller (three votes), the President of the City Council (three votes), and the five Borough Presidents (two votes each for Manhattan and Brooklyn, and one vote each for Queens, the Bronx, and Richmond). The Board members sat at a horseshoe-shaped mahogany table on a dais at one end of the room, facing the public, which occupied cream-colored, pewlike benches. All Board members were provided with a copy of the 1,425-page book and a glass of water, and the Mayor with an ebony gavel, as well. Throughout the hearings, the Mayor nearly always had something to say in reply to those who had something to say to the Board. The majority of those who showed up turned out to be municipal employees pleading for higher pay. At one stage in the proceedings, a man named Max Weintraub, who described himself as a stenographer in the Magistrates' Court in East New York, told the Board that he and seventeen other court stenographers were getting a bad deal. True, they had received small raises last year and the year before, bringing them up to around $3,500, but prior to that they had received the same salary for thirteen years and now the new budget made no provision at all to increase their pay. Moreover, according to Mr. Weintraub, court stenographers were given little opportunity to get ahead in the world. "Firemen can become lieutenants, patrol-men can become sergeants, we can become nothing—so here we are," he said. "Max, I know you boys work hard," the Mayor replied. "I know because I was a magistrate and I remember you. Many a new magistrate you broke in, including myself." He then told Weintraub that the city was simply too poor to grant him a raise this year and asked him to give his regards to the boys at the court.

About a score of speakers asked the Board to cut the budget. The rest wanted the city to spend more money, and some of them offered their own pet ideas of how to raise it—by licensing bicycles, baby carriages, bookies, and crap-game operators; by charging fees for police protection of payroll messengers; by imposing special taxes on the rich; by raising the transit fare and the price of ashes sold by the Sanitation Department; and by *making* Governor Dewey give more money to the city. By the fifth day, the members of the Board looked exhausted. The Borough Presidents of Manhattan and Queens took to dozing intermittently, and the Borough President of Brooklyn took to winking benevolently at elderly ladies in the front pews. The Mayor began to make frequent references to the grievous effects of public service upon a man's health. "Believe me, I'd rather see the flowers as they grow instead of in some funeral parlor," he remarked at one point. A Department of Sanitation man got up to describe the difficulties of his work on cranes and derricks and asked the Mayor to turn to an item on page 762 of the budget. "Just tell me what's on the page," the Mayor said wearily, taking a sip of water. "If we go on like this much longer, I'll be wrecking my wrist." But the people who had come to be heard kept on speaking. A man from the Department of Welfare wanted subway passes for social workers, officers of Parent-Teacher Associations protested against the cut in the allotment for school supplies, and a physician spoke up for more generous treatment of hospital psychiatrists. And so it went. At seven-fifteen that evening, the Mayor recognized the only remaining occupant of the benches—Myra Barnes, a retired schoolteacher from Staten Island, who, it developed, had come to complain not about the budget but about the dumping of garbage in her borough. She talked on for twenty minutes, and when she had finished, the Mayor banged his gavel on the table and declared the hearing adjourned. As the members of the Board started to leave, a man dashed into the room, clamoring that he had waited days to speak and had just left the room for a moment to call his wife to say he'd be late getting home. The Mayor and his colleagues resignedly took their seats again, and the man introduced himself as a climber-pruner for the Parks Department. He felt that since the city had two and a half million trees waiting to be pruned, its pruners should be better paid. The Mayor thanked him, and the hearing was adjourned, finally and officially, at seven-forty-five.

Three days later, the members of the Board of Estimate met again, this time in a closed session at which the Comptroller, I subsequently learned, brought the good news that he had underestimated the city's revenues for the year by about $2,000,000. But any substantial increase of the budget over that figure, he warned, would mean exceeding the limit set on real-estate taxation. In less than an hour, the Board decided to boost the budget $2,841,440—all for the benefit of schools, child-care centers, hospitals, and charitable institutions—and the following day, at an open meeting, it approved its own decision in a matter of minutes. Nothing was said about the problems of climber-pruners, court stenographers, or the dumping of garbage on Staten Island.

I had a brief talk with Mr. Patterson after the Board had approved the budget. He seemed very happy. His face was flushed with excitement and his jaws champed with even more than their accustomed vigor. "Have you read the book yet?" he asked eagerly. I was able to tell him truthfully that I had examined a number of its pages. "It isn't like last year's book," he said. "Last year, the Mayor and the Board did it over three times and then stuck in *eight* million. They barely touched it this year. Less than three million."

Within a week after the Board of Estimate had completed its labors, the City Council received the budget and passed it on to its Finance Committee for study. The Committee is headed by Colonel Charles E. Keegan, a Bronx Democrat who served as Military Governor of Bavaria in 1945, and it has nine other members, six of whom are also Democrats, two Republicans, and one a Communist—a political balance intentionally like that of the twenty-three-member Council. On May 1st, the Finance Committee held a public hearing on the budget in the Council Chamber, a few doors from the Board of Estimate's meeting place. In the chamber are a gallery for the public, a dais for the presiding officer, and desks and chairs for the Councilmen, arranged in a semicircle. When I got there, the gallery was empty, but all the members of the Committee were present except the Communist, Benjamin J. Davis, Jr., who was out marching in the May Day Parade. On the floor with them were five persons who wanted to be heard. Four of them representing municipal workers' unions, asked that the budget be passed without cuts. The fifth, a spokesman for the Citizens Budget Commission, thought he saw how reductions totalling $5,687,676 could be made. He wanted to cut out the appropriations for the upkeep of airports leased by the city to the Port of New York Authority, for Station WNYC (which, he said, the city should lease to a private operator), and for a number of other things. The hearing lasted only thirty-five minutes. After it was over, I asked Colonel Keegan how long it would take the Council to act on the budget. "Well," he said, "we're licked if we can't find anything to whittle out before May 22nd. That's our deadline, but we might be able to do the job in two weeks." He promised to let me know when the Finance Committee had finished its studies and was ready to report to the Council.

Mr. Cohen, who had also attended this desultory session, walked downstairs with me from the Council Chamber. He was in a cheerful mood. "This is the time *I* always used to make trouble when I was a member of the Council," he said. "I got in LaGuardia's hair. I got in Patterson's hair. I was trouble." He went on to say that if the Council should decide to make any changes, the budget would have to go back to the Mayor, who has the power of veto. If the Mayor should exercise that power, it would take a three-fourths vote of the Council to overrule him. I asked him what would happen if the city should be obliged to spend beyond its means. "Well, it's happened often enough in the past," he said. "When it does, the city pays the extra by issuing notes against future budgets."

At the foot of the stairs, we met a pudgy, bald man in shirtsleeves who was smoking a pipe. Cohen introduced him to me as Councilman Hart, of Brooklyn. I asked him whether he thought the City Council would cut the budget.

"What budget?" he asked.

"Why, you know, the city budget," said Cohen.

"Oh, *that*," said Councilman Hart, putting a hand on Cohen's shoulder. "Louie knows we wouldn't cut that. What the Council does about it is just a formality."

Shortly before lunchtime five days later, Colonel Keegan telephoned me to say that there was a change of plan and the Council was going to consider the budget that afternoon. Most of the Councilmen were already at their desks when I arrived, and I saw Councilman Hart among them, alternately puffing at his pipe and talking to Cohen. The gallery was filled with high-school boys and girls from a current-events class, many of whom were earnestly leaning over the rail to get a better view of the taxpayers' representatives in action. One of the Councilmen came over to me and said that action was being taken two weeks earlier than expected, because some of the city accountants who would have to compute the real-estate tax on the basis of the budget as finally approved had planned a fishing trip.

(Before taking off with their rods and reels, the accountants produced a set of figures that called for a nineteen-point rise in the city-wide tax rate—from $2.70 to $2.89 on each $100 of assessed valuation.)

When Council President Vincent Impellitteri got the meeting under way, Colonel Keegan reported that the Finance Committee had no changes to recommend in the budget and advocated its adoption. This precipitated an hour-long session of arguments, motion-making, and general confusion, in the course of which Councilman Phillips, a Republican of Queens, moved that the $161,000 allotted to Station WNYC for salaries be deleted. At this, Democratic Majority Leader Sharkey of Brooklyn got up and said that he had been opposed to the operation of WNYC under the LaGuardia administration but favored letting it run under the present one because it was now furthering "the cultural development of the people." Councilman Hart, who is also a Democrat, expressed pleasure that WNYC was not being used any longer as "an instrument of torture." The motion to deny funds for the station was defeated, 20-3. Councilman Goldberg, a Liberal of Brooklyn, moved to adjourn the meeting, saying that more time was needed to study the budget. Councilman (or Colonel) Keegan moved to table this motion. Councilman Goldberg was ruled out of order and replied by shouting that a motion to adjourn was always in order. "Likewise a motion to table!" Councilman Keegan shouted back. Councilman Goldberg said a motion to adjourn could not be tabled. His motion was tabled, 16-7.

When the Council got around to voting on the adoption of the Finance Committee's favorable report, Councilman Palestin of the Bronx, another Liberal, voted against it, and a moment later, before the voting was completed, stood up and said he wanted to change his vote and would be glad to tell his colleagues why. He explained that he had voted against adoption because the budget was so big and, he felt, was being steamrollered through without giving the Councilmen sufficient time to study it. He declared that the first he had heard of the budget was on May 5th, and here it was only May 6th. He wound up by saying, "Now that I have heard my own remarks, I think I will not change my mind after all and will still vote against adopting the report." The report was adopted, 16-7. Before a vote was taken on the budget itself, Councilman Sharkey said that Councilmen Goldberg and Palestin had had twenty days in which to study the document. "And if you had another twenty, or two hundred, you still wouldn't open that book!" he shouted. I looked at Budget Director Patterson, who was slouching in a chair across the room from me. His jaw was still, and he was staring disconsolately first at Goldberg and then at Palestin. The

Council President finally halted the wrangling by announcing that the vote on the budget would now be taken. The budget was adopted, 23-0.

After the meeting was adjourned, I went over to Patterson and congratulated him. "Thanks," he said, but he didn't look particularly happy. "How do you like *that*?" he asked irritably. "Everybody here had a copy of the book in front of him, and as far as I could see, not one of them even opened . . . Say"—he grabbed my arm and smiled proudly—"do you know that more than ninety-nine per cent of this budget stood as we made it? Well, that's that for a while," he added, tenderly gathering up a mess of papers and a copy of his book from underneath his chair.

Two days later, in his office, the Mayor signed a statement certifying that $1,031,961,754.73 was the amount approved to keep the city running during the next fiscal year. He did so at a two-minute ceremony attended only by Cohen and a meagre scattering of the press. The Mayor's large desk was bare except for the statement, two fountain pens in a stand, a clock, an ashtray, and, looming large far to his left, a copy of the budget. A moment after the Mayor had signed and a couple of photographers had taken his picture, a friend of his happened in and remarked, "It looks like a big book, Bill."

O'Dwyer grimaced. "It's *too* big, chum," he replied. "Don't think I like it. But it's a budget that makes the two ends meet. And all the blather in the world couldn't have made it one penny more or, believe me, one penny less."

No. 89

A DIFFERENT PRESCRIPTION [1]

by Charles E. Merriam

THE genuine reductions in American governmental costs will not be made by alarmists in a panic, but by careful examination of the underlying difficulties. I confess to a very genuine alarm at the activities of some well-intentioned citizens who are carrying on a crusade against high costs—sincerely but, as it seems to me, destructively. In the old days out in the country when a fire broke out, there was sometimes as much damage done by the amateur fireman as by the flames themselves.

I venture to offer to citizens and taxpayers, concerned as they should be about a sound fiscal policy, the following suggestions, which are widely different from those commonly presented, but which in my judgment and experience are likely to prove more useful in the long run.

[1] Charles E. Merriam, "A Different Prescription," *State Government* (June, 1932), Vol. 5, page 1. Reprinted by permission of the author and *State Government*.

1. *Abolish the spoils system* now found in 3,600 counties, 38 states [in 1932], and hundreds of cities; and enforce and develop the merit system where already found. The spoils system is the beginning of evil in governmental expenditures, and out of this come graft, corruption, and incompetence. Unless the spoils system can be abolished, not only will taxes mount higher and higher, and public services lag, but the industrial future of the nation will be seriously jeopardized by incompetent dealing with the vital economic affairs of the republic.

2. *Encourage the organization and training of responsible governing officials.* There are some 800 organizations of officials in the United States, some of which are very active although a few do little more than hold an annual banquet. The development of these responsible governing groups is full of promise for the future of American government.

3. *Reorganize the government units and departments* in such manner as to prevent the great wastes of overlapping and duplication. There are now in the United States more than 200,000 independent governing and taxing bodies. No one seems to know within a good many thousand just how many there are, but everyone knows there are too many, and that they are very expensive.

From another point of view, I venture to offer the following suggestions as to how governmental burdens may be lightened.

1. *Stop boycotting the governmental service.* There is throughout the United States a widespread and vociferous propaganda against government. This is not only the attitude of certain radicals, but of certain conservatives. This boycott of government and public life makes difficult the recruitment of the personnel necessary for government. It makes government inviting for spoilsmen, grafters, and racketeers and drives away many of those who might best serve the state. It produces higher costs and lower achievement levels. Unless we lift the boycott on government, there can be no substantial economy.

2. *Do not be misled by propagandists who say "economy" when they mean "immunity" from public regulation.* They wish to save money in order to conserve their own special privileges. We might save money by abolishing the Interstate Commerce Commission or the Federal Trade Commission, or by getting rid of the Public Utilities Commission of the state. But we might save a nickel and lose a dollar.

3. *Cultivate the forward look in government.* Unless our attitude toward government can become more flexible, there will be no permanent and substantial reduction in the expenditures of government. There may be panicky and foolish slashing of budgets, but there will not be that sound and prudent advance toward better use of the public money.

I have not been officially notified, as was Noah, of the coming flood, nor do I share the pessimism of Spengler in his gloomy prediction of the decline of western civilization. But unless I misread the signs of the times, our political and economic theory and practice must soon move up to a higher level and adjust themselves to the new conditions inexorably imposed on us by modern industrial and scientific development.

Chapter XXV

THE UNITED STATES IN ONE WORLD

[Two world wars have brought the United States into a major role in world affairs. As a nation, it is not possible, if it ever were possible, to withdraw into our own boundaries and let the rest of the world go by. The rest of the world is unable to go its way, unconcerned and unaffected by our policies—domestic as well as foreign. What we do and how we do it will determine, to a great extent, the course of civilization.

This means that the process of conducting our foreign relations and the nature of our foreign policy are of compelling significance to every American. This chapter makes no pretense of offering a systematic and complete picture of these matters. It does, however, present clearly certain aspects of and opinions about the conduct of our foreign affairs, the process of treaty making, the progress toward world law, and the problems of world government.

No. 90

FOREIGN AFFAIRS [1]

by The Commission on Organization of the Executive Branch of the Government

II. THE COMPLEXITIES OF THE PRESENT SITUATION

THE time is particularly appropriate to appraise the machinery of the Government for the conduct of foreign affairs. The United States emerged from the recent World War with a radically new role in world affairs. As a result, to-day's organizational requirements are drastically different from those of the prewar era. The executive branch to-day finds itself forced to develop positive foreign policies and programs, involving not merely the State Department but many other departments and agencies as well, and to deal cooperatively with other nations on a multilateral as well as a bilateral basis. The Congress, in addition, finds that the exercise

---

[1] The Commission on Organization of the Executive Branch of the Government, *Foreign Affairs*, A Report to the Congress (Washington, D. C., Government Printing Office, 1949), pp. 3-13, 17-21.

of its traditional powers in the domestic as well as in the international field has made it a participant in the conduct of foreign affairs on an unprecedented scale.

The problems of Government organization for the conduct of foreign affairs are, therefore, not confined to the State Department alone but involve the organization of the Presidency, the State Department and the Foreign Service, the departments and agencies other than the State Department, the interdepartmental relationships, and the relationships between the executive and legislative branches. The special problems in each of these cases will be discussed separately at a subsequent point. Accompanying the involvement of all these elements and contributing to the complexities of the situation is the increased size of the Government as a whole and of the State Department in particular.

Tangible manifestations of the foregoing are found on all sides. In the Presidency new factors affecting the conduct of foreign affairs include the Chief of Staff to the President and statutory interdepartmental bodies such as the National Security Council. The State Department itself in terms of appropriations is 12 times larger and in terms of personnel almost 5 times larger in 1948 than it was in 1938. In the interdepartmental field there are more than 30 committees concerned with economic, social, military, and other aspects of foreign affairs. Of 59 major departments and agencies in the executive branch, at least 46 are drawn into foreign affairs to a greater or lesser extent. Certain units are deeply involved, such as the National Military Establishment in connection with the administration of occupied areas abroad, the Economic Cooperation Administration in connection with financial assistance overseas, the Treasury Department in international financial matters, and the Commerce Department in connection with export control. Finally, Congressional participation in the conduct of foreign affairs has become particularly evident in the enhancement of the role of the House of Representatives in connection with appropriations for foreign programs.

A. *The Executive-Legislative Relationship Under the Constitution in the Conduct of Foreign Affairs*

The organization of the executive branch for the conduct of foreign affairs must necessarily be shaped to accord with the over-all governmental framework provided by the Constitution. The constitutional doctrine of separation of powers between the executive and legislative branches results in a duality of authority over foreign affairs which complicates the machinery of Government in that area, especially in contrast with the machinery of countries operating under the parliamentary system of government.

The difficulty caused by this duality of authority has been sharpened by the new position of the United States in world affairs. Prior to the recent World War, the Congress at times had considerable influence, of course, on foreign relations, but not on any continuous basis. The President, on the other hand, possessing relatively greater powers than in domestic affairs, largely controlled foreign affairs with only occasional reference to the Congress. Recent events have changed the situation and made the Congress a much more significant and regular participant in foreign affairs. As a consequence, the solutions of to-day's problems require joint legislative-executive cooperation on a scale heretofore unknown in American history.

The Constitution is not at all precise in its allocation of foreign affairs powers between the two branches. The President has the power to negotiate treaties, but only subject to confirmation by two-thirds vote of the Senate. The Constitution gives the President the power to appoint ambassadors and ministers, again subject to Senate confirmation. In addition, he is specifically empowered to receive ambassadors and ministers of other nations. Except for such powers, however, the executive authority must be derived from general constitutional provisions.

On the other hand, the Constitution gives the Congress certain explicit authority in the international field, including the powers to regulate foreign commerce, to fix import duties, and to declare war. Most important of all is its control over appropriation of funds. As the United States has assumed its new role in world affairs, and as domestic and foreign problems have involved more and more the same or closely related issues, all these congressional powers have assumed greater significance than in the prewar era.

It is one thing to suggest the need for the executive and legislative branches to cooperate in the conduct of foreign affairs and another to achieve such cooperation. One particular obstacle which should be frankly faced is the traditionally suspicious attitude of the Congress toward foreign affairs and toward the segment of the executive branch concerned with it.

This attitude appears to stem from three principal sources:

1. The fact that the State Department is the channel of communications between the United States and foreign nations. In that sense, the State Department represents foreigners. Furthermore, foreign affairs problems are usually troublesome and irritating, and they involve dollars or other commitments to other than the American electorate. In seeking to solve these problems the State Department is handicapped by the lack of any domestic constituency which will give the Congress credit for action taken or which will rise to the State Department's defense against congressional criticism.

2. The fact that the conduct of foreign affairs of necessity must frequently be on a secret and confidential basis. This is particularly true in the preliminary stages of a given matter where announcement of the intentions of the United States prior to consultation with other nations would result in embarrassments which would make it impossible to deal with those nations. This secrecy is resented by the Congress, which feels that secrecy is too often used to avoid congressional interference and control. The result is to afford a breeding ground for constant conflict.

3. The fact that up to about 1924 social prestige and protocol considerations were paramount in the minds and actions of the bulk of Americans concerned with foreign affairs. From this grew the conception of State Department and Foreign Service personnel as being primarily concerned with tea parties and striped pants. To-day, as a result of the Rogers Act of 1924 and the Foreign Service Act of 1946, and as a result of foreign affairs being injected as never before into the main stream of American life, this fact is no longer true, but the memory lingers on and will persist for at least another generation.

Given the present constitutional framework and the attitude of the legislative branch toward foreign affairs, the situation calls for mutual cooperation and restraint. The executive branch must appreciate the role of the Congress and the propriety of its participation in foreign affairs where *legislative* decisions are required. Similarly, the Congress should appreciate that leadership in the conduct of foreign affairs can come only from the executive side of the Government and that the Congress should not attempt to participate in *executive* decisions in the international field.

One serious procedural impediment to achieving satisfactory legislative-executive cooperation is the constitutional requirement of a two-thirds Senate vote for the confirmation of treaties. No thoughtful student of the conduct of foreign affairs can ignore the consequences of this provision. It is a serious trouble breeder between the executive branch and the Senate in that such an inherently rigid rule encourages circumvention by the executive by resort to the procedures of executive agreements and joint resolutions. Attempts to use these procedures, in turn, involve friction between the Senate and the House of Representatives. An especially bad result is that the emphasis is directed to the question of whether the proper procedure is being employed, instead of to the substance of the issues before the Congress. The question of a change in the present requirement of a two-thirds Senate vote is deemed, however, to be outside the province of this Commission.

*B. The Organization Within the Executive Branch for the Conduct of
Foreign Affairs*

The problem of organization within the executive branch for the conduct
of foreign affairs is, in the final analysis, the same problem as in the Government as a whole. First, despite the relatively greater authority assigned
by the Constitution to the President in the foreign affairs field, authority
or the power of command over the foreign affairs activities of the entire
executive branch is not satisfactorily vested in the President. Similarly,
at the departmental level, including the State Department, full authority
is not placed in the departmental or agency heads. Second, the line of
command and supervision over foreign affairs activities from the President
to the department and agency heads, and through them to their subordinate
units, is far from clear. Third, the staff services for foreign affairs activities
of the President, the Secretary of State, and the other department and
agency heads are utterly inadequate.

The present difficulties will be outlined in relation to:

1. The Presidency.
2. The interdepartmental relationships of the State Department and the
   other departments and agencies.

1. *The Presidency.* The President, as the single member of the executive
branch answerable to the electorate, is ultimately responsible to the American people for the formulation, execution, and coordination of foreign
policies. The emphasis is on "ultimately," because the President, either
personally or institutionally, can attempt to control only the very top and
crucial problems of foreign policy formulation, execution, and coordination.

To-day the authority of the President over the foreign affairs activities
of the executive branch is seriously hampered by both legal and practical
impediments. The legislative creation of new agencies and specific co-
ordinative bodies with foreign affairs powers, the existence of independent
regulatory agencies with executive functions, and the grant of foreign affairs
authority and funds to bureaus and offices below the level of the department
or agency head, all serve to lessen the efficiency of the executive branch
as a whole. Likewise these factors detract from the President's ability to
correct administrative weaknesses. They lessen the capabilities of the
departments and agencies to provide "self-coordination" and correspondingly throw a greater burden on the executive office of the President. They
also prevent the establishment of a direct and effective chain of command
from the Chief Executive down through the numerous segments of the
executive branch.

The Presidency, furthermore, is only casually organized to furnish staff assistance to the President in the conduct of foreign affairs. Better machinery is badly needed to bring competent and better rounded foreign affairs advice to the President and to force prompt resolution of interdepartmental disputes which, if left unsettled at lower levels, may impair the foreign relations of the United States. The Cabinet, moreover, it must be recognized, is not and cannot become an effective deliberative council of advisers to the President.

2. *The Relationship of the State Department to the Other Departments and Agencies.* Active participation of the departments and agencies other than the State Department in all phases of present-day foreign affairs imposes severe strains on the organizational structure of the Government. These other departments and agencies display an increasing tendency to establish policies or to make policy interpretations which are not coordinated with the foreign policies and interpretations of the State Department. The State Department, in turn, does not always coordinate its policies with over-all United States national policies. With the conduct of foreign affairs no longer the exclusive province of the State Department, coordinated action by the State Department and some 45 other units with foreign affairs activities is a sine qua non for efficient and effective dispatch of business. Until such action is achieved, the line of command and supervision from the President down through the department heads to subordinate levels will remain unclear, indecisive, and ineffective.

This new situation in the foreign affairs field does not mean, however, that the State Department has become just another executive department. Its statutory authority, basically unchanged since 1789, definitely fixes its role as a staff specialist and arm of the President in the conduct of foreign affairs and leaves its duties flexible and elastic. The other departments and agencies, in contrast, derive their foreign affairs authority through direct grants from the Congress which spell out the substantive tasks to be accomplished, usually in considerable detail. In essence, the State Department functions can be described as relating to the means or procedures of conducting foreign relations, whereas the organic statutes of the other departments and agencies pertain more to substantive matters, e.g., powers over fissionable materials, loans, communications, aviation, exports, imports, and the like. Coordination of all these varied activities obviously cannot be directed from the Presidential level. A large part must be delegated by the President to the State Department as his staff agency.

On certain crucial issues, however, coordination of foreign policy formulation and execution must come from the President or his executive office. To date the principal response to this need for high-level integration has been the development of specialized interdepartmental bodies at the cabinet level to advise the President on certain aspects of foreign affairs, such as national security and international finance. The absence of similar mechanisms in other important areas, particularly where foreign affairs touch upon domestic affairs, tends to give the President a partial and limited perspective in reaching decisions and to leave a substantial amount of policy execution to be coordinated on a "hit or miss" basis.

A final complicating factor in present-day governmental organization for the conduct of foreign affairs is the looseness and variation in organization of foreign affairs activities in the other departments and agencies. Some important departments have more than one bureau or office involved in foreign affairs but have no mechanism whereby the department head is able to coordinate the international activities of his own department. This results not only in confusion within a particular department but also places an added administrative burden upon the State Department which must seek not only to coordinate interdepartmental activity but activity within another department as well. Thus once again an important requirement of clear power of command and a clear chain of command is reemphasized.

III. ORGANIZATIONAL CONCEPTS

The conduct of foreign affairs to-day involves almost the entire executive branch—the President, the President's executive offices, the State Department, numerous other departments and agencies, and intricate interdepartmental machinery. In addition, it involves constant cooperation between the executive branch and the Congress. As a consequence the problems of organization are equally government-wide in scope, and organization reforms must be based on definite concepts of the part to be played by each segment of the Government.

The concepts for organization within the executive branch are, in summary, the following:

1. The decisions within the executive branch on the objectives of the United States in world affairs are ultimately decisions for the President only to make. He may, of course, delegate this power, but, as the sole elected member of the executive branch, he cannot divest himself of his final responsibility. When the President does delegate the power to make decisions, it must be recognized that it is impractical to make a blanket delegation to the State Department alone or to any other single department or agency.

2. The executive responsibility for the formulation and carrying out of foreign policies to achieve objectives is to-day that of the President with staff assistance from his executive office and the State Department. Under the President this responsibility is shared in various degrees by numerous departments and agencies throughout the executive establishment.

3. The responsibility for coordinating all the foreign affairs activities of the State Department and the other departments and agencies, whether in the decision-making process or in the processes of policy formulation and execution, ultimately is also that of the President. In delegating this responsibility the President may turn to the State Department, which is the specialist in foreign affairs, as, for example, to provide chairmen for inter-departmental committees, or he may turn elsewhere, depending on the balance of foreign and domestic implications in a particular problem.

4. The conduct of foreign affairs to-day involves the use of many means and instruments. Financial assistance, force or potential force, and propaganda are a few of the major ones. The utilization of these instruments similarly involves the performance of numerous supporting functions. A few examples are collection of information, evaluation of information through analysis and research, dissemination of information, employment of personnel, disbursement of funds, making of contracts, issuance of rules and regulations, and drafting of legislation.

5. The responsibility to-day for a decision as to which of several instruments to employ in the conduct of foreign affairs, together with the accompanying decisions as to when to employ them and as to the purposes to be accomplished thereby, carries with it two additional responsibilities. The first is for coordination throughout the executive branch in the choice of the instrument, the time of its use, and the purposes to be accomplished thereby. The second is for loyal teamwork between the State Department and the other departments and agencies instead of the evasion and back-biting that characterized these relationships during the recent war.

It is essential to recognize that in the discharge of this multifold responsibility, two different segments of the executive branch may perform functions which appear similar, but there should not and need not be duplication in the performance of identical functions in two parts of the Government. For example, if it is deemed to be of advantage to the United States that a democratic rather than a communistic government be in power in a foreign country, it may be found desirable to employ many instruments, including those of public information or propaganda, financial assistance, or other aids against outside interference. The medium of information may be in the State Department, the financial assistance instrument in the Economic Cooperation Administration, the Export-Import Bank and elsewhere, and other instruments may be in other branches of the Government.

All of these instruments, for example, involve the function of research and analysis of information. The State Department's research and analysis would relate to the state of public opinion of the country in question and the factors influential in forming public opinion; the Economic Cooperation Administration's research and analysis would be directed to the economic condition of the foreign country and the balance of international trade; and the military establishment's research and analysis would pertain to the status of communist military power on the borders of the country in question and the strategic disposition of United States forces in occupied areas nearby to strengthen the democratic elements in power in the country in question. Yet the performance of these functions involves no inevitable duplication of effort. For example, no duplication would occur in the case of financial assistance so long as the State Department economic and research units do not go over the same economic ground as those of Economic Cooperation Administration.

6. The effective discharge of the executive responsibilities in the conduct of foreign affairs (including the formulation of policies, employment of instruments to carry out policies, and coordination in both the formulation and execution stages) requires that authority be vested in the President and descend from him through a clear line of command to responsible department and agency heads with subordinate authority over cohesive executive agencies.

7. Decisions as to the conduct of foreign affairs to-day inevitably are decisions affecting our whole political, economic, and social life. The problem of organization for the conduct of foreign affairs is, therefore, but a segment of the larger problem of organization for the conduct of national affairs. Hence, governmental organization for the conduct of foreign affairs cannot be treated as a separate mechanism but must be regarded as an integral part of a larger mechanism.

No. 91

HOW THE UNITED STATES ENTERS INTO TREATIES WITH OTHER NATIONS [1]

by William V. Whittington

THE primary classification of the procedure by which the power to make treaties has been exercised is based upon a division of our history as an independent nation into three periods.

First, that period from the date of the Declaration of Independence in 1776 to March 1, 1781, during which time there was no constitution or other fundamental law in written form.

Second, that period from March 1, 1781, to March, 1789, during which

[1] William V. Whittington, "How the United States Enters into Treaties with Other Nations," *Congressional Digest* (August-September, 1938), Vol. 17, pp. 195-197. Reprinted by permission of the *Congressional Digest*, the Washington monthly published without editorial bias or advertising, featuring the congressional controversy of the month, pro and con.

time our Government operated under the Articles of Confederation adopted by the Continental Congress.

Third, that period from March, 1789, to the present, during which time the Government has operated under the Constitution.

It must be remembered that although the Articles of Confederation were adopted in November, 1777, the required acceptance by the thirteen States was not effected and the Articles did not become effective until 1781. In the meantime, however, there were concluded and brought into force two treaties.

The Continental Congress, which was vested with the power to appoint plenipotentiaries and to ratify treaties, delegated to Benjamin Franklin and certain others authority to negotiate with the Government of France for the conclusion of a treaty of amity and commerce and a treaty of alliance. These negotiations were of great importance in the revolutionary scheme. The two treaties were signed at Paris on February 6, 1778. It was not until late afternoon of Saturday, May 2, 1778, almost three months later, that these treaties were placed before the Continental Congress. On the following Monday, May 4, the Congress considered the treaties and approved them. These treaties with France are the only examples of treaty procedure during the first of our historic periods.

During the second period, beginning with the effective date of the Articles of Confederation in March, 1781, several treaties or agreements with foreign nations were concluded and entered into force, including agreements with France, Great Britain, the Netherlands, Prussia, and Morocco. Still another agreement, a consular convention with France negotiated by Thomas Jefferson and signed at Paris, was pending.

Under the Articles of Confederation it was necessary that nine States give their sanction to a treaty before it could become effective. We have referred to the fact that the Continental Congress delegated the authority and issued instructions directly to plenipotentiaries appointed by it. The Congress, pursuant to the terms of the Articles of Confederation, had control of foreign relations. As far as the making of treaties was concerned, the Congress then performed all those functions, including ratification of treaties, which now are performed by the Chief Executive. The President of the Congress was a presiding officer, without the executive powers now vested in the President under the Constitution.

The third of our historic periods began with the date on which the Constitution of the United States entered into force. Although the Constitution provided that it should enter into force when ratified by nine states, and the ninth ratification was effected in June, 1788, it was not until the first Wednesday in March, 1789, that the Constitution was declared to be in effect.

Many hundreds of treaties and agreements concerning nearly every conceivable phase of international relations have been concluded since that time. The provisions of the Constitution altered entirely the procedure for making treaties. In the field of treaty making, the President is the sole authority for entering into negotiations and for concluding agreements with foreign countries. The one limitation upon his authority is that set forth in paragraph 2 of section 2 of Article II of the Constitution, reading:

> He shall have power, by and with the advice and consent of the Senate, to make treaties, provided two-thirds of the Senate present concur.

It is necessary that we take the time to comment briefly upon the relative functions of the President and of the Senate in regard to the making of treaties.

It is sometimes incorrectly stated that the Senate ratifies a treaty. It is true that the Constitution provides that two-thirds of the Senators present shall give their advice and consent to the making of treaties, and failure of the Senate to give such advice and consent has prevented in a few instances the ratification of treaties. Nevertheless, the approval of a treaty by the required number of Senators does not ratify a treaty and is not mandatory upon the Executive.

Perhaps the principal factor to be borne in mind with respect to the Executive authority in the making of treaties is this: At every point until an international agreement becomes effective the authority of the President is sole and exclusive, with the one exception provided in the Constitution. The President's control, therefore, may be either positive or negative. With reference to the negative control, I quote a portion of an address delivered recently by Hunter Miller, Historical Adviser and Editor of Treaties of the Department of State:

> . . . He may refuse to permit a proposed treaty to be signed on behalf of the United States; if signed he may refuse to send it to the Senate; if sent to the Senate he may withdraw it at his pleasure; if acted on favorably by the Senate he may refuse to ratify it; and he may even ratify it and refuse to exchange the ratifications. At any stage in the making of a treaty, until it is internationally complete, the President may, in the exercise of his own discretion, bring the proceedings to an end.

Before proceeding to a study of the various types of agreements and the procedure for their negotiation, we should have a definition of terms.

As to the distinction between a bilateral and multilateral treaty, I believe there is no confusion. A bilateral treaty is, in its simplest terms, an agreement or contract between two governments with respect to certain matters of mutual interest. A multilateral treaty is one that has been signed and effected as between three or more governments and dealing with matters of more or less common interest to all of them.

In using the term "treaty" we do so with the language of the Constitution in mind. That is to say, those international agreements which are submitted to the Senate of the United States for its advice and consent to the ratification thereof are deemed to be treaties in the Constitutional sense. They may be called many other things by the nations interested. For instance, they may be referred to as treaties, or as conventions, or as protocols, acts, articles, contracts, or agreements; but it is convenient and proper to refer to them collectively as treaties.

The procedure in the making of bilateral treaties may be considered in two parts, the first being that up to and including signature, and the second being that which follows signature.

Probably the first question requiring attention is this: How do the two countries get together? There are, of course, many ways in which this may be done, but perhaps the most usual method is for one or the other of the governments to communicate to the other, through diplomatic channels, its desire to negotiate an agreement covering certain matters. In such case, it is customary for the government proposing the agreement to submit to the other a complete draft or text of the proposed arrangement.

Thereafter, the actual negotiations may take place in the capital city of either of the interested nations, or at any other place, as the competent authorities may consider most expedient. Let us say that the negotiations are carried on in Washington, D. C. In such case, the ambassador or minister or other qualified plenipotentiary of the foreign country will represent his government in the negotiations, and for that purpose will consult directly with the Secretary of State or other qualified officers within the Department of State. Throughout the negotiations, the representative of the foreign country may keep in touch with his government and will pursue the negotiations in accordance with instructions from his government.

It may be that the negotiations—that is to say, the discussions and consultations with a view to reaching an agreement with respect to subject matter and terminology—will be completed within a comparatively short time. On the other hand, these negotiations may and often do require months or even years, depending upon the complexity or controversial nature of the matters to be dealt with in the proposed treaty.

Eventually, we shall assume, an agreement is reached on all points. It is probable that the text of the agreement has been prepared in the languages of both countries, carefully compared and found to be identical so far as the substance of the provisions is concerned. The treaty then may be drawn up for signature, duplicate originals thereof being prepared in what is referred to as the *alternat*—that is, with parallel columns containing the two languages side by side, the language of one of the countries being in the left-hand column of one of the originals while in the other original that language will appear in the right-hand column. We shall refer to this again.

A time and a place are fixed for the signing of the treaty. Let us say the place is an office in the Department of State. Shortly before the time fixed for signature, the qualified plenipotentiary of the foreign nation and the Secretary of State of the United States will appear, and the documents will be placed in readiness for signature. Other interested officers of both governments may be present to assist in or to observe the procedure of signing. When all is in readiness, there having been a formal presentation of full powers, the treaty will be signed, and the respective seals of the plenipotentiaries will be affixed.

The treaty having been duly signed and sealed, the plenipotentiary of the foreign nation will retain one of the duplicate originals for transmission to the foreign office of his government, and the other duplicate original will be retained in the archives of the Department of State, subject to the further procedure required in regard to senatorial approval, and ratification.

The negotiations having been completed and the treaty having been concluded (that is, signed and sealed), we are prepared to consider the method by which the treaty is brought into force. For this purpose, it is believed that it would simplify matters greatly if we follow step by step the actual procedure in effecting a comparatively recent treaty—the treaty between the United States of America and Mexico terminating article VIII of the treaty of December 30, 1853 (the Gadsden Treaty).

This treaty was signed April 13, 1937. On April 19, 1937, the Secretary of State sent to the President a letter (or report), enclosing one of the signed and sealed originals of the treaty, for submission to the Senate of the United States. On April 22, 1937, the President sent to the Senate a message, together with the letter from the Secretary of State and the treaty. On that same date, the treaty was read the first time in the Senate and was referred to the Committee on Foreign Relations, and it was ordered that the treaty, together with the President's message and the accompanying letter of the Secretary of State, be printed in confidence for the use of the Senate. Accordingly, there was printed a confidential Executive document for the use of the Senate, copies thereof being furnished to the Treaty Division of the Department of State for confidential use.

It was on June 10, 1937, almost two months after the treaty was signed, that the Committee on Foreign Relations of the Senate submitted its Executive Report, recommending that the Senate "do advise and consent to the same." As of this date, the injunction of secrecy imposed by the Senate was removed and the treaty was made public. That did not mean that the treaty was approved by the Senate, but merely that copies thereof would be available for general distribution.

On June 29, 1937, about three weeks after the Committee on Foreign Relations had submitted its favorable report, the Senate of the United States gave its advice and consent to the ratification of the treaty, without amendment or reservation. Needless to say, in some cases the Senate has given its advice and consent only with certain reservations, which it has been necessary to communicate to the other government in order to ascertain whether the latter would accept them.

At this point, the function of the Senate ends. The remaining action is for the Executive. An instrument of ratification is prepared in the Treaty Division for the Signature of the President of the United States. This instrument recites the steps that already have been taken, then usually it sets forth the text of the treaty exactly, and concludes with a statement to the effect that the treaty is thereupon confirmed and ratified. In the case of the treaty with Mexico which we are considering, this instrument was signed and sealed by the President of the United States on July 15, 1937, a little more than two weeks after the Senate had given its advice and consent.

Meanwhile, the treaty was under consideration by the Government of Mexico in accordance with its own procedure. It was not until November 9, 1937, that the instrument of ratification of that Government was signed and sealed. It sometimes happens that the foreign government will ratify a treaty before its ratification by this Government.

Under the terms of the treaty, as is now customary with bilateral treaties, the ratifications were to be exchanged at a specified place and the treaty was to go into effect when such ratifications had been exchanged. The instruments of ratification of the treaty were exchanged formally in the Department of State at Washington, December 21, 1937. The treaty thereupon entered into effect internationally, despite the fact that under our national procedure the President had yet to proclaim it.

It is the practice of the Department of State at the present time to prepare instruments of ratification in duplicate, both being signed and sealed by the President. One of these is delivered to the foreign government; the other is placed in the archives with the original signed treaty. This has not always been the case, but as we have indicated already it would not be feasible to attempt an explanation of all the variations in procedure.

There is but one other step in our national procedure, namely, the promulgation of the treaty by the President. There is prepared in the Treaty

Division, for the President's signature, a proclamation commencing with the statement that a treaty of a certain kind with a certain country has been signed at a certain place and date, and then setting forth word for word the treaty as signed, and concluding that the treaty has been made public, "to the end that the same and every article and clause thereof may be observed and fulfilled with good faith by the United States of America and the citizens thereof." The President of the United States issued his proclamation of the treaty with Mexico on December 27, 1937, less than a week following the exchange of ratifications.

Thus terminates the procedure, as far as the effectiveness of the treaty is concerned, but that is by no means the end of the work that must be done. There remains the matter of publication, of recording, of distribution, and of various other labors, which are done by the Treaty Division of the Department of State.

No. 92

WE MOVE—SLOWLY—TOWARD WORLD LAW [1]
by A. H. Feller

THE other day the International Court of Justice, the World Court, handed down a historic opinion. It held that the United Nations has an international legal personality, like a state, and that just as states have the right to demand protection of their citizens from unlawful injury by other states, so the United Nations can demand protection for its officials.

This opinion doubtless made no particular impression on any average citizen; no more or less, perhaps, than the average American of Chief Justice Marshall's day was impressed by the opinion in *McCulloch v. Maryland,* which laid the foundation for the Federal powers under our Constitution. Yet the opinion of the World Court is a milestone in an extraordinary development of international law which has been getting under way almost unnoticed in the midst of the gloom and confusion of the contemporary political scene.

Most serious students of affairs are convinced that a secure world order is impossible without world law. How can we get such law? There are some who dream of a sudden act of law-giving, the appearance of some sort of international Hammurabi or Moses who will hand down the tablets of the law which a waiting multitude will enthusiastically embrace. The tablets are now to be inscribed with a constitution for a world government armed

[1] A. H. Feller, "We Move—Slowly—Toward World Law," *The New York Times Magazine* (June 5, 1949), pp. 10, 35, 37. Reprinted by permission of *The New York Times Magazine* and the author.

with all the apparatus, moral and physical, for imposing order and justice on the two billion inhabitants of the globe and the sixty or so states into which they are divided.

Others believe that this dream of a world constitution suddenly revealed from a new Sinai is just a dream, incapable of practical application in any foreseeable space of time. Many of these doubters have been engulfed by pessimism. They see nothing before the world but a continuation of the politics of force, of clashing alliances and uneasy truces based on balances of power and expediency.

Both camps usually ignore the system of law which now governs the conduct of nations. That system, which we call international law, has prevailed since the seventeenth century. It is a complicated structure, made up of rules embodied in treaties between states and of customary rules applied by foreign offices of governments and national and international courts. There has never been a legislature to make or an executive to enforce these rules. To the average man international law hardly exists. There are even a good many lawyers whose acquaintance with the subject is limited to the question, "Is international law really law?"

International law is a fragmentary and primitive system. This is not at all remarkable since it has grown up piecemeal through the actions of sovereign states in a disordered world. What is remarkable is that despite the absence of legislature or executive, despite its haphazard and erratic growth, it not only exists but has demonstrated a hardy vitality.

The notion that if it isn't enforceable it isn't law acquired a gloss of academic respectability in the last century. In the final analysis this sort of thinking holds that law only exists at the end of a policeman's club. The experience of mankind and particularly of our own country teaches a different lesson. There have been many communities plentifully endowed with legislatures, codes of law and law enforcement officers which have been as disorderly and anarchic as the international community. Contrast the lofty supremacy of the United States Supreme Court, which commands implicit obedience with only a single marshal at its command even though it gives judgment against powerful corporations, great states, the Federal executive and even the laws enacted by the Congress itself. Law is not just the rule enforced by the policeman; it is the rule obeyed by the citizen, and obeyed because of the necessities of his own existence in an organized society.

Both in theory and in practice, nations consider themselves bound by the rules of international law. Sometimes they will break the rules, just as individuals do in their own communities. But even the most flagrant law breaker among nations will not deny that there is an international law;

it will argue either that there is no rule to govern the case or that the rule means something different. Read nearly any exchange of diplomatic correspondence and you will see a legal argument—each party contending that the law is on its side. Even in the midst of a world war or the most intense ideological struggle, the nations still cling to at least the profession that they are bound by the rules of international law.

The trouble with international law is not that it isn't law, but that there isn't enough of it. The rules cover only a small part of the relations between states; many of the rules are vaguely defined or their meaning is disputed; there are too many loopholes, too many opportunities for quibbling and evasion. If the system is to furnish a secure foundation for the world community it must be developed until its content approximates that of national legal systems.

In fact, international law has been developing since its inception. Its early pre-occupation was with the status of diplomatic representatives and territorial waters, and later with the rules of warfare and neutrality. In this century there was much law making, through treaties, to cover new situations—international trade and commerce, aerial navigation, the control of the narcotics traffic, telecommunication, arbitration and judicial settlement of disputes. After 1922 the Permanent Court of International Justice added a solid body of doctrine through numerous decisions. The system has developed, but often too slowly, usually erratically, and twice in this century a world war has interrupted its progress just when it was gathering headway.

The Nineteen Thirties saw a substantial effort at codification under the League of Nations. Much work was done and in 1931 a conference at The Hague tried to bring some order into the fields of nationality, territorial waters and the responsibility of states. The attempt was pretty much a failure for technical and political reasons. Some people even thought that The Hague Conference did harm rather than good. For instance, it had been settled law for Anglo-Saxon countries that territorial waters extended only three miles from the shore. It was a surprise to discover that some European countries argued strenuously for a six- or twelve-mile limit. The rise of Hitler and the outbreak of the Second World War were as near fatal to international law as they were to freedom itself.

The revival began with the San Francisco Conference, where several delegates, particularly Senator Vandenberg, carried on a sturdy fight to prevent a purely political basis for the United Nations Charter and to bring the rule of law within its framework. The proponents of law won out. The first paragraph of the first article now proclaims as one of the purposes of the United Nations the settlement of international disputes "in conformity with the principles of justice and international law." Moreover, the

General Assembly is authorized to initiate studies and make recommendations for the purpose of encouraging the progressive development of international law and its codification.

The years since San Francisco have seen a burst of creative law-making without parallel in history. Foremost, perhaps, has been the crumbling of the old doctrine that international law is a system which concerns states alone. The few instances in which the system was applied in the past to individuals were either archaic, like the crime of piracy, or regional and transitory, like the minorities treaties after the First World War.

The Charter has begun a historic process of breaking through the barriers between the individual and the international legal systems. Its most striking innovation has been with regard to human rights and fundamental freedoms. The process of implementing the broad provisions of the Charter has brought forth the Universal Declaration of Human Rights. A binding Covenant of Human Right is in the making. The General Assembly has proposed to the nations a convention which makes genocide an international crime and imposes liability not just on states but on the responsible individuals. The provisions of the Charter for the right of petition to the Trusteeship Council by the inhabitants of the trust territories, and of visitation by the Council, are again instances where the individual is brought into direct contact with the international community.

This new current has been reinforced from another direction. The Nuremberg trials were a dramatic application of rules of international law to individual and corporate criminals. The principles which were there applied have not been permitted to fade into obscurity, as we shall see in a moment.

In the Anglo-American common law the decisions of courts are one of the most important ways in which law is developed. The same thing has been true in international law in the past, and will continue so in the future. The recent opinion of the World Court is a striking demonstration. The question was whether the United Nations could make claims against the states of Egypt, Israel and Transjordan for death or injuries caused to United Nations agents, including Count Bernadotte, during the hostilities in Palestine.

There is no express provision in the Charter which says that the United Nations has the standing to make an international claim, or that it has the right to demand protection for its agents. Ruling in favor of the United Nations on both of these points, the Court said that "in international law, the Organization must be deemed to have those powers which, though not expressly provided in the Charter, are conferred upon it by necessary implication as being essential to the performance of its duties."

Here we see the introduction into international law of a doctrine very much like the one announced by the United States Supreme Court when it held that the Federal Government is not confined to the express powers mentioned in the Constitution, but also possesses those "necessary and proper" to the exercise of the express powers. We cannot now foresee what the future applications of this new doctrine might be. None the less the opinion teaches some important lessons: international law is flexible enough to meet new situations; the processes of international adjudication are capable of making necessary adaptations; and the Court has strengthened both the legal foundations and the legal rights of the world community, as exemplified in the United Nations.

Now we are about to witness a conscious and well-prepared effort at large scale progressive development and codification. On April 12 there assembled in Lake Success for the first time the International Law Commission set up by the General Assembly and composed of fifteen distinguished scholars. It has before it three specific tasks: a Declaration on the Rights and Duties of States proposed by Panama, the consideration of the principles applied in the Nuremberg trials, and a proposal for the creation of an international criminal court. Beyond these, it is charged with surveying the entire field of international law and drawing up a plan of work for its progressive development and codification.

Two years of painstaking effort preceded the first meeting of the commission. No one who remembers the failure of the League's codification work has shown any easy optimism over this new start. The commission has received a flexible mandate; it can either propose conventions for adoption by states, or draw up reports which would be much like the restatements of law with which American lawyers are familiar. It has a membership of world-wide repute, under the chairmanship of Judge Manley O. Hudson, and competent assistance in the Legal Department of the United Nations. No one expects miracles or near miracles of law-making. The effort is one which must go on for years and its impact on the international scene will be slow, but hopefully and steadily evolutionary.

The difficulties of the task are, of course, increased by the current ideological and political conflict. Historic differences in the way of looking at law are now exacerbated by the great schism among the nations. Yet the largest measure of international cooperation so far attained has been in this field. The convention on genocide was adopted unanimously by the General Assembly; not a single dissenting vote was cast against the Declaration on Human Rights; and lawyers from all the major legal systems serve on the World Court and on the International Law Commission.

An English writer recently remarked that while the people of older civilizations think of institutions in terms of trees, which must be firmly rooted in the soil and then grow slowly, Americans tend to think of institutions as machines. When the machine does not go well, we want to throw it away and get a new model. If the system of international law is a machine it would certainly seem to many to be a rather creaky and rattletrap affair. Unfortunately, it cannot be changed as easily as an old model motor car; we just do not have another machine to take its place. In this case, at least, we will have to forego the machine analogy. The roots of the tree are already in the soil and it is growing. One of the major tasks of our time is to tend it so that it grows sturdily and soundly.

It is also essential to avoid creating once again the illusion that one particular institution is the answer to the problem of international peace. A sound system of world law will diminish the chances for war but will not in itself stop war. Law does not destroy violence unless it is bound up with an organized and stable society. On the other hand, no society can be stable unless it is founded on justice and the rule of law.

Here is where the world government enthusiast, the advocate of regional union, the supporter of an evolving United Nations, and even the pessimistic skeptic, can join hands. Whatever the future form of international society may be, it must have a legal basis. Each in his own way can work for the form of international society which holds for him the best hope of averting war and eliminating economic and social evils. All can work together for the growth of the rule of world law without which no system of world organization could long endure.

No. 93

THE ILLUSION OF WORLD GOVERNMENT [1]

by Reinhold Niebuhr

THE trustful acceptance of false solutions for our perplexing problems adds a touch of pathos to the tragedy of our age.

The tragic character of our age is revealed in the world-wide insecurity which is the fate of modern man. Technical achievements, which a previous generation had believed capable of solving every ill to which the human flesh is heir, have created, or at least accentuated, our insecurity. For the growth of technics has given the perennial problems of our common life a more complex form and a scope that has grown to be world-wide.

Our problem is that technics have established a rudimentary world community but have not integrated it organically, morally or politically. They

[1] Reinhold Niebuhr, "The Illusion of World Government," *Foreign Affairs* (April, 1949), Vol. 27, No. 3, pp. 379-388. Reprinted by permission of *Foreign Affairs*.

have created a community of mutual dependence, but not one of mutual trust and respect. Without this higher integration, advancing technics tend to sharpen economic rivalries within a general framework of economic inter-dependence; they change the ocean barriers of yesterday into the battle-grounds of to-day; and they increase the deadly efficacy of the instruments of war so that vicious circles of mutual fear may end in atomic conflicts and mutual destruction. To these perplexities an ideological conflict has been added, which divides the world into hostile camps.

It is both necessary and laudable that men of good will should, in this situation, seek to strengthen every moral and political force which might give a rudimentary world community a higher degree of integration. It was probably inevitable that the desperate plight of our age should persuade some well-meaning men that the gap between a technically integrated and politically divided community could be closed by the simple expedient of establishing a world government through the fiat of the human will and creating world community by the fiat of world government. It is this hope which adds a touch of pathos to already tragic experiences. The hope not only beguiles some men from urgent moral and political responsibilities. It tempts others into irresponsible criticisms of the necessarily minimal constitutional structure which we have embodied in the United Nations and which is as bad as its critics aver only if a better one is within the realm of possibilities.

Virtually all arguments for world government rest upon the simple pre-supposition that the desirability of world order proves the attainability of world government. Our precarious situation is unfortunately no proof, either of the moral ability of mankind to create a world government by an act of the will, nor of the political ability of such a government to integrate a world community in advance of a more gradual growth of the "social tissue" which every community requires more than government.

Most advocates of world government also assume that nations need merely follow the alleged example of the individuals of another age who are sup-posed to have achieved community by codifying their agreements into law and by providing an agency of some kind for law enforcement. This as-sumption ignores the historic fact that the mutual respect for each other's rights in particular communities is older than any code of law; and that machinery for the enforcement of law can be efficacious only when a com-munity as a whole obeys its laws implicitly, so that coercive enforcement may be limited to a recalcitrant minority.

The fallacy of world government can be stated in two simple propositions. The first is that governments are not created by fiat (though sometimes they can be imposed by tyranny). The second is that governments have only limited efficacy in integrating a community.

II

The advocates of world government talk of calling a world constitutional convention which would set up the machinery of a global constitutional order and would then call upon the nations to abrogate or abridge their sovereignty in order that this newly created universal sovereignty could have unchallenged sway. No such explicit abnegation has ever taken place in the history of the world. Explicit governmental authority has developed historically from the implicit authority of patriarchal or matriarchal tribal forms. Governments, so established, have extended their dominion over weaker neighbors. But the abridgment of sovereignty has always been indirect rather than direct; or it has been attained by the superimposition of power.

The notion that world government is a fairly simple possibility is the final and most absurd form of the "social contract" conception of government which has confused modern political thought since Hobbes. It must certainly be obvious by this time that the conception of a state of nature in which all men were at war with all, and of a subsequent social contract through which men established a power over themselves to avoid mutual annihilation, is a pure fiction. A small human community is as primordial as the individual. No group of individuals has ever created either government or community out of whole cloth. One reason why the social contract conception of government has a particular plausibility with us is because the United States came closer to a birth by "contract" than any other nation. But the preamble of our constitution declares that its purpose is to establish a "more perfect union." That is a very telling phrase which presupposes a previous union. This previous union was in fact established on the battlefield in a common struggle against a common foe; it needed only to be made "more perfect." It may be observed in passing that, though the 13 colonies had never enjoyed sovereignty, they did not find it too easy to submit what had only been potential, and not actual, sovereignty to the authority of the federal union. We fought a civil war before it was proved that they had in fact done this without reservations.

When the question is raised whether the nations of the world would voluntarily first create, and then submit to, a super-national authority, the possible reluctance of nations, other than Russia, to take this step is fortunately or unfortunately obscured by the Russian intransigeance. The Russians have declared again and again that they would leave the United Nations if the veto power were abolished. This means that Russia, as a prospective

minority in a world community, is not ready to submit her fate to the will
of a majority, even in such a loose organization as the United Nations. It is
therefore obvious that she would be even more unwilling to submit her
sovereignty to a more highly integrated constitutional order.

The proponents of world government have two answers to the problem
posed by Russian intransigeance. One is to assert that the Russians never
have had the chance to accept or reject a genuinely constitutional world
order; and that there are real possibilities of her acceptance of a constitution
which is not weighted against her. This answer contains in a nutshell the
rationalist illusion implicit in world government theories. It assumes that
constitutions can insure the mutual trust upon which community rests.
Actually, even the best constitution must, if it is democratic, set up some
kind of majority rule. It is not workable if there is not enough common
ground between majority and minority to assure that a majority will not
take advantage of a minority, or that the minority will not suspect the
majority of injustice, even though without cause. There are republics in
South America with quite nice constitutions in which a defeated minority
starts conspiracies against the government, usually through military channels, on the day after election.

The other answer to the problem of Russian intransigeance is a proposed
creation of a "world" government without Russia. Thus in the name of
"one world" the world would be divided in two. Proponents of world government are always ready with criticisms of the ambiguities in the Charter
of the United Nations, without recognizing that those ambiguities correspond
to the actual historical situation. The Security Council is, for instance, a
bridge of a sort between the segments of a divided world. They would
destroy that bridge for the sake of creating a more logical constitutional
system. This done, they look forward to one of two possibilities.

One is that Russia, faced with a united opposition, and concluding that
she would not have to sacrifice her Communist Government but only her
ambition to spread Communism, would ultimately capitulate and join the
world federation. This abstract approach to political problems is completely
oblivious of the dynamism of Communism.

The other course chosen by some advocates of world government is to
create such a government without Russia and to divide the world more consistently in the name of the principle of "one" world. If this should lead
to a world conflict they believe that the agonies of war will be assuaged for
us by our knowledge that we are at least fighting for a principle of ultimate
validity.

There is, of course, a possibility that a closer political integration of
the non-Communist nations may save the world from war by the creation

of an adequate preponderance of power in the west. But such an objective is not to be reached by loftily disavowing "power politics" in favor of "law." The world federalists who accept the inevitability of war walk bravely up the hill of pure idealism and down again into the realm of pure power politics. In this journey they rid themselves of the logical and moral ambiguities of the much despised quasi-constitutional system of the United Nations. Their brethren who are in a less exalted frame of mind will continue to put up with the Charter for the sake of preserving a bridge, however slight, between Russia and the west, making the best arrangements they can to restrain Russia, while trying at the same time to strengthen the existing world security agencies.

The ambiguities in the Charter of the United Nations which so outrage the advocates of world government are in fact the consequence of seeking to guarantee two, rather than one, objectives. The one objective is to preserve the unity of one world, even though it be seriously divided, and to provide a meeting ground between east and west where some of the tensions and frictions may be resolved. The other is to preserve the integrity of our "way of life" against a tyrannical system which we abhor. The Russians, in so far as they are honest devotees of a Marxist dream of world order, are presumably in the same position. Each of us hopes ultimately to create a world order upon the basis of our conception of justice. Neither of us is ready, at the moment, to submit our fate to a world authority without reservation, so long as the possibility remains that such an authority could annul a system of law and justice to which we are deeply committed.

III

So far we have considered only the difficulties of creating a world government by constitutional fiat. But a much more serious defect in world government theories is to be found in their conception of the relation of government to community. Governments cannot create communities for the simple reason that the authority of government is not primarily the authority of law nor the authority of force, but the authority of the community itself. Laws are obeyed because the community accepts them as corresponding, on the whole, to its conception of justice. This is particularly true of democratically organized communities. But it is well to observe that even in traditional, non-democratic communities of the past there was a discernible difference between tyranny and legitimate government. It consisted precisely in the fact that a legitimate government relied primarily upon the implicit consent of the community.

Even in a national constitutional system, such as our own, we have seen how limited is the power of law whenever a portion of the community adheres to moral standards which differ from those of the total community. We have had this experience both with the prohibition movement and with the question of civil rights for Negroes in southern states. And where is the police force, loyal to a world state, to come from? The police power of a government cannot be a pure political artifact. It is an arm of the community's body. If the body is in pieces, the arm cannot integrate it.

The priority of the community to its laws and its use of force does not mean that both law and force may not have limited efficacy in perfecting the organization and preserving the integrity of the community. Good constitutions provide for the rational arbitrament of many conflicting and competing forces which might otherwise tear the community apart. Preponderant force in one part of the community may also so shape the social forces of the total community that its use need not be perpetual. Thus the preponderant force of the northern states decided the issue whether our nation was a nation or merely a federation of states. But force is no longer necessary to guarantee the loyalty of the southern states to our union. The ancient empires of Egypt, Babylon and Persia were created through the preponderant force of a particular city-state; but they finally achieved a unity which did not require the constant application of force. It must be noted that this pattern of coalescence of communities gives us no analogy for the creation of a world community in democratic terms, that is, without the imposition of preponderant power. The best analogy for our present world situation is to be found in Greece rather than in Egypt or Babylon. The Greek city states never achieved the imperial unity of the oriental empires. The threat of Persia did finally prompt the organization of the Delian League; but the rivalry of Sparta and Athens for the hegemony in the League resulted in its disintegration. The unity of Greece was finally achieved under Philip and Alexander of Macedon. But this imperial unity was also a tyrannical nemesis for Greek culture. The analogy in present global terms would be the final unification of the world through the preponderant power of either America or Russia, whichever proved herself victorious in a final global struggle. The analogy teaches us nothing about the possibilities of a constitutional world state. It may teach us that though the perils of international anarchy are very great, they may still be preferable to international tyranny.

The coalescence of communities from city-states to empires in the ancient world, and from feudal entities to nations in the modern period, was frequently accomplished only by the imposition of preponderant power. The fact is particularly significant, since all of these communities could rely upon all sorts of "organic" factors for their force of cohesion which the rudimentary world community lacks. By organic factors, I mean such forces as the power of ethnic kinship, the force of a common history—particularly the memory of joint struggles against a common foe—a common language, a common culture and a common religion. We do have examples of ethnically and religiously pluralistic nations and empires, but they possess a basic homogeneity of some kind, underlying the differences. In modern India, where religious differences are thoroughgoing and highly localized, it proved impossible to construct a constitutional system which could allay the mutual fears of Hindus and Moslems. The birth in blood of these two nations, once the unifying force of an imperial power was removed, ought to teach our world planners more about the limited efficacy of constitutions than they have evidently learned. There were certainly more common elements in the situation in India than the world community will possess for a long time to come. Despite these common elements, the unity of India proved to be unattainable.

Sometimes the world planners recognize the absence of organic forces of cohesion in the world community. Thus Erich Kahler sees that a world constitution lacks the "substratum" of organic and historical forces, which characterize the constitutions of national governments. But he draws the conclusion that a world constitution "must create the substratum to which it is to be applied." The proposed method of creating the substratum, according to Mr. Kahler, is to use "regions" rather than "extant states" as electoral units in the world constitution, for "if we base the world government on the states, we will fail in the essential task of creating the substratum." The illusions of omnipotence which infect the thought of this kind of political idealism could not be more vividly portrayed. There is no explanation of how states, who have a sovereign voice, would be persuaded to grant this electoral power to "regions" which would have no such voice in a world constitutional convention. The idea probably is that there would be a nonrepresentative constitutional convention of "experts" and the hope is that sovereign states will meekly accept the dictum of the experts that regions offer a better "substratum" for the world community than extant states. Nor is any attempt made to deal with the difficulty that many of the regions which would hopefully be created are so little integrated that an electoral canvass would be completely meaningless in them.

The fact is that even the wisest statecraft cannot create social tissue. It can cut, sew and redesign social fabric to a limited degree. But the social fabric upon which it works must be "given."

IV

The international community is not totally lacking in social tissue; but it is very scant, compared with that of particular states. Let us briefly assess the various factors in it. Most important as a force of social cohesion in the world community is the increasing economic interdependence of peoples of the world. But it is important to contrast this economic interdependence immediately with the wide disparity in the economic strength of various nations. At the climactic dinner of the World Republic convention, held in Chicago in October 1948, Professor Urey, the atomic scientist, expressed the conviction that the "inclusion of the illiterate, poverty-stricken, overnumerous masses of the Far East" constituted the major problem of the world state. He believed that the white race would not tolerate being outvoted by Asiatics. He therefore proposed a system of weighted votes in favor of nations with high literacy and abundance of raw materials and industrial production. He felt certain that the more "enlightened" Orientals would not object to this procedure. But an objection, from Thomas Tchou, sitting two places to the left of Professor Urey, was immediately forthcoming. Weighted representation, he declared, was immoral. Thus the real problems have an inconvenient habit of peeking through, even at a dinner of a World Republic convention.

A second factor in the social tissue of the world community is the fear of mutual annihilation, heightened in recent years by the new dimension which atomic discoveries have given to mankind's instruments of death. We must not underestimate this fear as a social force, even as we must recognize that some culturally pluralistic communities of past history have achieved some cohesion through the minimal conviction that order is to be preferred to anarchy. But the fear of destruction in itself is less potent than the fear of specific peril from a particular foe. There is no record in history of peoples establishing a common community because they feared each other, though there are many instances when the fear of a common foe acted as the cement of cohesion.

The final and most important factor in the social tissue of the world community is a moral one. Enlightened men in all nations have some sense of obligation to their fellow-men, beyond the limits of their nation-state. There is at least an inchoate sense of obligation to the inchoate community of mankind. The desperate necessity for a more integrated world community has undoubtedly increased this sense of obligation, inculcated in the conscience of mankind since the rise of universal, rather than parochial, philosophies and religions. This common moral sense is of tremendous importance for the moral and religious life of mankind; but it does not have as much immediate political relevance as is sometimes supposed. Political co-hesion requires common convictions on particular issues of justice; and these are lacking. If there is a "natural law" which is "self-evident" to all men, it certainly does not contain very much specific content beyond such minimal rules as the prohibition of murder and theft and such general principles of justice as the dictum that each man is to have his due. There is little agreement on the criteria by which the due of each man is to be measured.

There is a special irony in the fact that the primary differences in the conceptions of justice in the world do not, however, spring from religious and cultural differences between east and west. They can, therefore, not be resolved by elaborate efforts at cultural syncretism between east and west. The primary differences arise from a civil war in the heart of western civ-ilization, in which a fanatical equalitarian creed has been pitted against a libertarian one. This civil war has become nationally localized. Russia has become the national center of the equalitarian creed, while America is the outstanding proponent of the libertarian one. The common use of the word "democracy," together with the contradictory interpretations of the meaning of that word, is the semantic symbol of the conflict. The idea that this conflict could be resolved by greater semantic accuracy is, however, one of the illusions of a too rationalistic culture which fails to understand the power of the social forces expressed in contradictory symbols.

In short, the forces which are operating to integrate the world community are limited. To call attention to this fact does not mean that all striving for a higher and wider integration of the world community is vain. That task must and will engage the conscience of mankind for ages to come. But the edifice of government which we build will be sound and useful if its height is proportionate to the strength of the materials from which it is constructed. The immediate political situation requires that we seek not only peace, but also the preservation of a civilization which we hold to be preferable to the universal tyranny with which Soviet aggression threatens us. Success in this double task is the goal; let us not be diverted from it by the pretense that there is a simple alternative.

We would, I think, have a better chance of success in our struggle against a fanatical foe if we were less sure of our purity and virtue. The pride and self-righteousness of powerful nations are a greater hazard to their success in statecraft than the machinations of their foes. If we could combine a greater degree of humility with our stubborn resolution, we might not only be more successful in holding the dyke against tyranny, but we might also gradually establish a genuine sense of community with our foe, however small. No matter how stubbornly we resist Russian pressure, we should still have a marginal sense of community with the Soviet Union, derived from our sense of being involved in a common fate of tragic proportions and from a recognition of a common guilt of mutual fear. If community in basic terms is established by various organic forces of history, it must finally be preserved by mutual forbearance and forgiveness.

There is obviously no political program which can offer us, in our situation, perfect security against either war or tyranny. Nevertheless we are not prisoners of historical destiny. We shall have constant opportunity to perfect instruments of peace and justice if we succeed in creating some communal foundation upon which constitutional structures can rest. We shall exploit our opportunities the more successfully, however, if we have knowledge of the limits of the will in creating government, and of the limits of government in creating community. We may have pity upon, but can have no sympathy with, those who flee to the illusory security of the impossible from the insecurities and ambiguities of the possible.

Chapter XXVI

SOME PROBLEMS OF LAW ENFORCEMENT

[WHEREVER people have lived together, there has been need for some rules governing their relationships with one another. Society always has had to prohibit certain kinds of anti-social conduct and enforce those prohibitions. In other words, law enforcement has always been looked upon as one of the legitimate functions of government.

Law enforcement is a gigantic task. National, state and local governments all are playing a part. The United States Department of Justice, the federal marshals, the secret service, state police, county sheriffs, chiefs of police, and courts at all levels are constantly carrying on the job of enforcing the rules that the community lays down.

Out of this welter of activity it is only natural that problems should arise. How can we prevent violations of the law and still preserve the rights of individuals? How can we modernize the law and the obsolete machinery now set up to enforce it? How can law enforcement be removed from politics? How can the lawyer criminal be dealt with? How can we get better judges? How should we reform the jury system? How can we overcome the barriers to law enforcement created by state lines? How can we facilitate settlement of small claims at minimum cost? How, in other words, can we secure reliable, efficient, and just enforcement of the law? These are the questions that are discussed in this chapter.]

No. 94

WHO'S WRONG WITH THE LAW? [1]

by Mitchell Dawson

"STRING 'em up! Burn 'em! Cut their hearts out!"

The rope tightens. The flames leap up. . . .

The Governor of California congratulates the avenging mob at San Jose: "That was a fine lesson to the whole nation. . . . I am checking San Quen-

---

[1] Mitchell Dawson, "Who's Wrong with the Law?", *The Atlantic Monthly* (May, 1934), Vol. 153, pp. 621-631. Reprinted by permission of the author and *The Atlantic Monthly*.

tin and Folsom prisons to find out what kidnappers they have. I am thinking of paroling them to those fine, patriotic citizens of San Jose, who know how to handle such situations. . . ."

"Congratulations on the stand you have taken," wires the pastor of New York's Church of the Heavenly Rest. (Later, the pastor admitted that his message was the result of being "deeply stirred," and that "it should not have been sent.")

Congratulations, pastor!

The spirit of the mob, aroused by frightful crimes, goes marching on. The Governor of Maryland impedes the course of swift, sure justice by calling out the troops. Twenty-one members of the state assembly—"almost all descendants of original Anglo-Saxon settlers"—denounce the Governor. Meanwhile the good citizens of St. Joseph, Missouri, hang and roast their man in spite of sixty-five National Guardsmen with armored tanks.

Editorial typewriters once more click out the old familiar tune: Now is the time, now is the time, now is the time for all good men . . . Something is fundamentally wrong. . . . The law has broken down. . . . Now is the time . . .

For what, gentlemen?

The cry goes up: "We need new laws, strong laws, hard laws, laws to end crime." Editors, preachers, judges, crime commissioners, and the good citizens of San Jose, point the finger of scorn at our laws. The courts are tied up by antiquated, weak, dilatory, and technical rules so that they cannot cope with the master minds of gunmen, kidnappers, bank robbers, ravishers, and street-corner bums.

In Illinois we have hard, strong penal laws. Murder and kidnapping are punishable by imprisonment or death; rape, robbery with a gun, and burglary with intent to commit a felony, by a maximum of life imprisonment; arson, by one to twenty years in the penitentiary; and other misdeeds by a sliding scale of fines and imprisonment, subject to commutation for good behavior. We have police also, and prosecutors, courts, and jails, all working overtime. Much of our procedure, it is true, dates back to mediaeval England. But in spite of that our criminal courts in Chicago, under the pressure of public opinion, are rapidly clearing their dockets.

Yet in Chicago robbery and burglary continue to flourish and people get shot as you might swat flies on the wall. From coast to coast it is the same: thousands of laws—hard laws, strong laws—thousands of police, thousands of prosecutors, thousands of courts, and hundreds of thousands of crimes.

This is the law the people built

It is built of blood and fire, of conflict, aggression, and reprisal. It was forged by the clamor of millions of ancestral voices: the voice of the tribe before the council fire howling for vengeance; the voice of the chieftain passing judgment of torture and death; the voice of fear building barriers about its belongings, its home, its lands, its wives, its maidservants and its manservants, its horses, cows, dogs, and asses, calling upon the tribe to curb the claws and fangs of rapacious neighbors; and the voice also of pity for the weak and justice for the wronged.

The law and its institutions are the fruits of centuries of collective living. Kings, princes, prelates, parliaments, presidents, governors, legislatures, and judges have all had a hand in its making, but behind them stand the people, ready at times to rise up and behead, hang, burn, and destroy in the passion of what they believe to be justice. Deep in their hearts lies a distrust of rulers and judges bred by centuries of injustice and oppression. Out of this grew the grand jury, the petit jury, the rule against self-incrimination, habeas corpus, the right to a change of venue, and other safeguards thrown about the accused.

Much of this legal machinery has, without question, become obsolete and inadequate for the handling of our increasingly complex social problems. Professors, police experts, criminologists, and lawyers have for years been suggesting improved methods for apprehending and trying criminals. Ideally, we should scrap the entire present system from police administration to the punishment or attempted reform of law violators, and build in its place a new structure in the light of more modern ideas as to ways and means of forestalling and controlling antisocial conduct. But the finest system in the world, whether devised by a practical criminologist or a social idealist, will not in itself reduce crime one iota without the spirit and will of the people behind it; and even a slight improvement is impossible as long as the nation, in the name of democracy, cherishes and applauds lawlessness and tolerates political corruption.

Our crime problem is not so much "What's wrong with the law?" as "Who's wrong, and why?"

This is the cop
Who enforces the law the people built

"Now, about this crime business," said a well-known hoodlum to Senator Copeland when he was in Chicago with the Senate subcommittee on racketeering and kidnapping, "all you need is honest cops and a little cooperation from the courts."

The average policeman must have bitterly resented the public's cynical approval of this gibe. He is in disrepute for conditions which he is power-less to change. The individual cop is no worse than the rest of us. He has a wife and children. He stands up to get shot at, and quite often is killed. His pay isn't large and sometimes it's delayed.

He may start out as a rookie with high ambitions to make a record for himself by catching crooks and cleaning up his precinct. He may dream of promotion through sheer merit, of becoming step by step a sergeant, lieu-tenant, captain, and chief amid the plaudits of all good citizens.

But he is soon disillusioned. He discovers that there are certain "joints" that must be left alone because they "kick in" to somebody with protection money, and that there are persons whom it is useless to arrest because they have somehow acquired "immunity" from punishment. This is lesson num-ber one—the lesson of political corruption. It is further illuminated by the flamboyant success of certain lieutenants and captains (not all of them, by any means) who "sport" big cars and invest in stocks, bonds, or apart-ment buildings.

Our ambitious young cop sees evidence all around him of the profits of the "shakedown" and the "fix." He learns to keep his mouth shut for fear of being exiled to "the sticks." Yet in spite of these conditions he may still have confidence in the civil service system (established in most of our large cities for the purpose of protecting the rank and file of the police and ensuring their orderly promotion), only to realize eventually, if he is bright, that it too is dominated by the machine of the party in power.

He may even resist all temptation to take part in the corruption which surrounds him. Thousands of policemen do. But the chances are that he will succumb to another influence just as insidious and vicious—the spirit of lawlessness. Going about his business from day to day, hauling in bums, pickpockets, holdup men, housebreakers, reds, and drunks, he learns from his brothers in arms to consider his prisoners as obstinate criminal cattle to be pushed and poked and yanked around in order to make them dread forever the sight of the police. No matter how kindly he may otherwise be, he discovers that all's fair in the war on crime. He becomes familiar with the ritual of the "goldfish" room, where prisoners are threatened and beaten with rubber hose, tortured by glaring lights, kept awake for endless hours, and assailed with questions and suggestions until they confess. "You gotta give 'em the works," he is told, and, his faith in the integrity of courts, juries, and prosecutors being weakened by his own actual experience with corruption and inefficiency, he accepts this doctrine of lawlessness with enthusiasm.

To anyone who doubts the prevalent use of the third degree by the police, let me recommend the Report on Lawlessness in Law Enforcement of the National Commission on Law Observance and Enforcement appointed by President Hoover, which presents a multitude of actual instances and concludes that such lawlessness not only brutalizes the police and hardens the prisoner, but impairs the efficiency of the police by leading them to rely on force rather than wits in solving crimes. This is demonstrated by the fact that the Boston police, with little or no use of the third degree, have obtained much better results than the Chicago force with its habitual resort to torture.

Corruption and lawlessness begin at the top and work down. The enforcement of law and order in most of our cities is controlled by a politically appointed commissioner or superintendent, and through him by the bosses of the dominant party, who thereby acquire a tremendous influence over the lives, property, and happiness of the citizens. How brutally, corruptly, and inefficiently they wield it should be apparent to any reader of the day's news.

In spite of such handicaps, here and there a few zealous men, who regard police work as a profession, have succeeded in putting in practice improvements in the technique of crime detection and have tried to encourage the morale of their co-workers and win the public's respect. But they struggle like ants in a sand pit.

> *This is the culprit*
> *Who is caught by the cop . . .*

Youth, growing up in the light of the flaring beacons of lawlessness and corruption, shrugs its shoulders: "Only saps work. You can't get a job, anyway. What's your racket, kid?"

What's your racket, gentlemen, you who howl for the cutting of school taxes, the reduction of teaching staffs, the shortening of the school year, and the curtailment of every school activity except the three R's—what's *your* racket?

Organized crime, organized labor, organized business, organized politics, organized exploitation, parallel and interlock. When trouble breaks, the "big shot" escapes abroad or gets off with a Senate investigation or a light sentence for income tax evasion. The little shots—our Tonys and Joes and Ikes—take the heavy "raps" and go to Sing Sing or Joliet or find permanent surcease via the electric chair.

These are the children, boys, girls, young men, young women, in the streets, alleys, basements, "athletic" clubs, pool rooms, dance halls, barrooms, dives, on the march to detention homes, reformatories, jails. Onward, ever onward, presses the eager, adventurous throng, lured by the hope of easy, gaudy living.

Among them are many mental and emotional misfits who constitute a separate problem. Some of these crippled personalities are discovered and isolated at an early age, but many go about without restraint until they become entangled in the processes of the law. Our social agencies have made progress in the care and treatment of mental defectives, but the law and the courts have been slow to accept the recommendations of psychiatrists.

Indifference, greed, stupidity, shoddy education, and the example of corruption and lawlessness in high places—these are the culprits.

"Lycurgus left none of his laws in writing," says Plutarch, "for he resolved the whole business of legislation into the bringing up of youth."

> *This is the prosecutor*
> *Who flays the culprit . . .*

He begins his career usually as an assistant district attorney or as state's attorney, with little experience in trial work. He learns his courtroom tactics in conflict with seasoned criminal lawyers who delight in springing on him all the tricks and chicanery of their trade. He thinks he must fight fire with fire and dirt with dirt. If he discovers the coercion and intimidation of witnesses by defendants and their friends, he feels justified in keeping the state's witnesses incommunicado and holding over them the threat of criminal prosecution.

The prosecutor is further incited to lawlessness by the clamor of editors, ministers, crime commissioners, and business men for more and stiffer sentences. The necessity of satisfying these good people and assuaging the public appetite for melodrama drives him and his assistants to seek convictions by fair means or foul. The prosecutor joins with the police in using the third degree; in court he violates the rules of evidence, and by improper and inflammatory remarks to juries lays the ground for numerous reversals.

Through his control over the grand jury and the initiation of criminal complaints, the prosecutor wields a power superior to the police, and if he is strong and shrewd he may very well become the dominant political personage in his county. Politics, in fact, is the keynote of all his activities. He probably began as a bright boy running errands for a precinct captain, canvassing voters, or handing out sample ballots; or he may have been related to an influential politician. In either case he saw the advantages of legal training and stepped out of law school into political office of some kind, working his way up through the system to nomination for prosecutor on the party ticket.

In his campaign for election he invariably follows the well-known formula of promising to clean up vice, racketeering, gangs, and gambling, and by constant repetition he may even convince himself that he will suppress crime altogether. But the moment he assumes office he is forced to abandon all but a pretense of an honest and independent administration. In the first place, he has to accept the staff of inexperienced and frequently incompetent assistants assigned to him by the party bosses. And, secondly, the men who nominated him are after him at once to "nol pros" this case and that, to give some hoodlum a break, or to let a confessed criminal plead guilty to a lesser offense than the one he is accused of so that he will take a lighter sentence and perhaps walk out of jail on probation. At the same time the forces of bribery and corruption begin to play upon the weaker members of his staff and find ways and means of gaining their ends no matter how honest the prosecutor himself may be.

Organized gangs recognize the prosecutor's bark, but fear his bite very little. They are in far greater danger from the guns of an outraged police force than from the loud reiteration of the prosecutor that he will drive crime out of his county. Nor can anyone improve the situation very much as long as the office of prosecutor remains a political prize.

This is the lawyer
Who fights the prosecutor . . .

This is the lawyer, aye, and the entire bar, including your humble servant. Most of us won't sully our hands with the criminal law. It's a dirty business. You can't touch tar without getting smirched. A defendant in a criminal case expects you to get him off by hook or by crook, but mostly by crook. If you are unwilling to adopt the devious and crooked ways of crime itself, you can't be the defendant's best advocate, so you turn him down. At least that is how the argument runs.

Most criminal lawyers, therefore, belong to a race apart. Heroes in the public eye; almost but not quite pariahs among "good people." Hardy and shrewd, they know their legal tricks, their police, prosecutors, judges, and gentlemen of the jury. Above all they are realistic—champions hired to get results.

The lower-grade criminal lawyer has his hook-up with gangs and keeps his petitions for habeas corpus written up in blank ready to fill in with the necessary data, so that he can "spring" a client from the lock-up the minute the police nab him. He knows who will furnish bail. He knows who knows which judges and how to pull the strings. He asks his clients no foolish questions. If someone intimidates witnesses and bribes jurors, that's their business, not his. He may indulge in fixing cases, but you can't prove it on him. His philosophy is short and simple: "Give the customers what they pay for."

You may call this sort of unscrupulous practitioner a lawyer criminal, if you like, but he can turn the phrase neatly on other members of the bar: "How about our respectable legal friends who advised public utility magnates and others in the intricacies of floating rotten bonds? And how about eminent counsel who connive among themselves for so-called 'friendly' receiverships to keep the looting of failing corporations and the consequent fees within the magic circle of the insiders?"

The code of ethics of the lawyers is actually higher than that of the business world which supports them. It includes many niceties and is scrupulously observed by the bulk of the bar. Serious infractions of ethics usually lead to disbarment. The lawyers, on the whole, like the ministers, doctors, tradespeople, laborers, and the police, are a decent, hard-working lot. But they labor under the narrow and often antisocial necessities of advocacy.

Some lawyers, in fact, maintain a distinct cleavage between their personal conduct and their conduct on behalf of clients. They would not steal a nickel or raise a finger in violation of the letter of the law, but they will, and do, without compunction disclose to buccaneers of business ways of evading the spirit of restrictive statutes. Their concern, like that of their supposedly criminal confreres, is to give the customers what they pay for, and they will ignore every consideration of social good if it conflicts with the aims and ambitions of a powerful client. Lawyers of this sort would doubtless subscribe to the notorious view of Lord Brougham expressed during the excitement of a trial:

> An advocate, by the sacred duty which he owes his client, knows, in the discharge of that office, but one person in the world, *that client and none other*. To save that client by all expedient means—to protect that client at all hazards and costs to all others, and amongst others to himself—is the highest and most unquestioned of his duties; and he must not regard the alarm, the suffering, the torment, the destruction, which he may bring upon any other. Nay, separating even the duties of a patriot from those of an advocate, and casting *them*, if need be, to the wind, he must go on reckless of the consequences, if his fate it should unhappily be, to involve his country in confusion for his client's protection.

This low and servile conception of the duties of an advocate has been generally repudiated by the legal profession. Yet the spirit of it survives among a minority who have so identified themselves with the interests of their clients that they retain no clear conception of the public good. They are the lawyers who aided and abetted the gentlemen denounced by the President in his message at the opening of the . . . [73rd] Congress:

> I am speaking of those individuals who have evaded the spirit and purpose of our tax laws, of those high officials of banks or corporations who have grown rich at the expense of their stockholders or the public, of those reckless speculators with their own or other people's money whose operations have injured the values of the farmers' crops and the savings of the poor.

There are fortunately signs that the honest, capable, and diligent majority of the bar have been so aroused by the general outcry for a house cleaning that they may rid themselves not only of the "lawyer criminal," but also of those other malefactors who through a highly developed legal technique and political connections have assisted in looting the public in the numerous ways that democracy affords.

> *This is the jury*
> *Who favor the lawyer . . .*

The culprit is said to be entitled to trial before a jury of his peers. They are too often just that and no more. Therein lies the vice of our jury system as it is administered. Our twelve men may be good and true, but they are not necessarily bright.

Certain trades and professions are notably missing from the jury panel. The police, firemen, teachers, soldiers, lawyers, doctors, and ministers are exempt by law from jury service in most of our states. Bankers, high executives, politicians, and their friends are exempt in practice. Sometimes their names are drawn, but they usually manage on one ground or another to be let off. No one can really blame them. The profitless frittering away of the time and energy of veniremen by lawyers, the courts, and their attachés is notorious. A busy man is appalled at the prospect of abandoning his own affairs even for a few weeks to take part in the drab and inefficient business of the courts.

Occasionally an intelligent and conscientious citizen called for jury service will not try to get excused, and may even look forward with some zeal to participating in the administration of justice. Such a venireman, however, finds himself herded about with other victims, often in badly ventilated and uncomfortable rooms; and when he is finally called to court for examination as a prospective juror he is certain to be challenged by one side or the other if he reveals the slightest ability to form opinions of his own. In fact, unless he conceals this dangerous faculty, he may fail altogether to enjoy the doubtful pleasure of sitting as a juror in any case. If he plays dumb and is accepted and sworn in as a juror, his experience will be illuminating but not edifying. He must sit in silence and listen to constant bickering over evidence and to arguments of counsel that insult his intelligence. Of course, there are exceptions. He may be lucky enough to be picked as juror in a case defended by a brilliant and inspired advocate. But that happens only once in a lifetime.

Whether the I.Q. of the average jury is lower than that of the police, the lawyers, and the court attendants, we do not know. That it is somewhat lower seems reasonable to suppose. But it should be remembered that the jury is the great alibi for prosecutors and judges. It is invariably blamed for every "miscarriage of justice," as in the case of the acquittal of the Touhy gang of alleged kidnappers by a Minneapolis jury.

The function of the jury is strictly limited to deciding the guilt of the defendant upon the particular evidence brought before it. It is not permitted to consider extrinsic circumstances presented in the newspapers but excluded from court. In cases of business fraud a verdict of acquittal in a supposedly air-tight case may be due to the inability of the jury to grasp intricate evidence, but in cases of murder, robbery, kidnapping, and crimes of violence generally, it is just as likely to be due to the failure of the state to prove the defendant's guilt beyond a reasonable doubt.

How far the jury system has been tampered with by the fingers of corruption we do not know. In Boston last fall twenty-five former jurors admitted accepting from twenty-five dollars to seventy-five dollars each for holding out for the acquittal of defendants. Two men were sent to jail in Jersey City a few months ago for offering to fix juries in criminal cases, and several others were indicted for jury-fixing in Passaic County last summer.

The drawing of veniremen may also be manipulated by political organizations, so that the men called for service will be of a class and character amenable to influence. The evidence of such practices in Detroit was so strong that the State of Michigan revised its jury panel system.

We have no means, however, of gauging the extent of the corruption and manipulation of juries. It is a secret locked in the hearts of innumerable individual jurors, but they certainly are not immune to the influence of the lawless forces that surround them.

This is the judge
Who instructs the jury . . .

Judge Thomas Taylor, Jr., upon retiring at the age of seventy-two from the bench of the Circuit Court of Cook County, Illinois, after nearly fifty years of the finest type of judicial service, had this to say:

We have many able men at the bar. It is a pity they will not be able to get on the bench. We do need something here. It is a calamity. I could name three hundred or four hundred of the best lawyers, fit for the bench, but no one of them will ever have the ghost of a show. Our people will not select men who are the best for them. They are plastic in the hands of the politicians.

Judges come up through the political route. The young lawyer becomes a precinct captain and a good organizer. In time he gets close to the ward committee-man.

He then tries out for the Municipal Court. After a few years here the ambitious ones aspire to the Circuit and Superior bench. Their success is at no time dependent on their ability as judges. *We get good ones only by chance.*

Judge Taylor states facts that are beyond dispute. It speaks well for the human race that we have as many fine, conscientious judges as we do. Quite often, lawyers who have shown no sign of great legal ability, or interest in public service, will demonstrate excellent judicial qualities after their elevation to the bench.

Unfortunately the work of the good judge is seldom broadcast. He labors day after day in court, in chambers, and at home, sometimes late into the night, reading and considering in the hope that by the grace of God he may arrive at just conclusions. But there is no drama for the public in the quiet researches of the human spirit. They go without acclaim. The name of the good judge seldom registers on the minds of the vast electorate, and when his term expires he is wholly at the mercy of the politicians who nominated or appointed him.

Sometimes a judge may renounce all political alliances and play directly for the support of the public, but very few judges can remain long on the bench if they utterly spurn the hands that boosted them up. This does not mean that cases are generally decided in judicial chambers before they are tried, as a large part of the public cynically believes. But it does mean that intervention through politicians is repeatedly sought by the relatives and friends of criminal defendants, and that the judges are besieged from day to day by requests from politicians, big and little, for leniency and special consideration in cases that are coming up before them.

We also have evidence in our great cities that some of the judges of the "lower" courts have tolerated or participated in the organized exploitation of accused persons, as revealed in Judge Seabury's investigation; that some judges have belonged to political organizations that were closely tied up with gangsters and racketeering; and that others have paid political debts through the appointment of receivers and their attorneys.

The aspirant for judicial office must travel the same path as the aspirant for the job of prosecutor. Very often he has been a state's attorney or district attorney, and he retains the point of view in criminal trials that he acquired in that office. He may separate his political activities from his function as a judge, but the chances are that his adjustment to the expediencies of politics will continue to have some effect upon his conduct. This is demonstrated in the common judicial practice of approving deals made between the prosecutor and attorney for the defendant, the toleration of innumerable continuances which discourage the witnesses for the state, the perversion of the ancient remedy of habeas corpus, the approval of insufficient and badly secured bail bonds, laxity in granting probation, and the distortion of many legal processes which in themselves would be adequate if properly administered.

> *This is the boss*
> *Who names the judge . . .*

He runs the show and gets things done for the electorate in a way that no one else will or can. He never turns a voter down. He formerly dispensed food, coal, and clothing to the needy through his party organization, and during the last few years he has claimed credit for getting such things for his constituents from unemployment relief agencies, although they could very well have been obtained without him. Quite recently he has tried desperately to control the distribution of jobs by the CWA as a means of keeping voters in line.

According to William B. Munro, who has studied the boss in his natural habitat, he is a necessary and almost indispensable part of our political system, not only furnishing direct contact between the citizenry and public administrative agencies, but also acting as liaison officer between the executive and legislative, yes, and the judicial branches of our government.

In return for helping his constituents, he asks only for their support at the polls. But the upkeep of his organization requires a large and constant supply of money, which he secures by indirect levies upon the entire public. He may still gather some funds through the time-honored sale of police and court protection, but his greatest revenue comes by dealing in licenses, franchises, tax rebates, public contracts, and through campaign contributions from business men, utility magnates, and job holders.

Give the boss power, and the rest of the boys may have the glory. He seldom seeks office except perhaps to grace the latter days of his life, so that he may leave to his children the tradition that their father was held in high honor and esteem.

That the boss and his lieutenants name the judges is a commonplace.

Judicial office is a political job whether filled by election or by appointment. While there is evidence that somewhat better men are obtained through the appointive system because of the focusing of responsibility, it is still apparent that a seat on the bench is considered principally as a reward for political service.

Bar association officers and committees again and again have besought party bosses to select their nominees for judicial office from a list of lawyers of unquestioned ability and reputation, but such efforts are vain. The boss knows what he is about and will never alter his purely political attitude toward the bench unless forced by the overwhelming pressure of public opinion expressed in votes.

> *These are the people*
> *Who stand for the boss*
> *Who names the judge*
> *Who instructs the jury*
> *Who favor the lawyer*
> *Who fights the prosecutor*
> *Who flays the culprit*
> *Who is caught by the cop*
> *Who enforces the law the people built*

"We, the people of the United States, in order to . . . establish justice . . ."

So said our forebears, bitter from the memory of Old World tyrannies and the cruelties of king-made judges like Jeffreys and Stubbs. The founders of our democracy stripped their judges of wigs and robes, aggrandized the jury of their peers, and sought by every possible means to protect the citizen against judicial usurpation and oppression.

And as the people spread out across the mountains and the western plains, they carried with them a relentless contempt for the pomp and dignity associated with the woolsack and the mace. Their ideal was justice—plain, swift, and sure. The outlaw—killer or horse thief—was caught and hanged without ceremony by the posse comitatus, or shot on sight by an outraged citizen. Rifle, shotgun, and six-shooter became implements of daily life, like the axe, the plough, and the scythe.

The hordes that poured in on us from the ends of the earth, with customs and traditions conflicting and diverse, eagerly embraced the ideals of democracy, which seemed to them to include not only the aversion for superimposed authority, but the right of the citizen to bear arms and to appropriate whatever property or privileges he could be the first to lay hands on. It was in this spirit that the processes of government and law

enforcement were ultimately converted both by native-born and by naturalized citizens into an organized system of plunder and political spoils. It
is against this spirit that we now begin to see signs of revolt.

The President issued a clear call for a new deal for justice in speaking
before the Federal Council of Churches in December:

> A thinking America . . . seeks a government that will be sufficiently strong
> to protect the prisoner and at the same time to crystallize a public opinion so
> clear that government of all kinds will be compelled to practise a more certain
> justice. The judicial function of the government is the protection of the
> individual and of the community through quick and certain justice. That
> function in many places has fallen into a state of disrepair. It must be a
> part of our programme to reëstablish it.

And in his address at the opening of Congress he roundly denounced
public malefactors whether operating within or without the letter of the
law:

> These violations of ethics and these violations of law call on the strong
> arm of the government for their suppression; they call also on the country
> for an aroused public opinion.

The American Bar Association at its annual meeting last summer anticipated the President's call to action by formulating a National Bar Programme for the purpose of arousing lawyers throughout the nation to a
concerted effort to solve, among other things, the problem of criminal law
enforcement. Since then the president of the association has sent out a
questionnaire to 1450 local and state bar associations asking for specific
data on the reasons for the failure of the law and courts to control and
abate crime.

The will to reform is, of course, futile without concrete plans. We must
have a programme of constructive action with the objective of divorcing
every part of the machinery of justice from the control of party politics
and of inspiring the entire nation not merely with respect for the law but
with the zeal to enforce it. Such a programme might well include:

1. A nation-wide reform of criminal procedure through the adoption by
the states of the modern code devised by the American Law Institute and
recommended by the American Bar Association, which would speed up the
work of the courts and eliminate useless technicalities. Many of its provisions could be adopted by the courts on their own initiative without legislative sanction.

2. The revamping of our police systems with a view to removing them
from the control of local politics, adopting more scientific methods of train-

ing, increasing administrative efficiency, and using every modern facility for the identification and apprehension of criminals. Consideration should also be given to Attorney-General Cummings's suggestion for the development of state constabularies, independent of county lines, working in coordination with each other and the federal authorities.

3. Federal laws for the control of the manufacture and sale of firearms and explosives, stringently limiting the right to bear arms and requiring the keeping of records which would enable the police to trace the pedigree of every dangerous weapon. Other federal laws, where practical and constitutional, to cover interstate criminal activities, not at present subject to federal prosecution.

4. A new attitude toward the problem of youthful delinquency, which goes to the root of our troubles. This would require a thorough change in educational methods in directions indicated by progressive pedagogues, the increased development of constructive habit-forming activities, the teaching of social ethics rather than merely abstract virtues, the consistent and periodical medical and psychiatric examination of all children from an early age, together with the keeping of behavior records, and the adoption throughout the nation of modern methods in the treatment of juvenile offenders. And to carry out such plans we should institute a stern and implacable offensive against the false and shortsighted educational economies which have made such disastrous headway during the depression.

5. The office of public prosecutor must be removed from politics. We should try to inspire a more clinical attitude on the part of the agencies of the state in handling offenders. Every criminal court should have a public defender and an independent staff of doctors and psychiatrists, dominated neither by the prosecutor nor by the defense, with the duty of ascertaining and reporting scientific facts to the court. The recommendations of such a body should largely determine the treatment of law violators.

6. The bar must eliminate the lawyer criminal. It is already tackling the job. The standards of conduct of defense attorneys are also likely to improve with a more scientific attitude on the part of the state.

7. The jury system need not and probably ought not to be abolished. But its function should be limited to a determination of facts. It should have no power to pass upon the moral, emotional, or mental responsibility of a defendant or his treatment and punishment. The problem of obtaining a higher grade of jurors and combating jury tampering is squarely up to the lawyers.

8. We must demand and get better judges. The problem of judicial selection is dealt with in one of the planks of the American Bar Association

platform for 1934. Its solution rests upon establishing a technique which will restrict the choice of judges to a qualified list approved by the bar.

9. As to the boss, our only immediate hope is to restrict his influence as far as possible and to use him for more constructive ends.

We have no need of Jeremiahs. The nation is already aroused, but we must find ways of directing the very real and widespread indignation against our law-enforcing agencies into effective action; and above all we must inspire the oncoming generation with an ardent spirit for justice which will burn bright and transcendent in every heart.

No. 95

BARBED-WIRE ENTANGLEMENTS [1]

by John A. Warner

" JUMPING over lines to beat a rap for crimes" seems to be the modern version of the offender's game of "hide and seek" with the forces of law and order. The lines are the invisible dividers separating state from state. The players in the game are the law-breakers versus the police. The challenger seeks immunity in the neutral corner over the boundary, and the opposition players, by statutory rules, dare not remove him from that neutral corner without the consent of the extraditing governor who constitutes the official referee. These umpires are often responsible for decisions which are difficult to reconcile. Moreover, since the rule book is cumbersome, technical, abstruse—the work of many different authors— months of deliberation are often required before a final decision can be reached. Such delay more often favors the sought-after than the seeker. A study of crime prevention teaches that swift apprehension coupled with sure punishment deters crime in no small degree, but the problem of inter-state rendition very frequently makes it impossible to act upon this knowledge.

The problem becomes particularly acute when the offense is one classified as a misdemeanor. In such cases, there is little inclination to spend time or funds in securing the return of the offender, although his offense may equal a felony in gravity. It is sometimes stated that crimes of misdemeanor grade are less serious than felonies and that less attention should therefore be paid to punishing them, but efficient police will not agree with that theory. So closely allied are the two classes that one sometimes wonders

[1] John A. Warner, "Barbed-Wire Entanglements," *State Government* (January, 1935) Vol. 8, pp. 285-287. Reprinted by permission of the author and *State Government*.

why the arbitrary division was made. Is a man less criminal because he succeeded in stealing only one hundred dollars' worth of property than he would have been had he been able to steal material valued at one hundred and one dollars?

The formidable barrier of state lines is seriously interfering with efficient police practice and procedure. The laborious process of requisition and extradition plus a tendency of localities to consider that the flight of criminals is "good riddance to bad rubbish," result in a condition whereby offender after offender goes unpunished for his acts against society.

State rendition laws as well as local regulations on the subject differ widely, and until some simplified and unified system is adopted, the ends of justice will continue to be defeated—in felony as well as in misdemeanor cases. A few states have amended their statutes in order to simplify the process of rendition. New York, for instance, recently prescribed that a fugitive wanted by some other state might waive his right to rendition process before a magistrate of a court of record. Whereas, of course, this is highly desirable for other states which may take advantage of New York's concession, New York itself may be balked in similar circumstances by the failure of these other states to provide a waiver clause. Until there is uniformity within all states, no general benefit may be gained by the police and prosecuting officers of the nation at large.

Many technical volumes have been written about the fugitive problem, and many court decisions on this subject—including some by the United States Supreme Court—have been handed down. It is, therefore, perhaps presumptuous for the police forces of the country to offer suggestions for the solution of the problem. It must be admitted, however, that police agencies are very often criticized for their failure to apprehend criminals, and that one outstanding reason for such failure is the intricate machinery of interstate return of offenders. While such disparity and lack of co-operation exist among the state laws, most misdemeanants and a goodly percentage of felons will continue to enjoy "out-of-state" immunity.

Another factor involved is the expense of preparing papers and of traveling to the capital of the asylum state to present these papers before reaching the place of the offender's incarceration. At times this may constitute a severe financial burden on the county, city, village, or town.

Since many so-called minor offenders committing crimes near the border lines of states seem aware of the protection offered after migration, there is a general trend toward that sort of immunity. The popularity of this form of escape has become increasingly apparent with the development of the modern system of police communication. The system exists between approximately seven hundred police departments in the states of Massachusetts, Connecticut, Rhode Island, New York, New Jersey, Pennsylvania, Delaware, and Ohio. This vast network of police teletypewriters distributes the alarms and messages from each of the states mentioned to all of the others. Supplementing this teletypewriter system, of course, are the police radio messages—many thousands of which are daily traveling the ether waves.

A study of message traffic via the teletypewriter—involving the transmission of about two hundred and fifty thousand police messages each year—indicates that the majority of the crimes are in the misdemeanor class. It also indicates that, because of the technical difficulties involved in the arrest of misdemeanants outside of the state where the crime was committed, the offender is seldom apprehended after his flight across the state lines.

When, however, with the aid of modern rapid means of communication, an asylum state does arrest a fugitive, the demanding state often fails to exercise the same vigor in securing his return as it manifested in seeking his arrest.

Both the interstate compact clause of the constitution and the so-called "Interstate Compact Act" of the 73rd Congress authorize the states to enter into agreements which would simplify interstate rendition and materially aid in the prompt return of fugitives. A study of the possibilities of such interstate compacts in the field of criminal justice might well be undertaken in the various states by legislators, crime commissions, and others interested in the subject. Undoubtedly such compacts could be broad enough to include interstate rendition on the basis of certification by the demanding state, and they might even recognize the authority of out-of-state police officials in the execution of process and apprehensions of offenders.

Another act of the 73rd Congress has made it a federal crime for felons or witnesses in criminal proceedings to flee from one state to another, but the assistance of federal authorities is necessary for the return of fugitives under this act. Strictly speaking, a criminal so apprehended is under the custody and control of the federal authority, and is subject to prosecution for the federal crime of flight. There is no definite provision for his being delivered to state authorities for prosecution under their statutes. Undoubtedly this act will be invoked in order to secure the return of criminals to a jurisdiction in which they can be tried for their original crime, but apparently the federal prosecution will always have priority.

Until the states realize the deficiencies of present rendition laws, interstate crime control will remain in an elementary stage. Simplification and uniformity of these laws are necessary if the police forces of the country are to do the work expected of them by press and public in the apprehension of law violators. At some future time uniform state legislation may be passed which will follow the lines of federal deportation proceedings, applicable in the case of alien offenders. In other words, states should be able to return to each other undesirable persons who have crossed state boundaries in order to escape trial and punishment for an offense committed elsewhere.

No. 96

TWELVE GOOD MEN—AND "UNTRUE!" [1]

by Upton Close

FOR the first time we have an official "low-down" on the American jury The Ruth Commission of Pennsylvania, armed by the Legislature with authority to subpoena, has put scores of ex-jurors on the stand and made them tell what really happens behind locked jury-room doors.

One result of the Commission's first year of work is that 117 individuals in Pennsylvania, ranging from professional criminals to court employees, lawyers and politicians, are under indictment by Judge Curtis Bok's special "blue ribbon" grand jury. But punishment of offenders turned up is incidental. Of first importance to everyone who must some day resort to the law, and to every American who wants justice, are the Commission's factual survey of shocking practices existing all over the United States, and its careful, common-sense recommendation of reform.

The Commission's report, going to press as this is written, and previewed only by this writer, was very nearly smothered by the bosses in Pennsylvania, who cut off funds with the hope that the findings could not be published. We shall have the report only because the fearless young director of the Commission, Chet Keyes, anticipating this strategy, wisely contracted for the printing even before the report was compiled, and put aside each month a sum now sufficient to publish the book.

It all began with a series of newspaper articles by Dave Wittals in the *Philadelphia Record,* exposing the probation racket in that city. The Legislature took notice, and Governor Earle appointed State Senator Rev. Frank W. Ruth to be chairman of a commission to investigate. That was a lucky choice. The good name of Ruth, pastor of a small-town Dutch Reformed Church, a man above reproach and beyond approach, saved the Commission from scorching when politicians turned on the heat.

[1] Upton Close, "Twelve Good Men—and 'Untrue!'" *The Christian Science Monitor* (July 20, 1938), pp. 1-2, 13. Reprinted by permission of *The Christian Science Monitor.*

The Ruth report covers a great deal of legal ground, but perhaps its most significant feature is the exposure of jury conduct. Most common of the sins of juries, says the report, is the tendency to regard lightly misconduct in office. A mayor sharing the proceeds of prostitution, a police chief collecting from illicit liquor dealers, political bosses conspiring to deprive the American citizen of his right to vote freely, seem to arouse the sporting instincts of jurors willing to have the verdict determined by the flip of a coin or pulling straws.

The Commission's post-mortems on amazing verdicts brought out the case —only slightly more ludicrous and outrageous than others—of the coin-flipping foreman at Easton.

"Let's get this over with!" he urged his fellow members as soon as the bailiff had locked them in. "It's all very confusing—none of us really knows whether to acquit or convict. Why not leave it to Lady Luck? She's always fair! I'll toss for each of you. If it's heads you're for acquittal; tails you're for conviction—O.K.?" It being a sporting proposition, all eleven agreed. The foreman outdid himself. He tossed for each of his fellow jurors, one at a time. All eleven came up heads. That decided the verdict and the jury filed into court with it. Some of the jurors had misgivings but didn't like to accuse the foreman of cheating. They didn't know then that he was a political henchman of the accused!

Jurors in one instance confessed to agreement in order to get to a lodge dance on time, in another instance to see a ball game. The ease with which one or two determined jurors can swing the remainder was evidenced by testimony after testimony. The ordinary, easily influenced juror seems to assume that his fellows who take definite stands right off know more about the case than himself.

The reasoning of the great American juror would baffle an ancient Greek Sophist or medieval logician. Certainly it did baffle several Philadelphia lawyers connected with the investigation. In one prominent case, a jury of conservative citizens received evidence, including a confession, of a fatal assault, committed by a young lady defendant. But the extraneous introduction of testimony which, in the minds of the jurors, offended the religious faith in which the defendant was reared made them decide to overlook the killing, although forgiveness was no part of their prerogative. Later, when the Commission subpoenaed the jurors in this case to find out why they had disregarded legal fact, it got such explanations as these: "There was a lot of argument—I did not know what it was all about." "I not understand English." "How do I know what happened, I wasn't there—see?" "The foreman was very stubborn."

And here is the foreman's logic: "We are not going to convict of murder!

. . . If we let her go free she will worry more about her wicked act and really suffer more than if she served a few years' imprisonment."

Is this typical of what goes on in a murder trial jury? The Commission's work shows that such warping of logic and placing of prejudice above duty are common.

Jury justice suffers, too, because courts forget the surprising ignorance of many jurors in such fundamental matters as court language and procedure. Ex-jurors in whose hands had lain the disposition of men's liberty and property admitted under oath to the Ruth Commission that they had reached verdicts without knowing who was the plaintiff and who the defendant, never having absorbed the meaning of the words from clerks, court, or lawyers.

Often, too, the juror is asked to perform unreasonable feats of memory. In one Pennsylvania case, a jury was asked to bring back verdicts against 53 defendants of varying degrees of guilt, being tried together, without so much as a written note on the evidence produced or the impressions made by the defendants at the trial. The baffled jurors couldn't remember them apart! Who could?

In states such as Kansas, jurors are provided, when they go into closet, with all trial exhibits and clerk's transcript of the testimony—material technical, rambling, contradictory and complicated, but, at least, something to refer to. In many states, however, the juror's only whack at trial exhibits is when they are waved under his confused remembrance of what witnesses, lawyers, and court said throughout the trial, which may have lasted many days.

In one case, jurors got to arguing over the phrase "undue influence," used by the judge, and found that none of them knew what it meant! Of course, they were forbidden a dictionary—all reference books are forbidden. They had not been told that they might go back and ask the judge, and, even had they known, that would have required a court session and formal re-entry and re-exit from the courtroom. A jury wants to get the thing over. And, after all, even jurors have their pride!

How much justification exists for the tradition (rather than law) that jurors may not take notes or carry memoranda into the jury room is uncertain. There is, of course, the danger that memoranda may be partial, or "loaded" from the outside. Yet a judge, or panel of judges, when serving in the function of the jury, works from copious notes. The unfortunate juror, however, is required to recall from memory the gist of 50 contradictory statements! And though he may not have notes, he may have seen newspapers, screaming sensational guesses.

The commission found that the barest start has been made in rendering simple, fundamental instruction to jurors. The judges of Northampton County, Pennsylvania, have prepared vest-pocket printed booklets for jurors. Words in common legal use have been avoided until after their meaning and effect have been stated. In some western states mimeographed instructions are provided. The Commission urges the improvement and standardization of such instructions.

Damaging to justice as ignorance may be, actual corruption is less forgivable. The Commission found it to be a custom in some counties for a defendant to look up prospective jurors directly or otherwise. Amazing industry was shown by one embezzler suspect. His first trial brought conviction, but he won retrial on a technicality. By direct visit or through intermediaries he got pretty well around to the members of two complete panels of 90 each, with disastrous expense to the State. Trial two resulted in a hung jury, trial three in acquittal—his assiduity brought results!

The Commission found the most startling and widespread jury malpractice to be service under false name. This is prevalent in large cities, and our "best citizens" are collaborators in it. A busy man or woman receives a summons to jury duty and goes to a "friend with influence" to get him out of it. The friend says: "Sure, forget it—just leave it to me!" What happens is that a henchman or favorite of the local boss turns up for jury duty, answers to the name of the impaneled citizen, and serves throughout the life of the panel for his $3 to $5 a day—meanwhile being in a perfect position to "throw" cases damaging to his political machine.

In Philadelphia and several lesser Pennsylvania cities, juror substitution has become so common as to be almost accepted practice by court officials. It has a charity angle! A Ward boss tries to have on hand a few "jury tours" for faithful unemployed voters who need to add to their relief dole.

In a sardonic case reported from Oregon the defendant's wife was on the jury—unknown to all save the defendant and his unscrupulous attorney. But when certain secrets the defendant had hidden from his spouse came out in court, the poor fellow rushed to his lawyer with the demand that he "get that woman off the jury at once!" She was in a fine position to revenge a wife's wounded pride.

The Commission received another shock when it subpoenaed jurors who had brought in a verdict of acquittal in a flagrant larceny case. Jurors testified that they followed the foreman, who blithely admitted that he had once done four years for larceny and shied away from causing such distress to a fellow being.

This case pointed up an evil existing in many states: The foreman is chosen or designated at the beginning of the trial, making him a marked man to those seeking to influence the verdict. In Kansas, for opposite instance, the jury chooses its foreman after it receives commitment of the case.

Legal qualification requirements for juries, varying in the 48 states, add up to a huge joke at the expense of society. Twenty-four states require the juror to possess "good moral character" or "one or more of the qualities of good moral character"! Thirty states, that the juror be "generally reputed to be intelligent." Eighteen states ask no positive qualities at all, but specify, more or less, against a person with a criminal record. Some say that he must be "not an idiot." Some states exempt World War veterans if honorably discharged after nine months' service. If dishonorably discharged, they can become jurors!

Men of learned professions—doctors, lawyers, and teachers—are usually exempt by statute or get off by custom. No wonder the report says: "By the time the higher type get excused, one out of three or four capable jurors remain. Our methods of selection blow away the wheat and save the chaff."

The panels from which juries are chosen are commonly made up of names drawn by lot from voters' registration lists, tax books, or even telephone directories. This proceeding is designed to insure impartiality of choice, but it offers no guarantee of the fitness to serve of any juror so drawn. In some instances politics enters into the selections, as in Berks County, Pennsylvania, where the panel is "nominated" by the big party bosses: one Republican, one Democrat. The Commission believes that a fundamental reform—procuring of good jury timber—can be brought about by pre-examination of names for fitness by a semi-judicial, semi-citizens' board. In Los Angeles, such a board has been established.

After that comes the reform of the business of challenging prospective jurors. Attorneys have a certain number of peremptory challenges—varying in the various states—whereby they can dismiss jurors without revealing any reason. Aside from this, they can ask the judge to dismiss any prospective juror whom they can cajole or bluff into admitting that he has set ideas about the case in hand. Naturally, the common result is a battle between contending attorneys, each trying to seat jurors sympathetic to his own argument. Actual fitness to serve becomes a secondary consideration.

Instead of this scandalous lawyers' game, the Commission would have the judge provided with a brief on each summoned citizen, procured by investigators who cannot know on what case he will serve. Secondly, it would have the reasonableness of all challenges ruled on by the judge. The right of peremptory challenge would be eliminated.

After an improved method of selecting juries, two final reforms are recommended. Bewildered by the inconsistency and even brutality of the law in fixing punishments, jurors frequently return arbitrary verdicts of not guilty or guilty in lesser degree than proved. If all states had the indeterminate sentence law now being tried by California, without minimum and maximum, leaving length of punishment to decision of an expert penal board according to merit, juries would bring in more honest convictions.

The last reform—which alone had wide discussion prior to the Ruth Commission's work—would authorize a "majority verdict" of ten or nine jurors. This is being tried now in a few places in civil cases. It saves many hung juries and consequent retrial costs and time. It enables the jury to get past one or two stubborn members, and makes "fixing" harder, since at least three jurors instead of one must be reached.

Americans are not purposely careless about a matter which touches us so closely as the administration of justice. But they have been at a loss to know how reforms can be made. The Ruth Commission's report gives a layman's-language picture of the abuses that exist, and the common-sense ways to correct them.

Mr. Chet Keyes and his co-workers have laid the problem out so that you in your county and state and I in mine and every voter in his can take hold of it. American justice will be just what the American public demands— and deserves.

No. 97

JUSTICE—QUICK AND CHEAP [1]

by Joe P. Faulkner

HOUSEWIVES, homeowners, motorists, neighborhood tradesmen, and many others are exposed daily to an enormous variety of petty injustices, unaware that with little effort these wrongs can be righted swiftly, fairly, and at almost no expense.

Popularly called "Poor Man's Courts," because patrons are served at marked-down costs, these tribunals to-day exist in virtually every section of the country. They function primarily to permit collection of small refunds, debts, damages, and payments that would cost more than they are worth to pursue elsewhere.

Monuments to our government's genuine interest in the little problems of all its people, whether they live in one-room, cold-water walk-ups or in sumptuous penthouses, these simple, economical courts for Mr. and Mrs. Average Citizen are known by various names in different parts of the country. The most descriptive name is Small Claims Courts. But they also

[1] Joe P. Faulkner, "Justice—Quick and Cheap," *Good Housekeeping* (January, 1949), Vol. 128, No. 1, pp. 42-43, 142. Reprinted by permission of Hearst Magazines, Inc., and the author.

are called Conciliation Courts, Wage Claims Courts, Small Claims Procedural Courts, Small Claims Departments of District, Municipal, or Justice's Courts, Small Causes Courts, and Arbitration Courts. A phone call to your courthouse will identify the one nearest your home.

Whatever the title, procedure is similar, if not identical. You merely outline your trouble to the clerk. He, and sometimes even the judge, will assist in details, writing them in simple, nontechnical language. You sign an affidavit. A hearing date is set. Your opponent is notified. Then you literally tell it to the judge. He asks you what you want, asks your adversary why he doesn't give it to you, tries to guide you both toward an amicable, equitable settlement. If conciliation fails, he hears the evidence and makes an on-the-spot decision.

Lawyers aren't necessary. Some states, notably California, bar them. Iowa ruled they could appear only by court permission. In most places they are optional. The judge gives free counsel to both sides and permits you to tell your story in your own words. You aren't put on a witness stand and ordered to answer yes or no.

There are no juries. You automatically waive this Constitutional right. There are no rules of evidence, no pleadings, no written complaints and answers, no motions, no petitions, no complicated, obfuscating formalities and technicalities.

Expense to litigants is small. Some places, as the District of Columbia, charge nothing if payment would cause hardship. Most states have $1 filing fees. New York, for ordinary cases, charges $1.25. For wage claims you pay only the actual cost of mailing a summons to your opponent. Registered letters, costing 27 cents, usually are sent; sometimes, ordinary 3-cent letters. All fees are returned if you win your case—tacked onto your judgment. In abolishing fictitious costs, these courts have decided that a United States postman is just as reliable as any professional process server, messenger, constable, or marshal.

If you are unable to attend these courts during the day, you may do so at night in many regions. In Washington, D. C., at least one weekly night session is mandatory by law.

Procedure differs mainly in maximum size of claims that may be filed. In some states, such as Oregon and Vermont, the limit is $20. In Chicago, it's $200. Most states have $50 maximums. Libel and slander suits are not allowed; only civil cases are accepted. Generally, no one person may press more than two actions a day. Corporations, partnerships, societies, and associations may not sue. This is to prevent the courts from becoming massive collection agencies.

Women sue for slight amounts, small but perhaps needed for necessities.

They come to recover for lost laundry, even handkerchiefs, and apparel damaged or ruined by cleaners. Judges' benches are used as clothes racks. Dresses, slips, coats, and even shoes are piled up for personal inspection. Frequently housewives take garments to the court, and actually try them on there, to demonstrate shrinkage or stretching.

What woman hasn't found broken dishes, cracked mirrors, or ripped upholstery after the moving men left? What moving man hasn't faced inability to collect for inexpensive jobs? Though the loss is bitter, it's usually accepted, because ordinary court costs would exceed possible recovery. In Small Claims Courts, these injustices are corrected.

Car owners collect for dented fenders, broken headlights, garage overcharges. Garage operators collect small bills. Many judges keep miniature autos in their desks, take them out in disputed cases, and have controversial accidents or smashups reenacted in court, to determine responsibility in a case involving perhaps $6.50.

Diners collect for unremovable spots caused by careless waiters. Other suits may be over broken spectacles, imperfect bath brushes, or a wide assortment of items valued at sums considered trivial in full-dress tribunals. The smallest case on record is for five cents. It was filed by a Brooklyn man, who claimed he was charged a dime for what actually was a nickel glass of orange juice.

Animals, poultry, and food are brought into court as evidence. A Massachusetts woman carried a droopy chicken before the judge to prove that her neighbor had sold her a sick bird. An elderly Philadelphia couple brought their "fresh" anniversary cake to show it was moldy. They collected the $4.35 purchase price. Dogs and cats are led in to demonstrate their gentleness when pet owners are sued for the price of new clothes by persons alleging "unprovoked attacks by vicious beasts."

In these cafeterialike courts, where 10-minute decisions are served while you wait, verdicts are strictly enforced. Although procedure is shorn of customary technicalities, decisions are reached according to ordinary substantive law.

When a decision is ignored, the challenger is warned. Continued defiance lands him in jail. Released, he finds the decision still holds. The warning-jailing process is repeated until the decision is obeyed. Garnishees and attachments may be issued, but seldom are.

Thousands of people would be ruined if forced to pay a judgment of even $20 in one lump sum. In all except wage-claim cases, installment payments, scaled to prevent hardships, are permitted.

Appeals are discouraged and infrequent. When Minnesota established her Small Claims procedure, appeals were prohibited. Los Angeles required a defendant who appealed to a higher court (where lawyers are needed) to pay $15 toward the plaintiff's counsel fee if he lost the appeal. In New York City, where almost 24,000 Small Claims cases are heard in a representative year, about one in 1,000 is appealed—a goal higher courts would delight to achieve.

Operating costs are small. Most of these courts are divisions of higher tribunals, whose judges take turns presiding over the lower branches. Added costs are chiefly for clerical expenses.

Small Claims procedure originated more than a century ago in Norway and Denmark, when those countries had one sovereign. North Dakota, in 1893, attempted to transplant these forums in American soil. The experiment failed because of improper planning.

By curious coincidence, Kansas and Ohio established this country's first successful Small Claims procedure on the same day of the same year, March 15, 1913. Cleveland opened a conciliation branch of its municipal court for claims up to $35, but neglected to provide enforcement measures. This flaw soon was corrected, and the limit of suits was raised to $50. Cases up to $100 were ruled acceptable if circumstances warranted this ruling.

Kansas' Small Debtors Court resulted when a Topeka charwoman appealed to the State's Attorney General because a businessman refused to pay her $3 wages for a week's work.

By 1920 such courts existed in Oregon, Illinois, Minnesota, Washington State, Massachusetts, and Pennsylvania. Dr. Herbert Harley, secretary of the American Judicature Society, who helped pioneer these courts, declared they represented "the only really new and promising advance in the administration of justice in this country in seventy years." He added, "On them depends the future of our jurisprudence."

The following year California and North and South Dakota joined in nullifying the prevailing belief that justice was a luxury for the wealthy. Outpacing all other legal movements, Small Claims procedure progressed to include Idaho, Iowa, Nevada, Vermont, New Jersey, Maryland, Connecticut, Rhode Island, Colorado, Utah, New York, Michigan, New Hampshire, and the District of Columbia.

Yet proportionately few people know of the existence, function, and easy accessibility of these unique courts. Not to be confused with charity, they are open to everybody. A legal axiom is: "Justice delayed is justice denied." The late William Howard Taft, former United States Chief Justice, was more explicit. He said, "The inevitable effect of the delays incident to the machinery required in the settlement of controversies in judicial tribunals is to oppress and put to a disadvantage the poor litigant, and give a great advantage to his wealthy opponent."

With justice on the assembly-line basis, the conveyor belt inevitably brings around humor, pathos, and a smörgåsbord variety of cases. Sometimes a witness suddenly starts to cross-examine his opponent—or even the judge. Simultaneous wordy *blitzkriegs* are common. And when the judge raps his gavel and roars for order, a litigant sometimes blurts, "Now, Judge, how can I hear him with you talking?"

Others in court, awaiting their call, frequently become embroiled in private quarrels, provoking into action the courtroom's riot squad. But judicial harshness seldom enters Small Claims environs. The informal, homey atmosphere is soothing, and it relaxes taut, frightened nerves.

Alien propaganda that our government exists for the privileged is dealt a solar-plexus blow by this genuinely American procedure, where over-the-counter justice is given the little man and woman at bargain-basement rates.

Chapter XXVII

MONEY AND CREDIT, BANKING, AND SECURITIES

[MODERN economy is a money economy. The exchange of commodities is based upon money and credit, not barter, and power over money and credit gives a considerable amount of control over the stability of commerce and the distribution of wealth. As a result the currency question is drawn into the conflict of interests that furnishes the substance of politics. There is no way to take the question of money and credit out of the public forum and into the laboratory. Nor is this any less true of the question of control over banks, be they of the savings, commercial or investment type. Whether or not they have power to issue notes or affect credit, the public will never permit them to be removed from at least a certain amount of control designed to protect the people against fraud. The question as to what kind of banking system we shall have—how much public supervision, control or ownership there shall be—can escape public scrutiny no more than can the question as to what kind of system of money and credit we shall have.

In addition, in recent years, another question of a similar character has assumed considerable importance, namely, the amount of control government should exercise over the sale of private securities. Since 1911, and especially since 1920, this matter has been one which the people have been unwilling to leave completely in private hands. To-day the government, both national and state, exercises considerable control in this field.

There are, of course, no pat answers to the questions that one can raise relative to public control of money and credit, banking and the securities market. This chapter is designed to indicate what some of the problems are, what government has done about them, and what it might do.]

No. 98

GOVERNMENT MANAGEMENT OF CURRENCY AND CREDIT [1]

by John Parke Young

THE tendency for governments to regulate increasingly economic life has nowhere been more marked than in the field of currency and credit. Whether the phrase "managed currency" be used or not, currencies all over the world have been subjected to more and more control and management. As in other fields, controversy has waged over how far regulation should go, what can be accomplished by it, and the devices to be employed.

The earliest types of currency regulation had to do merely with physical characteristics of coins and protection against counterfeiting. When paper money was issued, if the government established rules they were intended primarily to assure redemption in specie, which was considered the end of governmental responsibility. Regulation was later extended to include bank deposits, but the duty of government as to the safety of deposits was accepted less explicitly —partly because the problem was not easy. Banks were sometimes required to keep certain cash reserves—a fraction of the money they were supposed to have on deposit. Only since . . . World War [I], in most cases only during the last . . . [twenty years], have governments made serious efforts to control the value and functioning of money, apart from the devices mentioned above aimed at setting rough limits to depreciation.

When we pass from an endeavor on the part of government simply to assure the general safety or validity of money, to efforts to regulate its value and to guide its functioning in our economic system, we arrive at one of the most important and most difficult of economic problems. The major role money plays in modern highly specialized society, the profound effects of price level fluctuations, and particularly the intimate relation of monetary matters to interest rates and the business cycle, make the question of special consequence. The broader aspects of the monetary problem have come to be recognized in governmental circles principally as a result of the Great Depression. Many governments are to-day endeavoring to deal with it from the standpoint of its broader implications.

Society has traveled a long distance from the simple state wherein the

[1] John Parke Young, "Government Management of Currency and Credit," *The Annals* of the American Academy of Political and Social Science (November, 1939), Vol. 206, pp. 100-108. Reprinted by permission of *The Annals* of the American Academy of Political and Social Science. The footnotes in the original version are omitted here.

individual was fairly self-sufficient, and has become extremely dependent upon trade—buying and selling. It has developed a complicated existence in which monetary values and price movements occupy a pre-eminent position. Wages, incomes, and values of nearly all kinds are expressed in terms of money. The vast industrial machine in which goods are produced in huge quantities by specialized processes and distributed to the four corners of the world is utterly dependent upon money, functioning according to monetary costs and prices. Our society is organized down to the smallest detail, upon a financial or monetary basis. The proper functioning of the monetary mechanism is thus a matter of no small consequence.

What is "proper functioning," and just what do we expect of the monetary system? In other words, what is the goal or objective of monetary regulation?

Here we are confronted with the facts that the problem of money and prices has theoretical aspects that tax even the best economists, and that there is a wide range of opinion on actions to be taken. It formerly was thought that the well-known quantity theory of money was a fairly simple proposition and a rather complete explanation of prices. If we expanded the volume of money, other things being equal, prices would tend to rise. What could be more obvious. "Other things being equal," however, was a catchall phrase often used to obviate further analysis.

This is not the place for a labored discussion of the theory of money, but as Keynes and others have pointed out, the problem of money involves the whole gamut of economic theory. An expansion of money tends not only to raise prices but also to lower the rate of interest, increase production, and put men to work. Short of full employment and full production, however, it may have little effect upon prices. Furthermore, whether the individual decides to spend his money or save it, to hold his assets in the form of money or in the form of real wealth, affects the whole stream of economic activity. Depending upon whether confidence is high or low, monetary expansion may or may not mean economic expansion or a rise of prices.

Thus the story goes and the debate begins. Does monetary expansion lead to maladjustments and an unstable condition? Does it upset the balance or relationship between savings and expenditures which absorb savings, such as those for plant and equipment? Does it excessively stimulate the capital goods industries, and again at times fail entirely to stimulate these industries? Do we really want a stable price level? One thing is agreed— the consequences that flow from an expansion or contraction of money affect almost every phase of economic life. But this is of little help in formulating a currency program and discovering where we are trying to go.

The implications from monetary theory regarding governmental policy are great. Should the government pursue a spending program, endeavoring thereby to expand the flow of money and income? (See the views of John Maynard Keynes, Lauchlin Currie, and others.) If we stabilize the volume of money, will economic stability follow? (See the discussions on neutral money and an equilibrium rate of interest by K. Wicksell, L. von Mises, and F. A. Hayek.) Should we constantly adjust the volume of money to the volume and condition of business, and are price movements a guide to the amount needed? (See the views of Carl Snyder, Irving Fisher, W. I. King, and others.) Is the demand and supply of gold the chief factor in price and business stability, and should we attempt to adjust the supply of gold through alterations in the gold content of money? (See James Harvey Rogers, G. F. Warren and F. A. Pearson.) Is parity with gold and foreign exchange stability a prime objective of monetary policy? (See E. W. Kemmerer and others.) Considering world economic developments of the past ten years and the difficulties of the gold standard, has gold ceased to be able to perform useful functions and should it be completely demonetized? (See Frank Graham, C. R. Whittlesey, and others.) These are a few of the questions confronting currency administrators.

While these questions remain unanswered with anything approaching unanimity, governments have proceeded with more and more management. The phrase "managed currency" has been used with various meanings and has usually referred to an irredeemable paper currency, with little or no specific backing, regulated by some governmental agency, as opposed to the semi-automatic functioning of the gold standard. Strictly speaking, however, no currency is entirely unmanaged, and the question to-day is largely one of how much management and what kind should be imposed, of the probabilities of impartial and competent management, and particularly of the effectiveness and the consequences of control devices. Looking around the world, we find that practically all currencies are now subjected to a fairly large amount of governmental regulation.

The aims which in actual practice are sought are usually rather hazily recognized, but in general are to maintain as great a degree of foreign exchange stability as possible, and at the same time to maintain as much price and domestic economic stability as possible; or to put it negatively, to avoid actions which it is felt might upset conditions. Measures toward these ends are usually taken rather clumsily and gropingly. Moreover, it must be admitted that a considerable amount of management by governments is opportunistic, or akin to blind wandering. The objectives are complicated by the needs of treasuries and the fact that most governments are operating under deficits which tend toward currency expansion.

Particularly under war conditions are currency objectives subordinated to the raising of revenue. Thus the immediate currency problem for a large part of the world is that of holding inflation in check.

The present trend toward currency management has been stimulated by the economic confusion of recent years and the necessity of taking action of some kind. It is true that much of the confusion is in itself due to unfortunate currency policies. China turned to a managed currency when her silver standard broke down. Great Britain started the ball rolling by leaving gold in 1931. Then came a period of currency chaos throughout the world unprecedented in history. It has also been a period of currency revolution, when ideas have been radically altered.

A managed currency is not the opposite of the gold standard. (Unless we define the gold standard in its completely rigid and 100-per-cent automatic sense.) The problem is not one of the gold standard versus the non-gold standard, but one of regulating the currency and credit system and the flow of money so as to yield the desired price and economic stability—in so far as this can be accomplished by currency devices.

Gold movements under the former system tended to regulate currency and economic conditions, largely by expanding or contracting bank reserves. Gold, however, has long been recognized as an imperfect regulator of such conditions. The continual inflation and deflation which took place under the gold standard sometimes became disastrous. To-day gold has little influence in currency and credit systems, and the attempt is being made to provide stability by other devices. Since the breakdown of the gold standard, few nations have shown much interest in restoring gold. Some economists would abandon gold permanently. Others feel that in spite of its shortcomings, gold has a place in currency systems.

Although surrounded by superstition and ghosts, gold can be useful in settling foreign balances and in providing exchange stability. The recent huge importation of gold into the United States, however, has not been to settle balances, but on the contrary has itself been an unbalancing item. With the world in a chaotic condition and with little interest in the gold standard, there is slight prospect of any near term arrangements wherein gold would be used extensively to clear balances between nations.

Because of the high price which the United States has established for gold and the fact that this country will absorb gold at this price without limit, the metal is now being mined in very large amounts. Most of the world's monetary gold has come to America (Gold imports for the past five years [1934-1939] have averaged $1,509,000,000. In 1938 the United States acquired $1,974,000,000 of gold, and during the first eight months of 1939 about $2,500,000,000.), and with gold production at new peaks, this country's reserves of approximately seventeen billion dollars continue to mount. If the gold standard should not be restored in the rest of the world (and such restoration appears uncertain), the United States will have had unloaded upon it most of the world's monetary gold in exchange for real values. Dug from the ground in South Africa, it is being buried in the ground in America after having been paid for with American Dollars.

While fixed exchange rates, which the gold standard helps to provide, have important advantages, the cost of maintaining such rates may under certain circumstances become excessive. Measures to maintain fixed rates in terms of gold may involve deflation, falling commodity prices, and a lack of prosperity. Currency policy, therefore, may be faced with a decision between fixed rates and domestic well-being. Thus, France prior to 1936 held the franc steady in the foreign exchange markets, but because of this suffered more acutely at home. Since 1931 Great Britain has felt that a stable pound in terms of gold would require sacrifices not compensated for by the gains, and has therefore not pegged the pound at a fixed level, although she has through her stabilization fund endeavored to provide as much foreign exchange stability as practicable. The United States and several other leading countries also have stabilization funds which endeavor to prevent fluctuations in exchange—fulfilling a function formerly performed more or less automatically by gold. (The gold standard, however, included arrangements tending toward equilibrium in the balance of payments at the fixed rates. The absence of such arrangements under a system of controlled exchange rates is likely to lead eventually to disturbance and difficulty. This was one of the difficulties in the years leading up to the currency collapse of 1931. The gold-standard mechanism during that period had been restricted or disregarded.)

It can be seen that the problem of gold is not an easy one for currency administrators. Particularly is this true in the case of the United States, with its enormous stock of gold, a high fixed price for the metal, and the rest of the world not on gold.

Regarding a practical currency program for the United States at the present time, we find two fairly well defined schools of thought. One group believe that booms and depressions can to a large extent be moderated through the use of monetary measures, and that monetary policy therefore should be directed toward flattening out the business cycle. The other group feel that the business cycle is basically a non-monetary matter, and that while at certain times monetary measures may contribute toward economic stability, under most circumstances monetary maneuvers are harmful, impeding necessary adjustments in the economic system and leading to nervousness and uncertainty in the business world. They feel (with varying emphasis) that monetary policy should concern itself primarily with such things as the quality of the assets behind currency and credit and with maintenance of parity with gold, thus contributing to confidence and order in international affairs.

The first group, on the other hand, would expand the volume of money in periods of depression and falling prices, and conversely contract the volume in periods of boom and rising prices. The reasoning is that the immediate cause of recession is a shrinkage in the demand for goods, and that this shrinkage, if left alone, feeds on itself, becoming continually worse. The shrinkage in demand is reflected in a decline in prices, in a contraction in the volume of money, and in a slowing down of the rate of turnover and the flow of income.

It is argued that the government should at such times endeavor to stabilize demand by expanding the circulating media; that such expansion of money will tend to expand spending, i.e., to revive demand; and that one of the best guides as to whether demand is stable is an index of the general price level, an index that reflects the average prices of all goods bought and sold, including securities and services. If the price level rises, it indicates that demand is outstripping supply; while if it falls, it indicates the opposite. It follows that monetary policy should ordinarily aim to maintain a relatively stable price level and that this should be accomplished by expanding or contracting the circulating media. Inflation and deflation—those great disrupters of economic life—cannot be seriously disturbing if the currency volume is controlled, expanded if deflation sets in and contracted if inflation begins. It is like steering a car—if the car starts to veer in one direction, the wheel should be turned toward the other direction; if it is turned too far it should be turned back, the aim being to keep the car constantly in the center of the road. This viewpoint, with variations, is held by a large number of outstanding economists.

The opposing view is also held by a large number of distinguished economists. The Board of Governors of the Federal Reserve System in March, 1939, issued a statement disagreeing with certain proposals, based on the reasoning of group one, to use monetary devices to stabilize business. This statement said:

> Experience has shown, however, that (1) prices cannot be controlled by changes in the amount and cost of money; (2) the Board's control of the amount of money is not complete and cannot be made complete; (3) a steady average of prices does not necessarily result in lasting prosperity; and (4) a steady level of average prices is not nearly as important to the people as a fair relationship between the prices of the commodities which they produce and those which they must buy.

Economists favoring this latter position point out that price movements are not solely the result of changes in the volume of money. Changes in the velocity of money, or the rapidity with which it turns over, are continually taking place, reflecting many forces of a nonmonetary nature which lead to a rise or fall of prices. We must go behind the velocity, they say. Furthermore, the relationships between the prices of commodities, between costs and selling prices, are exceedingly important from the standpoint of prosperity or depression.

The differences of opinion on the currency question are to a considerable extent those of emphasis, and there is basically much more agreement than might appear on the surface. Practically all are agreed that the former gold standard was far from perfect, that fluctuations of the price level were often the source of serious trouble, and that efforts to remedy this condition deserve most careful attention. There is little dispute over the fact that an intimate relationship exists between monetary and credit matters and the ups and downs of business. It is also agreed that the state of confidence exerts a powerful influence upon currency movements, upon savings and the flow of income. Probably no economist would dispute the fact that the velocity of money reflects nonmonetary forces; yet one group would deal with a disrupting change in velocity as merely a symptom of some nonmonetary movement, and to be discovered and treated as such. Another group would agree that velocity is a symptom but would remedy matters by monetary devices, that is, by compensating changes in the volume of money—not necessarily to the exclusion of other remedies.

Those who fear a large amount of currency management realize the grave conditions which can come from mismanagement and political manipulation. Those who welcome it are impressed with the grave conditions which have in actual fact resulted from lack of regulation or from uninformed actions. Events of the past ten years provide ample evidence of this. The former currency systems were unable to meet the strains of current developments, including the high-pitched international economy, however irrational it may be. As a result, whether we like it or not, positive regulation is here and will remain.

It is clear that currency devices are very powerful forces for good or evil, and that currency and credit systems have not functioned well when left to gold and so-called automatic devices. The degree to which the problem can be solved by government is still unknown. In view of the profound effects of currency disturbances, the currency question offers a challenge to the resourcefulness and ability of government. When it is remembered that prices and monetary incomes are at the heart of our economic system and that currency matters have much to do with economic and social conditions in general, perhaps with the survival of free institutions and enterprise, the currency problem is seen to be one of the major problems of to-day.

No. 99

ISSUES IN THE FIELD OF BANKING [1]

by Marshall Edward Dimock

THE financial institutions of the United States and the controls they exercise have undergone marked changes during the past generation. The sources of financial credit have multiplied, established institutions such as commercial banks have experienced a shift of function, and at all points the admixture of public and private activities has covered an increasingly wider area. Consequently, as financial credit and monetary controls have become more prominent, they have also become considerably more complex. Thus "the monetary system is one of the most complicated parts of the economic order," observe the authors of a Brookings study, "with much mingling of monetary and nonmonetary functions in the same agencies, and much overlapping of functions between governmental and private agencies." Governmental intervention in this field has gone a good deal beyond mere implementation and assistance and to-day also includes major regulation and a large degree of direct public ownership and operation of financial institutions, as represented by the Reconstruction Finance Corporation among many others. If one seeks a knowledge of what financial policies and their mechanisms would achieve, therefore, the emphasis will not linger over the old labels private and public, but will focus rather on functions and interrelationships.

Between tax (fiscal) and credit (monetary) policies there is, of course, the closest kind of connection. Not only that, but in the history of the United States dominant opinion has changed markedly on the question of which of these two approaches by government is best designed to achieve economic and financial stability. Three distinct periods may be noted. The big issue of the first three quarters of the nineteenth century was "sound" money and took many forms: gold versus silver, paper money versus a fixed metallic content, redeemability in a fixed unit of gold—all revolving around creditor-versus-debtor interests. Early in the present century, however, emphasis shifted from the currency of exchange issue to the second phase,

[1] Marshall Edward Dimock, *Business and Government* (New York: Henry Holt and Company, Inc., 1949), pp. 559-560, 572-575. Reprinted by permission of the publisher. The footnotes in the original version are omitted here.

the use of banking policy as an automatic regulator. Lower or higher interest rates controlled through a central system were to iron out the fluctuations of the business cycle. Since the onset of the third period which started in the 1930s, ". . . much less attention has been given to the control of the cost and abundance of bank credit as a technique of monetary policy. Instead, interest now centers in fiscal policy, in the use of treasury deficits and surpluses as a direct method of forcing an increase of the flow of money in a depression period and checking it in a boom." Despite this new emphasis, however, the mechanisms of credit have lost none of their former importance, as both fiscal and monetary controls are essential to stability and progress and neither in isolation will suffice. . . .

The extent to which the nation's credit institutions have been changing in recent years is well illustrated in a comment by O. M. W. Sprague when he points out that "The word 'commercial' does not definitely characterize the operations of banks which are commonly known as commercial banks, although it does distinguish them from savings and mortgage banks as well as from banks and bankers primarily engaged in the business of marketing securities and in the management of trusts." These various functions may, however, be undertaken by commercial banks, and in recent years there has been a striking tendency for banks to engage in virtually every type of financial business. Nevertheless, the conventional distinction between commercial and other types of banks will provide the basis for differentiating the commercial banks heading up to the Federal Reserve Board . . . from the business of marketing securities as regulated by the Securities and Exchange Commission. . . .

The distinction becomes more clear when one considers the wide range of credit institutions found in to-day's economy. Thus, "over the past century or so, numerous types of financial enterprises have been developed, which together constitute the mechanism of the money market. *These agencies include commercial banks, investment banks, savings banks, insurance companies, corporate trustees, investment companies, security exchanges, etc.*"

. . . The Federal Reserve System and the Federal Deposit Insurance Corporation, it is now realized, were merely the beginnings of banking reform and not the ultimate. The issues which are hotly contested to-day provide ample evidence of this fact. Are there too many banks? The number of state commercial banks has been reduced by well over half since 1920. Should they be weeded out still further and should it be made more difficult to start small banks? Greater financial stability is the chief argument in favor of limitation; freedom of local enterprise and from all that Wall Street implies is the principal argument against it. The question has long been a major political issue—the case of *McCulloch v. Maryland* revolved about it in 1819—and there is every indication that it will continue as such. A National Industrial Conference Board study made in 1932 showed that there were 24,939 banks of all kinds, that four fifths were in towns of 10,000 or less, and that their average capitalization was only $44,000.

The second big issue is branch banking, or chain banking as it is sometimes called. The largest bank in the United States—the Bank of America started by Giannini on the West Coast and in 1949 under investigation as a monopoly—is a branch banking operation. The main arguments in favor of it are a greater degree of financial stability deriving from large size, accompanied by equally good service in small towns. The objections are concentrated financial power far removed from local centers, the draining off of community resources to distant financial capitals, and the loss of local controls built around the reputations of local citizens. As early as the 1920s branch banking was a major issue debated by Congress. Foreign experts are almost unanimous in their belief that America will eventually be forced to adopt the branch bank solution.

A third issue is whether all banks should be required to affiliate with the Federal Reserve System and the FDIC. The argument here is that a universally supported system is necessary to financial stability and that there is no reason why all units should not join. Against it is the contention that freedom of enterprise would be diminished, and that the necessity of affiliation has not and cannot be demonstrated. The issues of states' rights and fear of federal domination also figure prominently in this controversy; once all banking is brought under the same roof, it is held, regimentation could no longer be effectively resisted. Those who take this stand, however, give insufficient weight to the fact that the American banking system to date has been operated under a high degree of industry self-government.

The banking structure of the United States is characterized by extremes. There are more small independent units than in other comparable countries and there are also more giants. A fourth issue, therefore, is the charge that concentration has taken place, that some banks have become so large as to wield undue influence over industry and commerce and that they encourage industrial concentration, inter-locking directorates, and other evils of monopoly. This charge is not leveled against commercial so much as against investment banking . . . but it is heard nonetheless. It was brought out in the TNEC hearings, for example, that six of the country's billion dollar corporations are banking institutions—Chase National, National City Bank of New York, Guaranty Trust, Bank of America, Continental Illinois, and Banker's Trust—four of them being located in New

York City. Ranking below the "poorest" of these billion dollar corporations —the Banker's Trust Company with assets of $1.03 billion—were 18 states of the American Union, each with total taxable property of less than a billion dollars.

A final issue is the complaint that the Federal Reserve System, in attempting to stabilize economic conditions, unreasonably restricts the independence of private management. So pervasive has the influence of the Board of Governors and the Federal Open Market Committee become that the Brookings study refers to the "managerial activities" of the Federal Reserve— the same term that was applied to the control of the Interstate Commerce Commission over railways. Three recent policies of the System have apparently caused some criticism: increasing the requirements concerning reserves to be maintained by member banks, increasing member banks' holdings of federal securities, and low interest rates. The first two policies, it is claimed, restrict the percentage of funds left for high interest-bearing loans and investments, and low interest rates also tend to reduce bank earnings. These criticisms would be more impressive were it not for the fact that "net profits of banks reached new high levels (during World War II) as the increase in asset volume more than compensated for lower yields."

Lurking behind all of these questions is a problem of a different character: how effective are the Federal Reserve System and the FDIC likely to be in warding off another serious depression? At one time there was a good deal of optimism about the ability of the Federal Reserve System to insulate the country against violent economic fluctuations, but this was before 1930. As for the future, at least three observations may be made at this time: (1) Although financial controls alone cannot ward off depressions, such controls are an essential part of any over-all plan to promote equilibrium. (2) Judging from the relevant experience of other countries, a further tightening up of banking organization and central controls seems indicated if stabilization is to be effected. And (3), certainly as important as the question of whether the Federal Reserve System has sufficient authority is the issue of whether such authority will be courageously used when it is needed, because the crosscurrents of pressure groups and politics tend to neutralize such energetic measures. With a national debt of $256 billion and an annual interest charge of $5 billion, the United States could be involved in very serious trouble if another major depression were to take place; such an emergency might test our credit and business structure to its very roots.

No. 100

PROTECTING INVESTORS IN SECURITIES [1]

by Theodore W. Glocker

MANY million dollars are lost each year by investors in American securities. The Senate Committee on Currency and Banking estimated in 1933 that the loss from security investment in the United States had been twenty-five billion dollars during the previous ten years. Legislation protecting investors has been enacted in recent years by practically all states and by the Federal Government. The extent of this legislation and its effectiveness in removing the causes for losses of investors will be discussed.

Among the reasons for losses from security investment may be mentioned: (1) fraudulent practices by dishonest promoters, (2) bad faith on the part of accredited investment bankers, (3) manipulation of prices of securities by brokers and speculators, (4) betrayal of security holders by officers and directors of corporations, (5) wide fluctuation in economic conditions, and (6) ignorance and greed of investors.

The responsibility of governments to protect their citizens against fraud is generally recognized. The principle of *caveat emptor* is not applicable to investments. When buying food or clothes, the customer has a chance to learn by trial and error. In the case of investments, however, there may be error but no chance for another trial after one's money is lost.

The need for protection against purveyors of worthless securities is evident when one becomes familiar with their highly efficient methods. "Sucker lists" are carefully prepared and sold to dealers engaged in this business. School teachers, physicians, dentists, and clergymen are favorite victims. Whenever farmers in some section of the country have a good crop, impressive looking, high pressure salesmen descend on them from neighboring cities to gather part of their surplus cash. These salesmen study and take advantage of the weaknesses of prospective customers. They appeal to gambling proclivities and to the natural desire to get something for nothing. They stimulate the greed of prospects by glowing descriptions of large profits made in other enterprises, and flatter their vanity by telling them that they have been selected for solicitation because of their superior

[1] Theodore W. Glocker, "Protecting Investors in Securities," *The Annals* of the American Academy of Political and Social Science (November, 1939), Vol. 206, pp. 68-74. Reprinted by permission of *The Annals* of the American Academy of Political and Social Science.

intelligence. Hasty and ill-considered decisions to buy are encouraged by statements that only a few shares are left or that the price of the stock will rise in a few days.

The victim of these schemes has the right to sue in civil court to recover losses suffered through misrepresentation. One great difficulty is to prove intent to defraud. An oil promoter may actually own a tract of land near an oil field. He may have started drilling, and possibly there may be oil on his land. On one occasion a promoter who thought he had sold worthless securities repurchased them in a hurry at a higher price, because, overnight, his oil well became a gusher. Another difficulty is to discover the whereabouts of the swindler, who flits quickly from place to place and has probably departed for parts unknown before the victim discovers his loss.

Kansas was the first state to pass, in 1911, legislation designed to regulate the sale of fraudulent and low-grade securities, and has been followed by practically all other states. The phrase "blue-sky laws" has been applied to this type of laws to indicate that they have been enacted to regulate securities worth no more than a section of bright blue sky.

The states vary widely in their blue-sky laws. They may be roughly classified in three groups. In the first group are such states as New York, New Jersey, and Maryland, whose antifraud laws empower the attorney general in case of fraud to enjoin the sale of the securities and to prosecute guilty persons in criminal courts. Many injunctions stopping the sale of securities have been obtained by vigilant attorney-generals. However, there have been very few criminal convictions, and many fly-by-night dishonest dealers escape to other jurisdictions. Fear of conviction may cause restitution of part of the funds taken from defrauded customers, but much of the lost money is never recovered.

In the second group are those states which have created commissions to grant licenses to dealers. An applicant for a license must submit a personal history and this is checked in suspicious cases. The main purpose of the law is to permit only honest dealers to do business. However, indirectly it provides a check on the quality of new securities, since the commission must keep in touch with the transactions of dealers, may require information, as under the Pennsylvania law, concerning each of the issues sold by the dealer, and, if it finds intent to deceive or defraud, may stop the sale. The dealer's license may also be revoked, and he is subject to fine and imprisonment.

A third group of states require, sometimes in addition to registration of dealers, approval of the sale of securities by state officials. Certain types of securities are exempt, but detailed information is required regarding other types, and approval of their sale may be withheld if there is evidence of misrepresentation, or if the sale will work a fraud upon the purchaser.

Prevention of fraud is the primary purpose of laws licensing dealers and requiring approval of the sales of securities by state commissions, and in this respect such laws are preferable to antifraud laws which attempt to punish the guilty and to reimburse the victim after loss has occurred. Nevertheless, such laws impose burdensome restrictions on legitimate dealers, whereas many dishonest ones do not apply for licenses or inform state commissions concerning securities which they are selling. However, failure of dishonest dealers to conform to the law may attract the attention of the authorities and thus lead to detection of their fraudulent activities.

There are serious defects in the administration of the blue-sky laws of the various states. First, effectiveness of their enforcement has sometimes been lowered by the poor quality of politically appointed administrative officers and by political pressure on their policies. The most serious defect of state legislation has been its limitation to intrastate transactions. Dishonest dealers may do no business in the state where they are located, but sell securities in other states by mail, telegraph, telephone, and newspaper advertisements. Some states are helping others by amending their legislation so that it covers not only sales of securities to persons within the state but also sales to persons outside the state.

The Federal law forbidding use of the mail to defraud has supplemented state legislation and has greatly strengthened government control over fraudulent transactions in securities. Federal officers have been alert to detect the use of the mail by dishonest dealers in securities, and have been able to follow their trail from state to state. "Stop orders" preventing use of the mail may be issued by the Postmaster-General, and cases may be prosecuted in criminal courts. Jurisdiction of the Federal Government has been extended by the Federal Securities Act of 1933, which makes illegal all fraudulent interstate transactions, involving use of mail, telegraph, telephone, radio, express, or other means of communication or transportation. The Securities Act was passed primarily to require accredited investment bankers to provide complete and accurate information to their customers. However, in administering the law, the Securities and Exchange Commission discovers and aids in the punishment of many cases of fraud.

Many who favor government elimination of fraudulent promoters oppose government regulation of accredited dealers. Prior to World War . . . [I] there was not a great need for regulation of reputable investment bankers. Some dealers claimed that they assumed the attitude of a trustee in their relations with their customers and endeavored to map out a program of investment suitable to the latter's needs. The American Investment Bankers Association adopted ethical rules of conduct for members, and at its annual meetings responsibility of the dealer in securities for the welfare of customers was repeatedly emphasized. Members of leading, long-established firms took pride in the reputation of their organizations for conservatism and integrity.

Between 1922 and 1929 the attitude of dealers changed, and frequently little or no consideration was given to the welfare of the customer. As a rule, accredited investment bankers do not indulge in direct misstatements, but during this period unfavorable factors were often omitted in bond circulars, and figures in balance sheets and profit-and-loss statements were juggled to give a favorable impression. Sales commissions of dealers were sometimes too high for the less conservative types of securities, and stocks and bonds were sold for more than they were worth. Highly speculative securities were also sold to customers whose small capital did not permit sufficient diversification to justify the risk involved.

There were several reasons for the change in the attitude of bankers. First, their close personal relationship with customers was lost as a result of the great increase and the change in the type of persons purchasing securities. The campaigns to sell Liberty Bonds during the war popularized the idea of buying bonds, and the rich capitalists and the large financial institutions that were the chief customers during the pre-war period were submerged in a mass of ignorant and avaricious purchasers who wanted safety and 12 per cent.

A second reason was optimism. At a time when even bankers believed that a long era of prosperity lay ahead, the distinction between conservatism and speculation could not easily be maintained.

A third reason was the inexperience of commercial bankers, stock brokers, and many others who entered the business at that time. Moreover, even the old-time bankers were not well acquainted with foreign bonds and common stocks, types of securities which they began to sell in large quantities during that period.

A fourth reason was the dominance of avarice and the lowering of moral standards which takes place so often in a period of great prosperity.

Finally, a very important reason was the need for keeping busy the vast machinery for marketing securities. The large distributing houses had established branches or outlets in many communities. An efficient machine had been created capable of disposing of an issue of securities worth fifty or one hundred million dollars in a few hours after opening of the public sale. There were not enough good bonds to keep busy the small army of salesmen in the various cities, and bankers had recourse to low-grade securities in order that the machine might be kept working.

Investors have secured protection through legislation designed for other purposes. State regulation of finances of insurance companies is designed to aid policyholders, and state and Federal regulation of commercial banks is intended to protect depositors. However, stockholders benefit if such legislation strengthens the financial soundness of these institutions. As a part of the process of securing cheap rates for consumers, the Interstate Commerce Commission is given power to disapprove new issues of railway securities, and many state public utility commissions exercise similar control over the finances of local operating utilities. An unsound financial structure means, as a rule, high rates, because if a company is over-bonded or over-capitalized, its security holders may be able to prevent rates from being lowered by contending that such action would endanger payment of dividends and interest and might cause bankruptcy. The sounder financial structure of railways and utilities resulting from such regulation should make their securities safer investments.

The Federal Public Utility Holding Company Act was passed in 1935, partly to help the investor, but in large part to strengthen the power of state commissions to regulate rates. The large holding companies secured funds to purchase control over new local subsidiaries by siphoning the earnings of old ones, forcing them to make upstream loans and to pay unearned dividends and exorbitant fees for technical advice to the parent companies. Accounts were juggled to hide the extent of these transactions. The state commissions had no control over these large interstate holding companies, yet were prevented by them from lowering rates for service because of the artificial decrease in the earnings of subsidiaries. To remedy this situation the Federal Public Utility Holding Company Act gave the Securities and Exchange Commission drastic power to simplify the capitalization and regulate the finances of these holding companies, and to control relations between parent companies and their subsidiaries. The low price of utility holding company securities following 1935 has been attributed to the act. However, if administered in moderation, the law should ultimately help investors by forcing adoption of conservative financial policies and reducing the risk of bankruptcy.

States, counties, and cities should protect purchasers of their bonds from unwise financial policies of their legislative bodies and executive officers. Following periods of default and repudiation of state bonds during the last century, constitutional limitations were placed on state debt. These restrictions have sometimes been irksome, particularly during recent years, when such restrictions have prevented some states from borrowing funds to match grants of the Federal Government for unemployment relief. Nevertheless, with a few exceptions, state bonds have enjoyed a high credit rating during the past fifty years, including even the period of the recent depression, and for this situation these constitutional limitations may be partly responsible.

Supervision of borrowing policies of most local governments seems to be badly needed. The bonds of more than two thousand local governments were in default during the depression following 1929. Many statutory limitations have been imposed on local indebtedness and have been circumvented by local governments, sometimes with the connivance of state legislatures. Some states are creating state or local boards to supervise the borrowing and other financial policies of counties and cities, and such supervision should greatly improve the quality of the bonds of local governments.

In addition to the above-discussed legislation indirectly affecting certain nonfraudulent stocks and bonds, some state commissions administering blue-sky laws have attempted to check the purchase of nonfraudulent highly speculative securities on the ground that such sales would "work a fraud" to investors. However, until the passage of the Federal Securities Act in 1933, laws regulating the sale of securities were usually intended primarily to prevent fraud.

While certain provisions of the Securities Act are designed to strengthen the power of state and Federal officials to control fraud, its primary purpose is to prevent certain unfair practices in the sale of nonfraudulent stocks and bonds. Investment bankers are said frequently to omit or twist unfavorable facts in their advertisements of new securities so as to give a favorable impression. To prevent this practice, security dealers are made civilly liable to investors for misrepresentations and omissions, and the Securities and Exchange Commission withholds its approval of the sale of a new issue until satisfied that prospective customers will be given full and correct information. The Commission makes no attempt to decide concerning the soundness of securities sold to the public. Rather it seeks to secure pertinent, accurate, and complete facts which investors can use in making their own decisions.

With the exception of the stocks and bonds of local operating utilities, the Federal Act of 1933 applies to securities not regulated by other government agencies. Thus, it regulates only interstate transactions, and exempts the securities of railroads, banks, insurance companies, and domestic governments. Sales aggregating less than $100,000 are also not covered by the law.

There has been much criticism of the Federal Securities Act. Bankers claim that the provision imposing civil liability for unintentional misrepresentations and omissions is unduly harsh. However, the law cannot be considered very unjust, since it is merely transferring a loss from the investor to the banker whose carelessness caused it. The act should induce investment bankers to specialize in a single field of business, to become thoroughly familiar with that field, and to make painstaking investigations of corporations whose securities they offer to the public. With this increase in knowledge, bankers originating new issues should tend to become more conservative, and therefore security investment should become safer.

Fear of liability on the part of dealers and the high cost of securing the required information are said to have been the causes of the decline in public sale of new securities since the passage of the act. However, this decrease may be also explained by the stagnation of the capital-goods industries.

The extent to which the investing public will use the information obtained by the Securities and Exchange Commission may be questioned. Very few persons have the knowledge or the patience to analyze the mass of facts and figures contained in the registration statement. This information is digested in the prospectus used by the dealers in advertising the securities, but the law has increased the length of this prospectus, and in so doing may discourage the reading of it by investors. However, the long registration statements are studied by financial reporters, investment counselors, and other experts, and their opinion should exercise some influence on a considerable group of investors.

The Securities Act and similar government regulations tend to eliminate desirable as well as undesirable promotions. One wonders whether certain flourishing industries would exist to-day if present laws had been in effect at the time of their origin. Since a promoter does not usually possess definite information about cost of production, probable demand, and other facts concerning a new venture, he must sell its securities largely on the basis of optimistic generalizations, rosy-tinted by his hopes and desires. If, because of the Securities Act, his promises must be neutral in tone and his statements limited to cold facts and figures, the chances of selling such securities are quite slim. In the future, highly speculative enterprises may have to be financed to a considerable degree by private subscription, and new commodities and services may have to be developed largely by existing corporations. At any rate, slower progress may be the price which society must pay for conservatism and greater security.

After securities have been sold to an investor he continues to need protection, and to provide this protection, the Securities Exchange Act was passed in 1934. One purpose of the act is to vest power in the Securities and Exchange Commission to correct unfair practices on security markets. "Washed sales," "matched orders," or any other series of transactions likely to raise, lower, or stabilize prices are made illegal. No one is permitted to acquire a substantial control of the floating supply of any security so as to affect its price, and "pools" may not be organized for the purpose of manipulation. Dealers, brokers, and their employees must refrain from misleading statements and from dissemination of information intended to affect security markets. Persons injured by such price manipulations may sue for damages, and for violation of the act, brokers must be suspended from operating on stock exchanges.

A second purpose of the law is to require corporations whose securities are listed on exchanges to supply full information at frequent intervals regarding their operation and finances.

A third purpose is to check misuse of credit by operators on security exchanges. To achieve this last purpose, the Federal Reserve Board is authorized to fix the margin of cash required for loans having securities as collateral, and is given control over agencies extending such credit.

Investors should be protected from the exploitation of corporations by their officers and directors. These officials may manipulate statements of earnings and withhold important information in order to make a profit from the purchase and sale of the securities of a corporation. They may vote themselves high salaries and bonuses, sell property to the corporation at inflated values, make contracts for their company favoring other corporations in which they are interested, or fail to liquidate hopelessly unprofitable businesses through their reluctance to relinquish good salaries.

The Securities and Exchange Act attempts to control speculation by officers and directors in the shares of their own company. If the stocks and bonds of a corporation are listed on an exchange, its officials must state, monthly, the amount of its securities which they own. They cannot sell short the stock of their company, and must turn into its treasury all profits obtained by the selling of such securities within six months after their purchase.

One cause of the exploitation of corporations is the lack of control over directors by stockholders. Yet, how can twenty-five million stockholders, comprising three or four million separate individuals, exercise any real control over their respective companies? Some corporations are requesting their stockholders to vote yes or no on propositions presented in proxy statements. However, many fail to vote, and few possess sufficient detailed knowledge of the corporation to render intelligent decisions.

Another cause of these evils is ownership of an insufficient amount of the securities of a corporation by its directors. The suggestion has been made that each director of a corporation should own a minimum amount of its common stock. Some object to this regulation on the ground that it would cause many able men to refuse to serve as directors. However, such men could serve, perhaps, in an advisory capacity, and voting power could be vested in salaried directors owning a considerable number of shares of stock in the corporation. Serious consideration must be given by our business leaders to methods of correcting the weaknesses of corporate administration. Otherwise, Federal regulation of corporate affairs, with all the objectionable features of government supervision, may be inevitable.

The most efficient forms of legislation can replace only in a very small degree the exercise of good judgment by investors, and three factors make the exercise of such good judgment rather infrequent. First, successful practice of the art of investment is difficult, and many investors know as little about it as a child of six years does about original sin. Secondly, the desire to take a chance is strong in most of us. Thirdly, the avarice of investors militates against exercise of good judgment. We may laugh at the ignorance of the widow who asks for securities which are absolutely safe and yield 10 per cent. Yet, during the period of economic optimism from 1922 to 1929 we sought the same impossible combination, allowing the prospect of a high yield to blind us to the risk involved.

Education of the investor is recommended by most writers on this subject. However, educating the investor is a big job, which must be performed continuously, and at present there exists no agency whose primary function is education of the investing public. The Securities and Exchange Commission could perform a fine service by creating a department to do such educational work. The mass of information which is available in the reference rooms of the Commission for the use of financial experts could be digested and presented in diluted form to investors and an effort made to instill in the minds of the people correct points of view regarding investments.

Chapter XXVIII

GOVERNMENT AND BUSINESS·

[THE transformation of American economy from one based on the Jeffersonian ideal of sturdy independent yeomen to one founded on a mass production industrial system has profoundly affected the relation of government to business and industry. Although as yet we have formulated no general rationale of this relationship, it cannot be denied that regulation of the economy has increased both in scope and intensity in the last 75 years. This trend has been little affected by changes in political administration. Both Republican and Democratic Presidents and Congresses have advocated and adopted new regulations of business activity or expanded the scope of already existing controls.

Each new inroad government has made in the economic sphere has renewed the debate over how far it ought to go. Some people argue that government ought to own and operate all basic industries and closely supervise and regulate the rest. Others argue that government should restrict itself simply to preserving competition and preventing unfair practices. These two positions represent the extremes; in between lies a multiplicity of positions.

Unfortunately the debate as to the role of government has been tied to the question of democracy. Adherents of each of the extreme positions have argued that unless their views are accepted, democracy cannot exist. This confuses the issue. Democracy is a term used to describe a system of government, not an economy. When we say, "This is a democracy," we answer the question, "Who exercises the public power?" We are not answering the question, "What should be the limits of public power?" (We must be careful that when one question is asked we do not give the answer to another and different question.)

In the United States we have already answered the question, "Who shall exercise the public power?" by saying, "The people or representatives accountable to the people." We are, in other words, committed to democratic government. Therefore, the answer to the different question, "What should be the role of government in the economic life of the community?" will depend upon (1) what the people desire, (2) whether these desires can possibly be satisfied and (3) what, given the circumstances, will fulfill those desires.

It may be foolish or it may be wise to extend public power over the economic domain. Under some circumstances it is the one; under some, the other. There are no ready-made formulas to tell us which. Our decisions will depend much more upon what the economists than what the political scientists have to tell us. Only the economists can give us the necessary historical background, description and analysis of our current economic circumstances.

The contributions that follow here typify the kind of approach essential to the proper study of government-in-the-economy. They can do no more than open a window, however, to give us a look-in on one of the greatest complexities of our day.]

No. 101

THE MYTH OF RUGGED AMERICAN INDIVIDUALISM [1]

by Charles A. Beard

"THE House of Bishops would be as much at sea in Minneapolis as at Atlantic City." This bit of delicious humor, all too rare in America's solemn assemblies, sparkled at a tense moment in the late conference of the Episcopalian magnates at Denver when the respective merits of the two cities as future meeting places were under debate. But the real cause of the caustic comment seems to have been a heated discussion, led by the Honorable George W. Wickersham, over a dangerous proposal to modify, not the Volstead act, but the sacred creed of rugged American individualism.

That contest had been precipitated by the report of a special commission in which occurred these highly inflammatory words:

It is becoming increasingly evident that the conception of society as made up of autonomous, independent individuals is as faulty from the point of view of economic realism as it is from the standpoint of Christian idealism. Our fundamental philosophy of rugged individualism must be modified to meet the needs of a cooperative age.

This frightful conclusion flowed from a fact statement which the commission summarized in the following language:

Side by side with such misery and idleness, there are warehouses bursting with goods which cannot be bought; elevators full of wheat while bread lines haunt our cities; carefully protected machinery lying idle, while jobless men throng our streets; money in the banks available at low rates.

These shocking passages Mr. Wickersham read to the assembled delegates with considerable indignation, and denied their truth. Then he added an

---

[1] Charles A. Beard, "The Myth of Rugged American Individualism," *Harper's Magazine* (December, 1931), Vol. 164, pp. 13-22. Reprinted by permission of the author and *Harper's Magazine.*

illuminating exposition all his own. "I think this is an expression of a social philosophy that is expressed by the Soviet Government of Russia. It is a negation of the whole concept of American civilization. I think it would be a sad day when the American people abandon the principles on which they have grown to greatness." Coming to specifications, he particularly attacked a point in the report, that "compulsory unemployment insurance is feasible." Realizing that Mr. Wickersham was a specialist in individualism, since he was the chief author of a collective report from which each individual signer apparently dissented, the congregated deputies at Denver voted down the proposal that the commission's statement should be taken as "representing the mind of the Church," and substituted a mere pious recommendation that it should be given "careful consideration" by members of the Church. Such, at least, is the story reported in the press.

This is only one of many straws in the wind indicating a movement to exalt rugged individualism into a national taboo beyond the reach of inquiring minds. From day to day it becomes increasingly evident that some of our economic leaders (by no means all of them) are using the phrase as an excuse for avoiding responsibility, for laying the . . . depression on "Government interference," and for seeking to escape from certain forms of taxation and regulation which they do not find to their interest. If a smoke screen big enough can be laid on the land, our commercial prestidigitators may work wonders—for themselves.

Still more direct evidence confirms this view. For example, in the autumn of 1930, a New York bank published, as a kind of revelation from on high, a slashing attack on "Government interference with business," written by that stanch English Whig, Macaulay, a hundred years ago; and a few weeks later one of the leading advertising firms took a whole page in the *New York Times* to blazon forth the creed anew under the captivating head: "Cheer Up! Our Best Times Are Still Ahead of Us!" And the whole gospel was summed up in these words from Macaulay: "Our rulers will best promote the improvement of the people by strictly confining themselves to their own legitimate duties—by leaving capital to find its most lucrative course, commodities their fair price, industry and intelligence their natural reward, idleness and folly their natural punishment—by maintaining peace, by defending property, by diminishing the price of law, and by observing strict economy in every department of the State. Let the Government do this—the people will assuredly do the rest." In other words, here was put forth in the name of American business, with all the pontifical assurance that characterized Macaulay's shallowest sophistry, the pure creed of historic individualism, and here was served on the Government and people of the United States a warning revelation of confident expectations.

A year later, in a release to the press, Mr. Otto Kahn discussed the subject of planning and intimated that the fortunate position of France to-day is to be ascribed to the fact that the French Government interferes less with business than does the Government of Germany or Great Britain, with the implication that the United States might profit from this experience. About the same time the Honorable Newton D. Baker made a long address at Williamstown which was evidently designed to show that nothing important could be done in the present crisis by the Federal Government, except perhaps in the way of tariff reduction by international agreement. And now comes from Chicago the announcement that a number of rugged business men are forming a national association to combat Government in business, to break up this unholy alliance. There is not a professional lunching-and-dining fellowship in America that is not now applauding to the echo such ringing cries as "Let Us Alone," "Take Government Out of Business," "Hands Off," "Unburden Capital." With an eye on such straws in the wind, [former] President Hoover publicly state[d] that all notions about planned economy come out of Russia, thus placing such distinguished men as Gerard Swope and Owen D. Young under the horrible Red ban. As one of the high-powered utility propagandists recently explained, the best way to discredit an opponent is to pin a Red tag on him—without reference to his deserts, of course.

Hence it is important to ask, calmly and without reference to election heats, just what all this means. In what way is the Government "in business" and how did it get there? Here we climb down out of the muggy atmosphere of controversy and face a few stubborn facts. They are entered in the indubitable records of the Government of the United States and are as evident as the hills to them that have eyes to see. Let us catalogue a few of them *seriatim* for the first time in the history of this adventure in logomachy.

1. *Government Regulation of Railways, from 1887 to the last Act of Congress.* How did the Government get into this business? The general cause was the conduct of railway corporations under the rule of rugged individualism—rebates, pools, stock watering, bankruptcy-juggling, all the traffic will bear, savage rate slashing, merciless competition, and the rest of it. If anyone wants to know the facts, let him read the history of railroading in the sixties, seventies, and early eighties, or, if time is limited, the charming illustrations presented in Charles Francis Adams' "A Chapter of Erie." And what was the immediate cause of the Government's intervention? The insistence of business men, that is, shippers, who were harassed and sometimes ruined by railway tactics, and of farmers, the most rugged of all the rugged individualists the broad land of America has pro-

duced. And the result? Let the gentle reader compare the disastrous rail-way bankruptcies that flowed from the panic of 1873, including bloodshed and arson, with the plight of railways now, bad as it is. Government regu-lation is not a utopian success, but it is doubtful whether any of our great business men would like to get the Government entirely out of this business and return to the magnificent anarchy of Jay Gould's age. . . .

2. *Waterways.* Since its foundation the Government has poured hun-dreds of millions into rivers, harbors, canals, and other internal improve-ments. It is still pouring in millions. Some of our best economists have denounced it as wasteful and have demonstrated that most of it does not pay in any sense of the word. But President Hoover, instead of leaving this work to private enterprise, insist[ed] on projecting and executing the most elaborate undertakings, in spite of the fact that some of them . . . [were] unfair if not ruinous to railways. Who . . . [was] back of all this? Business men and farmers who want[ed] lower freight rates. There is not a chamber of commerce on any Buck Creek in America that will not cheer until tonsils are cracked any proposal to make the said creek navigable. Dredging companies want the good work to go on, and so do the concerns that make dredging machinery. Farmers are for it also and they are, as already said, the ruggedest of rugged individuals—so rugged in fact that the vigorous efforts of the Farm Board to instill cooperative reason into them have been almost as water on a duck's back.

3. *The United States Barge Corporation.* Who got the Government into the job of running barges on some of its improved waterways? Certainly not the Socialists, but good Republicans and Democrats speaking for the gentlemen listed under 2 above.

4. *The Shipping Business.* . . . World War [I] was the occasion, but not the cause of this departure. For more than half a century the politicians of America fought ship subsidies against business men engaged in the ship-building and allied industries. At last, under the cover of war necessities, the Government went into the shipping business, with cheers from business. Who is back of the huge expenditures for the merchant marine? Business men. Who supports huge subsidies under the guise of "lucrative mail con-tracts," making a deficit in postal finances to be used as proof that the Government cannot run any business? Business men clamor for these mail subsidies and receive them. Who put the Government into the business of providing cheap money for ship-building? Business men did it. Those who are curious to know how these things were done may profitably read the sworn testimony presented during the investigation of W. B. Shearer's patriotic labors on behalf of the ship-building interests, especially the ex-hibits showing how money was spent like water "educating" politicians.

Who wants navy officers on half pay to serve on privately owned ships? Business men. Who wants the Government to keep on operating ships on "pioneer" lines that do not pay? Business men. And when the United States Senate gets around to investigating this branch of business, it will find more entertainment than the Trade Commission has found in the utility inquest.

5. *Aviation.* The Government is "in" this business. It provides costly airway services free of charge and subsidizes air mail. Who is behind this form of Government enterprise? Gentlemen engaged in aviation and the manufacture of planes and dirigibles. Then the Government helps by buying planes for national defense. Who is opposed to air mail subsidies? A few despised "politicians."

6. *Canals.* Who zealously supported the construction of the Panama Canal? Shippers on the Pacific Coast who did not like the railway rates. Also certain important shipping interests on both coasts—all controlled by business men. Who insisted that the Government should buy the Cape Cod Canal? The business men who put their money into the enterprise and found that it did not pay. Then they rejoiced to see the burden placed on the broad back of our dear Uncle Sam.

7. *Highway Building.* Who has supported Federal highway aid—the expenditures of hundreds of millions on roads, involving the taxation of railways to pay for ruinous competition? Everybody apparently, but specifically business men engaged in the manufacture and sale of automobiles and trucks. Who proposes to cut off every cent of that outlay? Echoes do not answer.

8. *The Department of Commerce, its magnificent mansion near the Treasury Department, and its army of hustlers scouting for business at the uttermost ends of the earth.* Who is responsible for loading on the Government the job of big drummer at large for business? Why shouldn't these rugged individualists do their own drumming instead of asking the taxpayers to do it for them? Business men have been behind this enormous expansion, and Mr. Hoover, as Secretary of Commerce, outdid every predecessor in the range of his activities and the expenditure of public money. Who proposes to take the Government out of the business of hunting business for men who ought to know their own business?

9. *The Big Pork Barrel—appropriations for public buildings, navy yards, and army posts.* An interesting enterprise for the United States Chamber of Commerce would be to discover a single piece of pork in a hundred years that has not been approved by local business men as beneficiaries. When Ben Tillman shouted in the Senate that he intended to steal a hog every time a Yankee got a ham, he knew for whom the speaking was done.

10. *The Bureau of Standards.* Besides its general services, it renders valuable aid to business undertakings. Why shouldn't they do their own investigating at their own expense, instead of turning to the Government?

11. *The Federal Trade Commission.* Who runs there for rulings on "fair practices"? Weary consumers? Not often. Principally, business men who do not like to be outwitted or cheated by their competitors. If we are rugged individualists, why not let every individualist do as he pleases, without invoking Government intervention at public expense?

12. *The Anti-Trust Acts.* Business men are complaining against these laws on the ground that they cannot do any large-scale planning without incurring the risk of prosecution. The contention is sound, but who put these laws on the books and on what theory were they based? They were the product of a clamor on the part of farmers and business men against the practices of great corporations. Farmers wanted lower prices. Business men of the smaller variety objected to being undersold, beaten by clever tricks, or crushed to the wall by competitors with immense capital. And what was the philosophy behind the Sherman Act and the Clayton Act? Individualism, pure and undefiled. "The New Freedom" as President Wilson phrased it in literary language. "Break up the trusts and let each tub stand on its own bottom." That was the cry among little business men. As lawyers put it in their somber way, "the natural person's liberty should not be destroyed by artificial persons known as corporations created under the auspices of the State." Whether any particular business man is for or against the anti-trust laws depends upon his particular business and the state of its earnings.

13. *The Tariff.* On this tender subject it is scarcely possible to speak soberly. It seems safe to say, however, that if all the business men who demand this kind of "interference"—with the right of capital to find its most lucrative course, industry and intelligence their natural reward, commodities their fair price, and idleness and folly their natural punishment—were to withdraw their support for protection, cease their insistence on it, then the politicians would probably reduce the levy or go over to free trade; with what effect on business no one can correctly predict. At all events there are thousands of business men who want to keep the Government in the business of protecting their business against foreign competition. If competition is good, why not stand up and take it?

14. *The Federal Farm Board.* This collectivist institution . . . [was] the product of agrarian agitation on the part of our most stalwart individualists, the free and independent farmers; but President Hoover sponsored it and signed the bill that created it. Now what . . . [was] its avowed purpose as demonstrated by the language of the statute, the publications of the Farm

Board, and the activities carried out under its auspices? It . . . [was] primarily and fundamentally intended to stabilize prices and production through cooperative methods. And what . . . [did] the Board . . . [do]? It . . . encouraged the development of cooperation as distinguished from individualism among farmers; it . . . financed cooperative associations; it . . . denounced individualistic farmers who insist[ed] on growing as much as they please[d], and . . . tried to get them to increase their earnings by a common limitation of production. If the Agricultural Marketing Act mean[t] anything, if the procedure of the Farm Board . . . [was] not a delusion, then cooperation . . . [was] to be substituted for individualism in agricultural production and marketing. If there . . . [was] ever to be a rational adjustment of supply to demand in this field, the spirit and letter of President Hoover's measure . . . [had to be] realized through organized action by millions of farmers under Federal auspices. The other alternative is simon-pure individualism: let each farmer produce what he likes, as much of it as he likes, and sell it at any price he can get. But under the happy title "Grow Less—Get More," the Farm Board . . . [gave] instructions to farmers: "One thing the successful manufacturers learned long ago was that they could not make money when they produced more than they could sell at a profit." The obvious moral is for farmers to get together under Government leadership or hang separately. [The Agriculture Adjustment Act, provision for farm credit, price support, and other government action in recent years is further evidence supporting Mr. Beard's thesis.]

15. *The Moratorium and Frozen Assets.* . . . [Another] form of Government interference with "the natural course" of economy . . . [was] the suspension of payments due the United States from foreign powers on account of lawful debts and the proposal to give public support to "frozen assets." What was the source of inspiration here? American investment bankers having got themselves into a jam in their efforts to make easy money . . . [demanded] Government assistance. In 1927 one of the most distinguished German economists told the writer . . . that the great game in his country, as in other parts of Europe, was to borrow billions from private bankers in the United States, so that it would ultimately be impossible to pay reparations, the debts due the Federal Government, *and* then the debts owed to private parties. The expected result? American bankers would then force their Government to forego its claims for the benefit of private operators who wanted to make bankers' commissions and eight or ten per cent on their money. . . .

And what is a "frozen asset"? It is a gaudy name for a piece of paper representing a transaction in which the holder expected to get a larger return than was possible on a prudent, rock-bottom investment. . . . Why should there be Federal interference to save investors from reaping the fruits of their folly and greed? No reason, except that the latter want the Government to bring home their cake so that they can eat it. The trouble is that American capital, in finding "its most lucrative course," has fallen into a slough, and if it gets out with its gains intact the Government must bring a derrick to hoist it. [The trend Mr. Beard analyzed has continued—whatever opinion one may have of it. Note, for example: the NRA, the Federal Securities Act, the Taft-Hartley Act, the Social Security Act, and legislation providing farm price supports and subsidies to shipping.]

In this survey of a few leading economic activities of the Federal Government the emphasis is not critical; so far as the present argument is concerned, any or all of these functions may be justified with respect to national interest. Indeed it is difficult to find any undertaking of the Government which is not supported by some business men on the ground of national defense. In the early days of our history even those statesmen who generally espoused free trade or low tariffs were willing to concede the importance of making the nation independent in the manufacture of munitions of war. And in the latest hour, subsidies to the merchant marine, to aviation, and to waterways development are stoutly defended in the name of preparedness. Transforming a creek into a river navigable by outboard motor boats can be supported by military engineers on the theory that it gives them practice in their art. No; the emphasis here is not critical. The point is that the Federal Government does not operate in a vacuum, but under impulsion from without; and all of the measures which put the Government into business have been supported by rugged individualists—business men or farmers or both. The current tendency to describe the Government as a meddling busybody, prying around and regulating for the mere pleasure of taking the joy out of somebody's life, betrays an ignorance of the facts in the case. The Government of the United States operates continually in the midst of the most powerful assembly of lobbyists the world has ever seen—the representatives of every business interest that has risen above the level of a corner grocery; and there is not a single form of Government interference with business that does not have the approval of one or more of these interests—except perhaps the taxation of incomes for the purpose, among other things, of paying the expenses of subsidizing and regulating business.

For forty years or more there has not been a President, Republican or Democrat, who has not talked against Government interference and then supported measures adding more interference to the huge collection already accumulated. Take, for instance, President Wilson. He made his campaign in 1912 on the classical doctrine of individualism; he blew mighty blasts in the name of his new freedom against the control of the Government by corporate wealth and promised to separate business and Government, thus setting little fellows free to make money out of little business. The heir of the Jeffersonian tradition, he decried paternalism of every kind. Yet look at the statutes enacted under his benign administration: the trainmen's law virtually fixing wages on interstate railways for certain classes of employees; the shipping board law; the Farm Loan Act; Federal aid for highway construction; the Alaskan railway; the Federal Reserve Act; the Water Power Act; and all the rest of the bills passed during his régime. Only the Clayton anti-trust law can be called individualistic. No wonder Mr. E. L. Doheny exclaimed to Mr. C. W. Barron that President Wilson was a college professor gone Bolshevist! And why did Democrats who had been saying "the less government the better" operate on the theory that the more government the better? Simply because their mouths were worked by ancient memories and their actions were shaped by inexorable realities.

Then the Republicans came along in 1921 and informed the country that they were going back to normalcy, were determined to take the Government out of business. Well, did they repeal a single one of the important measures enacted during the eight years of President Wilson's rule? It would be entertaining to see the Sanhedrim of the United States Chamber of Commerce trying to make out a list of laws repealed in the name of normalcy and still more entertaining to watch that august body compiling a list of additional laws interfering with "the natural course of business" enacted since 1921. Heirs of the Hamiltonian tradition, the Republicans were not entitled to talk about separating the Government from business. Their great spiritual teacher, Daniel Webster, a pupil of Hamilton, had spoken truly when he said that one of the great reasons for framing the Constitution was the creation of a government that could regulate commerce. They came honestly by subsidies, bounties, internal improvements, tariffs, and other aids to business. What was the trouble with them in the age of normalcy? Nothing: they just wanted their kind of Government intervention in the "natural course of industry." Evidently, then, there is some confusion on this subject of individualism, and it ought to be examined dispassionately in the light of its history with a view to discovering its significance and its limitations; for there is moral danger in saying one thing and doing another—at all events too long.

Historically speaking, there are two schools of individualism: one American, associated with the name of Jefferson, and the other English, associated with the name of Cobden. The former was agrarian in interest, the latter capitalistic. Jefferson wanted America to be a land of free, upstanding farmers with just enough government to keep order among them; his creed was an agrarian creed nicely fitted to a civilization of sailing ships, ox carts, stagecoaches, wooden plows, tallow dips, and home-made bacon and sausages; and since most of the people in the United States, during the first century of their independence, were engaged in agriculture, they thought highly of Jefferson's praise of agriculture and his doctrine of anarchy plus the police constable. Cobden's individualism was adapted to capitalist England at the middle of the nineteenth century—early industrial England. At that moment his country was the workshop of the world, was mistress of the world market in manufactured commodities, and feared no competition from any foreign country. English capitalists thus needed no protective tariffs and subsidies and, therefore, wanted none. Hence they exalted free trade to the level of a Mosaic law, fixed and eternal. They wanted to employ labor on their own terms and turn working people out to starve when no profitable business was at hand; so they quite naturally believed that any Government interference with their right to do as they pleased was "bad." Their literary apologist, Macaulay, clothed their articles of faith in such magnificent rhetoric that even the tiredest business man could keep awake reading it at night.

Closely examined, what is this creed of individualism? Macaulay defines it beautifully in the passage which the New York bank and our happy advertising agency quoted so joyously. Let the Government maintain peace, defend property, reduce the cost of litigation, and observe economy in expenditure—that is all. Do American business men want peace all the time, in Nicaragua, for instance, when their undertakings are disturbed? Or in Haiti or Santo Domingo? Property must be defended, of course. But whose property? And what about the cost of litigation and economy in expenditures? If they would tell their hired men in law offices to cut the costs of law, something might happen. As for expenditures, do they really mean to abolish subsidies, bounties, and appropriations-in-aid from which they benefit? Speaking brutally, they do not . . . ; they prefer to cut off a few dollars from the Children's Bureau.

Then comes Macaulay's system of private economy: let capital find its most lucrative course alone, unaided: no Government tariffs, subsidies, bounties, and special privileges. That is the first item. Do American business men who shout for individualism believe in that? Certainly not. So that much is blown out of the water. Macaulay's next item is: let commodities find their fair price. Do the gentlemen who consolidate, merge, and make price understandings want to allow prices to take their "natural course"? By no means; they are trying to effect combinations that will hold prices up to the point of the largest possible profit. [And, the farmers demand price support for farm products.] Macaulay's third item is: let industry and intelligence receive their natural reward. Whose industry and intelligence and what industry and intelligence? When these questions are asked all that was clear and simple dissolves in mist.

Then there is Macaulay's last item: let idleness and folly reap their natural punishment. That was a fundamental specification in the bill of Manchesterism. Malthus made it a law for the economists: the poor are poor because they have so many babies and are improvident; nothing can be done about it, at least by any Government, even though it enforces drastic measures against the spread of information on birth control. Darwin made a natural science of it: biology sanctified the tooth and claw struggle of business by proclaiming the eternal tooth and claw struggle of the jungle. If the Government will do nothing whatever, all people will rise or sink to the level which their industry or idleness, their intelligence or folly commands. No distinction was made between those who were idle because they could find no work and those who just loved idleness for its own sake—either in slums or mansions. Those who hit bottom and starved simply deserved it. That is the good, sound, logical creed of simon-pure individualism which Herbert Spencer embedded in fifty pounds of printed matter. To him and all his devotees, even public schools and public libraries were anathema: let the poor educate themselves at their own expense; to educate them at public expense is robbery of the taxpayer—that industrious, intelligent, provident person who is entitled to keep his "natural reward."

Do any stalwart individualists believe that simple creed now? Not in England, where Liberals, professing to carry on the Cobden-Bright tradition, vote doles for unemployed working people. Why not let idleness and folly get their natural punishment? Why not, indeed? There must be a reason. Either the individualists betray their own faith, or, as some wag has suggested, they are afraid that they might find themselves hanging to a lantern if they let the idle and the foolish starve, that is, reap the natural punishment prescribed by Macaulay. Nor do American individualists propose to let nature take her course in this country. There is no danger of revolution here; as Mr. Coolidge has said, "we have had our revolution"; yet business men agree with the politicians on feeding the hungry. It is true that they seem to be trying to obscure the issues and the facts by talking about the beneficence of private charity while getting most of the dole from public treasuries; but that is a detail. Although our rugged individualists advertise Macaulay's creed, their faith in it appears to be shaky or their courage is not equal to their hopes. Then why should they try to delude themselves and the public?

There is another side to this stalwart individualism that also deserves consideration. Great things have been done in its name, no doubt, and it will always have its place in any reasoned scheme of thinking. Individual initiative and energy are absolutely indispensable to the successful conduct of any enterprise, and there is ample ground for fearing the tyranny and ineptitude of Governments. In the days of pioneering industry in England, in our pioneering days when forests were to be cut and mountain fastnesses explored, individualism was the great dynamic which drove enterprise forward. But on other pages of the doom book other entries must be made. In the minds of most people who shout for individualism vociferously, the creed, stripped of all flashy rhetoric, means getting money, simply that and nothing more. And to this creed may be laid most of the shame that has cursed our cities and most of the scandals that have smirched our Federal Government.

That prince of bosses, Croker, put the individualist creed in its bare logical form when he said that he was working for his own pocket all the time, just as "every man in New York is working for his pocket." Fall, Doheny, and Sinclair were all splendid individualists; they explained that they hoped to make money out of their transactions, even while they covered their operations with the mantle of patriotism—national defense. Tammany judges, Connolly and his iron pipe, Doyle with his split fees, and policemen growing rich on vice are all individualists of the purest brand. W. B. Shearer collecting money from ship-building concerns to make a naval scare so that they might increase their profits belongs to the same school. Britten, bringing a fleet to Montauk Point to boom real estate in which he is interested, does nothing reprehensible under the Manchester creed; his capital is finding "its most lucrative course." Wilder and Bardo, representing shipping interests, when they spend money in Washington "educating" members of Congress, are following the law of the game. They are perfect individualists. The ruinous chaos in coal and oil is to be attributed to the same Darwinian morality. Finally, Al Capone, with his private enterprise in racketeering, . . . [was] a supreme individualist: he want[ed] no Government interference with his business, not even the collection of income taxes; if he . . . [were] "let alone" he . . . [would] take care of himself and give some money to soup kitchens besides.

The cold truth is that the individualist creed of everybody for himself and the devil take the hindmost is principally responsible for the distress in which Western civilization finds itself—with investment racketeering at one end and labor racketeering at the other. Whatever merits the creed may have had in days of primitive agriculture and industry, it is not applicable in an age of technology, science, and rationalized economy. Once useful, it has become a danger to society. Every thoughtful business man who is engaged in management as distinguished from stock speculation knows that stabilization, planning, orderly procedure, prudence, and the adjustment of production to demand are necessary to keep the economic machine running steadily and efficiently. Some of our most distinguished citizens—Owen D. Young, Gerard Swope, Nicholas Murray Butler, and Otto Kahn, for example—have, in effect, warned the country that only by planning can industry avoid the kind of disaster from which we are now suffering; on all sides are signs of its coming—perhaps soon, perhaps late, but inevitably.

And all of them know that this means severe restraints on the anarchy celebrated in the name of individualism. The task before us, then, is not to furbish up an old slogan, but to get rid of it, to discover how much planning is necessary, by whom it can best be done, and what limitations must be imposed on the historic doctrine of Manchesterism. And to paraphrase Milton, methinks puissant America, mewing her mighty youth, will yet kindle her undazzled eyes at the full midday beam, purge and unscale her long abused sight, while timorous and flocking birds, with those that love the twilight, flutter about, amazed at what she means, and in their envious gabble would prognosticate a year of sects and schisms.

No. 102

THE CONTROL OF BIG BUSINESS [1]

by Walton H. Hamilton

. . . . .

OUR anti-trust laws express the common sense of another age. Toward the close of the nineteenth century a nation which had been composed of farmers and small business men was confronted by a crisis. A revolution in the ways of production which had been gaining momentum with the passing decades was no longer to be ignored. The hand trades were giving way to manufacture; the machine process was transforming the ways of production; businesses were becoming great corporations; captains of industry were coming into possession of wealth and power; and the strange and wicked city was dominating the country. A society made up of almost self-sufficient farms, with its complement of local trade, was being transformed into an articulate, even if rather unruly, industrial system. In the whirl of change small traders who saw their enterprises crowded to the wall cried out against the iniquities of big business. The public, which distrusted size as much as it feared extortionate price, realized that untoward things

[1] Walton H. Hamilton, "The Control of Big Business," *The Nation* (May 25, 1932), Vol. 134, pp. 591-593. This article was reprinted in Henry Hazlitt (Ed.) *A Practical Program for America* (New York: Harcourt, Brace and Company, 1932), and is reprinted here by permission of the author, *The Nation*, and Harcourt, Brace and Company.

were going forward. An industrialism which had got its start by stealth came on with such a rush as to leave the people bewildered. The world was no longer as it used to be—and ought to be.

In the emergency a policy had to be formulated. In the task it seemed to occur to no one, at least among those in strategic places, to ask whether industrialism was not rather different from anything society had known before, and whether experimentation might not be used to contrive for it a suitable scheme of control. Instead, the thinkers and the statesmen of the times brought to the problem the best wisdom they could muster—and this wisdom was the product of a social experience which was passing. If the farmer found difficulty in making ends meet, or the small merchant was threatened with extinction, or the customer had his pocket picked by the extortionate dealer, or the workingman put in his long hours for a pittance, it was all because the system of free competition was not working.

At the time, the case for an enforced competition seemed to be quite reasonable. Fact may be on time, but thought usually arrives on the scene a little late. The people talked quite grandly about every man being "the architect of his fate"; and they believed quite sincerely in the creed of "each for himself and the devil take the hindmost." In that climate of opinion only individualistic notions of the province of government and the control of industry could gain currency. Moreover, a long experience with petty trade had produced its own economic policy, and the sense of the man in the street was confirmed by the wisdom in the learned books. It was perfectly clear that the competition of seller with seller and of buyer with buyer gave assurance of efficient service, high quality, and fair price. The interests of one party to a trade—seller, lender, or employer—were balanced by the interests of the other party—buyer, borrower, or employee. Nor could any trader help himself at the expense of his customer, for his desire for gain was checked by the rivalry of others for the very dollars he was trying to secure. The ups and downs in prices which came in the wake of competition attracted or repelled capital, and thus in each industry kept the capacity-to-produce adjusted to the demand for the product. In fact, free enterprise was "a great and beneficent system" which kept industries organized, eliminated the inefficient, gave survival to the fit, insured to labor good working conditions and fair wages, and protected the consumer. For all "the blessings of free competition," as the Supreme Court of the nineties called them, a single provision had to be made. Trades were to be kept open, if need be through a legally enforced competition, and an automatic, self-regulating system could be depended upon to secure for the public all the business system had to give. The thing to be done seemed obvious;

and an attempt was made to stay the development of large-scale enterprise and to make big business behave as if it were petty trade.

So it was that in the name of laissez faire the law was invoked. For some time, even if not from time immemorial, the common law had forbidden "conspiracies in restraint of trade," and a number of States had in the decades following the Civil War aimed statutes at the growing evil of monopoly. In 1890 the Sherman Act, designed to prohibit combinations in "commerce among the several States," was enacted into law. In 1914 the Clayton and the Federal Trade Commission acts were passed in an attempt to extend and to strengthen the federal anti-trust act. The great majority of the States—almost all in the South and West—passed their little Sherman acts.

The resort to law carried its own peculiar hazards. The ideas of common sense had to be translated into the language of legislation; the ends of public policy had to be vindicated through a process of litigation. Economists and statesmen might talk of an enforced competition, but the judiciary gave its attention to "conspiracies in restraint of trade." The language of the statutes caused the courts to consider modern industrial mergers in the light of precedents from a pre-industrial era. The decisions of a former age were invoked in suits to punish offenders or to "dissolve" monopolies; the litigation had to go forward, from issue to issue and from court to court, under a formal code of procedure never designed to draw a line between desirable and undesirable forms of industrial organizations. The cases were heard before benches of judges far more experienced in the discipline of the law than in business, and far better acquainted with Cooley on Blackstone than with texts on the economics of monopoly. It is hardly strange that questions of anti-social practices were subordinated to the antecedent questions of decorous procedure, and that ingenious attorneys found ways to "wear the case out" before the larger issues were raised.

It is small wonder that the resort to law has not been a conspicuous success. Our era of federal "trust-busting" covers a period of more than forty years. In this period has occurred the greatest movement in the concentration of productive wealth known to history. Yet the statisitcs of the Department of Justice present a most illuminating picture of law enforcement at work. A little more than two score criminals have been jailed, and eight have fallen afoul of the law for contempt—a matter of a little more than one person a year. A little under 1,400 persons have had to pay fines aggregating about $1,750,000—or roughly 40 offenders and $50,000 a year. A number of States have derived far more revenue from trust-busting than has the federal government. Yet the prosecution of cases has not been a profitmaking enterprise; the fines collected have fallen far short of the costs of administration. On its face this record is a glorious tribute of respect paid by men of big business to the letter, if not to the spirit, of the anti-trust acts.

This does not mean that the statutes have been without their effect upon the practices of business. They have been ineffectual in preventing corporations from acquiring the physical properties of their competitors and in staying the progress of industrial combination. They have put serious obstacles in the way of agreement among rival manufacturers to restrict output and to maintain price. The barriers have not been insuperable; captains of industry are anxious to live within the law, but they also love to have their own way, and the art of doing both is not unknown to able lawyers. If resourcefulness has often failed the emergency, the credit is not always due to the law. The ups and downs of business strain the morale of all industrial groups; and lapses into the established ways of competition are due more often to a break in discipline from within than to the vigilance of public officials. It is of interest that a number of gigantic corporations have escaped the toils of the law, and that severe penalties have often fallen upon small businesses and upon trade unions. Even where they have not been effective, the acts have been at least a petty nuisance to the interests affected.

But the roots of failure are far more fundamental than a resort to law to give effect to a public policy. The course of industrialism has come with too much of a rush to be stayed; its forces have been too turbulent to be subdued by legislative fiat and court decree; business men have been too powerful to allow their activities to be crowded into the grooves chiseled out long ago for a simpler industry. The universe of petty trade was one sort of place; the world of big business is quite another. In the small town the trader knew his customers personally; he could enlarge his business as his market expanded; his out-of-pocket expenses furnished adequate bases for his prices. As invention brought changes in technical processes, time allowed an easy accommodation. Under the prevailing system a knowledge of the future intent of customers and of the hidden plans of rivals is essential to a sound policy. The business judgments of to-day determine the capacity-to-produce of to-morrow; yet, in an impersonal market, the demand may go to a rival or pass on to another ware. In many lines of business overhead costs have become dominant; and as fixed charges are spread over a large or a small output, the market determines the unit cost of production rather than the unit cost the market. In adapting the capacity-to-produce of an industry to the demand for goods, a far neater and less wasteful adjustment is demanded than the separate judgments of business rivals can effect. They must respond just enough and not too much to market trends, and the unity in action essential to order cannot be secured by a policy of competition.

In fact, the competitive system at work presents problems unknown to the competitive system in books. The good people of the nineties were disturbed because rivals might get together and conspire to impose extortionate prices upon their customers; and that danger still exists. But quite as important is the bill of costs which competition imposes upon the producers. It makes for plant waste and surplus capacity; it fails to articulate tidy establishments into orderly industries. A capacity which cries to be used and overhead costs which click on with the clock lead as often as not to an overdone competition which drives prices relentlessly down. In its wake comes a plague of bankruptcies, irregular employment, and wages too low to support a decent standard of life. Under such conditions there is no chance to get answered, or even to have raised, the larger questions of policy which affect all who have a stake in the industry. It makes all who are concerned—executives, salaried officials, investors, laborers, and consumers—creatures of an undirected industrialism.

The cry to-day is for a revision of the statutes; and yet that revision is no easy matter. An influential group demands that trade agreements be submitted to an official body, such as the Federal Trade Commission, and that advance opinions be given upon the legality of the proposed practices. The proposal has much to recommend it; the bother is that it will probably fail in operation. The spokesman for the government is likely to be guided in his advice by what the courts have said in the past, and to hand down general and platitudinous statements which have little relation to the novel practices for which approval is sought. A business must meet changing conditions; its policies must be adapted to the course of events as they emerge; a declaration that a policy on paper is legal can hardly apply to the policy as it works out in practice. Another group demands the right to "exchange information" and promises to abstain from a regulation of output and a control of price. The bother is that if discipline can be sustained and resourceful lawyers can be retained, the practice prayed for is all that is needed to effect a rather far-reaching monopoly. A third group boldly demands the repeal of the acts and offers no constructive scheme with which to replace them. It insists upon enlarging the control of business over industry when recent events have proved the incapacity of business for the proper exercise of the control it already possesses. The anti-trust statutes are a declaration that business is affected with a public interest; the moral commitment of that declaration is much too important to be lost.

But no mere expedients can get to the heart of the problem. The demand for change comes from an industrial world; it is not to be met with the devices and procedures of a craft society. The simple idea of the uniformity of all trades, which underlies current legislation, must give way to an accommodation of public control to the varying necessities of different industries. For our businesses are not all alike; banking, railroads, power, and radio-broadcasting have already been accorded their own schemes of control. The methods of production and of marketing in various other trades—building, retailing, milk, coal, textiles, cotton-planting—have their own peculiarities with which the problem of industrial direction must come to grips. In all cases, if there is to be order, if the nuisance of bankruptcy is to be abated, if workingmen are to have regular jobs and adequate wages, there must be some central direction. The formal control, or understanding, must certainly extend to capacity, probably to output, and possibly to price. In all cases, if there is to be flexibility, there must be some local control.

This general end is to be served by no simple and uniform economic organization. We have ceased to think in terms of panaceas; and neither a return to the good old competitive system of our fathers nor the adoption of a ready-made, hand-me-down substitute will meet current need. If our industries are to become instruments of national well-being, we must employ a varied program of economic control. Three distinct types of organization seem to be promising. Industries which produce non-essentials and can win only a limited trade against the allurements of unlike wares demand little public control; their activities may well be intrusted to the capricious solicitude of the market. Industries, such as railroads and power, which are linked with all the activities of the economic order demand a large social oversight; this may be met either by an administration commission or by public ownership. Industries, such as coal and steel, which have distinctive groups of customers may be organized from within under a control in which producers and consumers alike share. Industries must be kept going and their dependents must be given adequate livings; consumers must be accorded protection against an anti-social restriction of output and a monopoly element in price. This problem is not to be solved by any "either this or that" formula; its solution demands clear vision, full knowledge, and neat adjustments.

The plain truth of the matter is that the rewriting of the anti-trust laws is the beginning, not the end, of the problem. We may indulge in tinkering and console ourselves with make-believe and pretense; but the fundamental question stands out in clear-cut relief. To-day a lack of harmony exists between the technology of industry and its organization. An economic order in which the productive processes belong to big business and the arrangements for its control to petty trade cannot abide. We cannot banish depression and summon order by invoking the ideas which the people of the 1890's borrowed from a small-town culture. We must devise a scheme adequate to the task of the direction of great industry. In a world of change a society cannot live upon a wisdom borrowed from our fathers.

No. 103

THE PRIORITIES OF GOVERNMENT [1]

by Marshall Edward Dimock

WHAT any institution is capable of doing is restricted by the same practical limitations and considerations as apply to the individual. In both cases, although goals may be set at will, there are practical bounds to what may be acceptably accomplished. Neither business nor government —nor any other institution, for that matter—has inherent characteristics or "essences" different from those of other institutions. On the contrary, according to hypotheses verified by pragmatic tests, it seems to have been established that certain characteristics and limitations are found in all kinds of institutional life. The implications of these social truths for the present study have far-reaching consequences.

Jeremy Bentham, one of the earliest of modern political economists to view government and business broadly and in their total cultural setting, distinguished between Agenda which he defined as the irreducible minimum of functions to be undertaken by the state in maintaining a vital economy, and Non-Agenda which is the area to be reserved to private enterprise and to individuals. The dividing line, said Bentham, is a practical one, being that division of labor which contributes most to the happiness and well-being, the pleasure, and the greatest good of the greatest number of people in a given society. A re-emphasis and re-application in present-day society of this demarcation of functions between public and private institutions would greatly improve the chances of achieving the vital economy that was Bentham's aim.

A corollary of Agenda and Non-Agenda is that government cannot be all things to all people and perform all functions equally well. Or putting it another way, if government concentrates on those functions which it is best fitted to undertake and which redound most to the general advantage, it will

---

[1] Marshall Edward Dimock, *Business and Government* (New York: Henry Holt and Company, Inc., 1949), pp. 800-815. Reprinted by permission of the publisher. The footnotes in the original version are omitted here.

of necessity resist the temptation to act where some other group or individual is more competent.

What is the Agenda of the state in the middle of the twentieth century? An answer which has been suggested is that government should concentrate on matters of common concern which give most promise of producing an environment in which economic groups can operate with the greatest advantage to themselves and to society. But having staked out such a rule, many questions of application remain to be decided. For example, should the responsibility of government in the economic field include the guidance, planning, and stabilization of economic processes? The determination of major goals through cooperative effort? The use of tax and credit controls? The giving of assistance? The regulation of major concentrations of economic power? The operation of services commonly thought to be more appropriately administered by public than by private means? The conservation and development of natural resources? A mere listing of the range of possibilities illustrates the vastness of the field in which priorities must be established so that some may be emphasized and others avoided or delegated to non-governmental groups.

Before a rational decision can be made relative to Agenda and Non-Agenda, therefore, it must first be clear what the broad objectives or goals are which society would pursue. There must be some kind of positive affirmation such as "The goal of the political economy is the combining of stability and progress," or "The objective of the political economy is to reconcile and Insure a vigorous democratic government and a strong system of business enterprise."

THE GUIDELINES OF FUTURE POLICY

Once the goals have been determined—and not until then—the priorities begin to fall into place. Experience indicates certain so-called legitimate or inherent functions of government which supply an obvious and incontestable need. Beyond this, the determination of broad policies for the economy becomes more important than the detailed administration of any program, so that cooperative planning, aimed jointly at stabilization and progress, becomes the first priority. Other things being equal, control-without-ownership is preferable to control-through-ownership. Regulation should be reduced to a minimum if for no other reason than that it burdens the administration of government, complicates its structure, and reduces the attention that can be given to the first priority of creating a balanced setting for individual enterprise. Where government ownership is unavoidable it should not be allowed to assume such proportions as again to detract from government's primary concern; which might mean that extensions of government ownership should be avoided or, alternatively, that lower levels of government and corporate agencies of government might be entrusted with most of the burden.

What to do about government assistance to industry and agriculture involves discrimination between simple programs which are easily administered and constitute no serious encumbrance to higher priorities and those which do have this effect. Programs related to conservation or to some other major goal obviously have a stronger justification than those that do not. And all subsidy programs, especially, should be scrutinized with reference to their disrupting effect on desired equilibriums as contrasted with whatever social benefits they may offer. Cooperatives imposed no burden on government and hence are unobjectionable from the standpoint of government's ability to concentrate on first things first. But cooperatives must be taken into account in any over-all planning operations and any beneficial or injurious effects on other parts of the economy must be considered. And finally, it should be remembered that the importance of priorities is relative to the complexity of the economy and the degree of centralization that exists. In a deconcentrated, decentralized situation, government easily assumes all of these burdens and hence the problem of priorities is less acute. With increasing concentration and centralization, however, the more essential it becomes that priorities be established and adhered to. One of the best ways of solving a country's economic problems, therefore, is to secure as high a degree of decentralization as can be obtained consonant with the technological advantages deriving from mass-production methods.

CONCLUSIONS RELATIVE TO AGENDA

Since the grand strategy of the political economy should be to create the conditions most conducive to stability and progress, obviously the federal government should emphasize policy and planning more than regulation and ownership, the reverse of which is presently true. There is a danger to which this type of analysis is exposed, however, in that it is not categories as different as apples and barrel staves that are under question but *the aspects of government's relation to the economy which overlap and together form the end result which society desires to produce.* It does not take much demonstration to prove that all of the economic functions here considered—assistance, regulation, ownership and operation, and the promotion of cooperative enterprises—involve planning in the broadest sense of the term. Moreover, each of them may or may not contribute to the objective of simultaneously producing stability and progress in the economic structure.

Certainly much planning is involved in the meticulous regulation of transportation and communication. . . . In fact, the degree of specificity in those and other fields is a main reason for objecting to the government assuming an unreasonable degree of managerial supervision in derogation of the principle of unity of management. The trend toward increased planning has been commented on by Raymond T. Bye, who points out that in the early stages of capitalism, industry was unplanned and decentralized; then as the corporate device superseded simpler forms of organization, industry was increasingly planned and government interfered at many points; until, at length,

> The deeper meaning of all this is that the various processes of industry are gradually being brought under centralized control. . . . The planning is being done partly by the large corporation and trade associations which dominate their respective branches of production, and partly by the state, through such agencies as the Federal Power Commission, the Interstate Commerce Commission, the Securities and Exchange Commission, the National Labor Relations Board, and many others, federal, state, and local.

Unfortunately, this type of planning is piecemeal, uncoordinated, and often at variance with larger objectives.

A major obstacle in the way of simplification of controls and the establishment of rational priorities is that democratic government, for better or worse, is government by pressure groups, so that government's economic policies and programs are directly traceable to the successful pressures which various interests exert on legislatures and administrators. There is no central board of strategy in the government to determine the compatibility of a proposed economic measure with those which have preceded it or with the over-all goals of the economy. Moreover, programs once started are hard to discontinue because of the dogged defense of any administrative agency by the interests responsible for creating it. This has been shown, case by case, in Pendleton Herring's study, *Public Administration and the Public Interest.*

The inconsistencies and planlessness of the resulting situation, concludes Bye, mean:

> Laws affecting industry are enacted under the pressure of special interest instead of being framed with regard to the smooth functioning of the whole economy. Such laws are often in direct opposition to each other. . . . Because private business does not fully employ all our labor, we embark upon programs of public works intended to fill up the gap, while at the same time we enact measures designed to raise the wages of workers and thereby discourage an increase in private employment.

To correct this situation does not require a minor dictatorship. It merely involves a better organization of the government to make it more responsible, but so far the pressure groups and the public have been lukewarm even to this moderate proposal.

Simultaneously, therefore, with any expanded planning activity directed toward the economy, the processes and policies of government must also be boldly and constructively planned. This need has been underscored by one close to the Washington scene for many years:

> . . . a great deal more attention needs to be paid to seeing that these various functions and policies of the government mesh smoothly with the operations of the price-enterprise system. For government action affects the action of business, labor and agriculture and *vice versa.* The object of both is to conserve the health of the American economy and to accelerate its growth. But they can do these things only if they work in concert. *This requires that the economic policies of the government itself, no less than those of business men and laborers and farmers and consumers, must be aware of and responsive to some mutual economic aims.* Otherwise we shall all be acting at cross-purposes.

Is it any wonder that double-barreled executives, equally proficient in the fields of policy and administration, are in peak demand in Washington?

THE ROLE OF MAJOR GOVERNMENT REGULATION

It seems clear that in a mixed economy no one pattern of business-government relation may be expected to suffice. The economy is too complicated, the various problems differ too widely in character, and democracy seems to prefer variety to standardization. From the standpoint of safeguarding freedom of enterprise, diversity is doubtless both inevitable and desirable. Nevertheless, the bewildering array of policies and governmental methods does greatly add to the difficulties of clarifying the operations of government and of enabling it to focus on broad over-all stabilization and planning. For example, both judicial and administrative methods are employed to enforce competition through the application of the antitrust laws; direct price fixing occurs in the case of public utilities, milk, and coal; production is sometimes limited as in the case of agriculture and petroleum; subsidies are employed in certain areas of agriculture, and in shipping and aviation; the whole field of finance is regulated by boards and commissions and in addition the government itself operates an imposing number of banking and insurance ventures; the legal and bargaining status of organized labor have been strengthened and in most areas of industrial relations, administrative and judicial controls have been established; licensing occurs in radio, water power, and natural gas; the cooperative movement is actively encouraged through the Department of Agriculture; industrial self-government and cartelization have been stimulated by experiments such as the NRA; natural resources are both regulated and publicly administered; government ownership and operation have steadily increased at all levels, and especially in recent years at the top; tax policies are widely used for broad economic and specific regulatory purposes; and planning has been on the increase since the early 1930s.

This is not to suggest that complexity can be avoided because the progress of society seems to breed increasingly intricate arrangements, and due to the cause-and-effect relationship operating here, complexity in society and the economy is inevitably paralleled by complexity in government. Nevertheless, the picture drawn above does call attention to the fact that to-day major regulation is the largest area of governmental policy and administration relative to the economy and that hence the greatest possibilities of simplification may exist in this quarter.

Moreover, even within the category of regulation, as observed in previous chapters, wide varieties of policy and method are presently employed. So numerous are the areas of regulation that some have received but slight emphasis in this study. For example, during the great depression of the 1930s the plight of the bituminous coal industry became so serious that it was subjected "to a special regulatory regime which embraced perhaps the most complex venture in price fixing ever undertaken by any single governmental agency in the United States." Also during the same period, stringent federal prohibitions against the interstate shipment of oil produced in violation of state proration laws added a large new area to the ambit of federal control. More recently, the field of atomic energy has been made a monopoly of the federal government.

Is there no relief from the complexity of regulation? So intricate is the problem that it is hard even to encompass the whole of it in one's mind at the same time. And even when the problem has been surrounded, what workable alternatives present themselves? No regulation, better regulation, less regulation, or inherently circumscribed monopolies under private or public direction seem to exploit the available possibilities. Where regulation can be withdrawn without injury to the public interest, this step should by all means be taken without delay, but there seem to be few instances in which such a course seems possible. Less regulation also holds promise of reducing government's burdens and relaxing controls, but here too the opportunities so far give virtually no cause for encouragement, one reason being that once a certain degree of control has been established, the public uncritically assumes that any relaxation will be accomplished at its expense. Nevertheless, both of these possibilities deserve to be fully explored in individual instances.

The main alternatives seem to boil down to improvements in regulatory policy and administration plus the use of limited monopolies so organized and empowered as to be virtually free thereafter from additional outside controls. . . .

THE PROSPECTS AND POSSIBILITIES OF REGULATION

Of all the areas of business-government relations in the United States to-day, administrative regulation will probably undergo more critical analysis and possible change in coming years than any other. Corresponding foreign experience is one reason for predicting such a development, but an even more compelling one is the ferment of critical appraisal which has been at work amongst those in a position to direct public opinion for at least a generation—from about the time of the electric power investigation of 1928.

Two major areas in the field of regulation are likely to receive most attention. First, the interested public is concerned about the problems of valuation, rate-making, and profits and the solution here . . . is far from clear. The question is: Can valuation law and procedure be adequately clarified and simplified so as to give satisfaction and, withal, can commission regulation be strengthened and at the same time simplified and improved?

The second large question is also of concern to the general public but more directly it affects the managements of regulated enterprises: Can the problem of divided authority be solved so as to allow regulated enterprises to operate as ordinary business concerns and public corporations are supposed to, enjoying unity of management and an opportunity for initiative and enterprise? The problem is underscored in an article by James M. Herring appearing in *The Annals*. In the nature of the regulatory system, says Herring,

> . . . the placing of a regulatory body in the position of watchdog over the operations of men engaged in business for private profit, a body which enjoys many of the privileges of a supermanagement agency, is bound to engender suspicion and ill-will and to lead to subterfuge to accomplish what detailed statutes and administrative regulation are designed to prevent.

It seems a safe prediction that unless a satisfactory solution of this basic difficulty is found, administrative regulation will lose its place in public confidence.

Minor government regulation, as in the inspection of barber shops or eating establishments, presents relatively little trouble. The present interest centers on major regulation as exemplified by the fixing of valuations of public utilities for rate-making purposes. Here the question is: Can a basis be found for retaining some kinds of major regulation by regulatory commissions, as at present, and transferring others out of the regulatory field entirely, thus avoiding the two major objections referred to above?

Several bases on which to make a division do suggest themselves, such as between a monopoly and a nonmonopoly, or an industry in which prices are fixed and one in which they are not. Another distinction which has possible merit draws a line between regulation involving the establishment of a valuation and that which does not. On this basis railroads, communications, and other public utilities would fall into the category where valuation is involved, leaving banking, insurance, investment banking, stock markets, the milk industry, and oil and coal to constitute the second category where valuation is not a factor. This suggested division also seems to be justified by the fact that in the latter category, regulation affects a whole industry broadly—bank examiners, for example, make the rounds of all banks—whereas in the case of the public utilities, regulation is an individual matter of establishing particular valuations, particular rates, and particular profits. In consequence, there is more danger of invading the prerogative of the paid management in the case of the utilities than in the case of banking and other industries where valuation is not involved.

If a substitute for commission regulation could be found for the control of industries where valuation is a factor, the commissions could then concentrate on the regulation of businesses falling into the second category where valuation is absent. Valuation theory and practice are now so involved that some experts, even after years of experience, have concluded that the matter is well-nigh hopeless. If major regulation were confined to businesses where valuation does not enter, therefore, the burden of government would be immeasurably reduced—perhaps, in the regulatory field, by as much as 50 per cent—and a much better job would be done. And even if banking, insurance, investment banking, stock markets, the milk industry, and oil and coal were the only objects of regulation, the task would still be a large one.

In order to control those industries removed from commission regulation, the device of internal as contrasted with external control might be adopted. Concretely, this means that the necessary restrictions and policies are written into the utility's charter, which may then simply be withdrawn in case of non-compliance. The most important of these restrictions is the limitation on earnings and the establishment of a definite basis for determining total investment. The public utility trust in Great Britain, the mixed enterprise throughout the world, and the government-owned corporation in the United States and elsewhere accomplish regulation by this means. Except in the case of the government corporation, the private ownership of properties would be retained when the transfer was made from commission regulation. Nor is there any question that the managements of these enterprises would be much happier than at present because they would then enjoy unity of management and freedom from constant outside interference. In a dynamic economy, the need is to substitute administrative efficiency for regulation. Although regulation coincides with America's views of property ownership, it does not exactly square with America's insistence on efficient and progressive management.

THE ABILITY OF A PEOPLE TO GOVERN

Whether stability can be combined with progress and whether the economic goals decided on by Americans are the right goals or the wrong ones, will depend on the capabilities of the government and those who run it as well as on the comprehension of those who administer the various other parts of the economy. The future relations of business and government, therefore, will depend largely on how rapidly our governmental machinery and leadership can be improved to meet the tensions and challenges of the morrow.

In recent years a more constructive attitude than in the past has appeared toward government even on the part of those who most strongly oppose its interferences. The official journals of business no longer solicit articles on such topics as "A Plea for Inefficiency in Government," arguing that "the best public servant is the worst one." Business has learned that bad government leads to chaos, and chaos to tyranny; that bad government is wasteful and causes high taxes; that good government is essential to economic stability; that the better government is the more responsible it is, and the more responsible it is, the safer are the people's rights and liberties. In short, it is now recognized that governmental interference cannot be prevented by undermining the efficiency of government or by causing people to distrust democratic government. Governmental interference can be reduced only by placing able and responsible people in both industry and government.

Industry, therefore, has adopted a more sympathetic and constructive attitude toward the improvement of government. Symptomatic of the change was a plan to reorganize Congress drawn up by businessman Robert Heller of Cleveland, endorsed by businessmen associated with the National Planning Association, and published by that organization in 1945 under the title, *Strengthening the Congress*. This study had a direct bearing on the actual reorganization of Congress effected by the Legislative Reorganization Act of 1946. It is instances of this kind that cause one to hope that it may be possible to combine a vigorous democracy with a strong and independent economic system.

The internal security of a nation is no more sure than its security from the outside; business credit is no sounder than government credit; the protection of life and property is no better than the law enforcement agencies of government succeed in making it; and the economy is kept in balance largely—but by no means wholly—because of the wisdom of governmental policies. No businessman, labor leader, or farm leader, therefore, can afford to be less interested in the policies and efficiency of government than in his own institutional programs. Appreciation of this is a sure evidence that America is coming of age. It does not alter the fact, of course, that American government is suffering from generations of insufficient public interest and attention, during which the whole thought and effort of the people was turned inward on business and the economy. Government, for the most part, was either neglected or reviled by the wielders of economic power. In consequence, we as a people face a deficiency in this quarter, and institutional effectiveness in government has not kept pace with the rapid increase of domestic and international problems which government is expected to solve.

To discuss all of these matters in the present volume and to suggest possible solutions is not within the realm of possibility. Only the more important areas of government that seem to need attention will be mentioned, therefore, in the hope that enough interest will be aroused to cause further study.

The greatest need, perhaps, is to make government in the United States more responsible so that the people can be sure not only that what they authorize their agents to do will actually be done, but also that unwanted action will not be taken. Enhanced responsibility entails an improvement in the machinery of political parties, elections, representation, and pressure groups—subjects that are interestingly and constructively discussed by Odegard and Helms in *American Politics* and by V. O. Key in *Politics, Parties, and Pressure Groups*. The single greatest requirement, perhaps, is to secure better teamwork and party responsibility in the relations of the legislative and executive branches; here one may read with profit Thomas Finletter's *Can Representative Government Do the Job?* or George Galloway's *Congress at the Crossroads*.

Government is subject to the same forces inducing change that tend to refashion the economy. The machinery of government, therefore, must be periodically reviewed and tuned up if it is to keep pace with the times. In *The Need for Constitutional Reform*, W. Y. Elliott sets forth some of the more prominent aspects that need to be looked into, including simplification of the 150,000 and more separate units of government in the United States and the development of regional governments.

The administrative structure of government carries the bulk of the load so far as programs affecting the economy are concerned and hence the efficiency of the executive branch is a matter of concern. The principal aspects of this problem are dealt with in *Elements of Public Administration* edited by F. M. Marx, and in Leonard D. White's *Introduction to the Study of Public Administration.* These same studies also call attention to the need for improving leadership in government if modern problems are to be skillfully handled.

Power is a pivotal factor in all institutional life, as there have been many occasions to remark in the course of this study, but nowhere is power so omnipresent as in government. Analytical and rewarding studies of this problem are Charles E. Merriam's *Political Power: Its Composition and Incidence,* and R. M. MacIver's recent book, *The Web of Government.*

Pressure groups, political parties, legislative reform, constitutional change, efficient administration, adequate leadership, popular control of institutional power—these are the areas of American governmental life that have been singled out for special mention. Although they are by no means the only subjects deserving of such scrutiny, improvement in these areas would do much to strengthen democratic institutions. More efficient governmental processes would attract better men to its service, lead to more consistent and farsighted legislation, and produce more orderly and effective administration, all of which would do more to stabilize the economy and keep it healthy than any other single factor. One is reminded of the importance attributed to this matter by Ernest L. Bogart, an economist whose natural sympathies and interests would not lead him to overemphasize government's role in the economy. The aim of society, said Bogart,

> . . . is the promotion of the common welfare. Government is a most important and powerful agency in achieving this result, and has positive and beneficent contributions to make. . . . If political democracy and economic liberalism are to survive, it will be because they can prove their capacity to meet the problems of to-day. Government must be admitted as a partner if it is not to be master.

The last part of this statement, at least, is no exaggeration. Furthermore, history proves that sustained efficiency can be the means of preventing violent upheavals because once things get out of order, it requires more of a wrench to put them right again.

SUMMARY

It is the virtue of a mixed economy that it attempts to combine liberty and equality, stability and progress. It avoids the extremes and hews to the center of the road. It is non-authoritarian. Experience everywhere proves, however, that like any other, a mixed economy must define its goals and perfect its methods of business-government coordination if its efficiency is to be sustained and if drifting and depression are to be avoided.

The economic objectives America should seek are maximum employment, maximum production, and maximum purchasing power. To accomplish these purposes will require voluntary but close collaboration by consumers and the leaders of industry, labor, and agriculture acting cooperatively with their government. A form of limited planning is indicated in which objectives will be voluntarily arrived at and execution accomplished by the four economic groups listed above, with government acting merely as intermediary and upholder of the public interest in case of need. These goals should be general rather than detailed, but they must also be as specific as possible, getting into such things as priorities relative to major economic developments. Also to be determined is what standard of living is possible, by major areas of interest, and what standard the country will attempt to achieve. The test of this voluntary program is whether stability can be combined with economic progress and whether the economy remains free and liberal and government democratic and popularly controlled.

The need is to keep the economy on an even keel and to avoid the disastrous effects that new and deeper depressions might have. Among other things, this will require a new type of leadership in all segments of the economy—leaders who are broadsighted and farsighted, who will not choose immediate gain if it cuts off future advantage, who have a sense of social responsibility as well as of team responsibility.

If broad and farsighted goals are to be attained, government must plan its own operations as well as help to plan the economy. This means establishing an Agenda of essential functions and assigning to them an order of priority. The top priority is to create a stable and free environment in which groups and individuals may work. This goal involves a variety of activities in which planning, policy, and stabilization measures should receive highest rating, with regulation, assistance, and direct service fitting into the picture as the strategy requires. But care should be taken that government not attempt to do too much lest it fail to do well the things that are essential.

The cooperative movement imposes no appreciable burden on government and seems to serve the joint objectives of stability and progress. It must, however, be reckoned as part of any public program to establish economic goals, priorities, and coordinating techniques. Subsidies must be carefully scrutinized for their possible disturbing effect on competition and balance in the economy. Government ownership and operation may be undertaken by subordinate agencies and instrumentalities in order not to overburden the central machinery primarily responsible for policy and stabilization. Before such an Agenda and such priorities could be put into effect, however, it appears certain that internal improvements in the operation of government itself would be required.

Regulation is presently the major aspect of the business-government relationship in the United States and it is said to represent the typical American preference for moderation. This is true, so far as property ownership and profit-making are concerned, but there is some doubt as to whether regulation also encourages initiative and unity of management, other goals highly regarded by Americans. Accordingly major regulation might be confined to those areas of the economy where valuation, rate-making, and meticulous managerial oversight are not entailed—as in banking and insurance, for example. Where close regulatory duties are involved, however, as in the public utilities industries, a substitute method of operation and control might be found preferable. In a form of enterprise represented by the British public corporation, restrictions written into the charter obviate the necessity of independent regulatory bodies and give the utility greater freedom and initiative.

Finally, government must be better planned, organized, and administered if it is to aid materially in stabilizing the economy. Government must be made a better planning agency for policy and legislation, must be held accountable for carrying out programs voted by the people, must secure better teamwork between the President and Congress, reduce superfluous governmental units, modernize its machinery of administration and its constitutional structure, and see to it that power is held effectively in leash.

The reconciliation of private and public interest is the most fascinating study in the world. The problem is as old as man and yet it will always remain young in consequence of always being currently involved. The old thoughtless and automatic reaction against government is gradually dropping out of the picture as the reasons for public intervention are better comprehended. It is better to understand *why* government interferes, even though one heartily disapproves, than blindly to inveigh against such action.

"To-day," say the authors of *America's Needs and Resources,* "we undoubtedly place more emphasis on stability and security than we did a generation ago, and less on initiative and opportunity." Our basic individual attitudes and values are said to be changing due to the pressures engendered by complexity. These changes will certainly affect the course of America's economic destiny because in the last analysis it is people who make progress. The challenge to Americans in the last half of the twentieth century, therefore, is to adapt themselves to the cooperative kind of existence that complexity seems to dictate and at the same time retain that vigor of initiative and independence which Americans rightly esteem.

Chapter XXIX

GOVERNMENT AND PUBLIC SERVICE ENTERPRISES

[IT has been long recognized in the United States that those public service enterprises known as public utilities present special problems of regulation and control. Because of their naturally monopolistic character, the close relationship of their services to the public well-being, and the fact that government has conferred upon them its own power of eminent domain, public utilities for years have been subjected to close scrutiny and regulation.

The policy issues which are now before the American people do not, then, revolve about the question of whether or not to regulate the public utility. Rather they concern the most effective means of regulation and the jurisdictions most capable of administering a regulatory program. The problems and issues, both political and economic, that demand consideration in determining the most effective means and jurisdictions for regulating public utilities are extremely complex. Some of the most important are discussed in the following essays.]

No. 104

TECHNIQUES OF PUBLIC CONTROL—AN APPRAISAL OF METHODS [1]

by Robert M. Cooper

WITHIN recent years the public utility problem has assumed an increasingly significant place in the field of political as well as legal science. In certain respects the problem is universal in the sense that it is common to most systems of government. It will suffice merely to indicate that the governments of Great Britain, France, Germany, Italy, Sweden, Norway, and Switzerland, as well as the United States, have, through a variety of devices, recognized the fundamental problems created by business

[1] Robert M. Cooper, "Techniques of Public Control—An Appraisal of Methods," *The Annals* of the American Academy of Political and Social Science (January, 1939), Vol. 201, pp. 1-16. Reprinted by permission of *The Annals* of the American Academy of Political and Social Science. The views expressed in this article are to be attributed to the author alone, and not to the Department of Justice, with which he is connected.

"affected with a public interest" whose services are characterized "by public convenience and necessity."

The basis of the public utility problem, in its political aspect, is the desire to eliminate or control the enormous potential power which these enterprises possess by virtue of natural, social, or economic factors or their privileged position as compared with other, purely private businesses. Since public utility enterprise frequently assumes monopolistic form, either through natural economic circumstances or by direct governmental sanction, its operations lie beyond the reach of the automatic checks and restraints of the free competitive market. Similarly, many other economic principles, such as the law of supply and demand, are more or less inapplicable to public utility services, which are either indispensable or reasonably necessary to large portions of the public. To provide a substitute for these economic forces and competitive restraints, public authorities have been compelled to establish artificial devices for the protection of the consumer, on the one hand, from inferior services and unreasonable rates, and for the protection of the utility, on the other hand, from destructive and predatory practices.

During the past fifty years, both state and Federal governments have attempted to deal with the problem of the public utility enterprise through the increasingly familiar process of administrative regulation. Following a period of legislative hesitation, Congress has finally subjected most public utilities to a more or less constant regulation or control by means of one or more administrative agencies established for that single purpose. It may be said with little exaggeration that the rise of the "administrative commission" has been the outstanding development in the American system of government during this period. For the purposes of this discussion the general pattern of public utility regulation may be concisely stated. The general legislative policies and administrative standards are specifically set forth in the legislation creating the regulatory tribunal, whose duty it is to apply these standards and policies to concrete situations involving the operations of the utility sought to be regulated. Theoretically at least, the administration of these legislative standards provides a ready substitute for the normal checks of the competitive market and supplies a control device to offset the privileged position and potential power of such enterprises.

Following this general pattern, Congress has authorized the Interstate Commerce Commission to exercise extensive control over the rail and motor carrier industries; the Secretary of Agriculture to regulate certain activities of meat packers and the operations of stockyard companies; the Federal Communications Commission to regulate the operations and practices of the telephone, telegraph, and radio industries; the Federal Power Commission to control navigation and regulate the development of water power, as well as the interstate transmission and sale of electric energy and natural gas; the United States Maritime Commission to regulate the operations of water carriers engaged in interstate, foreign, and intercoastal commerce; and more recently, the Civil Aeronautics Authority to regulate the operations of air carriers engaged in interstate and foreign transportation.

It would be misleading to imply that these tribunals are the only Federal agencies exercising a supervisory control over public utility operations, or that such a description represents a complete survey of Federal control of such enterprises. But such a survey, if intended to be inclusive, is necessarily fraught with difficulties. One difficulty arises from the fact that in addition to the agencies just enumerated, there are various other tribunals whose authority and power extend to public utility enterprises as well as other private businesses. In addition to the Department of Justice, such agencies are the Securities and Exchange Commission, the Federal Trade Commission, the National Labor Relations Board, the National Mediation Board, and the . . . Wages and Hours Administrator.

Another difficulty which tends to prevent a more accurate description of public utility regulation by either the state or Federal Government is the fact that the public utility concept is no longer a definite and fixed category into which businesses may be classified with certainty. From a legal viewpoint, the public utility concept has become little more than an attempted rationalization of judicial opinion which has permitted certain types of control in one industry and condemned them in others. With a few noteworthy exceptions, the approach to the public utility problem by local governments has been similar to that of the Federal Government. The vast majority of states have established regulatory tribunals patterned after the example of the more successful Federal tribunals, with more or less extensive authority over the local operations of such industries as electric light, heat, and power companies; gas companies; street and interurban railways; motor vehicle carriers; telephone and telegraph companies; and water companies. Whatever difficulties may be encountered in measuring the precise extent of national and local public utility control, it cannot be doubted that both governments have in the main resorted to the device of administrative regulation in their attempt to meet the problem of the public utility enterprise.

In view of the extensive use of the regulatory commission in this country, it is not surprising to find a growing public sentiment that the process of administrative control is an inevitable device for solving the public utility problem. As a nation, we are rapidly developing a political attitude which accepts the regulatory commission as a permanent institution within the structural framework of our government. Unfortunately, however, this attitude frequently appears to be more the result of habit and familiarity than of rational examination. Before the stamp of inevitableness is placed exclusively upon any particular solution to such a complex problem as that of the public utility enterprise, two lines of inquiry should be carefully pursued. First, how effective is the regulatory commission and what are its outstanding defects? Second, are there any possible alternatives which would in whole or in part eliminate those defects?

In the main, the defects of administrative regulation fall into two classes —those which are minor since they may be corrected, and those which are inherent in the process of regulation. The minor deficiencies need not detain us longer than to observe that such shortcomings as the quality of personnel, the lack of sufficient appropriations, poorly drafted legislation, insufficient jurisdictional authority, lack of initiative and responsibility on the part of commissions, and improperly conducted public relations are matters of a temporary nature which may be completely eliminated by intelligent foresight and experience. Of more vital concern to those interested in the broader aspects of the public utility problem are those fundamental defects which seem to be inherent in the administrative process because of its essential characteristics and objectives. The very existence of these inherent deficiencies represents a serious compromise with the basic philosophy and purposes of the entire scheme of public utility regulation.

From beginning to end, the regulatory process operates in an atmosphere of more or less intense antagonism. In certain respects this is its outstanding defect as a permanent device for meeting the public utility problem. The idea that one group of officials may be set up to check, supervise, and control the commercial operations of another group of individuals without encouraging subterfuge, evasion, sharp practices, and animosity is inconceivable under a system of capitalistic economy. Although this antagonistic attitude is frequently driven below the surface of observation, its presence is none the less real. On the one hand, the regulatory commission is charged with the primary duty of securing efficient, widespread, economical services for the consuming public. On the other hand, the management of the public utility enterprise is forced to concern itself chiefly with securing the highest possible return to the owners of the industry. This is not to say that the regulatory commission condemns the profit motive, or that public utility management ignores the public interest in providing efficient service at low rates. It is clear, however, that the essential purposes of the two groups are socially and economically incompatible if carried to their logical conclusion.

Neither the commissions nor the public utilities have long succeeded in carrying their objectives to the stage of final accomplishment, with the result that the process of regulation has come to resemble more a half-hearted compromise than an effective instrument of control. If the profit motive continues to dominate the desires of public utility management—and there is every reason to believe that it will—antagonism and animosity are likely to grow until the entire scheme of regulation breaks down under their destructive force. While the law has definitely placed the public utility enterprise in the category of public interest for the purposes of public control, these judicially recognized prerequisites of social and economic welfare have had but little effect upon motives of public utility management.

Another more familiar defect of the regulatory process involves a consideration of the controversial subject of judicial control. Relying in part upon the Third Article of the Constitution and in part upon the due process clauses of the Fifth and Fourteenth Amendments, the judiciary has established itself as the ultimate protector of the rights and property of economic enterprise. This essentially American doctrine of judicial superiority has had an incalculable effect upon the process of administrative regulation. There are many who believe that the failure of the administrative process to function more successfully is directly due to unwarranted interference by the judiciary. Through a great variety of technical distinctions and judicial niceties, the courts have subjected the decisions of regulatory commissions to a supervision which frequently destroys the far-reaching advantages of administrative expertness and specialized knowledge presumably possessed by public officials. Judicial supervision has done much to cripple the legitimate exercise of administrative discretion which is the very essence of the regulatory device. There are few practices more disastrous to the sound functioning of the regulatory process than these frequent excursions by the judiciary into strange fields where their tools are antiquated and their knowledge only partially adequate.

Within recent years the courts have become more and more interested in the procedural elements of the regulatory process. The decisions of the Supreme Court in the cases of Jones v. Securities and Exchange Commission and Morgan v. United States are viewed with some apprehension by administrative officials. While it may be true that the techniques of certain administrative procedures are in need of improvement, any wholesale attempt on the part of the judiciary to impose its traditional methods upon the regulatory commission should be met with immediate opposition. Today there is a serious danger that the regulatory commission may become too "judicially minded" to perform its duties in accordance with the accepted standards of sound administration. This danger increases with each attempt of the courts to impose their methods upon the regulatory agency. It should not be forgotten that the rise of the administrative tribunal was in large measure due to the complete inadaptability of traditional judicial procedure to meet the exacting demands of the regulatory process. Although the Chief Justice of the United States was considering other problems of government at the time, his observation that "our government is the most successful contrivance the world has ever known for preventing things from being done" has particular applicability to the growth of judicial supervision over administrative action.

A further inherent deficiency of the regulatory device, intimately related to that of judicial control, is the administrative process of rate making. The problem of controlling rates—and hence indirectly the income—of a commercial enterprise frequently involving hundreds of millions of dollars is a delicate task at best. But here again the courts have imposed such restrictions upon the exercise of the rate-making function that the task has become doubly burdensome. Commencing with the Smyth v. Ames doctrine, limiting regulatory control to the establishment of those rates which will yield a "fair return" upon the "fair value" of the property dedicated to the public service, the courts have developed a bewildering collection of valuation formulae which have rendered intelligent administration of the rate-making authority practically impossible. Placing its chief emphasis upon the "hypothetical" concept of reproduction cost as an essential element of present value, the Federal judiciary has grasped at first one formula and then another, with the result that the valuation problem has become the focal point of public utility litigation. The growth of valuation litigation, in addition to causing serious delays in administration, has confused the regulatory tribunal to such an extent that there has been a positive reluctance to exercise its statutory authority over rates except in the most extreme cases. For this reason, administrative rate making and control has tended to become more sporadic than continuous, more uncertain than scientific.

It makes little difference whether one considers this judicial supervision over the rate-making process as an unwarranted usurpation by the courts or an essential safeguard for the protection of the legal rights of private enterprise. The fact remains that there exists to-day a fundamental conflict between administrative rate control and judicial requirements which has proved detrimental to the sound functioning of the regulatory process.

Another inherent defect in the process of administrative regulation arises from the American doctrine of federalism. The nation-wide conduct of public utility operations has little relation to the constitutional division of powers between the Federal and state governments. Since no state can be considered as an isolated unit, socially, economically, or physically, situations are constantly developing which require the intervention of a central rather than a local control in order to secure uniformity of action. Frequently the Federal Government is without constitutional power to intervene in such matters. In other situations the constitutional power resides in the Federal Government, although the logical solution to the problem would appear to be in the direction of a varying local control.

The ultimate success of any regulatory program is subject to the unyielding principle that the area of administrative control must coincide with the area of commercial operation of the enterprise sought to be regulated. Constitutional federalism is more often than not at odds with this principle. The problem of Federal and state jurisdiction goes much deeper than the mere need for liberal interpretation of the Constitution. There can be no doubt that the Constitution contemplates a more or less well-defined division of authority between the two political entities; but the theory of dual sovereignty is seldom adaptable to the actual operations of the public utility enterprise, whose activities are dictated by economic circumstances rather than the exigencies of political federalism. A possible solution to this difficult problem appears to be in the direction of cooperation between the two governments.

Within recent years numerous experiments in Federal-state cooperation have been undertaken with rather encouraging results. A number of Congressional acts have authorized the establishment of joint boards, composed of state and Federal officers, to administer jointly the regulatory features of national laws dealing with matters of local concern. In other situations Congress has authorized state commissioners to sit with the Federal agency during hearings on matters in which the local authorities might be interested. In a few instances Congress has employed the principle of supplementary legislation, which permits each government to operate within its respective sphere of sovereignty but partially avoids the jurisdictional problem by the formulation of similar legislative objectives. Another more recent method of cooperation is the system of Federal loans and grants-in-aid to local public authorities engaged in activities which affect the general welfare of the Nation. By this device the local agency assumes the basic responsibility of administering the legislative program, and the Federal Government renders financial assistance on condition that certain national policies be made a part of the local program. Despite the increasing application of these cooperative efforts by the Federal Government to avoid the "gaps" of constitutional federalism, its practical restrictions still stand as a serious threat to the effectiveness of the regulatory device.

One of the most persistent criticisms of the regulatory process is its ultimate tendency to divide or separate managerial responsibility. The continuing success as well as the efficient operation of any commercial enterprise depends primarily upon its ability to certalize responsibility and establish a unified management. The regulatory process is at odds with this principle by seeking to divide the responsibilities of management between the administrative agency and the public utility official. It is a mistake to assume that the effectiveness of the regulatory device can be measured *solely* by the extent of interference with the legitimate functions of management. Such administrative intervention, although necessary to effectuate many legislative policies, may act as a barrier to the normal accomplishments of progressive management. When considerations of public interest compel the regulatory commission to share actively in managerial responsibility, there is a grave danger that initiative and elasticity of operation may be subordinated to other, less consequential factors. In many situations the rigidity and inflexibility of administrative rules, due in part to legislative pre-definition and in part to judicial control of discretion, tend to sap the vitality of the regulated enterprise. During the initial stages of a regulatory program, administrative control is normally restricted to certain obvious abuses and evils which have grown up with the industry as a back-wash of unsound competitive practices. These regulatory activities resemble a "house cleaning" of undesirable practices, and seldom approach the realm of managerial responsibility. But as regulation increases in intensity and drives further into the sphere of management, there is a dangerous tendency toward a preservation of the status quo within the industry. When administrative control supplants managerial initiative and responsibility, regulatory standards which were intended to be merely minimal in character and quality tend to become the accepted criteria of public service. Perhaps the process of regulation may be so modified that this tendency to divide responsibility can be eliminated, but it should be recognized that the adoption of such adjustments in the regulatory device may involve a serious compromise with the present philosophy of public control.

One should be cautious in assuming that these deficiencies, fundamental as they are, represent a failure of administrative regulation to solve the public utility problem. Such an assumption would oversimplify the elements involved in an evaluation of such an extremely complex process. On the whole, however, the Federal regulation of public utilities appears to be more a success than a failure. In this respect the vitality of the administrative process has been demonstrated by its practical results. Federal regulation has gone far toward accomplishing its objectives, despite its shortcomings and serious handicaps. The effectiveness of local regulation is much more difficult to measure, because of the many varying factors which accompany the administration of local policies and the lack of reliable information as to their activities. But with respect to both Federal and local regulatory control, one may indulge in some interesting speculation as to how much more effectively the public utility problem could be met if devices not possessing such defects were utilized.

As previously suggested, the regulatory commission is a pre-eminently American method of meeting the public utility problem. Great Britain is rapidly abandoning the administrative commission for what are considered to be more efficient instruments of public control. Among European nations, the independent regulatory tribunal never achieved a position of lasting importance. In view of the more recent British experiments and the general satisfaction with other methods of public control throughout the world, an examination of these alternative devices against a background of American regulatory experience would appear to be most timely. The succeeding discussion of the operation of alternative methods is not intended to be a suggestion that they be utilized in this country in preference to any other system of control. I have no desire to advocate or seek the substitution of any of these devices for the present system of regulation. This discussion is merely a survey of the various methods which have been more or less generally employed to solve the public utility problem; but even a cursory consideration of these new techniques of social control may shed new light on the entire field of government regulation as we are accustomed to deal with the problem in America.

The rise and growth of the cooperative movement is one of the most significant developments in our social and economic history. From a functional aspect, the cooperative is not unlike many other economic organizations established to perform certain commercial or industrial services; but in other respects it is radically different. The cooperative is based upon two fundamental principles—production for use rather than profit, and substantial equality of ownership by the consumers. It is an economic organization which belongs to the people who use its services, the control of which rests equally with all the members, and the gains of which are distributed to the members in proportion to the use they make of its services.

The outstanding success of the cooperative movement abroad, particularly in Sweden, has led to its limited but relatively rapid adoption in this country. Although the American cooperative has been utilized most frequently in connection with agricultural production and distribution, its increasing use in such public utility services as electric power and light, water supply, and telephone is of more than passing significance. The nonprofit and democratic aspects of the cooperative movement tend to avoid the economic maladjustments which inevitably flow from the concentration of corporate power and the separation of ownership from control under a capitalistic economy. In one of his famous dissenting opinions, Mr. Justice Brandeis characterized the cooperative as a device "which leads directly to the freedom and equality of opportunity which the Fourteenth Amendment aims to secure," and further intimated that the rise of the movement represented an advance from "economic absolutism" of corporate domination to the ideal of an "industrial democracy."

As compared with the deficiencies of the regulatory devices, the cooperative enterprise presents some interesting contrasts. In the first place, the cooperative movement eliminates the defects which have their origin in the constant conflict between the profit motive and the ultimate objectives of administrative regulation. The cooperative is operated entirely on a public service basis—with little or no emphasis on the profit element—since consumer and owner are one and the same. The objectives of management, consumer, and owner are identical.

In the second place, the problem of judicial control as well as the cumbersome valuation-for-rate-making process is practically unknown to the cooperative enterprise, since its operations are the result of voluntary agreement between the management and the consumer. In the third place, since the public utility cooperative serves only a limited number of consumers rather than the public at large, and is thus not ordinarily subject to regulatory jurisdiction, the management of the enterprise is free to develop its own commercial policies. In this respect the cooperative is as free as private enterprise to develop the incentives and initiative of progressive management, with the assurance that such operations will not be detrimental to the public interest.

A final observation may be made with respect to the cooperative movement. From a psychological viewpoint, the cooperative acts as a stimulus to representative government by creating a sense of responsibility among the members and broadening their economic outlook. The tendency of the cooperative movement to arouse the public to their rights as well as their duties under a democratic government is a circumstance which has as yet been neither fully realized nor appreciated in this country. Its potential application to the public utility problem is only gradually being recognized.

Another method frequently utilized as a public utility control device is the program of public competition. There can be no doubt that it is an extremely effective method for creating and enforcing adequate public service standards. The theory of government competition has the virtue of going right to the heart of the public utility problem—the absence of competitive checks and restraints. In this respect it is a possible substitute for administrative regulation, just as regulation is a substitute for the forces of the competitive market. Unlike the regulatory device, government competition attacks the problem through the normal avenues of the capitalistic economy. In both instances, government provides the instruments of control, which in one case operate by means of an artificial standard of political authority, and in the other through the familiar competitive channels of commercial enterprise. Under these circumstances it is difficult to rationalize much of the contemporary argument against the use of government competition. It it quite obvious that a program of government competition could be administered with such intensity as to force rates down to the point of confiscation, or with such extravagance as to require unnecessarily high standards of service. But these arguments are hardly valid criticisms of the method per se, since they involve self-serving assumptions and may be applied with equal force to any method of social control, including the regulatory device.

Much of the resentment against competition by public authorities arises from the fact that it necessitates the entrance of government as a trader in the realm of commercial and industrial relationships. While this contention may have some merit with respect to purely private businesses, it seems strangely irrelevant when applied to the public utility enterprise, whose services are predominantly public in character. Certainly it must be conceded that government is entitled to utilize and should use the most effective method at its disposal for safeguarding and protecting the public interest. If public competition is a more effective device than regulatory control, misleading assumptions concerning the "sanctity of private enterprise" should not be permitted to halt its utilization in the public utility field. In any event, the choice between these methods of control is not aided by the characterization of public competition as "immoral," "unethical," or "unfair."

As in the case of the regulatory device, the Federal Government is presumably limited in its utilization of government competition by constitutional restrictions, although here the lines are not sharply drawn. Until rather recently, the commercial activities of the Federal Government were so clearly related to government use and consumption or so closely confined to its territorial jurisdiction, that few questions of constitutional power arose in the courts. The activities of such Federal agencies as the Emergency Fleet Corporation, [and] . . . the War Finance Corporation [(World War I) as well as the office of Price Administration and the Board of Economic Warfare (World War II)] were hardly considered to be indicative of a permanent policy. But it should be noted that the creation of these agencies, even on a temporary basis, represented a conscious recognition of the proper role of government during periods when the economic forces of production and distribution become unbalanced. The public utility problem to-day, as always, is no less real than the general commercial and industrial problem during . . . war.

The two outstanding experiments of the Federal Government with the competitive device are those operations associated with the Inland Waterways Corporation and the Tennessee Valley Authority. The first of these agencies is not so well known, and was established to regulate water carriers and operate a barge line on the Mississippi River in competition with other shipping and railroad enterprises. Although its liquidation has been recommended on several occasions, the corporation still operates as a serious competitive check on the transportation rates not only in the Mississippi Valley but throughout the entire Nation on long distance traffic.

The Tennessee Valley Authority is a more familiar Federal Agency, and a description of its functions need not detain us long here. Established for the primary purpose of erecting dams and hydroelectric plants along the navigable waters of the Tennessee Valley, its operations have been constantly extended into the electric power and distribution fields until to-day its services and rates act as an exceedingly effective competitive yardstick in the power industry throughout the entire Tennessee Valley from Little Rock to Asheville and from Cincinnati to Birmingham. Although the Supreme Court has sustained the validity of certain of these competitive activities by the TVA, the extent to which the Federal Government would be permitted to go in utilizing the competitive device on a wide scale without violating constitutional limitations remains a very much mooted question. It should be noted, however, that many of these constitutional restrictions can be avoided by the method of Federal and state cooperation, previously referred to in connection with the regulatory device. By the system of Federal loans and grants-in-aid to local authorities for the construction and operation of public utility enterprises, the government is in a position to assist in the establishment of the competitive device in areas where it cannot operate directly in the event that questions of constitutional power are raised. The Supreme Court has recently sustained the method of cooperative effort, and there is little doubt that it will be extensively used in the future.

But apart from these experiments in Federal-state cooperation, the competitive device has been most frequently utilized in the past by local governments. Local public competition in the case of electric power, gas, and water supply has proved to be an exceedingly effective method of maintaining high public service standards at low rates in many municipalities throughout the country. But since the line of demarcation between government competition and public ownership in the case of local authorities is at best uncertain, a further discussion of these matters will be reserved until later.

From an administrative standpoint, the utilization of the competitive method as a control device avoids many of the outstanding deficiencies of the regulatory process. Although the spirit of antagonism between the public authority and the private utility enterprise is probably more intense in the case of the competitive method, it does not materially alter the effectiveness of the device as it does of the regulatory process. Furthermore, the problem of judicial control is practically eliminated when the competitive method is employed, since the judiciary does not ordinarily have any power over the operations of public corporations. Due to the fact that the competitive method operates directly through the normal channels of the capitalistic economy, the administrative tendency to interfere with the independence and initiative of progressive management is completely avoided.

From an economic viewpoint, however, the competitive method presents several serious problems. The systematic utilization of public competition results in a duplication of plants and services, the additional cost of which must ultimately be borne by the consuming public. The principle of natural monopoly within limited areas is universally recognized in the case of certain utility enterprises such as the telephone industry. To permit a duplication of services in such circumstances involves an unnecessary waste and destruction of investment values which would ordinarily offset any advantages to be gained from such public control. However, the principle of natural monopoly even in those circumstances should be conditioned by the constant possibility of government competition. The threat of potential competition involves none of the disadvantages previously suggested, but its presence is frequently a decisive factor in the effort to obtain an adequate public service at reasonable cost.

Despite the fact that we live in a country where public ownership is a common spectacle, this method of social control is still considered by many to be the stepchild of socialism, communism, or fascism—depending upon the current political aversion of the writer or speaker. Social action is dictated and controlled by the practical demands of social necessity. Public ownership is one method of dealing with the public utility problem which is frank in its recognition of the true "public service" character of the functions to be performed. A recognition of the public service function entails no compromise with the ideals of democratic government and no unwarranted interference with the prerogatives of private enterprise. Although it is not the purpose of this paper to discuss the merits or demerits of the public ownership program, a brief consideration of the various factors which have caused its adoption in the public utility field may raise some interesting questions concerning its effectiveness as a control device.

The first and most significant reason for the utilization of the public ownership device is the desire to eliminate the profit motive from the management of the public service enterprise. Enough has already been said to indicate the nature of the conflict between the interests of owners and consumers, and that the desire to secure high returns on invested capital is frequently incompatible with the right of the public to obtain indispensable services at fair rates. The program of government ownership establishes a public trusteeship in which the profit motive is subordinated to the public service motive among those responsible for the management of the enterprise. In the past, private management has been conspicuous in its failure to recognize the dominant public interest in the nature of the utility enterprise and the conduct of its affairs. Then, too, private utility operators have consistently ignored the fact that government has made substantial contributions to the industry in the nature of free use of natural resources and public lands, the right of eminent domain, protection from wasteful competition, and even pecuniary gifts and bounties. The movement toward government ownership has received its chief impetus from the constant failure of private management to assume voluntarily this necessary sense of public trusteeship.

A second and equally significant reason for the extension of public ownership is the growing public dissatisfaction with existing service policies and practices of many utility enterprises. Many factors, including the persistent profit motive, have contributed to this failure to provide adequate as well as widespread utility services. Private management is frequently reluctant to extend the market for its services over wider areas unless there is little risk involved in the undertaking. The lack of a definite expansion program by many utility enterprises has virtually isolated large sections of the country from the benefits and conveniences of modern public service facilities. There are many who believe that this restrictive market policy has had a tendency to retard the economic development and advancement of the entire Nation. The failure of the electric power industry to expand its operations into rural areas was one of the chief reasons for the creation of the TVA and its subsequent program of rural electrification. In 1936 only about 11 per cent of the farms of the Nation had access to an electric power system, as compared with 90 per cent in Germany, 50 per cent in Scandinavia, 66 per cent in New Zealand, and almost 100 per cent in the Netherlands. Similarly, the rise of the cooperative telephone company in the West was symptomatic of the unwillingness of private management to expand its market into new areas. Independently of other causes which will be discussed later, it seems rather clear that the rapid growth of public ownership in Western Europe is largely explained by the fact that the people had more confidence in the ability of local government to provide efficient, adequate, and widespread service than they had in private enterprises.

The third reason for the employment of the public ownership device relates to the services performed by those enterprises which have entered an era of declining profitability. In the case of those enterprises where profits are rapidly approaching the vanishing point and new capital cannot be attracted to the industry, government is frequently forced to take over the whole industry or at least some of its weaker units. To-day there is much talk of the Federal Government's taking over the railroads because of their present precarious financial condition. Public authorities were faced with a similar situation when the turnpike superseded the canals, and even later, when the railroads destroyed the profitability of the toll-road ventures. In such situations government must first decide whether the service involved is worthy of continuation. If the service has been largely superseded by more efficient or less costly substitutes, there is no particular reason why it should be perpetuated even under a system of subsidies. On the other hand, if the service is still necessary to the economic or social well-being of the community, government should not hesitate to save the industry from complete or partial disintegration. With the exception of the railroad situation, this aspect of the public ownership program is relatively unimportant to our problem, since its utilization is generally considered to be an emergency device rather than a permanent plan of public control.

A final reason for resort to the public ownership program involves a consideration of the role of government as a pioneer in new and untried commercial fields. Frequently private enterprise is either unwilling or unable to take the initiative in supplying new services or facilities which appear to be necessary to the public interest. Under these circumstances government assumes the burden of developing and performing the service in question. The construction of highways, the provision of educational facilities, the transmission of the mails, and the development of a merchant marine are all examples of pioneering government ownership. Occasionally these enterprises are transferred to private management when they become profitable, but more often they remain under public operation and gradually assume every aspect of a traditional governmental function. It is significant to note that when government assumes the role of pioneer or risk bearer, there is seldom any objection on the part of private enterprise. Yet it must be recognized that the same fundamental principles of public control are involved whether the government operates a postal system or an electric power system; in both cases the public authority is supplying an indispensable service to the public, although for different but equally cogent reasons.

The preceding analysis of the causes and reasons for the rise of the movement toward public ownership would appear to indicate that as a method of control it avoids many of the deficiencies of the regulatory process. This is particularly true with respect to the subordination of the profit motive and the elimination of judicial supervision, especially in the direction of rate making. Public ownership avoids many of the shortcomings of administrative regulation by bridging over the constant clash of conflicting interests—between consumer and investor, between the courts and administration, between managerial initiative and administrative restrictions, and, above all others, between the public interest and industrial individualism.

But from these observations it is not meant to imply that government ownership is by any means the perfect instrument of social control. As a universal method of solving the public utility problem, it carries its own more or less serious deficiencies. As in the case of the competitive devices, future interpretations of the Fifth and Tenth Amendments to the Constitution may prevent the Federal Government from utilizing a program of public ownership as a general method of control, just as a more restricted construction of the Fourteenth Amendment may prohibit state and local governments from employing the same method. Moreover, the transition from private enterprise to public ownership may involve the creation of new problems which have their origin in the traditional shortcomings of government institutions, such as: the lack of commercial or industrial experience; disunity of management due to an excess of democratic controls; external financial supervision; questionable accounting practices; inflexibility of organization and procedure; inadequately managed public relations; and the presence of political influences. Many of these problems, if they exist at all, are remediable and may be solved by the revamping of administrative organizations under the guidance of an enlightened public opinion. Others are more deep-rooted and may involve a fundamental change in the science of government. With respect to these problems the British experiments in the public ownership of public utilities are of vital interest to those who search for new tools of social regulation.

While the Federal Government and various local authorities in this country have been reshaping and improving the regulatory device, Great Britain has blazed new trails in the inauguration of a vast program of public ownership experiments in the public utility field. . . . [This was true even before the recent nationalization. As long ago as 1939 the government owned about]

60 per cent of the electrical distribution; 40 per cent of the gas supply; 80 per cent of the local transport, including trams, railways, subways, and buses; 90 per cent of the water supply; and the entire radio broadcast system. The British program is built around three fundamental ideals or assumptions: first, that responsible administration is superior to regulation as a method of social control; second, that voting stockholders and speculative profits are undesirable elements in the public utility enterprise; and third, that the officials of the public utility are trustees of the public interest. Relying upon these basic principles, two somewhat different but highly effective organizations have been developed to meet these new demands—the public utility trust and the mixed undertaking.

The significant features of the public utility trust are the following: Its organization is corporate in form and monopolistic in character. The stock is held by the investing public, although they possess no voting rights by virtue of such ownership. The earnings of the trust are fixed by statute, being limited to from 3 to 5 per cent of the capitalization, its stock thus assuming the characteristics of a bond with a fixed and guaranteed interest rate. Excess earnings beyond the statutory rate are utilized to effectuate rate reductions. Sinking fund requirements are frequently established whereby the stock may be retired at periods varying from twenty to sixty years. The flotation of additional securities is subject to the approval of the Treasury.

The directors of the public utility trust are usually designated as "trustees" and are appointed by the government. The trustees are selected primarily on the basis of their ability and interest in public affairs, regardless of their political affiliations. It is expected that the trustees will represent and protect the interests of the four groups primarily concerned with the enterprise—consumer, investor, labor, and government. Selected by the trustees, the managerial function is vested in a general manager, who has wide discretion in the organization and development of commercial policies. The salaries of the trustees and the manager are established by statute and are sufficiently compensatory to attract men of considerable ability. The employees are subject to a merit system and only the more desirable features of the Civil Service law.

The interrelation between the government and the corporation is one of the most significant aspects of the public utility trust. The British practice has followed the policy of relative independence by placing the trust in a position of semi-autonomy. The Minister whose department activities are most closely related to the function of the trust is charged with an ex-officio responsibility in relation to its operations and activities. The Minister merely exercises a general power of surveillance and a reserved authority to investigate; he has no power to interfere with the managerial policy of the trust. In these respects the Minister merely acts as an advisory connecting link between the legislative body and the trustees. The outstanding examples of the British public utility trust are the London Transport Board, the Central Electricity Board, and the British Broadcasting Corporation— each of which varies only slightly from the pattern just described.

Although the mixed undertaking has points in common with the trust, such as its corporate form and monopolistic position, the two organizations are strikingly different.

The mixed undertaking is essentially a joint adventure in which government and private investors are joined to conduct a public service enterprise. The ownership, the management, and the profits are divided between the government and private interests, in proportion to the amount of capital each has contributed to the undertaking. The government owns a portion of the stock representing its investment, elects and appoints some of the executives, depending upon the proportion of the investment, and decides controversies arising between government and private directors. In these respects it is a cooperative enterprise in which public and private interests are safeguarded through a series of managerial checks. The proportion of government participation varies in those countries where the mixed undertaking is utilized; in France it is fixed by law at 40 per cent, in Germany it is usually above 50 per cent, and in Great Britain the percentage is dependent upon the type of enterprise involved. But in each instance the government reserves the right to veto any action arising out of fundamental disagreement between government and private representatives. Because of the remarkable success of the public utility trust and the comparative newness of the mixed enterprise, only a few of the latter undertakings are to be found in Great Britain at the present time.

The outstanding British examples of the mixed enterprise are the Manchester Ship Canal, the Southampton Harbor Board, and the Anglo-Persian Oil Company.

A comparison of the relative advantages of these two methods of public ownership gives rise to much uncertainty as to the problem of choice. On the one hand, the mixed undertaking permits government to participate in the operation and management of the utility enterprise with a minimum expenditure of public funds. This circumstance is becoming an increasingly important consideration, particularly where the program is to be carried out on a broad scale. The extent of participation may be varied in accordance with the needs of the enterprise and the public interest involved. As a solution to the American railroad problem, the mixed undertaking presents some interesting possibilities. Furthermore, the organization of the mixed enterprise allows the freedom and independence of managerial initiative which many governmental institutions are said to lack. However, the potential power of governmental veto with regard to matters of fundamental disagreement may serve as a serious check on developments in those directions. Finally, the mixed undertaking offers some unique advantages as an effective method of public control. The representatives of the government are familiar with the details and operations of the enterprise, since they are a part of the organization. Because of this association, government is able to obtain any information it requires, and is placed in a position where it may readily control or supervise capitalization, accounting practices, profits, and earnings, as well as service standards. The potentialities of this method of control will probably be fully appreciated only by the administrative official who has been literally bound, tied, and gagged in his attempt to obtain necessary information from private management.

On the other hand, the public utility trust possesses some significant advantages over both the mixed undertaking and the American public corporation. In the first place, the trust is semi-autonomous; government interference with managerial initiative is reduced to the bare minimum once the organization has been established. In the second place, the elimination of the profit motive effectively removes another source of trouble which could still arise in connection with the mixed enterprise. Finally, it is the only method of public ownership which makes no compromise with the fundamental postulate that the function of the public utility enterprise is predominantly public in character. The sense of public trusteeship is its outstanding characteristic.

By way of conclusion, the following observations may be made regarding the choice of control devices. In America, administrative regulation as a method of public utility control is on trial as it has never been before. Unless the antagonisms and conflicting interests can be eliminated from the regulatory process, the movement toward alternative methods, including social ownership, is certain to be given greater impetus. Private utility management, if it is so inclined, is in a crucial position to make regulation work. The denial of the profit motive as a dominant factor in the operation of the enterprise, the development of a spirit of cooperative effort and understanding between management and the administrative commission, and an enduring sense of public trusteeship—all of these represent the initial steps which must be taken to render the regulatory device an effective and desirable instrument of public control.

The principal lesson to be learned from the recent experiments in public ownership—both here and abroad—is that the effectiveness of any program of social control must depend in the last analysis upon good administration.

The public utility problem, in whatever form it is found, is primarily a question of distributing controls. The locus of ownership is merely an incidental aspect of the whole problem. Government is forced to resort to extreme measures only when its normal instruments of authority are dulled by constant impact with powerful resistance and deep-rooted hostility. When the use of sharper and more effective tools of political authority becomes necessary, new problems of administration and protection are certain to follow. The reconciliation of these new concepts of public interest with the older political ideals of freedom and individual initiative is surely one of the most urgent tasks that face democratic government to-day.

No. 105

THE REGULATORY AGENCY: DETACHED TRIBUNAL OR POSITIVE ADMINISTRATOR? [1]

by James C. Charlesworth

IT was unfortunate that the Interstate Commerce Commission was conceived in a spirit that made it appropriate to name Judge Thomas M. Cooley as its first chairman. A man preoccupied with constitutional limitations would inevitably shape a regulating body into a judicial tribunal rather than into a positive, directive administrative agency. The work of this unit and of the independent commissions subsequently created in its image has never quite recovered from the judicialized procedure that he and his colleagues instituted.

THE IMPLICIT ASSUMPTION OF A TRUNCATED SOVEREIGNTY

It was regrettable that the Interstate Commerce Commission should be constituted as a referee rather than as a manager-regulator, but it was the natural expression of the political philosophy of the period. At that time the doctrine of the limited state and the legal sphere of anarchy for the citizen and especially for the enterprising business corporation was in almost undisputed ascendancy, both in England and in America. The government was a truncated sovereign. It faced the double disadvantage of its own lack of strength and pervasiveness, and the energy, single-purposed leadership, and ruthlessness of the typical railroad management.

This referee concept, as long as it lasted, prevented the development of

[1] James C. Charlesworth, "The Regulatory Agency: Detached Tribunal or Positive Administrator?", The Annals of the American Academy of Political and Social Science (May, 1942), Vol. 221, pp. 17-20. Reprinted by permission of The Annals of the American Academy of Political and Social Science. The footnotes in the original version are omitted here.

positive railroad administration by the government. It was not a separate managing bureau, but the public itself that was to plead the customers' case, and it was not pleaded before the government, but before a detached, stateless, sovereignty-ignoring tribunal. The public and the utility hammered out their argument in an arena of equal combat, and, on the theory that justice can be obtained only in the courts, Cooley and his imitators pretended to build up a case law after the manner of Henry II's trouping judges.

This phase has now happily passed. The new contrition of the courts, the financial plight of the railroads and other utilities, the new sense of dignity and responsibility in the kinetic branches of the government, not to mention the growing importance of military preparedness, have collectively contrived to change the regulator from judge to manager. "Regulation *of* operation" no longer describes the real state of affairs. At this time, regulation *is* operation.

This new state of command unfortunately is not reflected, however, in the typical documentary treatment of the regulatory commissions. In the usual treatise, the emphasis on litigation would persuade one that the principal business of commissions is still that of defining their jurisdictions, whereas the truth is more likely to be that 98 per cent of their energy is being thrown into the application of known law to known conditions.

TYPICAL WRITTEN TREATMENT OF THE SUBJECT

The typical treatment of regulatory commissions in books and journals of political science consists of a historical record of their statutory creation and amendment, an examination of their constitutional relationship to the three sovereign branches of government, a commentary on the independence of their members, and a discussion of whether they currently represent business or the public.

When political science first emerged as a separate discipline in the United States and a body of relevant literature was being prepared by its sponsors, the sources to which they repaired were three: the statutes of Congress and of state legislatures; the opinions of the courts; and the turgid philosophy of the German professors from whom they had just received their Ph.D.'s. Before their successors in the 1920's could depart from this easy and authoritative habit of elucidating first principles, much patient grubbing had to be done. Administrators had to be watched at their daily tasks, party bosses observed, legislators and judges scrutinized in their informal moments—by humble but brilliant souls who wished to find out how the government worked rather than how it was ordained.

Some such second generation of preconceptionless investigators is what is now indicated for the regulatory commissions. Instead of the usual constitutional polemics as to whether a member of a commission is primarily legislator, judge, or administrator, or whether as a Protean executive he is all three, it is now time that we consider how these organizations apply known law to known facts. Our problem is no longer areas of jurisdiction, but areas of positive responsibility. The new desiderata are not litigation and adjudication, but control and prevention. It is true that judicial procedure lays down the boundaries of the subject, but the boundaries by this time are so extended that we may well find enough to do to exploit the interior.

RELATIVE UNIMPORTANCE OF LITIGATION

To illustrate the primacy of the administrative over the litigious aspects of the work of the regulatory commissions, let us look at the latest available report of the Interstate Commerce Commission, the prototype of this species of governmental agency. During the year covered by the document, the United States Supreme Court had decided, with and without opinions, fourteen cases touching on the powers and procedure of the Commission. In eleven cases it upheld procedural orders, and in one case set one aside. In the other two cases it upheld one and rejected one interpretation by the Commission of its jurisdiction. No cases were decided primarily on rate fixing or property evaluation.

There were only two cases, then, wherein administrative decisions were vetoed by another branch of the government. These will get the attention of the constitutional lawyer, or would get it if they contained new principles, but meanwhile 102,164 boilers were inspected, 8,565 of which were found defective. The Bureau of Accounts made 279 general and 18 special investigations. One hundred and sixty-five certificates were granted for new railroad construction, 6 applications were rejected, and 24 dismissed. The Bureau of Finance authorized an issuance of $854,000,000 in securities and authorized RFC loans in the amount of $82,000,000. The Bureau of Formal Cases decided 406 cases and dismissed 117. The Bureau of Informal Cases handled 6,536 letters and authorized refunds in 2,663 cases. The Bureau of Inquiry concluded 43 cases in district courts, obtained 8 indictments, and filed one complaint and 20 informations. The Bureau of Motor Carriers reviewed 9,593 reports. It approved 2,589 applications and denied, dismissed, or allowed to be withdrawn 5,966. Its Section of Complaints disposed of 416 formal cases, and its Section of Law and Enforcement closed 3,545 complaints. Its Section of Traffic reviewed 65,411 motor tariff publications for common carriers and 2,993 minimum rates for contract carriers. It rejected 2,317 schedules. The Bureau of Traffic (railroads) suspended 114 sets of rates, declined to suspend 282 sets, and rejected or allowed to be withdrawn 72 pleas for suspension. To do all this, the Commission uses nearly three thousand employees and spends $8,900,000 annually.

The leading cases involving the formula to be employed in making evaluations for rate-fixing purposes are known to every college senior majoring in political science, economics, or transportation, but how much publicity is given to the fact that, because of a shortage of staff personnel, evaluations by the Commission are two and one-half years to ten years behind the fact, and getting farther behind all the time? Who checks up on things like this?

The plain fact is that our writers who are preoccupied with court intervention in the work of regulatory commissions are not interested in commission regulation at all, but in construction of the powers of Congress.

Just as the best way to keep assessment cases out of the courts is to get good assessors, so the best way for regulating commissions to avoid protracted formal hearings and to escape obtruding judges is to develop a good administration. One shrewd administrative decision might well obviate the dialectic of six lawyers.

EXECUTIVE FREEDOM EMPHASIZED IN RECENT ORGANIZATIONS

Several approaches have been made toward a recognition of the importance of positive administration in the regulating agencies. One of these approaches is a growing awareness of the distinction among the legislative, judicial, executive, and administrative functions of the agency. Thus, the President neglected to name a board for the Federal Alcohol Administration created in 1935, but turned over the responsibility to an administrator in the Bureau of Internal Revenue. In 1937 the President recommended favorable Congressional action on the proposal of the President's Committee on Administrative Management to insert the administrative functions of the independent establishments into the relevant executive departments. Congress declined to do this, but the next year it eliminated separate enforcement procedure for the Federal Trade Commission, and provided that its orders were to be final and that the business corporations acted against must appeal rather than the Commission. Also in 1938 it created a Civil Aeronautics Authority, collegially composed, with an administrator ultimately responsible to the President, and a separate Air Safety Board.

The Bituminous Coal Division of the Department of the Interior, a line unit, now exercises the functions of the abolished National Bituminous Coal Commission. The Fair Labor Standards Act of 1938 is enforced by a Wage and Hour Division in the Department of Labor, and its administrator exercises rule-making powers. The famous Morgan cases illustrate the operation of this principle in the enforcement of the Packers and Stockyards Act. Indeed, early in 1939 the practice of one-man adjudication of regulatory questions was so well recognized that the Attorney General's Committee on Administrative Procedure, in "selecting the agencies for study . . . confined itself to those agencies which in a substantial way affect private interests by their power to make rules and regulations or by their power of adjudication in particular cases," and yet found fifty such agencies appropriate for study.

ADMINISTRATIVE, NOT JURISDICTIONAL, ANALYSIS NEEDED

These developments indicate a tendency to free the hands of the executive from judicial procedural restraints, however, more than they represent an effort to improve routine, uncontested administration. Our next objective in this governmental area should be an examination of the possibility of making administrative practice (and by this is not meant hearings and other quasi-judicial procedure) more efficient and more uniform among the several regulating agencies. Among the questions which could be asked—and answered—might be these:

1. What types of reports from utilities are really necessary?
2. What joint field work can be done by the several agencies?
3. What rules and regulations can be written into a code applicable to all?
4. What forms of action are most effective?
5. What principles of organization are generally applicable?
6. Should reports to the public be made more uniform?

The greatest example of all, to illustrate the effect of a demand by an informed public opinion that emphasis on administrative efficiency supplant considerations of control, is the evolution of war materials production management. When the real war emergency arrived, the Office of Production Management, the Supply Priorities and Allocations Board, the Office of Price Administration, with associate directors and ex-officio Cabinet members dividing the responsibility and slowing the work, were fortunately readily recognized as inadequate, and were succeeded by the hierarchical, unified, nondeliberative, and powerful organization under Donald M. Nelson.

There is good reason for the belief that if we were faced with the same emergency in the regulation of utilities and business as in production of war materials, we should as promptly set about to minimize the adjudicatory aspects of our regulatory bodies and to improve their administrative effectiveness.

No. 106

DEFECTS AND REMEDIES IN ADMINISTRATIVE ADJUDICATION [1]

by Roland L. Redmond

THE regulation of private rights by administrative agencies necessarily includes some degree of power to adjudicate questions concerning the conduct of persons within the regulated field. This function is customarily associated with judicial action, and no aspect of administrative law has evoked more criticism than the methods employed in making administrative adjudications. As this paper is primarily concerned with the process of adjudication within administrative agencies, I propose to review briefly the practices of the several existing agencies and to discuss the nature of the criticisms most commonly made and the remedies which have been proposed. I will leave to others the more difficult question of the extent to which the decisions of administrative agencies should be subject to judicial review.

Few persons realize the number and the variety of administrative agencies now in existence, or the very different procedures they employ in adjudicating matters in their respective fields. The study of administrative agencies of the Federal Government made by the Attorney General's Committee on Administrative Procedure revealed no fewer than twenty seven governmental units currently exercising power to determine private rights and obligations. Some of these units had several separate functions which were discharged by bureaus or suborganizations. If these semi-independent units were included, the total number of administrative agencies would be increased to fifty-one. The heads or subdivisions of the regular executive departments of the Government exercise twenty-nine of these functions, and the remaining twenty-two are exercised by independent agencies or commissions. In addition, all the states and substantially all American municipalities have a number of administrative agencies, so that the total for the entire country can probably be counted only in terms of thousands.

VARIED EXISTING PROCEDURE

The procedure followed by administrative agencies of the Federal Government in adjudicating matters within their scope is likewise very varied.

[1] Roland L. Redmond, "Defects and Remedies in Administrative Adjudication," *The Annals* of the American Academy of Political and Social Science (May, 1942), Vol. 221, pp. 138-144. Reprinted by permission of *The Annals* of the American Academy of Political and Social Science.

It ranges from a determination of a single head of an executive department, who may act with or in certain cases without a hearing as he sees fit, to formal hearings on notice before a board or commission. In the latter case, the administrative determination is usually preceded by an investigation or a preliminary hearing.

The general practice of each administrative agency seems to have been influenced by the fact that prior to 1880 administrative functions were considered as directly related to the executive branch of the Government. Power to regulate certain activities was granted to the head of an executive department, and to implement these regulations he was sometimes authorized to adopt rules; but little thought was apparently given as to whether such rules were legislative in character, although it is now quite clear that they partake more of the legislative than the executive function.

In the last sixty years, and particularly during the First World War and in the last decade, the tendency has been in the other direction, and, with notable exceptions, Congress has inclined to create independent administrative agencies, usually consisting of a board or commission of several persons, and to entrust them with broad power to legislate through the formulation of rules and regulations. This difference has profoundly influenced the procedure of these agencies in the adjudicative field as well as in the performance of their other functions.

The numerous duties imposed upon the independent administrative agencies and the number of instances in which the rights of individuals might require adjudication make it impossible for the entire board or commission to sit as trial judges. Various expedients have been employed to solve this difficulty. In some cases a single commissioner has been appointed to preside at the taking of testimony in adversary proceedings subject to review by the whole commission or by a majority of its members. The most general practice, however, has been the appointment of an individual, usually an employee of the administrative agency, as a trial examiner.

This practice undoubtedly arose in the earlier period when the head of an executive department had perforce to delegate to subordinates the gathering of information on which to base administrative action. It is frequently justified as analogous to the appointment of special masters by courts of equity, and appears to have developed without formal legislative authorization. In any event, the trial examiner is the generally accepted solution which permits administrative agencies to dispose of a large volume of adversary proceedings and still have time to perform their more important executive and legislative functions.

Results of use of trial examiner. There is considerable variety among the different administrative agencies as to the weight to be given to the findings and conclusions of a trial examiner. Some agencies treat such findings as an appellate court would treat the findings of facts of a trial judge. In others, the trial examiner's findings and conclusions are considered as merely advisory and may be entirely disregarded. In the latter case, trial examiners do not feel the same responsibility to rule on the admissibility of evidence, and there is a noticeable tendency to admit all evidence which is offered, even when it appears irrelevant. This leads to voluminous records which are difficult and expensive to review on appeal, increases the length of the proceeding and therefore its cost, and obscures the real issues.

Another consequence of the use of trial examiners is to delay the entry of any order which might be called final or appealable. This may be prejudicial to the individuals involved, since the notice of hearing and the hearing itself may be public, and the findings and conclusions of the examiner may be published months before there is any action by the administrative agency that would give rise to a right of review. The consequences of publicity have become particularly important as administrative regulation has been gradually extended into the domain of ordinary business. The mere report that a hearing will be held on an alleged violation may seriously affect the reputation and the business of the defendant. Greater damage will result if the trial examiner finds the defendant guilty. Nevertheless, months may elapse before the administrative agency, which alone has power to make a final decision, will be able to review the trial examiner's report and publish its decision. If it reverses the trial examiner, the defendant is exonerated, but is left without redress for the damage suffered.

Preliminary investigations. In this connection it should also be noted that a number of administrative agencies have investigatory as well as adjudicative powers, and that even before a trial examiner is appointed or a date is fixed for hearing, the persons concerned may have been summoned to testify under oath at either public or private hearings. These preliminary investigations are usually held in private, even when aimed at a particular alleged violation. In the latter type of case some administrative agencies take the position that no right to a transcript of the testimony exists either in the persons being investigated or in the persons who have been called as witnesses, because the proceeding is supposed to be investigatory in character until charges are filed.

CRITICISMS OF ADJUDICATIVE PROCEDURE

With this cursory review of existing practice, let us examine the nature of the criticisms most commonly urged against the adjudicative procedure of administrative agencies. They may be summarized as follows:

1. Investigatory power unfairly used. The investigatory power is unfairly used as a preliminary to adversary proceedings. This criticism illustrates the confusion which results from merging dissimilar functions in an administrative agency. The right to determine the existing situation and the probable consequences of proposed action is essential to the discharge of the legislative function of an administrative body. For this purpose, it should be able to initiate public investigations which are not adversary in character, in the same manner as committees of Congress. A different type of investigatory power is equally necessary to discharge its regulatory function, which is more analogous to that of a district attorney or a grand jury. These latter investigations should be private until the agency concludes that sufficient evidence of a violation has been discovered to warrant a formal adversary proceeding by means of a public hearing on specific charges.

In granting investigatory powers to administrative agencies, Congress has not differentiated between these two different functions, and there undoubtedly have been instances in which investigations of the legislative type have been used to collect evidence for subsequent adversary proceedings. As pointed out above, publicity has become a very effective instrument of administrative regulation, because of the consequences it may entail to private business. It follows that a public investigation of the legislative type, in which the individual being investigated has no standing as a party and is not allowed to present evidence or to cross-examine witnesses, may represent a very real abuse if it is employed as a disciplinary measure or as a foundation for an adversary proceeding.

2. No bill of particulars. The current custom in adversary proceedings of stating the charges only in general terms and of refusing to give a bill of particulars prevents the accused from preparing an adequate defense. It is usual to charge a violation either in the words of the statute or of a particular ruling or regulation, and it frequently happens that the defendant has little or no idea of the real nature of the charges against him. A bill of particulars is perhaps not so necessary in an administrative proceeding as in a judicial proceeding, because the flexibility of administrative practice mitigates the hardship resulting from surprise. It is nevertheless true that in many instances the administrative agency could, without prejudicing its case, furnish the accused with a bill of particulars that would fully advise him of the nature of the charges.

3. Rules of evidence disregarded. It is common practice in administrative hearings to disregard not only the rules of evidence applicable to court proceedings but even the basic principles which determine what testimony is relevant and admissible. As a result, records of extreme length are not uncommon. Evidence which is incomplete or partly erroneous is admitted, subject to correction. Hearsay evidence is freely admitted, and there have been instances where persons have been allowed to testify as to rumor or gossip. Finally, there have been dramatic instances in which persons have been allowed to testify without identifying themselves, and in at least one instance, a masked witness was allowed to testify over the objection of the defendant.

These radical departures from the rules of evidence are of course exceptions, but they serve to point out the unfortunate tendency of certain trial examiners to celebrate a new-found freedom by making no effort to confine the evidence to relevant and admissible testimony. The problem seems to be one of degree. The criticism might well disappear if the administrative agencies exercised a reasonable restraint in admitting irrelevant or incompetent testimony.

4. *Trial examiners biased.* It is frequently charged that trial examiners are biased and invariably rule against the accused while extending great latitude to their fellow employees who appear in the role of prosecutors. This in many ways is the most serious and the most tangible criticism. With rare exceptions, the trial examiner is an employee of the administrative agency who has worked on other cases with the very men who will present the charges against the individual defendant. This common employment is naturally apt to create a bias which affects his conduct as the officer presiding at the hearing and making the findings and conclusions which form part of his report. Moreover, the report of such a trial examiner is then reviewed by the administrative agency, and its findings of fact, if supported by substantial evidence, are in many cases not subject to judicial review. The same bias which may influence the trial examiner may also exist on the part of the agency. In such a case the administrative agency, either directly or through its employees, may be said to act as prosecutor, judge, and jury.

REMEDIES SUGGESTED

Those who are dissatisfied with the way the administrative process has developed have not hesitated to suggest remedies as well as to criticize. These proposed reforms may be summarized as follows:

1. *Judicial review.* It is said that the decisions of administrative agencies should be subject to review by our regularly constituted courts and that this review should extend to the findings of fact as well as to conclusions of law. As this subject will be dealt with more fully by others, it is sufficient for the purpose of this paper, which is confined to a consideration of the process of adjudications within administrative agencies, to point out two serious objections to this proposal.

In the first place, one of the principal reasons for the creation of administrative agencies was the fact that judicial procedure, however appropriate in criminal proceedings and in the settlement of civil disputes, was inappropriate for speedy solution of the complex questions arising in the regulation of the relations of government and business. Administrative procedure was therefore designed to be more flexible, even if this resulted in depriving the defendant of some of the safeguards accorded him by judicial process. All the benefits of the flexibility of administrative procedure would disappear if it were to be subjected to a complete judicial review.

The second principal objective of administrative law was to supply another defect in the judicial process. Our judges could not be expected to be expert in or even conversant with all the different types of business that might be affected by governmental action. To supply this lack of expertness, it was felt that separate administrative agencies devoting themselves exclusively to one or more subjects of regulation would ultimately arrive at sounder decisions than had been reached by our regularly constituted courts. Complete judicial review would result in superimposing on an expert decision the conclusions of an admittedly inexpert group.

2. Review by special courts. It is proposed that administrative decisions should be subject to review by one or more special courts. This suggestion is not novel. In matters affecting custom duties, patents, and certain internal revenue taxes, equivalent bodies have been in existence for a number of years and have operated with considerable success. There is, however, serious question as to whether special courts could review all matters now within the jurisdiction of administrative agencies. The wide variety of administrative function makes it doubtful whether any single remedy may be appropriate in all cases. A controversy over the correct amount of duty payable upon the importation of goods, or the liability of a taxpayer for income, estate, or other taxes, is more susceptible of determination by the judicial method than such questions as whether an employer has been guilty of unfair practices in dealing with labor, or whether a broker has sought to manipulate the price of a security, or what is the fair price for bituminous coal in various parts of the United States.

This suggestion also involves the serious disadvantage of interposing between the administrative agency and the regularly constituted courts a further special appeal body. The special courts now in existence have disposed of a great volume of litigation very expeditiously, and comparatively few appeals from their decisions have been taken to the regularly constituted courts. They have therefore performed a most useful function; but there is no assurance that this would be true in more controversial fields where large discretionary powers have been delegated and the evolution of administrative policy is an important factor.

3. *Independent trial examiners.* A third proposal is that independent or semi-independent trial examiners should preside at the taking of testimony and that their findings of fact should be given the same weight by the administrative agency as an appellate court would give to the findings of a trial judge. This proposal, or some variant of it, has frequently been made. The most extreme suggestion would create a body of trial examiners completely independent of administrative agencies and, to a certain degree, independent of the executive branch of the government. The appointment of trial examiners who would hold office for a term of years and who would be subject to removal only for cause, might create a body so out of touch with current policy as to render ineffective the work of any administrative agency. Independent trial examiners, whose findings of fact could be set aside only if contrary to the weight of evidence, might be more restrictive than complete judicial review.

There are more moderate versions of this proposal, notably that suggested by the Attorney General's Committee on Administrative Procedure, whereby each administrative agency would nominate the persons to be appointed as trial examiners, but the actual appointing power would be vested in a semi-independent Office of Federal Administrative Procedure. . . .

THE FUNDAMENTAL ISSUE

The controversy over administrative procedure conceals a more fundamental issue. The proponents of the new administrative technique profess to believe that the real issue is the desirability of the economic reforms of the last decade which have been made effective by the administrative process. By this test, all those who criticize the present development of administrative law are labeled reactionaries, and the good faith of their arguments is called in question. This attitude is unfortunate, because it confuses a serious criticism of the means by which economic reforms have been carried out with the merits of the reforms themselves.

Unless these supporters of the administrative process are willing to defend the thesis that the ends justify the means, they must answer the question of whether the present type of administrative agency does not encroach to a dangerous degree upon the constitutional safeguard of the separation of governmental power into independent legislative, executive, and judicial branches. This separation of powers is one of the basic features of our constitutional organization, and it was adopted because history had demonstrated that an unlimited executive or legislative power led to the destruction of the political liberty of the individual citizen. The principle of separation of powers has not always been strictly observed, but as far as the Federal Government is concerned, the exceptions have been sporadic, and until recent years were confined to the field normally associated with executive action. Aside from the temporary powers granted during the First World War to various boards and administrators, there is no precedent for merging into a subdivision of the executive branch of the Government broad legislative and judicial functions.

The speed with which the First World War administrative agencies were able to cope with the economic problems arising out of that emergency undoubtedly suggested that similar agencies would be able to solve the economic problems created by the depression; but there is one vast difference between the problems created by a war and the problems created by economic maladjustments. The first are temporary in character and disappear with the conclusion of hostilities, whereas the second require a permanent solution. In the face of war conditions it may be necessary to forego a large measure of political liberty, but it is at least open to serious question whether a permanent surrender of political safeguards can be justified even to bring about highly desirable economic reforms.

Reformers are notoriously impatient, and the proponents of the economic reforms of the last decade have relied upon the new type of administrative process as the only means of bringing about rapidly those changes in our national economy which they felt would solve the problems created by the depression. They have disregarded, or at least minimized, the danger of granting to the executive branch of the Government such all-inclusive power. Nevertheless, we must remember that the precedent, once established, may be used for quite different purposes. We live in an era of change. We must anticipate that many of our economic and social concepts will be revised, but there is no assurance that the powers of the executive, enlarged by the new type of administrative agency, may not be used just as effectively for reactionary as for liberal purposes.

The real issue, therefore, is the wisdom of destroying one of the great safeguards of political liberty, merely to increase the speed with which economic reforms may be accomplished.

Chapter XXX

GOVERNMENT, LABOR, AND MANAGEMENT

[AFTER the Civil War, the United States rapidly became an industrial, urbanized nation. The West was opened up. Improved technology fostered the creation of great railway systems. The invention of the automobile brought expanses of highways. Great new cities were born. Monopoly organization came to be the form of capitalist production. The number of salaried and wage workers increased. And labor-management relations became a major problem of the nation.

In 1870, 44.8 per cent of the gainfully employed were industrial and other wage workers; 4.8 per cent were salaried workers. By 1950, the percentage in the first class had grown to more than 60 and in the second to more than 20. Thus more than three-fifths of all gainfully employed Americans are now wage workers and more than four-fifths are wage and salaried workers.

As the number of workers has increased, so has the number, complexity and poignancy of labor-management problems. And with more and harder problems to be solved have come added responsibilities for government. To-day government guarantees labor the right to organize and helps it secure equality of bargaining power at the same time that it protects management from unfair practices on the part of labor. It is expected to prevent strikes and lockouts in institutions and industries whose services and products are considered vital to community welfare. It is, in short, playing a role in labor-management relations undreamed of 70 years ago.

Reaching as it does, down into the pocketbooks of workers, across picket lines and through the briefs of corporation counsels, the government has been—and continues to be—attacked from all sides for the way it handles labor-management problems. Its critics may be understandably prejudiced. That they should be uninformed, however, is inexcusable and dangerous. How many of us, for example, know what a "yellow dog" contract is? What about the Mohawk Valley formula, primary and secondary boycotts, closed and open shops, lockouts and injunctions? Few of us know why we think labor organizations are good or bad. Few of us know why labor is or is not well organized. Few of us have considered what the proper role of government should be in relation to labor on the one hand and to management on the other. Yet we have to know about these things if we are to be informed critics. The following articles will help.]

No. 107

LET'S LOOK AT LABOR [1]

by William H. Davis

THE duty of labor and management in a democratic society is to perfect the democratic process within the field of production. Government's duty to workers and to management is not to interfere with the
development of such processes, but to promote it.

The democratic principle is rooted in persuasion. It was Plato who first
declared that the creation of an orderly world is the victory of persuasion
over force. From this it follows that the enduring progress of mankind
implies a continuous succession of such victories; that any resort to force
means at least temporary defeat. As A. N. Whitehead has put it, "The
worth of men consists in the liability to persuasion. They can persuade
and be persuaded by the disclosure of alternatives, the better and the
worse. . . . The recourse to force, however unavoidable, is a disclosure of
the failure of civilization, either in the general society or in a remnant of
individuals." The Declaration of Independence affirms this principle when
it declares that "governments derive their just powers from the consent of
the governed."

The duty to bring labor relations into line with this democratic principle
lies at the very heart of the problem that confronts our industrial life to-day.
Democratic ideas reached their fullest development in the thoughts and
writings of western civilization during the revolutionary period at the end
of the eighteenth and the beginning of the nineteenth century. As the
industrial revolution developed during the nineteenth century it was particularly in this field of labor relations that liberty, equality and fraternity
were most conspicuously absent. No one can fail to realize the importance,
therefore, of practical and resolute action to make the democratic principle effective in the relations between the employers of this country and
their workers. But what does this mean in practical terms?

First, the use of persuasion in labor relations calls for equality of bargaining power. Without such equality persuasion is at once driven from
the field by force. In the United States there has been, within recent years,
a real advance in the understanding and acceptance of that basic fact. Industrial relations commence with the individual worker and his employer.
In this simplest form of bargaining the individual worker is obviously at

[1] William H. Davis, "Let's Look at Labor," *The Survey Graphic* (February, 1939)
Vol. 28, pp. 106-108. Reprinted by permission of *The Survey Graphic*.

a disadvantage. The beginning of equality of bargaining power is the organization into a bargaining unit of workers in a single plant. Organization of workers for concerted action has been bitterly opposed by powerful interests in this country, even as recently as the years following World War [I]; but it may be said that to-day such concerted opposition is a thing of the past. Indeed, the recognition of the workers' right to self-organization, by the people of this country and by their government, has deeper roots than some people seem to think.

The right itself is one aspect of our fundamental civil liberties: freedom of assembly and freedom of speech. It was recognized as early as 1901 by the Industrial Commission appointed by President McKinley. In Theodore Roosevelt's administration it was recognized by the Anthracite Board of Conciliation in 1902. It was accepted by the War Labor Board under Mr. Taft during Wilson's administration. During the Coolidge administration it was incorporated by Congress in the Railway Labor Act of 1926. It was referred to as "not to be disputed" by Mr. Justice Hughes, speaking for the Supreme Court in 1930. During the Hoover administration it was affirmed in the Norris-La Guardia Anti-Injunction Act of 1932 and in the Interstate Railways Bankruptcy Act of March 3, 1933; and during the . . . [Roosevelt terms] it . . . [was] incorporated in the National Industrial Recovery Act, the Amended Railway Labor Act, and in the Wagner Act.

It is clear that this right of the workers to organize for collective action is in no way limited to a single plant or locality. It is a right that has no limit of place, purpose, or extent, until it comes into conflict with the equally fundamental rights of others or with the common welfare. The extent of union organization is, therefore, a thing that lies primarily within the choice of the workers themselves; and whatever opposition remains to the extension of organization beyond the limits of a single plant or company is no longer based upon denial of the right, but rather on arguments of expediency. It has no power to stop the wider extension of unionization.

But when the workers in an industry have spread their organization beyond the individual plants to cover a competitive area, and still further when national or federated unions are formed, the balance of bargaining power shifts from the employer to the workers. As a mere matter of self-defense, employers in turn have to combine. The history of trade union movements in this country and abroad shows that the organization of employers, initiated in each case as a defensive measure, may follow either the path of opposition to, and concerted action to break down, organization of the workers; or it may follow the path of collective dealings with the labor organizations.

Choice of the first path has led to violence and continued conflict. This is inevitable under a democratic government, which lacks the power to put down the conflict that arises when a free people are interfered with in the exercise of rights they hold "unalienable."

The second path—organization of the employers as well as of the workers for collective bargaining on an industry-wide scale—has led, on the other hand, in the democratic countries abroad and in some industries in America, to stabilized and satisfactory labor relations. This development represents the maturity of labor relations in a democracy. It is the final balance of equality of bargaining power between the parties. Any step beyond it introduces governmental regulation with a corresponding departure from the democratic principle of persuasion.

Collective bargaining on this scale is vastly different in character and results from the narrower bargaining between an individual employer and his own workers. For collective bargaining on this wider scale the organization of the workers, as of the employers, must extend beyond the individual plant or company. Either by industry-wide organization or by federation or other common action of the different unions in an industry, the organization of the workers must be at least as wide as the extent of the industry within the competitive area. In this fact lies the possibility of a practical solution of all those disputes (nearly one half of the total number of labor disputes in America) that flow out of the efforts of the workers to build up strong labor unions and the opposition of the employers to such organization efforts.

The wider scope of bargaining, with its accompanying need for a wider scope of organization, leads to an understanding and acceptance on the part of the employers of the value of strong and stable unions, capable of carrying out the agreements they make and able to maintain throughout the industry the standards agreed to by the associated employers. This enables each associated employer to know with certainty what his labor costs will be during the term of the agreement and so reduces the danger of competition from rival producers operating on a lower wage scale. Readily available evidence shows that this general extension of trade unionism has substantially eliminated inter-union disputes and has reduced to insignificance the question of the closed shop. There is also abundant evidence that collective bargaining on this scale, which because of the numbers of men and the magnitude of the interests involved carries with it a peculiarly heavy responsibility, leads to the orderly conduct of the negotiations leading up to the basic agreements or their modifications, and almost always to a peaceful outcome of these negotiations. In addition to this, agreements negotiated on this scale commonly provide for settlement of any disputes arising under them without resort to strikes or lockouts, thereby minimizing that final cause of interruption of the productive process. In short, this matured system of industrial relations is one in which the democratic principle of persuasion is fully applied and which by its clearly recorded achievements, as in Great Britain and Sweden, has demonstrated its practical value to both employers and workers.

Labor and management have a community as well as a diversity of interests, and as citizens they have interests beyond their bargaining with one another. And the bargains they make have their own effect upon the general welfare. That sound, mature industrial relations lead on to a nation-wide confederation and cooperative action on the part of both employer organizations and labor unions is clearly shown by the history of the labor movements in democracies abroad. In Great Britain, for example, the British National Confederation of Employers Organizations and the Trade Union Congress have become integral parts of the national life. They are consulted by government not only in regard to labor legislation, but in many matters affecting general economic or social conditions. The government looks to these bodies to settle by conference all problems of industrial relations that affect the general welfare; and in turn they serve as an agency for control and stabilization of industrial relations. Through them the desirability of avoiding mass conflicts that arouse hostile public opinion is impressed upon the employers' associations and labor unions, thus giving to the opinion of the community the ultimate power of control that is proper in a democracy.

What is the duty of a democratic government toward such a matured system of industrial relations? The hallmark of democracy is economy of coercion, and a democratic government should not interfere with the working of any established agency of collective bargaining unless and until the bargains concluded adversely affect the general welfare. But the government may usefully carry on activities supplementing and reinforcing the activities of employer and union organizations. Thus the government may properly provide agencies for voluntary mediation and conciliation, with established panels of trained arbitrators who may be brought into a dispute at the joint request of the contending parties; and experience has shown that the government should have a recognized power to set up, in industrial disputes of outstanding public importance, boards of inquiry with power to investigate the issues and make findings of fact and recommendations, but without power to impose their recommendations. Compulsory arbitration has been tried over and over again in England and on the Continent, but always with unsatisfactory results. It is plain, from the evidence, that compulsory arbitration so distorts the processes of persuasion that they become practically useless.

It seems clear, therefore, that the duty of government toward such a matured system of industrial relations as has been described, is to refrain from all interference with the bargaining processes, limiting governmental activities to wholly voluntary assistance.

But the duty of a democratic government may be quite different from this, where industrial relations are in the adolescent stage in which we see them to-day in most American industries. Experience shows that trade unionism in a weak and struggling condition tends to increase the number and bitterness of industrial conflicts, and that it is in the earlier stages of organization that charges and counter-charges of provocative action, intimidation and coercion are most frequent and most troublesome. In this country, as in every democracy, intimidation or coercion by violence or threats of violence is prohibited by the general law under the police powers of the state. There is no apparent reason for any legislation specifically forbidding such activities in the field of labor relations.

It is, however, quite clear, although it is sometimes overlooked, that an employer has, with respect to his employes, a unique power of intimidation and coercion—the power to promote and demote, to hire and discharge. No doubt such authority must rest ultimately with the employer, but, like other forms of power, it is subject to abuse. It may be used by the employer to interfere with the worker's freedom to discuss wages and working conditions or to meet with his fellow workers for such discussion. This constitutes a direct attack upon the worker's basic civil rights of free speech and free assemblage, and the coercion may be as real and tyrannical as was ever true of the abuse of political powers that brought about the revolutionary establishment of these civil liberties. Even if the employer does not abuse this power, the worker's fear that he may lose his job, or that he may be discriminated against, fundamentally restricts his freedom of action. It is this situation that has led to the prohibition, in our National Labor Relations Act, of any interference by employers with the free exercise of the workers' right to organize. A parallel situation led to the passage of similar legislation in Sweden in 1936, when Swedish employers, despite the established recognition of trade unionism among industrial workers, showed a disposition to interfere with the organization of white-collar employes.

The nature of the prohibitions in the National Labor Relations Act [and subsequent legislation] is such that they will become a dead letter if and when employers cease to interfere with the organization of the workers; but until that occurs these special protections are justified by the fact that the employer has a special power, possessed by no one else and not covered by the ordinary police regulations, to coerce his employes.

It is clear from the very nature of the democratic principle that the entire value of collective bargaining may be defeated—it may be turned from an instrument of service into an instrument of oppression—if democratic principles and procedure are not maintained within the bargaining organizations themselves. Monopoly or monopolistic practices in associations of employers or in associations of workers is always a matter of public concern. It should be noted, however, that such practices, including what we call "labor racketeering," call for agreements behind closed doors. The wide scope of maturely developed collective bargaining affords a very real protection against them, since the greater the number of persons involved in an agreement and the wider its extent, the more difficult it is to maintain it upon, or bend it to, unlawful or unsocial practices.

This brief review omits all discussion of the economic factors involved in labor relations. They are important elements in the effect of the collective bargains made between the employers and their workers, but they have no bearing on the validity of the proposition that democratic principles should be applied in labor relations. As thus simplified, it appears that the common duty of labor, management and government in this country is to encourage the growth of organization and collective bargaining to that mature state in which, in every important industry, basic standards of wages, hours and working conditions are negotiated by national unions or groups of unions with industry-wide associations of employers.

It is easy to state broad general principles, to quote the Bill of Rights in support of them. But the test of our philosophy of government is whether it can be made to work in controversial fields. Beyond tolerance, patience, understanding, the democratic duty toward labor demands deep-rooted faith in persuasion as the only weapon democracy can use in the struggle for sound industrial relations—the only weapon it needs.

No. 108

THE FUNCTION OF GOVERNMENT CONTROL IN LABOR RELATIONS [1]
by Glenn W. Miller

LABOR PROBLEMS AND ATTEMPTED SOLUTIONS

WHEREVER people work for a living, labor problems will arise out of the job relationship of employers and workers. Labor problems develop from irritating job situations, for which workers or employers or

---

[1] Glenn W. Miller, *American Labor and the Government* (New York: Prentice-Hall, Inc., 1948), pp. 3-24. Reprinted by permission of the publisher. The footnotes in the original version are omitted here.

the representatives of each cannot find a mutually satisfactory solution. In many instances, labor and management find themselves in conflict over the allocation of the joint product that each is to receive, over hours of work, hiring and layoff practices, seniority policies, dispute-settling procedures, and many other points. Such conflicts do not mean that employers and workers cannot work together effectively; their existence does mean that there will be many differences, arising from these divergent interests and points of view, that may tax the abilities of both factions and sometimes those of appropriate agencies of government before arrival at solutions that are acceptable to both of the parties directly concerned and to the public.

Although problems will arise wherever people work, the relative importance and complexity of individual issues varies with different industries, phases of the business cycle, geographical locations, types of economy, and other factors. For example, seasonality of unemployment is more pronounced in construction than in retail food distribution; unemployment is a serious problem during a depression but almost non-existent in a period of war prosperity; and economic insecurities such as unemployment or dependent old age are perplexing problems in a capitalistic society but may be less troublesome in a governmentally controlled economy. Again, the labor problems that plague an agricultural economy will give way with industrialization to different but probably more complex problems.

Thus, at any time, and in any economy, there arise a diversity of irritating situations that have been termed labor problems. In an economy with a large degree of individual freedom, there are three approaches to a solution for these problems. Employers, working alone or in groups, try to promote solutions that are to their liking and in their best interests. Workers, often acting as a group through their unions, urge action to their liking. Very frequently, the two directly interested groups are in conflict; if they cannot reach a solution or if they reach a socially undesirable one, it is the necessary and proper function of government—federal, state, or local—to take steps necessary to protect the interests of the public and the economically weak groups in society.

It is the purpose of this volume to examine the nature of, the principles underlying, and the limitations on governmental intervention in the field of labor relations. However, before turning to this subject, it is necessary to note the basic assumptions on which the treatment rests and examine briefly the interests of workers and employers and the conflicts that arise between them.

The basic assumptions on which the following discussion is founded are:

1. The present type of government, although not perfect, will continue

in the United States, and under it the protection of certain constitutional rights of individuals and the continuation or increase of the responsibility of government to the people will be paramount aims.

2. A "free enterprise," profit-motivated, economic system will continue. However, under a system of free enterprise there is need for some government restrictions to protect public interest, as in the regulation or prevention of monopoly. In some instances, such measures may not sufficiently protect public interest, and provision by the government of certain essential services, such as postal service or police or fire protection, may be necessary. Therefore, "free enterprise" should be considered to be a relative term that does not preclude government controls or services provided by the government, but does assume that these be kept at the minimum compatible with public welfare.

The attitude and interests of labor center around the fact that the workers' well-being is closely tied up with the sale of their one marketable resource, labor power. To complicate the problem of labor relations, the labor power of the worker is inextricably tied up with his everyday life. He cannot sell his labor without selling a part of his life as well. For that reason, the conditions under which work is performed are important. For example, poorly lighted, heated, or cleaned work places, inadequate provisions for eating, antagonistic attitudes and practices of supervisors toward unionization, or insufficient worker participation in determination of policy may bring unrest, high turnover, low output, and the like—in other words, labor problems. Thus it is that working conditions are very important to workers, to employers, and to the public. And thus it is that much space is devoted in union agreements and in state and federal legislation to the establishment of satisfactory conditions of work.

Probably more important to workers than the physical conditions under which the job is done is the price at which labor is sold. There is an almost continuous pressure on the part of workers for higher wage rates. In the opinion of workers, higher wage rates mean better living and the possibility of savings to provide an economic cushion for the time when sickness or other unexpected emergencies arise. It does not worry the average worker that economists cannot agree on whether higher wages, working through increased demand for goods, mean a higher level of economic activity or, on the other hand, through the causing of higher costs and higher prices, more danger of economic collapse. To the worker, in the short run at least, higher wage rates are almost universally desirable. Since the demands of workers and unions are usually in excess of the amount employers are willing to pay, the subject of wages consumes much time in union-employer discussions and occupies an important place in every union agreement.

Here, again, government intervention, in the form of controls of wage rates to be paid, has become very important.

There is another basic factor to be noted in trying to understand the attitude and policies of labor, organized and unorganized. An ever-present fear and disturbing condition is the insecurity of the average worker. This insecurity may be uncertainty of a steady job, physical risks involved in the work, the prospect of dependent old age, or a combination of a number of these elements. Much of the philosophy of labor, especially organized labor, can be traced to the omnipresent consciousness of insecurity. High wage rates offer an opportunity of savings, home ownership, and similar factors that may mean more security. Seniority provisions offer a greater degree of job security to older workers. Shorter hours of work are thought to provide a thinner spreading of the available work, thus combating unemployment. Restrictive rules applying to apprenticeship or union admission are methods of keeping the supply of union men in a favorable relationship to the jobs that are anticipated. The desire for safer working conditions is another manifestation of the same fear, although it is directed toward a different type of insecurity; so also is the general support by workers of social security legislation, providing a measure of governmental aid for periods of unemployment and for dependent old age. Probably no one factor is so important to an understanding of much of the attitude of workers as is that of the insecure position which they feel is theirs. To understand the frequently adamant stand taken by a union on some point at issue with an employer, worker insecurity, one of the outstanding characteristics of our capitalistic economy, must be kept in mind.

Accompanying these drives and interests that influence the general attitude of labor is the assumption of many workers and most union leaders that their interests are in conflict at many points with those of management. Workers are of the opinion that their interests and desires are not those of management, that they often will prove unacceptable to owners or managers. This attitude is implicit in the very existence of labor unions. Organizations of workers are formed to force consideration of demands even when there is opposition to the union position. Such a philosophy is not new; it showed itself in the form of unions before the start of the nineteenth century. That the aims pursued by unions were in some respects in conflict with those of employers was shown in employer appeals to the courts for assistance and in court rulings of the early nineteenth century holding union action to be a conspiracy to harm employers. The same philosophy was stated by the Supreme Court prior to 1900. In *Holden v. Hardy* the court held, in supporting certain state labor legislation, that the interests of "proprietors" and "operatives" were "to a certain extent, conflicting."

Coupled with the assumption of a conflict of basic interests is the realization that the bargaining power of workers acting as individuals is not equal to that of employers. This fact is especially true as mass-production industry brings larger and larger establishments in which the individual worker becomes of relatively smaller importance to the employer. Large scale business organization and the frequent occurrence of absentee ownership create a gap between owners and workers so that there is less chance of a mutual understanding of the problems that each faces. In addition, with the gradual decrease in the skill of the worker as jobs are broken down and machine methods and simple manual operations developed to replace more highly skilled manual operations, the worker has less to distinguish himself. The more highly skilled or trained a worker is and the smaller the size of the plant, the more individual bargaining power he enjoys. This assumption of unequal bargaining power underlies the organization of labor unions. A group acting as a unit has power, but a similar number of individuals acting separately has little coercive ability.

The interest and attitudes of employers are frequently in sharp conflict with those of workers. To employers, labor is one of the factors of production which they must combine with others to produce a salable product. The end goal is sale of the product at a profit, and low wages per unit of product are a means toward that end. Because high wage rates are so important to the worker, much conflict emerges over this issue. Employers in search of a low labor cost per unit of output desire a low wage, or, if forced to pay relatively high wages, a high level of output. To a considerable extent employers are inconsistent with their own practices when they expect high-level production from workers. Since a limited amount of product may offer the greatest profit, employers may find high production by limited numbers of workers more desirable than full-scale output.

Although the division of the joint product, that is, determining the amount that goes into wages and into the return to management and ownership, is the most common and highly publicized point of conflict between labor and management, there are many other irritating issues. Such questions as hours of work (clearly related to earning), seniority policies, methods of settling grievances, and numerous other problems arise from time to time to show the frequent divergence of labor's and management's aims.

Many of the conflicts that develop under a capitalistic economy arise out of the fact that workers or employers or frequently both are subject to economic forces beyond their control. For example, cyclical fluctuations are a force too large to be controlled by an employer. In trying to run a business during a depression period, the policies followed may bring up problems such as the adjustment of wage rates, spreading of work, or policy to be followed in layoffs and rehirings. During such a period, unions will be urging their policies in matters such as the above and also trying to maintain their membership and protect their members' interests, while employers will be trying at the same time to maintain profits, if possible, and if not, to minimize losses. Conflicts may ensue over the action that should be taken, but it may be that neither party is directly responsible for the problems at hand.

THE REASONS FOR GOVERNMENT INTERVENTION

It is clear from observation that the differences in the aims of workers and employers are so numerous and basic that a strict *laissez-faire* policy on the part of government is not practical. With conflicts inescapable and where one of the contestants is markedly weaker than the other, the weaker may be faced with a "take it or leave it" choice. In the past, and in many employments at the present time, this has meant that worker groups have been at a disadvantage. With the relatively strong development of unions in some industries the reverse situation is now and then found to be true. Whatever the relative bargaining power of the parties to the labor contract, it is necessary for government to provide protection for the weaker.

The position taken above is in conflict with the frequently voiced opinion that industry will, if left alone, conduct its affairs in a socially desirable manner. Neither the inherent benevolence of management nor the regulatory hand of competition brings socially desirable practices on a widespread scale. It is clear that a balancing of the bargaining power of labor and management by means of labor organizations or the intervention of government is necessary to control the action of many employers and make it conform to socially desirable standards. The situation also develops, on occasion, that a well-organized and powerful union acts in an anti-social manner. While many of the restrictive practices of unions can be understood and some can be defended, when the power of a union is used anti-socially it should be controlled as is that of any other group.

Even when bargaining power is relatively equal, government intervention may be needed. The struggle between two equally powerful organizations of labor and business may cause public hardship. A long and bitterly contested labor-management dispute may disrupt or stop production of necessary or highly desirable commodities. Even though the dispute is finally settled on a somewhat equitable basis, the public, labor, and management may have suffered unnecessary losses. Here, again, government intervention is socially desirable.

Thus the justification for the evolution of a body of government controls in the field of labor rests on the assumption that *laissez-faire* in economic relations frequently does not result in the greatest social good. Rather it results in exploitation of the weak by the strong or in costly strife that is harmful to workers, employers, and that vaguely defined body called the public. If these unsocial results be the product of labor disputes, it is the duty of government to do everything in its power to remove the conditions giving rise to labor-management friction and encourage settlement of disputes. However, for government to forbid strikes or other overt forms of labor disputes is not compatible with our democratic form of government, unless the prohibition is accompanied by provisions that will ensure more just solution of employer-employee problems that can no longer be settled by a test of bargaining strength. Even if such a policy were to be embarked upon, it would be defensible only in those instances where a work stoppage would cause immediate hardship to the public, as would be the case if public utility or hospital employees were to stop work. Government machinery to function in appeal cases would be difficult to establish and its functioning might well be unsatisfactory. Any departure from freedom of the right to strike is a threat to our way of life, although sufficient irresponsible action may make such a step necessary.

The entire basis of government labor controls can be seen to rest on a denial of the social efficacy of *laissez-faire*. If that theory of government relationship to economic life is denied, the question arises of how far to travel the road of government control, and in what direction. How much control can be exerted on economic life while still retaining a basically free enterprise, capitalistic economy? Every control that is enacted to limit or direct the free action of business or labor is a step away from our eulogized free economy. However, a certain amount, perhaps an increasing amount, of control is inescapable in the interest of public well-being. There is no clear line of demarcation between the field of permissible control and the area that must be left for free economic action. The division that is generally acceptable now is not the same as might have been acceptable twenty, or fifty, or one hundred years ago. And changing economic and social conditions will bring changes in public attitudes that may sanction an entirely different division of fields of action at some future date. There are, therefore, no set areas of government control and free private action that are permanent in any way.

The most important questions regarding governmental economic controls are whether they are directed at promoting social well-being and whether they are compatible with a democratic society. For almost any control measure, some parties insist that the traditions of the American type of economy, that is, a profit-motivated, privately owned and operated capitalism, are being violated. The fact remains that government enactments curbing the predatory activities of individuals by limiting the freedom of some to act as they choose offer to economically weak groups more freedom than they otherwise could realize. Complete equality before the law is not compatible with effective democracy. Some persons or groups have more bargaining power and ability to pursue their own interests than others. Equitable treatment may demand that the powerful be subjected to controls that will protect the weaker when there are conflicts of interest. Equal treatment before the law might prove to be markedly inequitable treatment. Judicious use of controls to protect or help the weak and inept, on the other hand, is requisite to effective democracy among groups of individuals with different degrees of intelligence and of social and economic power.

It must be recognized that government controls do not affect all persons similarly, for controls in most cases do not specify action or behavior that all persons must follow. Rather, minimum standards of behavior are set and persons are free to do as much better than the minimum as they choose. A minimum-wage law, for example, setting a . . . [seventy-five-cent] minimum per hour simply specifies that wages of less than . . . [seventy-five] cents cannot be paid, but any rate above that may be paid; any employer paying more than the minimum loses none of his liberty thereby, but one desiring to pay less than the minimum is denied that freedom. Again, a law requiring that employers bargain collectively with representatives of their workers does not affect the person who is already bargaining with his workers. Government controls thus affect adversely only those persons whose behavior is below the standards set. It is the person whose actions are below a socially desirable par that suffers; it is surprising that so many tears are shed on his behalf.

The above must not be taken as implication that all government labor controls are socially desirable or in the best interest of labor. In fact, . . . the bulk of legislation favorable to labor and tending to control employers' action has come since 1930. Prior to that time, the absence of labor legislation and the application to labor of enactments not intended as labor laws were harmful to the interests of workers. In many cases the force of public opinion and the pressure of business groups was sufficient to make the controls contrary to the interests of labor and to build in the minds of many union leaders a long-standing distrust of government controls. The application of the anti-trust laws to labor unions is a pertinent example.

The view has been taken above that government actions are necessary to protect public interest or the weaker party where direct negotiations fail to bring socially desirable solutions to labor problems. But what are the functions which government action should perform? What are the mal-adjustments for which solutions will most likely be needed from time to time? One need is the establishment of minimum standards of wages, hours, and conditions of work. Without standards being set to specify minima, many wage rates will be far below the figure requisite for adequate family support, even with full-time work. Moreover, if wages are not adequate for family support, the public, through charity, government relief, high rates of illness, unrest and dissatisfaction, crime, and so forth, will be burdened. In the past, even into the 1930's, the hours of work required have been longer than an equitable distribution of work, health conditions, or citizenship and family obligations would permit. Also, safety and health and other conditions on the job are often unreasonably low when minimum standards are not required. Such standards probably will be of little direct benefit to unionized or highly skilled workers in our economy, since they have sufficient bargaining power to guard their own interests. But for those whose skills or ability or organization do not give them the bargaining power necessary to protect their own interests, controls are necessary. Also for the public, which will suffer from the results of unduly low wages, long hours, or unhealthful working conditions, government intervention is impera-tive.

Controls are also necessary to protect the economically weak. Women and children have held, traditionally, a relatively weak bargaining position. This fact has played an important part in the willingness of legislators to enact protective legislation on matters like wages and hours for women and children long before they were willing to extend similar protection to men. Women and children have been in a weak bargaining position for at least two reasons. They are usually employed in relatively unskilled jobs and they have generally been outside of unions, sometimes by preference and sometimes because of union policy. For women, still a third factor may be worth noting: many of them look upon gainful employment as temporary, a prelude to marriage, or to tide the family over some financial difficulty. If a job is temporary, there is less incentive to be a hard bargainer.

Generally speaking, the unskilled are the workers who have least bargain-ing power, since their duties are not such as to distinguish them or make it important that any one or any group be kept because of special skill or ability. In addition, in the past the unskilled also have been, in most industries, the less effectively organized. For these reasons they will need protective legislation more than skilled workers. Such workers may need at least two types of government help and protection: first, wage and hour controls, and second, laws establishing minimum standards of employment. In addition, they needed in the past protection of their right to organize to protect or promote their own interests. Many employers have objected or still do object to organizations of their workers. Without intervention by the government, many persons who were most in need of organization found it impossible to associate in unions with other workmen. There are good reasons to believe that without government protection of the right to organize there would still be, to-day, many unable to join unions freely. Even with the strong protection in the National Labor Relations Act, many were not allowed free choice in joining unions.

The question may arise as to whether or not intervention guaranteeing to weaker persons or groups that which they could not gain unaided violates the rights of the economically stronger who are forbidden to do as much for themselves as they could do without controls. Probably it is true that the bulk of government labor controls appearing between 1930 and 1945 tended to establish protections for the economically weak. But in a democratic society the aim of the government must be to promote the greatest good for the greatest number of people. To protect the rights of one person, or group, at the expense of larger numbers of other persons is not compatible with democratic principles underlying our society. There are, it is true, limits to the extent to which the rights of minority groups can be subordinated, but there is no clear line of demarcation to follow on this question. Moreover, any division that is considered to be justifiable at one time and under given circumstances may, at another time and under other circumstances, be inapplicable.

GOVERNMENT CONTROLS ON COLLECTIVE BARGAINING

Another function that should be performed through government controls is facilitation of the settlement of disputes between labor and management. It is emphasized, however, that government intervention should not be countenanced unless a dispute cannot be settled by direct collective bargaining; controls should not, and cannot, in a democracy, take the place of direct bargaining between workers and their employers. Governmentally imposed settlements of disputes leave a residue of dissatisfaction and unrest. An excellent example of this fact is the nation's experience with quasi-compulsory dispute settlements during World War II and the widespread labor trouble after the war.

Although arbitrary settlement of disputes by government authority is incompatible with democracy, facilitating the successful conclusion of collective bargaining is highly desirable. It is obvious that industrial disputes are costly both to the disputants and to the public. Therefore, government, which should exist for the benefit of the governed, should take whatever steps are compatible with the maintenance of individual liberties to lessen the number of disputes and to encourage the settlement of those that do occur. For this purpose, however, no one policy will be applicable to all industries at any one time or to one industry at different times. For example, there is no similarity in the public interest involved in work stoppages in a public utility and in a cosmetic factory. Public interest does not demand that the same policy be followed in dealing with disputes in the two types of firms.

Again, it does not seem reasonable to adhere to the same policies with regard to dispute settlement in an emergency that are followed under less pressing circumstances. During both World Wars the policy of our government was, of necessity, much more stringent than preceding policies. Settlement, whether amicable or not, was demanded and in most cases secured. However, when the emergencies ceased, wartime policies became less defensible.

Another reason for government labor controls is to prevent racketeering and other irresponsible activities. Much discussion following World War II centered on the need to curb the irresponsible acts of unions. There is some basis for such argument. The unfortunate fact is, however, that, in the opinion of a majority of the middle and well-to-do classes and of legislators, there is a dual standard of behavior. Certain actions by business, such as holding goods for higher prices, are good business practice. However, when workers engage in comparable action and withhold labor for higher wages, much of the public insists that such action is anti-social and should not be allowed. In Professor Commons' words, "Restriction of output is practiced by both, but in one case it seems 'natural' and therefore right, because there is no profit; in the other case, it seems arbitrary and therefore wrong because it places a limit on national wealth."

Despite the fact that there is a dual standard of behavior set, there are many instances of union or employer action that are unjustifiable. The make-work policies of some unions can hardly be justified as anything more than a rather selfish interest in their members only, if the practice is viewed from the standpoint of society as a whole. Likewise, various practices of business cannot be defended.

While government controls are defensible in many instances, the double standard referred to makes such controls dangerous to the organized labor movement. It is so easy for legislators, administrators, and members of the judiciary to put into controls their own economic and social predilections that organized labor has traditionally entertained a strong and abiding mistrust of controls. This has been especially true of the American Federation of Labor and its member unions, whose policies and philosophies were well-set long before the Franklin Roosevelt administration ushered an era of pro-labor legislation by administrators and a hierarchy of courts sympathetic toward the new trend in government controls. Many of the newer unions do not share this point of view. The relatively young member unions of the Congress of Industrial Organizations have leaned heavily on political action and government controls to reach some of their objectives. Whatever the attitude of unions or employer groups, government action to forestall racketeering, and especially selfish action of any relatively small group, is a valid and necessary sphere of control.

GOVERNMENT ASSISTANCE IN MEETING ECONOMIC INSECURITIES

A final area of government labor control is the very broad and significant one of helping individuals cope with some of the insecurities that are so characteristic of our society. Some of these controls are directed at preventing the occurrence of the undesirable situations and others at easing the effects of the insecurity once it is present.

The insecurities that characterize our economy include unemployment, dependent old age, and physical risks of accident or occupational disease. To a considerable extent, they are a product of our economy. Unemployment and much of the dependence of age, for example, would not be problems where goods were produced and disposed of on the basis of a need for goods rather than the profit to be made from the production. On the other hand, in that kind of an economy, other problems, such as the maintenance of individual liberties, might be much more inadequately settled than in our type of economy. Thus, to say that certain problems are a product of a certain type of economy, such as that in which we live, is not to criticize ours as being worse than others nor to imply that the problems found are more numerous or more complex. It only points out the peculiar difficulties that are present or threaten to appear. The problem is to find controls that will lessen or ease the effects of certain insecurities in the economy but through measures that preserve, or change slowly, the basic organization of society. Considerable changes probably will occur over a period of time, but the great advantage is that they will come gradually and with neither violence in their introduction nor repercussions.

If it is correct that the object of economic controls is to eliminate or contribute to a solution of problems without changing the economy basically at any one time, there are limits on the action that can be taken. If a basically capitalistic economy in which the primary drive is profits is to be preserved, we cannot require of business actions that a relatively uncertain economic future will not warrant. For example, it would not be practical to require all employers to provide their workers a guaranteed annual wage. Some industries are relatively stable, but in others there are so many uncertainties beyond the control of the businessman that such a guarantee would be difficult if not impossible of fulfillment. Consequently, much of the legislation that seeks to provide security of income or employment calls for government assistance to private business or for outright government performance. As will be shown later, the attack of the 1930's on unemployment included direct government employment programs, plans to encourage greater private employment, and very strong pressure to encourage the passage by states of unemployment compensation laws financed by employers. A similar mixture of programs can be seen in government policy on many other problems. The unfortunate fact is that usually the government does not plan ahead adequately, but rather develops programs piecemeal to meet the most pressing problems. It will be seen that as a result of the fact that government controls are largely a result of pressures exerted by politically minded groups and have been developed piecemeal to meet particular problems, the government control program is quite inadequate in many respects.

Where controls are imposed in an effort to minimize the hardships of certain insecurities the problem of maintaining the basic economy is less complex. While not all programs laid out by government can be effectuated by private businesses without putting an impossible drain on their economic ability, many of them are practicable, especially when all competitors are treated alike.

The opinion has already been stated that it is impracticable to require all employers to provide guaranteed annual wages. The broad extension of such security seems outside the power of individual employers in many industries. However, there is experience to prove that some of the hardship of unemployment can be alleviated in our economy by the widespread development of unemployment compensation. The former measure calls for the elimination of an insecurity, and this seems beyond the ability of business— in so far as entire work forces are concerned; unemployment compensation, however, is not directed at elimination, but rather at the easing of the ill effects of the insecurity. Thus it seems clear that the more we try to eliminate insecurities rather than alleviate them, the more the bases of the economy must be affected. And the more basic the change, the greater the opposition to the change.

THE AREAS OF GOVERNMENT CONTROLS: FEDERAL

Before beginning an analysis of the background and provisions of current government controls, it is desirable to survey briefly the extent to which controls now apply in the field of labor relations. Many persons feel that social controls of business began very late in the United States and have developed slowly. However, the philosophy of a right to control business activity for the assumed best interests of society showed itself in the levying of tariffs and taxing of state bank notes before the twentieth century. And the passage of the Sherman Anti-Trust Act in 1890 indicated somewhat the same policy. These early developments were only the forerunners of a movement that was destined to grow much stronger.

While social controls of business came slowly in the United States, a great number of controls now influence the economy. Probably the days of strict *laissez-faire* have always been more of a fable than a fact. Even in the nineteenth century, tariffs and government subsidies were common. *Laissez-faire* meant to most pressure groups of the nineteenth century an absence of government controls that would be harmful to business. Legislation or other government policies to aid businessmen, however, were quite compatible with the prevailing theory of government's relation to business. For these reasons, it seems more accurate to say that the day of little or no social control of business is well past. Nevertheless, the philosophy of "leave business alone and it will put its own house in order" is still very strong. This attitude, coupled with a strong post-World War II swing toward economic conservatism, may become even stronger for short periods, but the trend, if we are to maintain a democratic society, must in the long run be toward more ready acceptance and widespread application of controls that promote the interests of the general public. A policy that respects and protects true economic and political democracy demands a definition of the proper sphere of business activity and the relationship of government to industry sufficiently flexible to change with changing economic conditions and needs.

An examination of current labor legislation will serve to show how far the nation has moved into the area of government control of economic matters. This control is a mixture of federal, state, and local legislation, of administrative policies and judicial attitudes. Since World War I, federal legislation has assumed especial importance; state legislation has long been more important than local. Because federal legislation has become so important it will be surveyed first.

Wages and hours are problems that have caused numerous conflicts between workers and their employers. Until the twentieth century the long-standing practice of this nation had been to leave the determination thereof to the contestants. As this policy was gradually abandoned, the states began first to determine minimum wages and maximum hours for women and children, who were deemed less able to care for themselves than were men. Due to numerous weaknesses in such legislation and to adverse court decisions, this narrow coverage on a state-wide basis did not prove to be an adequate type of regulation. Consequently, the federal government began to experiment with wage controls, at first for children and women, and at a later date for men, women, and children in certain occupations. Early attempts ran afoul of adverse opinions by the Supreme Court, so it was not until 1938 that legislation meeting the approval of a majority of the Court was finally enacted. This approval probably resulted more from a change in the philosophy of the judges of the Supreme Court than from a change in economic conditions or in the content of the legislation.

The right of workers to organize and bargain collectively has been an extremely bitter point of debate in the United States. To a rather large extent, employers and the public have regarded unions and union activity with suspicion. However, with the precedents of labor policy applied in the First World War and of experiments with railway labor policy, the federal government now attempts to guarantee to many millions of workers, if that is their desire, the right to organize and bargain collectively with their employers. Here, again, the earliest attempts at such a guarantee met with judicial disapproval, and even after that hurdle was cleared many workers were exempted.

The fact that labor disputes are numerous and costly is a common-place. Generally, open disputes with work stoppages are most likely to occur in a period of prosperity, especially one with the economic dislocations of rapidly rising prices and a tight labor market. Although the largest number and most expensive of stoppages occur under such circumstances, there are numerous disputes all over the nation every day in the week. Recognizing this fact, the federal government long has been active in resolving disputes that seem incapable of settlement by the parties directly concerned. Since the establishment of the Department of Labor, the services of professional labor relations conciliators have been made available in case of significant labor disputes. In addition, the federal government has set up special machinery to assist in reconciling disputes on the railroads or airlines of the nation, and other federal representatives do much unofficial work in promoting the settlement of disputes.

Both major wars that the United States has fought in the twentieth century have brought a very great increase in the number and intensity of disputes. Therefore, during both wars, special agencies have been created to supplement existing dispute-settling services. These have done their wartime jobs, and in both instances have been disbanded shortly after cessation of hostilities. Both, using pressures and policies that could be forced through under the patriotic fervor of war, found their effectiveness reduced by attitudes of unions, employers, and the public immediately after the wars.

Another field of federal control is that of attempts to decrease the economic insecurities of modern life or to ease their effects once insecurities have appeared. Uncertainties as to job tenure, a reasonably comfortable and independent old age, physical risks and the occurrence of sickness of the wage earner or his family, as well as fluctuations in tax levels, price levels, and so forth, make the worker's life very insecure. Although complete security cannot be expected as a result of any government policy, and complete security may not even be desirable, any widespread improvement in the degree of security will have to come from government action or action by business induced by the government. Therefore, an adequate degree of social security demands a government program. The federal government did not move into the field of social security legislation until it became apparent that state programs were developing so slowly and with such widespread variations that they were not adequately meeting the problem. The federal program of unemployment and old age security is relatively new, being largely a product of the 1930's.

Federal attempts at regulation of child labor met with a number of rebuffs, through adverse court decisions and the refusal of the states to ratify a constitutional amendment enabling the federal congress to enact child labor regulations. State legislation regulating child labor was common, but the wide variations in the laws and their administration brought the first attempt at federal control in 1916. However, it was not until 1938 that a federal child labor law of broad coverage was enacted which was allowed to stand by the Supreme Court. Federal regulation of child labor in covered occupations is now a part of the law of the land.

The authority of the federal government has been extended in still other areas. Railway and other interstate transportation workers are the subject of considerable legislation. In addition, labor conditions required of government contractors have exerted an influence by serving as a yardstick. Also, agencies of the government propose sample legislation that may affect the type and content of state legislation. Finally, the labor policies of the government toward its employees and those in effect in the District of Columbia will have an influence on the legislation of lesser political areas.

From this summary it is clear that the federal government now has legislation on the statute books that influences the economic well-being of the majority of the people. In the field of labor problems and labor-management relations the controls are relatively new, but they are likely to continue and to be expanded.

THE AREAS OF GOVERNMENT CONTROLS: STATE AND LOCAL

In addition to the increasing amount of federal legislation, there is in every state in the union a great variety of laws that affect labor relations and labor problems. While these laws are less important, relatively, than they were prior to 1930, they are still very significant because some fields of labor regulations are left entirely to the states, and, in other instances, workers who do not come under federal legislation must look to state enactments for protection.

For example, the bulk of the safety legislation of the nation is the product of state legislatures. Most workers are employed under safety conditions set or influenced by state legislation. Provisions normally pertain directly to health and safety conditions such as ventilating devices, access to fire escapes, provisions for drinking water, and cleanliness of the work place.

In a similar vein, all states have enacted workmen's compensation laws, which provide that if a workman is injured on the job he shall be paid certain weekly benefits for time lost and medical benefits as well. In addition, such laws provide set allowances for permanent disabilities, such as the loss of a member or function of the body, and a considerable number of states provide benefits for persons injured by occupational diseases as well as by accidents. Such legislation actually has resulted not only in the provision for medical and monetary benefits, but also in much more safety consciousness than would otherwise have been the case.

A number of states have enacted legislation dealing with collective bargaining rights and duties and with the settlement of disputes. These laws have attracted more attention than their number would seem to warrant. However, since they tend to be much less sympathetic to labor than recent national legislation of the 1930's, it is possible that some of the state laws may have served as examples for more restrictive federal laws in the first session of the conservative 80th Congress.

Many states have enacted anti-injunction laws, some being passed prior to the federal legislation, but a number being put on the statute books after the federal law in order to exercise control over state courts similar to that imposed by the nation's Congress on federal courts. Thus, the net result is that, through federal court restriction and the restrictions by state legislatures, the use of court injunctions against labor during industrial disputes is widely controlled. However, the issuance of injunctions under specified conditions is not prohibited, but careful stipulation of good injunction practice is made.

To every worker the wages and hours of his employment are important. Although the federal government succeeded in 1938 in putting on the statute books wages, hours, and child labor legislation that bore successfully the scrutiny of the Supreme Court, up until that time little successful regulation had been accomplished even by the states. The constitutionality of governmental determination of minimum wages was long in doubt, final court approval coming in 1937 in the third significant case appealed. At the present, state wages and hours legislation serves as a supplement to federal legislation in protecting some groups not covered by national controls. If state governments so desire, they can set higher standards than federal law and thereby affect workers under the jurisdiction of federal controls. However, they cannot undermine national regulations by setting lower standards.

A very wide area of state labor regulation is that of child labor. Federal controls of child labor were denied by the Supreme Court until the late 1930's. This general field of legislation includes a wide range of controls of wages and hours, safety conditions, school attendance, time of work, and other matters. State controls in this area have met with relatively little objection by the courts.

There are, of course, other labor regulations by state governments, but the preceding pages serve to indicate the general fields of state control and the expansion of federal regulations. In a like manner, the state has surpassed local government as an important source of regulation. The day of the relatively isolated community that could handle all labor problems on a local basis is past. Many, probably most, of the important issues that confront labor cannot be settled adequately by local policies or controls. However, the attitudes of the local police and ordinances on such subjects as public assembly, fair employment practices, settlement of local labor disputes, and the like, give the policies of local governments considerable importance.

COURT ATTITUDES AND GENERAL CONSIDERATIONS

The foregoing summary statement of the function and the nature and extent of current labor controls . . . points up the fact that our economy is affected continuously at every turn of the road by government regulations. Labor relations, wages, hours, working conditions, rights of workers, child labor, and dispute-settlement plans are either determined or affected by government action. The economy is far from one based on *laissez-faire,* and, although there will be shifts from time to time in government policy, the tendency probably will be toward a greater degree of social control of industry.

Not only have long strides been made in the extension of legislative controls, but another facet of government control also has changed markedly. The courts of the nation have shown a significant change in attitudes. Since 1935 the Supreme Court of the United States has validated many pieces of legislation that unquestionably would have been ruled invalid a few years ago. Justice Brandeis attributed to the courts as long ago as 1921 "a better realization of the facts of industrial life," which shift may have figured in the changed court attitudes of the 1930's. However, it seems more reasonable to attribute the change in Supreme Court rulings to the change in the membership of that body. It is doubtful if the members of the courts changed greatly in their understanding of "the facts of industrial life," but certainly court appointees of the late 1930's were more likely to be liberal in their economic attitudes than were most of their predecessors. If this be true, then the liberalization of the courts came from new members on the bench more than from new thinking by the veteran judges.

Whatever the reason for the change in judicial attitudes, the shift made possible much of the governmental regulation in labor relations that has just been summarized. For it is the courts of the land, and in the final analysis, the United States Supreme Court, who determine what controls may and may not be administered. Prior to 1935, the interpretations and rulings of the Court were instrumental in holding back many socially desirable pieces of legislation. Undoubtedly . . . the courts had solid technical grounds and precedent cases on which to base their decisions. There is no question, however, that in many instances a different ruling could have been handed down and bolstered by precedents.

It is clear that there is no longer a question of whether or not there will be legal controls in our economy. Governmental guidance or control is certain to continue. Despite this fact, certain questions do arise as to the extent and nature of the controls. One important problem is that of whether there should be an expansion or easing of controls; there is not the same need for guidance at all times and some flexibility is necessary. This need for flexibility is due largely to the fact that the extent of regulation is dictated largely by economic conditions. Economic collapse in depression periods, or the emergency of war, for example, bring a demand from many that governmental direction be imposed. With these demands, or lessened objection, legislative changes are likely to come about, since the great majority of all legislation is a result of the pressures of special interest groups.

If economic controls are inevitable, what should be the nature of the controls, from what source should they arise, and what effect will they have on the nature of our economic and political life? The controls that can be exercised may come either through judicial interpretation and application of the common law—the legal customs and traditions of our society—or, to some extent, from improvisation by administrators using existing legislation that does not adequately fit the situation in question. To some extent these stop-gap measures must always be used, since it is not possible to have legislation that meets all problems that arise.

Even though the contents of the statute books are placed there in many cases as the result of pressures exerted on legislators, legislation seems to be the most desirable form of control. Guidance coming from the common law and from administrative ruling is a product of the thinking and prejudices or opinions of one or a few persons. Such control is less democratic and less representative of the public than is that springing from the elected representatives of the people, despite the weaknesses that exist in our election process. There is an especial danger involved in relying too heavily on the common law. It is based on precedent, and the persons applying it are looking backward for means of dealing with current problems. Experience is not valueless, but the nation cannot progress by looking backward for cues as to how to conduct itself in dealing with current economic problems. At least some of the persons who have a part in shaping our legislative guides must have an eye to the problems of the day and of the future.

The conclusion should not be drawn that the courts do not have a function to perform. That function, and a very important one, is to interpret statutory enactments and determine whether the legislation is consonant with the Constitution of the United States. But the application of common law where no legislation exists amounts to lawmaking by the courts, a function which they should not perform, and one which, if performed, is not so representative as when done by the legislative bodies. Consequently, to maintain as great a degree of democracy as possible, the greatest portion of necessary controls should come from legislatures and the federal Congress.

What will be the effect of economic controls on our economic and political life? Must democracy and capitalism disappear with the increase in the area of control? The danger of losing the essence of our way of life increases with the extension of controls. But it is also true that without controls, and probably an increasing amount of controls, the danger is as great or greater. On the one hand, controls may take away the right to vote, or to worship according to one's own convictions, or to go into business, or to join a free labor union. The world has seen such controls in Fascist nations. On the other hand, so little guidance and control that the economically and politically powerful are allowed almost complete license may result in the less powerful losing many liberties. Neither extreme is in keeping with the avowed political and economic belief held in the United States.

The basic problem of economic controls—in so far as this study is concerned, labor controls—is in ensuring that the controls are as democratic as possible. We must keep and improve our democratic elections, broadening the suffrage to groups now unable to exercise their right to vote. We must do more to teach the public, by every available means, the political and economic issues at stake and the alternative methods of handling them. Then the representatives of the people must provide the rules of government needed to promote the interests of the public. And finally the controls must be dynamic. Conditions do not remain static; legislation must not remain so either. A piece of legislation that is perfectly logical and necessary at the time of its enactment may be greatly out of step with the needs of the public ten or fifteen years later.

Chapter XXXI

SOCIAL SECURITY

[IN America to-day, nearly everybody is for social security. Few people, however, know exactly what they mean by "social security." In fact, even experts who have formulated definitions do not agree on what the term implies.

In the article below Mary Ross dips into history to show how the shift from an agrarian to an industrial economy has affected the needs of Americans. She gives us, in short, the rationale of the Social Security Act of 1935. But what of the future? "There are trends affecting social security that I view with alarm," writes Prof. Edwin E. Witte in the second article. "I am particularly concerned," he explains, "because there is such hazy thinking about social security and what may properly be expected from it." He contends, for example, that it is a perversion of the concept of social security to look upon it as being primarily designed for the control of the business cycle, to insure full employment, or to redistribute income and purchasing power. "Its effects in these respects should be considered and discussed," he says, "but should not overshadow its major objective—the protection of the individual and the family against the immediate economic hazards confronting them." Without maintaining these protections, he warns, "the hope of fundamental remedies for economic ills is but illusory."

Prescriptions for that most crippling of all economic ills—unemployment—generally have called for ministering at a national level. Though the selection from the book by the W. E. Upjohn Institute for Community Research does not deny that national measures are the ones most likely to influence the level of employment, it points out that there are many steps which can be taken in any local community. In this book, *Full Employment in Your Community*, the first chapter of which is reproduced here, there are refreshing ideas for simultaneously strengthening our democracy and assuring Americans of some of the security for which they clamor.]

909

No. 109

WHY SOCIAL SECURITY? [1]

by Mary Ross

THE musket over the fireplace once stood for security in American homes. It meant game for the pot. It gave protection against unfriendly beasts and Indians. It was a first defense against hunger and danger in the new land.

Probably no families in the world ever have been as self-reliant as the Americans who wielded their muskets in the Colonies and on the frontier. They literally made their own living, for a family had little or nothing except what its members could do and make. A large family was an advantage, since then there were many hands to plant and weed and harvest, to chop wood, to carpenter, to spin and dye and weave, cook and sew. A widow with children was a matrimonial prize.

Our Thanksgiving celebrates the security of the colonists. Our turkeys are the descendants of the wild turkeys their muskets brought down; our cranberries, of the cranberries they found in the bogs. Our pumpkins, potatoes, and onions still commemorate the good harvest the Pilgrims gathered in 1623.

For 250 years and more many American families, like the first colonists, measured their security in terms of the things they could make and do for themselves. As the frontier stretched westward, covered wagons carried with them the habits and ideals that had conquered the wilderness at Jamestown and Massachusetts Bay.

Now automobiles plunge in days over the trails that a scout on horseback or a wagon could travel only in months, and airplanes cross the continent in a single hop. The ways in which American families live have changed as swiftly as the ways in which they travel.

Within the lifetime of people still living, the frontier has all but vanished. Change is so obvious that we are likely to take it for granted. It has come so quickly that it is hard to realize what it means to us who live to-day. . . . The following pages . . . outline some of the changes that have brought us to days when we reach for a pay envelope, not a musket, to get our food and protect our homes.

[1] Mary Ross, *Why Social Security?*, (Washington, D. C.: United States Government Printing Office, 1945.)

WORK MOVES TO THE CITY

As late as 1890, more than a third of the Nation's homes were on farms. Country families are bigger than city families. Hence it was not until 1920 that the census found a greater number of people in the towns and cities than on farms and in villages. To-day the farms have only about a fifth of the homes and less than a quarter of the population. In hardly more than a generation we have ceased to be predominantly a nation of country people.

Boys and girls left the farms because the road of opportunity led to the city. Not so many hands were needed on the farms. Machines were taking over work that muscles once had done. Science taught more efficient ways to use the land. Up to 1870 the farms had more than half the Nation's workers, not counting children. By 1940 they had less than one in six.

Farm efficiency has grown rapidly in recent years. Production per acre increased nearly 20 per cent between 1910 and 1930. Production per worker increased 40 per cent.

Young people from the farms went into the factories and mines. They helped build the railroads and the cities. There seemed no end to new jobs in the rapidly developing Nation. From 1870 up to 1910, each census found a larger percentage of the population "gainfully occupied."

As factories turned out more goods, more people were needed to sell them and to finance the making and selling. Since 1900 literally millions of men and women have found jobs in these fields—as salespeople, stenographers and clerks, telephone and telegraph operators, wholesale and retail dealers, bookkeepers, cashiers, and accountants, insurance agents, commercial travelers, stockbrokers, and bankers.

And as invention and science multiplied the output in one field after another, more of our energy could be turned into jobs which have to do with services, rather than things. There has been a growing number of restaurant and lunchroom keepers, janitors and elevator operators, barbers and manicurists, doctors, dentists, and trained nurses; of librarians, teachers, and other public servants; actors, authors, and artists; lawyers, chemists, and technical engineers.

Some of these added jobs represent services which families formerly had done for themselves at home. Others reflect our rising standards of living—more and better education, better health, more leisure, greater comfort and convenience in daily living.

MAKING A LIVING AND MAKING MONEY

The life in all these many occupations differs in one way from that of the farms where once most Americans made their living.

To-day we do [not] make a living. We buy it. We make money, and that money mostly determines the kinds of houses we live in, the food we eat and the clothes we wear, the security and independence we look to in hard times, sickness, and old age.

Even in the Colonies, of course, some things were bought and sold. Paul Revere was a silversmith as well as a soldier. But the colonists used money chiefly to buy the luxuries of those days, such as Paul Revere's porringers, or fine furniture, or tea, coffee, and spices.

Many Americans lived as did a New England farmer who wrote in his diary:

> My farm gave me and my whole family a good living on the produce of it and left me, one year and another, one hundred and fifty dollars, for I never spent more than ten dollars a year, which was for salt, nails, and the like. Nothing to eat, drink, or wear was bought, as my farm produced it all.

On the farms of our grandparents where soap and candles were made and hogs butchered for the smokehouse, a family still made a considerable part of its living without using money. Even to-day, an important part of the "income" of farm families comes in the things they raise and make for themselves.

But farmers, too, now must have money. They need it for the kinds of things we no longer make at home and also for the modern tools of their trade—for machines and gas and oil to run them with, for commercial fertilizers, for radios to follow weather and market reports.

In the towns and cities, money is the means of existence from day to day.

The home of a pioneer family was a little world in itself. Members of the family were their own farm and factory workers, butchers, bakers, and barbers; policemen and firemen; often their own doctors and nurses, and sometimes their own teachers as well.

As one of these occupations after another has gone out from under a family's roof, it has become possible for us to have more goods and services than a family can produce for itself. But most of a family's chance to have them depends on its ability to buy a living.

A FAMILY NO LONGER IS A FIRM

It is common to hear young people discussing when they can afford to marry and have children. That question would have astonished young people on the frontier.

A young man then could hardly afford *not* to marry. He needed a wife as a business partner, children as helpers. In early New England not only spinsters but bachelors were under a cloud. Bachelors, in fact, were regarded with suspicion. Usually they had to live where the court told them to. Single people had to attach themselves to a family to get a chance to work for their living.

Both the children and the old people earned their place at the family table.

As we have shifted from a land economy to a money economy, the work of the young and the old no longer has the same value in helping a family to make its living.

Children need more schooling. Once they learned from their chores, while doing the family's business, many of the things they needed to know as adults. Now work at home fails to give them the background they need for jobs in business, trades, and professions. State by State, we agreed that children must go to school.

Change in the work done at home and in our knowledge and standards of child care made children almost a luxury to a family, instead of an economic asset. Families are smaller, especially in the cities. There are fewer sons and daughters to care for the old people of future years.

Old people, like children, have lost much of their economic value to a household. Most American families no longer live in houses where one can build on a room or a wing to shelter aging parents and aunts and uncles and cousins. They no longer have gardens, sewing rooms, and big kitchens where old people can help make the family's living.

Old people were not "dependent" upon their relatives when there was need in a household for work they could do. They have become dependent since their room and their board cost money, while they have little to give in return. Now they need money of their own to keep the dignity and independence they had when their share in work was the equivalent of money.

The shift of work away from homes also explains the work of girls and women to-day. Women have always worked for their living. When work left the home, they followed it into factories and offices. By 1930 the census found a quarter of all the girls and women "gainfully occupied," not including housewives working without pay for their families.

Studies of employed women have shown again and again that they, like men, get jobs in order to support themselves and their families. In other words, they, too, have shifted from making a living to making money. It is among native-born white American women that the habit of wage work has grown up so rapidly.

Married women, like single women, find it necessary to work for wages. Between 1900 and 1930 the percentage of married women at gainful work increased six times as rapidly as that of single women of the same ages. Many married women carry the double job of housewife and wage earner.

Here again, studies show that they do it because their families need their money. Most of the work of wage-earning women represents not women's rights but women's duties.

During our lifetime it has become increasingly difficult for a family to pull together and go into business for itself in one way or another.

For years there was good land to the westward to be had for the taking. Homesteading was an outlet for the sturdy and ambitious. In towns, family shops and businesses were carried on with relatively small amounts of capital.

There is no more free land on which a living can be made. A farmer needs machines as well as skill and grit if he is to compete in the market. In the towns and cities, modern methods of production and merchandising have greatly increased the experience and capital needed to go into business and stay in business.

Individual enterprise, which so often meant family enterprise, now plays a minor part in earning our national income. Including the farmers, only about one in five of the gainfully occupied works for himself. As a people, we no longer work as individuals or families, but as employees.

LIFE IS SAFER, BUT LIVING LESS SECURE

The safety of life has never increased as rapidly at any time on record as in the past 50 years.

Take Massachusetts, for example, where there are records over a long period. A baby born in Massachusetts in 1789 had, on the average, an expectation of a life of about 35 years. In the next century the expectation of life at birth increased about 8 years; babies born in Massachusetts in 1890 had before them a life expectation of 42.5 years for men and 44.4 years for women. But between 1890 and 1930 those averages grew to more than 59 years for men and more than 62.5 for women. The gain in the 40 years following 1890 was twice as great as that of the whole century preceding.

This gain in average length of life has come almost wholly from success in saving the lives of babies, children, and young people. More of us live to reach middle age and old age. At the same time the birth rate has been declining. The result of these changes is that old people form an increasing percentage of the population.

While life became safer, the chance to earn a living became less secure. The growth of employment in basic industries began to slow up. Machines and improved methods made it possible to increase output without increasing the number of workers needed to produce it. Then, for the first time, one important field of work after another reached its peak in employment and began to decline—began to use a smaller number of workers.

Agriculture's *share* in the total employment of the Nation had been going down since 1870, but each census up through 1910 counted a larger *number* of agricultural workers. In the census of 1920 and the census of 1930 the number of workers was smaller. In 1930 there were 600,000 fewer farmers and farm workers than there had been 20 years before.

A similar change came in mining. Efficiency was growing. In 1930 two soft-coal miners could turn out as much as three had done in 1900. The peak in the census record of mine workers came in 1920. In the 10 years that followed, industrial activity was expanding, and new mine workers were needed for the gas wells and oil wells. But by 1930 the total number of miners had dropped by 100,000.

All through the prosperous years of the 1920's there were fewer workers on the payrolls of factories and steam railroads than there had been at the start of the decade. In 1930 the average number of factory workers was 1,500,000 less than that in 1920. The average number of employees of steam railroads had dropped by 500,000.

A man no longer had the same chance to continue through his working years in the occupation he had learned as a boy. The new openings in trade and the service occupations and professions often made specialized demands which workers from the older industries found it hard to meet. It was not likely to help a jobless miner, for example, to learn that more barbers were being employed.

This shift in occupations was particularly difficult for older men. From 1890 on, an increasing percentage of the men of 65 and over was reported as unoccupied.

With the census of 1920 a more general change appeared. In that year and in 1930 the reports showed a drop in the percentage of all men and boys of 16 and over in gainful occupations. In spite of the increasing employment of girls and women, these reports found a decline in the proportion of all Americans of 16 and over in gainful occupations.

Work has been shifting from place to place as well as from occupation to occupation. Manufacturing was declining in New England, for example, at the time when the growing automobile industry pushed it upward in the Central States. Often families must move to follow jobs or find them.

Americans always have moved in search of a living. The older migrations, however, were likely to be those of people who expected to found a new home, settle down, and grow up with the town. The quick shifts of recent years have split up families. They have weakened the old ties of kinship and neighborliness on which a family used to rely. The loss of neighborliness and the increasing size of stores and factories have weakened the personal ties between workers and their employers.

As work has become specialized, we also have developed occupations in which the demand for work shifts from season to season.

On family farms work was, and is, seasonal, in the sense that each season has its particular demands. But indoors and outdoors, there is something useful to be done each month of the year. The season for wood cutting comes when the fields are bare; for sewing, before or after pantry shelves are stocked with jellies and preserves.

But when factories began to turn out the clothing that families once had made during the spring and the fall sewing, factory workers entered jobs in which they were likely to be employed for only part of the year. A cutter or a machine operator may be an expert at his own job, but he finds it is hard to earn in some other way when the factory slows down or closes.

All these changes in the kinds and places and time of work have made the demand for workers changeable and uneven. As a result, many workers —especially industrial workers—often have been without jobs even in boom times.

The Committee on Economic Security found that in the years 1922-29 an average of 8 per cent of our industrial workers were unemployed. In the best of those years, nearly 1,500,000, on the average, were without jobs.

When hard times came, further millions lost their chance to earn a living. By 1932 and 1933 industrial unemployment had risen to about 39 per cent. That meant two industrial workers out of five—10,000,000 or more in all.

The word "unemployment" was not used in English dictionaries before 1888. "Unemployable" came into use only a year earlier.

As far as we can look back, men and women, of course, had lost one way of earning their living and had to find others. Groups of workers, like the hand weavers, had seen their work taken away by machines. But it is only recently that we have realized that there could be a widespread situation— even in good times—in which large numbers of people who needed to work and wanted to work had no chance to do so.

It was not until machines had knit our lives closely together in industry and trade that unemployment could weigh down families throughout a community or a nation. Only recently have we realized that the require-ments of work have become so specialized and exacting that at any one time some people cannot get any paid job.

In our present money economy, unemployment became a common hazard of family life like the epidemics which swept our cities three or four genera-tions ago. The livelihood of families can be cut off as quickly and unex-pectedly as their lives once were cut off by typhus, yellow fever, or cholera.

Unemployment is like a contagion also because it spreads. When a big factory shuts down, its whole neighborhood and city suffers. The livelihood of all who have been selling their goods and services to those wage earners is affected—storekeepers, landlords, doctors, barbers, owners of movie houses, and, in turn, the workers whom they employ and those who produce the goods they sell. When large numbers of people in one part of the country are without earnings, families on farms and in cities hundreds of miles away may find their living less secure.

Science and invention have given ordinary people ease and comfort and variety of which even rich people of earlier civilizations did not dream. A pair of fine stockings once was a present for a king or queen. But this progress has a price. It demands that we use our ingenuity to keep families independent, now that their living hinges on the judgment, skill, and good luck of many other people as well as of themselves. We have shown our ingenuity in making machines and scientific discoveries. The job now is to adapt our common life to the changes that came with our progress.

FAMILY SECURITY AND SOCIAL SECURITY

The words "social security" have become popular in the last ten years. Actually the right and duty of a community to protect its members is as old as the records of men. Primitive tribes have rules and customs to assure the safety of all.

Even pioneer American families, of course, relied on each other for help in trouble and emergencies. Barn raisings and corn huskings, which have lasted down to our times, are a survival of years when a household asked the neighbors' help in an emergency, knowing it would give its help when its turn came.

But communities did not rely wholly upon the willingness of people to help each other. They did not rely wholly even on the willingness of families to support their own members. The common law of England, for example, lays down the duties husbands and wives owe to family support.

Under later circumstances we have found many of the older family laws oppressive, such as the laws which restricted the right of a woman to her earnings, or her right to hold or will property, or to make decisions about her children. Those laws, however, were intended for the protection of families in the circumstances which existed when the laws were made. They held a family together as an economic unit.

The great English commentator, Blackstone, wrote: ". . . even the disabilities which the wife lies under are for the most part intended for her protection and benefit. So great a favorite is the female sex of the laws of England."

In the Colonies, drawing their traditions from England, a husband was obliged by law to support his wife in the manner justified by his circumstances. He was liable for the debts she had contracted before her marriage, as well as later ones. She had a right to inherit part of his estate when he died. In these ways, law and custom, as well as affection, protected the security of persons least able to get security for themselves.

Since a living was made in families, it was through families that a community made and enforced its security measures.

Many of these measures remain with us to-day. The security of children, wives, and aged parents does not depend on the willingness of their family to support them. It is written into our laws and enforced daily in our courts. It is a form of social security, because as a society we see to it that members of a family give this support when they can, whether they wish to or not.

SECURITY IN HEALTH AND SAFETY

As cities have grown up we have taken another series of steps for social security by banding together to pay for certain kinds of protection that no one family can provide for itself. We have police and fire departments, for example. We make fire laws governing the kinds of buildings that people may build in safety to themselves and their neighbors. We support public health departments. We set up traffic regulations to protect safety of life on the highways and streets.

We also have taken steps to aid helpless people who need a kind of care or an amount of protection that few families can provide for themselves. As our increasing scientific knowledge showed the need and the way, we built hospitals for the mentally sick and for people with tuberculosis. We made laws and opened clinics and special schools for crippled children.

At first these measures to help unfortunate people dealt chiefly with those who were dangerous to others, such as mental patients and people sick with communicable diseases. More recently we realize that it is public economy as well as kindness to make sure that other disabled people get care, since often they can recover enough to earn a living for themselves. It is cheaper to cure them than to care for them for years in institutions.

About forty years ago we began to realize that security in health and life must follow people out of their homes and into the factories.

Our greatest success has come in making life safe for children.

Up to about 1900 many children had gone along with their elders into the factories. In 1900 nearly a fifth of all the 10- to 16-year-old children were at work. This was a larger percentage than had been found in any previous census year.

Then State after State decided that factories were not places for children. Laws were passed to restrict child labor and to specify the conditions under which children might work, if at all. At the same time other laws made it compulsory for children to have more chance to go to school and stay in school. In 1930 less than one-twentieth of the 10 to 16-year-old children were in gainful work.

We have not yet lifted by any means all the burden of harmful labor from the shoulders of children, but most of it is gone. And in the twentieth century we have come far toward achieving what some of the colonists set themselves as a goal: the right of children to the security of an education. In 1932 President Hoover's Committee on Recent Social Trends declared that the fact that half the children of high-school age were in the high schools was "evidence of the most successful single effort which government in the United States has ever put forth."

In the past half century many States have passed laws to promote health and safety in work for adults as well as for children—laws governing hours of work, night work, dangerous work, and the like. These are conditions which workers no longer can control for themselves as they could when they worked at home.

SECURITY OF LIVELIHOOD

And in some ways we have taken steps toward assuring not only health and safety in work but also the money to which working families must look in order to buy their living.

When children were taken out of factories and put in school, it was obvious that some families suffered from the loss of the children's earnings. This was especially true in families where the father was incapacitated or dead. Widows with children were no longer a matrimonial prize.

In 1911, two States passed laws to give small money allowances to needy mothers, so that they could keep their children at home rather than put them in an institution. By the beginning of 1935, 45 States, Alaska, Hawaii, and the District of Columbia had mothers'-aid laws on their books.

Other laws looked to the earnings of adults.

By 1911 a majority of the States had passed laws establishing minimum wages for employees on public works.

By 1910 a tenth of the States had free public employment services. This kind of service was later established by many of the other States, and Federal interest in it dates from 1918.

In 1911 the State of Washington passed a workmen's compensation act. In the next ten years similar laws were enacted by more than forty other States. These laws required employers to insure their employees against injury. Under them the cost of industrial accidents, and to some extent the costs of sickness due to work, have become a part of the running costs of industry.

Under the old common law, injured workers had a right to try to collect damages from their employers. The workmen's compensation acts established a more just and orderly way to give workers what the common law admitted as their due.

Starting in the 1920's, many States took steps to provide some security for another large group of their people—the old people who were in need and who probably would never be able to earn their own living again. Alaska has had a law since 1915 to aid old residents in the Territory who are in need. By 1935, there were 28 States, as well as Alaska and Hawaii, which had such laws.

This wave of laws to pay regular allowances to needy old people did not come by accident or imitation. It came because of the growing percentage of old people in the population and the inability of the old to work for their living. Old age was becoming an increasingly serious problem to old people and their families and their towns and counties.

Most of the allowances given to old people under State laws alone were very small. Even so, they have helped many old people to stay in their own homes and to keep their self-respect when they share the homes of others. Giving allowances has been cheaper as well as more humane than caring for old people in poorhouses.

Regular assistance was not provided for all the needy aged or all the needy mothers and children even in the States which had passed such laws. Under some of the State laws a county chose whether or not it would take part in the State plan. When county and State funds ran low, even eligible applicants remained on waiting lists for months or years.

Mothers' aid and old-age allowances are not "pensions" in the sense in which we generally use that word. Widowed mothers and old people do not get assistance just because they are widowed or have reached a certain age. They must show that they are in need.

This kind of assistance is a modern way of meeting an old responsibility. It recognizes the obligation of our Government to provide basic security for these people who cannot earn it for themselves; and it offers a more just and orderly way of meeting that responsibility.

It is a better method than those which States and towns and counties long have used, such as giving baskets of food or tons of coal, or building orphanages and almshouses. It gives needy people a greater chance to choose how they will live. It provides them with what all of us now need to keep our freedom and self-respect—money for their own use.

One social historian has called measures like these social inventions. They are ways we have invented to fit our social life to the changes brought by mechanical and scientific inventions.

Unemployment compensation is a social invention which was first applied in the United States when Wisconsin passed its unemployment compensation law in 1932. Such a law differs from the kind of assistance just mentioned. It is like workmen's compensation—a form of social insurance. As workmen's compensation protects wage earners from the costs of accidents to life and limb at work, so unemployment insurance insures them against some of the costs of the accident of having no job at all. It is not charity or relief, but a means of preventing the need for relief. Like other kinds of insurance, it distributes the cost of a risk—in this case loss of wages—among large numbers of people and over a long period of time, instead of leaving the individual worker with a burden greater than he can bear.

For some time, people had realized that the same principle—social insurance—might well be applied to the problem of old-age security. This also had become too big a risk for individuals or families or even State governments to meet single-handed.

SAVING FOR A RAINY DAY

Our expression "saving for a rainy day" recalls the times when families stored wood in the shed and food in the cellar and pantry for seasons when it was difficult or impossible to go out to fetch them. Why do they not store money in the bank now for the time of unemployment or old age when wages stop?

There is an answer to that question in a study made by The Brookings Institution of family incomes and savings for one of our richest years, 1929, and in a later study made by the Office of Price Administration for the war year 1942. "Savings" in these studies include not only money put in the bank but payments on mortgages, life insurance premiums, and the like.

The Brookings Institution found that in 1929 families with incomes under $1,000 spent, on the average, more than they received. They drew on past savings or got outside help or went into debt. Families with incomes of less than $1,000 represented a fifth of all the families of the Nation in 1929.

Families with incomes of $1,000 to $1,500 kept even, on the average, but saved little, especially in the cities, where everything had to be bought and living costs were higher. These families represented another fifth of all families in that year.

Families with $1,500 to $2,000, accounting for nearly another fifth of the families, saved a little as a group, but not much. The reason is not hard to find. At 1929 prices, the study pointed out, a family income of $2,000 "may perhaps be regarded as sufficient to supply only basic necessities."

Thus in the rich year 1929, three-fifths of the families in the United States could put by nothing or only a little for the hard times that were coming.

More than 85 per cent of all the family savings in that year belonged to the richest tenth of all the families, those with incomes of $4,600 or more.

By 1942, the pressures of war had forced total family income in the United States far higher than in 1929. But the pattern of family income and saving shown by the OPA study was not very different.

In 1942, more than one-fifth of the families had money income of less than $1,000 and, as a group, were in the red for the year. About half the families had less than $2,000 in money income.

Total family savings in 1942, like total family income, had greatly increased, partly because of wartime pressures and partly because it was hard or impossible to buy things like automobiles and refrigerators. But again, nearly all the saving was done by families in comfortable circumstances. The half of the families with less than $2,000 made less than 3 per cent of all the family savings. About 58 per cent of all the savings, on the other hand, belonged to the richest 10 per cent of the families, those with money income of $5,000 or more.

Should families have saved more than they did?

Even low-income families to-day are likely to regard as necessities things which their parents may have done without, such as running water, electricity, haircuts, movies, a greater variety in clothing and diet. It costs more to be sick. Medical care is better and therefore more expensive. An employee who loses time from his job because of sickness often loses pay and sometimes loses the job as well.

But what would happen if all families did save as much as they could by doing without all but the barest necessities?

The families who now save little—those with low and moderate incomes —make up a large share of the markets on which our living depends. In 1929, 71 per cent of all the families and in 1942, 62 per cent, were under the $2,500 mark. Their spending is necessary to hold up the fabric of trade and industry on which the living of the Nation depends.

When a large part of the population cuts down spending, that fabric sags, and workers and others feel the weight of hard times. That is what happened in the early years of the depression when fear and necessity made people stop buying.

There seems no question of the willingness of American families to save when their incomes approach a comfortable level. But the evidence of this study shows that most families, and especially the families whose risks are greatest, have little to look to when a rainy day comes. Their security lies in the steadiness of their earning and the safety of what savings they are able to make for the years when they no longer can earn.

When trade and industry brought people together in towns and cities, it no longer was safe for each house to have its own well. The safety of the whole town made it necessary to have a town water supply.

The safety of all of us now depends also on regular earning and spending. Unless many people are buying what others are producing and selling, earnings are less, jobs are fewer, and all of us have less chance to earn. The well-being of families depends on the ability of other families to buy.

Family security, in short, once dependent on work done at home, has followed the work of the family out of the home. Social security is no longer home-made.

THE SOCIAL SECURITY ACT

The Social Security Act of 1935 grew out of these changes in American life. It brought together our past experience in meeting insecurity. It also set up a bulwark against some of the newer kinds of insecurity which threatened large numbers of us in this twentieth century. After 4 years' experience with the law, Congress extended and strengthened it in 1939.

Several parts of the act apply to people whose troubles we have recognized for many years—those who are too young or too old to earn, and those who are physically handicapped. The act authorizes Federal grants of money to help the States to give public assistance to needy old people, needy blind people, and children who have lost support or care because of the death, disability, or absence of one or both parents. The Federal Government meets about half the cost of the monthly payments the States make to these needy people. The act also authorizes grants to the States to help them provide services for child welfare, for crippled children, and for the health of mothers and children.

These parts of the Social Security Act use our national resources to help all the States do better what most or all of them had already undertaken to some degree. Nearly all the States are taking part in all these programs.

In addition, the act set up two entirely new national systems of protection against insecurity caused by loss of earning power. These systems cover millions of the men and women who depend on their wages to buy their living and consequently suffer when they are out of a job or too old to work. They cover nearly all jobs in factories, offices, mines, mills, stores, and other branches of industry and commerce—about half of all employment in an average week in ordinary times. In general, they do not cover work on farms or domestic service in private homes or any kind of government employment or work for certain charitable and other nonprofit organizations—such as schools and churches—or the jobs of people, like farmers and storekeepers, who have their own business and work for themselves.

In the Federal-State system of unemployment insurance, the Federal Government makes grants to States to pay the cost of administering the State's unemployment insurance law. Within 2 years after the Social Security Act was passed by Congress, every State and Alaska, Hawaii, and the District of Columbia had an unemployment insurance law. Under this system, now in full operation throughout the United States, industry and business share part of the costs of unemployment which formerly fell upon workers alone. Employers, and in a few States workers as well, make regular contributions under the State law to pay benefits to people who are able to work and available for work but cannot get a job for which they are fitted.

Under the laws of the States, whether or not a worker can draw unemployment benefits and, if so, the amount he gets and the number of weeks for which he can get it if he does not find a job depend generally on the amount of work he has had in employment covered by the State law and what he has earned in such jobs. The weekly benefits paid to unemployed workers generally replace half or less of what they would have earned. Though workers still carry a large part of the loss involved in being jobless, the benefits help them to keep on buying their living until they can find work again. In this way unemployment insurance also benefits business, which depends on what workers buy.

Unemployment insurance helps workers to bridge gaps between jobs. It is equally important to help unemployed workers find new jobs. Together these two protections—job insurance and job-finding service—make up our employment security program. Local offices of the United States Employment Service help workers to find jobs and employers to find workers, without charge to either. A worker who is receiving unemployment benefits must report to the employment office each week and must take any suitable job that is offered him or have his benefits stopped.

The employment security program helps to steady the income of wage earners during their working years. The Social Security Act also helps workers to build up an income for themselves and their families in old age or for the family if the worker dies.

In 1935, the act established a Federal old-age benefits system to pay benefits to retired wage earners after they reached the age of 65. Under the 1939 amendments, this system was broadened to include insurance protection to the family as well. Now it is called old-age and survivors insurance.

Under this Federal system, monthly benefits are paid to insured wage earners after they reach 65 years of age and stop work, to their wives at age 65, and to their children under age 18. When an insured wage earner dies, whatever his age, monthly benefits are paid to his family; that is, to his young children, to his widow at age 65, or at any age while she has a child in her care; or to his aged dependent parents if he leaves no widow or child. When no survivor is eligible for monthly benefits at the time of the wage earner's death, a lump-sum death payment may be made.

The amount of the benefit that is paid to a worker or to a member of his family depends on his past wages in jobs that come under this law. Workers and their employers contribute equally to the trust fund from which benefits are paid. . . .

Federal old-age and survivors insurance is different from the public assistance paid to needy old people and dependent children by the States with Federal help. Public assistance is paid to people who are in need and are otherwise eligible under the State law. People have a right to assistance only if they are in need. In contrast, insurance benefits are based on the workers' past wages and are paid regardless of any other savings or income the worker or family may have. These benefits help to *prevent* need. Through this insurance, millions of workers are building up a definite income which the United States Government will pay to them when they are old or to their families if they die.

Thus the Social Security Act helps to provide some income to people who are little able or unable to earn. In one way or another, the cost is spread over large numbers of people to provide some security for those of their number who are unfortunate at any one time. The act is a foundation on which all of us, working together, have begun to build security against risks which very few of us can meet alone. As time goes on and as we learn by experience, these protections may be further broadened and strengthened.

What we want to-day is what Americans have always wanted and worked for. The colonists and frontiersmen wanted independence and opportunity for themselves and their children. They wanted to make their own living and to take an active share in the life of their times. All that has changed to-day is the way we take to get these things. Our security is the security of the whole people.

No. 110

WHAT TO EXPECT OF SOCIAL SECURITY [1]

by Edwin E. Witte

SOCIAL SECURITY is to-day an immensely popular term. Everybody in public life is for social security and nearly all discussion of the subject concerns improvement and extension. It remains, however, a term of uncertain meaning, which conveys very different ideas to different people.

[1] Edwin E. Witte, "What to Expect of Social Security," *The American Economic Review* (March, 1944), Vol. XXXIV, No. 1, Part 2, Supplement, pp. 212-221. Reprinted by permission of *The American Economic Review* and the author.

To many Americans it means nothing more than old age pensions; to others, it is a socialized form of insurance protection against hazards whose normal consequences are poverty and dependency; to still others, a governmentally guaranteed minimum income in all contingencies of life; to others, again, an economic system which operates to afford plenty for everybody. These are only some of the concepts of social security widely prevalent in this country. This lack of precise meaning to some extent accounts for the popularity of social security. Social security is in fact more of an ideal than an institution or group of institutions. Yet if we are to intelligently discuss the place which social security should have in postwar America or how social security can be improved, we need to give an institutional content to the term.

What is called "social security" differs from country to country. Social security is a part of the total institutional pattern of the nations in which it exists and is most soundly conceived in conformity with such total patterns. It is something different in totalitarian countries like [pre-war] Germany and Japan from what it is in democratic countries like the United States and the nations of the British Commonwealth, and something else still in Soviet Russia. The existing governmental structure, the economic system which prevails, the stage of economic development attained, the history and traditions of the nation will all have their influence upon the social security institutions of the country and even upon what is considered to be social security. So will such social and economic factors as the state of family life, the economic position of women, the mobility of labor, the extent of union organization, and, above all, the nation's economic productivity. This holds true also for psychological factors such as the public attitude toward government, the degree to which security is valued as contrasted with the opportunities presented by risks, and the prevailing concepts of progress.

In this paper I shall use the term social security as it was defined in the report on *Approaches to Social Security,* published in 1942 by the International Labour Office. This includes within the term both social assistance and social insurance and also social security systems. Social security systems represent an integration of social insurance and social assistance. Social assistance stems from the old institution of poor relief and "expresses the obligation of the community toward its needy members." It includes noncontributory pensions to the aged and to invalids (the American old age assistance and aid to the blind), mothers' pensions (officially called "aid to dependent children" in this country), unemployment assistance, medical assistance, rehabilitation of the disabled, and general public assistance (or relief). It is financed from general tax sources and is free to the beneficiaries.

Social insurance, in contrast, "is situated between social assistance and commercial insurance." It is established by law and serves social purposes, but utilizes insurance principles. To-day it includes workmen's compensation (which is known as industrial accident insurance in continental Europe), sickness (or health) insurance, old age, invalidity and survivors' insurance, and unemployment insurance (or compensation).

As thus defined, social security is broader than social insurance, although the latter term is sometimes applied to the entire scope of social security. It is narrower than the English social services and the Scandinavian social policy, which include, besides the social security institutions which have been enumerated, such other governmental services as public education, public health and medical services, public housing developments, minimum wage legislation, and still other publicly financed and directed programs for the benefit of people in low income groups. It is also narrower than economic security, which includes in addition to social security many other institutions whose objective is economic stability and an assurance of a satisfying minimum income for everybody.

As I conceive social security, it is oriented toward family and individual welfare rather than the functioning of the economic system. It is social in the sense that it is provided for by law and is compulsory in at least some of its aspects. It is usually administered by public officials and is always strictly controlled by the government. Its approach, however, is from the point of view of the welfare of the family and the individual rather than that of the nation as an entity or of society in the abstract. Its concern is with the immediate hazards confronting the family and the individual, or, rather, with their economic consequences, not with ultimate causes, as they appear to an economist.

Such a concept of social security is consistent with the totality of our existing institutions and calls for no revolutionary changes. Far from being inconsistent with our free enterprise system and our democratic government, it is a bulwark to these basic institutions, vitally necessary, under present conditions, for their preservation and continued successful functioning. Such a concept of social security is also in accord with the past history of the development of social security in the United States and, more specifically, with the statements regarding social security which were made by the President, the Congressional committees in charge of the legislation, and the Committee on Economic Security, which drafted the measure, at the time of the enactment of the Social Security Act.

In its present connotation, the term social security does not seem to go back further than 1933, when the late Dr. Abraham Epstein expanded his Association for Old Age Security into the Association for Social Security. It did not come into general use until the House Ways and Means Committee, in order to emphasize that the measure it recommended was not the Administration's Economic Security bill, changed its title to the Social Security Act. As a group of institutions, however, social security goes back to the earliest Colonial days. Social security in this country, as in England, had its beginnings in the Elizabethan Poor Law, which was brought here by the earliest settlers. Its subsequent development, however, was quite different.

England was far ahead of us in becoming industrialized. Economic conditions there were such as to bring home to public consciousness much earlier than here, that unemployment and poverty are not always the fault of the unemployed and the poor. England's racial unity and its unitary government facilitated earlier action and a more orderly development of social security than in the United States. This has often been noted, but it is less familiar that the differing history, concepts, and conditions also account for most of the differences in the present content of social security legislation in the two countries. We have never had a Poor Law Commission or a Beveridge Report in the United States, but on the other hand, England to this day does not have a workmen's compensation act developed on social insurance principles. The major social security legislation of England had its origin in dissatisfaction with the poor law but had the same objective of relieving distress. Social insurance developed as a substitute for poor relief, and retains many aspects to this day which plainly point to this origin. Completely absent in the development of social security in England has been the police power approach, which regards social insurance as a form of labor legislation, justified as a regulation of employment relations in the interests of public welfare.

In contrast, social security in the United States has stemmed from labor legislation quite as much as from poor relief. Workmen's compensation developed as labor legislation, without even a realization at the time that it is social insurance. Unemployment compensation and health insurance were both first advocated as logical complements of workmen's compensation. For twenty years before the American Association for Social Security was organized, the American Association for Labor Legislation championed social insurance measures and cited the police power as their legal justification. It was not until the great depression had set in that the point of view that unemployment insurance should serve primarily as a relief institution had any popularity in this country. No unemployment insurance law was enacted until that time, but the legislation we got was something between the British unemployment insurance and American workmen's compensation. Similarly, health insurance proposals in this country have departed far from European models.

The great depression furnished the impetus for the swift advances in social security which we made in the thirties. But it was less dissatisfaction with the disgraceful administration of poor relief than sheer need for financial assistance to the local and state governments which brought the national government into the social security picture. By this time, the national government again does not concern itself with relief in any manner, and our relief laws and their administration have reverted pretty much to their predepression status. In many other respects also the depression now seems to have produced far less change in relation to social security than appeared to be the case a few years ago. Social security is approved of by everybody and there is very general agreement that it should be expanded and "liberalized." But there is very little interest in social security and a great lack of understanding as to what it is all about. Particularly, there is almost no appreciation on the part of the prospective beneficiaries that social security involves costs as well as benefits, while to businessmen social security is nothing more than a matter of taxes. The word insurance in the terms social insurance, old age and survivors' insurance, and unemployment insurance is one of the reasons for the popularity of these institutions in this country where everybody has an insurance policy. However, confusion and doubt are now being created by the view that social insurance is not "insurance" at all. Americans generally still regard private enterprise, initiative, and thrift as the best assurance of security. Unlike the British and despite all the gibes about the WPA, they believe that work is the best cure for unemployment and that government should provide employment when private industry cannot do so. They distrust their government, and, particularly, the "Washington bureaucrats." Yet it is a certainty that if serious trouble develops they, almost as one man, will turn to their government to help them and it will be the national government to which they will turn.

These are the broad outlines of the present American concepts and attitudes in relation to social security. This is the foundation now available on which we can and must build. This is not a very secure foundation— and not so much because our social security legislation is defective in content or poor in administration as a consequence of confused thinking about social security. This confusion is largely attributable to the absence of any precise concept of what the term means and of all popular understanding as to the values and limitations of the institutions which are described by this term.

It is the thesis of this paper that to improve this foundation it is essential, at the stage of the evolution of social security in which we now are in this country, that we give to this term the meaning the International Labour Office has adopted. Further, we need to make the American public understand that the objectives and values of social security are limited but very necessary for the preservation of our institutions and the welfare of all our people.

This requires giving social security a narrower meaning than "freedom from want." Freedom from want cannot be guaranteed through social security measures. The possibilities of providing even a minimum satisfying income to all people and in all contingencies of life depend first of all upon total production. . . . Personally, it is my view that full employment, as we now know it, is too costly to be a practical objective for peacetime, although I believe that we can and must organize our economy so that we will have a much greater production than we had prior to the war, and an ever increasing production. This is an essential for the attainment of freedom from want. Most economic goods and services are so ephemeral that production must be continuous; moreover, what is a minimum satisfying income and even freedom from want is variable and in a progressive society will ever rise. Social security cannot assure the high and rising level of production which is essential to the attainment of such an objective. It may even be organized in such a way as to hold back production. . . . It cannot become a substitute for industry, initiative, and invention, or for the proper organization and controls of our economic system.

This does not mean that social security does not matter, nor that social security proposals should be judged primarily on the basis of their probable effects upon the functioning of the economic system. It is my view that the economic planners who look upon social security as one means for reshaping the economic system towards ends they deem desirable are a greater menace to the improvement of our social security institutions than are the Townsendites—and, as I shall develop later, I do not underrate the still present dangers from that source. It is a perversion of the concept of social security to look upon it as being primarily designed for the control of the business cycle, to insure full employment, or to redistribute income and purchasing power. Its effects in these respects should be considered and discussed, but should not overshadow its major objective—the protection of the individual and the family against the immediate economic hazards confronting them. Economists, interested as they are in the functioning of the economic system as a whole, are prone to look upon this objective as secondary; and perhaps it is, but it surely is not unimportant. Without maintenance of individuals and families in all contingencies of life, the hope of fundamental remedies for economic ills is but illusory.

It is very certain also that the economic system will never function so as to render unnecessary any social security measures. There is want and suffering even at this time of abnormally great production. Full employment and maximum production do not keep people from growing old and do not guarantee that many old people will not be in want and from reasons which are not their fault. There is some unemployment even in wartime and everyone knows that, under the most favorable circumstances, there will be a much greater volume of unemployment in the transition period. Sickness and invalidity have little relation to employment conditions and industrial accidents actually increase with increases in employment. Regardless of the functioning of the economic system, many breadwinners will die young and when this happens their surviving small children usually will be in poverty; and we cannot afford to overlook the fact that the great majority of all our children, upon whom depends the future of our country, are in the homes of the poor. Finally, it needs to be said, lest we overlook it in this connection, that . . . [the war was] not . . . fought to establish in this country the Nazi concept that those who cannot contribute to the security of the state and are a drain upon its resources deserve no consideration. The care given dependents is one measure of the civilization attained and we mean to continue as a civilized and Christian country.

Equally unsound is the view that social security is principally a tax problem. This appears to be the predominant view in Congress and may well produce even greater havoc in the future than it has already created. In part, at least, this view has developed because in the United States we had to label the employer and employee contributions to the social insurance funds as "pay roll taxes"—which has not been done in any other country. The attitude toward taxes in this country has always been antagonistic, with an almost complete failure to appreciate that in its entirety it is a two-way, not a one-way, process. Social security is not, at least mainly, an additional cost to society, but an orderly redistribution of costs which the American people have to bear in any event. Even from the point of view of the government's expenditures alone, the costs of a well-conceived social security system will be offset to a very considerable extent by reduced relief and salvage costs.

It is equally, if not more, dangerous that the largest groups of prospective beneficiaries think of social security in terms of benefits only and that this has also been the attitude of most of its champions in the ranks of the academicians and social workers. This is again a typically American point of view. Our economic growth has been so great that we have not had to think very much about where the money is coming from. America is the land of plenty and there is widespread belief that we can do anything. This is so

infectious that it is not unnatural that even people who thoroughly understand what costs are involved, generally are willing to take the chance
of a possible financial breakdown in the future to get improvements now
about whose costs they do not dare to talk. England, while it has something
like "pay as you go" financing for old age insurance, provides for increasing
government, employer, and employee contributions as disbursements increase
with the lapse of the years. In contrast, when the Social Security Amendments were passed in 1939 no estimates of costs whatsoever were given
Congress and language was written into the act which can be interpreted
as implying that we should not look ahead more than five years. This . . .
[was] followed, in three successive years, by the "freezing of social security
taxes" (which . . . [was] really a reduction in taxes already levied), although no one claimed that the accruing costs . . . [did] not far exceed the
amounts collected from present taxes. Many of the people who understood
what . . . [was] happening still . . . [saw] nothing very alarming in these
developments because they . . . [were] confident that a future Congress
. . . [would] come to the rescue with large government contributions from
general tax sources. Time may justify their hopes, but it is a fact that
Congress to date has refused to [face the issue—even though the tax rate
was increased to one and one-half per cent in the Eighty-First Congress and
an increase to at least three per cent seems likely].

The greatest danger in this sort of an attitude lies not in the possibility
that present commitments may not be fulfilled, but in amendments which
will prove ruinous. The view that only benefits matter and that future
costs can be ignored is an invitation to the increase of benefits beyond all
present economic possibilities. . . . While the Townsend Plan will never
become law, there is a decided possibility that ere long we may have a
"Baby Townsend Plan"—and babies usually grow. As Elizabeth Brandeis
has put it, in a still unpublished article: social security properly conceived
is more of "a net to catch those that fall" than "an overly soft feather bed."
But there is danger that it may be converted into an institution which "may
demoralize not only workers, but statesmen, business leaders, and the public."
As the Romans discovered long ago, "it is relatively easy to provide 'bread
and circuses' for the populace," but once we adopt that type of social
security there is no stopping point.

I view with similar concern the playing down of the "insurance" in social
insurance, which has developed since the passage of the Social Security Act.
It is understandable that insurance company executives and actuaries should
look upon private insurance as the only kind of insurance meriting the
esteem and confidence which Americans attach to that term. It is even
clearer why certain politicians see political advantages in creating distrust

of the government's handling of the social security funds. It would be extremely unfortunate, however, if they persuaded the workers that their funds were not safe with the government. Equally dangerous is any weakening of the contributory principle. The several forms of social insurance differ from private insurance, but not more so than do the several kinds of private insurance from each other. It is anomalous, to say the least, that the very people who justified reducing the pay roll tax rates by denouncing reserves as having no place in social insurance also were responsible for the provisions in the Social Security Act Amendments of 1939 limiting benefits to currently insured and fully insured persons. These are clearly concepts taken from private insurance, and they are likely to work out in such a way that many millions of war workers will get nothing at all for their social security deductions from pay rolls.

I also do not accept the view that social security is nothing more than a relief institution. I include social assistance within the concept of social security. But I object to making of social insurance but another form of relief. In the English environment and with the background of the history of social security in England, the concept that social insurance is a substitute for poor relief may be adequate. In the United States, where social security developed from labor legislation as well as from relief, there is still value in retaining something of the police power approach, although it alone also is not adequate. It is a defeatist attitude to say that, because the hazards against whose consequences social insurance is designed to provide protection cannot be wholly prevented, no attempt should be made to utilize it for preventive purposes. Such a position is illogical and is bound to provoke much unnecessary opposition to proposals for the improvement of social security. It is also to be noted that the world over, social security is increasingly coming to mean not merely cash payments but also social services with a preventive objective.

This entire paper, I know, sounds like a jeremiad. It is not so intended. There are trends affecting social security that I view with alarm. I am particularly concerned because there is such hazy thinking about social security and what may properly be expected from it. But I do not despair of social security; and I have not lost my faith in social security. . . .

Advances in social security have been made, above all else, because all peoples long for security in a world that in their own experience has been very insecure. The quest for social security is but one manifestation of a much broader phenomenon of the present day and age, which includes all of the "four freedoms" and beyond these a desire for a secure world, and for the security of life itself. In the midst of great insecurity, security has come to be valued, perhaps, even more than opportunity. . . .

I have deliberately not discussed the specific proposals for postwar social security which are now before the country. . . . I have elsewhere suggested the organization of another Advisory Committee on Social Security, which, this time, should be sponsored by both of the Congressional committees concerned with social security legislation.

In addition to consideration of the details of the social security needed in postwar America, there is an equally great need, at this time, for a clarification of thought as to what social security is and what can be expected of it. . . . The leaders of both the Associations which have concerned themselves with the advancement of social security (John B. Andrews, of the American Association for Labor Legislation, and Abraham Epstein, of the Association for Social Security) have passed away. It is doubtful at the moment whether either of these Associations will be able to survive the passing of their founders, despite the very great need for an organization outside of the government for the improvement of social security. This fact makes it all the more important that we should all do what we can to advance the cause to which they devoted their lives.

No. 111

THE COMMUNITY AND THE FULL EMPLOYMENT PROBLEM [1]

A Report of the W. E. Upjohn Institute for Community Research

FOR some time the local community has been losing significance in the minds of those concerned with political, economic, and social affairs. This tendency is evident in the lack of enthusiasm in local elections, in the proneness to forget the local businessman in economic planning, and in the emphasis on national aid in supporting such programs as nursery schools, crime prevention, and old-age assistance. This trend is no doubt due in part to the ease of communication and travel and to the pressure of international ideas. It is well for people to become aware of common problems and goals throughout the world. In emphasizing national and world perspectives, however, one must not lose sight of local opportunities. One must not forget that many problems are local and must be attacked in the local community.

The community as referred to in this book is not limited to any political subdivision. It may cut across several political boundaries. As used in this

[1] The W. E. Upjohn Institute for Community Research, *Full Employment in Your Community* (Chicago: Public Administration Service, 1947), Ch. I, pp. 1-7. Reprinted by permission of the publisher.

context the community refers to a geographical area which is bound together by common economic and social ties. A community may be a large city or a suburb. It may be a small town together with the surrounding rural area. In the western states a community may include two or three counties, while on the eastern seaboard it may be only a small section of a county.

In recent years much has been spoken and written concerning the ideals of democracy, free enterprise, and full employment. The community and its relationship to these objectives will be dealt with briefly in these pages.

THE COMMUNITY AND DEMOCRACY

Outside of the home the ideals of democracy have their first expression in the community. Community institutions such as schools, churches, and playgrounds nurture the ideals of democracy.

Democracy has thrived in America during those periods when community life has been active. The New England town meetings were a significant development because they represented participation by individual citizens in the problems of the community and the nation. They represented the voice of a democratic people. This same technique is being used in our own generation to stimulate people to think and to express opinions on questions of local and national importance. If democracy is to be virile— and it must be virile to survive—it must be strengthened at its roots in the community.

THE COMMUNITY AND FREE ENTERPRISE

Like democracy, the capitalistic system with its components, the price system, the right of private property, the profit motive, free competition, and free enterprise, has been regarded as a characteristically American pattern of life. The right of free enterprise has been especially cherished. For many this is a basic right which must be preserved.

There is a tendency to associate the idea of free enterprise with great industrial organizations like General Motors, U. S. Steel, and duPont. These industries do represent the extent to which free enterprise may be developed. Yet such development is unusual rather than typical. Typical examples of free enterprise are the corner drugstore, the neighborhood grocery, and the hardware store. These businesses are born in the community, are nurtured by the community, and thrive or die in the community. The need for the business, the idea for its establishment, the financing, and the labor come from the local community. Such establishments are an integral part of the community. It would be difficult to find an American community without these evidences of free enterprise.

Even the large industries and businesses are rooted in the community.

They receive their initial impetus from the community and wax strong there. Even now it is difficult to divorce many such enterprises from their origin. For example, the Ford Motor Company has plants and representatives in many countries of the world, yet it is still associated with Detroit. Detroit is the community which gave this modern colossus its birth and early support. It is the community to which Ford "belongs."

In the future as in the past, enterprises which will take the places of the obsolescent businesses and industries of to-day will originate in local communities. There will be fewer failures in communities which know their resources and which can forecast future demands. There will be less waste of financial and human resources in a community which is conscious of the direction of its economic development.

THE COMMUNITY AND THE FULL EMPLOYMENT PROBLEM

Nearly all the material which has been written during the past few years on full employment has been concerned with measures to be taken at the national level. It cannot be denied that these national measures are the ones most likely to influence the level of employment. Booms and depressions appear to be governed by factors largely beyond the control of the local community.

However, it is also evident that national policies and national measures will not insure a high level of employment in any particular community. There are many steps which can be taken in any local community to improve the soundness of its economic base and to increase the opportunity of its own citizens for continuous and productive employment. It is a matter of common observation that communities vary markedly in the extent to which they have been able to offer economic opportunity and stability to their citizens.

Many of these differences may have been due to accidental factors of advantage and disadvantage rather than to the diligent efforts of the citizens of the more fortunate communities. There is now, however, an increasing conviction that these important matters must not be left to chance. It is the chief purpose of this book [*Full Employment in Your Community*] to enumerate as specifically as possible the measures which communities may take to strengthen, expand, and stabilize the local economy.

THE MEANING OF FULL EMPLOYMENT

The real objective of economic activity is obscured by the currently popular slogan "full employment." In order to remove some confusion regarding full employment it will be helpful to indicate first what full employment is not before stating what it is.

Kinds of Unemployment

Full employment does not mean that there will be no unemployment. It must be recognized that a certain amount of unemployment is inevitable in a society where consumers are free to buy what they please and where investors are free to invest or withhold the funds necessary to operate productive establishments.

There are persons in every community who are not employed but who cannot properly be considered as unemployed, for they do not desire to work. This group would include students, housewives, minors, and the aged. The truly unemployed fall into the following eight classifications:

Casual Unemployment. Casual unemployment is day-to-day unemployment of short duration. Such unemployment is experienced by the day worker or by the outdoor worker who cannot work when it rains.

Seasonal Unemployment. Seasonal changes cause unemployment. Such unemployment is common on the farm where many workers are laid off from harvest until spring planting, and it is necessary for them to find work elsewhere. Some industries, such as food processing, also experience seasonal fluctuations in activity and in employment.

Labor Reserve Unemployment. Because production is not constant in most industries and geographical areas, workers are drawn into the labor force of a community to meet peak production demands. After the peak is over, they are idle. Such idleness is classified as labor reserve unemployment.

Cyclical Unemployment. The most serious type of unemployment is that caused by business depression. Businessmen, unable to sell their products, are forced to lay off workers. Cyclical unemployment is relatively long in duration and substitute work is difficult to obtain during depression periods.

Technological Unemployment. Changes in mechanical processes and managerial techniques which result in increased productivity of labor cause labor displacement. This displacement is referred to as technological unemployment. The added productivity and wealth resulting from technological improvements may create more jobs in the long run. However, in a period such as the nineteen-twenties technological advance may be so rapid and widespread that adjustment of displaced workers may be slow and difficult.

Frictional Unemployment. Frictional unemployment is due to time lag and labor immobility in the economy. Demand for labor varies from month to month but labor supply is relatively inelastic; thus unemployment occurs. Labor may be needed in a particular locality and workers may be available in another locality. Immobility of labor is an obstacle to full employment.

Secular Unemployment. It has been thought by some economists that there are persistent forces at work which tend to reduce opportunity for investment and therefore to reduce production and employment. It is believed that savings tend to increase faster than ways of making productive use of those savings can be found. These forces naturally are less evident during boom periods when everything appears to be going well than during depressions when everything seems to have become disorganized. But if these persistent tendencies do exist, then it means that we shall have a continuous problem of keeping the wheels of our economic machine running fast enough to provide goods and productive employment for everyone. It should be emphasized that not all economists agree that there is any such long-term trend toward unemployment.

Unemployables. In every community there are those who want and need work but who are unable to work because of physical or psychological handicaps.

The Goal of Full Employment

Just as full employment does not mean that there will be no unemployment, it should be clear also that full employment does not mean working more hours, or more days, or more years; or generally working harder than people have been working; or that working should be compulsory. Working hours have been decreasing progressively for many years, and this is in no way considered contrary to the full employment objective. The fact that the goal is not simply the working of more hours is illustrated by a comparison between our world and the world of our grandfathers. In the days when every man tilled his own ground, raised his own food, built his own house, chopped his own firewood, and made his own clothing, it would hardly have occurred to anyone to consider unemployment as a problem. There was plenty of work, but relatively little to show for it.

"Full employment" as used . . . [here] means the opportunity to work for all who are able and willing to work and the maximum utilization of all other factors of production: land, capital, and enterprise. In some respects the expression "full employment" is misleading. The word "full" does not mean what it says, and "employment" as such is not our real objective.

The real goal of full employment is to provide an abundant supply of goods and services for all consumers. It will mean an increased standard of living for all people. Full production without full consumption is a meaningless goal. Production will always be dependent upon purchasing power and the desire to consume.

Full and continuous employment is not simply a pious or humanitarian wish. It is, rather, a goal of utmost importance to the democratic way of life. It is a necessary requirement for freedom or even survival, not only for the individual, but also for democracy. The preservation and expansion of industrial civilization and of the system of free enterprise are dependent upon our ability to provide every citizen with the opportunity to contribute to our national wealth and to share in that wealth.

Socio-economic Interdependence

The following chapters [not reprinted here] suggest some of the ways in which groups of citizens organized at the community level can work for full and stable employment. These measures are not only economic in character, but social as well. At the local level it is easy to see the interdependence of social and economic factors. Economic factors predominate perhaps in the creation of employment opportunities; but social factors directly affect the utilization of existing employment opportunities.

This social and economic interdependence is nowhere more evident than in the case of housing. A lack of housing can hamper the expansion of industries and interfere with the settling of new industries in the community.

In deciding whether to locate in a given community, some companies consider not only economic advantages such as a favorable market, adequate transportation facilities, and a good labor supply, but also the kind of community in which their employees will live. They take account of recreational facilities, schools, parks, and hospitals. It is sound business practice and not simply a humanitarian concern which prompts a consideration of such social and physical factors. Full employment is a socio-economic problem and the measures which are proposed in this book have this orientation.

PLANNING AT THE COMMUNITY LEVEL

Basically, planning means the capacity to take thought for the morrow, the capacity to envision distant goals and to direct action toward the achievement of those goals. Planning is common to all of us in our individual lives. It is common also in industry. In these situations, planning is considered desirable. There is a similar contribution which planning can make in the life of a community. Logically there is no such thing as "no plan"; the decision not to plan is in itself a plan. We have seen "planlessness" in the lives of individuals, of businesses, in local government, and in national government.

There are at the present time only a few states which do not have enabling acts for city or county planning. Local planning has become mandatory for cities over 10,000 population in Massachusetts. In California, county planning is mandatory. Many states have enabling legislation for regional planning also. It is to be hoped that the trend toward planning in the local situation may be continued, for it is an important approach to the problem of providing a more prosperous and more secure life for all citizens of the nation.

The planning activities contemplated in these enabling and mandatory acts are theoretically as broad and all-inclusive as the entire social and economic life of the community. In practice, however, the efforts of such official planning groups tend rather naturally to emphasize matters that are ordinarily the functions of local governments. The location of streets, zoning, subdivision control, and provision of municipal services receive more emphasis than industrial stabilization plans, labor-management cooperation, or market analysis.

The theme of this book [*Full Employment in Your Community*] is not synonymous with community planning in this sense. The focal point in this book is *expansion and stabilization of employment,* community planning being one important aspect of the activities necessary in working toward that objective.

Chapter XXXII

EDUCATION, HOUSING, AND HEALTH— GOVERNMENTAL RESPONSIBILITIES?

[TAKE off an evening and come along to a professor's house. He and his wife are having in a few friends—for sociability's sake, he says. Listen now to their sociable talk about the latest loyalty oath for teachers. The room tingles with tension; voices grow louder, arguments become invectives and ultimately confusion wins.

All of this amuses one of the guests, a local newspaper writer. He hasn't said anything; he's been too engrossed in enjoying the discovery that academicians, too, lose sight of reason and objectivity. But now, with a lofty impudence, he breaks in: "Really, now, aren't there more basic questions to be decided? What I mean is that in all this talk of communism and democracy we're forgetting about education. I suggest that we'd do well to teach more people to read." Before he has time to survey all the faces for reaction, a wife of one of the professors pipes up: "Well, I suggest there's far more to education than teaching of reading. If . . ."

A few miles away in this same university city, on a street in what is politely referred to as a "blighted area," you can find another kind of social gathering. Have a look into the poolroom—that is, if you can get in. Out piles a gang of 13- and 14-year-old boys. They're worked up to a feverish pitch. They talk agitatedly under their breaths and puff nervously on their cigarettes as they push past, on out into the street. You may wonder what they are up to, but your attention is drawn to two middle-aged men, cues in hand, waiting their turns at the table. One has a look of despair on his face. He's complaining: "The old lady yammers . . . when you gonna move us outa this hole? . . . my kids are yellin' . . . one got a cough and now they all got it . . . I dunno. . . ."

Out in a quiet suburb where neat little bungalows flank one another in uniform rows, a group of housewives are having their night out. The bridge game languishes as the talk flourishes. "Honestly, Claire," says one of the plumper women, "you're getting too terribly thin." You may wonder if she's sincere. However, Claire accepts the comment. "I know, but . . ." "But nothing," interrupts her plump friend, "you'd better get yourself to a doctor." "I know," says Claire, "but—well, we just can't afford it. . . ."

An evening of sociability? Yes, of a sort. Americans will always get together, some to shoot pool, some to run in the streets and others to play bridge or to discuss. But whatever they do, wherever you find them, you will hear them, sooner or later, talking about their problems.

In this country, only seven out of ten youths of high-school age are enrolled in school. Fifteen million people live in blighted areas; these plus other millions are not getting proper medical care.

Whose job is it to do something about these conditions? In our democracy, pledged to "promote the general welfare," such conditions are the concern of each and every one of us. How, then, do we tackle our responsibility of educating, housing and maintaining the good health of all our citizens? The following articles contain seeds of a solution. Planted, nurtured to full stature, pruned, crossed and re-crossed, these seeds may grow to bear fruit to-morrow in areas still uncultivated to-day.]

No. 112

EDUCATION IN A DEMOCRACY [1]

by Harold Benjamin

THE men who wanted to establish a high school in a little Western town forty years ago seemed to have the weaker arguments that day.

"If we set up this high school," they said, "we will attract a lot of new people to this town. We will increase property valuations. We will bring more trade to our local merchants. In spite of increased taxation, this high school will make our town more prosperous."

They said these things earnestly but somewhat abashedly. They were obviously ashamed to have to make such materialistic appeals to the voters at the school meeting, but at the same time they seemed fully convinced that only such appeals had any chance of affecting the final vote.

The opposition's arguments sounded much more effective.

"Sure we need a high school in this town," they said, "but we need paved streets more than we need a high school. Look at that mud out there. You can't drive a buckboard through some of it in the spring now, and in the summer the dust is fetlock-deep. We need an electric light plant too— probably more than we need a high school. Are we going to use coal oil forever? We need new fire equipment. You get a blaze started here in a high wind and this town will go up like a powder box. We need a new courthouse. Lane County's got a new courthouse, and we never heard Lane County is better than this county. We need all these things and more. Where are we going to get the money for what we need? We're

[1] Harold Benjamin, "Education in a Democracy," *The Annals* of the American Academy of Political and Social Science (September, 1949), Vol. 265, pp. 10-16. Reprinted by permission of *The Annals* of the American Academy of Political and Social Science. The footnotes in the original version are omitted here.

taxed now more than we can bear! Sure we need a new high school. We need a lot of things, but we have got to use some common sense. Where are you going to get the money for all these things this town needs?"

The outlook for the high school was admittedly very dark. The only doubt possible appeared to be the size of the majority in opposition to the proposal for the high school.

Then the Old Rancher got to his feet, twisting his battered hat nervously, seemingly so embarrassed that he could hardly be heard as he first addressed the chair.

But this seeming embarrassment was only an unconscious pose. This man had great prestige. He had worn the mantle of that prestige so long that he was unconscious of it, and his seeming humility was merely that of a man who did not want to be thought uppity, high-toned, or too big for his breeches. He had not been a humble man when he had ridden into the valley at the head of his wagons, a rifle under his left stirrup leather, and the end of his .44-40 holster tied to his right leg for an easy draw. He had not been a humble man as he built up his herds and broke the land for his fields. He was not humble to-day and not embarrassed even though his voice trembled at the beginning of his speech.

"I hear the boys tellin' what this town needs. This town needs this and that, they tell us. I'll tell you what this town needs more'n it needs anything else. It needs better and smarter folks, and the only way I know to get 'em is to educate 'em up to it. We've always figured in this valley that one man was as good as another, and sometimes a damn-sight better. How are these boys goin' to have a chance to be a damn-sight better unless we give 'em the best education we can?"

The old man's final sentences were cracking like pistol shots. His neighbors looked at one another with slight grins and voted for the new high school.

FRONTIER SCHOOLING

This scene was repeated many times with many variations but always with the same direction in the history of the American frontier. It was characteristic of the frontier that the men who walked or paddled or rode into new lands believed that democracy was not old but new, that its structure was not set long ago but was something which needed remodeling and sometimes drastic repair, and that its functions were not the same yesterday, to-day, and forever.

Men holding such beliefs were compelled to build schools—not replicas of something back in the old settlements, but schools that were new in their purposes and practices. They had to be new in their purposes and practices if one man was going to be given an equal break with another man so that he could demonstrate his individual worth, so that he could be as good as another man and sometimes better.

In this sense, the American concept of democracy was based squarely on the American concept of public education. Notions of government and schooling on this continent, European at first, came to be very un-European.

EUROPEAN AND AMERICAN CONCEPTS

In Europe, if a people were ruled by an aristocracy, whether of blood or of brains, it seemed all right for them to set up a double-barreled school system, with "higher" education for the higher classes to give them the special skills and the wisdom needed for good government, and "lower" instruction for the masses to train them in patterns of diligence, docility, and devotion to their divinely appointed leaders and institutions.

If, on the other hand, as in America, a people believed that they themselves should rule themselves, and if they sought to put this notion into practice, they were forced into militant support of a single system of free, public, compulsory, universal education. Only thus could they hope to give all children equality of opportunity to be as good as anyone else and as much better as the development of their unique capacities permitted.

The difference between European and American concepts of education and democracy was steadily widened throughout the nineteenth century. "To bring up the children of the poor in the principles of the Established Church and to make them content in that station of life to which it hath pleased God to call them" was an English formulation of the objective of mass education which was accepted by many Americans in 1800. By 1900 it was rejected by most of them with brusque contempt.

In 1798, a great English supporter of improved public education argued in dignified fashion that one of the blessings of schooling for the masses was that it set up a bulwark against the inroads of democratic ideas.

The principal argument which I have heard advanced against a system of national education in England is, that the common people would be put in a capacity to read such words as those of Paine, and that the consequences would probably be fatal to government. But on this subject I agree most cordially with Adam Smith in thinking, that an instructed and well-informed people would be much less likely to be led away by inflammatory writings, and much better able to detect the false declamation of interested and ambitious demagogues, than an ignorant people. One or two readers in a parish are sufficient to circulate any quantity of sedition; and if these be gained to the democratic side, they will probably have the power of doing much more mischief, by selecting the passages best suited to their hearers, and choosing the moments when their oratory is likely to have the most effect, than if each individual in the parish had been in a capacity to read and judge of the whole work himself; and at the same time to read and judge of the opposing arguments, which we may suppose would also reach him.

But in addition to this, a double weight would undoubtedly be added to the observation of Adam Smith, if these schools were made the means of instructing the people in the real nature of their situation; if they were taught, what is really true, that without an increase of their own industry and prudence no change of government could essentially better their condition; that, though they might get rid of some particular grievance, yet in the great point of supporting their families they would be but little, or perhaps not at all benefited; that a revolution would not alter in their favour the proportion of the supply of labour to the demand, or the quantity of food to the number of the consumers; and that if the supply of labour were greater than the demand, and the demand for food greater than the supply, they might suffer the utmost severity of want, under the freest, the most perfect, and best executed government, that the human imagination could conceive.

A knowledge of these truths so obviously tends to promote peace and quietness, to weaken the effect of inflammatory writings and to prevent all unreasonable and ill-directed opposition to the constituted authorities, that those who would still object to the instruction of the people may be fairly suspected of a wish to encourage their ignorance, as a pretext for tyranny, and an opportunity of increasing the power and the influence of the executive government.

One hundred and thirty-five years after Malthus wrote this statement, an American schoolman warned his fellow citizens:

In its fundamental purpose, it is only too manifest that the public-school system has not succeeded. Nor has it utterly failed. The production of a sound and intelligent citizen involves something more than teaching him to read. Indeed, unless something more than that is done, it is probably safer for people not to learn to read at all, for it only places a new and immensely powerful weapon in the hands of the demagogues and the literary psychopaths. But, until a very recent period, the schools have not been able to get and keep most pupils long enough to teach them much more than reading. Actually a formidable proportion of the whole voting strength of the nation cannot yet, in any true sense, read. They pass as literate. They can read highway signs and newspaper headlines, but they balk even at subtitles in the moving pictures. They cannot read discourse, especially expository discourse. They were not in school long enough to learn.

This was the great fear that haunted many leaders of European and American societies alike—that the common people might be educated too much, that they might learn to read the wrong things, that they might learn to think wrong thoughts, and that they might thereby become discontented with things as they were.

CONSEQUENCES OF FEAR

In England, this fear delayed the establishment of a national system of free elementary education for at least a century. As late as 1916 in the debates on the Fisher Act, a member of the House of Commons could inquire bitterly, "What is it that the Honorable Gentlemen would do? Would they stuff Latin and Greek down the throats of agricultural laborers' children with one hand while taking away their bread and butter with the other?" In the United States it furnished the backbone of opposition to the nineteenth-century battles for secular, free, compulsory, elementary education, and it is still observable in attacks on the public schools, in attacks on higher education, and in the hysterical activities of self-appointed textbook "purifiers."

The real argument against public schools and in favor of parochial schools has been for more than a century that children would learn godless things in the former and would learn only godly things in the latter. The main argument against free education has been that only the economically superior classes can be safely entrusted with schooling.

PREVAILING PRACTICES

In spite of these fears and arguments, however, for more than a century and a half the American people as a whole have steadily implemented their belief that an effective democracy requires an effective education for all its members and that men who have the right and duty to order their own ways for their own benefit must also accept the obligation of changing their ways through education in the direction of their own ideals. The American people have carried out this belief by setting up the most extensive system of public elementary schools in the world, by establishing secondary schools at an unprecedented rate of increase over the past half century, and by giving higher education to millions of young people who, under other societies, would have no opportunity to achieve more than simple literacy.

In practice, the Americans know that they still have a long way to go to achieve their goal of a completely universal education for a completely democratic society. Even on the elementary level, the American child's chances for education are tied to such factors as the locality in which he lives, his parents' economic and social levels, his color, his race, and his religion. On the secondary level, these conditions have even greater weight in reducing the democratic character of the education offered. In higher education, the inequalities caused by wealth, race, and religion are particularly severe and constitute one of the most pressing and serious problems faced by the American people to-day.

PUBLIC AND PRIVATE EDUCATION

The state is theoretically the supreme educational authority and agency in this country. In practice it delegates much of its responsibility to individuals and private agencies. The Supreme Court, furthermore, in interpreting the Fourteenth Amendment, has assumed the power to decide whether state educational legislation deprives any citizen of life, liberty, or property without due process of law. Thus the court declared unconstitutional an Oregon law of 1922 requiring attendance at public schools of all children eight to sixteen years of age, on the grounds that it abridged the liberty of parents to educate their children in specific faiths and that it deprived corporations (private schools) of their property, without due process of law. In other decisions the Supreme Court has further clarified the concept that although the state's authority is paramount in education, its requirements must be reasonable and must not without good cause restrict the liberty of parents in providing unusual types of education for their children.

The value of nonpublic schools in the total pattern of education in a democracy is probably best measured by this one main question: How well does the nonpublic school explore areas and develop instruments which public schools cannot or do not discover and utilize? Many of the features of our modern American educational system were first adopted and tested by private schools. Kindergartens, industrial arts courses, music programs, child health work, physical education, commercial training, and graphic arts were all pioneered by private schools before they were made parts of the public educational offering. Nursery schools are to-day being operated mainly by private agencies. After they are sufficiently developed and evaluated, they will be taken over in many cases by the public schools. Adult education is still largely a private enterprise in this country, although the greatest single system of education for adults is operated by the United States Department of Agriculture.

Democracy needs a continuous stream of cultivated idiosyncrasy, developed individuality, and tested variations from the norm if it is to be progressive and dynamic rather than crystallized and static. A wide variety of nonpublic education is necessary in achieving this objective.

EDUCATION, TOTALITARIAN OR DEMOCRATIC?

A totalitarian state must have education of the masses for mass goals. The state itself is regarded as being an end in itself, something to be worshiped and served for its own sake. Schools for totalitarian purposes must therefore be very different institutions from those of democratic societies. The totalitarian school must have cut-and-dried programs set by the national leaders and followed by teachers and pupils unquestioningly. This simple fact dooms any totalitarian system to steady intellectual and emotional deterioration. Its teachers become more and more obedient mechanics of word and action; its pupils become parrots and automatons.

A democratic society is composed of individuals, recognized and treated as such. It has no existence except in its people. It has no purposes except the welfare of its individual citizens. The democratic state is not regarded as a sacred, unchanging entity; it is merely an instrument whereby its citizens order and direct their individual ways in association with one another.

The school for a democratic society must therefore be one in which the learners change their individual ways in the direction of their own ideals. This is not to say that teachers and parents in a democracy have less educational influence than in an autocracy. They are, in fact, much more influential in the school for democracy. In every phase of the child's growth and development, in every learning activity, the educators for democracy must examine and re-examine, scrutinize and evaluate, review and revise, with never ceasing care and industry, the peculiar abilities and potentialities of every individual, the items of experience affecting the individual's development, and the various possible ways to be followed in making the democratic society a better and greater instrument of human welfare.

Teachers, parents, and citizens of a democracy in general have to understand modern educational purposes and procedures on the highest level of insight and performance. No other level is safe for democracy. The best educational practice possible is not too good for democracy.

SOME TOTALITARIAN DANGERS TO AMERICAN EDUCATION

In recent years the people of the United States have had to fight against totalitarian states with weapons of steel and flame. They are now engaged in an ideological struggle against another totalitarian regime, a struggle in which weapons of education, propaganda, political action, and economic pressure are used. Some of the people of the United States have been so frightened by these various conflicts that they have tended to do what timid, scared men often do—imitate their enemies.

Totalitarian regimes commonly have secret police which get much of their information from secret informers who are not compelled to confront in public those whom they accuse.

Totalitarian states are commonly very frightened by possible wrong thoughts on the part of public servants. They are especially concerned that teachers shall be politically "pure." They censor reading matter, particularly for schools, with nervous concern, lest an unapproved idea should infiltrate the official lines.

If the Old Rancher described at the beginning of this chapter were alive to-day, he could be given astonishing news. He could be told of certain fright reactions affecting American education which are imitations—unconscious, without doubt, but still fairly faithful copies—of totalitarian practices.

What might we report to the old man?

"We keep men from government service because they are said to have been seen with men of wrong and bad notions."

The old-timer would laugh. "That would keep a lot of us out of office. Most of the men I've known have had wrong ideas some of the time. When you come right down to it they've always had wrong ideas whenever they've thought different from me."

"A committee of the Congress has asked school systems and colleges throughout the country to submit lists of textbooks and supplementary readings in order to find out how much subversive literature is used in education," we could report further.

The old man's smile would fade. "The *Federal* Congress?" he would inquire with heavy emphasis. "What the hell has the Federal government got to do with the books used in our schools and colleges? Either you've got your wires crossed, young man, or some Congressmen have got theirs crossed! If any from our state have, we'll do our best to uncross 'em."

"We are requiring special oaths of loyalty from public servants, including teachers," we report.

"Everybody ought to take an oath of office, swear to do his duty, support the Constitution, enforce the laws," comments the Old Rancher.

"These oaths are in addition," we explain.

"What for?" inquires the old man. "You got an oath of office, haven't you? What more do you need? A man who would fudge on his oath of office wouldn't be worth a damn to you if you had him swear a dozen oaths. What's the matter with you folks? You scared about something?"

"Well, we have to be careful," we explain. "There's so much subversive thinking going on. We don't want the privilege of government service, the privilege of teaching, or the privilege of education being given to people who have wrong ideas, disloyal attitudes, or subversive notions."

The old man chuckles. "You young folks kind of make me laugh. *Privilege?* I suppose you talk about duty to the government and loyalty to your school boards too. I suppose you talk about people's rights to education. Education isn't a right or a privilege either. It's just common sense. If you want people to be better and smarter for your town or your state or your nation, you've got to educate 'em up to it. *Right? Privilege?* It's a necessity. It's a job. It's work. It's for everybody. It's what gives our folks room according to their size and strength. Stop crying about how scared you are of wrong ideas and start working on education. Maybe if you work hard enough on it, you'll get some new ideas and find out after a while they are right ideas. You'll be surprised."

No. 113

HOW MAY THE SCHOOLS FURTHER DEMOCRACY? [1]

by Harold Alberty

IT has often been pointed out that the schools in any culture tend to reflect the ideals and values of that culture. Certainly this is true of the American school system. The dream of universal secondary education seems capable of realization in our time. The extension of secondary education to include the thirteenth and fourteenth years is already well advanced. The trend is certainly in the direction of a unified system of schools which meets the needs of all children and youth from every walk of life. Furthermore, the teaching of patriotism through the continuous study of the American tradition has always been a major emphasis in our schools.

THE CONFUSED SCENE

We might be complacent and self-satisfied were it not for the fact that at the present time our way of life is being challenged and threatened from outside our borders. From within, we are confused about the direction which we, as a people, should go. On the world scene, the threat of total war is constantly in the foreground. Technological development has forever destroyed the security of nations. Science tells us plainly that there can be only *one* world. Yet clashing ideologies prevent the world from utilizing the fruits of technology for promoting human welfare. This constant threat of destruction through another world war cannot but color the attitudes and activities of people all over the world. The enormous programs of economic and military mobilization cannot fail to affect the outlook and security of youth.

[1] Harold Alberty, "How May the Schools Further Democracy?", *The Annals* of the American Academy of Political and Social Science (September, 1949), Vol. 201, pp. 17-24. Reprinted by permission of *The Annals* of the American Academy of Political and Social Science. The footnotes in the original version are omitted here.

On the national scene, which of course reflects the world temper, we are beset by indecision, conflict, and confusion. We want world organization, but we fear giving up our sovereignty as a nation. We want government to assume increased responsibility for social welfare, but this desire runs counter to our cherished ideals of personal freedom. We want increasing socialization of industry, but at the same time we want to protect the free enterprise system. We cherish freedom of speech, but we are prone to suppress those who differ from us. We have faith in the method of intelligence as a way of solving problems, but we fear inroads upon our traditional religious beliefs. We recognize the brotherhood of man, but continue to discriminate against those who differ from us in race or creed. We want to preserve our democracy, but in attempting to do this, we use undemocratic means which may contribute to its destruction.

This is the sort of world in which the youth of to-day are growing up. An educational program which is not based squarely upon a realistic interpretation of the problems which beset youth in this kind of a world is certainly not capable of playing a major role in the preservation and refinement of democracy. Counts puts the matter succinctly, in a recent statement:

> We in America, in my judgment, have never given adequate thought to the development of an education that is suited to our democracy, particularly in the present industrial age. If we ever do, the result will be something new in the history of education. It will express at the same time both the emphasis upon knowledge, understanding and enlightenment and the emphasis on the cultivation of the basic ethical values of democracy—devotion to equality, individual worth, intellectual freedom, political liberty, democratic processes, general welfare, and the mastery of relevant knowledges. All this must be done in terms of the realities of the contemporary age. The major difficulty which all democracies confront here is the achievement through the democratic process of an educational program designed to strengthen democracy.

The facts set forth above present a real challenge to democracy's schools. Educators and the public should examine critically the educational program and procedures of the schools in order to determine how to make them a vital force in undergirding and strengthening our democratic values and institutions.

BASIC DEMOCRATIC VALUES

It is the thesis of this paper that the school gets its sense of direction from the basic values of our democratic culture. In brief, these are held to be the following:

1. Democracy is a form of social organization which holds that the opti-

mal development of the individual—of all individuals—represents the highest good.

2. The optimal development of all can be realized only to the extent that people have faith in intelligence as a basis for solving individual and common problems.

3. Man can achieve his highest possible development only through acting in concert with his fellows, each individual sensitive to the effect of his acts upon others.

If the school is to give active support to these values, certain principles of democratic education become clear. These will be stated and discussed briefly:

EQUAL OPPORTUNITY

I. *The democratic school provides an educational environment conducive to the optimal development of all American children and youth regardless of intelligence level, race, or social or economic status.*

It was pointed out earlier that we have made rapid progress toward the application of this principle. However, much needs yet to be done. Only seven out of ten youth of high school age are now enrolled. About half of those enrolled drop out before completion of the high school program. In some sections of the country equal educational opportunities are not available to all. Our schools tend to be academic and not well adapted to the needs of large groups of young people. This is especially true of those who do not expect to enter college.

Before this principle can be made fully effective, we shall need to secure much more adequate financial support for schools. Furthermore, we shall need to pay more than lip service to equality of educational opportunity. This can be accomplished only by changing our attitudes toward races and religions, and by providing Federal aid to those states that cannot afford better schools but are willing to provide for educational opportunity for all.

EXAMINATION OF CONFLICTING VALUES

II. *The democratic school helps each student to develop a dynamic understanding of our democratic culture through the intelligent examination of the conflicting values and practices of the immediate and wider community.*

It was pointed out earlier that our culture is in confusion. We hold allegiances to conflicting values. The schools must help youth to clarify these values. Obviously, a program of education which seeks to impose ready-made answers to the problems of our day is wholly inadequate. To attempt such a program is contrary to our whole way of life. Neither can we succeed by insulating youth from the crucial problems which are characteristic of our civilization. Such a program will lead only to frustration and eventual disillusionment.

All too frequently, our schools have fostered the "ivory-tower" conception of education. The traditional subject-centered curriculum has been dedicated to imparting selected facts and information for the purpose of "training the mind." Slavery to the fixed course of study or the adopted textbook has kept teachers from helping youth to solve the problems of contemporary living. Furthermore, in these days of legislative investigations and "witch hunts," teachers have found it safer to remain aloof from the problems which are of real concern to youth. Teachers do not get fired for teaching Caesar's Gallic Wars or solid geometry.

Rugg points up the situation by enumerating the following five areas "shunned and neglected" in conventional school programs:

—Real Work, personally and socially useful
—Sex and Home Life
—Inferiority and the intimate problems of personal living
—The insistent controversial issues of the social system—Property and the struggle for power, Race Conflict, and the control of Public Opinion
—Religion

Controversial subjects. If the schools are to strengthen democracy, they must bring into the curriculum these "shunned" areas which Rugg mentions. The most important test of the appropriateness of problems is the interest and maturity of the learner. In another connection the writer of this article has listed some problems which impinge upon young people and are well within the range of interest and maturity of senior high school students:

1. What kind of an economic system is best suited to our culture?
2. How far should government go in the regulation and control of business?
3. What, if any, responsibility should the government assume in providing for each citizen a good standard of living, e.g., adequate housing, education, medical care, recreation and fruitful work?
4. What fundamental ideas underlie different systems of government, and what system is best for America?
5. What kind of international organization is best for maintaining world peace?
6. Should there be compulsory military training in time of peace?
7. What are the causes of marital difficulties and divorce and what should be done about the problem?
8. What should one do about the so-called conflict between science and religion?
9. How should one determine one's attitude toward religion?
10. How does a person go about the development of a philosophy of life?

11. How should a person determine standards of right and wrong?

12. What are the bases for determining truth in the different aspects of living?

13. What basic knowledge should the citizen have concerning health, sex hygiene, so-called social diseases, and birth control?

14. What should be our attitude toward different racial and minority groups?

15. Should parents try to impose their own set of values on their children?

On every problem mentioned, there is a great deal of controversy. People hold emotional allegiance to certain solutions of these problems. Should the public schools examine problems such as these? In the judgment of the writer, the democratic school has no choice in the matter. Rather, the issue is: Are young people to become intelligent about the crucial problems of our culture? If the answer is "yes," controversial issues cannot be kept out of the schools.

Will the public permit the school to deal with these problems? There is evidence to support an affirmative answer—provided teachers can demonstrate that they are competent to do so, and provided further that students be left free to make up their minds without "thought control."

This does not mean that the teacher must remain neutral. Such an attitude would be impossible. The teacher's opinion should be weighed along with all pertinent data. The teacher's main concern ought to be to protect the process of arriving at decisions intelligently. If we have faith in intelligence, we need not fear the outcome. Our way of life must be capable of critical examination. If it cannot stand such examination, it probably will not survive anyway.

SCHOOL ORGANIZATION

III. *The democratic school is so organized as to exemplify in its daily life the ideals and values which we cherish.*

It is a truism to say that the most effective learning takes place through direct, firsthand experience. We learn through doing. It is one thing to learn about democracy by reading abstract definitions in the textbook. It is quite another thing to learn about it through actually living democratically.

Traditionally, our schools have not been particularly sensitive to this problem. Curriculums have been set up, textbooks adopted, and assignments made with little or no regard for the student's own needs, problems, and interests. The teacher was supposed to know what the student needed. The student's job was to learn what was assigned to him, without asking a lot of silly questions. Elaborate schemes have been developed to get the student to learn. Artificial incentives in the form of grades, and subtle pedagogical tricks, sometimes known as "motivation," have been worked out whereby the uninteresting task is artificially attached to some important want of the student. Thus, the student is forced into learning mathematics in order to play football. That such methods often succeed is testimony of the plasticity of the human organism. That they often fail is known by every experienced teacher.

Our classrooms have been arranged in terms of an authoritarian conception of living. Seats and desks were screwed to the floor. The teacher's desk was sometimes on a raised platform, so placed as to facilitate command of the class. The taskmaster stood before the class and issued orders. Perhaps he lectured to the students on the virtues of democracy.

The situation described above, even though it belongs to the past, could easily be duplicated to-day in hundreds of schools throughout the land. Often the teacher who "has good discipline" is regarded by the administration of the school and by the public as being superior, even though that discipline is based on an autocratic conception of living.

Democratic school program. How does the democratic school organize itself for democratic living? We might paraphrase the principle of democracy stated earlier, to read: *The student achieves his highest possible development only through acting in concert with his fellow students, each one sensitive to the effect of his acts upon others.* It is the business of the school to create the conditions under which this principle can become operative. Some of these conditions are herewith set forth.

The teachers and administrators of the school work together to achieve the highest possible level of common agreement upon the philosophy, the purposes, the psychology, and the methodology of learning, the curriculum, the outcomes, and the program for the evaluation of outcomes. This they do by group thinking, planning, discussing, and experimenting in terms of the common problems which the group faces. In this process of program building, the public will participate at appropriate levels, to be determined by the nature of the problem. The resulting program is not externally imposed, but represents the combined intelligence of the group, and is arrived at through the active participation of all who have a stake in the outcome. Such a program may not satisfy the experts, but it has life.

The formulation of such a dynamic program certainly is antecedent to developing democratic values in the classroom. The teacher studies his students, and the stresses and strains that operate upon them in the immediate and wider environment. Together they plan the learning activities that make up the curriculum, not on the basis of opportunism, but on the basis of accepted criteria which have been arrived at cooperatively. Together teachers and students ask such questions as: Will the unit help us in our daily living? Are all or nearly all of the group interested in it? Can we carry out our individual interests as we work on the common problems? Are there materials available which will help us to solve our problems (e.g., books, movies, recordings)? Decisions arrived at in this manner have the dynamic quality of democracy in that they provide for active participation of all.

Teacher and administrator. In this process, the teacher plays quite a different role from that previously described. His authority derives from his own competence in the field of endeavor, rather than from external or legalistic prescriptions. He protects the integrity of the process by seeing to it that group decisions are carried out; he serves as a specialist when his particular talents will aid the group in moving forward; he co-ordinates the activities of the group and uses every opportunity to release the creative capacities of each student.

In turn, the students assume leadership in dealing with various aspects of the problem. Thus the leadership shifts from time to time in terms of the character of the situation. To illustrate: Suppose a group of ninth-graders were studying the recreational program of the city of Columbus. One phase of the study might be the interviewing of the city recreational director, and reporting back to the group the results of the interview. The teacher would serve as the leader in directing the planning, but a student would be the leader in reporting the interview. A group of students might make a map of the city, plotting recreational centers and playgrounds. In such an activity the group might select its own leader.

In the area of extraclass activities, the high schools have done an excellent job of promoting democracy. Through student councils, athletics, and club activities, students have been given an opportunity to practice democracy. The school of the future will extend such opportunities to the regular work of the classroom.

In organizing the life of the school, the administrator plays an important role. In the past, school administration was organized on a basis comparable to that of industry. Orders were issued at the top and handed down through subordinates to the teachers, who had little or no voice in policy making. The administrator, functioning as supervisor, made classroom visitations, took notes or filled in check lists on what he observed, and held conferences with the teacher during which he told the teacher what was wrong.

The newer idea of administration conceives its principal function to be that of giving leadership in co-ordinating the work of the teachers, carrying on in-service education programs, working cooperatively with the teachers in determining policies and programs—all directed toward the improvement of learning conditions in the school.

IV. *The democratic school utilizes all the resources of the community in promoting effective learning and enriched living.*

The "little red schoolhouse" usually carried on its monotonous activities quite apart from the life of the community. Many of the school buildings were so constructed that the students could not see out of the windows, on the ground that learning took place more effectively if the environment were free from all distractions. The school was *in* the community, but not a part of it. Often, the only contact with parents was the ubiquitous monthly report card setting forth in terms of percentages little Johnny's achievement in a host of different subjects. The youngsters were being prepared for adult life, which had little or no relation to their present daily living.

Under the impact of the philosophy of John Dewey, who proclaimed more than half a century ago that education is not merely a preparation for life, but *is* life, the schools began to break down the barriers that separated them from the community. At first the contacts were largely "extracurricular"; but gradually, as the new philosophy and psychology of education became better understood, schools began to see the value of organizing learning activities around the life of the community.

More than twenty-five years ago, Ellsworth Collings, working under the direction of William Heard Kilpatrick in rural schools in Missouri, virtually threw the fixed subject-centered curriculum out of the window, and organized the life of the school around the problems of the community. When subject matter was needed to help in solving a problem, it was brought in. For example, when a study of why Mr. Smith had typhoid in his home revealed the necessity for knowledge of hygiene and sanitation, the school library afforded opportunity for a systematic study of text and reference books on the subject. When the students attended a political rally at Joplin at which candidate Cox spoke on the League of Nations, and the need for a knowledge of current events and history became apparent, the students turned to their geographies, histories, and periodicals for material which would help to clarify the issues discussed.

Collings proved rather conclusively that a project curriculum was more effective *even in learning the so-called fundamentals.* In addition, it brought the immediate and wider community into the school and enriched the living not only of the students but also of the community.

A community school. From that small beginning, the community concept of education has grown slowly, often in the face of bitter opposition from those who are wedded to the academic curriculum. A striking example of a modern community school is Holtville, Alabama, where the avowed purpose of the school is "to improve living conditions—economic, social, recreational—in this rural community." A cannery has been built and is now being operated by teachers and students. Fruit, vegetables, and meat are canned, either on shares with the farmers assisting, or by the school upon the payment of a small fee. A meat refrigeration plant has been constructed and turned over to the students to operate. Students assist farmers in planting and pruning fruit trees, and the school maintains a spraying service for the use of the community. In the shops, farm implements are constructed and repaired.

While schools of this type are still the exception, there certainly is a healthy movement toward breaking down the barriers between school and community. The manner in which this is done is, of course, dependent upon the nature of the community in which the school is located. Not all schools need to operate canneries or repair farm machinery, but all schools need to use the ongoing life of the community as a laboratory for learning.

It is conceivable, of course, that a community school might not further democracy. It might even serve to perpetuate the class system, and become a tool for maintaining the status quo. However, with enlightened leadership, it provides the opportunity for helping to realize the goal of optimal development of all.

MEASURE OF EFFECTIVENESS

V. *The democratic school evaluates the effectiveness of its program, not in terms of ground covered, but in terms of the democratic values which give it direction.*

The traditional school measured its product by means of factual tests and examinations. The assumption was that the mind was a kind of storehouse for ideas which could be drawn upon in adult life. Education consisted of "passing" courses and accumulating units of credit. Certainly the school was concerned with character building and in having the students acquire good habits of work. These things were duly recorded on the report card as "deportment" and "effort." But this was a supplement to the daily grind of lesson learning. It did not count toward graduation.

Under the impetus of the Eight-Year Study, which showed clearly that students succeeded in colleges even though they did not possess the conventional pattern of lesson-learning credits, new types of tests were developed which indicated changes in the behavior of students in the direction of ability to solve problems, attitudes of cooperativeness and social sensitivity, growth in physical and emotional adjustment, and the like. Since it has long been recognized that the nature of the testing program of the school largely determines the curriculum, this was a significant forward step; for if the schools are to promote democracy, they must evaluate their product in terms of democratic values.

Along with this movement toward a more functional program of evaluation, the old-fashioned report card to parents is giving way to descriptive accounts of student progress toward democratic goals. These reports are much more intelligible to parents, and foster a cooperative program between school and home, designed to facilitate greater progress on the part of the student. Once parents become accustomed to this new type of reporting, they tend to forget the satisfactions which they once gained through telling the neighbors about Mary's "A" or 99 per cent grades. The colleges, too, are gradually learning that the grades which they thought were so essential in determining a student's fitness to pursue advanced study may not be so meaningful, after all. Even the students, whose principal incentive formerly was the grade they received or hoped to receive, learn that honest work is its own reward.

WE CAN DO IT

Can schools promote democracy? The answer is clear. We now know enough about the true meaning of democracy, about the dynamic psychology of learning, about the way the democratic process functions in the classroom, about reorganizing the curriculum in terms of individual and community problems, about effective methods of appraising and recording student progress toward democratic goals, to transform our public school system.

Dotted all over the land are "pilot" schools that are pointing the way. Can these gains be extended? Again the answer is clear. We can change our school system into a dynamic agency for maintaining and strengthening democracy if the professional educator and the public join hands in the cooperative enterprise of building solidly upon the firm foundations which are already laid.

No. 114

DEMOCRACY CAN'T LIVE IN THESE HOUSES [1]

by Paul H. Douglas

WHATEVER the federal government has done or proposes to do about housing, it is a dangerous fact that millions of Americans are shabbily sheltered and living in filthy, malignant slum areas that are growing both in size and in their threat to the physical and political health of our country. Any slum-clearance legislation passed by Congress would have to be followed up by action in states and cities, and by continuous Congressional action.

We Americans like to think of the typical home as a vine-clad cottage, with roses growing on trellises, and trees and grass in the yard; and with all this we associate the pleasing and lively sounds of healthy children at play. It is one of the glories of America that so many of our homes are of that kind—or, at least, equally attractive.

But it is one of our moral, political and economic responsibilities to do something to lift more homes at least to the minimum level for satisfactory living. The 15,000,000 or more Americans who live in the blighted areas are not inferior to the rest of us. They are only less fortunate. Imagine how you would feel if you and your family were housed as they are. Trouble does not come from men who live agreeable lives. It breeds among men who are frustrated, ashamed and envious.

Some people seem to think that slums are what they are because of the character and capacity of the people who live in them. That is not true. Environment to a considerable degree determines the way men act. The extremely strong or the extremely lucky can break free from the handicaps which surround them. Unfortunately not many have exceptional luck or strength.

Clifford R. Shaw made a careful study of bad localities in Chicago, and in his book, *Delinquency Areas,* he presents some facts that will bring you up short.

For example, he found slum areas in which years ago most of the residents were Irish. The juvenile delinquency rate was from 12 to 14 times that of normal neighborhoods. The Irish in these blighted areas began rising in the world, and moved out. Italians moved in. Juvenile delinquency

[1] Paul H. Douglas, "Democracy Can't Live in These Houses," *Collier's* (July 9, 1949), Vol. 124, No. 2, pp. 22-23, 50 ff. Reprinted by permission of *The Crowell-Collier Publishing Company* and the author.

among the Italian youth was almost exactly what it had been when the Irish were there. The Italians moved out and Jews moved in. The delinquency story was repeated. The Jews moved out, and Negroes moved in. Again, the delinquency rate in these blighted sections was some 12 to 14 times that of cleaner neighborhoods.

If I can interpret facts, this means that the living conditions, and not race or religion or color, largely determine delinquency rates.

When the Farm Security Administration began its relief activities in the days of the depression, only rural families who were completely down and out could qualify for its program. If a farmer had means or could get credit, Farm Security could not take him on. Failure was the qualification for getting in under Farm Security. In the South, and elsewhere, this meant that only those who generally were thought of as "shiftless" or "worthless" were assisted. And what do you think happened?

FAITH IN HUMAN NATURE JUSTIFIED

When the government helped them, about 90 per cent of these people moved swiftly to better living than they ever had known, and paid back the loans the government had made to them. Of those who did not make good, some were sick, and a few—perhaps 5 per cent—were shiftless and worthless.

Farm Security first found reasonably fertile land and reasonably habitable houses for those in need of help. Then it set them up with loans for equipment and work clothes, and even a few dollars for window curtains.

That window curtain item evoked some loud yells of protest, but it was wise. Curtains, bright colors, mean something to women. These people, who had not imagined they ever could have such a luxury as curtains, aspired to new heights of living when they saw them in their own homes. Hundreds of thousands of "shiftless" and "worthless" rural slum dwellers, who never had known the possibility or even the meaning of thrift, became thrifty producers and canners of food. Never before had they had a reason for storage shelves.

These people could not have done this by themselves, and private landlords could not have done it for them. They had to have help, and the national government was the only source from which effective help could come at that time.

The people who dwell in the urban slums to-day can't get out by themselves, either. They require help. Where is it to come from?

The fact that upward of 4,000,000 dwelling units exist in blighted areas—and many of them are very old—is pretty good evidence that private capital cannot solve the housing problem.

Private enterprise is always alert for profitable investment. It must make a profit in order to survive. If slums could have been cleared and decent dwellings put up for the slum families, at a profit to private investors, it would have been done. But private enterprise should not be expected to commit suicide by plunging into enterprises that cannot possibly pay out. Men who finance great private works do so, usually, partly with the money of other persons. They have no right deliberately to lose it, even for the worthiest of social causes.

I would favor solving the housing problem by private effort, if it could be done that way. But since it cannot, I think the national government must do it. When the soil resources of this nation were threatened by erosion, the national government properly set to work to save them. It must act similarly when human resources are threatened. States and municipalities generally have not the means to do what must be done.

Anyway, the problem, the responsibility and the danger are national.

A TIDE THAT DOES NOT TURN

Over the stretch of recent years the slums have been getting worse and worse. The rush of war workers to the cities while the war was on added immensely to the housing problem. There has been no corresponding flow back to the rural localities since the war ended, and none is likely. We are an industrial, and increasingly a city people. The situation is badly out of control, and will speedily grow worse, if all building is left to private capital.

Consider some facts and figures. Chicago has from 12 to 20 square miles of blighted areas. The best any private outfit could do when confronted with a problem like that is to make sample-size improvements—rebuild a few houses here, and repair some there. But that would not cleanse the slums. It would only create a few relatively clean spots, not large enough to contribute much toward general improvement.

The cost of land in slum areas, because they are congested centers, usually is vastly in excess of what the same land would be worth if developed along normal, decent residential lines. It is estimated that the cost of slum land in Chicago is commonly $2.75 a square foot, or approximately $120,000 an acre. That's more than $76,000,000 a square mile. In New York some slum land values are nearly twice these figures. How can private enterprise be expected to move in on such excessive values, and come out with the profit necessary for its life?

As nearly as I can figure, the average value of urban slum land, if it is used for normal dwelling construction, is about 50 cents a square foot. That's a little less than $22,000 an acre, or about $14,000,000 a square mile.

Appeals to public spirit and civic pride are not enough to clear the slums, no matter how high-minded businessmen may be. Only a major operation can rid our cities of these cancers, and only the national government can perform that operation.

You have seen some wonderful illustrations of private enterprise at work in our great cities—for example, the erection of Stuyvesant Town in New York. But, to assure a reasonable profit, the buildings had to be so high as to create other problems of congestion. And the number of persons benefited is a tiny portion of the total who need better shelter.

Perhaps you think of slums as evils confined to some of the big cities of the industrial North and Middle West. Listen to the solicitor general of Fulton County (Atlanta), Georgia:

> In Atlanta we have 137,000 people living in filthy, dirty slums, cesspools and human junk yards, breeding places for juvenile delinquency and disease, immorality and crime. Twenty per cent of the city's area contains 39 per cent of the population, and 59 per cent of the crimes committed in Atlanta come from that section. In the same area occurs 72 per cent of the city's juvenile delinquency, and 69 per cent of Atlanta's tuberculosis. . . .

The county health officer for Jefferson County (Birmingham), Alabama, is speaking:

> From all causes the death rate was 72 per cent higher in the area of lowest rental, as compared with the area of highest rental. The tuberculosis rate was 507 per cent higher. The infant mortality rate, or death of infant children, was 117 per cent higher. Stillbirths, or infants born dead, 136 per cent higher, and deaths of mothers from causes related to childbirths 128 per cent higher . . . the adult crime rate was 122 per cent higher . . . and there was an excess of 416 per cent in juvenile delinquency. The illegitimacy rate was 383 per cent higher in the low-rent areas. . . .

Similar facts come from almost every urban center of great size. The Detroit Housing Commission reports that the pneumonia death rate is three times greater in the slum area than elsewhere; infant mortality six times that of normal neighborhoods; the tuberculosis death rate 10½ times greater in the slums; and criminals in the blighted areas are 15 times as numerous as in better sections. This recitation of misfortune, misery and danger could go on and on. The situation is not mainly Northern or Southern, or Eastern or Western, and neither is the problem. It is national.

THE DANGER OF COMPLACENCY

Some of you may imagine that because you live in nice small towns where the refreshing air of heaven circulates freely, the cleansing rays of the sun penetrate every room and yard, and rats do not congregate nightly around garbage cans and outside privies, you are immune to the threat of the blighted areas. I beg you, if you imagine yourself safe, to stop and think. If, because of depression in some future decade, we should have dangerous unrest, the consequences would not be confined to the areas where the unrest is most likely to develop first. If some dreadful disease should begin in one area, it might spread anywhere.

Responsibility to do something to clear the blighted living areas is not limited to morality or to national pride. National internal security demands that something effective be done. National health demands it. Protection of your own health and protection of you and your family from crime require it.

A number of years ago several cases of elephantiasis were discovered in widely scattered parts of the United States. Health authorities, alarmed at this alien disease in our midst, began careful studies to learn the source of the trouble, and every case was traced to the city dump in Charleston, South Carolina.

Senator Burnet R. Maybank, later chairman of the Senate Committee on Banking and Currency, was mayor of Charleston when those cases of elephantiasis were traced to his city. That situation, plus a personal experience, started him on the lines of thought and of action that brought him to be one of the foremost figures in the United States in the fight to provide for all Americans the kinds of houses which minimum standards of decency and safety require.

One day the public health officer of Charleston reported to young Mayor Maybank that the mayor's laundress was ill with meningitis. That laundress had just returned to the Maybank home the weekly baskets piled with freshly washed and ironed linen and clothes. When the mayor told Mrs. Maybank the disturbing news, she placed those baskets of clothes and sheets and towels and what not in the yard and burned them. Incidentally, like the noble woman she was, she went to the laundress' home and helped to nurse her.

Mayor Maybank came to Washington and called on the President. He told the story of the Charleston dump. He told of his personal experience. He explained that the city was broke. It could not act alone, nor could its businessmen remove the dreadful peril of the dump. He is a mighty man when aroused, as all of us who serve with him on his committee are aware, and when he went back to Charleston he had a relief appropriation for clearing away the city's dump. It was a stinking, unsightly and horrible spot frequented by buzzards and rats and disease germs—but it was no worse than other city dumps.

He transformed it into one of the first public housing developments for Negroes; and the neat buildings stand to-day as evidence of what can be done, and what must be done on a vast scale for the public safety.

A census estimate in 1947 shows there are more than 4,000,000 dwelling units in the nation's slum areas. This indicates that close to 15,000,000 persons—Americans, even as you and I—are living in these blighted rat- and germ-infested areas, where sickness, crime and despair are bound to be common.

Even if you reduce this problem to terms of money, and nothing more, you will find that money spent to clean up the slums will result in dollars saved to cities. A committee of the American Bar Association reported: "Based on composite figures representing many leading American cities, it may be stated that such blighted areas yield only 6 per cent of the average city's total tax revenue while absorbing 45 per cent of its service costs. . . ." In Cleveland another study showed that the slum area cost two and a half times its proportional share for police protection, three times its share for public health services, about five times its share for social services, and nearly six times its share in fire protection.

SLUMS COST TAXPAYERS PLENTY

Make your study in almost any large city, and the facts you find will support my contention that the slums are costly to taxpayers in terms of dollars. But I think that one of the lesser reasons for getting rid of them.

In Cleveland, where certain slum areas were cleared and public housing erected, the city saved yearly about $25,000 on relief rents, $11,000 in fire protection costs and $25,000 on tuberculosis care. And the crime for the families who were moved from slum dwelling to public housing was cut by about 34 per cent. In New Haven, Connecticut, the delinquency rate for children between seven and seventeen in 317 families who were taken out of the slums and rehoused in a public project was cut in half.

Enough has been done in a few spots to illustrate the great good that will result when we do more, as a result of action by this Congress, and when year after year we continue to do more and more.

. . . the slums must be licked, the rise of new slums must be prevented, by eternal vigilance on the part of citizens, manifested in local and national action. The apparent cost of the entire job will rise into the billions, but the benefits will be inestimable. A government investment in slum clearance, which I support, is not a dollar investment in the narrow sense. It is an investment in American ways of living, and in ever-rising American aspirations. It is an investment in social and political stability. It is an investment in the fundamental resource of this free country—the people.

A primary function of our representative and free government is "to promote the general welfare." When our nation was young, that did not demand as much government activity as is required now. In those simple, frontier days men were much on their own. But it is foolish for us to talk now about "going back" to simpler days and simpler ways. The basic principles of representative government do not change, but the application of those principles is constantly changing. Otherwise, our free government would have perished long ago because of a failure to promote the public welfare as it must be promoted in each generation—in the bright light of existing conditions, not in the nostalgia afterglow of conditions as they once were.

I think our government has been dangerously slow in recognizing that decent housing is a basic necessity for the public welfare. The public must urge that more be done for those who are caught in the slums. There is no sense in waiting longer, because it now is plain that only governmental aid can solve this national problem.

Such aid is not a threat to our free enterprise system. On the contrary, it provides families with decent homes upon which a better system of free enterprise can be built. The choice before us is slum clearance and rehousing by cities and the nation, or mounting millions of Americans living in slums. Which is the real threat? Think it over, in all of its implications.

No. 115

JUSTICE AND THE FUTURE OF MEDICINE [1]

by Wendell Berge

LET me confess that I stand somewhat in awe of my subject. Justice, medicine, the future, are all mysteries about which man can know little. My profession is the law, which aspires to, even though it does not always attain, justice; about it I know enough to be very humble in my knowledge. Your profession is medicine; about it you are far more conscious than I of the vistas which have not been reached and the depths which have not been probed. The future hangs upon far too many things which are alien to your shop and to mine for either of us to boast that he can chart its course. If I am a layman in respect to medicine, you are laymen in regard to law. But the fact that we differ in calling and in experience is an asset. It enables us to speak our separate minds, to compare our

---

[1] Wendell Berge, "Justice and the Future of Medicine," *Public Health Reports* (January 5, 1945), Vol. 60, No. 1, pp. 1-16.

viewpoints, to sharpen our differences, to move toward a common understanding.

The law is no mean challenge to the human understanding. Yet my admiration goes out to you doctors for the greater mystery which you have set yourselves to unravel. For a casual Nature has spent countless aeons in putting together that bewildering organism we call Man, and a process of discovery has used up millenniums in finding out enough about how the trick was done to help Man over ills and aches toward health. It has taken courage, intelligence, a myriad of guinea pigs, and the sacrifice of a thousand ancient truths to come as far as you have on a trail which still leads into the unknown.

For the Man, of which medicine is mindful, is a curious and wonderful thing. A long course of cosmic, geologic, and biologic events has made of him the permutation of things which anatomically he is. Nature, a slow and uncertain workman, took a fraction of eternity in which to make tries, beat retreats, blunder along her creative way. She achieved in Man a result which, if nothing to brag about, is at least passable. The chances against his being here at all are as legion to one; the chance of his being exactly what he is—well, write your own odds.

But the biologic process alone did not create man. Every human being has a distinct culture stamped all over him. At work and at play he is beaten upon by a continuous stream of stimuli from the human life pulsing about him. In taking care of himself, finding a way of life, begetting posterity, going on a tear, his pursuit of happiness is pent in by the prevailing culture. Man cannot exist apart from the ways and the beliefs of the folk. We are all of us products alike of the earth and of culture. Adjustment to nature and to society, always in process yet never completed, is the condition of our life.

Thus the patient—a curious and stubborn bundle of organs and ailments and resistances—presents a series of enigmas which challenge the skills of the doctor. Man, upon whom all medicine converges, is ancient in contrast to the youthful art which serves him. He was established in his anatomical estate and fitted out with his physiological heritage long before the "physican" was so much as a word. He bears in structure and function, in organ and senses, the impress of all that the life back of him has met in the ages it has passed through and, to complicate the problem, he is infinitely variable. The mixture of genes, chromosomes, and unit characters into fresh combinations in every individual makes each of us a new experiment. In a word, the doctor's challenge is not a standardized man. My hat is off to the man of medicine for the sheer audacity of the task he has undertaken.

From the medicine man of old to the modern clinic is a long way. Again and again mystery after mystery has been probed; again and again the utterly impossible has won acceptance against ancient truth; again and again the reach of medicine has been enlarged. The doctor's craft, with triumph after triumph to its credit, is still on its way. Yet it is set within a larger problem of human well-being which up to now has hardly been explored. It will not be solved until we learn to make culture in all its color and drama an instrument of health.

Institutions of some sort must be set up to serve each of the great needs of life. A people must be fed, given laws, protected against the weather, held to a moral code, provided with escapes from the dullness of everyday existence, fitted out with the comforts and frivolities which make life worth living. As we jog down the centuries and over the globe the ways in which these great tasks are performed present a most kaleidoscopic picture. If the job be to appease the gods, educate the young, ward off plagues, each people has its own way of doing it. Nowhere is there a final answer; there is always bother and striving that it may be better done.

Now the health of the people is among the mightiest of these great tasks. Yet the problem of the adequacy of medical care is unusually baffling. For it is only the exceptional person who has experienced all the arts—technical, economic, cultural—which converge in it. A beginning of understanding lies in a recognition of a distinction between the technology of medicine and its organization. By technology I mean all of those arts of diagnosis, therapeutics, surgery, radiology, dentistry, and the like, which constitute the profession of medicine. By organization I mean all of the arrangements, social and economic, by which medical service is made available. It is idle to dispute as to which is the more important; for there must be a medicine to practice, and there must be arrangements for bringing physician and patient together. It is no veiled mystery as to which is the more backward. In the advance of the art of medicine, you have done a brilliant job. In the face of this advance it is all the more tragic that progress in the organization of medicine has lagged and, because of this lag, the nation has not had the full benefit of your superlative performance.

For backwardness in organization I am not disposed to pass out blame. But we should be quite frank in looking into reasons. You must be able to state your problem before you can solve it; and I wonder if a primary cause of the backwardness is not a failure to put the question clearly. Is not confusion found in attitude, in approach, at the very beginning of inquiry? To be specific, I profess no knowledge of the practice of medicine, and should I attempt to "lay down the law" as to how to treat an ailment you could—and quite properly—laugh me down. Yet, as a group, physicians have been little exposed to the discipline of the social sciences, and social organization is as intricate and as full of mysteries as the art of medicine itself. So when I hear a physician speaking about the organization of medicine in a tone of doctrinaire finality, I cannot fail to remark the contrast with the courageous and humble search for truth displayed in his own work. And when I hear the question put as a choice between private practice and socialized medicine, I cannot escape noting a confusion and dogmatism strikingly different from the scientific approach. As for the "either or" of private practice and socialized medicine, there is no such question. There are a myriad of schemes under which the doctor and the patient may be brought together—not a choice between just two.

Here, then, is the main reason for the great lag of organization behind art. Organization must be shaped in the full knowledge of the economic and social arts, yet it also must be shaped to the art of medicine and the distinctive service it renders. Advance, then, depends upon a range of understanding which neither you and your kind, nor I and my kind, alone possess. It demands a cooperation of professions which is not yet an accomplished fact. As we now take counsel together we are not going to clear up the problem. But this is the kind of thing, multiplied a myriad of times over, out of which will some day emerge the answer to the question of justice and the future of medicine.

Down through the centuries the common law has recognized the maintenance of the common health as one of the great tasks of society. In Europe, and in America, there never was such a thing, strictly speaking, as the private practice of medicine. From the earliest days the common law has made this clear. It is true that from days of old the doctor held no public office, but his service was, as the judges put it, "clothed with a public interest." At a time when any man, butcher, mercer, wheelwright, baker, fishmonger, or candlestick maker, was free to enter the trade of his choice, a license was required of the doctor. To secure his right to practice the candidate had to prove his knowledge, his integrity, his skills. The physician was not free to select or to reject patients at will. As one who followed a common calling he held himself ready to serve all in need to the limit of his capacity. Nor was inability to pay a valid excuse for the refusal of his service. The law recognized him as a kind of unofficial servant of the community and exempted him from the ordinary rules of the market. It wisely refused to crowd the relation of doctor and patient into the elementary forms of trade. The doctor rendered a service, the patient, if he was able, paid a fee, but the courts refused to regard the matter as a business deal.

On the contrary the law judged the relation by reference to the norm of common health. It was recognized that the patient, unversed in the mystery, was unable to judge the quality of service. Hence the doctor, in taking a case, assumed a trust unknown in respect to trade at large. The courts steadfastly refused to bring the rights and duties of the parties involved under the ordinary law of contract. And even in days when any old bargain was held valid, I have yet to discover a case in which a bungling physician was allowed to get off with a plea of *caveat emptor*.

The law went to lengths unknown elsewhere to make certain that the common health was served. In respect to the wares of trade the law of single price usually holds; a commodity is available to all who wish to purchase on exactly the same terms. To insure adequacy of service, a special rule of law was decreed for the physician; he was permitted to charge different fees to patients differently situated. The sliding scale, as much later it came to be called, served a definite social end. It elevated medicine above commerce, broke the pecuniary connection between the doctor's service and his reward, and gave legal recognition to the principle that persons were to be served according to their needs, that charges were to be assessed in terms of ability to pay.

Not so long ago, in my official work, the public character of the doctor's calling was vividly brought home. It is a matter of public record, so I might as well confess. I was one of "the small group of willful men" who instituted the antitrust suit of the United States against the American Medical Association. The occasion, you will recall, was a boycott by the Medical Society of the District of Columbia of certain physicians employed under a group health plan. The Society had expelled one physician, forced a second to break his contract, and denied hospital facilities to their patients. Had the issue been between rival schools of medical practice, I, as a layman, would not have been entitled to an opinion. But both group health and the medical society stood for orthodoxy; there was no difference there. Had the question been a choice between two out of many ways of organizing medical service, I could in time have arrived at my own answer. But I should have wanted to get all the facts, examine experience critically, and think hard and long before deciding. But the issue was far simpler; it was merely a question of a fair field and no favors between two rival—and it seems to me immature—plans for bringing doctors and patients together. To us the American Medical Association seemed to be attempting to keep group health from having an opportunity to prove or to disprove its case. And we were convinced—the courts have now agreed with us—that the tactics were clearly illegal.

As the case went forward, this notion of medicine as the instrument of the common health was the Government's mainstay. Again and again we had occasion to recite the public character of the physician's office. There was a time when an association of doctors acted with the delegated authority of the State itself. The Royal Society of Physicians held a charter from the English Crown which conferred upon it the right to license, to discipline its own members, to search for and to seize illegal drugs, and otherwise as a corporate body to secure the common health. When, much later, Congress issued a charter to the Medical Society of the District of Columbia, it described its rights and obligations in words almost identical with the charter of the Royal Society. However, it was careful to withhold from the new medical society all economic power over its members. It refused to confer upon it authority to fix any schedule of fees for service. And, to clinch the matter, it stated that the privilege accorded was for scientific and educational work and for "no other purpose" whatever.

The same legal recognition of the public interest marked the law which converged on the case. The American Medical Association, or rather its attorneys, argued at one time that medicine was not a trade; hence doctors, even as officers of an association, could not be guilty of restraint of trade. And at another time they claimed for the American Medical Association the immunities from antitrust which by acts of Congress have been accorded to the labor unions. If, as the Journal of the American Medical Association insisted, it was an insult to call medicine a trade, it is a little hard to see how dignity could be restored by calling its association a trade union. The freedom accorded the unions was intended to make possible collective bargaining with their employers, while here a collective bargain between physicians and their patients is just the thing the American Medical Association stood against.

But, just to get the record straight, never once in all the proceedings did the Department of Justice call medicine a trade. Instead, it lodged against the American Medical Association the charge of restraint of trade. Now, restraint of trade, like a hundred glib medical phrases, is a term of art; you can, no more than with a bit of medical nomenclature, discover its meaning by looking up its verbal parts in the dictionary. As irony would have it, it is medicine more largely than any other calling which has given us this rule against restraint of trade. A doctor sells his practice to another doctor. He covenants that for a period of 9 years and within a distance of 25 miles he will not engage in practice. For a reasonable time, say 2 years, he endures his idleness. But the itch to be up and at it grows, and sooner or later the old shingle is hung out. Then the other doctor, who has laid out good cash, becomes indignant, demands what he paid for, and calls for justice. The doctor who found it is not healthy to rust has his ready defense. Society needs his services. His contract is in restraint of trade, hence it is void as against public policy.

Sometimes the plaintiff wins, more often the defendant, but always the court pits the common health against private advantage. His service is of such public importance that a physician is not allowed by his own will and to his own advantage to swear away his right to practice. We were able to present more than 100 cases in which the rule against restraint of trade was applied to medicine. The rule emerged, in fact, very largely out of actions of doctor versus doctor.

With the victory of the Government in the Supreme Court the case is now closed. I advert to it only because it has current significance. It is, to borrow a term from your profession, a symptom of a pathological condition in the organization of medicine. The organization of medicine has not kept up with its technology. The fault is not individual, but institutional. The cleavage is not to be eradicated by invectives, by isolation from modern thought, by clinging stubbornly to that which was once good. It can be resolved only by an escape from folklore, a probing diagnosis, a conquest of prejudice, a drive at the very heart of the malady.

Let us briefly survey the great trends which converge upon medicine, for they decree a revision of means if the great ends of the Hippocratic oath are to be served.

First, the art of medicine has refused to stand still. The family doctor, with his bedside manner, his nostrums, his ponderous vocabulary to conceal his perplexities, his downright devotion to duty and sacrifice of self, was once the very epitome of the art of healing. He has been succeeded by the general practitioner who is the focus of a group of specialists, of which there are now more than a score, each with what a lawyer would call its own jurisdiction. The doctor's office, filled with gadgets and contraptions, has become a combination of consulting room, laboratory, and miniature hospital. A number of separate shops for X-rays, chemical tests, and pathological checkups have become necessary adjuncts. Access to a hospital has become a requirement of the individual physician. Consultation with his fellows has grown into an essential of practice. And behind all this is medicine which, as science and art, is on the march. Behind medicine stand optics, physics, chemistry, biology, and bacteriology, and still medicine continues to capture provinces which until recently lay beyond its frontiers.

Second, the community which the physician must serve has changed with the times. In the good old days the parson, the squire, and the doctor each held sway over his flock. Allegiance to the family doctor was a tie so firmly rooted that it took a crisis to break it. But our world no longer invites so durable, so personal, so exclusive a relationship. The machine, the corporation, and the pecuniary calculus have made over our work, our lives, our personal relationships. Our society has become urban, industrial, gregarious. We have become a new sort of wanderers, a race of modern nomads operating a material culture.

For most of us a job has come to replace an equity in the old homestead. For most of us livings, no longer taken directly from the farm, are pent in between the wages we receive and the prices we must pay. As individuals we are as stubborn as ever our ancestors were. But we act far less on our own and far more as managers, agents, or employees. Our industry is operated by corporations, our farmers band themselves into cooperatives, our workers, skilled and unskilled, gather into unions, even the great mass of our scientists make their discoveries while working for others. In our culture the group has come to be the regular thing.

Against such forces our minds cannot stand firm. Profound changes in habit, interest, and value have come in their wake. The standard of living has moved to a place of primacy among our everyday concerns. It makes the costs of medical service an inescapable problem. The care of the sick no longer can be absorbed by the family; it becomes an item of expense in the budget. If it is a wage earner who is ill, there is a double cost; absence from work means loss of earnings and bills are there to be paid. So medical service becomes a sheer economic necessity, for unless a man's capacity to work is maintained, he ceases to earn. Health thus becomes an aspect of the operation of the national economy.

Within this urban, industrial, wage-earning society, men and women are becoming increasingly conscious of what they want. Our workers demand health as a condition of their livelihoods. They insist upon adequate medical service at a price they can afford to pay, and in their newly-won self-respect they will refuse all charity.

Third, a changing medicine has not yet been adapted to its new world. The high objectives of the profession endure, for they are eternal. But they must be freshly applied. Our society cannot be served by an instrument designed to fit the family physician into the village community. Neither my time nor your patience will permit a prolonged analysis. Yet two or three soundings will reveal the nature and contours of a very insistent problem.

In the not so long ago the old-fashioned doctor could be depended upon to administer medicine for the community. He could see to it that needs were met, service was adequate, and costs were justly distributed. The physician of to-day is in no position to discharge this office. His practice comprehends, not the whole community, but a mere fraction of it. If he is a specialist, the fraction is highly selective. And the whole body of physicians, each operating by himself, has no collective instrument by which it can apportion the totality of service in accordance with general need.

Nor can it any longer take the specific responsibility of graduated charges. The sliding scale survives as a legacy from a simpler society and it has not yet been shaped to the circumstances of modern life. In the larger cities and even in smaller places, there is something of a trend toward fashionable, middle-class, or industrial-worker practice. Here obviously the sliding scale no longer operates, for different physicians serve persons in different income groups.

It is far more serious that charges as a whole are quite out of accord with the ordinary standard of living. As medicine has advanced, its arts have become more intricate. Yet very little attention has been given toward making up-to-date facilities available at prices the common people can afford to pay. It is not that on the whole physicians are paid too much; the statistics I have seen lead me to believe that their remuneration is quite inadequate. It is rather that there is waste, a failure fully to use facilities, a lack in getting the most out of a trained personnel.

The result is a national tragedy. The rich, who do not have to consider price, are often pampered with medical care which they may not need. Paupers are often indulged with a service which rises far above their ordinary way of life. The great middle class finds charges on the whole quite above its ability to pay. As a result, a great part of our population tries to reduce its demand for medical service to the minimum. A great volume of cases reach the doctors in an aggravated condition which, in an early stage, could have been easily handled. Necessary service is often secured at the cost of a heavy debt—a fact which does not make for health. And a far larger part of the people than I like to admit never become your patients.

Here then is challenge. The arts of medicine have advanced; the importance of medicine has been enhanced; it has become a necessity to the people and an essential in the operation of the industrial system. It has outgrown the organization into which, in days of petty trade, it was cast. The demand is for a vaster, more comprehensive, more reliable medical service. If an instrument of the common health can be provided on terms the people can afford, the people will rejoice. If you do not help them to it, the people will seize upon whatever agencies are at hand as a help in time of need, for the universal demand that the common health be served cannot much longer be stayed.

A new medical order is inevitable. Whether we shall cling to the old order or create a new one is not the question. The swift course of events has decreed that there can be no turning back. The question is rather what sort of medical order it is going to be and whether it is the best which wisdom and knowledge can contrive. Like every promising venture, it has its hazards. Is it to be shaped by the best understanding which law, medicine, and the social studies can bring to it? Or is it to be constructed by amateurs in ignorance but with good intentions?

I can understand how, in the face of a new venture, you wonder whether change may not fail to constitute progress. I am certain that there will be serious loss if you sit upon the side lines and allow whoever may come to power to shape this new medical order.

As medicine gropes for a new organization, we all hear much of the doubts and fears of the profession. Many doctors are fearful lest objectives which have been hard won and which they value highly be lost. Many do not see how things which to them are essential can be fitted into a new order. Let us consider a few of the current perplexities.

A great many physicians are justly fearful that the quality of service may be compromised. From the profession I have frequently heard the argument that when the Government undertakes to look after the health of the people, the service rendered is invariably poor. With this insistence on quality I fully concur. Nor do I dispute the fact that the new venture may provide a service that fails to meet the standards of the profession. But I cannot follow the argument that a causal relation exists between Government auspices and poor medicine. The truth is that the new system will bring medical care to hosts of people who before have had no access to it. For them there can be no falling off in quality: there has been no service to fall off in quality. Under a new system the provision of doctors and facilities almost always falls short of the new and enlarged demand. As a result, doctors with exacting notions discover much with which they can find fault.

But let us be fair and place the blame where it belongs. The shortcomings are not necessarily due to the new system. They are probably due to the shortage of personnel and equipment with which to work. It is hardly wise to blame untried arrangements, when there is a scarcity of doctors, nurses, clinical facilities, and drugs. No system can discharge its obligations if it lacks the men and materials with which to carry on.

Much is said, too, about the maintenance of a "personal relation" between doctor and patient. Like the law, medicine is practiced by persons and is practiced upon persons. The patient may be served by one or a number of physicians; the contact may endure for a single call, over a stretch of time, or for a long period of years. But in the practice of the profession, there is no escape from a personal relationship. The law has made this clear beyond a reasonable doubt. Not so long ago a declaratory judgment was sought in the District of Columbia against Group Health Association. The action was brought in behalf of the Medical Society, which argued that a corporation could not legally engage in the practice of medicine. The court replied that medicine can only be practiced by physicians and that Group Health, a corporation, did no more than furnish the auspices under which doctor and patient were brought together. Whatever the character of the organization, the relation is in essence personal.

An oft-repeated variant of the same theme is the insistence upon the right of the patient freely to choose his physician. As a patient I am quite willing to have this right qualified for my own good. A well-recognized principle of economics has it that freedom of choice should be limited where the consumer is not a proper judge of the quality of the ware. If there is one field where freedom of choice should be qualified, it is medicine. For medicine is not one thing but many things. Its services are of a highly technical character. If we are downright honest, you and I know that the layman possesses neither the facts about the distinctive competence of particular physicians nor trustworthy norms to guide his judgment. In a matter of medicine, I am not foolish enough to trust my own choice, and a check with some of my lawyer colleagues indicates that they agree with me. I have over the years, through the devious ways by which a layman gets a little practical knowledge, discovered a physician or two whose judgment I have reason to trust. And with me it is their choice, not mine, which goes.

How many patients have walked into your office whose ailments have been aggravated by an amateur's choice of a physician? If for a moment I can be quite rash, I venture to say that in medicine competence does not wholly accord with ability to attract patients, as in law it does not always rest on ability to attract clients. List, if you will, the six physicians in your city in which you repose the greatest confidence. Let me, from the records of the Bureau of Internal Revenue, list the six who have the highest incomes. It's dollars to doughnuts, isn't it, that the lists do not match? People go to Johns Hopkins or the Mayo Clinic not to be treated by a particular doctor, but to secure skillful service. A personal choice, for that matter, can be secured even under State medicine. But far more important to the patient is the assurance of a high standard of competence.

Nor is wide-open freedom fair to the physician. He should on sheer merit advance in his profession. In all justice his work should be judged, not by the laity, to whom medicine is still a mystery, but by men of his craft who can distinguish brilliant from routine work. "The free choice of a physician," I fear, has become a shibboleth which will not stand analysis.

Candor compels me to say that I feel much the same about the argument that group practice robs the physician of his incentive. In its usual form it runs that if a man is on his own, he will give his best; if he works for a salary, he will put in his hours and let it go at that. The age-old traditions of your honorable profession deny the truth of such an argument. Your code of medical ethics has always elevated the relief of suffering above the pursuit of gain. Its purpose has always been to save the physician from avarice, one of the seven deadly sins. It has long been a canon of yours that service is to be given to rich and poor alike, that quality is not to be tempered to the ability of the patient to pay. My limited experience indicates—and a number of colleagues to whom I have put the question concur—that the mightiest urge to which the physician responds is the pride, the drive, the keeping faith with his calling. A doctor cares, and cares mightily, about the respect of his fellows. A friend of mine tells me of his oculist who insisted he should stop in Baltimore and consult an oculist there. My friend, professing himself satisfied, saw no occasion for the consultation. Finally the oculist said, "Do I have to be brutally frank? I'm damn proud of that operation on your left eye; Dr. Blank is my old teacher, and I want an excuse for him to take a peek at my work." You know better than I that a conscientious and resourceful physician is not, if he can help it, going to allow a case to lick him, and if the case is tough and he loses, it hurts.

Now I do not say that material things are to the doctor of no account. Like the judge, the lawyer, the engineer, the university professor, he has a right to demand advancement, security, an income adequate to his standard of life. For the professional man such things are necessities. Without them the physician is not in a position to give his best.

But such values depend upon no one single way of organizing medicine. To say that a doctor will give his utmost if he acts as his own business agent, and that his incentive will be stifled if he receives a salary, is not borne out by experience. The time was when the great scientific advance was the work of the solo inventor. To-day the most creative of all work, the progress of science and the useful arts, is the product of men on salary. In the larger offices the great mass of lawyers now work on salary and work as hard and as heroically as the youngster who used to flaunt his own shingle in the breeze. It is true that the chance to become a partner is an incentive, but I would not rank it overly high, for work equally as good is done by the lawyers in the Government, where no such opportunity exists. In our institutions of higher learning, research as well as teaching falls to salaried employees and there you will observe an interest, excitement, devotion to duty, an urge to be up and doing. To return to medicine, how many thousands of our best doctors are to-day giving their all without stint in the service of the Army and the Navy?

Ambition, security, income are necessary things. They have in every age and among the most varied conditions of society driven men to accomplishment. If I were a youngster, I would rather leave the series of judgments which shape my career to men of my own profession than attempt to get ahead by translating my skills into the art of winning and holding patients. Most important of all, why is it that doctors are troubled by this doubt when university professors, lawyers in public service, officials who make of government a life work, never even raise the question. And why is it that, when the Government of England first undertook to offer medical service, there was quite a chorus which viewed with alarm the loss of incentive, while to-day such a doubt remains unvoiced? It is easy enough to answer the argument that a salary will kill the urge to serve; it is hard to understand why the question is ever asked.

It is too late to turn away from that fearful subject of the State as employer, for I am already discussing it. As for myself I have no more fear of a venture of the State into medicine than I have of a venture of the State into law. The venture into law is old—judges, public counsel, prosecuting attorneys, are examples. The venture into medicine, the pauper and the criminal aside, is new, but the traditions and high standards which have long operated in one realm can be established in the other. Our Federal Government, in most of its activities, has adhered to a very high standard of professional competence. If for a moment I may be personal, I have experienced the practice of law in a large private New York office and in the Department of Justice. The Government has never imposed upon me restrictions which I have felt to be a burden. If anything, I have enjoyed a greater freedom than I could have had in a private law office. It is true that frequently my own judgment is tempered by the opinions of my colleagues. But usually a consultation, as you call it, leads to a sounder decision than any one of us alone would make.

You are right in insisting that high standards of medical care must not be compromised. But standards are a professional matter. Their chief dependence is upon adequacy of resources. They are not inherent in any type of organization. Your current way, as well as State medicine, has its insidious dangers, and, since comparative merits are at issue, I am not content with any argument which points out vices in the one without looking at the faults of the other. As it is now practiced, medicine is exposed to the corroding ways of business. Witness the recent exposure of fee-splitting in the city of New York. Under another dispensation, medicine may be exposed to the strange ways of politics. Which is the greater temptation, I am not able to say. But politics is a thing from which no activity of man is free. It can be employed to achieve holy as well as unholy results. And the State is not, as some of my physician friends seem to fear, a ward heeler telling the doctor how to practice.

I am not, mind you, presenting a case for or against the prevailing system, State medicine, or any particular medical order. There is, as I said at the beginning, no such question as private practice versus socialized medicine. For practice is never private and all medicine has a social function. The question to be faced is harder, more intricate, far more detailed than any such antithesis suggests. First of all you must ask what you want medicine to do. That is easy, to furnish to the whole population an adequate service of quality upon terms it can afford. Next, you must contrive ways and means of seeing to it that the great variety of services we call medicine are called into play to serve the common health. Next, you must set up protections against the hazards you and I see so clearly. And finally, all of these arrangements must be brought together into a going organization. Such a result is not to be attained by an act of faith or a single trial. The conditions of health vary from city to country, from section to section. The needs of the people as locally felt must be met, and this means variety, flexibility, and capacity for adaptation. It means, seek—honestly, objectively, courageously—and ye shall find; knock at many doors until the right ones shall be opened to you.

There is no royal road to a modern medical order. Thus the system we seek is not a choice between private practice and socialized medicine. In following his private calling the physician is fulfilling a social service; in medicine "private" and "social" always have been and always will be associated. These terms, so frequently set down as opposites, have only the most evasive content. Private practice has no stabilized form; the private practice of the country doctor who rode his horse, made his rounds, and was monarch of all he surveyed is not the private practice of a modern urologist. And "socialized medicine" embraces systems as distinct as the charity of the medieval church, the Royal College of Physicians, the clinic of a modern university, the bureau of public health, and the Russian way. You can no more get anywhere with such terms than you can practice your profession with a general concept of disease as your stock in trade.

The question demands, not an easy answer, but painful, constructive, detailed thought. It demands, too, an indulgence in downright trial and error without which nothing worth while emerges. A few experiments—far fewer than the length and breadth and depth of the subject demands—have been blazing fresh trails. Increasing numbers of physicians have enjoyed practice on their own and on salary, and are prepared, from experience rather than in speculative terms, to assess debits and credits. In my pocket I have a letter from one such physician who sets down an illuminating comparison by no means to the disadvantage of salaried work.

Last but most important of all, the war has accelerated a trend long in the making. A host of physicians now in service are conscious of the shortcomings of "military medicine" and have scores of suggestions as to how it can be improved. But they have become aware of the tremendous possibilities which inhere in a medicine directly organized to perform its function. Millions of soldiers, returned from the front, are going to demand for themselves and for their families the instruments of health to which they are entitled.

The course of events moves fast and a new medical order seems inevitable. My fear is not that we will not get it; an awakened public, sparked by our veterans, will see to that. My fear is that we will not bring to its creation all the knowledge, wisdom, and understanding we possess. . . . On ways and means I am open to argument. . . . Of the necessity for distributing the cost of protection against illness I am wholly convinced, and I think the American people are adamant.

The medical order our stalwarts defend has already ceased to exist. A new medical order will come into being even though we do not will it, even, in fact, if we stubbornly resist it. For the medical order, like other institutions, cannot insulate itself against the impinging culture. It must make its response to the great pulsing tides which everywhere else enter our national life. The wiser physicians know that sheer opposition is not going to hold back the tide. They are putting forward—it seems to me a little timidly—proposals of their own. The other day the medical society right here in St. Louis voted approval of a plan for prepaid medical care, and the papers stated that a minority of doctors thought it did not go far enough. Timidity must be replaced by high resolve, and I am afraid that a very old adage which goes back at least as far as ancient Egypt applies here: "If you can't stop a movement, join it."

Seriously, support of the doctors is essential to the salvation of the movement. The organization of medicine is an affair of a couple of shops. It is a job for the craftsman in social order, but it must be shaped to the very life of the medical service it has to offer. If doctors oppose, or stand on the side lines, the layman will create a medical order which may prove to be indifferent or even blind to the values doctors prize most. If the doctors assume a role in its creation, they can see to it that no compromise is made with the standards of the profession.

The problem thus becomes one of creation. In respect to the selection of personnel, the standards of care, the carrying of risks, the methods of payment, the ways of remuneration, a score of ways are open. The form of organization may follow an agency of the State, the university pattern, the hospital set-up, or a combination of devices from all these. The Government may dominate the system, become one of a number of parties to its management, or be excluded from it altogether. The venture may fall into the legal form of a public health authority, a nonprofit-making corporation, a series of independent or interlocking corporations, a group of consumers cooperatives, a mutual association of the profession and the laity, or something else. Its direction may be lodged with a tripartite board, representing the Government, the public, and the profession, or the public and the profession, free from Government interference, may assume joint responsibility. It may or may not be State medicine; it cannot escape being social medicine.

It is man for whom medicine exists. Its function must be to keep a whole people in health. The doctor must be the focus, but upon his office a host of unlike services must converge. The physician must not stop with asking, "Of what is this man ill and what can I do about it?" He must also inquire, "Why and how did this man become ill in the way he did?" The quest leads beyond cure to all the conditions upon which personal well-being depends. Food, clothing, housing, recreation, family, occupation, social life are all terms in the equation of health. Nor must man's habitat be forgotten, for adaptation is a requisite of the life process. Many arts must converge into the new medicine; prevention, sanitation, the public health must become a part of it. At its hub must stand the doctor; it is he who must direct this vast apparatus of skills, specialized personnel, facilities to the service of the human being. The medical order I suggest, and which the American people are going to have, will be vaster and mightier than anything we now know.

Such a medical order, it seems to me, should be hailed enthusiastically by the physician. In respect to professional matters his word will prevail. His opportunities for service will be greatly enlarged. He will have access to facilities which only the exceptional physician can now afford. A shift in work now and then will keep him alive in his profession. He can get away occasionally for further training. And above all, he ought to be better able to turn his clinical work to permanent account.

In an abstract way I recognize the value of ivory-tower research. But, after all, the heat of the daily round has its own contribution to make. In our Antitrust Division we have in the last 5 years perhaps done more to blaze a path for the law than any law college faculty in the land. The result has not been due to any unusual ability of ours. We have simply been on the firing line and have had an opportunity to turn our clinical work to account. To me it seems that one of the great shortcomings of the prevailing medical system is that the practitioner is kept so busy with his patients that he cannot translate his work into medical discovery.

Thus, in the end, I return to my beginning. I can hand you no ready-made medical order on a silver platter. If I could, it would do you no good. I can only suggest to you, whose minds have long been busied with the subject, some reflections of a man of another profession. And I am positive that a service adequate to the times cannot be brought into being without the doctors' creative participation. As doctors and patients we face a crisis, and my appeal is to the ancient wisdom of the profession. The ends of medicine remain unchanged; ways and means must be found to adapt its practice to the conditions of present-day society. A new organization must be created that an ancient mission be not lost, that once again medicine shall be available to all in need and charges shall be graduated in accordance with ability to pay.

An instrument of the common health such as never before has been offered to a people is within our reach. This is no time for petty doubts and timid moves. In the face of a national challenge we must, as one of our great jurists said of the law, let our minds be bold.

Chapter XXXIII

GOVERNMENT AND FARM PROBLEMS

[In the United States of 1850 a farm could be obtained for little expenditure of capital, and only a small sum was needed to equip and operate it. Our rapidly expanding population could absorb the farmer's products and surpluses could be readily and easily exported. Given an ever-mounting demand for farm products, farmers sought and obtained government aid in increasing their production. Land was made available at slight cost through the homestead laws; irrigation projects put fertile but arid land into use. Bureaus were established to aid the farmer by placing the results of scientific investigation at his disposal and to help him battle those pests and diseases which destroyed his crops.

World War I further emphasized the trend towards increasing production, due to the inability of Europe to grow much of its own foodstuffs. The emphasis on producing was increased when we entered the war in 1917. It was in this period that we ploughed the "dust bowl" and planted the seeds of new crops and new conservation problems. The wartime activity also created an intense activity in farm land speculation. Farms were purchased at fabulously high prices and purchasers borrowed liberally on these new inflated values.

After 1920 we were confronted with a different set of circumstances. Demand for agricultural products declined, partly because of the loss of European markets and partly because of the slowing up of our annual population increase. Farming became an enterprise which required large amounts of capital; those who could not raise this money were forced, in an ever-increasing number, to become tenants. It was necessary to remove lands, especially those of sub-marginal productivity, from production. Some action had to be taken which would solve the capital and credit problems of our farmers.

Throughout the 1920s and 1930s, the farm problem was a major concern of the American people. Many remedies were tried: the Agricultural Marketing Act of 1929, the Agricultural Adjustment Act of 1933, the Bankhead Cotton Control Act, the Kerr Tobacco Act and the Bankhead Jones Acts of 1934-35, the Soil Conservation and Domestic Allotment Act of 1936, the Farm Security Act of 1937, the Agricultural Adjustment Act of 1938 plus much legislation designed to secure easier farm credit.

But the farm problem was still unsolved when we entered World War II. The New Deal program of the 1930s and the wartime boom partly alleviated the farmer's situation but the long term problem of finding markets to absorb the productive capacity of the American farmer still is unsolved.

The farmer wishes to improve his standard of living; he wants to increase his income. This drives him to produce more and more, and, because of the inelasticity of effective demand for farm products, creates surpluses and drives down prices. This forces the farmer to even greater production to increase his income. The American people are still groping for a solution to the problem. This chapter can do little more than present certain facts and opinions to stimulate ideas and provoke discussion.]

No. 116

SOME ESSENTIALS OF A GOOD AGRICULTURAL POLICY [1]

by Howard R. Tolley

THE "GOOD LIFE" FOR FARM PEOPLE—WHAT DOES IT MEAN TO THEM?

BEFORE one considers what is desirable in agricultural policy, it is appropriate to define "desirable" and to glance at the sources of policy. In the long run, the desires of the people themselves must be the determinant. It is they who issue the charters of policy. These charters are often mutually contradictory; sometimes they are no more than a vigorous negation of an unpopular policy, without approval of a substitute. Through the processes of legislation and administration, policy is hammered out into detailed form and becomes concrete in programs. Yet, in the last analysis, these concrete details are accepted or rejected by the people, so that policy rests ultimately upon their desires as a base.

If policy is looked at as an expression of popular will, the thing to do is to try to arrive at some understanding of what the people, the farm people in common with their fellow citizens of other groups, think it should try to achieve for them.

In the effort to understand what farm people want, few objects of study are more rewarding than the ways in which Government has attempted to meet the demand of farmers for equal economic status with other groups in an industrialized world. As the impact of the Machine Age began to be fully felt after the Civil War, the Farmers' Alliance succeeded the Granger movement, the Populists succeeded the Farmers' Alliance, and still other vehicles of agrarian unrest followed the Populist movement. The

[1] Howard R. Tolley, "Some Essentials of a Good Agricultural Policy," *Farmers in a Changing World; 1940 Yearbook of Agriculture* (Washington, D. C.: United States Government Printing Office, 1940), pp. 1161-1168.

Spanish-American and World Wars silenced the outcries briefly, but always they were renewed with increasing volume, because none of the responses of Government fully sufficed to right what the farmers regarded as their inferior economic position.   Throughout the earlier years, the clamor of the farmers was for regulation of railroads and trusts, for credit and currency reform, for innumerable other actions by Government, but always it was for some action that would restore the economic dignity enjoyed by agriculture before the Civil War.   In this century an extension of governmental efforts to comply with those demands has been apparent.

What are the common denominators in all these waves of action and reaction?   What does the farmer want in terms of his own life when he insists upon equality for agriculture?   What, in brief, does he regard as the elements that would go to make his life a good life?

Food, Clothing, and Shelter.   To start with the most common of all common denominators, the average rural American wants food.   He wants it three times a day and enough of it.   His unfavorable reaction to the existence of agricultural commodities in quantity too great to be distributed by our economic system while at the same time great numbers of persons suffer want has been clearly expressed in recent years.   Food, even more than houses or clothing, is the great fundamental necessity.

The inability of this country thus far to make its economy get food to those who need it and are willing to work for it is more dramatic than the corresponding inability to make houses and clothing available to those who need them.   Yet both failures are of the same character.   The disastrous effects of weakened purchasing power, perhaps aggravated by the imbalance of costs and prices, upon the housing and clothing industries have been clear to everyone in recent years.   The need and demand for more and better houses, for more and better clothing, has persisted.   It is unnecessary to pile up such evidence as the figures on housing shortages, even for those people who are well above the average in income, or the estimates of the acres that would be required to produce fibers to clothe the ill-clothed.

The Newer Fundamentals.   But to the classic triumvirate of past generations—food, clothing, houses—ours has added other necessities that it regards as so basic that they must be grouped with those three.   For one thing, it has become clear in the last few years that the great majority of people in this country need better medical care than has been available to them and that included in their broad demands for higher living standards is a desire for better health.   The success of governmental attempts to bring more nearly adequate medical facilities to rural people, the development of group-health movements, and the wide agitation for a new national health policy all indicate the genuineness of this desire and the need to satisfy it in one way or another.

For our times, too, it has become equally essential for people to have means of ready transportation. The expansion of living standards that has gone on steadily in the United States and is considered by most people the outstanding characteristic of this country is dependent in large part upon facility of movement. Hence, good roads and means of using them must now be included among the necessities if we are to move toward the spread of this higher standard of living among all the people. Means of communication are almost equally important, from this point of view, and are rapidly becoming more significant. It is impossible, too, to ignore the growing desire for devices for home and farm that will reduce the drudgery too often associated with farm life. Obviously, the rural people of this country, more than any other group, stand in need of the essentials enumerated in this and the preceding paragraphs.

"Not by Bread Alone." There is an intangible to be added to these tangibles, partly produced by them and in turn influencing them. Rural people, like everybody else, must feel at least some measure of security in the enjoyment of the fundamentals of the good life. This does not mean the kind of stability that conditions have imposed upon some other countries, the quiet of a strangulating economy or the rigidities of a society laid down in unchanging strata. It means that the average man wants to be able to look forward to the conduct of his life free from fear of events over which he has no control. If this assurance can be added to the elements outlined here, then truly the citizen will be prepared to live well.

For it is true that no man ever remains satisfied with bread alone, once he has achieved enough of that. In any passably adequate definition of the true desires of the people, therefore, those elements are to be included that do not contribute simply to material welfare.

Prominent among these essentials are schools. It is perhaps the greatest contradiction between the democratic theory and its practice that the rural schools of this country are as poor as they are. The country child to-day does not have the opportunity to obtain schooling as adequate as that afforded most city children. Yet from the rural areas come the majority of the country's children. The eagerness of rural people to take advantage of schools when they are available is attested from all sources and in turn attests that educational opportunity is one of the elements of the good life that they are striving to obtain for themselves.

The desire of farm people for improved transportation and communication for economic reasons has already been mentioned. Those two necessities are likewise important for a social reason. The drudgery of farm life is stressed no more often in modern writing dealing with agriculture than is the isolation, and this isolation is one of the most difficult barriers to the achievement of the good life individually and a strong, rich, homogeneous culture nationally. Greater opportunity to take part in social activities, however, involves other elements than transportation and communication. Indeed, nearly every factor involved in raising standards of living contributes to this greater opportunity, as do more leisure, the development of group participation in political and economic life, and many others. Of the urgent need for a better social life there seems to be no doubt, if the reaction of farm people when the opportunity is offered is a gage.

Thomas Jefferson wrote 130 years ago:

> I have often thought that nothing would do more good at small expense than the establishment of a small circulating library in every county to consist of a few well-chosen books, to be lent to the people of the county under such regulations as would secure their safe return in due time. These should be such as would give them a general view of other history and a particular view of that of their own country, a tolerable knowledge of geography, the elements of natural philosophy, of agriculture, and mechanics. Should your example lead to this it will do great good.

Few rural people even now have access to more than an infinitesimal part of the reservoirs of human thought stored in books new and old. Only infrequently are they able to have even the newspapers and periodicals that city people take for granted.

Many others of the softer threads woven into the rough fabric of living and enjoyed by other groups of our population are not for most farmers. Even the more well-to-do farmers may be without some of the advantages of city people merely because of the circumstances of rural life. For the poorer farmers this lack is aggravated by their poverty. The point is not that any particular activities are necessarily to be sponsored by the Government. If government makes it possible for people to have more leisure or greater income, the point would be the same. The provision of the opportunity for people to build a desirable life is what is important. It is not important whether this is done by government or otherwise; nor is it important whether government directly provides employment in cultural enterprises or merely makes it easier for people to share in them.

Very significant has been the development by rural people of their own means of self-expression, even when their material circumstances would apparently make it difficult for them to interest themselves in such things. Some investigators have cited the survival, through times of poverty and distress, of native folk arts such as square dances and handicrafts and the revival in late years of folk singing to illustrate the latent resources of our rural culture. Where highly commercialized agriculture has not altered the basic patterns of rural thought, these folk arts seem to flourish with vigor. Such response means that people are hungry for the interpretations of themselves and their own lives that the arts can give. The Nation may be only dimly aware of the richness of the cultural soil that awaits seeding. Here is a factor in the good life that farm people miss more than most others.

One of the great essentials for such a life is that a man have the opportunity to feel valuable, to feel that his work is of use and worth. Men do not like to feel that they are the victims of forces over which they have no control. The farmer, for instance, does not want to feel that great cyclic depressions will rob him of the chance to make a living or that other unmanageable disasters hang over him daily or yearly. In a sense, this is the same desire for security mentioned earlier. Not that men demand absolute assurance that their efforts will be successful; what they want is the assurance that they can work and struggle for some reasonably achievable end.

Finally, every man needs to feel that he is working with and is part of a group of his fellow men. Partly, this feeling arises from self-interest. The farmer has learned that he can ordinarily achieve more for himself as a member of a group than he can working alone. But, equally, cooperative endeavor in work, as in social activity, satisfies a deep-rooted desire.

There has been abundant evidence of this in recent years. There are the remarkable records of participation by farmers in the various referenda that have been held in connection with Government programs, and the eagerness with which farmers for a quarter century have availed themselves of the chances to get together afforded by the State and Federal extension services and other organizations. The pronounced development in the last 25 years of cooperative-marketing groups illustrates the desire of farmers to work together for collectively beneficial ends. Finally, there has been a strong response by farmers to the new opportunities offered them to participate in community undertakings, to function as members of committees dealing with farm problems and helping to administer farm programs, and in other group activities not previously available to them. They have almost uniformly seized the opportunity not merely to attend meetings and sessions but to function with enthusiasm and effectiveness, and have demonstrated clearly that the traditional individualism of the agriculturist is not of the kind that prohibits successful cooperation.

It seems clear that the opportunity to assume the full dignity of the mature citizen of a democracy is one of the things that people desire.

Therefore this opportunity should be included among the elements that make up the good life.

THE NATION'S STAKE IN THE GOOD LIFE ON THE FARM

Up to this point we have considered elements pertaining primarily to individuals and secondarily to farmers as a group. What is the Nation's interest in the attainment of the good life both by individual farmers and by agriculture as a whole? The Nation's principal interest in agriculture, aside from its interests in farmers as citizens like other citizens and in the production by farmers of an adequate supply of food and fibers, is that agriculture assume a status equal with those of other elements in the economy. A depressed agriculture obviously is a millstone about the Nation's neck. Agriculture must prosper if the Nation is to prosper—though the converse is true also, of course. The Nation also looks to agriculture to contribute to a well-rounded national culture, fully representative of the national life. Then, too, it must look primarily to agriculture for conservation of natural resources and for the cultivation of another resource—human values—among people engaged in agriculture. The Nation has a definite interest in the reinforcement of the sense of personal dignity, of the citizen's importance as a citizen. Indeed, this may be regarded as a dominant interest, for the health of any state depends upon the free intelligent functioning of its citizens.

The entire Nation, then, has a stake in seeing that its farm people have a chance at the good life. How far is it possible to say that the constituents of such a life, as roughly outlined, have so far been made attainable to the farmers of the United States? If the yardstick of what rural people want is applied to what they now have, much remains to be done before it can be said that any large number of them have attained very many of these elements of the good life or attained them in any large proportion.

For a generation or more the slogan of vocal farm groups has been "equality for agriculture." This has arisen from the feeling of farm people that they cannot now earn enough from their labor to enable them to buy for themselves, individually or as a group, to the same extent as other groups, these elements of a good life.

For instance, to take the denominator that is most readily usable, agriculture represents about 25 per cent of the population, yet has less than 10 per cent of the national money income, despite some progress in late years toward giving agriculture proportional status. Since farm families rear about one third of the Nation's children, it is obvious that many of those children, in a money economy such as now exists, start life at a grave disadvantage compared with other children in the Nation. It has been estimated that 22 per cent of American children suffer from malnutrition, and there is little evidence, even inferential, that rural children are much if any better off than urban in this respect. The prevalence of cash-crop farms as well as bitter poverty imposes an ill-balanced diet upon great groups of farm people. The evidence points to a relatively worse position for the farmer with respect to clothing and housing. As many as 50 per cent of farmers are believed to live in inadequate dwellings, and probably one third of them are poorly clothed.

Aside from the over-all inequity of the status of agriculture, there is imbalance within agriculture. . . . [Though the situation has improved considerably since 1935-36 when it was estimated that 24 per cent of all farm families had an income of less than $500 on which to live for a year and many were in dire physical need, the low income of many farm families to-day still presents a serious challenge.] Erosion still claims, despite great efforts, 3 billion tons of soil a year. So much for the material situation of agriculture. Figures upon many nonmaterial elements are hard to obtain, but it is known that rural school terms are shorter on an average than those of city schools and that teachers in rural schools are paid less than their urban colleagues. More than 70 per cent of the entire rural population is without public-library service. And observation shows that all too few country families have any opportunity to enjoy music, pictures, plays, or movies. As citizen and worker, the farmer is still without effective control over the fruits of his labor, and he is still unsure that he can act to make his needs and desires known.

In conclusion this may be emphasized: The wants and desires of those who people the countrysides of the Nation are not static and will not go unvoiced. Their conception of what makes up a good life will continue to evolve with the changing times, and their struggle to convert that concept into reality will go on.

FUNDAMENTALS OF A GOOD AGRICULTURAL POLICY

Once some agreement has been reached as to the elements that rural people regard as essential to living a good life, the next question that logically arises is, How are they to obtain these elements? In terms of this discussion, how do these desires become translated first into policy and then into action designed to obtain the things they want? There can be little debate as to the ways in which they have obtained in recent years such of these elements as they have obtained. The last decade has given convincing demonstration to farmers of the value of group organization that moves aggressively on their behalf. There is no doubt whatever that the disposition of agriculture is to continue and expand this type of action. Symptomatic of this state of mind is this statement by the editor of a farm periodical:

> The farmer to-day demands a standard of living in keeping to the contribution he makes to the national economy. He sees no reason why he should not enjoy most of those conveniences found in our cities and towns as a matter of course. But to obtain all those things takes money, far more money than farmers 40 years ago dreamed of having. Automobiles, tractors, radios, bath tubs, washing machines, refrigerators, etc., must be bought. To buy and maintain them the farmer must produce far above the animal needs of his family, and he must sell his products at a fair exchange value.
>
> When farm prices were low back in 1920-25, the farmer faced a choice. He could take what might be dished out to him and sink back into a state of chronic poverty. Or, he could make a fight for a share of the national income which would permit him to live in decency and on a level comparable to men in town who render a like service to the nation. In the good old traditional American spirit he decided to fight. He is demanding government aid, not because he believes in aid as such, but because it seems at the moment the only attack on his problem that will get results.

Thus farmers have learned that group pressure will yield certain results, and few will deny that in justice they richly deserve the results they have obtained. New devices of consultation, cooperation, and administration looking toward the satisfaction of these demands will become major components of agricultural policy in the future if that policy mirrors the wishes of the people.

Discussion of such questions as these inevitably brings up related questions as to the interrelation of the popular will, the legislative process, and the administrative process; perhaps even of the place, in this framework, of the judiciary and of the great body of technical competence available in contemporary culture. Where do all these things fit into the makings of national policy? Perhaps the matter will be clarified somewhat by this quotation from Charles A. Beard, setting forth what he calls a "bill of axioms or aphorisms for public administration":

> (1) The continuous and fairly efficient discharge of certain functions by government, central and local, is a necessary condition for the existence of any great society.
>
> (2) As a society becomes more complicated, as its division of labor ramifies more widely, as its commerce extends, as technology takes the place of handicrafts and local self-sufficiency, the functions of government increase in number and in their vital relationships to the fortunes of society and of individuals.
>
> (3) Any government in such a complicated society, consequently any such

society itself, is strong in proportion to its capacity to administer the functions that are brought into being.

(4) Legislation respecting these functions, difficult as it is, is relatively easy as compared with the enforcement of legislation, that is, the effective discharge of these functions in their most minute ramifications and for the public welfare.

(5) When a form of government, such as ours, provides for legal changes, by the process of discussion and open decision, to fit social changes, then effective and wise administration becomes the central prerequisite for the perdurance (continuance) of government and society—to use a metaphor—becomes a foundation of government as a going concern.

(6) Unless the members of an administrative system are drawn from various classes and regions, unless careers are open in it to talents, unless the way is prepared by an appropriate scheme of general education, unless public officials are subjected to internal and external criticism of a constructive nature, then the public personnel will become a bureaucracy dangerous to society and to popular government.

(7) Unless . . . an administrative system is so constructed and operated as to keep alive local and individual responsibilities, it is likely to destroy the basic well-springs of activity, hope, and enthusiasm necessary to popular government and to the flowering of a democratic civilization.

Can it not be said, in the light of these words, that policies are, in the first place, proposed by the people, and that, in the last place, they are judged by their effectiveness in the daily lives of the people? A corollary would seem to be that the more continuously and the more in detail policies are proposed and judged by the people, the better will be the chances of those policies for success. In other words, policies are outlined by the people in broad sweeping mandates, often inconsistent within themselves and usually very general in terms. The legislative branch of government gives these policies form and, to a certain extent, harmonizes them. The administrative arm develops and administers programs to give effect to the policies. But the "well-springs of activity, hope, and enthusiasm necessary to popular government" will be tapped throughout all these stages in "the flowering of a democratic civilization."

Policy, therefore, cannot be taken to mean simply a rule laid down by the people or their legislative or administrative representatives and then left to operate in a vacuum untouched by the necessities of circumstance. The mere statement of such a view seems to refute it. The realistic view is that policy making is a part of the daily, detailed living of the people and the functioning of their government in all its branches. If the formation of policy is conceived as being of this character, the powerful directive force of popular will throughout the process is apparent.

No. 117

PRESSURE FROM FARMERS [1]

by Stuart Chase

IN 1800, four out of five Americans lived on farms. Now only about one out of five lives there, approximately 25 million people. Another 20 per cent of the population live in rural areas, but do no commercial farming. They are storekeepers, mechanics, carpenters, agents, who serve, or live off, the farmer, according to your point of view. Thus fewer than half our people now make their home in the great open spaces. Yet the rural folklore is still strong. The homespun virtues of Calvin Coolidge made him the perfect symbol of leadership. Every morning on its editorial page *The New York Times* . . . celebrates the Old Oaken Bucket.

There are more than six million separate farms, mostly strung along the roads. In Europe farmers tend to live in the village and go out to their fields. Three American farms out of five are occupied by their owners, two by tenants. Tenantry has been increasing very rapidly.

In New England, where dairying predominates, the average size of a farm is 100 acres. In the corn and hog belt of the Middle West it is 160 acres; in the cotton belt, 80; and in the wheat fields of the Great Plains, where the combines wallow like tanks, it is 400 acres.

There are perhaps a million marginal farms where the soil is so thin or so eroded that most years people cannot make a living. They keep afloat on relief, unless the Farm Security Administration can help them find a better piece of land. There is a big increase at both ends of the scale. The practice of "twilight farming," where mill workers come home to tend the garden patch, was increasing even before the war. There is also a growing number of big factory farms, where migratory workers constitute the uncertain labor supply, and farming as a way of life has about disappeared. Since 1930 these big farms of more than 1,000 acres have increased 25 per cent, while little farms of under 50 acres have decreased 15 per cent.

After the collapse of farmland values and crop prices in 1920, following World War I, agriculture remained largely in the dumps all through the prosperous '20's. Prices for most crops were down. In the depression, the situation became revolutionary in some areas. Foreclosures were being halted with shotguns, as farmers took the law into their own hands.

[1] Stuart Chase, *Democracy Under Pressure* (New York: The Twentieth Century Fund, 1945), pp. 90-104. Reprinted by permission of the publishers. The footnotes in the original version are omitted here.

During the '20's they were given crop and mortgage loans on a small scale, a little tariff protection, and a veto by President Coolidge of the McNary-Haugen bill, which proposed helping them more substantially. Under President Hoover they got the Federal Farm Board, which disbursed $500,-000,000 to buy surplus crops. This looks generous until one remembers that values at the same time were dropping by the billions.

NEW DEAL FOR FARMERS

In 1933 the new Administration began giving farmers many of the things they had long been clamoring for: higher prices, cheaper credit, subsidies, mortgage relief. Most farmers were mighty glad to get this help after thirteen lean years, three of them altogether dreadful.

To give the farmers so many of the things they wanted, the New Deal had to increase central planning. In effect it organized agriculture as one stupendous business, with headquarters in Washington, and Henry Wallace in charge. By a curious irony the individualistic, freedom-loving, leave-me-alone farmers of the nation were the first major group to become integrated in an over-all national plan. Furthermore, their own organizations helped to draft the plan. The banks, the railroads, the insurance companies, the unemployed, received cash relief; but agriculture was in effect collectivized —lifted clean out of the free market and put in a market where prices, or production, or both, were controlled. If this seems a strong statement, look at the following record:

1. The AAA removed cotton, corn, rice, tobacco, wheat—the great staples —from the free market. The resulting control was comparatively democratic. Farmers first voted whether they wanted it, and then after the majority had voted yes—as they mostly did—the farmers themselves, in 2,500 local county boards, administered the Act.

The AAA procedure was roughly as follows. Experts in the Department of Agriculture figured out how much of a crop could be sold at prices to satisfy the farmer—say 12 million bales of cotton. Then they prorated the total to each cotton-growing state, where it was prorated to each cotton-growing county, where the local board prorated it to each cotton-growing farm. If the farmer held to his allotment, he was paid in Treasury checks for not growing more. When the Supreme Court declared this unconstitutional, the farmer was paid for taking conservation measures, improving his soil, rotating cover crops—which had the same effect of holding his cotton acreage to the allotted figure.

If exceptionally fine weather brought a bigger crop than estimated, the government took over the surplus, giving the farmer cash and taking the crop as security. If nature, on the other hand, was unfair to organized farmers, the government insured the farmer against loss. This did not apply to all crops, but to some of the big staples.

2. For crops which the AAA did not cover, the Food Stamp Plan bought up the surplus and held the price at levels satisfactory to the farmers.

3. Butter surpluses were purchased by a special government corporation, and warehoused in cold storage to maintain prices.

4. Various "marketing agreements" were entered into. Take milk, for instance. The milk marketing agreement amounted to a government-sponsored monopoly in which dairy farmers, creameries, distributors to doorsteps, united to control production and maintain prices in the New York milk shed or the Chicago milk shed.

5. For poor farmers the Farm Security Administration was established, to make them loans for seeds, fertilizer, tools, a mule, a house, and to put them on their feet again. A million were so helped.

6. A series of vast government credit agencies lent farmers billions of dollars at low rates of interest for first mortgages, second mortgages, crop loans, market loans, processing loans, cooperative loans. The government saved hundreds of thousands of farms from foreclosure in the depression.

7. The Department of Agriculture went after the middleman with a number of severe statutes. It also had some very mean surprises for speculators in agricultural commodities.

8. The Rural Electrification Administration brought electric power to more than a million farms.

MARRIED TO GOVERNMENT

The above is not a complete list, but it is enough, I think, to warrant Mr. Kiplinger's statement that "Farmers as a class have gotten themselves married to government and there is no possibility of divorce or separation." It warrants the conclusion of two Pennsylvania dirt farmers: "If the government should step out of the picture to-day, American farming would collapse," and the remark of a Washington correspondent in 1940: "Once the farm organizations stand united they can get anything out of Congress short of good growing weather."

This record also lends support to Dr. Polanyi's thesis. . . . He concluded . . . that neither "labor" nor "land" could remain indefinitely as a mere commodity on the automatic Market. Society would revolt against it. Certainly American agriculture has revolted in a big way since 1933, with crop after crop taken out of the free market to be managed collectively. It is interesting to note that this historical drive was paralleled by another one taking "labor" out of the free market via the Wagner Act, the Wages and Hours law, the National Labor Board, and a great increase in the area of collective bargaining.

Can six million farmers be thrown back on their own resources . . . ? Only in after dinner speeches and campaign oratory. The farmers are married to the government and there are no divorce laws in this court. When farm prices start slipping . . . as they did after World War I, the marriage knot will pull the tighter. Furthermore the Farm Bloc has blessed the union.

THE FARM BLOC

The business bloc started with the tariff, before 1800. The labor bloc started soon after the trusts, about 1900. The farm bloc in its present phase started with tractors in the 1920's; tractors encourage large-scale commercial farming. It became great and powerful after 1933. Some observers, such as Mr. Kiplinger, think it the smartest, best turned-out lobby in Washington. It controls at least fifteen million votes, "once the organizations stand united."

The "farm bloc" is a loose term covering at least three kinds of members: (1) Congressmen especially amenable to farm legislation; (2) general organizations theoretically representing all kinds of farmers, with their own Washington lobbies; (3) special crop organizations such as the American Livestock Association. This group goes whooping to town whenever it catches the whiff of Argentinian beef. There are three general organizations which count: the Grange, the Farmers Union, and the Farm Bureau Federation.

The Grange was born in 1867 and began lobbying for state railroad regulation almost at once. It helped establish the Interstate Commerce Commission. After that it tended to lapse into local good works, such as oyster suppers for those who could grow the largest pumpkins. It has 800,000 members and a vital part in rural life. But at present its political activity is minor, its leaders timid, worried and very conservative.

The Farmers Union is a progressive outfit of 92,000 members, who fight to help sharecroppers, to retain the Farm Security Administration, and who even join hands with the labor unions occasionally. Its function has been chiefly that of a gadfly, but it may have a considerable future. Its leaders know that the nineteenth century has gone.

DREAMS OF EMPIRE

The Farm Bureau Federation is the big shot, the NAM of agriculture. It is administered by a genial southerner named Ed O'Neal, who can make more Congressmen run faster than any man alive. The Federation came in with the tractors after the last war, and represents principally the big commercial farmers, who hire a lot of labor and who are interested in the land more as a source of profit than as a way of life. It claims 690,000 members, and thus must include many family-size farms as well as the hacienda boys.

One of its major goals was to achieve something called "parity." Bassett Jones has labeled parity a hermaphrodite statistical monster. It is based on the average prices farmers got for their crops from 1910 to 1914, when the crop pattern was very different, grades were often different, world conditions far different. It is obvious that "parity" and the free market have nothing in common, for it is a straight price-fixing program.

The Farm Bureau also favors cooperative marketing, when the cooperative is large enough to exercise a bit of monopoly. It favors conservation within reason, and tax reform. It helped draw the teeth of the Copeland pure food and drug bill. It almost killed the Administration's war subsidy program, because the Farm Bureau chiefs felt the program held down agricultural prices.

The Farm Bureau is tied up in a direct way with the Department of Agriculture. Some of its local representatives hold appointments as government County Agents—which raises the interesting question whether a lobby should be paid by the government to bring pressure on the government. Sometimes the Bureau dictates department policy. It would like to control the department completely, and is in a fair way to do so. It will take a man as tough as Henry Wallace to stand up against Ed O'Neal. The Bureau wants to plow under the small farmer, and the FSA which helps him, so that the big boys may have an abundant supply of cheap farm labor. This repeats on a larger scale the policy of the Associated Farmers of California, who apparently will not be satisfied until they can buy migratory workers on the hoof. Read *The Grapes of Wrath*.

The Farm Bureau neglects, when it does not oppose, farm laborers, little farmers and consumers. It is keen on interfering with the "law" of supply and demand when prices are down, but calls it an irrevocable process of nature when prices are up. Its strongest branches are in the South and Middle West, and it is trying to create a cotton and corn belt coalition to control the House to perpetuity. "As matters now stand," says *Fortune,* "few things in politics are as certain as Ed O'Neal's ability to get votes. . . . On the floor of the House the Farm Bureau can pass or stop *any* farm measure on which it makes a determined fight." The talented Ed works both sides of the street, Republicans and Democrats. He is not, however, quite so omnipotent in the Senate.

Fortune lists five methods by which the Farm Bureau manipulates Congress:

1. It rewards its friends with re-election. Local Bureau organizations get out the vote.

2. It makes it very unpleasant for Congressmen who oppose its measures.

3. It defends Congress against the President, which is duck soup for Congressmen. Ed is a spectacular critic of the "bureaucrats."

4. It offers prominence and publicity to friendly legislators.

5. It is very skillful at logrolling and trading with other pressure groups.

COTTON CARTEL

The Farm Bureau sages will thoughtfully take a wisp of hay out of their hair, and tell you they are for liberty, free enterprise, sturdy independence, thrift, early rising, and down with the beef trust and government interference. Then they excuse themselves to rush over to the Capitol to make sure that their trained seals are barking loudly against any tampering with their Cotton Cartel—which is as good an example as the next covering the farm bloc's tangible performance in the field of rugged independence.

The "cotton cartel" came in with the New Deal legislation. . . . Under its provisions the Commodities Credit Corporation must lend cotton growers up to 90 per cent of "parity" on their crops. "If prices go up, growers can reclaim their cotton for private sale. But if prices start downward, an artificial scarcity is created—which soon snaps them back. For eleven years cotton growers have unloaded their surpluses on the U. S. taxpayer, and have used the taxpayer's money to build a firm floor under cotton prices." In early 1944 the CCC held seven million bales in storage. "Textile manufacturers," continues *Time*, "squeezed between artificially higher cotton prices and OPA ceilings on their finished goods, protest that no cartel ever dared to manipulate supply and prices so brazenly."

The Farm Bureau uses all the slogans of rugged individualism as a smoke screen behind which it manipulates some of the smoothest monopolies known to man. If any American believes that the New Deal agricultural legislation was the product of dreamers, long-haired professors and agents from Moscow, he is a pretty good dreamer himself. It was the product primarily of local farmers crying to be delivered from free competition. Before you blame them, remember where cotton, wheat and beef were in 1932—6 cents a pound, 32 cents a bushel, and $3.20 a hundredweight, respectively.

LITTLE PIGS

For . . . years, Henry Wallace has been branded as the murderer of the "little pigs," which shambles has been perhaps Exhibit A in the indictment of the New Deal. The program was devised, according to Lowell Mellett, at a conference of corn and hog farmers from the midwestern states. The pig killing had the approval of the American Farm Bureau Federation, the National Grange, the National Farmers Union, the Corn Belt Meat Producers, and the Central Cooperative Exchange. The gentlemen have maintained a dignified silence all these years, and allowed Mr. Wallace to take the panning. I say panning rather than blame, for, as far as I can learn, the farm bloc was quite justified in asking for the slaughter. It was absolutely necessary unless farmers were to go flat broke in a year when there was not enough corn to bring in the pig crop.

When the Farm Bureau and other general organizations are not applying enough specific heat in Washington, flying columns of prune growers, raisin, citrus, wool, apple, peanut, potato, sugar growers will execute a giant pincer movement on the Capitol, "usually demanding that the government buy up their surpluses to boost the price."

HEADS-WE-WIN

The farm bloc folks not only want "parity"; they demand a 12 per cent bonus above this. They want 90 per cent of the price guaranteed by government loans. "They want these loans," says *The New York Times*, "on the principle of heads-the-farmer-wins-tails-the-taxpayer loses; for if the farmers' products go below this 90 per cent, the government is to take the loss; but if they go above, the farmer is to pocket the profit." This principle is on all fours with that of the real-estate bloc: if there is any profit in government housing we take it; if there is any loss, the taxpayer takes it. It is the sign of a nicely blocked government that prices are controlled in the interest of special groups, and on principles which, if applied to all groups, would lead to a complete breakdown of the economy.

It is easy to see, the *Times* continues, why we have a bloc government in Congress. "Each Congressman is elected from a particular state or district. Most of them feel responsible only to the voters of their particular district. They will play a particular local interest against the whole national interest if they think that the voters of their district are greedy or short-sighted enough to approve such action."

The farm bloc, like the other super-blocs, is seldom united for long. Its major cleavage is between big and little farmers. But the dairy versus the oleo interests, the livestock versus the poultry interests, do not train well together. Said the *Dairy Record* in 1941: "The dairy industry must set as its goal the complete extermination of oleomargarine." Even the mighty Farm Bureau stands on two legs which traditionally have never traveled long in the same direction: the cotton planters of the South, Democrats to a man; the big corn farmers of Iowa, black Republicans.

LIVING ON OUR CAPITAL

Farmers used to account for most of the national income, now in peacetime they account for only 10 per cent of it. More important than the national income, however, they account for 33 per cent of the nation's children. Without youngsters from the farms, cities would lose population rapidly.

Despite the fact that for most of their continental existence Americans have farmed for a living—farmers did not drop below 50 per cent of the population until 1880—and despite the fact that our folklore is based chiefly on the thrift and independence of rural life, we have not been very good farmers. We have been efficient croppers, but that is something else. An efficient cropper can tear the nutriment out of 160 acres in Ohio, and move on to tear it out of 160 acres in Iowa.

As farmers we have lived on our capital, the land. There were three million square miles of it, and many thought it would last forever. We have taken the life-giving elements out and not put an equivalent back. From farming for a living we turned to farming for a cash crop, with "cotton up to the front door." The price of paying off the mortgage was to take it out of the soil.

It is not a mere coincidence that when good new land was no longer to be had free on the frontier, the woes of the farmers multiplied, and presently they were storming Congress. A stern moralist might let them stew in their own juice. Why should taxpayers bail them out for their misuse of the land? The question is academic. You cannot allow 25 to 30 million citizens, men, women and children, to stew in their own juice without wrecking the stability of our society. We have all been takers, not givers. What the farmers have done to the land is no more than what others have done to the forests, the mineral deposits, the oil pools, fisheries, waters. Can you name any considerable river in the nation which is not an open sewer? We are all guilty. Even if we were not, we had better not get too haughty with our farmers if we want to go on eating.

THE FUTURE OF FARMING

The decline in the farm population, while the output of food has been increasing, shows again the effects of the power age. As new machines and methods have made two blades of grass grow where one grew before, the displaced farmers went into factories and boosted the standard of living by manufacturing things. Along in the 1920's, in this country, industry became so efficient that the number of factory workers began to decline. . . .

These displaced workers went into the service trades, which by 1930 had more people in them than agriculture and factory work combined.

This is the regular rhythm of the power age, the one sure employment guide in the postwar world. *For the long swing, most of the new civilian jobs will have to be found in the service trades.* The farm population will certainly fall below 20 per cent, the factory population will fall below its ratio of 23 per cent in 1940. "In 1943, with a farm population 10 per cent smaller than in 1918, the nation's farmers produced nearly 50 per cent more food on two per cent fewer acres. . . . In 1950, according to rough estimates of the Bureau of Agricultural Economics, the farmers of the nation could duplicate the 1943 record with a 10 per cent further reduction in both man power and crop land. . . ."

BACK TO THE LAND?

This accredited rhythm reduces to nonsense all back-to-the-land movements as a solution for mass unemployment. Some of us can go back to the land to raise fresh food for our own tables. We can make our victory gardens permanent if we so desire. But we must not forget that when the . . . demand for food relaxes, in so far as we raise our own stuff we deprive some regular farmer of a market. Back-to-the land was all right for veterans after the Civil War. It proved highly unsuccessful after World War I. It would be idiotic . . . [now], except in carefully selected cases. This will not stop demagogues from yelling for it. . . .

If we took our . . . war diet and enriched it with all the . . . food now sent abroad, we would not be far from a balanced diet for every American. Yet it has been produced with our present agricultural plant, way short of normal man power. Where is there room for millions of additional farmers? Only in somebody's fervid imagination. For another thing, the veterans will not be qualified. To run a modern self-supporting farm, it has been reliably estimated that a man needs not only all-round skills, but an **average capital equipment of $12,000.**

. . . furthermore, a flood of new processes will be released to make three blades grow where one grew before—hop pickers, cotton pickers, cylinders of gaseous ammonia which, released into irrigation waters, act as high-speed fertilizer. All sorts of new chemicals, gadgets and devices are ready to spread "agrological unemployment" if we try to crowd more people on the land than an adequate standard of national nutrition requires. . . .

The farm bloc can no more stand off the grapes of wrath than Congress can guarantee good growing weather. It will be as helpless as the business bloc or the labor bloc to save itself alone. A postwar world of full employment is a national matter, which can only be worked out by all Americans pulling together. Yet of all answers to the farm problem, full employment is the most conclusive and the most enduring. When city workers have jobs they buy the farmer's food.

There is no future for American farmers, big or little, in restricted output, high scarcity prices, cotton plowed under, eroding soils, jerking puppet strings in Congress. Their future lies in producing a strong, healthy diet for every last American, while getting some enjoyment out of life themselves, and saving the soil for the oncoming generations.

No. 118

THE FARMER'S IN THE WORLD [1]

from *The Reporter*

WHEN the stranger arrived, the afternoon sun was fast drying the mud on the streets and automobiles. Beyond, where the steaming black land crowded the crossroads town on every side, the sunlight loosened the flats and hillsides into running gumbo, and raised a richness in the cow yards, and caused the barns to warp and creak. It was late March: a time of enforced idleness and uneasy speculation, between the winter mending and the spring planting. A great many farmers were in town. One of them nodded to the stranger:

"Town looks busy," the stranger remarked.

The farmer nodded again.

"On a Tuesday, too," the stranger went on. "What kind of a winter did you have?"

"Terrible. Cold."

"Well, it's muddy enough around here now. I've always heard that that's a good sign."

"No. It ought to be drier. Planting may be held up."

"That's too bad."

"Well, it is and it ain't. Suppose we do have a big crop. Where we going to sell it?"

The stranger eased down beside the farmer.

"Europe?"

"Farmers over there had a big year in '48. Ought to have a bigger one this year."

"But we're still going to ship them all the wheat we can."

---

[1] ——, "The Farmer's in the World," *The Reporter* (April 26, 1949), Vol. I, pp. 20-22. Reprinted by permission of *The Reporter*.

The farmer frowned.

"Don't talk wheat around here, Mister. We don't raise wheat in this part of Iowa. Raise corn and feed it to the hogs. Hogs are the money."

"Well, we eat plenty of pork in the United States. That should keep you rich."

"Nobody's rich. I been dipping into my savings account."

"Far?"

"Some. I don't like to get into my bonds."

"Well, pork should make it up to you this year."

"Pork's the worst since before the war; down to nineteen and a half cents. It was twenty-four cents in '46."

"What was it in '34?"

"Two and a half cents," the farmer said quietly.

"Well?"

"Pork's down, Mister. That's all!"

There was a long pause.

"How's corn?" the stranger prompted again.

"Down."

"What are you going to do?"

The farmer considered the question.

"Raise hogs." He shifted his seat. "But I don't like the looks of things. The *Register and Tribune* in Des Moines says the country's somewhere between the boom and whatever's coming. Nobody knows where. What do you make of that?"

"That's what I heard in Chicago and the Tri-Cities. Are you worried?"

"Starting to be."

"Well, that doesn't sound like you think it's so bad."

"Oh, it's bad! I can get a new tractor now soon's I want it."

"Why, that's fine."

"No, I'd sooner have to wait. This way, it looks like we're working up another depression."

"But the government's economic commission says we're only in a 'twilight zone'—levelling off."

"Levelling off? Say, that sounds like it'll be here sooner than we thought."

"Maybe not. The President is asking for price controls the same as three or four years ago. He wants to fight inflation."

"Price controls?" The farmer stroked his chin. "Well, we do have to do something about the price of machinery, of course. Labor, too."

"What about food?"

"Food's fine."

"Do you know what they're saying about the price of food in the city?"

"I know what they're saying about a lot of things all over the world. This ain't any backwoods, Mister. We got the radio."

"Does it say that people in Des Moines, for instance, aren't eating as well this year?"

"Yep. I know that. I got a daughter there, working for the Equitable. I got another girl in Los Angeles and another one in Rome, Italy, married to a government man. I get the word."

"Well, if this thing grows, what'll you do?" persisted the stranger. "Holler for price supports?"

"We got a darn sight too much government already."

"Will you try acreage control again?"

"That's worse'n killing hogs."

"Well, what will you do?"

"We got the Farm Price Act from the last Congress."

The stranger looked surprised.

"Why, everybody knows that's government support at the wartime top!"

"Everybody knows it?"

"The Congress made enough stink about it."

"Now, hold on!" said the farmer, abruptly. "We don't want that. We don't want the people in the city to think we're trying to gouge them."

"Well, what do you want?"

"We want what's fair!"

The farmer sat back.

"We want to get back to normal," he went on, soberly. "We don't want any favors. We want steady prices, even if they're lower. That's fair."

"What if they won't steady?"

The farmer blinked.

"Then it's dog eat dog, I guess. We'll have to fight for what help we can get. The Farm Bureau says maybe we ought to ask for supports somewhere between 50 and 90 per cent of parity."

"But I thought you were against supports altogether?"

"That's right. But we may need them."

"Would you pay taxes to keep a price support under a delicatessen in New York?"

The farmer recognized a pat question when he heard it. "Hell, no!" he snorted, playing it straight. "We don't want Socialism in this country!"

"Do you think Truman's farm program sounds like Socialism?"

"No. Truman's a good man. I heard him talk at Dexter last September. He knows what the farmer wants."

"Who'd you vote for?"

"Dewey."

"Well," said the stranger, rather hastily, "it's nice to have had this talk with you. In the city you get out of touch."

"Yes, I suppose so."

"By the way, what's the name of this town?"

"Dallas Center, Mister. Eighteen miles from Des Moines."

"Pretty place."

"Well, it is and it ain't. . . ."

In most of the crossroads in Iowa's ninety-nine counties this spring, the farmers worried one another, or worried strangers, with talk like this. It helped pass the time while they waited for the reviving earth to thaw until it would crumble damply in the hand and be ready for planting. In Dallas Center, everyday conversation was often edgy. One reason was the long prairie winter which, although it had little of the record savagery of the great storms farther west, wore its customary chinks in barns and men. Then, there were the persistent rumors of depression from the cities, and the local signs that one might indeed be on the way—the recent drop in pork prices, for instance, or the January slump in the prices of grain, fats, and oils, or the slow recovery from the general price break of early 1948. Iowa's entrapment in the "twilight zone," both in the weather and in the economy, was a great irritant, of course. But the over-riding reason for Dallas Center's unrest was not in the future at all but in the past. It was the memory of '32-'34 and the dread that the whole Midwest might be headed once more for the days of eighteen-cent corn and two-bit wheat. That was the arch-fear, the farmer's true *Angst* this blustery spring.

One of the farmers who felt it strongest was an alert, friendly, middle-sized man named Maynard Menafee. Menafee was losing his will to fight the depression when the war came along. He now owns and farms ninety gently-rolling acres two miles northwest of Dallas Center, his listening post. In 1940, he was a tenant farmer with a wife, a small son, an open mind, an above-average farming skill, and a net worth a little short of $3,000 to recommend him. His net worth (the phrase is a favorite with administrators) is now some $45,000 and there are no debts. He has a small savings account, enough insurance, and some bonds laid away. He is infinitely better off than most people who worked out the war in the cities, for salaries, or the thousands who abandoned the land to work in the war factories—the people who never recovered from the plague of depression, drought, chinch bugs, and dust storms.

Menafee is not a typical Iowa farmer, because there is no such thing. Still, in broad outline, his success story is remarkably like that of some 200,000 other farmers now making crops around the Hawkeye State. He is a lucky man in that he was ready when the break came. He is a steady man, too: the provider, the balance; a man with heavy responsibilities toward the hungry in Paris, Brussels, Rome, and Berlin; a man who has been plucked from traditional middle-border isolation and stamped with a new kind of averageness by the automobile, the movie, the radio, and the newspaper, and yet a man whose curiosity and sympathy are far from average. His future is mixed up with those of the longshoreman in San Francisco, the foreman in Detroit, and the bushelman in Philadelphia. He is the fiercely independent dependent who has felt that government threatened his freedom even while it lifted him from the threat of peonage; who voted for Federal price supports while he longed for a world economy that would make price supports unnecessary; who hated the war that lifted the mortgage.

Menafee has been farming one place and another, on a subsistence level and above, since 1928. In 1931, a year after he had married a schoolteacher, he owned no farm machinery and was thankful to be sharecropping eighty acres of his grandfather's land. Two years later, when the names of banks and insurance companies were becoming Midwest expletives, he was trying to work four hundred acres he had rented in Guthrie County. He failed. The sheriff, armed with eviction notices, was just beginning to have more work than he could do when the Menafees moved to Dallas County and began working eighty acres on a grain-share rental basis. They raised enough corn to feed three cows, and lived on the $25 a month they earned from the sale of milk and eggs in Des Moines. Then, while Agriculture Secretary Henry Wallace plugged through his hog-killing and corn-ceiling programs, the dust began to roll up out of Kansas and Oklahoma. The summer of 1934 brought coppery, gritty gloom at noontime, a plague of chinch bugs, and blistering weeks without rain. If the depression had any distinct bottom on the prairie, this was it.

In the years from 1934 to 1939, Menafee inched his net worth up to $3,000—if you include a tractor on which he had not been able to make a payment in two years. In 1940, he became the first man in Dallas County to apply to the Farm Housing Administration for a property loan. He got it: $11,500 for ninety acres of land, a tiny house (in which he still lives), a barn, chicken house, corn crib, grainery, and machine shed; $500 for seed and farming equipment. That was the turning point. Menafee did not count on a war boom to lift him over. He had always wanted his own place and he bought it as soon as he possibly could. The boom was gratuitous, although it enabled Menafee to pay off his loan in six years. Without the war, it might easily have taken him the contract limit to accomplish the same end—forty years.

Now the white buildings of Menafee's electrified, mechanized, paid-for farm, shielded on the north by a screen of trees and fringed with ragged seedlings—Menafee's farm sits rock-solid in the mud. Beyond it in all directions, at the whim of the weather and the world, lies Menafee's state.

The principal fact about Iowa is a functional one: the farmers there are making progress almost as swift as that in the field of plastics. Menafee uses a new chemical spray called 2,4-D which has reduced his once back-breaking weeding problem to a day's work. Artificial insemination of cattle and the cross-breeding of hogs or poultry is not an unusual job for him. His sows are now bred with undershot jaws so that they can root for corn in frozen ground, so they will eat less food but put on greater poundage, or produce more milk for shoats. Some of Menafee's white hogs, which are likely to sunburn badly, are being bred to dark-skinned types for pigment. His chicken houses have thermostatic controls and red-glass windows—to keep the cannibalistic chicks from spotting a fleck of blood on an injured mate and picking it to pieces. He has an electric brooder. His cows are milked in one hour, and in squads of six, by octopus-like machines; and certain vines, like the low-growing kudzu, are ready to hold down his fallow acres and guard against another dust bowl. Menafee may buy a bewildering number of farm machines, of which combines, manure spreaders, corn picker, binders, silage cutters, sprayers, balers, loaders, grass-seeding pulverizers, electric litter-stirrers, and feed mixers are only a few. He already possesses an awesome array of apparatus that goes under the deceptive heading of "tractor equipment."

The Menafees spend most of their leisure time at organization or church functions, of course, or in watching their fourteen-year-old son, Myron, play basketball. Younger Iowans live a good deal of their social lives in their high-school auditoriums or in new-fangled places called "milk bars," listening gravely to bebop. The well-to-do elders have taken to wintering at home or in Florida, and here lies a strange turn in the traditional emigrant trail. For decades, Southern California has been the goal of the retired Iowa farmer. Inevitably, it has also become one of his central burying grounds, so that now all thoughts of that sunny land have become mixed up in the Iowa mind with dark premonitions of the crutch and the head-stone. Florida has no such stigma as yet, so many aging Iowans now go there. Better still, many now put their money into a second home on their own property, and rent the main house, or turn it over to their sons or sons-in-law. What has altered the time-tried migratory pattern of a whole region is nothing more complex than central heating and the sunlamp.

The sprayers, the sunlamp, and the host of other glittering, efficient gadgets make the Iowa farmer's life easier, but they do not quite shield him from a recurring feeling of apprehension. He is better off, he knows, than farmers in other continents—the Chinese farmers, for instance, or the Spanish and Italian and French farmers. Yet there are some clouds in the sky of Iowa. Menafee—and the other farmers there—can never quite forget 1931 and 1932. He is not sure that the horror of those years belongs to the past alone. He does not know whether he can count upon the ever-normal price system *forever,* whether the government can go on supporting prices; he doubts it when he tunes in his radio and hears of the airlift into Berlin. He knows far more than he did in 1931 about the world, about the connection between echelons of planes in Europe and droves of hogs in Iowa. It is more apparent than ever this sullen and restless spring that, in the last twenty years or so, the world with all its shadows has moved in on Iowa and Iowa has moved into the world. It is a very unsteady world.

Chapter XXXIV

DEMOCRATIC GOVERNMENT AND PLANNING

[THE world in which we live exhibits so much instability and conflict, both within nations and between them (two world wars and a severe economic depression in one generation), that increased planning for stability at home and for peace in the world has become a necessity. This in turn is bound to generate much argument as to the merits of planning and its relation to freedom and democratic government.

This dispute often takes the form of argument about whether it is good or bad to plan. Such argument is unrealistic. The question is not "plan or no plan" but how much planning and what kind of planning. No political or economic system is either completely planned or completely unplanned.

The American people do not want either complete laissez-faire or complete regimentation. Neither unregulated free enterprise nor communism is acceptable. They do want a positive program by which they, through a democratic and responsible government, can achieve security in employment, minimum standards in health, housing, and education, opportunity for recreation and creative living and at the same time preserve their freedom and democratic institutions.

Some of the planning, therefore, will relate to health, some to housing, some to full employment, some to conservation, some to education. The student of politics needs to distinguish the questions that relate to these matters and which are the province of the expert in economics, public health, conservation, or education from the questions that relate to politics or government. The primary concern of the student of politics is with the procedures of planning, the processes by which it is done and by which the plans are carried out. He wants to know to whom the planners and those who execute the plans are accountable for their actions. He wants to know whether there are to be adequate controls by the mass of the people over those who are going to determine the conditions of life in the community. To use Barbara Wooton's question: WHO IS GOING TO PLAN THE PLANNERS?]

No. 119

THE ROLE OF GOVERNMENT IN ECONOMIC PLANNING [1]

by Raymond T. Bye

IN the early stages of capitalism, industry was carried on by many small, competing enterprises, whose proprietors were free to formulate their own policies with very little interference from the state. Such a system of industry can be described as unplanned, because it was extremely decentralized, depending for its guidance not on the will of any controlling body, but on the ups and downs of prices, which, through their effects on profits, were supposed to keep production in rough balance with consumers' demand. It was a process of trial and error, comparable in some respects to life in the jungle, where many different plants and animals struggle for existence with no other guiding principle than the law of survival. Like the jungle, it was both wasteful and cruel. The waste appeared in the inefficiency of small business units, in errors of individual judgment leading to business failures, in competitive duplication of facilities, in unemployment and periodic depressions. The cruelty was evidenced by ruthless competitive practices, by intolerable factory conditions, by starvation wages, child labor, and poverty.

In an effort to correct these weaknesses, two developments ensued. In the first place, small individual proprietors were replaced by corporations, and these in turn by supercorporations, which subjected portions of industry to a considerable measure of central guidance. Competition was in some cases eliminated, in others tempered by mutual understandings and trade association rules. Similarly, the wage earners banded together into trade unions. In the second place, government stepped in to prevent abuses. Workers were protected by factory legislation, public utilities were regulated, trusts were restrained, banks were partly centralized, and so on. This evolution has continued, so that the character of the industrial system has been greatly changed.

The deeper meaning of all this is that the various processes of industry are gradually being brought under centralized control. Just as the jungle has been replaced by man's cultivated fields, so the chaos of thousands of

[1] Raymond T. Bye, "The Role of Government in Economic Planning," *The Annals* of the American Academy of Political and Social Science (November, 1939), Vol. 206, pp. 126-132. Reprinted by permission of *The Annals* of the American Academy of Political and Social Science.

competing enterprises is being replaced by organization. Little by little, industry is being *planned,* instead of being left to the automatic guidance of natural economic forces. The planning is being done partly by the large corporations and trade associations which dominate their respective branches of production, and partly by the state, through such agencies as the Federal Reserve System, the Interstate Commerce Commission, the Securities and Exchange Commission, the National Labor Relations Board, and many others, Federal, state and local.

However, such measures of planning as the above are separate and disconnected; they are not integrated into a unified whole. The result is that the processes of industry are not yet well articulated. Indeed, the plans effective in one part may work at cross-purposes to those in another. For example, anthracite and bituminous coal, natural and manufactured gas, petroleum, and electricity are all sources of fuel for the production of heat and power. Efficient utilization of our natural resources would require that these several industries be fitted together in such a way as to avoid waste and to conserve as much as possible for the future; yet they are notoriously disorganized. The anthracite industry is paralyzed, the bituminous industry chaotic and continually in the throes of labor disputes, the petroleum industry a confusion of exploitation, instability, and profligate waste, while the gas and electric industries, although better integrated and publicly regulated, have been characterized by financial mismanagement and exorbitant costs. These are typical of the results which naturally follow from a system of independent free enterprise.

The controls introduced into the situation by government are little better. Laws affecting industry are enacted under the pressure of special interests instead of being framed with regard to the smooth functioning of the whole economy. Such laws are often in direct opposition to each other. Witness the efforts of our Federal Government to persuade foreign governments to pay their debts to it, while at the same time protective tariffs are established to prevent the importation of goods by which alone these debts might be paid. Because private business does not fully employ all our labor, we embark upon programs of public works intended to fill up the gap, while at the same time we enact measures designed to raise the wages of workers and thereby discourage an increase in private employment.

If industry is ever to function smoothly and consistently, a greater measure of unity in its processes must be achieved. No other way to accomplish this seems possible than through planning of a more general sort than that which now prevails. Some kind of central guidance is needed.

Some business leaders, conscious of this need, have advocated that each industry develop its own program of planning, with only enough participation by government to give the plans its blessing and to prevent any flagrant abuses. Something of this sort was attempted by the National Recovery Administration, and similar schemes have been favored by prominent business leaders, such as Gerard Swope, and by the United States Chamber of Commerce.

Although many of the people who have advanced these proposals are men of high motives, such planning would almost inevitably degenerate into exploitation of the public. If each industry is allowed to plan for itself, there will be a strong temptation for it to suppress competition within its own ranks and to limit the output of its product, to the end that high prices, with resulting high profits, may be secured. This was what happened under the NRA, and it is what might be expected under any similar program.

Even at its best, independent planning by separate industries could not achieve balance in the economy as a whole. Railways must be co-ordinated with other kinds of transportation, and transportation facilities as a whole co-ordinated with the industries which employ their services. Fuel and raw materials industries must be co-ordinated with the manufacturing groups which use their products, and manufacturing industries in turn must be co-ordinated with the wholesale and retail establishments through which they find their outlets. In the end, the output of all the industries must be co-ordinated with the needs of consumers. Planning of this broad type can be done only by the Federal Government, for it alone is competent to deal with so vast a problem on a national scale. It alone is sufficiently catholic in its interests to represent all of the people, and sufficiently wide in its jurisdiction to control the various industries that must be included.

Under a dictatorial form of government, planning can readily become ruthless regimentation. This has been the case in Soviet Russia, where general economic planning is most fully developed, and in [pre-war] Germany and Italy. But the extreme suppression of the individual which is characteristic of these systems is largely political in character and is rooted in the traditions of the people. Russia has never known anything but autocracy, which was exercised long before the advent of the Communists; the Germans had always been used to a good deal of regimentation; and the traditions of democracy had not been so fully developed in Italy as among English-speaking peoples. Moreover, planning in these countries came about by revolution, not by evolution. If developed in a more orderly manner and kept within the framework of democratic institutions, it ought to be possible to achieve unity and co-ordination in our economic life without the sacrifice of essential liberties.

To accomplish this, the program of planning would have to meet two basic requirements. In the first place, it should retain the essential features of the existing price system. This means that demand and supply should be the guide for production to follow. The planning authorities should not decree what things were to be produced and what should be the output of the various industries and enterprises on the basis of arbitrary decisions or intuitive guesses, but should seek to achieve that balance in industry which would naturally result if production were nicely adjusted to demand. The difficulty with the present system of unplanned industry is that this adjustment is not well attained. The planning authorities could presumably replace the erroneous guesses of the thousands of enterprisers who now follow their individual judgments, by informed decisions based on adequate information. Thus they would enable business men to proceed with a program which would offer less risk and more assurance of a market for their outputs at prices which would cover their costs than they can possibly have at the present time.

Because planning of this sort would follow the natural tendencies of the present economic system, and thereby help business men toward correct policies instead of hindering them, it seems likely that it could enlist their willing cooperation. They would not have to be forced to conform to the plans if the plans proved by experience to reduce losses and to provide wise guidance. Similarly, the plans would help investors to place their savings in profitable rather than losing ventures, and they would help employees to find lucrative positions where their innate capacities could be more sure of a market and where employment would be more steady than is now the case. Therefore, investors and wage earners would also find it to their advantage to follow the plans, so that very little coercion would be needed. So far as the individual consumer is concerned, he would still be allowed to spend his money as he pleased, exercising his free choice among the commodities offered to him in the markets. It would not be necessary to regiment his consumption, but merely to forecast it intelligently.

The second requirement which a system of democratic planning would have to meet is that the organization through which the plans were drawn up and administrated would have to be genuinely representative. This means that every interested party would have to have some voice, through elected representatives, in making the decisions which would constitute the plans for industry. New machinery of government would have to be built up along these lines, thus carrying forward into a new sphere the traditions of representative democracy.

The development of a planning organization that would meet the above two requirements would have to be achieved by gradual experimentation. It is probably impossible to prescribe its detailed forms in advance. Some indication of the lines along which such machinery might be developed have, however, been suggested by other writers and may be briefly indicated here.

There might be set up in each industry an Industrial Planning Council, whose membership would be composed of people democratically chosen to represent investors, management, and labor in the industry concerned, and the consuming public at large. Existing trade and labor organizations in the several industries might be used as a starting point from which to develop suitable organizations for providing such representation. Some organization of investors might have to be worked out in order to provide for the selection of delegates from that group. Representatives of consumers might be appointed by the public authorities. . . . [The author points out that remnants of the code authorities of the National Recovery Administration might have been used to form a nucleus for planning councils.]

The function of these bodies would be to gather data concerning plant capacities, available labor and materials, and possible outputs in their respective branches of production. They would make estimates of the probable growth of the industry and of its requirements for new capital and labor. On the basis of these data they would formulate tentative plans for the industry. The plans would specify the output to be scheduled for the ensuing year or years, with quotas for the individual businesses contributing thereto, the requirements of the industry for fuel and raw materials, the estimated costs of production, and the probable selling prices at which the products could be disposed of. These plans would not be final, but would be submitted to the central planning authorities for their guidance. The plans would constitute a sort of proposal from the industry as to what it was prepared to do for the economy.

At the head of the planning organization there would be needed a National Economic Planning Commission. This would be an arm of the Federal Government, probably headed by a Cabinet officer. Its membership should be of the highest caliber, and it would need to have at its command a large staff of technical experts, economists, statisticians, accountants, stenographers, clerks, and other office workers. In a country as large as the United States, subsidiary state or regional planning commissions, organized on similar lines, would be needed. The Commission would need to be clothed with sufficient authority to compel corporations and individuals to supply it with such information concerning their businesses as it needed for the formulation of its plans, and to prescribe the forms on which these data were to be reported.

The function of the National Planning Commission would be to receive and scrutinize the tentative plans submitted to it by the Industrial Councils. Forming its judgments on the basis of these plans and on information derived from a national survey of productive capacity and consumptive needs, it would draw up superplans for the economy as a whole for one-year, five-year, and perhaps longer periods. These superplans would indicate expected output, volume of employment, capital replacements and extensions, and the probable costs, wages, selling prices, and profits in each of the several industries. They would indicate where the market for the products would be found, and they would provide for the utilization of all the resources and labor power available. Some scheme of employment offices would presumably be developed for supplying labor where it would be needed in industry. Monetary policy would also have to be formulated by the Commission, or in close collaboration with it, so as to maintain a reasonably stable level of prices and to direct credit into the channels where it was expected to go.

The result of all this would be a kind of industrial budget or schedule for the Nation, so designed as to make the fullest possible use of existing resources, provide full employment for labor at the best wages industry could afford, and co-ordinate the various branches of industry—in short, to provide balanced abundance for the United States.

The comprehensive plans drawn up by the National Planning Commission should not have binding effect until acted upon by Congress. Otherwise, the danger of dictatorial regulation would be real; but if the plans were embodied in a bill to be fully debated and amended in Congress before it became the law of the land, they would have the democratic character which it is important to preserve.

When the plans were adopted by Congress and approved by the President, they should be put into effect through appropriate administrative machinery. The organization needed for this purpose should parallel that for drawing up the plans in the first place, but should not be identical with it. A certain amount of separation between those who made the plans and those who carried them out would probably be desirable, although they should cooperate closely. Those who formulated the plans would need to be guided by the experience of those who administered them, and the administrators should have some voice in the formulation of plans for the future. So it would be wise to set up a National Planning Administration as an arm of the executive branch of the Government, linked closely to the National Planning Commission, and similar state or regional planning administrations and industrial administrations paralleling the corresponding planning commissions and industrial councils.

The industrial administrative bodies would be charged with the function of carrying out in detail the plans that applied to their particular industries. It is here that the delicate matter of securing conformity with the plans without entire loss of individual liberty and initiative would arise most acutely. Execution of the plans would probably necessitate the setting of production quotas for the different enterprises in each industry and the enforcement of compliance with the adopted schedules on the part of individual business men and groups. However, it is to be remembered that these groups would have had some voice in formulating the plans in the first place, so that the restrictions forced upon them at the execution stage would not be arbitrary or onerous.

There might or might not have to be some regulation of prices and wages; this would depend on how successfully the plans succeeded in anticipating the demand, investment, and production which would maintain balance in the various industries. It does not appear that there would be any necessity for the rationing of consumption or for the drafting of capital or labor. Consumers would still be free to spend their incomes as they pleased, choosing such commodities as were offered by the market; investors would still be free to purchase such securities as were made available under the plans, just as they are now free to choose such stocks and bonds as are offered by the various corporations which issue them; and labor would still be free to enter such occupations and accept such employment as was open. But in all these matters, more information would be available for their guidance than under the present system of industry.

Enterprisers would still be free to direct the technical operation of their plants according to their best judgment, to buy such materials and employ such labor as was available at existing prices and wages, and to make profits by the economies of low costs made possible by efficient production. The amount of interference in the details of their businesses need not be any greater than that to which railroads and other public utilities are now subject under government regulation.

Such a program of planning as is here advocated promises two great advantages. In the first place, decisions reached through the machinery of planning would be based on much more accurate and complete information than the industrial decisions of an unplanned economy. The planning authorities, empowered with the authority of government and provided with machinery for collecting and correlating statistics from every branch of industry and from every part of the country, would have resources for gathering information far greater than those at the disposal of any individual business organization, no matter how large.

In the second place, through the machinery of planning, the thousands of decisions which have to be made in industry about such important matters as new investments and capital expansion, production schedules, and the flow of materials and semifinished goods through the various processes of industry, could be co-ordinated into a unified picture. As long as these decisions are made independently, many mistakes are bound to occur. The present competitive system depends for co-ordination largely on the rectifying of such mistakes *after they occur,* through the corrective reactions of prices. However, the system is so interdependent that mistakes made in one part of it lead to errors elsewhere, in a cumulative chain, until there is a general breakdown. Balance is not restored until after a severe depression, which sooner or later is repeated. Planning should succeed in *preventing* mistakes. This will not be done to perfection, of course, but it ought to be possible to keep errors at a minimum and to prevent them from becoming cumulative. As a result, the system of planned economy should enable industry to be maintained smoothly at a higher level of productivity than the world has ever known.

One of the most conspicuous tendencies of modern times is the increasing control of central governments over the affairs of men. General economic planning involves a still further extension of such control. To many, this will be an argument against it, for they will see in it the final downfall of individual liberty and initiative. It is believed, however, that the democratic safeguards suggested in the foregoing paragraphs should suffice to protect the rights of the individual. If economic science has any practical significance for mankind, it must be found in the power which it gives to control and improve the functioning of economic life. The only agency which is qualified to exercise controls for society as a whole is the state itself. It is to be expected, therefore, that the state will continue to expand its regulation of industry. What is here advocated is that such control shall be planned instead of haphazard, and that the government which is to do the controlling shall retain its democratic character and be made as efficient as possible.

No. 120

SOCIAL AND ECONOMIC PLANNING [1]

by Alvin H. Hansen

SOME months ago I participated in a discussion on planning in the postwar world. Among the participants were some who expressed, in general abstract terms, vigorous opposition to planning in all forms. Theoretical arguments, drawn largely from Professor Hayek's book *The Road to Serfdom,* were expounded. There followed an address by a middle-of-the-road Republican Senator, well known for his common-sense approach to practical

[1] Alvin H. Hansen, *Economic Policy and Full Employment* (New York: McGraw-Hill Book Company, 1947), pp. 14-28. Reprinted by permission of the publisher.

problems, and utterly devoid of doctrinaire views. "I approach the topic," he said, "from the standpoint of the day-to-day problems that come before me as a member of Congress." Before he was through, he had touched upon many domestic and international problems upon which he was compelled, as a member of Congress, to have an opinion and about which something had to be done. For him it was not an abstract question about planning or not planning. For him some workable solution had to be found that might prove reasonably satisfactory, else up bobbed these questions again.

ATOMISTIC INDIVIDUALISM

The plain fact is that all advanced individual nations have moved very far away from the atomistic individualism of the mid-nineteenth century. Then economic opportunity meant essentially a chance to operate your own farm or small business. To-day economic opportunity means largely a chance to get a job. Then the bulk of the population lived in the country— on farms or in small villages. To-day they live in great urban centers. Industrialization and urbanization have come upon us with a speed that no one could have imagined in 1850. Torn from the old individualistic pattern of work and living into a society characterized by great factories and giant cities, modern man must erect a new social structure adapted to the changed conditions. In an industrialized and urbanized society, the individual cannot order his life alone. He can meet the problems of living only by joint action with his fellows. This is the great challenge of modern life—how to reconcile the rights and freedoms of the individual in a society in which group and community action is a necessary basis for successful living. This is the problem of democratic planning in the modern world.

Planning is, however, not something new. Its form and content have, it is true, changed. In the early days of our country, planning had to do, so far as economic matters were concerned, with creating an environment in which the citizens could successfully undertake to become small farmers, shopkeepers, or tradesmen. Essentially what was needed was a legal and economic environment favorable for the starting of a small enterprise. It became a primary responsibility of government to ensure the right to set yourself up in business. This right was not the product of automatic forces, as some naively suppose. This right was fought for in the great social and economic movements of the early nineteenth century. It was fought for in the antimonopoly movements, in the struggle for free banking, in the great Homestead movement which finally won the right to free land. The history of the first half of the nineteenth century was alive and glowing with great human programs—social plans to ensure and maintain economic opportunity.

A program to keep open the door for new enterprise remains also to-day a vital and necessary part of economic planning. Among other things, this means a revitalization of our antitrust laws and their enforcement, reform of our patent system, and an adequately financed Institute for Technical and Scientific Research to aid new and small business.

By and large the right to establish a business or to acquire free land was adequate, in the nineteenth century, to maintain economic opportunity and to ensure the right to "life, liberty, and the pursuit of happiness." This is no longer the case. In all modern countries the trend of technology, whether in industry, transportation, or distribution, restricts economic opportunity, for the overwhelming majority, to the getting of a job—not to establishing a business of their own. If, therefore, we are to keep open the door of economic opportunity, under modern conditions, it becomes necessary for modern society to undertake as a primary responsibility the maintenance at all times of adequate employment opportunities. Just as the right to free land was the watchword of economic opportunity a hundred years ago, so the right to useful, remunerative, and regular employment is the symbol of economic opportunity to-day. The Murray Full Employment bill is to-day's counterpart of the Homestead Act of a century ago. The Homestead movement of the 1840's represented a great struggle for human rights and economic opportunity. It was fought by the forces of reaction. But the issue could not be evaded. So also with the full-employment program to-day. It involves essential human rights—the right to life, liberty, and the pursuit of happiness. So long as 80 to 90 per cent of the population cannot earn a livelihood except by getting a job, the issue of full employment will not down.

The White Paper on Employment Policy, issued by the British Government in May, 1944, is the first formal acceptance by a leading nation of the primary aim and responsibility to maintain a high and stable level of employment. This was followed, in April, 1945, by a similar declaration by the Canadian Government. In setting as its aim a high and stable level of employment, the Canadian Government specifically stated that it was not selecting a lower target than "full employment." Rather, it was mindful that it was breaking new ground and that it needed full public understanding and support to achieve its high goal. A mere declaration will not achieve full employment.

We shall indeed encounter innumerable difficulties in the pursuit of a full-employment goal. The fact that this experiment will prove difficult will not permit us to escape it. The problems that we shall be compelled to face will command the ingenuity and resourcefulness of both practical statesmen and theoretical economists in many decades to come. What I wish to stress here is my deep conviction that the political democracies of our time must undertake this new responsibility. We have reached a stage in economic evolution in which social planning must go beyond providing the economic opportunity to set up a business. For the great majority of citizens, in the world in which we live, economic opportunity means the right to a job.

Free Enterprise and the Right to a Job. The old right and the new one are interrelated. Freedom to choose among job opportunities in a free society presupposes the right and the opportunity for as many citizens as possible to establish a private enterprise. This right and this opportunity are important, not only for those who can and wish to become independent entrepreneurs, but also for those who remain employees. This is true because only in a private-enterprise economy can the great mass of wage and salaried workers enjoy the essential freedom of choice of employment among thousands and thousands of different employers. In a totalitarian society there is only one employer—the state. It is a vitally important safeguard for the preservation of personal liberty that the citizens of a free society shall enjoy the opportunity to choose between numerous employers, including private entrepreneurs, cooperative societies, and governments, federal, state, and local.

Thus the goal of full employment, if it is to be achieved in a free society, involves planning to make the market economy function in a workable manner so as to provide adequate employment opportunities together with the privilege of choice between different employers.

Democratic Planning. If the democratic countries were not now planning and developing new institutional arrangements designed to make the market economy function more effectively than it did in the past, the future would be black indeed. Those who think that a reversion to the institutional arrangements of the nineteenth century would give us, in the world we live in, stability and prosperity are not realistic. They are nostalgic dreamers. They are fighting for a lost cause. We cannot meet the problems of to-day by institutions suitable to conditions that no longer exist. We need, and we are in fact devising, new plans both domestic and international.

The old market economy has broken down. It failed us utterly in the two decades between the two world wars. In England unemployment, never falling below 10 per cent, reached in some years 22 per cent of the labor force and averaged 14 to 15 per cent for the entire two decades. In the United States, taking account of the whole interwar period, the spotty twenties and the depressed thirties, unemployment averaged about 12 per cent, and in the worst years, 1932-1933, reached 24 to 25 per cent of the labor force.

All hopes for the restoration of the old prewar economy were dashed in the great depression which shook the entire world and fanned the flames of the ensuing terrible world conflagration. International economic cooperation was completely cast aside. Economic warfare became the rule. The old order was destroyed. A new economic structure can be erected only on the basis of new institutions. We must rebuild the market economy, in both the domestic and the international spheres, so as to prevent similar disastrous breakdowns in the future. We are confronted with the task of devising new machinery, suitable to modern conditions, under which the market economy can operate effectively at high and stable levels of income and employment.

TOTAL OUTLAY

Under the market economy, good employment opportunities depend upon an adequate demand for goods and services. As the British White Paper on Employment Policy put it: "A country will not suffer from mass unemployment as long as the total demand for its goods and services is maintained at a high level." "Demand" in economic terminology does not mean "need" or "desire"; it means "outlay" or "expenditure." Adequate total *demand* means an adequate volume of expenditure whether by individuals, business, or government for goods and services.

Some critics have had a field day pointing out that high total outlay will not cure pockets of unemployment in stranded areas; nor will it cure seasonal, frictional, and technological unemployment. They have pointed out that expenditures on land, old houses, securities already outstanding, and the like do not create employment. They have moreover noted that increased outlays, if wages are increased more rapidly than productivity, would merely result in high prices without increasing employment.

These criticisms, while accurate enough, are not very brilliant. They are old but important truths that we do well to remember. Neither the British nor Canadian Governments, nor the sponsors of the American full-employment proposals are naive enough to overlook these matters. The points raised have been discussed again and again, both in the theoretical and the applied literature. What needs *now* to be stressed is the all-important fact that the market economy cannot function even tolerably well unless the total outlay on goods and services, public and private, is maintained at a high and stable level. This is the central problem to which we must address ourselves if we really want the free-market economy to work. How can we ensure that the total outlay on goods and services will be adequate to provide continuing full employment?

The outlays on goods and services, as elaborated in nearly all current full-employment documents, can conveniently be divided into four categories: (1) private consumption expenditures, (2) private capital outlays, (3) current services of government, and (4) government capital outlays on public works and developmental projects.

PRIVATE CONSUMPTION

The first of these—private consumption expenditures—can be fairly closely estimated for different levels of employment. We know from all past experience that private consumer expenditures cannot be expected to reach a level adequate to employ the entire labor force. A rich society such as ours does not and will not spend all its income on consumers' goods. We need in the postwar period, it is estimated, a total outlay on goods and services of around 180 billion dollars to provide full employment. But we know from long-established patterns of spending and saving (taking account of probable postwar taxation) approximately what the maximum contribution is that consumers can be expected to make toward that needed outlay of 180 billion dollars. The probable maximum is not far from 120 billion dollars. This means that around 60 billion dollars must be expended by private business on capital outlays and federal, state, and local governments on current services or construction projects. Only a drastic change in the expected peacetime tax structure or really fundamental changes in social security and income distribution could alter these figures substantially.

PRIVATE INVESTMENT

Now while the maximum contribution to total outlay from consumer expenditures can be estimated with fair accuracy, we know very little about what may be expected from year to year in private capital outlays. In some years, private investment is high and in some low. It was 17 billion dollars in 1929, and it fell to only 2 billion dollars in 1932. Herein lies the essential explanation of the great depression. It is just this utter undependability of private capital outlays that makes the economic system so unstable.

COMMUNITY SERVICES

The third category—public outlays on current services—can also be set down as a pretty definite figure. We know what the yearly outlays are on education, police protection, and the usual current government services. From the long-run standpoint we may wish to raise the figure gradually, but from the short-run it does not and should not fluctuate materially. We know pretty accurately, therefore, what the contribution will be to total demand from this third category of outlay or expenditure.

PUBLIC INVESTMENT

The fourth category—public capital outlays on public improvement and development projects—like the second, is subject to wide variation. Government construction projects for the most part do not have to be made in any one year. We can plan a 50-billion-dollar program, more or less, according to our prospective needs, over a 6- to 8-year period, and we can vary the annual outlays according to the requirements of stability and full employment. If private capital outlays decline, public capital outlays can be stepped up. Thus the public sector can act as a balance wheel to the private sector. With adequate planning, much could be done to stabilize the construction industry as a whole, taking account of both the public and the private sectors. Public projects should be built in the usual case under private contract. Thus contractors would switch from private to public projects as private capital outlays declined and public outlays took up the slack. But the construction industry, privately owned and operated, would find a stabilized volume of outlays, public and private combined.

SOCIAL SECURITY AND TAXATION

Stabilization of the construction industry would go very far toward stabilizing the economy as a whole. But it cannot do the job alone. A broad and comprehensive system of social security and social welfare, combined with a progressive tax structure, acts steadily and continuously as a powerful stabilizing factor. It puts a floor under depression. It acts as a great irrigation system, distributing purchasing power widely over the entire country. Now that we have current collection at the source, cyclical variation in the standard income-tax rate can, I believe, serve as a useful and effective supplementary measure. Thus the three main measures upon which we must rely for stability and continuing full employment are (1) a comprehensive and flexible program of public improvement and develop mental projects, (2) a comprehensive system of social security, and (3) variation in the basic income-tax rate.

SUSTAINED EXPANSION AND THE BUSINESS CYCLE

Once these measures are adequately implemented to sustain and advance the level of income and employment, it will, I think, be discovered that the business cycle will become something very different from that experienced in the past. The cumulative features that have characterized the cycle for a hundred years would tend to disappear. Under the automatic forces that controlled the cycle in the past, once the downward movement got started, the cumulative process fed on itself. Unemployment spread fear among consumers and reduced the volume of expenditures. Falling prices and falling markets induced pessimism among businessmen and cut off new capital outlays. In contrast, a sustaining social-security and developmental program will tend to stop this cumulative process. Thus the cycle (within the framework of an adequate compensatory, developmental, social-security, and flexible tax program), shorn of its worst cumulative features, may become manageable and susceptible to social control.

THE NEED FOR PLANNING

Modern governments are just at the threshold of this great experiment. We are still in the kindergarten stage. The stabilization of the construction industry alone involves an immense amount of physical and fiscal planning. It involves city planning and programs of urban redevelopment. It involves a comprehensive housing program, including not only a 20-year plan for the demolition of substandard houses, but also a long-range program of new residential construction, public and private. It involves a national plan for regional resource development in every part of the country, taking account not only of the great river basins such as the Tennessee Valley, the Columbia, the Missouri, and the Arkansas, but of land and water resources up and down the country that need reclamation, development, and conservation. It involves a thorough modernization of our entire transportation facilities—roadways, airways, waterways, and railways. In these three great fields—urban redevelopment and housing, regional resource development, and transportation—public investment must play an important role if we are to rebuild America on lines commensurate with the potentialities of modern science and modern technology. As we look at the deplorable physical condition of our great cities, the substandard housing both urban and rural, the congested urban transportation facilities, and the wastage of natural resources, it becomes abundantly evident that our greatest deficiencies are precisely in those areas that require large public investment outlays. We need to undertake a great national program of development. And such development would open up new rich fields for private investment.

I have underscored the role of a comprehensive system of social security and social welfare in a program of stability and expansion. Education, health and nutrition, recreational facilities, and community cultural activities are essential parts of a broad national development program. Of what good are mere brick and mortar if we neglect to develop a healthy, trained, educated, and socially minded citizenry? In our great country we are seriously deficient, not only in terms of natural-resource development, but also in terms of human development. Forty per cent of our children grow up in areas deplorably deficient in educational facilities. A disquieting percentage of the young men drafted into the service were adjudged "functional illiterates" or were physically unfit for military duty. These are areas we must not neglect when we plan a well-balanced program of national development and public investment.

INTERNATIONAL PLANNING

Planning for the future, however, cannot stop short at our national boundaries. National planning for stability and expansion involves not only domestic but also international plans. It is to the credit of the leading governments of our generation that we have not drifted on to the end of the war without a program. We are on our way to building a set of new international institutions that fit the needs of the world we live in. While the war was still being fought, we held a whole series of international conferences—Atlantic City on Relief and Rehabilitation, Hot Springs on Food and Agriculture, Bretton Woods to devise a new international monetary system and to provide capital for international development, Dumbarton Oaks and San Francisco to give us a charter for a world government.

One of the main pillars of the United Nations Charter is the Social and Economic Council. Through this council the member nations will dedicate themselves to the continuing task of solving their common economic problems and of achieving international stability and expansion. This requires first and foremost full employment and economic stability within each country. Any country that fails at home cannot be a good neighbor in the family of nations. This is especially true of the great countries. There is nothing that the United States can do which will contribute more to international stability than to achieve a high and stable level of prosperity at home. Yet no country, at least none of the free countries that operate on the basis of a market economy, is immune to economic disturbance from the outside. Depression spreads, we have learned in the interwar years, with devastating effect from country to country. Collective action by the whole family of nations thus becomes necessary. The Social and Economic Council can play an important role toward achieving a workable international order.

The agreements made by 44 countries at Bretton Woods, together with the inclusion of the Social and Economic Council in the San Francisco Charter, are indications that there is overwhelming agreement throughout the modern world that new international institutions are necessary if we would escape a repetition of the disastrous experiences between the two world wars. We are determined not to let things drift again. We mean to try to become masters of our fate. We shall not achieve a hundred-percent perfection. But we can nonetheless set our standards high. We have become convinced, at long last, that the old machinery will not work. We are no longer afraid to try something new. This is the meaning of the International Monetary Fund, the International Bank for Reconstruction and Development, the International Organization for Food and Agriculture, the Social and Economic Council of the United Nations Charter; and with respect to domestic policy, this is the meaning of such documents as the British White Paper on Employment Policy, the Canadian Paper on Employment and Income, and the Employment Act of 1946 in the United States.

The catalogue of programs, which I have just listed, is impressive. I have discussed the international aspects of this program of planning for the future in some detail in my recent book, *America's Role in the World Economy*. I cannot particularize here. The list of institutions that are there described and that are on the way to realization presents a strong contrast to the confusion and frustration that characterized economic policy all over the world 25 years ago. We have learned, I am convinced, a great deal from the terrible experiences of the last two decades. In all the advanced countries we are reaching some degree of agreement about what we need to do to reshape our world in order to make it again a functioning and manageable system.

THE FREE SOCIETIES

In what I have said I have had in mind chiefly the problems confronting the free societies—the countries where economic life is ordered mainly on the basis of private enterprise, but with the state playing nonetheless a large and increasing role. It has been aptly called a "mixed system." It is no longer the old simon-pure private-enterprise economy. But its most characteristic feature continues nevertheless to be *the market* or *the price system*. This basic characteristic is common to all the free societies—to the United States, Great Britain, the Scandinavian countries, Holland, Belgium, France, Canada, Australia, and New Zealand. It is upon these countries, in particular, that the task devolves to rebuild by means of new institutions, appropriate to modern conditions, a workable world.

SECURITY AND PROGRESS

Such a world must combine security with progress. There are those who have sought to show that these two goals are in conflict. But I think it can convincingly be shown that this is a highly superficial view. The modern urbanized world, highly interdependent geographically and occupationally, is extraordinarily sensitive to instability. The modern social structure cannot survive the kind of economic instability, domestic and international, we have suffered in our generation. Amidst such chaotic upheavals progress cannot flourish. And, conversely, it is not possible to achieve a high degree of stability except in an expanding world.

The restrictive policies of trade unions are most evident in the highly unstable building industry. Instability promotes restriction and contraction. Foreign trade restrictions—import quotas, exchange control, etc.— multiply in periods of deep depression and mass unemployment. Restrictive practices of all kinds are the instinctive defensive mechanisms of a contracting market. Expansion makes it possible to achieve stability without making it necessary to resort to the contrived and artificial stability of restrictive practices.

If we hope to win social and economic stability, we must make sure that productivity and standards of living are continually on the increase. Large-scale governmental support for scientific and technical research deserves to be put high on the agenda of public investment projects. The development of new products, new methods, new industries is an essential condition, not only of expansion and full employment, but also of economic stability and social security. A stagnant society, incapable of raising the standards of living of its people, will not be a secure or stable society.

THE "ROAD TO SERFDOM"

And now a final word about "planning" and the so-called "road to serfdom." There are those who allege, led by Professors Mises and Hayek, that conscious planning is not compatible with personal freedom. They would rely upon the automatic forces alone. Only such institutions as are basic to the necessary automatic processes are acceptable to them. All other planning is regarded as "bad planning." That, at least, is the logic of the case, and it is in fact the position of Mises. Hayek, a little less rigid and doctrinaire in his thinking than Mises, is forced to abandon logical consistency in the face of the hard realities of the modern world. Thus, he admits, somewhat reluctantly, the necessity of social security and some other measures involving a minimum of social planning.

THE RULE OF LAW

Hayek fears a world that requires human management. He has a great deal to say about the "rule of law." Yet he confuses automatism in social life with the rule of law. He forgets that the very concept of the rule of law was developed in England just at the time when there was a vast amount of governmental control of economic life. It was precisely because this was the case that the rule-of-law concept was developed. The rule of law does not mean that human management is replaced by automatic forces. It means that the conscious management of social life is conducted under established canons that preclude *arbitrary* action. The rule of law substitutes rational principles of management for the arbitrary acts of arbitrary men.

The widespread acceptance of social and economic planning by all modern governments is evidence that the hard experiences of recent decades have driven home the lesson that the functioning of modern economic life cannot be left to automatic forces. But it does not mean that we thereby deliver ourselves up to the arbitrary management of irresponsible men. That is not now, and never has been, the method of political democracy. The plans we are devising, both domestic and international, are not ships let loose on an uncharted sea with instructions to the captains to steer as they see fit. Rational and democratic planning involves the development of rules of law that preclude arbitrary action by those who are chosen to administer the plans. This could be illustrated in any one of the plans, domestic or international, that I have reviewed. For example, while the International Monetary Fund does mean that we have abandoned the moorings of the old international gold standard, it will not leave us in international monetary matters adrift upon a sea of arbitrary decisions by the Governing Board of the Fund. New moorings to take the place of the old gold standard are established. Rules of law are set up which constitute a framework within which decisions are made.

In the decades that lie ahead, a major task of economic and social statesmanship must be undertaken precisely in this field. We must evolve rules of law under which the social planning of the future can be made a rational and democratic method of managing our social order. Only thus can we achieve the high goals of progress, stability, and full employment combined with the undying human values of personal and individual liberty. Without exception, all the great democracies are to-day embarked upon programs of social planning. In our own Anglo-Saxon tradition, the concept of social control *under law,* not control by irresponsible and arbitrary men, reaches far back into history. It antedates the age of modern capitalism. It reaches back into the early beginnings of local government. And it was never wholly lost sight of even in the heyday of *laissez-faire.* We have a rich heritage of legal and political tradition which gives us high confidence and faith that we can achieve the great social and economic goals we seek without losing our personal freedoms.

BIOGRAPHICAL NOTES

ALBERTY, HAROLD (b. 1890). Superintendent of Schools, Berea, Ohio, 1916-21; Assistant Superintendent of Schools, Cuyahoga County, Ohio, 1924-26; Professor of Education, Ohio State University, 1928—.

ANDERSON, WILLIAM (b. 1888). Professor of Political Science. Harvard University, 1915-16; University of Minnesota 1916—; President of the American Political Science Association, 1942. Director, Bureau for Research in Government, 1919-28. Minnesota State Planning Board, 1935-38. Minnesota Resources Commission, 1939-42. Social Science Research Council, 1932-36; Chairman, Committee on Public Administration, 1939-45; Chairman, Committee on Government, 1941-45. Author of many books and articles on political science.

BEARD, CHARLES A. (1874-1948). Professor of History and Government. Columbia University, 1904-17; Johns Hopkins University, 1940-41; President of the American Political Science Association, 1926, and of the American Historical Association, 1933. Director, Training School for Public Service, New York City, 1917-22. Director, Bureau of Municipal Research, New York, 1918-22. Adviser, Institute of Municipal Research, Tokyo, 1922. Adviser, Japanese Ministry of Home Affairs, 1923. Author of many books and articles on history and government.

BEARD, MARY R. (b. 1876). Author. Long experience in woman and labor movements; travel and study in Europe and Orient. Co-author (with her husband Charles A. Beard) of *The American Spirit, The Rise of American Civilization,* and author of several books and articles.

BELLOWS, HENRY A. (1885-1939). Publicity director. Member of English Department, University of Minnesota, 1910-12; manager of radio station WCCO, 1925-27; member, Federal Radio Commission, 1927; Vice-President, Columbia Broadcasting System, 1930-34; Director and Chairman of Legislative Committee, National Association of Broadcasters, 1928-35; Director of Public Relations, General Mills, Inc., 1936-39.

BENJAMIN, HAROLD (b. 1893). University Dean and Professor of Education. Taught at University of Oregon, 1922-25; Stanford University, 1925-27; University of Minnesota, 1927-36; University of Colorado, 1937-39; Dean of the College of Education, University of Maryland, 1939—. Among his many books in the field of education are *Man—The Problem Solver* and *Emerging Conceptions of the School Administrator's Task.*

BERGE, WENDELL (b. 1903). Lawyer. Officer of the Anti-Trust Division of the United States Department of Justice, becoming Head of that Division in 1943. Has contributed articles to many legal reviews and periodicals; author of *Cartels: Challenge to a Free World*.

BINKLEY, W. E. (b. 1883). Professor of Political Science. Ohio Northern University, 1920—. Also a member of the municipal council of Ada, Ohio, since 1935. Author of monographs and books, many of them like *Powers of the President* and *The President and Congress* concerned with the office and powers of the American chief executive.

BURNS, JAMES McGREGOR (b. 1918). Political Scientist. Legislative Assistant, United States Congress, 1939-40, with War Labor Board during World War II, Assistant Professor of Political Science, Williams College, 1947—. Author of *Congress on Trial*.

BYE, RAYMOND T. (b. 1892). Professor of Economics. University of Pennsylvania, 1916—. Author of *Principles of Economics, Getting and Earning: a Study of Inequality* (with R. H. Blodgett), and numerous other books and articles in the field of economics.

CALDWELL, LYNTON K. (b. 1913). Instructor and Assistant Professor of Government, Indiana University, 1940-44. Director of Research and Publications, Council of State Governments, 1944-47; Professor of Political Science, Syracuse University, 1947—. Author of *The Administrative Theories of Hamilton and Jefferson*.

CALROW, CHARLES J. (1877-1938). Architect and public official. Architectural and engineering draftsman to 1898; construction superintendent and practicing architect to 1917; captain and major, U. S. Corps of Engineers, 1918-19; member of and consultant to the City Planning Commission of Norfolk, Virginia; chairman, Civic Improvement Committee, Norfolk Association of Commerce; District Administrator, Civil Works Administration, Southeast Virginia, 1933-34; Natural Resources Committee consultant and Director of the Virginia State Planning Board, 1934-38.

CARTER, HUGH (b. 1895). Professor of Sociology. University of Pennsylvania, 1930—. State Director of research history of poor relief, 1928-29; Senior Housing Research Analyst, U. S. Housing Authority, 1939-40.

CHARLESWORTH, JAMES C. (b. 1900). Professor of Political Science. University of Pittsburgh, 1927-39; University of Pennsylvania, 1939—; Consultant to Pennsylvania Labor Department and the Pennsylvania Civil Service Commission.

CHASE, STUART (b. 1888). Writer. Investigator of meat-packing industry for the Federal Trade Commission, 1917-22; with Labor Bureau, Inc., 1922-39. Consultant to National Resources Commission, 1934; Resettlement Administration, 1935; Securities and Exchange Commission, 1939; the Tennessee Valley Authority, 1940-41. Author of many books on public questions, among them are: *The Tragedy of Waste, Men and Machines, The Economy of Abundance*, and *Rich Land, Poor Land*.

CHATTERS, CARL (b. 1898). Public administrator. City auditor, Flint, Michigan, 1932-39. Director of Finance, Flint, 1929-31. Director of Municipal Advisory Council of Michigan, 1931-32, and Executive Director of the Municipal Finance Officers Association of the United States and Canada, 1932-45; Comptroller, Port of New York Authority, 1946-47; Executive Director, American Municipal Association, 1948—. In addition to many articles on local finance, is the author of *Local Government Debt Administration* and *Government Accounting*.

CLOSE, UPTON—Josef Washington Hall (b. 1894). Author and lecturer. Investigating officer for U. S. Government in Shantung during Japanese invasion, 1916-19; newspaper correspondent in China, Japan, and Siberia, 1917-22; Chief of Foreign Affairs under Wu Pei Fu, 1922; lecturer on Oriental life and literature, University of Washington, 1922-26; speaker for National Industrial Conference Board. Frequent contributor to leading periodicals. Author of *Behind the Face of Japan* and *Ladder of History*.

COMMISSION OF INQUIRY ON PUBLIC SERVICE PERSONNEL. This commission was appointed in 1933 by the Social Science Research Council with the approval of President Franklin D. Roosevelt to examine the broad problems of personnel within the United States and to outline a program for future action. The committee was headed by Lotus D. Coffman, then President of the University of Minnesota, and was composed of four other members: Louis Brownlow, Director, Public Administration Clearing House, Chicago; Ralph Budd, President, Chicago, Burlington and Quincy Railroad; Arthur L. Day, Vice-President, Corning Glass Works; and Charles E. Merriam, Department of Political Science, University of Chicago.

COMMISSION ON THE ORGANIZATION OF THE EXECUTIVE BRANCH OF THE GOVERNMENT. Established by Congress, July 7, 1947, to make an exhaustive study of the executive branch of the government and to recommend changes in the administrative organization. Former President Herbert Hoover was named Chairman and Dean Acheson, now Secretary of State, Vice-Chairman. Other members of the Commission were Arthur S. Fleming, James Forrestal, George H. Mead, George D. Aiken, Joseph P. Kennedy, John L. McClellan, James K. Pollock, Clarence J. Brown, Carter Manasco, and James H. Rowe, Jr.

COMMITTEE ON POST WAR TAX POLICY. A non-partisan committee established at the suggestion of several leading economists. Its chairman was Roswell Magill, and the other members were Fred R. Fairchild, Professor of Economics at Yale, Rowland R. Hughes, Victor H. Stempf, and Thomas N. Tarlean. Professor H. L. Lutz, Professor of Public Finance at Princeton, was Director of Research.

COOPER, ROBERT M. (b. 1907). Lawyer and public official. Special attorney, Department of Justice, 1934-37; Department of Justice representative as a member of the U. S. Codification Board, 1937-38; Department of Justice representative, advisory council of the Marketing Laws Survey, 1938-39;

special assistant to the Attorney General of the United States, 1937—; assistant to the General Counsel of the Federal Communications Commission 1939—.

CORWIN, EDWARD S. (b. 1878). Professor of Political Science. Princeton University, 1905—. Visiting Professor of Political Science at Yenching University, Peiping, China, 1928-29. Advisor to Public Works Administration, 1936; Consultant to the Attorney General of the United States on constitutional questions, 1937. Has published a large number of articles on jurisprudence, constitutional law, and political science. Author of *John Marshall and the Constitution, The Twilight of the Supreme Court, The Constitution and What It Means To-day,* and *The President: Office and Powers.*

CUSHMAN, ROBERT E. (b. 1889). Professor of government. University of Illinois, 1915-19; University of Minnesota, 1919-23; Cornell University, 1923—. Member, The President's Committee on Administrative Management, 1936. Author, *American National Government* (with S. P. Orth); *The Independent Regulatory Commissions;* editor, *Leading Constitutional Decisions;* frequent contributor to legal and other periodicals.

DAVENPORT, FREDERICK M. (b. 1866). Professor of Law and Politics. Hamilton College, 1904-29. Member, New York State Senate, 1909-10, 1919-25; Progressive nominee for Governor of New York, 1914; member of Congress from New York, 1925-33; President, National Institute of Public Affairs; Chairman, Federal Personnel Council, U. S. Government, 1939—.

DAVIS, WILLIAM H. (b. 1879). Patent lawyer and public official. Deputy administrator and National Compliance Director, N.R.A., 1933-34; member, Federal Commission of Industrial Analysis, 1936; member, Emergency Board under Railway Labor Act, 1937; member, President's Commission on Industrial Relations in Great Britain and Sweden, 1938; member, New York City Housing Authority, 1939; Vice-chairman, National Defense Mediation Board, 1941, Chairman, same board, 1941-42; Chairman, National War Labor Board, 1942 and after.

DAWSON, MITCHELL (b. 1890). Lawyer and writer. Director and secretary-treasurer, Chicago Civic Broadcast Bureau, 1934-35; chairman, Public Relations Committee, Chicago Bar Association, 1934-37; chairman, Public Relations Committee of Section on Bar Organization Activities, American Bar Association, 1936-38; editor, *Chicago Bar Record;* Lecturer on newspaper law, Medill School of Journalism, Northwestern University, 1943-44; frequent contributor to leading periodicals.

DERN, GEORGE H. (1872-1936). Businessman, inventor, and public official. General manager, Consolidated Mercury Gold Mines, 1900-13; joint inventor of Holt-Dern ore roaster; member, Utah State Senate, 1915-23; Governor of Utah, 1925-32; chairman, Governor's Conference, 1929-30; Secretary of War of the United States, 1933-36.

DICKINSON, JOHN (b. 1894). Lawyer. Lecturer on Government. Harvard University and Radcliffe College, 1924-27; Professor of Politics, Princeton University, 1927-29; Professor of Law, University of Pennsylvania, 1929—; Assistant Secretary of Commerce, 1933-35; Assistant United States Attorney General, 1935-37; General Solicitor, Pennsylvania Railroad, 1937-41; General Counsel of Pennsylvania Railroad since 1941; author of numerous books and articles on legal and political subjects.

DIMOCK, MARSHALL E. (b. 1903). Professor of Public Administration. University of California, 1928-32; University of Chicago, 1932-41. Second Assistant Secretary of Labor, 1938-40; Consultant, National Resources Committee, 1935-39; Administrative Assistant, Immigration and Naturalization Service, 1940-42; Assistant Deputy War Shipping Administrator, 1942-44; Professor of Political Science, Northwestern University, 1944-48. Among his books in the field of political science are: *American Government in Action* and *Government and Business*.

DOOB, LEONARD (b. 1909). Professor of Psychology, Yale University, 1934—. Chief, Analysis Section, Coordinator of Inter-American Affairs, 1942-43; Chief Consulting Psychologist, Psychological Warfare branch, U. S. War Department, 1942-43; Policy Coordinator, Overseas Branch, Office of War Information, 1943-45. Author of *Propaganda* and *Public Opinion and Propaganda*.

DOUGLAS, PAUL H. (b. 1892). U. S. Senator. Professor of Economics, University of Washington, 1919-20; University of Chicago, 1925-48. Member, Illinois Housing Commission, 1931-33; Consumers Advisory Board, N.R.A., 1933-35; Alderman, Chicago City Council, 1939-42. Elected as United States Senator from Illinois in 1948. Author of several books and articles, many dealing with social welfare and social security problems.

DUMAS, J. N. (b. 1921). City hall reporter for the *Schenectady Gazette* and string correspondent for the New York *Herald Tribune* in Schenectady. Entered newspaper work in 1939 as part time reporter for Albany *Times Union* while attending journalism course at Siena College; staff writer of weekly paper published by U. S. Coast Guard, 1943-45.

EAGLETON, CLYDE (b. 1891). Professor of Government. University of Louisville, 1918-19; Southern Methodist University, 1919-23; New York University, 1923—. Chairman, United States National Committee of International Student Service; Technical expert, U. S. Delegation to Dumbarton Oaks and San Francisco Conferences; now on leave as consultant to U. S. State Department; International Law Editor, *New York University Law Quarterly;* member, Editorial Board, *American Journal of International Law.* Author of *International Government, The Forces That Shape Our Future,* and numerous articles on political subjects.

EDGERTON, HENRY W. (b. 1888). Judge. Private practice of law, 1914-21; Professor of Law, Cornell University, 1916-19, 1929-38; George Washington University, 1921-29; special assistant to United States Attorney General,

1934-35; Associate Justice, United States Court of Appeals for District of Columbia, 1938—.

EDWARDS, WILLIAM H. (b. 1901). Professor of Political Science. He has held professorships at the University of North Dakota and Sweet Briar College, Virginia, New Mexico State College, and is now Professor at and Head of the Social Science Department, State Teachers College, Brockport, New York. He is one of the first among the critics of orthodox state reorganization plans to have presented a clear choice between two fundamentally different systems and to have made a strong case for independent boards. Author of numerous articles on state reorganization and related questions.

FAULKNER, JOE P. (b. 1911). Reporter and rewrite man for *The New York Journal-American,* 1933—. Graduate of Southern Methodist University, 1932. Columnist for the *Dallas Dispatch,* 1932-3. Author of numerous magazine articles.

FELLER, A. H. (b. 1904). General Counsel and Director of Legal Affairs, Secretariat of United Nations, 1946—. Special Assistant to U. S. Attorney General, 1934-40. Visiting lecturer, Harvard University, 1937-38. Associate Professor of Law, Yale University, 1940-43. Author and contributor to periodicals.

FISCHER, JOHN (b. 1910). Rhodes Scholar at Oxford, 1933; with Associated Press, 1935-37. Held several government posts, 1938-43, including posts with Board of Economic Warfare, and head of Lend-Lease Administration in India. Associate editor of *Harper's,* 1944-47; editor of Trade Department at Harper and Brothers, 1947—. Author of *Why They Behave Like Russians,* and frequent contributor to periodicals.

FLYNN, JOHN T. (b. 1882). Author and journalist. City editor, *New York Globe,* 1920; managing editor, 1920-23; adviser to United States Senate Committee on Banking and Currency, 1933-34; lecturer in contemporary economics, 1935-36; member, Board of Higher Education, City of New York. Author of *Men of Wealth, As We Go Marching, Meet Your Congress,* and *The Road Ahead.*

GLASS, CARTER (1858-1946). United States Senator. Member, Virginia Senate, 1899-1903; member, State Constitutional Convention, Virginia, 1901; member, United States House of Representatives, 1902-18; Secretary of the Treasury of the United States, 1918-20; member, United States Senate, 1920-46.

GLOCKER, THEODORE W. (b. 1881). Professor of Economics. Instructor in economics, Johns Hopkins University, 1907-08; assistant director of research, Boston School of Social Work, 1908-09, Director of Research, 1909-12; Professor of Economics and Sociology, University of Tennessee, 1913-20; director, School of Business Administration, 1921-46; Dean of School of Commerce, 1947—.

GRAVES, W. BROOKE (b. 1899). Professor of Political Science, Temple University, 1925-42; Staff Officer of the United States Civil Service Commission, 1942—. Chairman, Philadelphia Federal Council of Personnel Administration; Research Consultant of Joint Legislative Committee on Finances of Pennsylvania. Author and contributor to many periodicals.

GROVES, HAROLD M. (b. 1897). Professor of Economics, University of Wisconsin. Member of Wisconsin Assembly, 1930; member, Wisconsin State Senate, 1934-36; member, Wisconsin State Tax Commission, 1932; member of Commission on Intergovernmental Fiscal Relations, U. S. Treasury Department, 1941-42. Author of *Financing Government, Federal, State, and Local Fiscal Relations, Production, Jobs, and Taxes,* and articles in the field of public finance.

HAINES, CHARLES GROVE (b. 1879). Professor of Political Science. Ursinus College, 1906-10; Whitman College, 1910-14; University of Texas, 1914-25; University of California, 1925—. Executive Secretary, League of the Pacific Northwest Municipalities, 1912-14; President, American Political Science Association, 1939. Commissioner, Department of Water and Power, Los Angeles, 1939. Author of *The American Doctrine of Judicial Supremacy, The Role of the Supreme Court in American Government and Politics,* and other books and articles on legal and political subjects.

HAMILTON, WALTON H. (b. 1881). Professor of Law. Professor of economics, University of Michigan, 1900-14; University of Chicago, 1914-15; Amherst College, 1915-23; Brookings Institution, 1923-28. Professor of law, Yale University, 1928—. Member, NRA Board, 1934-35; delegate of United States Government to International Labor Organization Conference, Geneva, 1935; special assistant to United States Attorney General, 1938-45.

HANSEN, ALVIN (b. 1887). Professor of Economics. University of Minnesota, 1919-37; Harvard University, 1937—. Economist with U. S. State Department, 1934-35; member of Advisory Council on Social Security, 1937-38; Special Adviser to the Federal Reserve Board, 1940-45. Author of many books in the field of economics, and a frequent contributor to periodicals.

HARRELL, C. A. (b. 1893). City Manager. Portsmouth, Ohio, 1930-31; Binghamton, New York, 1933-37; Schenectady, New York, 1937—. Consultant with the National Defense Commission, 1941; War Production Board, 1942. Author of many papers dealing with municipal government.

HIBSCHMAN, HARRY (b. 1879). Lawyer, lecturer, and author. Member of the Illinois and Washington bars. Deeply interested in the law of the press, and in modernizing and humanizing the law; frequent contributor to popular and legal periodicals.

HYNEMAN, CHARLES S. (b. 1900). Professor of Political Science. Syracuse University, 1928-30; University of Illinois, 1930-37; Professor of Government and Director, Bureau of Government Research, Louisiana State University, 1937-42; Director, School of Government and Public Affairs, Louisiana State University, 1938-42; Principal Administrative Analyst, U. S. Bureau of the Budget, 1942-43; Director, Foreign Broadcast Intelligence

Service of the Federal Communications Commission, 1944-46; Professor of Political Science at Northwestern University, 1947—.

JACOBSON, J. MARK (?-1938). Lawyer and Professor of Political Science. Instructor in political science, University of Wisconsin. Member of the New York Bar; member, Legal Division, National Labor Relations Board. Author of *The Development of American Political Thought* and numerous articles on political and legal subjects.

KEY, V. O., JR. (b. 1908). Professor of Political Science. University of California at Los Angeles, 1934-36; Johns Hopkins University, 1938-49; Head of Department of Political Science, Yale University, 1949—; staff member, Committee on Public Administration, Social Science Research Council, 1936-37; research technician, National Resources Committee, 1937-38; member, Baltimore Commission on Governmental Efficiency and Economy, 1940-42. Author of *The Administration of Federal Grants to the States, Politics Parties, and Pressure Groups,* and *Southern Politics.*

LASKI, HAROLD J. (b. 1893). Professor of Political Science. Lecturer in history, McGill University, 1914-16; at Harvard University, 1916-20; Harvard lecturer at Yale University, 1919-20; London School of Economics, 1920—. Vice-chairman, British Institute of Adult Education, 1921-30; member of the Fabian Society Executive, 1922-36; member of the Industrial Court, 1926—; member of the Lord Chancellor's Committee on Delegated Legislation, 1929; member of the Departmental Committee on Legal Education, 1932; member of the Council of Institute of Public Administration; member of the National Executive Committee of the British Labor Party. Author of many books and articles in the field of political science.

LERNER, MAX (b. 1902). Professor of Political Science. Assistant editor, *Encyclopedia of the Social Sciences,* managing editor, 1927-32. Member of faculty, Sarah Lawrence College, 1932-36. Director, Consumers' Division, National Emergency Council, 1934. Lecturer, Department of Government, Harvard University, 1935-36. Associate editor, *The Nation,* 1936-38. Professor, Williams College, 1938-43; Chief Editorial Writer, *PM.* Professor, Brandeis University, 1949—. Author of *It Is Later Than You Think, Ideas Are Weapons, Ideas for the Ice Age, The Mind and Faith of Justice Holmes,* and numerous articles.

LILIENTHAL, DAVID (b. 1899). Lawyer. Practiced law in Chicago, 1923-31. Director, Tennessee Valley Authority, 1934-41; Chairman, Tennessee Valley Authority, 1941-46. Chairman, Atomic Energy Commission, 1946-50.

LOEWENSTEIN, KARL (b. 1891). Professor of Political Science and Jurisprudence, Yale University, 1934-36; Amherst College, 1936—. Special Assistant to the U. S. Attorney General, 1942-44; Consultant, Office of U. S. Military Government for Germany in Berlin, 1945-46. Author of many books, including *Hitler's Germany, Brazil Under Vargas,* and *Political Reconstruction.*

MARSH, DONALD B. (b. 1911). Economist, Royal Bank of Canada and Professor of Economics at McGill University. Author of *Taxes Without Tears,* and several periodical articles on economic problems.

MARTIN, J. W. (b. 1893). Economist. Professor of Economics, Emory University, 1924-28; University of Kentucky, 1928—. Commissioner of Revenue, Kentucky, 1936-39. Consultant to the U. S. Treasury Department, 1941—. Contributor to professional journals.

MEIKLEJOHN, ALEXANDER (b. 1872). Philosopher and Educator. Professor at Brown University, 1899-1912; President, Amherst College, 1912-24; Professor, University of Wisconsin, 1926-38; Professor emeritus, 1938—. Author of several books on philosophy and education.

MERRIAM, CHARLES E. (b. 1874). Professor of Political Science, University of Chicago, 1900-1940; Professor emeritus, 1940—. Alderman, Chicago, 1909-11 and 1913-17; Republican candidate for mayor, 1911. President, Social Science Research Council, 1924-27; President, American Political Science Association, 1925. Member, Hoover Commission on Recent Social Trends, National Resources Board, 1933-34; President's Committee on Administrative Management. Author of a large number of books and articles dealing with American government and politics.

McBAIN, HOWARD LEE (1880-1936). Professor of Political Science. George Washington University, 1907-10; University of Wisconsin, 1910-13; Columbia University, 1913-36. Dean of the Graduate Faculties, Columbia University, 1929-36. Special counsel for New York City before State Constitutional Convention, 1915; member, Board of Education, City of New York, 1916-18; member and secretary, New York City Charter Commission, 1921-23; associate editor of *The National Municipal Review* and *Political Science Quarterly;* author of *The Living Constitution.*

MILLER, GLENN W. (b. 1911). Assistant Professor of Economics at Ohio State University. Author of *American Labor and the Government.*

MILLER, SPENCER, JR. (b. 1891). Public administrator. Assistant to Warden of Sing Sing Prison, New York, 1915-16; Director, Workers Education Bureau of America, 1921-42; member of faculty, School of Commerce, New York University, 1941—. New Jersey State Highway Commissioner, 1942—. Author and contributor to many periodicals.

MUNRO, WILLIAM BENNETT (b. 1875). Professor of Political Science. Williams College, 1901-04; Harvard University, 1904-29; California Institute of Technology, 1929-45; at present, Treasurer, California Institute of Technology. Editorial writer, *Boston Herald,* 1907-21; member, Cambridge Charter Commission, 1913-14; member, city of Boston Budget Commission, 1915; chairman, Commission on Data and Information for Massachusetts Constitutional Convention, 1917-18; President, American Political Science Association, 1927; author of numerous books and frequent contributor to literary and political reviews.

MURPHY, RUTH Z. Secretary, National Council on Naturalization and Citizenship, 1930-38; now Executive Vice-President of this council. Formerly, Chairman of the New York Committee on Naturalization. Author of several articles and studies in the field of naturalization problems and policies.

MYRDAL, GUNNAR (b. 1898). Professor and Lawyer. Practiced law for several years in Sweden and has been professor of economics at the University of Stockholm, 1931—. Member of the Swedish Senate for the Social Democratic Party. Director of the study of American Negro problems for the Carnegie Corporation of America, 1938-42. Author of many studies of economics and government.

NEVINS, ALLAN (b. 1890). Historian. Editorial writer, *New York Evening Post,* 1913-23; *The Nation,* 1913-18. Professor of American history, Cornell University, 1927-28; Columbia University, 1931—. Winner of two Pulitzer prizes for biography, 1932 and 1937. Author of many books and a frequent contributor to magazines.

NIEBUHR, REINHOLD (b. 1892). Clergyman. Professor of Applied Christianity, Union Theological Seminary, 1930—. Editor of *Christianity and Society* and *Christianity and Crisis.* Author of *Christianity and Power Politics, The Nature and Destiny of Man,* and other books and articles.

OUTLAND, G. E. (b. 1906). Educator. Former member of House of Representatives from California (1943-47). Director of Boys Work, Hale House, Boston, 1928-30; Neighborhood House, Los Angeles, 1933-34. On faculty of Yale University, 1935-37; Santa Barbara State College, 1937-42. Author of *Boy Transiency in America.*

OVERACKER, LOUISE (b. 1891). Professor of Political Science. Vassar College, 1920-22; Wilson College, 1924-25; Wellesley College, 1925—. Author of *The Presidential Primary, Money in Elections,* and *Presidential Campaign Funds.* Frequent contributor to various political science journals.

PHILLIPS, CABELL (BEVERLEY HATCHETT) (b. 1905). University of Richmond, 1926. Journalist in Washington for *Time,* Inc., *Chicago Herald-American, The New York Times.* Reporter for *Richmond Times-Dispatch* and other papers in the South and Middle West, 1926-36. Government information service in Washington. Editor, *Dateline: Washington;* contributor to *Public Opinion and Foreign Policy.* Author of many articles on topics of politics and national affairs.

PORTER, KIRK H. (b. 1891). Professor of Political Science. University of Iowa, 1918—; head of the Department of Political Science, 1940—. Author of *A History of the Suffrage in the United States,* (ed.) *National Party Platforms, State Administration,* and numerous articles on politics and administration.

RADIN, MAX (b. 1880). Professor of Law. Columbia University, 1918-19; College of City of New York, 1917-19; University of California, 1919-40. Member of the bar of New York, California, and the United States Supreme

Court. Author of several works on Roman law and legal history, and numerous articles in philological and legal periodicals.

RANNEY, JOHN C. (1915-50). Professor. Member of faculty of Department of Political Science, Smith College, 1943-50. Contributor to many professional journals.

REDMOND, R. L. (b. 1892). Lawyer. Practice in New York, 1919—. Trustee of Pierpont Morgan and New York Public Libraries.

REEVES, FLOYD W. (b. 1890). Professor of Educational Administration. Rural school teacher until 1912; public school administrator, 1912-20; Transylvania College, 1923-25; University of Kentucky, 1925-29; University of Chicago, 1929—; director, American Youth Commission, 1939—; chairman, Permanent Commission on College Cost of the Association of American Colleges, 1926-28; Director of Personnel, TVA, 1933-36; member of staff, President's Committee on Administrative Management, 1936; chairman, Advisory Committee on Education, 1936; member, Advisory Committee on Administrators of the President's Committee on Civil Service Improvement, 1939—. Author of *Education for To-day and To-morrow*, and frequent contributor to professional periodicals.

RIORDON, WILLIAM L. (1861-1909). Author and newspaper writer. Contributed numerous articles on the political views of George Washington Plunkitt, who was a New York State Senator and an important figure in the Tammany organization.

RODELL, FRED (b. 1907). Professor of Law. Legal adviser to Governor Pinchot of Pennsylvania, 1931-33; Yale Law School, 1933—; member, Committee on Public Law, Association of American Law Schools, 1935-36. Author of *Fifty-Five Men, Woe Unto You Lawyers,* and a frequent contributor to legal journals.

ROOSEVELT, FRANKLIN D. (1882-1945). Thirty-second President of the United States. Admitted to New York Bar, 1907; member, New York Senate, 1910-13 (resigned); Assistant Secretary of the Navy, 1913-20; Democratic Nominee for Vice President, 1920; Governor of New York, 1929-33; President of the United States, 1933-1945.

ROSS, LILLIAN (b. 1920). Staff writer for *The New Yorker Magazine,* 1945—. Graduate of Hunter College; studied at Cornell University; reporter for *PM* newspaper, 1943-44. Author of numerous magazine articles.

ROSS, MARY. Journalist and public official. Graduate of Vassar College, 1915, and the Columbia University School of Journalism, 1916. Reporter, *New York World;* writer and editor for the American Red Cross, World War I; book reviewer, *New York Herald Tribune,* 1924—; member, editorial staff, *Survey Graphic,* 1922-36; chief, Division of Publications and Review, Bureau of Research and Statistics, Social Security Board, 1936—. Frequent contributor to a number of periodicals.

SABINE, GEORGE H. (b. 1880). Professor of Philosophy. Stanford University, 1907-14; University of Missouri, 1914-23; Ohio State University, 1923-31;

Cornell University, 1931-40; Dean of the Graduate School at Cornell, 1940-44; Vice-President of the University, 1943-49. Author of *A History of Political Theory* and numerous articles in the fields of philosophy and political theory.

SCHOLZ, K. W. H. (b. 1886). Professor of Economics at the University of Pennsylvania, 1919—. Author of several books in the field of economics and frequent contributor to economic journals.

SMITH, ALFRED E. (1873-1944). Business executive, public official. Member, New York State Assembly, 1903-15; sheriff, New York County, 1915-17; President, Board of Aldermen, Greater New York, 1917-19; Governor of New York, 1919-20, 1923-28; Democratic Candidate for President of the United States, 1928; President, Empire State, Inc.; Director, New York Life Insurance Co.; Trustee, Catholic University of America; one of the founders of the American Liberty League.

SMITH, J. ALLEN (1860-1926). Lawyer and Professor of Political Science. Practiced law, Kansas City, Missouri, 1887-92; Marietta College, 1895-97; University of Washington, 1897-1926; Dean of the Graduate School, University of Washington, 1909-20. Author of numerous books and articles on political and economic subjects.

SMITH, T. V. (b. 1890). Professor of Philosophy, University of Chicago, 1927-48, Syracuse University, 1948—. Member of Illinois State Senate, 1935-38; Chairman, Illinois Legislative Council, 1937-38; Member of U. S. House of Representatives, 1939-41; Director of Education, Allied Control Commission in Italy, 1944. Among his books on political subjects are *Politics and People* and *The Promise of American Politics*.

STERN, EDITH M. (b. 1901). Free lance journalist and novelist. Graduate of Barnard College. Author of several novels and contributor to many of America's leading magazines.

STERN, WILLIAM A., 2ND (b. 1897). Lawyer. Chief Attorney of the Court of Claims Section of the U. S. Department of Justice. Prior to 1937 in private law practice in New York. Author of *Getting the Evidence*.

TOLLEY, H. R. (b. 1899). Agricultural Economist. Assistant Chief of Bureau of Agricultural Economics, U. S. Department of Agriculture, 1928-30; Professor of Agricultural Economics, University of California, 1930-36; Administrator of AAA, 1936-38; Chief of Bureau of Agricultural Economics, 1938—. Adviser to the U. S. Delegation to the United Nations Conference on Food and Agriculture, 1943. Author of *The Farmer Citizen at War* and many articles on agricultural economic problems and policies.

TREADWAY, WILLIAM E. (b. 1901). Lawyer and public official. Member, Indiana House of Representatives, 1934-38; member, Indiana State Tax Study Commission, 1935; member, Indiana Liquor Study Commission, 1936; Executive Secretary, Indiana Commission on Interstate Cooperation, 1938-41; Captain, Judge Advocate General's Department, United States Army, 1938-41; author of numerous articles in legal and academic journals.

W. E. Upjohn Institute for Community Research. Director, Harold C. Taylor. A privately sponsored nonprofit research organization, established in 1945. It is an activity of the W. E. Upjohn Employment Trustee Corporation which was founded in 1932 to administer a fund set aside by the late Dr. W. E. Upjohn to "carry on research into the causes and effects of unemployment and measures for the alleviation of unemployment."

Warner, John A. (b. 1886). Police officer. Entered the New York State Police at its organization in 1917 and served as Lieutenant of Troop "A," Batavia, New York, from June, 1917, to June, 1918; served as Captain of Troop "K" at White Plains, New York, from June, 1918, to December, 1923; appointed Superintendent, New York State Troopers, December, 1923, and held that position until his retirement in 1943.

Weidner, Edward (b. 1921). Political Scientist. Assistant Professor of Political Science, University of Minnesota, 1947-49; University of California, Los Angeles, 1949—. Research Associate, National Municipal League, 1944-45; Consultant, Governments Division, Bureau of the Census, 1945. Author of *The American County—Patchwork of Boards*, and *County Boards and Commissions*.

White, William Allen (1868-1944). Newspaper publisher, author. Proprietor and editor of the *Emporia Daily and Weekly Gazette*, 1895-1944. Sent to France as observer by American Red Cross, 1917; delegate, Russian Conference at Prinkipo; member, Republican National Convention, 1920, 1928, 1936; trustee, Rockefeller Foundation; president, American Society of Newspaper Editors; awarded gold medal for citizenship, Theodore Roosevelt Memorial Association.

Whittington, William V. (b. 1904). Lawyer; Legal Assistant, Treaty Division, Department of State. Administrative assistant and clerk, Department of State, 1924-30; member of the District of Columbia and Illinois bars; general law practice, Washington, D. C., 1928-30; technical-legal assistant, Treaty Division, Department of State, 1930-35; delegate of the United States to an international radio conference, Lisbon, Portugal, 1934; special assistant to Commissioner, Federal Communications Commission, 1935-37; Editor of Treaty Index, Treaty Division, Department of State, 1937-38; Legal Assistant, Treaty Division, Department of State, 1939—.

Willoughby, W. F. (b. 1867). Economist. Expert, U. S. Department of Labor, 1890-1901; special agent, U. S. Commission to Paris Exposition, 1900; received Cross Legion d'Honneur from French government; lecturer in economics, Johns Hopkins and Harvard, 1901; treasurer of Puerto Rico, 1901-07; secretary of Puerto Rico, and President of the executive council of the legislative assembly of Puerto Rico, 1907-09; assistant director, U. S. census, 1909-11; member, President's Committee on Economy and Efficiency, 1911-12; professor of jurisprudence and politics, Princeton, 1912-17; constitutional adviser to the Chinese Republic, 1914-16; director, Institute for Government Research, 1916-32.

WIRTH, LOUIS (b. 1897). Sociologist. Social work in Chicago, 1919-22; Professor of Sociology, Tulane University, 1928-30; University of Chicago, 1931—. Author of several books and articles on sociology and social research.

WITTE, EDWIN E. (b. 1887). Economist. Statistician, Industrial Commission of Wisconsin, 1912; secretary, Congressman John M. Nelson, 1912-14; special investigator, U. S. Commission on Industrial Relations, 1914-15; secretary, Industrial Commission of Wisconsin, 1917-22; chief, Wisconsin Legislative Reference Library 1922-33; acting director, Unemployment Compensation Division, Industrial Commission of Wisconsin, 1934; member, Wisconsin State Planning Board, 1935-38; member, Wisconsin Labor Relations Board, 1937-39; member of staff, University of Wisconsin, 1920—; chairman, Department of Economics since 1936; member (representing the public), on National War Labor Board, 1944-45. Has written extensively on social legislation.

YOUNG, JOHN PARKE (b. 1895). Economist. Examiner for the Federal Trade Commission, 1917-18; economist, U. S. Senate Commission of Gold and Silver Inquiry (field study of 16 European nations), 1923-25; professor of economics and sociology and chairman of department, Occidental College, 1926—; president, Young & Koenig, Inc., Los Angeles; member, Kemmerer Commission to Government of China, 1929; member, Board of Economic Survey of Port of Los Angeles, 1933; member, Board of Governors, Investment Counsellors' Association of Southern California; Associate Chief, Division of Foreign Economic Development, Department of State, 1943—. Author of numerous books and articles.